Foundations of Modern Macroeconomics

Third Edition

Ben J. Heijdra

OXFORD
UNIVERSITY PRESS

OXFORD
UNIVERSITY PRESS

Great Clarendon Street, Oxford, OX2 6DP,
United Kingdom

Oxford University Press is a department of the University of Oxford.
It furthers the University's objective of excellence in research, scholarship,
and education by publishing worldwide. Oxford is a registered trade mark of
Oxford University Press in the UK and in certain other countries

© Ben J. Heijdra 2017

The moral rights of the author have been asserted

First edition published in 2002
Second edition published in 2009
Third edition published in 2017

Impression: 4

Published in the United States of America by Oxford University Press
198 Madison Avenue, New York, NY 10016, United States of America

British Library Cataloguing in Publication Data
Data available

Library of Congress Control Number: 2017932967

ISBN 978–0–19–878413–5

Printed and bound by
CPI Group (UK) Ltd, Croydon, CR0 4YY

In memoriam

Jenny E. Ligthart

November 6, 1967 – November 21, 2012

Walter H. Fisher

December 9, 1961 – November 15, 2012

Preface

What can the book do for you?

As was the case for the first two editions of this book, this new edition tries to present a balanced overview of modern macroeconomic theory. I follow two guiding principles. First, I adopt a rather eclectic approach by paying attention not just to the most recent insights in the field but also to developments that are currently less popular. In doing so, I hope to provide students with a better overview of current *and* past debates in macroeconomic theory. History can teach us useful lessons, provided we are willing to listen! For example, I continue to include discussions of the IS-LM model, the adaptive expectations hypothesis, and the Solow-Swan growth model (to mention a few). Though these theories are currently less fashionable (and, as some economists argue, may even be "outdated"), it is my firm conviction that they nevertheless provide important insights. For example, to fully appreciate the importance of the rational expectations hypothesis, a good understanding of the adaptive expectations hypothesis (its immediate predecessor) is indispensable. Similarly, to really understand the contributions made in recent years by New Keynesian Dynamic Stochastic General Equilibrium (DSGE) economists, it is very useful to have a firm understanding of the IS-LM model. Also, a good grasp of the Solow-Swan model helps in appreciating the Ramsey model and the endogenous growth models formulated in the 1980s and 1990s. Of course, as the saying goes, "old habits die slowly" and the IS-LM model is still used extensively even though, as Blanchard has pointed out, many people may not even know they are using it (2000, p. 1405).

The second guiding principle concerns the expositional style of the book. In addition to introducing the different theories by verbal and graphical means, I have also aimed to successively develop "the tools of the trade" of modern macroeconomics. In this aspect the book is related to Allen's (1967) marvellous macroeconomic toolbook. So instead of only providing students with a verbal/intuitive understanding of the material (valuable as it is), I also explain the basic modelling tricks of modern macroeconomics. Where needed the full details of both the models and their solutions are presented. Students who have worked through the textbook (and its accompanying manual) should have little or no problems reading the recent journal literature in macroeconomics or building their own macro models.

How can the book be used?

Depending on the background of students, the book can be used in the undergraduate and/or the graduate curriculum. Part I, consisting of Chapters 1-9, can be used in an intermediate macroeconomics course in the undergraduate curriculum. For example, I use Chapters 1-6 in my seven-week macroeconomics course in the third-year of the bachelor program at the University of Groningen. Economics students in this course have been exposed to Blanchard et al. (2013) in their first two years, whilst econometrics students have studied Gärtner (2016) in their second year of studies. In addition, these students have studied basic mathematical methods at the level discussed, for example, in Hoy et al. (2011).

Parts II and III of the book consist of Chapters 10-19. They are aimed at advanced bachelor students, first-year master students, and beginning doctoral students. In the graduate curriculum, the book can be used as the main text in a first-semester macroeconomics course or as a supplementary text for an advanced graduate macro course. At the University of Groningen, for example, I use Chapters 12-15 in my half-semester macroeconomics course in the regular masters programs. In the research master courses I also cover Chapter 10 and most of Chapters 16-19. The book is also well-suited for beginning doctoral students with no (or insufficient) previous training in macroeconomic theory. Parts of Chapters 12-16 were used in the various graduate courses I have taught over the years for the Netherlands Network of Economics (NAKE), the Tinbergen Institute, CESifo, and the Institute for Advanced Studies (Vienna).

Intermezzos

The book contains a number of so-called intermezzos. I use the term 'intermezzo' in an extended and unusual sense. Recall that in music an intermezzo is a composition that is played in between acts of a play or movements of a much larger musical piece. In this book, the intermezzos do not make any sound but, like in music, they are 'small morsels in between big chunks'. They serve a number of purposes. First of all, they ensure that upon first reading students are not distracted by complex technical intricacies. Second, they allow for in-depth coverage of a number of key results in theoretical macroeconomics. Furthermore, in combination with the chapter appendices and the mathematical appendix at the end the book, they cover all technicalities necessary for a sound understanding of modern macroeconomics. Whereas the appendices are purely aimed at mathematical results, the intermezzos focus more on the fault line between mathematics and theoretical macroeconomics. Finally, the intermezzos serve as reference tools for readers who wish to reacquaint themselves with things they used to know but have forgotten.

Starred sections

In this edition I have also included sections marked with a superscript star (★). These sections contain material that is more difficult than the rest of the chapter in which they are located. Students may choose to skip the starred material when first reading the chapter. Upon completion of the book the successful student will find that most (or even all) stars have become invisible.

Changes for the Third Edition

The book has been thoroughly rewritten. Compared to the second edition, it has grown in size by about one hundred pages. The main changes are as follows.

- The current book includes forty-seven intermezzos, of which sixteen are new. All of these have been extensively checked and streamlined. They are numbered and carry an informative title. A List of Intermezzos is included in the preamble of the book which facilitates cross-referencing. The numbering system is as before, with the first digit denoting the chapter in which the intermezzo is located. The new intermezzos are 1.1, 1.2, 5.1, 5.2, 8.2, 8.3, 9.1, 12.2, 13.3, 16.1, 17.1, 18.1, 18.2, 19.1, 19.2 and 19.3.

- The new Chapter 2 deals exclusively with the open economy. It follows logically from the first chapter and contains material from Sections 1 and 2 of the old Chapter 10.

- Chapter 3 is a rewritten version of the old Chapter 2.

- Chapter 4 has been renamed to better reflect its contents. It contains a rewritten version of the old Chapter 4 as well as Section 3 (on the Dornbusch model) from the old Chapter 10.

- Chapter 5 is an expanded and rewritten version of the old Chapter 3. It now includes a small open economy model and explains the Dynare software package that can be used to solve rational expectations models.

- Chapter 6 is a lightly rewritten version of the old Chapter 5.

- Chapter 7 is a thoroughly edited and shortened version of the old Chapters 6 and 7. It also contains some new material on union- and efficiency-wage models in general equilibrium.

- Chapter 8 is an expanded version of the old Chapter 8. It now contains a section on endogenous job destruction.

- Chapter 9 has been renamed to better reflect its contents. In addition it has been expanded and now includes a discussion of dynamic inconsistency of individual choices resulting from present-biased (or quasi-hyperbolic) preferences.

- Chapters 10 and 11 are lightly edited versions of the old Chapters 11 and 12.

- The old Chapter 12 (on exogenous growth) has been split into two much expanded chapters. The new Chapter 12 deals exclusively with Solow-Swan style growth models. It has been expanded somewhat and now also features a section of the two-sector Meade-Uzawa model.

- Chapter 13 contains Sections 13.5–13.7 from the old Chapter 13. In addition it has been expanded dramatically. It now includes models with endogenous labour supply (using material from the old Chapter 15), search unemployment, and money balances entering the felicity function. This is the pivotal chapter in the book as the Ramsey-Cass-Koopmans model that it covers in all its guises plays a central role in the material that follows from there on.

- Chapter 14 is a lightly edited version of the old Chapter 14. Similarly, Chapters 15 and 16 are lightly edited versions of the old Chapters 16 and 17.

- Chapter 17 is brand new. It provides a brief (and mostly intuitive) discussion of the method of dynamic programming (DP). In addition it introduces the concept of complete markets and shows how one can construct a "representative agent" in such a setting. Whilst a deep knowledge of DP is not really essential to understand Chapters 18–19, it is indispensable if one wants to proceed to the more advanced literature in macroeconomics, e.g. the graduate textbook by Ljungqvist and Sargent (2012).

- Chapter 18 is the first chapter on the DSGE approach. It contains material from the old Section 15.5. It has been edited thoroughly and now includes discussions of the stochastic discount factor and shows how DSGE models can be simulated with the aid of the Dynare software package (introduced in Chapter 5).

- Chapter 19 is brand new. It contains a thorough discussion of the New Keynesian DSGE approach and finishes with a brief assessment of the state of the art at the time of writing. This assessment replaces the Epilogue from the second edition.

Visible means of support

It somehow seems impossible to produce a book of this size without generating (free of charge) some typos and errors. Needless to say, all such errors and typos will be published as I become aware of them. I will make the errata documents available through the website for the book:

$$\texttt{http://www.heijdra.org/fomm3}$$

So please let me know about any typos and/or errors that you may spot. This is what you can do for the book! The contact address is: info@heijdra.org. As a (weak substitute for a) reward, I will mention your name prominently on the website (as having contributed to the public good). Of course, your name will also feature in the Acknowledgements section in any future edition of the book.

The website also includes ready-to-use slides for all chapters in PDF format. Teachers who wish to adapt these slides to their own purpose or software platform can download the LATEX 2_ε code and all figures (in EPS and EMF formats) and proceed from there.

I have updated and streamlined the accompanying *Exercise and Solutions Manual* which is published by Oxford University Press. This hands-on exercise book contains a large number of problems plus model answers. These problem sets allow the interested student to further develop his/her skills.

Acknowledgements

In preparing the *third edition*, I received useful comments from many people, including Pieter Ijtsma, Gerard van der Meijden, Laurie Reijnders, Girum Dagnachew Abate, Wilma Huitema, Christien de Kort, Stine Celius, Kengo Tahara, Carolien Calkhoven, Mika Kortelainen, Matthijs Katz, Yoni Schirris, Bastiaan Quast, Jelle van Essen, Marc Boom, Annemarije Santman, Bart Rutjes, Lisan Spiegelaar, Gert-Jan Romensen, Jitka Vavra, and Vesa-Matti Heikkuri. One of the great privileges of working in a university is that – surrounded by young and enthusiastic people – one never really grows old. Life-long learning is the norm rather than the exception in academia. Over the years I have greatly benefited from the interaction with some outstanding colleagues. The collaboration with Fabian Kindermann (University of Bonn) has resulted in a significant upgrade of my computing skills – something that was long overdue. Since he is a great teacher of computational economics, I highly recommend his forthcoming textbook on Fortran computing (Fehr and Kindermann, 2017). My friend and colleague, Pim Heijnen (University of Groningen) not only accompanied me to the pub quite regularly (for work-related meetings) but also had a very significant effect on my computing skills. In addition, he suggested the cake-eating example of dynamic inconsistency (and hyperbolic discounting) that is discussed in Chapter 9. Another colleague, Allard van der Made, has been a great sounding board on mathematical issues. I also thank my Groningen colleagues Lammertjan Dam for discussions on the consumption-based asset pricing model employed in Chapters 18–19, Christiaan van der Kwaak for comments on Chapters 17 and 19, and Gerard Kuper for plowing through Chapter 18. Just as for the second edition, Jochen Mierau has read the entire manuscript and has provided useful advice on many aspects of the book (both content and exposition). To the extent that I have not followed some (or all) of their suggestions, this is not because I disagreed with them but rather because of a binding time constraint on my part.

As with the previous two editions of the book, Siep Kroonenberg has assisted at crucial instances with the more complicated aspects of the LaTeX 2_ε codes used to produce this book. Of course, Leslie Lamport and Donald E. Knuth are thanked implicitly too for producing, respectively, LaTeX 2_ε and TeX.

Over the years the following people from Oxford University Press have been of great assistance in the production and marketing of this book: Andrew Schuller, Rebecca Bryant, Sarah Dobson, Jennifer Wilkinson, Sarah Caro, Aimee Wright, T.W. Bartel, and Adam Swallow. During the fine-tuning of the book I benefited tremendously from the efforts of Katie Bishop, Elisa Cozzi, and Joshua Hey. I thank all of them for their efforts.

Dedication

I dedicate this new edition of the book to Jenny E. Ligthart and Walter H. Fisher who passed away during a *hebdomas horribilis* in November 2012. I first met Jenny in December 1992. I moved to the University of Amsterdam (where she was a Ph.D. student) in May 1993 and together with Rick van der Ploeg I ended up supervising Jenny's doctoral work. Following her successful thesis defence in November 1997 we continued to work together on various projects until her passing. I first met Walter in May 2002 when he invited me to the Institute for Advanced Studies (IHS) in Vienna. From 2006-2013 I held a Visiting Research Professorship at the institute and our collaboration became much more intensive. Jenny and Walter were much more than nice colleagues and co-authors to me. Over time they became close personal friends. Some of their work finds its way into this book. The loyalty and friendship I received from them does not. I will cherish their memory for as long as I live.

Ben J. Heijdra
University of Groningen, The Netherlands
February 2017

Contents

List of Figures

List of Tables

List of Intermezzos

Part I

Intermediate macroeconomics

Chapter 1

Review of the AD-AS model

The purpose of this chapter is to achieve three goals:

1. To (partially) refresh and extend the macroeconomic knowledge from first-year courses.

2. To investigate the effectiveness of monetary and fiscal policy on output, employment, the interest rate, and the price level.

3. To introduce the most important past and current schools of thought in macroeconomics.

In order to achieve these goals, we first have to discuss some elementary concepts relating to the *aggregate labour market* and the *demand for money*. It turns out that the most important differences of opinion between (most varieties of) Classical and Keynesian economists can be traced back to their respective assumptions regarding the labour market, expectation formation, and money demand.

1.1 The aggregate labour market

Our discussion of the labour market in this chapter is very basic. In Chapters 7–8 we return to this important topic in more detail. The stylized account of the labour market uses the devices of the aggregate demand for and supply of labour.

1.1.1 The demand for labour

The central element in the basic theory of labour demand is the production function. Perfectly competitive profit-maximizing entrepreneurs utilize this production function under the restriction that the capital stock is given in the short run. The production function is thus given by:

$$Y = F(N, \bar{K}), \tag{1.1}$$

where Y is real output, $\bar{K}$ is the given capital stock (machines, PCs, cars), N is the amount of labour employed, and $F(N, \bar{K})$ is the production function. The marginal products of labour and capital are denoted by $F_N \equiv \partial F(N, \bar{K})/\partial N$ and $F_K \equiv \partial F(N, \bar{K})/\partial \bar{K}$, respectively. Furthermore, we assume that the marginal product of labour (capital) declines as employment (capital) is increased, i.e. $F_{NN} \equiv \partial^2 F(N, \bar{K})/$

$\partial N^2 < 0$ ($F_{KK} \equiv \partial^2 F(N, \bar{K})/\partial \bar{K}^2 < 0$). Too many cooks in the kitchen spoil the broth. We also assume that the factors are cooperative in the sense that increasing one factor raises the marginal productivity of the other factor ($\partial^2 F(N, \bar{K})/\partial \bar{K} \partial N \equiv F_{KN} = F_{NK} \equiv \partial^2 F(N, \bar{K})/\partial N \partial K > 0$). The use of robot mixers in the kitchen thus enhances the productivity of the cooks. Finally, we assume constant returns to scale so that doubling all factors of production induces a doubling of output. More precisely, $F(\lambda N, \lambda \bar{K}) = \lambda F(N, \bar{K})$ with λ any positive constant.

Short-run profits are defined as revenues minus the wage bill:

$$\Pi \equiv PY - WN, \tag{1.2}$$

where Π is nominal profit, P is the price charged by the firm, and W is the nominal wage rate. In words, all revenue (PY) that is not paid to the variable production factor labour in terms of wages (WN) is considered profit, which is the reward that accrues to the owners of the capital stock (note that we ignore taxes for the moment).

We assume perfect competition on the aggregate goods market, so that the individual firm cannot exert any influence on the price it charges for its product. Hence, the only choice that is open to the firm (in the short run) is to determine the amount of production (Y) and employment (N) such that profit is maximized. By substituting the production function in the profit definition, we see that once employment is chosen, output is also automatically chosen. The problem for the firm is thus to choose N to maximize Π:

$$\max_{\{N\}} \Pi \equiv PF(N, \bar{K}) - WN. \tag{1.3}$$

The firm can do no better than to follow the following decision rule:

$$\frac{d\Pi}{dN} = 0: \qquad PF_N(N, \bar{K}) - W = 0, \tag{1.4}$$

where the second-order condition implies that (1.4) describes a maximum: $d^2\Pi/dN^2 = PF_{NN} < 0$ (because $P > 0$ and $F_{NN} < 0$ by assumption). The interpretation of (1.4) is clear; the firm should keep expanding its employment up to the point where the marginal unit of labour exactly breaks even (in the sense that the additional output produced by the marginal worker yields a revenue that exactly covers the wage that is paid to the worker). In terms of Figure 1.1, the profit maximum occurs at point A. (At points B and C the firm makes no profits.)

The decision rule (1.4) is a vitally important element in the macroeconomic labour market story. It is also relatively uncontroversial: virtually all macroeconomists believe in some version of equation (1.4). We can easily transform (1.4) into the demand for labour, a schedule which shows how much labour a firm wants to hire for a given real wage rate. Formally, we can view equation (1.4) as an implicit relationship between N^D (the superscript "D" stands for demand) on the one hand and the real wage, W/P, and the given capital stock, $\bar{K}$, on the other. The partial derivatives of this implicit relationship can be obtained by using the trick of implicit functions. First, we totally differentiate equation (1.4):

$$dF_N(N^D, \bar{K}) = d(W/P) \quad \Rightarrow \quad F_{NN}dN^D + F_{NK}d\bar{K} = d(W/P), \tag{1.5}$$

or, after rearranging terms:

$$dN^D = -\frac{F_{NK}}{F_{NN}}d\bar{K} + \frac{1}{F_{NN}}d(W/P). \tag{1.6}$$

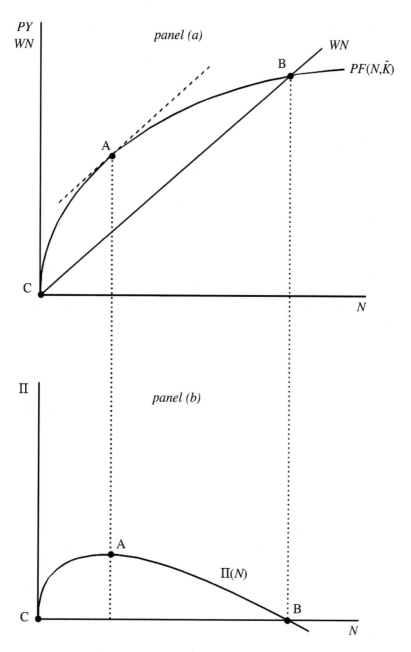

Figure 1.1: Short-run profit maximization

Since $F_{NN} < 0$, the marginal product of labour falls as more units of labour are employed. As a result, equation (1.6) states that a higher real wage ($d(W/P) > 0$) diminishes the demand for labour ($dN^D < 0$) ceteris paribus (i.e. holding $\bar{K}$ constant). Hence, $1/F_{NN}$ in equation (1.6) can be interpreted as the partial derivative of the implicit function between N^D and $(W/P, \bar{K})$ with respect to the real wage, W/P.

The partial derivative with respect to the capital stock is obtained in a similar fashion (and is equal to $-F_{NK}/F_{NN} > 0$). Since labour and capital are cooperative factors of production, increasing the capital stock raises the marginal product of labour. For a given real wage rate, the profit-maximizing firm thus hires more labour.

In summary, we can write:

$$N^D = N^D(W/P, \bar{K}) \quad N^D_{W/P} \equiv \frac{1}{F_{NN}} < 0, \quad N^D_{\bar{K}} \equiv -\frac{F_{NK}}{F_{NN}} > 0. \tag{1.7}$$

In terms of Figure 1.2, varying the real wage rate implies a movement along a given demand for labour curve, whilst increasing the capital stock shifts the demand curve to the right. A higher cost of labour or a lower capital stock necessitates a higher marginal productivity of labour and thus a lower demand for labour.

Intermezzo 1.1

The Cobb-Douglas production function and labour demand. In this intermezzo we discuss an often-used two-factor production function featuring constant returns to scale. The Cobb-Douglas function can be written as:

$$F(N, K) \equiv Z_0 K^\alpha N^{1-\alpha}, \qquad 0 < \alpha < 1, \tag{a}$$

where α is an efficiency parameter and Z_0 is a scaling factor. Several things are worth noting. First, it is easy to verify that this function features constant returns to scale:

$$F(\lambda N, \lambda K) = Z_0 (\lambda K)^\alpha (\lambda N)^{1-\alpha} = \lambda^{\alpha+1-\alpha} Z_0 K^\alpha N^{1-\alpha} = \lambda F(N, K). \tag{b}$$

Second, the marginal products of labour and capital are both positive:

$$F_N(N, K) = (1 - \alpha) Z_0 \left(\frac{K}{N}\right)^\alpha > 0, \tag{c}$$

$$F_K(N, K) = \alpha Z_0 \left(\frac{K}{N}\right)^{-(1-\alpha)} > 0. \tag{d}$$

Third, each factor features diminishing marginal productivity, and the factors are cooperative:

$$F_{NN}(N, K) = -\alpha(1 - \alpha) Z_0 \left(\frac{K}{N}\right)^\alpha \frac{1}{N} < 0, \tag{e}$$

$$F_{KK}(N, K) = -\alpha(1 - \alpha) Z_0 \left(\frac{K}{N}\right)^{-(1-\alpha)} \frac{1}{K} < 0, \tag{f}$$

$$F_{NK}(N, K) = \alpha(1 - \alpha) Z_0 \left(\frac{K}{N}\right)^\alpha \frac{1}{K} > 0. \tag{g}$$

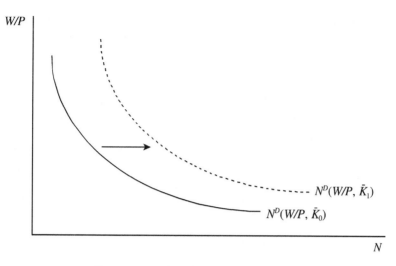

Figure 1.2: The demand for labour

Fourth, for a given capital stock $\bar{K}$ the competitive labour demand function can be written as:

$$N^D = \left(\frac{(1-\alpha)Z_0}{w} \right)^{1/\alpha} \bar{K},\tag{h}$$

where $w \equiv W/P$ is the real wage rate. The (absolute value of the) wage elasticity of labour demand—defined in general as $\varepsilon_D \equiv -F_N(N,\bar{K})/(NF_{NN}(N,\bar{K}))$—thus equals $\varepsilon_D = 1/\alpha$ for the Cobb-Douglas production function. Fifth, provided labour is paid its marginal product, the labour income share in production is constant, i.e. $wN/F(N,K) = 1 - \alpha$.

****

1.1.2 The supply of labour

In the previous section we implicitly assumed that firms can freely observe the actual values of the price level and the wage rate (P and W). This is realistic enough, because all the individual firm must do is to observe its *own* price and the wage paid to its *own* workers.

Matters are somewhat more complicated for the households, who are the suppliers of labour in our stylized account of the labour market. Indeed, in the decision about goods consumption and labour supply, the households may know their own nominal wage (W) with certainty, but they may not know how much they can actually consume with that wage. The household has to estimate the price of a whole basket of goods, a task inherently more difficult than the one facing the individual firm. The simplest way to introduce this asymmetry in information is to assume that the household forms a guess about the aggregate price level, denoted by P^e (where the superscript "e" stands for expected).

The household derives utility from goods consumption (denoted by C) and leisure $(1 - N^S)$. The household "owns" one unit of time, of which N^S units are spent working, so that time available for leisure is equal to $1 - N^S$. We write the utility function in general terms as $U(C, 1 - N^S)$ and assume positive but diminishing marginal utilities: $U_C > 0$, $U_{1-N} > 0$, $U_{CC} < 0$, and $U_{1-N,1-N} < 0$. Some extra consumption of goods and leisure is fun, but less so if you already consume a lot or have plenty of spare time to enjoy. In addition, we assume that indifference curves bulge toward the origin, i.e. $U_{CC}U_{1-N,1-N} - U^2_{C,1-N} > 0$.

The household chooses that combination of C and $1 - N^S$ for which the highest possible satisfaction is attained (as measured by $U(\cdot, \cdot)$), *given* the expected price level, P^e, and the (expected) budget restriction $P^e C = WN^S$. We assume that the household has no sources of income other than wages. Formally, we can thus write the problem for the household as follows:

$$\max_{\{C,N^S\}} U \equiv U(C, 1 - N^S) \quad \text{subject to} \quad P^e C = WN^S. \tag{1.8}$$

This problem looks rather prohibitive, but we can make it easier by substituting the level of consumption implied by the budget restriction ($C = (W/P^e)N^S$) into the utility function. The household then only has to choose the level of labour supply:

$$\max_{\{N^S\}} U \equiv U\left((W/P^e)N^S, 1 - N^S\right). \tag{1.9}$$

This yields a straightforward decision rule for the household:

$$\frac{dU}{dN^S} = 0: \quad (W/P^e)U_C - U_{1-N} = 0. \tag{1.10}$$

The first term on the left-hand side (i.e. $(W/P^e)U_C$) measures the marginal benefit of supplying one extra unit of labour to the labour market. By working more, the household obtains more income, especially if the real wage is high, and hence more consumption. The second term (i.e. U_{1-N}) measures the marginal cost of that extra unit. By supplying more labour, the household misses out on valuable leisure time. In an optimum the household sets the marginal benefit equal to the marginal cost of supplying an additional unit of labour.

In principle we could now proceed by investigating what happens to labour supply and consumption if the expected real wage rate is varied. Mathematically this is slightly more involved than for the labour demand equation, so that we first derive the basic intuition concerning labour supply by graphical means. (The mathematical derivation of labour supply is given in Chapter 7.)

In Figure 1.3 we plot consumption on the vertical axis and leisure on the horizontal axis. The initial expected real wage is $(W/P^e)_0$, and the budget line goes through $\bar{C}_0 (\equiv (W/P^e)_0)$ on the C-axis, and 1 on the $(1 - N^S)$-axis. The optimal consumption-leisure choice occurs at the point where an indifference curve has a tangency with the budget line. This occurs at point E_0, where consumption is C_0, leisure is $1 - N^S_0$, and the level of utility is U_0. By plotting the implied value of labour supply, N^S_0, against the expected real wage rate in Figure 1.4, we obtain the first point on the labour supply curve.

Suppose now that the expected real wage is a bit higher, say $(W/P^e)_1$. In terms of Figure 1.3 this implies that the budget line rotates in a clockwise fashion around the intersection point on the leisure axis. The new intersection on the consumption axis is at $\bar{C}_1 (\equiv (W/P^e)_1)$. For the case drawn, the new optimum choice occurs at

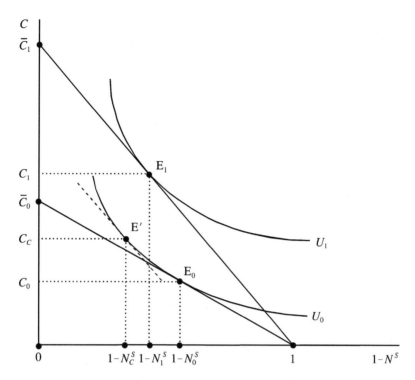

Figure 1.3: The consumption-leisure choice

point E_1, which lies above and to the left of the initial point E_0. Consumption is C_1, leisure is $1 - N_1^S$, and the level of utility is U_1. By plotting the implied value of labour supply, N_1^S, against the real wage rate in Figure 1.4, we obtain the second point on the labour supply curve. By connecting the two points we obtain the labour supply schedule, labelled $N^S (W/P^e)$, which for the case drawn slopes upward.

Unlike the labour demand curve, which always slopes downwards, the slope of the labour supply curve is not necessarily positive. The reason is that there are two, potentially offsetting, effects that confront the household when the expected real wage rises. The first effect is called the *pure substitution effect*. To determine this effect, we ask ourselves what combination of consumption and leisure the household would choose at the higher expected real wage if it were somehow restricted to remain at the initial level of utility U_0. In Figure 1.3, we see that the household would choose point E', where consumption is C_C, leisure is $1 - N_C^S$, and labour supply is N_C^S (the subscript "C" stands for compensated). The move from the initial point E_0 to the (hypothetical) compensated point E' constitutes the pure substitution effect (i.e. *SE*). Intuitively, the pure substitution effect says that a household will buy less of anything for which the price has risen. A rise in the expected real wage rate means that the price of leisure has gone up. Consequently, the household buys less of it. This gives us an interesting result: *the compensated labour supply curve is always upward sloping* (see $N^S(W/P^e, U_0)$ in Figure 1.4).

The second effect is called the *income effect*. It says that, for a given initial level of labour supply N_0^S, a higher expected real wage implies a higher expected real income, or, $(W/P^e)_1 N_0^S > (W/P^e)_0 N_0^S$. Provided leisure is a normal good the household would react to this higher income by purchasing *more* leisure, not less. Hence, the income effect (i.e. *IE*), which is represented by the move from point E' to E_1,

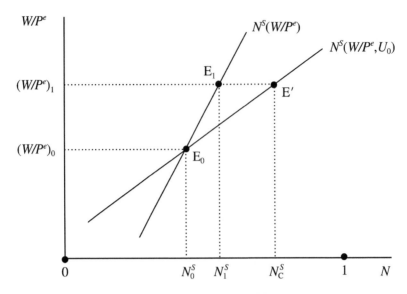

Figure 1.4: The supply of labour

works in the opposite direction to the pure substitution effect. As it happens, Figure 1.3 has been drawn for the case where the substitution effect dominates the income effect, so that labour supply slopes up. The other cases cannot be excluded on a priori grounds, however, and the issue can only be fully resolved by empirical means (see Chapter 7).

Mathematically, we can represent the labour supply curve in general form by:

$$W/P^e = g(N^S), \qquad g_N \gtreqless 0 \quad \Leftrightarrow \quad SE \gtreqless |IE|, \tag{1.11}$$

where $|IE|$ is the absolute value of the income effect and SE is the substitution effect. A higher real wage thus has two effects on labour supply. On the one hand, it makes leisure more expensive which induces households to have less leisure and work more hours (the SE). On the other hand, a higher real wage raises the income of households so they become lazier and work less hours (the IE).

Intermezzo 1.2

The Stone-Geary utility function and labour supply. In this intermezzo we study the optimal labour supply decision when the household's utility function is of the Stone-Geary form. In the present context, utility depends on consumption and leisure and can be written as:

$$U(C, 1 - N) \equiv (C + \gamma)^\beta (1 - N)^{1-\beta}, \qquad 0 < \beta < 1, \quad \gamma > 0, \tag{a}$$

where β and γ are taste parameters. (Note that (a) reduces to a Cobb-Douglas utility function if we assume that $\gamma = 0$.) It is easy to verify some of the key properties of the Stone-Geary utility function (for $C + \gamma > 0$ and $1 - N > 0$). First, marginal utility of consumption and leisure are both positive:

$$U_C(C, 1 - N) = \beta \left(\frac{1 - N}{C + \gamma}\right)^{1-\beta} > 0, \tag{b}$$

$$U_{1-N}(C, 1-N) = (1-\beta)\left(\frac{1-N}{C+\gamma}\right)^{-\beta} > 0, \tag{c}$$

Second, the marginal utilities are diminishing:

$$U_{CC}(C, 1-N) = -\frac{1-\beta}{C+\gamma}U_C(C, 1-N) < 0, \tag{d}$$

$$U_{1-N,1-N}(C, 1-N) = -\frac{\beta}{1-N}U_{1-N}(C, 1-N) < 0. \tag{e}$$

Third, the marginal utility of consumption is increasing in leisure and vice versa:

$$U_{C,1-N}(C, 1-N) = \frac{1-\beta}{1-N}U_C(C, 1-N)$$

$$= \frac{\beta}{C+\gamma}U_{1-N}(C, 1-N) > 0. \tag{f}$$

Fourth, for a household that maximizes $U(C, 1-N)$ subject to the budget constraint $C = w^e N$, where $w^e \equiv W/P^e$, the first-order condition is given by $w^e U_C(C, 1-N) = U_{1-N}(C, 1-N)$, or:

$$\frac{1-\beta}{\beta}\frac{C+\gamma}{1-N} = w^e. \tag{g}$$

The budget constraint can be rewritten in terms of spending on consumption goods and leisure:

$$C + w^e(1-N) = w^e, \tag{h}$$

and after combining (g) and (h) we easily find the Marshallian (uncompensated) consumption and labour supply choices:

$$C = \varepsilon w^e - (1-\beta)\gamma, \qquad N^S = \beta - \frac{\gamma(1-\beta)}{w^e}. \tag{i}$$

Fifth, in the text we write the optimal labour supply choice as $w^e = g(N^S)$. The functional form of $g(N^S)$ can be easily recovered from the second expression in (i):

$$g(N^S) \equiv \frac{\gamma(1-\beta)}{\beta - N^S}. \tag{j}$$

The $g(N^S)$ function is upward sloping and features a vertical asymptote at $N^S = \beta$. Since labour supply cannot be negative, it follows that $0 \leq N^S < \beta$. The (uncompensated) wage elasticity of labour supply – defined in general as $\varepsilon_S \equiv g(N)/(N g_N(N))$ – equals $\varepsilon_S = (\beta - N^S)/N^S$ for the Stone-Geary utility function considered here. Sixth, to find the Hicksian (compensated) labour supply function we make use of the expenditure function. In the present context the expenditure function is defined as follows:

$$E(P^e, W, U_0) \equiv \min_{\{C, 1-N\}} P^e C + W(1-N)$$

$$\text{subject to} \quad U_0 = U(C, 1 - N) \tag{k}$$

Intuitively, $E(P^e, W, U_0)$ represents the minimum amount of spending on consumption and leisure that gives rise to a certain utility level, U_0, taking as given the (expected) prices of goods and labour. For the utility function (a) we find that:

$$E(P^e, W, U_0) = -\gamma P^e + \left(\frac{P^e}{\beta}\right)^{\beta} \left(\frac{W}{1 - \beta}\right)^{1-\beta} U_0 \tag{l}$$

The expenditure function is an extremely convenient tool because Shephard's lemma tells us that the expression for the Hicksian demand for leisure is obtained by taking the partial derivative of $E(P^e, W, U_0)$ with respect to the price of leisure, W, i.e.:

$$1 - N_c^S \equiv \frac{\partial E(P^e, W, U_0)}{\partial W} = \left(\frac{P^e}{\beta}\right)^{\beta} \left(\frac{W}{1 - \beta}\right)^{-\beta} U_0, \tag{m}$$

where N_c^S is the Hicksian labour supply function. By noting that $w^e \equiv W/P^e$ and simplifying we find:

$$N_c^S = 1 - \left(\frac{1 - \beta}{\beta w^e}\right)^{\beta} U_0. \tag{n}$$

Clearly the Hicksian labour supply function is increasing in w^e. It is left as an exercise for the reader to prove that—in a diagram like Figure 1.4—through a given (w^e, N) point on the Marshallian labour curve passes a corresponding Hicksian labour supply curve that is flatter.

****

Equation (1.11) can be written in a more useful form by writing:

$$W/P = (P^e/P)g(N^S). \tag{1.12}$$

The interpretation is easy. If households overestimate the price level (i.e. $P^e > P$), they will demand a higher real wage for a given level of labour supply than if they had estimated the price level correctly. This is exactly the mechanism behind the Lucas Supply Curve that we discuss in Chapter 5.

1.1.3   Aggregate supply in the goods market: Adaptive expectations

We have developed a logically consistent description of the aggregate labour market consisting of equations (1.7) and (1.12). We must now assume something about the way in which households form their expectations. Since we shall return to this issue in Chapters 4 and 5 in more detail, we simply postulate two alternative assumptions regarding the expected price level: (i) the *adaptive expectations hypothesis* (AEH) and (ii) the *perfect foresight hypothesis* (PFH).

Under the AEH the expected price level is given in the short run, but moves slowly to correct for past expectational errors. Using t as an index for time (e.g.

years), the AEH mechanism is:

$$P_{t+1}^e = P_t + (1 - \lambda) [P_t^e - P_t], \qquad 0 < \lambda < 1. \tag{1.13}$$

This equation says that households expect the price in the future period $t + 1$ to be equal to the actual price in the current period t if their expectations proved correct in the current period. If, instead, they have mis-estimated the price level in the current period ($P_t^e \neq P_t$), they incorporate part of the expectational error in the revision of their expectation in the current period, where λ represents the speed with which households update their price expectations. We find it convenient to use the short-hand notation for the AEH:

$$\Delta P_{t+1}^e = \lambda [P_t - P_t^e], \qquad 0 < \lambda < 1, \qquad \text{(AEH)}, \tag{1.14}$$

where the Δ-operator stands for the change in a variable from one period to the next, i.e. $\Delta P_{t+1}^e \equiv P_{t+1}^e - P_t^e$. Equation (1.14) captures sluggish adjustment of expectations regarding the price level.

The second, diametrically opposed, assumption regarding expectations is the PFH. It simply states that households expect the price level that actually holds:

$$P_t^e = P_t, \qquad \text{(PFH)}. \tag{1.15}$$

The PFH can be seen as the deterministic counterpart to the rational expectations hypothesis (REH) discussed in Chapter 5.

The labour market description can be used, in combination with either the AEH or PFH, to describe the supply curve (AS) on the aggregate goods market. Obviously, the form of this AS curve depends on the particular expectations hypothesis used. We first consider the AS curve under the AEH. This is illustrated in Figure 1.5. Suppose that the initial price level is P_0 and that the expected price level is equal to this, i.e. $P_0^e = P_0$. In that case, households make no expectational error, supply the "correct" amount of labour, labour market equilibrium determines the right amount of employment and the correct real wage, and output is (via the short-run production function) equal to so-called potential output Y^*. In terms of Figure 1.5, north-west panel, the labour supply function (1.11) is given as $W = P_0^e g(N^S)$, and the labour demand function (1.7) is given implicitly by $W = P_0 F_N(N^D, \bar{K})$ (note that we have put the *nominal* wage, W, on the vertical axis). The equilibrium nominal wage is W_0 and employment is N^*, so that $Y^* = F(N^*, \bar{K})$. Now consider a higher actual price level, say P_1. The expected price level is still equal to P_0^e and the labour supply curve is unchanged. The demand for labour shifts up, to $W = P_1 F_N(N^D, \bar{K})$, so that labour market equilibrium is at point A, the nominal wage rate is W_1, employment is N_1 (greater than N^*), and output is Y_1 (greater than Y^*). This yields the second point on the AS curve. Employment and output are larger because the *actual* real wage is lower. This is due to the fact that households have underestimated the price level and consequently overestimated their real wage. Point B corresponds to a lower actual price level and a lower level of aggregate supply of goods; it can be derived in a similar fashion as point A. In the north-east panel of Figure 1.5, the curve labelled AS_{AEH} is upward sloping and passes through points B, E_0, and A.

The AS curve under the PFH is even easier to derive. Expected and actual prices always coincide, so labour supply is always based on the correct information (as is labour demand), employment is always equal to N^*, output is equal to Y^*, and the aggregate supply curve, AS_{PFH}, is vertical. This is also illustrated in Figure 1.5, where the equilibrium points associated with P_1 and P_2 are given by, respectively, points E_1 and E_2.

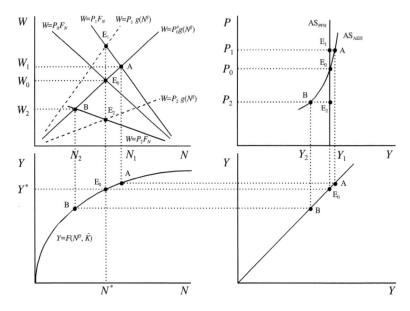

Figure 1.5: Aggregate supply and expectations

Before we move on, we find it instructive to give an analytical derivation of the AS curve. The labour demand and labour supply curves (1.7) and (1.11) may be written in terms of elasticities:

$$\frac{dN^D}{N^D} = \frac{d\bar{K}}{\bar{K}} - \varepsilon_D \left[\frac{dW}{W} - \frac{dP}{P} \right], \tag{1.16}$$

$$\frac{dN^S}{N^S} = \varepsilon_S \left[\frac{dW}{W} - \frac{dP^e}{P^e} \right], \tag{1.17}$$

where $\varepsilon_D \equiv -F_N/(NF_{NN})$ and $\varepsilon_S \equiv g(N)/(Ng_N)$ denote the wage elasticities of labour demand (expressed in absolute value) and labour supply, respectively.[1] We assume that the substitution effect dominates the income effect in labour supply, so that $\varepsilon_S > 0$. We furthermore assume equilibrium on the labour market, $N = N^D = N^S$, so that the above expressions for labour demand and labour supply can be used to solve for the real wage:

$$\frac{dW}{W} - \frac{dP}{P} = \frac{1}{\varepsilon_D + \varepsilon_S} \left[\frac{d\bar{K}}{\bar{K}} - \varepsilon_S \left(\frac{dP}{P} - \frac{dP^e}{P^e} \right) \right]. \tag{1.18}$$

If we substitute this result into the labour demand schedule and subsequently into the differentiated production function,

$$\frac{dY}{Y} = \frac{F_N}{Y}dN + \frac{F_K}{Y}d\bar{K} = \omega_N \frac{dN}{N} + (1 - \omega_N)\frac{d\bar{K}}{\bar{K}}, \tag{1.19}$$

where $\omega_N \equiv WN/PY$ stands for the national income share of wages, we obtain an expression for the relative change in the aggregate supply of goods:

$$\frac{dY}{Y} = \frac{\omega_N \varepsilon_D \varepsilon_S}{\varepsilon_D + \varepsilon_S} \left(\frac{dP}{P} - \frac{dP^e}{P^e} \right) + \frac{(1 - \omega_N)\varepsilon_D + \varepsilon_S}{\varepsilon_D + \varepsilon_S} \frac{d\bar{K}}{\bar{K}}, \quad \text{(AS)}. \tag{1.20}$$

---

[1]In the derivation of (1.16) we have made use of the following property of linear homogeneous production functions: $KF_{NK} = -NF_{NN}$. See Intermezzo 4.3 in Chapter 4 on production theory for further properties.

Ceteris paribus, a bigger capital stock boosts the marginal productivity of labour and thus the real wage. This attenuates the rise in the aggregate supply of goods. Anticipated price changes ($dP^e/P^e = dP/P$) do not affect real wages, employment, or the aggregate supply of goods. Unanticipated price changes, however, do affect these variables. For example, if the actual price level turns out to be bigger than the expected price level, the real wage falls and thus employment and the aggregate supply of output rise.

Expression (1.20) corresponds to the AS curve derived graphically in Figure 1.5. As we have derived above, under the PFH we clearly have a vertical AS curve which shifts to the right if the capital stock expands. Under the AEH, the expected price level is fixed in the short run so that the AS curve slopes upwards. In this case, the AS curve also shifts to the right if the capital stock rises. Over time, expectations regarding the price level may be adjusted which leads to shifts in the AS curve. For example, if in any period the actual price level rises above the expected price level, in subsequent periods the expected price level will be revised upwards. This lowers the purchasing power households expect from their wage income, so households decide to work fewer hours. This induces a rise in the real wage and thus a fall in labour demand and employment. Consequently, aggregate supply of output falls. This argument shows why a rise in the expected price level shifts the AS curve to the left.

1.1.4 Nominal wage rigidities

As we have seen above, the AEH assumption ensures that the nominal price level affects aggregate supply in the economy. We now consider an alternative assumption. Modigliani (1944) demonstrated that there is a way in which an upward-sloping (segment of the) aggregate supply curve can be generated even if we adopt the PFH. Modigliani assumes that *nominal* wages are inflexible downwards, but perfectly flexible in the upward direction. Workers hate wage cuts, but love a rise. In Figure 1.6, we assume that the rigid nominal wage is equal to W_0 and that P_0 is the price level at which full employment holds. We assume the PFH (1.15). The situation for price levels exceeding P_0 is straightforward. The nominal wage rises to keep the real wage constant and maintain full employment. The situation is different for a lower price level than P_0, however. For example, if $P = P_2$, the demand for labour is given by $W = P_2 F_N(N^D, \bar{K})$, but the effective supply of labour is the horizontal line segment $W_0 C$. Since we assume that the nominal wage rate is not allowed to fall, employment equals $N_2 (< N^*)$ and there are $N_2^S - N_2$ units of labour unemployed. By not allowing their wages to fall in nominal terms, the households end up partially pricing themselves out of the labour market.

1.2 Aggregate demand: Review of the IS-LM model

From our first-year course in macroeconomics, we recall that the demand side of the economy can be described by means of the IS-LM model. For the closed economy this model can be written as:

$$Y = C + I + G, \tag{1.21}$$

$$C = C(Y - T), \qquad 0 < C_{Y-T} < 1, \tag{1.22}$$

$$I = I(R), \qquad I_R < 0, \tag{1.23}$$

$$T = T(Y), \qquad 0 < T_Y < 1, \tag{1.24}$$

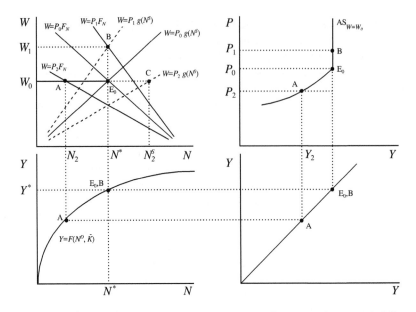

Figure 1.6: Aggregate supply with downward nominal wage rigidity

$$M/P = l(Y, R), \qquad l_Y > 0, \quad l_R \leq 0, \tag{1.25}$$

where I is investment, G is government spending, T represents taxes, and R is the rate of interest. Equation (1.21) is the usual national income accounting identity, (1.22) is the consumption function expressing C as a function of disposable income, $Y - T$, where C_{Y-T} denotes the marginal propensity to consume (MPC, in short) out of disposable income. The investment equation is given in (1.23). A higher rate of interest means that the cost of capital is high, leading entrepreneurs to lower the level of investment. Equation (1.24) shows that tax receipts depend on the level of income generated in the economy; T_Y stands for the marginal tax rate. Equations (1.21)–(1.24) implicitly define the IS curve, that is the combinations of R and Y for which there exists spending equilibrium. Finally, equation (1.25) is the money market equilibrium condition, equating the real money supply, M/P, to the real demand for money. This last schedule has proved a real bone of contention between the different schools of thought in macroeconomics, and consequently it warrants some further discussion.

1.2.1 The demand for money

Why do people hold money, even though it does not pay any interest? This is one of the unresolved questions in macroeconomic theory. Over the centuries, some of the finest minds in economics have broken their heads over this issue, and some (partial) answers are indeed available. Keynes claimed that the money theory proposed in his *General Theory* represented a radical break with the traditional wisdom of his days. In this section we show in what sense Keynes may have meant this statement.

    There are two main motives for holding money balances, the *transactions motive* and the *speculative motive*. The transactions motive runs as follows. People like to consume goods steadily over the course of the month (say), but usually only get their income paid once a month or once a week. Since cash is used as payment in many transactions, people need a certain amount of cash during the period in between pay cheques. They could, of course, put their income in the bank in an interest-earning savings account and get the necessary amount needed for transactions each day (hour, minute, second?), but that would involve a lot of trips to the bank and involve substantial transaction costs and a loss of valuable leisure time. A more reasonable approach would be for the households to decide on an optimal cash management problem: choose the number of trips to the bank such that the marginal costs and benefits of the savings account are equated. Out of this cash management problem we would certainly obtain an interest sensitivity of money demand, since interest represents the income foregone when wealth is held in the form of money. We would also expect that the transactions demand for money would depend positively on the real stream of transactions that the household wishes to conduct. Economy-wide we can proxy this effect on real money demand with the specification (1.25).

Intermezzo 1.3

Baumol's transactions theory of the demand for money. Let k be the number of transactions per period (month or week), so that average money holdings are given by $M/P = \frac{1}{2}Y/k$. Households choose the number of transactions and thus average money holdings by minimizing the sum of foregone interest on money holdings (the opportunity cost) and transactions costs: $\frac{1}{2}RY/k + ck$, where c denotes the cost per transaction (bank costs plus leisure time). Minimization by choice of k yields the first-order condition:

$$-\frac{RY}{2k^2} + c = 0.$$

The second-order condition is $RY/k^3 > 0$, confirming that the optimum is indeed a minimum. The first-order condition implies the following optimum number of transactions and demand for money:

$$k = \sqrt{\frac{RY}{2c}}, \quad \frac{M}{P} = \frac{Y}{2k} = \sqrt{\frac{cY}{2R}}.$$

Hence, the higher the cost per transaction, c, and the lower the opportunity cost of holding money, R, the higher the demand for real money balances. Money demand rises with the square root of income and is proportional to the price level.

****

Another motive for holding money that was stressed by Keynes is the so-called speculative motive (called "the demand for money to hold as an asset" by Modigliani (1944)). Money has two important properties: it is very liquid, and it is risk free in the absence of inflation (a euro is still a euro tomorrow). Other assets such as shares and bonds fluctuate in value (even in real terms, once corrected for inflation) and are hence both more risky and less liquid. Keynes (and Modigliani, 1944) suggests regressive expectations as a rationale behind the liquidity preference. The story runs as follows. If the rate of interest is very low then prices of bonds are very high (the price

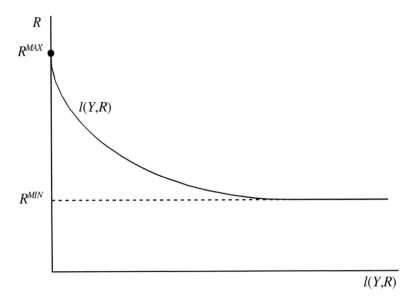

Figure 1.7: The liquidity preference function

of a consol that pays 1 euro indefinitely is $P_B = (1+R)^{-1} + (1+R)^{-2} + \cdots = 1/R$. Hence, bond prices and interest rates move in opposite directions). Investors expect that high prices of bonds cannot persist forever, and thus anticipate that bond prices will fall (P_B falls, or R rises). In other words, they expect a capital loss on bonds, which prompts them to hold most of their wealth in the form of money (we take into account the differences in riskiness of money and bonds to avoid the conclusion that the agents choose a corner solution: either all money or all bonds). The speculative demand for money thus motivated depends negatively on the interest rate, i.e. $l_R \le 0$.

Keynes suggested that, for a given output level Y, the liquidity preference function $l(Y, R)$ may have the form as drawn in Figure 1.7. If the rate of interest is very high ($R \ge R^{MAX}$), households will not hold any cash for speculative purposes. Bond prices are very low and capital gains on bonds are expected. So why hold money? On the other hand, Keynes argued, if the rate of interest is very low ($R \le R^{MIN}$) then people would become indifferent between holding their wealth in terms of money or bonds. The liquidity preference function would become perfectly elastic at that minimum rate of interest, R^{MIN}. This is called the liquidity trap, the consequences of which are studied below.

1.2.2 The IS-LM model

The money market is represented by equation (1.25). The LM curve represents all combinations of output Y and the rate of interest R for which the money market is in equilibrium. Formally, the properties of the LM curve can be found by using the implicit function trick once again:

$$d(M/P) = l_Y dY + l_R dR \qquad \Rightarrow \qquad dR = \frac{d(M/P) - l_Y dY}{l_R}. \tag{1.26}$$

The slope of the LM curve is thus $-l_Y/l_R \ge 0$, while the effect of the real money supply on the rate of interest is equal to $1/l_R \le 0$. Graphically, the LM curve is

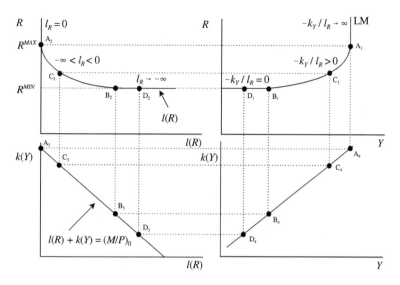

Figure 1.8: Derivation of the LM curve

derived as in Figure 1.8.[2] In that figure, the LM curve in the top right-hand panel is obtained by trying different interest rates and completing the dotted rectangles. For example, for $R = R^{MAX}$, the relevant rectangle is made up of points $A_1 A_2 A_3 A_4$.

We have shown with equation (1.26) that the LM curve, typically, slopes upwards and shifts to the right if real money balances expand. A higher interest rate lowers money demand, so national income must be higher to boost money demand back to the unchanged level of money supply. A higher money supply or a lower price level pushes up bond prices and thus lowers the interest rate. We note that the LM curve is vertical for high rates of interest, and horizontal for low rates of interest (provided we accept Keynes' liquidity preference function as drawn in Figure 1.7).

The IS curve represents combinations of output Y and the rate of interest R for which there exists aggregate spending balance. Formally, by using equations (1.21)–(1.24) we derive the IS curve as follows:

$$Y = C(Y - T(Y)) + I(R) + G \quad \Rightarrow$$
$$dY = C_{Y-T}(1 - T_Y)dY + I_R dR + dG, \tag{1.27}$$

or, after rearranging:

$$dY = \frac{dG + I_R dR}{1 - C_{Y-T}(1 - T_Y)}. \tag{1.28}$$

Increasing government spending stimulates output for a given level of the interest rate. Students are invited to derive the IS curve graphically as well.

1.2.3 The AD curve

As we know from first-year courses in macroeconomics, the demand side of the economy is in equilibrium if there is simultaneous spending and money market

---

[2]For the special case where the demand for money is additively separable and can be written as $k(Y) + l(R)$. This assumption facilitates the graphical derivation of the LM curve because it allows us to place $k(Y)$ and $l(R)$ in separate panels in Figure 1.8.

equilibrium. This demand-side equilibrium corresponds to the intersection of the IS and LM curves and is summarized by the AD curve, that is those combinations of output Y and the price level P for which there is money market equilibrium and spending equilibrium. By using (1.26) and (1.28), the expression for the AD curve can be obtained:

$$dY = \frac{dG + (I_R/l_R)(M/P)[dM/M - dP/P]}{1 - C_{Y-T}(1 - T_Y) + l_Y I_R/l_R}, \qquad \text{(AD)}. \qquad (1.29)$$

The AD curve can also be derived graphically. This is left as an exercise for the students.

The intuition is as follows. A higher price level erodes the real value of money balances and thus exerts an upward pressure on the interest rate. This depresses aggregate investment and thus lowers the aggregate demand for goods. Consequently, the AD curve generally slopes downwards. A higher level of public spending or a boost to the nominal money supply boosts aggregate demand and thus shifts out the AD curve. The former case induces a rise, while the latter case a fall, in the interest rate.

1.2.4   Effectiveness of fiscal policy

The output multiplier for public spending given in equation (1.28) equals the inverse of the marginal propensity to save out of income plus the marginal tax rate, i.e. $1/[1 - C_{Y-T}(1 - T_Y)]$, and thus exceeds unity.[3] This multiplier is relevant when the interest rate is exogenous (i.e., when we consider only the IS curve) or if investment does not depend on the interest rate. It was first derived by a colleague of John Maynard Keynes, namely Richard Kahn (1931). An instructive way to write this multiplier is as follows:

$$\frac{dY}{dG} = 1 + C_{Y-T}(1 - T_Y) + C_{Y-T}^2(1 - T_Y)^2 + C_{Y-T}^3(1 - T_Y)^3 + \cdots$$
$$= \frac{1}{1 - C_{Y-T}(1 - T_Y)}. \qquad (1.30)$$

Let us assume for the sake of argument a marginal propensity to consume of three quarters ($C_{Y-T} = 3/4$) and a marginal tax rate of one third ($T_Y = 1/3$). The impact effect of a one million euro bond-financed increase in public spending yields a one million euro increase in aggregate demand and national income. Of that increase in national income one sixth of a million is saved and another one third of a million is taken by the tax men. The remainder, i.e. half a million euros, is consumed and is the second-round boost to national income. Of that second-round boost one twelfth of a million is saved and one sixth of a million is brought to the tax men. A quarter of a million is left for consumption and induces the third-round boost to national income. This multiplier process is continued *ad infinitum* leading to a total increase in national income of two million euros (namely $1 + 0.5 + 0.25 + 0.125 + \cdots$) and corresponding to a Kahn multiplier of two. Hence, for every euro pumped by the government into the economy, national income expands by two euros.

---

[3]Since C_{Y-T} and T_Y are both between zero and one, it follows that $0 < C_{Y-T}(1 - T_Y) < 1$ so that the multiplier exceeds unity. Aggregate saving is defined as $S(Y) \equiv Y - C(Y - T(Y)) - T(Y)$ so that the marginal propensity to save out of income equals $S_Y \equiv (1 - T_Y)(1 - C_{Y-T})$, which clearly satisfies $0 < S_Y < 1$. The savings identity furthermore implies that $(1 - T_Y)C_{Y-T} \equiv 1 - (S_Y + T_Y)$, from which it follows that $0 < S_Y + T_Y < 1$. The multiplier can thus also be written as $dY/dG = 1/(S_Y + T_Y)$.

The magnitude of the Kahn multiplier is smaller if saving leakage and tax leakage are substantial, that is if the marginal propensity to consume is small and the marginal tax rate is large. For example, if the marginal tax rate is zero, the multiplier is four instead of two. For a small open economy, this multiplier is smaller again if there is a lot of import leakage (see Chapter 2).

Expression (1.29) shows the Keynesian multiplier for a bond-financed rise in public spending, which is relevant when the interest rate is endogenous (i.e., when we consider both the IS and the LM curve) and the price level is rigid (at least in the short run). This multiplier is thus only relevant under the assumption of sticky prices. The Keynesian multiplier is smaller in magnitude than the Kahn multiplier given by expression (1.30) on account of crowding out of private investment. This is captured by the additional positive term $l_Y I_R / l_R$ in the denominator of the Keynesian multiplier. The intuition is as follows. A bond-financed rise in public spending leads to a greater supply of government bonds and thus exerts a downward pressure on bond prices and an upward pressure on interest rates. This leads to a fall in private investment and a fall in aggregate demand and employment, so that the Keynesian multiplier is smaller in magnitude than the Kahn multiplier. The extent of crowding out is more significant if private investment is very sensitive to changes in the interest rate ($|I_R|$ large) while money demand is not very sensitive ($|l_R|$ small) to changes in the interest rate and sensitive to changes in national income (l_Y large).

1.3   Schools in macroeconomics

We now have all the ingredients that are needed to characterize the different schools of thought in macroeconomics. We briefly distinguish: (1) the classical economists, (2) the Keynesians, (3) proponents of the neo-Keynesian synthesis, (4) the monetarists, (5) the new classical economists, (6) the supply siders, and last but not least (7) the new Keynesians.

1.3.1   Classical economists

Names that spring to mind are Adam Smith [1723–1790], David Hume [1711–1776], David Ricardo [1772–1823], John Stuart Mill [1806–1873], Knut Wicksell [1851–1926], Irving Fisher [1867–1947], and Keynes [1883–1946] in the *Treatise on Money* of 1930. We can roughly characterize the classical view on money by the crude quantity theory of money. In terms of our model, the LM curve (1.25) is replaced by a special case in which money demand does not depend on the interest rate:

$$M = kPY. \tag{1.31}$$

Hence, there is no reason to hold money for speculative purposes ($l_R \equiv 0$), and the velocity of circulation, $1/k$, is constant. The classical view regarding the supply side of the economy is characterized by a strong belief in markets and the efficacy of the price mechanism. In terms of our model, this implies flexible wages and prices, perfect foresight, labour market clearing, and a vertical AS curve. See Figure 1.9. Hence, fiscal and monetary policy cannot affect the levels of employment and output.

The classical model can be seen as a special case of the IS-LM-AS model developed above, with $l_Y = k =$ constant and $l_R = 0$. This means that the LM curve is vertical, so that fiscal policy is useless in affecting employment and output. Increasing government spending leads to a higher rate of interest and full crowding out of private investment, but not to changes in the price level. Monetary policy, on

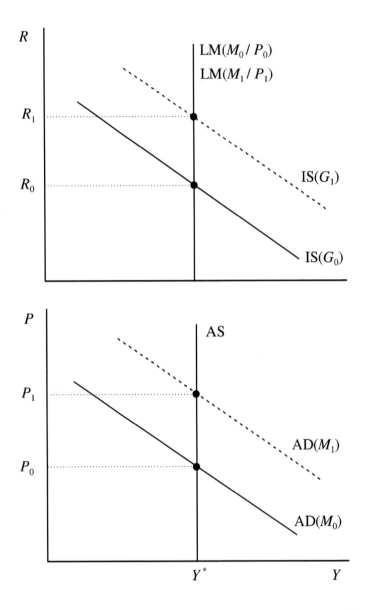

Figure 1.9: Monetary and fiscal policy in the classical model

the other hand, has no effects on the real sphere of the economy, and only leads to a higher price level. This property is called the neutrality of monetary policy. The classical economists thus believed in a dichotomy: the real and monetary sectors could essentially be studied separately. Demand-side policies merely affect the interest rate and/or the price level, while supply-side policies affect the real wage, employment, and output.

1.3.2   Keynesians

Will we ever know what Keynes really meant when he wrote the *General Theory*? Probably not, but a number of insights into what Keynes may have meant can be obtained by following Modigliani's (1944) suggestion that the main Keynesian innovations consist of the liquidity preference schedule and the assumption of nominal wage rigidity.

With respect to his liquidity preference theory of money, Keynes himself used the classical economists as scapegoats. In doing so, he used the gimmick of the liquidity trap. Suppose, Keynes argued, that the rate of interest is so low that the economy is on the horizontal part of the LM curve. Suppose, furthermore, that the level of spending at that interest rate is too low to support full employment of the factors of production, and that prices and wages are flexible. In terms of Figure 1.10, the rate of interest is R^{MIN}, and output is $Y_0 < Y^*$. Keynes came to the startling conclusion that the classical model is inconsistent in that case. Aggregate supply is vertical at $Y = Y^*$, but demand falls short of Y^*, and no amount of price/wage reductions will restore equilibrium. The self-correcting feature of the market, which is of course the hallmark of classical theory, simply does not work.

Monetary policy will not help, according to Keynes, because the additional money will simply be absorbed by investors with no noticeable effect on the interest rate. Fiscal policy, on the other hand, will work really well. In terms of Figure 1.10, the additional government spending will stimulate aggregate demand (corresponding to a shift in the IS curve) and hence employment and output.

Nowadays, the liquidity trap is seen as a nice way to get people to take notice of the Keynesian ideas. In fact, Keynes' classical colleague and contemporary, A. C. Pigou, quickly pointed out that Keynes' inconsistency result disappears once a wealth effect is introduced in the consumption function. In that case, the position of the IS curve will depend on real money balances M/P, the AD curve will slope downwards (and not be vertical, as Keynes suggested), and full employment will be restored provided prices and wages are flexible.

1.3.3   The neo-Keynesian synthesis

The neo-Keynesian synthesis was developed by neoclassical economists who allowed for a short run with Keynesian properties and a long run with classical properties. Since it contains classical and Keynesian elements, the approach is often referred to as the neoclassical synthesis. Names of neo-Keynesian synthesizers: Franco Modigliani [1918–2003], Paul Samuelson [1915–2009], James Tobin [1918–2002], Robert Solow [1924–], and in the 1950s and 1960s virtually all macroeconomists *except* Milton Friedman [1912–2006]. There are actually different versions of the neo-Keynesian synthesis, depending on the assumption made about the labour market. The first version maintains (as does Modigliani, 1944) that nominal wages are rigid downwards. This opens up the possibility of unemployment and an upward sloping section of the AS curve (see section 1.1.4 and Figure 1.6). To get some adjustment

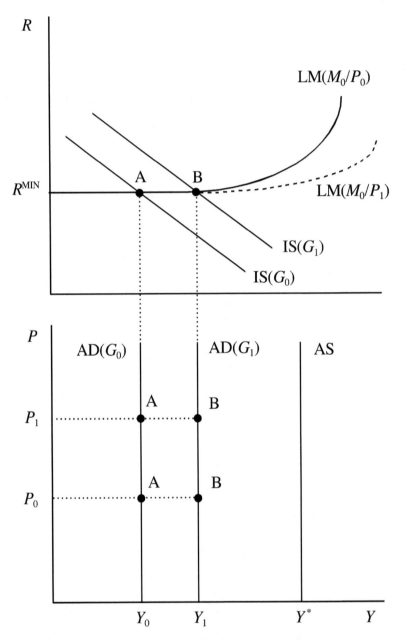

Figure 1.10: Monetary and fiscal policy in the Keynesian model

over time, we add a Phillips curve relationship to the model, i.e. $\dot{W} = \alpha u$ ($\alpha < 0$), where u is unemployment, defined as $u \equiv (N^S - N)/N^S$. Introduction of a Phillips curve thus makes the change in nominal wages dependent on the amount of unemployment. As a result, full employment will be restored after some time.

The second version of the neoclassical synthesis allows nominal wages to be fully flexible, but uses the AEH (1.14) to make the expected price level a slowly moving variable. The model corresponding to the neo-Keynesian synthesis corresponds to the AS curve (1.20), the AD curve (1.29), and the AEH (1.14). Again, full employment will eventually be restored, depending on the speed at which agents adapt to expectational errors. The effects of fiscal and monetary policy are illustrated in Figure 1.11. A bond-financed rise in public spending from G_0 to G_1 induces an outward shift of the IS curve and thus the AD curve. On impact, output rises above Y^* even though there is some crowding out of private investment on account of the rise in the rate of interest. The impact multiplier is, in fact, smaller than the Keynesian multiplier contained in expression (1.29). The reason is that the rise in aggregate demand caused by the increase in public spending causes the price level to rise from P_0 to P_1 on impact (through an upward move along the initial aggregate supply curve, AS($P^e = P_0$)). The higher price level induces a contraction in the supply of real money balances and thus causes a rise in the interest rate and a fall in aggregate demand (associated with the backward shift in the LM curve). Consequently, the short-run multiplier is smaller than the Keynesian multiplier. We thus conclude that the short-run employment and output multipliers for a bond-financed rise in public spending are lower if saving, tax, and import leakages are substantial, crowding out of private investment is substantial, and the price level rises a lot. The short-run effects on employment and output are small if the AD curve is relatively flat and the AS curve is relatively steep. In subsequent periods, households revise their expectations regarding the price level upwards. This lowers the expected real wage and the supply of labour. Hence, the AS curve shifts backwards over time until output and employment are cut back to their equilibrium levels. The long-run effect of the fiscal expansion is thus merely a rise in the price level with no effect on employment or output.

Figure 1.11 may also be used to investigate the effects of an expansion of the nominal money supply from M_0 to M_1 under the AEH. The outward shift of the LM curve lowers the interest rate and pushes up aggregate demand. Consequently, the AD curve shifts out. On impact the price level also rises, which attenuates the rise in national income. Over time the expected price level is revised upwards, and the AS curve shifts to the left until the original equilibrium of employment and output are reached again. In the short run a monetary expansion thus induces a boom in employment and output and a fall in the interest rate, but in the long run employment and output are unaffected and the price level rises in proportion with the rise in the nominal money supply. Although money is not neutral in the short run, it is neutral in the long run.

1.3.4 The monetarists

Names: Milton Friedman [1912–2006] and his friends. They assumed that the interest sensitivity of investment is very high (i.e. $|I_R|$ large) so that the IS curve is very flat. Consequently, fiscal policy leads to strong crowding out of private investment. Furthermore, the monetarists, like the classical economists, had strong sympathy for the quantity theory of money which implies a steep or vertical LM curve. In contrast to the classical economists, Friedman does *not* accept the REH. Instead, he adopted the AEH. Fiscal policy is, under monetarist assumptions, unable to influence em-

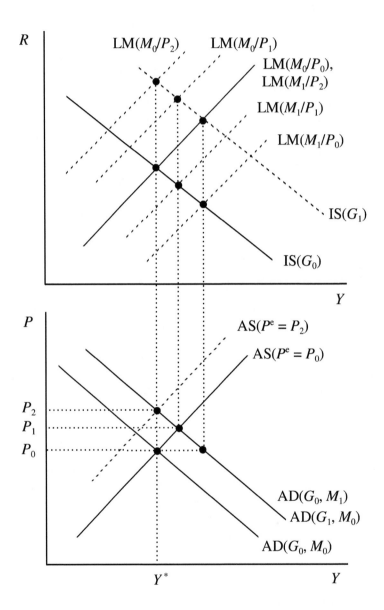

Figure 1.11: Monetary and fiscal policy in the neo-Keynesian synthesis model

ployment and output. This is why the monetarists were so vehemently against the Keynesians who believed in pump priming the economy in recessions.

Undoubtedly, the monetarists' assumptions imply that monetary policy has real effects. Indeed, from the quantity theory we have $M = kPY$, so that $dM > 0$ implies that $dPY = (1/k)dM > 0$. The distribution of the total effect (dPY) over real effects (dY) and nominal effects (dP) depends on the assumptions made about the labour market and the formation of expectations. Under the AEH there are temporary effects on real output. The policy maker may therefore be tempted to use a monetary expansion to combat unemployment. According to the monetarists, however, policy makers are typically not very good at timing monetary policy. There are long and variable time lags before a macroeconomic problem is recognized, before an appropriate macroeconomic policy is implemented, and before a policy has the required effect. As a result, monetary policy can actually accentuate business cycle fluctuations in the economy (if the policy is set too late, for example). This is why Friedman (1968) suggests that the central bank should follow a constant growth rule for some monetary aggregate and not tinker with monetary policy in order to try to influence aggregate demand and employment.

1.3.5 New classical economists

Names: Robert Lucas [1937–], Thomas Sargent [1943–], Robert Barro [1944–], and Edward Prescott [1940–]. Natural successors of the classical economists. These modern day classical economists stress mathematical techniques and are called "fresh water" economists, because they work (or used to) at universities near the big lakes in the Mid West (Chicago, Carnegie-Mellon, Minneapolis) and should be contrasted with the more Keynesian, "salt water" economists who work at US universities on the East Coast (Harvard, MIT, Yale, Princeton).

These new classical economists have shed themselves more thoroughly of the neo-Keynesian synthesis than the monetarists, and firmly back classical ideas such as flexible prices and wages, rational expectations or perfect foresight, the efficiency of the market, and full employment. All fluctuations that we observe in the economy are due not to nominal rigidities but to rational agents responding to the incentives as they observe them. Strong endorsement of rational expectations and microeconomic underpinning of macroeconomic relations, such as the consumption function, the investment function, and the labour market. An early gimmick that was used to get the profession's attention was the so-called policy ineffectiveness proposition (PIP), according to which the policy maker either cannot (strong PIP) or should not (weak PIP) use countercyclical policy–see also the discussion of the classical proposition that monetary policy is neutral at the end of section 1.3.1. This school of thought will be discussed in more detail in Chapter 5.

1.3.6 Supply siders

Names: Arthur Laffer [1940–] and Robert Mundell [1932–]. These are radical conservatives who despise government intervention in markets and emphasize the distorting effects of taxation, beautifully criticized by Krugman (1994). Their policy advice was quite simple: cut tax rates and thus stimulate the economy. They argued that there was no need to cut government spending because the tax cut would pay for itself. Reagan loved the story, especially as it suggested that you could have your cake and eat it: no need to restrain public spending on defence while having an excuse to substantially cut the tax rate.

The central element was the so-called Laffer curve, first drawn on the back of an envelope. This Laffer curve can be derived from a small modification of our model of the labour market, namely equations (1.7) and (1.12). Assume that there is only one tax, levied on labour income and paid by households, denoted by t_L, and that there is perfect foresight (so that $P^e = P$). The labour market model is then given by:

$$(1 - t_L)W/P = g(N^S), \qquad W/P = F_N(N^D, \bar{K}), \qquad N^D = N^S = N. \qquad (1.32)$$

It is easy to see (from (1.12)) that $1 - t_L$ plays the same role as P/P^e in the expression for the AS curve (1.20). Ignoring potential tax effects on capital accumulation (and setting $d\bar{K}/\bar{K} = 0$) we can write the relative change in national income as:

$$\frac{dY}{Y} = -\frac{\omega_N \varepsilon_D \varepsilon_S}{\varepsilon_D + \varepsilon_S} \frac{dt_L}{1 - t_L}. \qquad (1.33)$$

This expression can be used to find the relative change in revenue from the tax on labour in real terms (i.e. $T \equiv t_L WN/P = t_L \omega_N Y$):

$$\frac{dT}{Y} \equiv \omega_N \left(dt_L + t_L \frac{dY}{Y} \right) = \omega_N \left[dt_L - t_L \frac{\omega_N \varepsilon_D \varepsilon_S}{\varepsilon_D + \varepsilon_S} \frac{dt_L}{1 - t_L} \right], \qquad (1.34)$$

where we assume that the share of labour in value added (ω_N) is constant (i.e., $d\omega_N = 0$) as will be the case for a Cobb-Douglas production function (see Intermezzo 1.1). The first term within square brackets on the right-hand side shows the direct revenue (also called the tax-rate) effect of the labour tax for a given level of wage income. The second term within square brackets on the right-hand side shows the tax-base effect. If the labour tax rate is increased and labour supply slopes upwards ($\varepsilon_S > 0$), then labour supply and employment decrease. Hence, labour tax revenue will fall as well. We note that, for small labour tax rates ($t_L \approx 0$), the (negative) tax-base effect is dominated by the (positive) tax-rate effect on public revenue so that public revenue increases with the tax rate.

For large labour tax rates, however, the (positive) tax-rate effect can be dominated by the (negative) tax-base effect, especially if labour demand and labour supply are very elastic. In that case, labour tax revenue declines as the tax rate increases. Conversely, cutting the labour tax rate may actually boost revenue. Similar reasoning led Laffer to suggest that the revenue function would look like a parabola: for high tax rates the disincentive effect of the tax would be so strong that revenue would actually decline as the tax rate is increased further. This occurs beyond point A in Figure 1.12 at which tax revenue is maximized. If the tax rate is small, e.g. at point B, a rise in the tax rate boosts public revenue. Beyond point A, say at point C, a *reduction* in the tax rate would lead to an *increase* in tax revenue. Clearly, when the tax rate is zero or unity, tax revenue is zero.

Although Laffer's advice itself is logically consistent and appeals to wishful thinkers, it was empirically irrelevant: the US economy was at a point like B in Figure 1.12. As a result, huge deficits and a massive build-up of government debt occurred despite substantial tax cuts in the US during the Reagan years.

1.3.7 New Keynesians

Names: (1970s) George Akerlof [1940–], Edmund Phelps [1933–], John B. Taylor [1946–], Stanley Fischer [1943–], (1980s) Olivier-Jean Blanchard [1948–], Michael Woodford [1955–], and Greg Mankiw [1958–]. These are "salt water" economists who

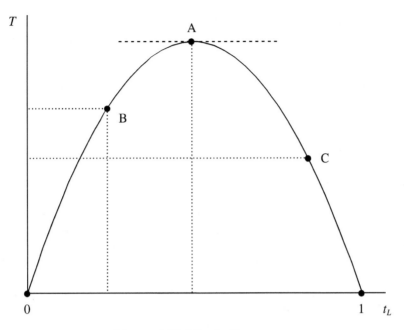

Figure 1.12: The Laffer curve

derive their main inspiration from the insights of John Maynard Keynes. Markets may not be as perfect as the classical economists suggest. Early new Keynesians accepted the REH but stressed the existence of nominal rigidities, arising from, for example, multi-period nominal wage contracts. Such rigidities invalidate the PIP of the new classical economists. Hence, new Keynesians argue that the government can and should stabilize the economy, even under REH.

The most recent wave of new Keynesian economics is more micro-based. The predominance of imperfect competition, coordination failures, and credit restrictions are stressed. Although it is too early to call in the jury for a verdict, it is clear that this is a very promising avenue of research. Chapter 11 gives some of the details.

1.4 Punchlines

In a closed economy, aggregate demand effects can be found with the aid of the IS-LM model (open economy issues are studied in Chapter 2). A rise in public spending sets in motion a multiplier process which leads to a larger rise in national income. However, the multiplier process is dampened by saving and tax leakages. In addition, there is crowding out of private investment on account of the higher interest rate. An expansion of the nominal money supply or a fall in the aggregate price level also increases aggregate demand and employment. In this case the interest rate falls so that private investment is boosted.

Aggregate supply is essentially determined by equilibrium in the labour market. Labour demand rises if there is a cut in the real wage or a boost to the capital stock. The wage elasticity of labour supply is positive if the substitution effect dominates the income effect in labour supply. Labour supply slopes downwards in the opposite case, with the income effect dominating the substitution effect. Due to asymmetry in information, firms observe the wages to be paid to workers while households have to form expectations regarding the aggregate price level when deciding on their labour supply. Hence, equilibrium employment and the aggregate supply of goods rises if the capital stock expands, the labour income tax falls, and if there is an unanticipated rise in the price level.

Macroeconomic equilibrium occurs when aggregate demand and aggregate supply of goods match up. The easiest case is the one assumed by classical economists: a quick clearing of all markets and perfect foresight. In that case, monetary policy is neutral in the sense that it cannot affect the real wage, employment, or output, neither in the short nor in the long run. A doubling of the money supply simply leads to a doubling of the aggregate price level. A fiscal expansion is fully crowded out by a fall in private investment on account of a rise in the interest rate, so that neither employment nor output is affected. Hence, only supply-side policies, such as changes in the capital stock or in the various tax rates, can affect employment and output. Modern day versions of the classical economists are the new classicals, also called the "fresh water" economists, who stress rational expectations in stochastic environments and microeconomic foundations of macroeconomic relationships. A related breed of macroeconomists are the supply siders who believe in cutting taxes as this would boost tax revenue and alleviate the need to cut public spending. The supply siders were very influential in the 1980s, but have largely been discredited.

The older variety of Keynesian economists assumed sticky prices in the short run, so that employment and output were mainly determined by aggregate demand in the short run. A recent school of new Keynesians give the microeconomic underpinnings by stressing imperfect competition, coordination failures, and credit restrictions. The neo-Keynesian synthesis allows for a Keynesian short run and classical long run by introducing the assumption of adaptive expectations regarding the price level. In the short run the multiplier associated with a fiscal expansion is further reduced due to the rise in the price level. This leads to a contraction in real money balances, a further rise in the interest rate, and thus a dampening of the expansion in aggregate demand. Over time households revise their expectations upwards. As a result, aggregate supply and employment fall until the original equilibrium is restored again. The long-run output and employment multipliers for a rise in government spending are thus zero because any expansion of aggregate demand is fully offset by reductions in private investment caused by a higher interest rate.

Monetarists are somewhere in between the classical and Keynesian economists. They allow for adaptive expectations, but believe in the ineffectiveness of fiscal policy and the potential harmfulness of using monetary policy to manage aggregate demand. Monetarists believe in long and variable time lags in monetary policy and therefore advocate a constant and modest rate of monetary growth. Clearly, monetarists are also deeply suspicious of using fiscal policy to fight unemployment.

Further reading

The classic statement of the IS-LM model is presented by Hicks (1937). Mathematical treatments of the IS-LM approach published in the 1970s include Branson (1972), Burrows and Hitiris (1974), and Turnovsky (1977). Even at present, most intermediate textbooks still contain a thorough discussion of the IS-LM model. The ones we are familiar with are: Burda and Wyplosz (2005), Mankiw (2007), Blanchard (2006), Carlin and Soskice (2006), Gärtner (2016), and Abel and Bernanke (2005). The expectations-augmented Phillips curve was proposed independently by Friedman (1968) and Phelps (1967). Phelps et al. (1970) is a classic collection of the first wave of articles aiming to improve the microeconomic foundations of macroeconomics. Gordon (1974) presents a nice overview of the discussion between the monetarist Friedman and his various critics. Students interested in the historical aspects of the quantity theory of money should consult Laidler (1991). Feldstein (1986) presents an interesting discussion of supply side economics. Mankiw and Romer (1991) present a number of key articles in the new Keynesian school. To celebrate the arrival of a new millennium a number of very interesting articles have appeared giving an overview of twentieth century developments in macro–see Blanchard (2000) and Woodford (1999). Snowdon, Vane, and Wynarczyk (1994) also present a good overview of the various schools of thought. Klamer (1984) contains interviews with some of the principal new classical economists and some critics of this approach. Students interested in a thorough treatment of labour demand should refer to Hamermesh (1993). Recently, a large literature has been developed on learning and expectations formation. An excellent but rather advanced textbook on this material is the one by Evans and Honkapohja (2001).

Chapter 2

The open economy

The purpose of this chapter is to discuss the following issues:

1. How do we add the international sector to the IS-LM model?

2. What is the Mundell-Fleming contribution?

3. What are the implications of openness on the effects of fiscal and monetary policy? How do the degree of capital mobility and the exchange rate system affect the conclusions?

4. How can we introduce short-run aggregate supply into the open economy model?

5. How are shocks transmitted across countries?

2.1   Some international bookkeeping

From national income accounting principles we know that for the open economy aggregate output can be written as:

$$Y \equiv C + I + G + (EX - IM), \tag{2.1}$$

where Y is aggregate output, C is private consumption, I is investment, G is government consumption, EX are exports, and IM are imports. Aggregate spending by domestic residents is called *absorption* and is defined as $A \equiv C + I + G$. Exports are added to domestic absorption in the calculation of aggregate output because foreigners also spend on our goods, but imports must be deducted because what we import (i.e. parts of C, I, and G) does not lead to domestic production.

In view of the definition of absorption A, equation (2.1) can also be written as:

$$Y \equiv A + (EX - IM), \tag{2.2}$$

which says that income equals aggregate spending by domestic residents plus *net* exports (the term in brackets).

We also recall that aggregate output in an economy can be measured in different manners. Particularly, total output produced within the country is measured by gross domestic product (GDP), whereas total output produced by residents of the country (anywhere in the world) is measured by gross national product (GNP).

For the first definition the relevant criterion is "where the output is produced" and for the second definition "by whom it is produced". The difference between GNP and GDP therefore depends on net factor payments received from abroad (such as income from capital in the form of interest and dividends, and labour income received by domestic residents from abroad). In practice we shall ignore the difference between the two concepts regarding aggregate output.

Yet another definition is obtained from (2.1) by adding international transfer receipts TR and deducting net taxes T (total taxes minus domestic transfers) on both sides:

$$Y + TR - T \equiv C + I + (G - T) + (EX + TR - IM), \tag{2.3}$$

where the left-hand side of (2.3) gives the definition of disposable income of residents. By noting that aggregate saving by the private sector S is defined as $S \equiv Y + TR - T - C$, equation (2.3) can be written as:

$$(S - I) + (T - G) \equiv (EX + TR - IM) \equiv CA. \tag{2.4}$$

The current account surplus CA is identically equal to the private sector savings surplus $S - I$ plus the government budget surplus $T - G$. The current account surplus measures the rate at which the aggregate economy is adding to its net external assets: by spending less than your income (as a nation) you build up claims on the rest of the world. Hence, ignoring valuation changes of the existing stock of net foreign assets (NFA) we have:

$$\Delta NFA \equiv CA, \tag{2.5}$$

or, equivalently,

$$\Delta NFA \equiv (S - I) + (T - G). \tag{2.6}$$

Hence, a country for which $S = I$ and $G > T$ is *out of necessity* running down its stock of net foreign assets (it is "borrowing from the rest of the world").

As a final step we must link the situation of the balance of payments to what happens in the financial sector by means of some elementary money accounting. In equation (2.6) the *aggregate* change in net foreign assets is determined (i.e. lumping together all sectors of the economy such as the central bank, commercial banks, treasury, and the non-bank private sector). We denote what happens to the central bank's net foreign asset position by ΔNFA^{cb}. The monetary authority's balance sheet can be written (in stylized form) as shown below.

Here NFA^{cb} includes foreign exchange reserves net of liabilities to foreign official holders, and DC includes securities held by the central bank (such as T-bills), loans, and other credit. High powered money consists of currency C^P (cash in vaults and currency in the hands of the public) plus commercial bank deposits at the central bank RE (so that $H \equiv C^P + RE$). High powered money is often referred to as "base money".

By taking first differences we can derive from the central bank's balance sheet that the change in the net foreign asset position of the central bank is equal to the difference between the rate of high powered money creation minus the rate of domestic credit creation:

$$\Delta NFA^{cb} \equiv \Delta H - \Delta DC. \tag{2.7}$$

Balance sheet of the central bank

Assets		Liabilities	
Net foreign assets	NFA^{cb}		
Domestic credit	DC	High powered money	H

Equation (2.7) demonstrates an important mechanism that was first suggested by the eighteenth century Scottish philosopher and economist David Hume. If the monetary authority intervenes in the foreign exchange market (by buying or selling foreign exchange) the stock of net foreign assets changes and, by (2.7), the stock of high powered money changes as well, i.e. $\Delta H = \Delta NFA^{cb}$. Hence, foreign exchange sales (purchases) automatically reduce (increase) the stock of high powered money (and, by the money multiplier, the money stock as well; see below).

The monetary authority can (temporarily) break this automatic link between H and NFA^{cb} by engaging in so-called *sterilization* operations. In terms of (2.7) the central bank can sterilize the effect of changes in its net foreign asset position by manipulating domestic credit, i.e. $\Delta H = 0$ if $\Delta DC = -\Delta NFA^{cb}$. For example, if the central bank sells foreign exchange reserves (so that $\Delta NFA^{cb} < 0$) and simultaneously uses an expansionary open market operation (a purchase of domestic bonds on the open market) of appropriate magnitude, so that $\Delta DC = -\Delta NFA^{cb} > 0$, then $\Delta H = 0$.

In a *fractional reserve* banking system, commercial banks are required to hold a fraction of their deposits in the form of reserves with the central bank (RE). The money stock, M^S, as measured by the sum of deposits at the commercial banks, D, plus currency, C^P, is then a multiple of the stock of high powered money:

$$M^S \equiv D + C^P = \mu H \quad \Leftrightarrow \quad \Delta M^S = \mu \Delta H, \tag{2.8}$$

where $\mu > 1$ is the money multiplier.[1]

2.2   The IS-LM model for a small open economy

Up to this point all we have done is manipulate some unexciting (but rather essential) identities. We can give the story some theoretical content by specifying the behavioural equations of the model. First, we write (2.2) in the form of a condition for spending equilibrium in the aggregate goods market as:

$$Y = A(R, Y) + G + X(Y, Q), \tag{2.9}$$

---

[1] Assume that the commercial banks are required by law to hold a fraction c_1 of their deposits as reserves with the central bank, $RE = c_1 D$, where $0 < c_1 < 1$. Suppose furthermore that the public desires a constant ratio between currency holdings and deposits, say $C^P/D = c_2$. Then, since $M^S \equiv D + C^P = (1 + c_2)D$ and $H = (c_1 + c_2)D$, we can derive that $M^S = \mu H$, where $\mu \equiv (1 + c_2)/(c_1 + c_2) > 1$. A higher legal reserve requirement or a lower desired currency-deposits ratio both decrease the money multiplier.

where $A(R, Y)$ is the part of domestic absorption that depends on the rate of interest R and the level of aggregate output Y, and G is the exogenous level of government spending. $X(Y, Q)$ is net exports ($\equiv EX-IM$) expressed as a function of output and the relative price of foreign goods $Q \equiv EP^*/P$, where E is the nominal exchange rate (domestic currency per unit of foreign currency), P^* is the foreign price level, and P is the domestic price level. We refer to Q as the *real exchange rate*. In view of the definition of the nominal exchange rate, a depreciation (or devaluation) of the domestic currency is represented by an increase in E.

Since investment depends negatively on the interest rate and the marginal propensity to consume out of current income is between zero and unity, we have that $A_R < 0$ and $0 < A_Y < 1$. Furthermore, the net export function satisfies $X_Y < 0$ (since imports depend positively on income) and $X_Q > 0$ (as it is assumed that the *Marshall-Lerner condition* holds–see also equations (2.38)–(2.39) below). Equation (2.9) is the open economy IS curve. Like its closed economy counterpart, it is downward sloping in (R, Y) space, but the import leakage makes it steeper than for the closed economy.

The money market can be modelled in the standard fashion.

$$M^D/P = l(R, Y), \tag{2.10}$$

$$M^S = \mu \left[NFA^{cb} + DC \right], \tag{2.11}$$

$$M^D = M^S = M, \tag{2.12}$$

where M^D and M^S are, respectively, money demand and supply. The money demand function features partial derivatives $l_R < 0$ and $l_Y > 0$ (see Chapter 1). Equations (2.10)–(2.11) define the open economy LM curve, which is upward sloping in (R, Y) space. The modification brought about by the recognition of the openness of the economy consists of the potential endogeneity of the money supply through changes in the stock of net foreign assets of the central bank. The model is closed by assuming that both domestic and foreign prices are fixed (and normalized to unity, i.e. $P^* = P = 1$), and by making an assumption regarding the degree of international capital mobility.

We can distinguish several degrees of "financial openness" of an economy. First, it can be assumed that the small open economy (SOE) has no trade in financial assets with the rest of the world (ROW). This extreme case is referred to as one of *capital immobility*. This case was relevant during the 1940s and early 1950s when many countries had capital controls. A second case is that of *perfect capital mobility*. Financial capital is perfectly mobile and flows to that location where it earns the highest yield. Domestic and foreign bonds are perfect substitutes and portfolio adjustment is instantaneous so that yields are equated across the world. This case is often deemed to be relevant to the situation from the 1980s onward. Finally, the intermediate case is referred to as one of *imperfect capital mobility*.

The balance of payments, B, can be written as the sum of the current account and the capital account. Ignoring net international transfers, the former coincides with the trade account:

$$B \equiv X(Y, Q) + KI(R - R^*) \equiv \Delta NFA^{cb}, \tag{2.13}$$

where B is the balance of payments, KI is net capital inflows (depending on the interest differential), and R^* is the interest rate in the ROW. If KI is positive this means that domestic residents are selling more financial assets (such as bonds) to the ROW

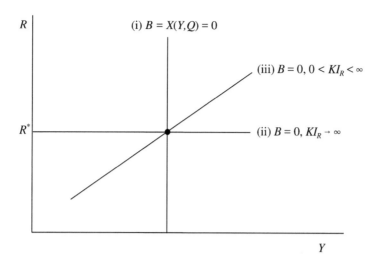

Figure 2.1: The degree of capital mobility and the balance of payment

than they are buying from the ROW. In that case the country as a whole is a net borrower from the ROW. The three assumptions regarding capital mobility that were mentioned above can now be made more precise.

(i) Capital Immobile Capital immobility means that $KI(R - R^*) \equiv 0$ no matter what the interest differential is. In this case, the balance of payments equilibrium coincides with equilibrium on the current account, i.e. $B = \Delta NFA^{cb} = X(Y, Q) = 0$.

(ii) Capital Perfectly Mobile With perfect capital mobility, arbitrage in the capital markets and the resulting capital flows ensure that $R = R^*$ always. This case can be represented mathematically by assuming that $KI_R \to \infty$.

(iii) Capital Imperfectly Mobile For the intermediate case of imperfect capital mobility, differences between R and R^* can exist in equilibrium and $0 < KI_R \ll \infty$.

Figure 2.1 shows the balance of payments (BP) curves in (R, Y) space for the different cases. In each case, the BP curve depicts combinations for R and Y for which the balance of payments is in equilibrium ($B = 0$). The slope of the BP curve can be obtained by differentiating (2.13):

$$\left(\frac{dR}{dY} \right)_{B=0} = -\frac{X_Y}{KI_R} \geq 0. \tag{2.14}$$

For case (i), the BP curve does not depend on the interest rate ($KI_R = 0$) and is thus vertical. In case (ii), $KI_R \to \infty$ so that the BP curve is horizontal. Finally, for case (iii), KI_R is positive but finite, so that the BP curve is upward sloping.

2.2.1 Fixed exchange rates and immobile capital

The IS curve is given by (2.9), the LM curve in (2.10)–(2.12), and the BP curve in (2.13) (with $B = 0$ and $KI \equiv 0$ imposed). For the case under consideration the

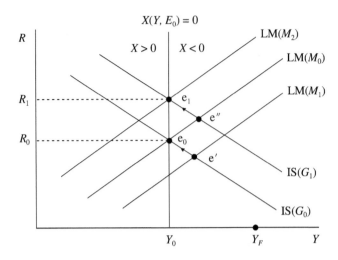

Figure 2.2: Monetary and fiscal policy with immobile capital and fixed exchange rates

macroeconomic system can be summarized by:

$$Y = A(R, Y) + G + X(Y, E), \tag{2.15}$$

$$\mu \left[NFA^{cb} + DC \right] = l(R, Y), \tag{2.16}$$

$$\Delta NFA^{cb} = X(Y, E), \tag{2.17}$$

where Y, R, and NFA^{cb} are endogenously determined whilst E, DC, and G are exogenous policy variables. Graphically the situation in the economy can be drawn as in Figure 2.2. The initial IS-LM-BP equilibrium is at point e_0 where output is Y_0 and the interest rate is R_0. For points to the right of the BP curve output and imports are too high and the current account is in deficit ($X < 0$), with the reverse holding for points to the left of the BP curve. It is assumed that output is below full employment output Y_F and that the policy maker wishes to conduct economic policy aimed at increasing employment and output.

Since the money supply is generally endogenous in the open economy, operating under fixed exchange rates, we must be precise about what is meant by *monetary policy*. An open market operation in the form of a purchase of bonds by the central bank leads to an increase in domestic credit $\Delta DC > 0$, and to an increase in the money supply (the right-hand side of (2.16)). In terms of Figure 2.2, the LM curve shifts from $LM(M_0)$ to $LM(M_1)$ in the short run. At point e', output is higher and the interest rate is lower than before the shock, but the current account is in deficit ($B = X < 0$). Since the country is spending more than it is earning, the demand for foreign exchange exceeds the supply of foreign exchange. The monetary authority is committed to maintaining a fixed exchange rate, however, and it must satisfy the excess demand for foreign exchange by running down its international reserves, i.e. $\Delta NFA^{cb} < 0$. In the absence of sterilization this means that the money stock starts to decrease again. This causes the LM curve to *gradually* shift to the left, and the economy moves along the IS curve back to point e_0. Ultimately, the initial increase in domestic credit is exactly offset by the loss in foreign exchange reserves, and only the composition (but not the size) of the central bank's portfolio has been changed as a result of the monetary policy.

Now consider what happens if the policy maker wishes to stimulate the economy by means of *fiscal policy*, consisting of a bond-financed increase in government spending. In this scenario the Treasury issues *new* bonds to pay for the additional government spending, thus ensuring that the money supply stays constant as the level of domestic credit is unchanged. The money raised by the bond sale is spent again on the additional government goods. Assume furthermore that government spending is entirely on domestically produced goods (a simplification that is relaxed below in section 2.3). In terms of Figure 2.2, the IS curve shifts from $IS(G_0)$ to $IS(G_1)$ and the new short-run equilibrium is at point e''. In view of the increase in output, imports are higher, the current account is in deficit ($X < 0$), and the money supply gradually declines (from M_0 to M_2) as the central bank foreign exchange reserves dwindle. The ultimate equilibrium is at point e_1, output is unchanged, and the interest rate is higher.

In conclusion, neither monetary nor fiscal policy can (permanently) raise the level of income in the absence of capital mobility. The balance of payments is only in equilibrium if the current account is, but the latter does not itself depend on the rate of interest. This very strong conclusion is modified once the extreme assumption of capital immobility is relaxed.

2.2.2 Fixed exchange rates and perfect capital mobility

With perfect capital mobility, the BP curve is horizontal and $R = R^*$ always. For this case the macroeconomic system is given by:

$$Y = A(R^*, Y) + G + X(Y, E), \tag{2.18}$$

$$\mu \left[NFA^{cb} + DC \right] = l(R^*, Y), \tag{2.19}$$

where the endogenous variables are Y and NFA^{cb}, whereas the exogenous variables are E, DC, and G. In terms of Figure 2.3, the initial equilibrium is at e_0. Monetary policy, consisting of an increase in domestic credit, shifts the LM curve from $LM(M_0)$ to $LM(M_1)$. At point e' the domestic interest rate is below the world interest rate and a massive capital outflow would occur, which worsens the capital account. Since output (and hence imports) is higher, the current account is also worse than at point e_0. The money supply will decrease (instantaneously) as investors purchase foreign exchange in order to buy profitable foreign financial assets. Since the exchange rate is fixed, the monetary authority sells them the required foreign exchange, which means that its stock of net foreign assets decreases, i.e. $\Delta NFA^{cb} < 0$. The adjustment occurs instantaneously, since all that happens is a portfolio reshuffling by investors. Hence, the economy stays at point e_0. The shift in LM due to the increase in domestic credit is immediately reversed by the loss of foreign exchange reserves, or, in terms of (2.7), $\Delta NFA^{cb} + \Delta DC \equiv \Delta H = 0$. Monetary policy is totally ineffective even in the short run.

Fiscal policy, on the other hand, is very effective in this case. Consider again a bond-financed increase in government spending. In terms of Figure 2.3, the IS curve shifts to the right from $IS(G_0)$ to $IS(G_1)$. This puts upward pressure on the domestic interest rate (at point e'') which causes massive net capital inflows. As investors from the ROW wish (in net terms) to buy domestic securities, the supply of foreign exchange outstrips the demand for foreign exchange. In order to maintain

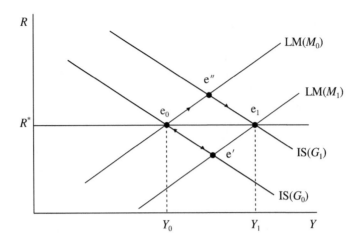

Figure 2.3: Monetary and fiscal policy with perfect capital mobility and fixed exchange rates

the fixed exchange rate, the central bank purchases the excess supply of foreign exchange and its stock of net foreign assets, and hence the money supply increases (instantaneously), i.e. $\Delta M^S = \mu \Delta NFA^{cb} > 0$. This causes the LM curve to shift from $LM(M_0)$ to $LM(M_1)$. Only at point e_1 are the domestic and foreign interest rates equated and is the money supply stabilized. Since capital is perfectly mobile, the shift from e_0 to e_1 occurs instantaneously. Hence, fiscal policy is highly effective in a small open economy operating under fixed exchange rates and experiencing perfect capital mobility.

2.2.3 Flexible exchange rates with perfect capital mobility

Under flexible exchange rates, variations in the value of the domestic currency (E) ensure that the balance of payments is always in equilibrium. Indeed, the exchange rate is endogenously determined by balance of payments equilibrium, since it implies that the demand for and supply of foreign exchange are equated:

$$B \equiv \Delta NFA^{cb} = 0 \qquad \Leftrightarrow \qquad X(Y, E) + KI(R - R^*) = 0, \qquad (2.20)$$

where we have set $P^* = P = 1$ so that $Q = E$ in the expression for net exports. Suppose that there is a current account deficit, so that exports are smaller than imports. Since exports give rise to a supply of foreign exchange, and imports cause a demand for foreign exchange, this means that $X < 0$ represents an excess demand for foreign exchange. This excess demand for foreign exchange is met by capital inflows, consisting of investors from the ROW buying domestic bonds. Since they have to pay for these bonds, the capital inflow gives rise to a supply of foreign exchange. In equilibrium, therefore, E adjusts until $X(Y, E) = -KI(R - R^*)$ since only then does demand equal supply in the foreign exchange market.

This has an important consequence for economic policy, since it implies that the monetary authority has control over the domestic money supply under flexible exchange rates. The reason is that the central bank, by allowing the exchange rate to float freely, does not need to intervene in the foreign exchange market. This means that its stock of net foreign assets is fixed, so that changes in domestic credit translate directly into changes in the money supply.

The equilibrium exchange rate follows from the IS-LM equilibrium with $R = R^*$ imposed. By using (2.9)–(2.12) and imposing $R = R^*$, equilibrium in the money market and the (demand side of the) goods market implies:

$$M = l(R^*, Y), \tag{2.21}$$

$$Y = A(R^*, Y) + G + X(Y, E), \tag{2.22}$$

where we have also substituted $P = 1$ in (2.21). Equation (2.21) represents money market equilibrium at the given world interest rate R^*. Since the money supply is constant, (2.21) determines a unique level of output that is independent of the exchange rate. In terms of Figure 2.4, this curve is drawn as $LL(M_0)$ in panel (b). Equation (2.22) represents domestic spending equilibrium at the world rate of interest. Since a high value for E (a weak domestic currency) stimulates net exports, (2.22) implies a positive relationship between output and the exchange rate that has been drawn as the schedule YY in panel (b) of Figure 2.4. Indeed, the slope of the YY schedule can be obtained from (2.22) as:

$$\left(\frac{dE}{dY} \right)_{YY} = \frac{1 - A_Y - X_Y}{X_Q} > 0. \tag{2.23}$$

Monetary policy is highly effective in this case. In terms of Figure 2.4, an increase in domestic credit shifts the LM curve in panel (a) from $LM(M_0)$ to $LM(M_1)$ and the LL curve from $LL(M_0)$ to $LL(M_1)$. At point e' the domestic interest rate is below the world interest rate, and a massive capital outflow occurs. There is excess demand for foreign exchange which leads to an instantaneous depreciation of the domestic currency (from E_0 to E_1 in panel (b)). This stimulates net exports as domestic goods are now cheaper to foreigners, and shifts the IS curve from $IS(E_0)$ to $IS(E_1)$. The new equilibrium, which is attained instantaneously, is at point e_1 where output is increased.

Fiscal policy, in the form of a bond-financed increase in government spending, turns out to be entirely ineffective (as was to be expected from the discussion surrounding the LL and YY curves). In terms of Figure 2.5, the fiscal impulse shifts the IS curve in panel (a) from $IS(G_0, E_0)$ to $IS(G_1, E_0)$, and the YY curve in panel (b) from $YY(G_0)$ to $YY(G_1)$. This puts upward pressure on domestic interest rates, and at point e' massive capital inflows occur leading to an excess supply for foreign exchange. In response, the domestic currency appreciates (E falls from E_0 to E_1), which leads to a deterioration of the current account and shifts IS back from $IS(G_1, E_0)$ to $IS(G_1, E_1)$, which coincides with $IS(G_0, E_0)$. In the new equilibrium, which is again attained instantaneously, output and the rate of interest are unchanged and the exchange rate has appreciated. Fiscal policy is completely ineffective under flexible exchange rates.

An immediate policy consequence of this ineffectiveness result is that the small open economy operating under flexible exchange rates is, in a sense, insulated from foreign spending disturbances (such as shocks to the demand for its exports), *provided* these shocks are uncoordinated and consequently have no effect on the world rate of interest. For example, if a spending bust occurs in Germany leading to a decrease in the demand for exports from Norway, the Norwegian exchange rate will depreciate and no output effects will occur under flexible exchange rates. Matters are different, of course, if a global shock hits the economy. If all countries, except Norway, pursue expansionary aggregate demand policies, the world interest rate

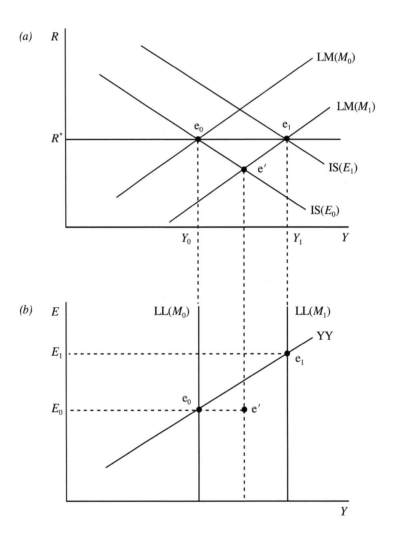

Figure 2.4: Monetary policy with perfect capital mobility and flexible exchange rates

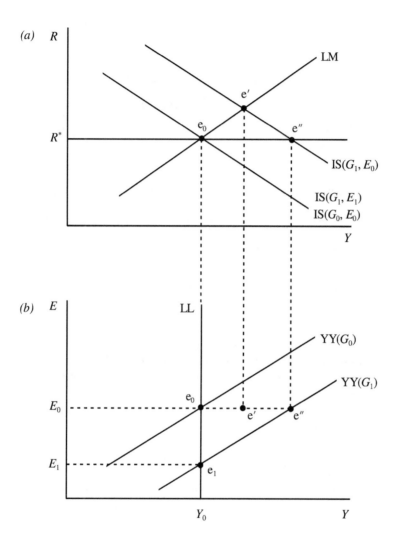

Figure 2.5: Fiscal policy with perfect capital mobility and flexible exchange rates

Table 2.1. Imperfect capital mobility under fixed and flexible exchange rates

Flexible exchange rates

	dG	dM	dR^*
dY	$-\dfrac{l_R X_Q/KI_R}{|\Delta|} \geq 0$	$\dfrac{X_Q(1-A_R/KI_R)}{|\Delta|} > 0$	$-\dfrac{l_R X_Q}{|\Delta|} > 0$
dR	$\dfrac{l_Y X_Q/KI_R}{|\Delta|} \geq 0$	$-\dfrac{X_Q(1-A_Y)/KI_R}{|\Delta|} \leq 0$	$0 < \dfrac{l_Y X_Q}{|\Delta|} \leq 1$
dE	$\dfrac{l_R X_Y/KI_R - l_Y}{|\Delta|} \lessgtr 0$	$\dfrac{1-A_Y-X_Y+A_R X_Y/KI_R}{|\Delta|} > 0$	$\dfrac{-A_R l_Y - l_R(1-A_Y-X_Y)}{|\Delta|} > 0$

Fixed exchange rates

	dG	dE	dR^*
dY	$\dfrac{1}{|\Gamma|} > 0$	$\dfrac{X_Q(1-A_R/KI_R)}{|\Gamma|} > 0$	$\dfrac{A_R}{|\Gamma|} < 0$
dR	$-\dfrac{X_Y/KI_R}{|\Gamma|} \geq 0$	$-\dfrac{(1-A_Y)X_Q/KI_R}{|\Gamma|} < 0$	$0 < \dfrac{1-A_Y-X_Y}{|\Gamma|} \leq 1$
dM	$\dfrac{l_Y - l_R X_Y/KI_R}{|\Gamma|} \gtrless 0$	$\dfrac{|\Delta|}{|\Gamma|} > 0$	$\dfrac{A_R l_Y + l_R(1-A_Y-X_Y)}{|\Gamma|} < 0$

Notes: $|\Delta| \equiv X_Q \left[l_Y(1-A_R/KI_R) - l_R(1-A_Y)/KI_R\right] > 0$
$|\Gamma| \equiv 1 - A_Y - X_Y + A_R X_Y/KI_R > 0$

will rise. This will affect the Norwegian economy even if it is operating under flexible exchange rates. In terms of Figure 2.6, the rise in R^* shifts the YY curve to the left and the LL curve to the right. The domestic currency depreciates, due to the capital outflows, and output increases. A global shock is transmitted to the small open economy through its effect on the world rate of interest. We return to the issue of shock transmission below—see Section 2.4.

2.2.4 Imperfect capital mobility

If financial capital is imperfectly mobile, we have a "weighted average" of the two previous extreme cases. In formal terms the model is given by the LM, IS, and BP curves:

$$M = l(R, Y), \tag{2.24}$$
$$Y = A(R, Y) + G + X(Y, E), \tag{2.25}$$
$$0 = X(Y, E) + KI(R - R^*). \tag{2.26}$$

The balance of payments curve is upward sloping (see (2.14)), and points to the left (right) of the BP curve are consistent with a balance of payments surplus (deficit). The IS, LM, and BP curves have been drawn in Figure 2.7, where the BP curve has been drawn flatter than the LM curve. Instead of discussing fiscal and monetary policy under fixed and flexible exchange rates by graphical means, we present the different comparative static effects in mathematical form in Table 2.1. The results in

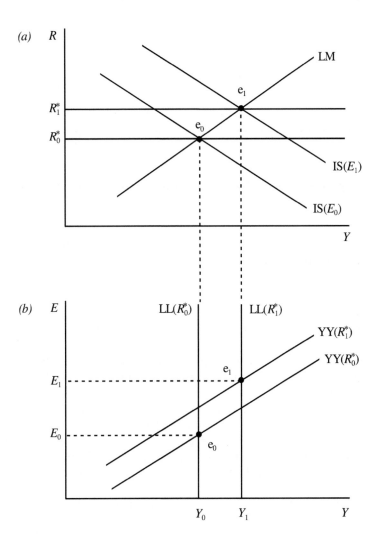

Figure 2.6: Foreign interest rate shocks with perfect capital mobility and flexible exchange rates

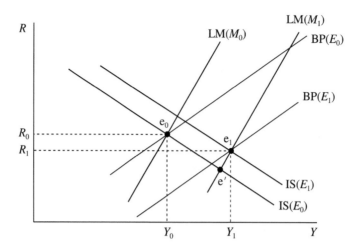

Figure 2.7: Monetary policy with imperfect capital mobility and flexible exchange rates

Table 2.1 are obtained as follows. First we totally differentiate the LM, IS, and BP curves. After some manipulations we obtain:

$$
\begin{bmatrix}
l_Y & l_R & 0 & -1 \\
1 - A_Y - X_Y & -A_R & -X_Q & 0 \\
X_Y/KI_R & 1 & X_Q/KI_R & 0
\end{bmatrix}
\begin{bmatrix}
dY \\ dR \\ dE \\ dM
\end{bmatrix}
=
\begin{bmatrix}
0 \\ dG \\ dR^*
\end{bmatrix}.
\tag{2.27}
$$

Of course, equation (2.27) cannot be used to solve for all four variables appearing on the left-hand side since we only have three equations. This "problem" is solved, however, by specifying the exchange rate regime. Under flexible exchange rates the money supply is exogenous (and the column for dM is moved to the right-hand side of (2.27)) and (2.27) determines dY, dR, and dE, as a function of the exogenous variables dM, dG, and dR^*. Under fixed exchange rates, on the other hand, the exchange rate is exogenous (and the column for dE is moved to the right-hand side of (2.27)) and (2.27) determines dY, dR, and dM, as a function of the exogenous variables dE, dG, and dR^*.

    In order to demonstrate the link between the mathematical results in Table 2.1 and the graphical representation in Figure 2.7, consider the case of monetary policy under flexible exchange rates. The increase in domestic credit shifts the LM curve from $LM(M_0)$ to $LM(M_1)$. At point e', output and imports are too high and net capital inflows too low, so that there exists a balance of payments deficit ($B < 0$), which manifests itself as an excess demand for foreign exchange. The domestic currency depreciates (E rises), the IS curve shifts from $IS(E_0)$ to $IS(E_1)$, and the BP curve shifts from $BP(E_0)$ to $BP(E_1)$. Both the current account and the capital account recover somewhat due to the depreciation and the slight increase of the domestic interest rate (that occurs in moving from e' to e_1). The new equilibrium is at e_1. Although it is impossible to deduce by graphical means alone, the results in Table 2.1 demonstrate that the ultimate effect on the domestic interest rate is negative.

    Of course, since the results of Table 2.1 are derived for any value of KI_R, the polar cases of immobile and perfectly mobile capital can be obtained as special cases from the table by setting $KI_R = 0$ and $KI_R \to \infty$, respectively. The students are advised to verify that this is indeed the case.[2]

2.3 Aggregate supply considerations

Up to this point we have assumed that domestic and foreign price levels are constant ($P = P^* = 1$). Whilst this may be appropriate under some conditions (e.g. in the very short run), it is nevertheless important to add a *supply side* to the Mundell-Fleming model of the small open economy. We use a model inspired by Argy and Salop (1979), Armington (1969), and Branson and Rotemberg (1980) to demonstrate the importance of supply-side effects. This model will also be used (in simplified form) in Section 2.4 on the transmission of shocks in a two-country model of the world. We restrict attention to the case of perfect capital mobility and flexible exchange rates.

2.3.1 The Armington approach

Now that we wish to model the production side of the economy, we have to be more precise about the various price indexes. There are two goods, a *domestic good* with price P, and a *foreign good* with price P^* in foreign currency (EP^* is the price of the foreign good in domestic currency). These goods are *imperfect substitutes* for each other (otherwise one would expect purchasing power parity (PPP) to hold, so that the real exchange rate, EP^*/P, would be identically equal to unity at all times). Real household consumption C and investment I are assumed to be determined by the usual macro-relations:

$$C = C(Y), \qquad I = I(R), \tag{2.28}$$

with $0 < C_Y < 1$ and $I_R < 0$. Real government spending G is exogenously given.

We now need to confront the issue of *sourcing* of the goods. For example, once the households know how much they wish to consume in the aggregate and in real terms, the next issue for them is to decide on where to purchase the goods (and the same holds for investment by firms and government consumption). The trick that was devised by Armington (1969) is to assume that, for example, C is in fact "constructed" out of domestically produced goods (labelled by C_d) and foreign produced goods (labelled by C_f). Since the two goods are assumed to be imperfect substitutes, we cannot simply add C_d and C_f to find C (a German apple is not quite the same as a Dutch apple, even though they are both round and taste good). A particularly simple way to capture the imperfect substitution idea is to assume that:

$$C = \Phi(C_d, C_f) \equiv \left(\frac{C_d}{\alpha}\right)^\alpha \left(\frac{C_f}{1-\alpha}\right)^{1-\alpha}, \tag{2.29}$$

with $0 < \alpha < 1$ denoting the relative weight given to domestically produced goods used in consumption. In the decision about sourcing, the households wish to attain

---

[2]For $KI_R = 0$ we find from Table 2.1 that $|\Delta| = \infty$, $|\Gamma| = -\infty$, and

$$KI_R \cdot |\Delta| = -X_Q \left[l_Y A_R + l_R (1 - A_Y)\right], \qquad KI_R \cdot |\Gamma| = A_R X_Y.$$

For $KI_R \to \infty$, we find that $1/KI_R \to 0$ and:

$$|\Delta| = X_Q l_Y, \qquad |\Gamma| = 1 - A_Y - X_Y.$$

the composite consumption level C (that is determined by (2.28) once Y is known) as cheaply as possible. Since the (domestic currency) prices of domestic and foreign goods are P and EP^*, respectively, the households decide on C_d and C_f such that total nominal consumption spending, $PC_d + EP^*C_f$, is minimized given the restriction imposed by (2.29). For a given level of total consumption, $C(Y)$, the optimal choices regarding domestic and foreign consumption goods (C_d and C_f) are given by:

$$C_d = \alpha Q^{1-\alpha}C(Y), \qquad C_f = (1-\alpha)Q^{-\alpha}C(Y), \tag{2.30}$$

where $Q \equiv EP^*/P$ is the real exchange. Furthermore, optimal nominal consumption spending can be written as $P_C C = PC_d + EP^*C_f$ where P_C is is a consumer price index (CPI):

$$P_C \equiv P^\alpha \left(EP^*\right)^{1-\alpha} \tag{2.31}$$

The interpretation of the results given in (2.30) is as follows. First, for a given real exchange rate, a rise in real income raises the demand for both domestic and foreign consumption goods equiproportionately. Second, for a given level of aggregate income, an increase in the real exchange rate (a real depreciation) increases the demand for domestic goods and decreases the demand for foreign goods.

Intermezzo 2.1

Imperfect substitution between domestic and foreign goods. In this intermezzo we study the Armington trick and derive the unit expenditure (or cost) function. For consumption we call this the consumer price index (CPI), but for investment (government consumption) it stands for the unit cost of constructing a given quantity of I (G) using domestic and foreign goods I_d and I_f (G_d and G_f) as inputs. Here we explain in detail how the expression for the consumer price index P_C is obtained. In the present context the expenditure function is defined as follows:

$$E(P, EP^*, C_0) \equiv \min_{\{C_d, C_f\}} \quad PC_d + EP^*C_f$$

$$\text{subject to} \quad C_0 = \Phi(C_d, C_f). \tag{a}$$

Intuitively, $E(P, EP^*, C_0)$ represents the minimum amount of spending on domestic and foreign consumption goods that gives rise to a certain level of composite consumption, C_0, taking as given the prices of domestic and foreign goods (expressed in the domestic currency). The Lagrangian associated with the minimization problem is $\mathcal{L} \equiv PC_d + EP^*C_f + \theta \left[C_0 - \Phi(C_d, C_f) \right]$ where θ is the Lagrange multiplier. The first-order necessary conditions are:

$$\frac{\partial \mathcal{L}}{\partial C_d} = P - \theta \Phi_{C_d}(C_d, C_f) = 0,$$

$$\frac{\partial \mathcal{L}}{\partial C_f} = EP^* - \theta \Phi_{C_f}(C_d, C_f) = 0,$$

$$\frac{\partial \mathcal{L}}{\partial C_f} = C_0 - \Phi(C_d, C_f) = 0.$$

For the Cobb-Douglas aggregation function (2.29) these conditions simplify to:

$$P = \alpha\theta\frac{C_0}{C_d},$$ (b)

$$EP^* = (1-\alpha)\theta\frac{C_0}{C_f},$$ (c)

$$C_0 = \left(\frac{C_d}{\alpha}\right)^\alpha \left(\frac{C_f}{1-\alpha}\right)^{1-\alpha}.$$ (d)

It follows from (b) that $C_d = \alpha\theta C_0/P$ and from (c) that $C_f = (1-\alpha)\theta C_0/(EP^*)$. Substituting these results into (d) gives:

$$C_0 = \left(\frac{\alpha\theta C_0}{\alpha P}\right)^\alpha \left(\frac{(1-\alpha)\theta C_0}{(1-\alpha)EP^*}\right)^{1-\alpha} = \theta C_0 P^{-\alpha}(EP^*)^{-(1-\alpha)},$$

or:

$$\theta = P^\alpha (EP^*)^{1-\alpha}.$$ (e)

Substituting (b) and (c) into the expression for total expenditure, $PC_d + EP^*C_f$, gives the expenditure function:

$$E(P,EP^*,C_0)\left[= PC_d + EP^*C_f\right] = \alpha\theta C_0 + (1-\alpha)\theta C_0 = \theta C_0.$$ (f)

The total expenditure needed to construct C_0 units of composite consumption is θC_0 so θ represents the unit cost of consumption. In the text
we denote θ by P_C. Note finally that by employing Shephard's lemma
we can find the derived demands for domestic and foreign consumption
goods:

$$C_d = \frac{\partial E(P,EP^*,C_0)}{\partial P} = C_0\frac{\partial P_C}{\partial P} = \alpha C_0\left(\frac{EP^*}{P}\right)^{1-\alpha},$$ (g)

$$C_f = \frac{\partial E(P,EP^*,C_0)}{\partial EP^*} = C_0\frac{\partial P_C}{\partial EP^*} = (1-\alpha)C_0\left(\frac{EP^*}{P}\right)^{-\alpha}.$$ (h)

****

By using the same approach for investment and government spending – such
that $I = \Phi(I_d,I_f)$ and $G = \Phi(G_d,G_f)$ – we obtain expressions for I_d, I_f, G_d, and G_f:[3]

$$I_d = \alpha Q^{1-\alpha}I(R), \quad I_f = (1-\alpha)Q^{-\alpha}I(R),$$ (2.32)

$$G_d = \alpha Q^{1-\alpha}G, \quad G_f = (1-\alpha)Q^{-\alpha}G.$$ (2.33)

Real exports are denoted by EX and are sold to the ROW at the same price that
domestic customers pay for these goods (P), and spending on imported goods (in

[3]We assume for the sake of convenience that I and G are similar composites as C. This assumption
ensures that the price indices for investment and government spending are the same as the CPI, so that
the real exchange rate does not affect relative prices within a country.

terms of domestic currency) equals $EP^*(C_f + I_f + G_f)$, so that the national income identity (2.1) can be written as:

$$PY \equiv P_C C + P_C I + P_C G + P\,EX - EP^* \left[C_f + I_f + G_f\right]$$
$$= P\,C_d + P\,I_d + P\,G_d + P\,EX \Rightarrow$$
$$Y \equiv C_d + I_d + G_d + EX, \tag{2.34}$$

which shows (more clearly than (2.1)) that only domestically produced goods enter into the aggregate production measure for the domestic economy. By looking in more detail at the sourcing issue we find that C_d, I_d, and G_d all depend on the real exchange rate—see equations (2.30), (2.32), and (2.33). In summary, we now have an IS equation (similar in form to (2.9)) in which the real exchange rate affects domestic spending equilibrium.

By defining net exports (in real terms) by $X \equiv EX - (EP^*/P)[C_f + I_f + G_f]$, noting (2.30)–(2.33) and assuming that the demand for exports depends on the real exchange rate,

$$EX = EX_0 \left(\frac{EP^*}{P}\right)^\beta = EX_0 Q^\beta, \qquad \beta \geq 0, \tag{2.35}$$

(where EX_0 represents all exogenous influences on the country's exports) we obtain the net export function defined by the model:

$$X\,(R,Y,Q,G,EX_0) \equiv EX_0 Q^\beta - Q(1-\alpha)Q^{-\alpha}\left[A(R,Y)+G\right], \tag{2.36}$$

where $A(R,Y) \equiv C(Y) + I(R)$. Several features are worth noting in the comparison between (2.36) and the net export function used throughout section 2.2 (i.e. $X(Y,Q)$). First, domestic absorption, and not just aggregate domestic income, appears in (2.36). Since domestic absorption depends on the rate of interest, and some investment goods are purchased from the ROW, the BP curve has a positive slope even under perfectly immobile capital (compare to section 2.2.1). A higher rate of interest chokes off aggregate investment, decreases imports of investment goods, and causes a trade account surplus. To restore equilibrium on the trade account, income (and hence imports) must rise.

A second feature of (2.36) is that we can now be more precise about the *Marshall-Lerner condition*. Indeed, by differentiating (2.36) with respect to the real exchange rate Q (holding EX_0 and $A(R,Y) + G$ fixed), we obtain:

$$\frac{X_Q}{Y} = \frac{\beta EX_0 Q^{\beta-1}}{Y} - \frac{(1-\alpha)^2 Q^{-\alpha}\left[A(R,Y)+G\right]}{Y} = \frac{\beta\omega_X - (1-\alpha)\omega_M}{Q}, \tag{2.37}$$

where $X_Q \equiv \partial X/\partial Q$. Note that $\omega_X \equiv EX/Y$, and $\omega_M \equiv Q[C_f + I_f + G_f]/Y$ are, respectively, the domestic output shares of exports and imports. This expression shows that net exports improve as a result of a real exchange rate depreciation if the following condition holds:

$$\frac{QX_Q}{Y} = \beta\omega_X - (1-\alpha)\omega_M > 0, \tag{2.38}$$

or, if the trade balance is initially in equilibrium (so that imports and exports are of equal magnitude and $\omega_M = \omega_X$), the condition is:

$$\beta + \alpha - 1 > 0. \tag{2.39}$$

This is the famous Marshall-Lerner condition: if the sum of the elasticities of export and import demand exceeds unity, a depreciation of the currency improves the trade account, so that $X_Q > 0$. The intuition behind the Marshall-Lerner condition is as follows. A depreciation of the currency (a rise in Q) makes domestic goods cheaper for the ROW and increases export earnings. This improves net exports. The rise in Q also makes foreign goods more expensive to domestic residents. If real imports were unchanged, *spending* on imports would rise because of the depreciation, which would worsen net exports. Domestic residents, however, substitute domestic goods for foreign goods, as a result of the depreciation, and this effect mitigates the rise in import spending and its adverse effect on net exports. The strength of the export effect is regulated by the export elasticity β and that of the import spending effect is regulated by $1 - \alpha$. The Marshall-Lerner condition ensures that the export effect dominates the import spending effect, which translates as $\beta > 1 - \alpha$ or, equivalently, $\beta + \alpha > 1$.

2.3.2 The extended Mundell-Fleming model

In this section we develop the extended Mundell-Fleming model of a small open economy which possesses the following main features. First, there is perfect mobility of financial capital. Second, exchange rates are fully flexible. Third, domestic and foreign goods are imperfect substitutes so the real exchange rate will generally differ from unity (as PPP fails). Fourth, on the supply side the labour market may be characterized by nominal or real wage rigidity. We analyse the extended Mundell-Fleming model in its loglinearized form.

2.3.2.1 Aggregate demand side

The aggregate demand side of the model consists of the IS, LM, and BP curves. The IS curve is derived as follows. First, by substituting the relevant expressions from (2.30) and (2.32)–(2.33) as well as (2.35) into (2.34), we obtain:

$$Y = \alpha Q^{1-\alpha} [C + I + G] + EX_0 Q^\beta, \tag{2.40}$$

which can be written in loglinearized form as:

$$\tilde{Y} = (1 - \omega_X) \left[\omega_C \tilde{C} + \omega_I \tilde{I} + \omega_G \tilde{G} + (1 - \alpha)\tilde{Q} \right] + \omega_X \left[\widetilde{EX}_0 + \beta \tilde{Q} \right], \tag{2.41}$$

where $\tilde{Y} \equiv dY/Y$, $\tilde{C} \equiv dC/C$, $\tilde{I} \equiv dI/I$, $\tilde{G} \equiv dG/G$, $\tilde{Q} \equiv dQ/Q$, $\widetilde{EX}_0 \equiv dEX_0/EX_0$. Note that $\omega_X \equiv EX_0 Q^\beta/Y$ is the output share of exports, and $\omega_C \equiv C/[A + G]$, $\omega_I \equiv I/[A + G]$, and $\omega_G \equiv G/[A + G]$ denote, respectively, the share of consumption, investment, and government spending in total domestic absorption ($\omega_C + \omega_I + \omega_G = 1$).

Next, we loglinearize the expressions for aggregate consumption and investment (see (2.28)) to obtain:

$$\tilde{C} = \varepsilon_{CY} \tilde{Y}, \qquad \tilde{I} = -\varepsilon_{IR} dR, \tag{2.42}$$

where $0 < \varepsilon_{CY} \equiv YC_Y/C \equiv MPC/APC < 1$ and $\varepsilon_{IR} \equiv -I_R/I > 0$ are, respectively, the income elasticity of the aggregate consumption function and (the absolute value of) the interest semi-elasticity of the investment function.[4] Note that ε_{CY} equals the

---

[4] We use the term semi-elasticity to indicate that ε_{IR} relates the *percentage* rate of change of investment to the *absolute* change in the interest rate. In the case of interest rates, the use of semi-elasticities is natural. For example, if $\varepsilon_{IR} = 2$, a one percentage *point* increase in the rate of interest (say a rise in r from 5 to 6% per annum) causes a fall in investment of 2%.

marginal propensity over the average propensity to consume, and is thus less than unity for the usual Keynesian consumption function.

Finally, by substituting the expressions from (2.42) into (2.41) and solving for $\tilde{Y}$ we find the IS curve:

$$\tilde{Y} = \frac{[\beta \omega_X + (1-\alpha)(1-\omega_X)]\tilde{Q} - (1-\omega_X)\omega_I \varepsilon_{IR} dR}{1 - \omega_C \varepsilon_{CY}(1-\omega_X)}$$
$$+ \frac{(1-\omega_X)\omega_G \tilde{G} + \omega_X \widetilde{EX}_0}{1 - \omega_C \varepsilon_{CY}(1-\omega_X)}, \tag{2.43}$$

where we note that the denominator is between zero and one (because $0 < \omega_C < 1$, $0 < \varepsilon_{CY} < 1$, and $0 < \omega_X < 1$). Domestic demand depends positively on the real exchange rate, government consumption, and exogenous exports, and negatively on the domestic interest rate.

The money market of the model is summarized by the LM curve $M/P = l(R, Y)$, which can be loglinearized to:

$$\tilde{M} - \tilde{P} = -\varepsilon_{MR} dR + \varepsilon_{MY} \tilde{Y}, \tag{2.44}$$

where $\varepsilon_{MY} \equiv Y l_Y / l > 0$ and $\varepsilon_{MR} \equiv -l_R / l > 0$ are, respectively, the income elasticity and (the absolute value of) the interest semi-elasticity of the money demand function.

Since we assume perfect capital mobility, the world interest rate determines the domestic rate ($R = R^*$), so that:

$$dR = dR^*. \tag{2.45}$$

2.3.2.2 Aggregate supply side

The aggregate supply side of the model summarizes the situation on the labour market and yields an expression for the aggregate supply of goods. Compared to its closed economy counterpart, the aggregate supply model for the open economy contains some novel elements. Domestic firms are perfectly competitive (and do not attempt to exploit the export demand function (2.35), as a monopolist would) and maximize short-run profit $\Pi \equiv PF(N, \bar{K}) - WN$, where N is employment, W is the nominal wage, and $\bar{K}$ is the given capital stock. The labour demand function is implicitly defined by the marginal productivity condition $PF_N(N, \bar{K}) = W$, which can be loglinearized to:

$$\tilde{P} + \tilde{F}_N = \tilde{W} \quad \Rightarrow \quad \tilde{N} = -\varepsilon_{NW}[\tilde{W} - \tilde{P}], \tag{2.46}$$

where $\varepsilon_{NW} \equiv -F_N/(NF_{NN}) > 0$ is the (absolute value of the) real wage elasticity of labour demand. It is assumed, following Branson and Rotemberg (1980), that the labour market is characterized by unemployment because the wage is too high. We model this by assuming that labour supply is perfectly elastic at a level of the nominal wage set according to a wage-setting rule of the form $W = W_0 P_C^\theta$, where W_0 is an exogenous parameter, P_C is the consumer price index (CPI) given in (2.31) above, and $0 \leq \theta \leq 1$. Depending on the assumed value of θ, three cases can be considered.

- If $\theta = 1$, workers are said to have a *real wage target*. They demand to be fully compensated for any changes in the CPI that may occur, i.e. $W/P_C = W_0$ is held constant and thus does not depend on the CPI.

- If $\theta = 0$, workers are said to have a *nominal wage target* in that they demand the nominal wage to be constant, i.e. $W = W_0$. Their real wage is W_0/P_C which falls if the CPI rises.

- If $0 < \theta < 1$, workers take the CPI into account but suffer from *money illusion* in the sense that they do not keep the real wage in terms of the CPI constant, i.e. $W/P_C = W_0 P_C^{\theta-1}$ which falls if the CPI rises.

Branson and Rotemberg (1980) suggest on the basis of empirical evidence that $\theta = 0$ is relevant for the US economy in which there is little or no indexing of nominal wages, and $\theta = 1$ is more relevant to the situation in the UK, Germany, Italy, and Japan, where wage indexing is much more common. Here we study the general case by allowing $0 \le \theta \le 1$. The wage setting rule in its most general form can be loglinearized to:

$$\tilde{W} = \tilde{W}_0 + \theta \tilde{P}_C. \tag{2.47}$$

Once the wage rate is set, domestic producers determine employment (by (2.46)), after which output is determined by the production function which can be loglinearized to:

$$\tilde{Y} = \omega_N \tilde{N}, \tag{2.48}$$

where $0 < \omega_N \equiv WN/(PY) < 1$ is the share of labour income in aggregate output. Rewriting (2.31) in terms of Q we find $P_C \equiv PQ^{1-\alpha}$ which we loglinearize to obtain:

$$\tilde{P}_C = \tilde{P} + (1-\alpha)\tilde{Q}. \tag{2.49}$$

By substituting (2.46)–(2.47) and (2.49) into (2.48) we obtain the AS curve:

$$\tilde{Y} = -\varepsilon_{YW}[\tilde{W}_0 + \theta\tilde{P}_C - \tilde{P}]$$
$$= -\varepsilon_{YW}[\tilde{W}_0 + \theta(1-\alpha)\tilde{Q} - (1-\theta)\tilde{P}], \tag{2.50}$$

where $\varepsilon_{YW} \equiv \omega_N \varepsilon_{NW}$ is the (absolute value of the) wage elasticity of output supply. The intuition behind the AS curve can be explained with the aid of Figure 2.8. In panel (a), labour demand (2.46) is depicted by the downward sloping line N^D. Labour supply is obtained by substituting (2.49) into (2.47) and solving for the real wage facing domestic producers, $\tilde{W} - \tilde{P}$. Mathematically, the real supply price of labour is given by the term in square brackets on the right-hand side of (2.50). In general, it depends negatively on $\tilde{P}$ and positively on $\tilde{Q}$. The initial labour supply curve is depicted by N_0^S, and the initial equilibrium is at point e_0 in panels (a) and (b), employment is N_0, and output is Y_0.

Next we consider what happens if the domestic price or the real exchange rate changes. Under nominal wage rigidity ($\theta = 0$), the labour supply curve only depends on $\tilde{P}$. In terms of panel (a), an increase in the domestic price level shifts the labour supply downward, to N_1^S, and moves the equilibrium to point e_1. Employment and output both increase. Workers demand a fixed *nominal* wage, so that a domestic price increase erodes the real producer wage which prompts firms to expand employment and output. This explains the positive sign for $\tilde{P}$ in (2.50) when $\theta = 0$.

Under real wage rigidity ($\theta = 1$), the real supply price of labour only depends on $\tilde{Q}$. An increase in the real exchange rate shifts labour supply up, from N_0^S to N_2^S, and shifts the equilibrium from e_0 to e_2. Employment and output both decrease. Workers

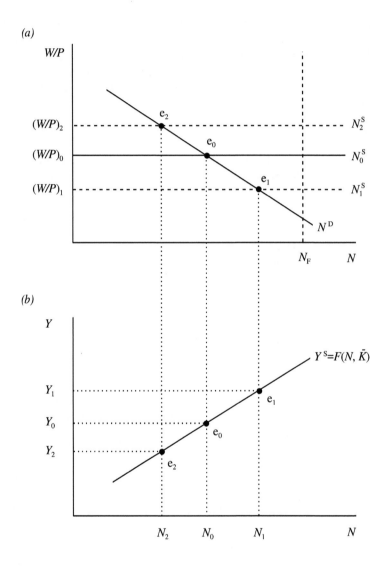

Figure 2.8: Aggregate supply in the open economy

Table 2.2. The extended Mundell-Fleming model

$$\tilde{Y} = \frac{(1-\omega_X)\left[-\omega_I\varepsilon_{IR}dR^* + \omega_G\tilde{G}\right] + \omega_X\widetilde{EX}_0}{1-(1-\omega_X)\omega_C\varepsilon_{CY}},\qquad\text{(T2.1)}$$

$$+\frac{\left[(1-\alpha)(1-\omega_X)+\beta\omega_X\right]\tilde{Q}}{1-(1-\omega_X)\omega_C\varepsilon_{CY}}$$

$$\tilde{M} - \tilde{P} = -\varepsilon_{MR}dR^* + \varepsilon_{MY}\tilde{Y},\qquad\text{(T2.2)}$$

$$\tilde{Y} = -\varepsilon_{YW}\left[\tilde{W}_0 + \theta(1-\alpha)\tilde{Q} - (1-\theta)\tilde{P}\right]\qquad\text{(T2.3)}$$

Notes: Endogenous variables are $\tilde{Y} \equiv dY/Y$, $\tilde{Q} \equiv dQ/Q$, $\tilde{P} \equiv dP/P$. Exogenous variables are dR^*, $\tilde{M} \equiv dM/M$, $\tilde{G} \equiv dG/G$, $\tilde{W}_0 \equiv dW_0/W_0$, $\widetilde{EX}_0 \equiv dEX_0/EX_0$. The absorption shares of consumption, investment, and government spending are given by, respectively, ω_C, ω_I, and ω_G. These shares add up to unity. The export share in GDP is ω_X. The income elasticity of aggregate consumption is ε_{CY}, the interest semi-elasticity of aggregate invest-ment is ε_{IR}, the income elasticity of money demand is ε_{MY}, the interest semi-elasticity of money demand is ε_{MR}, the wage elasticity of output supply is ε_{YW}, the real exchange rate export elasticity is β, the real exchange rate import spending elasticity is $1-\alpha$. Money il-lusion exists if $0 < \theta < 1$, real wage rigidity if $\theta = 1$, nominal wage rigidity if $\theta = 0$.

demand a fixed real consumer wage, W/P_C, and an increase in the real exchange rate raises the real producer wage which prompts firms to cut back employment and output. This explains the negative sign for $\tilde{Q}$ in (2.50) when $\theta = 1$.

Finally, under money illusion ($0 < \theta < 1$), aggregate supply depends positively on the domestic price level and negatively on the real exchange rate.

2.3.2.3 Full model

The full model consists of the IS curve (2.43), the LM curve (2.44), the BP curve (2.45), and the AS curve (2.50). For convenience, the equations are gathered in Table 2.2, where we have substituted the BP curve into the IS and LM curves. The en-dogenous variables are aggregate output $\tilde{Y}$, the domestic price level $\tilde{P}$, and the real exchange rate $\tilde{Q}$. Once the latter two are determined, the nominal exchange rate is also determined since $\tilde{E} \equiv \tilde{P} + \tilde{Q} - \tilde{P}^*$, where $\tilde{P}^*$ is exogenous due to the small open economy assumption. The other exogenous variables are $\tilde{M} \equiv dM/M$, $\tilde{G} \equiv dG/G$, dR^*, $\widetilde{EX}_0 \equiv dEX_0/EX_0$, and $\tilde{W}_0 \equiv dW_0/W_0$. The comparative static effects can be obtained in the standard fashion and have been collected in Table 2.3.

Graphically the comparative static effects can be illustrated as follows. Consider the case of a positive demand shock (say $\tilde{G} > 0$). In the standard Mundell-Fleming model with fixed prices and flexible exchange rates, such a shock does not affect aggregate output (and hence employment). This is the well-known insulation prop-erty of flexible exchange rates. The results in Table 2.3 suggest that this insulation property no longer holds for the augmented Mundell-Fleming model developed in this section (as $dY/dG > 0$), unless there exists nominal wage rigidity ($\theta = 0$). The basic intuition behind this result can be explained with the aid of Figure 2.9. In the left-hand side of Figure 2.9, the perfect-capital-mobility version of the LM curve is

Table 2.3. Wage rigidity and demand and supply shocks

	$\omega_G(1-\omega_X)\tilde{G}$ $\omega_X\widetilde{EX_0}$	$\tilde{M}$	$\varepsilon_{YW}\tilde{W_0}$
$\tilde{Y}$	$\frac{\theta(1-\alpha)\varepsilon_{YW}}{|\Delta|} \geq 0$	$\frac{(1-\theta)\delta_1\varepsilon_{YW}}{|\Delta|} \geq 0$	$-\frac{\delta_1}{|\Delta|} < 0$
$\tilde{Q}$	$-\frac{1+(1-\theta)\varepsilon_{MY}\varepsilon_{YW}}{|\Delta|} < 0$	$\frac{(1-\theta)\delta_2\varepsilon_{YW}}{|\Delta|} \geq 0$	$-\frac{\delta_2}{|\Delta|} < 0$
$\tilde{P}$	$-\frac{\theta(1-\alpha)\varepsilon_{MY}\varepsilon_{YW}}{|\Delta|} \leq 0$	$\frac{\theta(1-\alpha)\delta_2\varepsilon_{YW}+\delta_1}{|\Delta|} > 0$	$\frac{\delta_1\varepsilon_{MY}}{|\Delta|} > 0$
$\tilde{E}$	$-\frac{1+(1-\alpha\theta)\varepsilon_{MY}\varepsilon_{YW}}{|\Delta|} < 0$	$\frac{(1-\alpha\theta)\delta_2\varepsilon_{YW}+\delta_1}{|\Delta|} > 0$	$\frac{\delta_1\varepsilon_{MY}-\delta_2}{|\Delta|} \gtrless 0$
$\tilde{P}_C$	$-\frac{(1-\alpha)(1+\varepsilon_{MY}\varepsilon_{YW})}{|\Delta|} < 0$	$\frac{(1-\alpha)\delta_2\varepsilon_{YW}+\delta_1}{|\Delta|} > 0$	$\frac{\delta_1\varepsilon_{MY}-(1-\alpha)\delta_2}{|\Delta|} \gtrless 0$

Notes: $\delta_1 \equiv (1-\alpha)(1-\omega_X) + \beta\omega_X > 0$
$\delta_2 \equiv 1 - (1-\omega_X)\omega_C\varepsilon_{CY}, \quad 0 < \delta_2 < 1$
$|\Delta| \equiv \theta(1-\alpha)\varepsilon_{YW}\delta_2 + [1 + (1-\theta)\varepsilon_{MY}\varepsilon_{YW}]\delta_1 > 0$

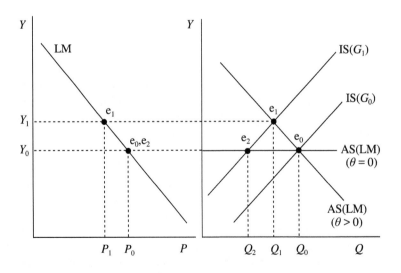

Figure 2.9: Aggregate demand shocks under wage rigidity

drawn. As we can easily deduce from (T2.2), ceteris paribus R^* and M, the LM curve represents a downward sloping relationship between the domestic price level and output. An increase in the world interest rate or the domestic money supply shifts the LM curve up.

Equation (T2.1) is the perfect-capital-mobility version of the IS curve. Ceteris paribus G, EX_0, and R^*, the IS curve represents an upward sloping relationship between output and the real exchange rate–see the right-hand panel in Figure 2.9. A second relationship between output and the real exchange rate is obtained by substituting the LM curve (T2.2) into the AS curve (T2.3) and solving for $\tilde{Y}$:

$$\tilde{Y} = \frac{-\varepsilon_{YW}\left[\tilde{W}_0 + \theta(1-\alpha)\tilde{Q} - (1-\theta)\left(\tilde{M} + \varepsilon_{MR}dR^*\right)\right]}{1 + (1-\theta)\varepsilon_{MY}\varepsilon_{YW}}, \qquad \text{AS(LM)}. \qquad (2.51)$$

As is illustrated in the right-hand panel of Figure 2.9, the AS(LM) curve is downward sloping for $0 < \theta \leq 1$ (real wage rigidity or money illusion) and horizontal for $\theta = 0$ (nominal wage rigidity). If there is real wage rigidity ($\theta = 1$), the AS(LM) curve is independent of the money supply and the world interest rate (because the price level does not affect the AS curve in that case). In contrast, if there is nominal wage rigidity ($\theta = 0$), the AS(LM) curve is independent of the real exchange rate and shifts up when the money supply or the world interest rate is increased.

2.3.2.4 Fiscal policy

In the right-hand panel in Figure 2.9, an increase in government spending shifts the IS curve up from IS(G_0) to IS(G_1). In the absence of nominal wage rigidity ($\theta > 0$), AS(LM) is downward sloping and the equilibrium shifts from e_0 to e_1. The real exchange rate appreciates (from Q_0 to Q_1), but not by enough to undo the expansionary effect of increased government spending on output. The domestic price level falls (see the left-hand panel) as does the nominal exchange rate ($\tilde{E} < \tilde{P} < 0$).

If there is nominal wage rigidity ($\theta = 0$), the AS(LM) curve is horizontal and the equilibrium shifts from e_0 to e_2. Output and the domestic price level are unchanged, and the real exchange rate appreciation exactly reverses the stimulative effect of the additional government spending. Since real output depends on what happens to the real producer wage (as producers do not have money illusion), nominal wages must be free to fall (along with the domestic price level) if there are to be any positive output effects. This explains why output effects are zero under nominal wage rigidity.

2.3.2.5 Monetary policy

The effects of monetary policy have been illustrated in Figure 2.10. To keep this figure uncluttered we ignore the nominal wage rigidity case and thus assume that $0 < \theta \leq 1$ so that the AS(LM) curve is downward sloping. The initial equilibrium is at point e_0. An increase in the money supply shifts the LM curve to the right in the left-hand panel, say from LM_0 to LM_1. If there is money illusion ($0 < \theta < 1$) then the AS(LM) curve shifts to the right, from AS(LM)$_0$ to AS(LM)$_1$, and the new equilibrium is at point e_1. The domestic price level increases (from P_0 to P_1), the real exchange rate depreciates (from Q_0 to Q_1), and output increases (from Y_0 to Y_1). The output increase results from the fact that the real supply price of labour falls, i.e., in terms of Figure 2.8(a), the net effect of the increases in P and Q is to shift the labour supply curve down.

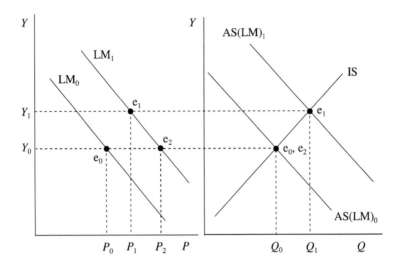

Figure 2.10: Monetary policy under wage rigidity

In contrast, if there is real wage rigidity ($\theta = 1$) then the money shock leaves the AS(LM) curve unaffected and nothing is changed in real terms, i.e. in the right-hand panel of Figure 2.10 the equilibrium stays at point e_0 and both output and the real exchange rate are unaffected. In the left-hand panel of Figure 2.10, the new equilibrium is at point e_2, and the domestic price increases from P_0 to P_2. Monetary policy cannot be used to affect output in this case.

2.4 Transmission of shocks in a two-country world

In section 2.3 we introduced a simple Mundell-Fleming type model with a rudimentary aggregate supply side. Some microeconomic foundations were provided for the supply side of the model and for the issue of sourcing. The model of section 2.3 was used to study a small open economy under flexible exchange rates and perfect capital mobility. One of the reasons so much attention was paid to the details of *sourcing* and *price indexes* is to be able to construct a (logically consistent) model of the world economy.

Assume that the world consists of *two countries* (or regions) that are identical in structure and look like the small open economy discussed in section 2.3. One immediate consequence of this assumption is that we must do away with the ad hoc export demand function (2.35). Indeed, we know from (2.30)–(2.33) that the domestic economy's demand for imports is given by:

$$C_f + I_f + G_f = (1 - \alpha) \left(\frac{EP^*}{P} \right)^{-\alpha} [C(Y) + I(R) + G]$$

$$= (1 - \alpha) \left(\frac{EP^*}{P} \right)^{-\alpha} [A(R, Y) + G]. \tag{2.52}$$

But the domestic economy's exports are (in a two-country world) just the foreign country's demand for imports which, in view of the symmetry assumption, take a form similar to (2.52):

$$EX \equiv C_f^* + I_f^* + G_f^* = (1 - \alpha) \left(\frac{EP^*}{P} \right)^{\alpha} [A(R^*, Y^*) + G^*], \qquad (2.53)$$

where stars denote foreign variables, e.g. C_f^* is the demand for domestically produced consumption goods by foreign residents. Several things are worth noting. First, the real exchange rate from the perspective of the foreign country is $P/(EP^*) \equiv 1/Q$. This explains the positive sign of the exponent on the real exchange rate in (2.53). Second, a comparison of (2.53) and (2.35) reveals that the two coincide if $\alpha = \beta$ and $EX_0 \equiv (1 - \alpha)[A(R^*, Y^*) + G^*]$. This shows that EX_0 is no longer exogenous in a two-country model – foreign absorption is endogenous. In loglinearized terms, we find:

$$\widetilde{EX_0} = \omega_C \varepsilon_{CY} \tilde{Y}^* - \omega_I \varepsilon_{IR} dR^* + \omega_G \tilde{G}^*. \qquad (2.54)$$

By setting $\beta = \alpha$ and substituting (2.54) in equation (T2.1) in Table 2.2, we obtain the IS curve for the domestic economy in a two-country setting:

$$\tilde{Y} = \frac{-\omega_I \varepsilon_{IR} dR^* + \omega_G \left[(1 - \omega_X)\tilde{G} + \omega_X \tilde{G}^* \right] + \omega_X \omega_C \varepsilon_{CY} \tilde{Y}^*}{1 - (1 - \omega_X)\omega_C \varepsilon_{CY}}$$
$$+ \frac{[(1 - \alpha)(1 - \omega_X) + \alpha \omega_X] \tilde{Q}}{1 - (1 - \omega_X)\omega_C \varepsilon_{CY}}. \qquad (2.55)$$

By comparing (T2.1) and (2.55), it is clear that the IS curve is augmented in a number of ways. First, the interest rate exerts a stronger effect on domestic production than before. The reason is that an decrease (increase) in the interest rate increases (decreases) investment in *both* countries, and since some investment goods are imported, spillover effects exist. Second, foreign government spending spills over into the domestic economy, both directly (via the term involving $\tilde{G}^*$) and indirectly (via the term with $\tilde{Y}^*$).

Of course, the foreign country also has an IS curve (labelled IS*) which is similar in form to (2.55). By making the appropriate substitutions, the IS* curve can be written as:

$$\tilde{Y}^* = \frac{-\omega_I \varepsilon_{IR} dR^* + \omega_G \left[(1 - \omega_X)\tilde{G}^* + \omega_X \tilde{G} \right] + \omega_X \omega_C \varepsilon_{CY} \tilde{Y}}{1 - (1 - \omega_X)\omega_C \varepsilon_{CY}}$$
$$- \frac{[(1 - \alpha)(1 - \omega_X) + \alpha \omega_X] \tilde{Q}}{1 - (1 - \omega_X)\omega_C \varepsilon_{CY}}. \qquad (2.56)$$

The real exchange rate affects foreign spending negatively because it is measured from the point of view of the domestic country (i.e. $Q \equiv EP^*/P$). By using (2.55)–(2.56) to solve for Y and Y^*, the following simplified expressions for IS and IS* are obtained:

$$\tilde{Y} = \frac{-(1 + \gamma)\omega_I \varepsilon_{IR} dR^* + \omega_G \left([1 - \omega_X(1 - \gamma)] \tilde{G} + [\gamma + \omega_X(1 - \gamma)] \tilde{G}^* \right)}{(1 - \gamma^2) [1 - (1 - \omega_X)\omega_C \varepsilon_{CY}]}$$
$$+ \frac{(1 - \gamma) [(1 - \alpha)(1 - \omega_X) + \alpha \omega_X] \tilde{Q}}{(1 - \gamma^2) [1 - (1 - \omega_X)\omega_C \varepsilon_{CY}]}, \qquad (2.57)$$

$$\tilde{Y}^* = \frac{-(1 + \gamma)\omega_I \varepsilon_{IR} dR^* + \omega_G \left([1 - \omega_X(1 - \gamma)] \tilde{G}^* + [\gamma + \omega_X(1 - \gamma)] \tilde{G} \right)}{(1 - \gamma^2) [1 - (1 - \omega_X)\omega_C \varepsilon_{CY}]}$$

$$- \frac{(1-\gamma)\left[(1-\alpha)(1-\omega_X) + \alpha\omega_X\right]\tilde{Q}}{(1-\gamma^2)\left[1 - (1-\omega_X)\omega_C\varepsilon_{CY}\right]}, \tag{2.58}$$

where $0 < \gamma \equiv \omega_X\omega_C\varepsilon_{CY}/[1 - (1-\omega_X)\omega_C\varepsilon_{CY}] < 1$.

Domestic output depends on both domestic and foreign government spending in this symmetric model of the world economy. It is, however, not a priori clear which effect dominates, the "own" effect (via $\tilde{G}$) or the spillover effect (via $\tilde{G}^*$). By comparing the coefficients for $\tilde{G}$ and $\tilde{G}^*$ in (2.57)–(2.58), it can be seen that the own effect is larger than the spillover effect provided the economies are not "too open", i.e. provided the share of exports in GDP is less than one-half ($\omega_X < \frac{1}{2}$). This requirement is intuitive, since a high value of ω_X implies that the two economies are more sensitive to foreign than to domestic influences (in colloquial terms, if the foreign country sneezes, the domestic country catches a cold if ω_X is high).

Since it is more convenient to work with a logarithmic version of the model (and in order to cut down on notation), we capture the salient aspects of equations (2.57) and (2.58) with, respectively, equations (T4.1) and (T4.2) in Table 2.4. The composite parameters ε_{YR}, ε_{YQ}, and ε_{YG} are related to the other parameters of the model according to:

$$\varepsilon_{YR} \equiv \frac{(1+\gamma)\omega_I\varepsilon_{IR}}{(1-\gamma^2)\left[1 - (1-\omega_X)\omega_C\varepsilon_{CY}\right]} > 0,$$

$$\varepsilon_{YQ} \equiv \frac{(1-\gamma)\left[(1-\alpha)(1-\omega_X) + \alpha\omega_X\right]}{(1-\gamma^2)\left[1 - (1-\omega_X)\omega_C\varepsilon_{CY}\right]} > 0,$$

$$\varepsilon_{YG} \equiv \frac{\left[1 - \omega_X(1-\gamma)\right]\omega_G}{(1-\gamma^2)\left[1 - (1-\omega_X)\omega_C\varepsilon_{CY}\right]} > 0,$$

$$0 < \eta \equiv \frac{\gamma + \omega_X(1-\gamma)}{1 - \omega_X(1-\gamma)} < 1,$$

where the final inequality follows from the condition $\omega_X < \frac{1}{2}$.

In order to discover how the two-country model works, we look at three prototypical cases. We start with the case with nominal wage rigidity in both countries ($\theta = \theta^* = 0$). Next we study the case with real rigidity in both countries ($\theta = \theta^* = 1$). Finally, we consider the Branson-Rotemberg case in which the domestic country features real wage rigidity ($\theta = 1$) and the foreign economy operates under nominal wage rigidity ($\theta^* = 0$).

2.4.1 Nominal wage rigidity in both countries

If there exists nominal wage rigidity in both countries, the relevant model is obtained from Table 2.4 by setting $\theta = \theta^* = 0$. The resulting model can be written in a compact format as:

$$y = -\varepsilon_{YR}R^* + \varepsilon_{YQ}q + \varepsilon_{YG}\left[g + \eta g^*\right], \tag{2.59}$$

$$y^* = -\varepsilon_{YR}R^* - \varepsilon_{YQ}q + \varepsilon_{YG}\left[g^* + \eta g\right], \tag{2.60}$$

$$m - p = \varepsilon_{MY}y - \varepsilon_{MR}R^*, \tag{2.61}$$

$$m^* - p^* = \varepsilon_{MY}y^* - \varepsilon_{MR}R^*, \tag{2.62}$$

$$y = -\varepsilon_{YW}\left[w_0 - p\right], \tag{2.63}$$

$$y^* = -\varepsilon_{YW}\left[w_0^* - p^*\right], \tag{2.64}$$

Table 2.4. A two-country extended Mundell-Fleming model

$$y = -\varepsilon_{YR}R^* + \varepsilon_{YQ}q + \varepsilon_{YG}\left[g + \eta g^*\right], \tag{T4.1}$$

$$y^* = -\varepsilon_{YR}R^* - \varepsilon_{YQ}q + \varepsilon_{YG}\left[g^* + \eta g\right], \tag{T4.2}$$

$$m - p = \varepsilon_{MY}y - \varepsilon_{MR}R^*, \tag{T4.3}$$

$$m^* - p^* = \varepsilon_{MY}y^* - \varepsilon_{MR}R^*, \tag{T4.4}$$

$$y = -\varepsilon_{YW}\left[w - p\right], \tag{T4.5}$$

$$y^* = -\varepsilon_{YW}\left[w^* - p^*\right], \tag{T4.6}$$

$$w = w_0 + \theta p_C, \tag{T4.7}$$

$$w^* = w_0^* + \theta^* p_C^*, \tag{T4.8}$$

$$p_C = p + (1 - \alpha)q, \tag{T4.9}$$

$$p_C^* = p^* - (1 - \alpha)q, \tag{T4.10}$$

Notes: All variables except the interest rate are in logarithms and starred variables refer to the foreign country. Endogenous variables are the outputs (y, y^*), the real exchange rate (q), the rate of interest (R^*), price levels (p, p^*), nominal wages (w, w^*), and consumer price indexes (p_C, p_C^*). Exogenous are government spending (g, g^*), the money stocks (m, m^*), and the wage targets (w_0, w_0^*). Elasticities of (T4.1)–(T4.2) can be recovered from (2.57)–(2.58).

which constitutes a simultaneous system of six equations determining six endogenous variables $(y, y^*, p, p^*, q, $ and $R^*)$ as a function of the exogenous variables $(g, g^*, m, m^*, w_0, $ and $w_0^*)$. In the appendix to this chapter, we use "brute force" and solve the system analytically by means of matrix inversion. Here, however, we use a more subtle approach which analyses the model by graphical means. The method exploits the structure of the model in such a way that the two-country equilibrium can be characterized by simple two-dimensional equilibrium loci. The one-million euro question is, of course, how one should go about this.

Figure 2.11 reveals the answer. The LM(AS$_N$) curve is obtained by substituting the AS$_N$ curve (2.63) (where "N" stands for nominal) into the LM curve (2.61) (the LM*(AS$_N^*$) curve is obtained in an analogous fashion). This is a useful thing to do because it gives us expressions for the domestic and foreign price and output levels in terms of a *single* endogenous variable (viz. the world interest rate) and the exogenous variables:

$$p = \frac{m + \varepsilon_{MR}R^* + \varepsilon_{YW}\varepsilon_{MY}w_0}{1 + \varepsilon_{YW}\varepsilon_{MY}}, \tag{2.65}$$

$$p^* = \frac{m^* + \varepsilon_{MR}R^* + \varepsilon_{YW}\varepsilon_{MY}w_0^*}{1 + \varepsilon_{YW}\varepsilon_{MY}}, \tag{2.66}$$

$$y = \frac{\varepsilon_{YW}\left[m + \varepsilon_{MR}R^* - w_0\right]}{1 + \varepsilon_{YW}\varepsilon_{MY}}, \qquad \text{LM(AS}_N\text{) curve} \tag{2.67}$$

$$y^* = \frac{\varepsilon_{YW}\left[m^* + \varepsilon_{MR}R^* - w_0^*\right]}{1 + \varepsilon_{YW}\varepsilon_{MY}}. \qquad \text{LM*(AS}_N^*\text{) curve} \tag{2.68}$$

The curves LM(AS$_N$) and LM*(AS$_N^*$) are drawn in the left-hand panel of Figure 2.11, and coincide in the initial equilibrium due to the symmetry assumption.

The goods market equilibrium schedule under nominal wage rigidity, GME$_N$, is

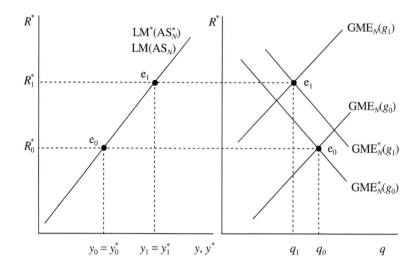

Figure 2.11: Fiscal policy with nominal wage rigidity in both countries

obtained by substituting (2.67) into the IS curve (2.59) and solving for R^* in terms of the real exchange rate and the exogenous variables (and similarly for GME_N^*, we substitute (2.68) into (2.60)):

$$R^* = \frac{(1 + \varepsilon_{YW}\varepsilon_{MY})\left[\varepsilon_{YQ}q + \varepsilon_{YG}(g + \eta g^*)\right] + \varepsilon_{YW}\left[w_0 - m\right]}{\varepsilon_{YR}(1 + \varepsilon_{YW}\varepsilon_{MY}) + \varepsilon_{YW}\varepsilon_{MR}}, \qquad \text{GME}_N \text{ curve}$$

(2.69)

$$R^* = \frac{(1 + \varepsilon_{YW}\varepsilon_{MY})\left[-\varepsilon_{YQ}q + \varepsilon_{YG}(g^* + \eta g)\right] + \varepsilon_{YW}\left[w_0^* - m^*\right]}{\varepsilon_{YR}(1 + \varepsilon_{YW}\varepsilon_{MY}) + \varepsilon_{YW}\varepsilon_{MR}}. \qquad \text{GME}_N^* \text{ curve}$$

(2.70)

In the right-hand panel of Figure 2.11, GME_N is upward sloping in (R^*, q) space because a real depreciation (a rise in q) stimulates domestic output and, consequently, the demand for real money balances. Money market equilibrium can only be restored if the interest rate is higher. Of course, the slope of GME_N^* is opposite in sign because $-q$ measures the real exchange rate from the foreign country's perspective.

That's it! We have "tamed" the six-equation simultaneous system (2.59)–(2.64) and can now represent its core properties with a simple, two-panel diagram. We are now ready to look at the effects of domestic and foreign fiscal and monetary policies.

2.4.1.1 Fiscal policy

Fiscal policy in the domestic country (represented by a rise in g) shifts up both GME_N and GME_N^* but, provided the own effect of government spending dominates (so that $\eta < 1$), the former shifts by more than the latter (i.e. $\partial R^*/\partial g$ is largest for GME_N). The new equilibrium is at e_1, the domestic economy experiences a real appreciation, and output in *both countries* rises. Hence, the fiscal stimulus in the domestic economy also stimulates the foreign economy. This is why this phenomenon is called a *locomotive policy*: one country is able to pull itself and the other country out of a recession by means of fiscal policy. Why does it work? The increased government spending in the domestic economy leads to upward pressure on domestic interest rates. The resulting capital inflows cause the domestic currency to appreciate, so that the demand for foreign goods is increased. This stimulates output in the foreign country. The resulting increase in the interest rate causes the price levels of both countries to rise by the same amount (see (2.65)–(2.66) above). Since nominal wages are fixed, the real producer wage falls in both countries, which explains the increase in output and employment.

For future reference we derive the expressions for the output multipliers (details are found in the appendix). First, we use (2.69) and (2.70) to derive the effect of domestic and foreign fiscal policy on the world interest rate:

$$\frac{dR^*}{dg} = \frac{dR^*}{dg^*} = \frac{(1+\eta)\varepsilon_{YG}(1+\varepsilon_{YW}\varepsilon_{MY})}{2\left[\varepsilon_{YR}(1+\varepsilon_{YW}\varepsilon_{MY})+\varepsilon_{YW}\varepsilon_{MR}\right]} > 0. \tag{2.71}$$

Next, we use (2.67), (2.68), and (2.71) to derive the output effects:

$$\frac{dy}{dg} = \frac{dy}{dg^*} = \frac{dy^*}{dg} = \frac{dy^*}{dg^*} = \frac{(1+\eta)\varepsilon_{YG}\varepsilon_{YW}\varepsilon_{MR}}{2\left[\varepsilon_{YR}(1+\varepsilon_{YW}\varepsilon_{MY})+\varepsilon_{YW}\varepsilon_{MR}\right]} \equiv \pi_N > 0. \tag{2.72}$$

The key thing to note is that own and foreign fiscal policy have the same output effects in both countries.

2.4.1.2 Monetary policy

Unlike fiscal policy, monetary policy in the domestic country does not benefit but harm the foreign country. This is illustrated with the aid of Figure 2.12. The increase in the domestic money stock shifts the domestic goods market equilibrium locus from $GME_N(m_0)$ to $GME_N(m_1)$ and the LM(AS) curve from $LM(AS_N)_0$ to $LM(AS_N)_1$. There is downward pressure on domestic interest rates, and the capital outflows lead to a depreciation of the currency. This shifts domestic demand towards domestically produced goods and away from foreign goods. Also, foreigners shift towards goods produced in the domestic economy. In view of (2.66), the foreign price level falls and consequently the real producer wage rises. This explains the fall in output and employment in the foreign country. For obvious reasons monetary policy is referred to as a *beggar-thy-neighbour policy*: the domestic economy is stimulated at the expense of the foreign economy.

In a similar fashion, an increase in the foreign money supply boosts foreign output and reduces domestic output. In this case the foreign country beggars its neighbour, the domestic economy.

2.4.2 Real wage rigidity in both countries

If both countries experience real wage rigidity, the relevant model is obtained from Table 2.4 by setting $\theta = \theta^* = 1$. Upon making the relevant substitutions, the model reduces to:

$$y = -\varepsilon_{YR}R^* + \varepsilon_{YQ}q + \varepsilon_{YG}\left[g+\eta g^*\right], \tag{2.73}$$

$$y^* = -\varepsilon_{YR}R^* - \varepsilon_{YQ}q + \varepsilon_{YG}\left[g^*+\eta g\right], \tag{2.74}$$

$$p = m - \varepsilon_{MY}y + \varepsilon_{MR}R^*, \tag{2.75}$$

$$p^* = m^* - \varepsilon_{MY}y^* + \varepsilon_{MR}R^*, \tag{2.76}$$

$$y = -\varepsilon_{YW}\left[w_0 + (1-\alpha)q\right], \qquad \text{AS}_R \text{ curve} \tag{2.77}$$

$$y^* = -\varepsilon_{YW}\left[w_0^* - (1-\alpha)q\right]. \qquad \text{AS}_R^* \text{ curve} \tag{2.78}$$

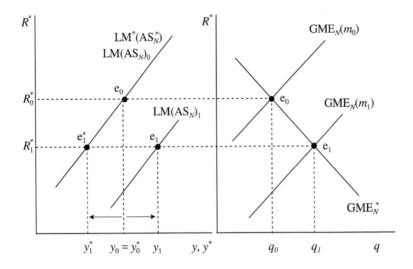

Figure 2.12: Monetary policy with nominal wage rigidity in both countries

Again relegating the brute-force method to the appendix, we study the model by graphical means. Under real wage rigidity, the aggregate supply curves in the two countries only depend on a single endogenous variable (the real exchange rate) and some exogenous variables. In the bottom panel of Figure 2.13, AS_R and AS_R^* have been illustrated.

The goods market equilibrium schedules for the two countries are obtained by equating the respective AS and IS curves (viz. (2.77) and (2.73) for the domestic country and (2.78) and (2.74) for the foreign country) and and solving for R^* in terms of the real exchange rate and the exogenous variables. The subscript "R" is used to indicate that real wages are rigid in the two countries:

$$R^* = \frac{\varepsilon_{YW} w_0 + \left[\varepsilon_{YQ} + (1-\alpha)\,\varepsilon_{YW}\right] q + \varepsilon_{YG}\left[g + \eta g^*\right]}{\varepsilon_{YR}}, \qquad \text{GME}_R \text{ curve}$$

(2.79)

$$R^* = \frac{\varepsilon_{YW} w_0^* - \left[\varepsilon_{YQ} + (1-\alpha)\,\varepsilon_{YW}\right] q + \varepsilon_{YG}\left[g^* + \eta g\right]}{\varepsilon_{YR}}. \qquad \text{GME}_R^* \text{ curve}$$

(2.80)

In the top panel of Figure 2.13, GME_R is upward sloping and GME_R^* is downward sloping.

Once again we have managed to represent the core properties of a six-equation simultaneous system of equations with a simple, two-panel diagram. Let us look at the effects of domestic and foreign fiscal and monetary policies.

2.4.2.1   Fiscal policy

In sharp contrast to our conclusion in the previous section, fiscal policy constitutes a beggar-thy-neighbour policy under real wage rigidity. This can be illustrated with the aid of Figure 2.13. The increase in government spending in the domestic country (g) produces an upward shift in both GME_R and GME_R^*, with the former experiencing the bigger shift because the "own" effect exceeds the "spillover" effect (i.e.

$\eta < 1$). To restore equilibrium, the interest rate rises and the real exchange rate appreciates (for the domestic country). The equilibrium shifts from e_0 to e_1 in the top panel of Figure 2.13.

The output effects in the two countries are opposite in sign. In the bottom panel of Figure 2.13, equilibrium in the domestic country shifts from e_0 to e_1 and output is stimulated. The equilibrium for the foreign country, in contrast, shifts from e_0 to e_1^*, and foreign output contracts! How does this work? Since the real consumer wage (W/P_C) is fixed, the producer wage (W/P) falls in the domestic economy and output and employment are stimulated. The opposite holds in the foreign country, where the real producer wage (W^*/P^*) rises. By raising g, the domestic policy maker causes a fall in q (a depreciation of the foreign currency) which prompts foreign workers to demand higher nominal wages in order to keep their real consumption wage (W^*/P_C^*) constant.

For future reference we derive the expressions for the various output multipliers. First we use (2.79) and (2.80) to derive the effect of domestic and foreign fiscal policy on the real exchange rate:

$$\frac{dq}{dg} = -\frac{dq}{dg^*} = -\frac{(1-\eta)\varepsilon_{YG}}{2\left[\varepsilon_{YQ} + (1-\alpha)\,\varepsilon_{YW}\right]} < 0. \tag{2.81}$$

Next, we use (2.77), (2.78), and (2.81) to derive the output effects:

$$\frac{dy}{dg} = -\frac{dy}{dg^*} = \frac{dy^*}{dg^*} = -\frac{dy^*}{dg} = \frac{(1-\eta)(1-\alpha)\varepsilon_{YW}\varepsilon_{YG}}{2\left[\varepsilon_{YQ} + (1-\alpha)\,\varepsilon_{YW}\right]} \equiv \pi_R > 0. \tag{2.82}$$

Equation (2.82) provides a clear statement of the beggar-thy-neighbour property of fiscal policy when both countries experience real wage rigidity.

2.4.2.2 Monetary policy

Not surprisingly, domestic monetary policy has no real effects under real wage rigidity. As none of the equilibrium loci (AR_R, AS_R^*, GME_R, and GME_R^*) are affected, the interest rate, output levels, and the real exchange rate are also unaffected. It thus follows that an increase in m causes an (equal) increase in the domestic price level ($dm = dp$) and the nominal wage rate ($dp = dw$). Since the real exchange rate is unaffected, the nominal exchange rate depreciates by the full amount of the change in the domestic price ($de = dp$).

In a similar fashion, and for exactly the same reasons, an increase in the foreign money supply has no real effects at all and just leads to nominal wage and price increases and a nominal depreciation of the foreign currency, i.e. $dw^* = dp^* = -de = dm^* > 0$.

2.4.3 Real wage rigidity in Europe and nominal wage rigidity in the United States

In an influential paper, Branson and Rotemberg (1980) argue (on the basis of empirical evidence) that nominal wage rigidity characterizes the US economy whilst real wage rigidity well describes the European countries. Letting Europe denote the home country and the US the foreign country (and ignoring the rest of the world for convenience), the model describing this configuration is obtained from Table 2.4 by setting $\theta = 1$ and $\theta^* = 0$.

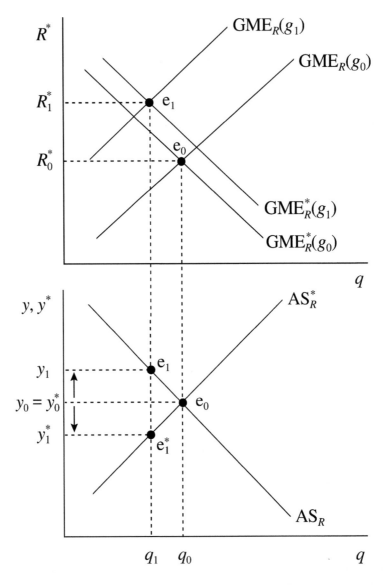

Figure 2.13: Fiscal policy with real wage rigidity in both countries

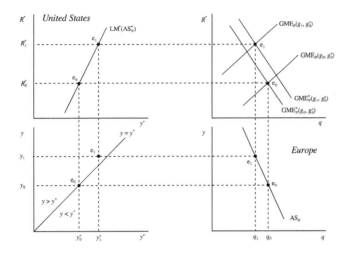

Figure 2.14: European fiscal policy with real wage rigidity in Europe and nominal wage rigidity in the United States

The analysis of the effects of fiscal and monetary policy can once again proceed by graphical means. Since Europe experiences real wage rigidity, it is fully described by GME_R and AS_R, which we restate for convenience:

$$R^* = \frac{\varepsilon_{YW}w_0 + \left[\varepsilon_{YQ} + (1-\alpha)\varepsilon_{YW}\right]q + \varepsilon_{YG}\left[g + \eta g^*\right]}{\varepsilon_{YR}}, \qquad GME_R \text{ curve}$$

$$\tag{2.83}$$

$$y = -\varepsilon_{YW}\left[w_0 + (1-\alpha)q\right]. \qquad AS_R \text{ curve}$$
$$\tag{2.84}$$

The US economy, on the other hand, experiences nominal wage rigidity, and is described by GME_N^* and $LM^*(AS_N^*)$:

$$R^* = \frac{(1+\varepsilon_{YW}\varepsilon_{MY})\left[-\varepsilon_{YQ}q + \varepsilon_{YG}(g^* + \eta g)\right] + \varepsilon_{YW}\left[w_0^* - m^*\right]}{\varepsilon_{YR}(1+\varepsilon_{YW}\varepsilon_{MY}) + \varepsilon_{YW}\varepsilon_{MR}}, \qquad GME_N^* \text{ curve}$$

$$\tag{2.85}$$

$$y^* = \frac{\varepsilon_{YW}\left[m^* + \varepsilon_{MR}R^* - w_0^*\right]}{1+\varepsilon_{YW}\varepsilon_{MY}}. \qquad LM^*(AS_N^*) \text{ curve} \qquad (2.86)$$

The different schedules have been drawn in Figures 2.14-2.16. In each case, the initial equilibrium is at e_0.

2.4.3.1 Fiscal policy

In Figure 2.14, a European fiscal expansion (a rise in g) leads to an upward shift of both GME_R and GME_N^*, with the former experiencing the larger shift (because $\eta < 1$ and $\varepsilon_{YW}\varepsilon_{MY} > 0$):

$$\left(\frac{\partial R^*}{\partial g}\right)_{GME_R} \equiv \frac{\varepsilon_{YG}}{\varepsilon_{YR}} > \frac{\eta\varepsilon_{YG}}{\varepsilon_{YR} + \frac{\varepsilon_{YW}\varepsilon_{MR}}{1+\varepsilon_{YW}\varepsilon_{MY}}} \equiv \left(\frac{\partial R^*}{\partial g}\right)_{GME_N^*}. \tag{2.87}$$

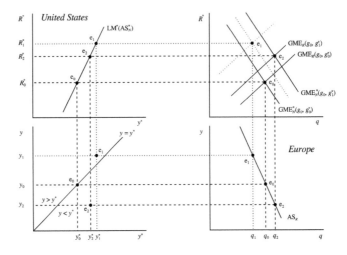

Figure 2.15: US fiscal policy with real wage rigidity in Europe and nominal wage rigidity in the United States

The real exchange rate of Europe appreciates and the new equilibrium is at e_1. We show in the appendix that the output multipliers are both positive:

$$\frac{dy}{dg} = (1-\alpha)\,\varepsilon_{YW}\varepsilon_{YG} \cdot \frac{(1-\eta)\,\varepsilon_{YR}\,[1+\varepsilon_{MY}\varepsilon_{YW}] + \varepsilon_{YW}\varepsilon_{MR}}{-|\Delta|} > 0, \tag{2.88}$$

$$\frac{dy^*}{dg} = \varepsilon_{MR}\varepsilon_{YW}\varepsilon_{YG} \cdot \frac{(1+\eta)\,\varepsilon_{YQ} + \eta\,(1-\alpha)\,\varepsilon_{YW}}{-|\Delta|} > 0, \tag{2.89}$$

where $|\Delta| < 0$. Both y and y^* increase, but it is not a priori clear which effect dominates. For reasonable parameter values, the effect on own output is likely to exceed the induced effect on foreign output, i.e. $dy/dg > dy^*/dg$. This is the case illustrated in Figure 2.14 (see the third quadrant). The European fiscal impulse constitutes a locomotive policy since it ends up simultaneously stimulating US output and employment.

A US fiscal expansion (a rise in g^*) shifts both GME_R and GME_N^*, but is not clear which shift dominates:

$$\left(\frac{\partial R^*}{\partial g}\right)_{\mathrm{GME}_R} \equiv \frac{\eta\varepsilon_{YG}}{\varepsilon_{YR}} \lesseqqgtr \frac{\varepsilon_{YG}}{\varepsilon_{YR} + \frac{\varepsilon_{YW}\varepsilon_{MR}}{1+\varepsilon_{YW}\varepsilon_{MY}}} \equiv \left(\frac{\partial R^*}{\partial g}\right)_{\mathrm{GME}_N}. \tag{2.90}$$

In Figure 2.15 we draw the case for which the shift in GME_N^* is dominant. The equilibrium shifts from e_0 to e_2. The rate of interest is higher, there is a real depreciation in Europe, but output falls because real producer wages in Europe rise. Output and employment in the US rise, so that the US fiscal expansion constitutes a beggar-thy-neighbour policy. It leads to lower output and higher unemployment in Europe.

In the appendix we derive the expressions for the general case:

$$\frac{dy}{dg^*} = (1-\alpha)\,\varepsilon_{YW}\varepsilon_{YG} \cdot \frac{-(1-\eta)\,\varepsilon_{YR}\,[1+\varepsilon_{MY}\varepsilon_{YW}] + \eta\varepsilon_{YW}\varepsilon_{MR}}{-|\Delta|} \gtreqless 0, \tag{2.91}$$

$$\frac{dy^*}{dg^*} = \varepsilon_{MR}\varepsilon_{YW}\varepsilon_{YG} \cdot \frac{(1+\eta)\,\varepsilon_{YQ} + (1-\alpha)\,\varepsilon_{YW}]}{-|\Delta|} > 0. \tag{2.92}$$

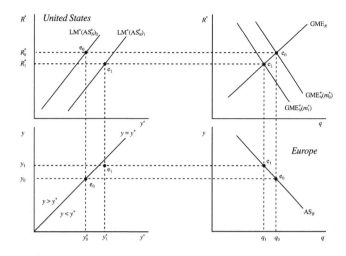

Figure 2.16: US monetary policy with real wage rigidity in Europe and nominal wage rigidity in the United States

2.4.3.2 Monetary policy

Monetary policy in Europe has no real effects: GME_R and AS_R are both independent of the European money supply (see above). In contrast, expansionary US monetary policy (a rise in m^*) constitutes a locomotive policy for Europe. This has been illustrated in Figure 2.16. The increase in the US money stock shifts GME_N^* down and $LM^*(AS_N^*)$ to the right. The equilibrium shifts from e_0 to e_1. The European real exchange rate appreciates and the interest rate falls. Both y and y^* rise, and the US monetary impulse thus stimulates both economies. By inflating the foreign price level, the real producer wage abroad falls. This explains why foreign output rises. Similarly, the real exchange rate appreciation causes European producer wages to falls, thus also enabling an increase in output there.

2.5 Punchlines

In this chapter we conclude our discussion of the IS-LM model that was commenced in Chapter 1, by discussing the contributions made by Mundell and Fleming (MF) and subsequent work in the area. In the MF framework it is explicitly recognized that most countries are open economies, i.e. they trade goods and financial assets with each other. There are two crucial aspects characterizing the open economy, namely its "financial openness" and the exchange rate system it maintains.

By financial openness we mean the ease with which domestic residents substitute domestic and foreign assets in their portfolios as yields between assets differ. If substitution is very easy then yields will equalize. This situation is often referred to as one of perfect capital mobility. At the other extreme, if domestic residents are not willing to hold foreign assets at all (or if there are strictures against it) then the economy is "financially closed" and there is said to be no capital mobility at all. The intermediate case, with imperfectly mobile capital, can also be distinguished.

There are two prototypical exchange rate systems. Under a system of fixed exchange rates, the monetary authority keeps the exchange rate for the domestic currency fixed by means of interventions on the foreign exchange market. Unless the policy maker engages in sterilization operations, the money supply will be endogenous under this regime. With a system of flexible exchange rates, the monetary authority does not intervene in the foreign exchange market. As a result the equilibrium exchange rate is endogenously determined by the forces of demand and supply in that market.

The results of monetary and fiscal policy depend both on the degree of capital mobility and on the exchange rate system. With immobile capital and under fixed exchange rates neither monetary nor fiscal policy can permanently affect aggregate output. With perfectly mobile capital and fixed (flexible) exchange rates, monetary policy is ineffective (effective) and fiscal policy is effective (ineffective) at influencing output. All these results are based on the assumption of a fixed price level.

In order to endogenize the price level we add a simple model of aggregate supply to the MF framework. The key features of this model are as follows. First, perfectly competitive firms set prices of the domestic good. Second, domestic and foreign goods are distinct and are imperfect substitutes for each other. Third, to give the model some Keynesian features it is assumed that the (real or nominal) consumer wage is fixed and that the demand for labour determines employment and output. Finally, because domestic consumers use both domestic and foreign goods, the consumer price index, upon which the wage claims are potentially based, depends on both the domestic and the foreign price (and thus on the nominal exchange rate).

Armed with this extended MF model we investigate the effects of monetary and fiscal policy under perfect capital mobility. Not surprisingly, the wage setting regime plays a crucial role. Under real (nominal) wage rigidity, monetary policy is ineffective (effective). With real wage rigidity fiscal policy boosts output, reduces the domestic price, and leads to an appreciation of both the nominal and the real exchange rate. In contrast, with nominal wage rigidity fiscal policy does not affect output and the domestic price and merely leads to an appreciation of the real and nominal exchange rate. All these results hold for a small open economy which faces an exogenously given world interest rate.

In order to endogenize the world interest rate we assume that the world consists of two identical countries which can each be described by the extended MF model. The two-country MF model shows how shocks are transmitted internationally. Depending on the configuration of wage-setting regimes in the two countries, macroeconomic policy initiatives may spill over across countries.

Further reading

The classic references on the open economy IS-LM model are Mundell (1968) and Fleming (1962). See Frenkel and Razin (1987) for a review article. Good textbook treatments are found in Branson (1972) and Turnovsky (1977). For two-country models see Cooper (1968), Dornbusch (1976b), Argy and Salop (1983), and Aoki (1981).

Appendix: Analysing two-country models

In this appendix we provide analytical solutions for the two-country model presented in Table 2.4. We exploit the symmetry of the model by utilizing the Aoki (1981) transformation. This transformation works as follows. Instead of working with the ten-equation system of Table 2.4, it works with two (much smaller) subsystems that are very easy to analyse, namely the *average* subsystem and the *difference* subsystem. For each set of variable x and x^*, the following transformed variables are defined:

$$x_a \equiv \frac{x + x^*}{2}, \qquad x_d \equiv \frac{x - x^*}{2}. \tag{A2.1}$$

Intuitively, x_a represents the world average of the variable, whilst x_d is the scaled difference between the domestic and foreign values of the variable. Of course, once we know x_a and x_d, we can recover the domestic and foreign values of x by noting that:

$$x \equiv x_a + x_d, \qquad x^* \equiv x_a - x_d. \tag{A2.2}$$

A.1 Symmetric case

For the symmetric case with $\theta = \theta^*$, the difference subsystem implied by Table 2.4 can be written in matrix format as:

$$\Delta_D \cdot \begin{bmatrix} y_d \\ q \\ p_d \end{bmatrix} = \begin{bmatrix} (1 - \eta)\,\varepsilon_{YG}g_d \\ m_d \\ -\varepsilon_{YW}w_{0d} \end{bmatrix}, \tag{A2.3}$$

where Δ_D is defined as follows:

$$\Delta_D \equiv \begin{bmatrix} 1 & -\varepsilon_{YQ} & 0 \\ \varepsilon_{MY} & 0 & 1 \\ 1 & \theta\,(1 - \alpha)\,\varepsilon_{YW} & -(1 - \theta)\,\varepsilon_{YW} \end{bmatrix}, \tag{A2.4}$$

where $y_d \equiv (y - y^*)/2$, $p_d \equiv (p - p^*)/2$, $g_d \equiv (g - g^*)/2$, $m_d \equiv (m - m^*)/2$, and $w_{0d} \equiv (w_0 - w_0^*)/2$. The difference subsystem determines the endogenous variables y_d, q, and p_d, as a function of the exogenous variables, g_d, m_d, and w_{0d}. The key thing to note is that Δ_D is only a three-by-three matrix, and is thus relatively easy to invert:

$$\Delta_D^{-1} \equiv \frac{1}{|\Delta_D|} \cdot \begin{bmatrix} -\theta\,(1 - \alpha)\,\varepsilon_{YW} & -(1 - \theta)\,\varepsilon_{YW}\varepsilon_{YQ} & -\varepsilon_{YQ} \\ 1 + (1 - \theta)\,\varepsilon_{YW}\varepsilon_{MY} & -(1 - \theta)\,\varepsilon_{YW} & -1 \\ \theta\,(1 - \alpha)\,\varepsilon_{YW}\varepsilon_{MY} & -[\theta\,(1 - \alpha)\,\varepsilon_{YW} + \varepsilon_{YQ}] & \varepsilon_{MY}\varepsilon_{YQ} \end{bmatrix}, \tag{A2.5}$$

where $|\Delta_D| \equiv -[\theta\,(1 - \alpha)\,\varepsilon_{YW} + \varepsilon_{YQ}[1 + (1 - \theta)\,\varepsilon_{YW}\varepsilon_{MY}]] < 0$.

The average subsystem implied by Table 2.4 can be written as:

$$\Delta_A \cdot \begin{bmatrix} y_a \\ R^* \\ p_a \end{bmatrix} = \begin{bmatrix} (1 + \eta)\,\varepsilon_{YG}g_a \\ m_a \\ -\varepsilon_{YW}w_{0a} \end{bmatrix}, \tag{A2.6}$$

where Δ_A is defined as follows:

$$\Delta_A \equiv \begin{bmatrix} 1 & -\varepsilon_{YR} & 0 \\ \varepsilon_{MY} & -\varepsilon_{MR} & 1 \\ 1 & 0 & -(1 - \theta)\,\varepsilon_{YW} \end{bmatrix}, \tag{A2.7}$$

where $y_a \equiv (y + y^*)/2$, $p_a \equiv (p + p^*)/2$, $g_a \equiv (g + g^*)/2$, $m_a \equiv (m + m^*)/2$, and $w_{0a} \equiv (w_0 + w_0^*)/2$. The average subsystem determines the endogenous variables y_a, R^*, and p_d, as a function of the exogenous variables, g_a, m_a, and w_{0a}. Again, matrix inversion is practicable:

$$\Delta_A^{-1} \equiv \frac{1}{|\Delta_A|} \cdot \begin{bmatrix} (1-\theta)\,\varepsilon_{YW}\varepsilon_{MR} & (1-\theta)\,\varepsilon_{YW}\varepsilon_{YR} & \varepsilon_{YR} \\ 1 + (1-\theta)\,\varepsilon_{YW}\varepsilon_{MY} & -(1-\theta)\,\varepsilon_{YW} & -1 \\ \varepsilon_{MR} & \varepsilon_{YR} & -(\varepsilon_{MR} + \varepsilon_{MY}\varepsilon_{YR}) \end{bmatrix}, \quad (A2.8)$$

where $|\Delta_A| \equiv (1-\theta)\,\varepsilon_{YW}\,[\varepsilon_{MR} + \varepsilon_{MY}\varepsilon_{YR}] + \varepsilon_{YR} > 0$.

The reduced-form expressions for q and R^* are obtained from the second row of (A2.3) and (A2.6), respectively:

$$q = \frac{-\,[1 + (1-\theta)\,\varepsilon_{YW}\varepsilon_{MY}]\,(1-\eta)\,\varepsilon_{YG}g_d + (1-\theta)\,\varepsilon_{YW}m_d - \varepsilon_{YW}w_{0d}}{\theta\,(1-\alpha)\,\varepsilon_{YW} + \varepsilon_{YQ}\,(1 + (1-\theta)\,\varepsilon_{YW}\varepsilon_{MY})}, \quad (A2.9)$$

$$R^* = \frac{[1 + (1-\theta)\,\varepsilon_{YW}\varepsilon_{MY}]\,(1+\eta)\,\varepsilon_{YG}g_a - (1-\theta)\,\varepsilon_{YW}m_a + \varepsilon_{YW}w_{0a}}{(1-\theta)\,\varepsilon_{YW}\,[\varepsilon_{MR} + \varepsilon_{MY}\varepsilon_{YR}] + \varepsilon_{YR}}. \quad (A2.10)$$

The real exchange rate only depends on the difference variables (g_d, m_d, and w_{0d}), and we immediately find the policy effects:

$$\frac{dq}{dg} = -\frac{dq}{dg^*} = \frac{-\,(1-\eta)\,\varepsilon_{YG}\,[1 + (1-\theta)\,\varepsilon_{YW}\varepsilon_{MY}]}{2\,[\theta\,(1-\alpha)\,\varepsilon_{YW} + \varepsilon_{YQ}\,(1 + (1-\theta)\,\varepsilon_{YW}\varepsilon_{MY})]} < 0, \quad (A2.11)$$

$$\frac{dq}{dm} = -\frac{dq}{dm^*} = \frac{(1-\theta)\,\varepsilon_{YW}}{2\,[\theta\,(1-\alpha)\,\varepsilon_{YW} + \varepsilon_{YQ}\,(1 + (1-\theta)\,\varepsilon_{YW}\varepsilon_{MY})]} \geq 0, \quad (A2.12)$$

where $dq/dm = -dq/dm^* = 0$ only for the case of real wage rigidity ($\theta = 1$).

The world interest rate only depends on the average variables (g_a, m_a, and w_{0a}) and the policy effects are thus given by:

$$\frac{dR^*}{dg} = \frac{dR^*}{dg^*} = \frac{[1 + (1-\theta)\,\varepsilon_{YW}\varepsilon_{MY}]\,(1+\eta)\,\varepsilon_{YG}}{2\,[(1-\theta)\,\varepsilon_{YW}\,[\varepsilon_{MR} + \varepsilon_{MY}\varepsilon_{YR}] + \varepsilon_{YR}]} > 0, \quad (A2.13)$$

$$\frac{dR^*}{dm} = \frac{dR^*}{dm^*} = \frac{-\,(1-\theta)\,\varepsilon_{YW}}{2\,[(1-\theta)\,\varepsilon_{YW}\,[\varepsilon_{MR} + \varepsilon_{MY}\varepsilon_{YR}] + \varepsilon_{YR}]} \leq 0, \quad (A2.14)$$

where $dR^*/dm = dR^*/dm^* = 0$ only for the case of real wage rigidity ($\theta = 1$). By setting $\theta = 0$, in (A2.13) we obtain (2.71) in the text. Similarly, by setting $\theta = 1$ in (A2.11) we obtain (2.81).

The comparative static effects for y, y^*, p, and p^* can be obtained by recognizing the results in (A2.2). By using (A2.6) and (A2.3) we find the following expressions for y_a and y_d:

$$y_a = \frac{(1-\theta)\,\varepsilon_{YW}\varepsilon_{MR}\,(1+\eta)\,\varepsilon_{YG}g_a + (1-\theta)\,\varepsilon_{YW}\varepsilon_{YR}m_a - \varepsilon_{YR}\varepsilon_{YW}w_{0a}}{(1-\theta)\,\varepsilon_{YW}\,[\varepsilon_{MR} + \varepsilon_{MY}\varepsilon_{YR}] + \varepsilon_{YR}}, \quad (A2.15)$$

$$y_d = \frac{\theta\,(1-\alpha)\,\varepsilon_{YW}\,(1-\eta)\,\varepsilon_{YG}g_d + (1-\theta)\,\varepsilon_{YW}\varepsilon_{YQ}m_d - \varepsilon_{YQ}\varepsilon_{YW}w_{0d}}{\theta\,(1-\alpha)\,\varepsilon_{YW} + \varepsilon_{YQ}\,(1 + (1-\theta)\,\varepsilon_{YW}\varepsilon_{MY})}. \quad (A2.16)$$

The fiscal policy effects can be obtained as follows:

$$\frac{dy}{dg} = \frac{dy_a}{dg} + \frac{dy_d}{dg} = \frac{(1-\theta)\,\varepsilon_{YW}\varepsilon_{MR}\,(1+\eta)\,\varepsilon_{YG}}{2\,[(1-\theta)\,\varepsilon_{YW}\,[\varepsilon_{MR} + \varepsilon_{MY}\varepsilon_{YR}] + \varepsilon_{YR}]}$$

$$+ \frac{\theta \left(1 - \alpha\right) \varepsilon_{YW} \left(1 - \eta\right) \varepsilon_{YG}}{2 \left[\theta \left(1 - \alpha\right) \varepsilon_{YW} + \varepsilon_{YQ} \left[1 + \left(1 - \theta\right) \varepsilon_{YW} \varepsilon_{MY}\right]\right]}, \tag{A2.17}$$

$$\frac{dy^*}{dg} = \frac{dy_a}{dg} - \frac{dy_d}{dg} = \frac{\left(1 - \theta\right) \varepsilon_{YW} \varepsilon_{MR} \left(1 + \eta\right) \varepsilon_{YG}}{2 \left[\left(1 - \theta\right) \varepsilon_{YW} \left[\varepsilon_{MR} + \varepsilon_{MY} \varepsilon_{YR}\right] + \varepsilon_{YR}\right]}$$

$$- \frac{\theta \left(1 - \alpha\right) \varepsilon_{YW} \left(1 - \eta\right) \varepsilon_{YG}}{2 \left[\theta \left(1 - \alpha\right) \varepsilon_{YW} + \varepsilon_{YQ} \left[1 + \left(1 - \theta\right) \varepsilon_{YW} \varepsilon_{MY}\right]\right]}, \tag{A2.18}$$

$$\frac{dy}{dg^*} = \frac{dy_a}{dg^*} + \frac{dy_d}{dg^*} = \frac{dy^*}{dg}, \tag{A2.19}$$

$$\frac{dy^*}{dg^*} = \frac{dy_a}{dg^*} - \frac{dy_d}{dg^*} = \frac{dy}{dg}. \tag{A2.20}$$

By setting $\theta = 0$ in (A2.17)–(A2.20) we obtain (2.72) in the text, and by setting $\theta = 1$ we obtain (2.82).

For the monetary policy effects we obtain from (A2.15)–(A2.16):

$$\frac{dy}{dm} = \frac{dy_a}{dm} + \frac{dy_d}{dm} = \frac{\left(1 - \theta\right) \varepsilon_{YW} \varepsilon_{YR}}{2 \left(1 - \theta\right) \varepsilon_{YW} \left[\varepsilon_{MR} + \varepsilon_{MY} \varepsilon_{YR}\right] + \varepsilon_{YR}}$$

$$+ \frac{\left(1 - \theta\right) \varepsilon_{YW} \varepsilon_{YQ}}{2 \left[\theta \left(1 - \alpha\right) \varepsilon_{YW} + \varepsilon_{YQ} \left(1 + \left(1 - \theta\right) \varepsilon_{YW} \varepsilon_{MY}\right)\right]}, \tag{A2.21}$$

$$\frac{dy^*}{dm} = \frac{dy_a}{dm} - \frac{dy_d}{dm} = \frac{\left(1 - \theta\right) \varepsilon_{YW} \varepsilon_{YR}}{2 \left(1 - \theta\right) \varepsilon_{YW} \left[\varepsilon_{MR} + \varepsilon_{MY} \varepsilon_{YR}\right] + \varepsilon_{YR}}$$

$$- \frac{\left(1 - \theta\right) \varepsilon_{YW} \varepsilon_{YQ}}{2 \left[\theta \left(1 - \alpha\right) \varepsilon_{YW} + \varepsilon_{YQ} \left(1 + \left(1 - \theta\right) \varepsilon_{YW} \varepsilon_{MY}\right)\right]}, \tag{A2.22}$$

$$\frac{dy}{dm^*} = \frac{dy_a}{dm^*} + \frac{dy_d}{dm^*} = \frac{dy^*}{dm}, \tag{A2.23}$$

$$\frac{dy^*}{dm^*} = \frac{dy_a}{dm^*} - \frac{dy_d}{dm^*} = \frac{dy}{dm}. \tag{A2.24}$$

Obviously, for $\theta = 1$ (real wage rigidity) money is neutral. For $\theta = 0$, we obtain the results described in the text.

In closing we note that the comparative static results for p and p^* can be obtained from (A2.6) and (A2.3) by using (A2.2). This is left as an exercise to the reader.

A.2 Asymmetric case

For the asymmetric case, with $\theta = 1$ and $\theta^* = 0$ the Aoki transformation does not yield a simplification, and we write the simultaneous system directly in terms of the original variables:

$$\Delta \cdot \begin{bmatrix} y \\ y^* \\ p \\ p^* \\ q \\ R^* \end{bmatrix} = \begin{bmatrix} \varepsilon_{YG} \left[g + \eta g^*\right] \\ \varepsilon_{YG} \left[\eta g + g^*\right] \\ m \\ m^* \\ -\varepsilon_{YW} w_0 \\ -\varepsilon_{YW} w_0^* \end{bmatrix}, \tag{A2.25}$$

where Δ is defined as:

$$
\Delta \equiv
\begin{bmatrix}
1 & 0 & 0 & 0 & -\varepsilon_{YQ} & \varepsilon_{YR} \\
0 & 1 & 0 & 0 & \varepsilon_{YQ} & \varepsilon_{YR} \\
\varepsilon_{MY} & 0 & 1 & 0 & 0 & -\varepsilon_{MR} \\
0 & \varepsilon_{MY} & 0 & 1 & 0 & -\varepsilon_{MR} \\
1 & 0 & 0 & 0 & (1-\alpha)\varepsilon_{YW} & 0 \\
0 & 1 & 0 & -\varepsilon_{YW} & 0 & 0
\end{bmatrix}
\tag{A2.26}
$$

After some manipulation, we find that:

$$
|\Delta| \equiv -\,(1-\alpha)\,\varepsilon_{YW}\Big[\varepsilon_{YW}\varepsilon_{MR} + \varepsilon_{YR}\left[1 + \varepsilon_{MY}\varepsilon_{YW}\right]\Big]
$$

$$
-\,\varepsilon_{YQ}\Big[\varepsilon_{YW}\varepsilon_{MR} + 2\varepsilon_{YR}\left[1 + \varepsilon_{MY}\varepsilon_{YW}\right]\Big] < 0.
\tag{A2.27}
$$

By using Cramer's Rule we obtain the policy effects on output in the two regions. The fiscal policy multipliers are reported in the text—see equations (2.88), (2.91), (2.89), and (2.92). The monetary policy effects are given by $dy/dm = dy^*/dm = 0$ and:

$$
\frac{dy}{dm^*} = \frac{(1-\alpha)\,\varepsilon_{YR}\varepsilon_{YW}^2}{-\,|\Delta|} > 0,
\tag{A2.28}
$$

$$
\frac{dy^*}{dm^*} = \frac{\varepsilon_{YR}\varepsilon_{YW}\left[(1-\alpha)\,\varepsilon_{YW} + 2\varepsilon_{YQ}\right]}{-\,|\Delta|} > 0.
\tag{A2.29}
$$

Chapter 3

Dynamics in aggregate demand and supply

The purpose of this chapter is to study the following four issues relating to the implicit dynamics present in macroeconomics models:

1. The AEH and stability of the IS-LM-AS model under the neo-Keynesian synthesis,

2. A theory of investment and the implied stock-flow interaction between investment and the capital stock,

3. A first view of the government budget restriction and the implied stock-flow interaction between the government deficit and debt or money, which allows a comparison of stability and effectiveness of money-financed and bond-financed increases in government spending, and

4. The concept of hysteresis or path dependence arising in a model where the equilibrium rate of unemployment is determined by the past rate of unemployment and temporary shocks have permanent effects.

3.1 What is stability?

Throughout this chapter the notion of stability will play a fundamental role. A *stable system* may be defined as one in which the unique equilibrium (also called stationary state) is eventually restored following a shock to one or more of the exogenous variables. Obviously, to operationalize this definition we must in each case indicate exactly what we mean by an equilibrium, and which variables we classify as exogenous. When the system has multiple equilibria (or stationary points), there may be stable and unstable equilibria. If there is a unique stable equilibrium, we shall choose that equilibrium as the relevant one and can still speak of a stable system.

The reason that economists like to focus attention on stable systems is that the alternative is unpalatable: unstable systems are not very useful for understanding the economy. An unstable system has no stable equilibria. Such an unstable system may very well have one or more unstable equilibria, but it is not likely to be at any of those equilibria at any point in time. Indeed, even if such a system starts in an equilibrium, a very small shock will permanently displace the system from that equilibrium. Therefore, only by pure coincidence would the system be in an equilibrium. Since economists know a lot more about equilibria than they do about disequilibrium situations, they like to study models that predict that the system converges along an equilibrium adjustment path to a stable equilibrium (see also Chapter 4). Note that this notion of equilibrium can also be extended to uncertain environments, in which case one would talk, for example, of stochastic steady states (see Chapter 5).

A very useful piece of methodological advice is contained in the so-called *correspondence principle*, which was transplanted from physics to economics by Paul Samuelson in his classic *Foundations of Economic Analysis* published in 1947. In words, the correspondence principle states that we should have confidence in, and use, only stable systems. As it will turn out, adherence to this principle often yields important information on the comparative static (or even comparative dynamic) predictions that can be derived from a theory. More precisely, the mathematical conditions that are necessary to have a stable system often enable macroeconomists to sign the steady-state multipliers for changes in government policy or other exogenous variables. We will give a number of applications of the correspondence principle during the course of this chapter.

In this chapter we restrict attention to models exhibiting a particular form of stability, the one that is most familiar to students of physical systems. All models discussed in this chapter display stability of a *backward-looking* kind. At a particular instant in time, the model determines the endogenous variables as a function of the exogenous variables and the predetermined state variables. Loosely put, history (as summarized by the state variables) determines the present situation. These backward-looking models are fairly mechanical, very much as switching on a machine will cause effects now and in the future but a machine will not switch itself on in anticipation of a future operation. In Chapter 4 we shall look at models exhibiting a completely different kind of stability, namely *forward-looking stability*. There history and the future jointly determine the current situation. Such forward-looking models are not considered in this chapter. These models arise in cases where economic psychology is relevant; for example, firms investing in anticipation of an investment subsidy being abolished in the future, consumers rushing to the store in the expectation of a future sales tax increase, or a little boy who starts salivating at the promise of a Chelsea bun.

We also look in Section 3.5 at a macroeconomic model for which the steady state is not uniquely defined. Instead, the equilibrium at which the economy finally settles down depends on the course of history, i.e. the equilibrium is path-dependent. Although this property seems eminently reasonable to historians and other social scientists, it must be stressed that the steady-state equilibrium of most economic models does *not* depend on the course of history. (Mathematically, path-dependent systems are characterized by a zero eigenvalue of the Jacobian matrix in the continuous-time case or a unit root in the discrete-time case. See the Mathematical Appendix for further details.) An interesting feature of models with the hysteresis property is that temporary shocks can have permanent effects. For example, a temporary adverse shock to the labour market can lead to a lasting increase in the rate of unemployment.

3.2 Adaptive expectations and stability

In Chapter 1 we saw that one variant of the neo-Keynesian synthesis model can be obtained under flexible wages and prices by assuming that price expectations are formed according to the adaptive expectations hypothesis (AEH). The model can be written in a very compact form as:

$$Y = AD(G, M/P), \tag{3.1}$$

$$Y = Y^* + \phi[P - P^e], \qquad \phi > 0, \tag{3.2}$$

$$\dot{P}^e = \lambda[P - P^e], \qquad \lambda > 0. \tag{3.3}$$

Equation (3.1) is the AD curve, which summarizes the simultaneous occurrence of money market equilibrium and spending equilibrium. The AD curve depends on two exogenous variables, namely government consumption, G (via the IS curve), and the nominal money supply, M (via the LM curve). The partial derivatives of the AD curve with respect to its arguments have been interpreted in Chapter 1 and follow immediately from equation (1.29):

$$AD_G \equiv \frac{1}{1 - C_{Y-T}(1 - T_Y) + l_Y I_R / l_R} > 0, \tag{3.4}$$

$$AD_{M/P} \equiv \frac{I_R / l_R}{1 - C_{Y-T}(1 - T_Y) + l_Y I_R / l_R} > 0, \tag{3.5}$$

where C_{Y-T} is the marginal propensity to consume, T_Y is the marginal tax rate, I_R is the interest sensitivity of investment, and l_Y and l_R denote, respectively, the income and interest sensitivity of money demand. We recall from Chapter 1 that $0 < C_{Y-T} < 1$, $0 < T_Y < 1$, $I_R < 0$, $l_Y > 0$, and $l_R < 0$. Clearly, aggregate demand rises if government spending or real money balances are increased. In the bottom part of Figure 3.1 the AD curves are downward sloping, i.e. $AD_P \equiv -(M/P^2) \cdot AD_{M/P} < 0$.

Equation (3.2) is the specification for aggregate supply in the goods market. Potential output, also called the full-employment level of output, Y^*, depends on supply-side variables. For example, potential output is an increasing function of the capital stock–see expression (1.20). Due to the fact that the expected and the actual price levels do not always coincide under the assumption of adaptive expectations, labour supply and consequently output can differ (in the short run) from their respective full-employment levels. The parameter ϕ follows from the AS curve (1.20):

$$\phi \equiv AS_P = \frac{\omega_N \varepsilon_D \varepsilon_S}{\varepsilon_D + \varepsilon_S} \frac{Y}{P} > 0, \tag{3.6}$$

where ω_N is the national income share of wages, and ε_D and ε_S denote the wage elasticity of, respectively, labour demand and labour supply. We recall from Chapter 1 that $0 < \omega_N < 1$ and $\varepsilon_D > 0$. Recall furthermore that, due to diminishing returns to labour, the demand curve for labour is downward sloping, and that ε_D is measured in absolute value terms. Finally, provided the substitution effect dominates the income effect in labour supply, we also have that the labour supply curve is upward sloping, i.e. $\varepsilon_S > 0$. Hence, the parameter ϕ determines the slope of the short-run AS curve–the higher a value of ϕ, the flatter the short-run AS curve, and the larger the output fluctuations that occur as a result of a given shift in aggregate demand. Indeed, by rewriting (3.2) somewhat, the AS curve can be written as:

$$P = P^e + \frac{1}{\phi}[Y - Y^*], \tag{3.7}$$

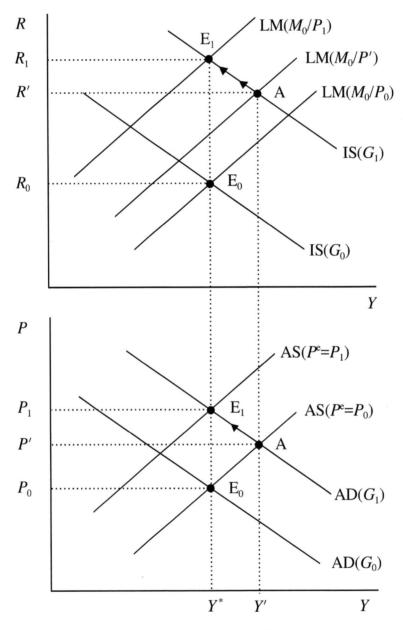

Figure 3.1: Fiscal policy under adaptive expectations

from which it follows readily that $(dP/dY)_{P^e=P_0} = 1/\phi$. In the bottom part of Figure 3.1, the curve labelled $AS(P^e = P_0)$ depicts the short-run aggregate supply curve when the expected price level is equal to P_0. Note that the difference between the full-employment level of output and the actual level of output, $Y^* - Y$, is sometimes called Okun's gap. It is also a measure of (involuntary) unemployment.

Finally, equation (3.3) is the continuous time version of the AEH expressed in equation (1.14). Agents revise their expectations regarding the price level if there is a discrepancy between the actual and the expected price level. The parameter λ is an indicator for the speed at which agents adapt their expectations (i.e. the promptness with which they correct their mistakes). A crucial aspect of the AEH is that the expected price level is a *state variable*, which means that its value is given at a particular instant in time. Hence, under the AEH the expected price level, P^e, is treated just like the capital stock, namely as something that is determined in the past. Suppose we want to compute the *level* of P^e at some particular time t. Just as the capital stock depends on past investment outlays, the expected price level $P^e(t)$ depends on actual price levels from period t into the indefinite past. To show that this is indeed the case, we solve the differential equation (3.3) to obtain the following expression for the expected price level:

$$P^e(t) = \int_{-\infty}^{t} \lambda P(\tau) e^{-\lambda(t-\tau)} d\tau. \tag{3.8}$$

The expected price level in period t, denoted by $P^e(t)$, depends on the entire path of (exponentially weighted) price levels in the past. Due to the discounting, distant prices have relatively little influence on the expectation of the current price level.

Intermezzo 3.1

The expected price level under the adaptive expectations hypothesis.
By explicitly recognizing the dependence on time, τ, equation (3.3) can be written in terms of a first-order differential equation for $P^e(\tau)$ featuring a constant coefficient, λ, and a time-varying forcing term, $P(\tau)$:

$$\dot{P}^e(\tau) + \lambda P^e(\tau) = \lambda P(\tau). \tag{a}$$

By multiplying both sides of (a) by the integrating factor, $e^{\lambda \tau}$, we find that:

$$\left[\dot{P}^e(\tau) + \lambda P^e(\tau)\right] e^{\lambda \tau} = \lambda P(\tau) e^{\lambda \tau} \qquad \Leftrightarrow$$

$$\frac{d}{d\tau} P^e(\tau) e^{\lambda \tau} = \lambda P(\tau) e^{\lambda \tau} \qquad \Leftrightarrow$$

$$dP^e(\tau) e^{\lambda \tau} = \lambda P(\tau) e^{\lambda \tau} d\tau. \tag{b}$$

Integrating both sides for $\tau \in (-\infty, t]$ gives:

$$\int_{-\infty}^{t} dP^e(\tau) e^{\lambda \tau} = \lambda \int_{-\infty}^{t} P(\tau) e^{\lambda \tau} d\tau$$

$$P^e(\tau) e^{\lambda \tau} \Big|_{-\infty}^{t} = \lambda \int_{-\infty}^{t} P(\tau) e^{\lambda \tau} d\tau$$

$$P^e(t) e^{\lambda t} - \lim_{\tau \to -\infty} P^e(\tau) e^{\lambda \tau} = \lambda \int_{-\infty}^{t} P(\tau) e^{\lambda \tau} d\tau. \tag{c}$$

But $\lim_{\tau \to -\infty} P^e(\tau)e^{\lambda \tau} = 0$ so we can rewrite (c), by taking $e^{\lambda t}$ to the other side, and obtain the expression for $P^e(t)$ as given in equation (3.8). Sargent (1987b, pp. 117–118) studies the case for which expected *inflation*, rather than the expected *price level*, is adjusted according to the AEH.

****

The neo-Keynesian model of aggregate demand and supply summarized by equations (3.1)–(3.3) can be solved quite easily for the short run, the transition period, and the long run. Graphically, the solution has already been discussed in Chapter 1 and is illustrated again in Figure 3.1. The initial situation is point E_0, where output is equal to its potential level ($Y = Y^*$), the rate of interest is equal to R_0, and the price level is equal to P_0. Now consider the following experiment in order to determine the stability of our model: does the economy automatically return to an equilibrium after a shock, say an increase in government spending? The (affirmative) answer is easily illustrated with the aid of the diagram. Following the increase in government spending ($dG > 0$), the IS curve and hence the AD curve both shift to the right. Expectations are given in the short run, so that the economy operates along the short-run aggregate supply curve through E_0. At point A the price level has increased from P_0 to P' and output has also increased (to Y'). Is there an equilibrium at point A or, more precisely from a mathematical point of view, is A a stationary point? Clearly, there is equilibrium in the sense that the AD curve and short-run AS curve intersect. Given their price expectations, households are happy to supply the amount of labour they do, and all markets clear. There is, however, a disequilibrium regarding expectations: at point A households base their plans on the expectation that the price is P_0 but the actual price level is higher ($P' > P_0$). The AEH suggests that this discrepancy will be eliminated over time. Hence, A is not a stationary point. As the expected price level is increased, the short-run AS curve will start to shift up and to the left and the economy will move along the new AD curve towards point E_1. Point E_1 is a point of full equilibrium, because all markets clear *and* there is an expectational equilibrium. Hence, point E_1 is both an equilibrium from an economic point of view and a stationary point. Consequently, the IS-LM-AS model is stable.

It is not always so easy to use graphical devices to demonstrate stability. For that reason the following, slightly more formal method, may be used. Recall that in the short run, the expected price level P^e is a predetermined, or state, variable. Consequently, we can use expressions (3.1)–(3.2) to solve for the short-run equilibrium values of the price level, P, and output, Y, conditional on the exogenous variables (G, M, and Y^*) and the predetermined state variable (P^e). Put differently, we know that (3.1)–(3.2) give rise to two *implicit* functions of the following form:

$$P = \Phi(G, M, Y^*, P^e), \qquad Y = \Psi(G, M, Y^*, P^e). \tag{3.9}$$

Of course we do not know the *explicit* functional forms of $\Phi(\cdot)$ and $\Psi(\cdot)$ but that is not a problem. All we need to know is the partial derivatives of these functions, and they can be easily obtained by employing the implicit function theorem. We briefly remind the reader how to do this. In the first step we totally differentiate equations (3.1)–(3.2) to obtain:

$$dY = AD_G dG + (1/P)AD_{M/P} dM - \alpha dP, \tag{3.10}$$

$$dY = dY^* + \phi \left[dP - dP^e \right], \tag{3.11}$$

where $\alpha \equiv (M/P^2)AD_{M/P} > 0$ is a composite parameter. In the second step we solve these two expressions for the change in the price level, dP, and in output, dY:

$$dP = \frac{AD_G dG + (1/P)AD_{M/P}dM - dY^* + \phi dP^e}{\phi + \alpha}, \tag{3.12}$$

$$dY = \frac{\phi AD_G dG + (\phi/P)AD_{M/P}dM + \alpha dY^* - \alpha\phi dP^e}{\phi + \alpha}. \tag{3.13}$$

Since both ϕ and α are positive, the denominator of (3.12) and (3.13) is guaranteed to be positive. In the final step we recover the partial derivatives of $\Phi(\cdot)$ and $\Psi(\cdot)$ by in each case letting one of dG, dM, dY^*, and dP^e be non-zero. For example, by using (3.12) we find that $\Phi_G = AD_G/(\phi + \alpha) > 0$, $\Phi_M = (1/P)AD_{M/P}/(\phi + \alpha) > 0$, $\Phi_{Y^*} = -1/(\phi + \alpha) < 0$, and $\Phi_{P^e} = \phi/(\phi + \alpha) > 0$. Hence, the first expression in (3.9) says that P is an increasing function of P^e, G, and M but a decreasing function of Y^*.

In a similar fashion we can deduce from (3.13) that $\Psi_G = \phi AD_G/(\phi + \alpha) > 0$, $\Psi_M = (\phi/P)AD_{M/P}/(\phi + \alpha) > 0$, $\Psi_{Y^*} = \alpha/(\phi + \alpha) < 0$, and $\Psi_{P^e} = -\alpha\phi/(\phi + \alpha) > 0$. Hence the Keynesian multiplier which is relevant when prices are sticky, i.e. AD_G, is weakened on account of the rise in the price level and the associated contraction in real money balances. The extent of this weakening is captured by the factor $\phi/(\phi + \alpha)$ which is positive but less than unity. We see that the flatter the AS curve, i.e. the smaller the change in the price level caused by a change in aggregate demand (the higher is ϕ), the smaller is the rise in the price level and the dampening of the short-run Keynesian multiplier. A very steep AS curve (a low value of ϕ) implies that a rise in government spending yields a relatively large boost to the price level and a small rise in employment and output.

The implicit function $P = \Phi(G, M, Y^*, P^e)$ (stated in (3.9)) is very useful for our stability analysis, because it summarizes all the effects that influence the price level, P, at a particular instant in time. By substituting this function into equation (3.3) we obtain:

$$\dot{P}^e = \lambda \left[\Phi(G, M, Y^*, P^e) - P^e \right] \equiv \Omega(P^e, G, M, Y^*), \tag{3.14}$$

where $\Omega(\cdot)$ is yet another implicit function relating the time rate of change in the expected price level to that price level and to the exogenous variables. The partial derivatives of this implicit function are once again obtained by employing the implicit function theorem. Indeed, by totally differentiating equation (3.3), and substituting (3.12), we obtain:

$$d\dot{P}^e = \lambda \left[dP - dP^e \right]$$
$$= -\frac{\lambda\alpha}{\phi + \alpha}dP^e + \frac{\lambda AD_G dG + (\lambda/P)AD_{M/P}dM - \lambda dY^*}{\phi + \alpha}, \tag{3.15}$$

from which we conclude that $\Omega_{P^e} = -\lambda\alpha/(\phi + \alpha) < 0$, $\Omega_G = \lambda AD_G/(\phi + \alpha) > 0$, $\Omega_M = (\lambda/P)AD_{M/P}/(\phi + \alpha) > 0$, and $\Omega_{Y^*} = -\lambda/(\phi + \alpha) < 0$.

Let us now return to the stability experiment mentioned above. We leave exogenous variables other than government spending unchanged (i.e. $dM = dY^* = 0$ and $dG > 0$) and determine the "law of motion" of the expected price level. The resulting *phase diagram* is found in Figure 3.2. From the expressions in (3.15) it is clear that $\dot{P}^e = \Omega(\cdot)$ is a decreasing function of P^e (since $\Omega_{P^e} < 0$). The initial equilibrium

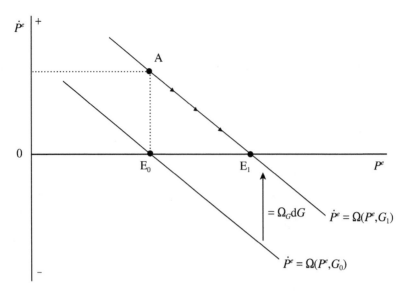

Figure 3.2: Stability and adaptive expectations

or steady state is given by point E_0. If government spending is increased, the $\dot{P}^e$ line shifts up and to the right (since $\Omega_G > 0$). Even though P^e is fixed in the short run, $\dot{P}^e$ jumps to a positive value (point A). The expected price level starts to rise, which is represented by the arrows along the new $\dot{P}^e$ line. Eventually, the economy reaches point E_1, which is the new equilibrium and steady state. This experiment shows that the crucial property that is needed for stability is that changes in the expected price level should taper off. More formally, stability implies (and is implied by) $\partial \dot{P}^e / \partial P^e \equiv \Omega_{P^e} < 0$. If this stability condition holds, the model is, of course, stable in the face of shocks to other kinds of exogenous variables as well.

In order to test one's understanding of the material it is useful to examine the stability of an alternative neo-Keynesian synthesis model, namely one where the nominal wage adjusts sluggishly in response to conditions in the labour market. This is left as an exercise.

3.3   Investment, the capital stock, and stability

In Section 3.2 we saw an example of stability analysis involving expectations. In this section and the next, we look at stability in a class of dynamic systems that stresses the interaction between stocks and flows. A very prominent example of interaction between stocks and flows is the one between the level of the capital stock and the rate of investment. This interaction is typically ignored in the IS-LM model, which renders the IS-LM model less useful for understanding transient and long-run issues. Notable exception to this ad hoc approach are Tobin and Buiter (1976) and Sargent (1987b). Before turning to the stability issue in the context of investment-capital dynamics, we first briefly introduce a theory of investment (by the typical firm) that is based on microeconomic foundations. This theory will be further developed in Chapter 4, but is used here to motivate the form of the investment function that is appropriate if dynamic issues are taken into account.

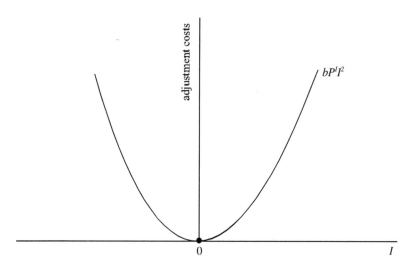

Figure 3.3: Adjustment costs of investment

3.3.1   Adjustment costs and investment

Firms invest in order to add units of capital to the stock they already have and to replace the worn out capital stock. They do this because they want to conduct their operations in the most profitable way. In Chapter 1 we have already described a very basic *static* model of producer behaviour. The objective of this section is to expand our basic model of producer behaviour to a *dynamic* setting. By doing so, the issue of optimal investment plans can be studied.

We make the following assumptions regarding the typical firm. First, the firm has static expectations regarding all prices and the interest rate. Second, technology is constant. Third, the firm is a perfect competitor in the markets for its inputs and its output. Fourth, the investment process is subject to *adjustment costs*. Adding new machines is disruptive to the production process and leads to lost revenue. For low levels of investment these adjustment costs are low, but these costs rise more than proportionally with the level of investment. The adjustment cost function is (for simplicity) assumed to be quadratic: $bP^I I^2$, where b is a positive constant, P^I is the price of new machines, and I is the level of gross investment by the firm. The adjustment cost function is illustrated in Figure 3.3. The production function is still given by $Y = F(N, K)$ and has the properties stated in Chapter 1.

Finally, we assume that the typical firm maximizes the present value of the net payments it can make to the owners of its capital stock (i.e. the shareholders), subject to the restrictions of the production function and the capital accumulation identity. The market rate of interest on bonds, R, is used as the discount factor. In Intermezzo 3.2 we demonstrate that this assumption is justified in a decentralized market setting with a well-functioning stock market.

Since the problem of the firm is essentially dynamic, all variables must be given a time index. In order to obtain the simplest possible expressions, the derivation proceeds in discrete time. Nominal cash flow at the beginning of period t, Π_t, is defined as:

$$\Pi_t = PF(N_t, K_t) - WN_t - P^I I_t - bP^I I_t^2, \tag{3.16}$$

where N_t is employment in period t, K_t is the capital stock at the beginning of period t, and I_t is the level of investment in period t. Note that the prices of goods and labour (P, P^I, W) have no time index because we assume that firms expect these to be constant over time. The first two terms on the right-hand side of (3.16) represent sales revenue minus the wage bill; they are familiar from Chapter 1. The third term represents the current outlays on new investment goods, and the fourth term represents the adjustment costs. The identity linking rates of investment and the capital stock is given in discrete time as:

$$K_{t+1} - K_t = I_t - \delta K_t, \qquad 0 < \delta < 1, \tag{3.17}$$

where δ represents the constant rate of physical deterioration of the capital stock due to wear and tear.

In period 0 ('today') the objective function of the firm, i.e. the present value of present and future cash flow streams, can be written as:

$$\bar{V}_0 \equiv \sum_{t=0}^{\infty} \left(\frac{1}{1+R} \right)^t \Pi_t$$

$$= \sum_{t=0}^{\infty} \left(\frac{1}{1+R} \right)^t \left[PF(N_t, K_t) - WN_t - P^I I_t - bP^I I_t^2 \right]. \tag{3.18}$$

Due to the dynamic nature of the problem, the firm must formulate plans regarding production now and in the indefinite future (Y_t, for $t = 0, 1, 2, \cdots, \infty$). It does so by choosing paths (for time periods $t = 0, 1, 2, \cdots, \infty$), for employment ($N_t$), investment ($I_t$), and the capital stock (K_{t+1}) such that (3.18) is maximized subject to (3.17).

Intermezzo 3.2

The cost of capital to the firm: Modigliani-Miller. Which rate should the firm use to discount its present and future profits? Does the firm's dividend policy matter to the valuation of its shares on the stock market? These and related questions were first analysed in a number of highly influential papers by Modigliani and Miller (1958), Miller and Modigliani (1961), and Miller (1977). Miller and Modigliani (1961, p. 413) consider the following scenario: suppose a firm wants to invest by buying a $100 machine. How should it finance this investment–by reducing dividends (and thus relying on retained earnings) or by issuing new shares? Their surprising answer is that, in an ideal economy characterized by perfect capital markets, rational behaviour, and perfect certainty, the firm's dividend policy does not matter. This is the famous *Modigliani-Miller theorem* (MMT hereafter). As it turns out this theorem also gives an answer to our first question concerning the appropriate discount rate for the firm.

Before giving a simple demonstration of the MMT it is important to emphasize the assumptions upon which its validity is based (Miller and Modigliani, 1961, p. 412). By *perfect capital markets* it is meant that no buyer or seller of securities has market power. There are no brokerage fees, transaction costs, and tax distortions. By *rational behaviour* it is meant that investors prefer more wealth to less and do not care about the form in which their wealth accrues (e.g. by cash payments or by valuation changes). Finally, by *perfect certainty* it is meant that all investors are fully aware of all future investment programmes and the future profits of every corporation. Presumably because these assumptions are rather stringent, the late Modigliani himself reputedly always added the proviso "to a first approximation" when talking about the validity of the MMT (see Blanchard and Fischer, 1989, p. 314 fn. 35).

Suppose that there are many firms (indexed with i), facing identical technology and adjustments costs, and that the shares of all firms are traded in the stock market. Assume furthermore that, apart from holding shares in the various companies, investors can also hold a one-period government bond which pays $(1 + R)$ euros per euro invested each period. We assume that the firms issue no (corporate) debt and that the interest rate, wages, and prices are constant, both at present and in the future. Under the assumptions made, the *fundamental principle of valuation* says that the yield per euro invested must be the same for all financial assets:

$$\frac{d_t^i + p_{t+1}^i - p_t^i}{p_t^i} = R, \tag{a}$$

where d_t^i is the dividend per share paid by firm i at the end of period t, p_t^i is the price of a share in firm i (exclusive of period $t-1$ dividend) at the start of period t. The left-hand side of (a) shows that the yield on one euro invested in shares of firm i consists of dividend plus capital gains expressed in terms of the price of a share in that firm. The right-hand side of (a) shows that this common yield on shares must be equal to the yield on one-period government bonds.

Note that (a) can be rewritten as:

$$p_t^i = \frac{1}{1+R} \left[d_t^i + p_{t+1}^i \right]. \tag{b}$$

This expression can be rewritten in terms of the value of the firm as a whole by defining $V_t^i \equiv p_t^i n_t^i$, where n_t^i is the number of shares of firm i at the beginning of period t:

$$\begin{aligned} V_t^i &= \frac{1}{1+R} \left[n_t^i d_t^i + n_t^i p_{t+1}^i \right] \\ &= \frac{1}{1+R} \left[n_t^i d_t^i + \left(n_t^i + n_{t+1}^i - n_{t+1}^i \right) p_{t+1}^i \right] \\ &= \frac{1}{1+R} \left[D_t^i + V_{t+1}^i - m_{t+1}^i p_{t+1}^i \right], \end{aligned} \tag{c}$$

where $D_t^i \equiv n_t^i d_t^i$ is total dividends paid at the end of period t to the n_t^i 'old' stockholders and $m_{t+1}^i \equiv n_{t+1}^i - n_t^i$ is the number of new shares sold during period t at the ex-dividend closing price p_{t+1}^i. Suppose that $P^I I_t^i (1 + b I_t^i)$ is the given firm's investment level (inclusive of adjustment costs) and that $X_t^i \equiv PF(K_t^i, N_t^i) - W N_t^i$ is the firm's gross profit, both measured at the beginning of period t. Then the amount of outside capital that the firm needs to finance its investment plans at the beginning of period $t+1$ is:

$$m_{t+1}^i p_{t+1}^i = P^I I_{t+1}^i (1 + b I_{t+1}^i) + D_t^i - X_{t+1}^i. \tag{d}$$

By substituting (d) into (c) we obtain the following expression for the value of the firm at the start of period t:

$$V_t^i = \frac{1}{1+R} \left[X_{t+1}^i - P^I I_{t+1}^i (1 + b I_{t+1}^i) + V_{t+1}^i \right]. \tag{e}$$

The crucial thing to note is that the level of dividends does not affect anything in (e)! Hence, the current value of the firm is independent of its current dividend policy. Solving (e) by repeated substitution of terms like V_{t+1}^i, V_{t+2}^i, etc., we find the following expression for V_t^i after T substitutions:

$$V_t^i = \sum_{s=t+1}^{t+T} \left(\frac{1}{1+R} \right)^{s-t} \Pi_s^i + \left(\frac{1}{1+R} \right)^T V_{t+T}^i, \tag{f}$$

where we have used the definition of cash flow, Π_s^i (cf. the one given in (3.16)). By letting $T \to \infty$ in (f) we obtain:

$$V_t^i = \sum_{s=t+1}^{\infty} \left(\frac{1}{1+R} \right)^{s-t} \Pi_s^i. \tag{g}$$

As is pointed out by Auerbach (1979b, p. 437), the expression in (g) holds provided the value of the firm grows at a slower rate than R so that $\lim_{T \to \infty} (1+R)^{-T} V_{t+T}^i = 0$ in (f). This is a so-called *No-Ponzi-Game* (NPG) condition which prohibits the firm from running a "chain letter scheme" by supporting dividend payments solely from new share issues. (We shall encounter NPG conditions in various setting throughout the book).

By dropping the now superfluous firm index i and noting that the firm also has some cash flow at the beginning of the period t, we find that the objective function of the firm can be written as:

$$\tilde{V}_t \equiv V_t + \Pi_t = \sum_{s=t}^{\infty} \left(\frac{1}{1+R} \right)^{s-t} \Pi_s. \tag{h}$$

By normalizing the planning period $t = 0$ we obtain the expression (3.18) in the text. Cash flows should be discounted by the cost of capital which, in the present setting, equals the rate of return on government bonds.

The Modigliani-Miller theorem has been extended and generalized over the last four decades. Useful extensions in a macroeconomic setting are Auerbach (1979b), Sinn (1987), and Turnovsky (1995, ch. 10). All these authors focus on the effect of real world taxes on the validity of the MMT.

****

Two things are noteworthy about the firm's optimization problem. First, the choices regarding investment and the capital stock are not independent because the capital accumulation identity (3.17) implies a path of the capital stock once a path for investment is chosen. Second, in the planning period, $t = 0$, the firm has an installed capital stock already, so that K_0 is not a choice variable to the firm. Formally, the maximization problem can be solved by means of the Lagrange multiplier method. The Lagrangian is:

$$\mathcal{L}_0 \equiv \sum_{t=0}^{\infty} \left(\frac{1}{1+R}\right)^t \left[PF(N_t, K_t) - WN_t - P^I I_t - bP^I I_t^2\right]$$
$$- \sum_{t=0}^{\infty} \left(\frac{1}{1+R}\right)^t \cdot \lambda_t \cdot [K_{t+1} - (1-\delta)K_t - I_t], \tag{3.19}$$

where λ_t is the Lagrange multiplier for the capital accumulation constraint that is relevant in period t (in order to simplify the notation these multipliers are weighted by the discount factor). The first-order conditions are (for $t = 0, \cdots, \infty$):

$$\frac{\partial \mathcal{L}_0}{\partial N_t} = \left(\frac{1}{1+R}\right)^t [PF_N(N_t, K_t) - W] = 0, \tag{3.20}$$

$$\frac{\partial \mathcal{L}_0}{\partial K_{t+1}} = \left(\frac{1}{1+R}\right)^t \left[\frac{PF_K(N_{t+1}, K_{t+1}) + \lambda_{t+1}(1-\delta)}{1+R} - \lambda_t\right] = 0, \tag{3.21}$$

$$\frac{\partial \mathcal{L}_0}{\partial I_t} = \left(\frac{1}{1+R}\right)^t \left[-P^I - 2bP^I I_t + \lambda_t\right] = 0. \tag{3.22}$$

(Note the timing of the Lagrange multiplier in the first-order condition for capital!)

Although (3.20)–(3.22) look monstrously difficult, they can nevertheless be readily interpreted. Note that $(1+R)^{-t} > 0$ so that the terms in square brackets on the right-hand sides of (3.20)–(3.22) must be zero to satisfy the first-order conditions. Hence, equation (3.20) amounts to the marginal productivity condition for the labour input that was already derived for the static case (see equation (1.4)). It is intuitively obvious why these two first-order conditions coincide: labour is a fully flexible factor of production, and the choice of how much labour to use is not a dynamic one.

Equations (3.21) and (3.22) can be combined to yield an expression for the optimal path of investment. First, (3.22) is used to get expressions for λ_t and λ_{t+1}:

$$\lambda_t = P^I [1 + 2bI_t], \quad \lambda_{t+1} = P^I [1 + 2bI_{t+1}]. \tag{3.23}$$

By substituting these expressions into (3.21), we obtain the first-order condition for investment:

$$PF_K(N_{t+1}, K_{t+1}) + \lambda_{t+1}(1-\delta) - \lambda_t(1+R) = 0 \Rightarrow$$
$$PF_K(N_{t+1}, K_{t+1}) + (1-\delta)P^I [1 + 2bI_{t+1}] - (1+R)P^I [1 + 2bI_t] = 0 \Rightarrow$$
$$I_{t+1} - \frac{1+R}{1-\delta} I_t + \frac{PF_K(N_{t+1}, K_{t+1}) - P^I(R+\delta)}{2bP^I(1-\delta)} = 0. \tag{3.24}$$

This equation is an unstable difference equation for investment, because the coefficient for I_t is greater than unity. The steady-state solution for investment is found by setting $\Delta I_{t+1} = 0$, or $I_{t+1} = I_t = I$:

$$I = \frac{1}{2b} \left[\frac{PF_K(N, K)}{P^I(R+\delta)} - 1\right]. \tag{3.25}$$

The intuition behind expression (3.25) is very simple. If the value of the marginal product of capital (PF_K) is greater than the rental price of capital (i.e. the opportunity cost of capital plus the depreciation charge, $(R + \delta)P^I$), the firm should invest. Note furthermore that in the absence of adjustment costs ($b = 0$), the firm has no well-defined optimal *investment* policy. In that case (3.25) reduces to $PF_K = P^I(R + \delta)$, which is a static condition determining the optimal *capital stock* for the firm. Hence, in the absence of adjustment costs, the firm has an infinite speed of investment and immediately adjusts its capital stock to the optimal level.

In Chapter 4 we shall demonstrate more formally that the steady-state investment plan (3.25) is also the optimal solution to the firm's maximization problem. Intuitively, the firm chooses the smoothest possible investment path in order to avoid very high adjustment costs in periods of high investment. An uneven path of investment, e.g. low now, high later, would have low adjustment costs now but very high adjustment costs later. Due to the fact that the adjustment cost function is convex (e.g. quadratic), these higher costs later dominate the low costs early on.

One final remark about expression (3.25) concerns the price of investment goods, P^I. The IS-LM model is essentially a one-good model, so one would expect that the investment good is actually the same as the consumption good and thus $P \equiv P^I$. There is, however, a reason why the two prices can diverge, even in a one-good setting. Suppose that the government wishes to stimulate investment. It could do so by subsidizing investment goods. In that case the price of investment goods faced by firms is equal to $P^I \equiv (1 - s_I)P$, where s_I is the subsidy. Equation (3.25) then becomes:

$$I = \frac{1}{2b}\left[\frac{F_K(N,K)}{(1 - s_I)(R + \delta)} - 1\right]. \tag{3.26}$$

It is clear from this expression that the investment subsidy is successful in stimulating investment, i.e. $\partial I/\partial s_I > 0$. We return to the important issue of how government policy can be used to stimulate private investment in Chapter 4.

3.3.2 Stability

The investment theory developed in the previous section may be summarized by the general functional form for investment:

$$I = I(R, K, Y), \qquad I_R < 0, \ I_K < 0, \ I_Y > 0, \tag{3.27}$$

where we assume that there is no investment subsidy (so that $P^I = P$). We also assume that the marginal product of capital (that appears in expression (3.26)) depends positively on Y and negatively on K. This is, for example, the case for the Cobb-Douglas production function, $Y = Z_0 K^\varepsilon N^{1-\varepsilon}$ (with $0 < \varepsilon < 1$), for which $F_K = \varepsilon Y/K$, $\partial F_K/\partial Y > 0$, and $\partial F_K/\partial K < 0$ (see Intermezzo 1.1 for more details on this type of production function). An alternative, more ad hoc derivation of this investment relationship is the so-called accelerator theory of investment. This proceeds by postulating a desired level of the capital stock, say $K^D(Y, R)$ with $K_Y^D > 0$ and $K_R^D < 0$, and assuming that investment takes place in order to close the gap between the desired and the actual level of the capital stock, say $I = b(K^D - K)$ with b now being the speed of adjustment. Clearly, this accelerator view of investment may also be seen as a special case of this general functional form for investment.

In order to investigate stability in the IS-LM model, we first simplify matters by postulating that the price level is constant, i.e. we assume that the AS curve is perfectly elastic at the given price level which we normalize to unity ($P = 1$).

Throughout this section we hold the money supply constant. The model of aggregate demand with dynamics in the capital stock can thus be written as:

$$Y = C(Y - T(Y)) + I(R, K, Y) + G, \tag{3.28}$$

$$M = l(Y, R), \tag{3.29}$$

$$\dot{K} = I(R, K, Y) - \delta K. \tag{3.30}$$

Equation (3.28) is the IS curve, (3.29) is the LM curve, and (3.30) is the capital accumulation identity (3.17) rewritten in continuous time and with (3.27) substituted. We assume that the IS curve is downward sloping in Figure 3.4, i.e. $0 < C_{Y-T}(1 - T_Y) + I_Y < 1$.

The capital stock is predetermined in the short run, so that the IS-LM equations (3.28)–(3.29) jointly determine short-run equilibrium values for output, Y, and the rate of interest, R, in terms of K and G:

$$Y = \Phi(\underset{-}{K}, \underset{+}{G}), \qquad R = \Psi(\underset{-}{K}, \underset{+}{G}), \tag{3.31}$$

where $\Phi(\cdot)$ and $\Psi(\cdot)$ are implicit functions. The pluses and minuses summarize the signs of the partial derivatives of these implicit functions. These are obtained in the standard manner by employing the implicit function theorem. The spending multiplier is, for example, given by:

$$\Phi_G = \frac{1}{1 - C_{Y-T}(1 - T_Y) - I_Y + I_R l_Y / l_R} > 0. \tag{3.32}$$

The positive output effect in investment ($I_Y > 0$) ensures that the multiplier is larger than its counterpart in the standard IS-LM model—see equation (3.4). In terms of Figure 3.4, an increase in government consumption shifts the IS curve to the right, and moves the equilibrium from point E_0 to point A. The remaining partial derivatives are given by:

$$\Phi_K = I_K \Phi_G < 0, \qquad \Psi_G = -\frac{l_Y}{l_R} \Phi_G > 0, \qquad \Psi_K = -\frac{l_Y I_K}{l_R} \Phi_G < 0. \tag{3.33}$$

The interested reader should verify that the move from E_0 to A in Figure 3.4 explains the signs of Φ_G and Ψ_G, whilst the move from E_0 to B explains the signs of Φ_K and Ψ_K. Clearly, a fiscal contraction or a higher capital stock lowers the interest rate and depresses aggregate demand and hence output.

It is immediately obvious that the stability issue is not as easy as for the case of price expectations under the AEH. Indeed, equation (3.30) says that $\dot{K}$ depends on K directly and indirectly via induced effects on Y and R. By using (3.31) in (3.30) we find that the function relating $\dot{K}$ to K and G can be written as:

$$\dot{K} = I(\Psi(K, G), K, \Phi(K, G)) - \delta K \equiv \Omega(K, G), \tag{3.34}$$

where the partial derivatives of $\Omega(K, G)$ are given by:

$$\Omega_K \equiv I_R \Psi_K + I_K + I_Y \Phi_K - \delta, \tag{3.35}$$

$$\Omega_G \equiv I_R \Psi_G + I_Y \Phi_G. \tag{3.36}$$

Recall that the stability requirement is that changes in the capital stock must taper off, i.e. stability requires that $\partial \dot{K} / \partial K \equiv \Omega_K < 0$ holds. But is Ω_K negative? Glancing

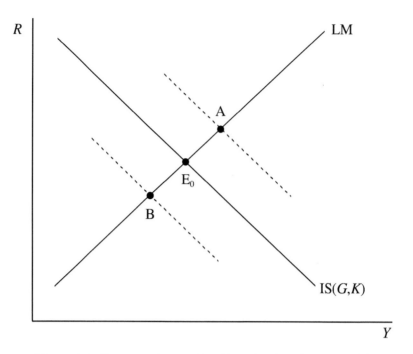

Figure 3.4: Comparative static effects in the IS-LM model

at (3.35), "stabilizing" influences exist because $I_K < 0$, $I_Y \Phi_K < 0$, and $-\delta < 0$. A high capital stock and (thus) a low level of aggregate demand both imply a low level of gross investment. In addition, a high capital stock implies a high level of depreciation. Hence, net investment is at a low level and the capital stock will fall in future periods back to its equilibrium value. However, a "destabilizing" influence is clearly the term $I_R \Psi_K > 0$. Intuitively, the destabilizing effect is due to the fact that a higher capital stock induces a lower interest rate (as $\Psi_K < 0$) and stimulates investment (as $I_R < 0$).

What would the well-trained economist do in such a situation where stability is not guaranteed? Typically, one would appeal to Samuelson's correspondence principle and simply assume stability, i.e. postulate that the destabilizing effect of $I_R \Psi_K > 0$ is dominated by the sum of the stabilizing effects $(I_K + I_Y \Phi_K - \delta) < 0$, so that Ω_K is negative and the $\dot{K}$ lines in Figure 3.5 are downward sloping. This is the approach taken here also.

Given that stability has been assumed, what happens if the government increases its expenditure on goods and services ($dG > 0$)? Equation (3.34) says that the $\dot{K}$ line may shift up or down depending on the sign of $\partial \dot{K} / \partial G \equiv \Omega_G$—recall that $I_R \Psi_G$ is negative whilst $I_Y \Phi_G$ is positive. A typical monetarist (see Chapter 1) would suggest a strong interest rate effect on investment ($|I_R|$ large), and a large effect on the interest rate but a small effect on output of a rise in government spending (Ψ_G large and Φ_G small). Consequently, a monetarist might suggest that Ω_G is negative. This is illustrated in Figure 3.5. According to the monetarist view, the $\dot{K}$ line shifts down, and in the long run the capital stock is crowded out by government spending.

A typical Keynesian might argue the reverse: $|I_R|$ small, Ψ_G small, and Φ_G large, so that $\Omega_G > 0$. This implies that the $\dot{K}$ line shifts up and to the right, so that the capital stock is stimulated in the long run by a rise in government spending. The Keynesian predictions regarding the effects on the rate of interest and output have

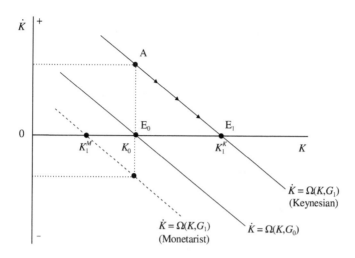

Figure 3.5: The effect on capital of a rise in public spending

been illustrated in Figure 3.6. In the short run the capital stock is fixed (at K_0) and the IS curve shifts to the right (from $IS(K_0, G_0)$ to $IS(K_0, G_1)$) as a result of the increase in government consumption. The economy moves from E_0 to A, and output and employment increase. Despite the higher interest rate, firms wish to add to their capital stock, i.e. net investment is positive at point A ($\dot{K} > 0$). Over time the capital stock increases and the IS curve gradually shifts to the left. In the new steady state, $\dot{K} = 0$, the capital stock is equal to K_1, $IS(K_1, G_1)$ is the relevant IS curve, and the equilibrium is at point E_1.

The long-run effect on output is guaranteed to be positive (though more so under the Keynesian assumptions). This can be shown as follows. In the long run it must be the case that $\dot{K}^{LR} = \Omega \left(K^{LR}, G \right) = 0$, where the superscript LR denotes long-run values. Hence, the long-run effect on the capital stock is given by:

$$\left(\frac{dK}{dG} \right)^{LR} = \frac{\Omega_G}{-\Omega_K}, \tag{3.37}$$

where stability ensures that the denominator is positive. To a Keynesian, the additional government spending "crowds in" the capital stock and the numerator is positive, and the reverse holds for a monetarist. By using the long-run capital stock effect (3.37) and the implicit function for output (the first expression in (3.31)), $Y^{LR} = \Phi \left(K^{LR}, G \right)$, we obtain the following long-run output multiplier for a rise in public spending:

$$\left(\frac{dY}{dG} \right)^{LR} = \Phi_K \left(\frac{dK}{dG} \right)^{LR} + \Phi_G$$

$$= \Phi_G \left[I_K \left(\frac{dK}{dG} \right)^{LR} + 1 \right]$$

$$= \frac{(\delta - I_K)\Phi_G}{-\Psi_K} > 0, \tag{3.38}$$

where we have used (3.33) and (3.36) to simplify the expression. In the stable case

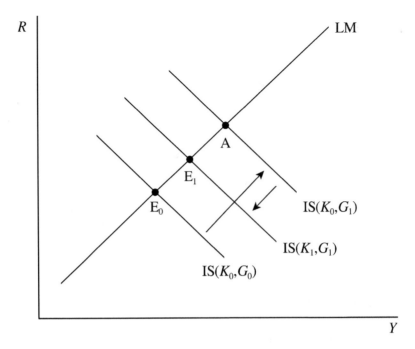

Figure 3.6: Capital accumulation and the Keynesian effects of fiscal policy

(with $-\Psi_K > 0$) Samuelson's correspondence principle thus yields useful information on the sign of the denominator. Since the numerator of expression (3.38) is positive as well (as $I_K < 0$ and $\Phi_G > 0$), output must rise in the long run. The Keynesian assumptions imply that investment is not very sensitive to the rate of interest while money demand is very sensitive to changes in the interest rate (a steep IS curve and a flat LM curve), and that investment reacts strongly to changes in output. In that case, crowding out of private investment is small relative to the output effect on investment. It thus follows that output and capital both rise after an increase in public spending. The monetarist assumptions are the opposite (a steep LM curve, a flat IS curve, and a small output effect on investment). Hence, a rise in public spending depresses capital and output rises by less in the long run.

This example must not be taken too seriously, of course, in view of the fact that it is highly implausible that the actual AS curve is horizontal (as was assumed in this section). It merely serves to illustrate the stability issues surrounding the stock-flow interaction between the capital stock and investment.

3.4   Wealth effects and the government budget constraint

Another example of stock-flow interaction are the intrinsic dynamics in the IS-LM models that arise once we allow for the wealth effects in consumption and money demand if the government issues extra bonds or prints more money to finance its deficit. Blinder and Solow (1973) suggest that this issue can be fruitfully studied with the aid of the IS-LM model with a fixed price level (horizontal AS curve). We again normalize the price level at unity, i.e. $P = 1$. Despite its simplistic treatment of aggregate supply, the Blinder-Solow extension of the IS-LM model is an important one, because the textbook IS-LM model is somewhat of a curious construct as it measures in one diagram both flow concepts (through the IS curve) and stock concepts (through the LM curve). In the textbook IS-LM model it is not really possible to even ask the question of how the effectiveness of, say, a fiscal expansion depends on the mode of government finance. It is for this reason that we now turn to the crucial question of allowing for the dynamics arising from private wealth and the government budget restriction.

The government can issue consols (bonds of infinite term to maturity) that promise the owner a fixed periodic payment of 1 euro from now to infinity. Such consols are popular wedding presents among economists, since they remind the partners to buy a rose each time the coupon is paid at the wedding anniversary. If the rate of interest is R, how much would an investor be willing to pay for such a bond? Obviously, the price of the bond, P_B, would be exactly equal to the present value of the stream of income derived from the bond, or, in continuous time:

$$P_B = \int_0^\infty 1 \cdot e^{-R\tau} d\tau = -\frac{1}{R} \cdot e^{-R\tau} \Big|_0^\infty = \frac{1}{R}. \tag{3.39}$$

If the government has issued B of such bonds in the past, then the payments it must make each period are equal to B times 1 euro. Hence, B represents both the number of consols in the hands of the public and the interest payments of the government to the public. If the government issues new consols ($\dot{B} > 0$), it receives $P_B \dot{B}$ in revenue from this bond sale. Furthermore, the government can meet its obligations by simply printing money ($\dot{M} > 0$). With goods prices fixed at unity, the government budget restriction can be written as:

$$G + B = T + \dot{M} + (1/R)\dot{B}. \tag{3.40}$$

The left-hand side represents the nominal spending level of the government inclusive of interest (i.e. coupon) payments to private agents. The right-hand side of the government budget restriction shows the three financing methods open to the government, namely taxation, money finance, and bond finance.

The level of taxation, T, depends on all income received by the households, i.e. inclusive of real interest receipts B:

$$T = T(Y + B), \quad 0 < T_{Y+B} < 1, \tag{3.41}$$

where T_{Y+B} is the marginal tax rate. The total amount of real private financial wealth in the economy, A, is the sum of the fixed capital stock, $\bar{K}$, the real money supply, and the real value of bond holdings by the public:

$$A \equiv \bar{K} + M + B/R. \tag{3.42}$$

As a final modification, Blinder and Solow (1973) suggest that both consumption and money demand depend positively on the level of wealth:

$$C = C(Y + B - T, A), \quad 0 < C_{Y+B-T} < 1, \quad C_A > 0, \tag{3.43}$$
$$M = l(Y, R, A), \quad l_Y > 0, \; l_R < 0, \; 0 < l_A < 1, \tag{3.44}$$

where C_A and l_A represent the wealth sensitivity of, respectively, consumption and money demand. Equation (3.43) is a mixture of two theoretical notions. As we shall see in Chapter 6, the forward-looking theory of consumption typically assumes households to have unlimited access to a perfect capital market. This suggests that private consumption should depend on total wealth (i.e. financial wealth plus human wealth, the present value of lifetime earnings) and, possibly, the rate of interest as well. Furthermore, bonds should not be counted as part of private wealth. In contrast, the Keynesian theory of consumption suggests a central role for current income. As we shall see in Chapter 6, however, there is an empirically plausible rationale for the specification adopted in (3.43). For now we simply use (3.43) without further comment and leave some of these issues as an exercise and for Chapter 6.

Money demand, given by the right-hand side of (3.44), is also different from the one used in equation (1.25). The rationale for this money demand function is a portfolio allocation model. The household chooses to allocate its total financial wealth, A, over the three different financial assets that exist in the model: bonds, claims to physical capital, and money. Under the assumption that claims to physical capital and bonds are perfectly substitutable, the rate of return on these assets must be the same (and equal to R). This explains why only R appears in (3.44). Obviously, if wealth rises, one would expect all components of the wealth portfolio to rise, including the demand for money. This explains the positive wealth effect in money demand.

3.4.1 Short-run macroeconomic equilibrium

In the short run, the money supply and the level of government debt are predetermined variables. The IS curve is obtained by combining (3.41)–(3.43) with the standard investment function, $I = I(R)$, and the national income identity for the closed economy, $Y = C + I + G$:

$$Y = C(Y + B - T(Y + B), \bar{K} + M + B/R) + I(R) + G. \tag{3.45}$$

The LM curve is given by equation (3.44). By total differentiation of (3.44) and (3.45), keeping $\bar{K}$ constant ($d\bar{K} = 0$) and noting (3.42), we obtain:

$$dY = \frac{dG + [C_{Y+B-T}(1 - T_{Y+B}) + C_A/R]\, dB + C_A dM}{1 - C_{Y+B-T}(1 - T_{Y+B})}$$
$$+ \frac{[I_R - C_A B/R^2]\, dR}{1 - C_{Y+B-T}(1 - T_{Y+B})}, \tag{3.46}$$

$$dR = \frac{-(l_A/R)\, dB + (1 - l_A)\, dM - l_Y dY}{l_R - l_A B/R^2}. \tag{3.47}$$

The IS curve is downward sloping and the LM curve slopes up, just as in the basic IS-LM model. The short-run equilibrium values of output, Y, and the rate of interest, R, can once again be expressed in terms of the key predetermined and exogenous variables:

$$Y = \Phi(G, B, M), \qquad R = \Psi(G, B, M), \tag{3.48}$$
$$\underset{+ \; ? \; +}{} \qquad \underset{+ \; + \; ?}{}$$

where $\Phi(\cdot)$ and $\Psi(\cdot)$ are implicit functions. By using (3.46) and (3.47), expressions for the partial derivatives can be obtained in the usual manner. For the implicit function for output we find:

$$\Phi_G = \frac{1}{1 - C_{Y+B-T}(1 - T_{Y+B}) + \xi l_Y} > 0, \tag{3.49}$$

$$\Phi_B = \frac{C_{Y+B-T}(1 - T_{Y+B}) + C_A/R - \xi l_A/R}{1 - C_{Y+B-T}(1 - T_{Y+B}) + \xi l_Y} \gtrless 0, \tag{3.50}$$

$$\Phi_M = \frac{C_A + \xi(1 - l_A)}{1 - C_{Y+B-T}(1 - T_{Y+B}) + \xi l_Y} > 0, \tag{3.51}$$

whilst for the implicit function for the interest rate we obtain:

$$\Psi_G = \frac{l_Y}{l_A B / R^2 + |l_R|} \Phi_G > 0, \tag{3.52}$$

$$\Psi_B = \frac{(l_A / R) \left[1 - C_{Y+B-T}(1 - T_{Y+B})\right]}{l_A B / R^2 + |l_R|} \Phi_G$$

$$+ \frac{l_Y \left[C_{Y+B-T}(1 - T_{Y+B}) + C_A / R\right]}{l_A B / R^2 + |l_R|} \Phi_G > 0, \tag{3.53}$$

$$\Psi_M = \frac{l_Y C_A - (1 - l_A) \left[1 - C_{Y+B-T}(1 - T_{Y+B})\right]}{l_A B / R^2 + |l_R|} \Phi_G \gtrless 0. \tag{3.54}$$

In these expressions, ζ is a positive composite parameter, defined as $\zeta \equiv [C_A B / R^2 + |l_R|] / [l_A B / R^2 + |l_R|] > 0$. The interpretation of these partial derivatives is facilitated with the aid of Figures 3.7-3.9. For example, in the top panel of Figure 3.7, the initial equilibrium is at point E_0. An increase in government spending shifts the IS curve from $IS(G_0, M_0)$ to $IS(G_1, M_0)$. At point A income is higher than before and there is an excess demand for money (an excess supply of bonds). This causes a fall in bond prices, i.e. a rise in the interest rate, which moves the economy to point E'. In terms of Figure 3.7, both output and the rate of interest are higher, hence $\Phi_G > 0$ and $\Psi_G > 0$. (The partial derivatives for changes in M and B are discussed below.)

In Figure 3.7 we have shown that an increase in government spending causes a short-run increase in output, Y, and the rate of interest, R. This is not the end of the story, of course, since we have not yet taken the government budget restriction into account. Blinder and Solow (1973) consider two extreme cases. In the first case, the government prints new money to finance the additional government spending. Consequently, the money stock changes over time to balance the government's books, i.e. $\dot{M} \neq 0$ and $\dot{B} = 0$. In the second case considered by Blinder and Solow (1973), the government balances its books by issuing additional bonds, i.e. $\dot{M} = 0$ and $\dot{B} \neq 0$. The questions that can be analysed now are: (i) is the model stable under both financing methods, and (ii) what is the relationship between the different output multipliers for government spending with respect to different modes of government finance. At first blush one would ignore wealth effects and suggest that a money-financed increase in government spending boosts output by more than a bond-financed rise in government spending, because it is associated with a fall in the interest rate and thus an additional boost to aggregate money demand as the LM curve shifts out. At second blush this may not turn out to be correct as the wealth effects in consumption and money demand affect the multipliers as well. We now investigate this in more detail.

3.4.2 Money finance

Under money finance the government budget restriction reduces to $\dot{M} = G + B - T(Y + B)$, where B is fixed. This government budget restriction thus represents a function relating $\dot{M}$ to government spending G and output Y. But output itself depends on G and M, via the output relationship $Y = \Phi(G, B, M)$ given in (3.48), so the implicit relationship between $\dot{M}$, G, and M can be written as:

$$\dot{M} = G + B - T(\Phi(G, B, M) + B) \equiv \Omega(M, G), \tag{3.55}$$

where we suppress the variable held constant (B) in this financing scenario in the implicit function $\Omega(M, G)$. The partial derivatives of the $\Omega(M, G)$ function are given

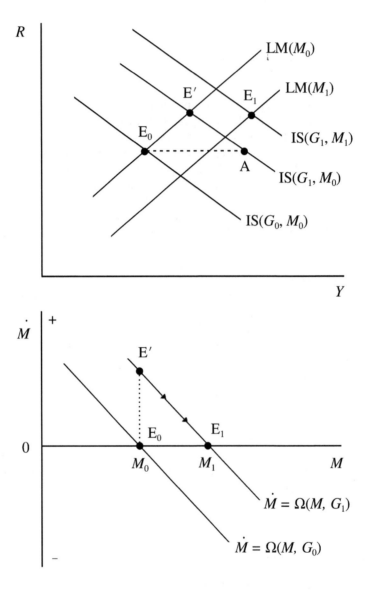

Figure 3.7: The effects of fiscal policy under money finance

by:

$$\Omega_M \equiv -T_{Y+B}\Phi_M < 0, \tag{3.56}$$

$$\Omega_G \equiv 1 - T_{Y+B}\Phi_G = \frac{(1 - C_{Y+B-T})(1 - T_{Y+B}) + \xi l_Y}{1 - C_{Y+B-T}(1 - T_{Y+B}) + \xi l_Y} > 0, \tag{3.57}$$

where we have used (3.49) to arrive at the second expression in (3.57). Hence, it is immediately obvious that the model is stable under money finance. Indeed, it follows from (3.56) that $\partial \dot{M}/\partial M \equiv \Omega_M < 0$ so that changes in the money stock dampen out over time. Furthermore, (3.57) shows that the initial effect of the fiscal impulse is to cause a budget deficit, i.e. $\partial \dot{M}/\partial G \equiv \Omega_G > 0$. The impact, transition, and long-run effects of a money-financed increase in government spending are illustrated in Figure 3.7. In the bottom panel, the stable adjustment path consists of a jump from E_0 to E' at impact, followed by a gradual move from E' to E_1 during transition. Not surprisingly, the money supply increases in the long run, from M_0 to M_1. From the diagram in the top panel it is obvious that the long-run effect on output exceeds the short-run effect, i.e. point E_1 lies to the right of point E'. The *steady-state* government budget restriction is obtained by setting $\dot{B} = \dot{M} = 0$ in (3.40) above. We find that $G + B = T(Y^{LR} + B)$, from which we easily derive the long-run output multiplier:

$$\left(\frac{dY}{dG}\right)^{LR}_{MF} \equiv \frac{1}{T_{Y+B}} > \Phi_G \equiv \left(\frac{dY}{dG}\right)^{SR}_{MF}, \tag{3.58}$$

where the subscript "MF" denotes money financing. Money finance leads to a stable adjustment process. Both the IS and the LM curve shift out leading to an expansion of output and tax revenue thereby reducing the government deficit until balanced budget and steady state are reached. Output has to rise by just enough to generate sufficient tax revenue to pay for the rise in government spending. This is why the long-run output multiplier for a money-financed increase in government spending is equal to one over the marginal tax rate.

3.4.3 Bond finance

Under bond finance the government budget restriction reduces to $(1/R)\dot{B} = G + B - T(Y + B)$ and M is fixed. But both Y and R depend on G and B, via the expressions stated in (3.48) above. Hence, it would appear that the implicit relationship between $\dot{B}$, B, and G is quite complex in this case:

$$\begin{aligned}
\dot{B} &= R \cdot [G + B - T(Y + B)] \\
&= \Psi(G, B, M) \cdot [G + B - T(\Phi(G, B, M) + B)] \\
&\equiv \Lambda(B, G),
\end{aligned} \tag{3.59}$$

where we have once again suppressed the variable held constant in the implicit function $\Lambda(B, G)$ (M in this scenario). Evaluated at a *steady-state*, however, the partial derivatives of the $\Lambda(B, G)$ function are not very complicated:[1]

$$\Lambda_B \equiv R[1 - T_{Y+B}(1 + \Phi_B)] \gtrless 0, \tag{3.60}$$

$$\Lambda_G \equiv R[1 - T_{Y+B}\Phi_G] > 0. \tag{3.61}$$

---

[1] These partial derivatives are obtained by totally differentiating the first line of (3.59) around an initial equilibrium in which $\dot{B} = 0$. This implies that the term $[G + B - T]dR = 0$ so that only the effects operating via the $\Phi(G, B, M)$ function feature in (3.60)–(3.61).

It follows from (3.60) that it is not at all obvious that the model is stable under bond finance. Recall that the model is stable if (and only if) changes in debt eventually dampen over time, i.e. $\partial \dot{B}/\partial B \equiv \Lambda_B$ is negative. The correspondence principle instructs us to only use stable models, so we must impose the following (necessary-and-sufficient) stability condition:

$$\Lambda_B \equiv \frac{\partial \dot{B}}{\partial B} < 0 \quad \Leftrightarrow 1 - T_{Y+B}(1 + \Phi_B) < 0 \quad \Leftrightarrow \quad \Phi_B > \frac{1 - T_{Y+B}}{T_{Y+B}} > 0. \quad (3.62)$$

This condition says that the wealth effect on aggregate demand, Φ_B, must be positive *and* sufficiently large in magnitude. In (3.50) we showed, however, that Φ_B cannot be signed a priori. This is because a rise in the level of debt boosts private wealth, private consumption, and thus aggregate demand and output (the outward shift of the IS curve), but it also increases money demand and thus depresses aggregate demand and output (inward shift of the LM curve). As was demonstrated by Blinder and Solow (1976a, p. 184), a necessary (but not sufficient) condition for stability is that the weighted wealth sensitivity of consumption, $C_A |l_R|$, exceeds the weighted wealth sensitivity of money demand, $l_A |l_R|$. Put differently, if $C_A |l_R| < l_A |l_R|$ then the stability condition (3.62) simply cannot be satisfied. To prove this rather subtle claim, we use (3.49)–(3.50) and substitute the definition of ξ, stated below (3.54), to find:

$$\frac{T_{Y+B}}{1 - T_{Y+B}} \Phi_B = C_{Y+B-T} T_{Y+B} \Phi_G + \frac{T_{Y+B}}{1 - T_{Y+B}} \Phi_G \frac{C_A |l_R| - l_A |l_R|}{l_A B/R + R |l_R|}. \quad (3.63)$$

Clearly, the first term on the right-hand side of (3.63) is between zero and one (because $0 < C_{Y+B-T} < 1$ and $0 < T_{Y+B}\Phi_G < 1$). If $C_A |l_R| < l_A |l_R|$ the second term is negative, so the left-hand side of (3.63) must be less than one thus violating the stability condition (3.62)![2]

But the condition, $C_A |l_R| > l_A |l_R|$, which of course implies that Φ_B is positive, is not sufficient for stability. This is because the additional debt also gives rise to additional government outlays on interest payments and the potential danger of a self-fuelling explosion of government debt. The interest payments must ultimately be financed by means of higher tax revenues for otherwise the government books will not be balanced (i.e. it must be the case that eventually $\dot{B} = 0$). This is why the marginal tax rate plays a crucial role in the necessary-and-sufficient stability condition (3.62). More precisely, with a high marginal tax rate, more tax revenues are generated for a given expansion of output and thus it is more likely that the deficit is eliminated and the build-up of government debt is arrested (i.e. stability is ensured).

The impact, transition, and long-run effects of a bond-financed rise in government spending are illustrated in Figure 3.8 for the stable case. From the diagram it is obvious that the long-run effect on output exceeds the short-run effect, i.e. point E_1 lies to the right of point E'. Mathematically, we derive the long-run output multiplier as follows. First, we totally differentiate the steady-state government budget restriction, $G + B = T(\Phi(G, B, M) + B)$, with respect to G and B to find the long-run effect on government debt:

$$\left(\frac{dB}{dG}\right)^{LR}_{BF} = \frac{\Lambda_G}{-\Lambda_B} = \frac{1 - T_{Y+B}\Phi_G}{T_{Y+B}(1 + \Phi_B) - 1} > 0, \quad (3.64)$$

---

[2]To see that this is the case, note that:

$$\frac{T_{Y+B}}{1 - T_{Y+B}} \Phi_B < 1 \quad \Leftrightarrow \quad \Phi_B < \frac{1 - T_{Y+B}}{T_{Y+B}},$$

where the second expression is easily seen to violate the stability condition (3.62).

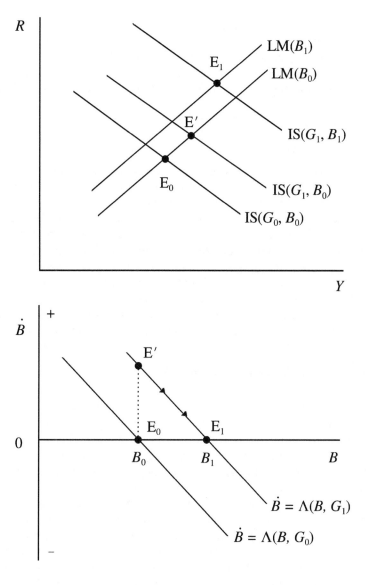

Figure 3.8: Fiscal policy under (stable) bond financing

where the sign follows from (3.61) and the stability condition (3.62). Next, we totally differentiate the implicit function for output, $Y = \Phi(G, B, M)$, with respect to Y, G, and B and substitute (3.64). After some straightforward manipulation we find the long-run output multiplier:

$$\left(\frac{dY}{dG}\right)_{BF}^{LR} \equiv \Phi_G + \Phi_B \frac{1 - T_{Y+B}\Phi_G}{T_{Y+B}(1 + \Phi_B) - 1} > \Phi_G \equiv \left(\frac{dY}{dG}\right)_{BF}^{SR}. \tag{3.65}$$

The inequality follows readily from the fact that Φ_B is positive (see (3.62)) and long-run government debt rises (see (3.64)).

As a final remark, consider the long-run multipliers under the two financing methods. It is obvious from (3.58) and (3.65) that, provided the stability condition (3.62) holds, the bond-financed output multiplier exceeds the money-financed multiplier:

$$\left(\frac{dY}{dG}\right)_{BF}^{LR} > \left(\frac{dY}{dG}\right)_{MF}^{LR}. \tag{3.66}$$

The intuition is straightforward. The long-run increase in output under bond finance must exceed the one under money finance, because the additional interest payments must also be financed by means of higher tax receipts and this requires a higher steady-state national income. This has been illustrated in Figure 3.9, where point E_0 indicates the initial equilibrium, point E' stands for new equilibrium that is attained immediately after government consumption is increased (the impact effect, which is common to both financing modes), and points E_M and E_B represent the long-run outcome under money finance and bond finance, respectively. Figure 3.9 clearly shows that bond finance (provided it is stable!) yields a bigger long-run multiplier than money finance even though the interest rate rises by more. Providing the intuition behind the shifts in the IS, LM, and tax schedules is left as an exercise.

3.5 A first look at hysteresis★

We now consider a special class of models that have the *hysteresis* property.[3] With hysteresis we mean a system whose steady state is not given, but can wander about and depends on the past path of the economy. Mathematically, we will see that this property implies that the Jacobian matrix of a continuous-time system has, apart from some "stable" eigenvalues (i.e. with a negative real part), a zero eigenvalue. For a discrete-time system there will be a unit root next to the other eigenvalues that are supposed to be smaller than one in absolute value. (See the Mathematical Appendix.) Systems with hysteresis can thus be viewed as being in the twilight zone between stable and unstable systems. Such systems are important in macroeconomics, because they allow us to depart from the rigid framework of equilibrium, a-historical economics. The best economic example of hysteresis is due to people becoming alienated from the labour market if they remain unemployed for a long enough period of time.

3.5.1 Alienation of the unemployed

So far, we have assumed that the equilibrium, steady-state, or potential level of output, Y^*, depends on the (exogenous) capital stock and supply-side policies (e.g. tax

---

[3]The material in this section is technically more advanced than the rest of this chapter and may be skipped upon first reading.

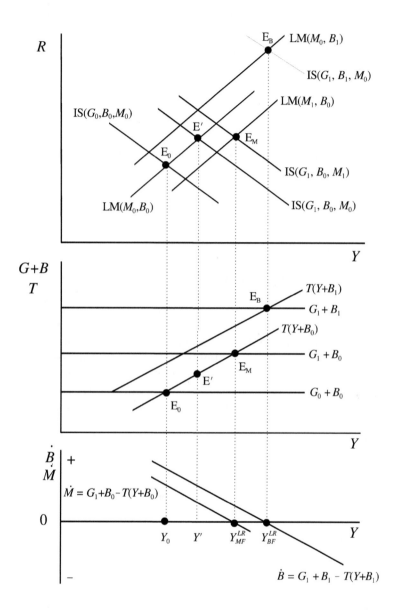

Figure 3.9: Long-run effect of fiscal policy under different financing modes

rates on labour). Associated with the potential level of output is an equilibrium, steady-state, or *natural* rate of unemployment. The implied natural rate of unemployment is a constant, albeit that it may depend on various tax rates, and does not depend on past history. Here we will develop a different model of aggregate supply. In order to do this, we depart from the concept of a path-independent natural rate of unemployment.[4] We will assume a discrete-time system. To prepare for the discussion to follow, we write the discrete-time counterparts to (3.12) and (3.13) in short-hand notation as:

$$dP_t = \frac{\phi dP_t^e + d\delta_t - dY_t^*}{\phi + \alpha},$$ (3.67)

$$dY_t = \frac{-\alpha\phi dP_t^e + \phi d\delta_t + \alpha dY_t^*}{\phi + \alpha},$$ (3.68)

where α is defined below equation (3.11), and $d\delta_t \equiv AD_G dG_t + (1/P)AD_{M/P}dM_t$ is an aggregate demand shock in period t. Similarly, the discrete-time version of the AEH can be written as:

$$dP_{t+1}^e = (1-\lambda)dP_t^e + \lambda dP_t,$$ (3.69)

where the expectational adjustment coefficient satisfies $0 < \lambda < 1$.

The alienation idea is rather simple: people that stay unemployed become alienated from the labour market, stop searching for a job, and no longer count as part of the potential work force. Plausible explanations are that long-term unemployed lose skills if they remain without a job or are stigmatized by firms. Hence, people that stay unemployed for long enough no longer add to downward wage pressure and become part of the natural rate of unemployment. We assume that the natural unemployment rate at any point in time is determined by the past unemployment rate. A simple, but convenient way to capture this hypothesis is to assume that the potential (or natural) output level at time $t + 1$, Y_{t+1}^*, is given by the actual output level at time t, Y_t, minus an exogenous adverse supply shock in period t, denoted by σ_t. In total derivative format we get $dY_{t+1}^* = dY_t - d\sigma_t$ and we can use expression (3.68) to write potential output in the next period as a function of the current levels of potential output, the expected price, the supply shock, government spending and the money supply:

$$dY_{t+1}^* = \frac{\phi d\delta_t - \alpha\phi dP_t^e + \alpha dY_t^* - (\phi + \alpha)d\sigma_t}{\phi + \alpha}.$$ (3.70)

Hence, a recession caused by tight monetary or fiscal policy or other falls in aggregate demand can lead to a future fall in potential output and thus a future rise in the corresponding natural unemployment rate.

By using (3.67) in (3.69) we obtain the discrete-time equivalent for the expression of next period's expected price level as a function of the current levels of the expected price, potential output, government spending, and the money supply:

$$dP_{t+1}^e = \frac{\lambda d\delta_t - \lambda dY_t^* + [(1-\lambda)\alpha + \phi]dP_t^e}{\phi + \alpha}.$$ (3.71)

---

[4]Indeed, this hysteresis effect is already present in the analysis of Phelps (1972, pp. 76–80).

3.5.2 History matters

The system defined by the difference equations (3.70) and (3.71) generates the dynamics in the potential level of output, Y_t^*, and the expected price level, P_t^e. It can be written in a single matrix expression as:

$$\begin{bmatrix} dY_{t+1}^* \\ dP_{t+1}^e \end{bmatrix} = J \cdot \begin{bmatrix} dY_t^* \\ dP_t^e \end{bmatrix} + \frac{1}{\phi + \alpha} \begin{bmatrix} \phi d\delta_t - (\phi + \alpha) d\sigma_t \\ \lambda d\delta_t \end{bmatrix}, \tag{3.72}$$

where the Jacobian matrix, J, is given by:

$$J = \frac{1}{\alpha + \phi} \begin{bmatrix} \alpha & -\phi\alpha \\ -\lambda & (1-\lambda)\alpha + \phi \end{bmatrix}. \tag{3.73}$$

It is not difficult to show that the two eigenvalues of J are given by, respectively, $\mu_1 = 1$ and $\mu_2 = \alpha(1-\lambda)/(\phi+\alpha)$.[5] The important thing to note is that $0 < \mu_2 < 1$, i.e. the unit root is accompanied by a stable root.

In order to analyse the dynamic properties of this system in more detail, we use a trick and write $JS = S\Lambda$, where Λ denotes the diagonal matrix of eigenvalues:

$$\Lambda \equiv \begin{bmatrix} 1 & 0 \\ 0 & \frac{\alpha(1-\lambda)}{\phi+\alpha} \end{bmatrix}, \tag{3.74}$$

and S is the matrix whose columns correspond to the eigenvectors of J.[6] It is easy to show that the matrix S and its inverse S^{-1} are given by:

$$S = \begin{bmatrix} -\alpha & \phi \\ 1 & \lambda \end{bmatrix} \quad \text{and} \quad S^{-1} = \frac{1}{\alpha\lambda + \phi} \begin{bmatrix} -\lambda & \phi \\ 1 & \alpha \end{bmatrix}. \tag{3.75}$$

Next, we premultiply both sides of (3.72) by S^{-1} and write the transformed system as:

$$Z_{t+1} = \Lambda Z_t + \Xi_t, \tag{3.76}$$

where the auxiliary variables Z_t and Ξ_t are defined as follows:

$$Z_t \equiv \begin{bmatrix} Z_{1,t} \\ Z_{2,t} \end{bmatrix} \equiv S^{-1} \cdot \begin{bmatrix} dY_t^* \\ dP_t^e \end{bmatrix}, \tag{3.77}$$

$$\Xi_t \equiv \frac{1}{\alpha + \phi} S^{-1} \cdot \begin{bmatrix} \phi d\delta_t - (\phi + \alpha) d\sigma_t \\ \lambda d\delta_t \end{bmatrix}$$

$$= \frac{1}{\alpha + \phi} \begin{bmatrix} 0 \\ 1 \end{bmatrix} d\delta_t + \frac{1}{\alpha\lambda + \phi} \begin{bmatrix} \lambda \\ -1 \end{bmatrix} d\sigma_t. \tag{3.78}$$

The transformed system (3.76) is much easier to analyse than the original system (3.72) because Λ is diagonal (whereas J is not), i.e. there are no simultaneity effects anymore. The transformed system in fact consists of two first-order difference equations stacked on top of each other.

---

[5]The easiest was to check this result is as follows. We know that the product of the two eigenvalues of J is given by the determinant, i.e. $\mu_1\mu_2 = |J| = \alpha(1-\lambda)/(\alpha+\phi)$, and the sum of the two eigenvalues is given by the trace, i.e. $\mu_1 + \mu_2 = \text{tr}(J) = [(2-\lambda)\alpha + \phi]/(\alpha + \phi)$. The solution mentioned in the text satisfies both equalities, so it must be the right one.

[6]In formal terms, since J has distinct eigenvalues, its eigenvectors are linearly independent so that J can be diagonalized as $S^{-1}JS = \Lambda$ (Strang, 1988, pp. 254–260). By pre-multiplying both sides of this expression by S, the result in the text is found. See also Azariadis (1993, pp. 34–38) and the Mathematical Appendix.

3.5.2.1   Aggregate demand shocks

First we restrict attention to demand shocks only. By setting $d\sigma_t = 0$ for all t, we find that (3.76) implies:

$$Z_{1,t} = Z_{1,t-1}, \tag{3.79}$$

$$Z_{2,t} = \mu_2 Z_{2,t-1} + \frac{1}{\phi + \alpha} d\delta_{t-1}. \tag{3.80}$$

Demand shocks do not affect the difference equation for $Z_{1,t}$ and we thus conclude from (3.79) that $Z_{1,t} = 0$ for all t.[7] Equation (3.80) is a stable difference equation (because $0 < \mu_2 < 1$) which can be solved by repeated substitution. After $T - 1$ such substitutions we find:

$$Z_{2,t} = \mu_2^T + \frac{1}{\phi + \alpha} \left[d\delta_{t-1} + \mu_2 d\delta_{t-2} + \mu_2^2 d\delta_{t-3} + \cdots + \mu_2^{T-1} d\delta_{t-T} \right]. \tag{3.81}$$

By letting $T \to \infty$, however, we find that the first term on the right-hand side of (3.81) goes to zero (as $0 < \mu_2 < 1$ so that $\mu_2^T \to 0$) so that we are left with:

$$Z_{2,t} = \frac{1}{\alpha + \phi} \sum_{i=0}^{\infty} \left[\frac{\alpha(1 - \lambda)}{\alpha + \phi} \right]^i d\delta_{t-1-i}, \tag{3.82}$$

where we have substituted the expression for μ_2 stated below equation (3.73). The solutions for the original, untransformed, variables are obtained by substituting $Z_{1,t} = 0$ and (3.82) into equation (3.77):

$$\begin{bmatrix} dY_t^* \\ dP_t^e \end{bmatrix} = SZ_t = \begin{bmatrix} -\alpha & \phi \\ 1 & \lambda \end{bmatrix} \begin{bmatrix} 0 \\ Z_{2,t} \end{bmatrix} = \begin{bmatrix} \phi \\ \lambda \end{bmatrix} \frac{1}{\alpha + \phi} \sum_{i=0}^{\infty} \left[\frac{\alpha(1 - \lambda)}{\alpha + \phi} \right]^i d\delta_{t-1-i}. \tag{3.83}$$

Hence, in contrast to economies in which hysteresis is not present, demand-side policies have real effects in the long run as well as in the short run. For example, the long-run effects of a sustained increase in government spending (i.e. $dM_t = 0$ and $d\delta_t \equiv AD_G dG$) on the actual and potential levels of output are easily seen to be equal to:[8]

$$\left(\frac{dY^*}{dG} \right)^{LR} = \frac{\phi}{\alpha + \phi} \sum_{i=0}^{\infty} \left[\frac{\alpha(1 - \lambda)}{\alpha + \phi} \right]^i AD_G = \frac{\phi}{\alpha\lambda + \phi} AD_G. \tag{3.84}$$

Clearly, temporary shocks to the aggregate demand for goods do not induce permanent effects on the levels of output. This can be seen by using (3.83) to derive the effect of a past demand shock on current potential output:

$$\frac{dY_t^*}{d\delta_{t-j}} = \frac{\phi}{\alpha + \phi} \left[\frac{\alpha(1 - \lambda)}{\alpha + \phi} \right]^{j-1} \tag{3.85}$$

Clearly, the effect of the shock wears off because the term in square brackets on the right-hand side goes to zero as j gets large.

---

[7]In principle $Z_{1,t} = \tilde{Z}_1$, with a non-zero $\tilde{Z}_1$ also solves (3.79). Assume, however, that the system was in a steady-state at some past time $t^* < t$. Clearly, at time t^* we have that $dY_t^* = dP_t^e = 0$ and thus that $Z_{1,t} = 0$ also. The only feasible solution is that $\tilde{Z}_1 = 0$.

[8]We use the fact that $0 < \mu_2 < 1$ so that the infinite sum converges, i.e.:

$$\sum_{i=0}^{\infty} \left[\frac{\alpha(1 - \lambda)}{\alpha + \phi} \right]^i = \sum_{i=0}^{\infty} \mu_2^i = \frac{1}{1 - \mu_2} = \frac{\alpha + \phi}{\alpha\lambda + \phi}.$$

3.5.2.2 Aggregate supply shocks

To demonstrate that temporary shocks to aggregate supply may in the presence of hysteresis indeed lead to permanent changes in output and the natural rate of unemployment, we solve the system of difference equations when there are adverse shocks to aggregate supply $d\sigma_t$ (and no demand shocks, i.e. $d\delta_t = 0$ for all t). Following the same steps as before, we find the following solutions for the transformed variables:

$$Z_t = \frac{1}{\alpha\lambda + \phi} \left[\begin{array}{c} \lambda \sum_{i=0}^{\infty} d\sigma_{t-1-i} \\ -\sum_{i=0}^{\infty} \left[\frac{\alpha(1-\lambda)}{\alpha+\phi}\right]^i d\sigma_{t-1-i} \end{array} \right]. \tag{3.86}$$

By using (3.77) we thus find the solutions for dY_t^* and dP_t^e:

$$\left[\begin{array}{c} dY_t^* \\ dP_t^e \end{array} \right] = SZ_t = \frac{1}{\alpha\lambda + \phi} \left[\begin{array}{cc} -\alpha & \phi \\ 1 & \lambda \end{array} \right] \left[\begin{array}{c} \lambda \sum_{i=0}^{\infty} d\sigma_{t-1-i} \\ -\sum_{i=0}^{\infty} \left[\frac{\alpha(1-\lambda)}{\alpha+\phi}\right]^i d\sigma_{t-1-i} \end{array} \right]. \tag{3.87}$$

We immediately observe an essential difference between aggregate supply and aggregate demand shocks. Although the effects of temporary shocks to aggregate demand fade out with time, the effects of temporary shocks to aggregate supply are permanent. Indeed, a supply shock j periods ago affects current potential output according to:

$$\frac{dY_t^*}{d\sigma_{t-j}} = -\frac{1}{\alpha\lambda + \phi} \left[\alpha\lambda + \phi \left(\frac{\alpha(1-\lambda)}{\alpha+\phi} \right)^{j-1} \right]. \tag{3.88}$$

The second term within the square brackets fades out as j increases, but the first term does not fade out and is the reason why temporary shocks have permanent effects.

3.6 Punchlines

We have extended the static IS-LM-AS model by adding some essential dynamic features to do with adaptive expectations, capital accumulation, and the build-up of government debt. Allowing for adaptive expectations in aggregate supply ensures that fiscal and monetary policy can have transient real effects. This is why this extension corresponds to a neo-Keynesian synthesis with a Keynesian short run and a classical long run. Hence, an expansion of aggregate demand leads in the short and medium run to a rise in output but as expectations catch up with the rise in prices the initial gains in output are wiped out. Money is thus neutral in the long run. Stability of the expectational adjustment process is guaranteed.

To allow for finite speeds of investment and sluggish adjustment in the capital stock, it is useful to introduce adjustment costs when investment takes place. In that case, employment still follows from the condition that the marginal productivity of labour must equal the real wage but the marginal productivity of capital no longer equals the user cost of capital (i.e. the rental charge plus the depreciation charge). Instead, investment is high if the gap between the marginal productivity of capital and the user cost of capital is large. This amounts to an investment function which states that investment increases if output rises and the capital stock or the interest rate declines. Such a specification also arises if one adopts an accelerator view of investment. Introducing this specification of investment and the capital accumulation identity into the basic model of aggregate demand, typically does not lead to instability. Under the Keynesian assumptions, i.e. investment not very sensitive, but money demand very sensitive to changes in the interest rate, a rise in public spending leads to higher levels of capital and output. However, under the monetarist assumptions, i.e. investment very sensitive, but money demand insensitive to changes in the interest rate, an increase in public spending crowds out capital. Output nevertheless still rises in the long run.

A third extension to allow for dynamics in the basic IS-LM-AS model is to incorporate wealth effects in consumption and money demand. This extension is essential, because the basic IS-LM framework compares apples with oranges as the IS curve refers to flow concepts while the LM curve relates to stock concepts. There is something fundamentally wrong with seeking equilibrium in both stock and flow concepts without allowing for a time dimension. To allow for this time dimension, we assume that consumption and money demand rise if wealth (consisting of claims to physical capital, real money balances and government bonds) increases. Consumption also depends on disposable income, where taxes are levied on both production and interest income. The government budget constraint states that the public sector financial deficit, i.e. primary public spending plus interest payments minus tax revenue, must be financed by printing money or issuing bonds. Since a money-financed increase in public spending induces downward pressure on the interest rate while a bond-financed increase in public spending induces upward pressure on the interest rate, one might think at first sight that money finance is more expansionary than bond finance. Surprisingly, this is not the case in the long run. In fact, provided the debt dynamics is stable, the long-run bond-financed multiplier is larger than the money-financed multiplier because national income must rise to generate sufficient tax revenue not only to cover the rise in public spending but also the interest on the accumulated government debt. The money-financed multiplier simply equals one over the marginal tax rate, whereas the bond-financed multiplier is larger than this. Money finance automatically leads to a stable process, since the initial government deficit is gradually eliminated as money supply expands, the interest rate falls, and national income and tax revenue rise. In contrast, bond finance may lead to a never-ending explosion of government debt if over time the build-up of government debt raises money demand and pushes up the interest rate so much that national income and tax revenue fall. The result is an ever-increasing government deficit. This instability can only be stopped if the wealth effect in consumption is strong enough, that is if the rise in private wealth and consumption boosts aggregate demand, national income and tax revenue sufficiently to ensure that the government deficit becomes smaller over time. Hence, to ensure stability under bond finance the wealth effect in consumption must be relatively strong compared to the wealth effect in money demand. By appealing to the Samuelsonian correspondence principle, a simple stability condition can be derived which ensures that debt will be stabilized in the long run.

Finally, we also provided an example of hysteresis, or path dependence of the steady state, by suggesting that the natural level of output depends on the past level of output. Alternatively, the natural unemployment rate is supposed to be determined by the past unemployment rate. This captures the phenomenon that the long-term unemployed become alienated from the labour market, stop searching for a job, and no longer exert downward wage pressure. Two lessons can be drawn from this analysis. First, permanent changes in fiscal and monetary policy have lasting effects on employment and output. Second, as far as supply-side policy and shocks are concerned, even temporary changes have permanent effects on employment and output. Temporary adverse supply shocks can thus lead to permanently higher levels of unemployment.

Further reading

Key readings in the adjustment cost approach to investment are Eisner and Strotz (1963), Lucas (1967), Gould (1968), and Treadway (1969). Abel (1990) gives an overview of this literature. The classic articles on the government budget constraint are Blinder and Solow (1973, 1976a, 1976b). See also Tobin and Buiter (1976), Turnovsky (1977), and Scarth (1988). For early applications of dynamic methods to the study of the macroeconomy readers are referred to Samuelson (1947), Baumol (1959), and Allen (1967). See Cross (1988) for a collection of papers dealing with hysteresis.

Chapter 4

Perfect foresight and economic policy

The purpose of this chapter is to investigate the effects of different economic policies when agents are blessed with perfect foresight. The specific goals for this chapter are the following:

1. To complete our discussion of the dynamic "forward-looking" theory of investment by firms that was commenced in Chapter 3.

2. To use the investment theory to determine how the government can use tax incentives (such as an investment subsidy) to stimulate capital accumulation. This is an example of fiscal policy where the government changes a relative price in order to prompt a substitution response.

3. To loosely embed the investment theory in an IS-LM framework and to investigate how anticipation effects influence the outcome of traditional budgetary policies.

4. To study how exchange rate expectations influence the effects of fiscal and monetary policy in a small open economy facing perfect financial capital mobility and operating under flexible exchange rates.

4.1 Dynamic investment theory

In Chapter 3 we sketched a theory of investment by firms that is based on forward-looking behaviour and adjustment costs of investment. For reasons of intuitive clarity, the model was developed in discrete time. It turns out, however, that working in continuous time is much more convenient from a mathematical point of view. The first task that must be performed therefore is to redevelop and generalize the model in continuous time.

4.1.1 The basic model

Assume that the real profit of the representative firm is given by what is left of revenue after the production factor labour and investment outlays have been paid:

$$\pi(t) \equiv F(N(t), K(t)) - w(t)N(t) - p^I(t)\left[1 - s_I(t)\right]\Phi(I(t)), \qquad (4.1)$$

where $\pi(t)$ is real profit in period t, $F(\cdot, \cdot)$ is the constant returns to scale production function, $w(t)$ is the real wage rate ($\equiv W(t)/P(t)$), $p^I(t)$ is the relative price of investment goods ($\equiv P^I(t)/P(t)$), $s_I(t)$ is the investment subsidy, and $\Phi(\cdot)$ is the adjustment cost function, with $\Phi_I > 0$ and $\Phi_{II} > 0$. By assuming that the good produced by the firm is the same as the investment good (the so-called single good assumption), we obtain the simplification $p^I(t) = 1$. In some cases it is convenient to assume that the adjustment cost function is quadratic:

$$\Phi(I(t)) = I(t) + b\left[I(t)\right]^2, \quad b > 0. \tag{4.2}$$

The capital accumulation identity is given by:

$$\dot{K}(t) = I(t) - \delta K(t), \quad \delta > 0. \tag{4.3}$$

The firm must choose a path for its output such that the present value of its profits is maximized. Since *real* profits are defined in (4.1), the appropriate discount rate is the *real* rate of interest on alternative financial assets. This real interest rate is denoted by r and is assumed to be constant over time throughout (the body of) this section. Under these assumptions, the net present value of the stream of profits now and in the future is given by:

$$V(0) \equiv \int_0^\infty \pi(t)e^{-rt}dt$$
$$= \int_0^\infty \left[F(N(t), K(t)) - w(t)N(t) - \left[1 - s_I(t)\right]\Phi(I(t))\right]e^{-rt}dt. \tag{4.4}$$

To the extent that shares of this company are traded in the stock exchange, and share prices are based on fundamentals and not on the speculative whims and fancies of irrational money sharks, its value on the stock market should equal $V(0)$ in real terms, or $P(0)V(0)$ in nominal terms.

The firm maximizes (4.4) under the restriction (4.3). With the aid of the Maximum Principle the solution to this problem can be found quite easily.[1] The current-value Hamiltonian can be written as:

$$\mathcal{H}_C(t) \equiv F(N(t), K(t)) - w(t)N(t) - \left[1 - s_I(t)\right]\Phi(I(t))$$
$$+ q(t)\left[I(t) - \delta K(t)\right]. \tag{4.5}$$

Formally, $q(t)$ plays the role of the Lagrange multiplier for the capital accumulation restriction. The economic interpretation of $q(t)$ is straightforward. It can be shown that $q(0)$ represents the shadow price of installed capital $K(0)$. In words, $q(0)$ measures by how much the value of the firm would rise ($dV(0)$) if the initial capital stock were increased slightly ($dK(0)$), i.e. $q(0) \equiv dV(0)/dK(0)$ (see Intermezzo 4.1 on Tobin's q below).

The firm can freely choose employment and the rate of investment at each instant, so that the following first-order conditions (for $t \in [0, \infty)$) should be intuitive:

$$\frac{\partial \mathcal{H}_C(t)}{\partial N(t)} = F_N(N(t), K(t)) - w(t) = 0, \tag{4.6}$$

---

[1]Note that the method sketched here is a generalization of the Lagrange multiplier method used in Chapter 3. An explanation of the Maximum Principle based mainly on pure economic intuition can be found in Dorfman (1969). Other excellent sources are Dixit (1990), Léonard and Long (1992), Chiang (1992), and Intriligator (1971). See also the Mathematical Appendix.

$$\frac{\partial \mathcal{H}_C(t)}{\partial I(t)} = q(t) - [1 - s_I(t)] \, \Phi_I(I(t)) = 0. \tag{4.7}$$

The interpretation of (4.6) is the usual one: the value-maximizing firm chooses the amount of labour such that the marginal product of labour equals the real wage rate. Note that (4.7) implies a very simple investment function:

$$[1 - s_I(t)] \, \Phi_I(I(t)) = q(t) \quad \Rightarrow \quad I(t) \equiv I(q(t), s_I(t)), \tag{4.8}$$

where $I_q \equiv \partial I(\cdot)/\partial q = 1/[(1 - s_I)\Phi_{II}] > 0$ and $I_s \equiv \partial I(\cdot)/\partial s_I = \Phi_I/[(1 - s_I)\Phi_{II}] > 0$. In words, higher values for q and s_I both imply a higher rate of investment. Indeed, for the quadratic adjustment cost function (4.2), the investment function has a very simple form:

$$\Phi_I(I(t)) = 1 + 2bI(t) = \frac{q(t)}{1 - s_I(t)} \quad \Rightarrow \quad I(t) = \frac{1}{2b}\left[\frac{q(t)}{1 - s_I(t)} - 1\right]. \tag{4.9}$$

The parallel with the expression derived in Chapter 3 (i.e. equation (3.26)) should be noted. Note that we have not used the symbol q for nothing: the investment theory developed here is formally known as Tobin's q-theory, after its inventor James Tobin (1969).

The first expression in equation (4.8) allows a very simple interpretation of the optimality condition for investment. It instructs the firm to equate the marginal cost of investment (equal to $(1 - s_I)\Phi_I$) to the shadow price of capital, which is the marginal benefit of investment. In other words, by spending money today on investment you add value to your company. This added value is measured by the shadow price.

Equations (4.6)–(4.7) are in essence static conditions of the form "marginal cost equals marginal benefit". The truly *intertemporal* part of the problem is solved by choosing an optimal path for the shadow price of capital. The first-order condition for this choice is:

$$\dot{q}(t) - rq(t) = \left[-\frac{\partial \mathcal{H}_C(t)}{\partial K(t)} \equiv \right] - [F_K(N(t), K(t)) - \delta q(t)]. \tag{4.10}$$

This condition can be written in several ways, two of which are:

$$\dot{q}(t) = (r + \delta)q(t) - F_K(N(t), K(t)), \tag{4.11}$$

and:

$$\frac{\dot{q}(t) + F_K(N(t), K(t))}{q(t)} = r + \delta. \tag{4.12}$$

Equation (4.12) allows for a very intuitive interpretation. The shadow return on the possession and use of physical capital is the sum of the shadow capital gain ($\dot{q}(t)$) and the marginal product of capital [$F_K(N(t), K(t))$], expressed in terms of the shadow price (to make it a *rate* of return). This shadow rate of return must equal the market rate of return on other financial assets (that are perfect substitutes for shares) *plus* the rate of physical deterioration of the capital stock. The depreciation costs must be counted as a cost item because capital evaporates over time, regardless of whether the firm uses the capital for production or not. Hence, in determining the optimal path for $q(t)$ the firm is guided by the implicit arbitrage equation (4.12).

We have developed Tobin's *marginal* q-theory of investment in this section. It is shown in Intermezzo 4.1 that, provided some more specific assumptions are made about the adjustment cost function, Tobin's *average* q-theory coincides with his marginal q-theory. Average q for the firm is defined as $\bar{q}(0) \equiv V(0)/K(0)$. In words, $\bar{q}$ represents the value that the stock market ascribes to each unit of installed capital of the firm (at replacement cost; see Intermezzo 4.1).

And this is exactly where the great beauty of the theory lies. In principle one can look up the stock market value of a firm from the financial pages in the newspapers, and divide this by the replacement value of its capital stock (slightly more work), and calculate the firm's q. The value of q that is obtained in this manner reflects all information that is (according to the stock market participants) of relevance to the particular firm (see Hayashi (1982) for further remarks).

Intermezzo 4.1

Tobin's q-theory of investment. In this intermezzo we demonstrate that Tobin's average and marginal q coincide under certain conditions. The proof is adapted from Hayashi (1982). Suppose that the profit function in equation (4.1) is adjusted by including the existing capital stock in the adjustment cost function:

$$\pi(t) \equiv F(N(t), K(t)) - w(t)N(t) - [1 - s_I(t)]\,\Phi\,(I(t), K(t)), \qquad \text{(a)}$$

where $\pi(t)$ is real profit, $w(t)$ is the real wage rate $[\equiv W(t)/P(t)]$, and $s_I(t)$ is the investment subsidy. The adjustment cost function is homogeneous of degree one in $I(t)$ and $K(t)$, so that $\Phi = \Phi_I I + \Phi_K K$ (see also Intermezzo 4.3). The partial derivatives of $\Phi\,(\cdot)$ are given by $\Phi_I > 0$, $\Phi_K < 0$, $\Phi_{II} > 0$, $\Phi_{IK} < 0$, and $\Phi_{KK} > 0$. Hence, adjustment costs are decreasing in the capital stock. Large firms experience less disruption for a given level of investment than small firms.

The firm is assumed to maximize the present value of profits, using the (time-varying) real interest rate $r(t)$ as the discount factor. Equation (4.4) is altered to:

$$V(0) \equiv \int_0^\infty \Big[F(N(t), K(t)) - w(t)N(t)$$
$$- [1 - s_I(t)]\,\Phi\,(I(t), K(t)) \Big] e^{-R(t)} dt, \qquad \text{(b)}$$

where $V(0)$ is the real stockmarket value of the firm, and $R(t)$ is a discounting factor that depends on the entire path of short interest rates up to t:

$$R(t) \equiv \int_0^t r(\tau)d\tau \;\Rightarrow\; \frac{dR(t)}{dt} = r(t). \qquad \text{(c)}$$

As the saying goes, variety is the spice of life, so let us solve the optimization problem with the regular (rather than the current-value) Hamiltonian (see the Mathematical Appendix for the difference between the two). The regular Hamiltonian is given by:

$$\mathcal{H}(t) \equiv \Big[F(N(t), K(t)) - w(t)N(t) - [1 - s_I(t)]\,\Phi\,(I(t), K(t)) \Big] e^{-R(t)}$$
$$+ \lambda(t)\,[I(t) - \delta K(t)],$$

where $\lambda(t)$ is the co-state variable. The first-order conditions for this problem are:

$$\frac{\partial \mathcal{H}(t)}{\partial N(t)} = 0: \quad F_N(N(t), K(t)) = w(t), \tag{d}$$

$$\frac{\partial \mathcal{H}(t)}{\partial I(t)} = 0: \quad \lambda(t)e^{R(t)} = [1 - s_I(t)]\, \Phi_I(I(t), K(t)), \tag{e}$$

$$\frac{d\lambda(t)}{dt} = -\frac{\partial \mathcal{H}(t)}{\partial K(t)}: \quad \Longleftrightarrow$$

$$[\dot{\lambda}(t) - \delta\lambda(t)]\, e^{R(t)} = -F_K(N(t), K(t))$$
$$+ [1 - s_I(t)]\, \Phi_K(I(t), K(t)), \tag{f}$$

where we have already deleted the (non-zero) exponential term $e^{-R(t)}$ from (d). By defining $q(t) \equiv \lambda(t)e^{R(t)}$, so that $\dot{q}(t) \equiv e^{R(t)}\dot{\lambda}(t) + r(t)q(t)$, we find that (e) and (f) can be rewritten as:

$$q(t) = [1 - s_I(t)]\, \Phi_I(I(t), K(t)), \tag{g}$$

$$\dot{q}(t) = (r(t) + \delta)\, q(t) - F_K(\cdot) + [1 - s_I(t)]\, \Phi_K(\cdot). \tag{h}$$

Expressions (d), (g) and (h) generalize, respectively, (4.6), (4.7), and (4.10) to the case of a linear-homogeneous adjustment cost function and a time-varying rate of interest.

Recall that $t = 0$ is the planning period. We want to establish a relationship between the real stockmarket value of the value-maximizing firm, $V(0)$, and the installed capital stock in the planning period, $K(0)$. We note from (b) that $V(0)$ is the present value of cash flows, $\pi(t)$, defined in (a). Cash flow in period t can be written as:

$$\pi(t) = F(N(t), K(t)) - w(t)N(t) - [1 - s_I(t)]\, \Phi(I(t), K(t))$$
$$= F_N(\cdot)\, N(t) + F_K(\cdot)\, K(t) - w(t)N(t) - [1 - s_I(t)]\, \Phi(\cdot)$$
$$= F_K(\cdot)\, K(t) - [1 - s_I(t)]\, \Phi(I(t), K(t)), \tag{i}$$

where we have used the linear homogeneity of F (i.e. Euler's theorem, which implies that $F = F_N N + F_K K$) in going from the first to the second line, and expression (d) in getting from the second to the third line. Next we note that:

$$\frac{d}{dt}[q(t)K(t)] \equiv q(t)\dot{K}(t) + K(t)\dot{q}(t)$$
$$= q(t)I(t) + [r(t)q(t) - F_K(\cdot) + [1 - s_I(t)]\, \Phi_K(\cdot)]\, K(t)$$
$$= [1 - s_I(t)]\, \Phi_I(\cdot)\, I(t) + r(t)q(t)K(t) - F_K(\cdot)\, K(t)$$
$$+ [1 - s_I(t)]\, \Phi_K(\cdot)\, K(t), \tag{j}$$

where we have used (4.3) and (h) to get from the first to the second line, and (g) to get from the second to the third line. But the linear homogeneity of Φ implies that $\Phi = \Phi_I I + \Phi_K K$, so that (j) can be simplified even more:

$$\frac{d}{dt}[q(t)K(t)] = r(t)q(t)K(t) - F_K(\cdot)\, K(t) + [1 - s_I(t)]\, \Phi(\cdot)$$

$$= r(t)q(t)K(t) - \pi(t), \tag{k}$$

where we have used (i) to arrive at the final expression. Multiplying both sides of (k) by $e^{-R(t)}$ we obtain:

$$\frac{d}{dt}\left[q(t)K(t)e^{-R(t)}\right] = -\pi(t)e^{-R(t)}. \tag{l}$$

By taking dt to the other side and integrating for $t \in [0, \infty)$ we obtain:

$$\int_0^\infty d\left[q(t)K(t)e^{-R(t)}\right] = -\int_0^\infty \pi(t)e^{-R(t)}dt \equiv -V(0) \Rightarrow$$

$$\lim_{t\to\infty} q(t)K(t)e^{-R(t)} - q(0)K(0) = -V(0) \Rightarrow$$

$$V(0) = q(0)K(0), \tag{m}$$

where we note that $R(0) = 0$ (so that $e^{-R(0)} = 1$) and arrive at the final expression by imposing the transversality condition, according to which $\lim_{t\to\infty} q(t)K(t)e^{-R(t)} = 0$. Expression (m) is the one we were after. It says that a firm with an installed capital stock of $K(0)$ at time $t = 0$ will have a stockmarket value of $q(0)$ times $K(0)$. Hence, $q(0)$ represents the stock market value of one unit of installed capital. Note, finally, that (m) also implies that Tobin's marginal and average q coincide in this case. Tobin's marginal q measures by how much the stockmarket value of the firm would rise if the installed capital stock would increase slightly, i.e. it is $dV(0)/dK(0)$. Tobin's average q measures the stockmarket value per unit of capital, i.e. it is $V(0)/K(0)$. In this model the two concepts coincide. Hayashi (1982) discusses cases where this is no longer the case.

****

4.1.2 Fiscal policy: Investment subsidy

The model can now be used to investigate the immediate, transitional, and long-run effects of governmental efforts to stimulate investment. Omitting the (now almost superfluous) time index, the model consists of equations (4.3) (with the investment function given in (4.8) substituted), (4.11), and (4.6):

$$\dot{K} = I(q, s_I) - \delta K, \tag{4.13}$$

$$\dot{q} = (r + \delta)q - F_K(N, K), \tag{4.14}$$

$$w = F_N(N, K). \tag{4.15}$$

Despite its simplicity, the model allows several economically interesting variations to be considered within the same framework. Clearly, in view of (4.15), some assumption must be made about the real wage rate w. At least three types of labour market assumptions can be distinguished: (i) the model is interpreted at firm level and the real wage is assumed to be exogenously given (and constant); the model is interpreted at the level of the aggregate economy and (ii) full employment of labour is postulated or (iii) a macroeconomic labour supply equation is added to it (e.g. equation (1.11) with $P^e = P$). We consider these three cases in turn.

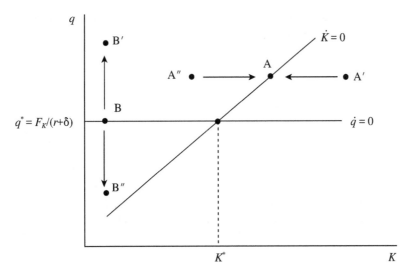

Figure 4.1: Investment with constant real wages

4.1.2.1   Constant real wages

If the real wage rate is constant, the assumption of perfect competition in the goods market (and the implied homogeneity of the production function) renders the model very simple indeed. Of course, aside from the microeconomic interpretation given above, this case is also relevant for an entire economy with rigid real wages. Since the production function is homogeneous of degree one (constant returns to scale), the marginal products of labour and capital are homogeneous of degree zero (see Intermezzo 4.3 below). This implies that $F_N(N, K)$ can be written as $F_N(1, K/N)$, which depends on the capital-labour ratio only. Equation (4.15) can be rewritten as $w = F_N(1, K/N)$, and uniquely determines the K/N ratio for the firm. This ratio is constant over time because w is assumed to be constant. This also implies that the marginal product of capital is constant, since $F_K(N, K) = F_K(1, K/N) = F_K$, a constant.

By assuming a constant real wage, the labour demand equation can be ignored, and the model consists of equations (4.13)–(4.14). The qualitative content of the model can be summarized graphically by means of Figure 4.1. The $\dot{K} = 0$ line represents all combinations of K and q such that the capital stock is in equilibrium. In view of (4.13), this implies that gross investment is exactly equal to replacement investment along the $\dot{K} = 0$ line, i.e. $I(q, s_I) = \delta K$. Formally, we obtain from (4.13):

$$d\dot{K} = I_q dq + I_s ds_I - \delta dK, \qquad I_q > 0, \ I_s > 0. \tag{4.16}$$

which implies that the slope of the $\dot{K} = 0$ line is:

$$\left(\frac{\partial q}{\partial K} \right)_{\dot{K}=0} = \frac{\delta}{I_q} > 0. \tag{4.17}$$

In words, a higher capital stock necessitates a higher level of steady-state gross investment. This is only forthcoming if q is also higher.

Equation (4.16) also implies that an increase in the investment subsidy shifts the $\dot{K} = 0$ line down and to the right:

$$\left(\frac{\partial q}{\partial s_I} \right)_{\dot{K}=0} = -\frac{I_s}{I_q} < 0. \tag{4.18}$$

The after-subsidy cost of investing falls and as a result firms are willing to invest the same amount for a lower value of q.

For points off the $\dot{K} = 0$ line, the dynamics of the capital stock is also provided by equation (4.16):

$$\frac{\partial \dot{K}}{\partial K} = -\delta < 0. \tag{4.19}$$

The graphical interpretation is as follows. At point A the capital stock is in equilibrium. If K is slightly higher (say at A$'$ to the right of point A), (4.19) predicts that depreciation exceeds gross investment so that the capital stock falls over time, i.e. $\dot{K} < 0$. This dynamic effect is indicated by a horizontal arrow towards the $\dot{K} = 0$ line. Obviously, for points to the left of the $\dot{K} = 0$ line, the arrows point the other way (see point A$''$). The basic insight is, of course, that the capital accumulation process is self-correcting, i.e. for a given value of q, K has an automatic tendency to return to the $\dot{K} = 0$ line.

The $\dot{q} = 0$ line represents all points for which the firm's investment plans are in equilibrium. By differentiating (4.14) we obtain:

$$d\dot{q} = (r + \delta)dq + qdr, \tag{4.20}$$

where we have used the fact that the marginal product of capital is constant. From (4.20) it is clear that the $\dot{q} = 0$ line is horizontal:

$$\left(\frac{\partial q}{\partial K}\right)_{\dot{q}=0} = 0. \tag{4.21}$$

This is intuitive: since both the rate of interest and the marginal product of capital are constant (and hence independent of K), q itself is also constant and independent of K in the steady state. If the (exogenous) rate of interest rises, future marginal products of capital are discounted more heavily, so that the steady-state value of q falls:

$$\left(\frac{\partial q}{\partial r}\right)_{\dot{q}=0} = -\frac{q}{r+\delta} < 0. \tag{4.22}$$

For points off the $\dot{q} = 0$ line, the dynamic behaviour of q is also provided by (4.20):

$$\frac{\partial \dot{q}}{\partial q} = r + \delta > 0. \tag{4.23}$$

The graphical interpretation is as follows. At point B the value of q is consistent with an equilibrium investment plan. Now take a slightly higher value of q, say the one associated with point B$'$, directly above point B. Clearly, in view of the fact that both r and F_K are constant, this higher value of q can only satisfy the arbitrage equation (4.12) if a (shadow) capital gain is expected, i.e. if $\dot{q} > 0$. The opposite holds at points below the $\dot{q} = 0$ line (say point B$''$, as is indicated with the arrows in Figure 4.1). Intuitively, therefore, the q-dynamics is inherently unstable. Slight moves away from the $\dot{q} = 0$ line are not self-correcting but reinforcing.

By combining the information regarding the K-dynamics and q-dynamics, the forces operating on points in different regions of Figure 4.1 are obtained and summarized by the arrows. For example, at point B$'$ there are automatic forces shifting the (q, K) combination in a north-easterly direction. In Figure 4.2, a number of representative *trajectories* have been drawn. Note especially what happens if a trajectory

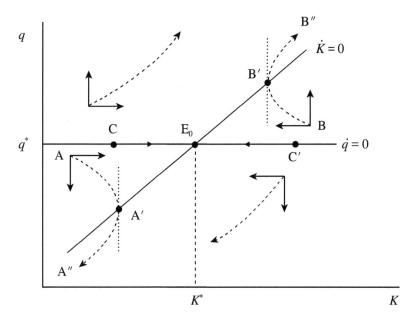

Figure 4.2: Derivation of the saddle path

crosses through the $\dot{K} = 0$ line. Take point A, for example. As the (q, K) combination moves in a south-easterly direction, it gets closer and closer to the $\dot{K} = 0$ line. As it reaches this line (at point A'), however, the value of q keeps falling and the level of gross investment becomes too low to sustain the given capital stock. As a result, the trajectory veers off in a south-westerly direction towards point A'' (never to be heard of again).

From the different trajectories that have been drawn in Figure 4.2, it can be judged that the model appears to be very unstable: all trajectories seem to lead away from the steady-state equilibrium point at E_0. There is, however, one path that does give rise to stable adjustment, namely the $\dot{q} = 0$ line itself. Consider, for example, point C. It lies on the $\dot{q} = 0$ line (so there are no forces operating to change the value of q over time), but it lies to the left of the $\dot{K} = 0$ line. But, the K-dynamics is stable, so the capital stock will automatically rise towards its level at point E_0. A similar conclusion holds for point C'.

In conclusion, for each given initial level of the capital stock, *there is exactly one path towards the steady-state equilibrium*. And this is very fortunate indeed, because one would have an embarrassment of riches if this were not the case. Indeed, suppose that the model were globally stable, so that "all roads lead to Rome", i.e. all (q, K) combinations would eventually return to point E_0. That would lead to a very troublesome conclusion, namely that the shadow price of capital (q) is not determined at any point in time!

The particular type of stability that is exemplified by the model is called *saddle-point stability*: there is exactly one stable adjustment path (called the saddle path) that re-establishes equilibrium after a shock. Technically speaking, the requirement that the economy be on the saddle path has more justification than just convenience: ultimately, an exploding solution is seen by agents not to be in their own best interests, so that they have good reason to restrict attention to the saddle-path solution. The remainder of this chapter will be used to demonstrate the remarkable predictive content of models incorporating saddle-point stability.

Consider the case of an *unanticipated and permanent increase in the investment subsidy*. This means that at some time t_A the government announces that s_I will be increased "as of today". In other words, the policy change is implemented immediately. For future reference, the implementation date is denoted by t_I. Hence, an unanticipated shock is a shock for which announcement and implementation dates coincide, i.e. $t_A = t_I$. The effects of the policy measure can be derived graphically with the aid of the phase diagram in the top panel of Figure 4.3. We have already derived that an increase in s_I shifts the $\dot{K} = 0$ line to the right, so that the ultimate equilibrium will be at point E_1. How does the adjustment occur? Very simple. Since E_0 is on the $\dot{q} = 0$ line (which is also the saddle path for *this* model), the higher subsidy gives rise to higher gross investment (because $I_s > 0$) and the adjustment path is along the saddle path from E_0 to E_1. Note that the capital stock adjusts *smoothly*, due to the fact that adjustment costs make very uneven investment plans very expensive. The adjustment over time has also been illustrated in Figure 4.3.

As a second "finger exercise" with the model, consider an unanticipated and permanent increase in the exogenous rate of interest r as illustrated in Figure 4.4. Equation (4.22) shows that this shock leads to a downward shift in the $\dot{q} = 0$ line because future marginal products of capital are discounted more heavily. What does the adjustment path look like now? Clearly, the new equilibrium is at point E_1 and the only path to this point is the saddle path going through it. Since K is fixed in the short run, the only stable adjustment path is the one with a "financial correction" at the time of the occurrence of the shock (at time t_A): q jumps down from point E_0 to point A directly below it. The intuition behind this financial correction is aided by solving the unstable differential equation for q, stated in equation (4.14) above, forward in time. Intermezzo 4.2 derives the general solution:

$$q(t) \equiv \int_t^\infty F_K(\tau) \exp\left[-\int_t^\tau [r(s) + \delta]\, ds \right] d\tau. \tag{4.24}$$

Hence, as was already hinted at above, q represents the discounted value of present and future marginal products of capital, so that an increase in r (either now or in the future) immediately leads to a revaluation of this stream of returns. After the immediate financial correction, the adjustment proceeds smoothly along the saddle path towards the ultimate steady-state equilibrium point E_1.

Intermezzo 4.2

Tobin's q as the present value of marginal products of capital. Recognizing the possible time dependence of the interest rate and the marginal product of capital, we write the differential equation for Tobin's q as:

$$\dot{q}(\tau) - [r(\tau) + \delta]\, q(\tau) = -F_K(\tau). \tag{a}$$

Clearly, equation (a) is an unstable differential equation because $r(\tau) + \delta$ is assumed to be positive. However, we can still compute the *forward-looking solution* to this expression. Technically, the trick that we use is very similar to the one used in Intermezzo 3.1, i.e. we find a suitable integrating factor and solve the differential equation by integration. Experience suggests that the correct integrating factor is $e^{-\bar{R}(t,\tau)}$, where $\bar{R}(t, \tau)$ is defined as:

$$\bar{R}(t, \tau) \equiv \int_t^\tau [r(s) + \delta]\, ds. \tag{b}$$

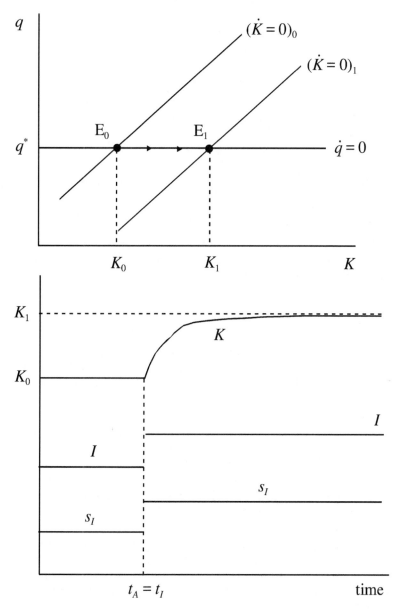

Figure 4.3: An unanticipated and permanent increase in the investment subsidy

From this expression we can derive readily that $\bar{R}(t,t) = 0$ and $d\bar{R}(t,\tau)/d\tau = r(\tau) + \delta$. Following steps similar to those in Intermezzo 3.1. we derive:

$$[\dot{q}(\tau) - [r(\tau) + \delta] q(\tau)] e^{-\bar{R}(t,\tau)} = -F_K(\tau) e^{-\bar{R}(t,\tau)} \qquad \Leftrightarrow$$

$$\frac{d}{d\tau} q(\tau) e^{-\bar{R}(t,\tau)} = -F_K(\tau) e^{-\bar{R}(t,\tau)} \qquad \Leftrightarrow$$

$$dq(\tau) e^{-\bar{R}(t,\tau)} = -F_K(\tau) e^{-\bar{R}(t,\tau)} d\tau. \qquad (c)$$

Integrating (c) for $\tau \in [t, \infty)$ we obtain:

$$\int_t^\infty dq(\tau) e^{-\bar{R}(t,\tau)} = -\int_t^\infty F_K(\tau) e^{-\bar{R}(t,\tau)} d\tau$$

$$q(\tau) e^{-\bar{R}(t,\tau)} \Big|_t^\infty = -\int_t^\infty F_K(\tau) e^{-\bar{R}(t,\tau)} d\tau$$

$$\lim_{\tau \to \infty} q(\tau) e^{-\bar{R}(t,\tau)} - q(t) e^{-\bar{R}(t,t)} = -\int_t^\infty F_K(\tau) e^{-\bar{R}(t,\tau)} d\tau. \qquad (d)$$

But the transversality condition implies that $\lim_{\tau \to \infty} q(\tau) e^{-\bar{R}(t,\tau)} = 0$, i.e. we restrict attention to the fundamental replacement value of installed capital. Furthermore, we have that $\bar{R}(t,t) = 0$. By substituting these results in (d) we obtain equation (4.24).

****

As a final example of how the model works, consider the case where the firm hears at time t_A that interest rates will rise permanently at some future date t_I. This is an example of a so-called *anticipated shock*. Formally, an anticipated shock is one that is known to occur at some later date. Obviously, the only real news reaches the agent at time t_A. Everything that happens after that time is known to the agent. What happens to the value of q can already be gleaned 'from (4.24). Discounting of future marginal products becomes heavier (than before the shock) after the rate of interest has actually risen, i.e. for $t \geq t_I$. Hence, q must fall at the time the news becomes available. But by how much? This is best illustrated with the aid of Figure 4.5. Consider the following intuitive/heuristic solution principle: a discrete adjustment in q must occur at the time the news becomes available (i.e. at t_A), and there cannot be a further discrete adjustment in q after t_A. Intuitively, an *anticipated* jump in q would imply an infinite (shadow) capital gain or loss (since there would be a finite change in q in an infinitesimal amount of time). Hence, the solution principle amounts to requiring that all jumps in q occur when something truly unexpected occurs (which is at time t_A). Obviously, at t_A there is an infinite capital loss, but it is unanticipated.

With the aid of this solution principle, the adjustment path can be deduced. We start our detective task at time t_I and work backward in time toward t_A. At the time of the interest rate increase the (q, K) combination must be on the new saddle path, i.e. at point B on the line labelled $(\dot{q}=0)_1$. If it were to reach B too soon (say at time $t < t_I$) or too late ($t > t_I$), equilibrium would never be re-established without further jumps in q that are prohibited. Between t_A and t_I the dynamic forces determining q and K are those associated with the old equilibrium E_0 (see the arrows). Working

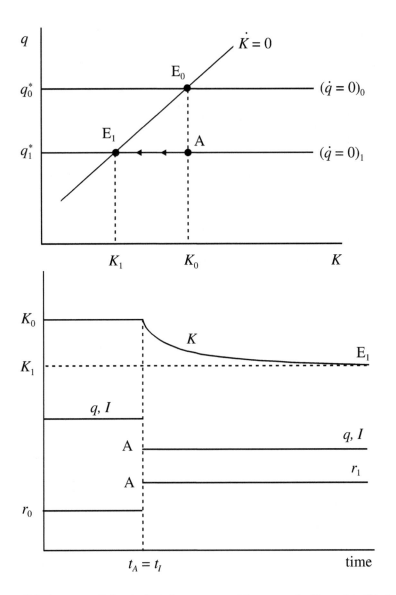

Figure 4.4: An unanticipated and permanent increase in the rate of interest

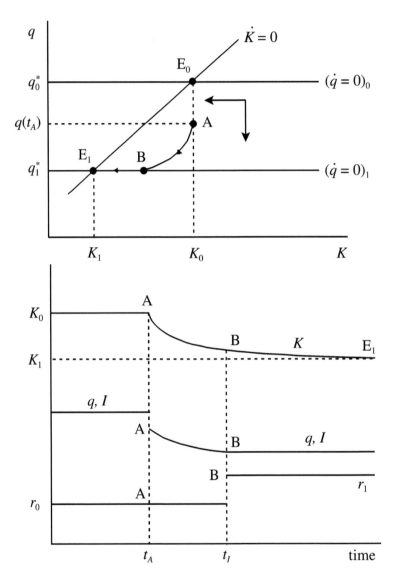

Figure 4.5: An anticipated and permanent increase in the rate of interest

backwards, there is exactly one trajectory which starts at time t_A at point A and arrives at point B at the right time, t_I. Hence, the unique path that re-establishes equilibrium after the shock is the one comprised of a discrete adjustment at t_A from E_0 to A, followed by gradual adjustment from A to B in the period before the interest rate has risen, arrival at point B at t_I, followed by further gradual adjustment in the capital stock from B to E_1.

In comparison with the case of an unanticipated rise in the interest rate, the paths of q and investment are more smooth in the anticipated case (compare Figures 4.4 and 4.5, lower panel). The reason is, of course, that the firm in the case of an anticipated shock has an opportunity to react to the worsened investment climate in the future.

4.1.2.2 Full employment in the labour market

Up to now we have interpreted the model given in (4.13)–(4.15) as applying to a single firm facing a constant real wage. Suppose that we reinterpret the model at a macroeconomic level, i.e. I and K now represent economy-wide gross investment and the capital stock, respectively, and the interpretation of q is likewise altered. Assume furthermore that the economy is characterized by full employment in the labour market, and that labour supply equal unity so that $w = F_N(1, K)$ is the market clearing wage rate, and the macroeconomic marginal product of capital is given by $F_K(1, K)$. The model now consists of the following two equations:

$$\dot{K} = I(q, s_I) - \delta K, \tag{4.25}$$
$$\dot{q} = (r + \delta)q - F_K(1, K). \tag{4.26}$$

It is clear that the major change caused by our reinterpretation is that the marginal product of capital is no longer constant as it depends on the capital stock. Intuitively, since the labour input is fully employed ($N = 1$), the economy experiences diminishing returns to capital, since $F_{KK} < 0$. This also causes the $\dot{q} = 0$ line to be affected:

$$\left(\frac{\partial q}{\partial K} \right)_{\dot{q}=0} = \frac{F_{KK}}{r + \delta} < 0. \tag{4.27}$$

Intuitively, steady-state q is downward sloping in K because the more capital is used, the lower is its marginal product. As a result, the discounted stream of marginal products (which is q) falls.

In Figure 4.6, the saddle path is derived graphically. The dynamic forces are much more complicated in this case. This is because the steady-state level of q and the q-dynamics itself are now both dependent on K. In addition to trajectories from points like A and C, there are now also trajectories from points like B and D that pass through the $\dot{q} = 0$ line. The major alteration compared to our earlier case is that the saddle path no longer coincides with the $\dot{q} = 0$ line.

As a first policy measure, consider an *anticipated abolition* of the investment subsidy, as was for example the case in the Netherlands in the late 1980s. Using the intuitive solution principle introduced above, the effects of this announced policy measure can be derived with the aid of Figure 4.7. The ultimate effect of the abolition of the subsidy is to increase the relative price of investment goods and to shift the $\dot{K} = 0$ line up and to the left. In the long run the economy ends up at point E_1, with a lower capital stock and a higher value of q (due to the higher steady-state marginal product of capital). Since the capital stock is given at time t_A, discrete adjustment in q must occur at the time of the announcement t_A, and the economy must

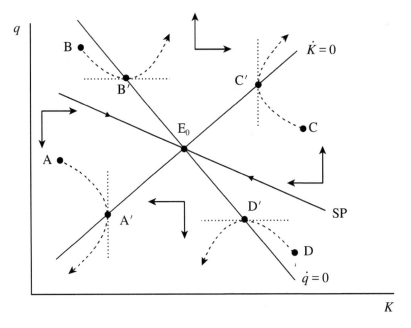

Figure 4.6: Investment with full employment in the labour market

be on the new saddle path at the time of implementation t_I, the adjustment path must look like the one sketched in the diagram. At t_A there is a financial correction that pushes the economy from E_0 to A directly above it ($K = K_0$ at impact). Between t_A and t_I the economy moves in a north-easterly direction towards point B, where it arrives at t_I. After that, there is gradual adjustment from B to the new steady state at E_1.

The striking (though intuitive) conclusion is that investment goes up initially! Firms in this economy rush to put in their investment orders in order to be able to get the subsidy while it still exists. This is of course exactly what happened in the Dutch case. The adjustment paths for all variables have been drawn in the lower panel of Figure 4.7. The conclusion of this experiment must be that anticipation effects are very important and can give rise to (at first glance) unconventional dynamic adjustment.

4.1.2.3   Temporary or permanent investment subsidy?

Suppose that the policy maker wishes to stimulate the economy and has decided to do so by creating investment incentives in the form of an investment subsidy. If the policy maker desires the maximum stimulus to emerge for a given subsidy, should he introduce a permanent or a temporary investment subsidy? Intuition would suggest that a temporary subsidy would have a larger impact on current investment because firms would squeeze in their investments while the subsidy exists. This is an intertemporal substitution argument: firms are tempted to bring forward their intertemporal investment plans to "make hay while the sun shines". It turns out that our simple model in fact predicts this kind of response.

The temporary subsidy is announced and introduced at time $t_A = t_I$ and simultaneously announced to be abolished again at some fixed time in the future t_E ($> t_I$ of course). The duration of the shock is thus given by $t_E - t_I$. Our heuristic solution

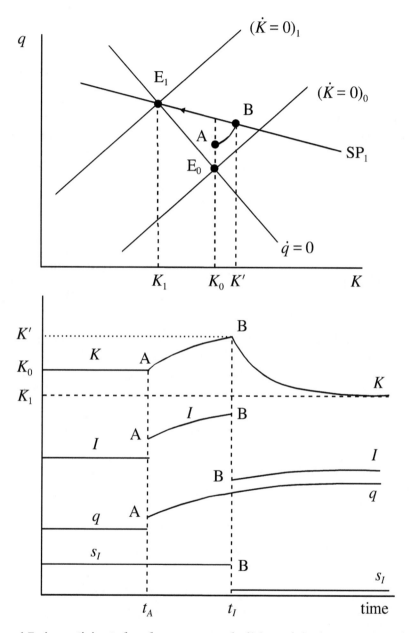

Figure 4.7: An anticipated and permanent abolition of the investment subsidy

principle can again be used to graphically derive the adjustment path with the aid of Figure 4.8. Working backwards in time, the following must hold: (i) at t_E the economy must be on the saddle path towards the eventual steady-state equilibrium E_0; (ii) between t_A and t_E the dynamic forces operating on q and K are those associated with the equilibrium E_1 (which would be relevant if the subsidy were permanent). The arrows are drawn in Figure 4.8. At t_A the capital stock is given (at K_0) and the discrete financial adjustment must take place.

Using all this information, the adjustment path is easily seen to consist of a jump from E_0 to A at time t_A, gradual adjustment from A to B between t_A and t_E, followed by gradual adjustment from B to E_0 after t_E. The time paths for all variables are drawn in the lower panel of Figure 4.8.

Of course, the path associated with an *unanticipated and permanent* subsidy is an immediate jump at t_A from E_0 to A' followed by gradual adjustment from A' to E_1. This shows that the effect on current investment (i.e. $I(t_A)$) is highest for a temporary investment subsidy (compare points A and A'). This is because, for a given investment subsidy, the value of q falls by less in the case of a temporary subsidy. Hence, if the policy maker is concerned about stimulating current investment, a temporary investment subsidy is one way to achieve it.

Intermezzo 4.3

Some production theory: the two-factor production function. If $Y = F(N,K)$ is a linear homogeneous production function, it possesses several very useful properties (see e.g. Ferguson, 1969, pp. 94–96):

(P1) $F_N N + F_K K = Y$ (Euler's theorem);

(P2) F_N and F_K are homogeneous of degree zero in N and K, hence;

(P3) $N F_{NN} + K F_{NK} = 0$ and $K F_{KK} + N F_{KN} = 0$;

(P4) $\sigma_{KN} \equiv F_N F_K / (Y F_{KN})$ is the substitution elasticity between capital and labour.

Also, Young's theorem ensures that $F_{NK} = F_{KN}$. Armed with these useful properties equations (4.29) and (4.30) can be derived. First, totally differentiate $F_N(N,K)$:

$$dF_N = F_{NN} dN + F_{NK} dK. \tag{a}$$

But (P3) ensures that $F_{NN} = -(K/N)F_{NK}$, so that (a) can be written as:

$$dF_N = -(K/N)F_{NK} dN + F_{NK} dK = -F_{NK} K \left[\frac{dN}{N} - \frac{dK}{K} \right] \Rightarrow$$

$$\frac{dF_N}{F_N} = \frac{F_{NK} K}{F_N} \left[\frac{dK}{K} - \frac{dN}{N} \right]. \tag{b}$$

It remains to be shown that $F_{NK} K / N$ can be written in terms of an income share and the substitution elasticity defined in (P4):

$$\frac{F_{NK} K}{F_N} = \frac{F_K K}{Y} \cdot \frac{F_{NK} Y}{F_N F_K} = \frac{1 - \omega_N}{\sigma_{KN}}. \tag{c}$$

Combining (c) and (b) yields (4.29). Note that we have used (P1) and (c) to derive that $F_K K / Y = 1 - F_N N / Y = 1 - w N / Y = 1 - \omega_N$. The derivation of (4.30) is left as an exercise.

****

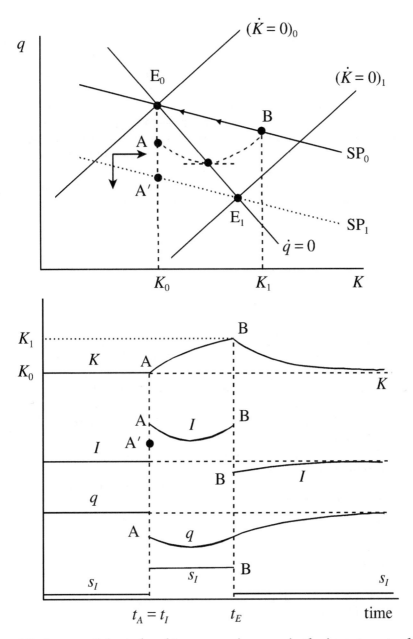

Figure 4.8: An unanticipated and temporary increase in the investment subsidy

4.1.2.4   Interaction with the labour supply decision

As a final application of the model, we now consider the general case where the model is interpreted at a macroeconomic level, and equations (4.13)–(4.15) are appended with a labour supply equation of the form familiar from Chapter 1:

$$w(1 - \theta_L) = g(N), \tag{4.28}$$

where θ_L is the tax rate on labour income, and we assume that $g_N > 0$, i.e. the substitution effect dominates the income effect in labour supply.

What happens to investment and employment if the tax on labour is reduced? And how do these effects occur over time? Obviously, in order to examine the effect on investment, the effect on the steady-state value of q must be determined. As is clear from (4.14), we need to know what happens to the marginal product of capital, F_K. Similarly, in order to study the consequences of labour market equilibrium, we must confront labour supply (4.28) with labour demand (4.15), where the latter depends on the marginal product of labour, F_N. Since the economy is operating under perfect competition, the production function is linear homogeneous (constant returns to scale), and F_N and F_K depend only on K/N. The expressions for F_N and F_K can be linearized as follows (see Intermezzo 4.3 below):

$$\tilde{F}_N = \frac{1 - \omega_N}{\sigma_{KN}} [\tilde{K} - \tilde{N}] = \tilde{w}, \tag{4.29}$$

$$\tilde{F}_K = -\frac{\omega_N}{\sigma_{KN}} [\tilde{K} - \tilde{N}], \tag{4.30}$$

$$\tilde{N} = \varepsilon_S [\tilde{w} - \tilde{\theta}_L], \tag{4.31}$$

where $\tilde{F}_K \equiv dF_K/F_K$, $\tilde{F}_N \equiv dF_N/F_N$, $\tilde{N} \equiv dN/N$, $\tilde{K} \equiv dK/K$, $\tilde{w} \equiv dw/w$, $\tilde{\theta}_L \equiv d\theta_L/(1 - \theta_L)$, $\omega_N \equiv NF_N/Y$, $\varepsilon_S \equiv g(N)/(Ng_N) > 0$, and $\sigma_{KN} \equiv F_N F_K/(YF_{NK}) \geq 0$. In words, a variable with a tilde represents the proportional rate of change in that variable, ω_N is the share of income paid out to the factor labour, ε_S is the labour supply elasticity (see Chapter 1) that is assumed to be positive, and σ_{KN} (≥ 0) is the substitution elasticity between capital and labour. Intuitively, it measures how easy it is to substitute one factor of production for the other. The easier the substitution, the higher the value for σ_{KN}. Note that we have already imposed that the labour market is in equilibrium.

By using (4.29) and (4.31), the equilibrium employment level and the wage rate can be written as functions of $\tilde{K}$ and $\tilde{\theta}_L$:

$$\tilde{w} = \frac{(1 - \omega_N)[\tilde{K} + \varepsilon_S \tilde{\theta}_L]}{\sigma_{KN} + (1 - \omega_N)\varepsilon_S}, \tag{4.32}$$

$$\tilde{N} = \frac{\varepsilon_S(1 - \omega_N)\tilde{K} - \varepsilon_S \sigma_{KN} \tilde{\theta}_L}{\sigma_{KN} + (1 - \omega_N)\varepsilon_S}. \tag{4.33}$$

By substituting (4.33) into (4.30), the expression for $\tilde{F}_K$ is obtained:

$$\tilde{F}_K = -\frac{\omega_N[\tilde{K} + \varepsilon_S \tilde{\theta}_L]}{\sigma_{KN} + (1 - \omega_N)\varepsilon_S}. \tag{4.34}$$

This expression is particularly important. It says that the marginal product of capital increases if the tax on labour is reduced. The reason is that a decrease in the labour tax stimulates employment (since $\varepsilon_S > 0$), which means that capital becomes more productive (since $F_{NK} > 0$).

The immediate, transitional, and long-run effects of a permanent and unanticipated reduction in the labour income tax are illustrated in Figure 4.9. As the labour tax falls, the marginal product of capital rises (for all levels of the capital stock) and the $\dot{q} = 0$ line shifts up and to the right. The economy jumps from E_0 to A, and the value of q jumps from q_0 to q'. Entrepreneurs observe a very good business climate and feel a strong incentive to expand business by investing. The economy moves smoothly along the saddle path from A to E_1. The situation in the labour market is depicted in Figure 4.10. The immediate effect of the tax reduction is an expansion of labour supply from N_0^S to N_1^S. Employment is immediately stimulated and rises from N_0 to N'. This is not the end of the story, however. Due to the fact that more capital is put in place (factories are expanded) labour becomes more productive as well. In terms of Figure 4.10, the labour demand schedule starts to gradually shift up and to the right, and employment expands further. The ultimate steady-state equilibrium is at E_1. The time paths for the main macroeconomic variables have been sketched in the bottom panel of Figure 4.9.

4.2 A dynamic IS-LM model

Tobin's q-theory has become very popular among macroeconomists. The reason is that it allows for a very simple description of the dynamics of the investment process, and gives predictions that are not grossly contradicted by empirical evidence. In this section we discuss Blanchard's (1981) version of the IS-LM model which loosely incorporates the q-theory along with the assumptions of fixed prices and slow quantity adjustment. This allows us to study the macroeconomic effects of traditional fiscal policy in an explicit forward-looking framework. The model that is used is described by the following equations:

$$Y^D = aq + (1 - b)Y + G, \quad a > 0, \ 0 < b < 1, \tag{4.35}$$

$$\dot{Y} = \sigma \left[Y^D - Y \right], \quad \sigma > 0, \tag{4.36}$$

$$\frac{M}{P} = kY - lR_S, \quad k > 0, \ l > 0, \tag{4.37}$$

$$R_S = R_L - \frac{\dot{R}_L}{R_L}, \tag{4.38}$$

$$\frac{\dot{q} + \pi}{q} = R_S, \tag{4.39}$$

$$\pi = -\alpha_0 + \alpha_1 Y, \quad \alpha_0 > 0, \ \alpha_1 > 0, \tag{4.40}$$

where Y^D is real spending on goods and services, q is Tobin's average q, Y is the level of real production (and income), G is an index of fiscal policy, $\dot{Y}$ [$\equiv dY/dt$] is the time rate of change in output, R_S is the rate of interest on short-term bonds, R_L is the interest rate on consols (see Chapter 3), M is the nominal money supply, and P is the fixed price level which we normalize to unity ($P = 1$). We refer to R_S and R_L as, respectively, the "short rate" and the "long rate".

Equations (4.35)–(4.36) together describe a dynamic IS curve. Equation (4.35) shows that spending depends on Tobin's average q, both because of its positive effect on investment and (potentially) because of positive wealth effects in consumption.[2] Furthermore, spending depends on income and on an index of fiscal policy G.

---

[2]Recall that qK is the value of the nation's capital stock. To the extent that domestic households own the firms, qK is part of wealth which may affect consumption. Strictly speaking, household bond holdings

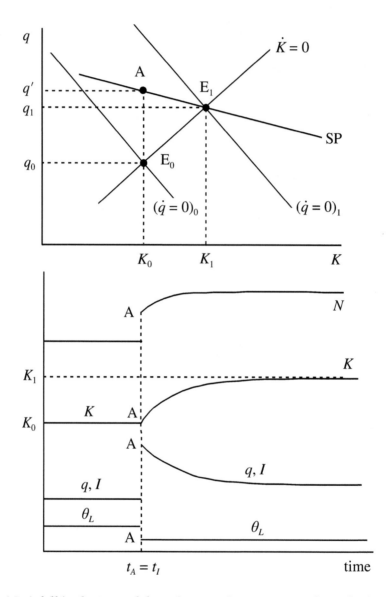

Figure 4.9: A fall in the tax on labour income: investment and employment effects

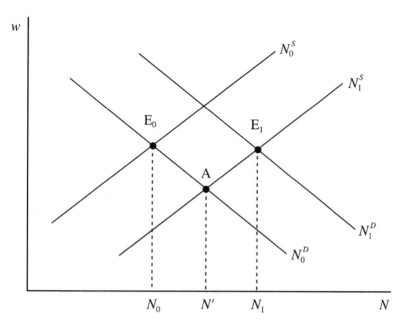

Figure 4.10: The short-run and long-run labour market effects

Equation (4.36) shows the dynamic behaviour of output. If demand exceeds production ($Y^D > Y$) then inventories are run down and output is gradually increased. Unlike in the standard IS-LM model, output is now modelled as a state variable which can only move gradually over time.

Equation (4.37) is a linear money demand equation (ignoring the wealth effect). The demand for real money balances depends negatively on the short rate of interest and positively on income. In discrete time, the short rate of interest is the rate of interest on single-period bonds. Such bonds have no capital gain/loss because they mature after a single period. In continuous time, the short rate represents the rate of interest on a bond with an infinitesimal term to maturity. Hence, there are no capital gains/losses in this case either.

Equation (4.38) is the arbitrage equation between short bonds and consols. It is derived as follows. We assume that the two types of financial instruments are perfect substitutes, so that their respective rates of return must equalize. For short-term bonds this rate of return is R_S since there are no capital gains/losses. For consols there may, however, be capital gains/losses. Recall from Chapter 3 that the price of consols is the inverse of the rate of interest on consols, i.e. $P_B \equiv 1/R_L$. The rate of return on a consol is equal to the sum of the coupon payment (1 euro each period) plus the expected capital gain ($\dot{P}_B$) expressed in terms of the price of the consol (P_B):

$$\text{return on consol} \equiv \frac{1 + \dot{P}_B}{P_B} = \frac{1 - (1/R_L^2)\dot{R}_L}{1/R_L} = R_L - \frac{\dot{R}_L}{R_L}, \qquad (4.41)$$

where we have used $P_B \equiv 1/R_L$ and $\dot{P}_B = (-1/R_L^2)\dot{R}_L$ to arrive at the final expression. This rate of return on consols must be the same as the short rate of interest:

$$R_L - \frac{\dot{R}_L}{R_L} = R_S. \qquad (4.42)$$

and the real money supply should also affect consumption (as in the Blinder-Solow model studied in Chapter 3) but this effect is ignored by Blanchard.

Equation (4.42) is known as the *term structure of interest rates*.

Equation (4.39) is another arbitrage equation. Since q measures the value of shares, the rate of return on shares is the sum of the periodic dividend payment (π) plus the expected capital gain on shares ($\dot{q}$), expressed in terms of the share price (q) itself:

$$\text{return on share} \equiv \frac{\pi + \dot{q}}{q}. \tag{4.43}$$

Since shares and the other non-monetary financial assets are perfect substitutes, the rate of return on shares must be the same as the short rate of interest. This is what (4.39) says. Finally, equation (4.40) is an ad hoc relationship between profit (or dividends) and output. If output is high, the marginal product of capital is also high (for a given capital stock) and so are profits. Conversely, if output is low, then the firm may not be able to meet its fixed cost so that profit may be negative.

The model can be condensed to two equations by means of simple substitutions:

$$\dot{Y} = \sigma \left[aq - bY + G \right], \tag{4.44}$$

$$\dot{q} = \frac{kY - M}{l} q - \alpha_1 Y + \alpha_0. \tag{4.45}$$

Clearly, the model gives rise to a non-linear system of differential equations in Y and q. The exogenous variables are G and M. Once the paths for Y and q are known, the paths for the remaining variables can be solved also. The dynamic properties of the model can be studied with the aid of the phase diagrams in Figure 4.11.

Equation (4.44) shows that the $\dot{Y} = 0$ line is linear and upward sloping. Increasing government spending shifts the $\dot{Y} = 0$ line down and to the right, and the dynamic forces operating on points off the $\dot{Y} = 0$ line are stabilizing, i.e. for a given level of q, output automatically returns to the equilibrium line over time. In summary:

$$\left(\frac{\partial q}{\partial Y} \right)_{\dot{Y}=0} = \frac{b}{a} > 0, \quad \left(\frac{\partial q}{\partial G} \right)_{\dot{Y}=0} = -\frac{1}{a} < 0, \quad \frac{\partial \dot{Y}}{\partial Y} = -\sigma b < 0. \tag{4.46}$$

The $\dot{q} = 0$ line is slightly more complicated due to its non-linearity. By using (4.45) we find that the $\dot{q} = 0$ can be written as follows:

$$q = \frac{\alpha_1 Y - \alpha_0}{(kY - M)/l}. \tag{4.47}$$

The denominator on the right-hand side is the short interest rate which must be positive. Indeed, if R_S were negative, people would just hold their wealth in the form of money balances, kept in an old sock in some cupboard. In terms of Figure 4.11, only output values exceeding M/k are thus feasible. It is not difficult to see that the slope of the $\dot{q} = 0$ line depends on the relative strength of two effects: if Y increases, both profits and the short rate of interest rise. The profit effect increases steady-state q but the interest rate effect decreases it. As a result, the net effect on the steady-state value for Tobin's q is not a priori clear. Using (4.47) and taking derivatives we find:

$$\left(\frac{\partial q}{\partial Y} \right)_{\dot{q}=0} = \frac{\alpha_1}{R_S} - \frac{\alpha_1 Y - \alpha_0}{R_S} \frac{k}{l R_S}$$

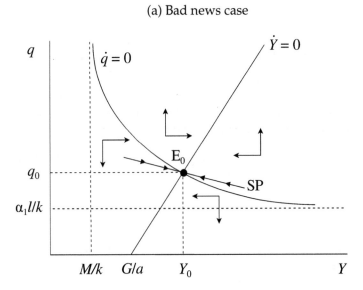

(a) Bad news case

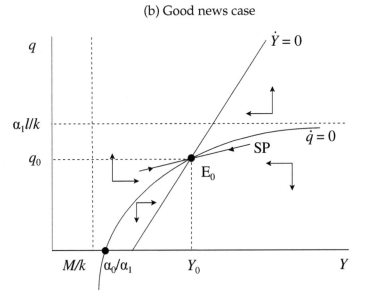

(b) Good news case

Figure 4.11: Dynamic IS-LM model and the term structure of interest rates

$$= \frac{1}{R_S} \left[\alpha_1 - \frac{qk}{l} \right] \lessgtr 0, \tag{4.48}$$

where the first term in the square brackets represents the profit effect and the second term is the interest rate effect. Depending on the parameter values, the model describes either one of two cases, both of which have been illustrated in Figure 4.11. Using the terminology of Blanchard (1981), we distinguish:

Bad news case If $M/k > \alpha_0/\alpha_1$ then q has a lower bound of $\alpha_1 l/k$ and $\lim_{Y \downarrow M/k} q = +\infty$. The profit effect of output is dominated by the interest rate effect and the $\dot{q} = 0$ line is downward sloping, as in Figure 4.11(a).

Good news case If $M/k < \alpha_0/\alpha_1$ then q has an upper bound of $\alpha_1 l/k$ and $\lim_{Y \downarrow M/k} q = -\infty$. The profit effect of output dominates the interest rate effect and the $\dot{q} = 0$ line is upward sloping, as in Figure 4.11(b).

Note that for both cases, equation (4.47) implies that an increase in the money supply shifts the $\dot{q} = 0$ line up and to the right:

$$\left(\frac{\partial q}{\partial M} \right)_{\dot{q}=0} = \frac{q}{l R_S^2} > 0. \tag{4.49}$$

Finally, the dynamic adjustment in Tobin's q can be deduced in a straightforward fashion from equation (4.45):

$$\frac{\partial \dot{q}}{\partial q} = R_S > 0. \tag{4.50}$$

In terms of Figure 4.11, points above (below) the $\dot{q} = 0$ line are associated with capital gains (losses) on shares. Hence, the dynamics of q for points off the $\dot{q} = 0$ line is destabilizing. The dynamic behaviour of the model can once again be determined graphically with the aid of Figure 4.11. In both cases the model is saddle-point stable, and the initial equilibrium is at E_0, with output equal to Y_0 and Tobin's q equal to q_0. The saddle path is downward (upward) sloping in the bad (good) news case.

Now consider what happens if the policy maker announces a permanent fiscal expansion to be implemented some time in the future (hence $t_I > t_A$). In the interest of brevity we restrict attention to the bad news case. In the top part of Figure 4.12 the $\dot{q} = 0$ line is drawn as a linear line for convenience. The initial equilibrium is at point E_0. Using the heuristic solution principle used extensively in this chapter, the adjustment path is easily derived. At time t_A there is a stockmarket correction and q jumps from q_0 to q'. Agents know that output will expand in the future and as a result short interest rates will eventually rise also. Even though profits increase also, the interest rate effect dominates in this case, so that the discounted value of profits (i.e. q) must fall. Between t_A and t_I, output, profits, and the short rate actually fall. This is because aggregate spending (Y^D) has collapsed due to the fall in q (recall that the additional government spending has not yet materialized). At time t_I the economy arrives at point B and the fiscal impulse is implemented. The $\dot{Y} = 0$ locus shifts to the right and demand exceeds production ($Y^D > Y$). This leads to a gradual increase in production (and thus profits and the short rate) along the saddle path from B to E_1. Ultimately, the economy ends up with a higher level of output and a lower value of q.

What happens to the other variables over time has been illustrated in the lower panel of Figure 4.12. The path of the short rate of interest is implied by the path for

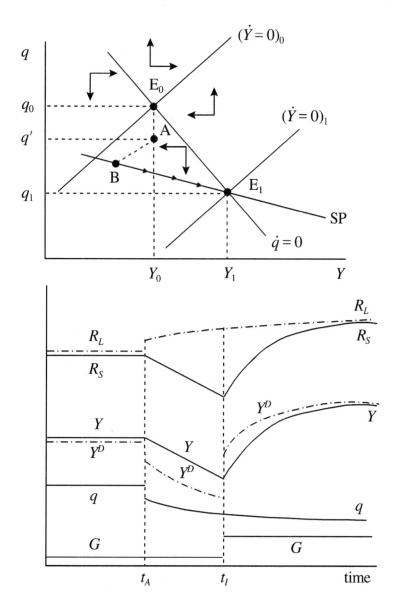

Figure 4.12: Anticipated fiscal policy

income Y and the LM curve (4.37) and has already been discussed. The long rate of interest must satisfy (4.38). We know that in the long run both the short and the long rate must rise, i.e. $\frac{dR_L(\infty)}{dG} = \frac{dR_S(\infty)}{dG} > 0$. In view of the solution principle, R_L can only jump at time t_A since no anticipated infinitely large capital gains/losses are allowed. If R_L were to jump down to a level below R_S, equilibrium would never be restored since then $\dot{R}_L = R_L(R_L - R_S) < 0$, and R_L would continue to fall over time (whereas its steady-state level is higher than before the shock). Hence, R_L must jump up at time t_A to a level above R_S (but below its new steady-state level). Thereafter, $\dot{R}_L = R_L(R_L - R_S) > 0$, and R_L gradually starts to rise further over time towards its new steady-state level.

The lesson we learn from this policy experiment cannot be overemphasized. In the presence of forward-looking agents endowed with perfect foresight the announcement of expansive fiscal policy to take place in the future will actually give rise to a recession in the short run. This is not because the government consumes less in the short run (which it does not) but because agents are fully aware of what will happen to output, Tobin's q, and interest rates in the future, and condition their plans accordingly.

4.3   Exchange rate expectations and fiscal and monetary policy

As a final example of perfect foresight macroeconomics we study a small open economy operating under flexible exchange rates and facing perfect (financial) capital mobility. We augment the analysis conducted in Chapter 2 by explicitly incorporating forward-looking behaviour in international financial markets. In our earlier chapter we have been somewhat inconsistent in our discussion of the economy operating under flexible exchange rates. The nature of this inconsistency can be gleaned by looking at the *uncovered interest parity* condition. Consider a domestic investor who has €100 to invest either at home, where the interest rate on short-term bonds is R_S, or in the US, where the interest rate on such bonds is R_S^*. If the investor chooses to purchase a domestic bond, he will get €100·$(1 + R_S)$ at the end of the period, so that the gross yield on his investment is equal to $1 + R_S$. If, on the other hand, the investor purchases the US bond, he must first change currency (from euros to dollars), and purchase US bonds to the amount of €100/E_0 US dollars, where E_0 is the nominal exchange rate at the beginning of the period (the dimension of E is, of course, € per \$). At the end of the period he receives $(€100/E_0) \cdot (1 + R_S^*)$ US dollars, which he converts back into euros by taking his dollars to the foreign exchange market, thus obtaining $(1 + R_S^*)\cdot(€100/E_0) \cdot E_1 = €100 \cdot (1 + R_S^*) \cdot (E_1/E_0)$ euros. Of course, the investor must decide at the beginning of the period on his investment, and he does not know the actual exchange rate that will hold at the end of the period. The *estimated* gross yield on his foreign investment therefore equals $(1 + R_S^*) \cdot (E_1^e/E_0)$, where E_1^e is the exchange rate the investor expects at the beginning of the period to hold at the end of the period. If the investor is risk-neutral, he chooses the domestic (foreign) bond if $1 + R_S > (<)(1 + R_S^*) \cdot (E_1^e/E_0)$, and is indifferent between the two investment possibilities if the expected yields are equal.

The point of all this is that the expected yield differential between domestic and foreign investments depends not only on the interest rates in the two countries (R_S and R_S^*) but also on what is expected to happen to the exchange rate in the period of the investment:

$$\text{yield gap} \equiv (1+R_S) - (1+R_S^*)\frac{E_1^e}{E_0} = (1+R_S) - (1+R_S^*)\left(1+\frac{\Delta E^e}{E_0}\right)$$

$$= (1+R_S) - \left(1+R_S^* + \frac{\Delta E^e}{E_0} + R_S^*\frac{\Delta E^e}{E_0}\right) \approx R_S - \left(R_S^* + \frac{\Delta E^e}{E_0}\right),$$

(4.51)

where we have used the fact that $E_1^e \equiv E_0 + \Delta E^e$ in the first line. The cross-term $R_S^*\Delta E^e/E_0$ can be ignored because it typically is of second-order magnitude (i.e., very small). Equation (4.51) can be written in continuous time as:

$$\text{yield gap} = R_S - (R_S^* + \dot{e}^e),$$

(4.52)

where $e \equiv \ln E$, so that $\dot{e}^e \equiv de^e/dt \equiv \dot{E}^e/E$. Expressions (4.51) and (4.52) are intuitive. If the domestic currency is expected to appreciate during the period ($\dot{e}^e < 0$), then the domestic currency yield on the US bond is reduced because the dollar earnings on the bond are expected to represent fewer euros than if no appreciation is expected. In the case of perfect capital mobility, arbitrage will ensure that the yield differential is eliminated, in which case (4.52) reduces to the famous uncovered interest parity condition:

$$R_S = R_S^* + \dot{e}^e.$$

(4.53)

4.3.1 The Dornbusch model

In Chapter 2 we simply postulated that $R_S = R_S^*$ under perfect capital mobility. This would, of course, be correct if investors never expect the exchange rate to change. Whilst this may be reasonable under a (tenable) fixed exchange rate regime, it is a somewhat unfortunate and inconsistent assumption to adopt about investors' expectations in a regime of freely flexible exchange rates. Investors know that the exchange rate can (and generally will) fluctuate, and consequently will form expectations about the change in the exchange rate. In a seminal contribution to the literature, Dornbusch (1976a) fixed this embarrassing problem by introducing the perfect foresight assumption in an otherwise standard Mundell-Fleming model of a small open economy facing perfect capital mobility and sticky prices.

The Dornbusch model is summarized in Table 4.1. Equations (T1.1) and (T1.2) are, respectively, the IS curve and the LM curve for a small open economy.[3] Uncovered interest parity is given in equation (T1.3), and equation (T1.4) is the Phillips curve. If output is higher than its full employment level $\bar{y}$, prices *gradually* adjust to eliminate Okun's gap. The adjustment speed of the price level is finite, due to the assumption of sticky prices. This means in formal terms that $0 < \phi \ll \infty$. Finally, equation (T1.5) represents the assumption of perfect foresight. Agents' expectations regarding the path of the exchange rate coincide with the actual path of the exchange rate.

The model exhibits long-run monetary neutrality, as $\dot{p} = 0$ implies that $y = \bar{y}$ and $\dot{e} = 0$ implies that $R_S = R_S^*$, so that (T1.2) shows that $m - p$ is constant. In the long run, the domestic price level and the nominal money supply move together. Furthermore, there is also a unique equilibrium real exchange rate, defined by (T1.1)

---

[3]Note that we could have introduced the *real* interest rate, $R_S - \dot{p}$, in the IS equation (T1.1) as investment is likely to depend on the real rather than the nominal interest rate. In the interest of simplicity, however, we have abstracted from this slight complication.

Table 4.1. The Dornbusch Model

$$y = -\varepsilon_{YR} R_S + \varepsilon_{YQ} \left[p^* + e - p \right] + \varepsilon_{YG} g, \tag{T1.1}$$

$$m - p = -\varepsilon_{MR} R_S + \varepsilon_{MY} y, \tag{T1.2}$$

$$R_S = R_S^* + \dot{e}^e, \tag{T1.3}$$

$$\dot{p} = \phi \left[y - \bar{y} \right], \tag{T1.4}$$

$$\dot{e}^e = \dot{e}. \tag{T1.5}$$

Notes: All variables except the domestic and foreign interest rates are in logarithms and starred variables refer to the foreign country. Endogenous variables are domestic output y, the nominal exchange rate e, the domestic rate of interest R_S, and the domestic price level p. Exogenous are government spending g, the money stock m, the foreign interest rate R_S^*, domestic full employment output $\bar{y}$, and the foreign price level p^*. The coefficients satisfy: $\varepsilon_{YR} > 0, \varepsilon_{YQ} > 0, \varepsilon_{YG} > 0, \varepsilon_{MR} > 0, \varepsilon_{MY} > 0$, and $\phi > 0$.

---

with $y = \bar{y}$ and $R_S = R_S^*$ substituted. This equilibrium real exchange rate is not affected by monetary policy, but can be affected by fiscal policy.

But we are really interested in the short-run dynamics implied by the model. To study this, we must first reduce the model to two differential equations in e and p. This task is achieved in the following way. In the first step we solve the IS-LM equations (T1.1)–(T1.2) for output and the short-term interest rate, conditional on the exogenous variables (g, m, p^*), the nominal exchange rate e, and the domestic price level p. We thus obtain *quasi-reduced-form expressions* for output and the domestic interest rate:

$$y = \frac{\varepsilon_{MR} \varepsilon_{YQ} \left[p^* + e \right] - \left[\varepsilon_{YR} + \varepsilon_{MR} \varepsilon_{YQ} \right] p + \varepsilon_{MR} \varepsilon_{YG} g + \varepsilon_{YR} m}{\varepsilon_{MR} + \varepsilon_{MY} \varepsilon_{YR}}, \tag{4.54}$$

$$R_S = \frac{\varepsilon_{MY} \varepsilon_{YQ} \left[p^* + e \right] + \left[1 - \varepsilon_{MY} \varepsilon_{YQ} \right] p + \varepsilon_{MY} \varepsilon_{YG} g - m}{\varepsilon_{MR} + \varepsilon_{MY} \varepsilon_{YR}}. \tag{4.55}$$

The quasi-reduced-form expressions are quite convenient because they summarize how the instantaneous equilibrium values of output and the interest rate depend on the dynamic variables (e and p) and the exogenous variables. The signs of the coefficients for e and p can be explained with the aid of Figure 4.13. Consider an economy facing a price level of p_0 and a nominal exchange rate of e_0. The initial equilibrium is at point A. If the nominal exchange rate increases to e_1 (a depreciation) and the price level stays unchanged then the IS curve shifts to the right, and the equilibrium shifts to point B. It follows that y and R_S are both increasing functions of e. Next we consider what happens if the price level increases to p_1 whilst the exchange rate stays equal to e_0. There are now two effects. On the one hand, real money balances decrease and the LM curve shifts to the left, which leads to upward pressure on the interest rate. On the other hand the domestic price increase also leads to an appreciation of the *real* exchange rate which shifts the IS curve to the left, decreases output and hence the (transactions) demand for money. This money-demand effect causes downward pressure on the interest rate. We assume for simplicity that the money-supply effect dominates the money-demand effect, i.e. the parameters are such that $0 < \varepsilon_{MY} \varepsilon_{YQ} < 1$. In terms of Figure 4.13 this means that point C lies northwest from point A.

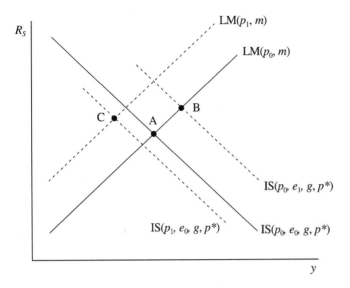

Figure 4.13: Understanding the quasi-reduced-form expressions for y and R_S

In the second step of the derivation of the system of differential equations we substitute (4.54)–(4.55) and (T1.5) into (T1.3) and (T1.4), to obtain the dynamic representation of the model:

$$
\begin{bmatrix} \dot{e} \\ \dot{p} \end{bmatrix} = \begin{bmatrix} \dfrac{\varepsilon_{MY}\varepsilon_{YQ}}{\varepsilon_{MR} + \varepsilon_{MY}\varepsilon_{YR}} & \dfrac{1 - \varepsilon_{MY}\varepsilon_{YQ}}{\varepsilon_{MR} + \varepsilon_{MY}\varepsilon_{YR}} \\[2ex] \dfrac{\phi\varepsilon_{MR}\varepsilon_{YQ}}{\varepsilon_{MR} + \varepsilon_{MY}\varepsilon_{YR}} & -\dfrac{\phi\left[\varepsilon_{YR} + \varepsilon_{MR}\varepsilon_{YQ}\right]}{\varepsilon_{MR} + \varepsilon_{MY}\varepsilon_{YR}} \end{bmatrix} \begin{bmatrix} e \\ p \end{bmatrix}
$$

$$
+ \begin{bmatrix} \dfrac{\varepsilon_{MY}\varepsilon_{YQ}p^* + \varepsilon_{MY}\varepsilon_{YG}g - m}{\varepsilon_{MR} + \varepsilon_{MY}\varepsilon_{YR}} - R_S^* \\[2ex] \dfrac{\phi\left[\varepsilon_{MR}\varepsilon_{YQ}p^* + \varepsilon_{MR}\varepsilon_{YG}g + \varepsilon_{YR}m\right]}{\varepsilon_{MR} + \varepsilon_{MY}\varepsilon_{YR}} - \phi\bar{y} \end{bmatrix}. \tag{4.56}
$$

The only sign that is ambiguous in the Jacobian matrix on the right-hand side of (4.56) is the one for $\partial\dot{e}/\partial p$. But with the assumption (made above) of a dominant money-supply effect we find that $\partial\dot{e}/\partial p > 0$.

The model can be analysed with the aid of Figure 4.14. The $\dot{e} = 0$ line is obtained by taking the first equation in (4.56), setting $\dot{e} = 0$, and solving it for e as a function of p and the exogenous variables:

$$
e + p^* = \frac{-(1 - \varepsilon_{MY}\varepsilon_{YQ})p - \varepsilon_{MY}\varepsilon_{YG}g + m + (\varepsilon_{MR} + \varepsilon_{MY}\varepsilon_{YR})R_S^*}{\varepsilon_{MY}\varepsilon_{YQ}}. \tag{4.57}
$$

Along the $\dot{e} = 0$ line the domestic interest rate equals the foreign interest rate ($R_S = R_S^*$). It is downward sloping in view of our assumption (made above) that $\varepsilon_{MY}\varepsilon_{YQ} < 1$. For points above the $\dot{e} = 0$ line the nominal (and the real) exchange rate is too

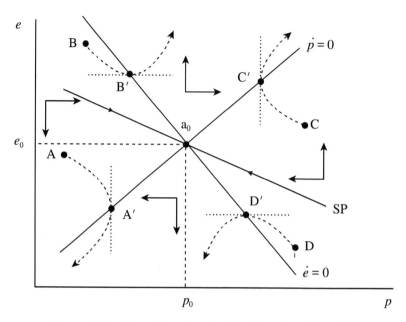

Figure 4.14: Phase diagram for the Dornbusch model

high, output is too high, and the domestic rate of interest is higher than the world rate ($R_S > R_S^*$). Uncovered interest parity predicts that an exchange rate depreciation is expected and occurs ($\dot{e}^e = \dot{e} > 0$). The opposite holds for points below the $\dot{e} = 0$ line. These dynamic forces on the nominal exchange rate are indicated by vertical arrows in Figure 4.14. More formally we can derive the same result by noting that (4.56) implies:

$$\frac{\partial \dot{e}}{\partial e} = \frac{\varepsilon_{MY}\varepsilon_{YQ}}{\varepsilon_{MR} + \varepsilon_{MY}\varepsilon_{YR}} > 0, \tag{4.58}$$

which shows that the interest parity condition introduces an unstable element into the economy in the sense that exchange rate movements are magnified, rather than dampened, according to (4.58).

The $\dot{p} = 0$ line is obtained by taking the second equation in (4.56) and solving it for e as a function of p and the exogenous variables:

$$e + p^* = \frac{(\varepsilon_{YR} + \varepsilon_{MR}\varepsilon_{YQ})p - \varepsilon_{MR}\varepsilon_{YG}g - \varepsilon_{YR}m + (\varepsilon_{MR} + \varepsilon_{MY}\varepsilon_{YR})\bar{y}}{\varepsilon_{MR}\varepsilon_{YQ}}. \tag{4.59}$$

Along the $\dot{p} = 0$ line there is full employment ($y = \bar{y}$). It is upward sloping because an increase in the domestic price level reduces output via the real balance effect. To restore full employment, the nominal exchange rate must depreciate. For points to the right of the $\dot{p} = 0$ line, output is below its full employment level ($y < \bar{y}$) and the domestic price level is falling. The opposite holds for points to the left of the $\dot{p} = 0$ line. The dynamic forces operating on the price level are indicated by horizontal arrows in Figure 4.14. In formal terms, the second equation of (4.56) shows that the real side of the model exerts a stabilizing influence on the economy:

$$\frac{\partial \dot{p}}{\partial p} = -\frac{\phi(\varepsilon_{YR} + \varepsilon_{MR}\varepsilon_{YR})}{\varepsilon_{MR} + \varepsilon_{MY}\varepsilon_{YQ}} < 0. \tag{4.60}$$

The long-run steady-state equilibrium is at point a_0 in Figure 4.14, where $\dot{p} = \dot{e} = 0$ so that both $R_S = R_S^*$ and $y = \bar{y}$ hold.

What about the stability of this steady-state equilibrium? Will a shock away from a_0 eventually and automatically be corrected in this model? The answer is an emphatic "no" unless we invoke the perfect foresight hypothesis. The dashed trajectories drawn in Figure 4.14 eventually all turn away from the steady-state equilibrium. There is, however, exactly one trajectory which does lead the economy back to equilibrium. This is the saddle path, SP. If and only if the economy is on this saddle path, will the equilibrium be reached. Since agents have perfect foresight they know that the economy will fall apart unless it is on the saddle path (p and/or e will go to nonsense values). Consequently, they expect that the economy must be on the saddle path, and by their behaviour this expectation is also correct. If anything unexpected happens, the nominal exchange rate immediately adjusts to place the economy on the new saddle path. Since the price level is sticky, it cannot jump instantaneously and consequently the nominal exchange rate takes care of the entire adjustment in the impact period.

4.3.1.1 Fiscal policy

As an example of adjustment, consider the case of an *unanticipated and permanent expansionary fiscal policy*. In terms of Figure 4.15, the increase in g shifts the $\dot{p} = 0$ line to the right and the $\dot{e} = 0$ line to the left, leaving the long-run price level unchanged. At impact the exchange rate adjusts downward from point a_0 to a_1. There is no transitional dynamics, and the Dornbusch model predicts exactly the same adjustment pattern as the traditional Mundell-Fleming approach does in this case. Since there is no need for a long-run price adjustment the assumption of price stickiness plays no role in the adjustment process, and because the fiscal impulse is unanticipated, the interest parity condition does not introduce transitional dynamics into the exchange rate in this case. Students are advised to verify that the announcement of a future permanent increase in government spending leads to an immediate appreciation of the currency, followed by falling prices and a further appreciation of the exchange rate, in the period between announcement and implementation of the policy. Once government spending has gone up, the price level starts to rise again and the exchange rate appreciates further. In the long run, the equilibrium is at a_1, with a permanently lower exchange rate and the same price level, and the adjustment path is a_0 to a' at impact, gradual movement from a' to a'' between announcement and implementation, followed by gradual movement from a'' to a_1 after implementation.

4.3.1.2 Monetary policy

An *unanticipated and permanent expansionary monetary policy* produces the famous overshooting result. In terms of Figure 4.16, an increase in the money supply shifts both the $\dot{e} = 0$ line and the $\dot{p} = 0$ line to the right, leaving the long-run equilibrium real exchange rate unchanged (recall that money is neutral in the long run). In the short run, however, prices are sticky and the exchange rate makes a discrete adjustment from e_0 to e'. The depreciation of the currency leads to an increase in the demand for aggregate output ($y > \bar{y}$) and the domestic price level starts to rise. A gradual adjustment along the saddle path SP_1, with an appreciating real exchange rate, leads the economy back to the long-run equilibrium. The nominal exchange rate actually overshoots its long-run target in the impact period. The intuition behind this result is that agents expect a long-run depreciation of the nominal exchange

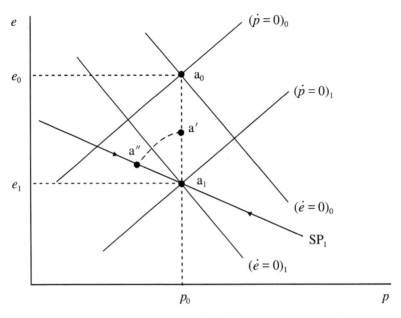

Figure 4.15: Fiscal policy in the Dornbusch model

rate, and hence domestic assets are less attractive. There is a net capital outflow and the spot rate depreciates. The exchange rate overshoots in order for investors in domestic assets to be compensated (for the fact that $R_S < R_S^*$) during adjustment by an exchange rate appreciation. Hence, point a_1 must be approached from a north-westerly direction.

4.3.2 Price stickiness and overshooting

The finite speed of adjustment in the goods market (a distinctly Keynesian feature) plays a crucial role in the exchange rate overshooting result illustrated in Figure 4.16. To demonstrate that this is so, suppose, for example, that $\phi \to \infty$, so that (T1.4) predicts that $y = \bar{y}$ always, as prices adjust infinitely fast. This means that we can solve (T1.1)–(T1.2) for the domestic rate of interest and price level as a function of the nominal exchange rate e and the exogenous variables. For the domestic interest rate we obtain:

$$R_S = \frac{(\varepsilon_{YQ}\varepsilon_{MY} - 1)\bar{y} + \varepsilon_{YQ}(p^* + e) + \varepsilon_{YG}g - \varepsilon_{YQ}m}{\varepsilon_{YR} + \varepsilon_{YQ}\varepsilon_{MR}}, \tag{4.61}$$

which, together with (T1.5), can be substituted into (T1.3) to get the expression for the rate of depreciation of the exchange rate under perfectly flexible prices:

$$\dot{e} = \frac{(\varepsilon_{YQ}\varepsilon_{MY} - 1)\bar{y} + \varepsilon_{YQ}(p^* + e) + \varepsilon_{YG}g - \varepsilon_{YQ}m}{\varepsilon_{YR} + \varepsilon_{YQ}\varepsilon_{MR}} - R_S^*. \tag{4.62}$$

This is an unstable differential equation in e only (it does not feature the price level, p). In terms of Figure 4.17, the only stable solution, following an unanticipated increase in the money supply, is an immediate discrete adjustment of the exchange rate from e_0 to e_1. Consequently, both immediately before and immediately after the

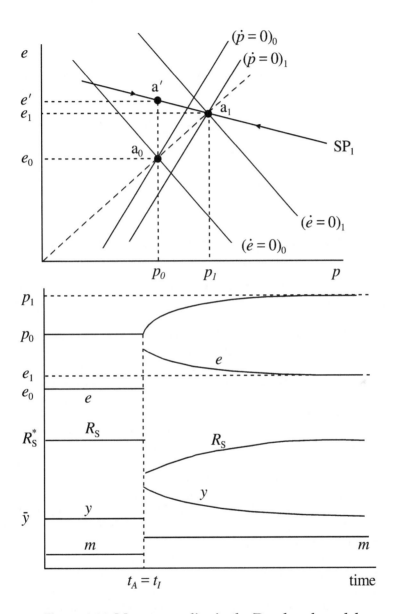

Figure 4.16: Monetary policy in the Dornbusch model

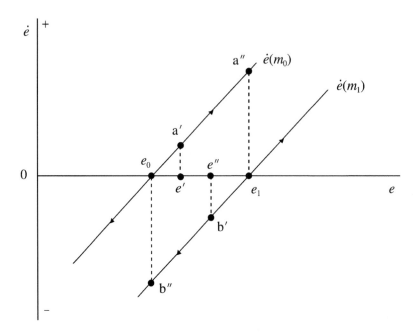

Figure 4.17: Exchange rate dynamics with perfectly flexible prices

shock, the exchange rate is constant ($\dot{e} = 0$) so that the domestic rate of interest stays equal to the world rate at all times ($R_S = R_S^*$). Unanticipated monetary policy does not lead to overshooting if prices are perfectly flexible.

This does not mean, of course, that overshooting is impossible when the price level is fully flexible. In some cases, anticipation effects can also cause overshooting of the exchange rate. Assume that the monetary impulse is announced at time t_A to be implemented at some later time t_I ($> t_A$). If agents have perfect foresight, the adjustment path will be an immediate depreciation at time t_A from e_0 to e', followed by gradual further depreciation between t_A and t_I, represented by the movement from point a' to a'' along the $\dot{e}(m_0)$ line. Exactly at time t_I, the money supply is increased (as was announced), the $\dot{e} = 0$ line shifts to the right to $\dot{e}(m_1)$, and the exchange rate settles at its new equilibrium level e_1. Agents anticipate a depreciation of the currency in the long run since the money supply increases. There can be no anticipated jumps in the exchange rate, since these would imply infinitely large expected capital gains/losses, so that one side of the market would disappear. Consequently, interest parity dictates adjustment, and the exchange rate starts to depreciate immediately.[4] There is still no overshooting in this case.

Matters are different if the monetary impulse is implemented immediately ($t_A = t_I$) but is of a temporary nature. Specifically, it is announced (and believed by the agents) that the money supply will be decreased to its old level at some time t_E in the future. In that case, the adjustment path is given by an immediate depreciation at $t_A = t_I$ from e_0 to e'', followed by gradual appreciation between t_A and t_E (described by the movement from point b' to b''). At the time the money supply is decreased again, the exchange rate has fallen back to its initial level, the $\dot{e} = 0$ line

---

[4]The smaller the difference between implementation and announcement dates ($t_I - t_A$), the larger is the jump in the exchange rate at impact. This can be seen intuitively, by noting that if ($t_I - t_A$) → 0, the jump is instantaneous from e_0 to e_1, and if ($t_I - t_A$) → ∞, the policy measure is postponed indefinitely, and nothing happens to the exchange rate.

shifts from $\dot{e}(m_1) = 0$ to $\dot{e}(m_0) = 0$, and equilibrium is restored. A temporary monetary expansion causes the exchange rate to overshoot its long-run (unchanged) level. Agents expect no long-run depreciation but the domestic interest rate is temporarily below the world rate of interest, so that interest parity predicts that $\dot{e} < 0$ along the transition path.

4.4 Punchlines

The key concept that is developed in this chapter is that of saddle-point stability. To illustrate this concept we develop Tobin's q theory of investment in continuous time. This theory, which was also discussed briefly in discrete time in Chapter 3, is quite attractive because it is very simple but nevertheless yields predictions which accord with intuition and (some of the) empirical evidence. In the q theory, investment by firms depends on the shadow price of installed capital goods, which is called Tobin's marginal q. This shadow price is a forward-looking concept, and it incorporates all the information that is of relevance to the firm. Under some conditions Tobin's marginal q coincides with average q, which can be measured in a relatively straightforward fashion by looking at the stockmarket value of the firm.

In order to understand the capital dynamics implied by Tobin's q theory, we study the effect of an investment subsidy in a number of different settings. In the simplest possible setting we interpret the theory at the level of an individual firm for which the real wage rate and thus the marginal product of capital is constant. In a more complex setting we interpret the theory as pertaining to the economy as a whole. This necessitates an assumption about the labour market. We consider two cases; one with a fixed supply of labour and the other with an elastic labour supply. The latter case allows for a discussion of the effects of a labour income tax on employment, investment, and the capital stock.

Since the q theory is inherently forward looking, the effects of a policy shock depend critically on whether the shock is anticipated or not. A policy shock is unanticipated (anticipated) if the time of implementation coincides with (postdates) the time of announcement. An anticipated shock which affects either the marginal product of capital or the interest rate will have an immediate effect on investment because Tobin's q is the present value of present and future marginal capital productivity. Graphically the model can be shown to be saddle-point stable, i.e. there is a unique trajectory towards the new equilibrium following a shock. At impact the capital stock is predetermined (accumulated in the past) but Tobin's q can jump to incorporate new information.

The model gives rise to some interesting policy implications. For example, an anticipated abolition (or reduction) of the investment subsidy leads to an investment boom at impact because firms rush to put in their investment orders to get the subsidy while it still exists. Similarly, a temporary investment subsidy causes a larger impact effect on investment than a permanent subsidy does. Intuitively this happens because firms bring forward their intertemporal investment plans in order to "make hay while the sun shines". The fact that these predictions accord with intuition lends the theory some credibility.

Another attractive feature of Tobin's q theory is that it is easily incorporated in the IS-LM model. In doing so one of the objections raised against that model, namely that it contains only rudimentary dynamics, is substantially weakened. By also modelling gradual output adjustment and a simple (forward-looking) term structure of interest rates, the dynamic IS-LM model gives rise to a rich array of intertemporal effects. For example, with an anticipated increase in government consumption it is possible that output falls during the early phase of the transition. This is because the downward jump in Tobin's q causes a fall in investment and aggregate demand which is not counteracted because the additional government consumption has not yet materialized. In the long run, of course, output rises beyond its initial level.

In the last part of this chapter we introduce forward-looking elements in a sticky-price model of a small open economy facing perfect capital mobility. A striking feature of this model is that an unanticipated and permanent monetary expansion may produce overshooting of the exchange rate. Intuitively, agents expect a long-run depreciation of the nominal exchange rate which, ceteris paribus, makes domestic assets less attractive than foreign assets. There is a net capital outflow and the spot exchange rate depreciates. During transition the domestic interest rate falls short of the world interest rate. As a result the exchange rate overshoots its long-run equilibrium value because part of the yield on domestic assets consists of a gradual appreciation of the exchange rate. The overshooting result caused a big stir in the late 1970s because it provided an economically intuitive rationale for the large swings that are often observed in the exchange rate. Large changes in the exchange rate need not be due to the behaviour of irrational currency speculators after all!

Further reading

The material on the investment subsidy is motivated in part by the analyses of Abel (1982) and Summers (1981). Abel (1981) shows how the investment model can be generalized by allowing for a variable utilization rate of capital. The recent investment literature stresses the irreversibility of investment and/or non-convex adjustment costs. Key articles are: Abel and Eberly (1994), Abel et al. (1996), Dixit and Pindyck (1994), and Caballero and Leahy (1996). A good survey is Caballero (1999).

Sargent (1987b) and Nickell (1986) develop a dynamic theory of labour demand based on adjustment costs on the stock of labour. Hamermesh and Pfann (1996) present a survey of this literature. Saddle-point equilibria naturally arise in the open economy context. Key papers are Dornbusch (1976a) and Buiter and Miller (1981, 1982), and a good survey is Scarth (1988, ch. 9).

Chapter 5

Rational expectations and economic policy

In this chapter we continue our investigation of forward-looking expectations mechanisms. We move to an economic setting in which market participants experience stochastic shocks. More specifically the purpose of this chapter is to discuss the following issues:

1. What do we mean by rational expectations (also called model-consistent expectations)?

2. What are the implications of the rational expectations hypothesis (REH) for the conduct of macroeconomic policy? What is the meaning of the so-called policy-ineffectiveness proposition (PIP)?

3. What are the implications of the REH for the way in which we specify and use macroeconometric models, and what is the Lucas critique?

4. To what extent can countercyclical economic policy be conducted in a small open economy facing perfect financial capital mobility when agents are blessed with rational expectations?

5. What is the lasting contribution of the rational expectations revolution?

5.1 What are rational expectations?

5.1.1 The basic idea

More than half a century ago, John Muth published an article in which he argued forcefully that economists should be more careful about their informational assumptions, in particular about the way in which they model expectations. Muth's (1961) point can be illustrated with the aid of the neoclassical synthesis model under the adaptive expectations hypothesis (AEH) that was discussed in Chapter 3. Consider Figure 5.1, which illustrates the effects of monetary policy over time. The initial equilibrium is at point E_0, with output equal to its full-employment level $\bar{Y}$ and the price level equal to P_0. There is an expectational equilibrium, because $P = P^e$ at point E_0. If the monetary authority increases the money supply (in a bid to stimulate the

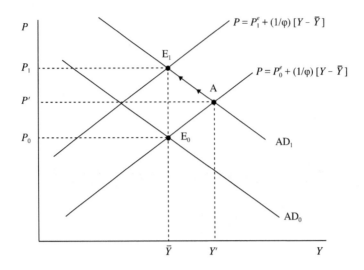

Figure 5.1: Monetary policy under adaptive expectations

economy), aggregate demand is boosted (the AD curve shifts from AD_0 to AD_1), the economy moves to point A, output increases to Y', and the price level rises to P'. In A there is a discrepancy between the expected price level and the actual price level. This discrepancy is slowly removed by an upward revision of the expected price level, via the adaptive expectations mechanism (e.g. equation (1.14)). In the diagram this is represented by a gradual movement along the new AD curve towards point E_1, which is the new full equilibrium.

The adjustment path of expectations is very odd, however, because agents (e.g. households supplying labour) make *systematic mistakes* along this path. The time paths for the actual and expected price levels are illustrated in Figure 5.2, as is the expectational error ($P^e - P$). The initial shock causes an expectational error that is slowly eliminated. All along the adjustment path, the error is negative and stays negative, and agents keep guessing wrongly.

This is very unsatisfactory, Muth (1961) argued, because it is diametrically opposed to the way economists model human behaviour in other branches of economics. There, the notion of rational decision making (subject to constraints) occupies centre stage, and this does not appear to be the case under the AEH. As a result, Muth proposed that: "...expectations, since they are informed predictions of future events, are essentially the same as the predictions of the relevant economic theory" (1961, p. 316).

With respect to the model illustrated in Figure 5.1, this would mean that agents hear at time t_0 that the money supply has been increased from M_0 to M_1, use the relevant economic theory (equations (3.1)–(3.2)), calculate that the correct price level for the new money supply is P_1, adjust their expectations to that new money supply ($P_1^e = P_1$), and supply the correct amount of labour. As a result, the economy jumps from E_0 to E_1, output is equal to $\bar{Y}$ and the price level is P_1. Of course, this adjustment story amounts to the perfect foresight hypothesis (PFH) version of the policy-ineffectiveness proposition (PIP). Since there is no uncertainty in the model, forecasting is not difficult for the agents. They realize that a higher money supply induces a higher price level and thus adjust their wages upwards. As a result, the real wage, employment, and output are unaffected.

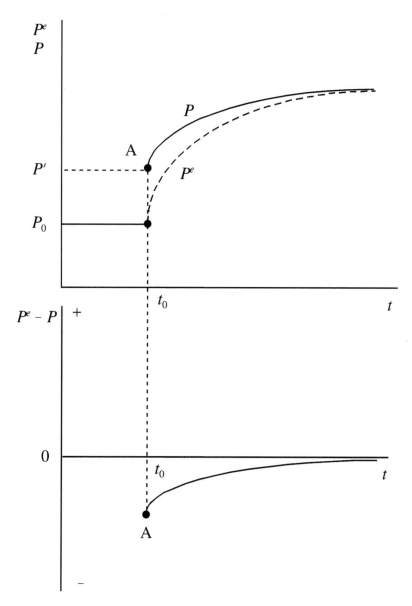

Figure 5.2: Expectational errors under adaptive expectations

In reality all kinds of chance occurrences play an important role. In a macroeconomic context one could think of stochastic events such as fluctuation in the climate, natural disasters, shocks to world trade (German reunification, OPEC shocks, the Gulf War), etc. In such a setting, forecasting is a lot more difficult. Muth (1961) formulated the rational expectations hypothesis (REH) to deal with situations in which stochastic elements play a role. The basic postulates of the REH are: (i) information is scarce and the economic system does not waste it, and (ii) the way in which expectations are formed depends in a well-specified way on the structure of the system describing the economy.

In order to clarify these postulates, consider the following example of an isolated market for a non-storable good (so that inventory speculation is not possible). This market is described by the following linear model:

$$Q_t^D = a_0 - a_1 P_t, \quad a_1 > 0, \tag{5.1}$$

$$Q_t^S = b_0 + b_1 P_t^e + U_t, \quad b_1 > 0, \tag{5.2}$$

$$Q_t^D = Q_t^S \quad [\equiv Q_t], \tag{5.3}$$

where P_t is the price of the good in period t, Q_t^D is the quantity demanded, Q_t^S is the quantity supplied, and P_t^e is the price level that suppliers expect in period $t-1$ to hold in period t. The random variable U_t represents all stochastic elements that impinge on the supply curve. If the good in question is an agricultural commodity, for example, then U_t could summarize all the random elements introduced in the supply decision by the weather, crop failures, animal diseases, insect plagues, etc.

Equation (5.1) shows that demand only depends on the actual price of the good. In other words, the agents know the price of the good, and there are no stochastic events occurring on the demand side of the market, such as random taste changes, income fluctuations, etc. Equation (5.2) implies that there is a production lag: suppliers must decide on the production capacity before knowing exactly what will be the price at which they can sell their goods. They make this decision on the basis of all information that is available to them. In the context of this model, the information they possess in period $t-1$ is summarized by the so-called *information set*, Ω_{t-1}:

$$\Omega_{t-1} \equiv \left\{ P_{t-1}, P_{t-2}, ...; Q_{t-1}, Q_{t-2}, ...; a_0, a_1, b_0, b_1; U_t \sim N(0, \sigma^2) \right\}. \tag{5.4}$$

What does this mean? First, the agents know all prices and quantities up to and including period $t-1$ (they do not forget relevant past information). Obviously, the information set Ω_{t-1} does not include P_t, Q_t, and U_t. Second, the agents know the structure of the market they are operating in (recall: "...the relevant economic theory" is used by agents). Hence, the model parameters a_0, a_1, b_0, and b_1 are known to the agents as is the structure of the model given in (5.1)–(5.3). Third, although the actual realization of the stochastic error term U_t is not known for period t, the probability distribution of this stochastic variable is known. For simplicity, we assume that U_t is distributed as a normal variable with an expected value of zero ($E(U_t) = 0$), no autocorrelation ($E(U_t U_s) = 0$ for $t \neq s$), and a constant variance of σ^2 [$\equiv E(U_t - E(U_t))^2$], where $E(\cdot)$ is the *unconditional expectations* operator. This distributional assumption is written in short-hand notation as $N(0, \sigma^2)$. Recall from first-year statistics that the normal distribution looks like the symmetric bell-shaped curve drawn in Figure 5.3. Fourth, past realizations of the error terms are, of course, known. Agents know past observations on Q_{t-i} and P_{t-i}, and can use the model (5.1)–(5.3) to find out what the corresponding realisations of the shocks must have been (i.e. U_{t-i}).

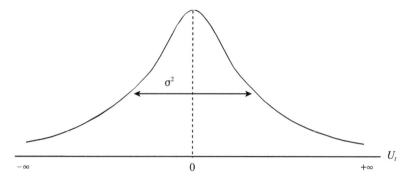

Figure 5.3: The normal distribution

The REH can now be stated very succinctly as:

$$P_t^e = E\left(P_t \mid \Omega_{t-1}\right) \equiv E_{t-1} P_t, \tag{5.5}$$

where E_{t-1} is short-hand notation for $E(\cdot \mid \Omega_{t-1})$, which is the *conditional expectation* operator. In words, equation (5.5) says that the *subjective* expectation of the price level in period t formed by agents in period $t-1$ (P_t^e) coincides with the conditional *objective* expectation of P_t, given the information set Ω_{t-1}.

How does the REH work in our simple model? We obtain the answer in a number of steps. First, equilibrium outcomes are calculated. Hence, (5.3) is substituted into (5.1) and (5.2), which can then be solved for P_t and Q_t in terms of the parameters and the expected price P_t^e:

$$P_t = \frac{a_0 - b_0 - b_1 P_t^e - U_t}{a_1}, \tag{5.6}$$

$$Q_t = b_0 + b_1 P_t^e + U_t. \tag{5.7}$$

Equation (5.6) is crucial. It says that the actual price in period t depends on the price expected to hold in that period, and the realization of the stochastic shock U_t. More precisely, a higher expected price level or a positive supply shock (bigger P_t^e or U_t) boosts the supply of goods, and thus the equilibrium price level must fall in order to clear the market. The REH postulates that individual agents can also calculate (5.6) and can take the conditional expectation of P_t:

$$\begin{aligned} E_{t-1} P_t &= E_{t-1} \left[\frac{a_0 - b_0 - b_1 P_t^e - U_t}{a_1} \right] \\ &= \frac{a_0 - b_0}{a_1} - \frac{b_1}{a_1} E_{t-1} P_t^e - \frac{1}{a_1} E_{t-1} U_t. \end{aligned} \tag{5.8}$$

Consider the three terms on the right-hand side of (5.8) in turn. The first term is obvious: the conditional expectation of a known constant is that constant itself. The second term can similarly be simplified: P_t^e is a known constant, so that $E_{t-1} P_t^e = P_t^e$. The third term can be simplified by making use of our knowledge concerning the distribution of U_t. Since U_t is not autocorrelated, the conditional expectation of it is equal to its unconditional expected value, i.e. $E_{t-1} U_t = 0$. As a result of all these simplifications, $E_{t-1} P_t$ can be written as:

$$E_{t-1} P_t = \frac{a_0 - b_0}{a_1} - \frac{b_1}{a_1} P_t^e. \tag{5.9}$$

But the REH states in (5.5) that the objective expectation, $E_{t-1}P_t$, and the subjective expectation, P_t^e, coincide. Hence, by substituting $E_{t-1}P_t = P_t^e$ into (5.9) we obtain the solution for P_t^e:

$$P_t^e = \frac{a_0 - b_0}{a_1} - \frac{b_1}{a_1}P_t^e \Rightarrow P_t^e = E_{t-1}P_t = \frac{a_0 - b_0}{a_1 + b_1}. \tag{5.10}$$

The final expression is the rational expectations solution for the *expected* price level. The actual price level P_t is stochastic (of course, since it depends on the stochastic supply shock U_t). By substituting (5.10) into (5.6), the expression for P_t is obtained:

$$P_t = \bar{P} - \frac{1}{a_1}U_t, \tag{5.11}$$

where $\bar{P} \equiv (a_0 - b_0)/(a_1 + b_1)$ is the equilibrium price that would hold if there were no stochastic elements in the market. Equation (5.11) says that the actual price P_t fluctuates randomly around $\bar{P}$. The expectational error is equal to $P_t - E_{t-1}P_t = -(1/a_1)U_t$, and exhibits no predictable pattern. Also, the average of this error is zero, so that agents do not make systematic mistakes. If there is an expected negative supply shock, for example due to an agricultural disaster, the price level rises.

What would have been the case under the AEH? Can we derive an equation for P_t under the AEH that we can then compare to the REH expression in (5.11)? The answer is "yes of course", but only after using some technical tricks to get rid of terms involving P_t^e and P_{t-1}^e. Here goes. Obviously, under AEH, the expectational errors do display a predictable pattern. Recall (from (1.14)) that the AEH says that the expected price level can be written as a weighted average of last period's actual price level and last period's expected price level:

$$P_t^e = \lambda P_{t-1} + (1 - \lambda)P_{t-1}^e, \qquad 0 < \lambda < 1. \tag{5.12}$$

By using (5.6), once for P_t and once more for P_{t-1} we find:

$$P_t = \frac{a_0 - b_0 - b_1 P_t^e - U_t}{a_1}, \tag{5.13}$$

$$P_{t-1} = \frac{a_0 - b_0 - b_1 P_{t-1}^e - U_{t-1}}{a_1}. \tag{5.14}$$

Now comes the trick: multiply (5.14) by $1 - \lambda$ and deduct the result from (5.13) to get:

$$P_t - (1 - \lambda)P_{t-1} = \frac{\lambda(a_0 - b_0)}{a_1} - \frac{b_1}{a_1}[P_t^e - (1 - \lambda)P_{t-1}^e] - \frac{1}{a_1}[U_t - (1 - \lambda)U_{t-1}]. \tag{5.15}$$

But, according to (5.12), the first term in square brackets on the right-hand side is equal to λP_{t-1}, so after gathering terms we can rewrite (5.15) as:

$$P_t = \frac{\lambda(a_0 - b_0)}{a_1} + \left[1 - \lambda\frac{a_1 + b_1}{a_1}\right]P_{t-1} - \frac{1}{a_1}[U_t - (1 - \lambda)U_{t-1}], \tag{5.16}$$

and more compactly as:

$$P_t - \bar{P} = \mu[P_{t-1} - \bar{P}] - \frac{1}{a_1}V_t, \tag{5.17}$$

where $\mu \equiv 1 - \lambda \frac{a_1 + b_1}{a_1}$ is a composite parameter, $\bar{P} = (a_0 - b_0)/(a_1 + b_1)$ is the deterministic equilibrium price, and $V_t \equiv U_t - (1 - \lambda)U_{t-1}$ is a composite stochastic term. The trick works! But before getting carried away on a wave of pure joy we must first check a technical feature of this AEH solution for the price path. Indeed, even abstracting from the random term, V_t, the difference equation for the price level must be stable for this model to be of any use under the AEH (remember the correspondence principle). In particular, the stability condition requires μ to be less than unity in absolute value. Expressed in terms of the expectational adjustment parameter, λ, the stability condition is thus $0 < \lambda < \min[1, 2a_1/(a_1 + b_1)]$.[1]

The key thing to note about equation (5.17) is that the equilibrium price, P_t, displays a clearly recognizable pattern under the AEH: P_t depends on its own lagged value P_{t-1}, and the composite error term V_t displays autocorrelation (i.e., $E(V_t V_{t-1}) = -(1 - \lambda)\sigma^2$). It is not difficult to show that the expectational error under the AEH can be written as follows:

$$P_t^e - \bar{P} = -\frac{\lambda}{a_1} \sum_{i=0}^{\infty} \mu^i U_{t-1-i}. \tag{5.18}$$

To help understand (5.18), consider the effect of an isolated supply shock in period $t - 1$, i.e. set $U_{t-1-i} = 0$ for $i \geq 1$. Repeated use of (5.18) shows that this shock will affect the expectational errors from period t onward, i.e. $P_t^e - \bar{P} = -(\lambda/a_1) U_{t-1}$, $P_{t+1}^e - \bar{P} = -(\lambda\mu/a_1) U_{t-1}$, $P_{t+2}^e - \bar{P} = -(\lambda\mu^2/a_1) U_{t-1}$, etcetera. Of course, because the model is stable, the effect of U_{t-1} will ultimately die down, but depending on the magnitude of μ this may take a long time indeed.

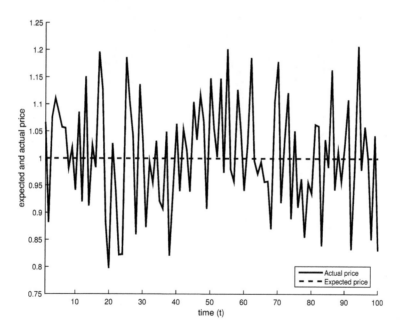

Figure 5.4: Actual and expected price under REH

[1]The function $\min[x, y]$ is the minimum-value function, i.e. $\min[x, y] = x$ if $x \leq y$ and $\min[x, y] = y$ if $x > y$.

The issue can be further illustrated with the aid of Figures 5.4 and 5.5, which show the paths of the actual price level, P_t, and the expected price level, P_t^e, under, respectively, the REH and the AEH. The diagrams were produced as follows. First, the computer was instructed to draw 100 (quasi-) random numbers from a normal distribution with mean zero and variance $\sigma^2 = 0.01$. These random numbers are the supply shocks of the model (that is, U_t for $t = 1, \cdots, 100$). The parameters of demand and supply were set at $a_0 = 3$, $a_1 = 1$, $b_0 = 1$, and $b_1 = 1$, which implies that the deterministic equilibrium price is $\bar{P} = 1$. Obviously, from (5.10) we find that under the REH, $P_t^e = \bar{P} = 1$. This is the dashed line in Figure 5.4. The actual price level under the REH is given by (5.11), and is drawn as a solid line fluctuating randomly around the dashed line. In Figure 5.5 the expected and actual price levels have been drawn for the same stochastic U_t terms as before but assuming that the AEH is valid. To generate these numbers we set $\lambda = 0.8$ and assume that $P_0^e = P_0 = \bar{P}$ and $U_0 = 0$. Not surprisingly, there is a clear pattern in the way expectations continually lag behind actual price movements (as (5.12) of course suggests theoretically).

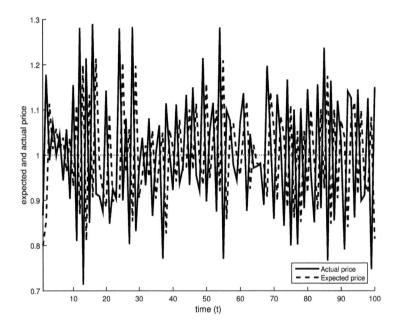

Figure 5.5: Actual and expected price under AEH

5.1.2 Do we really believe the idea?

In the previous section we have postulated the REH in the form of a statement like (5.5). Muth (1961) offers an intuitive defence for the equality of conditional and subjective expectations. First, if the conditional expectation of the price level based on the model ($E_{t-1}P_t$) were considerably better at forecasting P_t than the subjective expectation of suppliers (P_t^e), there would be an opportunity for making larger than normal profits for an alert "insider", i.e. someone who does use the information contained in the model. This insider could, for example, start his/her own business, engage in inventory speculation (in the case of storable goods), or operate a consulting firm specialized in selling forecasting services to the existing suppliers.

It has unfortunately proved very difficult indeed to come up with a formal model of this "market for information". This is because (i) information is costly to get, and (ii) is at least partially a public good. Agents that possess information can, by their actions in the market place, unwittingly reveal the content of this information to agents who have not acquired it. As a result, there may be a strong "free-rider" problem in the market for information. Using this type of argument, Grossman and Stiglitz (1980) conclude that it is impossible for the market for information to be efficient. Other authors investigate the question whether agents can learn to converge to rational expectations—see, for example, Friedman (1979), DeCanio (1979), and Pesaran (1987). The conclusions of this literature suggest that is not always the case. To quote DeCanio, "the economical use of information will not necessarily generate rational expectations" (1979, p. 55).

So there are good reasons to believe that the use of the REH cannot be justified as an outcome of an informational cost-benefit analysis. Yet, many economists today accept the REH as the standard assumption to make in macro-models involving uncertainty. The reason for this almost universal acceptance is again the correspondence principle. Since we know little about actual learning processes, and the REH describes an equilibrium situation, it is the most practical hypothesis to use. Of course, the equilibrium described by models involving the REH is inherently stochastic. For that reason, REH solutions for models can be referred to as *stochastic steady-state solutions*.

5.2 Applications of the REH in macroeconomics

The idea behind rational expectations remained unused for a decade, before new classicals like Robert Lucas, Thomas Sargent, Neil Wallace, and Robert Barro applied it to macroeconomic issues. They took most of their motivation from Friedman's (1968) presidential address to the American Economic Association, and consequently focused on the role of monetary policy under the REH.

Their basic idea can be illustrated with a simple loglinear model, that is based on Sargent and Wallace (1975):

$$y_t - \bar{y} = \phi(p_t - E_{t-1}p_t) + u_t, \qquad \phi > 0, \tag{5.19}$$

$$y_t = \alpha + \beta(m_t - p_t) + \gamma E_{t-1}(p_{t+1} - p_t) + v_t, \qquad \beta > 0, \quad \gamma > 0, \tag{5.20}$$

$$m_t = \mu_0 + \mu_m m_{t-1} + \mu_y y_{t-1} + z_t, \qquad 0 \le \mu_m \le 1, \tag{5.21}$$

where $y_t \equiv \ln Y_t$, $\bar{y} \equiv \ln \bar{Y}$, $m_t \equiv \ln M_t$, and $p_t \equiv \ln P_t$ are, respectively, actual output, full-employment output, the money supply, and the price level, all measured in logarithms. The random terms are given by $u_t \sim N(0, \sigma_u^2)$, $v_t \sim N(0, \sigma_v^2)$, and $z_t \sim N(0, \sigma_z^2)$. They are assumed to be independent from themselves in time, $E(u_t u_s) = E(v_t v_s) = E(z_t z_s) = 0$ for $t \ne s$, and from each other, $E(u_t z_t) = E(u_t v_t) = E(v_t z_t) = 0$.

Equation (5.19) is the expectations-based short-run aggregate supply curve, i.e. it is the loglinear stochastic counterpart to equation (3.2) above. If agents underestimate the price level ($p_t > E_{t-1}p_t$), they supply too much labour and output expands. Equation (5.20) is the AD curve. The real balance term, $m_t - p_t$, reflects the influence of the LM curve, i.e. the Keynes effect, and the expected inflation rate,

$E_{t-1}(p_{t+1} - p_t)$, represents a Tobin effect.[2] The intuition behind the Tobin effect is as follows. Investment depends on the real interest rate, so that, for a given level of the nominal interest rate, a higher rate of expected inflation implies a lower real rate of interest, and a higher rate of investment and hence aggregate demand.

Finally, equation (5.21) is the *policy rule* followed by the government. This specification nests two interesting special cases: (i) a monetarist like Friedman would advocate a constant money supply (since there is no real growth in the model) and would set $\mu_m = \mu_y = 0$, so that $m_t = \mu_0 + z_t$; (ii) a Keynesian like Tobin would believe in a countercyclical policy rule, i.e. $\mu_m = 0$ but $\mu_y < 0$. If output in the previous period is low (relative to its full-employment level, for example), then the monetary authority should stimulate the economy by raising the money supply in this period. The interpretation of the error term in the money supply rule is not that the monetary authority deliberately wishes to make the money supply stochastic, but rather that the central bank has imperfect control over this aggregate. We could also allow money supply to depend on other elements of the information set, i.e. $p_{t-1}, p_{t-2}, \cdots,$ $m_{t-2}, m_{t-3}, \cdots, y_{t-2}, y_{t-3}, \cdots$, but that does not affect the qualitative nature of our conclusions regarding the effectiveness of monetary policy whatsoever.

How do we solve the model given in (5.19)–(5.21)? It turns out that the solution method explained above can be used in this model also. First, we equate aggregate supply (5.19) and demand (5.20) and solve for the price level:

$$p_t = \frac{\alpha - \bar{y} + \beta m_t + \phi E_{t-1} p_t + \gamma E_{t-1}(p_{t+1} - p_t) + v_t - u_t}{\beta + \phi}. \tag{5.22}$$

Second, we take expectations of p_t, conditional on the information set Ω_{t-1}:

$$E_{t-1} p_t = \frac{\alpha - \bar{y} + \beta E_{t-1} m_t + \phi E_{t-1} E_{t-1} p_t}{\beta + \phi}$$
$$+ \frac{\gamma E_{t-1} E_{t-1}(p_{t+1} - p_t) + E_{t-1}(v_t - u_t)}{\beta + \phi}. \tag{5.23}$$

But the conditional expectation of a conditional expectation is just the conditional expectation itself, i.e. we only need to write E_{t-1} once on the right-hand side of (5.23). The shock terms v_t and u_t are not autocorrelated, so the conditional expectation of these shocks is zero, i.e. $E_{t-1} v_t = 0$ and $E_{t-1} u_t = 0$. In other words, knowing the actual realization of these shocks in the previous period (v_{t-1} and u_{t-1}), as the agents do, does not convey any information about the likely outcome of these shocks in period t. After substituting all these results into (5.23), one obtains a much simplified expression for $E_{t-1} p_t$:

$$E_{t-1} p_t = \frac{\alpha - \bar{y} + \beta E_{t-1} m_t + \phi E_{t-1} p_t + \gamma E_{t-1}(p_{t+1} - p_t)}{\beta + \phi}. \tag{5.24}$$

By deducting (5.24) from (5.22), a very simple expression for the price surprise is obtained:

$$p_t - E_{t-1} p_t = \frac{1}{\beta + \phi}(v_t - u_t) + \frac{\beta}{\beta + \phi}(m_t - E_{t-1} m_t). \tag{5.25}$$

---

[2] To see that $p_{t+1} - p_t$ represents the inflation rate we note that $p_{t+1} - p_t \equiv \ln(P_{t+1}/P_t)$. Next we note that for values of x close to $x_0 = 1$, we have that $\ln x \approx x - 1$. Hence, $\ln(P_{t+1}/P_t) \approx P_{t+1}/P_t - 1 = \Delta P_{t+1}/P_t$, where the final expression is the inflation rate.

Only unanticipated shocks to AD and AS, and unanticipated changes in the money supply can cause agents to be surprised. Indeed, (5.21) implies that $m_t - E_{t-1}m_t = z_t$, so that (5.25) and (5.19) imply the following expression for output:

$$y_t - \bar{y} = \frac{\phi v_t + \beta u_t + \beta \phi z_t}{\beta + \phi}. \tag{5.26}$$

The similarity between expressions (5.11) and (5.26) should be obvious. Equation (5.26) represents the stochastic steady-state solution for output. Given the model and the REH, output fluctuates according to (5.26).

Equation (5.26) has an implication that proved very disturbing to many economists in the early 1970s. It says that monetary policy is completely ineffective at influencing output (and hence employment): regardless of the policy rule adopted by the government (passive monetarist or activist Keynesian), output evolves according to (5.26) *which contains no parameters of the policy rule!*[3] This is, in a nutshell, the basic message of the policy-ineffectiveness proposition (PIP). In the words of Sargent and Wallace:

> In this system, there is no sense in which the authority has the option to conduct countercyclical policy. To exploit the Phillips curve, it must somehow trick the public. By virtue of the assumption that expectations are rational, there is no feedback rule that the authority can employ and expect to be able systematically to fool the public. This means that the authority cannot exploit the Phillips curve even for one period. (1976, p. 177)

Of course, the PIP caused an enormous stir in the ranks of the professional economists. Indeed, it seemed to have supplied proof that macroeconomists are useless. If macroeconomic demand management is ineffective, then why should society fund economists engaging themselves in writing lengthy scholarly treatises on the subject of stabilization policy?

Intermezzo 5.1

The method of undetermined coefficients in a rational expectations model. Rational expectations models can often be solved by employing a "guess and verify" method. Intuitively, this method of undetermined coefficients, as it is commonly called, works as follows. First we guess a functional form for the candidate solution. This guess will contain parameters whose values are, of course, unknown at this stage. In the second step we incorporate the candidate solution into the model and derive the solution that is implied by the guess. Finally, in the third step we verify that the implied solution and the initial guess can be made consistent with each other in a unique fashion. If that is so, then the candiate solution turned out to be correct and the unique REH solution of the model is obtained. In the remainder of this intermezzo we solve the model given in (5.19)–(5.21) using the method of undetermined coefficients. As

---

[3]The REH solution for the price level will, of course, depend on the parameters of the policy rule. This is demonstrated in Intermezzo 5.1 where the method of undetermined coefficients is used to derive the solution.

a by-product of this exercise we also obtain the REH solution for the price level.

The fundamental expectational difference equation (FEDE) of the model is obtained by substituting (5.21) into (5.22):

$$p_t = \frac{\alpha - \bar{y} + \beta[\mu_0 + \mu_m m_{t-1} + \mu_y y_{t-1} + z_t] + \phi E_{t-1} p_t}{\beta + \phi}$$
$$+ \frac{\gamma E_{t-1}(p_{t+1} - p_t) + v_t - u_t}{\beta + \phi}. \tag{a}$$

Equation (a) looks like an ugly beast but it does suggest a suitable trial solution of the form:

$$p_t = \pi_0 + \pi_m m_{t-1} + \pi_y y_{t-1} + \pi_z z_t + \pi_v v_t + \pi_u u_t, \tag{b}$$

where the values of the π_j coefficients are to be determined. Equation (b) is a reasonable guess because, at the very least, it contains all the variables that are included in the FEDE given in (a), namely a constant term, m_{t-1}, y_{t-1}, z_t, v_t, and u_t. This concludes step 1 of the derivation.

In step 2 we squeeze out every bit of information contained in (b). A direct implication of (b) is that:

$$E_{t-1} p_t = \pi_0 + \pi_m m_{t-1} + \pi_y y_{t-1}, \tag{c}$$

where we have used the fact that $E_{t-1} z_t = E_{t-1} v_t = E_{t-1} u_t = 0$. Furthermore, since the π_j coefficients are time-invariant it follows from (b) that:

$$p_{t+1} = \pi_0 + \pi_m m_t + \pi_y y_t + \pi_z z_{t+1} + \pi_v v_{t+1} + \pi_u u_{t+1}, \tag{d}$$

so that:

$$E_{t-1} p_{t+1} = \pi_0 + \pi_m E_{t-1} m_t + \pi_y E_{t-1} y_t, \tag{e}$$

where we note that $E_{t-1} z_{t+1} = E_{t-1} v_{t+1} = E_{t-1} u_{t+1} = 0$. From equation (5.19) we derive that:

$$E_{t-1} y_t = \bar{y}, \tag{f}$$

since $E_{t-1}(p_t - E_{t-1} p_t) = E_{t-1} u_t = 0$. And from (5.21) we obtain:

$$E_{t-1} m_t = \mu_0 + \mu_m m_{t-1} + \mu_y y_{t-1}, \tag{g}$$

as $E_{t-1} z_t = 0$. Substituting (f)–(g) into (e) we obtain:

$$E_{t-1} p_{t+1} = \pi_0 + \pi_m \mu_0 + \pi_y \bar{y} + \mu_m \pi_m m_{t-1} + \mu_y \pi_m y_{t-1}. \tag{h}$$

Step 2 is completed by substituting (c) and (h) into (a) and gathering terms:

$$p_t = \frac{\alpha - \bar{y} + \beta \mu_0 + \phi \pi_0 + \gamma \bar{y} \pi_y + \gamma \mu_0 \pi_m}{\beta + \phi}$$

$$+ \frac{\beta\mu_m + \pi_m\left(\phi - \gamma\left(1 - \mu_m\right)\right)}{\beta + \phi} m_{t-1} + \frac{\beta\mu_y + \left(\phi - \gamma\right)\pi_y + \gamma\mu_y\pi_m}{\beta + \phi} y_{t-1}$$

$$+ \frac{\beta}{\beta + \phi} z_t + \frac{1}{\beta + \phi} v_t - \frac{1}{\beta + \phi} u_t. \tag{i}$$

Equation (i) is the implied solution we were looking for.

In step 3 we check whether or not (i) and (b) can be made consistent with each other by suitable choice of the π_j coefficients. This amounts to the following set of restrictions that must hold:

$$\pi_0 = \frac{\alpha - \bar{y} + \beta\mu_0 + \phi\pi_0 + \gamma\bar{y}\pi_y + \gamma\mu_0\pi_m}{\beta + \phi}, \tag{j}$$

$$\pi_m = \frac{\beta\mu_m + \pi_m\left(\phi - \gamma\left(1 - \mu_m\right)\right)}{\beta + \phi}, \tag{k}$$

$$\pi_y = \frac{\beta\mu_y + \left(\phi - \gamma\right)\pi_y + \gamma\mu_y\pi_m}{\beta + \phi}, \tag{l}$$

$$\pi_z = \frac{\beta}{\beta + \phi}, \qquad \pi_v = \frac{1}{\beta + \phi}, \qquad \pi_u = -\frac{1}{\beta + \phi}. \tag{m}$$

From (k) we find the unique solution for π_m:

$$\pi_m = \frac{\beta\mu_m}{\beta + \gamma\left(1 - \mu_m\right)}. \tag{n}$$

By using (n) in (l) we find the unique solution for π_y:

$$\pi_y = \frac{\beta\mu_y}{\beta + \gamma\left(1 - \mu_m\right)}. \tag{o}$$

Finally, by using (n) and (o) in (j) we obtain the unique solution for π_0:

$$\pi_0 = \frac{\alpha - \bar{y}}{\beta} + \frac{\left(\beta + \gamma\right)\mu_0 + \gamma\bar{y}\mu_y}{\beta + \gamma\left(1 - \mu_m\right)}. \tag{p}$$

Since all π_j coefficients are uniquely determined we have found the REH solution for the price level:

$$p_t = \frac{\alpha - \bar{y}}{\beta} + \frac{\left(\beta + \gamma\right)\mu_0 + \gamma\bar{y}\mu_y}{\beta + \gamma\left(1 - \mu_m\right)} + \frac{\beta\mu_m}{\beta + \gamma\left(1 - \mu_m\right)} m_{t-1}$$

$$+ \frac{\beta\mu_y}{\beta + \gamma\left(1 - \mu_m\right)} y_{t-1} + \frac{\beta z_t + v_t - u_t}{\beta + \phi}. \tag{q}$$

****

On top of this came the second strike of the new classicals against the then predominantly Keynesian army of policy-oriented macroeconomists. Lucas (1976) argued that the then popular large macroeconometric models (with a strong Keynesian flavour) are useless for the exact task for which they are being used, namely the evaluation of the effects of different types of economic policy. This so-called *Lucas critique* can be illustrated with the aid of our model. Suppose that the economy has operated under the policy rule (5.21) for some time, that agents know and understand it, and that the economy is in a stochastic steady state, so that output follows the stochastic process given by (5.26).

By solving (5.21) for z_t and substituting the result into (5.26), it is clear that output can be written as follows:

$$y_t - \bar{y} = \zeta_0 + \zeta_1 y_{t-1} + \zeta_2 m_t + \zeta_3 m_{t-1} + \psi_t, \tag{5.27}$$

where ζ_0, ζ_1, ζ_2, and ζ_3 are composite coefficients and ψ_t is a composite stochastic variable:

$$\zeta_0 \equiv -\frac{\beta\phi\mu_0}{\beta+\phi}, \qquad \zeta_1 \equiv -\frac{\beta\phi\mu_y}{\beta+\phi}, \qquad \zeta_2 \equiv \frac{\beta\phi}{\beta+\phi}, \tag{5.28}$$

$$\zeta_3 \equiv -\frac{\beta\phi\mu_m}{\beta+\phi}, \qquad \psi_t \equiv \frac{\phi v_t + \beta u_t}{\beta+\phi}. \tag{5.29}$$

An econometrician trying to obtain estimates for the ζ-parameters would run a regression of the form (5.27) and would find a well-fitting model. Under rational expectations and with a given monetary policy rule there will be a stable relationship between, on the one hand, current output and, on the other hand, lagged output and the current and lagged money supply. But can the policy maker use knowledge of this relationship to stimulate the economy? An innocent but popular interpretation might suggest that a monetary expansion would yield an expansion of output and employment (because the estimate for ζ_2 is undoubtedly positive). Indeed, many economists use simulations of econometrically estimated models to give policy recommendations. Lucas pointed out, however, that the model would be useless for policy simulations because its coefficients are not invariant to the policy rule under the REH, i.e. the ζ-parameters are mixtures of *structural* parameters (like β and ϕ) and *policy-rule* parameters (μ_0, μ_m, and μ_y). Indeed, suppose that the government would switch from a passive to a strong countercyclical viewpoint, reflected in a change from $\mu_y = 0$ to a large negative value for the parameter μ_y. Predictions with the model based on the existing estimates of the ζ-parameters would seriously misrepresent the real effects of this policy switch, due to the fact that the actual ζ-parameters would change. For example, an increase in $|\mu_y|$ would increase the actual value of $|\zeta_1|$.

Of course, Lucas is right *in principle*. Provided one compares only stochastic steady states, the effects mentioned by him will indeed obtain. But in practice the Lucas critique may be less relevant, especially in the short run. As we have argued above, very little is known about the learning processes that may prompt agents to converge to a rational expectations equilibrium. To the extent that it may take agents some time to adapt to the new policy rule, it may well be that both (5.27) and (5.21) give the wrong answers. This may explain why econometrically estimated full-scale models embodying the REH are still relatively scarce.[4]

5.3 Should we take the PIP seriously?

Shortly after the publication of Sargent and Wallace's (1976) seemingly devastating blow to advocates of (Keynesian) countercyclical policy, it was argued that the PIP

---

[4]In Chapters 18 and 19 we discuss calibrated stochastic general equilibrium models under the REH.

is not the inevitable outcome of the REH (that, of course, made a lot of Keynesians happy again, and may have promoted the broad acceptance of the REH). The crucial counter-example to the PIP was provided by Stanley Fischer (1977), a new-Keynesian economist. With the benefit of hindsight, his argument is predictable, especially in view of Modigliani's (1944) influential interpretation of Keynes' contribution. Fischer asks a very simple question: what happens with the PIP if money wages are rigid, for example due to nominal wage contracts?

5.3.1 One-period nominal wage contracts

Fischer's (1977) model is very simple. The AD curve is monetarist in nature:

$$y_t = m_t - p_t + v_t, \tag{5.30}$$

which can be seen as a special case of (5.20) with $\alpha = \gamma = 0$ and $\beta = 1$. The supply side of the economy consists of workers signing one-period or two-period nominal wage contracts, after which the demand for labour curve determines the actual amount of employment. We first consider the case of one-period wage contracts. We assume that workers aim (and settle) for a nominal wage contract for which they *expect* full employment in the next period, when the wage contract is in operation. This is illustrated in Figure 5.6. Workers know the supply and demand schedules for labour, and estimate the market clearing real wage, $\bar{\omega}$. Since the contract is specified before the price in period t is known, the workers use the expected price level to determine the market clearing real wage. If their price expectation is p_t^e, then expected full employment occurs at point E_0. If the actual price level in period t is higher ($p_t^0 > p_t^e$) then employment occurs at point A. Employment is higher than full employment, $\bar{n}_t$, because the actual real wage rate, $w_t - p_t^0$, is lower than the full employment real wage rate, $\bar{\omega}$. In the opposite case, with $p_t^1 < p_t^e$, the real wage rate is too high and the economy settles at point B.

Let $w_t(t-1)$ denote the (logarithm of the) nominal wage that is specified at the end of period $t-1$, to hold in period t. Since the real wage that clears the labour market is equal to $\bar{\omega}$, it follows that $w_t(t-1)$ is set as:

$$w_t(t-1) = \bar{\omega} + E_{t-1} p_t, \tag{5.31}$$

where we can simplify notation further by normalizing $\bar{\omega} = 0$. The supply of output depends negatively on the actual real wage:

$$y_t = -[w_t(t-1) - p_t] + u_t, \tag{5.32}$$

so that (5.31) and (5.32) imply a Lucas-type supply curve:

$$y_t = [p_t - E_{t-1} p_t] + u_t. \tag{5.33}$$

Note that (5.33) is a special case of (5.19) with $\bar{y} = 0$ and $\phi = 1$.

Regarding the shocks to aggregate demand and supply, Fischer assumes that they are independent from each other but display autocorrelation, i.e.:

$$u_t = \rho_u u_{t-1} + \varepsilon_t, \quad |\rho_u| < 1, \qquad v_t = \rho_v v_{t-1} + \eta_t, \quad |\rho_v| < 1, \tag{5.34}$$

where $\varepsilon_t \sim N(0, \sigma_\varepsilon^2)$ and $\eta_t \sim N(0, \sigma_\eta^2)$ are uncorrelated white noise terms (often referred to as *innovations*). Finally, we assume that the monetary policy rule adopted by the policy maker has the following form:

$$m_t = \mu_{u1} u_{t-1} + \mu_{u2} u_{t-2} + \mu_{v1} v_{t-1} + \mu_{v2} v_{t-2}. \tag{5.35}$$

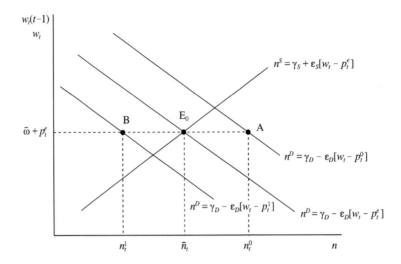

Figure 5.6: Wage setting with single-period contracts

Hence, in period t the policy maker reacts only to aggregate demand and supply shocks that occurred in periods $t-1$ and $t-2$. (Reacting to shocks that occurred in the more distant past do not affect the model so we can safely set $\mu_{ui} = \mu_{vi} = 0$ for $i = 3, 4, \cdots, \infty$.)

Not surprisingly, in view of the similarities with our earlier model, Fischer's one-period contract model implies that the PIP is valid. The REH solution is constructed as follows. First, solving (5.30) and (5.33) for p_t yields:

$$p_t = \tfrac{1}{2} \left[m_t + v_t - u_t + E_{t-1} p_t \right]. \tag{5.36}$$

This is the price level at which the AD curve intersects with the Lucas supply curve. By taking conditional expectations on both sides of (5.36) we obtain:

$$E_{t-1} p_t = \tfrac{1}{2} \left[E_{t-1} m_t + E_{t-1} v_t - E_{t-1} u_t + E_{t-1} p_t \right]. \tag{5.37}$$

Subtracting (5.37) from (5.36) yields the expression for the expectational error:

$$p_t - E_{t-1} p_t = \tfrac{1}{2} \left[(m_t - E_{t-1} m_t) + (v_t - E_{t-1} v_t) - (u_t - E_{t-1} u_t) \right]. \tag{5.38}$$

What does the surprise term (5.38) look like? First, (5.35) implies that agents know the money supply in period t once they have lagged information (there is no stochastic element in the policy rule). Hence, $m_t - E_{t-1} m_t = 0$. Second, the fact that the AD and AS shocks are autocorrelated implies that agents can use information on the shocks in the previous period (i.e. v_{t-1} and u_{t-1}) to forecast the shocks in period t:

$$E_{t-1} u_t = \rho_u u_{t-1}, \qquad E_{t-1} v_t = \rho_v v_{t-1}. \tag{5.39}$$

By using these forecasts in equation (5.38), and substituting the price surprise into (5.33), the REH solution for output is obtained:

$$y_t = \tfrac{1}{2} \left[\eta_t - \varepsilon_t \right] + u_t. \tag{5.40}$$

The coefficients of the policy rule (i.e. μ_{ui} and μ_{vi}) do not influence the path of output, so that PIP holds. In other words, anticipated monetary policy is unable to cause deviations of output from its natural level. It will, of course, affect the path of equilibrium prices under rational expectations:[5]

$$p_t = [\mu_{u1} - \rho_u] u_{t-1} + [\mu_{v1} + \rho_v] v_{t-1} + \tfrac{1}{2} [\eta_t - \varepsilon_t]. \tag{5.41}$$

5.3.2 Overlapping wage contracts

Now consider the case where nominal contracts are decided on for two periods. We continue to assume that nominal wages are set such that the expected real wage is consistent with full employment. Hence, in period t there are two nominal wage contracts in existence. Half of the workforce is on the wage contract agreed upon in period $t - 1$ (to run in periods t and $t + 1$), and the other half has a contract formulated in period $t - 2$ (to run in periods $t - 1$ and t). In symbols:

$$w_t(t - 1) \equiv E_{t-1} p_t, \quad w_t(t - 2) \equiv E_{t-2} p_t. \tag{5.42}$$

Notice the difference in the information set used for the two contracts.

The economy is perfectly competitive, so that there is only one output price, and aggregate supply is equal to:

$$y_t = \tfrac{1}{2} \left[-(w_t(t - 1) - p_t) + u_t \right] + \tfrac{1}{2} \left[-(w_t(t - 2) - p_t) + u_t \right], \tag{5.43}$$

where the first term in brackets on the right-hand side is the output of firms with workers on one-year old contracts, and the second term is the output of firms with workers on two-year old (expiring) contracts. By substituting (5.42) into (5.43), we obtain the aggregate supply curve for the two-period contract case:

$$y_t = \tfrac{1}{2} [p_t - E_{t-1} p_t] + \tfrac{1}{2} [p_t - E_{t-2} p_t] + u_t. \tag{5.44}$$

Hence, this supply curve has two surprise terms, differing in the information set. The rest of the model consists of the aggregate demand curve (5.30) and the money supply rule (5.35).

The model can be solved by repeated substitution. Because the derivations are non-trivial and somewhat tedious we show the details in Intermezzo 5.2 where we find that the REH solution for output can be written as follows:

$$y_t = \tfrac{1}{2} [\eta_t + \varepsilon_t] + \tfrac{1}{3} [\mu_{u1} + 2\rho_u] \varepsilon_{t-1} + \tfrac{1}{3} [\mu_{v1} + \rho_v] \eta_{t-1} + \rho_u^2 u_{t-2}. \tag{5.45}$$

This is the crucial counter-example to the PIP. It is the black swan that disproves the proposition that all swans are white. Equation (5.45) contains the policy parameters μ_{u1} and μ_{v1}, so that output can be affected by monetary policy even under rational expectations. As Fischer puts it, the intuitive reason for his result is that "...between the time the two-year contract is drawn up and the last year of operation of that contract, there is time for the monetary authority to react to new information about recent economic disturbances" (1977, p. 199). Because of the two-period contracts, half of the workers have implicitly based their contract wage on "stale" information.

But Fischer's blow to the new classicals was made even more devastating by the following. Clearly, output *can* be affected by monetary policy. But *should* it be affected, and if so, how? Equation (5.45) implies that output fluctuates stochastically,

---

[5]Upon reading Intermezzo 5.1 the interested reader can derive equation (5.41) as the solution to (5.36) by noting (5.35) and using the following trial solution:

$$p_t = \pi_0 + \pi_u u_{t-1} + \pi_v v_{t-1} + \pi_\varepsilon \varepsilon_t + \pi_\eta \eta_t.$$

so some measure of the degree of fluctuations over time is required. An often-used measure is the *asymptotic variance* of y_t, designated by σ_y^2 (see Intermezzo 5.3). Intuitively, the asymptotic variance measures the severity of the fluctuations in output. Using standard (but somewhat tedious) techniques, the asymptotic variance of the output path described by (5.45) can be written as:

$$\sigma_y^2 \equiv \sigma_\varepsilon^2 \left[\tfrac{1}{4} + \frac{\rho_u^4}{1 - \rho_u^2} + \tfrac{1}{9} \left(\mu_{u1} + 2\rho_u \right)^2 \right] + \sigma_\eta^2 \left[\tfrac{1}{4} + \tfrac{1}{9} \left(\mu_{v1} + \rho_v \right)^2 \right]. \tag{5.46}$$

So, to the extent that fluctuations in output are a good proxy for loss of economic welfare, the policy maker could attempt to minimize the asymptotic variance of output by choosing its reaction coefficients μ_{u1} and μ_{v1} appropriately. It turns out that the optimal values for these parameters are equal to:

$$\mu_{u1} = -2\rho_u, \quad \mu_{v1} = -\rho_v. \tag{5.47}$$

Intuitively, the policy parameters should be set at values that neutralize the effects of the shocks that occur in period $t - 1$, namely ε_{t-1} and η_{t-1}. In view of (5.45), the coefficients given in (5.47) do exactly that. Of course, not all output fluctuations can be eliminated by the policy maker. This is because both the first and the fourth term on the right-hand side of (5.45) cannot be affected by the policy maker. For the first term this is because the policy maker has no better information about the innovations in the present period than the public possesses. For the fourth term it is because u_{t-2} was known when the oldest contracts were signed in period $t - 2$, and is thus incorporated in the oldest contract.

Intermezzo 5.2

Solving the two-period overlapping wage contract model. The REH solution for the two-period contract model is obtained as follows. First, (5.30) and (5.44) can be solved for p_t:

$$p_t = \tfrac{1}{2}[m_t + v_t - u_t] + \tfrac{1}{4}[E_{t-1}p_t + E_{t-2}p_t]. \tag{a}$$

By taking expectations conditional upon period $t - 2$ information of both sides of (a), we obtain:

$$\begin{aligned} E_{t-2}p_t = &\tfrac{1}{2} \left[E_{t-2}m_t + E_{t-2}v_t - E_{t-2}u_t \right] \\ &+ \tfrac{1}{4} \left[E_{t-2}E_{t-1}p_t + E_{t-2}E_{t-2}p_t \right]. \end{aligned} \tag{b}$$

We already know that $E_{t-2}E_{t-2}p_t = E_{t-2}p_t$, but what does $E_{t-2}E_{t-1}p_t$ mean? In words, it represents what agents expect (using period $t - 2$ information) to expect in period $t - 1$ about the price level in period t. But a moment's contemplation reveals that this cannot be different from what the agents expect about p_t using $t - 2$ information, i.e. $E_{t-2}E_{t-1}p_t \equiv E_{t-2}p_t$. This is an application of the so-called law of iterated expectations. In words this law says that you do not know ahead of time how you are going to change your mind. Only genuinely new information makes you change your expectation. Hence, (b) can be solved for $E_{t-2}p_t$:

$$E_{t-2}p_t = E_{t-2}m_t + E_{t-2}v_t - E_{t-2}u_t. \tag{c}$$

Similarly, by taking expectations conditional upon period $t - 1$ information of both sides of (a), we obtain:

$$E_{t-1}p_t = \tfrac{1}{2}\left[E_{t-1}m_t + E_{t-1}v_t - E_{t-1}u_t\right]$$
$$+ \tfrac{1}{4}\left[E_{t-1}E_{t-1}p_t + E_{t-1}E_{t-2}p_t\right]. \tag{d}$$

Obviously, $E_{t-1}E_{t-1}p_t = E_{t-1}p_t$, but what does $E_{t-1}E_{t-2}p_t$ mean? In words, it represents what agents expect (using period $t - 1$ information) to expect in period $t - 2$ about the price level in period t. But $E_{t-2}p_t$ is known in period $t - 1$, so that $E_{t-1}E_{t-2}p_t \equiv E_{t-2}p_t$ (the expectation of a constant is the constant itself). By substituting (c) into (d), the solution for $E_{t-1}p_t$ is obtained:

$$E_{t-1}p_t = \tfrac{2}{3}E_{t-1}m_t + \tfrac{1}{3}E_{t-2}m_t + \tfrac{2}{3}\left[E_{t-1}v_t - E_{t-1}u_t\right]$$
$$+ \tfrac{1}{3}\left[E_{t-2}v_t - E_{t-2}u_t\right]. \tag{e}$$

If we now substitute (c) and (e) into (a), the REH solution for the price level is obtained:

$$p_t = \tfrac{2}{3}E_{t-1}m_t + \tfrac{1}{3}E_{t-2}m_t + \tfrac{1}{2}(v_t - u_t) + \tfrac{1}{6}E_{t-1}(v_t - u_t)$$
$$+ \tfrac{1}{3}E_{t-2}(v_t - u_t). \tag{f}$$

This can be substituted into the AD equation (5.30) to obtain the expression for y_t:

$$y_t = \tfrac{1}{3}\left(m_t - E_{t-2}m_t\right) - \tfrac{1}{2}(v_t - u_t) - \tfrac{1}{6}E_{t-1}(v_t - u_t)$$
$$- \tfrac{1}{3}E_{t-2}(v_t - u_t) + v_t, \tag{g}$$

where we have used the fact that $E_{t-1}m_t = m_t$.

The monetary surprise $(m_t - E_{t-2}m_t)$ must now be calculated. Using (5.35), we find that:

$$m_t = \mu_{u1}u_{t-1} + \mu_{v1}v_{t-1} + \mu_{u2}u_{t-2} + \mu_{v2}v_{t-2}, \tag{h}$$

and:

$$E_{t-2}m_t = \mu_{u1}E_{t-2}u_{t-1} + \mu_{v1}E_{t-2}v_{t-1} + \mu_{u2}E_{t-2}u_{t-2} + \mu_{v2}E_{t-2}v_{t-2}$$
$$= \mu_{u1}\rho_u u_{t-2} + \mu_{v1}\rho_v v_{t-2} + \mu_{u2}E_{t-2}u_{t-2} + \mu_{v2}E_{t-2}v_{t-2}, \tag{i}$$

where we have used (5.39), and note that $E_{t-2}u_{t-2} = u_{t-2}$ and $E_{t-2}v_{t-2} = v_{t-2}$. Equations (5.34) implies that $E_{t-2}u_{t-1} = \rho_u u_{t-2}$ and $E_{t-2}v_{t-1} = \rho_v v_{t-2}$. Using (h) and (i) we thus find:

$$m_t - E_{t-2}m_t = \mu_{u1}\left[u_{t-1} - \rho_u u_{t-2}\right] + \mu_{v1}\left[v_{t-1} - \rho_v v_{t-2}\right]$$
$$= \mu_{u1}\varepsilon_{t-1} + \mu_{v1}\eta_{t-1}. \tag{j}$$

Equation (j) can be understood at an intuitive level. Agents can perfectly forecast the money supply *one* period ahead (i.e. $E_{t-1}m_t = m_t$) but not *two* periods ahead. That is because in period $t - 1$ an innovation in the demand and supply shock occurs (equal to ε_{t-1} and η_{t-1}, respectively) that the monetary policy maker will react to (provided $\mu_{u1} \neq 0$ and $\mu_{v1} \neq 0$).

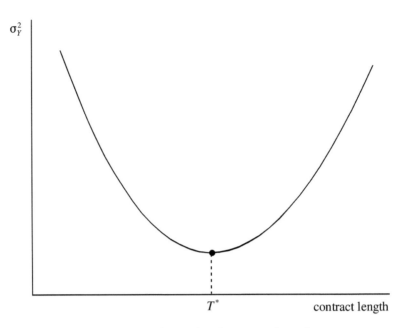

Figure 5.7: The optimal contract length

In other words, the innovation that occurs in period $t - 1$ is not fore-castable by agents who have signed their contract in period $t - 2$.

If we substitute (j) into (g), the final expression for output is obtained:

$$
\begin{aligned}
y_t &= \tfrac{1}{3} \left[\mu_{u1} \varepsilon_{t-1} + \mu_{v1} \eta_{t-1} \right] + \tfrac{1}{2} (v_t + u_t) - \tfrac{1}{6} E_{t-1} (v_t - u_t) \\
&\quad - \tfrac{1}{3} E_{t-2} (v_t - u_t) \\
&= \tfrac{1}{3} \left[\mu_{u1} \varepsilon_{t-1} + \mu_{v1} \eta_{t-1} \right] + \tfrac{1}{2} (\rho_v v_{t-1} + \eta_t + \rho_u u_{t-1} + \varepsilon_t) \\
&\quad - \tfrac{1}{6} (\rho_v v_{t-1} - \rho_u u_{t-1}) - \tfrac{1}{3} (\rho_v^2 v_{t-2} - \rho_u^2 u_{t-2}) \\
&= \tfrac{1}{2} \left[\eta_t + \varepsilon_t \right] + \tfrac{1}{3} \left[\mu_{u1} + 2\rho_u \right] \varepsilon_{t-1} + \tfrac{1}{3} \left[\mu_{v1} + \rho_v \right] \eta_{t-1} + \rho_u^2 u_{t-2}.
\end{aligned}
$$
$$ \text{(k)} $$

In going from the first to the second line we use (5.34)–(5.39), and note that $E_{t-2} v_t = \rho_v^2 v_{t-2}$ and $E_{t-2} u_t = \rho_u^2 u_{t-2}$. In going from the second to the third line, we have used the fact that $v_{t-1} = \rho_v v_{t-2} + \eta_{t-1}$ and $u_{t-1} = \rho_u u_{t-2} + \varepsilon_{t-1}$. The reason why we make these substitutions is that we want to express the output solution *as much as possible* in terms of current and lagged innovation terms (ε_{t-i} and η_{t-i}) for which we know the statistical properties.

****

Chadha (1989) has extended Fischer's (1977) analysis to the multi-period overlap-ping contract setting using the insights of Calvo (1982) that are discussed in detail below in Chapter 11. In his model, he is able to analyse contracts of any particular duration (not just one-period and two-period contracts as in Fischer's model). He is furthermore able to express the asymptotic variance in output as a function of the contract length. This diagram is given in Figure 5.7. The conclusion is very surprising indeed: there is an optimal contract length of $T^* > 0$, which Chadha estimates to be around 3.73 quarters for the US economy (1989, p. 492). Hence, intuitively, contracts act as "shock absorbers" of the economy.

There are a number of other reasons why PIP fails–see Buiter (1980) for an interesting discussion. For example, private agents may not have rational expectations, or there may be nominal price stickiness. Furthermore, even though anticipated monetary policy may not be able to cause deviations of output from its natural level, anticipated monetary policy may affect the natural rate itself. A theoretic (albeit empirically not so relevant) example is the Mundell-Tobin effect: a higher monetary growth rate depresses the real interest rate, and this boosts capital accumulation and the natural level of output.

Intermezzo 5.3

Asymptotic variance. Rational expectations models often use the asymptotic variance of output as a welfare measure. Intuitively, the asymptotic variance measures the degree of fluctuations over time in output. An economy with violent (mild) fluctuations has a high (low) asymptotic variance. Suppose that the path for output is described by the following equation:

$$y_t = \lambda y_{t-1} + x_t + \varepsilon_t, \quad |\lambda| < 1, \tag{a}$$

where y_t is output, x_t is some (vector of) deterministic exogenous variable(s), and ε_t is a white noise stochastic error term with mean zero and variance σ_ε^2. How would a Martian judge the degree of fluctuations in output, not knowing any realizations of output and the error term, but in full knowledge of equation (a) and the stochastic process of the error terms. The answer is that he would calculate the asymptotic variance:

$$\sigma_y^2 \equiv E_{t-\infty} \left[y_t - E_{t-\infty} y_t \right]^2, \tag{b}$$

where the notation $E_{t-\infty}$ formalizes the idea of no information about the actual realizations mentioned above. It is as if the Martian makes his calculations at the beginning of time.

The asymptotic variance of output implied by the process in (a) is calculated as follows. First, we write $E_{t-\infty} y_t = \lambda E_{t-\infty} y_{t-1} + x_t$ and work out the square:

$$
\begin{aligned}
\left[y_t - E_{t-\infty} y_t \right]^2 &= \left[\lambda y_{t-1} + x_t + \varepsilon_t - \lambda E_{t-\infty} y_{t-1} - x_t \right]^2 \\
&= \left[\lambda \left(y_{t-1} - E_{t-\infty} y_{t-1} \right) + \varepsilon_t \right]^2 \\
&= \lambda^2 \left[y_{t-1} - E_{t-\infty} y_{t-1} \right]^2 + \varepsilon_t^2 + 2\lambda \varepsilon_t \left[y_{t-1} - E_{t-\infty} y_{t-1} \right],
\end{aligned} \tag{c}
$$

where we have used the fact that $E_{t-\infty} x_t = x_t$ and $E_{t-\infty} \varepsilon_t = 0$. Taking expectations of both sides of (c) yields:

$$
\begin{aligned}
E_{t-\infty} \left[y_t - E_{t-\infty} y_t \right]^2 &= \lambda^2 E_{t-\infty} \left[y_{t-1} - E_{t-\infty} y_{t-1} \right]^2 \\
&+ E_{t-\infty} \varepsilon_t^2 + 2\lambda E_{t-\infty} \varepsilon_t \left[y_{t-1} - E_{t-\infty} y_{t-1} \right].
\end{aligned} \tag{d}
$$

The second term on the right-hand side is the variance of the error term ($\sigma_\varepsilon^2 \equiv E_{t-\infty}\varepsilon_t^2$), and the third term is zero because the error term is independent of lagged output. The term on the left-hand side is the asymptotic variance of y_t, and the first term on the right-hand side is λ^2 times the asymptotic variance of y_{t-1}. Because the process in (a) is stationary ($|\lambda| < 1$), these two asymptotic variances are identical. Using all this information, the final expression for the asymptotic variance becomes:

$$\sigma_y^2 = \lambda^2 \sigma_y^2 + \sigma_\varepsilon^2 \quad \Rightarrow \quad \sigma_y^2 = \frac{\sigma_\varepsilon^2}{1 - \lambda^2}. \tag{e}$$

Intuitively, the asymptotic variance of output is a multiple of the variance of the error term due to the persistence effect via lagged output. If λ is close to unity, there is a lot of persistence and the variance multiplier is very large.

****

5.4 Rational expectations in a small open economy★

As a final example of rational expectations macroeconomics we study a small open economy facing perfect (financial) capital mobility and operating under flexible exchange rates. More specifically we consider a discrete-time version of the Dornbusch model that was discussed in detail in Chapter 4. The macro-economy is described by the following set of equations:

$$y_t = \alpha - \eta R_t + \delta[p_t^* + e_t - p_t], \quad \eta > 0, \quad 0 < \delta < 1, \tag{5.48}$$
$$m_t - p_t = \beta - \lambda R_t + y_t, \quad \eta > 0, \tag{5.49}$$
$$R_t = R_t^* + E_t e_{t+1} - e_t, \tag{5.50}$$
$$p_{t+1} - p_t = \phi[y_t - \bar{y}], \quad \phi > 0, \tag{5.51}$$

where all variables except the domestic and foreign interest rates are in logarithms, starred variables refer to the foreign country, and the subscript denotes time periods. The endogenous variables are domestic output y_t, the nominal exchange rate e_t (expressed in € per $), the domestic rate of interest R_t, and the domestic price level p_t. The exogenous variables are the foreign interest rate R_t^*, domestic full employment output $\bar{y}$, and the foreign price level p_t^*. (We leave the status of the money supply open at this stage.) The model is obtained by re-expressing the continuous-time version of the Dornbusch model (given in Table 4.1) in discrete time and by imposing some simplifications. Specifically, we ignore the fiscal policy index and we have imposed some notational simplifications.

Equations (5.48) is the open-economy IS curve expressing (the demand for) output as a function of the interest rate and the real exchange rate. Equation (5.49) is the LM curve representing money market equilibrium. Real money demand depends negatively on the interest rate and positively on output. The output elasticity of money demand is set equal to unity. Uncovered interest parity is given in equation (5.50). It shows that any gap between the domestic and foreign interest rate, $R_t - R_t^*$, must equal the (rationally) expected rate of depreciation of the domestic currency,

$E_t e_{t+1} - e_t$. Finally, equation (5.51) is an old-fashioned Phillips curve showing that the rate of price change is proportional to the difference between actual and full-employment output. The adjustment speed of the price level is positive but finite, due to the assumption of sticky prices.

The small open economy under consideration is facing two types of exogenous stochastic shocks that originate from the rest of the world, namely a foreign price shock and a world interest rate shock. To keep things simple we assume:

$$p_t^* = \bar{p}^* + v_t, \tag{5.52}$$
$$R_t^* = \bar{R}^* + u_t, \tag{5.53}$$

where $\bar{p}^*$ and $\bar{R}^*$ are constants. The shocks are (i) independent (from each other and through time) and (ii) normally distributed with zero mean and constant variances, i.e. $v_t \sim N(0, \sigma_v^2)$ and $u_t \sim N(0, \sigma_u^2)$. The price shock impinges on the IS curve (5.48) whilst the interest rate shock affects the uncovered interest parity condition (5.50).

In order to prepare for the dynamic analysis to come we follow the usual steps. First we use equations (5.48)–(5.49) to derive the quasi-reduced form expressions for y_t and R_t:

$$y_t = \frac{\lambda\alpha - \eta\beta + \delta\lambda \left[\bar{p}^* + v_t + e_t\right] - (\delta\lambda + \eta)p_t + \eta m_t}{\lambda + \eta}, \tag{5.54}$$

$$R_t = \frac{\alpha + \beta + \delta \left[\bar{p}^* + v_t + e_t\right] + (1 - \delta)p_t - m_t}{\lambda + \eta}. \tag{5.55}$$

Second, we substitute (5.53) and (5.55) into (5.50) to obtain the fundamental expectational difference equations for the nominal exchange rate:

$$E_t e_{t+1} = \left[1 + \frac{\delta}{\lambda + \eta}\right] e_t + \frac{1 - \delta}{\lambda + \eta} p_t + \frac{\alpha + \beta + \delta \left[\bar{p}^* + v_t\right] - m_t}{\lambda + \eta} - \bar{R}^* - u_t. \tag{5.56}$$

Note that the coefficient for the current exchange rate e_t exceeds unity alerting us to the fact that the uncovered interest parity condition is "destabilizing". Finally, we substitute (5.52) and (5.54) into (5.51) to obtain the fundamental difference equation for the domestic price level:

$$p_{t+1} = \frac{\delta\lambda\phi}{\lambda + \eta} e_t + \left[1 - \phi\frac{\delta\lambda + \eta}{\lambda + \eta}\right] p_t + \frac{\lambda\phi\alpha - \eta\phi\beta + \delta\lambda\phi \left[\bar{p}^* + v_t\right] + \eta\phi m_t}{\lambda + \eta} - \phi\bar{y}.$$
$$\tag{5.57}$$

For price changes to be a stabilizing influence, the coefficient for the current price level p_t must be between unity in absolute value. It clearly is less than unity, but if ϕ is very large it may be less than -1 which would be destabilizing. This explains why we need to make an additional assumption regarding the speed of price adjustment below.

The description of the model is completed once an assumption is made regarding the money supply process. We proceed in the following way. In subsection 5.4.1 we first consider the benchmark version of the model, that of the unmanaged economy in which the policy maker is passive and keeps the money supply constant. In subsection 5.4.3 we consider the more challenging case in which monetary policy is used to stabilize the economy.

5.4.1   Unmanaged economy

In the absence of activist monetary policy, $m_t = \bar{m}$, and the dynamic system describing exchange rate and price fluctuations can be written in the following compact matrix expression:

$$
\begin{bmatrix} E_t e_{t+1} - \hat{e} \\ p_{t+1} - \hat{p} \end{bmatrix} = \Delta \begin{bmatrix} e_t - \hat{e} \\ p_t - \hat{p} \end{bmatrix} + \begin{bmatrix} (\delta_{11} - 1)v_t - u_t \\ \delta_{21} v_t \end{bmatrix},
\tag{5.58}
$$

where $\hat{e}$ and $\hat{p}$ are the deterministic steady-state values for, respectively, the nominal exchange rate and the domestic price level:

$$
\hat{e} = \frac{\delta\left[\bar{m} - \beta - \bar{p}^*\right] - \alpha + (1 - \delta)\bar{y} + (\lambda\delta + \eta)\bar{R}^*}{\delta},
\tag{5.59}
$$

$$
\hat{p} = \bar{m} - \beta - \bar{y} + \lambda\bar{R}^*,
\tag{5.60}
$$

and Δ is the Jacobian matrix (featuring typical element δ_{ij}):

$$
\Delta \equiv \begin{bmatrix} 1 + \dfrac{\delta}{\lambda + \eta} & \dfrac{1 - \delta}{\lambda + \eta} \\[2ex] \dfrac{\delta\lambda\phi}{\lambda + \eta} & 1 - \dfrac{\phi(\delta\lambda + \eta)}{\lambda + \eta} \end{bmatrix}.
\tag{5.61}
$$

Intuitively, $\hat{e}$ and $\hat{p}$ are the equilibrium values for the exchange rate and the price level that would be reached if there would never be any stochastic shocks at all (i.e. $u_t = v_t = 0$ for all t).

5.4.1.1   Stability

The first task at hand concerns the stability analysis. As this is far from trivial in a simultaneous discrete-time model we show some of the details here. Since the domestic price level is a predetermined ("sticky") variable, and the exchange rate is a non-predetermined ("jumping") variable, the parameters must be such that the model is saddle-point stable. In a discrete-time setting this requires that Δ features one stable root, say $|\xi_1| < 1$, and one unstable root, say $\xi_2 > 1$. Note that the Jacobian matrix in (5.61) can be written as $\Delta \equiv I + \Delta^*$ where Δ^* is given by:

$$
\Delta^* \equiv \Delta \equiv \begin{bmatrix} \dfrac{\delta}{\lambda + \eta} & \dfrac{1 - \delta}{\lambda + \eta} \\[2ex] \dfrac{\delta\lambda\phi}{\lambda + \eta} & -\dfrac{\phi(\delta\lambda + \eta)}{\lambda + \eta} \end{bmatrix}.
\tag{5.62}
$$

The determinant and trace of Δ^* are given by:

$$
|\Delta^*| = -\frac{\delta\phi}{\lambda + \eta} = \chi_1\chi_2 < 0, \qquad \mathrm{tr}\,\Delta^* = \frac{\delta - \phi(\delta\lambda + \eta)}{\lambda + \eta} = \chi_1 + \chi_2,
\tag{5.63}
$$

where χ_1 and χ_2 are the characteristic roots of Δ^*. It follows from the first expression that these roots have opposite signs, i.e. $\chi_1 < 0$ and $\chi_2 > 0$. The characteristic roots of $\Delta \equiv I + \Delta^*$ are given by $\xi_1 = 1 + \chi_1$ and $\xi_2 = 1 + \chi_2$ (see Section A.7.4 in the Mathematical Appendix) so that $\xi_1 < 1$ and $\xi_2 > 1$ for sure. But saddle-path stability in the discrete-time case also requires that the stable root satisfy $\xi_1 > -1$ which is the case if and only if $\chi_1 > -2$. Without an additional restriction on the ϕ parameter it is not possible to prove that saddle-point stability holds in this discrete-time model.

To further investigate the conditions under which the model is saddle-point stable we need to consider the roots of the characteristic equation of Δ which can be written as:

$$\Psi(s) = s^2 - s \cdot \text{tr}\Delta + |\Delta| \tag{5.64}$$

$$= s^2 - s \cdot [2 + \text{tr}\Delta^*] + 1 + \text{tr}\Delta^* + |\Delta^*|. \tag{5.65}$$

where we have used the fact that $\text{tr}\Delta = 2 + \text{tr}\Delta^*$ and $|\Delta| = 1 + \text{tr}\Delta^* + |\Delta^*|$ to arrive at the second expression. By definition we have that $\Psi(\xi_1) = \Psi(\xi_2) = 0$. In Figure 5.8 the solid line depicts the characteristic equation (a parabola that opens up) for the case in which $0 < \xi_1 < 1$ and $\xi_2 > 1$. But, depending on the magnitude of ϕ several cases are consistent with saddle-point stability. To see why this is so, we first define the following critical values for ϕ:

$$\bar{\phi}_l \equiv \frac{\lambda + \eta + \delta}{\delta\lambda + \eta + \delta}, \qquad \bar{\phi}_u \equiv \frac{2(\lambda + \eta) + \delta}{\delta\lambda + \eta + \delta/2}, \tag{5.66}$$

where we note that $\bar{\phi}_l$ is such that $\Psi(0) = 0$ and $\bar{\phi}_h$ is such that $\Psi(-1) = 0$. Four cases can be distinguished. Regardless of the magnitude of ϕ, the unstable root satisfies $\xi_2 > 1$ so that part is boring. The attention is focused on the sign and magnitude of the stable root, ξ_1.

- *Case 1*: low price flexibility. For $0 < \phi < \bar{\phi}_l$ we find $\Psi(0) = |\Delta| > 0$ and thus $0 < \xi_1 < 1$.

- *Case 2*: first knife-edge case. For $\phi = \bar{\phi}_l$ we find $\Psi(0) = |\Delta| = 0$ and thus $\xi_1 = 0$. This case is illustrated with the dashed line in Figure 5.8.

- *Case 3*: high price flexibility. For $\bar{\phi}_l < \phi < \bar{\phi}_u$ we find $\Psi(0) = |\Delta| < 0$ and $\Psi(-1) > 0$ and thus $-1 < \xi_1 < 0$. See the dash-dotted line in Figure 5.8.

- *Case 4*: second knife-edge case. For $\phi = \bar{\phi}_u$ we find $\Psi(0) = |\Delta| < 0$ and $\Psi(-1) = 0$ and thus $\xi_1 = -1$. See the dotted line in Figure 5.8.

The trick that we use to designate these cases is the following. First, for $\phi = \bar{\phi}_l$ we find that $|\Delta| = 0$ so that the stable root is equal to zero, i.e. $\xi_1 = 0$. Since $|\Delta| = 1 + \text{tr}\Delta^* + |\Delta^*|$ we find (by using (5.63)) that $\frac{\partial|\Delta|}{\partial\phi} = -\frac{\delta(1+\lambda)+\eta}{\lambda+\eta} < 0$. In other words, $|\Delta|$ is decreasing in ϕ and it follows that for $\phi < \bar{\phi}_l$ we have $|\Delta| > 0$ so that $0 < \xi_1 < 1$. Similarly, for $\phi > \bar{\phi}_l$ we have $|\Delta| < 0$ so that $\xi_1 < 0$. Now we must ensure saddle-point stability by requiring that $\phi \leq \bar{\phi}_h$ so that $\Psi(-1) \geq 0$.

5.4.1.2 Solution

Assuming that the price adjustment parameter ϕ is such that $0 < \phi < \bar{\phi}_u$ the issue of saddle-point stability has been settled and we can derive the REH solution for the model. We solve the model by using the method of undetermined coefficients—see Intermezzo 5.1 for a simple and intuitive introduction to this method.[6] Again the derivations are far from trivial so we show some of the details here.

---

[6]Here we follow the approach suggested by Campbell (1994). See Appendix B.2 of Chapter 18 for another application of this method. In Chapters 18 and 19 we will discuss a number of solutions methods that are much more general.

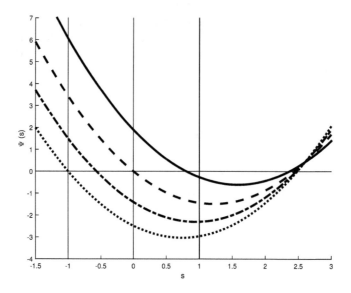

Figure 5.8: Price flexibility and the characteristic roots of Δ

In the first step we postulate a trial solution which expresses e_t in terms of the state variables p_t, u_t, and v_t:

$$e_t - \hat{e} = \pi_{e0} + \pi_{ep}(p_t - \hat{p}) + \pi_{eu}u_t + \pi_{ev}v_t, \qquad (5.67)$$

where the π_{ej} parameters are to be determined. It follows from (5.67) that for period $t+1$ we have:

$$e_{t+1} - \hat{e} = \pi_{e0} + \pi_{ep}(p_{t+1} - \hat{p}) + \pi_{eu}u_{t+1} + \pi_{ev}v_{t+1}, \qquad (5.68)$$

so that:

$$E_t e_{t+1} - \hat{e} = \pi_{e0} + \pi_{ep}(p_{t+1} - \hat{p}), \qquad (5.69)$$

where we have used the fact that $E_t u_{t+1} = E_t v_{t+1} = 0$ and $E_t p_{t+1} = p_{t+1}$ (see equation (5.57)).

In the second step we substitute (5.69) and (5.67) into (5.58) to obtain:

$$\left[\begin{array}{c} \pi_{e0} + \pi_{ep}(p_{t+1} - \hat{p}) \\ p_{t+1} - \hat{p} \end{array} \right] = \Delta \left[\begin{array}{c} \pi_{e0} + \pi_{ep}(p_t - \hat{p}) + \pi_{eu}u_t + \pi_{ev}v_t \\ p_t - \hat{p} \end{array} \right]$$
$$+ \left[\begin{array}{c} (\delta_{11} - 1)v_t - u_t \\ \delta_{21}v_t \end{array} \right]. \qquad (5.70)$$

The key thing to note is that equation (5.70) gives two solutions for p_{t+1} that must both hold for *all* possible values of the triple (p_t, u_t, v_t). Indeed, recalling that the typical elements of Δ are denoted by δ_{ij} we find that the first row of (5.70) implies:

$$p_{t+1} - \hat{p} = \frac{(\delta_{11} - 1)\,\pi_{e0} + (\delta_{11}\pi_{ep} + \delta_{12})(p_t - \hat{p}) + (\delta_{11}\pi_{eu} - 1)u_t}{\pi_{ep}}$$
$$+ \frac{(\delta_{11}(1 + \pi_{ev}) - 1)\,v_t}{\pi_{ep}}, \qquad (5.71)$$

whilst the second row yields:

$$p_{t+1} - \hat{p} = \delta_{21}\pi_{e0} + (\delta_{21}\pi_{ep} + \delta_{22})(p_t - \hat{p}) + \delta_{21}\pi_{eu}u_t + \delta_{21}(1 + \pi_{ev})v_t. \quad (5.72)$$

Equating the two expressions for p_{t+1} and gathering terms gives:

$$0 = \theta_0 + \theta_p(p_t - \hat{p}) + \theta_u u_t + \theta_v v_t, \quad (5.73)$$

where the π_{ej} parameters must be set such that $\theta_0 = \theta_p = \theta_u = \theta_v = 0$. This gives the following set of restrictions:

$$\theta_0 \equiv \left[\frac{\delta_{11} - 1}{\pi_{ep}} - \delta_{21}\right]\pi_{e0} = 0, \quad (5.74)$$

$$\theta_p \equiv \frac{\delta_{11}\pi_{ep} + \delta_{12}}{\pi_{ep}} - (\delta_{21}\pi_{ep} + \delta_{22}) = 0, \quad (5.75)$$

$$\theta_u \equiv \frac{\delta_{11}\pi_{eu} - 1}{\pi_{ep}} - \delta_{21}\pi_{eu} = 0, \quad (5.76)$$

$$\theta_v \equiv \frac{\delta_{11}(1 + \pi_{ev}) - 1}{\pi_{ep}} - \delta_{21}(1 + \pi_{ev}) = 0. \quad (5.77)$$

Although this set of restrictions may look like an insurmountable obstacle to the uninitiated, it turns out that they are relatively easy to solve. The trick is to start with the right equation. Note that π_{ep} appears in all expressions but that it is the *only* unknown parameter in (5.75). Hence this is the logical place to start. Solving (5.75) for π_{ep} gives $\delta_{11}\pi_{ep} + \delta_{12} = (\delta_{21}\pi_{ep} + \delta_{22})\pi_{ep}$ or:

$$0 = \delta_{21}\pi_{ep}^2 + (\delta_{22} - \delta_{11})\pi_{ep} - \delta_{12}. \quad (5.78)$$

This is a quadratic equation in π_{ep} which has two distinct roots:

$$\pi_{ep}^{(1)} = \frac{\delta_{11} - \delta_{22} + \sqrt{(\delta_{22} - \delta_{11})^2 + 4\delta_{12}\delta_{21}}}{2\delta_{21}} > 0, \quad (5.79)$$

$$\pi_{ep}^{(2)} = \frac{\delta_{11} - \delta_{22} - \sqrt{(\delta_{22} - \delta_{11})^2 + 4\delta_{12}\delta_{21}}}{2\delta_{21}} < 0, \quad (5.80)$$

where the signs follow from the fact that $\delta_{12} > 0$ and $\delta_{21} > 0$. We seem to have hit a brick wall as there are two solutions whilst the method of undetermined coefficients requires a single unique solution for π_{ep}! So which one should we take, the positive or the negative solution?

To answer this question we note that the coefficient for p_t in (5.71) can be written as:

$$\pi_{pp} \equiv \delta_{11} + \frac{\delta_{12}}{\pi_{ep}} = 1 + \frac{\delta}{\lambda + \eta} + \frac{1 - \delta}{\lambda + \eta}\frac{1}{\pi_{ep}}. \quad (5.81)$$

For the positive root, $\pi_{ep} = \pi_{ep}^{(1)}$, this coefficient exceeds unity for sure leading to an explosive trial path for the price level. Hence, there is a strong presumption that we must select the negative root, $\pi_{ep} = \pi_{ep}^{(2)}$, as the unique value for π_{ep} that is consistent with saddle-point stability. But a hunch is not enough. It remains to be proved that $\pi_{ep}^{(2)}$ is associated with a stable value for π_{pp}. Note that (5.72) implies that

$\pi_{pp} = \delta_{21}\pi_{ep} + \delta_{22}$ so the result to be proved is that $|z| < 1$ where $z \equiv \delta_{21}\pi_{ep} + \delta_{22}$. By multiplying (5.78) by δ_{21} and using the definition of z we obtain:

$$
\begin{aligned}
0 &= \delta_{21}^2\pi_{ep}^2 + (\delta_{22} - \delta_{11})\delta_{21}\pi_{ep} - \delta_{12}\delta_{21} \\
&= (z - \delta_{22})^2 + (\delta_{22} - \delta_{11})(z - \delta_{22}) - \delta_{12}\delta_{21} \\
&= z^2 - z \cdot \text{tr}\Delta + |\Delta| \equiv \Psi(z).
\end{aligned}
$$

Under saddle-path stability $\Psi(z)$ has two roots, namely $z^{(1)} = \xi_1$ (such that $|\xi_1| < 1$) and $z^{(2)} = \xi_2 > 1$. To obtain a stable price path we must select the first of these roots, i.e. $\pi_{pp} = \xi_1$ and $|\pi_{pp}| < 1$. Since $\pi_{ep} = \delta_{12}/(\pi_{pp} - \delta_{11})$, $\delta_{12} > 0$, and $\delta_{11} > 1$, it follows that π_{ep} is negative (as we suspected above). In summary we have now established the following results:

$$
\pi_{ep} = \frac{\delta + \phi(\delta\lambda + \eta) - \sqrt{[\delta + \phi(\delta\lambda + \eta)]^2 + 4\delta(1-\delta)\lambda\phi}}{2\delta\lambda\phi} < 0, \tag{5.82}
$$

$$
\pi_{pp} = \xi_1 = 1 - \phi\frac{\delta\lambda(1 - \pi_{ep}) + \eta}{\lambda + \eta}, \qquad |\pi_{pp}| < 1. \tag{5.83}
$$

Now that we have selected the appropriate value for π_{ep}, equations (5.74), (5.76), and (5.77) can be solved for, respectively, π_{e0}, π_{eu} and π_{ev}:

$$
\pi_{e0} = 0, \tag{5.84}
$$

$$
\pi_{eu} = \frac{1}{\delta_{11} - \delta_{21}\pi_{ep}} = \frac{\lambda + \eta}{\lambda + \eta + \delta[1 - \lambda\phi\pi_{ep}]} > 0, \tag{5.85}
$$

$$
\pi_{ev} = -\frac{\delta[1 - \lambda\phi\pi_{ep}]}{\lambda + \eta}\frac{1}{\delta_{11} - \delta_{21}\pi_{ep}} = -\frac{\delta[1 - \lambda\phi\pi_{ep}]}{\lambda + \eta + \delta[1 - \lambda\phi\pi_{ep}]} < 0. \tag{5.86}
$$

For future reference we note that $1 + \pi_{ev} = \pi_{eu}$. Because we have found unique values for π_{e0}, π_{ep}, π_{eu}, and π_{ev} we have obtained the unique rational expectations solution of the model. The saddle path is given by:

$$
e_t - \hat{e} = \pi_{ep}(p_t - \hat{p}) + \pi_{eu}u_t + \pi_{ev}v_t. \tag{5.87}
$$

Note that (5.87) expresses e_t as a downward sloping function of p_t (as $\pi_{ep} < 0$). Since p_t is predetermined at time t, a positive world interest rate shock ($u_t > 0$) leads to an immediate depreciation of the currency (as $\pi_{eu} > 0$) whilst a positive world price shock ($v_t > 0$) has the opposite effect on the exchange rate (as $\pi_{ev} < 0$).

What about the remaining endogenous variables? By using (5.54)–(5.55), (5.87), and noting that $m_t = \bar{m}$ we find the equilibrium paths for output and the domestic interest rate:

$$
y_t - \bar{y} = \frac{\delta\lambda\pi_{eu}[u_t + v_t] - [\delta\lambda(1 - \pi_{ep}) + \eta](p_t - \hat{p})}{\lambda + \eta}, \tag{5.88}
$$

$$
R_t - \bar{R}^* = \frac{\delta\pi_{eu}[u_t + v_t] + [1 - \delta(1 - \pi_{ep})](p_t - \hat{p})}{\lambda + \eta}, \tag{5.89}
$$

where we have used the fact that $1 + \pi_{ev} = \pi_{eu}$ to simplify these expressions. Finally, by using (5.88) in (5.51) we find the expression for next period's price level:

$$
p_{t+1} - \hat{p} = p_t - \hat{p} + \phi\frac{\delta\lambda\pi_{eu}[u_t + v_t] - [\delta\lambda(1 - \pi_{ep}) + \eta](p_t - \hat{p})}{\lambda + \eta}. \tag{5.90}
$$

It is clear from (5.88)–(5.89) that both output and the domestic interest rate fluctuate randomly as a result of the foreign price- and interest rate shocks. The output results critically depend on the assumption of price stickiness. Indeed, if prices were perfectly flexible ($\phi \to \infty$), then output would equal its full employment level at all times and international shocks would only affect the domestic interest rate and price level, as well as the exchange rate. Indeed, denoting variables with a tilde as the REH solutions under perfect price flexibility, it is easy to show that:[7]

$$\tilde{y}_t = \bar{y}, \tag{5.91}$$

$$\tilde{R}_t - \bar{R}^* = \frac{\delta}{(1+\lambda)\delta + \eta}[u_t + v_t] \tag{5.92}$$

$$\tilde{p}_t - \hat{p} = \frac{\delta\lambda}{(1+\lambda)\delta + \eta}[u_t + v_t] \tag{5.93}$$

$$\tilde{e}_t - \hat{e} = \frac{\delta\lambda + \eta}{(1+\lambda)\delta + \eta}u_t - \frac{\delta}{(1+\lambda)\delta + \eta}v_t. \tag{5.94}$$

5.4.1.3 Measures of economic fluctuations

As was pointed out above, the early rational expectations literature often uses the asymptotic variance of output as a measure of economic welfare—see Section 5.3.2. In Intermezzo 5.3 we explained how an asymptotic variance can be calculated in the context of a simple single-equation stochastic process. In this section we show how the asymptotic variance of output (and various other measures of variability) can be computed for the much more complicated sticky-price model.

We start by writing equation (5.90) in short-hand notation as:

$$p_{t+1} - \hat{p} = \pi_{pp}(p_t - \hat{p}) + \pi_{pu}u_t + \pi_{pv}v_t, \tag{5.95}$$

and taking the unconditional expectations of both sides:

$$E_{t-\infty}(p_{t+1} - \hat{p}) = \pi_{pp}E_{t-\infty}(p_t - \hat{p}), \tag{5.96}$$

where we have used the fact that $E_{t-\infty}u_t = E_{t-\infty}v_t = 0$. By deducting (5.96) from (5.95), noting $E_{t-\infty}\hat{p} = \hat{p}$, and squaring the resulting expression, we obtain:

$$[p_{t+1} - E_{t-\infty}p_{t+1}]^2 = \pi_{pp}^2[p_t - E_{t-\infty}p_t]^2 + \pi_{pu}^2u_t^2 + \pi_{pv}^2v_t^2$$
$$+ 2\pi_{pu}\pi_{pp}[p_t - E_{t-\infty}p_t]u_t + 2\pi_{pv}\pi_{pp}[p_t - E_{t-\infty}p_t]v_t$$
$$+ 2\pi_{pu}\pi_{pv}u_tv_t. \tag{5.97}$$

Finally, after taking the unconditional expectation of both sides of (5.97) we obtain:

$$E_{t-\infty}[p_{t+1} - Ep_{t+1}]^2 = \pi_{pp}^2E_{t-\infty}[p_t - E_{t-\infty}p_t]^2 + \pi_{pu}^2E_{t-\infty}u_t^2 + \pi_{pv}^2E_{t-\infty}v_t^2$$
$$+ 2\pi_{pu}\pi_{pp}E_{t-\infty}[p_t - E_{t-\infty}p_t]u_t + 2\pi_{pu}\pi_{pv}E_{t-\infty}u_tv_t$$
$$+ 2\pi_{pv}\pi_{pp}E_{t-\infty}[p_t - E_{t-\infty}p_t]v_t, \tag{5.98}$$

---

[7]By setting $\tilde{y}_t = \bar{y}$, equations (5.48)–(5.49) and (5.52) can be used to obtain quasi-reduced-form expressions for $\tilde{R}_t$ and $\tilde{p}_t$. Using the former one in (5.50) and noting (5.53), the expectational difference equation for the nominal exchange is obtained:

$$E_te_{t+1} - \hat{e} = \left[1 + \frac{\delta}{\delta\lambda + \eta}\right](e_t - \hat{e}) + \frac{\delta}{\delta\lambda + \eta}v_t - u_t.$$

This equation can be solved by using the trial solution $e_t - \hat{e} = \pi_{e0} + \pi_{eu}u_t + \pi_{ev}v_t$.

which can be rewritten as:

$$\text{var}(p_{t+1}) = \pi_{pp}^2 \text{var}(p_t) + \pi_{pu}^2 \text{var}(u_t) + \pi_{pv}^2 \text{var}(v_t) + 2\pi_{pu}\pi_{pp}\text{cov}(p_t, u_t)$$
$$+ 2\pi_{pv}\pi_{pp}\text{cov}(p_t, v_t) + 2\pi_{pu}\pi_{pv}\text{cov}(u_t, v_t), \tag{5.99}$$

where $\text{var}(x_t) \equiv E_{t-\infty}[x_t - E_{t-\infty}x_t]^2$ is the asymptotic variance of x_t and $\text{cov}(x_t, y_t)$ $\equiv E_{t-\infty}[x_t - E_{t-\infty}x_t][y_t - E_{t-\infty}y_t]$ is the asymptotic covariance between x_t and y_t.

The expression in (5.99) can be simplified quite a bit. First, by assumption $\text{var}(u_t)$ $= \sigma_u^2$ and $\text{var}(u_t) = \sigma_v^2$. Second, because both u_t and v_t are not autocorrelated by assumption $(E_{t-\infty}u_t u_s = E_{t-\infty}v_t v_s = 0$ for all $s \neq t)$ it follows that the asymptotic covariance between the price and the stochastic shock terms is zero, i.e. $\text{cov}(p_t, u_t) =$ $\text{cov}(p_t, v_t) = 0$. Third, since u_t and v_t are independent from each other $(E_{t-\infty}u_t v_t =$ $0)$, it follows that $\text{cov}(u_t, v_t) = 0$. Fourth, since the stochastic process in (5.95) is stationary (because $|\pi_{pp}| < 1$) the asymptotic variances of p_{t+1} and p_t are identical, i.e. $\text{var}(p_{t+1}) = \text{var}(p_t)$. Fifth, equation (5.90) implies that $\pi_{pv} = \pi_{pu}$. Incorporating all these simplifications we thus obtain the following expression for the variability of the price level:

$$\text{var}(p_t) = \frac{\pi_{pu}^2}{1 - \pi_{pp}^2}\left[\sigma_u^2 + \sigma_v^2\right]. \tag{5.100}$$

Note that the denominator is positive (as $|\pi_{pp}| < 1$) and may be quite small (if $|\pi_{pp}|$ is close to unity). Hence, the individual variances σ_u^2 and σ_v^2 may be blown up substantially because $1/(1 - \pi_{pp}^2)$ can be quite large.

To find the asymptotic variance of y_t we write (5.88) in short-hand notation as:

$$y_t - \bar{y} = \pi_{yp}(p_t - \bar{p}) + \pi_{yu}[u_t + v_t]. \tag{5.101}$$

Going through similar steps as before we easily find that the asymptotic variance of output is given by:

$$\text{var}(y_t) = \pi_{yp}^2 \text{var}(p_t) + \pi_{yu}^2[\sigma_u^2 + \sigma_v^2]$$
$$= \left[\pi_{yu}^2 + \pi_{yp}^2 \frac{\pi_{pu}^2}{1 - \pi_{pp}^2}\right][\sigma_u^2 + \sigma_v^2], \tag{5.102}$$

where we have used (5.100) to get from the first to the second line. In the sticky-price model output displays fluctuations both because of the *direct* effect of the international shocks and because of their *indirect* effect operating through the domestic price level. This conclusion stands in stark contrast to the case with perfectly flexible prices for which the variability in output is zero (this follows readily from (5.91)).

5.4.2   Introduction to Dynare

In the previous subsection we have analysed the key properties of a discrete-time sticky-price model of a small open economy. In addition we solved this model under rational expectations by making use of the method of undetermined coefficients. We were able to derive conditions under which the model is saddle-path stable, to prove that the saddle-path is downward sloping, and to prove stability of the price adjustment process. By now the reader should be convinced that matters can become analytically intractable quite rapidly. Even though the dynamical system in (5.58) only contains two equations, a lot of hard work was needed to prove the relevant features of the model. For higher-dimensional systems the pen-and-paper method used above will fail for sure.

Fortunately there now exists a very useful (and free) software package that does all the hard work for us at lightning speed. As is explained on the Dynare website:[8]

> Dynare is a software platform for handling a wide class of economic models, in particular dynamic stochastic general equilibrium (DSGE) and overlapping generations (OLG) models. The models solved by Dynare include those relying on the rational expectations hypothesis, wherein agents form their expectations about the future in a way consistent with the model.

The DSGE and OLG models mentioned in the quotation are studied below—see Chapters 19 and 16. Here we illustrate the use of Dynare in the context of the sticky-price model given in (5.58). In doing so we prepare the way for much more complicated Dynare applications to come in this and subsequent chapters.

Dynare comes in three flavours, a version that runs under Matlab (licensed software), one that operates under Octave (which is free software), and a stand-alone version written in C++ (also free of charge). Throughout the book we restrict attention to the Matlab implementation of Dynare. Pratap (2017) is an excellent primer on Matlab, whilst Adjemian et al. (2011) is a very extensive Dynare Reference Manual. Dynare, like life itself, is based on the give-and-take principle. It needs information from you (as the programmer) and in return it will give you lots of interesting output.

5.4.2.1 What Dynare needs from you

The central component of any Dynare application is the so-called *model file* which must have the file extension mod. Table 5.1 lists the Dynare code for the sticky-price model. The model file is called Program05_01.mod as is indicated in the commented line at the top. (Note that any line that starts with a percentage sign (%) is ignored by Dynare and that Dynare statements are terminated by a semi-colon (;) even if they run across several lines.)

Let us run through the different components of the model file. There are four Dynare related blocks of statements. In *Block 1* the variables and parameters are defined. The command var defines the endogenous variables (y_t, R_t, e_t, p_{t+1}, p_t^*, and R_t^* in (5.48)–(5.53)), varexo defines the exogenous variables (u_t and v_t), and parameters defines the structural parameters and constants of the model (α, β, η, δ, λ, ϕ, $\bar{m}$, $\bar{y}$, $\bar{R}^*$, and $\bar{p}^*$).

Dynare is a numerical (rather than symbolic) package so it needs numbers to work with. In *Block 2* all parameters defined in the previous block are given actual values. In addition starting values for some endogenous variables are also provided. These values are mostly "cooked", i.e. the constants are chosen to get nice round figures for the endogenous variables and the parameters are not based on empirical estimates but rather are meant to illustrate the workings of Dynare. Note, however, that $\bar{R}^* = 5$, implying that world interest rates fluctuate randomly around a value of five percent per annum. Furthermore, $e_0 \equiv \ln(E_0) = -0.12$ implying a euro-dollar

---

[8]See http://www.dynare.org. This website is a veritable goldmine. It not only provides download links to the software package and the supporting manuals but also contains news of upcoming Dynare events, working papers, and other resources. With Dynare you'll never walk alone.

Table 5.1. A Dynare model file for the sticky-price model

```
% Discrete-Time Dornbusch Overshooting Model with Rational Expectations
%
% Dynare model file: Program05_01.mod
%

%-----------------------------------------------------------------
% Block 0. Housekeeping
%-----------------------------------------------------------------

close all;

%-----------------------------------------------------------------
% Block 1. Define the variables and parameters
%-----------------------------------------------------------------

var y R e p pstar Rstar ;
varexo u v ;
parameters alpha beta eta delta lambda phi m_bar y_bar Rstar_bar
pstar_bar;

%-----------------------------------------------------------------
% Block 2. Parameter values
%-----------------------------------------------------------------

eta         =   0.1;
delta       =   0.8;
lambda      =   0.5;
phi         =   0.2;
pstar_bar   =   1;
y_bar       =   1;
Rstar_bar   =   5;
m_bar       =   1;
alpha       =   1.596;
beta        =   1.5;

y0          =   y_bar;
R0          =   Rstar_bar;
p0          =   1;
e0          =   -0.12;


%-----------------------------------------------------------------
% Block 3. Model
%-----------------------------------------------------------------

model (linear);
   y        = alpha - eta * R + delta *(pstar + e - p(-1)) ;
   m_bar    = beta + p(-1) - lambda * R + y ;
   R        = Rstar + e(+1) - e ;
   p        = p(-1) + phi *(y - y_bar) ;
   pstar    = pstar_bar + v ;
   Rstar    = Rstar_bar + u ;
end;
```

Table 5.1, continued

```
%---------------------------------------------------------------
% Block 4. Computation
%---------------------------------------------------------------

% Compute initial steady state and verify the calibration

initval;
  y        = y0;
  R        = R0;
  p        = p0;
  e        = e0;
  pstar    = pstar_bar;
  Rstar    = Rstar_bar;
end;

steady;

% Compute the characteristic roots

check;

% Define the stochastic shock processes

shocks;
var u; stderr 1;
var v; stderr 0.2;
end;

% Simulate the stochastic model

stoch_simul;
```

exchange rate of $E = 0.887$, i.e. 88.7 euro cents per US dollar, which is roughly the spot rate at the time of writing this sentence (June 2015).

Block 3 contains the core of the Dynare code, namely a statement of the model in a format that Dynare can understand. The equations of the model are found between the statements `model (linear)` and `end`. The equations are separated from each other by semi-colons. Dynare does not "know" which variables are considered to be predetermined so it needs a little help here from the programmer. In particular the program is instructed that the price level is a predetermined variable by adopting the following timing convention. Instead of writing p_{t+1} and p_t appearing in (5.51) as `p(+1)` and `p`, we must write these variables as `p` and `p(-1)`, i.e. prices must be measured at the end (rather than the beginning) of the period. In doing so Dynare "knows" that `p(-1)` (i.e. p_t) must be treated as a predetermined variable. Note that for non-predetermined (jumping) variables Dynare uses the same notation as in the theoretical model, that is `e` and `e(+1)` designate, respectively, e_t and e_{t+1}.

In *Block 4* the actual computations are done. The Dynare command `steady` computes the deterministic steady state, using the starting values stated between the commands `initval` and `end`.[9] Furthermore, the command `check` computes the characteristic roots of the Jacobian matrix (ζ_1 and ζ_2). In between the commands `shocks` and `end` we specify the stochastic process for the shock terms (u_t and v_t). The statement `var u; stderror 1` means that we set the standard error of u_t equal to unity, i.e. $\sigma_u = 1$. And `var v; stderror 0.2` means that $\sigma_v = 0.2$. Since we assume u_t and v_t to be independent there is no need to specify a value for the covariance (which is zero by default). The last command in Block 4 is `stoch_simul`. As the name suggests it solves the stochastic rational expectations model.

5.4.2.2   What Dynare gives you

In order to run Dynare using the model file `Program05_01.mod` we start up Matlab, navigate to the directory where the model file is located, and, at the Matlab prompt, we enter the command `dynare Program05_01`. In Table 5.2 we show (a lightly edited version of) what will be written to the computer screen. We have added the labels (T2.1)–(T1.7) to facilitate the discussion of these results.

In block (T2.1) of Table 5.2 we see that Dynare needs to do a lot of preparatory things before it can actually start the required computing. The details of these preliminary tasks need not concern us here. In block (T2.2) Dynare tells us that, for the parameter values adopted, the eigenvalues are equal to $\zeta_1 = 0.8043$ and $\zeta_2 = 2.362$. The ϕ value chosen thus corresponds to Case 1 mentioned above (that of low price flexibility). Since Dynare knows that there is one forward-looking variable (namely `e(+1)` in the language it can understand) and one unstable root, it gives the green light: "The rank condition is verified".

In block (T2.3) Dynare reports the deterministic steady-state results ($\hat{y}$, $\hat{R}$, $\hat{e}$, $\hat{p}$, $\bar{p}^*$, and $\bar{R}^*$), and in block (T2.4) the covariance matrix of the shocks is listed featuring σ_u^2 and σ_v^2 on the main diagonal. The first really interesting set of results is given in block (T2.5). There Dynare reports what it calls "policy and transition function". They are the rational expectations solutions for the different variables. For example, the column for `p` is the computed counterpart to equation (5.95) which it rewrites as:

$$p_{t+1} = \hat{p} + \pi_{pp}(p_t - \hat{p}) + \pi_{pu} u_t + \pi_{pv} v_t. \tag{5.103}$$

---

[9]Note that by specifying `model (linear)` in Block 3 we tell Dynare that the model is linear in the variables. In such a case there is no requirement to specify starting values for the endogenous variables, i.e. the model will also run without values for `y0`, `R0`, `p0`, and `e0`.

Table 5.2. Output from the Dynare model file `Program05_01.mod`

```
>> dynare Program05_01

(T2.1)
Configuring Dynare ...
[mex] Generalized QZ.
[mex] Sylvester equation solution.
[mex] Kronecker products.
[mex] Sparse kronecker products.
[mex] Local state space iteration (second order).
[mex] Bytecode evaluation.
[mex] k-order perturbation solver.
[mex] k-order solution simulation.
[mex] Quasi Monte-Carlo sequence (Sobol).
[mex] Markov Switching SBVAR.

Starting Dynare (version 4.4.3).
Starting preprocessing of the model file ...
Found 6 equation(s).
Evaluating expressions...done
Computing static model derivatives:
 - order 1
Computing dynamic model derivatives:
 - order 1
 - order 2
Processing outputs ...done
Preprocessing completed.
Starting MATLAB/Octave computing.

(T2.2)
EIGENVALUES:
        Modulus           Real          Imaginary

        0.8043           0.8043             0
        2.362            2.362              0


There are 1 eigenvalue(s) larger than 1 in modulus
for 1 forward-looking variable(s)

The rank condition is verified.

(T2.3)
STEADY-STATE RESULTS:

y          1
R          5
e          -0.12
p          1
pstar      1
Rstar      5

MODEL SUMMARY

  Number of variables:          6
  Number of stochastic shocks: 2
  Number of state variables:    1
  Number of jumpers:            1
  Number of static variables:   4
```

Table 5.2, continued

```
(T2.4)
MATRIX OF COVARIANCE OF EXOGENOUS SHOCKS

Variables       u          v
u            1.000000   0.000000
v            0.000000   0.040000

(T2.5)
POLICY AND TRANSITION FUNCTIONS
                y          R          e          p        pstar
Rstar
Constant     1.000000   5.000000  -0.120000   1.000000   1.000000
5.000000
p(-1)       -0.978665   0.042669  -0.217998   0.804267
0            0
u            0.282199   0.564398   0.423298   0.056440            0
1.000000
v            0.282199   0.564398  -0.576702   0.056440
1.000000        0


(T2.6)
THEORETICAL MOMENTS

VARIABLE      MEAN    STD. DEV.   VARIANCE
y            1.0000     0.3030     0.0918
R            5.0000     0.5756     0.3313
e           -0.1200     0.4392     0.1929
p            1.0000     0.0969     0.0094
pstar        1.0000     0.2000     0.0400
Rstar        5.0000     1.0000     1.0000


(T2.7)
MATRIX OF CORRELATIONS

Variables       y        R        e        p      pstar    Rstar
y            1.0000   0.9475   0.8637   0.3128   0.1863   0.9314
R            0.9475   1.0000   0.8931   0.6000   0.1961   0.9806
e            0.8637   0.8931   1.0000   0.4923  -0.2626   0.9637
p            0.3128   0.6000   0.4923   1.0000   0.1165   0.5827
pstar        0.1863   0.1961  -0.2626   0.1165   1.0000   0.0000
Rstar        0.9314   0.9806   0.9637   0.5827   0.0000   1.0000


(T2.8)
COEFFICIENTS OF AUTOCORRELATION

Order       1        2        3        4        5
y        -0.0979  -0.0787  -0.0633  -0.0509  -0.0409
R         0.0043   0.0035   0.0028   0.0022   0.0018
e        -0.0237  -0.0190  -0.0153  -0.0123  -0.0099
p         0.8043   0.6468   0.5202   0.4184   0.3365
pstar    -0.0000  -0.0000  -0.0000  -0.0000  -0.0000
Rstar     0.0000   0.0000   0.0000   0.0000   0.0000


Total computing time : 0h00m03s
>>
```

Hence, what Dynare calls the constant is actually $\hat{p}$ (not what we would call π_{p0}). Note that $\pi_{pp} = 0.8043$ and $\pi_{pu} = \pi_{pv} = 0.0564$. The column for e reports the parameters of the saddle path, i.e. Dynare finds that $\pi_{ep} = -0.2180$, $\pi_{eu} = 0.4233$, and $\pi_{ev} = -0.5767$.

In blocks (T2.6)–(T2.8) Dynare reports what it calls the "theoretical moments", i.e. the means and variances of the different endogenous variables (in (T2.6)), the correlations between the variables (in (T2.7)), and the autocorrelation of these variables (in (T2.8)). It calls these measures "theoretical" because they are directly based on the computed policy functions and the theoretical properties of the shocks (u_t and v_t). (Dynare also has the option to compute "empirical moments", in which case it computes the means and variances by generating quasi-random vectors for u_t and v_t not unlike what we did in the context of the Muth model above.) Note from (T2.6) that there is huge amount of turbulence in this toy economy, e.g. the asymptotic standard deviation of output is a whopping thirty percent of steady-state output, and exchange rates also fluctuate wildly. Note that the asymptotic standard deviation of prices is rather modest owing to the fact that we have postulated a low degree of price flexibility.

A rather interesting message is displayed by Dynare at the end of Table 5.2. The entire computation takes the machine three seconds! Compare this to the time and effort required to derive these same results with the analytical pen-and-paper method employed above and it becomes obvious why Dynare is such a popular software package!

5.4.3 Managed economy

In this section we briefly study to what extent countercyclical monetary policy can be used in the sticky-price model under rational expectations. We assume that the policy maker employs the following countercyclical monetary policy rule:

$$m_t = \bar{m} - \mu\left[y_{t-1} - \bar{y}\right], \qquad \mu > 0. \tag{5.104}$$

If output in period $t - 1$ falls short of (exceeds) its full employment level then the policy maker increases (decreases) the money supply in period t. Since the model has a rather Keynesian flavour (as prices are sticky) there is a strong presumption that countercyclical policy should not only be possible in this model but also desirable in the sense that it leads to a lower asymptotic variance of output.

To verify this presumption we need to solve the model under rational expectations. The pen-and-paper method would proceed as follows. First, we note that the economy is now represented by a three equation system of expectational difference equations taking the following form:

$$
\begin{bmatrix} E_t e_{t+1} - \hat{e} \\ p_{t+1} - \hat{p} \\ m_{t+1} - \bar{m} \end{bmatrix} = \Delta \begin{bmatrix} e_t - \hat{e} \\ p_t - \hat{p} \\ m_t - \bar{m} \end{bmatrix} + \begin{bmatrix} (\delta_{11} - 1)v_t - u_t \\ \delta_{21}v_t \\ -\mu\delta_{21}v_t \end{bmatrix}, \tag{5.105}
$$

Table 5.3. A Dynare model file with a monetary policy rule

```
% Discrete-Time Dornbusch Overshooting Model with Rational Expectations
%
% Dynare model file: Program05_02.mod
%

%------------------------------------------------------------
% 0. Housekeeping
%------------------------------------------------------------

close all;

%------------------------------------------------------------
% 1. Define the variables and parameters
%------------------------------------------------------------

var y R e p m pstar Rstar ;
varexo u v ;
parameters alpha beta eta delta lambda phi m_bar y_bar Rstar_bar
pstar_bar mu ;

%------------------------------------------------------------
% 2. Parameter values
%------------------------------------------------------------

eta         =   0.1;
delta       =   0.8;
lambda      =   0.5;
phi         =   0.2;
pstar_bar   =   1;
y_bar       =   1;
Rstar_bar   =   5;
m_bar       =   1;
alpha       =   1.596;
beta        =   1.5;
mu          =   0.5;

y0          = y_bar;
R0          = Rstar_bar;
p0          = 1;
e0          = -0.12;


%------------------------------------------------------------
% 3. Model
%------------------------------------------------------------

model (linear);
    y       = alpha -eta * R + delta *(pstar + e - p(-1)) ;
    m       = beta + p(-1) - lambda * R + y ;
    R       = Rstar + e(+1) - e ;
    p       = p(-1) + phi *(y - y_bar) ;
    m       = m_bar - mu * (y(-1) - y_bar);
    pstar   = pstar_bar + v ;
    Rstar   = Rstar_bar + u ;
end;
```

Table 5.3, continued

```
%-------------------------------------------------------------------
% 4. Computation
%-------------------------------------------------------------------

% Compute initial steady state and verify the calibration

initval;
   y     = y0;
   R     = R0;
   p     = p0;
   e     = e0;
   m     = m_bar;
   pstar = pstar_bar;
   Rstar = Rstar_bar;
end;

steady;

check;

shocks;
var u; stderr 1;
var v; stderr 0.2;
end;

stoch_simul;
```

where the Jacobian matrix (featuring typical elements δ_{ij}) is given by:

$$\Delta \equiv \begin{bmatrix} 1 + \dfrac{\delta}{\lambda + \eta} & \dfrac{1 - \delta}{\lambda + \eta} & -\dfrac{1}{\lambda + \eta} \\[2ex] \dfrac{\delta \lambda \phi}{\lambda + \eta} & 1 - \dfrac{\phi (\delta \lambda + \eta)}{\lambda + \eta} & \dfrac{\phi \eta}{\lambda + \eta} \\[2ex] -\dfrac{\mu \delta \lambda}{\lambda + \eta} & \dfrac{\mu (\delta \lambda + \eta)}{\lambda + \eta} & -\dfrac{\mu \eta}{\lambda + \eta} \end{bmatrix}. \tag{5.106}$$

The characteristic polynomial of Δ is:

$$\Psi(s) = s^3 - s^2 \cdot \text{tr}\Delta + s \cdot \Gamma - |\Delta|, \tag{5.107}$$

where $\Gamma \equiv \sum_{i=1}^{3} M_{ii}$, and M_{ij} is the minor of element δ_{ij} (i.e. the determinant of the two-by-two submatrix obtained by deleting row i and column j from Δ). Clearly $\Psi(s)$ is a cubic equation which, in principle, features three characteristic roots, say ζ_1, ζ_2, and ζ_3. Since there is one jumping variable (e_t) and two predetermined variables (p_t and m_t), the model is saddle-point stable provided there is one unstable root (say $\zeta_2 > 1$) and two stable roots (featuring $|\zeta_1| < 1$ and $|\zeta_3| < 1$). Since it is much harder to characterize the roots of a cubic equation than it is for a quadratic equation not much analytical progress can be made here. Of course it is still possible to use the method of undetermined coefficients. As the reader will be asked to verify in a question in the book manual, the appropriate trial solution expresses e_t in terms of the variables p_t, m_t, u_t, and v_t:

$$e_t - \hat{e} = \pi_{e0} + \pi_{ep}(p_t - \hat{p}) + \pi_{em}(m_t - \bar{m}) + \pi_{eu}u_t + \pi_{ev}v_t, \tag{5.108}$$

where the π_{ej} parameters are to be determined.

The upshot of the discussion thus far is that the analytical pen-and-paper method grinds to a screeching halt even for a relatively low-dimensional model such as is given here. Of course Dynare has no trouble with this model at all. Indeed, the model file reported in Table 5.3 will do the job for us. Compared to Program05_01.mod only five adjustments need to be made to obtain Program05_02.mod:

- The money supply must be declared as an endogenous variable (see the var line in Block 1)

- The parameter μ must be declared (see the parameters line in Block 1)

- A value for μ must be given (see Block 2)

- The equation for the money supply rule must be specified in the model section.

- A starting value for the steady-state money supply is (optionally) given in the initval section.

Table 5.4 lists selected portions of the output from Program05_02.mod. The most notable features are as follows. First, there are indeed two stable characteristic roots ($\xi_1 = 0.8713$ and $\xi_3 = -0.3376$) and one unstable root ($\xi_2 = 2.5500$) as is required for saddle-point stability. Second, as we observe from the computed policy functions, Dynare confirms that the trial solution (5.108) is actually the correct one. Third, the asymptotic standard deviation is reduced a little bit under an active monetary policy of the form given in (5.104). As we conjectured above, as a result of its Keynesian feature of backward-looking price stickiness, the PIP does not hold in this model.

5.5   Punchlines

To most economists, one of the unsatisfactory aspects of the adaptive expectations hypothesis (AEH) is that it implies that agents make systematic mistakes along the entire adjustment path from the initial to the ultimate equilibrium. In the early 1960s, John Muth argued that such an outcome is difficult to reconcile with the predominant notion adopted throughout economics, namely that agents use scarce resources (like information) wisely. He formulated the rational expectations hypothesis (REH) which, in essence, requires the subjective expectation of households regarding a particular variable to be equal to the objective expectation for that variable conditional upon the information set available to the agent.

Muth's idea was introduced into the macroeconomic literature in the early 1970s by a number of prominent new classical economists. They argued that under the REH, monetary policy is ineffective (at influencing aggregate output and employment) because agents cannot be systematically fooled into supplying too much or too little labour. This is the so-called policy ineffectiveness proposition (PIP) which caused a big stir in the ranks of professional macroeconomists in the mid 1970s. Another implication of the REH is that, according to the Lucas critique, the then predominant macroeconometric models are useless for the task of evaluating the effects of different macroeconomic policies.

As was quickly pointed out by proponents of the New Keynesian school, the REH does not necessarily imply the validity of the PIP. Stanley Fischer demonstrated that if nominal wage contracts are set for more than one period in advance (and are not indexed) then even under rational expectations, monetary policy can (and indeed

Table 5.4. Selected output from the Dynare model file `Program05_02.mod`

```
>> dynare Program05_02


STEADY-STATE RESULTS:

y              1
R              5
e              -0.12
p              1
m              1
pstar          1
Rstar          5

EIGENVALUES:
          Modulus              Real            Imaginary

           0.3376            -0.3376                0
           0.8713             0.8713                0
            2.55               2.55                0


There are 1 eigenvalue(s) larger than 1 in modulus
for 1 forward-looking variable(s)

The rank condition is verified.


POLICY AND TRANSITION FUNCTIONS
                   y            R            e            p            m
Constant      1.000000     5.000000    -0.120000     1.000000     1.000000
y(-1)        -0.294165     0.411670    -0.316248    -0.058833    -0.500000
p(-1)        -0.860444     0.279112    -0.040666     0.827911            0
u             0.261480     0.522960     0.392220     0.052296            0
v             0.261480     0.522960    -0.607780     0.052296            0


THEORETICAL MOMENTS

VARIABLE      MEAN     STD. DEV.    VARIANCE
y            1.0000     0.2977      0.0886
R            5.0000     0.5496      0.3021
e           -0.1200     0.4216      0.1777
p            1.0000     0.0853      0.0073
m            1.0000     0.1489      0.0222
pstar        1.0000     0.2000      0.0400
Rstar        5.0000     1.0000      1.0000


Total computing time : 0h00m06s
>>
```

should) be used to stabilize the economy. Hence, the validity of the PIP hinges not so much on the REH but rather on the type of model that is used. If the REH is introduced in a classical model then the implications are classical whereas a Keynesian model with the REH yields Keynesian implications.

It is almost universally agreed that the PIP cannot be taken seriously, except perhaps as an extreme position taken to promote a discussion. Furthermore, due to the fact that Fischer and others demonstrated that the REH does not necessarily imply the PIP, acceptance of the REH as a modelling device is also almost universal. The Lucas critique is valid, but its empirical short-run relevance is seriously doubted by both theoretical econometricians (Favero and Hendry, 1992) and applied policy modellers. A reason for this lukewarm reception may be the absence of a credible theory of how agents learn new policy rules.

In the last part of this chapter we revisit the sticky-price model of a small open economy facing perfect capital mobility that was introduced in the previous chapter. In this discrete-time Dornbusch model the economy is continually hit by stochastic shocks originating from the rest of the world. Under rational expectations the model is saddle-path stable provided the domestic price is sufficiently sticky. The saddle path is a downward sloping relationship between the spot exchange rate and the predetermined price level with the international shocks acting as shift factors. With sticky prices both quantities and all "prices" (the exchange rate and the domestic interest and inflation rates) fluctuate as a result of the international shocks. The flexibility of exchange rates and the domestic interest rate does not insulate the small open economy from international shocks. In contrast, with perfectly flexible prices (the absence of price stickiness) these shocks would have no effect at all on output, and the entire adjustment would be borne by adjustments in the exchange rate as well as the domestic interest rate and price level.

The chapter demonstrates that the analytical analysis of discrete-time stochastic models quickly becomes intractable. Whereas in continuous-time models it suffices to establish the *signs* of characteristic roots, in discrete-time models the *absolute magnitudes* of these roots (relative to unity) are crucial. This explains why the use of numerical methods is virtually unavoidable, even in relatively low-dimensional systems of expectational difference equations. Fortunately an easy-to-use software package is available in the form of Dynare. This package is introduced in the context of the Dornbusch model in which the policy maker, instead of staying passive, follows a countercyclical monetary policy rule to reduce output fluctuations.

Further reading

The classic articles setting out the rational expectations approach in a macroeconomic context are Lucas (1972, 1973), Sargent (1973), Sargent and Wallace (1975, 1976), and Barro (1976). Papers stressing the stickiness of wages or prices include Fischer (1977), Phelps and Taylor (1977), Barro (1977), Gray (1976, 1978), and Taylor (1979, 1980). For good surveys of the rational expectations literature, see Shiller (1978), McCallum (1980), Maddock and Carter (1982), Sheffrin (1996), and Attfield et al. (1985). General solution methods for linear rational expectations models are discussed by, among others, Taylor (1986), Blanchard and Kahn (1980), King and Watson (1998, 2000), Klein (2000), and McCallum (1998). Several key articles on the rational expectations approach are collected in Lucas and Sargent (1981), Miller (1994), and Hoover (1992). The interested reader should also consult the collections of essays by Lucas (1981) and Sargent (1993). See Frydman and Phelps (1983) for a collection of essays on learning under rational expectations. On non-uniqueness in linear rational expectations models, see Blanchard and Kahn (1980, p. 1308), and McCallum (1983a, 1999).

As was acknowledged by Lucas himself, an early statement of the Lucas critique is found in Marschak (1953). For an early application of the rational expectations hypothesis to finance, see Samuelson (1965). McCallum (1983b) presents a model of the liquidity trap and finds the rational expectations solution. The pre-REH literature on optimal stabilization policy is well surveyed by Turnovsky (1977, chs. 13-14). See also the classic analysis by Poole (1970) on the optimal choice of policy instruments within the stochastic IS-LM model. For an early analysis of economic policy under rational expectations, see Fischer (1980b).

Michel Juillard and colleagues have developed Dynare, a software package designed to perform computer simulations for stochastic dynamic general equilibrium models. At the time of writing, the most recent version of Dynare is version 4.4.3. It can be downloaded free of charge from the Dynare website:

`http://www.dynare.org.`

On this website you also find the Reference Manual, see Adjemian et al. (2011).

Chapter 6

The government budget deficit

The purpose of this chapter is to discuss a number of issues relating to the government budget constraint. The specific goals for this chapter are:

1. To explain and assess the validity of the Ricardian equivalence theorem.

2. To explain the notion of tax smoothing and the golden financing rule.

3. To show how the fiscal stance of the government should be measured.

An important secondary aim of this chapter is the introduction and analysis of a simple two-period optimizing model of household consumption (and labour supply) behaviour. In this chapter the forward-looking theory of household behaviour is shown to be very a useful tool with which the intuition behind the Ricardian equivalence theorem can be explained. But, as shall be demonstrated below, the ideas introduced here are much more widely applicable. Concepts such as intertemporal utility optimization and consumption smoothing form vital elements of modern microeconomically founded macroeconomics.

6.1 Ricardian equivalence

The Ricardian equivalence theorem was formulated, as the name suggests, by the British classical economist David Ricardo (1817, p. 245), who immediately dismissed it as being irrelevant in practice. In an influential paper, however, the new classical economist Robert Barro (1974) forcefully argued that the Ricardian equivalence theorem is worthy of professional attention and yields important policy prescriptions.

Loosely speaking, the Ricardian equivalence theorem can be stated as follows: for a given path of government spending the particular method used to finance these expenditures does not matter, in the sense that real consumption, investment, and output are unaffected. Specifically, whether the expenditures are financed by means of taxation or debt, the real consumption and investment plans of the private sector are not influenced. In that sense government debt and taxes are equivalent.

In other words, government debt is simply viewed as delayed taxation: if the government decides to finance its deficit by issuing debt today, private agents will save more in order to be able to redeem this debt in the future through higher taxation levels. Consequently, if the Ricardian equivalence theorem is valid, the Blinder and Solow (1973) model (discussed extensively in Chapter 3) is seriously flawed.

In that model real private consumption (in equation (3.43)) depends on net wealth, *which includes government debt!* Under Ricardian equivalence, government debt in the hands of the public should not be counted as net wealth since it is exactly matched by the equal-sized liability in the form of future taxation. In order to explain and evaluate the Ricardian equivalence theorem we first need to build a simple dynamic model of household consumption.

6.1.1   A simple model

Suppose that historical time from now into the indefinite future is split into two segments. The first segment (called period 1) is the present, and the second segment (called period 2) is the future (obviously, by construction, there is no period 3). There is perfect foresight on the part of both households and the government. We look at the behaviour of the representative household first. It lives as long as the government does, and achieves utility by consuming goods in both periods. Labour supply is exogenous and household income consists of exogenous "manna from heaven". Lifetime utility V is given by:

$$V = U(C_1) + \frac{1}{1+\rho}U(C_2), \qquad \rho > 0, \tag{6.1}$$

where C_t is consumption in period t ($= 1, 2$), $U(\cdot)$ is the instantaneous utility (or "felicity") function, and ρ is the pure rate of time preference, representing the effects of "impatience". The higher ρ, the heavier future instantaneous utility is discounted, and the more impatient is the household. The felicity function has the usual properties, i.e. $U'(\cdot) > 0$ and $U''(\cdot) < 0$. At the end of period 0 (i.e. the "past"), the household has financial assets amounting in real terms to A_0 over which it also receives interest payments at the beginning of period 1 equal to $r_0 A_0$, where r_0 is the real rate of interest on period 0 savings. The exogenous non-interest income payments are denoted by Y_1 and Y_2, respectively, so that the *periodic budget restrictions* in the two periods are:

$$A_1 = (1 + r_0)A_0 + (1 - \theta_1)Y_1 - C_1, \tag{6.2}$$
$$A_2 = (1 + r_1)A_1 + (1 - \theta_2)Y_2 - C_2 = 0, \tag{6.3}$$

where r_1 is the interest rate on savings in period 1, θ_1 and θ_2 are the proportional tax rates on non-asset income in the two periods, and $A_2 = 0$ because it makes no sense for the household to die with a positive amount of financial assets ($A_2 \leq 0$), and it is also assumed that it is impossible for the household to die in debt ($A_2 \geq 0$). (Below, we modify the model and show that households with children may wish to leave an inheritance.) Note that (6.2)–(6.3) incorporate the assumption that interest income is untaxed.

If the household can freely borrow or lend at the going interest rate r_1, then A_1 can have either sign, and equations (6.2)–(6.3) can be consolidated into a single *lifetime budget restriction*. Technically, this is done by substituting out A_1 from (6.2)–(6.3):

$$[A_1 =] \quad \frac{C_2 - (1 - \theta_2)Y_2}{1 + r_1} = (1 + r_0)A_0 + (1 - \theta_1)Y_1 - C_1 \quad \Rightarrow$$

$$C_1 + \frac{C_2}{1 + r_1} = (1 + r_0)A_0 + H, \tag{6.4}$$

where the right-hand side of (6.4) represents total wealth, which is the sum of initial *financial wealth* inclusive of interest received, $(1 + r_0)A_0$, and *human wealth, H*:

$$H \equiv (1 - \theta_1)Y_1 + \frac{(1 - \theta_2)Y_2}{1 + r_1}. \tag{6.5}$$

Equation (6.4) says that the *present value* of consumption expenditure during life must equal total wealth.

In order to demonstrate the Ricardian equivalence theorem, we need to introduce the government and its budget restriction. We start as simple as possible by assuming that the government buys goods for its own consumption (G_1 and G_2), and finances its expenditure by taxes and/or debt. There is no money in the model, so money financing is impossible. The government, like the household, exists for two periods, and can borrow or lend at the interest rate r_1. In parallel with (6.2)–(6.3), the government's periodic budget restrictions are:

$$[D_1 \equiv] \quad r_0 B_0 + G_1 - \theta_1 Y_1 = B_1 - B_0, \tag{6.6}$$
$$[D_2 \equiv] \quad r_1 B_1 + G_2 - \theta_2 Y_2 = B_2 - B_1 = -B_1, \tag{6.7}$$

where D_t and B_t denote, respectively, the deficit and government debt in period $t (= 1, 2)$, respectively, and $B_2 = 0$ because the government, like the household, cannot default on its debt and is assumed to remain solvent (no banana republic!). Using the same trick as before, equations (6.6)–(6.7) can be consolidated into a single government budget restriction:

$$[B_1 =] \quad (1 + r_0)B_0 + G_1 - \theta_1 Y_1 = \frac{\theta_2 Y_2 - G_2}{1 + r_1} \quad \Rightarrow$$
$$(1 + r_0)B_0 + G_1 + \frac{G_2}{1 + r_1} = \theta_1 Y_1 + \frac{\theta_2 Y_2}{1 + r_1}, \tag{6.8}$$

where the left-hand side of (6.8) represents the present value of the net liabilities of the government, and the right-hand side is the present value of net income of the government (i.e. the tax revenue).

Since government bonds are the only financial asset in the toy economy, household borrowing (lending) can only take the form of negative (positive) holdings of government bonds. Hence, equilibrium in the financial capital market implies that:

$$A_t = B_t, \tag{6.9}$$

for $t = 0, 1, 2$. Formally, equilibrium in the capital market determines the equilibrium interest rates, r_0 and r_1.

The first demonstration of the Ricardian equivalence theorem is obtained by solving the consolidated government budget restriction (6.8) for $(1 + r_0)B_0$, and substituting the result into the lifetime household budget restriction (6.4) taking (6.9) into account:

$$\begin{aligned}
C_1 + \frac{C_2}{1 + r_1} &= (1 + r_0)B_0 + (1 - \theta_1)Y_1 + \frac{(1 - \theta_2)Y_2}{1 + r_1} \\
&= \theta_1 Y_1 + \frac{\theta_2 Y_2}{1 + r_1} - G_1 - \frac{G_2}{1 + r_1} + (1 - \theta_1)Y_1 + \frac{(1 - \theta_2)Y_2}{1 + r_1} \\
&= Y_1 - G_1 + \frac{Y_2 - G_2}{1 + r_1} \equiv \Omega. \tag{6.10}
\end{aligned}$$

The final expression shows that the tax parameters drop out of the household's lifetime budget restriction altogether. Only the present value of (exogenously given) government spending affects the level of net wealth of the household. Consequently, the choices of C_1 and C_2 do not depend on the tax parameters θ_1 and θ_2 either. The way in which the government finances its expenditure has no real effects on consumption.

So if consumption plans are unaffected by the timing of taxation, then what is? The answer is, of course, household saving. In order to demonstrate this, and to facilitate the subsequent discussion, we use a specific functional form for the felicity function $U(\cdot)$, one that yields very simple expressions for the optimal consumption and saving plans:

$$U(C_t) = \ln C_t. \tag{6.11}$$

(The most general version of the two-period consumption model is studied in Intermezzo 6.1.) The household chooses C_1 and C_2 such that (6.1) is maximized subject to (6.10) and given the felicity function (6.11). Again the optimality conditions can be obtained by using the Lagrange multiplier method. The Lagrangian is:

$$\mathcal{L} \equiv \ln C_1 + \frac{1}{1+\rho} \ln C_2 + \lambda \left[\Omega - C_1 - \frac{C_2}{1+r_1} \right], \tag{6.12}$$

so that the first-order conditions are:

$$\frac{\partial \mathcal{L}}{\partial C_1} = \frac{1}{C_1} - \lambda = 0, \tag{6.13}$$

$$\frac{\partial \mathcal{L}}{\partial C_2} = \frac{1}{(1+\rho)C_2} - \frac{\lambda}{1+r_1} = 0, \tag{6.14}$$

and the third condition, $\partial \mathcal{L}/\partial \lambda = 0$, yields the budget restriction (6.10).[1] By combining (6.13)–(6.14), the so-called *consumption Euler equation* is obtained:

$$\lambda = \frac{1}{C_1} = \frac{1+r_1}{(1+\rho)C_2} \quad \Rightarrow \quad \frac{C_2}{C_1} = \frac{1+r_1}{1+\rho}. \tag{6.15}$$

In words, equation (6.15) can be understood as follows. Assume, for example, that the interest rate exceeds the pure rate of time preference, i.e. $r_1 > \rho$. Then it follows from (6.15) that the household finds it optimal to set $C_2/C_1 > 1$, i.e. $C_2 > C_1$. The household wishes to enjoy relatively high consumption in the second period. This is understandable in view of the fact that a low value of ρ (relative to r_1) implies that the household has a lot of patience, and hence a strong willingness to postpone consumption. This is the intertemporal substitution mechanism in consumption.

Equation (6.15) determines the *optimal time profile* of consumption, i.e. it shows consumption in the future relative to consumption now. The *level* of consumption is obtained by substituting (6.15) into the household budget restriction (6.10):

$$C_1 = \frac{1+\rho}{2+\rho} \Omega, \qquad C_2 = \frac{1+r_1}{2+\rho} \Omega. \tag{6.16}$$

---

[1] The *optimized* value of the Lagrange multiplier has a straightforward economic interpretation. It represents the marginal lifetime utility of lifetime wealth, i.e. $\lambda = dV/d\Omega$. In words, if a Martian gives the household $d\Omega$ extra lifetime wealth then optimal consumption plans will be changed and as a result lifetime utility will rise by $dV = \lambda d\Omega$.

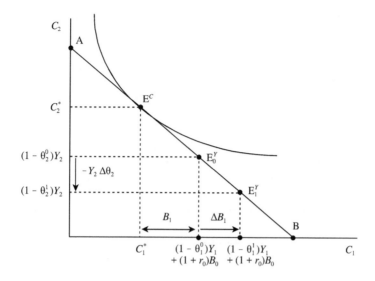

Figure 6.1: Ricardian equivalence experiment

The expression for household saving (S_1) is determined by the identity $S_1 \equiv A_1 - A_0 = B_1 - B_0$, or:

$$S_1 = r_0 B_0 + (1 - \theta_1)Y_1 - \frac{1+\rho}{2+\rho}\,\Omega, \tag{6.17}$$

from which we see immediately that the tax rate θ_1 does not vanish from the expression for household saving in the first period.

Now consider the following Ricardian experiment. The government reduces the tax rate in the first period ($\Delta\theta_1 < 0$) but keeps its goods consumption (G_1 and G_2) constant. The tax cut may be quite substantial so we do not rely on differentiation—we use the notation $\Delta\theta_1$ rather than $d\theta_1$ to alert the reader to this fact. We proceed under the assumption—verified below—that the interest rate stays constant, i.e. $\Delta r_1 = 0$. Then equation (6.17) implies that

$$\Delta S_1 = -Y_1 \, \Delta\theta_1 > 0, \tag{6.18}$$

(because $\Delta\Omega = 0$) but the government budget restriction (6.8) implies that taxes in the second period must be increased:

$$Y_1 \, \Delta\theta_1 + \frac{Y_2}{1+r_1} \, \Delta\theta_2 = 0 \quad \Rightarrow \quad \Delta\theta_2 = -\frac{(1+r_1)Y_1}{Y_2} \, \Delta\theta_1 > 0, \tag{6.19}$$

as the present value of government liabilities are unchanged by assumption. Hence, the reaction of the household to this Ricardian experiment is to increase its saving in the first period ($\Delta S_1 > 0$) in order to be able to use the extra amount saved plus interest in the second period to pay the additional taxes ($\Delta\theta_2 > 0$). In Figure 6.1, the Ricardian experiment has been illustrated graphically.

The initial *income endowment* point is at E_0^y. It represents the point at which the household makes no use of debt in the first period (i.e. $A_1 = B_1 = 0$) and simply consumes according to (6.2)–(6.3). Since the household can freely lend/borrow at the going rate of interest r_1, however, it can choose any (C_1, C_2) combination along the budget line AB. Suppose that the optimal consumption point is at E^C, where there is a tangency between an indifference curve and the budget line. The optimal consumption levels are given by C_1^* and C_2^*, respectively. The household saves B_1 in the first period, and receives $(1+r_1)B_1$ in interest income in the second period. As a result of the Ricardian experiment ($\Delta\theta_1 < 0$), non-asset income rises in the first period and falls in the second period, but the net wealth of the household (Ω) is unchanged. Hence, all that happens is that the income endowment point shifts *along* the given budget line in a south-easterly direction to E_1^y. The optimal consumption point does not change, however, since nothing of importance has changed for the household. Hence, the only thing that happens is that the household increases its saving (by an amount ΔB_1) in the first period and it does so by purchasing more bonds from the government. Demand for and supply of government debt expand by the same amount so that no change in the interest rate, r_1, is required to maintain capital market equilibrium.

There are many theoretical objections that can be levelled at the Ricardian equivalence theorem. In the next subsections we discuss the most important theoretical reasons causing Ricardian equivalence to fail. The interested reader is referred to the symposium on the budget deficit (published in the *Journal of Economic Perspectives*) for further details; see in particular the contributions by Barro (1989) and Bernheim (1989).

Intermezzo 6.1

The two-period consumption model. Because the two-period consumption model has played such an important role in the macroeconomic literature, it pays to have a very good understanding of its basic properties. Assume that the representative household's lifetime utility function is given in general terms by:

$$V = V(C_1, C_2), \tag{a}$$

where C_t is consumption in period t, and we assume positive but diminishing marginal utility of consumption in both periods, i.e. $V_1 \equiv \partial V/\partial C_1 > 0$, $V_2 \equiv \partial V/\partial C_2 > 0$, $V_{11} \equiv \partial^2 V/\partial C_1^2 < 0$, and $V_{22} \equiv \partial^2 V/\partial C_2^2 < 0$. Note that (6.1) is a special case of (a) incorporating a zero cross derivative $V_{12} \equiv \partial^2 V/\partial C_1 \partial C_2$. In the general case considered here, no such restriction is placed on V_{12}. To avoid uninteresting corner solutions, however, we assume that indifference curves bulge towards the origin, i.e. $V_{11}V_{22} - V_{12}^2 > 0$.

Abstracting from taxes, the household's periodic budget identities are given by $A_1 + C_1 = (1+r_0)A_0 + Y_1$ and $C_2 = (1+r_1)A_1 + Y_2$ which can be consolidated to yield the lifetime budget constraint:

$$C_1 + \frac{C_2}{1+r_1} = (1+r_0)A_0 + \left[Y_1 + \frac{Y_2}{1+r_1}\right] \equiv \Omega, \tag{b}$$

where Y_t is exogenous non-interest income in period t, A_0 is initial financial wealth, Ω is initial total wealth (i.e. the sum of financial and human wealth), and r_t is the interest rate in period t. The household chooses C_1 and C_2 in order to maximize lifetime utility (a) subject to the lifetime budget constraint (b). The first-order conditions are given by (b) and the Euler equation:

$$\frac{V_1(C_1, C_2)}{V_2(C_1, C_2)} = 1 + r_1, \tag{c}$$

where we indicate explicitly that V_i in general depends on both C_1 and C_2 (because $V_{12} \neq 0$ is not excluded a priori).

Equations (b)–(c) define implicit functions relating consumption in the two periods to the interest rate and total wealth which can be written in general terms as $C_t = C_t(\Omega, r_1)$ for $t = 1, 2$. To find the partial derivatives of these implicit functions we employ our usual trick and totally differentiate (b)–(c) to obtain the following matrix expression:

$$\Delta \begin{bmatrix} dC_1 \\ dC_2 \end{bmatrix} = \begin{bmatrix} 1 \\ 0 \end{bmatrix} d\Omega + \begin{bmatrix} \frac{C_2}{(1+r_1)^2} \\ V_2 \end{bmatrix} dr_1, \tag{d}$$

where the matrix Δ on the left-hand side of (d) is defined as:

$$\Delta \equiv \begin{bmatrix} 1 & \frac{1}{1+r_1} \\ V_{11} - (1+r_1)V_{12} & V_{12} - (1+r_1)V_{22} \end{bmatrix}, \tag{e}$$

and we have already incorporated Young's theorem according to which $V_{12} = V_{21}$ (Chiang, 1984, p. 313). The second-order conditions for utility maximization ensure that the determinant of Δ is strictly positive (see Chiang (1984, pp. 400–408) for details), i.e. $|\Delta| > 0$. This means that the implicit function theorem can be used (Chiang, 1984, p. 210).

Let us first consider the effects of a marginal change in wealth. We obtain from (d):

$$\frac{\partial C_1}{\partial \Omega} = \frac{V_{12} - (1+r_1)V_{22}}{|\Delta|} \gtrless 0, \tag{f}$$

$$\frac{\partial C_2}{\partial \Omega} = \frac{(1+r_1)V_{12} - V_{11}}{|\Delta|} \gtrless 0. \tag{g}$$

Several observations can be made regarding these expressions. First, the effect of wealth changes on consumption in both periods is ambiguous in general. Second, if lifetime utility satisfies $V_{12} \geq 0$ then $\partial C_t / \partial \Omega > 0$ for $t = 1, 2$, and present and future consumption are both normal goods. Third, if $V_{12} < 0$ then either present consumption or future consumption may be an inferior good ($\partial C_i / \partial \Omega < 0$). It follows from (b), however, that at most one good can be inferior, i.e.:

$$\frac{\partial C_1}{\partial \Omega} + \frac{1}{1+r_1} \frac{\partial C_2}{\partial \Omega} = 1. \tag{h}$$

Next we consider the effects of a marginal change in the interest rate r_1. It follows from the budget restriction (b) that a change in r_1 not only changes the relative price of future consumption (on the left-hand side of (b)) but also affects the value of human wealth (and thus total wealth) given in square brackets on the right-hand side of (b). Indeed, in view of the definition of Ω, we find $\partial\Omega/\partial r_1 = -Y_2/(1+r_1)^2 < 0$, i.e. an increase in the interest rate reduces the value of human wealth because future wage income is discounted more heavily. By taking this human-wealth effect into account we obtain the following partial derivatives from (d):

$$\frac{\partial C_1}{\partial r_1} = \frac{V_{12} - (1+r_1)V_{22}}{|\Delta|}\frac{A_1}{1+r_1} - \frac{1}{|\Delta|}\frac{V_2}{1+r_1} \gtrless 0, \tag{i}$$

$$\frac{\partial C_2}{\partial r_1} = \frac{(1+r_1)V_{12} - V_{11}}{|\Delta|}\frac{A_1}{1+r_1} + \frac{1}{|\Delta|}V_2 \gtrless 0, \tag{j}$$

where we have used the second period budget identity, $(1+r_1)A_1 = C_2 - Y_2$, to simplify these expressions. Again several observations can be made regarding the expressions in (i)–(j). First, without further restrictions on V_{12} and A_1 the effects are ambiguous. By differentiating the lifetime budget equation (b) we find:

$$\frac{\partial C_1}{\partial r_1} + \frac{1}{1+r_1}\frac{\partial C_2}{\partial r_1} = \frac{A_1}{1+r_1}, \tag{k}$$

from which we deduce that for an agent who chooses to save in the first period ($A_1 > 0$), either present or future consumption (or both) rise if the interest rate rises. Second, if $A_1 > 0$ and $V_{12} \geq 0$ then $\partial C_1/\partial r_1 \gtrless 0$ and $\partial C_2/\partial r_1 > 0$. Third, if the agent's utility maximum happens to coincide with its endowment point (so that $A_1 = 0$) then it neither saves nor dissaves in the first period and it follows that $\partial C_1/\partial r_1 < 0$ and $\partial C_2/\partial r_1 > 0$.

In the literature it is often assumed that the utility function is *homothetic*. A homothetic utility function can be written as $V(C_1, C_2) = G(H(C_1, C_2))$, where $G(\cdot)$ is a strictly increasing function and $H(C_1, C_2)$ is homogeneous of degree one in C_1 and C_2 (see e.g. Sydsæter and Hammond, 1995, p. 573). We recall the following properties of such functions from Intermezzo 4.3 in Chapter 4: (P1) $H_1 C_1 + H_2 C_2 = H$, (P2) H_1 and H_2 are homogeneous of degree zero in C_1 and C_2, (P3) $H_{12} = -(C_1/C_2)H_{11} = -(C_2/C_1)H_{22}$ and thus $H_{11} = (C_2/C_1)^2 H_{22}$, and (P4) $\sigma_{12} \equiv -d\ln(C_1/C_2)/d\ln(H_1/H_2) = H_1 H_2/(HH_{12}) \geq 0$. Since $H_{11} < 0$ and $H_{22} < 0$ it follows from (P3) that $H_{12} > 0$ and from (f)–(g) that present and future consumption are both normal goods. To see why this is the case, we note that (c) simplifies to $H_1/H_2 = 1 + r_1$ so that V_{11}, V_{12}, and V_{22} in (d)–(f) are replaced by, respectively, H_{11}, H_{12}, and H_{22}.

To study the effect of a change in the interest rate we note that the first-order condition (c) becomes $H_1/H_2 = 1 + r_1$. Since H_1 and H_2 are homogeneous of degree zero, this Euler equation pins down a unique C_1/C_2 ratio as a function of $1 + r_1$. By loglinearizing the Euler equation (c) and the budget restriction (b) (holding $(1+r_0)A_0$, Y_1, and Y_2 constant) we obtain the following expression:

$$\begin{bmatrix} \omega_1 & 1-\omega_1 \\ -1 & 1 \end{bmatrix}\begin{bmatrix} dC_1/C_1 \\ dC_2/C_2 \end{bmatrix} = \begin{bmatrix} A_1/\Omega \\ \sigma_{12} \end{bmatrix}\frac{dr_1}{1+r_1}, \tag{l}$$

where $\omega_1 \equiv C_1/\Omega$ and $1 - \omega_1 \equiv C_2/[(1+r_1)\Omega]$ are the budget shares of, respectively, first- and second-period consumption. Solving (l) we obtain the comparative static effects:

$$\frac{\partial C_1}{\partial r_1} = \frac{C_1}{1+r_1}\left[(1-\omega_1) - \frac{Y_2}{(1+r_1)\Omega} - (1-\omega_1)\sigma_{12}\right], \qquad \text{(m)}$$

$$\frac{\partial C_2}{\partial r_1} = \frac{C_2}{1+r_1}\left[(1-\omega_1) - \frac{Y_2}{(1+r_1)\Omega} + \omega_1\sigma_{12}\right], \qquad \text{(n)}$$

where we have also used $(1+r_1)A_1 = C_2 - Y_2$. The three terms appearing in square brackets on the right-hand sides of (m) and (n) represent, respectively, the *income effect*, the *human-wealth effect*, and the *substitution effect* (see also Obstfeld and Rogoff (1996, p. 30) for this terminology). We illustrate these effects in Figures A and B.

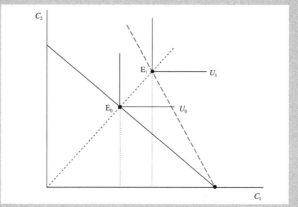

Figure A: Special case with $\sigma_{12} = Y_2 = 0$

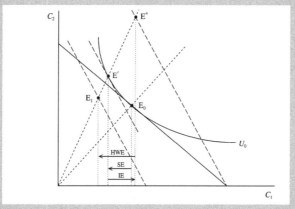

Figure B: General case $\sigma_{12} > 0$ and $Y_2 > 0$

In both figures, the ultimate effect of an increase in the interest rate r_1 is given by the move from E_0 to E_1. This total effect can be decomposed in the usual Hicksian fashion. In doing so we exploit the fact that for homothetic utility functions the slope of the indifference curves is the same along a straight ray from the origin. In Figure A we study a very simple case for which the substitution elasticity between current and future consumption is zero ($\sigma_{12} = 0$, so that indifference curves are right angles), and for which there is no future non-interest income ($Y_2 = 0$). The increase in the interest rate rotates the budget constraint in a clockwise fashion, and moves the optimum point from E_0 to E_1. Both C_1 and C_2 increase, and the move from E_0 to E_1 is due to the income effect (IE) only.

In Figure B we study the general case, for which $\sigma_{12} > 0$ and $Y_2 > 0$. Again the increase in r_1 changes the optimum from E_0 to E_1. Two wealth expansion paths are drawn in Figure B, one for the old and one for the new interest rate. The move from E_0 to E' is the substitution effect (SE) and the move from E' to E'' is the income effect (IE). If the household were to have no non-interest income in the second period ($Y_2 = 0$) this would be all as the human-wealth effect would be absent. If Y_2 is positive, however, the increase in the interest rate reduces human wealth and shifts the budget restriction inward. Hence, the human-wealth effect (HWE) is represented by the move from E'' to E_1.

****

6.1.2 Distorting taxes

Up to this point we have assumed that non-interest income in the two periods is exogenous. It is easy to imagine that, for example due to an endogenous labour supply decision, this type of income depends on the tax rate on labour income (see Chapter 1 and below). If that is the case, we should write the non-asset income points as $Y_1(\theta_1, \theta_2)$ and $Y_2(\theta_1, \theta_2)$, and the path of taxes may directly influence the income endowment point, and potentially also the level of net household wealth. Consequently, Ricardian equivalence should be expected to fail. In the remainder of this section we show how labour supply can be endogenized in a dynamic setting.

In the two-period setting, the intertemporal labour supply model could take the following format. We change the lifetime utility function (6.1) to:

$$V = U(C_1, 1 - N_1) + \frac{1}{1+\rho} U(C_2, 1 - N_2), \qquad \rho > 0, \tag{6.20}$$

where N_t is labour supply (and $1 - N_t$ is leisure) in period t. Just as in Chapter 1, the household has a time endowment of unity, which it must allocate over leisure and work. The felicity function is given by:

$$U(C_t, 1 - N_t) = \ln \left(C_t^\varepsilon [1 - N_t]^{1-\varepsilon} \right), \qquad 0 < \varepsilon < 1. \tag{6.21}$$

To keep matters simple, the *sub-felicity function*, $u(C_t, 1 - N_t) \equiv C_t^\varepsilon [1 - N_t]^{1-\varepsilon}$, takes the Cobb-Douglas form, implying that the *intra*temporal substitution elasticity between consumption and leisure is equal to one.[2] As a result, the felicity function itself is loglinear in C_t and $1 - N_t$.

---

[2]The intratemporal substitution elasticity, $\sigma_{C,1-N}$, measures the degree of substitutability between con-

The periodic budget constraints are still given by (6.2)–(6.3), but with Y_t replaced by $w_t N_t$, where w_t is the gross (before-tax) real wage rate in period t.[3] The lifetime budget constraint is thus:

$$C_1 + \frac{C_2}{1+r_1} = (1+r_0)A_0 + (1-\theta_1)w_1 N_1 + \frac{(1-\theta_2)w_2 N_2}{1+r_1}. \tag{6.22}$$

As it turns out, a rather useful trick is to treat the labour supply decision as a purchase decision of leisure. Intuitively, by supplying N_t units of labour to the labour market, the household implicitly "buys" $1 - N_t$ units of leisure from itself. Straightforward manipulation of (6.22) yields the consolidated budget constraint in terms of spending on goods and leisure:

$$C_1 + (1-\theta_1)w_1[1-N_1] + \frac{C_2 + (1-\theta_2)w_2[1-N_2]}{1+r_1} = (1+r_0)A_0 + \bar{H} \equiv \bar{\Omega}, \tag{6.23}$$

where $\bar{\Omega}$ is redefined total wealth and $\bar{H}$ is redefined human wealth:

$$\bar{H} \equiv (1-\theta_1)w_1 + \frac{(1-\theta_2)w_2}{1+r_1}. \tag{6.24}$$

Intuitively, $\bar{H}$ is the after-tax market value of the household's time endowment in present-value terms.

The household chooses C_1, C_2, $1-N_1$, and $1-N_2$ in order to maximize (6.20) subject to (6.23) and noting the felicity function (6.21). The Lagrangian for this optimization problem is:

$$\mathcal{L} \equiv \varepsilon \ln C_1 + (1-\varepsilon) \ln(1-N_1) + \frac{\varepsilon}{1+\rho} \ln C_2 + \frac{1-\varepsilon}{1+\rho} \ln(1-N_2)$$

$$+ \lambda \left[\bar{\Omega} - C_1 - (1-\theta_1)w_1[1-N_1] - \frac{C_2 + (1-\theta_2)w_2[1-N_2]}{1+r_1} \right], \tag{6.25}$$

and the (interesting) first-order conditions are:

$$\frac{\partial \mathcal{L}}{\partial C_1} = \frac{\varepsilon}{C_1} - \lambda = 0, \tag{6.26}$$

$$\frac{\partial \mathcal{L}}{\partial [1-N_1]} = \frac{1-\varepsilon}{1-N_1} - \lambda(1-\theta_1)w_1 = 0, \tag{6.27}$$

$$\frac{\partial \mathcal{L}}{\partial C_2} = \frac{\varepsilon}{(1+\rho)C_2} - \frac{\lambda}{1+r_1} = 0, \tag{6.28}$$

$$\frac{\partial \mathcal{L}}{\partial [1-N_2]} = \frac{1-\varepsilon}{(1+\rho)[1-N_2]} - \frac{\lambda(1-\theta_2)w_2}{1+r_1} = 0. \tag{6.29}$$

---

sumption and leisure in the same time period. For a linear homogeneous subfelicity function, $\sigma_{C,1-N}$ is defined as:

$$\sigma_{C,1-N} \equiv \frac{u_C u_{1-N}}{u \cdot u_{C,1-N}}.$$

For $u(C_t, 1-N_t)$ we easily obtain $\sigma_{C,1-N} = 1$. See also Intermezzo 4.3 in Chapter 4 for a definition of the substitution elasticity in the context of production theory.

[3]In the absence of physical capital, labour is the only production factor and the constant returns to scale production function can be written as $Y_t = w_0 N_t$. Perfectly competitive firm behaviour ensures that $w_t = w_0$ for $t = 1, 2$, i.e. in the absence of technological change w_0 and thus the real wage rates, w_1 and w_2, are constants.

(As before, the condition, $\partial \mathcal{L} / \partial \lambda = 0$, just gives us back the budget restriction (6.23).)

It is clear from (6.26)–(6.29) that the solutions for C_t and $1 - N_t$ can all be expressed in terms of the Lagrange multiplier, λ, and the relevant relative price terms. We can thus use the following solution method. First, we substitute the first-order conditions into (6.23) and solve for $1/\lambda$. After some steps we obtain:

$$\bar{\Omega} = C_1 + (1 - \theta_1) w_1 [1 - N_1] + \frac{C_2 + (1 - \theta_2) w_2 [1 - N_2]}{1 + r_1}$$

$$= \frac{\varepsilon}{\lambda} + \frac{1 - \varepsilon}{\lambda} + \frac{\varepsilon}{\lambda (1 + \rho)} + \frac{1 - \varepsilon}{\lambda (1 + \rho)} = \frac{2 + \rho}{1 + \rho} \frac{1}{\lambda} \quad \Leftrightarrow$$

$$\frac{1}{\lambda} = \frac{1 + \rho}{2 + \rho} \bar{\Omega}. \tag{6.30}$$

Hence, in this simple dynamic consumption-labour-supply model, the Lagrange multiplier, representing the marginal utility of lifetime wealth, is inversely related to the total wealth level itself.

In the second step, we use (6.30) in (6.26)–(6.29) to obtain the solutions that we are looking for:

$$C_1 = \varepsilon \frac{1 + \rho}{2 + \rho} \bar{\Omega}, \qquad C_2 = \varepsilon \frac{1 + r_1}{2 + \rho} \bar{\Omega}, \tag{6.31}$$

$$(1 - \theta_1) w_1 [1 - N_1] = (1 - \varepsilon) \frac{1 + \rho}{2 + \rho} \bar{\Omega}, \tag{6.32}$$

$$(1 - \theta_2) w_2 [1 - N_2] = (1 - \varepsilon) \frac{1 + r_1}{2 + \rho} \bar{\Omega}. \tag{6.33}$$

Several points are worth noting about these expressions. First, the consumption expressions in (6.31) are very similar to the ones for the basic model as stated in (6.16). The key difference lies in the fact that only part of total wealth, $\varepsilon \bar{\Omega}$, enters the expressions in (6.31). This is not surprising, in view of the fact that the household now spends on goods *and* leisure in the extended model. Note, however, that the Euler equation for consumption implied by the two expressions in (6.31) is the same as in the basic model (see (6.15) above). Second, the expressions in (6.32)–(6.33) show that the household spends constant fractions of total wealth on leisure. Note furthermore that (6.32) and (6.33), taken in combination, imply an Euler equation for leisure demand (and thus implicitly for labour supply) in the two periods:

$$\frac{1 - N_2}{1 - N_1} = \frac{1 + r_1}{1 + \rho} \cdot \frac{1 - \theta_1}{1 - \theta_2} \cdot \frac{w_1}{w_2}. \tag{6.34}$$

The optimal intertemporal division of leisure consumption is governed by the product of three ratios on the right-hand side of (6.34), namely the interest-impatience ratio (first term), the relative-tax ratio (second term), and the relative gross-wage ratio (third term). Holding constant the last two ratios, an increase in the interest rate boosts the interest-impatience ratio and induces the household to adopt a steeper time profile for leisure, i.e. to postpone current leisure consumption to the future (and to work relatively hard in the current period). Similarly, holding constant the interest ratio, an increase in either the relative tax ratio or the relative gross-wage ratio prompts households to work relatively hard in the current period (when taxes are relatively low or gross wages are relatively high). The mechanism just described is called the intertemporal substitution effect in labour supply. It plays a vital role in the real business cycle models studied in Chapter 18 below.

By using (6.32)–(6.33) and (6.23)–(6.24), we find that the labour supply model yields the following expressions for pre-tax non-interest income in the two periods:

$$Y_1 \equiv w_1 N_1 = w_1 \frac{1 + \varepsilon(1 + \rho)}{2 + \rho} - \frac{1 - \varepsilon}{1 - \theta_1} \frac{1 + \rho}{2 + \rho} \left[(1 + r_0) A_0 + \frac{(1 - \theta_2) w_2}{1 + r_1} \right],$$

(6.35)

$$Y_2 \equiv w_2 N_2 = w_2 \frac{1 + \rho + \varepsilon}{2 + \rho} - \frac{1 - \varepsilon}{1 - \theta_2} \frac{1 + r_1}{2 + \rho} \left[(1 + r_0) A_0 + (1 - \theta_1) w_1 \right].$$

(6.36)

As was asserted at the beginning of this section, both Y_1 and Y_2 depend in a rather complicated fashion on, among other things, the tax rates in the two periods. It follows that the Ricardian tax cut experiment in general will not only affect household saving (as in the basic model) but will also change the labour supply decisions and thus the macroeconomic equilibrium.

Intermezzo 6.2

Ricardian equivalence in a small open economy. As a second example of the effects of distorting taxes on the validity of the Ricardian equivalence theorem, we consider the case of a small open economy in which interest income is taxed. In such an economy, households and the government can borrow or lend at an exogenously given world interest rate, r_t. Denoting net foreign assets owned by domestic households by F_t, the financial capital market equilibrium condition (6.9) changes to:

$$A_t = B_t + F_t.$$

(a)

Households can thus hold their financial wealth in the form of governments bonds or in net financial assets (or both). The two types of assets are perfect substitutes so their rates of return equalize. Assume that non-interest income is exogenous (as in the basic model) but that there is a comprehensive income tax, and that interest income from all sources is also taxable (i.e., a residence-based interest income tax). Equations (6.2)–(6.3) are modified to:

$$A_1 = A_0 + (1 - \theta_1) [Y_1 + r_0 A_0] - C_1,$$ (b)
$$A_2 = A_1 + (1 - \theta_2) [Y_2 + r_1 A_1] - C_2 = 0.$$ (c)

By eliminating A_1 from (b)–(c) and noting (a), we obtain the consolidated household budget restriction:

$$C_1 + \frac{C_2}{1 + r_1 (1 - \theta_2)} = [1 + r_0 (1 - \theta_1)] [B_0 + F_0]$$
$$+ (1 - \theta_1) Y_1 + \frac{(1 - \theta_2) Y_2}{1 + r_1 (1 - \theta_2)}.$$

(d)

Assuming a utility function as in (6.1), the household's Euler equation is now given by:

$$\frac{U'(C_1)}{U'(C_2)} = \frac{1 + r_1 (1 - \theta_2)}{1 + \rho}.$$

(e)

The future tax rate affects the intertemporal price of future consumption and thus influences the optimal choice between current and future consumption. We should thus expect that Ricardian equivalence no longer holds in this setting. Hence, this is yet another example of Ricardian non-equivalence caused by the fact that a distorting tax is being changed in the Ricardian experiment.

The proof on Ricardian non-equivalence proceeds as follows. The budget restrictions for the government, (6.6)–(6.7), are given by:

$$B_1 = (1 + r_0) B_0 + G_1 - \theta_1 [Y_1 + r_0 (B_0 + F_0)], \tag{f}$$
$$B_2 = (1 + r_1) B_1 + G_2 - \theta_2 [Y_2 + r_1 (B_1 + F_1)] = 0. \tag{g}$$

Using (f)–(g), we find that the consolidated government budget constraint is:

$$G_1 + \frac{G_2}{1 + r_1 (1 - \theta_2)} = -[1 + r_0 (1 - \theta_1)] B_0 + \theta_1 [Y_1 + r_0 F_0]$$
$$+ \frac{\theta_2 [Y_2 + r_1 F_1]}{1 + r_1 (1 - \theta_2)}. \tag{h}$$

Next we look at the solvency condition faced by the nation as a whole. National solvency follows automatically from the fact that both households and the government are solvent economic agents. We note from (a) that $F_t = A_t - B_t$. By substituting (b)–(c) and (f)–(g) into this expression we can derive expressions for the path of net foreign assets in the two periods:

$$F_1 = (1 + r_0) F_0 + Y_1 - C_1 - G_1, \tag{i}$$
$$F_2 = (1 + r_1) F_1 + Y_2 - C_2 - G_2 = 0. \tag{j}$$

Eliminating F_1 from these expressions we find the national budget constraint:

$$(1 + r_0) F_0 = M_1 + \frac{M_2}{1 + r_1}, \tag{k}$$

where $M_t \equiv C_t + G_t - Y_t$ is net imports, i.e. domestic consumption minus domestic production of goods. To the extent that the nation initially possesses net foreign assets ($F_0 > 0$) it can afford to be a net importer of goods in present value terms.

In Figure A, the broken line NBC_{MAX} represents the maximum attainable private consumption bundles implied by the national budget constraint in the hypothetical case that the government does not consume anything (i.e. $G_t = 0$). It is the maximum size of the national cake available for private consumption. The actual national budget constraint with positive levels of government consumption is denoted by NBC.

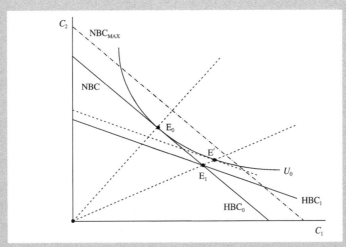

Figure A: Ricardian equivalence and interest-income taxation

Now consider the usual Ricardian experiment of a tax cut in the current period ($\Delta\theta_1 < 0$), matched by a tax increase in the future ($\Delta\theta_2 > 0$). Assume for simplicity that initially the future tax is zero, i.e. $\theta_2 = 0$. In that case the household budget constraint (d), denoted by HBC_0 in Figure A, coincides with the national budget constraint, NBC. The household chooses the consumption point E_0, which is at the intersection of HBC_0 and the implicit Euler equation (e).

The Ricardian experiment leaves that national budget constraint (k) unaffected but changes both the intercept and the slope of the household budget constraint (d). The increase in θ_2 raises the relative price of future consumption, and the household chooses the consumption point E_1. Of course, by definition E_1 must be located on both the national budget constraint, NBC, and the new household budget constraint, HBC_1. The Ricardian experiment is not neutral because current consumption increases and future consumption falls. The future tax distorts the savings decision and creates a welfare loss for the household. Expressed in terms of future consumption, the welfare loss is given by the vertical distance between the dashed line tangent to U_0 at point E' and the HBC_1 line.

****

6.1.3 Borrowing restrictions

In the basic case considered in Section 6.1.1 we have assumed that households can borrow/lend at the same rate of interest as the government. In practice this is unlikely to be the case, as is evidenced by the prevalence of credit rationing of young agents with high earning potential but no tangible appropriable collateral (slavery is not allowed, so future labour income typically cannot serve as collateral). Furthermore, households are more risky to lend to than (stable) governments, suggesting that the former may pay a larger risk premium than the latter. It turns out that borrowing restrictions can invalidate the Ricardian equivalence proposition.

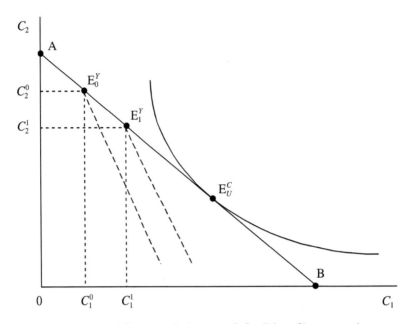

Figure 6.2: Liquidity restrictions and the Ricardian experiment

For simplicity we return to the basic model (with exogenous labour supply) and assume that a household is unable to borrow altogether but can lend money at the going interest rate r_1. In the case discussed so far, this would be no problem because the household chose to be a net *lender* in the first period. Let us now augment the scenario by assuming that income is low in the first period and high in the second period. This case has been drawn in Figure 6.2. The income endowment point is E_0^Y, and the optimal consumption point *in the absence of borrowing restrictions* is E_U^C. This point is not attainable, however, since it involves borrowing in the first period, which is by assumption not possible for the household. The effective choice set is consequently only $AE_0^Y C_1^0 0$ and the optimal consumption point (C_1^0, C_2^0) is at the kink in the budget line (at point E_0^Y).

If we now conduct the Ricardian experiment of a tax cut in the first period matched by a tax increase in the second, the income endowment point shifts along the unrestricted budget line AB, say to point E_1^Y. As a result, the severity of the borrowing constraint is relaxed and the optimal consumption point (C_1^1, C_2^1) is at point E_1^Y. The effective choice set has expanded to $AE_1^Y C_1^1 0$, and real consumption plans (and household utility) have changed for the better.

Obviously, a similar story holds in the less extreme case where the borrowing rate is not infinite (as in the case discussed here) but higher than the rate the government faces. In that case the budget line to the right of the income endowment point is not vertical but downward sloping, and steeper than the unrestricted budget line AB (see the dashed line segments). As a result, the Ricardian experiment still leads to an expansion of the household's choice set and real effects on the optimal consumption plans.

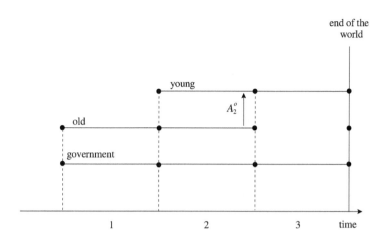

Figure 6.3: Overlapping generations in a three-period economy

6.1.4   Finite lives

Everybody knows that there are only two certainties in life: death and taxes. Hence, one should feel ill at ease if Ricardian equivalence only holds if households live forever. In the examples discussed so far, households, the government, and the entire economy last for two periods, which effectively amounts to saying that, like the government, the household has an infinite life. Suppose that we change the model slightly by introducing two representative households, that each live for only two periods, and that the government and the economy last for three periods. The old household lives in periods 1 and 2, whilst its offspring, the young household, lives in periods 2 and 3. The structure of the overlapping generations is drawn in Figure 6.3.

   We describe the *old generation* first. They are assumed to possess the following lifetime utility function:

$$V^o = \ln C_1^o + \frac{1}{1+\rho} \ln C_2^o + \alpha V^y, \qquad \alpha \geq 0, \tag{6.37}$$

where the superscript "o" designates the old generation, and "y" the young generation. Equation (6.37) says that if $\alpha > 0$, the old generation loves its offspring, in the sense that a higher level of welfare of the young also gives rise to a higher welfare of the old. The old can influence the welfare of the young by leaving an inheritance. Assume that this inheritance, if it exists, is given to the young just before the end of period 2 (see Figure 6.3). The inheritance is the amount of financial assets left over at the end of the old generation's life, i.e. A_2^o. Clearly, it is impossible to leave a negative inheritance, so that the only restriction is that $A_2^o \geq 0$.

   The consolidated budget restriction of the old generation is derived in the usual fashion. The periodic budget restrictions are:

$$A_1^o = (1+r_0)A_0^o + (1-\theta_1)Y_1^o - C_1^o, \tag{6.38}$$
$$A_2^o = (1+r_1)A_1^o + (1-\theta_2)Y_2^o - C_2^o, \tag{6.39}$$

from which A_1^o can be eliminated to yield:

$$C_1^o + \frac{C_2^o + A_2^o}{1 + r_1} = (1 + r_0)A_0^o + H^o \equiv \Omega^o, \tag{6.40}$$

where Ω^o is total wealth and H^o denotes human wealth of the old generation:

$$H^o \equiv (1 - \theta_1)Y_1^o + \frac{(1 - \theta_2)Y_2^o}{1 + r_1}. \tag{6.41}$$

Equation (6.40) says that the present value of consumption expenditure (including the bequest to the young) during life must equal total wealth. Equation (6.41) implies that tax changes in periods 1 and 2 affect the old household via its human wealth.

In order to determine the optimal size of the bequest from the perspective of the old generation, we need to know the link between the size of the inheritance and lifetime utility of the young generation, i.e. we must find the relationship between V^y and A_2^o, which we write as $V^y = \Phi(A_2^o)$. By studying the optimal choices made by the young generation we can find the functional form for $\Phi(A_2^o)$.

By assumption the *young generation* has no offspring (presumably because "the end of the world is nigh"), does not love the old generation, and hence has the standard utility function which only depends on own consumption levels:

$$V^y = \ln C_2^y + \frac{1}{1 + \rho} \ln C_3^y. \tag{6.42}$$

Its consolidated budget restriction is derived in the usual fashion. The periodic budget restrictions are:

$$A_2^y = (1 - \theta_2)Y_2^y - C_2^y, \tag{6.43}$$
$$A_3^y = (1 + r_2)[A_2^o + A_2^y] + (1 - \theta_3)Y_3^y - C_3^y = 0, \tag{6.44}$$

from which A_2^y can be eliminated to yield:

$$C_2^y + \frac{C_3^y}{1 + r_2} = A_2^o + H^y \equiv \Omega^y, \tag{6.45}$$

where Ω^y is total wealth and H^y is the amount of human wealth of the young generation:

$$H^y \equiv (1 - \theta_2)Y_2^y + \frac{(1 - \theta_3)Y_3^y}{1 + r_2}. \tag{6.46}$$

The optimal plan for the young generation is to choose C_2^y and C_3^y such that (6.42) is maximized subject to (6.45). The solutions are similar to those given in (6.16):

$$C_2^y = \frac{1 + \rho}{2 + \rho} \Omega^y, \qquad C_3^y = \frac{1 + r_2}{2 + \rho} \Omega^y. \tag{6.47}$$

By substituting these optimal plans into the lifetime utility function (6.42), we obtain the expression relating optimal welfare of the young generation as a function of the exogenous variables, including the inheritance A_2^o:

$$V^y = \ln \left(\frac{1 + \rho}{2 + \rho} \right) + \frac{1}{1 + \rho} \ln \left(\frac{1 + r_2}{2 + \rho} \right) + \frac{2 + \rho}{1 + \rho} \ln(A_2^o + H^y) \equiv \Phi(A_2^o), \tag{6.48}$$

where we have used the definition of Ω^y. Clearly, the marginal utility (to the young) of a bequest is positive:

$$\Phi'(A_2^o) = \frac{2+\rho}{1+\rho} \frac{1}{A_2^o + H^y} > 0. \tag{6.49}$$

Note that the marginal utility of a bequest is diminishing in total lifetime wealth of the young. Hence, if the young generation lives during very prosperous economic times and has a high level of human wealth then a given-sized bequest received from the old generation has less of an impact that if times were bleak during the young generation's life.

Now that we know the functional form of $\Phi(A_2^o)$, we can return to the decision problem faced by the *old generation*. This generation is aware of the relationship given in (6.48), and uses it in the decision regarding its own optimal plan. Hence, the old generation chooses C_1^o, C_2^o, and A_2^o such that (6.37) is maximized subject to (6.40), (6.48), and the inequality restriction $A_2^o \geq 0$. The first-order conditions are obtained by postulating the Lagrangian:

$$\mathcal{L} \equiv \ln C_1^o + \frac{1}{1+\rho} \ln C_2^o + \alpha \Phi(A_2^o) + \lambda \left[\Omega^o - C_1^o - \frac{C_2^o + A_2^o}{1+r_1} \right], \tag{6.50}$$

so that the first-order conditions are:

$$\frac{\partial \mathcal{L}}{\partial C_1^o} = \frac{1}{C_1^o} - \lambda = 0, \tag{6.51}$$

$$\frac{\partial \mathcal{L}}{\partial C_2^o} = \frac{1}{(1+\rho)C_2^o} - \frac{\lambda}{1+r_1} = 0, \tag{6.52}$$

$$\frac{\partial \mathcal{L}}{\partial A_2^o} = \left[\alpha \Phi'(A_2^o) - \frac{\lambda}{1+r_1} \right] \leq 0, \quad A_2^o \geq 0, \quad A_2^o \frac{\partial \mathcal{L}}{\partial A_2^o} = 0. \tag{6.53}$$

(The fourth condition, $\partial \mathcal{L}/\partial \lambda = 0$, yields the budget restriction (6.40).) Equation (6.53) is the Kuhn-Tucker condition for the optimal inheritance A_2^o that must be used because of the inequality restriction (see e.g. Chiang (1984, ch. 21) and the Mathematical Appendix). The mathematical details need not worry us too much at this point because the economic interpretation is straightforward. If $\alpha = 0$ (unloved offspring), then the first expression in equation (6.53) implies that $\partial \mathcal{L}/\partial A_2^o = -\lambda/(1+r_1) < 0$ (a strict inequality, because (6.51) shows that $\lambda = 1/C_1^o > 0$). The complementary slackness condition, $A_2^o \partial \mathcal{L}/\partial A_2^o = 0$, thus implies that $A_2^o = 0$. In words, no inheritance is given to offspring that are unloved. More generally, if α is so low that $\partial \mathcal{L}/\partial A_2^o < 0$, giving an inheritance would detract from the old generation's lifetime utility, which means that the inheritance is set at the lowest possible value of $A_2^o = 0$. Weakly loved offspring also do not receive an inheritance!

Hence, if there is to be a positive inheritance ($A_2^o > 0$) then it must be because the first expression in (6.53) holds with equality, i.e. $\alpha \Phi'(A_2^o) = \frac{\lambda}{1+r_1}$. By using (6.49) and (6.52) we thus obtain:

$$\frac{\alpha(2+\rho)}{A_2^o + H^y} = \frac{1}{C_2^o}. \tag{6.54}$$

Furthermore, (6.51)–(6.52) can be combined to yield the familiar Euler equation for consumption.

$$C_2^o = \frac{1+r_1}{1+\rho} C_1^o. \tag{6.55}$$

Finally, by using (6.40) and (6.54)–(6.55), the solutions for optimal consumption and the (positive) inheritance can be solved:

$$C_1^o = \frac{(1+\rho)\left[\Omega^o + H^y/(1+r_1)\right]}{(2+\rho)(1+\alpha)}, \tag{6.56}$$

$$C_2^o = \frac{(1+r_1)\Omega^o + H^y}{(2+\rho)(1+\alpha)}, \tag{6.57}$$

$$A_2^o = \frac{\alpha(1+r_1)\Omega^o - H^y}{1+\alpha}. \tag{6.58}$$

Several things are worth noting. First, if α is very large (unbounded love for the offspring) the old generation consumes next to nothing, and the bequest approaches its maximum value of $(1+r_1)\Omega^o$. Second, the optimal bequest is decreasing in the human wealth of the young. i.e. $\partial A_2^o/\partial H^y < 0$. Of course, by the same logic it follows that consumption of the old generation in both periods of life is increasing in H^y ($\partial C_1^o/\partial H^y > 0$ and $\partial C_2^o/\partial H^y > 0$).

It can now be demonstrated that, *provided the optimal bequest stays positive*, Ricardian equivalence holds in this economy despite the fact that households have shorter lives than the government! To prove this surprising result we proceed as follows. Since there are now three periods, the government budget restriction is given by:

$$(1+r_0)B_0 + G_1 + \frac{G_2}{1+r_1} + \frac{G_3}{(1+r_1)(1+r_2)} = \theta_1 Y_1^o + \frac{\theta_2(Y_2^o + Y_2^y)}{1+r_1}$$
$$+ \frac{\theta_3 Y_3^y}{(1+r_1)(1+r_2)}. \tag{6.59}$$

As before, the left-hand side of (6.59) represents the present value of net liabilities of the government whilst the right-hand side is the net present value of the government's tax income.

Consider the following Ricardian experiment: the government reduces the tax rate in period 1 ($\Delta\theta_1 < 0$) and raises it in period 3 ($\Delta\theta_3 > 0$), such that (6.59) holds for an unchanged path of government consumption, i.e.:

$$0 = Y_1^o \,\Delta\theta_1 + \frac{Y_3^y}{(1+r_1)(1+r_2)}\,\Delta\theta_3 \qquad \text{(balanced-budget).} \tag{6.60}$$

Taken in isolation this experiment makes the old wealthier and the young poorer. But what do (6.56)–(6.58) predict will be the result of this Ricardian experiment? Clearly, from (6.56) we have that:

$$\Delta C_1^o = \frac{1+\rho}{(2+\rho)(1+\alpha)}\left[\Delta\Omega^o + \frac{1}{1+r_1}\Delta H^y\right]. \tag{6.61}$$

But (6.40)–(6.41) predict that:

$$\Delta\Omega^o = -Y_1^o\,\Delta\theta_1 > 0, \tag{6.62}$$

and (6.46) implies that:

$$\Delta H^y = -\frac{Y_3^y}{1+r_2}\,\Delta\theta_3 = (1+r_1)Y_1^o\,\Delta\theta_1, \tag{6.63}$$

where we have used (6.60) to relate $\Delta\theta_3$ to $\Delta\theta_1$. Hence, it follows from (6.62)–(6.63) that $\Delta\Omega^o + (1/(1+r_1))\Delta H^y = 0$, and (6.61) is reduced to:

$$\frac{\Delta C_1^o}{\Delta\theta_1} = 0, \tag{6.64}$$

and, of course, also (by (6.57)):

$$\frac{\Delta C_2^o}{\Delta\theta_1} = 0. \tag{6.65}$$

The Ricardian experiment does not affect the consumption plans of the old generation at all! Apparently they do not feel wealthier as a result of the experiment. What is the intuition behind this result? The answer is found by totally differentiating equation (6.58) and noting (6.62)–(6.63):

$$\Delta A_2^o = \frac{\alpha(1+r_1)\Delta\Omega^o - \Delta H^y}{1+\alpha}$$

$$= \frac{-\alpha(1+r_1)Y_1^o - (1+r_1)Y_1^o}{1+\alpha}\Delta\theta_1 = -(1+r_1)Y_1^o\,\Delta\theta_1 > 0. \tag{6.66}$$

The entire tax cut is simply added to the inheritance. In period 1 the old generation buys government bonds (that have just been emitted by the government to finance its deficit, hence there is no upward pressure on the interest rate!) on which it receives interest. The additional bonds plus interest are added to the inheritance so that the young generation is able to meet its higher tax bill. Equations (6.45)–(6.47) and (6.66) therefore predict that the consumption of the young generation is unchanged as well:

$$\Delta\Omega^y = \Delta A_2^o - \frac{Y_3^y}{1+r_2}\Delta\theta_3$$

$$= -(1+r_1)Y_1^o\Delta\theta_1 - \frac{Y_3^y}{1+r_2}\cdot-\frac{Y_1^o(1+r_1)(1+r_2)}{Y_3^y}\Delta\theta_1 = 0, \tag{6.67}$$

which implies that

$$\Delta C_2^y = \Delta C_3^y = 0. \tag{6.68}$$

In conclusion, the fact that individual lives are finite does not mean that Ricardian equivalence automatically fails. Provided future generations are linked to the current generation through operative (positive) bequests, the unbroken chain of connected generations ensures that Ricardian equivalence holds. Of course, once a single link of the chain snaps (zero bequests, childless couples), generations are no longer linked and Ricardian equivalence does not hold in general. In closing we note that leaving no inheritance is the optimal feasible strategy if the degree of "altruism" α is low, or if future income growth is high.[4] Students should test their understanding of this material by showing that Ricardian equivalence also fails, even if there are positive inheritances, if there is an inheritance tax that is varied in the experiment.

6.1.5   Some further reasons for Ricardian non-equivalence

Distortionary taxes, borrowing constraints, and finite lives may invalidate the Ricardian equivalence theorem. A fourth reason why this theorem may fail is the occurrence of *net population growth*, by which we mean the future arrival of new agents

---

[4]Barring transfers in the opposite direction, i.e. from child to parent.

that are not connected—via operative bequests—to agents who are currently alive. Intuitively, the burden of future taxation is borne by more shoulders, so that the burden per capita is lower for future generations than for current generations. Hence, one expects real effects from a Ricardian experiment that shifts taxation to the future. (We demonstrate this with a formal model in Chapter 13 below.)

A fifth reason why Ricardian equivalence may fail has to do with issues such as irrationality, myopic behaviour, and lack of information. Households may not be as farsighted and rational as we have assumed so far, and may fail to fully understand the implications of the government budget restriction. Furthermore, they may simply not have the cognitive power to calculate an optimal dynamic consumption plan, and simply stick to static "rule of thumb" behaviour like "spend a constant fraction of current income on consumption goods".

A sixth reason why Ricardian equivalence may fail has to do with the "bird in the hand" issue. A temporary tax cut, accompanied by a rise in government debt, acts as an insurance policy and thus leads to less precautionary saving and a rise in private consumption (Barsky et al., 1986). The main idea is that the future rise in the tax rate reduces the variance of future after-tax income, so that risk-averse households have to engage in less precautionary saving. A temporary tax cut thus has real effects, because it is better to have one bird in the hand than two in the bush. This critique of Ricardian debt equivalence relies on the absence of complete private insurance markets. A related reason for failure of debt equivalence is that people are uncertain of what their future income and thus also what their future bequests will be (Feldstein, 1988). People may thus value differently, on the one hand, spending a sum now, and, on the other hand, saving the sum of money and then bequeathing.

Finally, a frequently stated but incorrect "reason"and popular argument is that government debt matters in as far as it has been sold to foreigners. The idea is that in the future our children face a burden, because they have to pay higher taxes in order for the government to be able to pay interest on and redeem government debt to the children of foreigners. A rise in government debt is thus thought to constitute a transfer of wealth abroad. However, the original sale of government debt to foreigners leads to an inflow of foreign assets whose value equals the present value of the future amount of taxes levied on home households which is then paid as interest and principal to foreigners. Hence, this critique of Ricardian debt equivalence turns out to be a red herring.[5]

6.1.6 Empirical evidence

The Ricardian equivalence theorem has been the subject of many empirical tests ever since its inception by Barro (1974). Much of the relevant literature was surveyed by Bernheim (1987) and Seater (1993). There is a substantial part of the empirical literature that finds it hard to reject the Ricardian equivalence theorem. Nevertheless, the jury is still out as solid tests with microeconomic data still have to be performed. Even though Seater (1993) concludes that debt equivalence is a good approximation, Bernheim (1987) in his survey comes to the conclusion that debt equivalence is at variance with the facts. Even though debt equivalence is from a theoretical point of view invalid, and according to most macroeconomists empirically invalid as well, one might give the supporters of Ricardian debt equivalence, for the time being, the benefit of the doubt when they argue that the Ricardian proposition is from an

---

[5]It must be stressed that in Intermezzo 6.2 Ricardian equivalence fails **not** because we study an open economy but because a distorting interest-income tax is varied in the experiment.

empirical point of view not too bad. Hence, in the following section we see what role there is for government debt if Ricardian equivalence is assumed to hold.

6.2 The theory of government debt creation

Is there any role for government debt if it barely affects real economic outcomes such as investment and consumption? According to the neoclassical view of public finance the answer is yes. Government debt can be quite useful to mitigate the intratemporal distortions arising from government policy. In particular, government debt may be used to smooth tax rates and thus to minimize the distortiveness of the tax system and to reduce fluctuations in private consumption over time. Such neoclassical views on public finance give prescriptions for government budget deficits and government debt that are more or less observationally equivalent to old-fashioned Keynesian views on the desirability of countercyclical policy. After a simple discussion of the intertemporal aspects of the public sector accounts, we review the principle of tax smoothing in a simple two-period model. In the light of this discussion we are able to comment on the golden rule of public finance as well as some other rules of thumb.

6.2.1 A simple model of tax smoothing

Assume that the policy maker can only raise revenue by means of a distorting tax system (e.g. labour taxes). Assume furthermore, that there are costs associated with enforcing the tax system, so-called "collection costs", and suppose that we can measure the welfare loss of taxation (L_G) as a quadratic function of the tax rates (θ_1 and θ_2), and a linear function of income levels in the two periods (Y_1 and Y_2):

$$L_G \equiv \tfrac{1}{2}\theta_1^2 Y_1 + \tfrac{1}{2}\frac{\theta_2^2 Y_2}{1+\rho_G}, \qquad \rho_G > 0, \tag{6.69}$$

where ρ_G is the (policy maker's) political pure rate of time preference. We continue to assume that household income is exogenous. Intermezzo 6.3 provides a simple example in which direct collection costs are absent but a labour-income tax gives rise to a welfare loss that is approximately quadratric in the tax rate and linear in the income measure. This intermezzo also clarifies how a labour income tax distorts the labour supply choice.

The government budget restrictions (6.6)–(6.7) are generalized somewhat by distinguishing between consumption and investment expenditure by the government, denoted by G_t^C and G_t^I, respectively ($t = 1, 2$):

$$(D_1 \equiv) \quad r_0 B_0 + G_1^C + G_1^I - \theta_1 Y_1 = B_1 - B_0, \tag{6.70}$$

$$(D_2 \equiv) \quad r_1 B_1 + G_2^C - R_2^I - \theta_2 Y_2 = B_2 - B_1 = -B_1, \tag{6.71}$$

where D_t is the deficit in period t and R_2^I is the gross return on public investment obtained in period 2. The net *rate* of return, r_1^G, on such investments can determined by employing the definition $R_2^I \equiv (1 + r_1^G) G_1^I$, or:

$$r_1^G \equiv \frac{R_2^I - G_1^I}{G_1^I}. \tag{6.72}$$

Obviously it makes no sense for the government to invest in period 2 since the world ends at the end of that period (hence $G_2^I = 0$). Note furthermore that (6.70)–(6.71) also imply the following relationship between the deficits in the two periods and the initial debt level:

$$D_1 + D_2 + B_0 = 0. \tag{6.73}$$

To the extent that the initial debt level is positive ($B_0 > 0$), the sum of the deficits in the two periods must be negative (i.e. amount to a surplus). The consolidated government budget restriction can be obtained in the usual fashion:

$$[B_1 =] \quad (1+r_0)B_0 + G_1^C + G_1^I - \theta_1 Y_1 = \frac{\theta_2 Y_2 + (1+r_1^G)G_1^I - G_2^C}{1+r_1} \quad \Rightarrow$$

$$\Xi_1 = \theta_1 Y_1 + \frac{\theta_2 Y_2}{1+r_1}, \tag{6.74}$$

where Ξ_1 is the present value of the net liabilities of the government:

$$\Xi_1 \equiv (1+r_0)B_0 + G_1^C + \frac{G_2^C}{1+r_1} + (r_1 - r_1^G)\frac{G_1^I}{1+r_1}. \tag{6.75}$$

We immediately see the *golden rule of government finance*: as long as $r_1^G = r_1$, government investment expenditure can be debudgeted from the government budget constraint. In words, public investments that attain the market rate of return do not give rise to a net liability of the government and hence do not necessitate present or future taxation. They can be financed by means of debt without any problem (more on this below).

Intermezzo 6.3

Welfare loss of taxation. In this intermezzo we compute the welfare loss of a labour income tax. We use a simple static model and show that this loss is (approximately) quadratic in the tax rate. The example is meant to clarify and motivate the form of the objective function of the policy maker as it is postulated in equation (6.69) in the text.

The representative household has a Cobb-Douglas utility function featuring consumption, C, and leisure, $1 - N$:

$$U = C^\varepsilon (1 - N)^{1-\varepsilon}, \qquad 0 < \varepsilon < 1, \tag{a}$$

where U is utility. The household budget constraint is given by:

$$PC - (1-\theta)WN = 0, \tag{b}$$

where P is the price of the consumption good and W is the before-tax rate. The labour income tax is given by θ, so $\bar{W} \equiv (1-\theta)W$ is the after-tax wage rate. The key thing to note is that the household has no non-labour income at all.

To study the welfare cost of the labour income tax we follow the expenditure function approach of Diamond and McFadden (1974). In formal terms, the expenditure function is defined in this case as:

$$E(P, \bar{W}, U_0) \equiv \min_{\{C,N\}} PC - \bar{W}N \quad \Big| \quad U_0 = C^\varepsilon (1 - N)^{1-\varepsilon} \tag{c}$$

$$= -\bar{W} + \left(\frac{P}{\varepsilon}\right)^{\varepsilon} \left(\frac{\bar{W}}{1-\varepsilon}\right)^{1-\varepsilon} U_0. \tag{d}$$

Expression (d) is obtained by using the Lagrange multiplier method to solve the constrained minimization problem contained in (c) and substituting the results for C and $1 - N$ back into the objective function, $PC - \bar{W}N$. Intuitively, $E(P,\bar{W},U_0)$ represents the minimum possible amount of spending on C and $-N$ such that, at given prices P and $\bar{W}$, the utility level U_0 is attained. Assume that in the initial situation there is no labour income tax, so that $W = \bar{W}$. Obviously, since there is no non-labour income, it follows that $E(P,W,U_0) = 0$. (If there would be non-labour income, say equal to Y_0, then the budget constraint (b) would be modified to $PC - \bar{W}N = Y_0$ and we would have that $E(P,W,U_0) = Y_0$.) *Shephard's lemma* is a very useful property of the expenditure function. It says that the Hicksian (utility-constant) consumption demand and labour supply are obtained by differentiating the expenditure function with respect to the relevant price:

$$C^D(\bar{W}/P, U_0) = \frac{\partial E(P,\bar{W},U_0)}{\partial P} = \left(\frac{\varepsilon}{1-\varepsilon}\frac{\bar{W}}{P}\right)^{1-\varepsilon} U_0, \tag{e}$$

$$N^S(\bar{W}/P, U_0) = -\frac{\partial E(P,\bar{W},U_0)}{\partial \bar{W}} = 1 - \left(\frac{\varepsilon}{1-\varepsilon}\frac{\bar{W}}{P}\right)^{-\varepsilon} U_0, \tag{f}$$

where the superscripts "D" and "S" stand for, respectively, demand and supply.

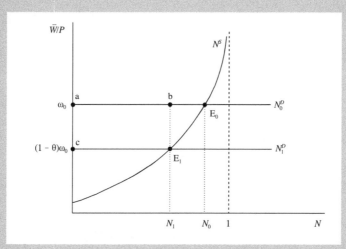

Figure A: Labour market equilibrium

Labour is assumed to be the only factor of production. The perfectly competitive representative firm faces the constant returns to scale production function, $Y = \omega_0 N$, where ω_0 is a positive constant. Profit maximization yields a horizontal labour demand function, i.e. the demand price of labour is:

$$\frac{W}{P} = \omega_0, \tag{g}$$

and excess profit is zero (thus rationalizing the absence of non-labour income for the representative household). The situation on the labour market has been illustrated in Figure A, where N_0^D is the initial labour demand curve and N^S is the Hicksian labour supply curve. Since there is no tax initially, the market clearing real wage rate equals ω_0 and the equilibrium occurs at point E_0.

Now consider the situation in the presence of a positive labour income tax, θ. Since the after-tax wage to consumers is plotted on the vertical axis, labour demand is now given by N_1^D and $\bar{W}/P = (1-\theta)\,\omega_0$. In a Hicksian sense, labour market equilibrium occurs at point E_1, where employment is equal to N_1. We define the Hicksian tax revenue, expressed in units of the consumption good, as:

$$T(\theta, \omega_0, U_0) \equiv \theta \omega_0 N_1 = \theta \omega_0 N^S((1-\theta)\,\omega_0, U_0). \tag{h}$$

This tax revenue is represented by the area abE_1c in Figure A. The welfare loss due to the tax is measured by the area aE_0E_1c:

$$
\begin{aligned}
\text{welfare loss} &\equiv \int_{(1-\theta)\omega_0}^{\omega_0} N^S(s, U_0)\,ds \\
&= \int_{(1-\theta)\omega_0}^{\omega_0} \left[1 - \left(\frac{\varepsilon}{1-\varepsilon}\right)^{-\varepsilon} s^{-\varepsilon} U_0 \right] ds \\
&= \theta \omega_0 - \left(\frac{1}{\varepsilon}\right)^{\varepsilon} \left(\frac{\omega_0}{1-\varepsilon}\right)^{1-\varepsilon} U_0 \left[1 - (1-\theta)^{1-\varepsilon} \right] \\
&= E(1, (1-\theta)\,\omega_0, U_0) - E(1, \omega_0, U_0) \\
&= E(1, (1-\theta)\,\omega_0, U_0), \tag{i}
\end{aligned}
$$

where we have set $P = 1$ in the various expressions because the consumption good acts as the numeraire commodity. In going from the third to the fourth third line we have used the fact that $E(1, \omega_0, U_0) = 0$ (see above). The welfare loss thus represents the amount of lump-sum income one would have to give the representative household in order to attain the initial utility level U_0 at the tax-inclusive real wage rate, $(1-\theta)\,\omega_0$. We can now follow Diamond and McFadden (1974, p. 5) and define the *excess burden* (or deadweight loss) associated with the tax as follows:

$$EB \equiv E(1, (1-\theta)\,\omega_0, U_0) - T(\theta, \omega_0, U_0). \tag{j}$$

Intuitively, the excess burden measures the difference between the amount needed for compensation of the household and the revenue that is collected from the household.

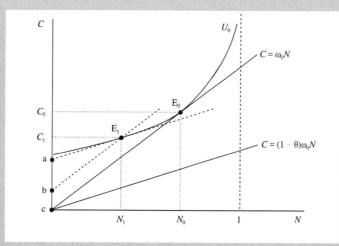

Figure B: Optimal consumption and labour supply

The excess burden can be represented graphically with the aid of Figure B. In that figure, the indifference curve is given by:

$$C = (1 - N)^{(\varepsilon-1)/\varepsilon} U_0^{1/\varepsilon}, \tag{k}$$

and the pre-tax and post-tax budget lines are given by, respectively, $C = \omega_0 N$ and $C = (1 - \theta)\,\omega_0 N$. Clearly, the indifference curve is upward sloping and convex, and labour supply cannot exceed unity. The initial equilibrium is at point E_0 whilst the new (compensated, utility-constant) equilibrium is at point E_1. Point E_1 is found by finding the point of tangency between the indifference curve and a line parallel to the post-tax budget line. The vertical intercept represents the expenditure needed to attain U_0 at the new after-tax wage rate, i.e. the line segment ac is equal to $E(1, (1 - \theta)\,\omega_0, U_0)$. Note that, by construction, we have that $E(1, (1 - \theta)\,\omega_0, U_0) = C_1 - \omega_0 N_1 + T(\theta, \omega_0, U_0)$. Next we draw a line through point E_1 that is parallel to the initial budget line. This line has the general form $C = z + \omega_0 N$. Since this line passes through the new compensated equilibrium point (C_1, N_1), we must have that $z = E(1, (1 - \theta)\,\omega_0, U_0) - T(\theta, \omega_0, U_0)$. It thus follows that the line segment bc in Figure A represents the excess burden of the tax, whereas the line segment ab is the compensated tax revenue.

It remains to derive the relationship between the excess burden and the tax rate. By using (d), (f), (h), and (j) we find after some manipulation that:

$$EB = -\omega_0 + \left(\frac{1}{\varepsilon}\right)^\varepsilon \left(\frac{\omega_0}{1 - \varepsilon}\right)^{1-\varepsilon} U_0 f(\theta), \tag{l}$$

where $f(\theta)$ is defined as:

$$f(\theta) \equiv \frac{1 - \varepsilon\theta}{(1 - \theta)^\varepsilon}, \qquad \text{for } 0 \leq \theta < 1. \tag{m}$$

It is straightforward to find that $f(0) = 1$, $f'(0) = 0$, and $f''(0) = \varepsilon(1-\varepsilon)$, so a quadratic approximation of $f(\theta)$ around $\theta = 0$ gives $f(\theta) \approx 1 + \frac{1}{2}\varepsilon(1-\varepsilon)\theta^2$. Using this result in (l) yields:

$$
EB \approx -\omega_0 + \left(\frac{1}{\varepsilon}\right)^\varepsilon \left(\frac{\omega_0}{1-\varepsilon}\right)^{1-\varepsilon} U_0 \left[1 + \frac{1}{2}\varepsilon(1-\varepsilon)\theta^2\right]
$$

$$
= E(1,\omega_0,U_0) + \frac{1}{2}\theta^2(1-\varepsilon)\left(\frac{\varepsilon\omega_0}{1-\varepsilon}\right)^{1-\varepsilon} U_0
$$

$$
= \frac{1}{2}\theta^2(1-\varepsilon) Y_0, \tag{n}
$$

where we have used the fact that $E(1,\omega_0,U_0) = 0$ in going from the first to the second line, and $C_0 = Y_0 = \left(\frac{\varepsilon\omega_0}{1-\varepsilon}\right)^{1-\varepsilon} U_0$ in going from the second to the third line. The ultimate expression in (n) shows that the excess burden is quadratic in the tax rate and linear in output.

****

The (exogenously given) growth rate of income in this economy is defined as $\gamma \equiv (Y_2 - Y_1)/Y_1$, so that we can write $Y_2 = (1+\gamma)Y_1$, and everything can be written in terms of Y_1. Specifically, the welfare loss function (6.69) can be rewritten as:

$$
L_G \equiv \left[\frac{1}{2}\theta_1^2 + \frac{1}{2}\frac{1+\gamma}{1+\rho_G}\theta_2^2\right] Y_1, \tag{6.76}
$$

whilst the consolidated budget constraint (6.74) becomes:

$$
\xi_1 = \theta_1 + \frac{1+\gamma}{1+r_1}\theta_2, \tag{6.77}
$$

where $\xi_1 \equiv \Xi_1/Y_1$ is net government liabilities expressed as a share of income in the first period:

$$
\xi_1 \equiv g_1^C + \frac{1+\gamma}{1+r_1}g_2^C + \frac{r_1 - r_1^G}{1+r_1}g_1^I + (1+r_0)b_0, \tag{6.78}
$$

and where $g_t^C \equiv G_t^C/Y_t$, $g_1^I \equiv G_1^I/Y_1$, and $b_0 \equiv B_0/Y_1$.

The policy maker is assumed to minimize the welfare loss due to distortionary taxation (6.76), subject to the revenue requirement restriction (6.77) and taking as given ξ_1. We thus assume that government consumption and investment spending are exogenous. i.e. only the taxation decision is "on the table" in this model. The Lagrangian is:

$$
\mathcal{L} \equiv \left[\frac{1}{2}\theta_1^2 + \frac{1}{2}\frac{1+\gamma}{1+\rho_G}\theta_2^2\right] Y_1 + \lambda \left[\xi_1 - \theta_1 - \frac{1+\gamma}{1+r_1}\theta_2\right], \tag{6.79}
$$

where λ is the Lagrange multiplier. The key first-order conditions are:

$$
\frac{\partial \mathcal{L}}{\partial \theta_1} = \theta_1 Y_1 - \lambda = 0, \tag{6.80}
$$

$$\frac{\partial \mathcal{L}}{\partial \theta_2} = \frac{1+\gamma}{1+\rho_G}\theta_2 Y_1 - \lambda\frac{1+\gamma}{1+r_1} = 0, \tag{6.81}$$

and the third condition, $\partial \mathcal{L}/\partial \lambda = 0$, yields the revenue requirement restriction (6.77). By combining (6.80)–(6.81), the Euler equation for the government's optimal taxation problem is obtained:

$$\theta_2 = \frac{1+\rho_G}{1+r_1}\theta_1. \tag{6.82}$$

This expression is intuitive: a short-sighted government (ρ_G greater than r_1) would choose a low tax rate in the current period and a high one in the future ($\theta_2 > \theta_1$). In doing so, the "pain" of taxation is postponed to the future. The opposite holds for a very patient policy maker. This is called the *tax-tilting* effect by Ghosh (1995, p. 1034).

Equations (6.77) and (6.82) can be combined to solve for the levels of the two tax rates:

$$\theta_1 = \frac{(1+r_1)^2\xi_1}{(1+r_1)^2 + (1+\gamma)(1+\rho_G)}, \tag{6.83}$$

$$\theta_2 = \frac{(1+\rho_G)(1+r_1)\xi_1}{(1+r_1)^2 + (1+\gamma)(1+\rho_G)}. \tag{6.84}$$

Since b_0 is predetermined and $b_2 = 0$, the optimal path of government debt is fully characterized by $b_1 \equiv B_1/Y_2$ which, by using (6.70), can be written as:

$$(1+\gamma)b_1 = (1+r_0)b_0 + g_1^C + g_1^I - \theta_1. \tag{6.85}$$

For given values of b_0, g_1^C, g_2^C, and g_1^I, the value of ξ_1 follows readily from (6.78), and equations (6.83)–(6.85) determine the optimal choices for θ_1, θ_2, and b_1. We observe that the existing debt, b_0, exerts an influence on the optimal tax rates only via ξ_1. In that sense it is only of historical significance: the debt was created in the past and hence leads to taxation now and in the future.

The optimal taxation problem is illustrated in Figure 6.4. The straight line through the origin is the Euler equation (6.82), and the downward sloping line is the revenue requirement line (6.77). The concave curves are iso-welfare loss curves (i.e. combinations of θ_1 and θ_2 for which L_G is constant). The closer such a curve is to the origin, the smaller is the welfare cost of taxation. The given revenue is raised with the smallest possible welfare loss at the point of tangency between a given revenue requirement line and an iso-welfare loss curve. This happens at point E.

6.2.2 Implications from the tax smoothing model

In this subsection we employ a special case of the tax-smoothing theory that is obtained by assuming that $r_1 = \rho_G$. In that case, the tax-tilting effect is absent and (6.83)–(6.84) predict that the two tax rates are equal in the two periods:

$$\theta_1 = \theta_2 = \frac{1+r_1}{2+r_1+\gamma}\xi_1. \tag{6.86}$$

Debt is used to keep the tax rates constant (perfectly smoothed over time), hence the name "tax smoothing". In order to facilitate the graphical interpretation of the tax smoothing optimum and to derive some of its key implications, we use equation

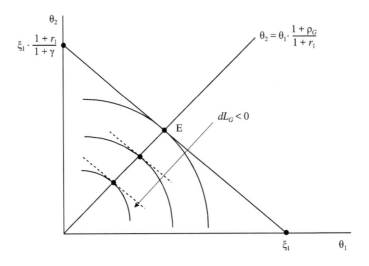

Figure 6.4: Optimal taxation

(6.70) and express the deficit in the first period in terms of national income in that period:

$$d_1 = r_0 b_0 + g_1^C + g_1^I - \theta_1, \tag{6.87}$$

where $d_1 \equiv D_1/Y_1$. Similarly, in view of (6.73), the adding-up constraint can be written as $d_1 + (1+\gamma) d_2 + b_0 = 0$, so that the deficit in the second period satisfies:

$$d_2 = -\frac{b_0 + d_1}{1+\gamma}, \tag{6.88}$$

where $d_2 \equiv D_2/Y_2$. We can now define the *spending point* as that (θ_1, θ_2) combination along the revenue requirement line for which $d_1 = 0$. As is clear from (6.87), the first-period tax exactly covers government spending on goods and interest payments on pre-existing debt in the first period. For points along the revenue requirement line that lie south-east from the spending point, the first period tax is more than high enough to cover first-period spending and, as a result, there is a first-period surplus ($d_1 < 0$). The opposite holds for points north-west of the spending point. In Figure 6.5 it is assumed that the spending point is at E_0^S on the revenue-requirement line RRL$_0$. Since the *optimal taxation point* E_0^T lies north-west from the spending point E_0^S, there is a first-period deficit equal to d_1^a in the lower panel. Note that DL$_0$ is the deficit locus, i.e. the graphical representation of equation (6.87).

With the aid of this simple model a number of "rules of thumb" can be derived for the government's finances.

Rule #1 Government investment projects exactly earning the market rate of return can be financed by means of debt. As was mentioned above, if $r_1^G = r_1$ then public investments do not feature in the expression for ζ_1—see (6.78). Hence, if the government decides to increase g_1^I then optimal taxes are unchanged but the deficit and public debt both increase, i.e. $\Delta d_1 = (1+\gamma)\Delta b_1 = \Delta g_1^I$. In terms of Figure 6.5, in such a scenario the spending point moves from E_0^S to E_1^S, the deficit line shifts to DL$_1$, the optimal taxes remain unchanged, and the increase

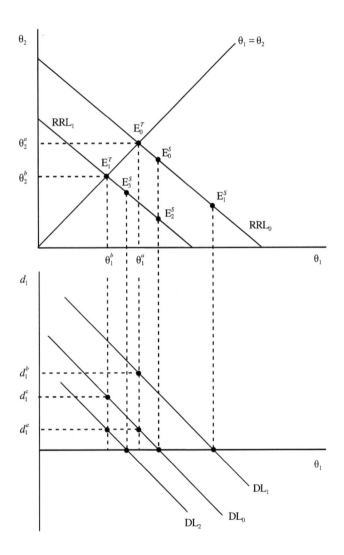

Figure 6.5: Optimal taxation, tax smoothing, and deficit financing

in infrastructural government spending is accommodated by an increase in the first-period deficit from d_1^a to d_1^b.

Rule #2 Public consumption spending and losses on public investment projects should be financed by means of taxation. Of course, by the same logic, profits on public investments must be used to reduce taxes.

Rule #3 The composition of a given level of ξ_1 does not matter. Consider, for example, a *temporary* rise in government consumption, i.e. an increase now that is exactly offset by a decrease in the future, or $(1+r_1)\Delta g_1^C = -(1+\gamma)\Delta g_2^C$. Since ξ_1 is unchanged, optimal tax rates are unchanged and debt financing is called for. In terms of Figure 6.5 the change only shifts the spending point (say from E_0^S to E_1^S) but leaves the optimal taxation point unaffected. The temporary increase in government spending is thus accommodated by an increase in the first-period deficit (and hence debt). This is a neoclassical policy prescription that looks a lot like old-fashioned Keynesian countercyclical policy. During (temporary) recessions government consumption may be higher and there is no harm in letting the debt increase a little bit provided future government consumption is curbed appropriately. (Of course, the tax smoothing model employed here does not include a description of the macro-economy so the similarity between the neoclassical and Keynesian prescriptions is only suggestive.)

Rule #4 If there is a change in the government's net liabilities, ξ_1, then it is optimal to adjust both tax rates immediately. For example, assume that the government credibly announces that it will lower its consumption spending in the future ($\Delta g_2^C < 0$). Then *both* tax rates should be lowered immediately. In terms of Figure 6.5, the revenue requirement line shifts from RRL_0 to RRL_1, the optimal taxation point shifts to E_1^T, and the spending point moves from E_0^S to E_2^S directly below it. The first-period deficit increases from d_1^a to d_1^c as a result. Mathematically, we obtain $\Delta d_1 / \Delta g_2^C = -(1+\gamma)/(2+r_1+\gamma)$.

Rule #5 If the government decides to implement a so-called "balanced decline" of the public sector, for which $\Delta g_1^c = \Delta g_2^c = \Delta g < 0$, then both tax rates should be reduced and there is no effect on the first-period deficit, i.e. $\Delta \theta_1 = \Delta \theta_2 = \Delta g$ and $\Delta d_1 = 0$. In terms of Figure 6.5 the spending point shifts from E_0^S to E_3^S, the optimal taxation point moves from E_0^T to E_1^T, and the deficit line shifts from DL_0 to DL_2.

6.3 Punchlines

In this chapter two concepts, both relating to the government budget constraint, are introduced and analysed, namely the so-called Ricardian equivalence theorem (RET) and the theory of tax smoothing.

Starting with the first of these, the RET can be defined as follows. *For a given path of government spending*, the particular financing method used by the government (bonds or taxes) does not matter. More precisely, when the RET is valid, the financing method of the government does not affect real consumption, investment, output, and welfare, and government debt is seen as a form of delayed taxation. It must be stressed that the RET is not a statement about the effects of government consumption but rather deals with the way these expenditures are paid for by the government.

The intuition behind the RET is quite simple. If the government cuts taxes today and finances the resulting deficit by means of debt, then households will realize that, since total resources claimed by the government have not changed in present value terms, eventually the tax will have to be raised again sometime in the future. To ensure that it will be able to meet its future tax bills, the household reacts to the tax cut by saving it. The tax cut does not affect the lifetime resources available to the households and thus does not affect their consumption plans either.

Although the RET was not taken seriously by David Ricardo himself, it was (and still is) taken seriously by most new classical economists. A lot of objections have, however, been raised against the strict validity of the RET. First, if the Ricardian experiment involves changing one or more taxes which distort economic decisions (for example, because labour supply is endogenous and reacts to the timing of taxes) then the RET will fail. Intuitively, the lifetime resources available to the households will in that case depend on the particular time path of taxes and not just on the present value of taxes.

Second, if the household is unable to borrow freely, for example because future labour income cannot be used as collateral, then the RET fails. Again, the reason for this failure is that the household choice set (and the severity of the household's borrowing constraints) is affected by the time path of taxes chosen by the government.

Third, if households have finite lives whilst the government (and the economy as a whole) is infinitely lived, the RET may or may not be valid. It turns out that it matters whether the overlapping generations which populate the economy are altruistically linked with each other or not. Generations are altruistically linked if they care about each other's welfare (like children caring for their parents or vice versa). In the absence of intergenerational altruism, the the RET fails. Intuitively, a tax cut now matched (in present value terms) by a tax hike later on will make present generations wealthier and future generations poorer. With intergenerational altruism it is possible that the RET holds because transfers between generations will take place. Intuitively, a tax cut today will be passed on to future generations in the form of an (additional) inheritance.

Other objections to the RET relate to net population growth, informational problems (irrationality, myopia, and lack of information), and the so-called "bird in the hand" fallacy. The upshot of the discussion is that there are ample theoretical reasons to suspect that the RET is not strictly valid. Unfortunately, as is often the case, the empirical evidence regarding the approximate validity of the RET is inconclusive.

Even if one is willing to assume that the RET is valid, this does not mean that public debt has no role to play in the economy. Indeed, according to the theory of tax smoothing the government can use public debt to smooth its tax rates over time. To the extent that these tax rates are distorting the behaviour of private agents, tax smoothing is socially beneficial because it minimizes the distortions of the tax system as a whole. A number of intuitive "rules of thumb" follow from the theory.

Further reading

Although he did not use the term as such, the notion of Ricardian equivalence was introduced to modern macroeconomists by Barro (1974). Buchanan (1976) coined the term "Ricardian equivalence theorem," and O'Driscoll (1977) documents Ricardo's own misgivings about the result that is now known under his name. For good survey articles on Ricardian equivalence, see Bernheim (1987) and Seater (1993). Bernheim and Bagwell (1988) are very critical of the dynastic approach used by Barro and argue that it should not be used to study the effects of public policies. They take the altruistic approach as given, and demonstrate that there will be strong inter-family linkages in such a setting (due to marriages, etcetera). This in turn will produce neutrality results that are unrealistically strong (such as the equivalence of distorting taxes and lump-sum taxes, and the inability of governments to engage in redistribution). Arguing backwards, they conclude that there must be something wrong with the dynastic approach itself.

The earliest contributions to the macroeconomic theory of tax smoothing are by Prescott (1977) and Barro (1979). Subsequent contributions to the literature include Lucas and Stokey (1983), Kingston (1984, 1991), Roubini (1988), Huang and Lin (1993), Ghosh (1995), and Fisher and Kingston (2004, 2005). As was pointed out by Sargent (2001), in a stochastic framework the optimal time path of taxes depends critically on whether or not the government is able to issue state-contingent debt. Whereas the tax smoothing literature typically assumes government spending to be exogenous, Judd (1999) presents an analysis of the joint determination of optimal taxation and spending in a deterministic setting.

Readers interested in the various issues surrounding the government budget constraint and the deficit are referred to Buiter (1985, 1990). The intertemporal consumption model used in this chapter is due to Fisher (1930). Further results on the two-period consumption model are presented by Obstfeld and Rogoff (1996, ch. 1). See Deaton (1992) and Attanasio (1999) for advanced surveys of intertemporal consumption theory.

Chapter 7

A closer look at the labour market

In the previous chapters we have demonstrated that the aggregate labour market forms a crucial component of most short-run macroeconomic models. Up to this point the focus has been on identifying the determinants of aggregate demand and supply on that market. In this chapter and the next we delve a little deeper into the labour market. More specifically, the goal of this chapter is to discuss the following issues:

1. What are some of the most important stylized facts about the labour market in advanced capitalist economies?

2. How can we explain some of these stylized facts with the standard model of the labour market used so far? How do these theories fall short of providing a full explanation?

3. How does the tax system affect the macroeconomic labour market and which side of the market ends up bearing the tax burden?

4. What models of trade union behaviour exist, and what do they predict about unemployment?

5. What do we mean by efficiency wages and how do they lead to equilibrium unemployment?

7.1 Some stylized facts

The stylized facts about the labour market in advanced capitalist countries can be subdivided into the two categories of *time series* evidence and *cross-section* information. The main indicator of labour market performance is the unemployment rate. Ever since the Great Depression of the 1930s this has been at the forefront of macroeconomic research. The following stylized facts about unemployment can be established for most countries in the Western world (see Layard et al. (2005, ch. 1) for further details).

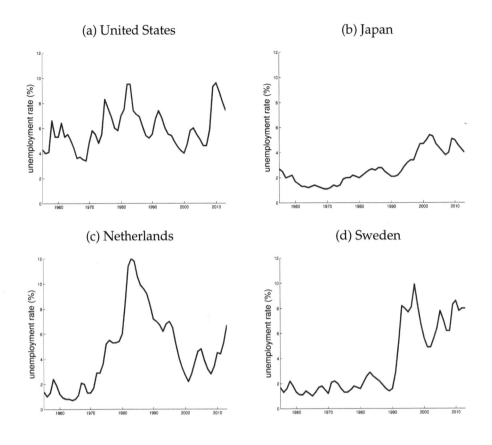

Figure 7.1: Postwar unemployment in selected OECD countries

Stylized Fact 1: The unemployment rate fluctuates over time   In Figure 7.1 we
plot the unemployment rate for a number of regions and countries for the post-war
period.[1] Several things are worth noting. First, in all countries depicted the unemployment rate fluctuates quite a lot over time. Second, in the two European countries
unemployment was relatively low and stable up until the time of the first oil shock
in 1973. After that, for about a decade the employment rate followed a steady trend
upward in the Netherlands, peaking in the early eighties after which a downward
trend in the unemployment rate is clearly visible. Interestingly, Sweden experienced
a low and steady unemployment rate until the beginning of the 1990s after which it
experienced an upward trend (as the Dutch did a decade before). Third, the impact
of the great financial crisis is clearly visible for all countries from 2009 onward.

**Stylized Fact 2: Unemployment fluctuates more between business cycles than
within business cycles**   In Figure 7.2 we plot the unemployment rate for the US
and the UK for extended periods of time.[2] The Great Depression truly deserves its

---

[1]The data for 1955-1990 are taken from Layard et al. (2005, pp. 526–528). Subsequent data are gathered
from various issues of the *OECD Employment Outlook*. Where possible we make use of standardized
unemployment data.

[2]The data for the period until 1993 have been taken from Mitchell (1998a, pp. 163, 165, 168–169) for the
United Kingdom and from Mitchell (1998b, pp. 112, 114) for the United States. The data for the period

name, especially in the US. Unemployment was very high for a prolonged period of time and peaked at close to 25%! Another thing to note is that, if unemployment were purely a business-cycle phenomenon, one would expect a much more regular pattern than the one observed in these figures. To put the same argument somewhat differently, the time series of unemployment displays a lot of *persistence*; much more than is consistent with the business cycle. To demonstrate this phenomenon, we follow Layard et al. (2005, p. 77) and regress unemployment on its own lagged variable and a constant. For the UK during the period 1856-2014 we find:

$$\hat{U}_t = \underset{(2.97)}{0.7305} + \underset{(20.88)}{0.8575}\, U_{t-1}, \qquad \bar{R}^2 = 0.734, \tag{7.1}$$

whilst for the US during the period 1891-2014 we obtain:

$$\hat{U}_t = \underset{(2.64)}{1.0157} + \underset{(18.30)}{0.8548}\, U_{t-1}, \qquad \bar{R}^2 = 0.731, \tag{7.2}$$

where U_t is the actual unemployment rate at time t and $\hat{U}_t$ is the unemployment rate predicted by the regression equation. The numbers in parentheses are the estimated t-statistics of the coefficient estimates and $\bar{R}^2$ is the coefficient of determination corrected for the degrees of freedom (i.e. the sample proportion of the variability in the dependent variable that is explained by the model). In both countries the coefficient for lagged unemployment is high (and close to unity) and highly significant. This suggests a lot of persistence in the unemployment time series. High persistence implies that it takes a long time before the effects of a particular shock die out (see equation (7.6) below).

Stylized Fact 3: The duration of unemployment spells differs between countries Even if countries have exactly the same unemployment rate, the composition of this labour market indicator may be quite different. In particular, in most European countries a substantial fraction of the unemployed have been jobless for more than one year. In contrast, in the United States (at least in the years before the great financial crisis) such long-term unemployment is much less severe. Broadly speaking, in the United States the inflow from employment to unemployment (the rate of job losses) is much higher than in Europe, but so is the outflow from unemployment to employment (the rate of job finding). As a result unemployment spells are shorter in the United States than in the European countries. We shall return to the topic of unemployment duration in Chapter 8.

Stylized Fact 4: In the very long run unemployment shows no trend This fact has been graphically illustrated in Figure 7.2. Although there are sharp peaks and deep troughs, there does not seem to be any noticeable trend in the unemployment rate for the US and the UK. This is all the more remarkable in view of the enormous productivity gains that have been made in the last century and a half. Apparently, the nineteenth century Luddite fear of physical capital permanently pushing workers into unemployment has proved unfounded.

More formally, and in terms of equations (7.1)–(7.2), the coefficient of the lagged unemployment rate is high but less than unity. Ultimately, there are mechanisms at work whereby unemployment returns to some average level. The convergence to this average level is very slow, however, as can be demonstrated as follows. From

---

1994-2014 have been taken from OECD (2001, Table 21), OECD (2006, Table A), and OECD (2015).

(a) United Kingdom, 1855–2014

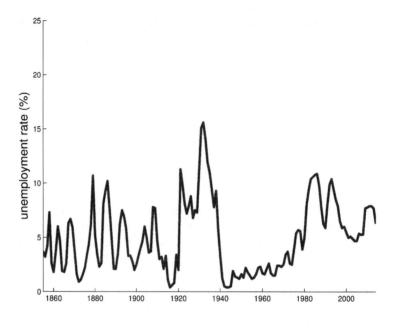

(b) United States, 1890–2014

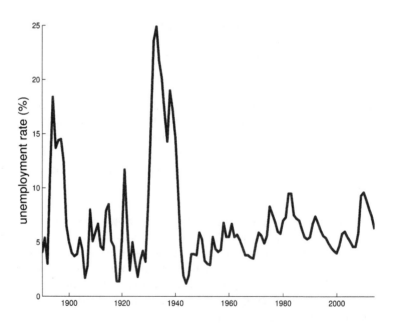

Figure 7.2: Unemployment over the centuries

equations like (7.1)–(7.2) we can determine the long-term steady-state unemployment rate $\bar{U}$. First, we write the equations in general form as:

$$U_t = \alpha_0 + \alpha_1 U_{t-1}, \qquad 0 < \alpha_1 < 1, \tag{7.3}$$

where α_0 is the intercept and α_1 is the coefficient for the lagged dependent variable. Next we note that in the steady state, $U_t = U_{t-1} = \bar{U}$, so that it follows from (7.3) that $\bar{U} = \alpha_0 / (1 - \alpha_1)$. Using the estimates from (7.1), for example, we find that $\bar{U} = 0.7305 / (1 - 0.8575) = 5.13\%$ for the UK.[3] From (7.3) we can compute the adjustment speed by solving the difference equation for U_t. Suppose that the unemployment rate at time $t = 0$ (the reference period) is equal to U_0. Then (7.3) can be solved by repeated substitutions of the kind:

$$U_1 = \alpha_0 + \alpha_1 U_0,$$
$$U_2 = \alpha_0 + \alpha_1 U_1 = \alpha_0 + \alpha_1 [\alpha_0 + \alpha_1 U_0]$$

$$\vdots \quad \vdots$$

$$U_t = \alpha_0 \left[1 + \alpha_1 + \alpha_1^2 + \ldots + \alpha_1^{t-1} \right] + \alpha_1^t U_0. \tag{7.4}$$

This expression can be rewritten in the following (more elegant) form:[4]

$$U_t - \bar{U} = [U_0 - \bar{U}] \alpha_1^t. \tag{7.5}$$

Equation (7.5) can be used to determine how long it takes for any discrepancy between U_0 and $\bar{U}$ to be eliminated. Suppose that the unemployment rate is currently U_0 and the long-run unemployment rate is $\bar{U}$. How many periods does it take, for example, before *half* of the difference $[U_0 - \bar{U}]$ is eliminated? The answer, which we denote by t_H, is called the half-life of the adjustment. Intuitively, we can use t_H as an indicator for the adjustment speed in the system. It is calculated as follows:

$$U_{t_H} - \bar{U} \equiv [U_0 - \bar{U}] \alpha_1^{t_H} = \tfrac{1}{2} [U_0 - \bar{U}] \quad \Rightarrow$$
$$\alpha_1^{t_H} = \tfrac{1}{2} \quad \Rightarrow$$
$$t_H \ln \alpha_1 = -\ln 2 \quad \Rightarrow \quad t_H = -\frac{\ln 2}{\ln \alpha_1}. \tag{7.6}$$

For the UK this amounts to $t_H = -\ln 2 / \ln 0.8575 = 4.51$ years (see (7.1)). Hence, it takes almost five years before half of the difference between the actual and the long-run unemployment rate is eliminated.

Stylized Fact 5: The level of the unemployment rate differs a lot between countries   As we can see from Figure 7.1 the level of the rate of unemployment differs a lot even between supposedly similar advanced OECD countries like the US, Japan, the Netherlands, and Sweden. And even within Europe there are marked differences, with Sweden currently experiencing high unemployment compared to the Netherlands (where it used to be the other way around in the 1980s).

---

[3] We ignore the fact that we are using estimates for α_0 and α_1, and should really be constructing confidence intervals for $\bar{U}$.

[4] The trick is to write the term in square brackets as:

$$1 + \alpha_1 + \alpha_1^2 + \cdots + \alpha_1^{t-1} = \frac{1 - \alpha_1^t}{1 - \alpha_1}.$$

By using this result plus the definition of $\bar{U}$ (stated below equation (7.3)), equation (7.5) is obtained.

Stylized Fact 6: Few unemployed have themselves chosen to become unemployed
Only a very small minority of the unemployed have quit a job in order to become
unemployed (for example, to search for a new job). The vast majority of unemployment occurs because the workers are laid off by their employer. This fact will prove
important in Chapter 8, where we discuss search behaviour.

**Stylized Fact 7: Unemployment differs a lot between age groups, occupations, re-
gions, races, and sexes**   There is a lot of heterogeneity in several dimensions. For
example, women experience much higher unemployment rates than men, and the
young have higher unemployment rates than older workers. Furthermore, unemployment depends a lot on the educational attainment of workers. Broadly speaking,
the unemployment rate is lower when the level of educational attainment is higher.

As these stylized facts show, there is quite a lot to be explained about the labour
market. The remainder of this chapter proceeds as follows. In Section 7.2 we demonstrate how the standard labour market story used so far can explain some of the stylized facts. We also show in which important aspects it fails to provide an adequate
explanation. One of these failures concerns the observed (relative) inflexibility of the
real wage rate with respect to demand and productivity shocks. For that reason we
discuss two theories that can explain real wage inflexibility in the final two sections
of this chapter.

7.2   Standard macroeconomic labour market theory

7.2.1   Skilled and unskilled labour

Up to this point we have modelled the labour market in the same way one would
model the market for peanuts, i.e. by postulating aggregate demand and supply
schedules (for labour in this case; see Chapter 1). A high level of aggregation is the
hallmark of macroeconomics, and one might be tempted to conclude that for that
reason the macro approach cannot be used to account for the evidence unearthed in
the previous section. Fortunately, such a negative conclusion is unwarranted.

For example, suppose that one wishes to use the standard approach to explain
why low-education workers experience a higher unemployment rate than high-education workers (see Stylized Fact 7). The way this problem is typically approached by
macroeconomists is to distinguish two types of labour. Call the low-education workers "unskilled" labour (denoted by N_U) and the high-education workers "skilled"
labour (N_S). The production function of the representative firm is given by:

$$Y = G(N_U, N_S, \bar{K}) \equiv F(N_U, N_S), \tag{7.7}$$

where Y is output, and the capital stock is fixed in the short run at $\bar{K}$. Hence,
$F(N_U, N_S)$ is the short-run production function featuring positive but diminishing
marginal products, i.e. $F_U \equiv \partial F/\partial N_U > 0$, $F_S \equiv \partial F/\partial N_S > 0$, $F_{UU} \equiv \partial^2 F/\partial N_U^2 < 0$,
and $F_{SS} \equiv \partial^2 F/\partial N_S^2 < 0$. In addition, we assume that short-run isoquants bulge
toward the origin, i.e. $\Delta \equiv F_{SS}F_{UU} - F_{SU}^2 > 0$, where $F_{SU} \equiv \partial^2 F/\partial N_S \partial N_U$. Whereas
$G(N_U, N_S, \bar{K})$ features constant returns to scale to the three factors of production,
$F(N_U, N_S)$ exhibits decreasing returns to the two types of labour.

The representative firm maximizes profit by choosing the optimal production
level. With perfect competition in the output market and both input markets, the

output price P and the wage rates W_U and W_S are taken as given by the firm and the choice problem is:

$$\max_{\{N_U,N_S\}} \Pi \equiv PF(N_U, N_S) - W_U N_U - W_S N_S, \tag{7.8}$$

which yields the usual marginal productivity conditions:

$$PF_U(N_U, N_S) = W_U, \qquad PF_S(N_U, N_S) = W_S. \tag{7.9}$$

In words, the value of the marginal product of each type of labour must be equated to its wage rate. Obviously, the expressions in equation (7.9) can be used to derive the demand functions for the two types of labour. By total differentiation of the two equations, we obtain the following matrix expression:

$$\begin{bmatrix} dN_S \\ dN_U \end{bmatrix} = \frac{1}{\Delta} \begin{bmatrix} F_{UU} & -F_{SU} \\ -F_{SU} & F_{SS} \end{bmatrix} \begin{bmatrix} dw_S \\ dw_U \end{bmatrix}, \tag{7.10}$$

where $w_S \equiv W_S/P$ and $w_U \equiv W_U/P$ are the real wages rates on, respectively, skilled and unskilled labour, and Δ is a positive constant defined in the text below equation (7.7). Equation (7.10) can be used to find all the comparative static results of the demand functions for the two types of labour which we write as follows:

$$N_S^D = N_S^D(w_S, w_U), \qquad N_U^D = N_U^D(w_S, w_U). \tag{7.11}$$

Clearly, the "own" real wage effects are guaranteed to be negative because both labour types feature a diminishing marginal product:

$$N_{SS}^D \equiv \frac{\partial N_S^D}{\partial w_S} = \frac{F_{UU}}{\Delta} < 0, \qquad N_{UU}^D \equiv \frac{\partial N_U^D}{\partial w_U} = \frac{F_{SS}}{\Delta} < 0. \tag{7.12}$$

The "cross" real wage effects, however, cannot be signed without making an additional assumption. In particular, we assume that skilled and unskilled labour are *gross substitutes* in the short-run production function. This implies that F_{SU} is negative, and the cross partial derivatives are both positive:

$$N_{SU}^D \equiv \frac{\partial N_S^D}{\partial w_U} = -\frac{F_{SU}}{\Delta} > 0, \qquad N_{US}^D \equiv \frac{\partial N_U^D}{\partial w_S} = -\frac{F_{SU}}{\Delta} > 0. \tag{7.13}$$

In words, if unskilled labour becomes dearer, the demand for skilled labour increases, and similarly if skilled labour becomes more expensive, the demand for unskilled labour increases. This is because the two factors can be used as substitutes in the production process. (Intermezzo 7.1 studies the issue of short-run gross substitutability or complementarity in more detail.)

In order to close the model as simply as possible, we assume that the supply curves of the two types of labour are perfectly inelastic.

$$N_S^S = \bar{N}_S, \qquad N_U^S = \bar{N}_U. \tag{7.14}$$

The equilibrium in the two labour markets can be drawn as in Figure 7.3.

If wages are perfectly flexible, full employment is attained in both markets. This is the case at points E_0^S and E_0^U, respectively. In the left-hand panel the demand for skilled labour—conditional on the market-clearing wage rate for unskilled labour—is denoted by $N_S^D(w_S, w_U^*)$. It intersects with skilled labour supply at point E_0^S. Similarly, in the right-hand panel the demand for unskilled labour—conditional on the

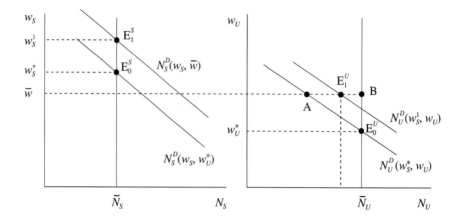

Figure 7.3: The markets for skilled and unskilled labour

market-clearing wage rate for skilled labour—is denoted by $N_U^D(w_S^*, w_U)$. This curve intersects with the unskilled labour supply curve at point E_0^U.

How can this model provide an explanation for the high unemployment rate among unskilled workers? A simple explanation runs as follows. Suppose that there is a minimum wage law, which states that the *real* wage of *any* worker (irrespective of that worker's skill level) must not fall below $\bar{w}$. This minimum wage is assumed to be at a level below the market clearing real wage in the market for skilled labour ($\bar{w} < w_S^*$), but above the equilibrium real wage in the unskilled labour market ($\bar{w} > w_U^*$). As a result, the minimum wage is binding in the market for unskilled labour, and unemployment emerges in that market equal to the segment AB in the right-hand panel of Figure 7.3. This is the partial equilibrium effect of the minimum wage. But it is not the end of the story, however, since the (artificially) high real wage of unskilled workers prompts the representative firm to substitute skilled for unskilled labour. In the left-hand panel the demand for skilled labour shifts to the right (from $N_S^D(w_S, w_U^*)$ to $N_S^D(w_S, \bar{w})$), the new equilibrium is at E_1^S, and the equilibrium skilled real wage rate rises to w_S^1. The higher equilibrium wage for skilled labour partially offsets the initial unemployment effect by stimulating the demand for unskilled labour a little. Indeed, in the right-hand panel, demand shifts from $N_U^D(w_S^*, w_U)$ to $N_U^D(w_S^1, w_U)$ and the new equilibrium is at E_1^U. Unemployment is equal to the segment E_1^UB.

In summary, the introduction of a binding minimum wage has the following effects. All skilled workers obtain higher wages. Some unskilled workers also receive a higher wage than before (namely the minimum wage) but others are unemployed. In conclusion, since minimum wages exist in most advanced countries, even our very simple standard model can be used to derive sensible conclusions about the labour market. In particular, high minimum wages constitute a potential explanation for Stylized Fact 7: unemployment among unskilled workers is high because this type of labour is simply too dear. Most economists agree that this is partially true, but that other elements also play a role.

In this subsection we have developed a very simple representation of the bottom end of the labour market. There is unemployment in the market for unskilled labour because this type of labour is too expensive: the marginal product of this type of labour is simply too low, given the existence of a binding minimum wage, to be consistent with full employment.

A number of policy options exist to solve this type of unemployment. First, the minimum wage could be abolished. This will obviously work, but may cause politically undesirable income distribution effects, social unrest, etc. Hence, some package of transfers to unskilled workers may be unavoidable. Second, unskilled labour could be subsidized. In terms of Figure 7.3, this amounts to shifting the demand for unskilled labour up and to the right. The demand for unskilled labour is artificially stimulated to make the minimum wage less of a disequilibrium wage. Third, the government can directly employ some unskilled workers at the going minimum wage. Again, the demand for unskilled labour shifts to the right, and unemployment is reduced. The problem with this option is that the jobs that are created tend to be "dead-end" jobs (like having three men guarding the Town Clerk's bicycle). For all three options discussed so far, there is a revenue requirement on the part of the government. To the extent that the additional tax revenue that is needed can only be raised in a distorting fashion (see Chapter 6), the net benefits to society are far from obvious. This is especially the case for the third option, since nothing of value to society may be created in dead-end jobs.

A fourth option may be more attractive. The government could invest in (re-) training projects specifically targeted at unskilled workers. By making unskilled labour more productive, it is possible to stimulate the demand for those workers and reduce unemployment. In the terminology of Chapter 6, a golden rule of financing could be used: to the extent that the rate of return on public investment in (re-) training schemes equals the market rate of return, such schemes may even be financed by means of debt, thus obviating the need for distorting taxation. The return to making unskilled workers more productive includes two components. First, as the unemployment rate falls, spending on unemployment benefits falls, thus reducing the government's revenue requirement. Second, as the previously unemployed find work, they also start to pay taxes, thus further reducing the government's revenue requirement.

Intermezzo 7.1

Some production theory: the three-factor production model. In this intermezzo we study the three-factor production model, when one of the factors is constant in the short run. A three-factor production function is *weakly separable* in production factors x_1 and (x_2, x_3) if it can be written as:

$$Y = F(x_1, Z), \qquad Z = G(x_2, x_3). \tag{a}$$

We assume that both $F(x_1, Z)$ and $G(x_2, x_3)$ are linear homogeneous in their respective arguments, so doubling x_1 and Z results to a doubling of Y, whilst doubling x_2 and x_3 results in a doubling of Z. Note that Z can be interpreted as a composite input, that is produced by combining primary inputs x_2 and x_3. We know (from Intermezzo 4.3) that:

$$Y = F_1 x_1 + F_Z Z, \qquad Z = G_2 x_2 + G_3 x_3, \tag{b}$$

where $F_1 \equiv \partial F/\partial x_1 > 0$, $F_Z \equiv \partial F/\partial Z > 0$, $G_2 \equiv \partial G/\partial x_2 > 0$, and $G_3 \equiv \partial G/\partial x_3 > 0$. We know also that:

$$F_{11} x_1 + F_{1Z} Z = 0, \qquad F_{Z1} x_1 + F_{ZZ} Z = 0, \tag{c1}$$
$$G_{22} x_2 + G_{23} x_3 = 0, \qquad G_{32} x_2 + G_{33} x_3 = 0, \tag{c2}$$

where $F_{11} \equiv \partial^2 F/\partial x_1^2 < 0$, $F_{1Z} = F_{Z1} \equiv \partial^2 F/\partial x_1 \partial Z > 0$, $F_{ZZ} \equiv \partial^2 F/\partial Z^2 < 0$, $G_{22} \equiv \partial^2 G/\partial x_2^2 < 0$, $G_{23} = G_{32} \equiv \partial^2 G/\partial x_2 \partial x_3 > 0$, and $G_{33} \equiv \partial^2 G/\partial x_3^2 < 0$. The two functions have the usual property that isoquants bulge toward the origin:

$$F_{11} F_{ZZ} - F_{1Z}^2 > 0, \qquad G_{22} G_{33} - G_{23}^2 > 0. \tag{d}$$

Finally, we define the substitution elasticities of the two functions in the usual way:

$$\sigma_F \equiv \frac{F_1 F_Z}{Y F_{1Z}} > 0, \qquad \sigma_G \equiv \frac{G_2 G_3}{Z G_{23}} > 0. \tag{e}$$

We wish to have loglinearized expressions for the marginal products of the three factors, $F_i \equiv \partial Y/\partial x_i$. We show the derivations for F_1 and F_2 in detail. Clearly, $F_1 \equiv F_1[x_1, G(x_2, x_3)]$ is a function of all three inputs. Totally differentiating we get:

$$dF_1 = F_{11} dx_1 + F_{1Z} dG(x_2, x_3) = F_{11} dx_1 + F_{1Z}[G_2 dx_2 + G_3 dx_3].$$

Dividing both sides by F_1 we obtain:

$$\frac{dF_1}{F_1} = \frac{x_1 F_{11}}{F_1} \frac{dx_1}{x_1} + \frac{x_2 F_{1Z} G_2}{F_1} \frac{dx_2}{x_2} + \frac{x_3 F_{1Z} G_3}{F_1} \frac{dx_3}{x_3}$$
$$\tilde{F}_1 = \frac{x_1 F_{11}}{F_1} \tilde{x}_1 + \frac{x_2 F_{1Z} G_2}{F_1} \tilde{x}_2 + \frac{x_3 F_{1Z} G_3}{F_1} \tilde{x}_3, \tag{f}$$

where $\tilde{F}_i \equiv dF_i/F_i$, and $\tilde{x}_i \equiv dx_i/x_i$. The terms on the right-hand side of (f) can be re-expressed in a more intuitive format. Starting with the first term, we obtain:

$$\frac{x_1 F_{11}}{F_1} = -\frac{Z F_{1Z}}{F_1} \frac{F_Z}{F_Z} \frac{Y}{Y} = -\frac{Y F_{1Z}}{F_1 F_Z} \cdot \frac{Z F_Z}{Y} = -\frac{1 - \omega_1}{\sigma_F}, \tag{g1}$$

where we have used the first expression in (c1) in the first step. Note that $\omega_1 \equiv x_1 F_1/Y$ and $1 - \omega_1 \equiv Z F_Z/Y$ are the income shares of, respectively, x_1 and the composite input Z. In a similar fashion we get:

$$\frac{x_2 F_{1Z} G_2}{F_1} = \frac{Y F_{1Z}}{F_1 F_Z} \cdot \frac{Z F_Z}{Y} \cdot \frac{x_2 G_2}{Z} = \frac{(1 - \omega_1) \omega_2}{\sigma_F}, \tag{g2}$$

$$\frac{x_3 F_{1Z} G_3}{F_1} = \frac{Y F_{1Z}}{F_1 F_Z} \cdot \frac{Z F_Z}{Y} \cdot \frac{x_3 G_3}{Z} = \frac{(1 - \omega_1)(1 - \omega_2)}{\sigma_F}, \tag{g3}$$

where $\omega_2 \equiv x_2 G_2 / Z$ and $1 - \omega_2 \equiv x_3 G_3 / Z$. By substituting (g1)–(g3) into (f) we thus obtain:

$$\tilde{F}_1 = -\frac{1 - \omega_1}{\sigma_F} \tilde{x}_1 + \frac{(1 - \omega_1)\omega_2}{\sigma_F} \tilde{x}_2 + \frac{(1 - \omega_1)(1 - \omega_2)}{\sigma_F} \tilde{x}_3. \tag{h}$$

The marginal product of x_1 depends negatively on the quantity of x_1 used, and positively on the quantities used of the other two factors.

Next we turn to the marginal product of the second production factor, x_2. Note that $F_2 \equiv F_Z [x_1, G (x_2, x_3)] \cdot G_2 (x_2, x_3)$ (by the product rule) so upon total differentiation we obtain:

$$dF_2 = G_2 F_{Z1} dx_1 + \left[G_2^2 F_{ZZ} + F_Z G_{22} \right] dx_2 + \left[G_2 G_3 F_{ZZ} + F_Z G_{23} \right] dx_3$$

$$\frac{dF_2}{F_2} = \frac{x_1 G_2 F_{Z1}}{F_Z G_2} \frac{dx_1}{x_1} + \frac{x_2 G_2^2 F_{ZZ} + x_2 F_Z G_{22}}{F_Z G_2} \frac{dx_2}{x_2}$$

$$+ \frac{x_3 G_2 G_3 F_{ZZ} + x_3 F_Z G_{23}}{F_Z G_2} \frac{dx_3}{x_3}. \tag{i}$$

The coefficients on the right-hand side of (i) can once again be simplified substantially:

$$\frac{x_1 F_{Z1}}{F_Z} = \frac{x_1 F_1}{Y} \cdot \frac{Y F_{Z1}}{F_1 F_Z} = \frac{\omega_1}{\sigma_F}, \tag{j1}$$

$$\frac{x_2 G_2^2 F_{ZZ} + x_2 F_Z G_{22}}{F_Z G_2} = -\frac{x_2 G_2}{Z} \cdot \frac{Y F_{1Z}}{F_1 F_Z} \cdot \frac{x_1 F_1}{Y} - \frac{Z G_{23}}{G_2 G_3} \cdot \frac{x_3 G_3}{Z}$$

$$= -\left[\frac{\omega_1 \omega_2}{\sigma_F} + \frac{1 - \omega_2}{\sigma_G} \right], \tag{j2}$$

$$\frac{x_3 G_2 G_3 F_{ZZ} + x_3 F_Z G_{23}}{F_Z G_2} = -\frac{x_3 G_3}{Z} \cdot \frac{Y F_{1Z}}{F_1 F_Z} \cdot \frac{x_1 F_1}{Y} + \frac{Z G_{23}}{G_2 G_3} \cdot \frac{x_3 G_3}{Z}$$

$$= (1 - \omega_2) \left[-\frac{\omega_1}{\sigma_F} + \frac{1}{\sigma_G} \right], \tag{j3}$$

where we have used (c1)–(c2) to simplify the expressions. Hence, by using (j1)–(j3) in (i) we get:

$$\tilde{F}_2 = \frac{\omega_1}{\sigma_F} \tilde{x}_1 - \left[\frac{\omega_1 \omega_2}{\sigma_F} + \frac{1 - \omega_2}{\sigma_G} \right] \tilde{x}_2 + (1 - \omega_2) \left[-\frac{\omega_1}{\sigma_F} + \frac{1}{\sigma_G} \right] \tilde{x}_3. \tag{k}$$

The marginal product of x_2 depends negatively on the quantity of x_2 used, and positively on the quantities used of factor x_1. The effect of factor x_3 is ambiguous.

Finally, for $F_3 \equiv F_Z [x_1, G (x_2, x_3)] G_3 (x_2, x_3)$ we obtain:

$$\tilde{F}_3 = \frac{\omega_1}{\sigma_F} \tilde{x}_1 + \omega_2 \left[-\frac{\omega_1}{\sigma_F} + \frac{1}{\sigma_G} \right] \tilde{x}_2 - \left[\frac{\omega_1 (1 - \omega_2)}{\sigma_F} + \frac{\omega_2}{\sigma_G} \right] \tilde{x}_3. \tag{l}$$

We reach a similar conclusion as for factor x_2. The marginal product of x_3 depends negatively on the quantity of x_3 used, and positively on the quantities used of factor x_1. The effect of factor x_2 is ambiguous.

Up to this point we have been silent about the identity of the three factors. Three different cases can now be considered:

1. The factors are $x_1 = \bar{K}$, $x_2 = N_U$, and $x_3 = N_S$. The productivity conditions are $w_U = F_2$ and $w_S = F_3$. The income shares are $\omega_K \equiv \bar{K}F_K/Y = \omega_1$, $\omega_U \equiv N_U F_U/Y = (1 - \omega_1)\omega_2$, and $\omega_S \equiv N_S F_S/Y = (1 - \omega_1)(1 - \omega_2)$.

2. The factors are $x_1 = N_S$, $x_2 = N_U$, and $x_3 = \bar{K}$. The productivity conditions are $w_U = F_2$ and $w_S = F_1$. The income shares are $\omega_S = \omega_1$, $\omega_U = (1 - \omega_1)\omega_2$, and $\omega_K = (1 - \omega_1)(1 - \omega_2)$.

3. The factors are $x_1 = N_U$, $x_2 = N_S$, and $x_3 = \bar{K}$. The productivity conditions are $w_U = F_1$ and $w_S = F_2$. The income shares are $\omega_U = \omega_1$, $\omega_S = (1 - \omega_1)\omega_2$, and $\omega_K = (1 - \omega_1)(1 - \omega_2)$.

Case 1. Using the productivity conditions stated in (7.9) and (k)–(l) we find the following system determining the demands for the two types of labour as a function of factor prices and the given capital stock:

$$
J_1 \begin{bmatrix} \tilde{N}_U \\ \tilde{N}_S \end{bmatrix} = \begin{bmatrix} \tilde{w}_U - \dfrac{\omega_1}{\sigma_F}\tilde{\bar{K}} \\ \tilde{w}_S - \dfrac{\omega_1}{\sigma_F}\tilde{\bar{K}} \end{bmatrix},
\tag{m}
$$

where w_i is the real wage rate for labour of type i, and $\tilde{w}_i \equiv dw_i/w_i$. The Jacobian matrix, J_1, is defined as:

$$
J_1 \equiv \begin{bmatrix} -\dfrac{\omega_1\omega_2\sigma_G + (1 - \omega_2)\sigma_F}{\sigma_F\sigma_G} & \dfrac{(1 - \omega_2)[\sigma_F - \omega_1\sigma_G]}{\sigma_F\sigma_G} \\[3mm] \dfrac{\omega_2[\sigma_F - \omega_1\sigma_G]}{\sigma_F\sigma_G} & -\dfrac{\omega_1(1 - \omega_2)\sigma_G + \omega_2\sigma_F}{\sigma_F\sigma_G} \end{bmatrix}.
\tag{n}
$$

After some manipulation we find that $|J_1| = \omega_1/(\sigma_F\sigma_G) > 0$. Since $J_1^{-1} = \text{adj}(J_1)/|J_1|$ we find that equation (m) can be solved:

$$
\begin{bmatrix} \tilde{N}_U \\ \tilde{N}_S \end{bmatrix} = \begin{bmatrix} -\dfrac{\omega_1(1 - \omega_2)\sigma_G + \omega_2\sigma_F}{\omega_1} \\[3mm] \dfrac{\omega_2[\omega_1\sigma_G - \sigma_F]}{\omega_1} \end{bmatrix} \tilde{w}_U
$$

$$
+ \begin{bmatrix} \dfrac{(1 - \omega_2)[\omega_1\sigma_G - \sigma_F]}{\omega_1} \\[3mm] -\dfrac{\omega_1\omega_2\sigma_G + (1 - \omega_2)\sigma_F}{\omega_1} \end{bmatrix} \tilde{w}_S + \begin{bmatrix} 1 \\ 1 \end{bmatrix} \tilde{\bar{K}}.
\tag{o}
$$

Using the definitions of the income shares for case 1, we find that $\omega_1 = \omega_K$, $\omega_2 = \omega_U/(1 - \omega_K)$, and $1 - \omega_2 = \omega_S/(1 - \omega_K)$. Hence, the expression in (o) can in principle be rewritten in observable income shares. Note that the sign of the cross effects $\partial N_U/\partial w_S$ and $\partial N_S/\partial w_U$ is determined by the sign of $\omega_K\sigma_G - \sigma_F$, which itself depends on the capital income share and on the two substitution elasticities. If $\omega_K\sigma_G > \sigma_F$ then skilled and unskilled labour are *gross substitutes* in production in the short run. Vice versa, if $\omega_K \sigma_G < \sigma_F$ they are *gross complements* in the short-run production function.

Cases 2 and 3 are left as exercises to the reader. It is not difficult to show that the two types of labour must be gross complements in short-run production in cases 2 and 3.

****

7.2.2 The effects of taxation

Before leaving the standard model of the aggregate labour market, we turn to an analysis of the effects of taxation on employment and the real wage rate. This analysis was commenced in Chapter 1 (see section 1.3.6 on the supply siders) and is completed here. In addition to considering flat tax rates on consumption and the use of labour by firms, we also study the effects of progressivity of the labour income tax. Attention is restricted to the short run, i.e. the capital stock is assumed to be constant (and equal to $\bar{K}$). There is only one type of labour, and the representative firm maximizes short-run profit which is defined as:

$$\Pi \equiv PF(N, \bar{K}) - W(1 + \theta_E)N, \tag{7.15}$$

where θ_E is an *ad valorem* tax levied on the firm's use of labour (e.g. the employer's contribution to social security). The usual argument leads to the marginal productivity condition for labour, $F_N(N^D, \bar{K}) = w(1 + \theta_E)$ where N^D is the competitive demand for labour and $w \equiv W/P$ is the gross real wage. The first-order condition can be linearized:

$$\tilde{N}^D = -\varepsilon_D \left[\tilde{w} + \tilde{\theta}_E \right], \tag{7.16}$$

where $\varepsilon_D \equiv -F_N/(N F_{NN})$ is the absolute value of the labour demand elasticity ($\varepsilon_D > 0$), $\tilde{N}^D \equiv dN^D/N^D$, $\tilde{\theta}_E \equiv d\theta_E/(1 + \theta_E)$, and $\tilde{w} \equiv dw/w$.

Most income tax systems in use in the developed countries are *progressive*, in the sense that the tax rate rises with the tax base (labour income in this case). Since we wish to investigate the effects of progressivity on the labour supply decision by households, we specify the general tax function $T(WN^S)$. The marginal income tax rate θ_M facing households coincides with the derivative of this function with respect to labour income, i.e. $\theta_M \equiv dT(WN^S)/d(WN^S)$. In the absence of taxable income from other sources, the average income tax rate is simply $\theta_A \equiv T(WN^S)/(WN^S)$. The key thing to note is that, in general, both θ_M and θ_A depend on the tax base, WN^S.

The household's utility function is assumed to be of the usual kind:

$$U = U(C, 1 - N^S), \tag{7.17}$$

with $U_C > 0$, $U_{1-N} > 0$, $U_{CC} < 0$, $U_{1-N,1-N} < 0$, and $U_{CC}U_{1-N,1-N} - U_{C,1-N}^2 > 0$. In addition to facing (progressive) income taxes, the household also has to pay an *ad valorem* tax on consumption goods (e.g. a value-added tax, θ_C), so that the household budget restriction is:

$$P(1 + \theta_C)C = WN^S - T(WN^S). \tag{7.18}$$

The household maximizes utility by choosing the optimal level of consumption and labour supply. The Lagrangian is:

$$\mathcal{L} \equiv U(C, 1 - N^S) + \beta \left[WN^S - T(WN^S) - P(1 + \theta_C)C \right], \tag{7.19}$$

and the first-order conditions for utility maximization are:

$$\frac{\partial \mathcal{L}}{\partial C} = U_C - \beta P(1 + \theta_C) = 0, \tag{7.20}$$

$$\frac{\partial \mathcal{L}}{\partial N^S} = -U_{1-N} + \beta \left[W - \frac{dT(WN^S)}{d(WN^S)} \frac{d(WN^S)}{dN^S} \right]$$

$$= -U_{1-N} + \beta W(1 - \theta_M) = 0, \tag{7.21}$$

where we have used the definition of the marginal income tax rate to arrive at the ultimate expression in (7.21). By solving (7.20) and (7.21) for β we obtain the expansion path:

$$\beta = \frac{U_C}{P(1 + \theta_C)} = \frac{U_{1-N}}{W(1 - \theta_M)} \quad \Rightarrow$$

$$\frac{U_{1-N}}{U_C} = \frac{w(1 - \theta_M)}{1 + \theta_C}, \tag{7.22}$$

where we have used the definition of the gross real wage, $w \equiv W/P$. Equation (7.22) drives home a very important point: in the optimum the marginal rate of substitution between leisure and consumption depends on the marginal (and not on the average) income tax rate facing households! This result follows from the assumption that labour is *perfectly divisible*, i.e. the household can freely choose the number of minutes of its time endowment that it wants to supply to the labour market. This is called the labour supply choice at the intensive margin.

In order to facilitate the discussion to come, we assume that the utility function (7.17) is homothetic (see Intermezzo 7.1 above) and define the substitution elasticity between consumption and leisure *along a given indifference curve* as follows:

$$\sigma_{CM} = \frac{\text{\%ge change in } C/(1 - N^S)}{\text{\%ge change in } U_{1-N}/U_C} \equiv \frac{d\ln(C/(1 - N^S))}{d\ln(U_{1-N}/U_C)} \geq 0, \tag{7.23}$$

where we have used the fact that $d\ln x = dx/x$ represents the proportional change in variable x. Intuitively, σ_{CM} measures how "easy" it is (in utility terms) for the household to substitute consumption for leisure. A household with a very low value of σ_{CM}, finds substitution very difficult, whereas a household with a high σ_{CM} is quite happy to substitute consumption for leisure. In graphical terms, the former household has sharp kinks in its indifference curves,[5] whereas the latter has relatively flat indifference curves. The substitution elasticity can be used in the linearization of (7.22):

$$d\ln\left(\frac{U_{1-N}}{U_C}\right) = \tilde{w} - \tilde{\theta}_M - \tilde{\theta}_C = \frac{1}{\sigma_{CM}}\left[\tilde{C} - \widetilde{(1 - N^S)}\right] \quad \Rightarrow$$

---

[5]This does not imply that this household is kinky. It just means that the household is very reluctant to deviate from a fixed proportion between consumption and leisure. In case $\sigma_{CM} = 0$, the indifference curves are right angles, and nothing will make the household deviate from a fixed proportion between consumption and leisure.

$$\tilde{C} + \frac{1}{\omega_L}\tilde{N}^S = \sigma_{CM}\left[\tilde{w} - \tilde{\theta}_M - \tilde{\theta}_C\right], \tag{7.24}$$

where $\tilde{\theta}_M \equiv d\theta_M/(1-\theta_M)$, $\tilde{\theta}_C \equiv d\theta_C/(1+\theta_C)$, and $\omega_L \equiv (1-N^S)/N^S$ is the initial ratio of leisure to labour supply. By using the definition of the average tax rate, θ_A, the budget restriction (7.18) can be rewritten as $(1+\theta_C)C = (1-\theta_A)wN^S$. By linearizing this expression we obtain:

$$\tilde{C} + \tilde{\theta}_C = \tilde{w} - \tilde{\theta}_A + \tilde{N}^S, \tag{7.25}$$

where $\tilde{\theta}_A \equiv d\theta_A/(1-\theta_A)$. Hence, the average income tax rate influences the budget restriction of the household.

By solving (7.24)–(7.25) for the change in labour supply, the following expression is obtained:

$$\begin{aligned}
\tilde{N}^S &= (1-N^S)\left[\sigma_{CM}\left[\tilde{w} - \tilde{\theta}_M - \tilde{\theta}_C\right] - \left[\tilde{w} - \tilde{\theta}_A - \tilde{\theta}_C\right]\right] \\
&= \varepsilon_{SW}^c\left[\tilde{w} - \tilde{\theta}_M - \tilde{\theta}_C\right] + \varepsilon_{SI}\left[\tilde{\theta}_A + \tilde{\theta}_C - \tilde{w}\right] \\
&= \varepsilon_{SW}\left[\tilde{w} - \tilde{\theta}_C\right] - \varepsilon_{SW}^c\tilde{\theta}_M + \varepsilon_{SI}\tilde{\theta}_A, \tag{7.26}
\end{aligned}$$

where $\varepsilon_{SW}^c \equiv \sigma_{CM}(1-N^S)$ is the *compensated* wage elasticity, and $-\varepsilon_{SI} \equiv -(1-N^S)$ is the income elasticity. The compensated wage elasticity corresponds to the substitution effect and is always non-negative (because $\sigma_{CM} \geq 0$ and $0 < N^S < 1$). As its name suggests the income elasticity of labour supply corresponds to the income effect and is always negative. The total effect of a change in the gross wage is measured by the *uncompensated* wage elasticity, $\varepsilon_{SW} \equiv \varepsilon_{SW}^c - \varepsilon_{SI} = (\sigma_{CM} - 1)(1-N^S)$, which may be positive, zero, or even negative, depending on the magnitude of σ_{CM}. If the elasticity of substitution between leisure time and consumption exceeds unity (i.e. $\sigma_{CM} > 1$), then the substitution effect dominates the income effect and thus labour supply is an increasing function of the real wage. Otherwise, the income effect dominates the substitution effect, and labour supply slopes backwards. Empirical studies report that the wage elasticity of labour supply (ε_{SW}) is fairly small for males, but bigger for females (see Pencavel, 1986 and Killingsworth and Heckman, 1986).

The demand and supply equations of the standard model of the labour market (expanded with various tax rates) are given in linearized form by, respectively, equations (7.16) and (7.26). There are several ways to close the model. For example, the *equilibrium* interpretation postulates flexible wages and assumes continuous market clearing. Since we also wish to discuss the effect of different tax rates on unemployment, the *disequilibrium* interpretation requires the real wage to be fixed at a level that is too high for market clearing. In Table 7.1 we summarize the effects of the different taxes on employment, the gross real wage rate, and unemployment for both the equilibrium and disequilibrium interpretations of the model.

7.2.2.1 Tax effects with flexible wages and a clearing labour market

In this subsection we assume that the wage rate is flexible and clears the labour market. Mathematically, we have that $\tilde{N} = \tilde{N}^D = \tilde{N}^S$ so that (7.16) and (7.26) can be rewritten as:

$$\tilde{N} = -\varepsilon_D\left[\tilde{w} + \tilde{\theta}_E\right], \tag{7.27}$$

$$\tilde{N} = \varepsilon_{SW}\left[\tilde{w} - \tilde{\theta}_C\right] - \varepsilon_{SW}^c\tilde{\theta}_M + \varepsilon_{SI}\tilde{\theta}_A. \tag{7.28}$$

Table 7.1. Taxes and the competitive labour market

	(a) Flexible wage			(b) Fixed consumer wage		
	$\tilde{w}$	$\tilde{N}$	dU	$\tilde{w}$	$\tilde{N}$	dU
$\tilde{\theta}_M$	$\dfrac{\varepsilon^c_{SW}}{\varepsilon_{SW}+\varepsilon_D}$	$-\dfrac{\varepsilon_D\varepsilon^c_{SW}}{\varepsilon_{SW}+\varepsilon_D}$	0	0	0	$-\varepsilon^c_{SW}$
$\tilde{\theta}_A$	$-\dfrac{\varepsilon_{SI}}{\varepsilon_{SW}+\varepsilon_D}$	$\dfrac{\varepsilon_D\varepsilon_{SI}}{\varepsilon_{SW}+\varepsilon_D}$	0	1	$-\varepsilon_D$	$\varepsilon^c_{SW}+\varepsilon_D$
$\tilde{\theta}_M=\tilde{\theta}_A$	$\dfrac{\varepsilon_{SW}}{\varepsilon_{SW}+\varepsilon_D}$	$-\dfrac{\varepsilon_D\varepsilon_{SW}}{\varepsilon_{SW}+\varepsilon_D}$	0	1	$-\varepsilon_D$	ε_D
$\tilde{\theta}_E$	$-\dfrac{\varepsilon_D}{\varepsilon_{SW}+\varepsilon_D}$	$-\dfrac{\varepsilon_D\varepsilon_{SW}}{\varepsilon_{SW}+\varepsilon_D}$	0	0	$-\varepsilon_D$	ε_D
$\tilde{\theta}_C$	$\dfrac{\varepsilon_{SW}}{\varepsilon_{SW}+\varepsilon_D}$	$-\dfrac{\varepsilon_D\varepsilon_{SW}}{\varepsilon_{SW}+\varepsilon_D}$	0	1	$-\varepsilon_D$	ε_D
$\tilde{w}_C$	$-$	$-$	$-$	1	$-\varepsilon_D$	$\varepsilon_{SW}+\varepsilon_D$

Notes: (a) coefficients satisfy $\varepsilon_D>0$, $\varepsilon^c_{SW}>0$, $\varepsilon_{SI}>0$;
(b) for a dominant substitution effect, $\varepsilon_{SW}\equiv\varepsilon^c_{SW}-\varepsilon_{SI}>0$;
(c) stability condition is $\varepsilon_{SW}+\varepsilon_D>0$.

Solving these expressions for $\tilde{N}$ and $\tilde{w}$ we find:

$$\tilde{w} = \frac{\varepsilon_{SW}^c \tilde{\theta}_M - \varepsilon_{SI}\tilde{\theta}_A - \varepsilon_D\tilde{\theta}_E + \varepsilon_{SW}\tilde{\theta}_C}{\varepsilon_D + \varepsilon_{SW}}, \tag{7.29}$$

$$\tilde{N} = -\varepsilon_D \cdot \frac{\varepsilon_{SW}^c \tilde{\theta}_M - \varepsilon_{SI}\tilde{\theta}_A + \varepsilon_{SW}\tilde{\theta}_E + \varepsilon_{SW}\tilde{\theta}_C}{\varepsilon_D + \varepsilon_{SW}}. \tag{7.30}$$

For the sake of convenience, the various comparative static effects have been summarized in panel (a) of Table 7.1. We now consider the labour market effects of several tax policy initiatives.

First, suppose that the policy maker wishes to make the tax system more progressive, without however, changing the average tax rate. In terms of Table 7.1(a), this means that $\tilde{\theta}_M > 0$ and all other tax rates remain constant ($\tilde{\theta}_A = \tilde{\theta}_E = \tilde{\theta}_C = 0$). Due to the higher marginal tax rate, households supply less labour at the same gross real wage rate, and labour supply shifts to the left, say from N_0^S to N_1^S in Figure 7.4. The equilibrium moves from E_0 to E_1, and the gross wage rate increases.[6] These results have been reported in the row for $\tilde{\theta}_M$ in Table 7.1(a). Obviously, because the labour market clears there is no effect on unemployment.

Note that part of the tax increase is shifted from households to the firms, namely the line segment BE_1. This tax shifting phenomenon can be explained with the aid of Figure 7.4. Following the tax shock, the price of labour paid by firms rises from w_0 to w_1. The price of labour that is received by households, however, falls from w_0 to w'. Note that with the original marginal tax rate, N_1 units of labour would have been supplied at the wage w'. It thus follows that the line segment AB represents the part of the tax increase that is borne by households, whilst BE_1 is the part borne by firms. The degree of tax shifting depends on the elasticities of the demand and supply curves. For example, if labour demand is perfectly elastic (horizontal) then households bear the full burden. At the opposite extreme, firms bear the full burden if labour supply is vertical (and $\varepsilon_{SW} = 0$).

As a second policy shock, consider the case in which the policy maker increases the average income tax ($\tilde{\theta}_A > 0$), whilst keeping the marginal tax on labour and all other taxes unchanged ($\tilde{\theta}_M = \tilde{\theta}_E = \tilde{\theta}_C = 0$). Now the effects on the labour market are completely different. The situation (for the case with $\varepsilon_{SW} > 0$) is depicted in Figure 7.4. As a result of the higher average tax, households feel poorer (due to the income effect) and decide to supply more labour. This shifts the labour supply curve to the right, say from N_0^S to N_2^S, and the equilibrium moves from E_0 to E_2. As a result of the tax increase, the gross real wage falls and employment rises. What is the degree of tax shifting in this case? Because the taxes affecting labour supply via the substitution effect (i.e. θ_M and θ_C) are unchanged, the traditional incidence analysis is not relevant. It is nevertheless possible to decompose the total effect on wages into a part borne by households and a part borne by firms. If labour supply were inelastic ($\varepsilon_{SW} = 0$), then N' units of labour would be supplied inelastically after the tax shock, labour market equilibrium would be at point F, and the wage would fall from w_0 to w''. With elastic labour supply ($\varepsilon_{SW} > 0$), however, labour market equilibrium occurs at point E_2 and the wage settles at w_2. Hence, because of the wage effect in labour supply, firms have to pay w_2 instead of w''. Hence, the

---

[6]This holds regardless of the sign of ε_{SW}, provided the stability condition $\varepsilon_{SW} + \varepsilon_D > 0$ is satisfied. In terms of Figure 7.4, the labour supply curve can be downward sloping ($\varepsilon_{SW} < 0$) but it must be steeper than the labour demand curve. Otherwise, high wages would be associated with excess demand for labour. There is no plausible real wage adjustment mechanism that would lead to stability in that case.

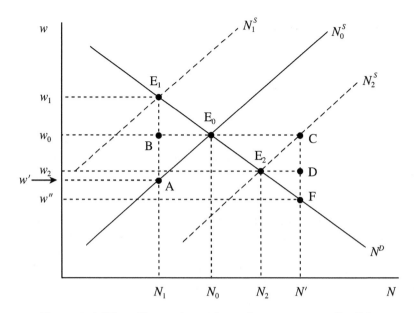

Figure 7.4: The effects of taxation when wages are flexible

line segment DF represents the part of the tax effect on wages that is borne by firms, whilst CD is the part borne by households.

7.2.2.2   Tax effects with rigid consumer wages and unemployment

Assume now that (for whatever reason) the real consumer wage is exogenously fixed above the level consistent with full employment. The real consumer wage is defined as the real wage after income taxes and the tax on goods have been taken into account, i.e. $w_C \equiv w(1 - \theta_A)/(1 + \theta_C)$. In loglinearized form we have that:

$$\tilde{w}_C \equiv \tilde{w} - \tilde{\theta}_A - \tilde{\theta}_C. \tag{7.31}$$

In view of this definition, equations (7.16) and (7.26) can be rewritten in terms of the exogenous real consumer wage:

$$\tilde{N}^D = -\varepsilon_D \left[\tilde{w}_C + \tilde{\theta}_A + \tilde{\theta}_E + \tilde{\theta}_C \right], \tag{7.32}$$

$$\tilde{N}^S = \varepsilon_{SW} \tilde{w}_C + \varepsilon_{SW}^c \left[\tilde{\theta}_A - \tilde{\theta}_M \right]. \tag{7.33}$$

By assumption the real consumer wage is too high for full employment, so that the minimum transaction rule[7] says that employment is determined by the demand for labour, i.e. $N = N^D$ which implies in loglinearized form that $\tilde{N} = \tilde{N}^D$. The unemployment rate is defined as $U \equiv (N^S - N^D)/N^S \approx \ln N^S - \ln N^D$, so that we have for the change in the unemployment rate:

$$dU = \tilde{N}^S - \tilde{N}^D. \tag{7.34}$$

Equations (7.32)–(7.34) determine employment, labour supply, and the unemployment rate as a function of the tax rates and the exogenous real consumer wage. Equation (7.31) can be used to determine what happens to the gross real wage.

---

[7]This rule states that the short side of the market determines the quantity that is actually traded. Market exchange is voluntary and nobody is forced to trade more than he/she wishes. The actual amount traded is thus the minimum of demand and supply.

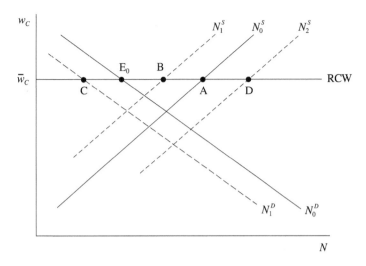

Figure 7.5: The effects of taxation with a fixed consumer wage

Consider first what happens if the marginal tax rate on labour is increased ($\tilde{\theta}_M >$ 0), leaving all other taxes unchanged ($\tilde{\theta}_A = \tilde{\theta}_E = \tilde{\theta}_C = 0$). For the given real consumer wage, labour supply is decreased and labour demand is unchanged. Consequently, unemployment is reduced. Some of the unemployed hours of labour are no longer supplied due to the disincentive effect of the higher marginal tax rate. This policy experiment has been illustrated in Figure 7.5, where RCW depicts the real consumer wage, N_0^S is the initial labour supply curve, and N_0^D is the initial labour demand curve. The economy is initially at E_0 and unemployment is given by the line segment $E_0 A$. The tax shock shifts the labour supply curve to the left, say from N_0^S to N_1^S. Provided the shock is not too large, the consumer-wage restriction remains binding and point B lies to the right of point E_0. There is no effect on employment and the reduction in unemployment is represented by the horizontal segment BA. It follows from (7.31) that the gross wage rate remains constant, i.e. $\tilde{w} = 0$ (since $\tilde{w}_C = \tilde{\theta}_A = \tilde{\theta}_C = 0$).

As a second policy shock, consider the case in which the policy maker increases the average income tax ($\tilde{\theta}_A > 0$), whilst keeping the marginal tax on labour and all other taxes unchanged ($\tilde{\theta}_M = \tilde{\theta}_E = \tilde{\theta}_C = 0$). There are several effects. It follows from (7.32) that labour demand shifts to the left, say from N_0^D to N_1^D in Figure 7.5. Similarly, we find from (7.33) that labour supply shifts to the right, say from N_0^S to N_2^S. The employment point moves from E_0 to C and unemployment increases from $E_0 A$ to CD. Why is employment reduced in such a dramatic fashion? The answer is furnished by (7.31), which implies that $\tilde{w} = \tilde{\theta}_A > 0$ (since $\tilde{w}_C = \tilde{\theta}_C = 0$). Taken in isolation an increase in the average tax rate leads to a reduction in the consumer wage which can only be undone by an increase in the gross wage rate. And since labour demand is at the short side of the market the increase in the gross wage rate translates directly into an employment reduction.

The students are advised to work through the remaining entries of Table 7.1(b), and verify their understanding by drawing pictures.

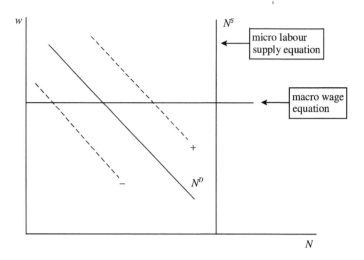

Figure 7.6: Labour demand and supply and the macroeconomic wage equation

7.2.3 The Holy Grail of macroeconomics

There exists a fundamental tension in the labour market theories that are based on perfectly competitive behaviour and flexible wages. From microeconometric research we know that the labour supply curve of (especially male) workers is highly inelastic (almost vertical). Macroeconometric research, on the other hand, shows that employment does fluctuate, for example due to productivity or demand shocks, without significant wage fluctuations occurring. In terms of Figure 7.6, this implies that the macroeconomic supply equation is not vertical but (almost) horizontal. What could be the microeconomic rationale behind such a horizontal real wage equation? In other words, why are real wages inflexible? A number of theories have been proposed to answer this question. In the remainder of this chapter we study two of these in detail, namely a theory based on the wage setting power of labour unions (in Section 7.3) and a theory based on wages acting as an incentive and motivation device for workers (in Section 7.4).

7.3 Trade unions and the labour market

The typical layman's sentiment about trade unions probably runs as follows. Powerful trade unions are just like monopolists. They sell labour dearly, cause high real wages, and hence are really to blame for low employment and high unemployment. In this section we evaluate this sentiment using the tools of neoclassical economics. We proceed as follows. First, in subsection 7.3.1 we study trade union behaviour in a partial equilibrium setting, i.e. we consider the case with a single representative union interacting with a single representative firm. Second, in subsection 7.3.2 we investigate a general equilibrium model of the dual economy in which firms operating in the primary sector are unionized and firms in the secondary sector are not. Under certain conditions the layman's sentiments about trade unions are shown to be correct.

7.3.1 Unions in partial equilibrium

We study the interaction between a single perfectly competitive firm and a single union. The firm is obliged to buy its labour inputs from the union. In order to prepare for the things to come we first characterize the objective functions of the two parties, starting with the description of union behaviour.

The trade union has a registered membership of T workers whose labour market interests it represents. We assume that labour is *indivisible*, i.e. the worker is either employed on a full-time basis and works for $L = \bar{L}$ hours, or he is unemployed in which case $L = 0$. Each unemployed worker receives the unemployment benefit B from the government. The worker enjoys both consumption C and leisure $1 - L$ and has a direct utility function which we write as $\Phi(C, 1 - L)$. Under the assumption that workers have no non-labour income and do not save or borrow, it follows that an unemployed worker attains the utility level $u^u(b) \equiv \Phi(b, 1)$ where $b \equiv B/P$ is the real dole payment and P is the price level. In contrast, an employed worker receives wage income $W\bar{L}$, where W is the nominal wage rate. As a result he achieves the utility level $u^e(w) \equiv \Phi(w\bar{L}, 1 - \bar{L})$, where $w \equiv W/P$ is the real wage rate.[8]

All individuals are identical and in each period the union randomly selects T^e of its members to be employed during that period. It follows that each worker has the probability $\frac{T^e}{T}$ of being employed in a particular period. Obviously, the probability of being unemployed is given by $1 - \frac{T^e}{T}$. Following Booth (1995, p. 91) we assume that the objective function of the representative trade union, $V(w, L)$, is the expected utility of a representative union member:

$$V(w, T^e) \equiv \frac{T^e}{T} \cdot u^e(w) + \left[1 - \frac{T^e}{T}\right] \cdot u^u(b). \tag{7.35}$$

Of course the union cannot employ more members than it has, i.e. $T^e \leq T$ is a feasibility constraint. But by employing T^e of its members, who each work for $\bar{L}$ hours, the union effectively supplies $N \equiv T^e \bar{L}$ hours of labour to the firm so that the union's objective function can be rewritten in a more convenient form as:

$$V(w, N) \equiv \frac{N}{N^{\max}} \cdot u^e(w) + \left[1 - \frac{N}{N^{\max}}\right] \cdot u^u(b), \tag{7.36}$$

where $N^{\max} \equiv T\bar{L}$ is the maximum amount of hours the union can supply, and $\frac{N}{N^{\max}}$ and $1 - \frac{N}{N^{\max}}$ represent the probabilities of, respectively, being employed or unemployed in a particular period.

The representative firm is modelled in the standard fashion. The short-run production function is written as $Y = AF(N, \bar{K})$, where Y is output, $\bar{K}$ is the fixed capital stock, A is a productivity index, and $F(\cdot, \cdot)$ features constant returns to scale and positive but diminishing marginal labour productivity ($F_N > 0 > F_{NN}$). Nominal short-run profit of the firm is defined as $\Pi \equiv PY - WN$ so that the (short-run) real profit function can be written as:

$$\pi(w, N) \equiv AF(N, \bar{K}) - wN. \tag{7.37}$$

---

[8] In the jargon of microeconomics, $\Phi(C, 1 - L)$ is the direct utility function, and $u^e(w)$ and $u^u(b)$ are indirect utility functions. An indirect utility function differs from a direct utility function in that it depends on prices and income rather than on quantities. The two are intricately linked, however. Indeed, the indirect utility function is obtained by substituting the optimal quantity choices of the household back into the direct utility function.

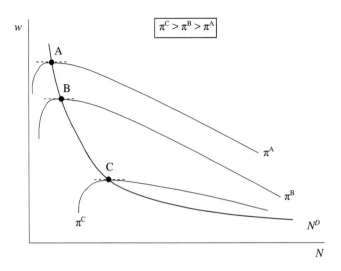

Figure 7.7: The iso-profit locus and labour demand

All models discussed in this section can be solved graphically. In order to do so, however, a number of graphical schedules must be derived. First, the labour demand schedule is obtained by finding all (w, N) combinations for which profit is maximized by choice of N. Formally, we have $\pi_N \equiv \partial \pi / \partial N = 0$, which yields:

$$\pi_N = AF_N(N, \bar{K}) - w = 0 \qquad \Leftrightarrow \qquad N^D = N^D(w, A, \bar{K}), \tag{7.38}$$

where $N_w^D \equiv \partial N^D(\cdot)/\partial w < 0$, $N_A^D \equiv \partial N^D(\cdot)/\partial A > 0$, and $N_{\bar{K}}^D \equiv \partial N^D(\cdot)/\partial \bar{K} > 0$. The labour demand curve is downward sloping in (w, N) space—see Figure 7.7.

The second graphical device that is needed to characterize the firm is the *iso-profit curve*. It represents the combinations of w and N for which profits attain a given level. It can be interpreted as the firm's indifference curve. The slope of an iso-profit curve can be determined in the usual fashion:

$$d\pi = 0: \Rightarrow \pi_w dw + \pi_N dN = 0 \Rightarrow \left(\frac{dw}{dN}\right)_{d\pi=0} = -\frac{\pi_N}{\pi_w}. \tag{7.39}$$

We know from equation (7.37) that $\pi_w = -N < 0$, so that the slope of an iso-profit line is determined by the sign of π_N. But $\pi_N \equiv AF_N - w$, and $F_{NN} < 0$, so that π_N is positive for a low employment level, becomes zero (at the profit-maximizing point), and then turns negative as employment increases further. Hence, in terms of Figure 7.7, the iso-profit curves are upward sloping to the left of the labour demand schedule, downward sloping to the right of labour demand, and attain a maximum for points on the labour demand schedule. In Figure 7.7 a number of iso-profit curves have been drawn, each associated with a different level of profit. Clearly, for a given level of employment N, the level of profit is increased if the wage rate falls, i.e. $\partial \pi / \partial w = \pi_w < 0$. Hence, the level of profit increases the further down the demand for labour curve the firm operates, i.e. $\pi^A < \pi^B < \pi^C$.

Trade union behaviour can also be represented graphically. The third schedule to be derived concerns the union's indifference curve. Obviously, the union will not be able to supply any workers to the firm if the wage rate is so low – relative to the unemployment benefit and the value of leisure – that at an unemployed union

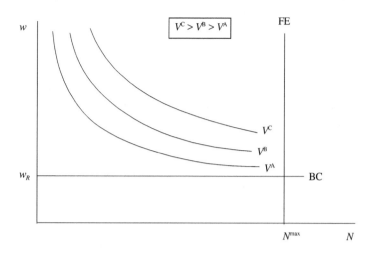

Figure 7.8: Indifference curves of the union

member is better off than an employed member, i.e. if w is such that $u^u(b) > u^e(w)$ all union members will refuse to work and will just collect the dole. By implicitly defining the reservation wage, w_R, such that $u^e(w_R) = u^u(b)$, it follows that the wage rate bargained by the union must satisfy the restriction $w \geq w_R$. In terms of Figure 7.8, this restriction is represented by the horizontal line BC (which stands for benefit curve, because the level of b has an important influence on its location). Furthermore, as was mentioned above the union is unable to supply any more workers than its current membership. Hence, there is an additional restriction $N \leq N^{\max}$, which is the full employment line FE in Figure 7.8. The feasible region is thus given by all combinations of w and N such that $w \geq w_R$ and $0 \leq N \leq N^{\max}$. The slope of an indifference curve of the union is determined in the usual way:

$$dV = V_w dw + V_N dN$$
$$= \frac{N u^e_w}{N^{\max}} dw + \frac{u^e(w) - u^u(b)}{N^{\max}} dN = 0 \qquad \Rightarrow$$
$$\left(\frac{dw}{dN}\right)_{dV=0} = -\frac{u^e(w) - u^u(b)}{N u^e_w} < 0, \qquad\qquad (7.40)$$

where $u^e_w \equiv \partial u^e(w)/\partial w$. Hence, the union's indifference curves are downward sloping (because $u^e_w > 0$ and $u^e(w) > u^u(b)$). Furthermore, union utility rises in a north-easterly direction (because $V_w > 0$ and $V_N > 0$), i.e. $V^C > V^B > V^A$ in Figure 7.8.

7.3.1.1 The monopoly model of the trade union

Perhaps the oldest trade union model is the monopoly model developed by Dunlop (1944). As its name suggests, the trade union is assumed to behave like a monopolistic seller of labour. It faces the firm's demand for labour (defined implicitly in (7.38)) and sets the real wage such that its utility (7.36) is maximized. Formally, the problem facing a monopoly union is as follows:

$$\max_{\{w\}} V(w, N) \quad \text{subject to} \quad \pi_N(w, A, N, \bar{K}) = 0, \tag{7.41}$$

where the restriction $\pi_N = 0$ ensures (by equation (7.38)) that the monopolistic union chooses a point on the labour demand function. In words, the demand for labour acts like the "budget restriction" for the monopolistic union. By substituting the labour demand function (given in (7.38)) into the union's utility function, the optimization problem becomes even easier:

$$\max_{\{w\}} V\left(w, N^D(w, A, \bar{K})\right), \tag{7.42}$$

so that the first-order condition is:

$$\frac{dV}{dw} = 0: \quad V_w + V_N N_w^D = 0, \tag{7.43}$$

which implies that $V_w / V_N = -N_w^D$. The slope of the union's indifference curve should be equated to the slope of the demand for labour.[9] For future reference we rewrite the expression in (7.43) in a much more intuitive form:

$$V_w + V_N N_w^D = \frac{N}{N^{\max}} \cdot u_w + \frac{1}{N^{\max}} \cdot [u^e(w) - u^u(b)] N_w^D$$

$$= \frac{N}{w N^{\max}} \cdot \left[w e_w^e + [u^e(w) - u^u(b)] \frac{w N_w^D}{N} \right] = 0$$

$$\Rightarrow \quad \frac{u^e(w) - u^u(b)}{w u_w^e} = \frac{1}{\varepsilon_D}, \tag{7.44}$$

where $\varepsilon_D \equiv -w N_w^D / N$ is the absolute value of the labour demand elasticity. Equation (7.44) can be seen as a kind of markup rule familiar from monopolistic pricing in the goods market.[10] The monopoly union sets the wage for its employed members in such a way that their utility is a markup factor times the utility of its unemployed members. Note that the unemployment benefit is the foundation upon which the union can build its wage claim.

The monopoly union solution is illustrated in Figure 7.9. The wage rate is set at w^M, the union attains a utility level V^M, and employment is N^M. The union has $(N^{\max} - N^M)$ of its members unemployed. How does this unemployment level compare to the competitive solution? If there were no unions and this was the only firm in the economy, then the effective labour supply would coincide with the BC line. The forces of the free market would force the wage rate down to $w = w_R$, so that point C in Figure 7.9 represents the competitive point. Employment is equal to N^C which is greater than employment with monopoly unions, i.e. $N^C > N^M$. Hence, in a partial-equilibrium sense, the monopoly union causes more unemployment than would be the case under perfect competition, and the layman's sentiments mentioned in the introduction are confirmed (see more on this below).

---

[9]It is possible that the union cannot choose this interior solution because the firm would make too little profit there. In such a case a corner solution is attained, and (7.43) does not hold with equality. We ignore this case here.

[10]A monopolistic firm facing marginal cost c and the demand curve $q = p^{-\varepsilon}$ sets its price such that $(p - c)/p = 1/\varepsilon$. By defining the wage elasticity of the indirect utility function as $\varepsilon_U \equiv w u_w^e(w)/u^e(w)$ we can rewrite (7.44) as:

$$\frac{u^e(w) - u^u(b)}{u^e(w)} = \frac{\varepsilon_U}{\varepsilon_D}.$$

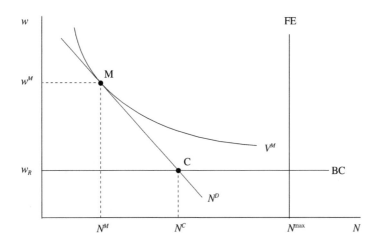

Figure 7.9: Wage setting by the monopoly union

In the monopoly union model the trade union unilaterally picks the wage and the firm unilaterally chooses the level of employment it wants at that wage. In the next union model this setting is made more realistic by assuming that the firm and the union bargain over the wage rate.

7.3.1.2 The "right-to-manage" model

The right-to-manage (RTM) model was first proposed by Leontief (1946). The firm still has "consumer sovereignty" in the sense that it can unilaterally determine the employment level (hence the name "right to manage"), but there is bargaining between the firm and the union over the real wage. The outcome of the bargaining process is modelled as a so-called generalized Nash bargaining solution (see e.g. Binmore and Dasgupta, 1987, and Booth, 1995, pp. 150–151). According to this solution concept, the real wage that is chosen after bargaining maximizes the geometrically weighted average of the gains to the two parties. In logarithmic terms we have:

$$\max_{\{w\}} \Omega \equiv \beta \ln \left[V(w, N) - V^{\min} \right] + (1 - \beta) \ln \left[\pi(w, N) - \pi^{\min} \right]$$

$$\text{subject to } \pi_N(w, A, N, \bar{K}) = 0, \tag{7.45}$$

where $V^{\min} \equiv u^u(b)$ is the fall-back position of the union, $\pi^{\min}$ is the fall-back position of the firm, and β represents the relative bargaining strength of the union ($0 \leq \beta \leq 1$). Obviously, the monopoly union model is obtained as a special case of the RTM model by setting $\beta = 1$. We have already argued that the union has no incentive to accept wages lower than the reservation wage w_R, where utility of the union is at its lowest value of $V(w_R, N) = u^u(b)$. This rationalizes the fall-back position of the union. For the firm a similar fall-back position will generally exist. To the extent that the firm has fixed costs, minimum profit must be positive, i.e. $\pi^{\min} > 0$.

The maximization problem is simplified substantially if we substitute the constraint (the labour demand function) into the objective function. Indeed, by substituting the second expression in (7.38) into (7.45) we obtain:

$$\max_{\{w\}} \Omega \equiv \beta \ln \left[V(w, N^D(w, A, \bar{K})) - V^{\min} \right] + (1 - \beta) \ln \left[\pi(w, N^D(w, A, \bar{K})) - \pi^{\min} \right],$$

(7.46)

for which the first-order condition is:

$$\frac{d\Omega}{dw} = \beta \cdot \frac{V_w + V_N N_w^D}{V - V^{\min}} + (1 - \beta) \cdot \frac{\pi_w + \pi_N N_w^D}{\pi - \pi^{\min}} = 0.$$

(7.47)

The numerator of the first term on the right-hand side of (7.47) can be simplified to:

$$V_w + V_N N_w^D = \frac{N}{wN^{\max}} \cdot \left[wu_w^e - \varepsilon_D \left[u^e(w) - u^u(b) \right] \right],$$

(7.48)

where we recall that $\varepsilon_D \equiv -wN_w^D/N$ is the absolute value of the labour demand elasticity. Furthermore, the numerator of the second term on the right-hand side of (7.47) becomes:

$$\pi_w + \pi_N N_w^D = \pi_w = -N,$$

(7.49)

since the solution lies on the labour demand curve, so that $\pi_N = 0$. By substituting (7.48)–(7.49) into (7.47), and simplifying, we obtain:

$$\frac{\beta}{V - V^{\min}} \left[V_w + V_N N_w^D \right] = -\frac{1 - \beta}{\pi - \pi^{\min}} \pi_w \Rightarrow$$

$$\frac{N}{wN^{\max}} \left[wu_w^e - \varepsilon_D \left[u^e(w) - u^u(b) \right] \right] = \frac{(1 - \beta)(V - V^{\min})}{\beta(\pi - \pi^{\min})} N \Rightarrow$$

$$wu_w^e - \varepsilon_D \left[u^e(w) - u^u(b) \right] = \frac{(1 - \beta)wN}{\beta(Y - wN - \pi^{\min})} \left[u^e(w) - u^u(b) \right],$$

(7.50)

where we have used the definition of π (in (7.37)) and the fact that $V - V^{\min} = (N/N^{\max})(u^e(w) - u^u(b))$ in the final step. Continuing the derivation, we find the real wage expression for the RTM model (in a form directly compatible to (7.44)):

$$\frac{u^e(w) - u^u(b)}{wu_w^e} = \frac{1}{\varepsilon_D + \phi}, \qquad \phi \equiv \frac{(1 - \beta)\omega_N}{\beta(1 - \omega_N - \omega_\pi)} \geq 0,$$

(7.51)

where $\omega_N \equiv wN/Y$ is the share of labour income in total income, and $\omega_\pi \equiv \pi^{\min}/Y$ is the share of the minimum profit level in total income.

    Equation (7.51) shows that the real wage markup that rolls out of the bargaining process is lower than under the monopoly union model (unless the union has all the bargaining power, in which case $\beta = 1$, $\phi = 0$, and (7.44) and (7.51) coincide). The RTM solution can be illustrated with the aid of Figure 7.10. For ease of reference, the monopoly solution M and associated iso-profit curve π^M have also been drawn. The RTM solution lies on the labour demand curve, but at a wage level below that for the monopoly solution. It is indicated by point R where the profit level of the firm is $\pi^R > \pi^M$. Compared to the competitive solution (at point C), there is still less employment and thus more unemployment. Compared to the monopoly solution, however, unemployment is lower.

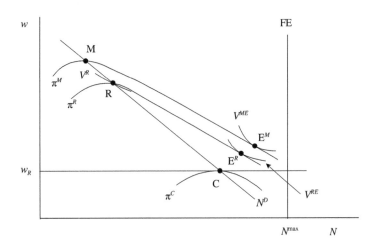

Figure 7.10: Wage setting in the right-to-manage model

The exact location of point R depends on the bargaining strength of the union, as represented by the parameter β. The higher β is, the closer point R lies to point M. On the other hand, if β is very low, then ϕ is very large (see (7.51)) and the wage is close to the competitive solution, i.e. $w \approx w_R$. Hence, depending on the magnitude of β, R can be anywhere on the labour demand curve between points M and C.

A major problem with the RTM solution is that the chosen wage-employment outcome is Pareto-inefficient, i.e. it is possible to make one of the parties involved in the bargain better off without harming the other party. This can be demonstrated with the aid of Figure 7.10. At point R, the union attains a utility level of V^R and the firm has a profit level of π^R. The firm is indifferent for all (w, N) combinations along the iso-profit curve π^R, but the union's utility strictly increases if a point off the labour demand curve is chosen. Indeed, the efficient solution occurs at the point where there is a tangency between the iso-profit curve π^R and an indifference curve for the union. This occurs at point E^R, where the union attains a utility level $V^{RE} > V^R$. (For the same reason, point M is also inefficient, but point C is efficient. Verify these claims.)

Economists are not particularly fond of inefficient solutions, especially in the "small numbers" case–that we are considering here–with only two parties bargaining. One would expect that the two parties would be sufficiently smart to eliminate the type of inefficiency that exists in the RTM and monopoly model. For that reason, the efficient bargaining model was developed by McDonald and Solow (1981).

7.3.1.3   The efficient bargaining model

McDonald and Solow (1981) analyse the case where the union and the firm bargain simultaneously over wages and employment. Again the bargaining problem can be analysed within a generalized Nash bargaining setup. Now the negotiations lead to the maximization of Ω by choice of the appropriate wage-employment combination:

$$\max_{\{w,N\}} \Omega \equiv \beta \ln \left[V(w, N) - V^{\min} \right] + (1 - \beta) \ln \left[\pi(w, N) - \pi^{\min} \right]. \qquad (7.52)$$

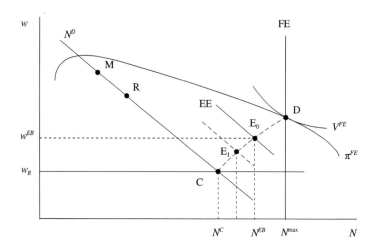

Figure 7.11: Wages and employment under efficient bargaining

The first-order conditions for this problem are:

$$\frac{\partial \Omega}{\partial w} = \frac{\beta}{V - V^{\min}} \cdot V_w + \frac{1 - \beta}{\pi - \pi^{\min}} \cdot \pi_w = 0, \tag{7.53}$$

$$\frac{\partial \Omega}{\partial N} = \frac{\beta}{V - V^{\min}} \cdot V_N + \frac{1 - \beta}{\pi - \pi^{\min}} \cdot \pi_N = 0. \tag{7.54}$$

By combining (7.53)–(7.54), the so-called *contract curve* is obtained:

$$-\frac{1 - \beta}{\pi - \pi^{\min}} = \frac{\beta}{V - V^{\min}} \frac{V_w}{\pi_w} = \frac{\beta}{V - V^{\min}} \frac{V_N}{\pi_N} \quad \Rightarrow \quad \frac{V_N}{V_w} = \frac{\pi_N}{\pi_w}. \tag{7.55}$$

In words, the contract curve (CD in Figure 7.11) represents the locus of (w, N) combinations for which efficient bargaining solutions are obtained. For any point on the contract curve, there is no (w, N) combination that makes one party better off without simultaneously harming the other party. In graphical terms, the contract curve represents all tangency points between iso-profit curves and union indifference curves.

One immediate implication of the efficient bargaining model is that the real wage exceeds the marginal product of labour. Indeed, (7.55) says that $\pi_N = V_N \pi_w / V_w < 0$ (since $V_N > 0$, $V_w > 0$, and $\pi_w < 0$). Hence:

$$\pi_N \equiv AF_N(N, \bar{K}) - w < 0 \quad \Leftrightarrow \quad w > AF_N(N, \bar{K}). \tag{7.56}$$

Hence, with the exception of the competitive solution, efficient contracts are not on the labour demand curve. Of course, we have already discussed three points on the contract curve, namely points C, E^R, and E^M in Figure 7.10. Of these only point C is on the labour demand curve.

In Figure 7.11, the entire contract curve is drawn as the dashed line connecting points C and D. We assume that full employment is possible in principle. This means that the profit level associated with the full employment level on the contract curve (point D) exceeds the fall-back profit level of the firm (i.e. $\pi^{FE} > \pi^{\min}$). In that case, the entire line segment CD constitutes the contract curve.

As it stands, the model is not yet fully specified because it does not yield a prediction about any *particular* wage-employment outcome—all (w, N) combinations along the line CD are efficient. McDonald and Solow (1981, p. 903) suggest closing the model by postulating a so-called "fair share" rule. After repeated interactions in the past, the union and the firm have somehow settled on a "fair" division of the spoils. In terms of the model, the *equity locus* (EE) is implicitly defined as:

$$wN = w_N^f Y = w_N^f AF(N, \bar{K}), \qquad 0 < w_n^f < 1, \tag{7.57}$$

where w_N^f is the "fair" share of the spoils going to the union (the firm gets $1 - w_N^f$ of output in the form of profits). The slope of the equity locus can be determined in the usual fashion:

$$N dw + w dN = w_N^f AF_N dN \quad \Rightarrow \quad \left(\frac{dw}{dN}\right)_{EE} = \frac{w_N^f AF_N - w}{N} < 0, \tag{7.58}$$

where the sign follows from the fact that $\pi_N \equiv AF_N - w < 0$ (for each N between N^C and $N^{\max}$ the equity locus lies above the labour demand function, $w > AF_N$, so that a fortiori $w > w_N^f AF_N$). The equity locus is downward sloping and shifts up and to the right if labour's share of the pie (w_N^f) is increased.

By combining the equity locus EE and the contract curve CD, the equilibrium wage-employment combination is obtained at E_0. A very surprising conclusion is reached. Compared to the competitive solution (point C), employment is higher (and unemployment is lower) under the efficient bargaining model ($N^{EB} > N^C$). The layman's sentiment, mentioned in the introduction to this chapter, is only partially correct. Wages are higher than in the competitive solution ($w^{EB} > w_R$) but employment is also higher than in the competitive solution. The intuition behind this result is that the union prevents the firm from grabbing the maximum profit level (at point C), and instead turns some of this profit into jobs for union members.

Armed with this intuition, the second conclusion that can be drawn on the basis of the efficient bargaining model is perhaps less paradoxical than it may appear at first sight. Wage moderation, as modelled by a smaller share of the pie for labour (w_N^f down), turns out to be bad for employment! Graphically, a lower w_N^f shifts the EE locus down and to the left, shifting the equilibrium from E_0 to E_1. The power of the firm is de facto increased, and the wage-employment combination is forced closer to the competitive solution.

It is fair to say that the efficient wage bargaining model yields some rather surprising conclusions. The problem with the model appears to be its tenuous empirical relevance. Although simultaneous bargaining over wages and employment is efficient, it is hardly ever observed in practice. It therefore appears that the RTM model (which includes the monopoly model as a special case) has a closer affinity to reality than the efficient bargaining model. In other words, in the real world the relevant case appears to be that firms and unions negotiate over the wage rate, but that the firm can unilaterally determine the employment level.

7.3.2 Unions in general equilibrium

In a partial equilibrium setting it is clear that trade unions typically end up not employing all their members. If all firms in the economy would be unionized then there would be no other option for the unemployed union members than to stay at home

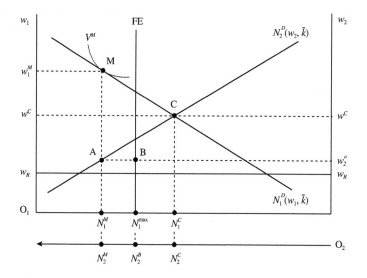

Figure 7.12: Unions and wage dispersion in a two-sector model

and wait for better luck next time. The general equilibrium results would be identical to the partial equilibrium results! But this is not a very realistic scenario. In most countries there are sectors that are heavily unionized and others that are not unionized at all. In this more realistic scenario the general equilibrium repercussions of union wage setting are much more interesting.

To investigate some of the issues that arise in a general equilibrium context, it is instructive to study the effects of trade union behaviour in a two-sector setting. This allows us to study the spillover effects that unions may have on the non-unionized sector of the economy. Suppose that labour is homogeneous, but that there are two sectors in the economy. The first sector, called the *primary sector*, is unionized, and the second, called the *secondary sector*, has a competitive system of wage determination. The total labour force is fixed, and equal to $\bar{N}$. Employment and the real wage rate in sector i are denoted by, N_i and w_i. Firms in both sectors are perfectly competitive and produce a homogeneous good using the short-run production function $Y_i = F(N_i, \bar{k})$ where $\bar{k}$ is the fixed capital stock (assumed to be of the same size for all firms). The competitive labour demand in sector i is defined implicitly as:

$$w_i = F_N(N_i, \bar{k}) \quad \Leftrightarrow \quad N_i^D = N_i^D(w_i, \bar{k}). \tag{7.59}$$

In Figure 7.12 the situation on the labour market is depicted in an Edgeworth box diagram. Employment in the primary sector is measured from left to right with the origin at O_1. Employment in the secondary sector is measured from right to left with origin O_2. The size of the box is equal to the total supply of labour $\bar{N}$. In the absence of unions, and with perfect mobility of labour between the two sectors, the common wage rate would be at the market clearing competitive level w^C, and employment in the two sectors would be N_1^C and N_2^C, respectively.

Now consider the effect of unionization. To keep things as simple as possible we consider the case where there is a single monopolistic union.[11] The union has a membership of $N_1^{\max}$ (in labour hours) and FE is the full employment locus. As

---

[11]This is equivalently to assuming that the primary sector is composed of a large number of identical union-firm pairs. Normalizing this large number to unity yields the case considered in the text.

we discovered above, the union set the wage rate w_1^M where there is a tangency between the labour demand curve and a union indifference curve. Employment in the primary sector is equal to N_1^M which falls short of N_1^{max}. If the jobless workers would be trapped in the primary sector then there would be unemployment equal to $N_1^{max} - N_1^M$. But in the two-sector model there are other options available to the unemployed worker.

Recall that an unemployed worker implicitly receives the reservation wage, w_R (in the form of the unemployment benefit b and leisure). But if all unemployed primary sector workers would supply their labour to the secondary sector, then employment in that sector would be equal to N_2^M and the wage rate would be w_2^a which is strictly greater than the reservation wage w_R. Unemployed primary sector workers are better off moving to the secondary sector.

We thus learn an important lesson. With free intersectoral mobility of labour the union causes identical workers to receive different wages in the two sectors but it does not cause unemployment. Put differently, there is *full employment* of labour at the aggregate level, but wage disparity between the primary and secondary sectors (such that $w_1^M > w_2^a$). Workers in the secondary sector would rather work in the primary sector (because wages are higher there), but are prevented from getting work there because of the union's wage-setting power.

Unemployment re-emerges in the two-sector model if intersectoral labour mobility is less than perfect. Consider the following scenario. From an ex ante perspective, labour is fully mobile across sectors. At the beginning of each period, workers must choose between two options. Option 1 is to accept a job in the secondary sector at the going wage rate w_2. Option 2 is to enter the primary sector, join the union, and enter the "queue of workers" waiting for a job in that sector. Only a fraction of the workers in the queue obtain a job (at wage rate w_1^M which exceeds w_2) while the rest of them remain unemployed and receive the unemployment benefit b (they cannot turn around and join the secondary sector by assumption!).

In equilibrium each worker must be indifferent between the two options, i.e. the following equality must hold:

$$u^e(w_2) = \frac{N_1}{N_1^{max}} u^e(w_1) + \left[1 - \frac{N_1}{N_1^{max}}\right] u^u(b). \tag{7.60}$$

Here the left-hand side represents the certain utility one obtains by taking a job in the secondary sector and receiving the wage w_2. The right-hand side of (7.60) is the expected utility of a worker who decides to take a gamble on joining the union and entering the primary sector. With probability $\frac{N_1}{N_1^{max}}$ he obtains a job and gets the utility level $u^e(w_1)$ whilst with probability $1 - \frac{N_1}{N_1^{max}}$ he is unemployed and gets utility $u^u(b)$. Intuitively, the arbitrage equation (7.60) pins down the intersectoral allocation of labour and thus the membership of the union.

In summary, the equilibrium in the two-sector model with imperfect labour mobility is characterized by:

$$\frac{u^e(w_1) - u^u(b)}{w_1 u_w^e(w_1)} = \frac{1}{\varepsilon_D}, \tag{7.61}$$

$$w_1 = F_N(N_1, \bar{k}), \tag{7.62}$$

$$w_2 = F_N(N_2, \bar{k}), \tag{7.63}$$

$$u^e(w_2) = \frac{N_1}{N_1 + U_1} u^e(w_1) + \left[1 - \frac{N_1}{N_1 + U_1}\right] u^u(b), \tag{7.64}$$

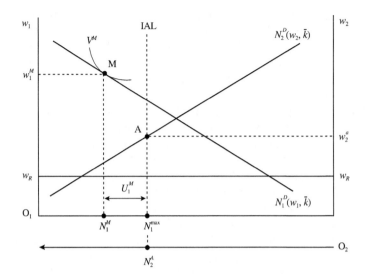

Figure 7.13: Unions and unemployment in a two-sector model

$$\bar{N} = N_1 + U_1 + N_2, \tag{7.65}$$

where the endogenous variables are w_1, w_2, N_1, U_1, and N_2. The exogenous variables are the unemployment benefit b, total labour supply $\bar{N}$, and the capital stock per firm $\bar{k}$. Equation (7.61) is the wage setting rule of the monopoly union, (7.62)–(7.63) show that employment in each sector must be on the labour demand equation. Equation (7.64) is obtained from (7.60) by noting that $N_1^{max} = N_1 + U_1$. Finally, (7.65) is the equilibrium condition.

The unemployment equilibrium is illustrated in Figure 7.13. The employment levels are N_1^M and N_2^A, respectively, and equilibrium "wait unemployment" equals U_1^M. As a result of the intersectoral labour mobility friction, wages in the secondary sector are higher than with full mobility because the U_1^M hours-worth of disappointed union members are barred from entering the secondary sector and driving down wages there.

7.3.3 Unions and real wage rigidity

Recall that one of the reasons for being interested in models of union behaviour in the first place is to investigate their potential in explaining the (near) horizontal real wage equation (see Figure 7.6). What happens, for example, if there is a productivity shock in the two-sector general equilibrium model of the previous subsection? Given the assumptions underlying that model, such a shock will lead to an upward shift in both labour demand curves. The monopoly union sets its real wage according to (7.61). So if the demand elasticity ε_D is constant (as is, for example, the case for a Cobb-Douglas production function), then the productivity shock has no effect on the real wage rate chosen by the monopoly union, i.e. w_1 is unchanged and employment N_1 is increased in response to the productivity shock. The model thus predicts a rigid real wage in the unionized sector. In contrast, in the secondary (non-unionized) sector both the real wage and the employment level will be affected by the productivity shock.

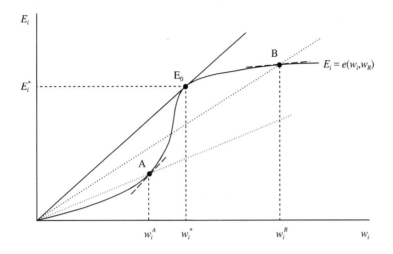

Figure 7.14: Efficiency wages

7.4   Efficiency wages and the labour market

As is argued by Stiglitz (1986, p. 182), the basic hypothesis underlying the group
of efficiency wage theories is that the net productivity of workers is a function of
the wage rate they receive. In that case firms may not lower the wage even if there
is excess supply of labour because they may fear that the adverse effect on worker
productivity outweighs the reduction in the wage per worker, thus increasing actual
total labour cost. As a result, there may be unemployment even in a world populated by non-unionized and perfectly competitive firms. The law of demand and
supply is repealed. Furthermore, since the relationship between wages and worker
productivity may differ between industries, wages (for otherwise identical workers)
may also differ across industries, thus repealing the law of one price.

Stiglitz (1986) mentions five structurally different explanations for the link between the wage a worker gets and his productivity. First, it has been argued in the
development economics literature that there is a direct link between productivity
and the level of nutrition, especially at low levels of nutrition. This link gives rise
to an S-shaped wage-productivity curve as is drawn, for example, in Figure 7.14.
The second theory leading to efficiency wage effects is based on labour turnover.
The lower the wage, the higher the rate of labour turnover. To the extent that the
firm must incur training costs for new workers, this mechanism gives rise to a link
between the wage and the worker's productivity. The third theory is based on imperfect information on the part of the firm about the characteristics of the worker.
By paying a high wage the firm obtains a high-quality labour force. The fourth
theory is based on the imperfect information that the firm has about the workers'
actions and the cost of monitoring them. Unemployment works as a disciplining
device (Shapiro and Stiglitz, 1984): if workers are caught shirking on the job, they
are fired and become unemployed (for some time). Note that there are other (potentially more efficient) means by which the firm can induce the good behaviour of
its work force. An example is the use of bonding. Upon entering employment in
the firm, the worker pays a bond upfront, to be forfeited to the firm if he is caught
shirking. Apart from the moral hazard problem that the firm may have (wrongfully

accusing the worker of shirking, leading to the forfeit of her/his bond), poor workers may have no way to borrow the money for the performance bond. Hence, to the extent that poor/unskilled workers have restricted access to the capital market, this theory may explain why these groups experience a higher unemployment rate (Stiglitz, 1986, p. 186). The fifth theory suggests that workers' performance depends on whether they believe they are being treated fairly. In this sociological theory the workers are particularly interested in their wage relative to that of other workers. In his insightful survey article, Katz (1986) adds a sixth reason why firms may be willing to pay efficiency wages, namely to prevent unionization. Loosely put, in this union-threat model a firm can prevent its unionization by paying its workers a wage that is equal to what these workers would receive in the presence of a union *minus* the cost to the workers of organizing such a union.

In the remainder of this section we consider a generic efficiency-wage model in which a worker's effort level is assumed to increase in the wage he receives. This reduced-form approach has the virtue of being relatively simple to analyse.

7.4.1 Efficiency wages in partial equilibrium

Assume that there are many identical perfectly competitive firms that are indexed by $i = 1, \ldots, M$, where M is a large number so that each firm is tiny with respect to the market it operates in. Firm i produces homogenous output Y_i using a short-run production function of the following type:

$$Y_i = AF(L_i, \bar{k}), \tag{7.66}$$

where A is an exogenous productivity index, $\bar{k}$ is the fixed capital stock, and L_i is the *effective* labour input, i.e. the total number of efficiency units of labour employed by the firm:

$$L_i \equiv E_i T_i \bar{L}. \tag{7.67}$$

It is important to recognize the dimension of L_i. Firm i has T_i workers who are each employed for $\bar{L}$ hours per unit of time. The effort level of a worker in firm i is denoted by E_i. In standard models of labour demand, E_i is assumed to be constant (typically equal to unity). In contrast, the basic insight of efficiency wage theories is that effort responds to the economic incentives offered to the worker. To make this notion more precise we assume that E_i depends positively on the real wage paid in firm i (w_i) and negatively on the (implicit or explicit) real wage that can be obtained elsewhere (the *reservation wage*, w_R):

$$E_i \equiv e(w_i, w_R), \tag{7.68}$$

where $e(\cdot)$ is the effort function featuring partial derivatives $e_w \equiv \partial e/\partial w_i > 0$ and $e_{w_R} \equiv \partial e/\partial w_R < 0$. The idea is simple: if you pay your workers well (as did pioneer car maker Henry Ford), they are likely to display a lot of effort. Conversely, "if you pay peanuts, you get (lazy) monkeys". By letting $N_i \equiv T_i \bar{L}$ denote the number of worker-hours that are employed in firm i, we can rewrite the short-run production function as $Y_i = AF(E_i N_i, \bar{k})$. The firm maximizes real short-run profit, which is defined as follows:

$$\pi_i \equiv AF(E_i N_i, \bar{k}) - w_i N_i, \tag{7.69}$$

where w_i is the real hourly wage rate paid by firm i. The firm chooses its level of employment (N_i) **and** its wage rate (w_i) in order to maximize profit. The first-order conditions are:

$$\frac{\partial \Pi_i}{\partial N_i} = AE_i F_L(E_i N_i, \bar{k}) - w_i = 0, \tag{7.70}$$

$$\frac{\partial \Pi_i}{\partial w_i} = \left[AF_L(E_i N_i, \bar{k})e_w(w_i, w_R) - 1 \right] \cdot N_i = 0, \tag{7.71}$$

where $F_L \equiv \partial F / \partial (E_i N_i)$ is the marginal product of labour measured in efficiency units. By substituting these two conditions, the expression determining the *efficiency wage* for firm i is obtained:

$$\frac{w_i e_w(w_i, w_R)}{e(w_i, w_R)} = 1. \tag{7.72}$$

This expression is often referred to as the *Solow condition*, after one of its discoverers Robert Solow (1979). In words it says that the firm should find the wage for which the elasticity of the effort function equals unity. The firm should keep increasing its wage rate as long as the effort rises faster than the wage rate (and the wage per unit of effort keeps falling). In terms of Figure 7.14, the optimum is at point E_0. This is the only point where the tangent of the effort curve goes through the origin, thus ensuring that the unit-elasticity condition (7.72) is satisfied.[12]

In order to further characterize the optimal wage set by the firm we follow Summers (1988) by postulating that the effort function (7.68) takes the following form:

$$E_i = (w_i - w_R)^\varepsilon, \qquad 0 < \varepsilon < 1, \tag{7.73}$$

where ε measures the strength of the productivity-enhancing effects of high wages which we call the *leap-frogging effect*. This effort function is illustrated in Figure 7.15. Of course this function is not S-shaped but it does capture the relevant (concave) part of the function depicted in Figure 7.14 where the point satisfying the Solow condition is located. Note that the effort function is vertical at point A and that the Solow condition is satisfied at point E_0 in Figure 7.15. In view of (7.72) and (7.73), the efficiency wage chosen by firm i is easily calculated:

$$\frac{w_i}{E_i} \frac{\partial E_i}{\partial w_i} = 1 \quad \Rightarrow \quad \frac{w_i^* - w_R}{w_i^*} = \varepsilon \quad \Leftrightarrow \quad w_i^* = \frac{w_R}{1 - \varepsilon}. \tag{7.74}$$

The firm pays a constant markup ($1/(1 - \varepsilon)$) times the value of the outside option as given by the reservation wage. At the efficiency wage the optimal effort level is equal to:

$$E_i^* = \left(\frac{\varepsilon w_R}{1 - \varepsilon} \right)^\varepsilon. \tag{7.75}$$

Once the efficiency wage, w_i^*, and the optimal effort level, E_i^*, have been determined, the number of worker-hours N_i^* that are employed by firm i is implicitly determined by equation (7.70):

$$AE_i^* F_L(E_i^* N_i^*, \bar{k}) = w_i^*. \tag{7.76}$$

---

[12]The ray from the origin has slope E_i / w_i. At point E_0 this ray is tangent to the effort curve, i.e. $E_i / w_i = e_w$ or $w_i e_w / E_i = 1$ at that point. At point A (B) the effort curve is steeper (flatter) than the ray from the origin and $w_i e_w / E_i > 1$ (< 1). Hence, w_i^A is too low, and w_i^B is too high.

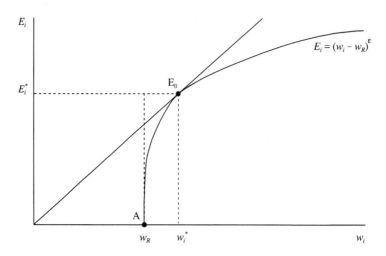

Figure 7.15: A tractable effort function

Since, by assumption, firms face the same technology and effort function, it follows that firms make identical choices regarding the real wage, effort level, and employment, i.e. $w_i^* = w^*$, $E_i^* = E^*$, $L_i^* = L^*$, and $N_i^* = N^*$.

Simple as it is, the partial equilibrium model already teaches us two things. First, holding constant the reservation wage w_R, a productivity shock has no effect on the efficiency wage chosen by the firms, and thus only affects employment. Indeed, it follows from (7.76) that $dN_i^*/dA = -F_L/\left(AE_i^* F_{LL}\right) > 0$, i.e. a positive (negative) productivity shock leads to an expansion (contraction) of employment. Hence, this model provides a partial equilibrium reason for the horizontal real wage equation drawn in Figure 7.6. Second, from the structure of the model there is no reason at all to expect that full employment will prevail. Indeed, the aggregate demand for labour-hours is given by MN^* which may well fall short of the aggregate supply of labour hours, $\bar{N} \equiv \bar{T}\bar{L}$, where $\bar{T}$ is the number of workers in this economy. Loosely put, the wage rate cannot do two things at the same time. In the efficiency wage model, the optimal wage minimizes the firm's labour cost per efficiency unit of labour. It is not set in such way as to guarantee full employment of labour. Of course this argument is based on partial equilibrium reasoning so the next task at hand is to embed the efficiency wage model in a general equilibrium context.

7.4.2 Efficiency wages in general equilibrium

Up to this point we have not yet determined the reservation wage, w_R. By definition w_R refers to some kind of outside option that a worker in a particular firm faces. To keep the model as simple as possible we once again study a two-sector economy. In Figure 7.16 the situation on the labour market is depicted in an Edgeworth box diagram. In the primary sector there are M active firms. In order to economize on notation we normalize the number of firms to unity ($M = 1$). It follows that the optimal choices made in the primary sector are fully characterized by:

$$w_1^E = \frac{w_R}{1 - \varepsilon}, \tag{7.77}$$

$$E_1^E = \left(\frac{\varepsilon w_R}{1-\varepsilon}\right)^\varepsilon, \tag{7.78}$$

$$w_1^E = A E_1^E F_L(E_1^E N_1^E, \bar{k}), \tag{7.79}$$

where w_1^E, E_1^E, and N_1^E denote the optimal choices in the primary sector for, respectively, the wage, the effort level, and the employment level. The superscript thus denotes that the efficiency-wage solutions are used whilst the subscript designates the primary sector. We know from our discussion above that the employment level lies on the conditional labour demand curve evaluated at the optimal effort level, i.e. $w_1 = A E_1^E F_L(E_1^E N_1, \bar{k})$ implicitly defines the curve $N_1^D = N_1^D(w_1, E_1^E, \bar{k})$ that has been drawn in Figure 7.16. In that figure the efficiency wage solution is located at point E.

In the second sector firms are assumed to have no access to efficiency wages, i.e. it is assumed that worker effort in that sector is constant (at $E_2 = \bar{E}_2$) irrespective of the wage rate. We assume that $\bar{E}_2$ is quite low compared to E_1^E so that worker productivity is low in the secondary sector. In the absence of efficiency wage considerations the competitive labour demand in the secondary sector is defined implicitly as:

$$w_2 = A\bar{E} F_L(\bar{E}_2 N_2, \bar{k}) \quad \Leftrightarrow \quad N_2^D = N_2^D(w_2, \bar{E}_2, \bar{k}). \tag{7.80}$$

Just as for the primary sector, we have normalized the number of firms in the secondary sector to unity. In Figure 7.16 the labour demand equation $N_2^D(w_2, \bar{E}_2, \bar{k})$ schedule has been drawn with respect to the origin at O_2.

We recall from our discussion surrounding unions in general equilibrium (in Section 7.3.2) that equilibrium unemployment will be zero in the absence of intersectoral mobility frictions. Something similar is the case here. Those workers who cannot find a job in the primary sector will find employment for sure in the secondary sector. Efficiency wage theory yields rigid wages in the primary sector but no unemployment.

Just as for the union case, unemployment re-emerges in the two-sector model if intersectoral labour mobility is less than perfect. We consider the same friction as before. From an ex ante perspective, labour is fully mobile across sectors. In particular at the beginning of each period, workers must choose between two options. Option 1 is to accept a job in the secondary sector at the going wage rate w_2. Option 2 is to join the group of workers chasing after a job in the primary sector. Only a fraction of the workers in this group obtain a job and receive the wage rate w_2^E while the rest of them remain unemployed and receive the unemployment benefit b (they cannot turn around and join the secondary sector by assumption!).

In equilibrium each worker must be indifferent between the two options, i.e. the following equality must hold:

$$u^e(w_2) = p_1^E u^e(w_1^E) + \left(1 - p_1^E\right) u^u(b), \qquad p_1^E \equiv \frac{N_1^E}{N_1^E + U_1^E}, \tag{7.81}$$

where p_1^E represents the ex ante probability of finding a job in the primary sector. The left-hand side of (7.81) represents the certain utility one obtains by taking a job in the secondary sector and receiving the wage w_2. The right-hand side of (7.60) is the expected utility of a worker who decides to take a gamble by entering the primary sector. With probability p_1^E he obtains a job and gets the utility level $u^e(w_1^E)$ whilst with probability $1 - p_1^E$ he is unemployed and gets utility $u^u(b)$. Intuitively, the

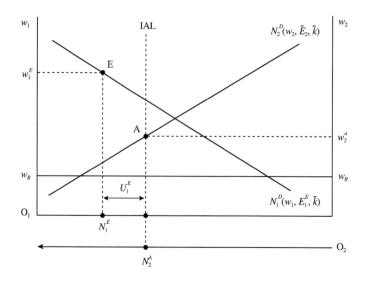

Figure 7.16: Efficiency wages and unemployment in a two-sector model

arbitrage equation (7.60) pins down the intersectoral allocation of labour. In terms of Figure 7.16 the IAL curve represents the optimal allocation of labour over the two sectors. Employment in the primary sector is N_1^E, there are U_1^E unemployed worker-hours in that sector, and employment in the secondary sector is equal to N_2^A.

So what is the reservation wage of a worker in the primary sector? Recall that w_R represents the value of the outside option for the individual worker, i.e. it represents what a worker would get if he is not employed by firm i. By assumption this worker cannot move to the secondary sector in the current period. But the worker does know what other firms in the primary sector are paying and is assumed to be able to rejoin the pool of unemployed instantaneously and find a job at some other firm.[13] It follows that w_R is a weighted average of the average wage paid by other firms in the primary sector ($\bar{w}_1$) and the unemployment benefit (b):

$$w_R = p_1^E \bar{w}_1 + (1 - p_1^E) b. \tag{7.82}$$

But equation (7.82) is not the end of the story. As we showed above, all firms in the primary sector set the same efficiency wage, i.e. $\bar{w}_1 = w_1^E$. By substituting this into (7.82), and using (7.77) we obtain the expressions w_R and w_1:

$$w_1^E = \frac{w_R}{1 - \varepsilon} = \frac{1 - p_1^E}{1 - \varepsilon - p_1^E} b. \tag{7.83}$$

Up to this point we have shown step-by-step which conditions must be satisfied in the two-sector model. Of course, in general equilibrium everything is determined simultaneously as everything depends in principle of everything else. Gathering all the previous results it is clear that the equilibrium in the two-sector model with imperfect labour mobility and efficiency wages in the primary sector is fully characterized by:

$$w_1 = \frac{1 - \frac{N_1}{N_1 + U_1}}{1 - \varepsilon - \frac{N_1}{N_1 + U_1}} b, \tag{7.84}$$

---

[13]In contrast, in section 7.3.2 above we implicitly assumed that a worker could only join a single union.

$$E_1 = \varepsilon w_1^\varepsilon, \tag{7.85}$$

$$w_1 = AE_1 F_L(E_1 N_1, \bar{k}), \tag{7.86}$$

$$w_2 = A\bar{E} F_L(\bar{E} N_2, \bar{k}), \tag{7.87}$$

$$u^e(w_2) = \frac{N_1}{N_1 + U_1} u^e(w_1) + \left[1 - \frac{N_1}{N_1 + U_1}\right] u^u(b), \tag{7.88}$$

$$\bar{N} = N_1 + U_1 + N_2, \tag{7.89}$$

where the endogenous variables are w_1, E_1, N_1, U_1, w_2, and N_2. The exogenous variables are the unemployment benefit b, total labour supply $\bar{N}$, and the capital stock per firm $\bar{k}$. Equation (7.84) is obtained from (7.83) by substituting the definition of the job-finding probability, p_1. Equation (7.85) is obtained by substituting the expression for the reservation wage—stated in (7.83)—into (7.78). Expressions (7.86)–(7.87) show that employment in each sector must be on the labour demand equation. Equation (7.89) is obtained from (7.81) by using the definition of p_1. Finally, (7.89) is the equilibrium condition.

7.5 Punchlines

We started this chapter by establishing some stylized facts about the labour market in advanced capitalistic economies. In such economies, unemployment shows a lot of fluctuations over time which are quite persistent (more so than the business cycle). Across countries the duration of unemployment spells can differ quite a lot, with long-term unemployment much more prevalent in Europe than in the US. Looking at very long data sets reveals that there is no long-run trend in the unemployment rate. The unemployment rate differs between apparently similar countries suggesting an explanatory role for dissimilar labour market institutions. The majority of job loss (inflow into unemployment) is due to layoffs by firms, not voluntary quitting by workers. Finally, the unemployment rate differs between age groups, occupation, regions, races, and sexes.

The standard labour market model employed in the early chapters of this book can easily be augmented to explain some of these stylized facts. For example, the lower unemployment rate among high-education workers vis-à-vis low-education workers can be modelled by distinguishing two types of workers, namely skilled and unskilled, and by assuming that there is a minimum (real) wage which is binding for the latter type of workers. In that case there is unemployment in the market for unskilled workers. The unemployment is directly caused by the binding minimum wage. Abolishing the minimum wage would solve the unemployment problem because the unskilled wage rate would fall to clear the market.

The standard model is also quite useful to study the impact of taxation on the aggregate labour market. We consider a wide array of taxes, namely a progressive system of (labour) income taxes, a payroll tax, as well as a tax on consumption. In the standard model with flexible wages, taxes affect equilibrium wages and employment but do not give rise to unemployment. Ceteris paribus the average income tax rate, an increase in the marginal income tax chokes off labour supply and leads to lower employment, a higher producer wage, and a lower consumer wage. On the other hand, if the marginal tax is kept unchanged and the average tax is increased then labour supply increases (because leisure is a normal good), both producer and consumer wages fall, and employment rises. Simple expressions can be derived which show which side of the labour market ends up paying the tax (so-called tax incidence).

If the consumer wage is assumed to be fixed above the market clearing level then employment is demand determined and unemployment emerges. Now, the effects of the tax system on both the level of employment and the unemployment rate can be traced. Raising the marginal income tax or lowering the average tax both lead to a reduction in the unemployment rate. In the former case labour demand (and hence employment) is unchanged but labour supply drops off. In the latter case labour demand (and employment) is boosted and labour supply falls.

Although the standard labour demand model is thus quite flexible there is one stylized fact for which it cannot easily furnish a credible explanation, namely the fact that the real wage appears to be rather rigid in the face of productivity and demand shocks. The standard model can be made consistent with this rigidity by assuming a highly elastic labour supply curve, but that assumption is grossly at odds with microeconometric evidence. For that reason, a number of economists have started to look for alternative reasons for real wage rigidity.

The first rationale for real wage rigidly is provided by the macroeconomic theory of trade unions. Three of the most important models of trade union behaviour have been studied, namely the monopoly union model, the right-to-manage model, and the efficient bargaining model. The objective function of the union is the expected (or average) utility of the union's members.

In the monopoly union model, the union unilaterally picks a wage rate such that union utility is maximized subject to the proviso that the solution lies on the labour demand curve. The union thus acts as the monopolistic seller of labour, exploiting the downward-sloping labour demand curve of the firm. The optimal wage choice of the union can be represented as a simple markup expression involving unemployment benefit and the elasticity of the labour demand function. The union's choice implies that both the wage and the unemployment rate are above their respective competitive levels. Productivity shocks typically lead only to employment changes so that the model is consistent with real wage rigidity. (The proviso must be made because a union which is fully employed is only interested in higher wages so that positive productivity shocks do not translate into employment expansions.)

In the right-to-manage model, the firm is still allowed to decide on employment but the wage is the outcome of a bargaining process between the union and the firm. Using the concept of generalized Nash bargaining, the resulting wage can again be written in a markup format. In addition to unemployment benefit and demand elasticity an additional component entering the markup solution is the relative bargaining strength of the union. An attractive feature of the right-to-manage model is that it contains the monopoly union solution and the competitive solution as special (extreme) cases. An unattractive feature of the right-to-manage solution is that it is Pareto inefficient, i.e. it is possible to make one of the parties involved in the bargaining strictly better off without making the other party worse off.

The efficient bargaining model solves this problem by assuming that the firm and the union bargain over both the wage and the employment level. The outcome of this bargaining process is a range of efficient wage-employment combinations. When combined with a "fair share" rule, dividing output over the two parties, the model predicts a unique wage-employment solution. Interestingly, wage and employment are higher than under the competitive solution as the union turns profits into jobs. Wage moderation, consisting of a smaller share of the output going to labour, is bad for employment because the wage-employment solution moves closer to the competitive solution.

A second rationale for real wage rigidity is provided by the theory of efficiency wages. The basic hypothesis underlying this theory is that the net productivity of workers is a function of the wage rate they are paid. A famous example of efficiency wages is provided by the case of Henry Ford, who paid very high wages and achieved a very high level of productivity as a result. The implications of the efficiency-wage hypothesis are quite far-reaching. First, the law of demand and supply is no longer relevant. Even if there is excess supply of labour, the firm may not lower its wage rate because the adverse effect on its workers' productivity may outweigh the beneficial reduction in the wage bill. Furthermore, the law of one price is also repealed. Since the effort-wage relationship may differ across industries, wages may also differ for otherwise identical workers.

In the final part of this chapter we developed a simple general-equilibrium model in which efficiency wages lead to real wage rigidity and a positive equilibrium unemployment rate. Crucial determinants of the equilibrium unemployment rate are the level of the unemployment benefit, the so-called leapfrogging coefficient (summarizing the productivity-enhancing effect of high wages), and the degree of intersectoral labour mobility.

Further reading

All serious students of the macroeconomic labour market should take notice of Layard et al. (2005) and Boeri and van Ours (2013). Nickell and Layard (1999) survey the effects of labour market institutions on unemployment. On European unemployment, see the studies by Bean (1994) and by Machin and Manning (1999). An outstanding textbook on the economics of labour markets is the one by Cahuc et al. (2014). Key readings on the efficiency wage theory are collected in Akerlof and Yellen (1986). Katz (1986), Stiglitz (1986), and Weiss (1991) present very good critical surveys. Solow (1979) is an early contribution to the literature. Hoel (1990) studies the impact of progressive income taxes in an efficiency wage model. Raff and Summers (1987) argue convincingly that Henry Ford's introduction of the five-dollar day in 1914 had all the results stressed by efficiency wage theories: productivity and profits increased, and workers queued for jobs at the Ford Motor Company. See also Brinkley (2003, ch. 8) for background details on Ford's decision to increase wages dramatically. On dual labour markets, see McDonald and Solow (1985), Bulow and Summers (1986), Atkinson (1994), and Saint-Paul (1996). For a good survey article on tax incidence in macro models, see Kotlikoff and Summers (1987). For good surveys of the economic literature on trade unions, see Oswald (1982, 1985), Farber (1986), Pencavel (1991), and Booth (1995). Manning (1987) embeds the union model in a sequential bargaining framework. Koskela and Vilmunen (1996) study the effects of income taxes in a union model. See Cross (1988) for an interesting collection of articles on hysteresis. Union-based models have been used to explain unemployment persistence, see for example Gottfries and Horn (1987). Lindbeck and Snower (1988) is a good reference to the insider-outsider literature. Calmfors and Driffill (1988) suggest that the unemployment rate may have something to do with the degree of corporatism that exists in the economy, and that unemployment tends to be low for the extreme cases when (1) unions are small and weak or (2) when there is a small number of highly centralized unions. The former cannot do much damage and the latter tend to internalize the government budget constraint in setting their wage claims. A national union cannot overbid its own wage claim (Layard et al., 2005, p. 30). There is a third approach to real wage rigidity which goes by the name of implicit contract theory. A key paper is Azariadis (1975). Good surveys on this literature are Azariadis (1981), Azariadis and Stiglitz (1983), and Rosen (1985). Bénassy (1993b) has shown that implicit contract theory does provide a rationale for real wage rigidity but not for (involuntary) unemployment. In fact, implicit contract models typically predict overemployment rather than unemployment. For that reason it is no longer at the top of the research agenda of most macroeconomists studying the labour market.

Chapter 8

Search in the labour market

In this chapter we abandon the notion of an aggregate labour market altogether. Instead we look directly at the determinants of the two principal labour market flows, namely the flow from unemployment to employment (job finding) and the reverse flow (job destruction). The keyword for this chapter is two-sided search. Unemployed workers are looking for a job, and firms with a vacancy are searching for a worker. The search process is costly because it takes time and resources. The specific purpose of this chapter is to discuss the following issues:

1. How can we model the search behaviour of workers and firms?

2. What does the resulting search equilibrium look like? And how does the model explain the duration of unemployment?

3. What is meant by efficient unemployment? What does the Hosios condition say about this concept?

4. How does taxation affect the equilibrium unemployment rate? How can we reduce the equilibrium unemployment rate?

5. How do job-specific shocks give rise to endogenous job destruction?

8.1 Search in the labour market

The labour market in many countries is characterized by huge gross flows of workers leaving a job and entering unemployment and vice versa. For example, for the US the flow of workers entering or leaving a job amounts to 7 million per month (Blanchard and Diamond, 1989, p. 1)! It would be tempting to argue that these enormous flows, due to the simultaneous occurrence of job creation and job destruction, are bound to cause problems. There are a lot of workers looking for jobs, and vice versa. At a macroeconomic level, however, it appears that (at least in the US) the labour market is relatively efficient at matching jobs and workers. As we saw in Chapter 7, US unemployment seems to be relatively low and stable (in non-crisis times). The modern theory of search behaviour in the labour market is specifically aimed at describing this matching process that takes place in the labour market. This theory is radically different from the previous labour market theories discussed so far in that the notion of an aggregate labour market is abandoned. As Diamond (1982b, p. 217) explains, rather than assuming that the market is the mechanism by which workers and jobs are brought together, the modern approach assumes that there is a search process which stochastically brings together unemployed workers and vacant jobs in a pair-wise fashion. This two-sided search process takes time and consequently causes loss of output. When a worker and a job meet each other, negotiations take place to determine the wage.

8.1.1   A canonical two-sided search model

In this section we present the canonical two-sided search model.[1] The modern theory of search makes use of the so-called *matching function*. This is a hypothetical concept, not unlike the production function, which turns out to be very convenient analytically. A matching function determines the number of job vacancies that are filled ("matches"), each instant, as a function of the number of unemployed job-seeking workers and the number of vacancies that exist (plus exogenous variables). Firms have jobs that are either *filled* or *vacant*. It is assumed that only vacant jobs are on offer. The firm is not searching for workers to replace existing (but unsatisfactory) workers. Workers either have a job or are unemployed, and only the unemployed engage in search. There is no on-the-job search in the model discussed in this section. By making these assumptions, the two activities of production of goods and trade in labour are strictly separate activities.

Firms and workers know the job-matching technology, and know that there is an exogenously given *job destruction process*.[2] At each moment in time, a proportion of the existing filled jobs are destroyed, say because of firm-specific shocks making previously lucrative jobs unprofitable. In equilibrium, there is thus a constant inflow into unemployment, and the model predicts an *equilibrium unemployment rate* that is strictly greater than zero.

It is assumed that there are many firms and many workers, and that every agent behaves as a perfect competitor. The fixed labour force consists of N workers, and each worker who has a job supplies one unit of labour. (There is no decision on hours of work by the worker, and the effort of each worker is constant.) The unemployment rate is defined as the fraction of the labour force without a job, and is denoted by U. The vacancy rate is the number of vacancies expressed as a proportion of the labour force, and is denoted by V. Hence, at each moment in time, there are UN unemployed workers and VN vacant jobs "trying to find each other".

The number of successful matches at each instant in time depends on UN and VN according to the matching function:

$$MN = G(UN, VN), \tag{8.1}$$

where MN is the total number of matches, so that M is the matching *rate*, and $G(UN, VN)$ is a linearly homogeneous function that can be rewritten as $G(UN, VN) = NG(U, V)$. We assume that $G_U > 0$, $G_V > 0$, $G_{UU} < 0$, $G_{VV} < 0$, and $G_{UU}G_{VV} - G_{UV}^2 > 0$. The intuitive idea behind (8.1) is that at each instant MN meetings occur between an unemployed worker and a firm with a job vacancy. Which particular worker meets which particular job vacancy is selected randomly.

Consider a small time interval dt. During that time interval, there are $MNdt$ matches and VN vacant jobs, so that the probability of a vacancy being filled during

---

[1]The exposition given in this section closely follows Pissarides (1990, ch. 1). We focus on an intuitive discussion of the model. More formal discussions of the matching model can be found in Mortensen and Pissarides (1999a,1999b). In Chapter 13 a macroeconomic matching model is constructed and analysed.

[2]In Section 8.3 we endogenize the job destruction rate along the lines suggested by Mortensen and Pissarides (1994) and Pissarides (2000, ch. 2)

dt equals $(MN/VN)dt$. By defining $q \equiv MN/VN = M/V$, we can use equation (8.1) to write q as:

$$q \equiv \frac{G(UN, VN)}{VN} = \frac{VN \cdot G(U/V, 1)}{VN} = G(U/V, 1) \equiv q(\theta), \tag{8.2}$$

where $\theta \equiv V/U$ is the vacancy-unemployment ratio that plays a crucial role in the analysis. Obviously, since $q(\theta)dt$ measures the probability that a vacancy will be filled in the time interval dt, $q(\theta)$ can be interpreted as the *instantaneous* probability of a vacancy being filled, and the expected duration of a job vacancy is $1/q(\theta)$. All these results are derived more formally in Intermezzo 8.1 below.

In view of the assumptions about $G(U, V)$, the following properties of the $q(\theta)$ function can be demonstrated:

$$\frac{dq}{d\theta} = -\frac{G_U}{\theta^2} < 0, \tag{8.3}$$

and

$$\varepsilon_q(\theta) \equiv -\frac{\theta}{q}\frac{dq}{d\theta} = \frac{G_U}{\theta q} \Rightarrow 0 < \varepsilon_q(\theta) < 1, \tag{8.4}$$

where $\varepsilon_q(\theta)$ is the absolute value of the elasticity of the $q(\theta)$ function.[3]

Unemployed workers also find a match in a stochastic manner. For workers, the instantaneous probability of finding a firm with a vacancy is given by MN/UN, the number of vacancies expressed as a fraction of the number of unemployed workers. This instantaneous probability can be written in terms of θ also:

$$\frac{G(UN, VN)}{UN} = \frac{VN \cdot G(UN/VN, 1)}{UN} = (V/U) \cdot G(U/V, 1) = \theta q(\theta) \equiv f(\theta). \tag{8.5}$$

The $f(\theta)$ function has the following elasticity:

$$\varepsilon_f(\theta) \equiv \frac{\theta}{f}\frac{df}{d\theta} = \left[q(\theta) + \theta\frac{dq}{d\theta}\right]\frac{\theta}{\theta q(\theta)} = 1 + \frac{\theta}{q}\frac{dq}{d\theta} = 1 - \varepsilon_q(\theta) > 0. \tag{8.6}$$

Since $f(\theta)$ represents the instantaneous probability of an unemployed worker finding a job, the expected duration of unemployment equals $1/f(\theta) = 1/(\theta q(\theta))$. This is intuitive, since unemployed workers find it easier to locate a job (and hence expect a shorter duration of unemployment) if θ is high, i.e. if there are relatively many vacancies. The definitions of $q(\theta)$ and $f(\theta)$ in (8.2) and (8.5) show that there is an intricate connection between the process linking workers to jobs, and the one linking jobs to workers. This is obvious, since workers and vacancies meet in pairs.

The variable θ is the relevant parameter measuring labour market pressure to both parties involved in the labour market. This parameter plays a crucial role because the dependence of the search probabilities on θ implies the existence of a *trading externality*. There is *stochastic rationing* occurring in the labour market (firms with unfilled vacancies, workers without a job) which cannot be solved by the price mechanism, since worker and vacancy must first get together before the price mechanism can play any role. The degree of rationing is, however, dependent on the situation in the labour market, which is summarized by θ. If θ rises, the probability of rationing

---

[3] The trick is to write (8.1) as $MN = [G_U U + G_V V] N$, which implies $q = G_U/\theta + G_V$. Hence, $\varepsilon_q(\theta) = G_U/(q\theta) = 1 - G_V/q$, which is between 0 and 1 because $0 < G_V < q$.

is higher for the average firm and lower for the average worker. The particular external effect that is present in the model is called the *congestion* or *search externality* by Pissarides (1990, p. 6).

As was pointed out above, it is assumed that there is an exogenously given job destruction process that ensures that a proportion δ_m of all filled jobs disappears at each instant. In a small time interval dt, the probability that an employed worker loses his/her job and becomes unemployed is thus given by $\delta_m dt$ (of course, by the same token, the probability that a filled job is destroyed is also equal to $\delta_m dt$). Hence, the average number of workers that become unemployed in a time interval dt equals $\delta_m(1 - U)Ndt$, and the average number of unemployed who find a job is given by $f(\theta)UNdt$. In the steady-state the unemployment rate is constant, so that the expected inflow and outflow must be equal to each other:

$$\delta_m(1 - U)Ndt = f(\theta)UNdt. \tag{8.7}$$

By assuming that the labour force N is large, expected and actual inflows and outflows can be assumed the same, so that (8.7) can be solved for the actual equilibrium unemployment rate:

$$U = \frac{\delta_m}{\delta_m + f(\theta)}, \tag{8.8}$$

which implies that $\partial U / \partial \delta_m > 0$ and $\partial U / \partial \theta < 0$.

8.1.1.1 Firms

Each firm is extremely small, has a risk-neutral owner, and has only one job, which is either filled or vacant. If the job is filled, the firm hires physical capital K at a given interest rate r, and produces output $F(K, 1)$. The production function is constant returns to scale and satisfies $F_K > 0 > F_{KK}$ and $F_L > 0 > F_{LL}$. If the job is vacant, on the other hand, the firm is actively searching for a worker and incurs a constant search cost of c per time unit. As was pointed out above, the probability that the firm finds a worker in time interval dt is given by $q(\theta)dt$. Since each firm only has one job, the number of jobs and firms in the economy coincide, and the free entry/exit condition determines the number of jobs/firms.

Let J_O denote the present value of the profit stream originating from a firm with an occupied job, and let J_V designate the same for a firm with a vacancy. With a perfect capital market the firm can borrow freely at the given interest rate, and the following steady-state *arbitrage equation* holds for a firm with a vacancy:

$$rJ_V = -c + q(\theta) [J_O - J_V]. \tag{8.9}$$

In words, equation (8.9) says that a vacant job is an asset of the firm. In equilibrium, the value of this asset must be such that the capital cost rJ_V is exactly equal to the return from the asset. The return consists of two parts, i.e. the constant search cost that must be incurred each time unit $(-c)$ plus the expected capital gain due to the fact that the vacant job can be filled in the future (with instantaneous probability $q(\theta)$). The capital gain is the difference in value of a filled and a vacant job, i.e. $J_O - J_V$.

Since anyone who is prepared to incur the constant search cost each time unit can set up a firm (with a vacancy) and start looking for a worker, free entry of firms will occur until the value of a vacant job is exactly equal to zero. Conversely, if a vacant job is worth a negative amount, exit of firms takes place and vacancies disappear. This implies the following expression:

$$J_V = 0 \quad \Leftrightarrow \quad 0 = -c + q(\theta)J_O \quad \Leftrightarrow \quad J_O = \frac{c}{q(\theta)}. \tag{8.10}$$

The final expression is intuitive. The expected duration of a vacancy is $1/q(\theta)$ during which the search cost c must be incurred. In equilibrium the number of jobs/firms must be such that the expected profit of a filled job is exactly equal to the expected cost of the vacancy.

For a firm with a filled job, the following steady-state arbitrage equation can be derived:

$$rJ_O = [F(K,1) - (r+\delta_k)K - w] - \delta_m J_O, \tag{8.11}$$

where $r + \delta_k$ is the rental charge on capital goods, δ_k is the depreciation rate of capital, and w is the real wage rate. Equation (8.11) says that the asset value of a filled job is J_O and its capital cost equals rJ_O. This must equal the return from the filled job, which consists of two parts. The first part is the surplus created in production, i.e. (the value of) output that remains after the production factors capital and labour have been paid (the term in square brackets). The second part is the expected capital loss due to job destruction ($\delta_m J_O$).

The size of each firm with a filled job is determined in the usual manner. The firm chooses the amount of capital it wants to rent such that the value of the firm is maximized. In terms of (8.11) we can write this problem as:

$$\max_{\{K\}} \ (r+\delta_m)J_O \equiv F(K,1) - (r+\delta_k)K - w \quad \Rightarrow \quad F_K(K,1) = r + \delta_k. \tag{8.12}$$

This is the usual condition equating the marginal product of capital to the rental charge on capital. Since both the interest rate r and the capital depreciation rate are constant, equation (8.12) fixes a unique capital intensity K^* and thus ensures that the marginal product of labour (which we call job productivity) is a constant, $p \equiv F_L(K^*, 1)$. Finally, by linear homogeneity of the production function we obtain the result that $F(K^*, 1) - (r + \delta_k)K^* = p$ so that equation (8.11) can be rewritten as follows:

$$rJ_O = [p - w] - \delta_m J_O. \tag{8.13}$$

It is important to recognize that job productivity p is constant in this chapter because both the interest rate r and the depreciation rate are.

Finally, by combining (8.10) and (8.13) we obtain the job creation condition:

$$\frac{p - w}{r + \delta_m} = \frac{c}{q(\theta)}. \tag{8.14}$$

The left-hand side of (8.14) represents the value of an occupied job, equalling the present value of rents (accruing to the firm during the job's existence) using the risk-of-job-destruction-adjusted discount rate, $r + \delta_m$, to discount future rents. The right-hand side of (8.14) is the expected search costs. With free exit/entry of firms, the value of an occupied job exactly equals the expected search costs.[4]

---

[4] If there were no search costs for the firm ($c = 0$), the model would yield the standard productivity condition for labour ($p = F_L = w$). With positive search costs, however, the factor labour receives less than its marginal product. This is because the marginal product of labour must be sufficiently large to cover the capital cost of the expected search costs.

8.1.1.2 Workers

The worker is risk neutral, lives forever, has a time preference rate equal to r, and consequently only cares about the expected discounted value of income (Diamond, 1982b, p. 219). A worker with a job earns the wage w, whilst an unemployed worker obtains the exogenously given "unemployment benefit" b. This may consist of a real transfer payment from the government but may also include the pecuniary value of leisure. Let Y_E denote the present value of the expected stream of income of a worker with a job, and let Y_U denote the same for an unemployed worker. Then the following steady-state arbitrage equation can be derived for a worker without a job:

$$rY_U = b + f(\theta)\left[Y_E - Y_U\right]. \tag{8.15}$$

In words, equation (8.15) says that the asset Y_U is the human wealth of the unemployed worker. The capital cost of the asset must be equal to the return, which consists of the unemployment benefit, b, plus the expected capital gain due to finding a job, i.e. $Y_E - Y_U$. As Pissarides (1990, p. 10) points out, rY_U can be interpreted in two ways. First, it is the yield on human wealth of an unemployed worker during search. It measures the minimum amount for which the worker would be willing to stop searching for a job, and hence has the interpretation of a *reservation wage*. The second interpretation is that of "normal" or "permanent" income: the amount that the unemployed worker can consume whilst still leaving his/her human wealth intact.

For a worker with a job the steady-state arbitrage equation reads as follows.

$$rY_E = w - \delta_m\left[Y_E - Y_U\right]. \tag{8.16}$$

The permanent income of an employed worker differs from the wage rate because there is a non-zero probability of job destruction causing a capital loss of $Y_E - Y_U$.

By solving (8.15)–(8.16) for rY_U and rY_E, the following expressions are obtained:

$$rY_U = \frac{(r + \delta_m)b + \theta q(\theta)w}{r + \delta_m + \theta q(\theta)}, \tag{8.17}$$

$$rY_E = \frac{\delta_m b + [r + \theta q(\theta)]\,w}{r + \delta_m + \theta q(\theta)} = \frac{r(w - b)}{r + \delta_m + \theta q(\theta)} + rY_U, \tag{8.18}$$

where the second expression in (8.18) shows that $w \geq b$ must hold for anybody to be willing to search for a job.

Intermezzo 8.1

Some statistical theory. The search-theoretic approach makes use of some statistical techniques that may not be immediately obvious. In this intermezzo some important notions are reviewed. Further details can be found in Ross (1993, ch. 5).

A very convenient probability distribution is the exponential distribution. A continuous random variable X is exponentially distributed if its probability density function has the form:

$$\phi(x) = \begin{cases} \lambda e^{-\lambda x} & x \geq 0 \\ 0 & x < 0, \end{cases} \tag{a}$$

where $\lambda > 0$. The cumulative distribution function is given by:

$$\Phi(x) \equiv \int_{-\infty}^{x} \phi(y)dy = \begin{cases} 1 - e^{-\lambda x} & x \geq 0 \\ 0 & x < 0 \end{cases} \tag{b}$$

The cumulative distribution function $\Phi(x)$ measures the probability that the random variable X attains a value less than or equal to x, or in symbols:

$$\Phi(x) \equiv P\{X \leq x\}. \tag{c}$$

The exponential distribution has the following properties. First, $E(X) = 1/\lambda$, the expected value of X is $1/\lambda$. Second, the variance of X is $V(X) \equiv E(X^2) - [E(X)]^2 = 1/\lambda^2$. Third, the random variable X is *memoryless*. Suppose that X is the lifetime of some light bulb. Then, if the light bulb is still working at some time t, the distribution of the remaining amount of time that it will continue to shine light is the same as the original distribution. Colloquially speaking, the light bulb does not "remember" that it has already shone for t periods. Formally, a random variable is memoryless if the following holds:

$$P\{X > s + t \mid X > t\} = P\{X > s\}. \tag{d}$$

The memoryless property implies a very simple expression for the *failure rate* function (often called the *hazard rate* function). The failure rate function $fr(t)$ represents the conditional probability density that a t-year old item (such as a light bulb or a human being) fails. It is defined as:

$$fr(t) \equiv \frac{\phi(t)}{1 - \Phi(t)}. \tag{e}$$

For the exponential distribution, the memoryless property implies that the distribution of remaining life for a t-year old item is the same as for a new item. As a result, the failure rate function should be constant. Using (a)–(c), we find that this is indeed the case:

$$fr(t) \equiv \frac{\phi(t)}{1 - \Phi(t)} = \frac{\lambda e^{-\lambda t}}{e^{-\lambda t}} = \lambda. \tag{f}$$

We shall have the opportunity to use this property in economically very interesting applications in the present chapter and in Chapter 15.

The search-theoretic approach also makes extensive use of the notion of a *Poisson process*. A Poisson process is a *counting process* with a number of properties. A stochastic process $\{M(t), t \geq 0\}$ is called a counting process if $M(t)$ represents the number of "events" that have occurred up to time t. For example, if $M(t)$ represents the number of goals scored by one's favourite soccer star by time t, an "event" consists of your star hitting the back of the net once more. In the context of matching, $M(t)$ represents the number of all matches that have occurred by time t. The counting process $M(t)$ must satisfy: (i) $M(t) \geq 0$; (ii) $M(t)$ is integer valued; and (iii) if $s < t$, then $M(t) - M(s) \geq 0$; and (iv) for $s < t$, $M(t) -$

$M(s)$ equals the number of events that have occurred in the interval (s,t) (Ross, 1993, p. 208).

A Poisson process is a specific kind of counting process. Formally, the counting process $\{M(t), t \geq 0\}$ is called a Poisson process with rate λ (> 0) if: (i) $M(0) = 0$; (ii) the process has independent increments; (iii) the number of events in any interval length t is Poisson distributed with mean λt. Hence,

$$P\{M(t+s) - M(s) = m\} \equiv e^{-\lambda t} \frac{(\lambda t)^m}{m!}, \tag{g}$$

for $m = 0, 1, 2, 3, \cdots$. For our purposes it is important to know something about interarrival times. Suppose that we have a Poisson process $M(t)$, and that the first event has occurred at time T_1. We define T_n as the elapsed time between the $(n-1)$st and the nth event (for $n > 1$), and refer to T_n as the interarrival time. Of course, T_n is stochastic. A very useful property of the Poisson process is that T_n ($n = 1, 2, 3, \cdots$) are independent identically distributed exponential random variables with parameter λ and hence have a mean of $1/\lambda$ (Ross, 1993, p. 214).

Within the context of the matching model this is a very handy property. Since interarrival times are distributed exponentially, the hazard rate $fr(t) = \lambda$ is constant and λdt represents the probability that a failure will take place in the time interval dt. Note that a "failure" implies that a match has occurred in this context. Hence, λ can be interpreted as the instantaneous probability of a match occurring.

As is stressed by Pissarides (2001), job matching is by definition a pair-wise event (namely between a firm with a vacancy and an unemployed worker), so that the rates of transition for jobs and for workers are related Poisson processes. For example, as is shown in (8.9), a firm with a vacancy faces a Poisson process with instantaneous probability $q(\theta)$ of meeting an unemployed worker (a match) and striking a deal with this worker. Similarly, as is shown in (8.15), the unemployed worker also faces a Poisson process, but one with instantaneous probability $f(\theta) \equiv \theta q(\theta)$ of meeting a firm with a vacancy that he/she is able to strike a deal with. For job destruction a similar connection between the firm and its worker exists—see equations (8.11) and (8.16).

****

8.1.1.3 Wages

What happens when a job seeker encounters a firm with a vacancy? Clearly there is a *pure economic rent* created by the encounter, existing of the sum of the foregone expected search costs by the firm. But how is this surplus shared between the two parties? In this search context, it is clearly not possible to refer to some going market wage rate, because the concept of an aggregate labour market with impersonal exchange has been abandoned. The exchange that takes place between the two parties is one-on-one, and the division of the rent is a matter of bargaining. Fortunately, as we saw in Chapter 7, there is a useful solution concept in two-person bargaining situations, called the *generalized Nash bargaining* solution.

We assume that all firm-worker pairings are equally productive, so that the wage rate is the same everywhere. This allows us to focus on the *symmetric* equilibrium solution of the model, which is reasonable because the aim of this chapter is to discuss the macroeconomic implications of search theory, not to develop an empirically adequate description of the labour market. We furthermore assume that each firm-worker pair that is involved in wage negotiations takes the behaviour of other such pairings as given.

Consider a particular firm-worker pairing i. What does the firm get out of a deal? Obviously the firm changes status from a firm with a vacancy (with value $J_V^i = 0$, due to free exit/entry) to a firm with an occupied job (with value J_O^i). Hence, it follows from (8.13) that the expected gain to the firm is:

$$J_O^i = \frac{p - w_i}{r + \delta_m}. \tag{8.19}$$

Equation (8.19) shows what the firm is after: it wants to squeeze as much surplus as possible out of the worker by bargaining for a wage w_i far below the marginal product p of the worker.

What does the worker get out of the deal? If a deal is struck, the worker changes status from unemployed to employed worker, which means that the net gain to the worker is:

$$r \left[Y_E^i - Y_U \right] = w_i - \delta_m \left[Y_E^i - Y_U \right] - rY_U, \tag{8.20}$$

where Y_U does not depend on w_i, but rather on the expectation regarding the wage rate in the economy as a whole (see equation (8.17)). If the worker does not accept this job offer (and the wage on offer w_i) then he must continue searching as one of many in the "pool of the unemployed". The relevant wage rate that the unemployed worker takes into account to calculate the value of being unemployed is not w_i but rather the *expected* wage rate elsewhere in the economy.

Using the generalized Nash bargaining solution, the wage w_i is set such that Ω is maximized:

$$\max_{\{w_i\}} \quad \Omega \equiv \beta \ln[Y_E^i - Y_U] + (1 - \beta) \ln[J_O^i - J_V], \qquad 0 < \beta < 1, \tag{8.21}$$

where $J_V \ (= 0)$ and Y_U can be interpreted as the "threat" points of the firm and the worker, respectively. The relative bargaining strengths of the worker and the firm are given by, respectively, β and $1 - \beta$. The usual rent-sharing rule rolls out of the bargaining problem defined in (8.21):

$$\frac{d\Omega}{dw_i} = \frac{\beta}{Y_E^i - Y_U} \cdot \frac{dY_E^i}{dw_i} + \frac{1 - \beta}{J_O^i - J_V} \cdot \frac{dJ_O^i}{dw_i} = 0 \Rightarrow$$

$$\frac{\beta}{r + \delta_m} \cdot \frac{1}{Y_E^i - Y_U} - \frac{1 - \beta}{r + \delta_m} \cdot \frac{1}{J_O^i - J_V} = 0 \Rightarrow$$

$$Y_E^i - Y_U = \frac{\beta}{1 - \beta} \cdot \left[J_O^i - J_V \right]. \tag{8.22}$$

This rent-sharing rule can be turned into a more convenient *wage equation* in two ways.

First, by substituting (8.19)–(8.20) into (8.22) and imposing $J_V = 0$ (due to free exit/entry) we obtain:

$$(1-\beta)Y_E^i = \beta J_O^i + (1-\beta)Y_U \Rightarrow$$

$$(1-\beta)\frac{w_i + \delta_m Y_U}{r+\delta_m} = \beta\frac{p-w_i}{r+\delta_m} + (1-\beta)Y_U \Rightarrow$$

$$(1-\beta)\left[w_i + \delta_m Y_U\right] = \beta\left[p-w_i\right] + (1-\beta)(r+\delta_m)Y_U \Rightarrow$$

$$w_i = (1-\beta)rY_U + \beta p. \tag{8.23}$$

The worker gets a weighted average of his/her reservation wage (rY_U) and marginal product ($p = F_L$). The stronger is the bargaining position of the worker, the larger is β and the closer is the wage to the marginal product of labour.

The second expression for the wage equation is obtained as follows. We know that job productivity is the same for each firm with an occupied job (this is because they all choose the same capital stock, so that $K_i = K$). Hence, the wage rate chosen by firm i is also the same for all firms, $w_i = w$. This implies that rY_U can be written as follows:

$$rY_U = b + \theta q(\theta)\left[Y_E - Y_U\right] = b + \theta q(\theta)\frac{\beta}{1-\beta}J_O$$

$$= b + \theta q(\theta)\frac{\beta}{1-\beta}\frac{c}{q(\theta)} = b + \frac{\beta\theta c}{1-\beta}, \tag{8.24}$$

where we have used the rent-sharing rule (8.22) and the free-entry condition (8.10) to arrive at the final expression. This result is intuitive. In words, it says that the reservation wage rY_U is increasing in the unemployment benefit b, the relative bargaining strength of the worker β, the employers' search cost c, and the tightness in the labour market θ. By substituting (8.24) into (8.23) we obtain the alternative wage equation:

$$w = (1-\beta)b + \beta\left[p + \theta c\right]. \tag{8.25}$$

Workers get a weighted average of the unemployment benefit and the surplus, which consists of the marginal product of labour plus the expected search costs that are saved if the deal is struck (recall that $c\theta \equiv cV/U$ represents the average hiring costs per unemployed worker).

8.1.2   Market equilibrium

We now have all the necessary ingredients of the model. For convenience, the full model is summarized by the following three equations which together determine the equilibrium values for the endogenous variables, w, θ, and U.

$$\frac{p-w}{r+\delta_m} = \frac{c}{q(\theta)}, \tag{8.26}$$

$$w = (1-\beta)b + \beta\left[p + \theta c\right], \tag{8.27}$$

$$U = \frac{\delta_m}{\delta_m + f(\theta)}. \tag{8.28}$$

The exogenous variables are p, c, and b, whilst δ_m and β are structural parameters. Equation (8.26) is a form of the zero profit condition implied by the assumption of free exit/entry of firms, and (8.27) is the wage-setting equation that rolls out of the Nash bargaining between a firm with a vacancy and an unemployed job seeker. Finally, (8.28) is the expression for the equilibrium unemployment rate. This equation is also known as the *Beveridge curve* (Blanchard and Diamond, 1989).

The model is recursive. First, equations (8.26)–(8.27) determine equilibrium values for w and θ as a function of the exogenous variables and parameters. Second, (8.28) determines the unemployment rate, U, as a function of θ. Once θ and U are known, the total number of jobs is given by $(1 - U)N + \theta UN$, and employment equals $L = (1 - U)N$.

The graphical representation of the model is given in Figure 8.1. In panel (a) the ZP curve is the zero-profit condition (8.26). It is downward sloping in (w, θ) space:

$$\left(\frac{dw}{d\theta}\right)_{ZP} = \frac{(r + \delta_m)c}{q(\theta)^2}q'(\theta) < 0. \tag{8.29}$$

Intuitively, a reduction in the wage increases the value of an occupied job and thus raises the left-hand side of (8.26). To restore the zero-profit equilibrium the expected search cost for firms (the right-hand side of (8.26)) must also increase, i.e. $q(\theta)$ must fall and θ must rise.

Also in panel (a), the WS curve is the wage-setting curve (8.27). This curve is upward sloping in (w, θ) space:

$$\left(\frac{dw}{d\theta}\right)_{WS} = \beta c > 0. \tag{8.30}$$

Intuitively, the wage rises with θ because the worker receives part of the search costs that are foregone when he strikes a deal with a firm with a vacancy (see above). By combining ZP and WS$_0$ in panel (a), the equilibrium wage, w^*, and vacancy-unemployment ratio, θ^*, are determined–see point E$_0$ in panel (a).

In panel (b) of Figure 8.1, the straight line from the origin, labelled LMT$_0$, depicts the equilibrium vacancy-unemployment ratio (i.e., the indicator for labour market tightness) by writing it in the form $V = \theta^* U$. The line labelled BC depicts the Beveridge curve (8.28), rewritten in (V, U) space:

$$U = \frac{\delta_m}{\delta_m + f(V/U)}. \tag{8.31}$$

The slope of the Beveridge curve is:

$$\left(\frac{dV}{dU}\right)_{BC} = -\frac{1}{\theta}\frac{f\,\varepsilon_f}{\delta_m + f\,[1 - \varepsilon_f]} < 0, \tag{8.32}$$

where f and ε_f are given, respectively, in (8.5) and (8.6). The Beveridge curve is downward sloping (since $f > 0$ and $0 < \varepsilon_f < 1$). Intuitively, for a given unemployment rate, a reduction in vacancy rate leads to a fall in the instantaneous probability of finding a job (f), i.e. for points below the BC curve the unemployment rate is less than the rate required for flow equilibrium in the labour market ($U < \delta_m/(\delta_m + f)$). To restore flow equilibrium the unemployment rate must rise.

8.1.3 Comparative static effects

In order to demonstrate some of the key properties of the model we now perform some comparative static experiments. The first experiment has some policy relevance and concerns the effects of an increase in the unemployment benefit b. It is

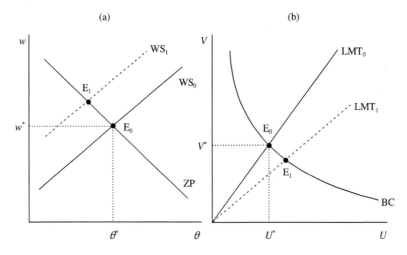

Figure 8.1: Search equilibrium in the labour market

clear from (8.27) that an increase in b leads to upward pressure on the wage rate as the fall-back position of workers in the wage negotiations improves. In terms of Figure 8.1, the wage setting equation shifts up from WS_0 to WS_1 and the equilibrium shifts from E_0 to E_1 in panel (a). The equilibrium wage rate increases and the vacancy-unemployment ratio decreases. Intuitively, the policy shock causes the value of an occupied job to fall. In panel (b) of Figure 8.1, the reduction in the vacancy-unemployment ratio is represented by a clockwise rotation of the LMT line, from LMT_0 to LMT_1. Since nothing happens to the Beveridge curve, the equilibrium shifts from E_0 to E_1 in panel (b), the vacancy rate falls, and the unemployment rate rises.

As a second comparative static experiment we consider what happens when the exogenous rate of job destruction δ_m rises. This shock is more complicated than the first one because it affects both the incentive for firms to create vacancies and the Beveridge curve itself. Indeed, it follows from equation (8.31) that:

$$\frac{\partial U}{\partial \delta_m} = \frac{1 - U}{\delta_m + f\left[1 - \varepsilon_f\right]} > 0, \tag{8.33}$$

i.e. an increase in the job destruction rate δ_m shifts the Beveridge curve to the right. It is clear from equation (8.26) that, ceteris paribus the wage, the increase in the job destruction rate reduces the value of an occupied job as the rents accruing to the firm are discounted more heavily. Hence, in terms of panel (a) of Figure 8.2, the ZP curve shifts to the left from ZP_0 to ZP_1. Since nothing happens to the wage-setting curve, the equilibrium in panel (a) shifts from E_0 to E_1 and both the wage and the vacancy-unemployment ratio fall. In panel (b) of Figure 8.2, the LMT curve rotates in a clockwise fashion from LMT_0 to LMT_1. As was noted above, the direct effect of an increase in the job destruction rate is to shift the Beveridge curve outward, say from BC_0 to BC_1 in panel (b). We show in Intermezzo 8.2 that the outward shift in the Beveridge curve dominates the clockwise rotation in the LMT curve (provided a very mild sufficient condition is satisfied) so that the new equilibrium E_1 lies in a north-easterly direction from the initial equilibrium E_0 so that both the unemployment and vacancy rate increase.

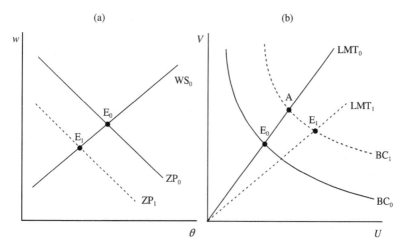

Figure 8.2: The effects of a higher job destruction rate

Intermezzo 8.2

Comparative static effects in the matching model of unemployment.
In section 8.1.3 we graphically derive some results regarding shocks to
the unemployment benefit, b, and the job destruction rate, δ_m. Here we
derive these results analytically. First we loglinearize equations (8.26)–
(8.27). After some manipulation we obtain:

$$\begin{bmatrix} \varepsilon_q(w-p) & -1 \\ -\beta c\theta & 1 \end{bmatrix} \begin{bmatrix} \tilde{\theta} \\ dw \end{bmatrix} = \begin{bmatrix} (p-w)\left[\tilde{c} + \left(\frac{\delta_m}{r+\delta_m}\right)\tilde{\delta}_m\right] \\ (1-\beta)db + \beta c\theta\tilde{c} \end{bmatrix}, \quad \text{(a)}$$

where ε_q is defined in (8.4), $\tilde{\theta} \equiv d\theta/\theta$, $\tilde{c} \equiv dc/c$, and $\tilde{\delta}_m \equiv d\delta_m/\delta_m$.
Solving (a) yields the solutions for $\tilde{\theta}$ and dw:

$$\tilde{\theta} \equiv \tilde{V} - \tilde{U} = \frac{-(p-w+\beta\theta c)\tilde{c} - (p-w)\left(\frac{\delta_m}{r+\delta_m}\right)\tilde{\delta}_m - (1-\beta)db}{\varepsilon_q(p-w) + \beta c\theta},$$

$$\text{(b)}$$

$$dw = (p-w)\left[\frac{-\beta\theta c\left[(1-\varepsilon_q)\tilde{c} + \frac{\delta_m}{r+\delta_m}\tilde{\delta}_m\right] + \varepsilon_q(1-\beta)db}{\varepsilon_q(p-w) + \beta c\theta}\right]. \quad \text{(c)}$$

It follows that an increase in the unemployment benefit ($db > 0$) raises the
wage ($dw > 0$) and reduces the vacancy-unemployment ratio ($\tilde{\theta} < 0$) as
is illustrated in Figure 8.1. An increase in the job separation rate ($\tilde{\delta}_m > 0$)
leads to a reduction in both the wage and the vacancy-unemployment
ratio ($dw < 0$ and $\tilde{\theta} < 0$) as is illustrated in Figure 8.2. Finally, an increase in the search costs ($\tilde{c} > 0$) reduces both the wage and the vacancy-
unemployment ratio ($dw < 0$ and $\tilde{\theta} < 0$). Students are invited to draw
the corresponding graph and to provide the economic intuition.

It remains to show that an increase in the job destruction rate raises both the unemployment and vacancy rates, as is asserted in the discussion surrounding Figure 8.2. By loglinearizing (8.31) we obtain:

$$\tilde{V} = \frac{1}{1 - \varepsilon_q} \tilde{\delta}_m - \frac{\delta_m + f\varepsilon_q}{f(1 - \varepsilon_q)} \tilde{U}, \tag{d}$$

where $\tilde{U} \equiv dU/U$, $\tilde{V} \equiv dV/V$, and where ε_q and f are given, respectively, in (8.4) and (8.5). By using (b) and (d) (and setting $\tilde{c} = db = 0$) we obtain a system in $\tilde{V}$ and $\tilde{U}$:

$$\begin{bmatrix} 1 & \frac{\delta_m + f\varepsilon_q}{f(1 - \varepsilon_q)} \\ 1 & -1 \end{bmatrix} \begin{bmatrix} \tilde{V} \\ \tilde{U} \end{bmatrix} = \begin{bmatrix} 1 \\ -\frac{\delta_m}{r + \delta_m} \frac{(1 - \varepsilon_q)(p - w)}{\varepsilon_q(p - w) + \beta c\theta} \end{bmatrix} \frac{\delta_m}{1 - \varepsilon_q}. \tag{e}$$

Solving (e) yields the following expressions:

$$\tilde{V} = \frac{f}{\delta_m + f} \cdot \left[1 - \frac{\delta_m + f\varepsilon_q}{f} \frac{\delta_m}{r + \delta_m} \frac{p - w}{\varepsilon_q(p - w) + \beta c\theta} \right] \tilde{\delta}_m \gtrless 0, \tag{f}$$

$$\tilde{U} = \frac{f}{\delta_m + f} \cdot \left[1 + \frac{\delta_m}{r + \delta_m} \frac{(1 - \varepsilon_q)(p - w)}{\varepsilon_q(p - w) + \beta c\theta} \right] \tilde{\delta}_m > 0. \tag{g}$$

Unemployment unambiguously rises but the effect on the vacancy rate is ambiguous in general. It is not difficult to show, however, that the term in square brackets on the right-hand side of (f) is positive if a rather weak sufficient condition is satisfied. First we note that (8.26) gives rise to the following result:

$$\frac{p - w}{\varepsilon_q(p - w) + \beta c\theta} = \frac{r + \delta_m}{\varepsilon_q(r + \delta_m) + \beta f}. \tag{h}$$

By using (h) the term in square brackets on the right-hand side of (f) can be simplified to:

$$\begin{aligned} [\cdot] &= 1 - \frac{\delta_m + f\varepsilon_q}{f} \frac{\delta_m}{r + \delta_m} \frac{r + \delta_m}{\varepsilon_q(r + \delta_m) + \beta f} \\ &= \frac{f\left[r\varepsilon_q + \beta f\right] - \delta_m^2}{f\left[\varepsilon_q(r + \delta_m) + \beta f\right]} \\ &= \frac{fr\varepsilon_q + f^2\left[\beta - (\delta_m/f)^2\right]}{f\left[\varepsilon_q(r + \delta_m) + \beta f\right]}. \end{aligned} \tag{i}$$

The denominator in (i) is positive, and, since $fr\varepsilon_q > 0$, a *sufficient* condition for the numerator to be positive also is $\beta > (\delta_m/f)^2$ or:

$$\beta > \left(\frac{U}{1 - U} \right)^2, \tag{j}$$

where we have used the fact that $U = \delta_m/(\delta_m + f)$. Provided the relative bargaining power of the worker (β) is not very small, the inequality in (j) is satisfied and the term in square brackets on the right-hand side of (f) is positive. In fact, the sufficient condition is quite weak. Even for the relatively high unemployment rate of 25% ($U = 0.25$) the condition is satisfied if $\beta > 1/9$. See, also Pissarides (1990, p. 16) who derives a more stringent sufficient condition.

In section 8.2.1 we modify the model to take into account the effects of taxation on the labour market. An increase in the labour income tax rate operates just like an increase in the unemployment benefit so the results follow immediately. Keeping all exogenous variables other than the payroll tax constant we find by differentiating (8.36) and (8.41):

$$
\begin{bmatrix} \varepsilon_q \frac{w(1+t_E)-p}{1+t_E} & -1 \\ -\frac{\beta c\theta}{1+t_E} & 1 \end{bmatrix} \begin{bmatrix} \tilde{\theta} \\ dw \end{bmatrix} = \begin{bmatrix} w \\ -\frac{\beta[p+c\theta]}{1+t_E} \end{bmatrix} \tilde{t}_E, \tag{k}
$$

where $\tilde{t}_E \equiv dt_E/(1+t_E)$. Solving (k) yields the solutions for $\tilde{\theta}$ and dw:

$$
\tilde{\theta} = -\frac{w(1+t_E) - \beta[p+\theta c]}{\varepsilon_q[p-w(1+t_E)]+\beta c\theta}\tilde{t}_E < 0, \tag{l}
$$

$$
dw = -\frac{\beta}{1+t_E}\frac{\theta cw(1+t_E)+\varepsilon_q[p-w(1+t_E)][p+\theta c]}{\varepsilon_q[p-w(1+t_E)]+\beta c\theta}\tilde{t}_E < 0, \tag{m}
$$

where it follows from (8.41) that the numerator of (l) is positive.

In section 8.2.2 we study the effects of an increase in the deposit on labour, b. Keeping all exogenous variables other than the deposit constant we find by differentiating (8.45) and (8.48):

$$
\begin{bmatrix} \varepsilon_q(w-p-rs_H) & -1 \\ -\beta c\theta & 1 \end{bmatrix} \begin{bmatrix} \tilde{\theta} \\ dw \end{bmatrix} = \begin{bmatrix} -1 \\ \beta \end{bmatrix} rds_H. \tag{n}
$$

Solving for $\tilde{\theta}$ and dw yields:

$$
\tilde{\theta} = \frac{1-\beta}{\varepsilon_q(p+rs_H-w)+\beta\theta c} rds_H > 0, \tag{o}
$$

$$
dw = \frac{\beta[\theta c + \varepsilon_q(p+rs_H-w)]}{\varepsilon_q(p+rs_H-w)+\beta\theta c} rds_H > 0. \tag{p}
$$

****

8.1.4 Efficiency

The matching model described in this section incorporates a *trading externality*. The matching probability of unemployed workers and firms with a vacancy depends on the number of traders in the market, i.e. on U and on V. When an unemployed worker and a firm with a vacancy meet and strike a deal (by agreeing on a particular wage rate), they do not take into account that in doing so they affect the labour market tightness ratio, V/U, and thus alter both the job-finding rate and the worker-finding rate for other participants in the labour market. The critical question is now whether the Nash-bargained wage rate internalizes the external effect, and produces an efficient outcome, or not? Put differently, is search unemployment efficient or not?

In a celebrated paper, Hosios (1990) argues in very general terms that the search equilibrium is Pareto efficient if, for each agent, the social contribution to and private gain from participating in the matching process are equal to each other. In the context of our particular model, the matching function features constant returns to scale and the equilibrium is efficient provided the *Hosios condition* is satisfied:[5]

$$\beta = \varepsilon_q(\theta), \tag{8.34}$$

where β is the bargaining weight of workers and $\varepsilon_q(\cdot) \equiv G_U U / G$ is the elasticity of the matching function with respect to unemployment (see also (8.4) above).

As is explained in detail by Pissarides (2000, p. 185), the Hosios condition must be seen as a knife-edge condition which is very unlikely to hold in real economies. This can be demonstrated most easily in the special case with a Cobb-Douglas matching function, $M = U^{\varepsilon_q} V^{1-\varepsilon_q}$ for which the elasticity is a constant and the Hosios condition reduces to $\varepsilon_q = \beta$. But these coefficients are completely independent and are thus unlikely to be equal to each other: β is the "bargaining strength" of the worker whereas ε_q is an aspect of the matching technology. In conclusion, the decentralized matching model is likely to be inefficient.

8.2 Applications of the canonical search model

In this section we use the canonical model developed above to study two policy issues. First, we continue our study of the effects of taxation on the labour market. Second, we study the idea of treating workers like empty beer bottles. Specifically, we look at what happens if employers must pay (receive) a deposit if they lay off (hire) a worker.

8.2.1 The effects of taxation

We assume that there are two separate taxes levied on labour. First, the employer must pay an *ad valorem* tax on the use of labour (a payroll tax), which is denoted by t_E. Second, the household faces a proportional tax on labour income, denoted by t_L.

The effects of the employers' tax on labour are as follows. First, equation (8.11) is modified to:

$$rJ_O = F(K,1) - (r + \delta_k)K - w(1 + t_E) - \delta_m J_O, \tag{8.35}$$

so that the marginal productivity condition for capital (equation (8.12)) is unaffected, but the free entry/exit condition (8.14) is modified to:

$$\frac{p - w(1 + t_E)}{r + \delta_m} = \frac{c}{q(\theta)}. \tag{8.36}$$

The effects of the labour income tax are as follows. First, since the unemployment benefit is untaxed and exogenous, equation (8.15) is unchanged, but the after-tax real wage rate $w(1 - t_L)$ appears in (8.16), so that (8.17)–(8.18) are modified to:

$$rY_U = \frac{(r + \delta_m)b + \theta q(\theta)w(1 - t_L)}{r + \delta_m + \theta q(\theta)}, \tag{8.37}$$

---

[5]A formal derivation of this condition is presented in Chapter 13.

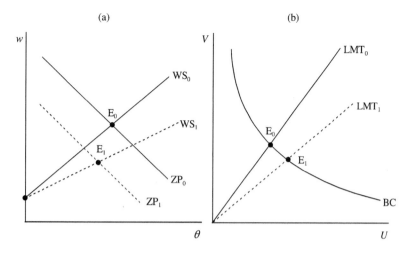

Figure 8.3: The effects of a payroll tax

$$rY_E = \frac{\delta_m b + [r + \theta q(\theta)] \, w(1 - t_L)}{r + \delta_m + \theta q(\theta)} = \frac{r \, [w(1 - t_L) - b]}{r + \delta_m + \theta q(\theta)} + rY_U, \tag{8.38}$$

where the second expression in (8.38) shows that $w(1 - t_L) \geq b$ must hold for anybody to be willing to search, i.e. the labour income tax must not be too high.

The second effect of the income tax operates via the wage bargaining process. By following the derivation in section 8.1.1.3, the rent-sharing rule (8.22) is modified to:

$$Y_E^i - Y_U = \frac{\beta}{1 - \beta} \frac{1 - t_L}{1 + t_E} \left[J_O^i - J_V \right], \tag{8.39}$$

so that the wage equation (8.23) becomes:

$$w_i = (1 - \beta) \frac{rY_U}{1 - t_L} + \beta \frac{p}{1 + t_E}, \tag{8.40}$$

and (8.25) can be written as:

$$w = (1 - \beta) \frac{b}{1 - t_L} + \beta \frac{p + \theta c}{1 + t_E}. \tag{8.41}$$

The core part of the model consists of the Beveridge curve (8.28), the zero-profit curve (8.36), and the wage-setting curve (8.41). It is possible to explain the intuition behind the comparative static effects of the various tax rates by graphical means. (The formal derivations are found in Intermezzo 8.2.)

First we consider in Figure 8.3 the effects of an increase in the payroll tax, t_E. It follows from (8.36) that the zero profit curve shifts to the left (from ZP_0 to ZP_1 in panel (a)) as a result of the shock. Ceteris paribus the gross wage rate, the tax increase reduces the value of an occupied job so that the zero profit equilibrium is consistent with a lower vacancy-unemployment ratio. The payroll tax also features in the wage-setting equation. Indeed, it follows from (8.41) that the increase in the payroll tax puts downward pressure on the wage rate. Intuitively this is because the firm is interested in the net surplus of the match (equal to $(p + \theta c)/(1 + t_E)$), i.e. it takes the payroll tax into account. Part of this surplus features in the wage which thus falls on that account. In terms of Figure 8.3, the wage-setting curve rotates in a

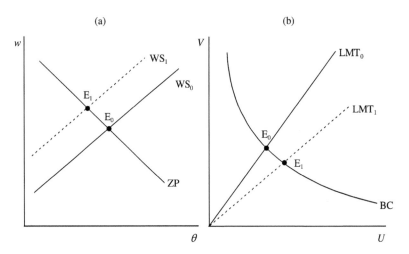

Figure 8.4: The effects of a labour income tax

clockwise fashion from WS_0 to WS_1 in panel (a). The equilibrium shifts from E_0 to E_1, and both the wage rate and the vacancy-unemployment ratio fall (see Intermezzo 8.2). In panel (b) the LMT curve rotates in a clockwise fashion from LMT_0 to LMT_1 and the equilibrium shifts from E_0 to E_1. The equilibrium vacancy rate falls and the unemployment rate increases.

As a second comparative statics exercise we now consider the effects of an increase in the labour income tax, t_L. The effects of this shock are illustrated in Figure 8.4. The increase in the labour income tax has no effect on the zero-profit curve but the wage-setting equation shifts up from WS_0 to WS_1 in panel (a). Intuitively, it follows from (8.41) that the tax increase raises the tax-inclusive value of the outside option $(b/(1 - t_L))$ for the household in the wage bargaining process because the unemployment benefit is untaxed. This leads, ceteris paribus, to upward pressure on the wage rate. In panel (a) the equilibrium shifts from E_0 to E_1, the gross wage rate increases, and the vacancy-unemployment ratio falls. In panel (b) the LMT curve rotates in a clockwise fashion from LMT_0 to LMT_1, the equilibrium shifts from E_0 to E_1, and equilibrium vacancies fall whilst the unemployment rate rises. The tax shock works in exactly the same way as an increase in the unemployment benefit.

8.2.2 Deposits on workers?

Some people return empty bottles to the store because they find it unacceptable from an environmental point of view to litter them. Most people, however, are less interested in this noble pursuit of a responsible attitude towards the natural environment, and only return the bottles because there is money to be made in the form of a deposit that will be refunded. One could argue that a similar system should be tried in the labour market. Why not have the firm pay a deposit when it fires a worker, to be refunded when it (re-) hires that (or another) worker? It turns out that this question can be analysed in the search-theoretic framework developed in this chapter.

Suppose that a firm that hires a worker receives a fixed once-off payment of s_H from the government, but that a firm that fires a worker must pay s_H to the government. Clearly, equation (8.9) would be modified to reflect this payment:

$$rJ_V = -c + q(\theta)[J_O + s_H - J_V]. \tag{8.42}$$

If a firm with a vacancy finds a worker, its capital gain will be $J_O - J_V$ *plus* the payment from the government. Free exit/entry of firms will then imply the following expression for the value of an occupied job:

$$J_V = 0 \quad \Rightarrow \quad J_O = \frac{c}{q(\theta)} - s_H. \tag{8.43}$$

Equation (8.43) shows that the deposit acts like a lump-sum subsidy to firms with a vacancy and thus stimulates job creation. The expected search costs $c/q(\theta)$ are reduced by the lump-sum payment received from the government.

For a firm with a filled job, the steady-state arbitrage equation reads as follows:

$$rJ_O = F(K,1) - (r + \delta_k)K - w - \delta_m [J_O + s_H]. \tag{8.44}$$

If the job is destroyed, the firm not only loses the value of the occupied job, but must also pay back the deposit on its worker to the government. As a result, the expected capital loss is $\delta_m(J_O + s_H)$. (Since the job destruction rate δ_m is exogenous, the firm can do nothing to reduce the probability of an adverse job-destroying shock.) The marginal productivity condition for capital (8.12) still holds so that job productivity is still constant and equal to $p \equiv F_L = F(K,1) - (r + \delta_k)K$. By combining this result with (8.43)–(8.44) we obtain the new zero profit condition (the counterpart to (8.14)):

$$(r + \delta_m)\left[\frac{c}{q(\theta)} - s_H\right] = p - w - \delta_m s_H \quad \Rightarrow$$

$$\frac{c}{q(\theta)} = \frac{p - w + r s_H}{r + \delta_m}. \tag{8.45}$$

Not the deposit itself but its capital value $r s_H$ acts like a subsidy on the use of labour.

The rent-sharing rule (equation (8.22)) is modified to reflect the payment the firm receives if it employs the worker:

$$Y_E^i - Y_U = \frac{\beta}{1 - \beta} \left[J_O^i + s_H - J_V\right], \tag{8.46}$$

so that the wage equation (8.23) becomes:

$$w_i = (1 - \beta)rY_U + \beta [p + r s_H]. \tag{8.47}$$

Since the reservation wage is still given by (8.24), the wage equation (8.47) can be rewritten for the symmetric case (with $w_i = w$) as:

$$w = (1 - \beta)b + \beta [p + r s_H + \theta c]. \tag{8.48}$$

The model consists of equations (8.28), (8.45), and (8.48).

In Figure 8.5 we illustrate the effects of an increase in the deposit, s_H. It follows from (8.45) that the zero profit curve shifts up (from ZP_0 to ZP_1 in panel (a)) because the interest payments the firm earns on the deposit increase the value of an occupied job. These interest payments, however, also influence the wage rate via the wage-setting equation (8.48). Hence, the wage-setting equation shifts up from WS_0 to WS_1 in panel (a). It is shown in Intermezzo 8.2 that both the wage and the vacancy-unemployment ratio rise as a result of the shock, i.e. point E_1 lies to the north-east of the initial equilibrium E_0. In panel (b) the LMT curve rotates in a counterclockwise fashion from LMT_0 to LMT_1 and the equilibrium shifts from E_0 to E_1. The equilibrium vacancy rate rises and the unemployment rate falls.

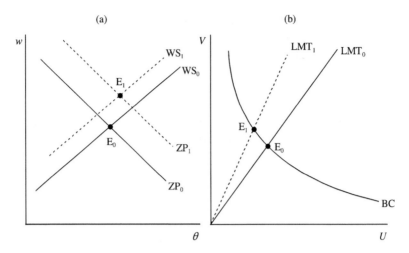

Figure 8.5: The effects of a deposit on labour

8.3 Endogenous job destruction*

Up to this point we have assumed that the job destruction rate δ_m is constant so that the only endogenous variable determining the steady-state unemployment rate is the job finding rate $f(\theta)$ which itself depends on the job creation process—see equation (8.8). As is pointed out by Pissarides (2000, p. 37), however, the empirical evidence strongly suggests that the job destruction rate is not constant but should be seen as an endogenous variable responding to exogenous shocks. He also argues that most job destruction is due to idiosyncratic shocks. In this section we study the model of Mortensen and Pissarides (1994) which endogenizes the job destruction process. Just as for the canonical model we restrict attention to the steady-state unemployment equilibrium and develop the model intuitively.

8.3.1 Basic assumptions

In order to generate a mechanism by which existing matches can be terminated voluntarily, it is assumed that labour productivity fluctuates idiosyncratically, i.e. at the level of the single-job firm. In particular, the production function facing the individual firm takes the form $F(K, N)$ where K is the firm's rented capital stock, $N \equiv xL$ measures employment in terms of efficiency units of labour, and $L = 1$ as the firm employs a single worker. By assumption, the random variable x satisfies $0 \leq x \leq 1$. Any changes in x correspond to idiosyncratic shocks. In order to streamline the discussion somewhat we incorporate the optimal capital rental decision of the firm upfront. Since the technology features constant returns to scale, it follows that $F(K, x) = KF_K(K, x) + xF_N(K, x)$. Active firms will rent capital such that $F_K(K, x) = r + \delta_k$. Since r and δ_k are both constant by assumption, this condition fixes the K/x ratio for active firms and explains why the marginal product of labour is also constant, i.e. $F_N(K, x) = p$. The net product (or "market value") of a job, $F(K, x) - KF_K(K, x)$, can thus be written as px.

   If a firm with a vacancy meets a worker and creates a new job, then it is assumed to be able to choose its start-up job productivity level, i.e. the firm can choose the value of x at the moment of job creation. Of course, profit maximization implies that it will set $x = 1$. As in the canonical model idiosyncratic shocks hit existing jobs at the Poisson rate δ_m. It is assumed that for existing firms at each moment in time a new value of x is drawn from a probability distribution function $\Phi(x)$ on the unit interval. The new value of x can be higher or lower than the old value. At each moment in time the firm can either accept the new value of x and continue production or destroy the job. The destruction choice is irreversible: the firm cannot rehire a worker it has just fired a moment before.

Before going into the details of the model we first explain the job-scrapping rule intuitively. Let $J_O(x)$ be the value of an occupied job with productivity parameter x and let J_V denote the value of a vacancy (equal to zero under free exit and entry). Then the firm retains the job if $J_O(x) \geq J_V = 0$. As the value of an occupied job is increasing in the idiosyncratic productivity level, $J_O'(x) \geq 0$ (see below), it follows that the optimal strategy for the firm is to choose a *reservation productivity* R such that $J_O(R) = 0$. To summarize, the job scrapping rule works as follows. If the firm is hit by a shock such that $x < R$ then the job is destroyed immediately and the worker becomes unemployed. Otherwise, if $x \geq R$ then the job is retained. The probability of job destruction following a shock is therefore $\Phi(R)$.

For readers who are a bit rusty on statistics and distribution functions, consider the simplest possible case where x is distributed according to the uniform distribution, i.e. $\Phi(x) = 0$ for $x < 0$, $\Phi(x) = x$ for $0 \leq x \leq 1$, and $\Phi(x) = 1$ for $x \geq 1$. The top panel of Figure 8.6 shows the cumulative distribution function for positive values of x. Denoting the probability density by $\phi(x) \equiv \Phi'(x)$ we find that $\phi(x) = 1$ for $0 \leq x \leq 1$ and is zero elsewhere. If the reservation productivity is R then jobs are scrapped for all values of $x \in [0, R)$ and jobs are maintained for $x \in [R, 1]$.

The steady-state unemployment rate can be computed as follows. In a small time interval dt, the probability that an employed worker loses his/her job and becomes unemployed is thus given by $\delta_m \Phi(R)dt$. Hence, the average number of workers that become unemployed in a time interval dt equals $\delta_m \Phi(R)(1 - U)Ndt$, and the average number of unemployed who find a job is given by $f(\theta)UNdt$. In the steady-state the unemployment rate is constant, so that the expected inflow and outflow must be equal to each other, $\delta_m \Phi(R)(1 - U)Ndt = f(\theta)UNdt$. Since the labour force N is large, expected and actual inflows and outflows are the same, so that the steady-state equilibrium unemployment rate is given by:

$$U = \frac{\delta_m \Phi(R)}{\delta_m \Phi(R) + f(\theta)}. \tag{8.49}$$

This expression generalizes (8.8). There are now two mechanisms explaining the unemployment rate. The job destruction mechanism works via $\Phi(R)$. Ceteris paribus θ, an increase in the reservation productivity R increases the rate of job destruction which leads to an upward shift of the Beveridge curve, $\partial U / \partial R > 0$. The job creation mechanism operates via the job finding rate $f(\theta)$. Just as in the canonical model, an increase in θ leads to an increase in the job-finding rate and a reduction in equilibrium unemployment, i.e. $\partial U / \partial \theta < 0$.

In the remainder of this section we discuss how the equilibrium values for R and θ follow from the maximizing behaviour of firms and workers facing stochastic rationing. We follow the same approach as for the canonical model.

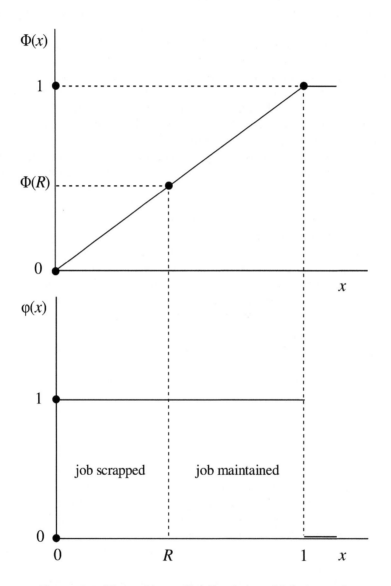

Figure 8.6: The uniform distribution and job scrapping

8.3.2 Model

8.3.2.1 Firms

The value of a vacancy is given by:

$$rJ_V = -c + q(\theta)[J_O(1) - J_V],\tag{8.50}$$

where c is the cost of searching and $q(\theta)$ is the instantaneous probability of a vacancy being filled. Note that the capital gain upon finding a worker is given by $J_O(1) - J_V$ because any new job is created at the maximum productivity level, $x = 1$. The zero-profit condition $J_V = 0$ yields:

$$J_O(1) = \frac{c}{q(\theta)}.\tag{8.51}$$

The value of a firm with an occupied job with productivity level $x \in [R, 1]$ is given by:

$$rJ_O(x) = [x - w(x)] + \delta_m \int_0^1 [\max\{J_O(z), 0\} - J_O(x)]d\Phi(z).\tag{8.52}$$

The left-hand side is the asset value of the job and the right-hand side represents its return. The first return component is the difference between the market value of the job minus the wage that the firm pays to its worker. The second term summarizes the scrapping choice that the firm needs to make. For each z such that $z \in [R, 1]$ the firm continues its operations and gets a capital gain (or loss) of $J_O(z) - J_O(x)$ whilst for $z \in [0, R)$ it destroys the job and makes a capital loss of $-J_O(x)$. The integral term thus represents the expected capital gain.

Note that since $J_O(z) < 0$ and $\max\{J_O(z), 0\} = 0$ for $z \in [0, R)$ the second term on the right-hand side of (8.52) can be rewritten as:

$$\int_0^1 [\max\{J_O(z), 0\} - J_O(x)]d\Phi(z) = -\int_0^R J_O(x)d\Phi(z) + \int_R^1 [J_O(z) - J_O(x)]d\Phi(z)$$

$$= -\Phi(R)J_O(x) + \int_R^1 [J(z) - J_O(x)]d\Phi(z).\tag{8.53}$$

By using (8.53) in (8.52) an alternative expression for $J_O(x)$ is obtained:

$$rJ_O(x) = px - w(x) + \delta_m \left[\int_R^1 J_O(z)d\Phi(z) - J_O(x)\right].\tag{8.54}$$

8.3.2.2 Workers

The value of an unemployed job-seeker's human wealth is given by:

$$rY_U = b + f(\theta)[Y_E(1) - Y_U],\tag{8.55}$$

where b is the unemployment benefit and $f(\theta) \equiv \theta q(\theta)$ is the instantaneous probability of finding a job and getting a capital gain equal to the change in human wealth, $Y_E(1) - Y_U$. As we noted before, any new job is created at value $x = 1$ so $Y_E(1)$ features in the capital gains term in (8.55).

Next we turn to the value of an employed worker's human wealth. For a worker productivity level x this value is given by:

$$rY_E(x) = w(x) + \delta_m \int_0^1 [\max\{Y_E(z), Y_U\} - Y_E(x)]\, d\Phi(z)$$

$$= w(x) + \delta_m \int_R^1 [Y_E(z) - Y_E(x)] d\Phi(z) - \delta_m \Phi(R)[Y_E(x) - Y_U], \quad (8.56)$$

where we have eliminated the max $\{\cdot\}$ function in going from the first to the second line by using the same reasoning as before. As in the canonical model, the worker's permanent income $rY_E(x)$ differs from the wage rate $w(x)$ because of the status changes that result from the idiosyncratic shocks. The second term on the right-hand side of (8.56) gives the expected capital gain for all $z \in [R, 1]$, i.e. for all shocks under which the job remains open. The third term is the expected capital loss for all other shocks $z \in [0, R)$ when the job is destroyed and the worker becomes unemployed.

8.3.2.3 Wages

Wages are renegotiated every time a productivity shock arrives. For each $x \in [R, 1]$ the wage is determined by generalized Nash bargaining. For each agent, the threat point is the option to look out for an alternative match partner. The wage rate $w_i(x)$ that rolls out of the negotiations is such that Ω is maximized:

$$\max_{w_i(x)} \quad \Omega = \beta \ln[Y_E^i(x) - Y_U] + (1 - \beta) \ln[J_O^i(x) - J_V]. \quad (8.57)$$

Since what goes to the worker must come from the firm, $\partial Y_E^i(x)/\partial w(x) = -\partial J_O^i(x)/\partial w(x)$, so that the first-order condition yields the rent-sharing rule:

$$Y_E^i(x) - Y_U = \frac{\beta}{1-\beta}[J_O^i(x) - J_V]. \quad (8.58)$$

In Intermezzo 8.3 we show that the following wage equation can be derived:

$$w(x) = (1 - \beta)b + \beta[px + c\theta]. \quad (8.59)$$

This expression generalizes equation (8.25) from the canonical model. The wage depends positively on the job's productivity but not on the productivities achieved in other firms. Note furthermore that the equilibrium wage rate does not take future wage fluctuations into account. Agents are risk neutral, and there is Nash bargaining at each value of x.

Since $J_O(R) = 0$ by definition, it follows from the rent-sharing rule that $Y_E(R) = Y_U$. Hence, the reservation productivity R is jointly rational: neither party wants to sustain a match when the productivity is below R. As such, all job separations are privately efficient (but not socially efficient due to search externalities).

Intermezzo 8.3

Some tedious derivations for the matching model of unemployment.
Two expressions for the wage equation can be derived from the rent-sharing rule (8.58). First we use (8.56) to find the expression for $Y_E^i(x)$:

$$(r + \delta_m)Y_E^i(x) = w_i(x) + \delta_m \int_R^1 Y_E(z)d\Phi(z) + \delta_m \Phi(R)Y_U. \quad (a)$$

Second, we use (8.54) to find:

$$(r + \delta_m)J_O^i(x) = px - w_i(x) + \delta_m \int_R^1 J_O(z)d\Phi(z). \quad (b)$$

Next, by substituting (a)–(b) into (8.58) and noting that $J_V = 0$ we find:

$$(1 - \beta) \left[w_i(x) + \delta_m \int_R^1 Y_E(z)d\Phi(z) - (r + \delta_m[1 - \Phi(R)])Y_U \right]$$

$$= \beta \left[px - w_i(x) + \delta_m \int_R^1 J_O(z)d\Phi(z) \right], \tag{c}$$

which can be solved for $w_i(x)$:

$$w_i(x) = (1 - \beta) \left[(r + \delta_m[1 - \Phi(R)])Y_U - \delta_m \int_R^1 Y_E(z)d\Phi(z) \right]$$

$$+ \beta \left[px + \delta_m \int_R^1 J_O(z)d\Phi(z) \right]. \tag{d}$$

By symmetry $w_i(x) = w(x)$ for all i so that $Y_E^i(x) = Y_E(x)$ and $J_O^i(x) = J_O(x)$. The rent-sharing rule (8.58) implies:

$$\int_R^1 (1 - \beta)Y_E(z)d\Phi(z) - \int_R^1 \beta J_O(z)d\Phi(z) = \int_R^1 (1 - \beta)Y_U d\Phi(z)$$

$$= (1 - \beta)[1 - \Phi(R)]Y_U. \tag{e}$$

From (8.55), the rent-sharing rule for new jobs, and the zero-profit condition (8.51) we have:

$$rY_U = b + \theta q(\theta)\frac{\beta}{1 - \beta}J_O(1) = b + \frac{\beta\theta c}{1 - \beta}. \tag{f}$$

By substituting (e)–(f) into (d) we obtain the wage equation (8.59).

The job creation condition (8.60) is derived as follows. By using the wage equation (8.59) the job value equation (8.54) can be written as:

$$(r + \delta_m)J_O(x) = (1 - \beta)[px - b] - \beta c\theta + \delta_m \int_R^1 J_O(z)d\Phi(z). \tag{g}$$

The reservation threshold condition $J_O(R) = 0$ implies:

$$(1 - \beta)[pR - b] = \beta c\theta - \delta_m \int_R^1 J_O(z)d\Phi(z). \tag{h}$$

Substitution of (h) into (g) yields:

$$J_O(x) = \frac{(1 - \beta)p[x - R]}{r + \delta_m}. \tag{i}$$

By combining (i) with the zero-profit condition (8.51) we obtain the job creation condition (8.60).

The job destruction condition (8.61) is derived as follows. Given the expression for $J_O(x)$ in (i) we can write:

$$\int_R^1 J_O(z)d\Phi(z) = \frac{(1 - \beta)p}{r + \delta_m} \int_R^1 [z - R]d\Phi(z). \tag{j}$$

By substituting (j) into (h) we obtain the job destruction condition (8.61). By using (f) in (8.61) we find (8.65).

****

8.3.3 Market equilibrium

We now have all the ingredients of the model. The full model is summarized by the following four equations:

$$(1 - \beta)\frac{p\,[1 - R]}{r + \delta_m} = \frac{c}{q(\theta)}, \tag{8.60}$$

$$pR + \frac{\delta_m}{r + \delta_m} \int_R^1 p[z - R]d\Phi(z) = \frac{\beta c\theta}{1 - \beta} + b, \tag{8.61}$$

$$U = \frac{\delta_m \Phi(R)}{\delta_m \Phi(R) + f(\theta)}, \tag{8.62}$$

$$w(x) = (1 - \beta)b + \beta[px + c\theta]. \tag{8.63}$$

The endogenous variables are the labour market tightness indicator θ, the reservation productivity R, the unemployment rate U, and the productivity dependent wage schedule $w(x)$. The exogenous variables are the unemployment benefit b, the firm's search cost c, the marginal product of labour p, and the interest rate r. Note that the model is block recursive. Equations (8.60)–(8.61) can be used to find the equilibrium values for for R and θ. Using these values equation (8.62) determines the equilibrium unemployment rate whilst (8.63) fixes the wage schedule. Equations (8.62)–(8.63) need no further comment as they have been discussed above.

Equation (8.60) is the job creation condition. It has been derived in Intermezzo 8.3. Intuitively it says that the firm's share of the expected net surplus of a new job (left-hand side) must equal the expected recruitment cost (right-hand side). In Figure 8.7 the job creation condition is represented by the JC locus. The slope of the JC curve is given by:

$$\left(\frac{dR}{d\theta}\right)_{JC} = \frac{c}{p\,[q(\theta)]^2}\frac{r + \delta_m}{1 - \beta}q'(\theta) < 0, \tag{8.64}$$

where the sign follows from the fact that $q'(\theta) < 0$. Intuitively, a higher value of θ implies higher expected search costs because the expected duration of a vacancy increases. To restore the job creation equilibrium the reservation productivity must go down so that a greater proportion of existing jobs survive.

Equation (8.61) is the job destruction condition—see Intermezzo 8.3 for its derivation. Intuitively this expression says that the reservation product plus the *option value* of continuing the match (left-hand side) must equal the foregone income plus expected returns from search (right-hand side). It is shown in Intermezzo 8.3 that in equilibrium the job creation condition can be formulated alternatively as:

$$\frac{\delta_m}{r + \delta_m}p \int_R^1 [z - R]d\Phi(z) = rY_U - pR, \tag{8.65}$$

where rY_U can be interpreted as the "reservation wage" of unemployed workers. This expression is useful because it establishes a very important property of the model, namely $pR < rY_U$, i.e. the reservation productivity falls short of the reservation wage. This is because jobs have an option value: firms will keep some jobs that generate negative profits in the short run as there is a probability that productivity will improve in the future. This is known as labour hoarding. In Figure 8.7 the job destruction condition is represented by the JD locus. The slope of this curve is given by:

$$\left(\frac{dR}{d\theta}\right)_{JD} = \frac{\beta c}{(1 - \beta)p}\left[1 - \frac{\delta_m}{r + \delta_m}[1 - \Phi(R)]\right]^{-1} > 0. \tag{8.66}$$

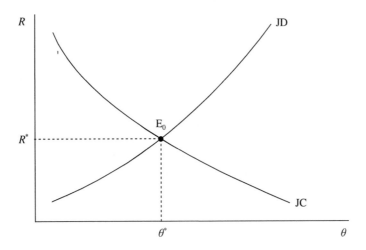

Figure 8.7: Job creation and destruction in the labour market

Intuitively, a higher value of θ increases wages which results in a lower reservation productivity so that a higher proportion of jobs are destroyed at each time. In Figure 8.7 the equilibrium is at point E_0 where $\theta = \theta^*$ and $R = R^*$.

As was pointed out by Pissarides (2000, p. 40) the traditional depiction of the Beveridge curve (8.62) in (V, U) space—as we used above in Figures 8.1 to 8.5—is no longer helpful when job destruction is endogenous. This is because this curve now depends on both θ and R (rather than just θ as for the canonical model). In (V, U) space, changes in R would have to be represented by shifts in the Beveridge curve. Fortunately there is an alternative method by which the effects on unemployment and vacancies of changes in the exogenous variables can be visualized—see Figure 8.8.

In the top panel of Figure 8.8 the UR locus depicts all combinations of R and U for which there is unemployment equilibrium. Formally this locus is obtained by combining the job creation condition and the Beveridge curve. Indeed, it follows from (8.60) that θ depends negatively on R along the job creation locus. Consequently for each point on the JC locus we can write the job finding rate as a decreasing function $f(R)$ of the reservation productivity, i.e. $f'(R) < 0$. Substituting $f(R)$ into (8.62) gives the mathematical expression for the UR locus:

$$U = \frac{\delta_m \Phi(R)}{\delta_m \Phi(R) + f(R)}. \tag{8.67}$$

The slope of the UR locus can easily be determined:

$$\left(\frac{dU}{dR} \right)_{UR} = \delta_m \frac{f(R)\Phi'(R) - \Phi(R)f'(R)}{[\delta_m \Phi(R) + f(R)]^2} > 0, \tag{8.68}$$

where the sign follows from the fact that $\Phi'(R) > 0$ and $f'(R) < 0$. So if the joint equilibrium of job creation and destruction gives rise to a labour market tightness index equal to θ_0^* and a reservation productivity of R_0^* then in the top panel of Figure 8.8 the equilibrium unemployment rate will be equal to U_0^*. In the lower panel of that figure the LMT_0 locus depicts the function $V = \theta_0^* U$. Hence, the vacancy rate is given by V_0^* in the bottom panel.

Armed with the diagrammatic apparatus we are able to investigate the steady-state effects of shocks in the exogenous variables. For reasons of space we restrict attention to the case of an increase in the unemployment benefit. It follows from (8.61) that the job destruction locus in Figure 8.7 shifts up whilst the job creation line stays put as b does not feature in (8.60). Without cluttering the diagram we can thus conclude that R^* will increase and θ^* will fall. In the top panel in Figure 8.8 the reservation productivity changes from R_0^* to R_1^*, the equilibrium shifts from E_0 to E_1, and unemployment increases from U_0^* to U_1^*. In the bottom panel of Figure 8.8 the decrease in θ, say from θ_0^* to θ_1^*, causes a clockwise rotation of the labour-market tightness locus, say from LMT_0 to LMT_1. We conclude that the unemployment rate increases and that the vacancy rate decreases. The latter effect is, however, not unambiguous as it depends on the magnitude of the change in θ.

8.4 Punchlines

In this chapter we discuss the search and matching approach to the labour market. This is by far the most technically demanding theory of the labour market discussed in this book thus far because it abandons the notion of an aggregate labour market altogether and instead directly models the flows of labour that occur in the economy, namely the movements of workers from unemployment into jobs and vice versa.

Because the theory is inherently quite demanding, we start by developing a simple canonical search model. The central elements in the model are the following. First, there are frictions in the process by which job-seeking unemployed workers come into contact with firms that are looking for a worker to fill a vacancy. These frictions are costly and time consuming. Second, the crucial analytical device that makes the model tractable is the so-called matching function. (This function plays a similar role in the flow approach to the labour market that the neoclassical production function plays in the theory of factor productivity and growth.) The matching function relates the probabilities of workers meeting firms (and firms meeting workers) as a function of an aggregate labour market tightness variable. This tightness indicator is the ratio of vacancies and unemployed workers.

If the vacancy-unemployment ratio is high (low) then the probability that an unemployed job seeker finds a firm with a vacancy is high (low) and expected duration of the search for a job is low (high). The matching function also explains the conditions facing the other party on the market. Indeed, if the vacancy-unemployment ratio is high (low), then there are many (few) firms trying to locate an unemployed worker so that the probability that an individual firm is successful is low (high) and the expected duration of the firm's search process is high (low).

The third key ingredient of the search model concerns the wage formation process. Once a firm with a vacancy meets an unemployed worker a pure economic rent is created consisting of the sum of foregone expected search costs by the firm and the worker. This surplus must be divided somehow between the firm and the worker. The typical assumption in this literature is that the two parties bargain over the wage.

The fourth ingredient of the model is the so-called Beveridge curve which relates the equilibrium unemployment rate to the (exogenous) job destruction rate (regulating the flow into unemployment) and the workers' job finding rate (regulating the

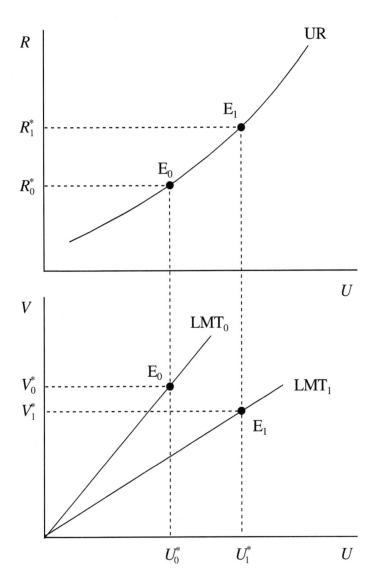

Figure 8.8: The effects of a higher unemployment benefit

flow out of unemployment). The job destruction rate is strictly positive because previously profitable firm-worker matches are destroyed due to idiosyncratic shocks.

The model yields a general equilibrium solution for, inter alia, the unemployment rate and the vacancy rate as a function of the exogenous variables. We perform various comparative static experiments. For example, an increase in the job destruction rate leads to an increase in both the unemployment and vacancy rates and to a decrease in the vacancy-unemployment ratio. The matching model incorporates a trading externality which is unlikely to be internalized by the Nash-bargained wage outcome. As a result, equilibrium unemployment is likely to be inefficient.

Next we apply the canonical search model in a number of different policy settings. First, we show how the search equilibrium is affected by the tax system. Second, we show that a worker-deposit scheme can be used to affect the equilibrium unemployment rate. (Under the scheme the firm receives a grant from the government when it hires a worker but must repay the grant when the job is destroyed again.)

Finally, we study an extension to the canonical model which endogenizes the job destruction rate. Job productivity has a deterministic and a stochastic component. Existing jobs are hit by idiosyncratic shocks which may make them so undesirable to both parties that the job is terminated. There is a reservation productivity below which jobs are scrapped. In the extended model the equilibrium unemployment rate depends on the two endogenous processes of job destruction and job creation.

Further reading

Key references to the modern search-theoretic literature are Mortensen (1978, 1982a, 1982b, 1986, 1989), Diamond (1984a, 1984b), Pissarides (1990, 1994), Mortensen and Pissarides (1994), and Blanchard and Diamond (1994). A good place to start reading this challenging literature is Pissarides (2000). Mortensen and Pissarides (1999a, 1999b) present good (but advanced) surveys of the literature. Pissarides (2001, 2011) present very accessible discussions. Rogerson et al. (2005) present a general survey of search-theoretic models of the labour market.

Hosios (1990) studies the welfare-theoretic properties of the search model. Microeconomic evidence on the job destruction/creation process is presented by Davis et al. (1996). For a very extensive survey of the matching function, see Petrongolo and Pissarides (2001). Mortensen and Pissarides (2001) and Heijdra and Ligthart (2002, 2009) study the effects on taxation in a matching model.

Chapter 9

Dynamic inconsistency in public and private decision making

The purpose of this chapter is to discuss the following issues:

1. What do we mean by dynamic inconsistency?

2. When is economic policy dynamically inconsistent and hence not credible?

3. How can reputation effects come to the rescue if optimal monetary policy is inconsistent?

4. Why does it sometimes pay to appoint a conservative to head the central bank?

5. How can the taxation of capital give rise to dynamic inconsistency?

6. Are individual consumers dynamically inconsistent? And how can inconsistent consumers commit themselves?

9.1 Dynamic inconsistency

9.1.1 A classic tale

As anyone with more than a fleeting interest in literature knows, Ulysses had a hard time getting back to his island of Ithaca after helping the Greeks win the war against the Trojans. Apparently the Greeks had forgotten to suitably thank the gods upon winning the war, and this had irritated them to such an extent that they decided to make the Greeks suffer. To cut a long story short, it took Ulysses ten years plus a lot of trouble to get home. During this journey he and his men have to pass the island of the Sirens. These Sirens were excellent singers but had a dangerous streak to them. As the witch Circe warns Ulysses:

> Your next encounter will be with the Sirens, who bewitch everybody that approaches them. There is no home-coming for the man who draws near them unawares and hears the Sirens' voices; no welcome from his wife, no little children brightening at their father's return. For with the music

of their song the Sirens cast their spell upon him, as they sit there in a meadow piled high with the mouldering skeletons of men, whose withered skin still hangs upon their bones. (Homer, 1946, p. 190 [Book XII, lines 36-110])

Ulysses is facing a difficult choice. He would like to listen to the Sirens (who would not?) but he does not want to end up as a skeleton just yet. Fortunately Circe also suggests a solution to the decision problem Ulysses faces. As Ulysses later tells his men, their ears should be plugged with beeswax so that they cannot hear the Sirens, and:

> I alone . . . might listen to their voices; but you must bind me hard and fast, so that I cannot stir from the spot where you will stand me, by the step of the mast, with the rope's end lashed round the mast itself. *And if I beg you to release me, you must tighten and add to my bonds.* (Homer, 1946, p. 193 [Book XII, lines 110-164]; emphasis added)

The plan is executed, they sail past the Sirens' island, and Ulysses instructs his men to release him. He wants to go the island. His men, suitably instructed, ignore his pleas and add to his bonds. They escape the perilous Sirens with no additional problems.

Ulysses' decision problem is a classic example of dynamic inconsistency, and Circe's suggestion constitutes a smart solution to the problem. The *optimal* policy for Ulysses and his men is to listen to the Sirens and continue the journey to Ithaca. After all, they are good singers. Unfortunately, this policy is *inconsistent*, since it leads to death and decay, and Ithaca will not be reached. Circe's solution is to make Ulysses *commit* himself to his long-term goal of reaching Ithaca by plugging the ears of his crew, and tying himself to the mast. By giving up his authority for a brief spell, he and his men are better off as a result. The commitment solution is consistent but *suboptimal*, as his men don't get to hear the music.[1]

9.1.2   A neoclassical tale

Dynamic inconsistency also features prominently in the economics literature. One of the simplest examples of dynamic inconsistency concerns the conduct of monetary policy with an expectations-augmented Phillips curve (Kydland and Prescott, 1977). Our version of their example makes use of the Lucas supply curve. Aggregate supply of goods y depends on the full employment level of output $\bar{y}$, the inflation surprise $\pi - \pi^e$, and a stochastic error term ε (with properties $E(\varepsilon) = 0$ and $E(\varepsilon^2) = \sigma^2$):

$$y = \bar{y} + \alpha [\pi - \pi^e] + \varepsilon, \quad \alpha > 0, \tag{9.1}$$

where y and $\bar{y}$ are both measured in logarithms. If the actual inflation rate, π, exceeds the expected inflation rate, π^e, workers have overestimated the real wage, labour supply is too high, and output is higher than its full-employment level.

We assume that agents hold rational expectations (REH, see Chapter 5), so that the expected inflation rate coincides with the mathematical expectation of the actual

---

[1]One wonders why Ulysses did not tie all his men but one to the mast, and plug that one man's ears with beeswax. That way a higher level of welfare would have been attained and consistency would have been ensured. Homer does not explain. Perhaps the mast only held one person, or the entire crew was needed to sail the boat.

inflation rate predicted by the model, i.e. $\pi^e \equiv E(\pi)$. The policy maker is assumed to have an objective function (often referred to as a *social welfare function*) which depends on inflation and an output target y^* that is higher than the full employment level of output ($y^* > \bar{y}$). Although this may appear odd, the policy maker deems the full-employment level of output to be too low from a societal point of view. This is, for example, due to the existence of distorting taxes, imperfectly competitive markets, or unemployment benefits.[2] The cost function of the policy maker is given by:

$$\Omega \equiv \tfrac{1}{2}[y - y^*]^2 + \tfrac{\beta}{2}\pi^2, \quad \beta > 0, \tag{9.2}$$

where β measures the degree of inflation aversion of the policy maker. The higher β, the higher the welfare costs associated with inflation, and the stronger is the inflation aversion. The policy maker cannot directly influence the expectations held by the private agents and consequently takes π^e as given in its optimization problem. There is *information asymmetry* in the sense that the policy maker can observe the realization of the supply shock, ε, but the public cannot. As a result, the policy-ineffectiveness proposition (PIP) fails and economic policy has real effects (see Chapter 5). The policy maker chooses the inflation rate and output level such that social costs (9.2) are minimized subject to the Lucas supply curve (9.1). The Lagrangian for this problem is:

$$\mathcal{L} \equiv \tfrac{1}{2}[y - y^*]^2 + \tfrac{\beta}{2}\pi^2 + \lambda[y - \bar{y} - \alpha(\pi - \pi^e) - \varepsilon], \tag{9.3}$$

so that the first-order conditions are:

$$\frac{\partial \mathcal{L}}{\partial y} = [y - y^*] + \lambda = 0, \tag{9.4}$$

$$\frac{\partial \mathcal{L}}{\partial \pi} = \beta\pi - \alpha\lambda = 0. \tag{9.5}$$

By combining (9.4)–(9.5) we obtain the "social expansion path", giving all combinations of inflation and output for which social costs are minimized:

$$y - y^* = -(\beta/\alpha)\pi \quad \Leftrightarrow \quad \pi = -(\alpha/\beta)[y - y^*]. \tag{9.6}$$

This downward-sloping line has been drawn in Figure 9.1. Graphically the line represents all points of tangency between an iso-cost curve of the policy maker and a Lucas supply curve. In view of the definition of the social welfare function (9.2), the iso-cost curves are concentric ovals around the bliss point E, where $\pi = 0$ and $y = y^*$. The slope of the iso-cost curves is obtained in the usual fashion:

$$d\Omega = 0: \quad \frac{d\pi}{dy} = -\frac{y - y^*}{\beta\pi}. \tag{9.7}$$

It follows that the iso-cost curve is horizontal ($d\pi/dy = 0$) for $y = y^*$ and is vertical ($d\pi/dy \to \infty$) for $\pi = 0$.

By combining (9.1) and (9.6), we obtain the expression for inflation under *discretion*, denoted by π_D:

$$\pi = \pi^e + (1/\alpha)[y - \bar{y} - \varepsilon] = \pi^e + (1/\alpha)[-(\beta/\alpha)\pi + y^* - \bar{y} - \varepsilon] \quad \Rightarrow$$

---

[2]Obviously, the first-best policy would be to remove these pre-existing distortions directly. It is assumed that this is impossible, however, so that monetary policy is used as a second-best instrument to boost output. See Persson and Tabellini (1989, p. 9).

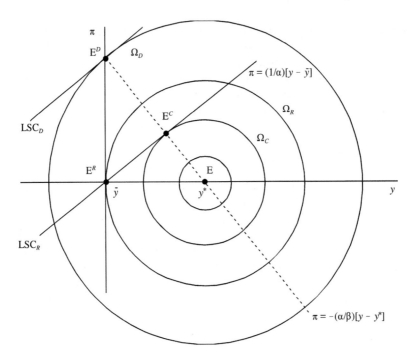

Figure 9.1: Consistent and optimal monetary policy

$$(1 + \beta/\alpha^2)\pi = \pi^e + (1/\alpha)\,[y^* - \bar{y} - \varepsilon] \;\Rightarrow$$

$$\pi_D = \frac{\alpha^2 \pi^e + \alpha\,[y^* - \bar{y} - \varepsilon]}{\alpha^2 + \beta}. \tag{9.8}$$

We use the term "discretion" because the policy maker chooses the optimal inflation rate in each period as it pleases, i.e. after it has observed the supply shock ε. Equation (9.8) says that inflation under discretion is high if expected inflation is high, if the ambition of the policy maker (i.e. $y^* - \bar{y}$) is large, and if there is a negative aggregate supply shock ($\varepsilon < 0$, which is the case, for example, with an OPEC shock).

This is not the end of the story, of course, since under rational expectations agents in the private sector know that the policy maker will choose the inflation rate π_D under discretion, so that they will form expectations accordingly:

$$\pi_D^e \equiv E\,(\pi_D) \;\Rightarrow\; \pi_D^e = \frac{\alpha^2 \pi_D^e + \alpha\,[y^* - \bar{y}]}{\alpha^2 + \beta} \;\Rightarrow$$

$$\pi_D^e \equiv \frac{\alpha}{\beta}\,[y^* - \bar{y}], \tag{9.9}$$

where we have used $E\,(\varepsilon) = 0$ (agents do not observe the supply shock but expect it to be zero). Equation (9.9) is the rational expectations solution for the expected inflation rate. By substituting (9.9) into (9.8) and (9.6), respectively, we obtain the expressions for actual inflation and output under discretionary monetary policy:

$$\pi_D = \frac{\alpha}{\beta}\,[y^* - \bar{y}] - \frac{\alpha}{\alpha^2 + \beta}\,\varepsilon, \tag{9.10}$$

$$y_D = \bar{y} + \frac{\beta}{\alpha^2 + \beta}\,\varepsilon. \tag{9.11}$$

These results are intuitive. Equation (9.10) says that under the REH the actual inflation rate is high if the output ambition of the policy maker is high or if there are negative supply shocks. Equation (9.11) shows that, for example, a negative supply shock is *partially* accommodated by expansionary monetary policy (only partially as $\beta/(\alpha^2 + \beta) < 1$).[3] This is especially the case if the policy maker has "leftist" preferences, i.e. has a low aversion towards inflation, represented by a low value of β. A left-wing policy maker attaches a greater importance to the stabilization of output (and hence, employment) fluctuations. A similar conclusion is obtained if the Lucas supply curve is very flat. In that case, α is very large and a large degree of accommodation takes place.

The problem with the discrete solution is that it is *suboptimal*! This can be demonstrated graphically with the aid of Figure 9.1. The discrete solution is represented by point E^D, where we have drawn the Lucas supply curve, LSC_D, for a realization of the supply shock equal to $\varepsilon = 0$. Suppose, however, that the policy maker could announce to the public that it would choose a zero inflation rate, i.e. $\pi = 0$. If the public believes this announcement, the REH implies that expected inflation will also be zero, i.e. $\pi^e = 0$, so that the relevant Lucas supply curve would be the one through the origin (i.e. LSC_R which passes through point E^R). Through this point, there is an iso-cost curve Ω^R that is closer to the bliss point E, and consequently involves strictly lower social costs, i.e. $\Omega^R < \Omega^D$. Hence, for this case the solution is:

$$\pi_R = \pi_R^e = 0, \tag{9.12}$$
$$y_R = \bar{y} + \varepsilon, \tag{9.13}$$

where we have used the subscript "R" to designate that this is policy under a *rule*. Instead of choosing the optimal inflation and output combination each period, the policy maker follows a simple money growth rule that ensures that the inflation rate is zero, as promised. Equation (9.13) shows that no accommodation of supply shocks is possible under this rule (obviously, since accommodation would lead to inflation, which violates the promise). The advantage is that there is no inflation under the rule, as (9.12) shows.

The problem with this optimal policy is that it is *inconsistent*! This can also be illustrated with the aid of Figure 9.1. The solution under the inflation rule $\pi_R = 0$ is given at point E^R, and the relevant Lucas supply curve goes through that point (LSC_R). But the policy maker has an even more attractive option than E^R if it faces LSC_R, namely the "cheating" point E^C, where there is a tangency between LSC_R and the iso-cost curve Ω^C. In the cheating solution, the policy maker creates an inflation surprise $\pi > \pi_R = \pi_R^e = 0$ in order to boost output $y > \bar{y}$.

Formally, the cheating solution for inflation, denoted by π_C, is obtained by substituting $\pi^e = \pi_R = 0$ into (9.8):

$$\pi_C = \frac{\alpha \left[y^* - \bar{y} - \varepsilon \right]}{\alpha^2 + \beta}, \tag{9.14}$$

so that output is:

$$y_C = \frac{\beta}{\alpha^2 + \beta} \bar{y} + \frac{\alpha^2}{\alpha^2 + \beta} y^* + \frac{\beta}{\alpha^2 + \beta} \varepsilon. \tag{9.15}$$

---

[3]With a completely passive central banker, output would be $y = \bar{y} + \varepsilon$, i.e. the full supply shock would enter output. In contrast, under the discretionary solution, output is equal to y_D in (9.11). By creating inflation, only a fraction, $\beta / \left[\alpha^2 + \beta \right]$, of the supply shock enters output. Monetary policy thus accommodates the shock somewhat.

The upshot of this is, of course, that the solution under the zero-inflation rule is not *credible*. Only if the policy maker is able to commit himself by being tied to the "mast" of zero inflation (like Ulysses), does the rules solution have credibility.

Before turning to one possible commitment mechanism, we summarize the argument up to this point. There are three possible options that the policy maker has in the current setup. It can pursue discretionary policy (equations (9.10)–(9.11)), follow a zero-inflation rule (equations (9.12)–(9.13)), or cheat (equations (9.14)–(9.15)). By substituting the different solutions for output and inflation into the welfare cost function (9.2) (assuming $\varepsilon = 0$ for simplicity), we obtain the following expressions:

$$\Omega_C = \tfrac{1}{2} \frac{\beta}{\alpha^2 + \beta} \left[\bar{y} - y^* \right]^2, \tag{9.16}$$

$$\Omega_R = \tfrac{1}{2} \left[\bar{y} - y^* \right]^2, \tag{9.17}$$

$$\Omega_D = \tfrac{1}{2} \frac{\alpha^2 + \beta}{\beta} \left[\bar{y} - y^* \right]^2, \tag{9.18}$$

from which we infer that $\Omega_D > \Omega_R > \Omega_C > 0$. The cheating solution is closest to the bliss point, is credible but it violates the REH. The rules solution is optimal and satisfies REH, but is open to temptation and is hence not credible. Finally, the solution under discretion is suboptimal, satisfies REH, and is credible.

9.1.3 Reputation as an enforcement mechanism

In the previous subsection we have shown that the only policy which is both credible and consistent with rational expectations is the suboptimal discretionary policy. Given the structure of the problem, it appears that the economy is likely to end up in the worst possible equilibrium. In an influential article, however, Barro and Gordon (1983b) have demonstrated that *reputation effects* can come to the rescue, and prevent this worst-case scenario from materializing. Their argument can be made with the aid of the model developed in section 9.1.2. In order to keep the discussion here as simple as possible, we assume that there are no stochastic shocks ($\varepsilon \equiv 0$). There is repeated interaction between the policy maker and the public (represented, for example, by the unions who set the nominal wage rate).

The cost function of the policy maker consists of the present value of the costs incurred each period, and is defined as:

$$V \equiv \Omega_0 + \frac{\Omega_1}{1+r} + \frac{\Omega_2}{(1+r)^2} + \cdots = \sum_{t=0}^{\infty} \frac{\Omega_t}{(1+r)^t}, \tag{9.19}$$

where r is the real discount factor (e.g. the real rate of interest), and Ω_t is the cost incurred in period t:

$$\Omega_t \equiv \tfrac{1}{2} \left[y_t - y^* \right]^2 + \tfrac{\beta}{2} \pi_t^2, \tag{9.20}$$

and the Lucas supply curve is given by:

$$y_t = \bar{y} + \alpha \left[\pi_t - \pi_t^e \right], \quad \alpha > 0. \tag{9.21}$$

It is assumed for simplicity that both y^* and $\bar{y}$ are constant over time and thus do not feature a time subscript.

As in section 9.1.2, there are again a number of choices that the policy maker can make. A discretionary policy involves setting inflation according to (9.10) in each period (with $\varepsilon = 0$ imposed). This yields a cost level of Ω_D in each period (see (9.18)), so that the present value of social costs equals V^D:

$$V^D \equiv \frac{1+r}{r} \Omega_D. \tag{9.22}$$

Now consider what happens if the policy maker chooses to follow a *constant-inflation rule*, $\pi_t = \pi_R$, where we generalize the previous discussion by allowing the constant inflation rate π_R to be non-zero. If this inflation rate is believed by the public, it will come to expect it, so that the expected inflation rate will also be equal to π_R in each period, so that output will equal $\bar{y}$ in each period. By substituting these solutions into (9.20) the periodic cost level under the rule is obtained:

$$\Omega_R(\pi_R) = \Omega_R + \tfrac{\beta}{2}\pi_R^2, \tag{9.23}$$

where Ω_R is the welfare cost under the zero-inflation rule as defined in (9.17), and we have indicated that under the more general inflation rule, the cost level depends positively on the chosen inflation level. By substituting (9.23) into (9.19), the present value of costs incurred under the rule $V^R(\pi_R)$ is obtained:

$$V^R(\pi_R) \equiv \frac{1+r}{r} \left[\Omega_R + \tfrac{\beta}{2}\pi_R^2 \right]. \tag{9.24}$$

Finally, as before, the cheating solution is derived by determining the optimal choice for the policy maker given that the public expects it to stick to the announced inflation rate π_R. By substituting $\pi^e = \pi_R$ into equation (9.8), and setting $\varepsilon = 0$, the expression for the cheating inflation rate π_C is obtained:

$$\pi_C = \frac{\alpha^2 \pi_R + \alpha \left[y^* - \bar{y} \right]}{\alpha^2 + \beta}, \tag{9.25}$$

which implies that output under cheating is given by:

$$y_C = \frac{\beta}{\alpha^2 + \beta} \bar{y} + \frac{\alpha^2}{\alpha^2 + \beta} y^* - \frac{\alpha\beta}{\alpha^2 + \beta} \pi_R. \tag{9.26}$$

By substituting (9.25)–(9.26) into (9.20), the periodic cost level associated with cheating is obtained:

$$\Omega_C(\pi_R) = \tfrac{1}{2} \left[\frac{\beta}{\alpha^2 + \beta} [\bar{y} - y^*] - \frac{\alpha\beta}{\alpha^2 + \beta} \pi_R \right]^2$$

$$+ \tfrac{\beta}{2} \left[\frac{\alpha^2}{\alpha^2 + \beta} \pi_R + \frac{\alpha}{\alpha^2 + \beta} [y^* - \bar{y}] \right]^2, \tag{9.27}$$

where Ω_C depends on the chosen inflation level under the rule. Obviously, (9.27) and (9.16) coincide for $\pi_R = 0$, and $\Omega_C(\pi_R)$ is greater than Ω_C for any non-zero value of π_R.

We are now in a position to introduce the policy maker's *reputation* into the analysis. Suppose that the public trusts the policy maker in period t, if it has kept its promise in the previous period $t-1$ (in the sense that it did as it was expected to do). If that is the case, the public expects that the rule will be followed in period t so that inflation will be set at π_R. On the other hand, if the policy maker did not keep its promise in period $t-1$, the public loses trust in the policy maker, and instead expects the discrete solution to obtain in period t. In formal terms, the postulated mechanism adopted by the public can be written as follows:

$$\pi_t^e = \begin{cases} \pi_R & \text{if } \pi_{t-1} = \pi_{t-1}^e \\ \pi_{D,t} & \text{if } \pi_{t-1} \neq \pi_{t-1}^e. \end{cases} \tag{9.28}$$

Equation (9.28) implies that the public adopts the tit-for-tat strategy in the repeated prisoner's dilemma game that it plays with the policy maker. If the policy maker "misbehaves" it gets punished by the public for one period. To see that this is indeed the case, consider the following possible sequences of events. We start in period 0 and assume that the policy maker has credibility in that period (i.e. in period -1 it has kept its promise), and so expected inflation in period 0 equals the level specified by the rule, i.e. $\pi_0^e = \pi_R$.

The first scenario that the policy maker can follow in period 0 is to keep its promise, and to produce inflation equal to π_R. The public observes this inflation rate, concludes that the policy maker is trustworthy, and continues to expect that inflation will be set according to the rule. By sticking to its promise, the policy maker has maintained its reputation, and no punishment takes place.

The second scenario that the policy maker can follow is to cheat in period 0. It has an incentive to do so since the periodic cost level attained in period 0 is then given by (9.27) which is lower than periodic cost under the rule as given in (9.23). In fact, the *temptation* that the policy maker is subjected to in period 0 can be calculated:

$$T(\pi_R) \equiv \Omega_R(\pi_R) - \Omega_C(\pi_R)$$

$$= \tfrac{1}{2} [\bar{y} - y^*]^2 + \tfrac{\beta}{2} \pi_R^2 - \tfrac{1}{2} \left[\frac{\beta}{\alpha^2 + \beta} [\bar{y} - y^*] - \frac{\alpha\beta}{\alpha^2 + \beta} \pi_R \right]^2$$

$$- \tfrac{\beta}{2} \left[\frac{\alpha^2}{\alpha^2 + \beta} \pi_R + \frac{\alpha}{\alpha^2 + \beta} [y^* - \bar{y}] \right]^2, \tag{9.29}$$

where we have used (9.27) and (9.23), and $T(\pi_R)$ is the temptation to cheat if the policy rule stipulates an inflation rate π_R. In Figure 9.2 we have plotted this quadratic temptation function. Several points of this function are easy to find. If the rule inflation rate $\pi_R = 0$, $T(0)$ is equal to:

$$T(0) \equiv \Omega_R - \Omega_C = \tfrac{1}{2} \frac{\alpha^2}{\alpha^2 + \beta} [y^* - \bar{y}]^2, \tag{9.30}$$

and $T(\pi_R) = 0$ if the rule inflation equals the discrete inflation rate π_D given in (9.10) (with $\varepsilon = 0$ imposed):

$$T(\pi_D) = 0. \tag{9.31}$$

The inflation rate under discretion is also the point where temptation is minimized. For higher inflation rates, the $T(\pi_R)$ curve starts to rise again.

But under the second scenario, the policy maker is punished in period 1, because it did not keep its promise in period 0. The public has lost confidence in the policy maker, and expects the discrete solution for period 1. This causes costs in period 1 to be higher than they would have been, since $\Omega_D > \Omega_R(\pi_R)$, and these additional costs must be taken into account in the decision about whether or not to stick to the rule in period 0. From the point of view of the policy maker, the punishment it receives consists of the discounted value of the additional costs it incurs in period 1:

$$P(\pi_R) \equiv \frac{\Omega_D - \Omega_R(\pi_R)}{1 + r}$$

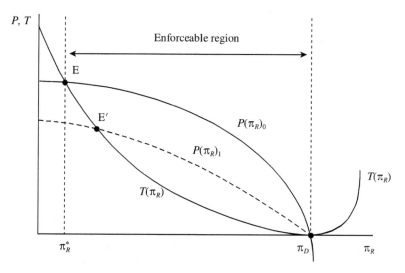

Figure 9.2: Temptation and enforcement

$$= \left[\tfrac{1}{2} \frac{\alpha^2 + \beta}{\beta} \, [\bar{y} - y^*]^2 - \tfrac{1}{2} [\bar{y} - y^*]^2 - \tfrac{\beta}{2} \pi_R^2 \right] \frac{1}{1+r}$$

$$= \left[\tfrac{1}{2} \frac{\alpha^2}{\beta} \, [\bar{y} - y^*]^2 - \tfrac{\beta}{2} \pi_R^2 \right] \frac{1}{1+r}, \tag{9.32}$$

where we have used (9.18) and (9.23). Again, a number of points on the punishment curve can be found easily. First, if the rule inflation $\pi_R = 0$, $P(0)$ is equal to:

$$P(0) = \tfrac{1}{2} \frac{1}{1+r} \frac{\alpha^2}{\beta} \, [\bar{y} - y^*]^2. \tag{9.33}$$

Assuming that the interest rate is sufficiently high ($r > \alpha^2/\beta$), it follows from the comparison of (9.33) and (9.30) that $P(0) < T(0)$. Furthermore, $P(\pi_R) = 0$ for the discrete inflation rate π_D:

$$P(\pi_D) = 0. \tag{9.34}$$

Finally, for rule inflation rates larger than π_D, $P(\pi_R) < 0$. The quadratic punishment function $P(\pi_R)$ has been drawn in Figure 9.2.

In period 1 the public expects the policy maker to produce the discretionary inflation rate π_D, and given this expectation it is also optimal for the policy maker to do so. Hence, in period 1 expected and actual inflation coincide, and confidence in the policy maker is restored (see (9.28)). As a result, the public expects the rule inflation rate to be produced in period 2. By assumption the policy maker does indeed produce the rule inflation, because we have investigated the effects of a single act of cheating by the policy maker. No further costs are associated with the cheating that takes place in period 0, and $P(\pi_R)$ and $T(\pi_R)$ fully summarize the relevant costs and benefits of a single act of cheating in period 0.[4]

---

[4]At the beginning of period 2 the policy maker faces exactly the same problem as at the beginning of period 0. Hence, if it pays to cheat in period 0 it also does in period 2. Vice versa, if it does not pay to cheat in period 0 then it also does not pay in period 2. For that reason we only need to check whether cheating pays for one deviation.

Clearly, if the temptation of cheating exceeds the punishment, the policy maker will submit to temptation and cheat. The public knows this and does not believe the rule at all in such a case. In technical terms, the rule inflation is then *not enforceable*. This immediately explains that the zero inflation rule is not enforceable. The temptation to cheat is simply too large for $\pi_R = 0$ to be enforceable. In terms of Figure 9.2, only rule inflation rates in the interval $[\pi_R^*, \pi_D]$ are enforceable. The *optimal enforceable* rule inflation rate is of course the lowest possible enforceable inflation rate π_R^* (point E). This is because for all rule inflation rates there are no inflation surprises (otherwise a punishment would occur) so that there are only costs associated with inflation and no benefits (through higher than full-employment output). Consequently, the lowest enforceable inflation rate minimizes these costs. Just as in the repeated prisoner's dilemma game analysed inter alia by Axelrod (1984), the enforcement mechanism in the form of loss of reputation ensures that the economy does not get stuck in the worst equilibrium with discretionary monetary policy.

The optimal enforceable rule inflation rate π_R^* can be calculated by equating $P(\pi_R)$ and $T(\pi_R)$ given in equations (9.29) and (9.32), respectively. After some manipulation we obtain:

$$\pi_R^* \equiv \left(\frac{\alpha\,[y^* - \bar{y}]}{\beta} \right) \cdot \frac{1-\zeta}{1+\zeta}, \qquad \zeta \equiv \frac{\alpha^2 + \beta}{\beta(1+r)}. \tag{9.35}$$

Hence, the optimal enforceable rule inflation rate is a weighted average of the unenforceable zero-inflation rule and the enforceable but suboptimal discretionary inflation rate π_D, which equals the term in round brackets (Barro and Gordon, 1983b, p. 113).[5]

As a final application of this model, consider what happens if the real interest rate r rises. In terms of Figure 9.2, nothing happens to the temptation line $T(\pi_R)$, but the punishment line $P(\pi_R)$ rotates in a counter-clockwise fashion around the discretionary point. As a result, the enforceable region shrinks, and the optimal enforceable rule inflation rate rises. This is intuitive. Due to the fact that punishment occurs one period after the offence, higher discounting of the future implies a smaller punishment ceteris paribus. This result is confirmed by the expression in (9.35).

9.2 The voting approach to optimal inflation

In a seminal paper, Rogoff (1985) asks himself the question why it is the case that central bankers are often selected from the conservative ranks of society. It turns out, once again, that the answer relies on the benefits of a commitment mechanism (like Ulysses' mast). In order to make the point as simply as possible, we utilize the model of section 9.1.2 with some minor modifications. Following Alesina and Grilli (1992), we use a median voter model to determine which person is elected to head the central bank and conduct monetary policy. Assume that person i has the following cost function:

$$\Omega_i \equiv \tfrac{1}{2}\,[y - y^*]^2 + \tfrac{\beta_i}{2}\,\pi^2, \tag{9.36}$$

where the only difference with (9.2) is that the degree of inflation aversion differs from person to person. The Lucas supply curve is still given by (9.1), so that if person

---

[5]We assume that the interest rate is not too low (i.e. $r > \alpha^2/\beta$) so that $0 < \zeta < 1$ and the optimal enforceable inflation rate is strictly positive. See also Figure 9.2.

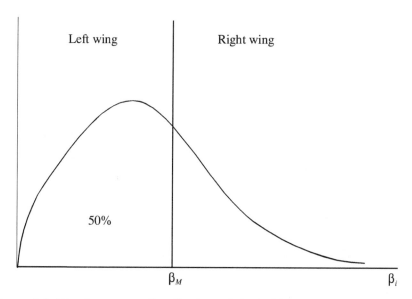

Figure 9.3: The frequency distribution of the inflation aversion parameter

i were elected to head the central bank, he would choose the discretionary inflation rate and associated output level (denoted by π_D^i and y_D^i, respectively). In view of (9.10)–(9.11), these would amount to:

$$\pi_D^i = \frac{\alpha}{\beta_i}\, [y^* - \bar{y}] - \frac{\alpha}{\alpha^2 + \beta_i}\, \varepsilon, \tag{9.37}$$

$$y_D^i = \bar{y} + \frac{\beta_i}{\alpha^2 + \beta_i}\, \varepsilon. \tag{9.38}$$

The preferences regarding inflation are diverse, and are summarized by the frequency distribution of β_i's as given in Figure 9.3. Agents with a very low value of β_i are called "left wing" in that they do not worry much about inflation but a great deal about output and employment stabilization. At the other end of the political spectrum, "right-wing" agents with a very high β_i have a strong aversion against inflation and worry very little about output stabilization.

We assume that the agents choose from among themselves the agent who is going to head the central bank. Voting is on a pairwise basis and by majority rule. The agent that is chosen has an inflation aversion parameter β. For this agent there exists no other agent i such that β_i is preferred by a majority of the people over β. Since there is a single issue (namely the choice of β) and preferences of the agents are single-peaked in β, the *median voter theorem* holds (see Mueller, 1989, pp. 65–66). In words this theorem says that the median voter determines the choice of β. The median voter has an inflation aversion parameter β_M that is illustrated in Figure 9.3. Exactly 50% of the population is more left wing than this voter and 50% is more right wing than the median voter.

But the median voter knows exactly what an agent with inflation aversion parameter β would choose, since that is given by (9.37)–(9.38) by setting $\beta_i = \beta$. By substituting (9.37)–(9.38) into the *median voter's cost function*, we obtain:

$$\Omega_M \equiv \tfrac{1}{2} E\left(\left(y_D^i - y^*\right)^2 + \beta_M \left(\pi_D^i\right)^2 \right)$$

$$= \tfrac{1}{2}E\left(\left(\bar{y}-y^* + \frac{\beta}{\alpha^2+\beta}\varepsilon\right)^2 + \beta_M\left(\frac{\alpha}{\beta}(y^*-\bar{y}) - \frac{\alpha}{\alpha^2+\beta}\varepsilon\right)^2\right)$$

$$= \tfrac{1}{2}\left[1+\beta_M\left(\frac{\alpha}{\beta}\right)^2\right](\bar{y}-y^*)^2 + \tfrac{1}{2}\frac{\beta^2+\beta_M\alpha^2}{(\alpha^2+\beta)^2}\sigma^2, \tag{9.39}$$

where we have used $E(\varepsilon)=0$, $E(\varepsilon^2)=\sigma^2$. The median voter minimizes his *expected* cost level by choice of β. The median voter cannot observe ε but knows exactly how agent β reacts to supply shocks in general. Hence, the median voter can determine which agent would (if chosen to head the central bank) minimize the expected value of his welfare costs. The first-order condition is given by: [1]

$$\frac{d\Omega_M}{d\beta} = -\tfrac{1}{2}2\beta_M\frac{\alpha^2}{\beta^3}(\bar{y}-y^*)^2$$

$$+\tfrac{1}{2}\frac{2(\alpha^2+\beta)^2\beta - 2(\beta^2+\beta_M\alpha^2)(\alpha^2+\beta)}{(\alpha^2+\beta)^4}\sigma^2 = 0 \Rightarrow$$

$$\frac{d\Omega_M}{d\beta} = -\frac{\beta_M}{\beta}\left(\frac{\alpha}{\beta}\right)^2(\bar{y}-y^*)^2 + \frac{(\beta-\beta_M)\alpha^2}{(\alpha^2+\beta)^3}\sigma^2 = 0. \tag{9.40}$$

Equation (9.40) implicitly defines the optimal β as a function of the parameters of the model and the median voter's inflation aversion parameter β_M. It is straightforward to show that the median voter chooses someone more conservative than himself, i.e. $\beta > \beta_M$. To see why this is the case, we rewrite (9.40) somewhat to get:

$$\beta - \beta_M = \frac{\beta_M(\alpha^2+\beta)^3(\bar{y}-y^*)^2}{\beta^3\sigma^2} > 0. \tag{9.41}$$

Hence, the median voter delegates the conduct of monetary policy to someone more inflation averse than himself, and in this manner commits himself to a lower inflation rate.

Furthermore, it is also possible to derive the following comparative static results with respect to the variance of the shocks (σ^2), the degree of inflation aversion of the median voter (β_M), and the ambitiousness of monetary policy ($y^*-\bar{y}$):

$$\frac{\partial\beta}{\partial\sigma^2} \equiv -\frac{\beta^3(\alpha^2+\beta)(\beta-\beta_M)}{\Xi_0} < 0, \tag{9.42}$$

$$\frac{\partial\beta}{\partial\beta_M} \equiv \frac{(\alpha^2+\beta)\left[(\alpha^2+\beta)^3(y^*-\bar{y})^2+\sigma^2\beta^3\right]}{\Xi_0} > 0, \tag{9.43}$$

$$\frac{\partial\beta}{\partial(y^*-\bar{y})} \equiv \frac{2\beta_M(\alpha^2+\beta)^4(y^*-\bar{y})}{\Xi_0} > 0, \tag{9.44}$$

where $\Xi_0 \equiv \beta^2\sigma^2\left[3\alpha^2(\beta-\beta_M)+\beta(\alpha^2+\beta)\right]$ is a positive constant.[6] In words, more uncertainty (a higher σ^2) and a more left-wing population (a lower β_M) both lead to the appointment of a more left-wing central banker (a lower β). Higher output ambition, however, leads to the appointment of a more conservative central banker.

---

[6]To derive these results, we first rewrite the first-order condition (9.40) as:

$$\Phi\left(\beta,\beta_M,\sigma^2,y^*-\bar{y}\right) \equiv -\beta_M(y^*-\bar{y})^2 + \frac{(\beta-\beta_M)\beta^3}{(\alpha^2+\beta)^3}\sigma^2 = 0.$$

It is easy to show that Φ_β is positive:

$$\Phi_\beta \equiv \frac{\beta^2\sigma^2\left[3\alpha^2(\beta-\beta_M)+\beta(\alpha^2+\beta)\right]}{(\alpha^2+\beta)^4} > 0.$$

9.3 Dynamic consistency and capital taxation

Up to this point the economic policy applications of the notion of dynamic inconsistency have all been in the area of monetary policy. This is not to say that this is
the only area where this phenomenon is encountered.[7] Indeed, the purpose of this
section is to demonstrate that exactly the same issues are relevant for fiscal policy
as well. We demonstrate this with the aid of a simple model of optimal taxation
and public goods adapted from Fischer (1980a). As in Chapter 6, time is split into
two periods, with period 1 representing the present and period 2 the future. The
representative household has the following utility function:

$$U \equiv \frac{C_1^{1-1/\varepsilon_C}}{1-1/\varepsilon_C} + \frac{1}{1+\rho}\left[C_2 + \alpha\,\frac{(1-N_2)^{1-1/\varepsilon_N}}{1-1/\varepsilon_N} + \beta\,\frac{G_2^{1-1/\varepsilon_G}}{1-1/\varepsilon_G}\right], \tag{9.45}$$

where C_t is goods consumption in period t ($=1,2$), ρ is the pure rate of time preference ($\rho > 0$), N_2 is labour supply in the future, and G_2 is the level of public goods
provision in the future. Notice that for simplicity, labour supply and public goods
provision are zero in the present period. Nothing of substance is affected by these
simplifications. At the beginning of period 1, there is an existing capital stock built
up in the past, equal to K_1. Capital does not depreciate and the constant marginal
product of capital is equal to b (see below). The resource constraint in the current
period is:

$$C_1 + [K_2 - K_1] = bK_1. \tag{9.46}$$

In words, (9.46) says that consumption plus investment in the present period must
equal production (and capital income). In the second period, total demand for goods
equals $C_2 + G_2$, which must equal production $F(N_2, K_2)$ plus the capital stock (which
can be consumed during period 2. Think of capital as "corn"). Assuming a linear
production function, the resource constraint in the second period is given by:

$$C_2 + G_2 = F(N_2, K_2) + K_2 = aN_2 + (1+b)K_2, \tag{9.47}$$

where a is the constant marginal product of labour.[8] By combining (9.46)–(9.47) and
eliminating K_2, we obtain the consolidated resource constraint:

$$C_1 + \frac{C_2 + G_2}{1+b} = (1+b)K_1 + \frac{aN_2}{1+b}. \tag{9.48}$$

9.3.1 The first-best optimum

Let us first study the so-called *command optimum*. Suppose that there is a benevolent
social planner who must decide on the optimal allocation by maximizing the utility

---

By using the implicit function theorem, we find that $\partial\Phi/\partial\sigma^2 = -\Phi_{\sigma^2}/\Phi_\beta$, where Φ_{σ^2} is given by:

$$\Phi_{\sigma^2} \equiv \frac{\beta^3\,(\beta - \beta_M)}{(\alpha^2 + \beta)^3}.$$

Combining results we obtain (9.42). The other comparative static effects are obtained in a similar fashion.

[7]Indeed, we came across dynamic inconsistency in Chapter 7 where we analysed the interaction between wage setting by the union and capital investment by the firm. There we showed that the future
wage offer of the union is dynamically inconsistent and thus not credible.

[8]Assuming a linear production function simplifies the exposition substantially. Technically, a linear
production function is obtained by imposing an infinite elasticity of substitution between capital and
labour, i.e. $\sigma_{KN} \to \infty$ (see Chapter 4). It also means that the demands for labour and capital are infinitely
elastic, and that both factors are *inessential*, in the sense that output can be produced with only one of the
two production factors.

of the representative household subject to the consolidated resource constraint (9.48). The Lagrangian for this optimal social plan is:

$$\mathcal{L} \equiv \frac{C_1^{1-1/\varepsilon_C}}{1-1/\varepsilon_C} + \frac{1}{1+\rho}\left[C_2 + \alpha\,\frac{(1-N_2)^{1-1/\varepsilon_N}}{1-1/\varepsilon_N} + \beta\,\frac{G_2^{1-1/\varepsilon_G}}{1-1/\varepsilon_G}\right]$$
$$+ \lambda \cdot \left[(1+b)K_1 + \frac{aN_2}{1+b} - C_1 - \frac{C_2+G_2}{1+b}\right], \tag{9.49}$$

which yields the first-order conditions:

$$\frac{\partial \mathcal{L}}{\partial C_1} = C_1^{-1/\varepsilon_C} - \lambda = 0, \tag{9.50}$$

$$\frac{\partial \mathcal{L}}{\partial C_2} = \frac{1}{1+\rho} - \frac{\lambda}{1+b} = 0, \tag{9.51}$$

$$\frac{\partial \mathcal{L}}{\partial G_2} = \frac{\beta G_2^{-1/\varepsilon_G}}{1+\rho} - \frac{\lambda}{1+b} = 0, \tag{9.52}$$

$$\frac{\partial \mathcal{L}}{\partial N_2} = -\frac{\alpha(1-N_2)^{-1/\varepsilon_N}}{1+\rho} + \frac{a\lambda}{1+b} = 0. \tag{9.53}$$

Equation (9.51) implies that the marginal utility of income (given by λ) is constant: $\lambda = (1+b)/(1+\rho)$. By substituting this value of λ into (9.50) and (9.52)–(9.53), the optimal values for C_1, N_2, and G_2 are obtained.

$$C_1 = \left(\frac{1+b}{1+\rho}\right)^{-\varepsilon_C}. \tag{9.54}$$

$$1 - N_2 = \left(\frac{a}{\alpha}\right)^{-\varepsilon_N}, \tag{9.55}$$

$$G_2 = \beta^{\varepsilon_G}. \tag{9.56}$$

Finally, by using (9.54)–(9.56) in the consolidated resource constraint, the level of consumption in the second period can be calculated:

$$C_2 = (1+b)^2 K_1 + a - (1+b)C_1 - G_2 - a(1-N_2)$$
$$= a + (1+b)^2 K_1 - (1+\rho)^{\varepsilon_C}(1+b)^{1-\varepsilon_C} - \alpha^{\varepsilon_N}a^{1-\varepsilon_N} - \beta^{\varepsilon_G}, \tag{9.57}$$

where we assume that the non-negativity restriction on consumption in the second period is non-binding (i.e. $C_2 > 0$). The command optimum is the best possible outcome for the representative household, given the availability of resources and the state of technology.

In practice, the policy maker may have direct control over the level of public goods provision G_2, but he/she is not likely to have direct control over the variables chosen by the representative household such as C_1, C_2, and N_2 (even in the former centrally planned Eastern bloc countries this proved to be difficult). This does not in and of itself imply that the first-best optimum cannot be attained in a decentralized economy. Indeed, if the government chooses G_2 optimally and has lump-sum taxes at its disposal, the first-best plan as given in (9.54)–(9.57) can be *decentralized*.

In the decentralized economy, households own the capital stock which they rent out to firms at an interest rate r. Households furthermore sell their labour to these firms, for which they receive a real wage w_2 (recall that they do not work in period 1). The budget restriction of the representative household in the first period is:

$$C_1 + [K_2 - K_1] = r_1 K_1, \tag{9.58}$$

where r_1 is the interest rate in period 1, so that $r_1 K_1$ is the interest income received by the household. This income is spent either on consumption goods or by purchasing additional investment goods. In the second period, the budget restriction is:

$$C_2 = w_2 N_2 + (1 + r_2)K_2 - Z_2, \tag{9.59}$$

where Z_2 is lump-sum taxes and r_2 is the real interest rate, both in period 2. The household does not invest in period 2 since the model world ends at the end of that period.

The representative firm produces output by hiring capital and/or labour from the representative household. Profit in period t is equal to:

$$\pi_t \equiv F(K_t, N_t) - w_t N_t - r_t K_t, \tag{9.60}$$

so that profit-maximizing behaviour implies that $r_t = F_K = b$ and $w_t = F_N = a$. In period 1 there is no labour supply and only capital is used, and in period 2 both labour and capital are used in production. Hence, for the linear production function we have:

$$r_1 = r_2 = b, \quad w_2 = a. \tag{9.61}$$

The real interest rate is constant and equal to b and the real wage in the second period is also constant and equal to a. Since both factors of production are paid exactly their respective marginal product, and the production function features constant returns to scale, the representative firm makes no profit.

The government purchases goods in period 2 and pays for these goods by lump-sum taxes levied on the representative household. Hence, the government budget restriction is:

$$G_2 = Z_2. \tag{9.62}$$

By substituting (9.61)–(9.62) into (9.58)–(9.59) and consolidating, we obtain:

$$C_1 + \frac{C_2 + G_2}{1 + b} = \frac{aN_2}{1 + b} + (1 + b)K_1. \tag{9.63}$$

The representative household maximizes its utility (9.45) by choice of C_1, C_2, and N_2, taking G_2 and its consolidated budget restriction (9.63) as given. Provided the government sets G_2 appropriately (i.e. at the level given in (9.56)) the thus chosen values of C_1, C_2, and N_2 coincide with the first-best optimum values given in (9.54)–(9.55) and (9.57). Hence, the social optimum can be decentralized if the government has access to lump-sum taxes.

9.3.2 The second-best problem

In practice the policy maker does not have (non-distorting) lump-sum taxes at its disposal. Instead, it must finance its spending by means of taxes on the different income categories. Suppose that t_L is the tax on labour income and t_K is the tax on capital income in the second period.[9] The household's budget restrictions become:

$$C_1 + [K_2 - K_1] = bK_1, \tag{9.64}$$

$$C_2 = a(1 - t_L)N_2 + [1 + b(1 - t_K)] K_2, \tag{9.65}$$

---

[9] A tax on capital income in the first period is abstracted from as it would amount to a lump-sum tax.

where we have already imposed the expressions in (9.61). By consolidating (9.64)–(9.65) we obtain:

$$C_1 + \frac{C_2}{1 + b(1 - t_K)} = \frac{a(1 - t_L)N_2}{1 + b(1 - t_K)} + (1 + b)K_1, \tag{9.66}$$

which is the counterpart to (9.63). The representative household maximizes its utility (9.45) by choice of C_1, C_2, and N_2, taking G_2 and its budget restriction (9.66) as given. The Lagrangian for this problem is:

$$\mathcal{L} \equiv \frac{C_1^{1-1/\varepsilon_C}}{1 - 1/\varepsilon_C} + \frac{1}{1 + \rho} \left[C_2 + \alpha \frac{(1 - N_2)^{1-1/\varepsilon_N}}{1 - 1/\varepsilon_N} + \beta \frac{G_2^{1-1/\varepsilon_G}}{1 - 1/\varepsilon_G} \right]$$
$$+ \lambda \left[(1 + b)K_1 - C_1 - \frac{C_2 - a(1 - t_L)N_2}{1 + b(1 - t_K)} \right], \tag{9.67}$$

which yields the first-order conditions:

$$\frac{\partial \mathcal{L}}{\partial C_1} = C_1^{-1/\varepsilon_C} - \lambda = 0, \tag{9.68}$$

$$\frac{\partial \mathcal{L}}{\partial C_2} = \frac{1}{1 + \rho} - \frac{\lambda}{1 + b(1 - t_K)} = 0, \tag{9.69}$$

$$\frac{\partial \mathcal{L}}{\partial N_2} = -\frac{\alpha(1 - N_2)^{-1/\varepsilon_N}}{1 + \rho} + \frac{a(1 - t_L)\lambda}{1 + b(1 - t_K)} = 0, \tag{9.70}$$

which can be solved for C_1, C_2, and N_2:

$$C_1 = \left(\frac{1 + b(1 - t_K)}{1 + \rho} \right)^{-\varepsilon_C}, \tag{9.71}$$

$$C_2 = a(1 - t_L) + (1 + b)\left[1 + b(1 - t_K) \right] K_1 \tag{9.72}$$
$$- (1 + \rho)^{\varepsilon_C} \left[1 + b(1 - t_K) \right]^{1-\varepsilon_C} - \alpha^{\varepsilon_N} \left[a(1 - t_L) \right]^{1-\varepsilon_N},$$

$$1 - N_2 = \left(\frac{a(1 - t_L)}{\alpha} \right)^{-\varepsilon_N}. \tag{9.73}$$

Finally, by substituting these optimal solutions back into the utility function, the *indirect utility function* is obtained:

$$V \equiv \frac{1}{\varepsilon_C - 1} \left(\frac{1 + b(1 - t_K)}{1 + \rho} \right)^{1-\varepsilon_C} + \frac{I_F}{1 + \rho}$$
$$+ \frac{\alpha}{1 + \rho} \frac{1}{\varepsilon_N - 1} \left(\frac{a(1 - t_L)}{\alpha} \right)^{1-\varepsilon_N} + \frac{\beta}{1 + \rho} \frac{G_2^{1-1/\varepsilon_G}}{1 - 1/\varepsilon_G}, \tag{9.74}$$

where I_F is *full income* of the representative household, which is defined as:

$$I_F \equiv a(1 - t_L) + \left[1 + b(1 - t_K) \right] (1 + b)K_1, \tag{9.75}$$

Full income represents the maximum amount of income the household could have in period 2, i.e. by not consuming anything in period 1 and by supplying the maximum amount of labour in period 2.

The government budget restriction in the absence of lump-sum taxes is:

$$G_2 = t_K b K_2 + t_L a N_2. \tag{9.76}$$

Government spending on public goods must be financed by the revenue from the capital and labour taxes. The policy maker maximizes indirect utility of the representative household (given in (9.74)) subject to the government budget restriction (9.76). The Lagrangian for the policy maker's problem is:

$$\mathcal{P} \equiv V(G_2, t_L, t_K) + \mu \left[t_K b K_2 + t_L a N_2 - G_2 \right], \tag{9.77}$$

where μ is the Lagrange multiplier associated with the government budget restriction (9.76). The first-order conditions for the policy maker's problem are the constraint (9.76) and:

$$\frac{\partial \mathcal{P}}{\partial G_2} = \frac{\partial V}{\partial G_2} - \mu = 0, \tag{9.78}$$

$$\frac{\partial \mathcal{P}}{\partial t_L} = \frac{\partial V}{\partial t_L} + \mu a \left[N_2 + t_L \frac{\partial N_2}{\partial t_L} \right] = 0, \tag{9.79}$$

$$\frac{\partial \mathcal{P}}{\partial t_K} = \frac{\partial V}{\partial t_K} + \mu b \left[K_2 + t_K \frac{\partial K_2}{\partial t_K} \right] = 0. \tag{9.80}$$

In Intermezzo 9.1 it is shown that the first-order conditions can be rewritten in the following, more intuitive, form:

$$\beta G_2^{-1/\varepsilon_G} = \eta, \tag{9.81}$$

$$\eta = \frac{1}{1 - \frac{t_L}{1 - t_L} \xi_L}, \tag{9.82}$$

$$\eta = \frac{1}{1 - \frac{t_K}{1 - t_K} \xi_K}, \tag{9.83}$$

where ξ_L is the uncompensated wage elasticity of labour supply ($\xi_L > 0$), ξ_K is the uncompensated interest elasticity of gross saving ($\xi_K > 0$), and $\eta \equiv \mu / (\partial V / \partial I_F)$ is the *marginal cost of public funds* (MCPF). Intuitively, the MCPF measures how much it "costs" to raise a euro of public revenue. If there are non-distorting taxes it costs exactly one euro to raise a euro, and the MCPF is unity. On the other hand, if taxes distort real decisions by the private sector, it costs more than one euro to raise one euro of public revenue and the MCPF exceeds unity.

Equation (9.81) is the modified Samuelson rule for the optimal provision of public goods (see Atkinson and Stern, 1974). In words, (9.81) says that the marginal benefits of public goods (the left-hand side of (9.81)) should be equated to the marginal cost of financing these public goods, i.e. the MCPF. If there are non-distorting taxes, $\eta = 1$, and society can afford the first-best optimum level of public consumption. With distorting taxes, $\eta > 1$, and fewer public goods are provided. Equations (9.82)–(9.83) determine the optimal mix of taxes. Indeed, by rewriting (9.82)–(9.83) we obtain:

$$\frac{t_L}{1 - t_L} = \left(1 - \frac{1}{\eta} \right) \frac{1}{\xi_L}, \tag{9.84}$$

$$\frac{t_K}{1 - t_K} = \left(1 - \frac{1}{\eta} \right) \frac{1}{\xi_K}, \tag{9.85}$$

Equations (9.84)–(9.85) are expressions for the so-called *Ramsey taxes* on capital and labour (named after the British economist Frank Ramsey). Intuitively, these taxes raise a given amount of government revenue in the least distorting fashion. In order to facilitate the interpretation of (9.84)–(9.85), suppose that labour supply is perfectly inelastic (i.e. $\zeta_L = 0$). Then we know that a tax on labour income works exactly like a (non-distorting) lump-sum tax. Equation (9.82) says that in that case the MCPF is unity, so that (9.85) says that capital should not be taxed at all, and the entire revenue should be raised by means of the labour tax. The reverse case holds if the savings function is very interest inelastic and the labour supply is very wage elastic. In that case capital should be taxed heavily and labour should be taxed lightly. In the general case, however, equations (9.84)–(9.85) say that both tax rates should be set at some positive level.

Intermezzo 9.1

Deriving the optimal spending and taxation rules. Equation (9.82) is derived as follows. First, we calculate $\partial V/\partial t_L$ from the indirect utility function given in (9.74):

$$\frac{\partial V}{\partial t_L} = -\frac{a}{1+\rho} + \frac{a}{1+\rho}\left(\frac{a(1-t_L)}{\alpha}\right)^{-\varepsilon_N} = -\frac{a}{1+\rho}N_2, \tag{a}$$

where we have used (9.73) in the final step. By substituting (a) into (9.79) we obtain:

$$-\frac{a}{1+\rho}N_2 + \mu a N_2\left[1 + \frac{t_L}{N_2}\frac{\partial N_2}{\partial t_L}\right] = 0 \Rightarrow$$

$$\eta\left[1 - \left(\frac{t_L}{1-t_L}\right)\zeta_L\right] = 1, \tag{b}$$

where $\eta \equiv \mu(1+\rho)$ is the marginal cost of public funds, and ζ_L is the uncompensated wage elasticity of labour supply:

$$\zeta_L \equiv \frac{\partial N_2}{\partial a(1-t_L)}\frac{a(1-t_L)}{N_2} = -\frac{1-t_L}{t_L}\frac{\partial N_2}{\partial t_L}\frac{t_L}{N_2} = \omega_H\varepsilon_N > 0, \tag{c}$$

where $\omega_H \equiv (1-N_2)/N_2$ is the leisure/work ratio. By rewriting (b), equation (9.82) is obtained.

Equation (9.83) is obtained in a similar fashion. First, we calculate $\partial V/\partial t_K$ from the indirect utility function given in (9.74).

$$\frac{\partial V}{\partial t_K} = -\frac{b}{1+\rho}(1+b)K_1 + \frac{b}{1+\rho}\left(\frac{1+b(1-t_K)}{1+\rho}\right)^{-\varepsilon_C}$$

$$= \frac{b}{1+\rho}\left[C_1 - (1+b)K_1\right] = -\frac{b}{1+\rho}K_2, \tag{d}$$

where we have used (9.71) and the definition of K_2 in the two final steps. By substituting (d) into (9.80) we obtain:

$$-\frac{b}{1+\rho}K_2 + \mu b K_2\left[1 + \frac{t_K}{K_2}\frac{\partial K_2}{\partial t_K}\right] = 0 \Rightarrow$$

$$\eta\left[1 - \left(\frac{t_K}{1-t_K}\right)\zeta_K\right] = 1, \tag{e}$$

where $\check{\zeta}_K$ is the uncompensated interest elasticity of gross saving:

$$\zeta_K \equiv \frac{\partial K_2}{\partial b(1-t_K)} \frac{b(1-t_K)}{K_2} = -\frac{1-t_K}{t_K} \frac{\partial K_2}{\partial t_K} \frac{t_K}{K_2} = \omega_C \varepsilon_C > 0, \qquad \text{(f)}$$

where ω_C is defined as:

$$\omega_C \equiv \frac{b(1-t_K)C_1}{[1+b(1-t_K)]K_2}. \qquad \text{(g)}$$

By rewriting (e), equation (9.83) is obtained.

****

9.3.3 Dynamic inconsistency of the optimal tax plan

The problem with the optimal tax plan calculated in the previous section is that it is dynamically inconsistent. In the first period the policy maker announces that it will tax both labour income and capital income in the second period. But it turns out that once the second period has commenced it is no longer optimal for the policy maker to stick to its plan. This can easily be demonstrated with the aid of the model. At the beginning of the second period, the representative household has a capital stock of K_2 and chooses C_2 and N_2 to maximize remaining lifetime utility,

$$U_2 \equiv C_2 + \alpha \frac{(1-N_2)^{1-1/\varepsilon_N}}{1-1/\varepsilon_N} + \beta \frac{G_2^{1-1/\varepsilon_G}}{1-1/\varepsilon_G}, \qquad (9.86)$$

subject to the budget restriction:

$$C_2 = a(1-t_L)N_2 + [1+b(1-t_K)]K_2. \qquad (9.87)$$

Following the usual steps, the solutions for C_2 and N_2 are obtained:

$$C_2 = a(1-t_L) + [1+b(1-t_K)]K_2 - \alpha^{\varepsilon_N}[a(1-t_L)]^{1-\varepsilon_N}, \qquad (9.88)$$

$$1-N_2 = \left(\frac{a(1-t_L)}{\alpha}\right)^{-\varepsilon_N}. \qquad (9.89)$$

By substituting (9.88)–(9.89) into (9.86) the indirect utility function for period 2 is obtained:

$$V_2 \equiv [a(1-t_L) + [1+b(1-t_K)]K_2] + \frac{\alpha}{\varepsilon_N - 1}\left(\frac{a(1-t_L)}{\alpha}\right)^{1-\varepsilon_N}$$

$$+ \beta \frac{G_2^{1-1/\varepsilon_G}}{1-1/\varepsilon_G}. \qquad (9.90)$$

Clearly, the expressions for future labour supply, as given in (9.73) and (9.89), coincide provided the same tax rate features in these expressions. Similarly, by noting that $K_2 = (1+b)K_1 - C_1$ and using (9.71) it is easy to show that (9.88) coincides with (9.72), again provided the policy maker keeps his word and produces the tax rates as given in (9.84)–(9.85).

The problem is that, from the perspective of period 2, the policy maker will set different tax rates. Intuitively, the reason is that once the capital stock K_2 is in place, taxing capital income is non-distorting (since the capital income is like a "sitting duck") and the optimal Ramsey tax solution is to set $t_L = 0$ (since the labour tax is distorting) and $t_K > 0$.[10] As a result of this, the optimal tax rates as given in (9.84)–(9.85) are not believed by the public.

Of course, there is a consistent solution to the problem. This solution is obtained by working backwards in time, starting in period 2. The public knows that the government will set $t_L = 0$ in period 2 and raise its revenue by means of the tax on capital income only. The public also knows that G_2 will be set according to the level given in (9.56) because the policy maker has a non-distorting tax at its disposal in period 2. As a result of the higher level of public spending and the higher capital tax, the public will save less in period 1.

9.4   Are consumers dynamically inconsistent?

Up to this point all examples giving rise to dynamic inconsistency concern cases where different actors engage in strategic interactions with each other. In the inflation example the interaction is between the monetary policy maker and the public, whereas in the optimal capital taxation case the interaction is between the tax office and the owners of the capital stock.

In this section we show that dynamic inconsistency can also arise in individual behaviour. As was shown in the classic paper by Strotz (1956), rational utility maximizing individuals endowed with perfect foresight may very well formulate plans over their lifetime that are dynamically inconsistent. Such an agent plans at time t do something at some later time $t + \tau$ but knows already that when time $t + \tau$ comes around he will not execute the plan made at time t. It must be stressed that Strotz's dynamic inconsistency result does not derive from the fact that the economic circumstances have changed unexpectedly between t and $t + \tau$, but rather because the individual's objective function itself gives rise to dynamically inconsistent choices.

To demonstrate the main argument the remainder of this section develops an elaborate example in which an individual must choose the optimal consumption plan over the life cycle. To keep things as simple as possible we assume that the individual does not work but owns a given amount of resources (say a 'cake') at the start of youth, denoted by E. The cake does not yield any interest but does not go off either. The individual lives and consumes for three periods, say youth (superscript y), middle-age (superscript m), and old-age (superscript o). In the first subsection we start by studying the decisions of a "regular" dynamically consistent individual. Once that case is fully understood we move in the second subsection to the discussion of a dynamically inconsistent consumer.

---

[10]Formally, the policy maker chooses G_2, t_L, and t_K in order to maximize (9.90) subject to the government budget restriction (9.76). By following the same steps as before it can be shown that these results follow. Notice also that the government's plan regarding public goods provision is also dynamically inconsistent. Provided enough revenue can be raised from the capital income tax, the policy maker will set G_2 at the first-best optimum level as given in (9.56). This is a higher level than was announced in the first period.

9.4.1   A dynamically consistent consumer

Consider an individual who has a lifetime utility function during youth of the type used in Chapter 6:

$$\Lambda^y \equiv U(C_y^y) + \frac{1}{1+\rho}U(C_y^m) + \left(\frac{1}{1+\rho}\right)^2 U(C_y^o), \tag{9.91}$$

where Λ^y is lifetime utility of somebody who is young in period 1, C_j^i is consumption during life phase i as chosen in life phase j, ρ is the pure rate of time preference ($\rho > 0$), and $U(x)$ is the felicity function (featuring $U'(x) > 0$, $U''(x) < 0$, and $\lim_{x\to 0} U'(x) = +\infty$). Consumption levels over the life cycle as chosen during youth are denoted by C_y^y, C_y^m, and C_y^o. We call a person with this type of lifetime utility function an *exponential discounter*.[11] We complete the characterization of preferences by noting that the felicity function is logarithmic:

$$U(x) \equiv \ln x. \tag{9.92}$$

There are two questions concerning the individual's life-cycle choices. First, what is the optimal way to consume the cake over the three periods of life? Second, are the choices made dynamically consistent? To answer these questions we note that the budget constraints are given by:

$$A_y^m = E - C_y^y, \tag{9.93}$$
$$A_y^o = A_y^m - C_y^m, \tag{9.94}$$
$$A_y^d = A_y^o - C_y^o, \tag{9.95}$$

where A_y^d stands for the size of the cake when the individual is dead (superscript d). In addition the size of the cake must be non-negative at all times:

$$A_j^i \geq 0. \tag{9.96}$$

We first consider the choices made during youth. The individual chooses C_y^y, C_y^m, C_y^o, A_y^m, A_y^o, and A_y^d in order to maximize (9.91) subject to the constraints (9.93)–(9.96). The Lagrangian for this optimization problem is:

$$
\mathcal{L}^y \equiv U(C_y^y) + \frac{1}{1+\rho}U(C_y^m) + \left(\frac{1}{1+\rho}\right)^2 U(C_y^o)
$$
$$
+ \lambda_1\left[E - C_y^y - A_y^m\right] + \lambda_2\left[A_y^m - C_y^m - A_y^o\right] + \lambda_3\left[A_y^o - C_y^o - A_y^d\right].
$$

The first-order necessary conditions for consumption over the life cycle are $\partial\mathcal{L}^y/\partial C_y^y = \partial\mathcal{L}^y/\partial C_y^m = \partial\mathcal{L}^y/\partial C_y^o = 0$ and give rise to:

$$U'(C_y^y) = \lambda_1, \tag{9.97}$$

$$\frac{1}{1+\rho}U'(C_y^m) = \lambda_2, \tag{9.98}$$

---

[11]Note that $(1+\rho)^{-t} = e^{-t \ln(1+\rho)}$ which explains why the discounting scheme is called exponential. In the continuous-time setting employed by Strotz (1956) we use the result that $\ln(1+\rho) \approx \rho$ (for small ρ) so that the discount factors are given by $e^{-\rho t}$.

$$\left(\frac{1}{1+\rho}\right)^2 U'(C_y^o) = \lambda_3. \tag{9.99}$$

The first-order necessary conditions for the cake size over time are slightly more complicated because the non-negativity constraints on A_t necessitates the use of Kuhn-Tucker conditions:

$$\frac{\partial \mathcal{L}^y}{\partial A_y^m} = \lambda_2 - \lambda_1 \leq 0, \qquad A_y^m \geq 0, \qquad A_y^m \frac{\partial \mathcal{L}^y}{\partial A_y^m} = 0, \tag{9.100}$$

$$\frac{\partial \mathcal{L}^y}{\partial A_y^o} = \lambda_3 - \lambda_2 \leq 0, \qquad A_y^o \geq 0, \qquad A_y^o \frac{\partial \mathcal{L}^y}{\partial A_y^o} = 0, \tag{9.101}$$

$$\frac{\partial \mathcal{L}^y}{\partial A_y^d} = -\lambda_3 \leq 0, \qquad A_y^d \geq 0, \qquad A_y^d \frac{\partial \mathcal{L}^y}{\partial A_y^d} = 0. \tag{9.102}$$

The assumption made above (that $\lim_{x \to 0} U'(x) = +\infty$) ensures that the consumer plans a positive amount of cake consumption in each period. But this, in turn, implies that A_y^m and A_y^o are both strictly positive so that (by complementary slackness) it follows from (9.100)–(9.101) that $\lambda_1 = \lambda_2 = \lambda_3$ and thus from (9.97)–(9.99) that:

$$\frac{U'(C_y^y)}{U'(C_y^m)} = \frac{1}{1+\rho}, \qquad \frac{U'(C_y^m)}{U'(C_y^o)} = \frac{1}{1+\rho}. \tag{9.103}$$

Finally, since λ_3 is strictly positive it follows from (9.102) by complementary slackness that $A_y^d = 0$, i.e. no cake is left uneaten.

For the logarithmic felicity function (9.92) we find that the expressions in (9.103) simplify to $C_y^m / C_y^y = C_y^o / C_y^m = 1/(1+\rho)$. Since the lifetime budget constraint is given by $E = C_y^y + C_y^m + C_y^o$ we thus get the following solutions for the optimal life-cycle consumption choices made during youth:

$$C_y^y = \frac{(1+\rho)^2}{2+\rho+(1+\rho)^2} E, \tag{9.104}$$

$$C_y^m = \frac{1+\rho}{2+\rho+(1+\rho)^2} E, \tag{9.105}$$

$$C_y^o = A_y^o = \frac{1}{2+\rho+(1+\rho)^2} E, \tag{9.106}$$

$$A_y^m = \frac{2+\rho}{2+\rho+(1+\rho)^2} E. \tag{9.107}$$

Because the individual is impatient (as $\rho > 0$), and the felicity function is logarithmic, cake consumption declines proportionally over the life cycle.

Are these choices dynamically consistent? Does the individual with a cake of size A_y^m (as given in (9.107)) choose the same consumption levels C_y^m and C_y^o (as given in (9.105)–(9.106)) when in middle-age? The answer is a resounding 'yes!'. To demonstrate this result note that the lifetime utility function in middle-age is given by:

$$\Lambda^m \equiv U(C_m^m) + \frac{1}{1+\rho} U(C_m^o), \tag{9.108}$$

whilst the constraints in middle-age are:

$$A_m^o = A_y^m - C_m^m, \qquad A_m^d = A_m^o - C_m^o. \tag{9.109}$$

The middle-aged individual chooses C_m^m, C_m^o, A_m^o, and A_m^d in order to maximize (9.108) subject to (9.109), (9.96), and taking A_y^m as given. The optimality conditions are given by:

$$\frac{U'(C_m^m)}{U'(C_m^o)} = \frac{1}{1+\rho}, \quad C_m^o = A_m^o, \quad C_m^m + A_m^o = A_y^m,$$
(9.110)

which for the logarithmic felicity function (9.92) yield the following solutions:

$$C_m^m = \frac{1+\rho}{2+\rho} \quad A_y^m = \frac{1+\rho}{2+\rho+(1+\rho)^2} E,$$
(9.111)

$$C_m^o = A_m^o = \frac{1}{2+\rho} \quad A_y^m = \frac{1}{2+\rho+(1+\rho)^2} E,$$
(9.112)

where we have used the expression for A_y^m from (9.107) to get from the first to the second expression in each case. The comparison between (9.111)–(9.112) and (9.105)–(9.106) reveals that the choices made in middle-age are the same as they were planned to be during youth ($C_y^m = C_m^m$, $C_y^o = C_m^o$, and $A_y^d = A_m^d = 0$). Exponential discounters are dynamically consistent individuals!

9.4.2 A dynamically inconsistent consumer

The exponential discounter has a very particular discounting scheme in the sense that immediate felicity gets weight unity, felicity one period later gets weight $1/(1+\rho)$, and felicity two periods later gets weight $1/(1+\rho)^2$. Psychological researchers have devoted a huge amount of research time to actually measure the way real people discount delayed rewards. They found strong evidence for the hypothesis that discounting is not exponential but hyperbolic, i.e. rewards that are τ periods away from the present are discounted with weight $(1+\alpha\tau)^{-\gamma/\alpha}$ with $\alpha > 0$ and $\gamma > 0$. The key feature of this discounting scheme is that discounting is much heavier for rewards that are close in time than is suggested by an exponential scheme.[12] Furthermore, as is pointed out by Harris and Laibson:

> In the short run, the hyperbolic discount rate is γ and in the long run the discount rate converges to zero. This reflects the robust experimental finding that people are very impatient in the short run (e.g., when postponing a reward from today to tomorrow) and very patient when thinking about long-run trade-offs (postponing rewards from 100 to 101 days) (2003, p. 261)

In a path-breaking paper Laibson (1997) uses the modelling insights from Phelps and Pollak (1968) and captures the salient features of hyperbolic discounting by postulating what he calls a quasi-hyperbolic discounting scheme. In the context of our toy

---

[12]Note that:

$$\lim_{\tau \to \infty} (1+\alpha\tau)^{-\gamma/(\alpha\tau)} = e^{-\gamma}.$$

It follows from this result that:

$$(1+\alpha\tau)^{-\gamma/\alpha} \approx e^{-\gamma\tau} \qquad \text{for large } \tau.$$

Hence, for distant-in-time events discounting is approximately exponential under the hyperbolic scheme.

model the lifetime utility functions during youth, middle-age, and old age are given by:

$$\Lambda^y \equiv U(C_y^y) + \frac{\delta}{1+\rho}U(C_y^m) + \delta\left(\frac{1}{1+\rho}\right)^2 U(C_y^o), \tag{9.113}$$

$$\Lambda^m \equiv U(C_m^m) + \frac{\delta}{1+\rho}U(C_m^o), \tag{9.114}$$

$$\Lambda^o \equiv U(C_o^o), \tag{9.115}$$

with $0 < \delta < 1$. Preferences of this form capture the gist of hyperbolic discounting in the sense that discounting between a current and a near-in-time reward is much heavier than discounting between two distant-in-time rewards. For this reason some authors prefer to use the term present-biased preferences to describe the discounting scheme adopted here —see O'Donoghue and Rabin (1999). Following-convention, however, from here on we will call a person with the type of lifetime utility function as stated in (9.113)–(9.115) a *hyperbolic discounter*.

As is pointed out by Laibson (1997, p. 451) there is a strong reason to believe that hyperbolic preferences lead to dynamically inconsistent choices. Indeed, preferences during youth are inconsistent with preferences during middle-age. During youth the marginal rate of substitution (MRS) between C_y^m and C_y^o is:

$$\frac{\partial \Lambda^y / \partial C_y^m}{\partial \Lambda^y / \partial C_y^o} = \frac{(1+\rho)U'(C_y^m)}{U'(C_y^o)},$$

whilst during middle-age the MRS between C_y^m and C_y^o is quite different:

$$\frac{\partial \Lambda^m / \partial C_m^m}{\partial \Lambda^m / \partial C_m^o} = \frac{(1+\rho)U'(C_m^m)}{\delta U'(C_m^o)}.$$

This – of course – means that the middle-aged individual will not execute the plans chosen in youth.

Let us now return to our three-period model and compute what happens over the life cycle of the hyperbolic discounter. We start by considering the optimal choices made during youth (ignoring the suspected dynamic inconsistency of these choices). The individual chooses C_y^y, C_y^m, C_y^o, A_y^m, A_y^o, and A_y^d in order to maximize (9.113) subject to the constraints (9.93)–(9.96). Following the same steps as before we find that the optimal choices are characterized by:

$$\frac{U'(C_y^y)}{U'(C_y^m)} = \frac{\delta}{1+\rho}, \quad \frac{U'(C_y^m)}{U'(C_y^o)} = \frac{1}{1+\rho}, \quad E = C_y^y + C_y^m + C_y^o. \tag{9.116}$$

For the logarithmic felicity function (9.92) we obtain the following closed-form solutions:

$$C_y^y = \frac{(1+\rho)^2}{\delta(2+\rho) + (1+\rho)^2} E, \tag{9.117}$$

$$C_y^m = \frac{\delta(1+\rho)}{\delta(2+\rho) + (1+\rho)^2} E, \tag{9.118}$$

$$C_y^o = A_y^o = \frac{\delta}{\delta(2+\rho) + (1+\rho)^2} E, \tag{9.119}$$

$$A_y^m = \frac{\delta(2+\rho)}{\delta(2+\rho) + (1+\rho)^2} E. \tag{9.120}$$

Not surprisingly, during youth the hyperbolic discounter consumes more and leaves a smaller cake for middle-age than a consumer with regular preferences (an exponential discounter)—compare (9.117) and (9.104). More importantly, it is easy to demonstrate that the choices for C_y^m and C_y^o as stated in (9.118)–(9.119) will not be executed!

The lifetime utility function in middle-age is given by (9.114) and the constraints are given by $A_m^o = A_y^m - C_m^m$ and $A_m^d = A_m^o - C_m^o$. The optimality conditions characterizing the optimal choices made during middle-age are:

$$\frac{U'(C_m^m)}{U'(C_m^o)} = \frac{\delta}{1+\rho}, \quad C_m^m + C_m^o = A_y^m. \tag{9.121}$$

For the logarithmic felicity function (9.92) we find the following closed-form expressions:

$$C_m^m = \frac{1+\rho}{1+\delta+\rho} A_y^m = \frac{1+\rho}{1+\delta+\rho} \frac{\delta(2+\rho)}{\delta(2+\rho) + (1+\rho)^2} E, \tag{9.122}$$

$$C_m^o = A_m^o = \frac{\delta}{1+\delta+\rho} A_y^m = \frac{\delta}{1+\delta+\rho} \frac{\delta(2+\rho)}{\delta(2+\rho) + (1+\rho)^2} E, \tag{9.123}$$

where we have used the expression for A_y^m from (9.120) to get from the first to the second expression in each case. The comparison between (9.118) and (9.122) reveals that the hyperbolic discounter over-eats during middle-age and thus saves too little for old age, i.e. $C_m^m > C_y^m$ and $A_m^o < A_y^o$ (this result follows readily from the fact that $(2+\rho)/(1+\delta+\rho) > 1$).

Unless the young individual can somehow commit himself to the plans made during youth, these plans will not be executed in the future. The question then arises, what does the hyperbolic discounter do in the absence of a commitment device? Two hypotheses are discussed in turn.

9.4.2.1 A naive hyperbolic discounter

Strotz (1956) introduces the term "naive" for the person who does not worry about the dynamic inconsistency of his plans and just executes the plan chosen in each period. In our toy model this means that youth consumption C_y^y will be set as in (9.117), middle-age consumption C_m^m will be set as in (9.122), and old-age consumption C_o^o as in (9.123).

9.4.2.2 A sophisticated hyperbolic discounter

A sophisticated planner realizes that he will not carry out the plans made during youth. Such a person – in a sense – splits himself up in current and future selves. From the perspective of youth there is the present self, the middle-aged self, and the old-age self. From the perspective of middle-age there is the middle-age self and the old-age self. In each life phase the current self plays a strategic game against future selves. The equilibrium concept that is used in the hyperbolic discounting literature is that of the subgame perfect Nash equilibrium (SPNE). This sounds like a very complicated concept but in our toy model it is easy to show how we can compute the SPNE for a hyperbolic discounter.

The key thing to note is that SPNE requires the choices that are made to be an equilibrium of every subgame of the original game. The solution is computed backwards in time. The old self has no future self and thus has no game to play. The middle-aged self plays a game against the old self. The young self plays a game against the middle-aged and old selves.

We work directly with the logarithmic felicity function to keep things simple. First consider the choice made during old age: utility is $\Lambda^o \equiv \ln C_o^o$ and the budget constraint is $A_m^o = C_o^o + A_o^d$. It follows that, when old, the person will choose $C_o^o = A_m^o$ and $A_o^d = 0$ and attain a utility level equal to:

$$\Lambda^o = \ln A_m^o. \tag{9.124}$$

Next consider the middle-aged self. The budget constraint is $A_y^m = C_m^m + A_m^o$ and utility is:

$$\Lambda^m \equiv \ln C_m^m + \frac{\delta}{1+\rho} \ln A_m^o,$$

$$= \ln C_m^m + \frac{\delta}{1+\rho} \ln(A_y^m - C_m^m), \tag{9.125}$$

where we have substituted the constraint faced by the middle-aged self to get from the first to the second line. The first-order necessary condition for utility maximization is:

$$\frac{1}{C_m^m} = \frac{\delta}{1+\rho} \frac{1}{A_y^m - C_m^m}, \tag{9.126}$$

from which we obtain the closed-form solutions:

$$C_m^m = \frac{1+\rho}{1+\delta+\rho} A_y^m, \tag{9.127}$$

$$A_m^o = \frac{\delta}{1+\delta+\rho} A_y^m. \tag{9.128}$$

Finally consider the young self. The budget constraint is $E = C_y^y + A_y^m$ and the utility function can be written as:

$$\Lambda^y \equiv \ln C_y^y + \frac{\delta}{1+\rho} \ln \left[\frac{1+\rho}{1+\delta+\rho} (E - C_y^y) \right]$$

$$+ \delta \left(\frac{1}{1+\rho} \right)^2 \ln \left[\frac{\delta}{1+\delta+\rho} (E - C_y^y) \right]. \tag{9.129}$$

Note that (9.129) is obtained by substituting (9.127)–(9.128) into (9.113) and noting the logarithmic felicity function (9.92). The first-order necessary condition characterizing the optimal choice of youth consumption (and thus of A_y^m) is:

$$\frac{1}{C_y^y} = \left[\frac{1}{1+\rho} + \left(\frac{1}{1+\rho} \right)^2 \right] \frac{\delta}{E - C_y^y}, \tag{9.130}$$

from which we readily obtain the closed-form solutions:

$$C_y^y = \frac{(1+\rho)^2}{\delta(2+\rho) + (1+\rho)^2} E, \tag{9.131}$$

$$A_y^m = \frac{\delta(2+\rho)}{\delta(2+\rho) + (1+\rho)^2} E. \tag{9.132}$$

Future selves will choose such that:

$$C_m^m = \frac{1+\rho}{1+\delta+\rho} \frac{\delta(2+\rho)}{\delta(2+\rho) + (1+\rho)^2} E, \tag{9.133}$$

$$C_o^o = \frac{\delta}{1+\delta+\rho} \frac{\delta(2+\rho)}{\delta(2+\rho) + (1+\rho)^2} E. \tag{9.134}$$

To summarize, the sophisticated hyperbolic discounter formulates a dynamically consistent life-cycle consumption profile that is given in (9.131)–(9.134).

The comparison between the consistent and optimal solution reveals that the former is suboptimal *from the perspective of youth*. Indeed, even though youth consumption is the same for both solutions (compare (9.131) and (9.117)), the middle-aged self over-eats and undersaves in the consistent solution. Hence, lifetime utility is higher for the optimal-but-inconsistent solution than for the time-consistent solution.[13]

In closing we note that in our toy model there exists a very simple to implement commitment device that the young self could employ. All he has to do is to give part of the cake (the amount A_y^o as given in (9.119)) to a friend who locks it up in a fridge, goes on holidays to a far-off destination during period 2 taking the key to the fridge, and returns the cake to its owner (the old-age self) in period 3. The middle-aged self will thus obtain less cake from the young self and will optimally choose to consume it all. Of course, in reality perfect commitment devices are hard or even impossible to come by. Laibson (1997) and co-authors mention and analyse several real world imperfect commitment strategies such as illiquid assets and the like.

9.5   Punchlines

The discussion in this chapter focuses on the phenomenon of dynamic inconsistency. The classic example of dynamic inconsistency and its potential resolution can be traced to the ancient Greek author Homer. In this chapter, however, we study examples of dynamic inconsistency in governmental economic policy. We study three examples, two of which deal with monetary policy and one with fiscal policy.

To prepare for the first two examples of dynamic inconsistency we develop a simple model in which the policy maker faces a (stochastic) Lucas supply curve and attempts to steer output towards a higher than full employment level by setting the inflation rate (using monetary policy instruments to do so). The cost function of the policy maker depends positively on the deviation of output from its target level and on the inflation rate. A simple parameter measures the relative aversion of the policy maker against inflation. The higher this parameter the more "right wing" we shall call the policy maker. There is informational asymmetry in the model because the policy maker can observe the realization of the stochastic supply shock in the Lucas

---

[13]The astute reader will have noticed that the naive and sophisticated solutions are identical. This is due to the fact that the felicity function is logarithmic, i.e. the intertemporal substitution elasticity is equal to unity ($\sigma = 1$). With an iso-elastic felicity function of the form:

$$U(x) \equiv \frac{x^{1-1/\sigma} - 1}{1 - 1/\sigma}, \quad \sigma \neq 1,$$

the naive and sophisticated solutions are different. The reader is asked to verify this in the Exercise and Solutions Manual.

supply curve but the public cannot. As a result of this asymmetry, monetary policy is effective at influencing output despite the fact that private agents formulate rational expectations.

We can distinguish three different solutions to the policy maker's optimization problem. Under the discretionary solution, the policy maker chooses inflation (and thus output) in each period. Since private agents know the structure of the model they can compute the rational expectations solution under discretion which then feeds back into the Lucas supply curve. The rational expectations solution for the discretionary policy has two features. First, the chosen inflation rate depends positively on the output ambition of the policy maker (the gap between target and full employment output) and negatively on the supply shock. Second, the degree of accommodation of supply shocks by monetary policy depends in an intuitive fashion on the political orientation of the policy maker. Indeed, a left-wing (right-wing) policy maker cares little (strongly) about inflation and cares strongly (little) about deviations in output from full employment.

The discretionary solution is suboptimal, however, in that the policy maker can steer closer to its bliss point under an alternative rule-based solution. The rule-based solution is as follows. The policy maker announces to the public that it will follow a monetary policy rule which produces zero inflation in every period. If the public believed that the policy maker would stick to its promise the expected inflation rate would also be zero and no output stabilization would take place.

The problem with the rule-based solution is, however, that it is dynamically inconsistent. A policy maker has a strong incentive to exploit the Lucas supply curve based on zero expected inflation and to accommodate supply shocks by producing surprise inflation. This is the so-called cheating solution which derives its name from the fact that the policy maker does not stick to its promises of no inflation. The cheating solution is closest to the policy maker's bliss point but it violates the rational expectations assumption.

The upshot of the discussion so far is that the only policy which is both believed by private agents (i.e. is said to be credible) and is consistent with rational expectations is the discretionary policy. Of all policies considered however, the discretionary policy yields the policy maker the lowest level of welfare (i.e. the highest level of social cost). It would seem that the economy gets stuck with the worst possible outcome.

In an ingenious paper, Barro and Gordon (1983b) have shown that the reputation of the policy maker can act as an enforcement device, making it possible that the superior rule-based equilibrium is credibly selected in equilibrium. These authors proxy the policy maker's reputation as follows. If the policy maker has kept its promise (whatever it was) in the previous period then the public will believe the policy maker's announcement that it will follow the monetary rule in the present period. In contrast, if the policy maker did not keep its promise in the previous period, the public discounts the policy maker's reputation and expects that the discretionary solution will be selected in the present period. This is an example of a "tit-for-tat" strategy adopted by the private agents in their repeated prisoner's dilemma game with the policy maker. The approach implies that a rule-based solution may be enforceable which features a positive inflation rate.

In the remainder of this chapter we give three more examples of dynamic inconsistency (and its possible resolution). In the first of these we show that in a voting model, the median voter will elect somebody to act as the central banker who is more conservative (and has a higher aversion against inflation) than he is himself. In doing so, the median voter commits himself to a lower inflation rate than he would have chosen had he himself been the monetary policy maker.

In the second example we develop a simple toy model of optimal taxation of labour and capital income when lump-sum taxes are not available. Two key results are derived. First, abstracting from issues of dynamic inconsistency, the optimal tax rates on both labour and capital are non-zero and these rates depend on the elasticities of the respective tax bases. Second, the optimal taxes are dynamically inconsistent. Once the future capital stock is in place, the tax base for capital income tax is inelastic and the policy maker can raise public revenue in a non-distorting fashion by not taxing labour income and taxing capital income as much as possible.

In the final example we show that dynamic inconsistency can also arise in individual behaviour. We develop a simple toy model in which a rational utility maximizing individual (endowed with perfect foresight) optimally consumes a cake over three periods. If the lifetime utility function is of the standard type (and exhibits exponential felicity discounting) then the consumer's plans are dynamically consistent. What is planned in youth will be executed in middle-age and old-age. If, on the other hand, the consumer has hyperbolic (or present-biased) preferences then consumption plans are dynamically inconsistent. Unless the consumer can somehow commit himself, plans made during youth will not be executed in later periods and the actual life choices will be suboptimal. In the toy model the consumer over-eats during middle-age and leaves too little of the cake for old-age.

Further reading

The key references to the reputational model of inflation are Barro and Gordon (1983a, 1983b), and Backus and Driffill (1985). See also Cukierman and Meltzer (1986) and Cukierman (1992). Klein (2008) presents a compact discussion of the time consistency literature and economic policy. Persson and Tabellini (1994a) present a collection of the most important articles. A number of monographs on the political economy approach to economic policy exist—see Persson and Tabellini (1989), Dixit (1996), Persson and Tabellini (2000), and Drazen (2000). For a review of the last two books, see Saint-Paul (2000). Readers interested in the optimal taxation literature are referred to Atkinson and Stiglitz (1980). Persson and Tabellini (1994b) study capital taxation in a model of a representative democracy. Van der Ploeg (1995) studies the political economy of monetary and fiscal policy in a dynamic macroeconomic model.

Early contributions to the dynamic inconsistency literature are Strotz (1956), Phelps and Pollak (1968), Pollak (1968), and Peleg and Yaari (1973). Tractable models of (quasi-)hyperbolic discounting were developed by Laibson and co-authors—see Laibson (1997), Harris and Laibson (2001, 2003, 2013), Angeletos et al. (2001), and Laibson et al. (2003). See also O'Donoghue and Rabin (1999) on present-biased preferences, and Lipman and Pesendorfer (2013) on temptation in general. For a review of the literature on time preference and discounting, see Frederick et al. (2002).

Part II

Towards advanced macroeconomics

Chapter 10

Money

The purpose of this chapter is to discuss the following issues:

1. What are the principal functions of money in advanced economies?

2. How can the role of money be captured in simple models?

3. What is the socially optimal quantity of money?

4. How does money affect the government budget constraint (nominal money growth as an inflation tax)?

10.1 Functions of money

When asked the question "What is money?", it will be answered with full confidence by any man or woman in the street. Indeed, the typical response one may expect from such a question would probably consist of the person in question taking out his/her wallet and showing a colourful piece of paper with some numbers printed on it and possibly the portrait of some past or present monarch or president. If the question had been asked a few centuries ago, the object produced from the wallet would probably have been made of some precious metal rather than (hard to counterfeit) paper but the intended answer would have been the same: money is the stuff which sits in one's wallet and can be used to purchase goods and services.[1]

Economists will show considerably less confidence if confronted with the same question and instead of formulating a straight answer will propose a number of functions performed by this elusive thing called "money". In other words, instead of designating what money "is" , economists describe what money "does", or more precisely what something must do in order for it to be called money. In broad terms three major functions of money can be distinguished: (1) money as a medium of exchange, (2) money as a medium of account, and (3) money as a store of value (McCallum, 1989a, pp. 16–18).

The various aspects of money can be illustrated with the aid of Figure 10.1. Suppose there are four agents (labelled 1 through 4) in the economy who each produce a unique commodity but like to consume not just their own product but also all other

---

[1] An exhaustive and highly readable historical treatment of the emergence of money in different societies is found in Einzig (1949). See also Davies (1994), Jevons (1875), Menger (1892), Fisher (1913), Wicksell (1935), and Jones (1976).

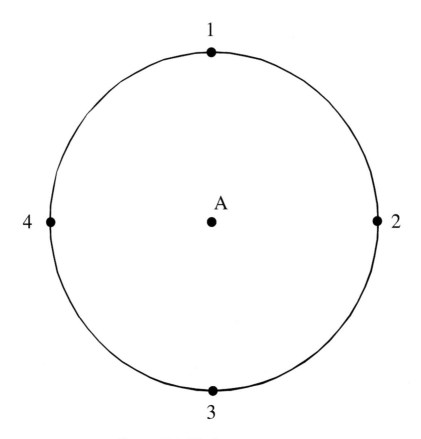

Figure 10.1: The barter economy

products in the economy. In a *barter* economy all agents formulate their supply of the own good and demands for the other goods, and meet at a central market place (which is located, say, at point A in Figure 10.1) in which the equilibrium *relative* prices are determined. Since there are four goods in our example, there are in total six relative prices which are determined.[2] Exchange takes place without the use of money, namely good 1 is directly exchanged ("bartered") for good 2, etc. Aside from obvious complications relating to indivisibilities of goods etc., a centralized market place would function perfectly well without money. Intuitively, without some kind of "friction" money is not likely to be a very useful thing to have.

In reality, of course, not all transactions take place in a centralized full-information setting and the process of trading becomes more complicated. Assume that the central market place in Figure 10.1 exists, but that the agent does not know beforehand which other trader he is going to meet there at any particular time. Suppose that at most two traders meet randomly at this market in each period. Then agents are confronted with a major problem due to the need for a double coincidence of wants. For example, agent 1 may find himself paired with agent 2 who may or may not want to trade with him. In fact, in the absence of money, an exchange of goods will only take place if agent 1 meets an agent who wants to have his good and who himself has a good which agent 1 is looking for. Hence, in such a setting it may take a lot of effort

---

[2]These are the rates at which the goods are exchanged pair-wise. Denoting p_{ij} as the relative price of good i in terms of good j, we have the following relative prices: p_{12}, p_{13}, p_{14}, p_{23}, p_{24}, and p_{34}. Obviously, we have that $p_{ij} \equiv 1/p_{ji}$.

and a long time before agent 1 can actually trade.

Even if agents are perfectly informed about the location of trading partners, the problem may still persist. Cass and Yaari (1966) present a case in which the double coincidence of wants always fails. Assume that agents only wish to consume their own good and the good produced by the agent located closest (in a clockwise direction), i.e. agent 1 would like to consume the bundle (1,2), agent 2 (2,3), agent 3 (3,4), and agent 4 (4,1). Assume that the goods are non-storable and that each agent can at most travel halfway towards his adjacent neighbours. This means that agent 1, for example, can attempt to trade with agents 4 and 2, agent 2 with 1 and 3, etc. It is easy to see, however, that no trading will actually take place. Agent 1, for example, cannot trade with 2 because the latter is not interested in good 1 at any price. Similarly, agent 1 will not trade with agent 4 for the same reason. The double coincidence of wants fails, all agents consume only their own good, and a situation of autarky persists.

Now assume there is a durable "thing" which is storable and can be transferred across agents at zero cost, and call this thing money. Then agents will actually be able to trade with each other by using this money rather than bartering. Agent 1, for example, sells his good to agent 4, and receives money for it with which he purchases good 2 from agent 2. Since the other agents do the same with their neighbours, an equilibrium can be attained in which all agents are better off (in welfare terms) as a result of the existence of a medium of exchange called money.

Of course, the circle model is a highly stylized account of the trading process but it is nevertheless useful because it motivates the following medium-of-exchange "test". Something serves the role of medium of exchange if its existence ensures that agents can attain a higher level of welfare.[3] In the "random-encounters" model and in the "circle" model money serves as a medium of exchange in the sense of this proposed definition. Indeed, in the former model the trading friction is reduced (but not totally eliminated)[4] by the existence of a medium of exchange, whereas in the latter the friction is completely eliminated.

There is nothing in the theory which suggests that the medium of exchange must be an intrinsically valuable commodity such as gold or silver (or rare shells) which enhance people's utility or can be put to productive uses. Indeed, an intrinsically low-valued good (such as paper) can also serve as a medium of exchange provided it is generally accepted in exchange. To the extent that gold and silver are better used for productive purposes, it is actually preferable for society to use intrinsically low-valued material as a medium of exchange (McCallum, 1989a, p. 17).

The second major function of money is that of *medium of account*. As was explained above, an economy with four distinct goods exhibits six distinct relative prices. For an economy with N different goods the number of distinct relative prices amounts to $N(N-1)/2$, which is a rather large number even for a modestly large N. If all goods are expressed in terms of money, and money is thus the medium of account, then only N different (absolute) prices for the different goods need be recorded. Denoting these absolute prices by p_i ($i = 1, \cdots, N$) the relative prices are then implied, e.g. $p_{ij} \equiv p_i/p_j$.

---

[3]This test is similar to (but more general than) the one suggested by McCallum (1983b). His requirement is more strict in that it requires the medium of exchange to expand production possibilities. Indeed, he calls this the "traditional presumption" (1983, p. 24).

[4]Agent 1 may meet an agent from whom he does not want to buy anything but who does want to buy good 1. The transaction takes place against money, which agent 1 can use at some later encounter. If agent 1 instead meets an agent who does not want good 1 and whose good agent 1 does not want, then no trade takes place. Hence, some frictions remain in the random-encounters model.

The third function of money is that of *store of value*. In a monetary economy money can be used to buy goods and vice versa, not only today but (more than likely) also tomorrow. Hence, a stock of money represents "future purchasing power". In the future the money can be exchanged for goods which can be consumed or used in the production process. Money is thus capable of being used as a store of value, but there are other assets (bonds, company shares, real estate, etc.) which typically outperform it in this role because they yield a positive rate of return whereas money (typically) does not.

Of the three major roles played by money, only the medium-of-exchange role is the distinguishing feature of money. Any commodity can serve as a medium of account (without at the same time serving as a medium of exchange) and there are various non-money assets which can serve as a store of value.

10.2 Modelling money as a medium of exchange

In Chapter 1 we discussed the Baumol (1952)-Tobin (1956) inventory-theoretic model of money demand–see Intermezzo 1.3. The basic idea behind that model is that money is held through the period between income receipts, despite the fact that it does not yield any interest, because it is needed to make purchases. The baker will sell you a loaf of bread in exchange for money but not for bonds. At a more general level the model suggests that money facilitates transactions. Of course, the Baumol-Tobin model is rather restrictive in its scope and is partial equilibrium in nature. The task of this section is to study how money as a medium of exchange can be cast in a general equilibrium framework. In what follows the Baumol-Tobin model is shown to be a special case of a more general framework in which money helps to "grease the wheels" of the economy by minimizing liquidity costs.

10.2.1 Setting the stage

Suppose an individual agent lives for two periods, "now" (period 1) and "in the future" (period 2), and possesses stocks of bonds (B_0) and money (M_0) that were accumulated in the past. The agent has fixed real endowment income in the two periods (Y_1 and Y_2, respectively) and consumes in the two periods (C_1 and C_2, respectively). The price of the good in the two periods is denoted by P_1 and P_2, respectively. The periodic budget identities are then given by:

$$P_1 Y_1 + M_0 + (1 + R_0) B_0 = P_1 C_1 + M_1 + B_1, \tag{10.1}$$
$$P_2 Y_2 + M_1 + (1 + R_1) B_1 = P_2 C_2 + M_2 + B_2, \tag{10.2}$$

where R_i is the nominal interest rate on bonds in period i. The left-hand side in these expressions represents the total resources available to the household whereas the right-hand side represents what these resources can be spent on.

Since the agent will not be around in period 3 and there is no bequest motive (see Section 6.1.4), he will not wish to die with positive stocks of money and/or bonds (i.e. $M_2 \leq 0$ and $B_2 \leq 0$). The financial sector will not allow him to die indebted ($B_2 \geq 0$) and the agent cannot create money ($M_2 \geq 0$). Hence, combining all these requirements yields $M_2 = B_2 = 0$, so that (10.1)–(10.2) can be combined into the following consolidated budget constraint:

$$[A \equiv] \ Y_1 + \frac{Y_2}{1 + r_1} + \frac{P_0}{P_1} m_0 + (1 + r_0) b_0 = C_1 + \frac{C_2}{1 + r_1} + \frac{R_1 m_1}{1 + R_1}, \tag{10.3}$$

where $m_t \equiv M_t / P_t$ is real money balances, $b_t \equiv B_t / P_t$ is real bonds (or real debt if b_t is negative), and r_t is the real rate of interest which is defined as:

$$r_t = \frac{P_t(1 + R_t)}{P_{t+1}} - 1. \tag{10.4}$$

If the price level is stable (rising, falling), the real interest rate equals (falls short of, exceeds) the nominal interest rate.

The agent has the usual lifetime utility function which depends on consumption in the two periods in a time-separable manner:

$$V = U(C_1) + \frac{1}{1 + \rho} U(C_2), \tag{10.5}$$

where $\rho > 0$ is the pure rate of time preference and $U(\cdot)$ has the usual properties (see Section 6.1.1). The household chooses consumption in the two periods (C_1 and C_2) and its desired money holding (m_1) in order to maximize (10.5) subject to (10.3) and the non-negativity condition on money holdings ($m_1 \geq 0$), and given the predetermined stocks of money and bonds (m_0 and b_0). The Lagrangian associated with this problem is:

$$\mathcal{L} \equiv U(C_1) + \frac{1}{1 + \rho} U(C_2) + \lambda \left[A - C_1 - \frac{C_2}{1 + r_1} - \frac{R_1 m_1}{1 + R_1} \right], \tag{10.6}$$

where λ is the Lagrangian multiplier. The first-order conditions consist of the consolidated budget constraint and:

$$\frac{\partial \mathcal{L}}{\partial C_1} = U'(C_1) - \lambda = 0, \tag{10.7}$$

$$\frac{\partial \mathcal{L}}{\partial C_2} = \frac{1}{1 + \rho} U'(C_2) - \frac{\lambda}{1 + r_1} = 0, \tag{10.8}$$

$$\frac{\partial \mathcal{L}}{\partial m_1} \equiv \lambda \cdot \left[\frac{-R_1}{1 + R_1} \right] \leq 0, \quad m_1 \geq 0, \quad m_1 \frac{\partial \mathcal{L}}{\partial m_1} = 0. \tag{10.9}$$

Equations (10.7)–(10.8) are exactly the same as in a model without money and in combination yield the usual Euler equation relating the optimal time profile of consumption to the divergence between the real interest rate and the rate of time preference. The existence of money does not affect this aspect of the intertemporal model. Equation (10.9) is new and warrants some further discussion. First consider the normal case with a strictly positive rate of interest ($R_1 > 0$) so that the term in square brackets in (10.9) is strictly negative and the complementary slackness condition suggests that no money is held by the agent:

$$m_1 = 0 \quad \text{if } R_1 > 0. \tag{10.10}$$

The intuition behind this result is that the opportunity cost of holding money consists of foregone interest, which is positive. Since money is not "doing" anything useful in the model developed thus far, the rational agent refrains from using money altogether.

The second, at first view rather *pathological*, case describes the situation in which the nominal interest rate is negative ($R_1 < 0$), so that the term in square brackets in (10.9) is positive. Now the agent wishes to hold as much money as possible. By simply holding these money balances they appreciate in value (relative to goods). To put it differently, money has a positive yield if the interest rate is negative.

$$m_1 \to \infty \quad \text{if } R_1 < 0. \tag{10.11}$$

Of course, negative nominal interest rates do not represent a particularly realistic phenomenon. We shall nevertheless have a need to return to this case in section 10.4.2 below where we discuss the optimal quantity of money argument. In the remainder of this section, however, we restrict attention to the normal case, i.e. we assume that the nominal interest rate is strictly positive. The challenge is then to modify the basic model in such a way that money will play a non-trivial role for the agent (and thus for the economy as a whole).

10.2.2 Shopping costs

In section 10.1 it was argued that money as a medium of exchange reduces the transactions costs associated with the trading process between agents. A particularly simple and elegant way to capture this aspect of money was suggested by McCallum (1983c, 1989a). He assumes that households value leisure time and that part of their time endowment is spent on "shopping around" for goods. Money is useful in the sense that it makes shopping easier, i.e. by using money the agent can save leisure time otherwise spent on shopping. We now modify our basic model to incorporate shopping costs.

Suppose that the household has a time endowment of unity, works a fixed amount of time units, $\bar{N}$, and spends S_t units of time on shopping. Then the agent enjoys $1 - \bar{N} - S_t$ units of leisure in period t. The utility function is modified to take into account that the agent likes leisure time:[5]

$$V = U(C_1, 1 - \bar{N} - S_1) + \frac{1}{1+\rho} U(C_2, 1 - \bar{N} - S_2), \quad \rho > 0. \tag{10.12}$$

The intertemporal budget constraint is still given by (10.3), with endowment income now representing real labour income, $Y_t \equiv (W_t/P_t)\bar{N}$, where W_t is the nominal wage rate in period t. The shopping technology is assumed to take the following form:

$$1 - \bar{N} - S_t = \psi(m_{t-1}, C_t), \tag{10.13}$$

where the $\psi(\cdot)$ function is assumed to have the following properties. First, for a given level of goods consumption, raising the level of real money balances results in a finite reduction of time spent shopping and thus an increase in available leisure, i.e. $\psi_m(\cdot) > 0$. Second, the reduction in shopping cost due to a given increase in money balances decreases as more money balances are used, i.e. $\psi_{mm}(\cdot) < 0$ or, in words, the shopping technology features diminishing marginal productivity of money balances. Third, increasing consumption requires more shopping costs but at a diminishing rate, i.e. $\psi_C(\cdot) < 0$ and $\psi_{CC}(\cdot) > 0$. Finally, the shopping costs are bounded, i.e. $0 < \psi(m_{t-1}, \infty) < \psi(m_{t-1}, 0) < 1 - \bar{N}$.

The household chooses C_t, S_t (for $t = 1, 2$), and m_1 (m_0 being predetermined) in order to maximize (10.12) subject to (10.3), (10.13), and the non-negativity constraint on money balances ($m_1 \geq 0$). The Lagrangian expression is:

$$\mathcal{L} \equiv U(C_1, 1 - \bar{N} - S_1) + \frac{1}{1+\rho} U(C_2, 1 - \bar{N} - S_2) \tag{10.14}$$

---

[5]Some people actually enjoy shopping. For them it is not lost leisure. They simply find it relaxing to visit book shops and shoe stores. We abstract from such people in this book.

$$+ \lambda \left[A - C_1 - \frac{C_2}{1+r_1} - \frac{R_1 m_1}{1+R_1} \right] + \sum_{t=1}^{2} \lambda_t \left[\psi(m_{t-1}, C_t) - (1 - \bar{N} - S_t) \right],$$

where λ_t are the Lagrangian multipliers associated with the shopping technology in the two periods. The first-order conditions consist of the constraints and:

$$\frac{\partial \mathcal{L}}{\partial C_1} = U_C(C_1, 1 - \bar{N} - S_1) - \lambda + \lambda_1 \psi_C(m_0, C_1) = 0, \tag{10.15}$$

$$\frac{\partial \mathcal{L}}{\partial C_2} = \frac{1}{1+\rho} U_C(C_2, 1 - \bar{N} - S_2) - \frac{\lambda}{1+r_1} + \lambda_2 \psi_C(m_1, C_2) = 0, \tag{10.16}$$

$$\frac{\partial \mathcal{L}}{\partial S_1} = -U_L(C_1, 1 - \bar{N} - S_1) + \lambda_1 = 0, \tag{10.17}$$

$$\frac{\partial \mathcal{L}}{\partial S_2} = -\frac{1}{1+\rho} U_L(C_2, 1 - \bar{N} - S_2) + \lambda_2 = 0, \tag{10.18}$$

$$\frac{\partial \mathcal{L}}{\partial m_1} \equiv -\lambda \frac{R_1}{1+R_1} + \lambda_2 \psi_m(m_1, C_2) \leq 0, \quad m_1 \geq 0, \quad m_1 \frac{\partial \mathcal{L}}{\partial m_1} = 0, \tag{10.19}$$

where $U_C(\cdot)$ and $U_L(\cdot)$ denote the marginal utility of consumption and leisure, respectively.

The first thing to note about these expressions concerns equation (10.19), which is the first-order condition for optimal money balances. Comparing this expression to its counterpart in the basic model (i.e. equation (10.9)) reveals that the existence of shopping costs indeed gives rise to an additional positive term in the first expression of (10.19), $U_L(C_2, 1 - \bar{N} - S_2)\psi_m(m_1, C_2)/(1+\rho)$ (we have used (10.18) to eliminate λ_2). This term represents the marginal utility of money balances. It must be stressed, however, that this does not in and of itself ensure that the agent will choose to hold positive money balances. Indeed, given the assumptions made so far, it is quite possible that $m_1 = 0$ is the best available option for the household. Specifically if the marginal utility of leisure and/or the marginal productivity of money balances are low, the first expression in (10.19) will be strictly negative so that the complementary slackness condition ensures that $m_1 = 0$ is optimal, as in the basic model. Intuitively, no money is held in that case because the agent does not really mind shopping (U_L low) and/or because money does not reduce shopping costs by much (ψ_m low).

In the remainder of this section we assume that ψ_m and/or U_L are high enough to ensure that a strictly positive amount of money is held by the agent. The first expression in (10.19) holds with equality and the Lagrange multipliers (λ_1 and λ_2) can be eliminated by substituting (10.17) into (10.15) and (10.18) into (10.16) and (10.19). We find the following optimality conditions:

$$\lambda = U_C(C_1, 1 - \bar{N} - S_1) + U_L(C_1, 1 - \bar{N} - S_1)\psi_C(m_0, C_1)$$

$$= \frac{1+r_1}{1+\rho} \cdot \left[U_C(C_2, 1 - \bar{N} - S_2) + U_L(C_2, 1 - \bar{N} - S_2)\psi_C(m_1, C_2) \right]$$

$$= \frac{U_L(C_2, 1 - \bar{N} - S_2)\psi_m(m_1, C_2)(1+R_1)}{(1+\rho)R_1}, \tag{10.20}$$

where λ represents the marginal utility of wealth (see Section 6.1.1). In planning his optimal consumption levels, the agent equates the marginal utility of wealth to the *net* marginal utility of consumption, which consists of the direct marginal utility of consumption ($U_C(\cdot)$ in the first and second lines of (10.20)) minus the disutility (since $\psi_C < 0$) caused by the additional shopping costs which must be incurred (the $U_L(\cdot)\psi_C(\cdot)$ terms). For consumption taking place in the future the expression is augmented by a net discounting factor (see the second line of (10.20)). The third line in (10.20) shows that the marginal utility of money balances ($U_L(\cdot)\psi_m(\cdot)$) must be equated to the opportunity costs associated with holding these balances expressed in utility terms (i.e. λ).

10.2.3   Money in the utility function

Inspection of equations (10.12)–(10.13) of the shopping-cost model reveals that this approach in effect amounts to putting money directly into the utility function, i.e. by substituting (10.13) into the felicity function $U(C_t, 1 - \bar{N} - S_t)$ we obtain an *indirect* felicity function, $\tilde{U}(C_t, m_{t-1}) \equiv U(C_t, \psi(m_{t-1}, C_t))$, which only depends on consumption and money balances. Hence, the shopping cost approach can be used to rationalize the conventional practice in macroeconomic modelling of putting money directly into the utility function.

Feenstra (1986) has provided further justifications for this practice by demonstrating that there exists a functional equivalence between, on the one hand, models with money entered as an argument into the utility function and, on the other hand, models in which money does not enter utility but instead affects "liquidity costs" which in turn show up in the budget restriction. Since the Baumol-Tobin model gives rise to such liquidity costs, Feenstra (1986) has demonstrated that, in a general equilibrium setting, it too is equivalent to a model with money in the utility function.

In a classic paper on the micro-foundations of monetary theory, Clower (1967) complained that (at least in models such as developed up to this point) money is not allowed to play a distinctive role in the economy. Indeed, by looking at the budget identities (10.1)–(10.2), it is clear that money enters these expressions in exactly the same way that goods and bonds do. Implicitly, this suggests that any item (be it goods, money, or bonds) can be directly exchanged for any other item, i.e. goods for bonds, bonds for money, etc. This makes Clower complain that: "...an economy that admits of this possibility clearly constitutes what any Classical economist would regard as a barter rather than a money economy.' The fact that fiat money is included among the set of tradeable commodities is utterly irrelevant; the role of money in economic activity is analytically indistinguishable from that of any other commodity" (Clower, 1967, p. 3). In a pure monetary economy, Clower argues, there is a single good, "money", which is used in all transactions, and "money buys goods and goods buy money; but goods do not buy goods" (1967, p. 5).

In the context of our basic model of section 10.2.1, Clower's idea can be formalized by requiring that spending on consumption goods cannot exceed cash balances carried over from the previous period.[6] The so-called *Clower* or *cash-in-advance constraint* thus amounts to:

$$P_t C_t \leq M_{t-1} \quad \Leftrightarrow \quad C_t \leq \frac{P_{t-1}}{P_t} m_{t-1}. \tag{10.21}$$

The basic model, augmented with the Clower constraint (10.21), can be solved as follows. To keep things simple, we assume that the Clower constraint holds with equality in the first period. Since m_0 is predetermined, the same then holds for consumption in the first period, i.e. $C_1 = P_0 m_0 / P_1$. The household chooses C_2 and m_1 in order to maximize (10.5), subject to (10.3) and (10.21). The Lagrangian is:

$$\mathcal{L} \equiv U\left(\frac{P_0}{P_1} m_0\right) + \frac{1}{1+\rho} U(C_2) + \lambda \left[A - \frac{P_0}{P_1} m_0 - \frac{C_2}{1+r_1} - \frac{R_1 m_1}{1+R_1}\right]$$

---

[6] For simplicity we assume that the cash-in-advance constraint does not affect purchases of bonds.

$$+ \lambda_2 \left[\frac{P_1}{P_2} m_1 - C_2 \right], \tag{10.22}$$

where λ_2 is the Lagrangian multiplier associated with the Clower constraint. The first-order conditions consist of the budget constraint (10.3) and:

$$\frac{\partial \mathcal{L}}{\partial C_2} \equiv \frac{1}{1+\rho} U'(C_2) - \frac{\lambda}{1+r_1} - \lambda_2 \leq 0, \quad C_2 \geq 0, \quad C_2 \frac{\partial \mathcal{L}}{\partial C_2} = 0, \tag{10.23}$$

$$\frac{\partial \mathcal{L}}{\partial m_1} \equiv -\lambda \frac{R_1}{1+R_1} + \lambda_2 \frac{P_1}{P_2} \leq 0, \quad m_1 \geq 0, \quad m_1 \frac{\partial \mathcal{L}}{\partial m_1} = 0, \tag{10.24}$$

$$\frac{\partial \mathcal{L}}{\partial \lambda_2} \equiv \frac{P_1}{P_2} m_1 - C_2 \geq 0, \quad \lambda_2 \geq 0, \quad \lambda_2 \frac{\partial \mathcal{L}}{\partial \lambda_2} = 0. \tag{10.25}$$

The marginal utility of wealth is strictly positive, i.e. $\lambda > 0$, so that (by (10.23)) the marginal utility of consumption is bounded. Since $\lim_{C_t \to \infty} U'(C_t) = 0$ by assumption, this implies that the consumer chooses a strictly positive consumption level in period 2, i.e. $C_2 > 0$ and (by the first inequality in (10.25)) $m_1 > 0$. Hence, the cash-in-advance constraint does indeed deliver the "goods" desired by Clower. Money is essential, not because it is valued intrinsically, but rather because households wish to consume in the second period. It can also be shown that the household will not hold excess cash balances. Since $m_1 > 0$, the first expression in (10.24) holds with equality, which ensures that the shadow price of cash balances is strictly positive:

$$\lambda_2 = \lambda \frac{P_2}{P_1} \frac{R_1}{1+R_1} > 0. \tag{10.26}$$

This implies that the first expression in (10.25) holds with an equality, i.e. the household will hold just enough cash to be able to finance their optimal consumption plan in the future. This result is not specific to our simple two-period model and easily generalizes to a multi-period setting.

As is the case for the shopping model and the Baumol-Tobin model, the cash-in-advance approach can also be shown to be equivalent to a utility-of-money approach. Indeed, as the Clower constraint always holds with equality ($C_t = (P_{t-1}/P_t) m_{t-1}$), the same results are obtained if the indirect felicity function $\tilde{U}(C_t, m_{t-1}) \equiv \min[C_t, m_{t-1}]$ is maximized subject to the budget constraint only (see Feenstra, 1986, p. 285). An important aspect of this indirect felicity function is that the substitution elasticity between consumption and money balances is zero. In this aspect the cash-in-advance formulation differentiates itself from both the shopping model and the Baumol-Tobin model.

10.3 Money as a store of value

In the basic model of section 10.2.1 above, both bonds and money can be used by the individual agent to transfer resources across time and both assets are thus capable of serving as a store of value, although the former does so in a superior fashion to the latter as it yields a higher rate of return. For that reason, money is not generally held in the basic model. It thus does not actually serve as a store of value even though it is technically capable of doing so.

Bewley (1980) presents a model in which money is used as a store of value. His approach can be illustrated with the aid of our basic model. The key assumption he makes is that money is the only asset available to the agent, i.e. $B_0 = B_1 = B_2 = 0$ in the budget equations (10.1)–(10.2). These can then be expressed in real terms as:

$$Y_1 + \frac{m_0}{1 + \pi_0} = C_1 + m_1, \quad Y_2 + \frac{m_1}{1 + \pi_1} = C_2, \quad m_1 \geq 0, \tag{10.27}$$

where $\pi_t \equiv P_{t+1}/P_t - 1$ is the inflation rate.[7] The agent chooses consumption in the two periods and money holdings (C_1, C_2, m_1) in order to maximize lifetime utility (10.5) subject to (10.27). The Lagrangian for this problem is given by:

$$\mathcal{L} \equiv U(C_1) + \frac{1}{1+\rho} U(C_2) + \lambda_1 \left[Y_1 + \frac{m_0}{1+\pi_0} - C_1 - m_1 \right]$$
$$+ \lambda_2 \left[Y_2 + \frac{m_1}{1+\pi_1} - C_2 \right], \tag{10.28}$$

where λ_1 and λ_2 are the Lagrangian multipliers associated with the two budget restrictions. The first-order conditions are the two budget constraints and:

$$\frac{\partial \mathcal{L}}{\partial C_1} = U'(C_1) - \lambda_1 = 0, \tag{10.29}$$

$$\frac{\partial \mathcal{L}}{\partial C_2} = \frac{1}{1+\rho} U'(C_2) - \lambda_2 = 0, \tag{10.30}$$

$$\frac{\partial \mathcal{L}}{\partial m_1} \equiv -\lambda_1 + \frac{\lambda_2}{1+\pi_1} \leq 0, \quad m_1 \geq 0, \quad m_1 \frac{\partial \mathcal{L}}{\partial m_1} = 0. \tag{10.31}$$

By substituting equations (10.29) and (10.30) into (10.31), the following expression is obtained:

$$\frac{\partial \mathcal{L}}{\partial m_1} \equiv \frac{U'(C_2)}{1+\rho} \cdot \left[\frac{1}{1+\pi_1} - \frac{(1+\rho)U'(C_1)}{U'(C_2)} \right] \leq 0, \tag{10.32}$$

$$m_1 \geq 0, \quad m_1 \frac{\partial \mathcal{L}}{\partial m_1} = 0.$$

The intuition behind (10.32) can be illustrated with the aid of Figure 10.2. The consolidated budget equation (see footnote 7) is drawn as the straight line segment AB with slope $dC_2/dC_1 = -1/(1+\pi_1)$. The indifference curve, V_0, has a slope of $dC_2/dC_1 = -(1+\rho)U'(C_1)/U'(C_2)$ and has a tangency with the budget line at point E^C. This is the privately optimal consumption point ignoring the non-negativity constraint on money holdings. If the income endowment point lies north-west of point E^C, say at E_0^Y, money is of no use as a store of value to the agent. In economic terms, the agent would like to be a net supplier of money in order to attain the consumption point E^C but this is impossible. Graphically, the indifference curve through E_0^Y (the dashed curve) is steeper than the budget line, the choice set is only $AE_0^Y D$, and the best the agent can do is to consume his endowments in the two periods. In mathematical terms, the slope configuration implies that $\partial \mathcal{L}/\partial m_1 < 0$ (lifetime utility rises by supplying money) and complementary slackness results in $m_1 = 0$.

---

[7] If m_1 is strictly positive, the first two expressions in (10.27) can be consolidated:

$$A \equiv Y_1 + (1+\pi_1)Y_2 + \frac{m_0}{1+\pi_0} = C_1 + (1+\pi_1)C_2,$$

which shows that the "implicit interest rate" on money satisfies $1 + r_t^M \equiv 1/(1+\pi_t)$, i.e. $r_t^M \equiv -\pi_t/(1+\pi_t) \approx -\pi_t$.

In the alternative case, for which the income endowment point lies south-east of the consumption point (say at E_1^Y) the agent saves in the first period by holding money and the first expression in (10.32) holds with equality so that the Euler equation becomes:

$$\frac{U'(C_2)}{U'(C_1)} = \frac{1+\rho}{1+r_1^M} = (1+\rho)(1+\pi_1), \tag{10.33}$$

where $r_1^M \equiv 1/(1+\pi_1) - 1$ is the implicit interest rate on money (see footnote 7). The upshot of the discussion so far is that money will be held under certain circumstances because it provides a means by which intertemporal consumption smoothing can be achieved.

Of course, the Bewley approach is rather specific and somewhat unrealistic in that interest-bearing financial instrument are widely available in modern market economies. This fact does not, in and of itself invalidate the argument, however, as the following example, inspired by Sargent and Wallace (1982) reveals. Suppose that there are poor agents (with low income endowments) and rich agents (with high income endowments) in the economy, and assume that both types of agents wish to save in the first period. Suppose furthermore that interest-bearing bonds exist but that they come in minimum denominations, say due to legal restrictions or otherwise, and assume there are no savings banks. In this setting the poor agents save too small an amount to be able to purchase even a single bond and they are thus forced to save by holding money. On the other hand, the rich agents will hold all (or part) of their saving in higher-yielding bonds. Aggregating over all agents in the economy, the indivisibility of bonds results in a positive demand for money to be held as a store of value.

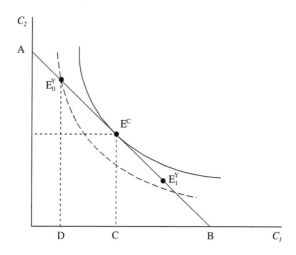

Figure 10.2: Money as a store of value

10.3.1 Overlapping-generations model of money

In the model of the previous section, money is used as a store of value by an individual agent provided there is some friction which prevents him from using higher-yielding assets for this task. The argument is based on a partial equilibrium investigation, and the first task of this section is to embed the notion of money as a store of value in a general equilibrium economy-wide model. Instead of using the legal restrictions argument of Sargent and Wallace (1982), we introduce an *intergenerational friction*, of the type first emphasized by Samuelson (1958), in order to motivate a meaningful role for money. This allows us to introduce and discuss the so-called *overlapping-generations* model of money, which has been extremely influential in modern monetary theory.

At time t the population consists of $N/2$ young agents and $N/2$ old agents and we normalize N to unity to simplify the notation. All agents live for two periods, so the young have two periods to live and the old only one. Agents receive an endowment, Y, when young, but do not have any endowment income when they are old. The output Y is potentially storable and for each unit stored in period t, $1/(1+\delta)$ units of output will be left over in period $t+1$, where $\delta > -1$. This storage technology nests several special cases. Particularly, if $\delta \to \infty$, goods spoil immediately and are thus non-storable. If $\delta = 0$, goods keep indefinitely, and if $-1 < \delta < 0$ goods reproduce without supervision by the storage process.[8]

The (representative) young agent can either consume his output in youth (C_t^Y, where the superscript denotes "young"), store it (K_t of which $K_t/(1+\delta)$ is available in period $t+1$), or trade it for fiat money. Since the money price of output is P_t, the last option yields the agent real money balances at the end of period t ($m_t \equiv M_t/P_t$). The budget identity facing a young agent in his youth is thus:

$$Y = C_t^Y + K_t + m_t. \tag{10.34}$$

Now consider the budget identity of an old agent in period t. This agent stored output in youth (K_{t-1}) as well as nominal money balances (M_{t-1}) with which he can purchase goods, facing the period-t price level (P_t). In addition, the agent receives a real transfer from the government (T_t), the amount of which he takes as given. The budget identity of an old agent is thus:

$$C_t^O = \frac{K_{t-1}}{1+\delta} + T_t + \frac{P_{t-1}}{P_t} m_{t-1}, \tag{10.35}$$

where the superscript denotes "old". But the agent who is young in period t will himself be old in period $t+1$, and will thus face a constraint similar to (10.35) but dated one period later in the last period of his life:

$$C_{t+1}^O = \frac{K_t}{1+\delta} + T_{t+1} + \frac{P_t}{P_{t+1}} m_t. \tag{10.36}$$

The lifetime utility function of the young agent in period t is given by:

$$V_t^Y = U(C_t^Y) + \frac{1}{1+\rho} U(C_{t+1}^O), \quad \rho > 0, \tag{10.37}$$

and the agent chooses C_t^Y, C_{t+1}^O, K_t, and m_t in order to maximize (10.37) subject to (10.34) and (10.36) as well as non-negativity conditions on money holdings and stored output ($M_t \geq 0$ and $K_t \geq 0$, respectively). The Lagrangian is:

$$\mathcal{L} \equiv U(C_t^Y) + \frac{1}{1+\rho} U(C_{t+1}^O) + \lambda_{1,t} \left[Y - C_t^Y - K_t - m_t \right]$$

---

[8]Samuelson gives the examples of rabbits and yeast for this case. In a more serious vein, a negative value for δ captures the notion of net productivity in the economy (1958, p. 468).

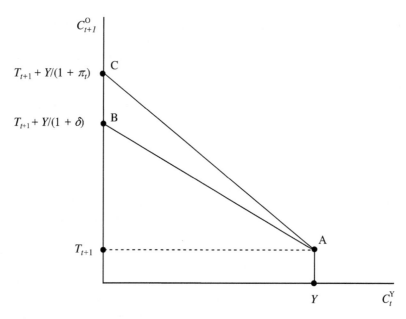

Figure 10.3: Choice set with storage and money

$$+ \lambda_{2,t} \left[\frac{K_t}{1+\delta} + T_{t+1} + \frac{P_t}{P_{t+1}} m_t - C_{t+1}^O \right], \tag{10.38}$$

where $\lambda_{1,t}$ and $\lambda_{2,t}$ are the Lagrangian multipliers of the budget identities in youth and old age respectively. The first-order conditions consist of the budget identities (10.34) and (10.36) and:

$$\frac{\partial \mathcal{L}}{\partial C_t^Y} = U'(C_t^Y) - \lambda_{1,t} = 0, \tag{10.39}$$

$$\frac{\partial \mathcal{L}}{\partial C_{t+1}^O} = \frac{1}{1+\rho} U'(C_{t+1}^O) - \lambda_{2,t} = 0, \tag{10.40}$$

$$\frac{\partial \mathcal{L}}{\partial m_t} \equiv -\lambda_{1,t} + \frac{\lambda_{2,t}}{1+\pi_t} \leq 0, \quad m_t \geq 0, \quad m_t \frac{\partial \mathcal{L}}{\partial m_t} = 0, \tag{10.41}$$

$$\frac{\partial \mathcal{L}}{\partial K_t} \equiv -\lambda_{1,t} + \frac{\lambda_{2,t}}{1+\delta} \leq 0, \quad K_t \geq 0, \quad K_t \frac{\partial \mathcal{L}}{\partial K_t} = 0, \tag{10.42}$$

where $\pi_t \equiv (P_{t+1} - P_t)/P_t = P_{t+1}/P_t - 1$ is the inflation rate. In view of our assumptions regarding the utility function, agents wish to consume in both periods of their lives so that $\lambda_{1,t} > 0$ and $\lambda_{2,t} > 0$. Equations (10.41)–(10.42) imply that, provided $\pi_t \neq \delta$, the young agent will choose a single type of asset to serve as a store of value, depending on which one has the highest yield. Particularly, if inflation is relatively low ($\pi_t < \delta$) then only money will be held ($K_t = 0$ and $m_t > 0$), and if it is relatively high ($\pi_t > \delta$) then only goods will be stored ($K_t > 0$ and $m_t = 0$). In terms of Figure 10.3, in the first case the storage technology is not productive enough and yields a budget line AB which lies below the budget line associated with holding money as a store of value (the line AC). The line configuration is switched in the second case with high inflation ($\pi_t > \delta$).

The behaviour of the old in period t is quite straightforward. Although they entered life (in period $t - 1$) possessing a utility function analogous to (10.37) (and designated by V_{t-1}^Y), their behaviour in period $t-1$ (their youth) constitutes "water under the bridge" in the sense that it cannot be undone in period t (it is irreversible or "sunk" in economic terms). All that remains for them is to maximize remaining lifetime utility, $U(C_t^O)$ subject to the budget identity (10.35). They simply consume their entire budget.

Following Wallace (1980) we assume that the government pursues a simple money supply rule:

$$M_t = (1+\mu)M_{t-1} \qquad \Leftrightarrow \qquad \frac{M_t - M_{t-1}}{M_{t-1}} = \mu, \qquad (10.43)$$

with $\mu > -1$ representing the constant rate of nominal money growth. The additional money is used to finance the transfer to the old, i.e. the government budget restriction is $M_t - M_{t-1} = P_t T_t$ which implies that the transfer in period $t+1$ is:

$$T_{t+1} = \frac{M_{t+1} - M_t}{P_{t+1}} = \frac{\mu M_t}{P_t}\frac{P_t}{P_{t+1}} = \frac{\mu m_t}{1+\pi_t}. \qquad (10.44)$$

Equilibrium in the model requires both money and goods markets to be in equilibrium in all periods. By Walras's Law,[9] however, the goods market is in equilibrium provided the money market is, i.e. provided demand and supply are equated in the money market:

$$m(T_{t+1}, \pi_t) = \frac{M_t}{P_t}, \qquad (10.45)$$

where $m(\cdot)$ is a function, representing the demand for money by the young in period t, which is implied by the first-order conditions (10.39)–(10.42). For example, if the felicity function in (10.37) is logarithmic, $U(x) \equiv \ln x$, then this money demand function has the following form:

$$m_t = \begin{cases} m(T_{t+1}, \pi_t) = \dfrac{Y - (1+\rho)(1+\pi_t)T_{t+1}}{2+\rho} & \text{if } \pi_t < \delta \\ 0 & \text{if } \pi_t > \delta. \end{cases} \qquad (10.46)$$

The model consists of (10.44) and (10.45) and we are looking for a sequence of price levels (P_t, P_{t+1}, etc.) such that the equilibrium condition (10.45) holds for all periods given the postulated money supply process (10.44). For the logarithmic felicity function the solution is quite simple and can be obtained by substituting (10.44) into the first line of (10.46), noting (10.45), and solving for the equilibrium level of real money balances:

$$m_t = \frac{Y}{2+\rho+\mu(1+\rho)} \qquad \Leftrightarrow \qquad P_t = \frac{2+\rho+\mu(1+\rho)}{Y}\cdot M_t. \qquad (10.47)$$

This expression, which is only valid if $\pi_t < \delta$, shows that real money balances are constant so that the price level is proportional to the nominal money supply. Since ρ, μ, and Y are all constant, it follows that the inflation rate is equal to the rate of growth of the money supply ($\pi_t = \mu$):

$$\pi_t \equiv \frac{P_{t+1} - P_t}{P_t} = \frac{\frac{2+\rho+\mu(1+\rho)}{Y}(M_{t+1} - M_t)}{\frac{2+\rho+\mu(1+\rho)}{Y}M_t} = \frac{M_{t+1} - M_t}{M_t} \equiv \mu. \qquad (10.48)$$

---

[9]Walras's Law states that in an economy with n markets, if $n-1$ of these markets are in equilibrium then the n-th market must also be in equilibrium. Another way to put it, the sum of the excess demand functions over all n market must sum to zero. See Patinkin (1987) for a further discussion.

So we reach the conclusion that, provided the money growth rate μ is less than the depreciation rate δ, intrinsically useless fiat money will be held by agents in a general equilibrium setting. Intuitively, money is the best available financial instrument to serve as a store of value as it outperforms the storage technology in that case. Of course, if the storage technology yields net productivity ($\delta < 0$) then the monetary equilibrium will only obtain if the money growth rate is negative ($\mu < \delta < 0$), i.e. if there is a constant rate of deflation of the price level. In contrast, if goods are perishable ($\delta \to \infty$) then the monetary equilibrium will always hold since money represents the only store of value in that case.

The existence of a monetary equilibrium is quite tenuous in the overlapping-generations model. Indeed, if $\mu > \delta$ then the storage technology outperforms money as a store of value and consequently the demand for real money balances will be zero (see the second line in (10.46)). Despite the fact that fiat money exists ($M_t > 0$) and is distributed to agents in the economy, it is not used by these agents as a store of value. This implies that money is valueless and the nominal price level is infinite, i.e. $1/P_t = 0$ for all t.

10.3.2 Uncertainty and the demand for money

In the basic model discussed in section 10.2.1 above, the respective yields on money and bonds are known by the agent who consequently only has to compare these yields in order to decide upon the optimal instrument to use as a store of value. In the basic model the yield on bonds is higher than that on money so that only the former are used as a store of value. In this section we introduce a friction into the basic model by assuming that the yield on bonds (though higher on average than that on money) is not known with certainty by the agent when making his decisions regarding consumption and saving in the first period. Sandmo (1970, p. 353) refers to this situation as one in which there exists *capital risk*; the investor is uncertain as to the yield on his investment. We assume that endowment income in both periods is known with certainty (there is no *income risk*). Furthermore, the yield on money is known with certainty so that money constitutes a "safe" asset from the point of view of the investor. To simplify the notation somewhat we define the yield on money as $1 + r_t^M \equiv 1/(1 + \pi_t)$. The periodic budget identities (10.1)–(10.2) can then be expressed in real terms as:

$$Y_1^* + \left(1 + r_0^M\right) m_0 + (1 + r_0) b_0 = C_1 + m_1 + b_1, \tag{10.49}$$

$$(1 + r_1^M) m_1 + (1 + \tilde{r}_1) b_1 = \tilde{C}_2, \tag{10.50}$$

where we have already incorporated the fact that $m_2 = b_2 = 0$ and we use a slightly different definition for $m_1 \equiv M_1/P_1 + Y_2/\left(1 + r_1^M\right)$. (We continue to refer to m_1 as money.) Note that Y_1^* represents the present value of present and future endowment income, capitalized at the risk-free rate, i.e. $Y_1^* \equiv Y_1 + Y_2/(1 + r_1^M)$. The tilde above r_1 denotes that the yield on bonds is a stochastic variable, the realization of which (r_1) will only be known to the agent at the end of the first period, i.e. after consumption and savings plans have been made (C_1, m_1, b_1).[10] This means (by (10.50)) that consumption in the second period is also a stochastic variable, i.e. $\tilde{C}_2$ appears in (10.50). In the terminology of Drèze and Modigliani (1972, p. 309) the model implies

---

[10]Of course, r_0 is not stochastic as it is a realization of $\tilde{r}_0$ which is known at the beginning of the first period.

that investing in bonds represents a *temporal uncertain prospect*, i.e. time must elapse before the uncertainty is removed.

Below it will turn out to be useful to write the budget identities (10.49)–(10.50) in a slightly different manner:

$$Y_1^* + A_1 = C_1 + \frac{\tilde{A}_2}{(1 + r_1^M)\omega_1 + (1 + \tilde{r}_1)(1 - \omega_1)}, \tag{10.51}$$

$$\tilde{A}_2 = \tilde{C}_2, \tag{10.52}$$

where $A_t \equiv (1 + r_{t-1}^M)m_{t-1} + (1 + r_{t-1})b_{t-1}$ represents total assets inclusive of interest receipts available at the beginning of period t and where $\omega_1 \equiv m_1/(m_1 + b_1)$ represents the portfolio share of money in the second period. In the first period the agent chooses consumption C_1 and the portfolio share ω_1, not knowing how high the value of his assets will be at the beginning of the second period because the yield on the risky investment is uncertain.

Since $\tilde{r}_1$ (and thus $\tilde{C}_2$ and $\tilde{A}_2$) is stochastic, the agent must somehow evaluate the utility value of the uncertain prospect $\tilde{C}_2$. The theory of *expected utility*, which was developed by von Neumann and Morgenstern (1944), postulates (as indeed its name suggests) that the agent will evaluate the expected utility in order to make his optimal decision, i.e. instead of using V in (10.5) as the welfare indicator the agent uses the expected value of V, denoted by $E(V)$.[11] We assume that the agent bases his decisions on a subjective assessment of the probability distribution of the yield on his investment, the density function of which is given by $f(\tilde{r}_1)$. We furthermore assume that $\tilde{r}_1$ is restricted to lie in the interval $[-1, \infty)$, with the lower bound representing "losing your entire investment principal and all" and the upper bound denoting "striking it lucky by hitting the jackpot". Finally, we assume that the parameters of the model and the stochastic process for $\tilde{r}_1$ are such that we can ignore the non-negativity constraint for money holdings. Since there is no sign restriction on bond holdings, this means that we only need to study an internal optimum.

The expected utility of the agent can now be written as follows:

$$E(V) \equiv \int_{-1}^{\infty} \left[U(C_1) + \frac{1}{1 + \rho} U(\tilde{C}_2) \right] f(\tilde{r}_1) d\tilde{r}_1$$

$$= U(C_1) + \frac{1}{1 + \rho} \cdot \int_{-1}^{\infty} U\left(S_1 \left[(1 + r_1^M)\omega_1 + (1 + \tilde{r}_1)(1 - \omega_1) \right] \right) f(\tilde{r}_1) d\tilde{r}_1, \tag{10.53}$$

where $S_1 \equiv A_1 + Y_1^* - C_1$. The agent chooses C_1 (and thus S_1) and ω_1 in order to maximize his expected utility, $E(V)$. Straightforward computation yields the following first-order conditions for ω_1:

$$0 = \int_{-1}^{\infty} U'(\tilde{C}_2)(A_1 + Y_1^* - C_1)(r_1^M - \tilde{r}_1)f(\tilde{r}_1)d\tilde{r}_1 \Leftrightarrow$$

$$0 = E\left(U'(\tilde{C}_2)(A_1 + Y_1^* - C_1)(r_1^M - \tilde{r}_1) \right), \tag{10.54}$$

and for C_1:

$$U'(C_1) = \frac{1}{1 + \rho} \cdot \int_{-1}^{\infty} U'(\tilde{C}_2) \left[(1 + r_1^M)\omega_1 + (1 + \tilde{r}_1)(1 - \omega_1) \right] f(\tilde{r}_1)d\tilde{r}_1 \Leftrightarrow$$

---

[11]The expected utility theory is discussed in more detail by Hirshleifer and Riley (1992).

$$U'(C_1) = \frac{1}{1+\rho} \cdot E\left(U'(\tilde{C}_2)\left[(1+r_1^M)\omega_1 + (1+\tilde{r}_1)(1-\omega_1)\right]\right). \tag{10.55}$$

Technically, (10.54) is the expression determining the optimal composition of the investment portfolio in terms of money (which has a certain yield r_1^M) and bonds (carrying a stochastic yield $\tilde{r}_1$). Intuitively (10.54) says that the expected marginal utility per euro invested should be equated for the two assets (see Sandmo, 1969, pp. 588, 590). Equation (10.55) is the Euler equation, determining the optimal time profile of consumption, generalized for the existence of capital uncertainty.

In order to simplify the discussion, we now assume that the agent has a felicity function, $U(C_t)$, which takes the following, iso-elastic form:

$$U(C_t) = \begin{cases} (1/\gamma)\left[C_t^\gamma - 1\right] & \text{if } \gamma \neq 0 \\ \ln C_t & \text{if } \gamma = 0, \end{cases} \tag{10.56}$$

where $\gamma < 1$ represents the *degree of risk aversion* exhibited by the agent (see below). (The function is called iso-elastic because the *marginal* utility function, $U'(C_1) \equiv C_t^{\gamma-1}$, features a constant elasticity, which we define as $\theta(C_t) \equiv -\frac{U''(C_t)C_t}{U'(C_t)} = 1 - \gamma$.) The first-order condition for ω_1 (given in (10.54)) collapses to:

$$0 = E\left[\tilde{C}_2^{\gamma-1}(A_1 + Y_1^* - C_1)(r_1^M - \tilde{r}_1)\right]$$
$$= E\left[(A_1 + Y_1^* - C_1)^\gamma\left[(1+r_1^M)\omega_1 + (1+\tilde{r}_1)(1-\omega_1)\right]^{\gamma-1}(r_1^M - \tilde{r}_1)\right]$$
$$= E\left[\left[(1+r_1^M)\omega_1 + (1+\tilde{r}_1)(1-\omega_1)\right]^{\gamma-1}(r_1^M - \tilde{r}_1)\right]. \tag{10.57}$$

In going from the first to the second line we have substituted the expression for $\tilde{C}_2$ from (10.50), and in the final step we have made use of the fact that A_1, C_1, and Y_1^* are non-stochastic variables. Equation (10.57) implicitly determines the optimal portfolio share, ω_1^*, as a function of r_1^M, γ, and parameters characterizing the probability distribution of $\tilde{r}_1$. The important thing to note is that ω_1^* maximizes the subjective mean return on the portfolio, r^*, which is defined (implicitly) as:

$$(1+r^*)^\gamma \equiv \max_{\omega_1} E\left[(1+r_1^M)\omega_1 + (1+\tilde{r}_1)(1-\omega_1)\right]^\gamma$$
$$= E\left(\left[(1+r_1^M)\omega_1^* + (1+\tilde{r}_1)(1-\omega_1^*)\right]^\gamma\right). \tag{10.58}$$

For the iso-elastic felicity function (10.56), the first-order condition for C_1 (given in (10.55)) collapses to:

$$C_1^{\gamma-1} = (1+\rho)^{-1}E\left(\tilde{C}_2^{\gamma-1}\left[(1+r_1^M)\omega_1 + (1+\tilde{r}_1)(1-\omega_1)\right]\right)$$
$$= (1+\rho)^{-1}(A_1 + Y_1^* - C_1)^{\gamma-1}E\left[(1+r_1^M)\omega_1 + (1+\tilde{r}_1)(1-\omega_1)\right]^\gamma$$
$$= (1+\rho)^{-1}(A_1 + Y_1^* - C_1)^{\gamma-1}(1+r^*)^\gamma$$
$$\Rightarrow \quad C_1 = c\left[A_1 + Y_1^*\right], \tag{10.59}$$

where c is the marginal propensity to consume out of total wealth:

$$c \equiv \frac{(1+r^*)^{\gamma/(\gamma-1)}}{(1+\rho)^{1/(\gamma-1)} + (1+r^*)^{\gamma/(\gamma-1)}}. \tag{10.60}$$

In going from the second to the third line in (10.59) we have made use of the expression for r^* in (10.58). The striking thing to note about (10.59)–(10.60) is that the optimal consumption plan for the first period looks very much like the solution that would be obtained under certainty. Indeed, in the absence of uncertainty about the bond yield, maximization of lifetime utility would give rise to the expression in (10.59)–(10.60) but with r^* replaced by $\max[\bar{r}_1, r_1^M]$, where $\bar{r}_1$ is the certain return on bonds. All is invested in the asset with the highest return in that case. Furthermore, in the case of a logarithmic felicity function ($\gamma = 0$), r^* drops out of (10.59)–(10.60) altogether and the capital risk does not affect present consumption at all (see Blanchard and Fischer (1989, p. 285) on this point).

With iso-elastic felicity functions, there thus exists a "separability property" between the savings problem (choosing when to consume) and the portfolio problem (choosing what to use as a savings instrument).[12] Since (as we shall see in subsequent chapters) modern macroeconomics makes almost exclusive use of such felicity functions, it is instructive to turn to a more detailed discussion of the pure portfolio problem. In doing so, we are not only able to characterize more precisely the factors influencing the choice of money versus bonds but it also allows us to introduce the liquidity preference theory of money that was developed by Tobin (1958). This so-called portfolio approach to money played a major role in macroeconomics in the 1960s and 1970s.

10.3.2.1   The portfolio decision

An important implication of the theory discussed above is that for a certain class of felicity functions, the expected-utility-maximizing household wishes to consume a fraction c of total wealth whilst saving the remaining fraction $1 - c$. Designating the amount to be invested by $S_1 = (1 - c)[A_1 + Y_1^*]$, the budget equation for the portfolio problem is $S_1 = m_1 + b_1$ and the household wishes to choose m_1 and b_1 such as to maximize expected utility of end-of-period wealth (to be consumed in the future), $E(U(\tilde{A}_2))$, where $\tilde{A}_2 \equiv S_1[(1 + r_1^M)\omega_1 + (1 + \tilde{r}_1)(1 - \omega_1)]$.

Stepping back somewhat from the specifics of our two-period model, the general form of the portfolio problem as analysed by Tobin (1958) and Arrow (1965) takes exactly this form. The investor chooses the portfolio share of money ω in order to maximize expected utility:

$$E(U(\tilde{Z})), \quad \tilde{Z} \equiv S\left[(1 + r^M)\omega + (1 + \tilde{r})(1 - \omega)\right], \tag{10.61}$$

where $\tilde{Z}$ is end-of-period wealth, S is the amount to be invested, and r^M is the risk-free rate (S and r^M are both exogenously given parameters). The first-order condition for this problem is:

$$E(U'(\tilde{Z}) \cdot (r^M - \tilde{r})) = 0. \tag{10.62}$$

Apart from a slight change of notation, equation (10.62) coincides with the first-order condition for ω_1 in the two-period model (see (10.54) above).

In order to further develop some intuition behind the first-order condition (10.62) we now turn to the *mean-variance model*, which can be seen as an approximation to

---

[12]This was first demonstrated by Samuelson (1969a, pp. 243–245) in a multi-period discrete-time setting and generalized to continuous time for a more general class of felicity functions by Merton (1971). See also the discussion by Drèze and Modigliani (1972, pp. 317–323) on the separability property in the context of a two-period model with both capital and income risk.

(or special case of) the model discussed so far.[13] The first step in the argument is to expand the utility function, $U(\tilde{Z})$, by means of a Taylor approximation around the expected value (or mean) of $\tilde{Z}$, denoted by $E(\tilde{Z})$:

$$U(\tilde{Z}) \approx U(E(\tilde{Z})) + U'(E(\tilde{Z})) \left[\tilde{Z} - E(\tilde{Z})\right] + \tfrac{1}{2}U''(E(\tilde{Z})) \left[\tilde{Z} - E(\tilde{Z})\right]^2$$
$$+ \tfrac{1}{6}U'''(E(\tilde{Z})) \left[\tilde{Z} - E(\tilde{Z})\right]^3 + \cdots. \tag{10.63}$$

Taking expectations on both sides of (10.63) yields the (approximate) expression for expected utility:

$$E(U(\tilde{Z})) \approx E(U(E(\tilde{Z}))) + E(U'(E(\tilde{Z})) \cdot [\tilde{Z} - E(\tilde{Z})])$$
$$+ \tfrac{1}{2}E(U''(E(\tilde{Z})) \cdot [\tilde{Z} - E(\tilde{Z})]^2) + \cdots$$
$$= U(E(\tilde{Z})) + \tfrac{1}{2}U''(E(\tilde{Z})) \cdot E([\tilde{Z} - E(\tilde{Z})]^2) + \cdots. \tag{10.64}$$

In going from the first to the second line in (10.64) we use the fact that the expected value of a constant is that constant itself. The expected utility associated with end-of-period wealth can thus be approximated by the utility of expected wealth (first term on the right-hand side in the second line), a term involving the variance of end-of-period wealth (second term), plus higher-order terms subsumed in the dots.

The second step in the argument amounts to ignoring all higher-order terms in (10.64) so that preferences of the investor are (assumed to be) fully described by only the mean and the variance of end-of-period wealth; hence the name of the mean-variance approach. In summary, we write expected utility as:

$$E(U(\tilde{Z})) = U(E(\tilde{Z})) - \eta E([\tilde{Z} - E(\tilde{Z})]^2), \tag{10.65}$$

where $\eta \equiv -\tfrac{1}{2}U''(E(\tilde{Z}))$. The sign of η fully characterizes the investor's attitude towards risk. Indeed, if $\eta = 0$, the variance term drops out of (10.65) altogether and the investor is only interested in the expected value of end-of-period wealth. Such an investor, who totally disregards the variance of end-of-period wealth, is called *risk neutral*. In the remainder of this section we focus attention on the portfolio behaviour of risk-averse investors, the case described by $\eta > 0$.

Intermezzo 10.1

Attitude to risk. The shape of the felicity function affects the investor's attitude to risk. For a risk neutral investor, the underlying utility function, $U(\tilde{Z})$, is simply a straight line from the origin ($U'(\tilde{Z}) > 0$ and $U''(\tilde{Z}) = 0$ in this case)–see Figure A.

In real life, most people do care whether the return they receive is certain (has a zero variance) or is subject to fluctuations and can be much higher or lower than expected (has a positive variance). *Risk-averse* investors are therefore characterized by a positive value of η. In terms of Figure A, a risk-averse investor has an underlying utility function which is concave ($U'(\tilde{Z}) > 0$ and $U''(\tilde{Z}) < 0$). In order to take on additional risk (a "bad" rather than a good) a risk-averse agent must be compensated in the form of a higher expected return, i.e. he must receive a *risk*

---

[13]See Hirshleifer and Riley (1992, pp. 69–73) for a further discussion.

premium. In formal terms the risk-premium, π_R, is such that the agent is indifferent between the risky prospect $\tilde{Z}$ and the certain prospect $E(\tilde{Z})$ (see Pratt, 1964):

$$U(E(\tilde{Z}) - \pi_R) = E(U(\tilde{Z})). \qquad \text{(a)}$$

In general π_R depends on the distribution of $\tilde{Z}$ but a simple example can be used to illustrate what is going on. Suppose that the distribution of $\tilde{Z}$ is such that $\tilde{Z} = Z_0 - h$ (point A) or $\tilde{Z} = Z_0 + h$ (point B) with equal probability $\frac{1}{2}$ so that $E(\tilde{Z}) = Z_0$. The risk premium associated with this distribution is found by applying equation (a).

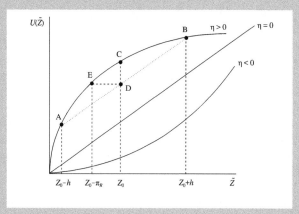

Figure A: Attitude towards risk and the felicity function

In terms of Figure A, the right-hand side of equation (a) is represented by point D which lies halfway along the straight line connecting points A and B. Concavity of the utility function ensures that the utility of the expected outcome, $U(E(\tilde{Z})) = U(Z_0)$, is higher than expected utility, $E(U(\tilde{Z}))$, i.e. point C lies above point D. To find the risk premium we must determine the certain prospect $(Z_0 - \pi_R)$ such that equation (a) holds. In Figure A this is done by going to point E, which lies directly to the left of point D. The horizontal distance between points D and E represents the risk premium π_R. In order to feel indifferent between, on the one hand, receiving $Z_0 - \pi_R$ for sure and, on the other hand, receiving $Z_0 - h$ or $Z_0 + h$ with equal probability, the risk-averse investor must receive a risk premium equal to π_R.

The third type of agent is also described by (10.65) but with a negative value for η inserted. Such an agent is called a *risk-lover* because he prefers an uncertain over a certain outcome when both have equal expected value. He thus enjoys the thrill of a gamble and, in view of equation (a), is willing to pay (rather than receive) a risk premium. In terms of Figure A, a risk-lover has a convex underlying utility function ($U'(\tilde{Z}) > 0$ and $U''(\tilde{Z}) > 0$).

****

Up to this point, we have described the agent's expected utility in terms of the variable $\tilde{Z}$ which is stochastic only because the return on the risky asset, $\tilde{r}$, is. Hence, the next step in our exposition of the mean-variance approach consists of postulating a particular probability distribution for $\tilde{r}$. A particularly simple and convenient distribution to choose in this context is the normal distribution:

$$\tilde{r} \sim N(\bar{r}, \sigma_R^2), \tag{10.66}$$

where "$\sim$" means "is distributed as", "N" stands for "normal or Gaussian distribution", $\bar{r}$ is the mean of the distribution, and σ_R^2 its variance. The advantage of working with the normal distribution lies in the fact that it is fully characterized by only two parameters, $\bar{r}$ and σ_R^2. All higher-order uneven terms, such as $E(\tilde{r} - \bar{r})^i$ (for $i = 3, 5, 7, \cdots$) are equal to zero as the distribution is symmetric around its mean. Furthermore, the higher-order even terms, such as $E(\tilde{r} - \bar{r})^i$ (for $i = 4, 6, 8, \cdots$) can be expressed in terms of $\bar{r}$ and σ_R^2 (Hirshleifer and Riley, 1992, p. 72). This implies that (10.64) can always be written as in (10.65) even without ignoring the higher-order terms, i.e. preferences are fully described by only two parameters. Another advantage of using the normal distribution is that it enables us to conduct simple comparative static experiments pertaining to $\bar{r}$ and σ_R^2 and the optimal portfolio choice below.

Armed with the distributional assumption in (10.66), the probability distribution of end-of-period wealth can be determined by noting the definition of $\tilde{Z}$ in (10.61). After some manipulation we derive that $\tilde{Z}$ is distributed normally (i.e. $\tilde{Z} \sim N(\bar{Z}, \sigma_Z^2)$) with parameters depending on the portfolio fraction of money ω:

$$\begin{aligned} \bar{Z} &\equiv E(\tilde{Z}) = S\left[(1 + r^M)\omega + (1 + \bar{r})(1 - \omega)\right], \\ \sigma_Z^2 &\equiv E([\tilde{Z} - E(\tilde{Z})]^2) = S^2(1 - \omega)^2 \sigma_R^2. \end{aligned} \tag{10.67}$$

By manipulating the portfolio share of money, the investor can influence both the expected value of, and the risk associated with, end-of-period wealth. For example, if only money is held in the portfolio ($\omega = 1$), end-of-period wealth equals $S(1 + r^M)$ for sure ($\sigma_Z = 0$). This determines point A in Figure 10.4. The top panel of that figure plots combinations of expected return (vertical axis) and risk (horizontal axis), whilst the lower panel plots the relationship between risk and the portfolio share of money.[14] At the other extreme, if no money is held at all ($\omega = 0$), expected end-of-period wealth equals $S(1 + \bar{r})$ and the standard deviation is $\sigma_Z = S\sigma_R$ (see point B). In order to have any non-trivial solution at all, the mean return on the risky asset must exceed that on money, otherwise a risk-averse agent would never hold any risky assets. Hence, $\bar{r} > r^M$ must be assumed to hold. This in turn ensures that point B lies north-east of point A in the top panel of Figure 10.4. By connecting points A and B in the top panel we obtain the upward-sloping constraint representing feasible trade-off opportunities between average return and risk. In the lower panel, σ_Z and ω are related by the second definition in (10.67) which can be rewritten as $1 - \omega = \sigma_Z / (\sigma_R S)$.

The final step in our exposition of the mean-variance model consists of introducing the appropriate indifference curve. According to (10.65), expected utility depends on both $\bar{r}$ and σ_R^2 and the indifference curve satisfies $dE(U(\tilde{Z})) = U'(\bar{Z})d\bar{Z} - 2\eta\sigma_Z d\sigma_Z = 0$ from which we derive:

$$\frac{d\bar{Z}}{d\sigma_Z} = \frac{2\eta\sigma_Z}{U'(\bar{Z})} > 0, \quad \frac{d^2\bar{Z}}{d\sigma_Z^2} = 2\eta\left[\frac{U'(\bar{Z}) - \sigma_Z U''(\bar{Z})(d\bar{Z}/d\sigma_Z)}{[U'(\bar{Z})]^2}\right] > 0. \tag{10.68}$$

---

[14]It is convenient to work with the standard deviation of $\tilde{Z}$ (rather than its variance) because it is in the same units as the mean of $\tilde{Z}$ which facilitates the economic interpretation to follow.

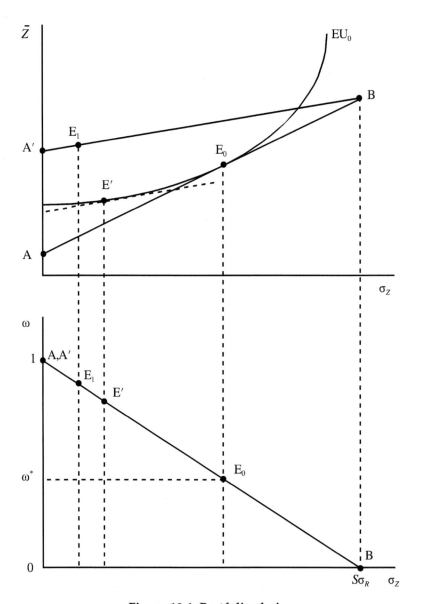

Figure 10.4: Portfolio choice

Hence, the typical indifference curve of a risk-averse agent is upward sloping and convex ($U'(\bar{Z}) > 0 > U''(\bar{Z})$); see for example the curve labelled EU_0 in the top panel in Figure 10.4. Since expected return is a "good" and risk is a "bad" for such an agent, expected utility increases if the indifference curve shifts in a north-westerly direction.

It is clear from the slope configuration in Figure 10.4 that a risk-averse investor will typically choose a *diversified portfolio*.[15] Rather than choosing the safe haven of only money (point A) it is optimal for him to "trade risk for return", i.e. to accept some risk by holding a proportion of his portfolio in the form of the risky asset. In exchange the investor receives a higher expected yield on his portfolio. In Figure 10.4 the optimum occurs at point E_0 where the indifference curve is tangential to the budget line.[16] In technical terms we have:

$$\left(\frac{d\bar{Z}}{d\sigma_Z}\right)_{IC} \equiv \frac{2\eta\sigma_Z}{U'(\bar{Z})} = \frac{\bar{r} - r^M}{\sigma_R} \equiv \left(\frac{d\bar{Z}}{d\sigma_Z}\right)_{BL}. \tag{10.69}$$

The left-hand side of (10.69) represents the slope of the indifference curve (subscript "IC") whereas the right-hand side is the slope of the budget line (subscript "BL").

Although (10.69) looks different from (10.62), it is not difficult to show that the former is merely a special case of the latter. Implicitly we work with a second-order expansion of utility, i.e. all cubic, quartic, and higher-order terms are ignored in (10.63) and we employ the utility function:

$$U(\tilde{Z}) \approx U(\bar{Z}) + U'(\bar{Z})[\tilde{Z} - \bar{Z}] - \eta[\tilde{Z} - \bar{Z}]^2, \tag{10.70}$$

so that marginal utility can be written as $U'(\tilde{Z}) \equiv dU(\tilde{Z})/d\tilde{Z} = U'(\bar{Z}) - 2\eta[\tilde{Z} - \bar{Z}]$ (recall that $\bar{Z}$, $U(\bar{Z})$, and $U'(\bar{Z})$ are constants). Equation (10.62) can thus be rewritten as:

$$
\begin{aligned}
0 &= E(U'(\tilde{Z}) \cdot (r_M - \tilde{r})) \\
&= E\left([U'(\bar{Z}) - 2\eta(\tilde{Z} - \bar{Z})] \cdot \left[\left(r^M - \bar{r}\right) - (\tilde{r} - \bar{r})\right]\right) \\
&= U'(\bar{Z})\left(r^M - \bar{r}\right) - U'(\bar{Z})E(\tilde{r} - \bar{r}) - 2\eta\left(r^M - \bar{r}\right)E(\tilde{Z} - \bar{Z}) \\
&\quad + 2\eta E((\tilde{Z} - \bar{Z})(\tilde{r} - \bar{r})) \\
&= U'(\bar{Z})\left(r^M - \bar{r}\right) + 2\eta\,\mathrm{cov}(\tilde{Z}, \tilde{r}), \tag{10.71}
\end{aligned}
$$

where we have used $E(\tilde{Z}) = \bar{Z}$ and $E(\tilde{r}) = \bar{r}$ in going from the third to the fourth line and where $\mathrm{cov}(\tilde{Z}, \tilde{r})$ is the covariance between $\tilde{Z}$ and $\tilde{r}$. In view of the definition of $\tilde{Z}$ in (10.62) we find that $\mathrm{cov}(\tilde{Z}, \tilde{r}) = S(1 - \omega)\sigma_R^2 = \sigma_Z\sigma_R$. By using this result in (10.71) we find that (10.71) (and thus (10.62)) coincides with (10.69).

Returning now to Figure 10.4, it is clear that a risk-averse agent will hold money even if its return is zero ($r^M = 0$) because it represents a riskless means of investing (at least, under the present set of assumptions). By going to the lower panel of Figure 10.4, the optimal portfolio share of money, ω^*, can be found which implies that the demand for money equals $\omega^* S$. Although S is given, ω^* (and hence money demand) depends on all the parameters of the model such as the yield on money, the mean and variance of the yield on bonds, and the preference parameter(s):

$$\omega^* = \omega^*(r^M, \bar{r}, \sigma_R^2, \eta). \tag{10.72}$$

---

[15]For a discussion of possible corner solutions, see Tobin (1958, pp. 77–78).

[16]The budget line is given by $\bar{Z} = S \cdot [1 + \bar{r} + \omega(r^M - \bar{r})]$ which can be written in terms of σ_Z by noting that $1 - \omega = \sigma_Z/(\sigma_R S)$.

The conventional method of comparative statics can now be used to determine the partial derivatives of the $\omega^*(\cdot)$ function.

The easiest way to derive these comparative static effects is to write the portfolio choice directly in terms of ω. The expected utility function is given by:

$$E(U(\tilde{Z})) = U(\bar{Z}) - \eta E([\tilde{Z} - \bar{Z}]^2),$$
$$= U\left(S\left[(1 + r^M)\omega + (1 + \bar{r})(1 - \omega)\right]\right) - \eta S^2(1 - \omega)^2 \sigma_R^2, \qquad (10.73)$$

where we have used (10.67) to arrive at the final expression. The first- and second-order conditions for the optimal portfolio decision are:

$$\frac{dE(U(\tilde{Z}))}{d\omega} = -U'(\bar{Z})S\left(\bar{r} - r^M\right) + 2\eta S^2(1 - \omega)\sigma_R^2 = 0, \qquad (10.74)$$

$$\frac{d^2E(U(\tilde{Z}))}{d\omega^2} = -2\eta S^2\left[\left(\bar{r} - r^M\right)^2 + \sigma_R^2\right] < 0, \qquad (10.75)$$

where we have used the fact that $U''(\bar{Z}) = -2\eta$. We write the first-order condition (10.74)—defining the optimal ω^*—as:

$$\Phi\left(\omega^*, r^M, \bar{r}, \sigma_R^2, \eta\right) \equiv -U'\left(S\left[(1 + r^M)\omega^* + (1 + \bar{r})(1 - \omega^*)\right]\right)S\left(\bar{r} - r^M\right)$$
$$+ 2\eta S^2(1 - \omega^*)\sigma_R^2 = 0, \qquad (10.76)$$

and note (from (10.75)) that $\partial\Phi/\partial\omega^* < 0$. Equation (10.76) can now be used to compute the comparative static effects.

First consider the effects of an increase in the yield on money r^M (i.e. a reduction in the inflation rate). By using the implicit function theorem we obtain from (10.76):

$$\frac{\partial\omega^*}{\partial r^M} = -\frac{\partial\Phi/\partial r^M}{\partial\Phi/\partial\omega^*} = \frac{SU'(\bar{Z}) + 2\eta\omega^*S^2\left(\bar{r} - r^M\right)}{2\eta S^2\left[(\bar{r} - r^M)^2 + \sigma_R^2\right]} > 0. \qquad (10.77)$$

In terms of Figure 10.4, the budget line shifts up and becomes flatter; see the line A'B in the top panel. We get the result, familiar from conventional microeconomic demand theory, that the ultimate effect on the portfolio share of money (and thus money demand) can be decomposed into income and pure substitution effects. On the one hand, an increase in r^M narrows the yield gap between money and the risky asset which induces the investor to substitute towards the safe asset and to hold a higher portfolio share of money. This is the pure substitution effect represented in Figure 10.4 by the move from E_0 to E'. On the other hand, an increase in r^M also increases expected wealth and the resulting income (or wealth) effect also leads to an upward shift in ω. Hence, both income and substitution effects work in the same direction and the new optimum lies at point E_1, where the move from E' to E_1 represents the income effect.

In formal terms, the total effect on ω^* of an increase in r^M can be expressed in the form of a conventional Slutsky equation:[17]

$$\frac{\partial\omega^*}{\partial r^M} = \left(\frac{\partial\omega^*}{\partial r^M}\right)_{dE(U)=0} + \omega^*S \cdot \frac{\partial\omega^*}{\partial\bar{Z}} > 0, \qquad (10.78)$$

---

[17]Sandmo (1977) derives comparative static effects for the more general case with one safe asset and many risky assets.

where the first term on the right-hand side represents the pure substitution or "compensated" effect and the second term is the income effect. These terms take the following form:[18]

$$\left(\frac{\partial \omega^*}{\partial r^M}\right)_{dE(U)=0} \equiv \frac{(1-\omega^*)\sigma_R^2}{(\bar{r}-r^M)\left[(r^M-\bar{r})^2+\sigma_R^2\right]} > 0, \tag{10.79}$$

$$\frac{\partial \omega^*}{\partial \bar{Z}} \equiv \frac{\bar{r}-r^M}{S\left[\sigma_R^2+(r^M-\bar{r})^2\right]} > 0. \tag{10.80}$$

The second, much more interesting, comparative static experiment concerns the effect on the money portfolio share of an increase in the expected yield on the risky asset. Throughout this book we have made use of money demand functions which are downward sloping in "the" interest rate, i.e. in terms of our model we have implicitly assumed that $\partial \omega^*/\partial \bar{r}$ is negative. The question is now whether this result is actually necessarily true in our model. In terms of Figure 10.5, an increase in $\bar{r}$ causes the budget line to rotate in a counter-clockwise fashion around point A. In contrast to the previous case, income and substitution effects now operate in opposite directions and the Slutsky equation becomes:

$$\frac{\partial \omega^*}{\partial \bar{r}} = \left(\frac{\partial \omega^*}{\partial \bar{r}}\right)_{dE(U)=0} + (1-\omega^*)S \cdot \frac{\partial \omega^*}{\partial \bar{Z}} \gtrless 0, \tag{10.81}$$

where $(\partial \omega^*/\partial \bar{r})_{dE(U)=0} = -(\partial \omega^*/\partial r^M)_{dE(U)=0} < 0$ and where $\partial \omega^*/\partial \bar{Z} > 0$ (see (10.80)). In terms of Figure 10.5, the pure substitution effect is the move from E_0 to E' and the income effect is the move from E' to E_1^1 if the substitution effect dominates or E_1^2 if the income effect dominates. It is thus quite possible that money demand depends positively on the expected yield on the risky asset in the portfolio model of Tobin (1958). Under the usual assumption of a dominant substitution effect (which we have employed time and again throughout this book), however, the portfolio approach does indeed deliver a downward-sloping money demand function as postulated by Keynes and his followers.

The third and final comparative static experiment concerns the effect on money demand of the degree of risk associated with the risky asset as measured by the standard deviation of the yield, σ_R. In terms of Figure 10.6, a number of things happen if σ_R rises. First, in the top panel the budget line becomes flatter and rotates in a clockwise fashion around point A. In order to get the same expected return, the investor must be willing to hold a riskier portfolio, i.e. to accept a higher value of σ_Z.

---

[18]These expressions are obtained as follows. First, we use (10.74) to rewrite the uncompensated effect (10.77) as:

$$\frac{\partial \omega^*}{\partial r^M} = \frac{(1-\omega^*)\sigma_R^2+\omega^*\left(\bar{r}-r^M\right)^2}{(\bar{r}-r^M)\left[(\bar{r}-r^M)^2+\sigma_R^2\right]}. \tag{A}$$

Next we note that the income effect on ω^* can be determined by writing (10.76) as:

$$\Phi\left(\omega^*,r^M,\bar{r},\sigma_R^2,\eta\right) \equiv -U'(\bar{Z})S\left(\bar{r}-r^M\right)+2\eta S^2(1-\omega^*)\sigma_R^2 = 0,$$

from which we derive:

$$\frac{\partial \omega^*}{\partial \bar{Z}} = -\frac{\partial \Phi/\partial \bar{Z}}{\partial \Phi/\partial \omega^*} = \frac{\bar{r}-r^M}{S\left[(\bar{r}-r^M)^2+\sigma_R^2\right]}. \tag{B}$$

Using (A) and (B) in (10.77) we obtain (10.79).

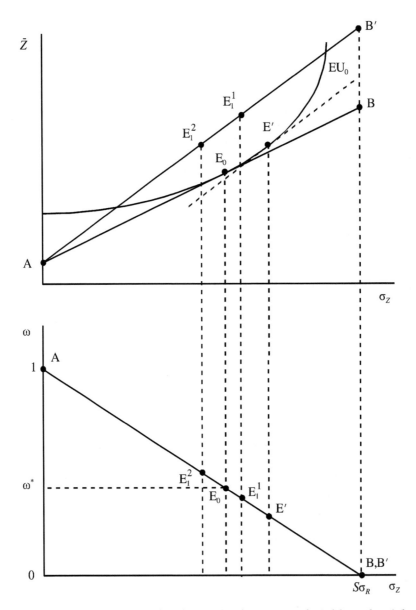

Figure 10.5: Portfolio choice and a change in the expected yield on the risky asset

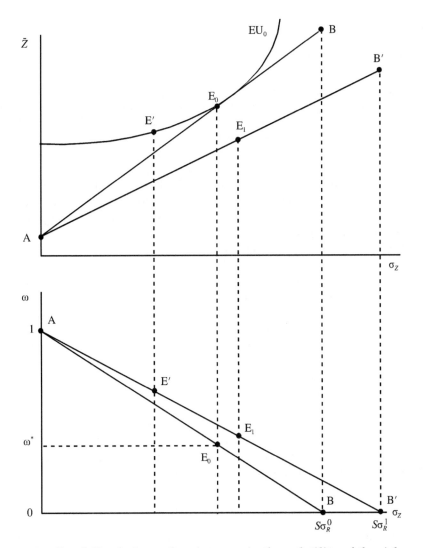

Figure 10.6: Portfolio choice and an increase in the volatility of the risky asset

In the bottom panel, the line relating the standard deviation of the portfolio to the portfolio share of money becomes flatter and rotates in a counter-clockwise fashion around point A. The Slutsky equation associated with the change in σ_R is:

$$\frac{\partial \omega^*}{\partial \sigma_R} = \left(\frac{\partial \omega^*}{\partial \sigma_R}\right)_{dE(U)=0} - (1 - \omega^*)S \cdot \frac{\bar{r} - r^M}{\sigma_R} \cdot \frac{\partial \omega^*}{\partial \bar{Z}} > 0, \tag{10.82}$$

where $\partial \omega^* / \partial \bar{Z}$ is given in (10.80) and the pure substitution effect is given by:

$$\left(\frac{\partial \omega^*}{\partial \sigma_R}\right)_{dEU=0} \equiv \frac{(1 - \omega^*)\left[2\sigma_R^2 + (r^M - \bar{r})^2\right]}{\sigma_R \left[\sigma_R^2 + (r^M - \bar{r})^2\right]} > 0. \tag{10.83}$$

The substitution effect dominates the income effect and money demand rises if the return on the risky asset becomes more volatile.

10.4   The optimal quantity of money

In the previous two sections we have reviewed the main models of money which have been proposed in the postwar literature. We now change course somewhat by taking for granted that money exists and plays a significant role in the economic process and by posing the question concerning the socially optimal quantity of money. If fiat money is useful to economic agents then how much of it should the policy maker bring into circulation? This question received an unambiguous answer from Friedman (1969). Social optimality requires marginal social benefits and costs of money to be equated. Since the production of fiat money (intrinsically useless tokens) imposes little or no costs on society, the money supply should be expanded up to the point where the marginal benefit of money is (close to) zero and agents are flooded with liquidity (money balances). This is the famous *full liquidity* result proposed by Friedman (1969) and others.[19]

Intuitively, people should not economize on resources which are not scarce from a social point of view (like fiat money). Since the opportunity cost of holding money is the nominal rate of interest on bonds, the strong form of the Friedman proposition requires the policy maker to manipulate the rate of money growth, μ_t, (and hence the inflation rate, π_t) such as to drive the *nominal* interest rate, R_t, to zero (Woodford, 1990, p. 1071). The nominal interest is itself the sum of the real rate of interest (r_t, which is largely determined by real factors according to Friedman) and the expected rate of inflation (π_t^e), i.e. $R_t = r_t + \pi_t^e$. Hence, in the steady state ($r_t = r$ and $\pi_t = \mu_t$) and with fulfilled expectations ($\pi_t^e = \pi_t$) the Friedman proposition requires a constant rate of decline in the money supply equal to the (constant) real rate of interest, i.e. $R_t = 0 \Leftrightarrow \mu_t = \pi_t = -r$.

The remainder of this section is dedicated to the following two issues. First, we demonstrate (a version of) the Friedman result with the aid of a simple two-period general equilibrium model. Second, we review the main objections which have been raised against the Friedman argument in the literature.

10.4.1   A basic general equilibrium model

In section 2 above we discussed several justifications for putting real money balances into the felicity function of households. We now postulate that the lifetime utility function of the representative agent can be written as follows:

$$V = U(C_1, m_1) + \frac{1}{1+\rho}U(C_2, m_2), \tag{10.84}$$

where m_t denotes real money balances held at the *end* of period t.[20] Abstracting from bonds, endogenous production, and economic growth, the budget identities in the two periods are given by:

$$P_1 Y + M_0 + P_1 T_1 = P_1 C_1 + M_1, \tag{10.85}$$

$$P_2 Y + M_1 + P_2 T_2 = P_2 C_2 + M_2, \tag{10.86}$$

where M_0 is given and $P_t T_t$ represents lump-sum cash transfers received from the government. The representative agent takes these transfers as parametrically given

---

[19]Other important contributors to the debate are Bailey (1956) and Samuelson (1968b, 1969a). An excellent survey of this vast literature is Woodford (1990).

[20]We thus change the timing of the utility-yielding effect of money in comparison to the arguments in section 2. We do so in order to simplify the argument and to retain consistency with Brock's (1975) model of which our model is a special case.

in making his optimal plans, but in general equilibrium they are endogenously determined.

We postulate a simple money supply process according to which the rate of nominal money growth is constant:

$$\frac{M_t - M_{t-1}}{M_{t-1}} = \mu, \tag{10.87}$$

where μ is a policy instrument of the government. The increase in the nominal money supply is disbursed to the representative agent in the form of lump-sum transfers:

$$P_t T_t = \Delta M_t, \tag{10.88}$$

where $\Delta M_t \equiv M_t - M_{t-1}$. The household chooses C_t and M_t (for $t = 1, 2$) in order to maximize (10.84) subject to (10.85)–(10.86). Employing the usual Lagrange multiplier method, and assuming an interior solution, the first-order conditions consist of the constraints (10.85)–(10.86) and:

$$\frac{U_C(C_1, m_1)}{P_1} = \frac{U_m(C_1, m_1)}{P_1} + \frac{1}{1+\rho} \frac{U_C(C_2, m_2)}{P_2}, \tag{10.89}$$

$$U_C(C_2, m_2) = U_m(C_2, m_2), \tag{10.90}$$

where $U_C(\cdot) \equiv \partial U(\cdot)/\partial C_t$ and $U_m(\cdot) \equiv \partial U(\cdot)/\partial m_t$. Equation (10.89) says that the marginal utility of spending one euro on consumption (the left-hand side) must be equated to the marginal utility obtained by holding one euro in the form of money balances (the right-hand side). The latter is itself equal to the marginal utility due to reduced transaction costs (first term) plus that due to the store-of-value function of money (second term). In the final (second) period, money is not used as a store of value so only the transactions demand for money motive is operative. This is what the expression in (10.90) says.

In the absence of goods consumption by the government, and public and private investment, the product market clearing condition says that endowment income equals private consumption in both periods:

$$Y = C_1 = C_2. \tag{10.91}$$

By multiplying the expression in (10.89) by M_1 and using (10.87), (10.90), and (10.91), the perfect foresight equilibrium for the economy can be written as:

$$[U_C(Y, m_1) - U_m(Y, m_1)] \cdot m_1 = m_2 \cdot \frac{U_C(Y, m_2)}{(1+\rho)(1+\mu)}, \tag{10.92}$$

$$U_C(Y, m_2) = U_m(Y, m_2). \tag{10.93}$$

These two equations recursively determine the equilibrium values for the real money supply. The trick is to work backwards in time. First, equation (10.93) is solved for m_2. Second, by using this optimal value, say m_2^*, in the right-hand side of (10.92), an equation determining m_1^* is obtained. Since the path of the nominal money supply is determined by the policy maker, the nominal price level associated with the solution is given by $P_t^* \equiv M_t / m_t^*$.

In our simple two-period model the solution method is quite simple, but the bulk of the literature on the optimal money supply is based on the notion of an infinitely lived representative agent for which a general solution is much harder to obtain. Indeed, in that literature the discussion is often based on simple special cases. In order to facilitate comparison with that literature and to simplify the exposition of our model, we now assume that the felicity function is *additively separable*:

$$U(C_t, m_t) \equiv u(C_t) + v(m_t), \tag{10.94}$$

with $u'(C_t) > 0$, $u''(C_t) < 0$, $v'(m_t) = 0$ for $m_t = m_t^*$ (a finite value), and $v''(m_t) < 0$. Marginal utility of consumption is positive throughout. Satiation with money balances is possible provided the real money supply is sufficiently high, i.e. the $v'(m_t)$ becomes negative for $m_t > m_t^*$.

By using (10.94) in (10.92)–(10.93) we obtain:

$$\left[u'(Y) - v'(m_1)\right] \cdot m_1 = m_2 \cdot \frac{u'(Y)}{(1+\rho)(1+\mu)} \tag{10.95}$$

$$u'(Y) = v'(m_2). \tag{10.96}$$

In Figure 10.7 these two equilibrium conditions have been drawn. Equation (10.96) is represented by the horizontal line TC, where "TC" stands for "terminal condition". Equation (10.95) is an Euler-like equation and is drawn in the figure as the upward-sloping EE line.[21] The equilibrium is at point E_0. Before going on to the issue of social optimality of the perfect foresight equilibrium at E_0, it is instructive to conduct some comparative dynamic experiments. An increase in the money growth rate, for example, leads to an upward shift in the EE line, say to EE_1 in Figure 10.7. The equilibrium shifts to E_1 and real money balances in the first period fall, i.e. $dm_1^*/d\mu < 0$. Hence, even though only the level of future nominal money balances is affected (M_1 stays the same and M_2 rises), the rational representative agent endowed with perfect foresight foresees the consequences of higher money growth and as a result ends up bidding up the nominal price level not only in the future but also in the present. A similar effect is obtained if the rate of pure time preference is increased.

10.4.2   The satiation result

We have seen that, in our simple two-period model, the privately optimal real money balances in the two periods are determined recursively by the expressions in (10.92)–(10.93) and can thus be expressed as implicit functions of taste and endowment parameters and the money growth rate, i.e. we can write $m_1^* = m_1^*(\rho, Y, \mu)$ and $m_2^* = m_2^*(\rho, Y, \mu)$. For the separable case of (10.94) these implicit functions feature the following partial derivatives with respect to the money growth rate: $\partial m_1^*/\partial \mu < 0$ and $\partial m_2^*/\partial \mu = 0$. Since the rate of money growth is a policy variable it follows that the policy maker has the instrument needed to influence the equilibrium of money balances, at least in the first period. By substituting $m_t^*(\cdot)$ and (10.91) into the utility function of the representative agent (10.94) we obtain:

$$V = u(Y) + v\left(m_1^*(\rho, Y, \mu)\right) + \frac{1}{1+\rho}\left[u(Y) + v\left(m_2^*(\rho, Y)\right)\right]. \tag{10.97}$$

---

[21]The slope of the EE line is:
$$\frac{dm_2}{dm_1} = \frac{(1+\rho)(1+\mu)\left[u'(Y) - v'(m_1) - m_1 v''(m_1)\right]}{u'(Y)} > 0.$$

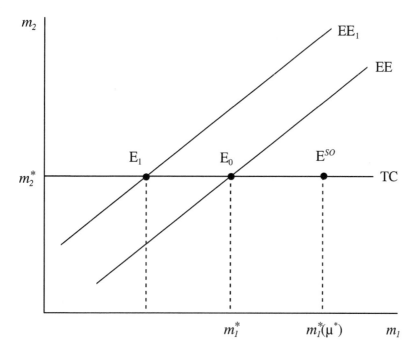

Figure 10.7: Monetary equilibrium in a perfect foresight model

A utilitarian policy maker can pursue a socially optimal monetary policy by choosing the money growth rate for which the welfare of the representative agent is at its highest level. By maximizing (10.97) by choice of μ we obtain (a variant of) the Friedman satiation result:

$$\frac{dV}{d\mu} = v'\left(m_1^*(\rho, Y, \mu^*)\right) \cdot \frac{dm_1^*}{d\mu} = 0 \ \Rightarrow \ v'\left(m_1^*(\rho, Y, \mu^*)\right) = 0, \qquad (10.98)$$

where μ^* is the optimal money growth rate. This optimal growth rate of the money supply induces the representative household to satiate itself with real money balances, i.e. to choose m_1^* such that the marginal utility of these balances is zero (and thus equal to the social cost of producing these balances). In terms of Figure 10.7, the social optimum is at point E^{SO} and corresponds to a higher level of real money balances and a lower money growth rate than at point E_0.

The satiation result does not hold in the final period, of course, as the terminal condition pins down a positive marginal utility of money balances needed for transaction purposes (see (10.93)). It is straightforward to generalize the Friedman result to a setting with an infinitely lived representative agent.[22] In that case terms like $(1+\rho)^{t-1}U(C_t, m_t)$ are added to the utility function in (10.84) and budget equations like $P_t Y + M_{t-1} + P_t T_t = P_t C_t + M_t$ are added to (10.85) (both for $t = 3, 4, 5, \cdots, \infty$). Equation (10.95) is then generalized to:

$$\left[u'(Y) - v'(m_t)\right] \cdot m_t = m_{t+1} \cdot \frac{u'(Y)}{(1+\rho)(1+\mu)}, \quad (t = 1, 2, 3, \cdots, \infty). \qquad (10.99)$$

The thing to note about (10.99) as compared to (10.95)–(10.96) is that the terminal condition is no longer relevant. Brock (1975, pp. 138–141) shows that the equilibrium

---

[22]Much of modern macroeconomic theory makes use of such a fictional agent. See Chapters 13–14 and 18–19.

solution to (10.99) will in fact be the steady-state solution for which $m_t = m_{t+1} = m^*$:

$$v'(m^*) = \left[1 - \frac{1}{(1+\rho)(1+\mu)}\right] u'(Y) \Rightarrow \tag{10.100}$$

$$\frac{dm^*}{d\mu} = \frac{u'(Y)}{(1+\rho)(1+\mu)^2 v''(m^*)} < 0. \tag{10.101}$$

Since both the endowment and real money balances are constant over time, lifetime utility of the infinite lived representative agent is equal to:

$$V = \sum_{t=1}^{\infty} \left(\frac{1}{1+\rho}\right)^{t-1} \cdot [u(Y) + v(m^*(\mu))]$$

$$= [u(Y) + v(m^*(\mu))] \cdot \frac{1}{1 - \frac{1}{1+\rho}}$$

$$= \frac{1+\rho}{\rho} \cdot [u(Y) + v(m^*(\mu))]. \tag{10.102}$$

Maximizing (10.102) by choice of μ yields the infinite-horizon generalization of equation (10.98):

$$\frac{dV}{d\mu} = \frac{1+\rho}{\rho} \cdot v'(m^*(\mu^*)) \cdot \frac{dm^*(\mu)}{d\mu} = 0. \tag{10.103}$$

Since $dm^*/d\mu < 0$, we find that the optimal money supply is such as to ensure that $v'(m^*) = 0$ for all periods. In view of (10.100), this is achieved if the money supply is shrunk at the rate at which the representative household discounts future utility:

$$\mu^* = -\frac{\rho}{1+\rho}. \tag{10.104}$$

Although there are no interest-bearing assets in our model, equation (10.104) can nevertheless be interpreted as a zero-nominal-interest-rate result (see Turnovsky and Brock, 1980). Indeed, the pure rate of time preference represents the psychological costs associated with waiting and $\rho/(1+\rho)$ ($\approx \rho$) can be interpreted as the real rate of interest. Furthermore, since real money balances are constant, the money growth rate μ^* also represents the rate of price inflation. The nominal rate of interest in the optimum is thus $R \equiv \rho/(1+\rho) + \pi = \rho/(1+\rho) + \mu^* = 0$.

10.4.3   Critiques of the full liquidity rule

The Friedman satiation rule, according to which the policy maker should use its money growth instrument in order to drive the marginal utility of real money balances to zero, has come under severe criticism in the literature. We now wish to demonstrate the two most important mechanisms by which the full liquidity result is invalidated. In order to do so we return to the two-period setting but we enrich the basic model of section 10.4.1 above by moving from an endowment to a production economy and by introducing (potentially) distorting taxes.

10.4.3.1   Introducing endogenous production

We assume that the representative household derives utility not only from consumption of goods and real money balances but also from leisure. Hence, equation (10.84) is replaced by:

$$V = U(C_1, 1 - L_1, m_1) + \frac{1}{1+\rho} U(C_2, 1 - L_2, m_2), \tag{10.105}$$

where the time endowment is unity, L_t is labour supply, and $1 - L_t$ is leisure in period t ($= 1, 2$). The household budget identities in the two periods are:

$$W_1(1 - \tau_1)L_1 + M_0 + P_1 T_1 = P_1 C_1 + M_1, \tag{10.106}$$
$$W_2(1 - \tau_2)L_2 + M_1 + P_2 T_2 = P_2 C_2 + M_2, \tag{10.107}$$

where M_0 is given, $P_t T_t$ represents lump-sum cash transfers received from the government, W_t is the nominal wage rate, and τ_t is the tax rate on labour. The household chooses C_t, L_t, and M_t in order to maximize (10.105) subject to (10.106)–(10.107). Writing the Lagrangian as:

$$\mathcal{L} \equiv \sum_{t=1}^{2} \left(\frac{1}{1+\rho} \right)^{t-1} U(C_t, 1 - L_t, m_t)$$
$$+ \sum_{t=1}^{2} \lambda_t \cdot [W_t(1 - \tau_t)L_t + M_{t-1} + P_t T_t - P_t C_t - M_t], \tag{10.108}$$

we easily find the (main) first-order conditions (for $t = 1, 2$):

$$\left(\frac{1}{1+\rho} \right)^{t-1} U_C(C_t, 1 - L_t, m_t) = \lambda_t P_t, \tag{10.109}$$

$$\left(\frac{1}{1+\rho} \right)^{t-1} U_{1-L}(C_t, 1 - L_t, m_t) = \lambda_t W_t (1 - \tau_t), \tag{10.110}$$

$$\frac{U_m(C_1, 1 - L_1, m_1)}{P_1} = \lambda_1 - \lambda_2, \tag{10.111}$$

$$\frac{1}{1+\rho} \frac{U_m(C_2, 1 - L_2, m_2)}{P_2} = \lambda_2. \tag{10.112}$$

To keep things simple we assume that production is subject to constant returns to scale and that the production function is given by $Y_t = L_t$. Perfectly competitive producers set price equal to marginal cost which implies that $P_t = W_t$, i.e. the real producer wage is equal to unity. As before, the government does not consume any goods so that the goods market clearing condition requires consumption by households to equal production in both periods. In summary, we have that:

$$C_t = Y_t = L_t, \quad W_t = P_t. \tag{10.113}$$

By using (10.109)–(10.113) we can write the first-order conditions characterizing the optimum as follows:

$$\frac{U_{1-L}(x_t)}{U_C(x_t)} = 1 - \tau_t, \quad t = 1, 2, \tag{10.114}$$

$$[U_C(x_1) - U_m(x_1)] \cdot m_1 = m_2 \cdot \frac{U_C(x_2)}{(1+\rho)(1+\mu)}, \tag{10.115}$$

$$U_C(x_2) = U_m(x_2), \tag{10.116}$$

where $x_t \equiv (C_t, 1 - C_t, m_t)$. The expressions in (10.114) are obtained by dividing (10.110) by (10.109) and noting (10.113) for each period. Equation (10.115) follows from (10.111)–(10.112) and (10.109) (for period $t = 1$). We have also used the definition of the money growth rate (given in (10.87)) to obtain an expression in terms of real money balances. Finally, (10.116) is obtained by combining (10.112) and (10.109) (for period $t = 2$).

Equation (10.114) shows that the household equates the marginal rate of substitution between leisure and consumption (left-hand side) to the real after-tax wage (right-hand side) in both periods. Equations (10.115)–(10.116) generalize (10.92)–(10.93) by accounting for an endogenous labour supply (and thus production) choice. Armed with this minor modification to our original model, the robustness of the full liquidity result can be examined.

10.4.3.2 Non-separability

The model is solved recursively by working backward in time, just as in section 10.4.1 above. We assume that both tax rates are constant. Equations (10.114) (for $t = 2$) and (10.116) then pin down optimal levels of consumption (and labour supply) and money balances for the final period (C_2^* and m_2^*, respectively) which are constant and independent of the rate of money growth μ. Given these values for C_2^* and m_2^*, equations (10.114) (for period $t = 1$) and (10.115) together constitute a system of implicit equations expressing C_1^* and m_1^* in terms of the rate of money growth μ (as well as ρ, τ_1, and τ_2, but these are held constant):

$$U_{1-L}(C_1, 1 - C_1, m_1) = (1 - \tau_1) U_C(C_1, 1 - C_1, m_1), \tag{10.117}$$

$$[U_C(C_1, 1 - C_1, m_1) - U_m(C_1, 1 - C_1, m_1)] \cdot (1 + \mu) \cdot m_1 = \frac{m_2^* U_C(x_2^*)}{1 + \rho}, \tag{10.118}$$

where we note that the right-hand side of (10.118) is constant. Denoting these implicit functions by $C_1^*(\mu)$ and $m_1^*(\mu)$, we obtain the following derivatives by means of standard techniques:

$$\frac{dC_1^*}{d\mu} = \frac{m_2^* U_C(x_2^*) [U_{1-L,m} - (1 - \tau_1) U_{Cm}]}{(1 + \rho)(1 + \mu)^2 |\Delta|}, \tag{10.119}$$

$$\frac{dm_1^*}{d\mu} = -\frac{m_2^* U_C(x_2^*) [U_{1-L,C} - U_{1-L,1-L} - (1 - \tau_1)(U_{CC} - U_{C,1-L})]}{(1 + \rho)(1 + \mu)^2 |\Delta|}, \tag{10.120}$$

where $|\Delta|$ is the (negative) Jacobian of the system and where the partial derivatives U_{CC}, U_{Cm}, $U_{C,1-L}$, $U_{1-L,1-L}$, and $U_{1-L,m}$ are all evaluated in the optimum point $(C_1^*, 1 - C_1^*, m_1^*)$.

The expression in (10.120) shows that the sign of $dm_1^*/d\mu$ is ambiguous in the generalized model. The existence of diminishing marginal utility of leisure and consumption ensures that $U_{1-L,1-L}$ and U_{CC} are both negative, but the cross-term, $U_{1-L,C} \equiv U_{C,1-L}$, can have either sign. Turnovsky and Brock (1980, p. 197) argue that it is reasonable to assume on economic grounds that $U_{C,1-L}$ is positive, i.e. the marginal utility of consumption rises with leisure. With that additional assumption it is clear that optimal money holdings in the current period fall as the money growth rate is increased, i.e. $dm_1^*/d\mu < 0$. This conclusion generalizes our earlier result obtained for the basic model of section 10.4.1 above (see (10.101)).

As the expression in (10.119) shows, the sign of $dC_1^*/d\mu$ is also ambiguous in general as it depends on the cross-partial derivatives $U_{1-L,m}$ and U_{Cm} which can have either sign and about which economic theory does not suggest strong priors. In economic terms the ambiguity arises because it is not a priori clear how (or even whether) the rate of money growth affects the marginal rate of substitution between consumption and leisure, i.e. how μ influences the consumption-leisure trade-off.

The issue can be investigated more formally by writing the marginal rate of substitution between leisure and consumption (for period $t = 1$) in a general functional form as $g(C_1, m_1)$:

$$g(C_1, m_1) \equiv \frac{U_{1-L}(C_1, 1 - C_1, m_1)}{U_C(C_1, 1 - C_1, m_1)}. \tag{10.121}$$

By partially differentiating $g(\cdot)$ with respect to m_1 we obtain the following result:

$$
\begin{aligned}
g_m(C_1, m_1) &= \frac{U_C U_{1-L,m} - U_{1-L} U_{Cm}}{[U_C]^2} \\
&= \frac{U_{1-L,m} - g(C_1, m_1) U_{Cm}}{U_C} \\
&= \frac{U_{1-L,m} - (1 - \tau_1) U_{Cm}}{U_C},
\end{aligned}
\tag{10.122}
$$

where we have used (10.114) in the final step). The expression in (10.122) shows the intimate link which exists between $g_m(C_1, m_1)$ and the sign of $dC_1^*/d\mu$ in (10.119): if the marginal rate of substitution between leisure and consumption rises (falls) with real money balances, $g_m(C_1, m_1) > 0\ (< 0)$, then an increase in the money growth rate leads to an increase (decrease) in goods consumption, i.e. $dC_1^*/d\mu > 0\ (< 0)$.

The upshot of the discussion so far is that C_2^* and m_2^* do not depend on the rate of money growth and that C_1^* and m_1^* do so but in an ambiguous fashion. By plugging $C_1^*(\mu)$ and $m_1^*(\mu)$ into the utility function (10.105) we obtain an expression for household utility in terms of the policy variable μ:

$$V \equiv U\left(C_1^*(\mu), 1 - C_1^*(\mu), m_1^*(\mu)\right) + \frac{1}{1 + \rho} U(C_2^*, 1 - C_2^*, m_2^*). \tag{10.123}$$

The policy maker selects the socially optimal money growth rate μ^* in order to maximize V, a problem which yields the following first-order condition:

$$\frac{dV}{d\mu} = \tau_1 U_C \cdot \frac{dC_1^*}{d\mu} + U_m \cdot \frac{dm_1^*}{d\mu} = 0, \tag{10.124}$$

where we have used equation (10.114) to simplify (10.124). Armed with this expression we can re-examine the validity of the Friedman full-liquidity result according to which μ^* should be set such as to drive the marginal utility of money balances to zero. Equation (10.124) shows the various cases under which this result continues to hold in our extended model. First, if there is no initial tax on labour in the first period ($\tau_1 = 0$) then the leisure-consumption choice is undistorted ($U_{1-L}/U_C = 1$ in that case) so that a change in the money growth rate does not create a first-order welfare effect even if it does affect consumption in the first period. In terms of (10.114), for $\tau_1 = 0$ the sign (or magnitude) of $dC_1^*/d\mu$ does not matter. The first term on the right-hand side of (10.124) drops out and, provided $dm_1^*/d\mu \neq 0$, the optimal money growth rate entails driving U_m to zero.

The second case for which the satiation result obtains is one for which the tax is strictly positive ($\tau_1 > 0$) but consumption is independent of the money growth rate

$(dC_1^*/d\mu = 0)$. This case was emphasized by Turnovsky and Brock (1980). In terms of (10.119) and (10.122) this holds if the marginal rate of substitution between leisure and consumption does not depend on μ. If that result obtains, the felicity function $U(\cdot)$ is said to be *weakly separable* in $(C_t, 1 - L_t)$ on the one hand and m_t on the other. It can then be written as:

$$U(C_t, 1 - L_t, m_t) = U\left(Z(C_t, 1 - L_t), m_t\right), \tag{10.125}$$

where $Z(\cdot)$ is some sub-felicity function. Note that (10.125) implies that the marginal rate of substitution between leisure and consumption only depends on the properties of $Z(\cdot)$, as $U_{1-L}/U_C = U_Z Z_{1-L}/(U_Z Z_C) = Z_{1-L}/Z_C$ and thus does not depend on m_t.

In summary, the Friedman satiation result holds in our model if (i) there is no initial tax on labour income ($\tau_1 = 0$), and (ii) if τ_1 is positive but preferences display the weak separability property. In general, however, (10.123) implicitly defines the optimal money growth rate and U_m will not be driven to zero. Turnovsky and Brock refer to (10.124) as a "distorted" Friedman liquidity rule (1980, p. 197).

10.4.3.3 The government budget restriction

The second major argument against the validity of the Friedman result is based on the notion that steady-state inflation (caused by nominal money growth) can be seen as a tax on money balances and thus has repercussions for the government budget constraint especially in a "second-best" world in which lump-sum taxes are not available to the policy maker. In such a world, Phelps (1973) argues, government revenue must be raised by means of various distorting taxes, of which the "inflation tax" is only one. The literature initiated by Phelps is often called the "public finance" approach to inflation and optimal money growth. Briefly put, the Phelps approach is an application to monetary economics of the optimal taxation literature in the tradition of Ramsey (1927).[23]

10.5 Punchlines

Money performs three major functions in the economy: it is a medium of exchange, it serves as a store of value, and it performs the role of a medium of account. Of these three functions, the first is the most distinguishing function of money. Despite the fact that every layman knows what money is (and what it can do) it has turned out to be difficult to come up with a convincing model of money. In the first part of this chapter we discuss some of the more influential models that have been proposed in the literature.

The medium of exchange role of money has been modelled by assuming that money reduces the transactions costs associated with the trading process between agents. In this view, the existence of money reduces the time needed for shopping. Since leisure is valued by the agents, the same holds for money. This so-called shopping cost approach is one way to rationalize the conventional practice in macroeconomic modelling of putting money balances directly into the household's utility function. The cash-in-advance approach is another possible rationalization for this practice.

---

[23] We briefly discussed Ramsey taxation in the context of Section 9.3 above.

The role of money as a store of value has been modelled in two major ways. In the first model, intrinsically useless money may be held if it allows agents to engage in intertemporal consumption smoothing *and* either (i) there are no other financial assets available for this purpose at all, or (ii) such assets exist but carry an inferior rate of return. The second model of money as a store of value is based on the notion that assets carrying a higher yield than money may also be more risky. In the simplest possible application of this idea, the yield on money is assumed to be certain and equal to zero (no price inflation) whilst the yield on a risky financial asset is stochastic. The risky asset carries a positive *expected* yield. The actual (realized) rate of return on such an asset is, however, uncertain and may well be negative. In such a setting the risk-averse household typically chooses a diversified portfolio, consisting of both money and the risky asset, which represents the optimal trade-off between risk and return.

In the second part of this chapter we take for granted that money exists and plays a useful role in the economic process and study the socially optimal quantity of money. If fiat money is useful to economic agents then how large should the money supply be? Friedman proposes a simple answer to this question: since fiat money is very cheap to produce, the money supply should be expanded up to the point where the marginal social benefit of money is (close to) zero. This is the famous *full liquidity* or *satiation* result. We first demonstrate the validity of the satiation result in a very simple two-period model of an endowment economy with money entering the utility function of the households. Next we extend the model by endogenizing the labour supply decision of households and demonstrate the various reasons why full liquidity may not be socially optimal.

Further reading

Good textbooks on monetary economics are Niehans (1978), McCallum (1989a), and Walsh (2010). Diamond (1984a), Kiyotaki and Wright (1993), and Trejos and Wright (1995) use the search-theoretic approach to model money. The demand for money by firms is studied by Miller and Orr (1966) and Fischer (1974). D. Romer (1986, 1987) embeds the Baumol-Tobin model in a general equilibrium model. Saving (1971) presents a model of money based on transactions costs. McCallum and Goodfriend (1987) give an overview of money demand theories. Fischer (1979) studies monetary neutrality in a monetary growth model. See also Chapter 14.

On the public finance approach to inflation, see Chamley (1985), Turnovsky and Brock (1980), Mankiw (1987), Gahvari (1988), Chari et al. (1996), Batina and Ihori (2000, ch.10), and Ljungqvist and Sargent (2012, ch. 26). On the unpleasant monetarist arithmetic argument, see Drazen and Helpman (1990), Sargent and Wallace (1993), and Liviatan (1984).

Chapter 11

New Keynesian economics

The purpose of this chapter is to discuss the following issues:

1. Can we provide microeconomic foundations behind the "Keynesian" multiplier?

2. What are the welfare-theoretic aspects of the monopolistic competition model? What is the link between the output multiplier of government consumption and the marginal cost of public funds (MCPF)?

3. Does monetary neutrality still hold when there exist costs of adjusting prices?

4. What do we mean by nominal and real rigidity and how do the two types of rigidity interact?

11.1 Reconstructing the "Keynesian" multiplier

The challenge posed by a number of authors in the 1980s is to provide microeconomic foundations for Keynesian multipliers by assuming that the goods market is characterized by monopolistic competition. This is, of course, not the first time such micro-foundations are proposed, a prominent predecessor being the fixed-price disequilibrium approach of the early 1970s (see Bénassy (1993b) for a survey of that literature). The problem with that older literature is that prices are simply assumed to be fixed, which makes these models resemble Shakespeare's *Hamlet* without the Prince, in that the essential market coordination mechanism is left out. Specifically, fixed (disequilibrium) prices imply the existence of unexploited gains from trade between restricted and unrestricted market parties. There are €100 bills lying on the footpath, and this begs the question why this would ever be an equilibrium situation.

Of course some reasons exist for price stickiness, and these will be reviewed here, but a particularly simple way out of the fixity of prices is to assume price-setting behaviour by monopolistically competitive agents.[1] This incidentally also solves Arrow's (1959) famous critical remarks about the absence of an auctioneer in the perfectly competitive framework.

---

[1]See the recent surveys by Bénassy (1993b), Silvestre (1993), Matsuyama (1995), and the collection of papers in Dixon and Rankin (1995).

11.1.1   A static model with monopolistic competition

In this subsection we construct a simple model with monopolistic competition in the goods market. There are three types of agents in the economy: households, firms, and the government. The representative household derives utility from consuming goods and leisure and has a Cobb-Douglas utility function:

$$U \equiv C^{\alpha}(1-L)^{1-\alpha}, \ 0 < \alpha < 1, \tag{11.1}$$

where U is utility, L is labour supply, and C is (composite) consumption. The household has an endowment of one unit of time and all time not spent working is consumed in the form of leisure, $1 - L$. The composite consumption good consists of a bundle of closely related product "varieties" which are close but imperfect substitutes for each other (e.g. red, blue, green, and yellow ties). Following the crucial insights of Spence (1976) and Dixit and Stiglitz (1977), a convenient formulation is as follows:

$$C \equiv N^{\eta} \left[N^{-1} \sum_{j=1}^{N} C_j^{(\theta-1)/\theta} \right]^{\theta/(\theta-1)}, \ \theta > 1, \eta \geq 1, \tag{11.2}$$

where N is the number of different varieties that exist, C_j is a consumption good of variety j, and θ and η are parameters. This specification, though simple, incorporates two economically meaningful and separate aspects of product differentiation. First, the parameter θ regulates the ease with which any two varieties (C_i and C_j) can be substituted for each other. In formal terms, θ represents the *Allen-Uzawa cross-partial elasticity of substitution* (see Chung, 1994, ch. 5). Intuitively, the higher is θ, the better substitutes the varieties are for each other. In the limiting case (as $\theta \to \infty$), the varieties are perfect substitutes, i.e. they are identical goods from the perspective of the representative household.

The second parameter appearing in (11.2), η, regulates "preference for diversity" (PFD, or "taste for variety" as it is often called alternatively). Intuitively, diversity preference represents the utility gain that is obtained from spreading a certain amount of production over N varieties rather than concentrating it on a single variety (Bénassy, 1996b, p. 42). In formal terms *average* PFD can be computed by comparing the value of composite consumption (C) obtained if N varieties and X/N units per variety are chosen with the value of C if X units of a single variety are chosen ($N = 1$):

$$\text{average PFD} \equiv \frac{C(X/N, X/N, \dots, X/N)}{C(X, 0, \dots, 0)} = N^{\eta-1} \equiv \phi(N). \tag{11.3}$$

The elasticity of this function with respect to the number of varieties (i.e. $N\phi'(N)/\phi(N)$) represents the *marginal* taste for additional variety[2] which plays an important role in the monopolistic competition model. By using (11.3) we obtain the expression for the marginal preference for diversity (MPFD):

$$\text{MPFD} = \eta - 1. \tag{11.4}$$

It is now clear how and to what extent η regulates the MPFD: if η exceeds unity MPFD is strictly positive and the representative agent exhibits a love of variety. The agent does not enjoy diversity if $\eta = 1$ and MPFD $= 0$ in that case.

---

[2]As is often the case in economics, the marginal rather than the average concept is most relevant. Bénassy presents a clear discussion of average and marginal preference for diversity (1996b, p. 42).

The household faces the following budget constraint:

$$\sum_{j=1}^{N} P_j C_j = WL + \Pi - T, \tag{11.5}$$

where P_j is the price of variety j, W is the nominal wage rate (labour is used as the numeraire later on in this section), Π is the total profit income that the household receives from the monopolistically competitive firms, and T is a lump-sum tax paid to the government. The household chooses its labour supply and consumption levels for each available product variety (L and C_j, $j = 1, \ldots, N$) in order to maximize utility (11.1), given the definition of composite consumption in (11.2), the budget constraint (11.5), and taking as given all prices (P_j, $j = 1, \ldots, N$), the nominal wage rate, profit income, and the lump-sum tax.

By using the convenient trick of *two-stage budgeting* (see Intermezzo 11.1 below), the solutions for composite consumption, consumption of variety j, and labour supply are obtained:

$$PC = \alpha \left[W + \Pi - T \right], \tag{11.6}$$

$$\frac{C_j}{C} = N^{-(\theta+\eta)+\eta\theta} \left(\frac{P_j}{P} \right)^{-\theta}, \quad j = 1, \ldots, N, \tag{11.7}$$

$$W(1 - L) = (1 - \alpha) \left[W + \Pi - T \right], \tag{11.8}$$

where P is the so-called *true price index* of the composite consumption good C. Intuitively, P represents the price of one unit of C given that the quantities of all varieties are chosen in an optimal (utility-maximizing) fashion by the household. It is defined as follows:

$$P \equiv N^{-\eta} \left[N^{-\theta} \sum_{j=1}^{N} P_j^{1-\theta} \right]^{1/(1-\theta)}. \tag{11.9}$$

Intermezzo 11.1

Two-stage budgeting and Dixit-Stiglitz preferences. As indeed its name strongly suggests, the technique of two-stage budgeting (or more generally, multi-stage budgeting) solves a relatively complex maximization problem by breaking it up into two (or more) much less complex subproblems (or "stages"). An exhaustive treatment of two-stage budgeting is far beyond the scope of this book. Interested readers are referred to Deaton and Muellbauer (1980, pp. 123–137) which contains a more advanced discussion plus references to key publications in the area.

We illustrate the technique of two-stage budgeting with the aid of the maximization problem discussed in the text. Since C and $1 - L$ appear in the utility function (11.1) and only C_j ($j = 1, ..., N$) appear in the definition of C in (11.2) it is natural to subdivide the problem into two stages. In stage 1 the choice is made (at the "top level" of the problem) between composite consumption and leisure, and in stage 2 (at the "bottom" level) the different varieties are chosen optimally, conditional upon the level of C chosen in the first stage.

Stage 1. We postulate the existence of a price index for composite consumption and denote it by P. By definition total spending on differentiated goods is then equal to $\sum_j P_j C_j = PC$ so that (11.5) can be re-written as:

$$PC + W(1 - L) = W + \Pi - T \equiv I_F, \tag{a}$$

which says that spending on consumption goods plus leisure (the left-hand side) must equal full income (I_F on the right-hand side). The top-level maximization problem is now to maximize (11.1) subject to (a) by choice of C and $1 - L$. The first-order conditions for this problem are the budget constraint (a) and:

$$\frac{U_{1-L}}{U_C} = \frac{W}{P} \Rightarrow \frac{W}{P} = \frac{1 - \alpha}{\alpha} \frac{C}{1 - L}. \tag{b}$$

The marginal rate of substitution between leisure and composite consumption must be equated to the real wage rate which is computed by deflating the nominal wage rate with the price index of composite consumption (and not just the price of an individual product variety!). By substituting the right-hand expression of (b) into the budget identity (a), we obtain the optimal choices of C and $1 - L$ in terms of full income:

$$PC = \alpha I_F, \qquad W(1 - L) = (1 - \alpha) I_F. \tag{c}$$

Finally, by substituting these expressions into the (*direct*) utility function (11.1) we obtain the *indirect* utility function expressing utility in terms of full income and a cost-of-living index:

$$V \equiv \frac{I_F}{P_V}, \tag{d}$$

where P_V is the true price index for utility, i.e. it is the cost of purchasing one unit of utility (a "util"):

$$P_V \equiv \left(\frac{P}{\alpha} \right)^\alpha \left(\frac{W}{1 - \alpha} \right)^{1-\alpha}. \tag{e}$$

Stage 2. In the second stage the agent chooses varieties, C_j ($j = 1, 2, ..., N$), in order to "construct" composite consumption in an optimal, cost-minimizing, fashion. The formal problem is:

$$\max_{\{C_j\}} N^\eta \left[N^{-1} \sum_{j=1}^N C_j^{(\theta-1)/\theta} \right]^{\theta/(\theta-1)} \quad \text{subject to} \quad \sum_{j=1}^N P_j C_j = PC, \tag{f}$$

for which the first-order conditions are the constraint in (f) and:

$$\frac{\partial C/\partial C_j}{\partial C/\partial C_k} = \frac{P_j}{P_k} \Rightarrow \left(\frac{C_k}{C_j} \right)^{1/\theta} = \frac{P_j}{P_k}, \text{ for } j, k = 1, 2, \dots, N. \tag{g}$$

The marginal rate of substitution between any two product varieties must be equated to the relative price of these two varieties. By repeatedly substituting the first-order condition (g) into the definition of C (given in (11.2)), we obtain the following expression for C_j:

$$C_j = \frac{N^{-\eta} C P_j^{-\theta}}{\left[\sum_{k=1}^{N} N^{-1} P_k^{1-\theta}\right]^{-\theta/(1-\theta)}}. \tag{h}$$

By substituting (h) into the constraint given in (f) the expression for the price index P is obtained:

$$\sum_{j=1}^{N} P_j C_j = \frac{N^{\theta/(\theta-1)-\eta} C \left[\sum_{j=1}^{N} P_j^{1-\theta}\right]}{\left[\sum_{j=1}^{N} P_j^{1-\theta}\right]^{-\theta/(1-\theta)}} = PC \Rightarrow$$

$$P \equiv N^{-\eta} \left[N^{-\theta} \sum_{j=1}^{N} P_j^{1-\theta}\right]^{1/(1-\theta)}. \tag{i}$$

By using this price index we can re-express the demand for variety j of the consumption good (given in (h)) in a more compact form as:

$$\frac{C_j}{C} = N^{-(\theta+\eta)+\eta\theta} \left(\frac{P_j}{P}\right)^{-\theta}, \quad j = 1, \ldots, N, \tag{j}$$

which is the expression used in the text (namely equation (11.7)).

It must be pointed out that we could have solved the choice problem facing the consumer in one single (and rather large) maximization problem, instead of by means of two-stage budgeting, and we would, of course, have obtained the same solutions. The advantages of two-stage budgeting are twofold: (i) it makes the computations more straightforward and mistakes easier to avoid, and (ii) it automatically yields useful definitions for true price indexes as by-products.

Finally, although we did not explicitly use the terminology, the observant reader will have noted that we have already used the method of two-stage budgeting before in Chapter 2. There we discussed the Armington approach to modelling international trade flows and assumed that a domestic composite good consists of a domestically produced good and a good produced abroad.

****

The firm sector is characterized by monopolistic competition, i.e. there are very many small firms each producing a variety of the differentiated good and each enjoying market power in its own output market. The individual firm j uses labour to produce variety j and faces the following production function:

$$Y_j = \begin{cases} 0 & \text{if } L_j \leq F \\ \dfrac{L_j - F}{k} & \text{if } L_j \geq F, \end{cases} \tag{11.10}$$

where Y_j is the marketable output of firm j, L_j is labour used by the firm, F is fixed cost in terms of units of labour, and k is the (constant) marginal labour requirement. The formulation captures the notion that the firm must expend a minimum amount of labour ("overhead labour") before it can produce any output at all (see Mankiw, 1988, p. 9). As a result, there are *increasing returns to scale* at firm level as average cost declines with output.

The profit of firm j is denoted by Π_j and equals revenue minus total costs:

$$\Pi_j \equiv P_j Y_j - W\left[kY_j + F\right], \tag{11.11}$$

which incorporates the assumption that labour is perfectly mobile across firms, so that all firms are forced to pay a common wage (W does not feature an index j). The firm chooses output in order to maximize its profits (11.11) subject to its price-elastic demand curve. We assume that it acts as a *Cournot* competitor in that firm j takes other firms' output levels as given, i.e. there is no strategic interaction between producers of different product varieties.

In formal terms, the choice problem takes the following form:

$$\max_{\{Y_j\}} \Pi_j = P_j(Y_j)Y_j - W\left[kY_j + F\right], \tag{11.12}$$

where the notation $P_j(Y_j)$ is used to indicate that the choice of output affects the price which firm j will fetch (downward-sloping demand implies $\partial P_j / \partial Y_j < 0$). The first-order condition yields the *pricing rule* familiar from first-year microeconomic texts:

$$\frac{d\Pi_j}{dY_j} = P_j + Y_j \cdot \frac{\partial P_j}{\partial Y_j} - Wk = 0 \Rightarrow$$

$$P_j = \mu_j Wk, \tag{11.13}$$

where μ_j is the markup of price over marginal cost (i.e. $MC_j = Wk$) and ε_j is the (absolute value of the) price elasticity of demand facing firm j:

$$\mu_j \equiv \frac{\varepsilon_j}{\varepsilon_j - 1}, \qquad \varepsilon_j \equiv -\frac{\partial Y_j}{\partial P_j} \frac{P_j}{Y_j}. \tag{11.14}$$

The higher is the elasticity of demand, the smaller is the markup and the closer is the solution to the perfectly competitive one (which sets $P_j = MC_j$). Clearly, the pricing rule in (11.13) is only sensible if μ_j is positive, i.e. demand must be elastic and ε_j must exceed unity.

The government does three things in this model: it consumes a composite good (G, given below), it levies lump-sum taxes on the representative household (T), and it employs civil servants (L_G). To keep things simple we assume that G is defined analogously to C in (11.2):

$$G \equiv N^\eta \left[N^{-1} \sum_{j=1}^{N} G_j^{(\theta-1)/\theta}\right]^{\theta/(\theta-1)}, \tag{11.15}$$

where G_j is the government's demand for variety j. It is assumed that the government is efficient in the sense that it chooses varieties G_j ($j = 1, ..., N$) in an optimal, cost-minimizing, fashion, taking a certain level of composite public consumption (G) as given. This implies that the government's demand for variety j is:

$$\frac{G_j}{G} = N^{-(\theta+\eta)+\eta\theta} \left(\frac{P_j}{P}\right)^{-\theta}, \quad j = 1, ..., N, \tag{11.16}$$

where the similarity to (11.7) should be apparent to all and sundry. Since C and G feature the same functional form, the price index for the public good is given by P in (11.9).

The total demand facing each firm j equals $Y_j \equiv C_j + G_j$, which in view of (11.7) and (11.16) shows that the demand elasticity facing firm j equals $\varepsilon_j = \theta$ so that the markup is constant and equal to $\mu_j = \mu = \theta/(\theta - 1)$. In this simplest case, the composition of demand does not matter. The model is completely symmetric: all firms face the same production costs and use the same pricing rule and thus set the same price, i.e. $P_j = \bar{P} = \mu W k$. As a result they all produce the same amount, i.e. $Y_j = \bar{Y}$, for $j = 1, \ldots, N$. A useful quantity index for real aggregate output can then be defined as:

$$Y \equiv \frac{\sum_{j=1}^{N} P_j Y_j}{P},$$
(11.17)

so that the aggregate goods market equilibrium condition can be written as in (T1.1) in Table 11.1 (we note that $PY = \sum_{j=1}^{N} P_j \left[C_j + G_j \right] = P \left[C + G \right]$).

Table 11.1. A simple macro model with monopolistic competition

$Y = C + G$	(T1.1)
$PC = \alpha I_F, \ I_F \equiv [W + \Pi - T]$	(T1.2)
$\Pi \equiv \sum_{j=1}^{N} \Pi_j = \frac{1}{\theta} PY - WNF$	(T1.3)
$T = PG + WL_G$	(T1.4)
$P = N^{1-\eta} \bar{P} = N^{1-\eta} \mu W k$	(T1.5)
$W(1 - L) = (1 - \alpha) I_F$	(T1.6)
$V = \dfrac{I_F}{P_V}, \quad P_V = \left(\dfrac{P}{\alpha} \right)^{\alpha} \left(\dfrac{W}{1 - \alpha} \right)^{1-\alpha}$	(T1.7)

For convenience, we summarize the model in aggregate terms in Table 11.1. Equation (T1.1) is the aggregate goods market clearing condition and (T1.2) is household demand for the composite consumption good (see (11.6)). Equation (T1.3) relates aggregate profit income (Π) to aggregate spending (PY) and firms' outlays on overhead labour (WNF). This expression is obtained by aggregating (11.11) over all active firms:

$$\Pi \equiv \sum_{j=1}^{N} P_j Y_j - \sum_{j=1}^{N} W k Y_j - WNF$$

$$= \sum_{j=1}^{N} P_j Y_j - \sum_{j=1}^{N} \frac{P_j Y_j}{\mu} - WNF$$

$$= \frac{1}{\theta} PY - WNF,$$

where we have used the rewritten pricing rule ($Wk = P_j/\mu$) to get from the first to the second line, and $1 - 1/\mu = 1/\theta$ to arrive at the final expression. The government budget restriction (T1.4) says that government spending on goods (PG) plus wage payments to civil servants (WL_G) must equal the lump-sum tax (T). By using the symmetric pricing rule in the definition of the price index (11.9) expression (T1.5) is obtained. Labour supply is given by (T1.6). Finally, (T1.7) contains some welfare indicators to be used and explained below in section 1.4.

Equilibrium in the labour market implies that the supply of labour (L) must equal the number of civil servants employed by the government (L^G) plus the number of workers employed in the monopolistically competitive sector:

$$L = L_G + \sum_{j=1}^{N} L_j. \tag{11.18}$$

Walras's Law ensures that the labour market is in equilibrium, i.e. (T1.1)–(T1.6) together imply that (11.18) holds.

There is no money in the model so *nominal* prices and wages are indeterminate. It is convenient to use leisure as the numeraire, i.e. W is fixed and everything is measured in wage units. The model can be analysed for two polar cases. In the first case, the number of firms is constant and fluctuations in profits emerge. This version of the model is deemed to be relevant for the short run and gives rise to short-run multipliers (Mankiw, 1988). In the second case, the number of firms is variable and exit/entry of firms ensures that profits return to zero following a shock. Following Startz (1989) this can be seen as the long-run version of the model.

11.1.2 The short-run balanced-budget multiplier

In the (very) short run, Mankiw (1988) argued, the number of firms is fixed (say $N = N_0$) and the model in Table 11.1 exhibits a positive balanced-budget multiplier. This can be demonstrated as follows. By substituting (T1.3) and (T1.4) into (T1.2), the aggregate consumption function can be written in terms of aggregate output and constants:

$$C = c_0 + \frac{\alpha}{\theta} Y - \alpha G, \tag{11.19}$$

where $c_0 \equiv \alpha [1 - N_0 F - L_G] w$ and $w \equiv W/P$ is the real wage. It follows from (T1.5) that $w = N^{\eta-1}/(\mu k)$, i.e. the real wage rate is constant in the short run.[3] The consumption function looks rather Keynesian and has a slope between zero and unity since $0 < \alpha < 1$ and $\theta > 1$. Additional output boosts real profit income to the household which spends a fraction of the extra income on consumption goods (and the rest on leisure). The consumption function has been drawn in Figure 11.1 for an initial level of government spending, G_0. By vertically adding G_0 to C, aggregate demand is obtained. The initial equilibrium is at point E_0 where aggregate demand equals production, and equilibrium consumption and output are, respectively, C_0 and Y_0.

Now consider what happens if the government boosts its consumption, say from G_0 to G_1, and finances this additional spending by an increase in the lump-sum tax, T. Such a balanced-budget policy has two effects in the short run. First, it exerts a negative effect on the aggregate consumption function (see (11.19)) because households have to pay higher taxes, i.e. the consumption function shifts down by αdG in Figure 11.1. Second, the spending shock also boosts aggregate demand one-for-one

---

[3]The number of product varieties (N) is fixed as are (by assumption) the markup (μ) and the marginal labour requirement (k).

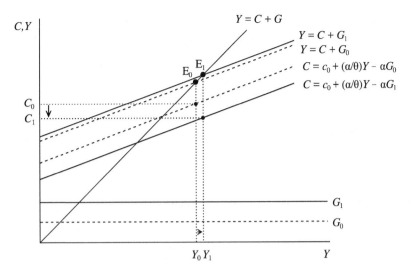

Figure 11.1: Government spending multipliers

because the government purchases additional goods. Since the marginal propensity to consume out of full income, α, is less than unity, this direct spending effect dominates the private consumption decline and aggregate demand increases (by $(1 - \alpha)dG$), as is illustrated in Figure 11.1. The equilibrium shifts from E_0 to E_1, output increases from (Y_0 to Y_1), but consumption falls (C_0 to C_1). Formally, the short-run income and profit multipliers are:

$$\left(\frac{dY}{dG}\right)^{SR}_T = \left(\frac{\theta d\Pi}{PdG}\right)^{SR}_T = (1 - \alpha)\left[1 + \sum_{i=1}^{\infty}(\alpha/\theta)^i\right] = \frac{1 - \alpha}{1 - \alpha/\theta} > 1 - \alpha, \quad (11.20)$$

where the subscript indicates that an increase in the lump-sum tax is used to balance the government budget ($d\,(T/P) = dG$). As the term involving the infinite summation shows, the output effect can be seen as resulting from a "multiplier-like" process. An increase in government spending increases aggregate demand on impact by $(1 - \alpha)dG$ and causes additional real profits to the tune of $\theta^{-1}(1 - \alpha)dG$. Although aggregate household consumption declines at impact by αdG, the rise in profit income mitigates this reduction somewhat. This furnishes a second round in the multiplier process, which ultimately converges to the expression given in (11.20). Under perfect competition, there is no profit effect and hence the ultimate effect of a change in government consumption coincides with the impact effect, $1 - \alpha$.

Although (11.20) looks like a Keynesian multiplier (and certainly was sold as one by the initial authors),[4] some features are distinctly un-Keynesian. For one, household consumption falls as a result of the increase in government consumption:

$$-\alpha < \left(\frac{dC}{dG}\right)^{SR}_T = \left(\frac{dY}{dG}\right)^{SR}_T - 1 = -\frac{\theta - 1}{\theta - \alpha}\alpha < 0, \quad (11.21)$$

which is at odds with the usual Haavelmo balanced-budget multiplier (see Haavelmo, 1945). Furthermore, it turns out that the same reason that makes households cut back consumption (i.e. the higher tax burden, which lowers full income) also makes them

---

[4]With the notable exception of Dixon (1987) who argued that the multiplier was more Walrasian than Keynesian.

cut back on leisure consumption (since leisure is a normal good, see (11.8)) and increase labour supply. By dividing (T1.6) by the first expression in (T1.2) we find that $w(1 - L) = (1 - \alpha)C/\alpha$. The aggregate employment effect is thus given by:

$$0 < w \cdot \left(\frac{dL}{dG}\right)_T^{SR} = -\frac{1-\alpha}{\alpha} \cdot \left(\frac{dC}{dG}\right)_T^{SR} = \frac{\theta-1}{\theta-\alpha}(1-\alpha) < 1-\alpha. \qquad (11.22)$$

Hence, the Keynesian multiplier is really explained by the fact that households supply more labour because they feel poorer. This is a mechanism more usually associated with the new classical school to be discussed below in Chapters 13 and 19.

11.1.3 The short-run multiplier in isolation

Mankiw (1988) uses an ingenious argument to mimic the effect of bond financing in a static model (like the one in Table 11.1). Suppose that the additional government consumption is not financed by additional taxes (as in the previous subsection) but instead is paid for by firing civil servants. As in the case of bond financing,[5] the representative household's budget constraint is unaffected by the spending shock, and the consumption function (11.19) is replaced by:

$$C = \alpha[1 - N_0 F]w + \frac{\alpha}{\theta}Y - \alpha\frac{T}{P}, \qquad (11.23)$$

where the real tax bill (T/P) is constant. The various multipliers are now:

$$\left(\frac{dY}{dG}\right)_{LG}^{SR} = \left(\frac{\theta d\Pi}{PdG}\right)_{LG}^{SR} = \left[1 + \sum_{i=1}^{\infty}(\alpha/\theta)^i\right] = \frac{1}{1-\alpha/\theta} > 1, \qquad (11.24)$$

$$\left(\frac{dC}{dG}\right)_{LG}^{SR} = \frac{\alpha}{\theta-\alpha} > 0, \quad w\left(\frac{dL}{dG}\right)_{LG}^{SR} = -\frac{1-\alpha}{\theta-\alpha} < 0, \qquad (11.25)$$

where the subscript indicates that a reduction in the civil service wage bill is used to balance the government budget $(-wdL_G = dG)$. The output multiplier exceeds unity (as in the traditional Keynesian cross-model). As the representative household is wealthier because of the additional profit income, consumption rises and labour supply (and hence employment) falls. The additional units of labour that are needed to produce the additional output are released from the public sector. The intersectoral re-allocation of labour (from the public to the private sector) dominates the reduction in labour supply so that aggregate output can expand.

11.1.4 The "long-run" multiplier

Startz (1989) suggested that the multiplier stories that were told in the previous two subsections are incomplete because they implicitly assume that there are €100 bills lying around on the footpath. Not all trading opportunities are exhausted in the short-run equilibrium that emerges following a public spending shock. Indeed, as both (11.20) and (11.24) demonstrate, additional profits emerge as a result of the increase in government spending. In the absence of barriers to entry, one would expect new firms to commence operations as long as super-normal profits persist.

---

[5]And with disconnected generations so that Ricardian equivalence does not hold; see section 6.1.4.

Following Heijdra and van der Ploeg (1996, p. 1291) we capture this idea with the following simple specification:

$$\dot{N} = \gamma_N \frac{\Pi}{P} = \gamma_N \cdot \left[\frac{Y}{\theta} - wNF \right], \qquad \gamma_N > 0, \tag{11.26}$$

where $\dot{N} \equiv dN/dt$ is the rate of change in the number of firms over time and γ_N is finite so that exit/entry occurs gradually over time.

To keep the discussion as simple as possible, it is assumed in the remainder of this section that the government employs no civil servants (i.e. $L_G = 0$) so that the government budget constraint reduces to $T = PG$. The goods market equilibrium (GME) condition is obtained by substituting (T1.2)–(T1.4) into (T1.1):

$$Y = \alpha \left[1 - NF \right] w + \frac{\alpha}{\theta} Y + (1 - \alpha) G$$

$$= \left[\frac{\alpha(1 - NF)}{\mu k (1 - \alpha/\theta)} \right] N^{\eta - 1} + \left[\frac{1 - \alpha}{1 - \alpha/\theta} \right] G, \qquad \text{(GME)}, \tag{11.27}$$

where we have solved for output and used the pricing rule (given in (T1.5) above) to relate the real wage to the number of firms in the second line of (11.27). For future reference we rewrite this pricing rule as follows:

$$w = \frac{N^{\eta - 1}}{\mu k}. \tag{11.28}$$

Finally, the zero-profit condition, ZP, which is obtained by setting $\Pi = 0$ in (T1.3), collapses to $Y = \theta w N F$ which can be re-expressed with the aid of the pricing rule (11.28) in terms of the number of firms:

$$Y = \frac{\theta F N^{\eta}}{\mu k}, \qquad \text{(ZP)}. \tag{11.29}$$

The intuition behind the short-run, transitional, and long-run effects of a tax-financed increase in public consumption can now be explained with the aid of Figure 11.2. In the top panel ZP represents combinations of output and the number of firms for which profits are zero. In view of (11.29) the ZP line goes through the origin and is upward sloping:

$$\left(\frac{dY}{dN} \right)_{ZP} = \eta \frac{Y}{N} > 0. \tag{11.30}$$

Furthermore, (11.26) shows that profits are positive (negative) for points to the left (right) of the ZP line so that the entry dynamics is as indicated by horizontal arrows. Still in the top panel, GME_0 represents the initial goods market equilibrium locus as defined in equation (11.27). In order to study the properties of the GME-locus we differentiate the first expression in (11.27) around an initial zero-profit equilibrium:

$$\left[1 - \frac{\alpha}{\theta} \right] \frac{dY}{Y} = \frac{\alpha w}{Y} \left[1 - NF \right] \frac{dw}{w} - \frac{\alpha w N F}{Y} \frac{dN}{N} + (1 - \alpha) \frac{dG}{Y}$$

$$= \left[1 - (1 - \alpha) \omega_G \right] \frac{dw}{w} - \frac{\alpha}{\theta} \left[\frac{dw}{w} + \frac{dN}{N} \right] + (1 - \alpha) \frac{dG}{Y}$$

$$= (\eta - 1) \left[\alpha + (1 - \alpha) \omega_C \right] \frac{dN}{N} - \frac{\alpha \eta}{\theta} \frac{dN}{N} + (1 - \alpha) \frac{dG}{Y}, \tag{11.31}$$

where we have used the zero-profit condition (in levels) in going from the first to the second line and the pricing rule in going from the second to the third line. The initial output shares of private and public consumption are given, respectively, by $\omega_C \equiv C/Y$ and $\omega_G \equiv 1 - \omega_C = G/Y$.

Equation (11.31) shows that, for a given number of firms, an increase in government consumption leads to an upward shift of the GME-locus. Note furthermore that the output-related profit effect appears on the left-hand side of (11.31). There are two distinct mechanisms by which a change in the number of firms affects the GME-locus, namely the *diversity effect* and the *fixed-cost effect*. The first term on the right-hand side of (11.31) represents the positive effect on aggregate demand of an increase in the real wage which occurs as a result of an increase in the number of firms provided the agents exhibit love of variety ($\eta > 1$). This is the diversity effect. The second term is potentially offsetting and represents the negative effect on aggregate demand of fixed costs: as the number of firms increases, total overhead costs rise and profits fall. This is the fixed-cost effect.

The overall effect of N on Y along the GME-locus is thus theoretically ambiguous because the diversity and fixed-cost effects work in opposite directions. Our usual ploy to be used in the face of ambiguity, the Samuelsonian correspondence principle (see Chapter 3), does not help to resolve this issue because the model is stable for all parameter values. Indeed, in view of (11.26) the stability condition ($\partial \dot{N}/\partial N < 0$) amounts to requiring that the ZP line is steeper than the GME line. We can derive the following condition:

$$\left(\frac{\partial Y}{\partial N}\right)_{GME} \equiv \left[\frac{(\eta - 1)\left[\alpha + (1 - \alpha)\omega_C\right] - \alpha\eta/\theta}{1 - \alpha/\theta}\right]\frac{Y}{N} < \eta\frac{Y}{N} \equiv \left(\frac{\partial Y}{\partial N}\right)_{ZP}$$

$$\Leftrightarrow (\eta - 1)\left[\alpha + (1 - \alpha)\omega_C\right] - \frac{\alpha\eta}{\theta} < \eta - \frac{\alpha\eta}{\theta}$$

$$\Leftrightarrow \frac{\eta - 1}{\eta}\left[\alpha + (1 - \alpha)\omega_C\right] < 1, \tag{11.32}$$

where the latter inequality holds as both terms on the left-hand side are strictly between zero and unity.[6]

Two often-used approaches lead to a resolution of the ambiguity regarding the slope of the GME-locus. In the first approach the ambiguity is resolved by ignoring the conceptual distinction between the price elasticity of demand (θ) and the preference for diversity (η) and imposing a single utility parameter to regulate these two effects. Technically, the standard Dixit and Stiglitz (1977, p. 298) formulation is used for composite consumption by setting $\eta = \mu \equiv \theta/(\theta - 1)$ in (11.2). Since $\theta > 1$ is required to guarantee a meaningful monopolistically competitive equilibrium (i.e. to ensure that $\mu > 1$), diversity preference is operative ($\eta > 1$) *and* strong enough to render the slope of the GME-locus positive:

$$\left(\frac{\partial Y}{\partial N}\right)_{GME}^{\eta = \mu} \equiv \frac{(1 - \alpha)\omega_C}{(\theta - 1)\left[1 - \alpha/\theta\right]}\frac{Y}{N} > 0. \tag{11.33}$$

This is the case drawn in Figure 11.2. An increase in government consumption shifts the GME locus from GME_0 to GME_1. At impact the number of firms is predetermined (at $N = N_0$) and output rises as the economy jumps from E_0 to E_1. This is

---

[6]For a more general utility function than (11.1), the stability condition does furnish additional information that is useful for comparative static purposes. See Heijdra and van der Ploeg (1996, p. 1291), Heijdra and Ligthart (1997, p. 817), and Heijdra et al. (1998, p. 86) for different examples.

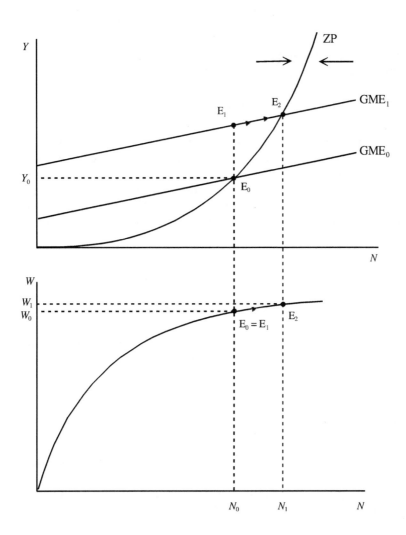

Figure 11.2: Multipliers and firm entry

the short-run multiplier given in (11.20). At point E_1 there are super-normal profits to be had and entry of new firms occurs. Gradually, the economy moves along GME_1 from E_1 to E_2 and both output and the number of firms increase towards their new equilibrium values. Furthermore, as the lower panel of Figure 11.2 shows, the real wage rate also increases during transition. So, even though the model may not be vintage Keynesian in its basic mechanism, it does have some Keynesian features since the real wage and aggregate output move pro-cyclically.

Whereas in the first approach the long-run output multiplier exceeds the short-run multiplier, this conclusion is reversed in the second approach. Startz (1989, p. 741) implicitly resolves the ambiguity concerning the slope of the GME locus by eliminating preference for diversity altogether, i.e. by setting $\eta = 1$ in (11.2). The GME locus is downward sloping in that case as entry of firms only does bad things to the economy (such as using up additional resources in the form of overhead labour):

$$\left(\frac{\partial Y}{\partial N}\right)_{GME}^{\eta=1} \equiv -\frac{\alpha/\theta}{1-\alpha/\theta}\frac{Y}{N} < 0. \qquad (11.34)$$

Furthermore, the pricing rule (11.28) implies a constant real wage in that case (recall that $w = N^{\eta-1}/(\mu k)$). In a diagram like Figure 11.2, the GME curve is downward sloping in the top panel and the wage curve is horizontal in the bottom panel. At impact the multiplier is as in (11.20) but during transition the increase in the number of firms leads to a reduction in aggregate output. The long-run effect on output is equal merely to the first round of the multiplier process in (11.20) (i.e. the impact effect of the shock):

$$0 < \left(\frac{dY}{dG}\right)_T^{LR,\eta=1} = (1-\alpha) < \frac{1-\alpha}{1-\alpha/\theta} \equiv \left(\frac{dY}{dG}\right)_T^{SR}. \qquad (11.35)$$

This prompts Startz (1989, p. 747) to conclude that "... in the long run the short-run multiplier is eliminated by free entry".

In the most general version of the model, with η unrestricted, the long-run multiplier can be computed by using the zero profit condition (11.29) to derive $dY/Y = \eta dN/N$ and by using this result in (11.31):

$$\left(\frac{dY}{dG}\right)_T^{LR} = \eta w \left(\frac{dL}{dG}\right)_T^{LR} = \frac{1-\alpha}{1 - \frac{\eta-1}{\eta}[\alpha + (1-\alpha)w_C]} > 1-\alpha, \qquad (11.36)$$

where the inequality follows from the fact that the denominator is strictly between zero and unity if $\eta > 1$ (see (11.32)). Hence, whereas fluctuations in profit income explain the multiplication of the impact effect in the short run, it is the preference for diversity effect which plays this role in the long run.

Although Startz (1989, p. 751 fn. 13) justifies the elimination of diversity preference by appealing to computational advantages, it is not an innocuous assumption at all, as the discussion above reveals. In essence, if the diversity parameter (η) is greater than unity there are economy-wide increasing returns to scale that help explain the "long-run" multiplier under free exit/entry of firms. Indeed, in the long run profits are zero and $Y = \theta w N F = wL$. The second equality implies that $N = L/(\theta F)$ which can be substituted into (11.29) to obtain the macroeconomic "production function":

$$Y = \frac{(\theta F)^{1-\eta}}{\mu k} L^\eta. \qquad (11.37)$$

Changes in the aggregate supply of the production factor(s) (labour in this case) are magnified more than proportionally. The importance of increasing returns to scale for Keynesian economics has been stressed time and again by seasoned warriors like Weitzman (1982, 1984, 1994) and Solow (1986, 1998), and allowing for preference for diversity is one particularly simple way to introduce scale economies.[7]

11.1.5 Welfare effects

In a famous passage in the *General Theory*, Keynes argued that seemingly useless government consumption could actually improve welfare for the agents in the economy:

> If the Treasury were to fill old bottles with bank-notes, bury them at suitable depths in disused coal-mines which are then filled up to the surface with town rubbish, and leave it to private enterprise on well-tried principles of *laissez-faire* to dig the notes up again (. . .), there need be no more unemployment and, with the help of the repercussions, the real income of the community, and its capital wealth also, would probably become a good deal greater than it actually is. (1936, p. 129)

In the jargon of modern economics, Keynes suggests in this quotation that the marginal cost of public funds (MCPF, see Chapter 9) is zero or even negative: useless spending turns out to be useful after all! To conclude this section we now investigate the link between fiscal policy multipliers and the welfare of the representative agent. It turns out that the monopolistic competition model has some Keynesian aspects in this regard although they are not quite as extreme as the quotation suggests.

One of the major advantages of macroeconomic models based on explicit microeconomic foundations is that they provide an explicit link between macroeconomic concepts (such as aggregate output, employment, etc.) and the level of welfare experienced by the representative household. To conduct the welfare analysis for the monopolistic competition model it is convenient to use the so-called *indirect utility function*, rather than the direct utility function given in (11.1). The indirect utility function is obtained by substituting the optimal plans of the representative household (namely (11.6) and (11.8)) into the direct utility function (11.1) (see Intermezzo 11.1 above for details):

$$V \equiv \frac{I_F}{P_V} \equiv \frac{w + \Pi/P - T/P}{P_V/P}, \quad \frac{P_V}{P} \equiv \frac{w^{1-\alpha}}{\alpha^\alpha (1-\alpha)^{1-\alpha}}. \tag{11.38}$$

Armed with this expression we can evaluate the welfare effects of expansionary fiscal policy. In the interest of brevity, we only analyse the short-run multipliers discussed above in subsections 1.2. and 1.3.

First consider the case in which the increase in government consumption is financed by means of a lump-sum tax increase. By substituting the expression for real aggregate profit income (T1.3) and the government budget constraint (T1.4) in (11.38) we obtain the following expression:

$$V \equiv \frac{[1 - NF - L_G]w + (1/\theta)Y - G}{P_V/P}. \tag{11.39}$$

---

[7]In the model developed here (and in most models in the literature) all scale economies are external to the firm in the long run. With a constant markup the zero profit condition in combination with markup pricing implies a unique (constant) optimal long-run firm size: $\bar{Y} \equiv F/[(\mu - 1)k]$. Hence, aggregate output expansion is solely due to increases in the number of firms in the long run.

Since N and thus also w, P, and P_V are constant in the short run, the welfare effect of a tax-financed fiscal expansion is simply the derivative of V with respect to G:

$$\left(\frac{dV}{dG}\right)_T^{SR} = \frac{P}{P_V}\left[\frac{1}{\theta}\left(\frac{dY}{dG}\right)_T^{SR} - 1\right] = -\frac{P}{P_V}\cdot\frac{\theta-1}{\theta-\alpha} < 0, \tag{11.40}$$

where we have substituted the output multiplier (given in (11.20)) to simplify the expression. Under monopolistic competition, there is an intimate link between the multiplier and the welfare effect of public spending which is absent under perfect competition. The intuition is that under monopolistic competition there is a distortion in the goods market and the economy is "too small" from a societal point of view. By raising government spending output rises and that in itself constitutes a move in the right, welfare-enhancing, direction. Of course government consumption must also be financed somehow (here by means of lump-sum taxes) so that the expansion is not costless. Indeed, (11.40) shows that the overall effect of a lump-sum financed fiscal expansion is negative.

So unless there are other reasons (such as public goods aspects due to government spending discussed by Heijdra and van der Ploeg, 1996) the government does not increase welfare as a result of its increased spending and Keynes' insight does not hold. This un-Keynesian element of the monopolistic competition model is explained by two of its key properties: (1) the real wage is flexible and clears the labour market, *and* (2) every unit of labour contributes to production in the economy.

The importance of the second property of the model can be demonstrated by studying the case (discussed in detail in subsection 1.3) in which the spending shock is financed by reducing the number of (unproductive) civil servants (i.e. $dG = -wdL_G$). In that case the lump-sum tax is constant and the relevant expression for indirect utility is:

$$V \equiv \frac{[1 - NF]\,w + (1/\theta)Y - T/P}{P_V/P}, \tag{11.41}$$

from which we obtain the welfare effect:

$$\left(\frac{dV}{dG}\right)_{L_G}^{SR} = \frac{P}{P_V}\frac{1}{\theta}\left(\frac{dY}{dG}\right)_{L_G}^{SR} = \frac{P}{P_V}\cdot\frac{1}{\theta-\alpha} > 0. \tag{11.42}$$

In this case only the beneficial effect of government-induced output expansion is operative and welfare rises. The intuition is the same as in Keynes' story: units of labour are shifted from socially unproductive to productive activities. The monopolistically competitive sector absorbs the former civil servants without prompting a change in the real wage.

Intermezzo 11.2

Multipliers and the marginal cost of public funds. There exists a simple relationship between the macroeconomic concept of the output multiplier and the public finance concept of marginal cost of public funds (MCPF). This link is particularly useful to study issues of optimal public spending and taxation. As was pointed out in Chapter 9, the MCPF measures how much it costs to raise a euro of public revenue. In the context of the monopolistic competition model, the MCPF is defined as follows:

$$MCPF \equiv -\frac{1}{U_C}\frac{dV}{dG}, \tag{a}$$

where U_C is the marginal utility of composite consumption. Intuitively, the minus sign appears on the right-hand side to convert benefits into costs (a negative benefit is equivalent to a positive cost!) and the division by U_C occurs in order to compare "likes with likes" and to render the MCPF dimensionless.

It is not difficult to show that U_C equals P/P_V. Recall that the representative household maximizes utility, $U(C, 1 - L)$, subject to the budget constraint, $I_F = PC + W(1 - L)$. The first-order conditions for this problem are $U_C = \lambda P$ and $U_{1-L} = \lambda W$, where λ is the Lagrange multiplier of the budget constraint representing the marginal utility of (full) income, i.e. $\lambda = dU/dI_F$ (see Intriligator, 1971, ch. 3). The indirect utility function (11.38) shows that $dV/dI_F = 1/P_V = dU/dI_F$. By combining these results we derive that $U_C = P/P_V$ so that (11.40) and (11.42) can be re-expressed in terms of the MCPF:

$$0 < \text{MCPF}_T^{SR} \equiv -\frac{1}{U_C}\left(\frac{dV}{dG}\right)_T^{SR} = \frac{\theta - 1}{\theta - \alpha} < 1, \tag{b}$$

$$\text{MCPF}_{L_G}^{SR} \equiv -\frac{1}{U_C}\left(\frac{dV}{dG}\right)_{L_G}^{SR} = -\frac{1}{\theta - \alpha} < 0. \tag{c}$$

Hence, it costs (more than zero but) less than one euro to raise a euro of revenue if lump-sum taxes are used (expression (b)) and the MCPF is even negative if useless civil servants can be made socially productive (expression (c)). Heijdra and van der Ploeg (1996) develop a more general monopolistic competition model and use the concept of the MCPF to derive the conditions under which optimal public spending is countercyclical.

****

11.2 Monopolistic competition and money

In the monopolistic competition model used throughout the previous section (and summarized in Table 11.1) money is abstracted from, and as a result *nominal* prices and the nominal wage are indeterminate although, of course, *relative* prices are determined within the model. The objective of this section is to introduce money into the model and study its properties. Although there are several ways to ensure that money plays a role in the model (see Chapter 10), we focus attention on the simplest of these and postulate that real money balances yield utility to the representative household. The utility function (11.1) is changed to:

$$U \equiv \left[C^\alpha (1-L)^{1-\alpha}\right]^\beta \left(\frac{M}{P}\right)^{1-\beta}, \quad 0 < \alpha, \beta < 1, \tag{11.43}$$

where M is nominal money balances. The household has an initial endowment of money, M_0, and the budget constraint (11.5) is changed to:

$$PC + W(1-L) + M = M_0 + W + \Pi - T, \tag{11.44}$$

which says that the sum of spending on consumption, leisure, and money balances (the left-hand side) must equal total wealth (the right-hand side of (11.44)).

The household chooses composite consumption (C), labour supply (L), and money balances (M) in order to maximize (11.43) subject to (11.44). The solutions are:[8]

$$PC = \alpha\beta I_F, \quad I_F \equiv M_0 + W + \Pi - T, \tag{11.45}$$
$$W(1-L) = \beta(1-\alpha)I_F, \tag{11.46}$$
$$M = (1-\beta)I_F. \tag{11.47}$$

The first two expressions are qualitatively the same as before (see (11.6) and (11.8)), although I_F now includes initial money balances. Furthermore, equation (11.47) shows that money demand is proportional to full income. For future reference we substitute the solutions (11.45)–(11.47) back into the direct utility function (11.43) to obtain the indirect utility function–see equation (T2.8) in Table 11.2 below.

Assuming a constant money supply (M_0), the money market equilibrium condition is:

$$M = M_0. \tag{11.48}$$

The rest of the model is unchanged and we summarize the main equations of the monetary monopolistic competition model in Table 11.2.

It is tempting (though wrong) to conclude from the form of the indirect utility function (T2.8) that the government could increase the welfare of the representative household by simply bringing more money into circulation (and boosting full income, I_F, in the process), for example by engineering a helicopter drop of money ($dM_0 > 0$). The reason why such a ploy would not work is that money is neutral in this model and the classical dichotomy holds (see Chapter 1). This can be demonstrated formally by noting that the equilibrium conditions (in Table 11.2) are homogeneous of degree zero in W, P, T, Π, I_F, and M_0 (see Dixon, 1987, p. 141). By substituting $\zeta W, \zeta P, \zeta T, \zeta \Pi, \zeta I_F$, and ζM_0 ($\zeta > 0$) into Table 11.2 the real equilibrium is unaffected. All that happens if the money supply is multiplied by ζ is that all nominal variables are increased equiproportionally and all real variables are unchanged. Hence, a helicopter drop of money does not succeed in raising household welfare because both I_F and P_V go up by the same proportional amount thus keeping V in (T2.8) unchanged. The upshot of this discussion is that monopolistic competition *in and of itself* does not introduce monetary non-neutrality. Put differently, if money is neutral in a model-economy without monopolistic competition then it is also neutral if monopolistic competition is introduced into the model (Silvestre, 1993, p. 122).

The model can be summarized with two equations. The goods market equilibrium (GME) locus is obtained by using (T2.2)–(T2.4) and (T2.7) in (T2.1). The money

[8]The demand for variety j of the composite consumption good is still given by (11.7).

Table 11.2. A simple monetary monopolistic competition model

$$Y = C + G \tag{T2.1}$$

$$C = \alpha\beta\frac{I_F}{P}, \quad \frac{I_F}{P} \equiv \frac{M_0}{P} + \frac{W}{P} + \frac{\Pi}{P} - \frac{T}{P} \tag{T2.2}$$

$$\frac{\Pi}{P} \equiv \frac{1}{\theta}Y - \frac{W}{P}NF \tag{T2.3}$$

$$\frac{T}{P} = G + \frac{W}{P}L_G \tag{T2.4}$$

$$\frac{P}{W} = \mu k N^{1-\eta}, \qquad \bar{P} = \mu k W \tag{T2.5}$$

$$\frac{W}{P}(1-L) = \beta(1-\alpha)\frac{I_F}{P} \tag{T2.6}$$

$$\frac{M_0}{P} = (1-\beta)\frac{I_F}{P} \tag{T2.7}$$

$$V = \frac{I_F}{P_V}, \qquad P_V = \left(\frac{P}{\alpha\beta}\right)^{\alpha\beta}\left(\frac{W}{\beta(1-\alpha)}\right)^{\beta(1-\alpha)}\left(\frac{P}{1-\beta}\right)^{1-\beta} \tag{T2.8}$$

---

market equilibrium (MME) locus is obtained by using the second expression of (T2.2) as well as (T2.3)–(T2.4) in (T2.7):

$$Y = \frac{\alpha[1 - NF - L_G]w + (1-\alpha)G}{1 - \alpha/\theta}, \qquad \text{(GME)}, \tag{11.49}$$

$$\frac{M_0}{P} = \frac{1-\beta}{\beta}\left[[1 - NF - L_G]w + \frac{1}{\theta}Y - G\right], \qquad \text{(MME)}. \tag{11.50}$$

The two loci provide a clear demonstration of the classical dichotomy. In the short run, N and thus w are fixed and GME determines equilibrium output. Since the money supply does not appear in (11.49), monetary policy cannot affect equilibrium output. According to (11.50), an increase in the money supply leads to an equiproportional increase in the price level.

The GME and MME loci can also be used to compute the short-run effects of a tax-financed increase in public consumption. An increase in G leads to a boost in output Y but a reduction in the demand for real money balances (as real full income falls). Since nominal money balances M_0 are constant, the price P rises to bring demand and supply of real money balances back into equilibrium. The nominal wage and prices of different varieties also rise equi-proportionally. In summary:

$$0 < \left(\frac{dY}{dG}\right)_T^{SR} = \frac{1-\alpha}{1-\alpha/\theta} < 1, \quad \left(\frac{dW}{W}\right)_T^{SR} = \left(\frac{dP}{P}\right)_T^{SR} = \left(\frac{d\bar{P}}{\bar{P}}\right)_T^{SR}, \tag{11.51}$$

$$\left(\frac{dM_0/P}{dG}\right)_T^{SR} = -\frac{M_0}{P^2}\left(\frac{dP}{dG}\right)_T^{SR} = -\frac{(1-\beta)(\theta-1)}{\beta(\theta-\alpha)} < 0.$$

As far as its monetary properties are concerned, the model is more classical than Keynesian if prices and wages are flexible.

11.3   Sticky prices and the non-neutrality of money

In the previous section it was demonstrated that the presence of monopolistically competitive agents in the economy does not in and of itself render money non-neutral. This is not to say that the introduction of price-setting agents in a macroeconomic model is merely a theoretical nicety yielding no novel insights or additional predictions. Indeed, in the first section of this chapter it was shown how the monopolistic competition model with flexible prices and wages generates results that are quite different from the standard competitive model. An additional advantage of assuming monopolistic, rather than perfect, competition is that one can do away with the fictional notion of the Walrasian auctioneer.

By modelling price-setting agents explicitly, it is also possible to study quite precisely the conditions under which such an agent would change his price (or keep it unchanged) following a shock in some nominal variable such as the money supply or the nominal wage rate (Rotemberg, 1987, p. 71). The key ingredient of the New Keynesian approach is to postulate that it costs the firm real resources in order to change its price. As a result, prices may not be adjusted after some nominal shock and money may be non-neutral. In the remainder of this section a number of the main macroeconomic price-adjustment models will be discussed. The key feature distinguishing these models lies in the nature of the price adjustment costs that are postulated.

As is pointed out by Rotemberg (1982, p. 522) there are two main reasons why prices may be costly to change. First, there may be administrative costs having to do with informing dealers, reprinting price lists, etc. Such costs tend to have the nature of a fixed cost per price change, independent of the magnitude of the change: it costs the same to reprint your restaurant menu card when you double or triple your prices. Such price adjustment costs are often referred to as *menu costs* in the new Keynesian literature. The second reason why prices may be costly to change is that there may be an implicit cost due to an adverse reaction of customers to large price changes. According to this view customers may prefer *frequent small* price changes over *infrequent but large* price adjustments. It is conventional to assume that such costs are increasing and convex in the price change.[9]

We now turn to a discussion of some of the most popular models of price setting. In the first model only menu costs play a role (subsection 11.3.1) whilst in the second we assume that price adjustment costs are quadratic (subsection 11.3.2). In subsection 11.3.3 we discuss an alternative setting in which price adjustment costs are random and are either infinite or zero in any particular period. The models in subsections 11.3.2–11.3.3 both give rise to a new Keynesian Phillips curve which is similar in form (though not in interpretation) to the expectations-augmented Phillips curve of Friedman and Phelps (see Roberts, 1995, pp. 979–980).

11.3.1   Menu costs

In this subsection we develop a simple monetary monopolistic competition model in which price-setting firms face small menu costs if they wish to changes their prices. The model is a simplified version of Blanchard and Kiyotaki (1987) in that the labour market is assumed to be competitive and populated by wage-taking agents (firms and the representative household). Hence, the nominal wage is flexible and labour

---

[9]Such costs are reminiscent of the adjustment costs often postulated in the theory of firm investment. See the discussion of Tobin's q-theory of investment in Chapters 3 and 4.

demand and supply are equated. The main advantage of assuming a competitive labour market is that it facilitates the exposition of the main results and identifies in a straightforward fashion some of the empirical problems the menu-cost argument runs into.

As in Blanchard and Kiyotaki (1987, p. 649) the representative household has a utility function which is additively separable in composite consumption and real money, on the one hand, and labour hours on the other:

$$U(C, M/P, L) \equiv U^1(C, M/P) - U^2(L)$$

$$= C^\alpha \left(\frac{M}{P} \right)^{1-\alpha} - \gamma_L \frac{L^{1+1/\sigma}}{1+1/\sigma}, \quad 0 < \alpha < 1, \quad \sigma > 0, \tag{11.52}$$

where $\gamma_L > 0$ is a simple scaling factor (to be used in the computer simulations below) and σ regulates the slope of the labour supply function (see below). The budget restriction is given by:

$$PC + M = WL + M_0 + \Pi - T \ (\equiv I), \tag{11.53}$$

where I represents total wealth of the household (including labour income). Composite consumption is defined by (11.2), and it is assumed that the diversity effect is absent (i.e. we set $\eta = 1$). This is a useful and innocuous simplification as it is assumed that the number of firms is constant. The household chooses consumption, money balances, and labour supply in order to maximize (11.52) subject to (11.53). Again a simple two-stage procedure can be used to find the solutions. In the first stage the household chooses C and M/P to maximize the sub-utility function $U^1(C, M/P)$ subject to the budget restriction $PC + M = I$. This yields the following expressions:

$$PC = \alpha I, \tag{11.54}$$

$$M = (1 - \alpha)I, \tag{11.55}$$

$$V^1(I/P) = \alpha^\alpha (1 - \alpha)^{1-\alpha} \frac{I}{P}, \tag{11.56}$$

where $V^1(I/P)$ is the indirect sub-utility function associated with $U^1(C, M/P)$.[10] In the second stage, the household chooses L and thus I in order to maximize $V^1(I/P) - U^2(L)$ subject to the definition of I (given on the right-hand side of (11.53)). This yields the expressions for labour supply and real household wealth including labour income:

$$L = \left(\frac{\alpha^\alpha (1 - \alpha)^{1-\alpha}}{\gamma_L} \right)^\sigma \left(\frac{W}{P} \right)^\sigma, \tag{11.57}$$

$$\frac{I}{P} = \left(\frac{\alpha^\alpha (1 - \alpha)^{1-\alpha}}{\gamma_L} \right)^\sigma \left(\frac{W}{P} \right)^{1+\sigma} + \frac{M_0 + \Pi - T}{P}. \tag{11.58}$$

By using the utility specification (11.52), there is no income effect in labour supply and only the substitution effect survives. The advantage of this specification is that it enables us to demonstrate the crucial role played by the elasticity of labour supply with respect to the real wage. If σ is very high, labour supply is highly elastic and

---

[10]It is obtained by substituting the optimal values for C and M/P into the direct sub-utility function $U^1(\cdot)$.

large labour supply changes result from only a small increase in the real wage. Conversely, if σ is low, labour supply is relatively inelastic and a large change in the real wage is needed to produce a given increase of labour supply.

Each firm in the monopolistically competitive sector faces a demand for its product from the private sector (see (11.7)) and from the government (see (11.16)). Since we abstract from diversity effects ($\eta = 1$), total demand facing firm j can be written as:

$$Y_j(P_j, P, Y) = \left(\frac{P_j}{P}\right)^{-\theta} \frac{Y}{N}, \tag{11.59}$$

where Y is aggregate demand:

$$Y = C + G = \frac{\alpha}{1 - \alpha} \frac{M}{P} + G, \tag{11.60}$$

and where we have used (11.54)–(11.55) to relate private consumption to real money balances.

For reasons that will become clear below, we use a slightly more general description of technology than before. Instead of (11.10) we use the following production function:

$$Y_j = \begin{cases} 0 & \text{if } L_j \leq F \\ \left[\dfrac{L_j - F}{k}\right]^{\gamma} & \text{if } L_j \geq F, \end{cases} \tag{11.61}$$

with $0 < \gamma \leq 1$. If γ is strictly less than unity, the marginal product of labour declines with output and the average cost curve of the firm is U-shaped (see Dixon and Lawler, 1996, p. 223). Of course, if $\gamma = 1$ (11.61) and (11.10) coincide.

Firm j chooses its price, P_j, in order to maximize its profit:[11]

$$\Pi_j(P_j, P, Y) \equiv P_j \cdot Y_j(P_j, P, Y) - W\left[k \cdot \left[Y_j(P_j, P, Y)\right]^{1/\gamma} + F\right]. \tag{11.62}$$

The optimal price of firm j must satisfy the following first-order condition:

$$\begin{aligned}
\frac{d\Pi_j(P_j, P, Y)}{dP_j} &= (P_j - MC_j) \cdot \frac{\partial Y_j(P_j, P, Y)}{\partial P_j} + Y_j(P_j, P, Y) \\
&= Y_j(P_j, P, Y) \cdot \left(1 + \frac{P_j - MC_j}{P_j} \cdot \frac{P_j}{Y_j(\cdot)} \frac{\partial Y_j(\cdot)}{\partial P_j}\right) \\
&= Y_j(P_j, P, Y) \cdot \left[1 - \theta \cdot \frac{P_j - MC_j}{P_j}\right] = 0,
\end{aligned} \tag{11.63}$$

where $MC_j \equiv (Wk/\gamma) Y_j(P_j, P, Y)^{(1-\gamma)/\gamma}$ is marginal costs of firm j and where we have substituted the price elasticity of demand (θ) in going from the second to the third line. An active firm is one which produces a positive amount of goods ($Y_j(\cdot) > 0$) and sets it price such that the term in square brackets on the right-hand side of (11.63) is equal to zero:

$$P_j = \mu MC_j \quad \Rightarrow \quad P_j = \frac{\mu k}{\gamma} WY_j^{(1-\gamma)/\gamma}, \qquad \mu \equiv \frac{\theta}{\theta - 1} > 1. \tag{11.64}$$

---

[11]The reason why we introduce the rather elaborate notation for demand $Y_j(P_j, P, Y)$ and profit $\Pi_j(P_j, P, Y)$ will be made apparent below.

This pricing rule generalizes the one derived in section 11.1 (i.e. equation (11.13)) by allowing for an upward-sloping marginal cost curve (if $\gamma < 1$). Apart from this generalization, another important thing to note is that in section 1 it was assumed that the firm sets its output level in a profit-maximizing fashion taking other producers' output levels as given (the Cournot assumption). In contrast, in this section the firm sets its price in an optimal (profit-maximizing) fashion, taking other producers' prices as given (the Bertrand assumption). In the absence of menu costs the two assumptions yield the same pricing rule. As is shown below, however, this equivalence does not necessarily hold in the presence of menu costs.

We now have all the ingredients of the model, though still abstracting from menu costs. The main equations have been collected in Table 11.3. Equation (T3.2) expresses consumption (and equilibrium real money balances) as a function of factors influencing real wealth. It is obtained by using (11.54)–(11.55) and (11.58), and substituting the government budget constraint $G = T/P$ (we again abstract from civil servants and set $L_G = 0$ in (T2.4)). Equation (T3.3) is the expression for aggregate profit income. It is obtained by substituting (11.64) into the definition of profit income (11.62) and simplifying by using the definition of Y in (11.17). Finally, (T3.4) is the price-setting rule in the symmetric equilibrium, and (T3.5) is the labour supply function.

Before turning to the implications of menu costs, we first study the properties of the model under perfect price flexibility. By studying the flex-price version of the models first, it is easier to understand the implications of menu costs later on. It is clear that money is neutral: multiplying W, P, and M_0 by $\zeta > 0$ does not change anything real and just changes all nominal variables (such as nominal wealth, I, and nominal profit, Π) equi-proportionally. As far as their monetary properties are concerned, the models of Tables 11.2 and 11.3 are thus similar in that they both exhibit monetary neutrality when prices and wages are flexible. There is an important difference between the two models, however, in the area of fiscal policy. Indeed, because there is no income effect in labour supply (see (T3.5)), fiscal policy is completely ineffective in the model of this section. Using the expressions in Table 11.3 it is easy to show that a tax-financed increase in public consumption leads to one-for-one crowding out of private consumption, no effect on output, real profits, employment, and real wages, and an increase in the price level. In that sense the model used here is even more classical than the one used in the previous section. In the next subsection we study if and to what extent the notion of menu costs can give this hyper-classical model a more Keynesian flavour.

11.3.1.1 The basic menu-cost insight

Sometimes the answer to an apparently simple question can be quite surprising. A beautiful example of this phenomenon is provided by Akerlof and Yellen's (1985a) question whether "small deviations from rationality make significant differences to equilibria". Alternatively, the question could be rephrased in terms of transaction costs: can small costs of changing one's actions have large effects on the economic equilibrium and social welfare? Nine out of ten people would probably answer this question with an unequivocal "no". The thought experiment would probably lead them to reject the notion that a small "impulse" can produce a "large effect". In terms of Matsuyama's (1995) terminology, most people are unfamiliar with the notion of macroeconomic complementarities and cumulative processes. It turns out, however, that the answer to Akerlof and Yellen's question can be quite a bit more complex.

In the context of our model, the task at hand is to investigate whether, following

Table 11.3. A simplified Blanchard-Kiyotaki model (no menu costs)

$$Y = C + G \tag{T3.1}$$

$$C = \frac{\alpha}{1-\alpha}\frac{M_0}{P} = \begin{cases} \alpha\left[\omega^{-\sigma}\left(\dfrac{W}{P}\right)^{1+\sigma} + \dfrac{M_0}{P} + \dfrac{\Pi}{P} - G\right] & (\text{if } \sigma < \infty) \\[2.2em] \alpha\left[\dfrac{W}{P}L + \dfrac{M_0}{P} + \dfrac{\Pi}{P} - G\right] & (\text{if } \sigma \to \infty) \end{cases} \tag{T3.2}$$

$$\frac{\Pi}{P} \equiv \frac{\mu - \gamma}{\mu}Y - \frac{W}{P}NF \tag{T3.3}$$

$$\frac{P}{W} = \frac{\mu k}{\gamma}\left(\frac{Y}{N}\right)^{(1-\gamma)/\gamma} \tag{T3.4}$$

$$\frac{W}{P} = \begin{cases} \omega L^{1/\sigma} & (\text{if } \text{œ} < \infty) \\ \omega & (\text{if } \text{œ} \to \infty) \end{cases} \tag{T3.5}$$

Notes: $\omega \equiv \gamma_L[\alpha^\alpha(1-\alpha)^{1-\alpha}]^{-1} > 0$ and $\mu \equiv \theta/(\theta-1)$.

a shock in aggregate demand, price stickiness can (a) be privately efficient and (b) exist in general equilibrium, whilst (c) the effect on social welfare can be large. If both parts (a) and (b) are demonstrated, Akerlof and Yellen's question is answered in the affirmative. Part (a) can be easily demonstrated to hold in our model and relies on a simple application of the *envelope theorem*. The proof of part (b) is more complex as it relies on the general equilibrium implications of price stickiness. Once (a) and (b) have been demonstrated, part (c) follows readily.

Intermezzo 11.3

The envelope theorem. The envelope theorem is extremely useful in economic theory. Broadly speaking the theorem says that the change in the objective function due to a change in an exogenous parameter is the same whether or not the decision variable is adjusted as a result of the change in the parameter. In more colloquial terms, the theorem says that objective functions are flat at the top (Rotemberg, 1987, p. 76).

Consider the formal demonstration by Varian (1992, pp. 490–491). Suppose that $f(x,z)$ is the objective function, x is the decision variable, and z is the (vector of) exogenous variables and parameters. The first-order condition for an optimum of $f(x,z)$ by choice of x is:

$$\frac{\partial f(x,z)}{\partial x} = 0. \tag{a}$$

But (a) can itself be interpreted as an implicit function relating the optimal choice for the decision variable (x^*) to the particular values of z, say $x^* = x^*(z)$. By plugging x^* back into the objective function we obtain the so-called optimal value function:

$$V(z) \equiv \max_{\{x\}} f(x,z) = f(x^*(z),z). \tag{b}$$

It is useful to note that we have in fact encountered many such optimal value functions throughout the book. For example, in this chapter the indirect utility function (11.38) is an example of a maximum value function: it expresses maximum attainable utility (the objective) in terms of full income and a true price index (the parameters that are exogenous to the household). Similarly, the true price index for the composite differentiated good (11.9) is an example of a minimum value function.

Using the optimal value function (b) we can determine by how much the objective function changes if (an element of) z changes by a small amount. By totally differentiating (b) we obtain:

$$\frac{dV(z)}{dz} = \left(\frac{\partial f(x,z)}{\partial x} \right)_{x=x^*(z)} \cdot \frac{dx^*(z)}{dz} + \frac{\partial f(x^*(z),z)}{\partial z}. \tag{c}$$

The second term on the right-hand side of (c) is the direct effect on the objective function of the change in z keeping the decision variable unchanged. The first term on the right-hand side is the indirect effect on the objective function that is induced by the change in x^* itself. The point to note, however, is that in the optimum the objective function is flat (i.e. (a) shows that $\partial f(\cdot)/\partial x = 0$ for $x = x^*$) so that the indirect effect is zero. Hence, equation (c) is reduced to:

$$\frac{dV(z)}{dz} = \frac{\partial f(x^*(z),z)}{\partial z} \equiv \frac{\partial V(z)}{\partial z}. \tag{d}$$

This is the simplest statement of the envelope theorem. The total and partial derivatives are the same, i.e. at the margin the change in the objective function is the same whether or not the decision variable is changed.

We close with an anecdote from times past. As is argued by Silberberg (1987), the discovery of the envelope theorem is due in part to a dispute between the famous economist Jacob Viner and his draftsman Dr Y. K. Wong. Viner was working on his famous paper about the relationship between short-run (AC_{SR}) and long-run average cost (AC_{LR}) curves (see Viner, 1931). He instructed Dr Wong to draw AC_{LR} in such a way that it was never above any portion of any AC_{SR} curve and that it would pass through the minimum points of all AC_{SR} curves. Dr Wong, being a mathematician, refused to do so and pointed out to Viner that his instructions were actually inconsistent. Unfortunately, Viner, not being a mathematician, could not understand Dr Wong's point and ended up drawing AC_{LR} through all the minima of the AC_{SR} curves (see his chart IV and footnote 16). Samuelson (1947), being both an economist and mathematician, ultimately solved the puzzle by pointing out that AC_{LR} is the envelope of all AC_{SR} curves. Wong was right after all! If this anecdote has any lesson at all, it must be that economists should also be reasonably good mathematicians to avoid falling into puzzles that cannot be solved by graphical means alone.

****

What happens to the optimal price of firm j if aggregate demand changes by a small amount? The answer is provided by the envelope theorem (see Intermezzo

11.3). In particular, (11.59) and (11.64) together yield an expression for the optimal price in terms of the parameters that are exogenous to firm j, i.e. $P_j^* = P_j(P, Y, W)$:

$$\frac{P_j^*}{P} = \left[\frac{\mu k}{\gamma} \cdot \frac{W}{P} \cdot \left(\frac{Y}{N} \right)^{(1-\gamma)/\gamma} \right]^{\gamma/[\gamma + \theta(1-\gamma)]}. \tag{11.65}$$

By substituting $P_j^*(\cdot)$ into (11.62) we obtain the maximum profit function of firm j:

$$\Pi_j^*(P, Y, W) \equiv P_j^*(\cdot) \cdot Y_j(P_j^*(\cdot), P, Y) - W \left[k \cdot [Y_j(P_j^*(\cdot), P, Y)]^{1/\gamma} + F \right]. \tag{11.66}$$

By differentiating this expression with respect to aggregate demand we obtain the result that it doesn't really matter to the profit of firm j whether or not it changes its price following a shock in aggregate demand:

$$\begin{aligned}
\frac{d\Pi_j^*(\cdot)}{dY} &= \left[\left[P_j^*(\cdot) - MC_j^*(\cdot) \right] \left(\frac{\partial Y_j(P_j, P, Y)}{\partial P_j} \right)_{P_j = P_j^*} + Y_j(P_j^*(\cdot), P, Y) \right] \frac{dP_j^*(\cdot)}{dY} \\
&\quad + \left[P_j^*(\cdot) - MC_j^*(\cdot) \right] \frac{\partial Y_j(P_j^*(\cdot), P, Y)}{\partial Y} \\
&= \left[\frac{\partial \Pi_j(\cdot)}{\partial P_j} \right]_{P_j = P_j^*} \frac{dP_j^*(\cdot)}{dY} + \left[P_j^*(\cdot) - MC_j^*(\cdot) \right] \frac{\partial Y_j(P_j^*(\cdot), P, Y)}{\partial Y} \\
&= \left[P_j^*(\cdot) - MC_j^*(\cdot) \right] \frac{\partial Y_j(P_j^*(\cdot), P, Y)}{\partial Y} \equiv \frac{\partial \Pi_j(\cdot)}{\partial Y},
\end{aligned} \tag{11.67}$$

where $MC_j^*(\cdot)$ is short-hand notation for the marginal cost of firm j evaluated at the optimum. Hence, to a first-order of magnitude, the effect on the profit of firm j of a change in aggregate demand is the same whether or not firm j changes its price optimally following the aggregate demand shock.

The envelope result can be illustrated with the aid of a diagram originally suggested by Akerlof and Yellen (1985a, p. 710). In Figure 11.3 firm j's price and profit level are put on the horizontal and vertical axes respectively. Initially aggregate demand is Y_0 and the optimal price is at the top of the "profit hill" at point A. The optimal price-profit combination is denoted by $(P_j^*(P, Y_0, W_0), \Pi_j^*(P, Y_0, W_0))$. Now consider what happens if aggregate demand expands, say from Y_0 to Y_1 ($> Y_0$). Ceteris paribus the nominal wage rate (W_0) and the price index for the composite consumption good (P),[12] the level of profit rises for all values of P_j and the entire profit function shifts up, say from $\Pi_j(P_j, P, Y_0, W_0)$ to $\Pi_j(P_j, P, Y_1, W_0)$.[13] The output expansion leads to an increase in marginal costs (provided $\gamma < 1$) and thus to an increase in the optimal price of firm j (see (11.64)–(11.65)). Hence, the top of the new profit hill (point B) lies north-east of the top of the old profit hill (point A).[14]

---

[12]We hold constant the prices charged by all other firms and conclude that this renders the price index, P, constant. In doing so, we ignore the fact that firm j's price also features in the price index P. This is allowed because there are many firms and each individual firm is extremely small and its price thus carries a small weight in the price index.

[13]Formally, (11.62) implies that $\partial \Pi_j(\cdot)/\partial Y = [P_j - MC_j]\partial Y_j/\partial Y$. A necessary condition for firm j to have positive profits (as drawn in Figure 11.3) is that its price must cover at least marginal cost, i.e. $P_j > MC_j$. Furthermore, (11.59) implies that firm j's demand expands if aggregate demand increases, i.e. $\partial Y_j/\partial Y > 0$. Combining these results yields $\partial \Pi_j(\cdot)/\partial Y > 0$. Firms like aggregate demand expansions because it raises

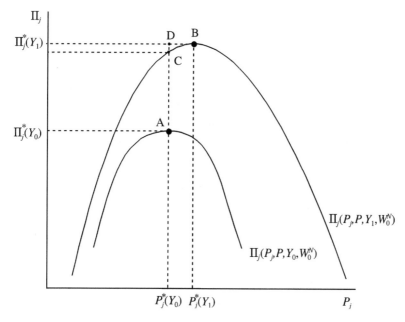

Figure 11.3: Menu costs

But this is not the end of the story. Following the shock to aggregate demand, firm j experiences a boost in the demand for its product and increases its production level accordingly. But this means that it needs to employ more workers. Since all firms are in exactly the same position as firm j they will also want to employ more workers so that aggregate demand for labour will rise. This is where the labour market comes in. Clearly, if the labour supply elasticity is very large ($\sigma \to \infty$), firm j (and all other firms) can obtain the additional units of labour at the initial nominal wage rate (W_0). In that case the real wage is rigid (see (T3.5)) and thus, if the price index P does not change neither will the nominal wage rate W. So all we need to show now is why the price index would be rigid.

Assuming for the time being that labour supply is infinitely elastic ($\sigma \to \infty$) it is possible to demonstrate the menu-cost insight graphically with the aid of Figure 11.3. For given values of P and W, the aggregate demand shock would increase the profits of firm j from $\Pi_j^*(P, Y_0, W_0)$ to $\Pi_j^*(P, Y_1, W_0)$ if it adjusted its price optimally (which is the move from A to B). If instead firm j keeps its price unchanged, the profit increase would be the vertical distance between points C and A, and the envelope theorem suggests that the profit loss due to non-adjustment of the price is of second order, i.e. the vertical distance DC in Figure 11.3 is very small. But that suggests that small menu costs can make non-adjustment of the price a profitable option for firm j. Indeed, provided the menu costs (Z) are larger than the vertical distance DC, keeping P_j unchanged is the optimal choice for firm j, i.e. P_j will be set equal to its

---

their profits.

[14]In contrast, if the marginal product of labour is constant ($\gamma = 1$), point B lies directly above point A. This strong result follows from the pricing rule (11.64) in combination with the fact that the demand elasticity (θ) and thus the gross markup (μ) of firm j are both constant. The optimal price is then proportional to the given nominal wage. As a result, for a given nominal wage there is no need for firm j to change its price and the envelope result (11.67) holds exactly.

old optimal level $(P_j^*(P, Y_0, W_0))$ if the following condition is satisfied:

$$\Pi_j(P_j^*(P, Y_0, W_0), P, Y_1, W_0) > \Pi_j^*(P, Y_1, W_0) - Z, \tag{11.68}$$

where the left-hand side of (11.68) is the profit level of firm j when it charges the old price and faces the higher aggregate demand, Y_1. The right-hand side of (11.68) is the net profit of firm j if it changes its price in the face of higher demand and incurs the menu cost. Since by assumption all firms are in exactly the same position as firm j, they also do not change their price if (11.68) holds and the maintained assumption that P is constant is thereby confirmed. Hence, for the infinitely elastic labour supply case ($\sigma \to \infty$) a menu-cost equilibrium exists for which an aggregate demand shock has no effect on prices and the nominal (and real) wage rate.

The effects of fiscal and monetary policy in a menu-cost equilibrium can be computed as follows. The model consists of equations (T3.1) and the second expression in (T3.2). Since aggregate profit income equals revenue minus the wage bill ($\Pi \equiv PY - WL$) we can write the system as:

$$Y = C + G, \tag{11.69}$$

$$C = \frac{\alpha}{1 - \alpha} \frac{M_0}{P} = \alpha \left[Y + \frac{M_0}{P} - G \right]. \tag{11.70}$$

Fiscal policy is highly effective in the menu-cost equilibrium:

$$\left(\frac{dY}{dG} \right)_T^{MCE} = 1, \quad \left(\frac{dC}{dG} \right)_T^{MCE} = \left(\frac{d(M_0/P)}{dG} \right)_T^{MCE} = 0, \tag{11.71}$$

where the superscript "MCE" stands for menu-cost equilibrium. The tax-financed increase in government consumption raises aggregate demand and thus each individual firm's demand and profit level. Due to the menu costs all firms keep their price unchanged, and because of the horizontal labour supply curve ($\sigma \to \infty$) the nominal wage does not change either. The firms can hire all the additional units of labour they need at the old real wage rate. The representative household receives the additional firm revenue in the form of additional wage payments and profit income. The additional income exactly covers the higher taxes levied by the government so that private consumption is unchanged and the output effect is simply the effect due to public consumption as in the original Haavelmo (1945) story. In view of the production function (11.61) the employment expansion can be written as:

$$w \cdot \left(\frac{dL}{dG} \right)_T^{MCE} = \frac{1}{\mu} \left(\frac{dY}{dG} \right)_T^{MCE} = \frac{\theta - 1}{\theta} > 0, \tag{11.72}$$

where $w \equiv W/P$ and we have used symmetry ($L_j = L/N$ for $j = 1, ..., N$) plus the fact that firms have set their prices as a markup over marginal cost in the *initial* (pre-shock) equilibrium.

Monetary policy, consisting of a helicopter drop of nominal money balances ($dM_0 > 0$), stimulates output, employment, and consumption, and the existence of menu costs thus destroys monetary neutrality:

$$P \left(\frac{dY}{dM_0} \right)^{MCE} = P \left(\frac{dC}{dM_0} \right)^{MCE} = \mu W \left(\frac{dL}{dM_0} \right)^{MCE} = \frac{\alpha}{1 - \alpha} > 0. \tag{11.73}$$

The increase in money balances leads to an increase in consumption spending and further multiplier effects via the expanded income of the representative household, i.e. after n rounds of the multiplier process spending has increased by $PdY = PdC = [\alpha + \alpha^2 + ... + \alpha^n]dM_0$ and the demand for money has increased by $dM = (1 - \alpha)[1 + \alpha + \alpha^2 + ... + \alpha^n]dM_0$. Since the marginal propensity to consume is less than unity, the multiplier process converges to the last expression in (11.73).

In summary, we have succeeded in demonstrating that with a very high labour supply elasticity ($\sigma \to \infty$, so that the labour supply curve is horizontal), small menu costs can lead to nominal price and wage inflexibility, which in turn drastically alters the qualitative properties of the model. Indeed, as was shown in the previous subsection, the flex-price version of the model possesses extremely classical properties in that money is neutral and fiscal policy only affects the price level. In contrast, in a menu cost equilibrium, both fiscal and monetary policy affect output and employment thus giving the model a much more Keynesian flavour. Below we demonstrate that both the *nominal rigidity* (price stickiness due to menu costs in price adjustment) and the *real rigidity* (constant real wage due to a horizontal labour supply curve) are of crucial importance in this result. Before doing so, however, we must demonstrate part (c) of our menu-cost investigation (see page 390 above) by demonstrating that there are first-order welfare effects associated with the aggregate demand effects that we have found.

As before, we use the indirect utility function to compute the welfare effects of aggregate demand shocks in a menu-cost equilibrium. By using (11.69)–(11.70) in (11.52) (with $\sigma \to \infty$ imposed) we find a number of alternative expressions for indirect utility:

$$
\begin{aligned}
V &= \alpha^\alpha (1 - \alpha)^{1-\alpha} \left[Y + \frac{M_0}{P} - G \right] - \gamma_L L \\
&= \alpha^\alpha (1 - \alpha)^{1-\alpha} \left[\frac{M_0 + \Pi}{P} - G \right] + \left[\alpha^\alpha (1 - \alpha)^{1-\alpha} \frac{W}{P} - \gamma_L \right] L \\
&= \alpha^\alpha (1 - \alpha)^{1-\alpha} \left[\frac{M_0 + \Pi}{P} - G \right].
\end{aligned}
\tag{11.74}
$$

In going from the first to the second expression we have used the definition for aggregate profit income ($\Pi \equiv PY - WL$), and in going from the second to the third expression we have used the labour supply equation (T3.5). Fiscal policy clearly has first-order welfare effects. Using the first line of (11.74) and noting (11.69) we derive:

$$
\begin{aligned}
\left(\frac{dV}{dG} \right)_T^{MCE} &= \alpha^\alpha (1 - \alpha)^{1-\alpha} \left(\frac{dC}{dG} \right)_T^{MCE} - \gamma_L \left(\frac{dL}{dG} \right)_T^{MCE} \\
&= -\frac{\gamma_L}{\mu} \frac{P}{W} = -\frac{\alpha^\alpha (1 - \alpha)^{1-\alpha}}{\mu} < 0,
\end{aligned}
\tag{11.75}
$$

where we have used the (11.71) and (11.72) to get from the first to the second line. The increase in government consumption raises output one-for-one but does not come for free (as in Keynes' story in section 11.1.5 above) as the representative household has to supply more hours of work. Since the labour market is competitive, the household derives no surplus from supplying labour; the additional wage income exactly compensates the household for having to work harder (Blanchard and Kiyotaki, 1987, p. 654). Hence, only the additional profit income mitigates the welfare loss due to additional government spending somewhat. Indeed, the welfare effect (11.75) can be restated in terms of MCPF as:

$$
0 < MCPF_T^{MCE} \equiv -\frac{1}{U_C} \cdot \left(\frac{dV}{dG} \right)_T^{MCE} = \frac{1}{\mu} = \frac{\theta - 1}{\theta} < 1,
\tag{11.76}
$$

where we have used the fact that the marginal utility of consumption equals $U_C = \alpha^\alpha (1-\alpha)^{1-\alpha}$. The existence of market power in the goods market mitigates but does not obliterate the social costs associated with a public spending shock.

Monetary policy also has first-order welfare effects in the menu-cost equilibrium. Indeed, using the final expression in (11.74) we derive:

$$
\begin{aligned}
\left(\frac{dV}{dM_0} \right)^{MCE} &= \alpha^\alpha (1-\alpha)^{1-\alpha} \left[\frac{1}{P} + \left(\frac{d(\Pi/P)}{dM_0} \right)^{MCE} \right] \\
&= \frac{\alpha^\alpha (1-\alpha)^{1-\alpha}}{P} \left[1 + P \left(\frac{dY}{dM_0} \right)^{MCE} - W \left(\frac{dL}{dM_0} \right)^{MCE} \right] \\
&= \frac{\alpha^\alpha (1-\alpha)^{1-\alpha}}{P} \left[1 + \frac{1}{\theta} \frac{\alpha}{1-\alpha} \right] > 0.
\end{aligned}
\tag{11.77}
$$

The term outside the brackets on the right-hand side of (11.77) represents the marginal utility of nominal income. Inside the square brackets on the right-hand side of (11.77) there are two effects which may be labelled, respectively, the *liquidity effect* and the *profit effect*. As is pointed out by Blanchard and Kiyotaki, the liquidity effect exists because even the competitive equilibrium (for which $1/\theta = 0$) is suboptimal if real money enters utility (1987, p. 654 fn. 13). As is explained in Chapter 10, the inefficiency results from the fact that people economize on a resource (fiat money) which is not scarce from a societal point of view. For that reason, ceteris paribus consumption, an increase in real money balances constitutes a welfare gain because it lowers the marginal utility of real money balances and brings the economy closer to Friedman's satiation point. This effect operates regardless of the nature of competition in the goods market.

In contrast to the liquidity effect, the profit effect in (11.77) is only operative under monopolistic competition (i.e. if $1/\theta$ is finite). This works via the profit income of households. An increase in the money stock boosts output and profit income, and this causes an additional welfare gain to the representative household over and above the liquidity effect. Since both effects work in the same direction, the total welfare effect of an increase in nominal money balances in a menu-cost equilibrium is unambiguously positive and first order.

11.3.1.2 Some simulations

In the previous subsection it was demonstrated (for the case with a horizontal labour supply curve, i.e. $\sigma \to \infty$), that with small menu costs both monetary and fiscal policy can have first-order effects on welfare. We have thus confirmed the basic menu-cost insight of Akerlof and Yellen (1985a, 1985b). In Tables 11.4 and 11.5 we present some numerical simulations with a more general version of the menu-cost model. In particular, we investigate the robustness of the menu-cost insight with respect to changes in key parameters such as the labour supply elasticity (σ), the markup (μ), and the elasticity of the marginal cost function ($\sigma_Y \equiv (1-\gamma)/\gamma$).

In order to perform the simulations, numerical values must be chosen for all the parameters that appear in Table 11.3. The following so-called *calibration approach* is adopted. We set up the model such that the parameters of special interest (σ, σ_Y, and μ) can be varied freely. We adopt a number of quantities/shares that are held constant (at economically reasonable values) throughout the simulations. In particular, the number of firms is $N_0 = 1000$ (large), the steady-state revenue share of overhead labour cost is $\omega_F \equiv WNF/PY = 0.05$, the output share of government consumption is $\omega_G \equiv G/Y = 0.1$, and the velocity of money is $v_M \equiv M_0/(PY)_0 = 6$. We assume that the initial money supply is $M_0 = 1$ and that initial output and employment are normalized at unity, $Y_0 = L_0 = 1$. For a given configuration of (σ, σ_Y, μ) it is possible to compute the initial steady state for the endogenous variables $(Y, C, P, W/P, L, \Pi/P)$ by using the calibration parameters (α, γ_L, F, k) appropriately, i.e. in such a way that the steady state is consistent with the share and parameter information we have imposed above.

Since this way of calibrating a theoretical model may not be familiar to all readers, we show in detail how we can retrieve the remaining variables and parameters. We denote the initial steady-state value with a subscript "0". It follows from (T3.1) that $C_0 = (1 - \omega_G)Y_0 = 0.9$ and $G_0 = \omega_G Y_0 = 0.1$. By rewriting the money velocity definition we find $P_0 = M_0/(v_M Y_0) = 1/6$. From (T3.2) we derive $\omega_C \equiv C/Y = \alpha v_M/(1 - \alpha)$ which can be solved for $\alpha = \omega_C/(\omega_C + v_M) \approx 0.13$. By defining the pure profit share as $1 - \varepsilon_L \equiv [\Pi/(PY)]_0$, it follows from (T3.3) and the definition of ω_F that $\varepsilon_L = \gamma/\mu + \omega_F$ (where $\gamma \equiv 1/(1 + \sigma_Y)$). By definition $\varepsilon_L \equiv [WL/(PY)]_0$ from which we derive an expression for the initial real wage $(W/P)_0 = \varepsilon_L$. We can make this expression for the real wage consistent with (T3.5) by setting $\gamma_L = (W/P)_0 \alpha^\alpha (1 - \alpha)^{1-\alpha}$. In view of the definition of ω_F we find that $F = (Y/N)_0/(W/P)_0 = (N_0 \varepsilon_L)^{-1}$. The value for k is retrieved from (T3.4)— $k = \gamma \left[\varepsilon_L \mu (Y/N)_0^{\sigma_Y}\right]^{-1}$ —and Π_0 is obtained from (T3.3). To give an example, for the case with $\mu \doteq 1.25$, $\sigma_Y = 0.1$, and $\sigma = 10^6$, the calibration approach yields the following results for the variables and parameters.

$$
\begin{array}{llll}
Y_0 = 1 & C_0 = 0.9 & G_0 = 0.1 & L_0 = 1 \\
N_0 = 1000 & (W/P)_0 = 0.777 & P_0 = 0.167 & \Pi_0 = 0.0371 \\
\alpha = 0.130 & \gamma_L = 0.528 & k = 1.867 & F = 6.433 \times 10^{-5}
\end{array}
\tag{11.78}
$$

In order to numerically investigate the menu cost insight, we follow Blanchard and Kiyotaki (1987, p. 658) by administering a non-trivial monetary shock, taking the form of a 5% increase in the money supply. We study the economy under two pure scenarios. In the *full-adjustment* case, all firms pay the menu cost and adjust the price of their product in the light of the higher level of aggregate demand. In contrast, in the *no-adjustment* case, all firms keep their price unchanged and expand output to meet the aggregate demand expansion.

Assuming that the menu cost takes the form of overhead labour (e.g. workers are employed to change price tags), under full adjustment, the model consists of equations (T3.1)–(T3.2) and (T3.4)–(T3.5) plus the augmented profit function:

$$
\Pi^{FA} = \frac{\mu - \gamma}{\mu} PY - WN(F + Z),
\tag{11.79}
$$

where the superscript "FA" stands for full adjustment. For a given value of Z, this system can be solved numerically for the endogenous variables Π^{FA}, Y, L, P, C, and W.

In contrast, in the no-adjustment case all firms keep their price unchanged ($P = P_0$) and the system consists of equations (T3.1)–(T3.2), (T3.5), and the profit function under no adjustment (superscript "NA"):

$$
\Pi^{NA} = P_0 Y - W\left[kY^{1/\gamma}N^{1-1/\gamma} + NF\right].
\tag{11.80}
$$

This system of equations can be solved numerically for the endogenous variables Π^{NA}, Y, L, C, and W.

In the final step, we compare profit levels under the two scenarios and find the lowest value of menu costs, Z_{MIN}, for which non adjustment of prices is an equilibrium, i.e. for which Π^{FA} just falls short of Π^{NA}. In Tables 11.4 and 11.5 we report a number of indicators for different parameter combinations. In Table 11.4 we consider four different values for the markup ($\mu \in \{1.1, 1.25, 1.5, 2\}$) and six different values for the labour supply elasticity ($\sigma \in \{0.2, 0.5, 1, 2.5, 5, 10^6\}$). In each case the entry labelled "menu costs" reports the revenue share of menu costs for which non-adjustment is an equilibrium for all firms, i.e. the entry equals:

$$\text{menu costs} = 100 \times \left[\frac{N_0 \, (W)^{NA} \, Z_{MIN}}{P_0 Y^{NA}} \right], \tag{11.81}$$

where $(W)^{NA}$ and Y^{NA} are, respectively, the nominal wage and output when the price is not adjusted. So, for example, if $\mu = 1.1$, $\sigma_Y = 0.1$, and $\sigma = 10^6$, the results in Table 11.4 show that menu costs amounting to no more than 0.20% of revenue will make non-adjustment of prices an equilibrium in the sense that $\Pi^{NA} > \Pi^{FA}$. The entry labelled "welfare gain" measures the gain in welfare (expressed in terms of an output share) which results from the monetary shock when there is no adjustment in prices:

$$\text{welfare gain} = 100 \times \left[\frac{V^{NA} - V_0}{U_C Y^{NA}} \right], \tag{11.82}$$

where $U_C \equiv \alpha^\alpha (1 - \alpha)^{1-\alpha}$ is the marginal utility of income, V_0 is initial welfare, and V^{NA} is welfare following the shock but in the absence of price adjustment. So, if $\mu = 1.1$, $\sigma_Y = 0.1$, and $\sigma = 10^6$, the monetary shock gives rise to a huge 29.1% rise in welfare. Finally, the entry labelled "ratio" is the ratio of the welfare gain and the macroeconomic menu costs. For the particular case considered here, the ratio is 146.12, so that a small menu cost gives rise to very large welfare effects.

In Table 11.4 we hold the elasticity of marginal cost constant (at $\sigma_Y = 0.1$) and consider various combinations of the markup (μ) and the substitution elasticity of labour supply (σ). Just like Blanchard and Kiyotaki (1987, p. 658) we find a number of key features in these simulations. First, the welfare measure does not vary a lot with the different parameter combinations. Second, for a given value of σ, the markup does not affect menu costs and the ratio very much. Third, for a given value of μ, menu costs are strongly dependent on the value of the labour elasticity. Take, for example, the empirically reasonable case for which the net markup is 25%, i.e. $\mu = 1.25$. If labour supply is infinitely elastic ($\sigma \to \infty$), menu costs of 0.2% of revenue suffice to make non-adjustment of prices optimal and the ratio is 145.73. This ratio drops very rapidly for lower, empirically more reasonable, values of σ. For example, if $\sigma = 1$ then only unreasonably high menu costs (amounting to 3.51% of revenue) can stop the firm from finding price adjustment advantageous. Intuitively, if labour supply is not very elastic, the output expansion under non-adjustment drives up wages (and thus production costs) very rapidly and thus makes it more likely that price adjustment is profitable.

In Table 11.5 we hold the markup constant (at $\mu = 1.25$) and consider various combinations of the elasticity of marginal cost (σ_Y) and the labour supply elasticity (σ). Essentially the same picture emerges from this table as from the previous one: the welfare gain is rather insensitive to (σ, σ_Y)-combinations, the value of σ_Y does not affect menu costs and the ratio very much, and the labour supply elasticity exerts a major effect on menu costs and the ratio.

Table 11.4: Menu costs and the markup

	$\mu = 1.10$			$\mu = 1.25$		
$\Delta M = 0.05$ $\sigma_Y = 0.1$	menu costs	welfare gain	ratio	menu costs	welfare gain	ratio
$\sigma = 0.2$	20.44	28.6	1.40	18.10	29.1	1.61
$\sigma = 0.5$	7.85	28.9	3.68	6.96	29.4	4.22
$\sigma = 1$	3.95	29.0	7.35	3.51	29.5	8.40
$\sigma = 2.5$	1.69	29.1	17.18	1.51	29.5	19.49
$\sigma = 5$	0.94	29.1	30.80	0.86	29.6	34.37
$\sigma = 10^6$	0.20	29.1	146.12	0.20	29.6	145.73

	$\mu = 1.50$			$\mu = 2$		
$\sigma = 0.2$	15.23	29.8	1.96	11.53	30.6	2.65
$\sigma = 0.5$	5.87	30.0	5.11	4.55	30.8	6.76
$\sigma = 1$	2.99	30.1	10.06	2.35	30.8	13.12
$\sigma = 2.5$	1.32	30.1	22.80	1.06	30.8	29.12
$\sigma = 5$	0.76	30.1	39.56	0.63	30.9	48.68
$\sigma = 10^6$	0.21	30.1	144.67	0.21	30.9	144.95

Table 11.5: Menu costs and the elasticity of marginal cost

	$\sigma_Y = 0$			$\sigma_Y = 0.05$		
$\Delta M = 0.05$ $\mu = 1.25$	menu costs	welfare gain	ratio	menu costs	welfare gain	ratio
$\sigma = 0.2$	17.44	29.2	1.67	17.72	29.2	1.65
$\sigma = 0.5$	6.61	29.4	4.45	6.76	29.4	4.35
$\sigma = 1$	3.17	29.5	9.31	3.34	29.5	8.84
$\sigma = 2.5$	1.19	29.5	24.73	1.36	29.5	21.69
$\sigma = 5$	0.52	29.6	56.72	0.70	29.6	42.23
$\sigma = 10^6$	$\rightarrow 0$	29.6	$\rightarrow \infty$	0.04	29.6	672.74

	$\sigma_Y = 0.1$			$\sigma_Y = 0.2$		
$\sigma = 0.2$	18.10	29.1	1.61	18.54	29.1	1.57
$\sigma = 0.5$	6.96	29.4	4.22	7.34	29.4	4.00
$\sigma = 1$	3.51	29.5	8.40	3.84	29.5	7.67
$\sigma = 2.5$	1.51	29.5	19.49	1.83	29.5	16.16
$\sigma = 5$	0.86	29.6	34.37	1.15	29.5	25.60
$\sigma = 10^6$	0.20	29.6	145.73	0.49	29.6	60.60

11.3.1.3 Evaluation

The simulation results graphically illustrate that the standard menu-cost model runs into trouble because non-adjustment of prices after a monetary shock is only an equilibrium if labour supply is highly elastic (Blanchard and Kiyotaki, 1987, p. 663). For an empirically reasonable value of the labour supply elasticity, there are very strong incentives to adjust prices and nominal frictions produce only small non-neutralities.[15] Ball and Romer (1990) argue that the menu-cost argument can be rescued if the economy has both real and nominal rigidities. By real rigidity they mean the phenomenon that "real wages or prices are unresponsive to changes in economic activity" (Ball and Romer, 1990, p. 183). Nominal rigidity can either take the form of small menu costs or departures from full rationality (as in Akerlof and Yellen, 1985a, 1985b). Taken in isolation, real rigidity does not imply price inflexibility. But in combination with nominal rigidity, a high degree of real rigidity translates into substantial effects of monetary shocks. In the model considered in the previous subsection, a high labour supply elasticity leads to substantial real rigidity. Indeed, for $\sigma \rightarrow \infty$, the real wage is constant (see equation (T3.5)) and thus completely insensitive to economic activity. Ball and Romer (1990) discuss a number of alternative models leading to real rigidities, such as the efficiency-wage model of the labour market and the imperfect-information customer-market model of the goods market.

Rotemberg (1987, pp. 80–81) has identified a number of problematic aspects of the menu-cost insight. First, the menu-cost equilibrium may not be unique. In the context of our model, his argument runs as follows. Recall that Z_{MIN} represents the minimum amount of menu costs for which it is profitable for an individual firm j not to adjust its price *given that all other firms also keep their prices unchanged!* But if one firm changes its price when $Z = Z_{MIN}$, it generally becomes profitable for *all* other firms to change their prices also, so we have two equilibria: the firms either all adjust their prices or they all keep them unchanged. Let us now define Z^*_{MIN} as the minimum amount of menu costs for which an individual firm j keeps its price unchanged *even if all other firms would change their prices.* Clearly, Z^*_{MIN} exceeds Z_{MIN}. Furthermore, if $Z \geq Z^*_{MIN}$ the menu cost equilibrium is unique. For the intermediate case, however, with $Z \in (Z_{MIN}, Z^*_{MIN})$ there are three equilibria: one with no firm adjusting, another with all firms adjusting, and an intermediate case in which a fraction ϕ of the firms adjusts ($0 < \phi < 1$). Rotemberg (1987, p. 90) argues that the multiplicity of equilibria is a weakness for any economic model. Essentially, with multiple equilibria it is impossible to predict the economy's reaction to particular policy shocks.

A second problem with the menu-cost insight is that it could equally well be applied to quantities instead of prices. Indeed, if there are costs of adjusting quantities (e.g. because capital has to be installed in advance of the price-setting decision, as in Shapiro, 1989, pp. 350–351) it may well be optimal for the firm to adjust its price and leave output unchanged (Rotemberg, 1987, p. 77).

Finally, as is argued by Rotemberg (1987, pp. 85–91) and Blanchard (1990, p. 822) an important practical disadvantage of the menu-cost approach to price adjustment is that it does not generalize easily to a dynamic setting.[16] For that reason we now turn to two approaches which do not have this disadvantage.

---

[15] As we show in Chapter 19, the competitive real business cycle (RBC) model runs into the same problem because it can only generate large output movements following real shocks if the (intertemporal) labour supply elasticity is very large.

[16] See Danziger (1999) for an example of a dynamic general equilibrium model with menu costs.

11.3.2 Quadratic price adjustment costs

In an influential article, Rotemberg (1982) has formulated a rather attractive dynamic model of price adjustment in which adjustment costs are assumed to be quadratic (just as in the investment literature surveyed in Chapters 3 and 4 above). Intuitively, his model solves the problem of dynamic price adjustments in two (conceptual) steps. In the first step, a path of "equilibrium" prices is determined consisting of the solution that firm j would choose if there were no costs of adjusting prices. Normalizing the current (planning) period by $t = 0$, this equilibrium path for firm j is denoted by the sequence $\{P_{j,\tau}^*\}_{\tau=0}^{\infty}$. In the second step, Rotemberg takes a quadratic approximation of the firm's profit function around this equilibrium path and incorporates adjustment costs. He shows that the dynamic objective function of the firm can then be written as follows:

$$\Omega_0 = \sum_{\tau=0}^{\infty} \left(\frac{1}{1+\rho}\right)^{\tau} \left[\left(p_{j,\tau} - p_{j,\tau}^*\right)^2 + c\left(p_{j,\tau} - p_{j,\tau-1}\right)^2\right], \tag{11.83}$$

where $(1+\rho)^{-1}$ is the firm's discount factor, c is a constant, $p_{j,\tau} \equiv \ln P_{j,\tau}$, and $p_{j,\tau}^* \equiv \ln P_{j,\tau}^*$. In the presence of price adjustment costs, the firm chooses a sequence of actual prices, $\{P_{j,\tau}\}_{\tau=0}^{\infty}$, in order to *minimize* the costs of deviating from the optimum that it would choose in the hypothetical case without price adjustment costs. Equation (11.83) shows that these "deviation costs" are composed of two terms. The first quadratic term on the right-hand side of (11.83) represents the *intra*temporal cost of setting the price at a "suboptimal" level, i.e. at a level different from $P_{j,\tau}^*$. The second quadratic term on the right-hand side of (11.83) parameterizes the *inter*temporal costs to the firm that are due to price adjustment costs. The higher is c, the more severe are the price adjustment costs.

The first-order condition for the optimal price in period τ is readily obtained by using (11.83) and setting $\partial \Omega_0 / \partial p_{j,\tau} = 0$:

$$\frac{\partial \Omega_0}{\partial p_{j,\tau}} = \left(\frac{1}{1+\rho}\right)^{\tau} \left[2\left(p_{j,\tau} - p_{j,\tau}^*\right) + 2c\left(p_{j,\tau} - p_{j,\tau-1}\right)\right]$$

$$- \left(\frac{1}{1+\rho}\right)^{\tau+1} \left[2c\left(p_{j,\tau+1} - p_{j,\tau}\right)\right] = 0. \tag{11.84}$$

After some straightforward manipulation we find that (11.84) can be simplified to:

$$p_{j,\tau+1} - \left[1 + (1+\rho)\frac{1+c}{c}\right] p_{j,\tau} + (1+\rho)p_{j,\tau-1} = -\frac{1+\rho}{c}p_{j,\tau}^* \tag{11.85}$$

Equation (11.85) is a second-order difference equation in $p_{j,\tau}$ with constant coefficients and a potentially time-varying forcing term $p_{j,\tau}^*$. In order to solve this equation we need two boundary conditions. The first is an initial condition which results from the fact that when the firm decides on its price $p_{j,\tau}$, the price it charged in the previous period ($p_{j,\tau-1}$) is predetermined. The second boundary condition is a terminal condition saying that the firm expects to charge a price close to $p_{t,\tau}^*$ in the distant future (see Rotemberg (1982, pp. 523–524) for details):

$$\lim_{\tau \to \infty} \left[\left(p_{j,\tau} - p_{j,\tau}^*\right) + c\left(p_{j,\tau} - p_{j,\tau-1}\right)\right] = 0. \tag{11.86}$$

It is shown by Kennan (1979, p. 1443) and Rotemberg (1987, p. 92) that the solution for the price in the planning period, $p_{j,0}$, can be written as:

$$p_{j,0} = \lambda_1 p_{j,-1} + (1 - \lambda_1) \left[\frac{\lambda_2 - 1}{\lambda_2} \sum_{\tau=0}^{\infty} \left(\frac{1}{\lambda_2} \right)^{\tau} p_{j,\tau}^* \right], \qquad (11.87)$$

where $0 < \lambda_1 < 1$ and $\lambda_2 > 1$.[17] The economic intuition behind the pricing-setting rule (11.87) is as follows. In the presence of price adjustment costs, the firm finds it optimal to adjust its price gradually over time. As a result, the optimal price in any period is the weighted average of the last period's price $p_{j,-1}$ and the long-run "target" price given in square brackets on the right-hand side of (11.87). This target price itself depends on the present and future equilibrium prices ($p_{j,\tau}^*$, for $\tau = 0, 1, ...$). In the special case where the equilibrium price is (expected to be) constant indefinitely, we have $p_{j,\tau}^* = p_j^*$ and it follows that the target price is equal to p_j^*. In the general case, however, the firm knows that it chases a moving (rather than a stationary) target because it recognizes future variability in the equilibrium price (say due to anticipated policy shocks).

11.3.3   Staggered price contracts

In a number of papers, Calvo has proposed an alternative approach to modelling sluggish aggregate prices (see e.g. Calvo, 1982, 1983, 1987 and Calvo and Végh, 1994). His basic idea, which derives from the early papers by Phelps (1978) and Taylor (1980), makes use of the notion that price contracts are staggered. Calvo (1987, p. 144) adopts the following price-setting technology. Each period of time "nature" draws a signal to the firm which may be a "green light" or a "red light" with probabilities π and $1 - \pi$, respectively. These probabilities are the same for all firms in the economy. A firm which has just received a green light can change its price optimally in that period but must maintain that price until the next green light is received.

In order to solve the pricing problem of a firm which has just received a green light we can follow the same approach as in the previous subsection. In the absence of the pricing friction firm j would always want to set its price equal to its equilibrium price P_j^*. But with the pricing friction the firm aims to minimize the deviation cost, Ω_0, given in equation (11.83) but with $c = 0$ (there are no price adjustment costs). By substituting the assumptions about the pricing technology into the objective function (11.83) we obtain:

$$\Omega_0 = \left(p_{j,0} - p_{j,0}^* \right)^2 + \frac{1}{1+\rho} \left[\pi \left(p_{j,1} - p_{j,1}^* \right)^2 + (1 - \pi) \left(p_{j,0} - p_{j,1}^* \right)^2 \right]$$

$$+ \left(\frac{1}{1+\rho} \right)^2 \left[\pi^2 \left(p_{j,2} - p_{j,2}^* \right)^2 + \pi(1 - \pi) \left(p_{j,1} - p_{j,2}^* \right)^2 \right.$$

$$+ (1 - \pi)^2 \left(p_{j,0} - p_{j,2}^* \right)^2 \left] + \text{higher-order terms.} \qquad (11.88) \right.$$

The interpretation of this expression is as follows. In the current period ($\tau = 0$) the firm has a green light so it can set its price. The first term on the right-hand side of (11.88) gives the cost of deviating from $p_{j,0}^*$ in the current period. In the next period ($\tau = 1$) the firm may or may not get a green light again. If it does (with probability π)

---

[17]Readers of the Mathematical Appendix will recognize that λ_1 and λ_2 are, respectively, the stable and unstable characteristic roots of the difference equation in (11.85).

it will again be able to set its price, taking into account the then relevant equilibrium price $p_{j,1}^*$. If it gets a red light, however, it will have to keep its price unchanged (at $p_{j,0}$) and face the deviation costs associated with this choice made in the previous period. In period $\tau = 2$ there are three different possibilities depending on when the firm last received a green signal.

Since the pattern should be clear by now and we are only interested in the price to be set by the firm in the planning period, we can rewrite (11.88) by gathering all terms involving $p_{j,0}$:

$$
\Omega_0 = \left(p_{j,0} - p_{j,0}^* \right)^2 + \frac{1-\pi}{1+\rho} \left(p_{j,0} - p_{j,1}^* \right)^2 + \left(\frac{1-\pi}{1+\rho} \right)^2 \left(p_{j,0} - p_{j,2}^* \right)^2 + \dots
$$
$$
= \sum_{\tau=0}^{\infty} \left(\frac{1-\pi}{1+\rho} \right)^\tau \left(p_{j,0} - p_{j,\tau}^* \right)^2 + \dots, \tag{11.89}
$$

where the remaining terms do not involve $p_{j,0}$. The pricing friction thus shows up in the discounting factor employed by the firm. The higher is the probability of a green light in any period, the less severe is the friction, and the lower is the weight attached to future equilibrium prices.

The firm chooses $p_{j,0}$ in order to minimize Ω_0. The first-order condition is given by $\partial \Omega_0 / \partial p_{j,0} = 0$ which can be written as:

$$
p_{j,0} \sum_{\tau=0}^{\infty} \left(\frac{1-\pi}{1+\rho} \right)^\tau = \sum_{\tau=0}^{\infty} \left(\frac{1-\pi}{1+\rho} \right)^\tau p_{j,\tau}^*. \tag{11.90}
$$

Since the infinite sum on the left-hand side of (11.90) converges to $(1+\rho)/(\pi+\rho)$ we can rewrite (11.90) as follows:

$$
p_0^n = \frac{\pi+\rho}{1+\rho} \sum_{\tau=0}^{\infty} \left(\frac{1-\pi}{1+\rho} \right)^\tau p_\tau^*, \tag{11.91}
$$

where p_0^n denotes the common "new" price set in period 0 by all firms facing a green light in that period. Note that we have assumed that all firms are identical so that the firm index no longer features in (11.91). The firms facing a red light in the planning period ($\tau = 0$) keep their prices as set in some past period using a rule like (11.91), i.e.:

$$
p_{-s}^n = \frac{\pi+\rho}{1+\rho} \sum_{\tau=0}^{\infty} \left(\frac{1-\pi}{1+\rho} \right)^\tau p_{\tau-s}^*, \tag{11.92}
$$

for $s = 1, 2, \dots \infty$. Since $\pi(1-\pi)^s$ is the fraction of firms which last adjusted prices s periods before the planning period, we can define the aggregate price level in the planning period as follows:

$$
p_0 = \pi p_0^n + \pi(1-\pi) p_{-1}^n + \pi(1-\pi)^2 p_{-2}^n + \pi(1-\pi)^3 p_{-3}^n + \dots
$$
$$
= \pi \sum_{s=0}^{\infty} (1-\pi)^s p_{-s}^n
$$
$$
= \pi p_0^n + (1-\pi) p_{-1}, \tag{11.93}
$$

where $p_{-1} \equiv \pi \left[p_{-1}^n + (1-\pi) \, p_{-2}^n + (1-\pi)^2 p_{-2}^n + \cdots \right]$. The actual aggregate price level in the planning period (p_0) is thus the weighted average of the aggregate price in the previous period (p_{-1}) and the newly set price (p_0^n). By substituting (11.91) in (11.93) we get the following expression for p_0:

$$p_0 = (1 - \pi)p_{-1} + \pi \left[\frac{\pi + \rho}{1 + \rho} \sum_{\tau=0}^{\infty} \left(\frac{1 - \pi}{1 + \rho} \right)^{\tau} p_{\tau}^* \right] \tag{11.94}$$

As is pointed out by Rotemberg (1987, p. 93), the pricing rule that results from the Calvo friction (given in (11.94)) is indistinguishable from the aggregate version of the pricing rule under adjustment costs (given in (11.87)). The nice thing about both pricing rules is that they can be readily estimated using time series data for actual economies. Rotemberg (1987, p. 93), for example, cites evidence that 8% of all prices are adjusted every quarter in the US, implying a mean time between price adjustments of about three years.[18]

11.4 Punchlines

We started this chapter by constructing a small general equilibrium model with monopolistic competition in the goods market. On the supply side of the goods market there are many small firms who each produce a slightly unique product variety and thus possess a small amount of market power. Each firm sets its price to optimally exploit its market power.

The model provides microeconomic foundations for the multiplier. In the short run the number of firms is fixed and a tax-financed increase in government consumption boosts output, though by less than one-for-one. The tax increase makes households poorer which prompts them to decrease consumption and leisure (and thus to increase labour supply). The increase in output raises profit income which partially mitigates the fall in consumption. In the long run the short-run increase in profits prompts entry of new firms which continues until all firms exactly break even (the Chamberlinian tangency solution). If households like product diversity then the increase in the number of product varieties causes an increase in the real consumer wage. The multiplier is not very Keynesian as the output expansion relies critically on the labour supply response (a new classical feature).

Under monopolistic competition, there exists an intimate link between the multiplier and the welfare effect of public spending which is absent under perfect competition. Under monopolistic competition there is a distortion in the goods market and the economy is "too small" from a societal point of view. By raising government spending output rises and that in itself constitutes a move in the right, welfare-enhancing, direction.

Next we introduce money into the model by assuming that households derive utility from real money balances. (This money-in-the-utility-function approach is discussed in detail in Chapter 10 and constitutes the simplest way to ensure that fiat money is held by economic agents.) Monopolistic competition in and of itself does not invalidate the classical dichotomy. Indeed, a helicopter drop of money balances

---

[18]The expected time of price fixity ($ETPF$) is:

$$ETPF = \pi \times 1 + \pi(1 - \pi) \times 2 + \ldots + \pi(1 - \pi)^{n-1} n + \ldots$$

$$= \pi \sum_{s=0}^{\infty} (1 - \pi)(1 + s) = 1/\pi.$$

See King and Wolman (1996, p. 10).

simply inflates all nominal variables equi-proportionally and leaves all real variables unchanged.

Money ceases to be a mere veil if prices are sticky. Here the assumption of monopolistic competition is essential because it explicitly recognizes that it is the individual firms (and not some anonymous auctioneer) who are responsible for setting prices in the economy. We study three major approaches under which price stickiness emerges as an equilibrium phenomenon. The menu-cost approach postulates the existence of small costs associated with changing prices. Since profit functions are flat at the top, it may be optimal for an individual firm not to increase its price in the wake of an expansionary (monetary or fiscal) shock and instead to expand its output. Provided labour supply is sufficiently elastic (and there is thus a sufficient degree of real rigidity) small menu costs (a source of nominal rigidity) can rationalize the fixity of both wages and prices in general equilibrium. In the menu-cost equilibrium, both fiscal and monetary policy are highly effective and money is not neutral. The Achilles heel of the menu-cost model is that it hinges on a highly elastic labour supply equation, a feature which is not supported by the empirical evidence.

A more pragmatic approach to price stickiness assumes that there are convex costs associated with changing prices. In this approach, the individual firm tries to steer the actual sequence of its price as close as possible to its "ideal" price path which would be attained in the absence of adjustment costs. The presence of adjustment costs ensures that the firm sets its actual price as a weighted average of last period's price and some long-run target price which is explicitly forward looking. At a macroeconomic level, the adjustment cost approach thus provides a microeconomic foundation for the expectations-augmented Phillips curve of Friedman and Phelps.

In the third approach to aggregate price stickiness, the pricing friction is stochastic. Each period of time "nature" draws a signal to the firm which may be a "green light" or a "red light" with given probabilities. These probabilities are the same for all firms in the economy. A firm which has just received a green light can change its price optimally (without adjustment costs) in that period but must maintain that price until the next green light is received. Although this theory differs substantially from the adjustment-cost approach at the microeconomic level, the two approaches give rise to an observationally equivalent macroeconomic pricing equation.

Further reading

Mankiw and Romer (1991) is a collection of key articles on new Keynesian economics. Also see Gordon (1990) and Benassi et al. (1994) for overviews of new Keynesian economics. On monopolistic competition as a foundation for the multiplier, see Ng (1982), Hart (1982), Solow (1986), Blanchard and Kiyotaki (1987), Dixon (1987), Mankiw (1988), and Startz (1989). Further contributions include Molana and Moutos (1992), Dixon and Lawler (1996), Heijdra and Ligthart (1997), and Heijdra et al. (1998). On the welfare properties of the monopolitically competitive equilibrium, see Mankiw and Whinston (1986). Bénassy (1991a, 1991b, 1993a), Silvestre (1993), and Matsuyama (1995) give excellent surveys of the early literature.

On price adjustment costs, see Mankiw (1985), Poterba et al. (1986), Parkin (1986), Sheshinski and Weiss (1993), Dixon and Hansen (1999), and Danziger (1999). Levy et al. (1997) present empirical evidence on the size of menu costs in supermarket chains. For the envelope theorem, see Dixit (1990). On the new Keynesian Phillips curve, see Ball et al. (1988) and Roberts (1995). The Calvo approach to price stickiness is widely used in monetary economics. See, for example, King and Wolman (1996, 1999), Clarida et al. (1999), Goodfriend and King (1997), Rotemberg and Woodford (1999), and Yun (1996). See also Chapter 19.

Kiyotaki (1988) and Bénassy (1993a) show that under monopolistic competition it may not be optimal for households to have rational expectations. There is a large literature on multiple equilibria and coordination failures. See Diamond (1982a, 1984a, 1984b), Howitt (1985), Shleifer (1986), Diamond and Fudenberg (1989, 1991), Cooper and John (1988), Weil (1989a), and Benhabib and Farmer (1994). An excellent survey of some of this literature is presented by Cooper (1999). The classic source on multiple equilibria and animal spirits is Keynes (1937).

Chapter 12

Exogenous economic growth—Solow-Swan

In this chapter we commence our study of macroeconomic growth processes. What mechanisms exist by which aggregate output that is produced in an economy grows over time? In order to prepare for things to come we start in this chapter with a very simple model in which the savings rate is exogenous. The specific purpose of this chapter is to discuss the following issues:

1. What are some of the most important stylized facts of economic growth?

2. How well does the Solow-Swan model explain these stylized facts?

3. What are the key implications of adding human capital to the Solow-Swan model?

4. How do fiscal policy and Ricardian equivalence work in the Solow-Swan model?

5. What does the growth mechanism look like in a two-sector model?

12.1 Stylized facts of economic growth

According to Kaldor (1961, pp. 178–179), a satisfactory theory of economic growth should be able to explain the following six "stylized facts" by which we mean results that are broadly observable in most capitalist countries.

> **Stylized Fact (SF1)**: *Output per worker shows continuing growth "with no tendency for a falling rate of growth of productivity."
>
> **Stylized Fact (SF2)**: Capital per worker shows continuing growth.
>
> **Stylized Fact (SF3)**: The rate of return on capital is constant.
>
> **Stylized Fact (SF4)**: *The capital-output ratio is constant.
>
> **Stylized Fact (SF5)**: *The production factors labour and capital receive constant shares of total income.
>
> **Stylized Fact (SF6)**: *There are wide differences in the rate of productivity growth across countries.

Note that not all these stylized facts are independent: (SF1) and (SF4) are easily seen to imply (SF2). In a similar fashion, (SF4) and (SF5) imply (SF3). Hence, the starred facts are fundamental. Paul Romer (1989, p. 55) argues that there is evidence which leads him to disbelieve (SF5), but the remaining facts can be considered stylized even four decades after Kaldor's original claims.

Paul Romer (1989, p. 55) suggests five more stylized facts that growth theorists should be able to explain:

> **Stylized Fact (SF7)**: In cross-section, the mean growth rate shows no variation with the level of per capita income.
>
> **Stylized Fact (SF8)**: The rate of growth of factor inputs is not large enough to explain the rate of growth of output; that is, growth accounting always finds a residual.
>
> **Stylized Fact (SF9)**: Growth in the volume of trade is positively correlated with growth in output.
>
> **Stylized Fact (SF10)**: Population growth rates are negatively correlated with the level of income.
>
> **Stylized Fact (SF11)**: Both skilled and unskilled workers tend to migrate towards high-income countries.

Although we shall have very little to say about the last three stylized facts, the other stylized facts will be referred to regularly.

12.2   The Solow-Swan model

The neoclassical growth model was developed independently by Solow (1956) and Swan (1956). The central element of their theory is the notion of an aggregate production function (which has already been used in earlier chapters). It can be written in a very general form as:

$$Y(t) = F(K(t), L(t), t), \tag{12.1}$$

where Y is aggregate output, K is the aggregate capital stock, L is aggregate employment, and t is the time index which appears separately in the production function to indicate that the technology itself may not be constant over time. We retain the assumption of perfectly competitive behaviour of firms which implies that the production function must obey constant returns to scale. We label this first property of technology (P1):[1]

$$F(\lambda K(t), \lambda L(t), t) = \lambda F(K(t), L(t), t), \qquad \text{for } \lambda > 0. \tag{P1}$$

It is assumed that the household sector as a whole (or the representative household) consumes a constant fraction of output and saves the rest. Aggregate saving in the economy is then:

$$S(t) = sY(t), \qquad 0 < s < 1, \tag{12.2}$$

---

[1] See Intermezzo 4.3 on production theory in Chapter 4 above.

where s is the constant propensity to save which is assumed to be exogenously given. In a closed economy, output is exhausted by household consumption $C(t)$ and investment $I(t)$:

$$Y(t) = C(t) + I(t), \tag{12.3}$$

where we have assumed that government consumption is zero for now. Aggregate gross investment is the sum of replacement investment, $\delta K(t)$ (where δ is the constant depreciation rate), and the net addition to the capital stock, $\dot{K}(t) \equiv dK(t)/dt$:

$$I(t) = \delta K(t) + \dot{K}(t). \tag{12.4}$$

We assume that labour supply is exogenous but that the population grows as a whole at a constant exponential rate n_L:

$$\frac{\dot{L}(t)}{L(t)} = n_L \qquad \Leftrightarrow \qquad L(t) = L(t_0)e^{n_L(t-t_0)}, \tag{12.5}$$

where $\dot{L}(t) \equiv dL(t)/dt$, and $L(t_0)$ is the population level in some past base year (of course, we can set $t_0 = 0$ and normalize $L(0) = 1$).

12.2.1 No technological progress

We first look at the case for which technology itself is time-invariant, so that the production function (12.1) has no separate time index:

$$Y(t) = F(K(t), L(t)). \tag{12.6}$$

In addition to linear homogeneity (property (P1)), we adopt the conventional assumption that the production function features positive but diminishing marginal products to both factors:

$$F_K, F_L > 0, \qquad F_{KK}, F_{LL} < 0, \qquad F_{KL} > 0. \tag{P2}$$

Recall from Intermezzo 4.3 that with constant returns to scale capital and labour must be cooperative factors of production, i.e. $F_{KL} > 0$. A more controversial assumption, but one we will make nevertheless, is that $F(\cdot)$ obeys the so-called *Inada conditions* (after Inada (1963)) which ensure that it has nice curvature properties around the origin (with K or L equal to zero) and in the limit (with K or L approaching infinity):[2]

$$\lim_{K \to 0} F_K = \lim_{L \to 0} F_L = +\infty, \qquad \lim_{K \to \infty} F_K = \lim_{L \to \infty} F_L = 0. \tag{P3}$$

As we shall demonstrate below (in Chapter 14), these conditions are far from innocuous and actually preclude a number of interesting non-standard cases.

The model consists of equations (12.2)–(12.5) plus the savings-investment identity, $S(t) \equiv I(t)$. Because the labour force grows, it is impossible to attain a steady state in *levels* of output, capital, etc., but this problem is easily remedied by measuring all variables in per capita or *intensive form*, i.e. we define $y(t) \equiv Y(t)/L(t)$,

---

[2]Ironically these are the two points about which we humans know the least. The question "Where do we come from and what are we heading for?" is perhaps better dealt with by theologians than by macroeconomists. The Inada conditions obviate the need for a deep study of theology.

$k(t) \equiv K(t)/L(t)$, etc. The model can then be condensed into a single differential equation in the per capita capital stock (see Intermezzo 12.1):

$$\dot{k}(t) = sf(k(t)) - (\delta + n_L)k(t),\tag{12.7}$$

where $f(k(t))$ is the intensive form of the production function:[3]

$$f(k(t)) \equiv F(K(t)/L(t), 1).\tag{12.8}$$

For example, in the Cobb-Douglas case we have $F(K, L) \equiv Z_0 K^\alpha L^{1-\alpha}$ from which we obtain $f(k) \equiv Z_0 k^\alpha$. We can obtain insight into the properties of the model by working with a phase diagram for $k(t)$—see Figure 12.1. In that figure, the straight line $(\delta + n_L)k(t)$ represents the amount of investment required to replace worn-out capital *and* to endow each existing worker with the same amount of capital. Since the work force grows, the line features the growth rate of the labour force, n_L.

Since the savings rate, s, is constant by assumption, the per capita saving curve has the same shape as the intensive-form production function. To draw this curve we need to know what happens for $k(t) = 0$ and $k(t) \to \infty$. We obtain from (12.8):

$$f'(k(t)) \equiv F_K(k(t), 1), \quad f''(k(t)) \equiv F_{KK}(k(t), 1),\tag{12.9}$$

about which the Inada conditions (P3) say all we need to know: $f(k(t))$ is vertical at the origin, is concave, and flattens out as more and more capital per worker is accumulated. Hence $f(k(t))$ and $sf(k(t))$ are as drawn in Figure 12.1.[4]

Intermezzo 12.1

Deriving the fundamental differential equation for the Solow-Swan model. We know that in the absence of a government and for a closed economy, output satisfies:

$$Y(t) = C(t) + I(t) = C(t) + S(t),\tag{a}$$

so that we obtain from the second equality:

$$S(t) = I(t).\tag{b}$$

Substituting (12.2) and (12.6) on the left-hand side of (b) and (12.4) on the right-hand side we obtain:

$$s \cdot F(K(t), L(t)) = \delta K(t) + \dot{K}(t).\tag{c}$$

Dividing both sides by the population size we get:

$$s \cdot \frac{F(K(t), L(t))}{L(t)} = \delta k(t) + \frac{\dot{K}(t)}{L(t)},\tag{d}$$

where $k(t) \equiv K(t)/L(t)$. The production function features constant returns to scale and can thus be written as:

$$F(K(t), L(t)) = L(t) \cdot F(K(t)/L(t), 1) = L(t) \cdot f(k(t)),\tag{e}$$

---

[3]Because (12.6) satisfies property (P1), we can write $\lambda Y = F(\lambda K, \lambda L)$. By choosing $\lambda = 1/L$ we thus find that $Y/L = F(K/L, 1)$.

[4]Barro and Sala-i-Martin (1995, p. 52) show that both inputs are *essential* if the properties (P1)–(P3) are satisfied. Hence, $F(0, L) = F(K, 0) = f(0) = 0$.

where we have used (12.8) in the final step. It remains to find a handsome expression for $\dot{K}(t)/L(t)$. From the definition of $k(t)$ we find:

$$\dot{k}(t) \equiv \frac{1}{L(t)} \cdot \dot{K}(t) - \frac{K(t)}{L(t)^2} \cdot \dot{L}(t)$$

$$= \frac{\dot{K}(t)}{L(t)} - n_L k(t), \tag{f}$$

where we have used (12.5) to arrive at the final result. Using (e) and (f) in (d) we thus obtain:

$$s \cdot f\left(k(t)\right) = \delta k(t) + \dot{k}(t) + n_L k(t). \tag{g}$$

Rearranging this expression somewhat we obtain the fundamental differential equation for the capital stock per worker as given in (12.7).

****

It follows in a straightforward fashion from the diagram that the model is stable. From any initial position $k(t)$ will converge to the unique equilibrium at point E_0. In the *steady state* capital per worker is constant and equal to $k(t) \stackrel{.}{=} k^*$. This implies that along the balanced growth path (BGP) the capital stock itself must grow at the same rate as the work force, i.e. $(\dot{K}(t)/K(t))^* = \dot{L}(t)/L(t) = n_L$. The intensive-form production function says that steady-state output per worker, y^*, satisfies $y^* = f(k^*)$ and is thus also constant. Hence, output itself also grows at the same rate as the work force along the BGP, i.e. $(\dot{Y}(t)/Y(t))^* = n_L$, and since the savings rate is constant, the same holds for the levels of saving and investment. In the *balanced growth path* we thus have:

$$\left(\frac{\dot{Y}(t)}{Y(t)}\right)^* = \left(\frac{\dot{K}(t)}{K(t)}\right)^* = \left(\frac{\dot{I}(t)}{I(t)}\right)^* = \left(\frac{\dot{S}(t)}{S(t)}\right)^* = \frac{\dot{L}(t)}{L(t)} = n_L. \tag{12.10}$$

Since the rate of population growth is exogenous, the long-run growth rate of the economy is exogenously determined and thus cannot be influenced by government policy or household behaviour. For example, an increase in the savings rate rotates the savings function counter-clockwise and gives rise to a higher steady-state capital-labour ratio but it does not affect the rate of economic growth along the balanced growth path. Note furthermore, that output per worker is constant in the balanced growth path, i.e. stylized fact (SF1) is not accounted for in this version of the Solow-Swan model.

Before turning to a detailed examination of the properties of the Solow-Swan model we first expand the model by re-introducing technological change into the production function.

12.2.2 Technological progress

Technical change can be *embodied* or *disembodied* (see Burmeister and Dobell, 1970, ch. 3). Embodied technical change is only relevant to newly acquired and installed equipment or workers and therefore does not affect the productivity of existing production factors. Disembodied technical progress takes place if, independent of

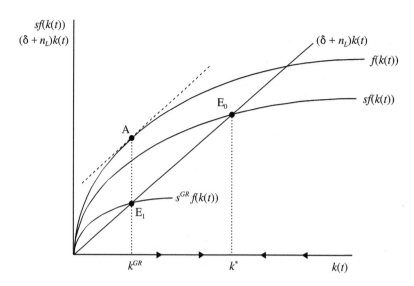

Figure 12.1: The Solow-Swan model

changes in the production factors, isoquants of the production function shift inwards as time progresses (Burmeister and Dobell, 1970, p. 66). Reasons for this inward shift may be improvements in techniques or organization which increase the productivity of new and old factors alike. Throughout this and the next two chapters we will restrict attention to cases of disembodied technical progress.

We can represent different cases of factor-augmenting disembodied technical change by writing the production function (12.1) in the following form:

$$Y(t) = F\left(Z_K(t)K(t), Z_L(t)L(t)\right), \tag{12.11}$$

where $Z_K(t)$ and $Z_L(t)$ only depend on time, and $Z_K(t)K(t)$ and $Z_L(t)L(t)$ are "effective capital" and "effective labour" respectively. Technical progress is purely labour augmenting if $\dot{Z}_K(t) \equiv 0$ and $\dot{Z}_L(t) > 0$, purely capital augmenting if $\dot{Z}_L(t) \equiv 0$ and $\dot{Z}_K(t) > 0$, and equally capital and labour augmenting if $\dot{Z}_K(t) \equiv \dot{Z}_L(t) > 0$.

Three different concepts of neutrality in the process of technical advance exist in the literature (Burmeister and Dobell, 1970, p. 75; Barro and Sala-i-Martin, 1995, p. 33). Technological change is (a) *Harrod neutral* if the relative input share $F_K K/(F_L L)$ is constant over time for a given capital-output ratio, K/Y, (b) *Hicks neutral* if this share is constant over time for a given capital-labour ratio, K/L, and (c) *Solow neutral* if this share is constant over time for a given labour-output ratio, L/Y. In terms of equation (12.11), the three cases correspond to, respectively, $Z_K(t) \equiv 1$, $Z_K(t) \equiv Z_L(t)$, and $Z_L(t) \equiv 1$.

Of course, for the Cobb-Douglas production function the three concepts of neutrality are indistinguishable, since (by redefining terms) we can write:

$$
\begin{aligned}
Y(t) &= [Z_K(t)K(t)]^\alpha \, L(t)^{1-\alpha} &&\Leftrightarrow \\
Y(t) &= K(t)^\alpha \, [Z_L(t)L(t)]^{1-\alpha} && \text{for } Z_L(t) \equiv Z_K(t)^{\alpha/(1-\alpha)} \Leftrightarrow \\
Y(t) &= Z(t)K(t)^\alpha L(t)^{1-\alpha} && \text{for } Z(t) = Z_K(t)^\alpha.
\end{aligned} \tag{12.12}
$$

For non-Cobb-Douglas cases, however, the different neutrality concepts have different implications for balanced growth. Barro and Sala-i-Martin (1995, pp. 54–55) show, for example, that technical progress must be Harrod neutral (labour augmenting) for the model to have a steady state with a constant growth rate. In a steady state we must have a constant capital-output ratio and it can be shown that for forms of technological progress that are not Harrod neutral, one of the factor shares approaches zero if the capital-output ratio is to be constant. So if we wish to have balanced growth *and* be able to consider a non-unitary substitution elasticity between capital and labour, we must assume Harrod-neutral technical progress. The remainder of the discussion in this section will thus assume that Harrod neutrality holds.

The production function is written as:

$$Y(t) = F\left(K(t), N(t)\right),\tag{12.13}$$

where $N(t)$ measures the effective amount of labour $(N(t) \equiv Z(t)L(t))$ and we assume that technical progress occurs at a constant exponential rate:

$$\frac{\dot{Z}(t)}{Z(t)} = n_Z, \quad Z(t) = Z(0)e^{n_Z t}.\tag{12.14}$$

Since the labour force itself grows exponentially at a constant rate n_L (see (12.5)), the *effective* labour force grows at a constant exponential rate $n_L + n_Z$, i.e.:

$$\frac{\dot{N}(t)}{N(t)} \equiv \frac{\dot{Z}(t)}{Z(t)} + \frac{\dot{L}(t)}{L(t)} = n_Z + n_L.\tag{12.15}$$

By measuring output and capital per unit of effective labour, i.e. $y(t) \equiv Y(t)/N(t)$ and $k(t) \equiv K(t)/N(t)$, and following the standard solution procedure explained above (in Intermezzo 12.1), the fundamental differential equation for $k(t)$ is obtained:

$$\dot{k}(t) = sf(k(t)) - (\delta + n_L + n_Z)k(t).\tag{12.16}$$

In the steady state, $k^* = sy^*/(\delta + n_L + n_Z)$, so that output and the capital stock grow at the same rate as the effective labour input. Hence, equation (12.10) is changed to:

$$\left(\frac{\dot{Y}(t)}{Y(t)}\right)^* = \left(\frac{\dot{K}(t)}{K(t)}\right)^* = \left(\frac{\dot{I}(t)}{I(t)}\right)^* = \left(\frac{\dot{S}(t)}{S(t)}\right)^* = \frac{\dot{N}(t)}{N(t)} = \frac{\dot{L}(t)}{L(t)} + \frac{\dot{Z}(t)}{Z(t)} = n_L + n_Z.\tag{12.17}$$

Hence, exactly the same qualitative conclusions are obtained as in the model without technological advance. Long-term balanced growth merely depends on the exogenous factors n_L and n_Z. Note that stylized fact (SF1) is accounted for as output per worker grows at an exponential rate n_Z along the balanced growth path.

12.3 Properties of the Solow-Swan model

In this section we study the most important properties of the Solow-Swan model. In particular, we look at (a) the golden rule and the issue of over-saving, (b) the transitional dynamics implied by the model as well as the concept of absolute versus conditional convergence, and (c) the speed of dynamic adjustment.

12.3.1 The golden rule of capital accumulation

One of the implications of the model developed thus far is that, even though long-term balanced *growth* is exogenous (and equal to $n \equiv n_L + n_Z$), the *levels* of output, capital, and consumption are critically affected by the level of the savings rate. In other words, even though s does not affect long-term growth it does affect the path along which the economy grows. This prompts the issue concerning the relative welfare ranking for these different paths. To the extent that the policy maker can affect s, he can also select the path on which the economy finds itself. We first consider steady-state paths and, to keep things simple, we assume that there is no technical progress (i.e. $n_Z = 0$ and $n = n_L$).

In the steady state, equation (12.7) implies a unique implicit relationship between the savings rate and the equilibrium capital-labour ratio which can be written as $sf(k^*) = (\delta + n)k^*$. By using the implicit function theorem we thus find that k^* depends on s:

$$k^* = k^*(s), \tag{12.18}$$

with $dk^*/ds = y^*/[\delta + n - sf'(k^*)] > 0$. Suppose that the policy maker is interested in steady-state per capita consumption which can be written as a function of the savings rate:

$$c^*(s) = (1 - s)f(k^*(s)) = f(k^*(s)) - (\delta + n)k^*(s). \tag{12.19}$$

In terms of Figure 12.1, $c^*(s)$ represents the vertical distance between the production function and the required-replacement line in the steady state. In Figure 12.2 we plot $c^*(s)$ for different savings-rates. Any output not needed to replace the existing capital stock per worker in the steady state can be consumed. Per capita consumption is at its maximum if the savings rate satisfies $dc^*(s)/ds = 0$, or:

$$\frac{dc^*(s)}{ds} = \left[f'(k^*(s)) - (\delta + n) \right] \cdot \frac{dk^*(s)}{ds} = 0. \tag{12.20}$$

In terms of Figure 12.1, per capita consumption is at its maximum at point A where the slope of the production function equals the slope of the required-replacement function. In view of (12.20), the *golden rule* savings rate, s^{GR}, satisfies:

$$f'\left(k^*(s^{GR})\right) = \delta + n. \tag{12.21}$$

The golden rule savings rate is associated with point E_1 in Figure 12.2. Burmeister and Dobell (1970, pp. 52–53) provide the economic intuition behind the result in (12.21). The produced asset (the physical capital stock) yields an own-rate of return equal to $f' - \delta$, whereas the non-produced primary good (labour) can be interpreted as yielding an own-rate of return $n_L = n$. Intuitively, the efficient outcome occurs if the rates of return on the two assets are equalized, i.e. if the equality in (12.21) holds.

Since $s^{GR}f(k^*(s^{GR})) = (\delta + n)k^*(s^{GR})$ we can rewrite the expression in (12.21) as:

$$s^{GR} = \frac{k^*(s^{GR}) \cdot f'(k^*(s^{GR}))}{f(k^*(s^{GR}))}. \tag{12.22}$$

Equation (12.22) shows that the golden rule savings rate is equal to the share of capital income in national income (which itself in general depends on the golden rule savings rate). In the Cobb-Douglas case, with $f(\cdot) = k(t)^\alpha$, α represents the capital income share so that the golden rule savings rate equals $s^{GR} = \alpha$.

We are now in a position to discuss the concept of *dynamic inefficiency*. We call an economy dynamically inefficient if it is possible to make everybody at least as well

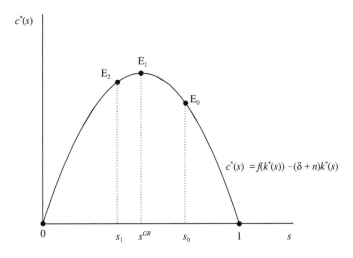

Figure 12.2: Per capita consumption and the savings rate

off (and some strictly better off) by reducing the capital stock. Consider the situation in Figure 12.2, and assume that the actual steady-state savings rate is s_0 so that the economy is at point E_0. Since this savings rate exceeds the golden rule savings rate ($s_0 > s^{GR}$), per capita consumption is lower than under the golden rule. It is not difficult to show that point E_0 is dynamically inefficient in the sense that higher per capita consumption can be attained by reducing the savings rate. Figure 12.2 shows that a reduction in the savings rate from s_0 to s^{GR} would move the steady state from E_0 to E_1 and lead to higher per capita steady-state consumption. With the aid of Figure 12.3 we can figure out what happens to per capita consumption during the transitional phase. The economy is initially at point E_0 and the initial steady-state capital-labour ratio is k_0^*. A reduction in the savings rate (from s_0 to s^{GR}) rotates the per capita consumption schedule in a counter-clockwise fashion and the economy jumps from E_0 to A at impact. Since the transition towards the golden-rule capital-labour ratio k^{GR} is stable, the economy moves from A to the new steady-state point E_1 as $k(t)$ falls towards k^{GR} during transition. Hence, as a result of the decrease in the savings rate, consumption is higher than it would have been, both during transition and in the new steady state. It follows that the reduction in s is Pareto improving, and we can conclude that savings rates exceeding s^{GR} are dynamically inefficient.

The same conclusion does not hold if the savings rate falls short of s^{GR} as the Pareto-optimality property cannot be demonstrated unambiguously. Consider an economy in which the savings rate falls short of its golden rule level, i.e. $s_1 < s^{GR}$. In terms of Figures 12.2 and 12.3, the economy is initially at point E_2. An increase in the savings rate from s_1 to s^{GR} still leads to an increase in steady-state per capita consumption. During transition, however, per capita consumption will have to fall before it can settle at its higher steady-state level prescribed by the golden rule. In terms of Figure 12.3, at impact the economy jumps from E_2 to B as the savings rate is increased. During part of the transition, consumption is lower than it would have been in the absence of the shock. Since we have no welfare function to evaluate the uneven path of per capita consumption, we cannot determine whether the increase in s is Pareto improving in this case.

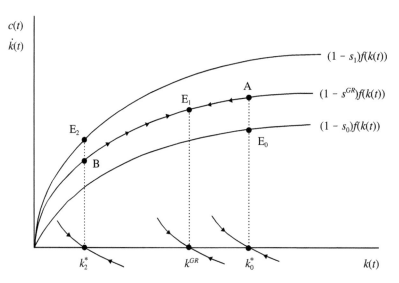

Figure 12.3: Per capita consumption during transition to its golden rule level

12.3.2   Transitional dynamics and convergence

Up to now attention has been focused on steady-state issues. We now return to the model with exogenous technical change, the fundamental equation of which is given in (12.16). By defining the growth rate of $k(t)$ as $\gamma_k(t) \equiv \dot{k}(t)/k(t)$, we derive from (12.16):

$$\gamma_k(t) \equiv s \cdot \frac{f(k(t))}{k(t)} - (\delta + n), \tag{12.23}$$

where $n \equiv n_L + n_Z$. In Figure 12.4 this growth rate is represented by the vertical difference between the two lines.[5] An immediate implication of (12.23), or Figure 12.4 for that matter, is that countries with little capital and low output (in efficiency units) grow faster than countries with a lot of capital and high output. The further away a country is from the steady state, the higher will be its growth rate. In other words, poor and rich countries should converge!

This suggests that there is a simple empirical test of the Solow-Swan model which is based on the convergence property of output in a cross-section of different countries. We take a group of closed economies (since the Solow-Swan model refers to the closed economy) and assume that they are similar in the sense that they possess the same structural parameters, s, n, and δ, and the same production function, so that in theory they have the same steady state. The so-called *absolute convergence hypothesis* (ACH) then suggests that poor countries should grow faster than rich countries. Barro and Sala-i-Martin (1995, p. 27), using a sample of 118 countries, regress the growth rate in per capita GDP during the period 1960–1985 on the logarithm of per capita GDP in the base year 1960. The results of their regression are dismal: instead of finding a negative effect as predicted by the ACH, they find a slight positive effect, i.e. countries that were rich in the base year ended up growing faster than poor countries did. Absolute convergence does not seem to hold and (Paul Romer's) stylized fact (SF7) is verified by the data.

---

[5]The Inada conditions ensure that $\lim_{k \to 0} sf(k)/k = \infty$ (vertical at the origin) and $\lim_{k \to \infty} sf(k)/k = 0$ (approaches horizontal axis asymptotically).

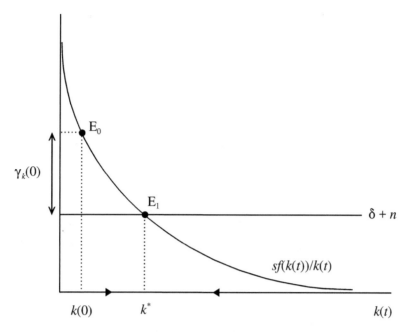

Figure 12.4: Growth convergence

This rejection of the ACH does not necessarily mean that the Solow-Swan model is refuted because one of the identifying assumptions underlying the regression results could be false. For example, if a rich country has a higher savings rate than a poor country, it could actually be further from its (higher) steady state than the poor country is from its steady state. The Solow-Swan model then predicts that the rich country will be growing faster than the poor country, as indeed the empirical results of Barro and Sala-i-Martin (1995) suggest. We demonstrate this result in Figure 12.5 where s_P and s_R are the savings rates of the poor and the rich country, respectively, and $(k^*)^P$ and $(k^*)^R$ are the corresponding steady states. If the poor country is initially at $k^P(0)$ and the rich country at $k^R(0)$, the former will grow slower than the latter (the vertical distance CD is larger than AB).

A refined test of the Solow-Swan model makes use of the *conditional convergence hypothesis* (CCH) according to which *truly similar* countries should converge. Barro and Sala-i-Martin (1995, pp. 27–28) show that convergence does appear to take place for the twenty original OECD countries and *a fortiori* for the different states in the US. This suggests that the CCH is not grossly at odds with the data, which is good news for the Solow-Swan model (and bad news for some of the endogenous growth models discussed in Chapter 14 below).

12.3.3   The speed of adjustment

The convergence property is not the only testable implication of the Solow-Swan model. Apart from testing *whether* economies converge, another issue concerns *how fast* they converge. In order to study this issue further we follow Burmeister and Dobell (1970, pp. 53–56) and Barro and Sala-i-Martin (1995, pp. 37–39, 53) by focusing on the Cobb-Douglas case for which $f(\cdot) = k(t)^\alpha$, and the fundamental differential equation (12.16) becomes:

$$\dot{k}(t) = sk(t)^\alpha - (\delta + n)k(t). \tag{12.24}$$

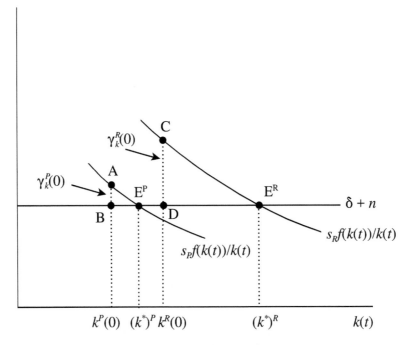

Figure 12.5: Conditional growth convergence

An exact analytical solution to this differential equation is not available because $k(t)$ enters non-linearly on the right-hand side of (12.24) (as $0 < \alpha < 1$). By using a first-order Taylor approximation around the steady-state capital intensity, k^*, we obtain:

$$sk(t)^\alpha \approx s\,(k^*)^\alpha + s\alpha\,(k^*)^{\alpha-1}\,[k(t) - k^*]$$
$$= (\delta + n)\,k^* + \alpha\,(\delta + n)\,[k(t) - k^*],\tag{12.25}$$

where we have used the fact that $s\,(k^*)^\alpha = (\delta + n)\,k^*$ in getting from the first to the second expression. Using (12.25) in (12.24) we obtain the linearized differential equation for $\dot{k}(t)$:

$$\dot{k}(t) = -\beta\,[k(t) - k^*],\qquad \beta \equiv (1-\alpha)(\delta + n) > 0.\tag{12.26}$$

Denoting the capital intensity in the base period by $k\,(0)$, the solution to (12.26) can be obtained by standard methods:

$$k(t) = k^* + [k(0) - k^*]\,e^{-\beta t},\tag{12.27}$$

where k^* is the steady-state capital intensity to which the economy converges in the long run, and where β measures the speed of convergence.

It is not difficult to deduce the speed of adjustment in the growth rate of output for the Cobb-Douglas case.[6] Indeed, dividing both sides of (12.26) by $k(t)$, noting that $\dot{k}(t)/k(t) = d\ln k(t)/dt$, $d\ln y(t)/dt = \alpha d\ln k(t)/dt$, and using the approximation $\ln\,(k(t)/k^*) = 1 - k^*/k(t)$, we find:

$$\frac{d\ln y(t)}{dt} = -\beta\,[\ln y(t) - \ln y^*],\tag{12.28}$$

---

[6]The more general case is covered by Barro and Sala-i-Martin (1995, p. 24).

which implies that:

$$\ln y(t) = \ln y^* + [\ln y(0) - \ln y^*] e^{-\beta t}. \tag{12.29}$$

Hence, β is the common (approximate) adjustment speed for $k(t)$, $\ln k(t)$, $y(t)$, and $\ln y(t)$ toward their respective steady-states.

The intuitive interpretation of β is as follows: $\zeta \times 100\%$ of the gap between $k(t)$ and k^* is eliminated after a time interval of t_ζ:

$$t_\zeta \equiv -\frac{\ln(1 - \zeta)}{\beta}. \tag{12.30}$$

Hence, the half-life of the adjustment ($\zeta = \frac{1}{2}$) equals $t_{1/2} = \ln 2/\beta = 0.693/\beta$.[7] Some back-of-the-envelope computations based on representative values of $n_L = 0.01$ (per annum), $n_Z = 0.02$, $\delta = 0.05$, and $\alpha = 1/3$ yield the value of $\beta = 0.0533$ (5.33% per annum) and an estimated half-life of $t_{1/2} = 13$ years. Transition is thus relatively fast, at least from a growth perspective.[8] As Barro and Sala-i-Martin (1995, p. 38) indicate, however, this estimate is far too high to accord with empirical evidence. They suggest that β is more likely to be in the range of 2% per annum (instead of 5.33%). So here is a real problem confronting the Solow-Swan model. In order for it to generate a realistic convergence rate of 2%, for given values of δ and n, the capital share must be unrealistically high (a value of $\alpha = \frac{3}{4}$ actually yields an estimate of $\beta = 0.02$)! One way to get the Solow-Swan model in line with reality is to assume a broad measure of capital to include human as well as physical capital. This is indeed the approach taken by Mankiw, Romer, and Weil (1992).

12.3.4 Human capital to the rescue

Mankiw, Romer, and Weil (1992, p. 415) start their analysis by using real world data to estimate the textbook Solow model. They show that, though the model appears to fit the data quite well, some of the parameter estimates are not entirely satisfactory. For example, the estimated capital coefficient is much larger than the actual capital share of about one third. So either their Cobb-Douglas technology assumption is inappropriate or there is a serious mis-measurement of the capital input. They adopt the latter stance and suggest that the convergence conundrum of the Solow-Swan model disappears if the production function is modified to include human capital:

$$Y(t) = K(t)^{\alpha_K} H(t)^{\alpha_H} [Z(t)L(t)]^{1-\alpha_K-\alpha_H}, \tag{12.31}$$

where $H(t)$ is the stock of human capital and α_K and α_H are the efficiency parameters of the two types of capital ($0 < \alpha_K, \alpha_H, \alpha_K + \alpha_H < 1$). In close accordance with the Solow-Swan model, productivity and population growth are both exponential ($\dot{Z}(t)/Z(t) = n_Z$ and $\dot{L}(t)/L(t) = n_L$) and the accumulation equations for the two types of capital and the production function can be written in effective labour units as:

$$\dot{k}(t) = s_K y(t) - (\delta_K + n)k(t), \tag{12.32}$$

---

[7]See also Chapter 7 where we compute the convergence speed of the unemployment rate in a discrete-time setting.

[8]Note that Sato (1963) actually complains about the startlingly low transition speed implied by the Solow-Swan model. His object of study is fiscal policy and business cycle phenomena. In this context convergence of 5% per annum is slow. Hence the different conclusion.

$$\dot{h}(t) = s_H y(t) - (\delta_H + n)h(t), \tag{12.33}$$
$$y(t) = k(t)^{\alpha_K} h(t)^{\alpha_H}, \tag{12.34}$$

where $k(t) \equiv K(t)/[Z(t)L(t)]$, $h(t) \equiv H(t)/[Z(t)L(t)]$, $y(t) \equiv Y(t)/[Z(t)L(t)]$, $n \equiv n_Z + n_L$, and s_K and s_H represent the propensities to accumulate physical and human capital, respectively. The depreciation rates of physical and human capital are denoted by, respectively, δ_K and δ_H.[9] The production functions of the two types of capital are assumed to be equal.

12.3.4.1 Stability

In order to study the stability properties of the model, we must first derive its phase diagram. The $\dot{k}(t) = 0$ line is obtained by substituting (12.34) into (12.32) and rearranging terms somewhat:

$$h(t) = \left(\frac{\delta_K + n}{s_K}\right)^{1/\alpha_H} \cdot k(t)^{(1-\alpha_K)/\alpha_H}, \tag{12.35}$$

where we note that the exponent for $k(t)$ exceeds unity $((1 - \alpha_K)/\alpha_H > 1)$. In terms of Figure 12.6, the $\dot{k}(t) = 0$ line passes through the origin and is convex. For points to the right (left) of the line, the physical capital stock falls (rises) over time. This has been indicated with horizontal arrows in Figure 12.6. In a similar fashion, the $\dot{h}(t) = 0$ line is obtain by using (12.34) in (12.33):

$$h(t) = \left(\frac{s_H}{\delta_H + n}\right)^{1/(1-\alpha_H)} \cdot k(t)^{\alpha_K/(1-\alpha_H)}, \tag{12.36}$$

where we observe that the exponent for $k(t)$ falls short of unity $(\alpha_K/(1 - \alpha_H) < 1)$. The $\dot{h}(t) = 0$ line passes through the origin and is concave. For points above (below) the line, the human capital stock falls (rises) over time—see the vertical arrows in Figure 12.6. Since there are decreasing returns to the two types of capital in combination $(\alpha_K + \alpha_H < 1)$ the model possesses a unique steady state for which $\dot{k}(t) = \dot{h}(t) = 0$, $k(t) = k^*$, and $h(t) = h^*$. By using (12.35)–(12.36) we obtain:

$$k^* = \left(\left(\frac{s_K}{\delta_K + n}\right)^{1-\alpha_H} \left(\frac{s_H}{\delta_H + n}\right)^{\alpha_H}\right)^{1/(1-\alpha_K-\alpha_H)}, \tag{12.37}$$

$$h^* = \left(\left(\frac{s_K}{\delta_K + n}\right)^{\alpha_K} \left(\frac{s_H}{\delta_H + n}\right)^{1-\alpha_K}\right)^{1/(1-\alpha_K-\alpha_H)}. \tag{12.38}$$

The configuration of arrows in Figure 12.6 confirms that the model is stable. Along the balanced growth path, $Y(t)$, $K(t)$, $H(t)$, and $C(t)$ all grow at the same exponential growth rate, n, just as in the standard Solow-Swan model discussed above.

12.3.4.2 Empirical performance

By substituting k^* and h^* into the (logarithm of the) production function (12.34) we obtain an estimable expression for per capita output along the balanced growth path:

$$\ln\left(\frac{Y(t)}{L(t)}\right)^* = \ln Z(0) + n_Z t - \frac{\alpha_K \ln(\delta_K + n_Z + n_L) + \alpha_H \ln(\delta_H + n_Z + n_L)}{1 - \alpha_K - \alpha_H}$$

---

[9]We use a slightly more general version of the Mankiw-Romer-Weil model by allowing δ_K to differ from δ_H. This model was also studied by Solow (1999, pp. 653–655).

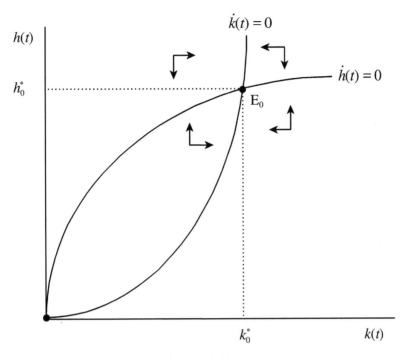

Figure 12.6: Augmented Solow-Swan model

$$+ \frac{\alpha_K}{1 - \alpha_K - \alpha_H} \ln s_K + \frac{\alpha_H}{1 - \alpha_K - \alpha_H} \ln s_H, \qquad (12.39)$$

where we recall that $\ln y(t) \equiv \ln \left(Y(t)/L(t) \right) - \ln Z(t)$ and we have used the second expression in (12.14) to write $\ln Z(t) = \ln Z(0) + n_Z t$. Mankiw, Romer, and Weil (1992, p. 417) suggest approximate guesses for $\alpha_K = \frac{1}{3}$ and α_H between $\frac{1}{3}$ and $\frac{4}{9}$. The latter guess is based on the observation that in the US manufacturing sector the minimum wage is between a third and a half of the average wage. By interpreting the minimum wage as the return to labour without any human capital (so-called "raw" labour), this means that between half and two thirds of the total payment to labour represents the return to human capital. Since an income share of $(1 - \alpha_K)$ is left after payments to owners of physical capital are taken care of, this implies $\frac{1}{2}(1 - \alpha_K) < \alpha_H < \frac{2}{3}(1 - \alpha_K)$ or $\frac{1}{3} < \alpha_H < \frac{4}{9}$.[10]

As a result of the inclusion of human capital, the model is much better equipped to explain large cross-country income differences for relatively small differences between, for example, savings rates (s_K and s_H) and population growth rates (n_L). This is apparent from equation (12.39). An increase in s_K, for example, induces higher income in efficiency units just as in the standard Solow-Swan model (see (12.32)) but also raises the stock of human wealth in efficiency units. By adding human capital to the model, the elasticity of s_K in (12.39) is of the order of unity rather than one half which is predicted by the standard Solow-Swan model. A similar conclusion holds for a change in n_L. An increase in n_L reduces income because both physical and human capital are spread out over more souls and the elasticity $\partial \ln \left(Y/L \right)^* / \partial n_L = -\left(\alpha_K + \alpha_H \right) / \left(1 - \alpha_K - \alpha_H \right)$ is not $-\frac{1}{2}$, as in the Solow-Swan

---

[10]Ingenious as it is, this approach to estimating the income share of human capital is not without dangers, especially in Europe where the minimum wage is policy manipulated rather than market determined.

model, but (for $\alpha_H = \frac{1}{3}$) a staggering -2! See Romer (2012) for a further numerical example.

Not surprisingly, the inclusion of a human capital variable works pretty well empirically; the estimated coefficient for α_H is highly significant and lies between 0.28 and 0.37 (Mankiw, Romer, and Weil, 1992, p. 420). The convergence property of the augmented Solow-Swan model is also much better. Indeed, for the special case with $\delta_K = \delta_H = \delta$, the convergence speed is given by $\beta \equiv (1 - \alpha_K - \alpha_H)(n + \delta)$ which can be made in accordance with the observed empirical estimate of $\hat{\beta} = 0.02$ without too much trouble. Hence, by this very simple and intuitively plausible adjustment the Solow-Swan model can be salvaged from the dustbin of history. The speed of convergence it implies can be made to fit the real world.

12.4   Macroeconomic applications of the Solow-Swan model

The Solow-Swan model can also be used to study traditional macroeconomic issues such as the effect of fiscal policy and the issue of debt versus tax financing and Ricardian equivalence. In order to keep things simple, we return to the standard Solow-Swan model in which there is only physical capital.

12.4.1   Fiscal policy in the Solow model

Suppose that the government consumes $G(t)$ units of output so that aggregate demand in the goods market is:

$$Y(t) = C(t) + I(t) + G(t). \tag{12.40}$$

Aggregate saving is proportional to after-tax income, so that (12.2) is modified to:

$$S(t) = s\,[Y(t) - T(t)], \tag{12.41}$$

where $T(t)$ is the lump-sum tax. Since $S(t) \equiv Y(t) - C(t) - T(t)$ any primary government deficit must be compensated for by an excess of private saving over investment, i.e. $G(t) - T(t) = S(t) - I(t)$. The government budget identity is given by:

$$\dot{B}(t) = r(t)B(t) + G(t) - T(t), \tag{12.42}$$

where $B(t)$ is government debt and $r(t)$ is the real interest rate which, under the competitive conditions assumed in the Solow-Swan model, equals the net marginal productivity of capital:[11]

$$r(t) = f'(k(t)) - \delta. \tag{12.43}$$

By writing all variables in terms of effective labour units, the model can be condensed to the following two equations:

$$\dot{k}(t) = f(k(t)) - (\delta + n)k(t) - c(t) - g(t)$$
$$= sf(k(t)) - (\delta + n)k(t) + (1 - s)\tau(t) - g(t), \tag{12.44}$$
$$\dot{b}(t) = [f'(k(t)) - \delta - n]\,b(t) + g(t) - \tau(t), \tag{12.45}$$

---

[11]This result is demonstrated more formally below. See section 13.1.2.

where $\tau(t) \equiv T(t)/N(t)$, $g(t) \equiv G(t)/N(t)$, and $b(t) \equiv B(t)/N(t)$. In the remainder of this subsection we assume that (i) government consumption per efficiency unit of labour is time-invariant, i.e. $g(t) = g$, and (ii) the economy is dynamically efficient, i.e. the initial capital stock, k_0^*, falls short of its golden-rule level so that the net interest rate is positive, $r_0^* - n \equiv f'(k_0^*) - \delta - n > 0$.

12.4.1.1 Tax-financed increase in government consumption

Under *pure tax financing* and in the absence of initial government debt ($\dot{b}(t) = b(t) = 0$), the government budget identity reduces to $\tau(t) \equiv g$, i.e. the tax is also time-invariant. By substituting this expression into (12.44) we obtain:

$$\dot{k}(t) = s\left[f(k(t)) - g\right] - (\delta + n)k(t). \tag{12.46}$$

The economy can be analysed with the aid of (12.46) alone—see Figure 12.7. In the absence of government consumption ($g = 0$), the unique (and stable) steady-state equilibrium is at point E_0. An increase in government consumption shifts the savings line down which results in multiple equilibria (or even no equilibria). Of these equilibria, the one at point A is unstable and that at E_1 is stable. Restricting attention to the stable equilibrium, we find that fiscal policy crowds out the physical capital stock in the long run, from k_0^* to k_1^*. At impact, the capital stock is predetermined ($k(0) = k_0^*$), private consumption and net investment (in efficiency units of labour) both fall ($dc(0)/dg = -(1-s) < 0$ and $d\dot{k}(0)/dg = -s < 0$) but output is unchanged ($dy(0)/dg = 0$). Over time, as the capital stock gradually falls towards its new steady-state value, output and private consumption per effective labour unit fall. The long-run effects are given by:

$$\frac{dy(\infty)}{dg} = \frac{f'(k_0^*)\,dk(\infty)}{dg} = -\frac{sf'(k_0^*)}{\delta + n - sf'(k_0^*)} < 0, \tag{12.47}$$

$$\frac{dc(\infty)}{dg} = (r_0^* - n)\frac{dk(\infty)}{dg} - 1 < -1, \tag{12.48}$$

where the sign in (12.47) follows readily from the fact that the required investment line is steeper than the savings line at the steady-state point E_0, i.e. $\delta + n > sf'(k_0^*)$, as can indeed be seen in Figure 12.7. Private consumption is crowded out more than one-for-one by public consumption in the long run.

12.4.1.2 Bond-financed tax cut

Next we consider the issue of *bond financing*. If the government increases its consumption without at the same time raising $\tau(t)$ by the same amount, a primary deficit will be opened up which, according to (12.45), will lead to an ever-increasing explosive process for government debt (since $r > n$ by assumption in (12.45)). In order to avoid this economically rather uninteresting result, we postulate a debt stabilization rule, a variation of which was suggested by Buiter (1988, p. 288):

$$\tau(t) = \tau_0 + \xi b(t), \quad \xi > r - n. \tag{12.49}$$

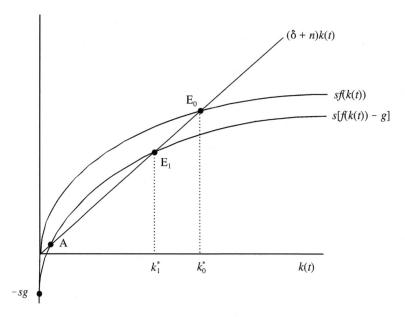

Figure 12.7: Fiscal policy in the Solow-Swan model

The tax thus depends positively on the outstanding stock of government debt. By substituting (12.49) into (12.45) we obtain a stable debt process:[12]

$$\dot{b}(t) = \left[f'(k(t)) - \delta - n - \xi \right] b(t) + g - \tau_0. \tag{12.50}$$

The dynamic properties of the economy can be illustrated with the aid of a phase diagram in (b, k) space—see Figure 12.8. By combining (12.44) and (12.49) and setting $g(t) = g$ we obtain the following expression:

$$\dot{k}(t) = sf(k(t)) - (\delta + n)k(t) + (1 - s)\left[\tau_0 + \xi b(t)\right] - g. \tag{12.51}$$

The slope of the $\dot{k} = 0$ line (evaluated at the steady state (k_0^*, b_0^*)) is obtained from (12.51) in the usual fashion:

$$\left(\frac{db(t)}{dk(t)} \right)_{\dot{k}(t)=0} = \frac{\delta + n - sf'(k_0^*)}{(1 - s)\xi} > 0. \tag{12.52}$$

The $\dot{k} = 0$ line is upward sloping, and points above (below) this line are associated with positive (negative) net investment, i.e. $\dot{k} > 0 \, (< 0)$. Ceteris paribus the capital stock, an increase in the level of debt raises tax receipts (by (12.49)), reduces consumption, and renders net investment positive. As a result, the new capital stock equilibrium features a higher capital stock. The dynamic forces are indicated by horizontal arrows in Figure 12.8.

The $\dot{b} = 0$ line is obtained from (12.50). It is horizontal if debt is zero in the initial steady state. In contrast, with a positive initial debt level, it is downward sloping because of the diminishing marginal productivity of capital:

$$\left(\frac{db(t)}{dk(t)} \right)_{\dot{b}(t)=0} = \frac{b_0^* f''(k_0^*)}{\xi - (r_0^* - n)} < 0. \tag{12.53}$$

---

[12]Equation (12.50) is stable because the coefficient for $b(t)$ on the right-hand side is equal to $(r - n) - \xi$, which is negative. Recall that r depends negatively on k, so $\xi > r - n$ cannot hold for all values of k if ξ is finite (as intended). We intend the inequality $\xi > r - n$ to hold in a sufficiently large region around the initial steady state.

For points above (below) the $\dot{b} = 0$ line there is a government surplus (deficit) so that debt falls (rises). This is indicated with vertical arrows in Figure 12.8. The Buiter rule thus ensures that the economy follows a stable (and possibly cyclical) adjustment pattern, as can be verified by graphical means. Local stability can also be investigated more formally by linearizing the model given by (12.50) and (12.51) around the steady-state, (k_0^*, b_0^*). After some manipulation we obtain the following system of first-order differential equations:[13]

$$\begin{bmatrix} \dot{b}(t) \\ \dot{k}(t) \end{bmatrix} = \begin{bmatrix} r_0^* - n - \xi & b_0^* f''(k_0^*) \\ (1-s)\xi & sf'(k^*) - (\delta + n) \end{bmatrix} \begin{bmatrix} b(t) - b_0^* \\ k(t) - k_0^* \end{bmatrix}. \tag{12.54}$$

The Jacobian matrix on the right-hand side of (12.54) is denoted by Δ, its typical elements are given by δ_{ij}, and λ_1 and λ_2 are its characteristic roots. For any square matrix, the trace and determinant equal, respectively, the sum and the product of the characteristic roots. Especially for two-by-two matrices this result is often quite useful to figure out the signs of the roots without actually computing them explicitly. To see that this is indeed the case, note that $\delta_{11} < 0$ and $\delta_{22} < 0$ so that $\text{tr}(\Delta) \equiv \lambda_1 + \lambda_2 = \delta_{11} + \delta_{22} < 0$ implying that the sum of the roots is negative. Furthermore, since $\delta_{12} < 0$ (for $b_0^* > 0$) and $\delta_{21} > 0$ it follows that $|\Delta| \equiv \lambda_1 \lambda_2 = \delta_{11}\delta_{22} - \delta_{12}\delta_{21} > 0$, so that the model is stable, i.e. λ_1 and λ_2 are both negative.

Now consider the typical Ricardian equivalence experiment, consisting of a postponement of taxation. In the model this amounts to a reduction in τ_0. This creates a primary deficit at impact ($g > \tau_0$) so that government debt starts to rise. In terms of Figure 12.8, both the $\dot{k} = 0$ line and the $\dot{b} = 0$ line shift up, the latter by more than the former. The new long-run equilibrium is at E_1, and government debt, the capital stock, and output (all measured in efficiency units of labour) rise as a result of the tax cut:

$$\frac{dy(\infty)}{d\tau_0} = \frac{f'(k_0^*) \, dk(\infty)}{d\tau_0} = -\frac{(1-s)(r_0^* - n)f'(k_0^*)}{|\Delta|} < 0, \tag{12.55}$$

$$\frac{db(\infty)}{d\tau_0} = \frac{sf'(k_0^*) - (\delta + n) + (1-s)b_0^* f''(k_0^*)}{|\Delta|} < 0. \tag{12.56}$$

Clearly, Ricardian equivalence does not hold in the Solow-Swan model. At impact, a temporary tax cut boosts consumption and depresses investment ($d\dot{k}(0)/d\tau_0 = -dc(0)/d\tau_0 = 1 - s > 0$) and thus has real effects.

12.5 Two-sector model

Up to this point we have assumed that output is homogeneous and can be used for consumption by households and the government and also for investment by firms.

---

[13]We write the non-linear system in general functional form as $\dot{b}(t) = \Phi(b(t), k(t))$ and $\dot{k}(t) = \Psi(b(t), k(t))$. A first-order Taylor approximation around (b_0^*, k_0^*) yields:

$$\dot{b}(t) \approx \Phi(b_0^*, k_0^*) + \Phi_b(b_0^*, k_0^*)[b(t) - b_0^*] + \Phi_k(b_0^*, k_0^*)[k(t) - k_0^*],$$
$$\dot{k}(t) \approx \Psi(b_0^*, k_0^*) + \Psi_b(b_0^*, k_0^*)[b(t) - b_0^*] + \Psi_k(b_0^*, k_0^*)[k(t) - k_0^*].$$

At the steady-state we have $\Phi(b_0^*, k_0^*) = \Psi(b_0^*, k_0^*) = 0$ so the first terms on the right-hand side drop out and the system can be written in matrix notation as:

$$\begin{bmatrix} \dot{b}(t) \\ \dot{k}(t) \end{bmatrix} = \begin{bmatrix} \Phi_b(b_0^*, k_0^*) & \Phi_k(b_0^*, k_0^*) \\ \Psi_b(b_0^*, k_0^*) & \Psi_k(b_0^*, k_0^*) \end{bmatrix} \begin{bmatrix} b(t) - b_0^* \\ k(t) - k_0^* \end{bmatrix}.$$

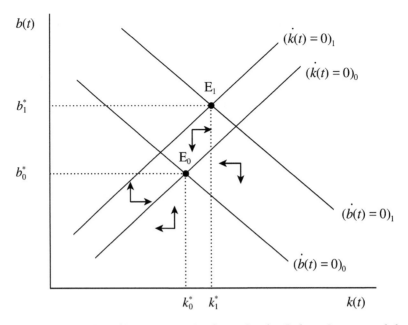

Figure 12.8: Ricardian non-equivalence in the Solow-Swan model

This is a rather unrealistic feature of the Solow-Swan model. Indeed, in reality consumption goods (apples, oranges, bread) are quite different from investment goods (machines, buildings, PCs). In this section we relax the single-good assumption and instead study (a version of) the two-sector growth model that was first proposed—almost simultaneously—by Meade (1961) and Uzawa (1961b, 1963). The Meade-Uzawa model recognizes two separate production sectors, namely a consumption good sector (with industry index $i = C$) and an investment good sector (with index $i = I$). In both sectors capital and labour are used to produce output. We abstract from technological progress to keep things simple. The technology in sector i is given by:

$$Y_i(t) = F^i(K_i(t), L_i(t)), \tag{12.57}$$

where Y_i is output, K_i is the capital input, and L_i is the labour input in sector $i \in \{C, I\}$. The production functions possess the usual properties, i.e. they exhibit constant returns to scale, positive but diminishing marginal products ($F_K^i \equiv \frac{\partial F^i}{\partial K_i} > 0$, $F_L^i \equiv \frac{\partial F^i}{\partial L_i} > 0$, $F_{KK}^i \equiv \frac{\partial^2 F^i}{\partial K_i^2} < 0$, $F_{LL}^i \equiv \frac{\partial^2 F^i}{\partial L_i^2} < 0$), and cooperative factors of production ($F_{KL}^i \equiv \frac{\partial^2 F^i}{\partial K_i \partial L_i} > 0$). In addition we assume that the relevant Inada conditions are satisfied. The intensive-form production functions are written as:

$$y_i(t) = f_i(k_i(t)), \tag{12.58}$$

where $y_i \equiv Y_i/L_i$ and $k_i \equiv K_i/L_i$. The marginal products of capital and labour can then be written as:[14]

$$F_K^i(K_i(t), L_i(t)) \equiv f_i'(k_i(t)), \tag{12.59}$$

---

[14]We use $\Gamma^i = F_K^i K_i + F_L^i L_i$, which follows from Euler's theorem, and $F_K^i = f_i'$ to derive the second expression.

$$F_L^i(K_i(t), L_i(t)) \equiv f_i(k_i(t)) - k_i(t) f_i'(k_i(t)). \tag{12.60}$$

Capital and labour are perfectly mobile between sector ensuring that the wage rate, W, and the rental rate on capital, R^K, are the same in both sectors. Profit of the representative firm in sector i is given by:

$$\Pi_i(t) = P_i(t) F^i(K_i(t), L_i(t)) - W(t) L_i(t) - R^K(t) K_i(t), \tag{12.61}$$

where P_i is the price of one unit of output produced in sector i. The firm is perfectly competitive and hires factors of production such that the value of the marginal product of each factor equals its rental rate:

$$P_i(t) F_K^i(K_i(t), L_i(t)) = R^K(t), \tag{12.62}$$

$$P_i(t) F_L^i(K_i(t), L_i(t)) = W(t). \tag{12.63}$$

Because there are constant returns to scale, (12.62)–(12.63) imply that profit is zero in each sector, i.e. $\Pi_i(t) = 0$. Note that the first-order conditions can be combined to obtain:

$$\omega(t) = \frac{F_L^i(K_i, L_i)}{F_K^i(K_i, L_i)}, \tag{12.64}$$

where $\omega(t) \equiv \frac{W(t)}{R^K(t)}$ is the relative price of labour which we refer to as the *wage-rental ratio*.

The equilibrium conditions on the markets for existing capital and labour can be written as:

$$K(t) = K_C(t) + K_I(t), \tag{12.65}$$

$$L(t) = L_C(t) + L_I(t). \tag{12.66}$$

At each moment in time the aggregate factor supplies ($K(t)$ and $L(t)$) are predetermined but the location of each factor's usage can be changed instantaneously in response to exogenous shocks.

Just as in the Solow-Swan model, aggregate saving is assumed to be proportional to aggregate output. Since the latter equals aggregate factor payments we thus have:

$$S(t) = s \left[R^K(t) K(t) + W(t) L(t) \right], \qquad 0 < s < 1, \tag{12.67}$$

where s is the exogenously given propensity to save. Of necessity, saving can only be used by buying investment goods, i.e.:

$$S(t) = P_I(t) Y_I(t). \tag{12.68}$$

At each moment in time, the savings decisions by households thus determine aggregate revenue in the investment goods sector.

The output of the investment goods sector augments the stock of capital according to:

$$\dot{K}(t) = Y_I(t) - \delta K(t), \tag{12.69}$$

where δ is the constant depreciation rate. The growth rate in the aggregate labour force is still given by (12.5) above.

Finally, aggregate output measured in terms of consumption goods is defined as follows:

$$Y(t) = Y_C(t) + \frac{P_I(t)}{P_C(t)} Y_I(t). \tag{12.70}$$

The full model is given in Table 12.1 for convenience. Since the derivation of these expressions is far from straightforward, Intermezzo 12.2 presents the details. The endogenous variables are aggregate per capita output, $y \equiv Y/L$, the capital intensities in the two sectors, k_I and k_C, the wage-rental ratio, ω, the macroeconomic capital intensity, $k \equiv K/L$, and the proportion of the work force that is employed in the investment goods sector, $l_I \equiv L_I/L$.

Table 12.1. The Meade-Uzawa growth model

$$y(t) = (1 - l_I(t))f_C(k_C(t)) + \frac{f'_C(k_C(t))}{f'_I(k_I(t))} l_I(t) f_I(k_I(t)) \tag{T1.1}$$

$$\omega(t) = \frac{f_C(k_C(t))}{f'_C(k_C(t))} - k_C(t) \tag{T1.2}$$

$$\omega(t) = \frac{f_I(k_I(t))}{f'_I(k_I(t))} - k_I(t) \tag{T1.3}$$

$$k(t) = (1 - l_I(t))k_C(t) + l_I(t)k_I(t) \tag{T1.4}$$

$$l_I(t)\frac{f_I(k_I(t))}{f'_I(k_I(t))} = s\left[k(t) + \omega(t)\right] \tag{T1.5}$$

$$\dot{k}(t) = l_I(t)f(k_I(t)) - (\delta + n_L)k(t) \tag{T1.6}$$

Notes: $y(t)$ is aggregate per capita output measured in terms of consumption goods, $k_i(t)$ is the capital intensity in sector i, $k(t)$ is the economy-wide capital-labour ratio, $\omega(t)$ is the wage-rental ratio, and $l_I(t)$ is the fraction of the work force employed in the investment goods sector. Capital depreciates at a constant rate δ and the population grows exponentially with rate n_L.

Along the balanced growth path the endogenous variables are all constant over time, i.e. $y(t) = y^*$, $k_i(t) = k_i^*$, $\omega(t) = \omega^*$, $l_i(t) = l_i^*$, and $k(t) = k^*$. Since the labour force grows at the exponential rate n_L, it thus follows that all level variables grow at that rate also:

$$\left(\frac{\dot{Y}(t)}{Y(t)}\right)^* = \left(\frac{\dot{K}_i(t)}{K_i(t)}\right)^* = \left(\frac{\dot{L}_i(t)}{L_i(t)}\right)^* = \left(\frac{\dot{K}(t)}{K(t)}\right)^* = n_L. \tag{12.71}$$

Of course, the steady state equilibrium solution is only of interest if we can demonstrate that it is stable. Whilst the stability proof is rather complicated for the most general case, it turns out to be quite straightforward for the special case with Cobb-Douglas technologies.

We assume from here on that the intensive-form production functions take the following form:

$$y_i(t) = Z_i k_i(t)^{\alpha_i}, \qquad 0 < \alpha_i < 1, \tag{12.72}$$

where Z_i is a sector-specific constant and α_i is the sector-specific efficiency parameter for capital. We assume that $\alpha_I \neq \alpha_C$ so the technologies are distinct. The fundamental differential equation is derived as follows. First, by using (12.72) in (T1.2)–(T1.3) we find the capital intensities in the two sectors conditional on the wage-rental ratio:

$$k_i(t) = \frac{\alpha_i}{1 - \alpha_i} w(t). \tag{12.73}$$

For a given wage-rental ratio, the sector with the highest efficiency parameter of capital features the highest capital intensity.

Second, by using (12.72) and (12.73) in (T1.4)–(T1.5) we obtain:

$$\frac{k(t)}{w(t)} = (1 - l_I(t)) \frac{\alpha_C}{1 - \alpha_C} + l_I(t) \frac{\alpha_I}{1 - \alpha_I}, \tag{12.74}$$

$$\frac{l_I(t)}{1 - \alpha_I} = s \left[\frac{k(t)}{w(t)} + 1 \right]. \tag{12.75}$$

Solving for $l_I(t)$ and $k(t)/w(t)$ we obtain:

$$l_I(t) = \frac{s(1 - \alpha_I)}{s(1 - \alpha_I) + (1 - s)(1 - \alpha_C)} \equiv l_I^*, \tag{12.76}$$

$$\frac{k(t)}{w(t)} = (1 - l_I^*) \frac{\alpha_C}{1 - \alpha_C} + l_I^* \frac{\alpha_I}{1 - \alpha_I} \equiv \kappa^*. \tag{12.77}$$

Clearly, $0 < l_I^* < 1$ and $\kappa^* > 0$. Since the savings rate and the efficiency parameters of the production functions are constant, it follows from these expressions that $l_I(t)$ and $w(t)/k(t)$ are both constant over time for the Cobb-Douglas case.

Third, by using (12.72)–(12.73) and (12.76) in (T1.1) we obtain a simple expression for per capita aggregate output:

$$y(t) = \left[1 - l_I^* + \frac{1 - \alpha_C}{1 - \alpha_I} l_I^* \right] Z_C k_C(t)^{\alpha_C}. \tag{12.78}$$

Per capita output is thus proportional to the intensive-form production function in the consumption goods sector. But this expression can be simplified even further by using (12.73) for $i = C$ and by noting (12.77):

$$y(t) = \left[1 - l_I^* + \frac{1 - \alpha_C}{1 - \alpha_I} l_I^* \right] Z_C \left[\frac{\alpha_C}{1 - \alpha_C} w(t) \right]^{\alpha_C}$$

$$= \left[1 - l_I^* + \frac{1 - \alpha_C}{1 - \alpha_I} l_I^* \right] Z_C \left[\frac{\alpha_C}{1 - \alpha_C} \frac{k(t)}{\kappa^*} \right]^{\alpha_C}. \tag{12.79}$$

Finally, by using (12.73) and (12.76)–(12.77) in (T1.6) we find that the economy-wide capital-labour ratio evolves according to:

$$\dot{k}(t) = l_I^* Z_I \left[\frac{\alpha_I}{1 - \alpha_I} w(t) \right]^{\alpha_I} - (\delta + n_L) k(t)$$

$$= l_I^* Z_I \left[\frac{\alpha_I}{1 - \alpha_I} \frac{k(t)}{\kappa^*} \right]^{\alpha_I} - (\delta + n_L) k(t). \tag{12.80}$$

This is the fundamental differential equation characterizing the transitional dynamics of (the Cobb-Douglas version of) the Meade-Uzawa model. It is the two-sector counterpart to equation (12.24) and its main properties are easily established. First, the model is stable and features a uniques economically interesting steady-state macroeconomic capital intensity, k^*. Steady-state per capita output, y^*, follows readily from (12.79). Second, the approximate speed of adjustment equals $\beta \equiv (1 - \alpha_I)(\delta + n_L)$ so it is the capital share parameter *in the investment goods sector* that is the crucial determinant of transition speed. So if this sector is highly capital intensive (and features a high value of α_I) then the Meade-Uzawa model may not be grossly at odds with the empirical convergence speed of two percent per annum mentioned in Section 12.3.3 above.

Perhaps the most important conclusion from the two-sector model is the following. Apart from details, the two-sector model provides a very similar description of the growth process as the much simpler one-sector model first suggested by Solow and Swan. This may explain why the Solow-Swan model has proven to be such a durable model. At the macroeconomic level it "explains a lot with very little", i.e. it gives a lot of bang for one's bucks.

Intermezzo 12.2

Some tedious derivations for the Meade-Uzawa model. The derivation of the expressions in Table 12.1 proceeds as follows. First we note that it follows from (12.62) and (12.59) that the relative price of investment goods is equal to:

$$\frac{P_I(t)}{P_C(t)} = \frac{f_C'(k_C(t))}{f_I'(k_I(t))}. \tag{a}$$

By using (12.58), (12.70), and (a) we obtain equation (T1.1):

$$y(t) \equiv \frac{Y(t)}{L(t)} = \frac{L_C(t)}{L(t)} \frac{Y_C(t)}{L_C(t)} + \frac{P_I(t)}{P_C(t)} \frac{L_I(t)}{L(t)} \frac{Y_I(t)}{L_I(t)}$$

$$= (1 - l_I(t))f_C(k_C(t)) + \frac{f_C'(k_C(t))}{f_I'(k_I(t))} l_I(t) f_I(k_I(t)), \tag{b}$$

where $l_I \equiv L_I/L$ is the proportion of the labour force employed in the investment goods sector (with the remainder, $1 - l_I$, employed in the consumption goods sector). Equations (T1.2) and (T1.3) are obtained by dividing (12.63) by (12.62) and noting (12.59)–(12.60). To obtain equation (T1.4) we divide (12.65) by (12.66):

$$k(t) \equiv \frac{K(t)}{L(t)} = \frac{K_C(t)}{L_C(t) + L_I(t)} + \frac{K_I(t)}{L_C(t) + L_I(t)}$$

$$= \frac{L_C(t)}{L_C(t) + L_I(t)} \frac{K_C(t)}{L_C(t)} + \frac{L_I(t)}{L_C(t) + L_I(t)} \frac{K_I(t)}{L_I(t)}$$

$$= (1 - l_I(t))k_C(t) + l_I(t)k_I(t). \tag{c}$$

To get equation (T1.5) we first combine (12.67) and (12.68) to get:

$$P_I(t)Y_I(t) = s[R^K(t)K(t) + W(t)L(t)]. \tag{d}$$

Dividing both sides by $R^K L$ gives:

$$\frac{P_I(t)Y_I(t)}{R^K(t)L(t)} = s[k(t) + \omega(t)]. \qquad (e)$$

The left-hand side of (e) can be simplified as follows:

$$\frac{P_I(t)Y_I(t)}{R^K(t)L(t)} = \frac{L_I(t)}{L(t)}\frac{P_I(t)y_I(t)}{R^K(t)} = l_I(t)\frac{P_I(t)f_I(k_I(t))}{P_I(t)f'_I(k_I(t))} = l_I(t)\frac{f_I(k_I(t))}{f'_I(k_I(t))}, \quad (f)$$

where we have used (12.62) for $i = I$ to arrive at the final expression. Substituting (f) into (e) yields equation (T1.5). Finally, equation (T1.6) follows from (12.69), (12.58), and (12.5) in the following fashion:

$$\frac{\dot{K}(t)}{L(t)} = \frac{L_I(t)}{L(t)}\frac{Y_I(t)}{L_I(t)} - \delta\frac{K(t)}{L(t)} \qquad \Leftrightarrow$$

$$\dot{k}(t) + n_L k(t) = l_I(t)f_I(k_I(t)) - \delta k(t). \qquad (g)$$

By rearranging (g) somewhat we obtain (T1.6).

****

12.6   Punchlines

We start this chapter by presenting some of the most important stylized facts about growth as they were presented over five decades ago by Kaldor. These are: (i) output per worker shows continuous growth, (ii) the capital-output ratio is constant, (iii) labour and capital receive constant shares of total income, and (iv) the rate of productivity growth differs across countries. Together these stylized facts also explain that (v) capital per worker grows continuously and that (vi) the rate of return on capital is steady.

Next we present the neoclassical growth model as it was developed by Solow and Swan in the mid 1950s. The key elements of this model are the neoclassical production function, featuring substitutability between capital and labour, and the "Keynesian" savings function according to which households save a constant fraction of their income. Although the Solow-Swan model is able to explain all of Kaldor's stylized facts, some economists are disturbed by its prediction that long-run growth is determined entirely by exogenous factors, such as the rate of population growth and the rate of labour-augmenting technological progress. For this reason the Solow-Swan model is often referred to as an "exogenous" growth model. The model does not feature Ricardian equivalence, i.e. public debt is not neutral. Further important features of the model are that it allows for the possibility of oversaving (dynamic inefficiency) and that it is consistent with the conditional convergence hypothesis according to which similar countries converge. The standard Solow-Swan model predicts too high a convergence speed, but this counterfactual prediction is easily fixed by incorporating human capital into the model.

In the final section of this chapter we study a two-sector growth model first proposed by Meade and Uzawa. This model assumes that consumption and investment goods are produced in different sectors featuring different technologies. Interestingly, at the macroeconomic level the Meade-Uzawa model looks very similar to the Solow-Swan model, at least for the case in which production functions are of the Cobb-Douglas type.

Further reading

The theory of exogenous economic growth is well surveyed by Burmeister and Dobell (1970), Wan (1971), Hamberg (1971), Hacche (1979), Barro and Sala-i-Martin (1995), and Acemoglu (2009).

On the two-sector model, see Meade (1961), Uzawa (1961, 1963), Solow (1961), and Inada (1964). See Drandakis (1963) for existence (causality) conditions. For a very good textbook treatment of the two-sector model, see Burmeister and Dobell (1970, chs. 4–5).

Chapter 13

Exogenous economic growth—Ramsey-Cass-Koopmans

The purpose of this chapter is to discuss the following issues:

1. How can we provide a microeconomic foundation for the savings decision by households?

2. What are the most important features of the growth model based on dynamically optimizing consumers?

3. How do fiscal policy and Ricardian equivalence work in the basic micro-founded growth model?

4. How do dynamically optimizing households choose their labour supply over time?

5. How do search frictions in the labour market lead to a positive equilibrium rate of unemployment in a world with hyper-rational consumers and firms?

6. What do we mean by monetary (super)neutrality?

13.1   The Ramsey-Cass-Koopmans model

In the previous chapter we employed an ad hoc savings function according to which aggregate saving is a constant fraction of income (see equations (12.2), (12.41), and (12.67)). Whilst the underlying consumption function works rather well empirically (in the sense that output and consumption are highly correlated), there are serious theoretical objections that can be raised against it. In Chapter 6, for example, it was shown that a forward-looking "representative" agent would condition consumption not on some measure of disposable income but rather on lifetime wealth, comprising the sum of financial and human wealth (see, for example, the expressions in (6.16)). In this chapter we investigate the implications for growth of the intertemporal utility maximization theory.

The intertemporal utility maximizing approach to consumption was pioneered by Frank Ramsey in the 1920s with some help from John Maynard Keynes—see Ramsey (1928). Ramsey's basic insights were embedded in a macroeconomic growth model in the 1960s by key contributers David Cass (1965) and Tjalling Koopmans (1965,

1967). The literature often refers to the model as the Ramsey model although a much more appropriate name would be the Ramsey-Cass-Koopmans (or RCK) model.

13.1.1 The representative household

Assume that the representative household has $L(t)$ members at time t, is infinitely lived,[1] and blessed with perfect foresight. The household experiences instantaneous utility (or "felicity") which depends on the consumption flow $c(t)$ per member of the household. The felicity function, $U(c(t))$, exhibits positive but diminishing marginal utility and thus satisfies $U'(c(t)) > 0$ and $U''(c(t)) < 0$. In addition the following Inada-style conditions are imposed:

$$\lim_{c(t)\to 0} U'(c(t)) = +\infty, \qquad \lim_{c(t)\to\infty} U'(c(t)) = 0. \tag{13.1}$$

The household derives no felicity from the consumption of leisure and is assumed to inelastically supply $L(t)$ units of labour to a competitive labour market, i.e. all household members work full time. (In Sections 13.5 and 13.6 this rather restrictive assumption is abandoned.) As before, labour supply grows over time at a constant exponential rate (i.e. $\dot{L}(t)/L(t) = n$).[2] The household's utility functional is defined as the discounted integral of present and future felicity. Normalizing the present by $t = 0$ ("today") we obtain:

$$\Lambda(0) \equiv \int_0^\infty U(c(t))e^{-\rho t}dt, \quad \rho > 0, \tag{13.2}$$

where $\Lambda(0)$ is lifetime utility and ρ is the pure rate of time preference. At time t, the household holds financial assets totalling $A(t)$ and yielding a rate of return of $r(t)$. The budget identity is thus given by:

$$C(t) + \dot{A}(t) \equiv r(t)A(t) + w(t)L(t), \tag{13.3}$$

where $w(t)$ is the real wage, $w(t)L(t)$ is household wage income, and $C(t) \equiv c(t)L(t)$ is aggregate household consumption. Equation (13.3) says that the sum of income from financial assets and labour (the right-hand side) is equal to the sum of consumption and saving (the left-hand side). By rewriting (13.3) in per capita form we obtain:

$$\dot{a}(t) \equiv [r(t) - n]\, a(t) + w(t) - c(t), \tag{13.4}$$

where $a(t) \equiv A(t)/L(t)$. As it stands, (13.4) is still no more than an identity, i.e. without further restrictions it is rather meaningless. Indeed, if the household can borrow all it likes at the going interest rate $r(t)$ it will simply accumulate debt indefinitely and thus be able to finance any arbitrary high consumption path. To avoid this economically nonsensical outcome, we need to impose a solvency condition:

$$\lim_{t\to\infty} a(t)\exp\left[-\int_0^t [r(\tau) - n]\, d\tau\right] = 0. \tag{13.5}$$

---

[1]Alternatively, one might assume a representative family dynasty, the finitely-lived members of which are linked across time via operative bequests. See Barro and Sala-i-Martin (1995, p. 60) and Chapter 6 for this interpretation.

[2]New, infinitely-lived family members are born into the household at each moment in time, leading to an exponential increase in total household labour supply.

Intuitively, equation (13.5) says that the household does not plan to "expire" with positive assets and is not allowed by the capital market to die hopelessly indebted.[3]

By integrating (13.4) over the (infinite) lifetime of the household and taking into account the solvency condition (13.5), we obtain the household lifetime budget constraint (see Intermezzo 13.1):

$$\int_0^\infty c(t)e^{-[R(t)-nt]}dt = a(0) + h(0), \tag{13.6}$$

where $a(0)$ is the initial level of financial assets, $h(0)$ is the initial level of human wealth,

$$h(0) \equiv \int_0^\infty w(t)e^{-[R(t)-nt]}dt, \tag{13.7}$$

and $R(t)$ is a discounting factor:

$$R(t) \equiv \int_0^t r(\tau)d\tau. \tag{13.8}$$

Equation (13.7) shows that human wealth is the present value of the real wage, i.e. the market value of each household member's (unit) time endowment. From the viewpoint of the household, the right-hand side of (13.6) is given and acts as a restriction on the time paths for consumption that are feasible.

Intermezzo 13.1

The household's lifetime budget constraint under perfect foresight. The household's lifetime budget constraint (13.6) is derived as follows. First we premultiply (13.4) by $e^{-[R(t)-nt]}$ to obtain:

$$[\dot{a}(t) - [r(t) - n]a(t)]e^{-[R(t)-nt]} = [w(t) - c(t)]e^{-[R(t)-nt]} \quad \Leftrightarrow$$

$$\frac{d}{dt}\left[a(t)e^{-[R(t)-nt]}\right] = [w(t) - c(t)]e^{-[R(t)-nt]}, \tag{a}$$

where we have used the fact that $dR(t)/dt = r(t)$ (Leibniz's rule; see the Mathematical Appendix) in going from the first to the second line. By integrating both sides of (a) over the interval $[0, \infty)$ we obtain:

$$\int_0^\infty da(t)e^{-[R(t)-nt]} = \int_0^\infty [w(t) - c(t)]e^{-[R(t)-nt]}dt$$

$$\lim_{t\to\infty} e^{-[R(t)-nt]}a(t) - a(0) = h(0) - \int_0^\infty c(t)e^{-[R(t)-nt]}dt, \tag{b}$$

where we have used (13.7) and have noted that $e^{-[R(0)-0n]} = 1$. The solvency condition (13.5) ensures that the first term on the left-hand side of (b) is equal to zero, i.e. equation (b) coincides with (13.6).

****

---

[3]Compare the discussion in Barro and Sala-i-Martin (1995, pp. 62–66). Strictly speaking (13.5) in equality form is an *outcome* of household maximizing behaviour rather than an a priori restriction. See also Intermezzo 13.2 for further details. By using (13.5) we avoid getting bogged down in technical issues. See also Section 6.1.1 for an intuitive discussion of the solvency condition in macroeconomics.

The consumer chooses a time path for $c(t)$ in order to attain a maximum lifetime utility level $\Lambda(0)$ (given in (13.2)), subject to the lifetime budget restriction (13.6). The Lagrangian for this optimization problem is given by:

$$\mathcal{L} \equiv \int_0^\infty U(c(t))e^{-\rho t}dt + \lambda \cdot \left[a(0) + h(0) - \int_0^\infty c(t)e^{-[R(t)-nt]}dt \right], \tag{13.9}$$

where λ is the Lagrange multiplier associated with the lifetime budget restriction (13.6). The optimized value of λ represents the marginal lifetime utility of wealth. The first-order conditions are (13.6) and:[4]

$$U'(c(t))e^{-\rho t} = \lambda e^{-[R(t)-nt]}, \quad t \in [0,\infty). \tag{13.10}$$

The left-hand side of (13.10) represents the marginal contribution to lifetime utility (evaluated from the perspective of "today", i.e. $t = 0$) of consumption in period t. The right-hand side of (13.10) is the lifetime marginal utility cost of consuming $c(t)$ rather than saving it. The marginal unit of $c(t)$ costs $e^{-[R(t)-nt]}$ from the perspective of today. This cost is translated into utility terms by multiplying it by the marginal utility of wealth.[5]

Since the marginal utility of wealth, λ, is constant (i.e. it does not depend on t), differentiation of (13.10) yields an expression for the optimal time profile of consumption:

$$\frac{d}{dt}U'(c(t)) = -\lambda e^{-[R(t)-nt-\rho t]} \cdot \left[\frac{dR(t)}{dt} - n - \rho \right] \quad \Leftrightarrow$$

$$U''(c(t)) \cdot \frac{dc(t)}{dt} = -U'(c(t)) \cdot [r(t) - n - \rho] \quad \Leftrightarrow$$

$$\theta(c(t)) \cdot \frac{1}{c(t)} \frac{dc(t)}{dt} = r(t) - n - \rho, \tag{13.11}$$

where we have used the fact that $dR(t)/dt = r(t)$ (see (13.8)) and where $\theta(\cdot)$ is the elasticity of marginal utility with respect to consumption, which is positive for all positive consumption levels because of the strict concavity of $U(\cdot)$:

$$\theta(c(t)) \equiv -\frac{U''(c(t))c(t)}{U'(c(t))}. \tag{13.12}$$

The *intertemporal substitution elasticity*, $\sigma(\cdot)$, is the inverse of $\theta(\cdot)$. By using this relationship, the expression in (13.11) can be rewritten to yield the consumption Euler equation:

$$\frac{1}{c(t)} \frac{dc(t)}{dt} = \sigma(c(t)) \cdot [r(t) - n - \rho]. \tag{13.13}$$

Intuitively, if $\sigma(\cdot)$ is low, a large interest gap $(r(t) - n - \rho)$ is needed to induce the household to adopt an upward-sloping time profile for consumption. In that case the willingness to substitute consumption across time is low, the elasticity of marginal utility is high, and the marginal utility function has a lot of curvature. The opposite holds if $\sigma(\cdot)$ is high. Then, the marginal utility function is almost linear so that a small interest gap can explain a large slope of the consumption profile.

---

[4]In deriving (13.10) we have applied Leibnitz's rule for differentiating under the integral sign to (13.9) to obtain $\partial \mathcal{L}/\partial c(t) = U'(c(t))e^{-\rho t} - \lambda e^{-[R(t)-nt]}$. In the optimum, $\partial \mathcal{L}/\partial c(t) = 0$ for all $c(t)$.

[5]See Dixit (1990, ch. 10) for intuitive discussions of apparently intractable first-order conditions.

Intermezzo 13.2

Deriving the Euler equation with the method of optimal control. In the main text we solve the household's optimization problem by using the Lagrangian method. We use this method because it gives rise to easily interpretable first-order conditions as given in (13.10). Of course the problem can also be solved by using the method of optimal control (see the Mathematical Appendix). The current-value Hamiltonian is:

$$\mathcal{H}_C \equiv U(c(t)) + \mu(t) \cdot \big[\, [r(t) - n]\, a(t) + w(t) - c(t) \big], \qquad \text{(a)}$$

where $c(t)$ is the control variable, $a(t)$ is the state variable, and $\mu(t)$ is the co-state variable. The household's asset holdings cannot become negative *in the limit*, so we write the terminal condition as:

$$\lim_{t \to \infty} a(t) \geq 0. \qquad \text{(b)}$$

The first-order conditions are given by:

$$\frac{\partial \mathcal{H}_C}{\partial c(t)} = 0, \qquad \text{(c1)}$$

$$\dot{a}(t) = \frac{\partial \mathcal{H}_C}{\partial \mu(t)}, \qquad \text{(c2)}$$

$$\dot{\mu}(t) - \rho\mu(t) = -\frac{\partial \mathcal{H}_C}{\partial a(t)}, \qquad \text{(c3)}$$

$$\lim_{t \to \infty} e^{-\rho t}\mu(t) \geq 0, \qquad \lim_{t \to \infty} e^{-\rho t}\mu(t) \cdot a(t) = 0. \qquad \text{(c4)}$$

Equation (c2) just gives us back the household budget identity (13.4). Equations (c1) and (c3) can be rewritten as:

$$U'(c(t)) = \mu(t), \qquad \text{(d1)}$$

$$-\frac{\dot{\mu}(t)}{\mu(t)} = r(t) - n - \rho. \qquad \text{(d2)}$$

Differentiating (d1) with respect to time we find $\dot{\mu}(t) = U''(c(t))\dot{c}(t)$. Using this expression as well as (d1) itself in (d2) we find:

$$\left[-\frac{\dot{\mu}(t)}{\mu(t)} = \right] \quad -\frac{U''(c(t))\dot{c}(t)}{U'(c(t))} = r(t) - n - \rho. \qquad \text{(e)}$$

Rearranging this expression somewhat (using (13.12)) we find the Euler equation (13.13).

To derive the solvency condition (13.5) we proceed as follows. First, we use (d2) to solve for $\mu(t)$:

$$\mu(t) = \mu(0) \cdot e^{-[R(t)-(n+\rho)t]}, \qquad \text{(f)}$$

where $R(t) \equiv \int_0^t r(\tau)d\tau$. Using (f) in the first expression of (c4) we find:

$$\lim_{t \to \infty} e^{-\rho t}\mu(0)e^{-[R(t)-(n+\rho)t]} = U'(c(0)) \cdot \lim_{t \to \infty} e^{-[R(t)-nt]} \geq 0, \qquad \text{(g1)}$$

where we have used the fact that $\mu(0) = U'(c(0))$ to arrive at the final expression. Since $U'(c(0))$ is strictly positive for a finite $c(0)$ and $e^{-[R(t)-nt]}$ is non-negative, condition (g1) is easily satisfied.

Using (f) in the second expression of (c4) we find:

$$\lim_{t\to\infty} e^{-\rho t}\mu(0) \cdot e^{-[R(t)-(n+\rho)t]} \cdot a(t) = U'(c(0)) \cdot \lim_{t\to\infty} a(t)e^{-[R(t)-nt]}$$

$$= 0. \tag{g2}$$

Since $U'(c(0)) > 0$, condition (g2) is seen to be equivalent to the solvency condition (13.5).

Finally, it is easy to deduce the relationship between the initial value of the co-state variable, $\mu(0)$, and the Lagrange multiplier used in the text, λ. From (d1) we observe that $\mu(0) = U'(c(0))$, whilst from (13.10) we find that $\lambda = U'(c(0))$. Since the same value for $c(0)$ features in both expressions, we find that $\lambda = \mu(0)$.

****

As it stands, (13.13) is of little use to us because $\sigma(c(t))$ still depends on consumption, rendering (13.13) difficult to work with and the derivation of a closed-form solution for consumption impossible. For this reason an explicit form for $U(c(t))$ is chosen. There are two useful functional forms, i.e. the *exponential utility* function:

$$U(c(t)) \equiv -\alpha e^{-(1/\alpha)c(t)}, \qquad \alpha > 0, \tag{13.14}$$

and the *iso-elastic* utility function:[6]

$$U(c(t)) \equiv \begin{cases} \dfrac{c(t)^{1-1/\sigma} - 1}{1 - 1/\sigma} & \text{for } \sigma > 0, \quad \sigma \neq 1, \\ \ln c(t) & \text{for } \sigma = 1. \end{cases} \tag{13.15}$$

It is not difficult to verify that the intertemporal substitution elasticities corresponding with these two functional forms are, respectively, $\sigma(c(t)) = \alpha/c(t)$ and $\sigma(c(t)) = \sigma$, so that the respective Euler equations are:

$$\frac{dc(t)}{dt} = \alpha\left[r(t) - n - \rho\right], \qquad \text{(exponential felicity)}, \tag{13.16}$$

$$\frac{1}{c(t)}\frac{dc(t)}{dt} = \sigma\left[r(t) - n - \rho\right], \qquad \text{(iso-elastic felicity)}. \tag{13.17}$$

So both these utility functions lead to very simple expressions for the Euler equation. But what about the closed-form solution for consumption itself?

We focus on the iso-elastic case, leaving the exponential case as an exercise for the reader. First we note that (13.17) can be integrated (between 0 and t) to yield future

---

[6]The second line in (13.15) is obtained from the first line by letting $1/\sigma$ approach unity. The trick is to use l'Hôpital's rule for calculating limits of the $0 \div 0$ type:

$$\lim_{(1/\sigma)\to 1} \left[\frac{c^{1-1/\sigma} - 1}{1 - 1/\sigma}\right] = \frac{-\lim_{(1/\sigma)\to 1} c^{1-1/\sigma}\ln c}{-1} = \ln c.$$

consumption $c(t)$ in terms of current consumption $c(0)$:

$$c(t) = c(0)e^{\sigma[R(t)-nt-\rho t]}. \tag{13.18}$$

By substituting this expression into the household budget constraint (13.6) we obtain in a few steps:

$$\int_0^\infty c(0)e^{\sigma[R(t)-nt-\rho t]}e^{-[R(t)-nt]}dt = a(0) + h(0) \quad \Leftrightarrow$$

$$c(0)\int_0^\infty e^{(\sigma-1)[R(t)-nt]-\sigma\rho t}dt = a(0) + h(0) \quad \Leftrightarrow$$

$$c(0) \equiv \frac{1}{\Delta(0)} \cdot [a(0) + h(0)], \tag{13.19}$$

where $\Delta(0)^{-1}$ is the propensity to consume out of total wealth, and $\Delta(0)$ is defined as:

$$\Delta(0) \equiv \int_0^\infty e^{(\sigma-1)[R(t)-nt]-\sigma\rho t}dt. \tag{13.20}$$

According to (13.19), consumption in the planning period is proportional to total wealth. Some special cases merit attention. If $\sigma = 1$ (so that $U(c(t))$ in (13.15) is logarithmic), $\Delta(0)^{-1} = \rho$ and, regardless of the anticipated path of future interest rates, the household consumes a constant fraction, ρ, of total wealth in the current period. Income and substitution effects of a change in the anticipated path for interest rates exactly cancel in this case (see also Section 6.1.1). Another special case is often used in the international context. If a country is small in world financial markets and thus faces a constant world interest rate $\bar{r}$ it follows from (13.8) that $R(t) = \bar{r}t$ and from (13.20) that $\Delta(0)^{-1} = \sigma\rho + (1-\sigma)(\bar{r}-n)$. (Of course restrictions on the parameters must ensure that $\Delta(0)$ remains positive.)

13.1.2   The representative firm

Perfectly competitive firms produce a homogeneous good by using capital and labour. Since there are constant returns to scale to the production factors taken together (see (P1) in Chapter 12) there is no need to distinguish individual firms and we can embrace the notion of a representative firm, which makes use of technology as summarized by the production function in (12.6). (We abstract from technical progress to keep things simple.)

The stockmarket value of the firm is given by the discounted value of its cash flows:

$$V(0) = \int_0^\infty \left[F(K(t), L(t)) - w(t)L(t) - (1-s_I)I(t) \right] e^{-R(t)}dt, \tag{13.21}$$

where $R(t)$ is the discounting factor given in (13.8), $I(t)$ is gross investment by the firm (see equation (12.4)), and s_I is an investment subsidy to be used below (in this section we assume $s_I = 0$). The firm maximizes its stockmarket value (13.21) subject to the capital accumulation constraint (12.4). Implicit in the formulation of the firm's choice set is the notion that it can vary its desired capital stock at will, i.e. there are no adjustment costs on investment (see Chapter 4 and below for a discussion of such costs). Indeed, by substituting (12.4) into (13.21) and integrating we find that the objective function for the firm can be written as:[7]

$$V(0) = K(0^-) + \int_0^\infty \left[F\left(K(t), L(t)\right) - (r(t) + \delta)K(t) - w(t)L(t) \right] e^{-R(t)} dt, \quad (13.22)$$

where $K(0^-)$ is the initial capital stock measured one second before the firm decides about $K(t)$ for $t \in [0, \infty)$. Equation (13.22) shows that the firm's decision about factor inputs is essentially a static one. Maximization of $V(0)$ by choice of $L(t)$ and $K(t)$ yields the familiar marginal productivity conditions for labour and capital:

$$F_L\left(K(t), L(t)\right) = w(t), \qquad F_K\left(K(t), L(t)\right) = r(t) + \delta. \quad (13.23)$$

By substituting the marginal productivity conditions (13.23) into (13.22) and noting the linear homogeneity property of the production function we find that $V(0) = K(0^-)$. In the absence of adjustment costs on investment the value of the firm equals the (replacement) value of its capital stock, and Tobin's q is unity.

By writing the production function in the intensive form (see (12.8)) we can rewrite the marginal products of capital and labour as follows:

$$F_K\left(K(t), L(t)\right) = f'(k(t)), \qquad F_L\left(K(t), L(t)\right) = f(k(t)) - k(t)f'(k(t)). \quad (13.24)$$

We now have all the ingredients of the model and we summarize them for the sake of convenience in Table 13.1. Equation (T1.1) is the rewritten Euler equation associated with an iso-elastic felicity function (see the expression in (13.17)). Equation (T1.2) combines equations (12.3)–(12.5) and is written in the intensive form. Finally, equation (T1.3) is obtained by combining the relevant conditions in (13.23) and (13.24).

Table 13.1. The Ramsey-Cass-Koopmans growth model

$$\dot{c}(t) = \sigma\left[r(t) - n - \rho\right]c(t), \qquad (T1.1)$$
$$\dot{k}(t) = f(k(t)) - c(t) - (\delta + n)k(t), \qquad (T1.2)$$
$$r(t) = f'(k(t)) - \delta. \qquad (T1.3)$$

Notes: $c(t)$ is per capita consumption, $k(t)$ is the capital-labour ratio, and $r(t)$ is the interest rate. Capital depreciates at a constant rate δ and the population grows exponentially with rate n.

13.1.3 The phase diagram

The model in Table 13.1 can be analysed to a large extent by means of its associated phase portrait which is given in Figure 13.1. The construction of this diagram warrants some additional comment. The $\dot{k}(t) = 0$ line represents points in $(c(t), k(t))$ space for which the per capita capital stock is in equilibrium. The Inada conditions

---

[7]In deriving (13.22) the key thing to note is:

$$\int_0^\infty \left[\dot{K}(t) - r(t)K(t)\right]e^{-R(t)}dt = \int_0^\infty d\left[K(t)e^{-R(t)}\right] = -K(0^-),$$

where we have used the fact that $\lim_{t\to\infty} K(t)e^{-R(t)} = 0$ in the final step.

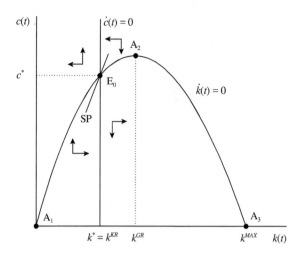

Figure 13.1: Phase diagram of the Ramsey-Cass-Koopmans model

ensure that it passes through the origin and is vertical there (see point A_1). Golden rule consumption occurs at point A_2 where the $\dot{k}(t) = 0$ line reaches its maximum:

$$\left(\frac{dc(t)}{dk(t)}\right)_{\dot{k}(t)=0} = 0: \quad f'(k^{GR}) = \delta + n. \tag{13.25}$$

The maximum attainable capital-labour ratio, k^{MAX}, occurs at point A_3, where per capita consumption is zero and total output is needed for replacement investment:

$$\frac{f\left(k^{MAX}\right)}{k^{MAX}} = \delta + n. \tag{13.26}$$

Finally, the capital dynamics can be most easily deduced by varying per capita consumption:

$$\frac{\partial \dot{k}(t)}{\partial c(t)} = -1 < 0. \tag{13.27}$$

The capital stock per worker rises (falls) for points below (above) the $\dot{k}(t) = 0$ line. This has been indicated by horizontal arrows in Figure 13.1.

The $\dot{c}(t) = 0$ line represents points for which the time profile of per capita consumption is flat. In view of (T1.1) this occurs at the point for which the interest rate equals the rate of time preference plus the rate of population growth, $r^{KR} \equiv \rho + n$, where the superscript "KR" refers to "Keynes-Ramsey", who were the first to discover this result. The Keynes-Ramsey interest rate is associated with a unique capital-labour ratio (see (T1.3)). Hence, $r^{KR} = f'(k^{KR}) - \delta$ and k^{KR} thus satisfies:

$$f'(k^{KR}) = \delta + n + \rho. \tag{13.28}$$

The comparison of (13.25) and (13.28) reveals that $f'(k^{KR})$ exceeds $f'(k^{GR})$, i.e. k^{KR} lies to the left of k^{GR}. Finally, we note that the expression determining the Keynes-Ramsey capital-labour ratio (namely (13.28)) is often referred to in the literature as the *modified golden rule*.

Consumption dynamics is obtained by substituting (T1.3) into (T1.1) and taking the derivative with respect to the capital intensity:

$$\frac{\partial \dot{c}(t)}{\partial k(t)} = \sigma c(t) f''(k(t)) < 0. \tag{13.29}$$

Per capita consumption rises (falls) for points to the left (right) of the $\dot{c}(t) = 0$ line. This has been indicated by vertical arrows in Figure 13.1.

The graphical representation of the model allows us to draw two important conclusions. First, the configuration of arrows suggests that the model is saddle-point stable, with $c(t)$ acting as the jumping variable and $k(t)$ as the predetermined (sticky) variable. Second, the economy features a unique steady state, with $c(t) = c^*$ and $k(t) = k^* = k^{KR}$. It follows that along the balanced growth path, output, capital, consumption, etcetera all grow at the rate of population growth, n, just as in the standard Solow-Swan model.

13.2   Properties of the Ramsey-Cass-Koopmans model

In this section we study the most important properties of the Ramsey-Cass-Koopmans model. In particular, we revisit the issue of over-saving, and study the model's transitional dynamics.

13.2.1   Efficiency

Perhaps the most important property of the Ramsey-Cass-Koopmans model is that it precludes the possibility of dynamic inefficiency and oversaving, phenomena which are possible in the Solow-Swan model. Intuitively, this result is perhaps not that surprising because there are no missing markets, distortions, and external effects in the model so there is no reason to suspect violation of the fundamental theorems of welfare economics.

The efficiency property of the Ramsey-Cass-Koopmans model can be demonstrated by proving the equivalence of the market outcome (discussed in the previous section) and the solution chosen by a benevolent social planner. Such a social planner would maximize lifetime utility of the representative agent ($\Lambda(0)$ given in (13.2)) subject to the production function (12.6) and the capital accumulation constraint (12.4).[8] We solve the planning problem using the method of optimal control (see Intermezzo 13.2 or the Mathematical Appendix).

The curent-value Hamiltonian associated with the command optimum is given by:

$$\mathcal{H}_C(t) \equiv U(c(t)) + \mu(t) \cdot [f(k(t)) - c(t) - (n + \delta)k(t)], \tag{13.30}$$

where $c(t)$ is the control variable, $k(t)$ is the state variable, and $\mu(t)$ is the co-state variable. The first-order necessary conditions characterizing the social optimum are:

$$\frac{\partial \mathcal{H}_C(t)}{\partial c(t)} = 0: \quad U'(c^{SO}(t)) = \mu(t), \tag{13.31}$$

---

[8] As well as an initial condition for the capital stock, non-negativity constraints for consumption and capital, and a transversality condition. See Blanchard and Fischer (1989, pp. 38–43) and Intriligator (1971, pp. 405–416).

$$-\frac{\partial \mathcal{H}_C(t)}{\partial k(t)} = \dot{\mu}(t) - \rho\mu(t): \qquad -\frac{\dot{\mu}(t)}{\mu(t)} = f'(k^{SO}(t)) - (\rho + n + \delta), \qquad (13.32)$$

where the superscript "SO" denotes socially optimal values. The socially optimal interest rate can be defined as $r^{SO}(t) \equiv f'(k^{SO}(t)) - \delta$, so that (13.31)–(13.32) can be combined to yield an easily interpretable expression for the optimal time profile of consumption:

$$\frac{1}{c^{SO}(t)}\frac{dc^{SO}(t)}{dt} = \sigma(c^{SO}(t)) \cdot [r^{SO}(t) - n - \rho], \qquad t \in [0, \infty). \qquad (13.33)$$

Equation (13.33) has exactly the same form as (13.13) so that the planning solution and market outcome coincide.[9] Hence, by removing the ad hoc saving function from the Solow-Swan model there is no possibility of oversaving any more.

13.2.2 Transitional dynamics and convergence

As was demonstrated graphically with the aid of Figure 13.1, the Ramsey-Cass-Koopmans model is saddle-point stable. An exact solution for the saddle path can in general not be obtained, however, rendering the study of the convergence properties of the model slightly more complicated than was the case for the Solow-Swan model. By linearizing the model around the initial steady state, E_0, however, the *approximate* transitional dynamics can be studied in a relatively straightforward manner.

After linearizing the model in Table 13.1 around the Keynes-Ramsey steady-state, $(c^*, k^*) = (c^{KR}, k^{KR})$, we obtain the following system of first-order differential equations:

$$\begin{bmatrix} \dot{c}(t) \\ \dot{k}(t) \end{bmatrix} = \begin{bmatrix} 0 & \sigma c^* f''(k^*) \\ -1 & \rho \end{bmatrix} \begin{bmatrix} c(t) - c^* \\ k(t) - k^* \end{bmatrix}. \qquad (13.34)$$

The Jacobian matrix on the right-hand side of (13.34) is denoted by Δ, and λ_1 and λ_2 are its characteristic roots. Since $\operatorname{tr}(\Delta) \equiv \lambda_1 + \lambda_2 = \rho > 0$ and $|\Delta| \equiv \lambda_1\lambda_2 = \sigma c^* f''(k^*) < 0$, it follows that the model is saddle-point stable, i.e. λ_1 and λ_2 have opposite signs. The absolute value of the stable (negative) characteristic root determines the approximate convergence speed of the economic system. After some manipulation we obtain the following expression:

$$\beta \equiv \frac{\rho}{2} \cdot \left[\sqrt{1 - \frac{4\sigma c^* f''(k^*)}{\rho^2}} - 1 \right]$$

$$= \frac{\rho}{2} \cdot \left[\sqrt{1 + \frac{4}{\rho^2} \cdot \frac{\sigma}{\sigma_{KL}} \cdot \frac{c^*}{k^*} \cdot (r^* + \delta) \cdot (1 - \omega_K)} - 1 \right], \qquad (13.35)$$

where β is the convergence speed, $r^* = r^{KR} = \rho + n$ is the Keynes-Ramsey interest rate, $\sigma_{KL} \equiv (1 - \omega_K)f'(k^*)/(-k^*f''(k^*))$ is the substitution elasticity between capital and labour in the production function, and $\omega_K \equiv k^*f'(k^*)/f(k^*)$ is the capital share in national income (all evaluated at the initial steady state). Recall that the Solow-Swan model predicts a convergence speed which exceeds the empirically

---

[9]We have also used the fact that the initial condition and the capital accumulation constraint are the same for the market and planning solutions. This implies that the *levels* of the interest rate, capital, and consumption also coincide for the two solutions.

Table 13.2. Convergence speed in the Ramsey-Cass-Koopmans model

	σ/σ_{KL}			
	0.2	0.5	1	2
$\omega_K = \frac{1}{3}$	4.23	7.38	10.97	16.08
$\omega_K = \frac{1}{2}$	2.41	4.39	6.70	10.00
$\omega_K = \frac{2}{3}$	1.25	2.44	3.88	5.96

relevant estimate of about 2% per annum by quite a margin (see section 12.3.3). Although it is not immediately apparent from the formula in (13.35) it turns out that the Ramsey-Cass-Koopmans model also predicts too high a rate of convergence for realistic values of the parameters. This can be demonstrated by means of the numerical simulations in Table 13.2. We choose the parameters that characterize the steady state of a fictional economy as follows. We set the rate of pure time preference at 3% per annum ($\rho = 0.03$), the rate of population growth at 2% ($n = 0.02$), and the depreciation rate of capital at 5% ($\delta = 0.05$). The steady state implies $r^* = \rho + n = 0.05$, $(k/y)^* = \omega_K/(r^* + \delta) = 10\omega_K$, and $(c/y)^* = 1 - (\delta + n)\omega_K/(r^* + \delta) = 1 - 0.7\omega_K$.

By varying the capital share (ω_K) and the ratio of elasticities of the felicity function and the production function (σ/σ_{KL}) we obtain a number of estimates for the convergence speed β. As is clear from the results in Table 13.2, the Ramsey-Cass-Koopmans model predicts even faster convergence than the Solow model! For example, if both the felicity function and the production function feature a unitary substitution elasticity (so that $\sigma/\sigma_{KL} = 1$) then for the realistic capital share of $\omega_K = \frac{1}{3}$, the convergence speed is a staggering 10.97% per annum. Only if the capital share is unrealistically high *and* the felicity function is relatively inelastic (so that σ/σ_{KL} is low) does the model come anywhere near to matching the empirically observed speed of convergence.

13.3 Macroeconomic applications of the Ramsey-Cass-Koopmans model

In this section we use the Ramsey-Cass-Koopmans model to study traditional macroeconomic issues such as (a) the effects of fiscal policy, and (b) the issue of debt versus tax financing and the validity of the Ricardian equivalence theorem.

13.3.1 Fiscal policy in the Ramsey-Cass-Koopmans model

In this section we investigate the effects of government consumption at impact, during transition, and in the long run. To keep things simple we assume that government consumption has no productivity-enhancing effects and, to the extent that it affects the welfare of the representative agent, does so in a weakly separable manner.[10] The only change that is made to the Ramsey-Cass-Koopmans model relates to

---

[10]See Turnovsky and Fisher (1995) for the more general cases. With weak separability we mean that the marginal utility of private consumption does not depend on the level of government consumption.

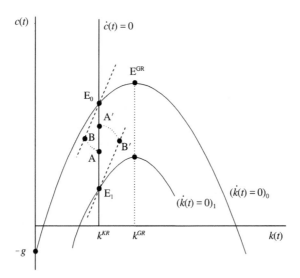

Figure 13.2: Fiscal policy in the Ramsey-Cass-Koopmans model

equation (T1.2) which is replaced by:

$$\dot{k}(t) = f(k(t)) - c(t) - g(t) - (\delta + n)k(t),\tag{13.36}$$

where $g(t) \equiv G(t)/L(t)$ is per capita government consumption. Government consumption withdraws resources which are no longer available for private consumption or replacement of the capital stock. As a result, for a given level of per capita public consumption, $g(t) = g$, the $\dot{k}(t) = 0$ line can be drawn as in Figure 13.2; see $(\dot{k}(t) = 0)_0$. Several conclusions can be drawn already. First, the existence of positive government consumption does not reinstate the possibility of dynamic inefficiency in the Ramsey-Cass-Koopmans model. The golden-rule capital stock per worker is not affected by g, although of course the golden-rule per capita consumption *level* is. Second, the issue of multiple equilibria also does not arise in the Ramsey-Cass-Koopmans model with government consumption. In contrast to the situation in the Solow model, provided an equilibrium exists in the Ramsey-Cass-Koopmans model it is unique and saddle-point stable.

An *unanticipated* and *permanent* increase in the level of government consumption per worker shifts the $\dot{k}(t) = 0$ line down, say from $(\dot{k}(t) = 0)_0$ to $(\dot{k}(t) = 0)_1$. Since the shock comes as a complete surprise to the representative household, it reacts to the increased level of taxes (needed to finance the additional government consumption) by cutting back private consumption. The representative household feels poorer as a result of the shock and, as consumption is a normal good, reduces it one-for-one:

$$\frac{dc(t)}{dg} = -1, \qquad \frac{dy(t)}{dg} = \frac{dk(t)}{dg} = 0,\tag{13.37}$$

for all $t \in [0, \infty)$. There is no transitional dynamics because the shock itself has no long-run effect on the capital stock and there are no anticipation effects. In terms of Figure 13.2 the economy jumps from E_0 to E_1.

With a *temporary* increase in g there are non-trivial transition effects. The representative household anticipates the temporarily higher taxes but spreads the negative effect on human wealth out over the entire lifetime consumption path. As a result, the impact effect on private consumption is still negative but less than one-for-one:

$$-1 < \frac{dc(0)}{dg} < 0. \tag{13.38}$$

In terms of Figure 13.2 the economy jumps from E_0 to point A. Immediately after the shock the household starts to dissave so that the capital stock falls, the interest rate rises, and (by (T1.1)) the consumption path rises over time. The economy moves from A to B which is reached at the time government consumption is cut back to its initial level again. This cut in g (and the associated taxes) releases resources which allow the capital stock to return to its constant steady-state level. As a result of the temporary boost in government consumption, the policy maker has managed to engineer a temporary decline in output per worker.

With an *anticipated* and *permanent* increase in g, the opposite effect occurs during transition. Consumption falls by less than one-for-one (as in (13.38)), but since the government consumption has not risen yet it leads to additional saving and a gradual increase in the capital stock, a reduction in the interest rate, and a downward-sloping consumption profile. At impact the economy jumps from E_0 to A', after which it gradually moves from A' to B' during transition. Point B' is reached at precisely the time the policy is enacted. As g is increased, net saving turns into net dissaving and the capital stock starts to fall. The economy moves from point B' to E_1.

13.3.2   Ricardian equivalence once again

Ricardian equivalence (see Chapter 6) clearly holds in the Ramsey-Cass-Koopmans model as can be demonstrated quite easily. The government budget identity (in per capita form) is given by:

$$\dot{b}(t) = [r(t) - n]\, b(t) + g(t) - \tau(t). \tag{13.39}$$

Like the representative household, the government must also remain solvent so that it faces an intertemporal solvency condition of the following form:

$$\lim_{t \to \infty} b(t) e^{-[R(t) - nt]} = 0, \tag{13.40}$$

where $R(t)$ is given in (13.8) above. By combining (13.39) and (13.40), we obtain the government budget restriction:[11]

$$b(0) = \int_0^\infty [\tau(t) - g(t)]\, e^{-[R(t) - nt]} dt. \tag{13.41}$$

To the extent that there is a pre-existing government debt ($b(0) > 0$), solvency requires that this debt must be equal to the present value of future primary surpluses. In principle, there are infinitely many paths for $\tau(t)$ and $g(t)$ (and hence for the primary deficit), for which (13.41) holds.

---

[11] By integrating (13.39) we obtain:

$$\lim_{t \to \infty} b(t) e^{-[R(t) - nt]} - b(0) = \int_0^\infty [g(t) - \tau(t)]\, e^{-[R(t) - nt]} dt,$$

where we have also used (13.8). The first term on the left-hand side is equal to zero provided the government solvency condition holds. By imposing this condition the government budget restriction (13.41) is obtained.

The budget identity of the representative agent is given in (13.4). It is modified to take into account that lump-sum taxes are levied on the agent:

$$\dot{a}(t) \equiv [r(t) - n]\, a(t) + w(t) - \tau(t) - c(t). \tag{13.42}$$

By using (13.42) in combination with the household solvency condition (13.5), the household budget restriction is obtained as in (13.6), but with a tax-modified definition of human wealth:

$$h(0) \equiv \int_0^\infty [w(t) - \tau(t)]\, e^{-[R(t)-nt]} dt. \tag{13.43}$$

By substituting the government budget restriction (13.41) into (13.43), the expression for human wealth can be rewritten as:

$$h(0) = \int_0^\infty [w(t) - g(t)]\, e^{-[R(t)-nt]} dt - b(0). \tag{13.44}$$

The path of lump-sum taxes completely vanishes from the expression for human wealth. Since $b(0)$ and the path for $g(t)$ are given, the particular path for the (non-distorting) lump-sum taxes does not affect the total amount of resources available to the representative agent. As a result, the agent's real consumption plans are not affected either.

By using (13.44) in (13.6), the household budget restriction can be written as:

$$\int_0^\infty c(t) e^{-[R(t)-nt]} dt = [a(0) - b(0)] + \int_0^\infty [w(t) - g(t)]\, e^{-[R(t)-nt]} dt. \tag{13.45}$$

This expression shows clearly why Barro (1974) chose the title "Are government bonds net wealth?" for his path-breaking article. Under Ricardian equivalence, government debt should not be seen as household wealth, i.e. $b(0)$ must be deducted from total financial wealth in order to reveal the household's true financial asset position, as is in fact done in (13.45).

13.4 An open-economy RCK model

13.4.1 Some model complications

Up to this point we have focused attention on the traditional closed-economy representation of the Ramsey-Cass-Koopmans (RCK) model. In a closed economy, the domestic interest rate clears the domestic rental market for *physical* capital and thus bears a close relationship with the capital-labour ratio; see equation (T1.3) in Table 13.1. In contrast, in an open economy which is small in world financial markets, the interest rate is determined abroad and is thus exogenous to the agents populating the tiny country in question. It is clear that the marginal productivity condition for capital (equation (T1.3)) can only hold for a small open economy if the physical capital stock is perfectly mobile across countries! Indeed, a small increase in the world interest rate must be accompanied by an immediate and instantaneous outflow of physical capital in order to restore equality between the domestic marginal product of capital and the world interest rate.

Apart from the fact that perfect mobility of physical capital is extremely unrealistic, it also has a very unfortunate implication in that it renders the convergence speed of the economy infinitely large! In technical terms, capital is changed from a slow-moving (predetermined) variable to a jumping variable. The traditional solution to this problem is to assume that physical capital is firm specific and thus cannot move costlessly and instantaneously. *Financial* capital, such as bonds and ownership claims of domestic assets, is of course perfectly mobile in this context so that yields on domestic and foreign assets are equalized. Formally, imperfect mobility of physical capital is modelled by assuming that the firm must incur installation costs associated with the investment process.

The small open economy assumption also causes a complication on the consumption side of the Ramsey-Cass-Koopmans model. Indeed, as was shown above, the representative household chooses its optimal consumption profile according to the Euler equation (T1.1). But if the rate of interest is exogenous (i.e. $r(t) = \bar{r}$, where $\bar{r}$ is the world interest rate) then consumption can only ever attain a steady state ($\dot{c}(t) = 0$) if the world interest rate happens to be equal to the exogenous population growth plus the rate of time preference, i.e. $\bar{r} = \rho + n$ must be satisfied. In any other case, the country either follows an ever-decreasing path of per capita consumption if its citizens are impatient ($\rho + n > \bar{r}$) or the country saves so much that it eventually ceases being small in world financial markets (with very patient citizens, $\rho + n < \bar{r}$). In order to avoid these difficulties we assume that the following "knife-edge" condition holds:

$$\rho + n = \bar{r}. \tag{13.46}$$

An immediate consequence of (13.46) in combination with (T1.1) is that per capita consumption of the representative household is completely smoothed over time, i.e. $\dot{c}(t)/c(t) = 0$ for all time periods.

We now consider the behaviour of the representative (domestic) firm facing adjustment costs for investment. The stockmarket value of the firm is still given by (13.21) but net and gross investment are now related according to a concave installation function:

$$\dot{K}(t) = \left[\Phi \left(\frac{I(t)}{K(t)} \right) - \delta \right] K(t), \tag{13.47}$$

where $\Phi(\cdot)$ captures the presence of installation costs associated with investment. We assume that the installation function satisfies the usual properties: $\Phi(0) = 0$, $\Phi'(\cdot) > 0$, and $\Phi''(\cdot) < 0$.[12]

The firm chooses time paths for investment, labour demand, and the capital stock in order to maximize $V(0)$ (given in (13.21) above) subject to the capital accumulation identity (13.47), an initial condition for the capital stock, and a terminal condition requiring the capital stock to remain non-negative:

$$\lim_{t \to \infty} K(t) \geq 0. \tag{13.48}$$

The current-value Hamiltonian for this problem is:

$$\mathcal{H}_C \equiv F(K(t), L(t)) - w(t)L(t) - (1 - s_I) I(t) + q(t) \cdot \left[\Phi \left(\frac{I(t)}{K(t)} \right) - \delta \right] \cdot K(t),$$

where s_I is the investment subsidy, $L(t)$ and $I(t)$ are control variables, $K(t)$ is the state variable, and $q(t)$ is the co-state variable. The first-order necessary conditions

---

[12]See Chapters 3 and 4 for an extensive discussion of the theory of investment based on adjustment costs. The installation function is just an alternative way to model adjustment costs. See Hayashi (1982) on this.

are the constraint (13.47) and:

$$w(t) = F_L\left(K(t), L(t)\right), \tag{13.49}$$

$$q(t)\Phi'\left(\frac{I(t)}{K(t)}\right) = 1 - s_I, \tag{13.50}$$

$$\dot{q}(t) = \left[r(t) + \delta - \Phi\left(\frac{I(t)}{K(t)}\right)\right] q(t)$$

$$- F_K\left(K(t), L(t)\right) + (1 - s_I)\frac{I(t)}{K(t)}, \tag{13.51}$$

$$\lim_{t \to \infty} e^{-R(t)}q(t) \geq 0, \qquad \lim_{t \to \infty} e^{-R(t)}q(t)K(t) = 0. \tag{13.52}$$

where $q(t)$ is Tobin's q (its current value, $q(0)$, measures the marginal (and average) value of installed capital, $K(0)$, i.e. $V(0) = q(0)K(0)$).

As was demonstrated in Chapter 2, gross domestic product in an open economy can be written as follows:

$$Y(t) \equiv C(t) + I(t) + X(t), \tag{13.53}$$

where $X(t)$ is net exports (i.e. the trade balance), and gross investment (inclusive of installation costs) appears in the national income identity. Note furthermore that we abstract from government consumption for convenience. Designating $A_F(t)$ as the stock of net foreign assets in the hands of domestic agents, gross national product is equal to gross domestic product plus interest earnings on net foreign assets, $\bar{r}A_F(t)$. The current account of the balance of payments is equal to net exports plus interest earnings on net foreign assets. The dynamic equation for the stock of net foreign assets is thus:

$$\dot{A}_F(t) = \bar{r}A_F(t) + X(t) = \bar{r}A_F(t) + Y(t) - C(t) - I(t), \tag{13.54}$$

which can be written in per capita form as:

$$\dot{a}_F(t) = \rho a_F(t) + y(t) - c(t) - i(t), \tag{13.55}$$

where we have used the fact that $\rho = \bar{r} - n$ (see (13.46)). Although the country can freely borrow from (or lend to) the rest of the world, it must obey an intertemporal solvency condition of the form:

$$\lim_{t \to \infty} a_F(t)e^{-\rho t} = 0. \tag{13.56}$$

Equations (13.55) and (13.56) in combination imply that there is a relationship between the initial level of net foreign assets per capita, a_{F0}, and the present value of future trade balances:

$$a_{F0} = \int_0^\infty \left[c(t) + i(t) - y(t)\right] e^{-\rho t}dt. \tag{13.57}$$

To the extent that the country possesses positive net foreign assets ($a_{F0} > 0$), it can afford to run present and future trade balance deficits. All that nation-wide solvency requires is that the present value of these trade balance deficits (the right-hand side of (13.57)) add up to the initial level of net foreign assets (left-hand side of (13.57)).

We now possess all the ingredients of the open-economy Ramsey-Cass-Koopmans model and we restate its key equations for the sake of convenience in Table 13.3.

Table 13.3. The Ramsey-Cass-Koopmans model for the open economy

$$\frac{\dot{c}(t)}{c(t)} = 0 \tag{T3.1}$$

$$q(t)\Phi'\left(\frac{i(t)}{k(t)}\right) = 1 - s_I \tag{T3.2}$$

$$\dot{q}(t) = \left[\rho + n + \delta - \Phi\left(\frac{i(t)}{k(t)}\right)\right]q(t) - f'(k(t)) + (1 - s_I)\frac{i(t)}{k(t)} \tag{T3.3}$$

$$\dot{k}(t) = \left[\Phi\left(\frac{i(t)}{k(t)}\right) - n - \delta\right]k(t) \tag{T3.4}$$

$$\dot{a}_F(t) = \rho a_F(t) + f(k(t)) - c(t) - i(t) \tag{T3.5}$$

Notes: $c(t)$ is per capita consumption, $k(t)$ is the capital-labour ratio, $q(t)$ is Tobin's q, $i(t)$ is gross investment per worker, s_I is an investment subsidy, and $a_F(t)$ is net foreign assets per worker.

Equation (T3.1) shows that per capita consumption is completely smoothed over time. As was pointed out above, this result is a direct consequence of the assumption expressed in (13.46). Equation (T3.2) implicitly determines the optimal investment-capital ratio as a function of (subsidy-adjusted) Tobin's q. Equation (T3.3) gives the dynamic evolution of Tobin's q and (T3.4) does the same for the capital stock per worker. Finally, (T3.5) is the current account equation which is obtained by substituting the intensive-form production function, $f(k(t))$, into (13.55).

13.4.2 Model solution and convergence speed

The model is quite unlike the growth models that were studied up to this point because it contains a zero root (originating from the consumption Euler equation (T3.1)) and thus displays hysteretic properties in the sense that the steady state depends on the initial conditions.[13] Technically, the model solution proceeds as follows. First, we note that equations (T3.2)–(T3.4) form an autonomous subsystem determining the dynamics of $i(t)$, $q(t)$, and $k(t)$. Second, once the solutions for investment and capital are known, they can be substituted into the nation-wide solvency condition (13.57) which can then be solved for per capita consumption.

Since the model is non-linear, it can only be solved analytically by first linearizing it around the steady state. We start with the investment system consisting of (T3.2)–(T3.4). To keep the model as simple as possible we postulate a convenient specific functional form for the installation function:

$$\Phi\left(\frac{i(t)}{k(t)}\right) \equiv \frac{1}{1 - \sigma_I}\left(\frac{i(t)}{k(t)}\right)^{1-\sigma_I}, \tag{13.58}$$

with $0 < \sigma_I < 1$. The parameter σ_I regulates the curvature of the installation function. The lower is σ_I, the closer $\Phi(\cdot)$ resembles a straight line, and the higher is the

---

[13]See Turnovsky (1995, ch. 12), Sen and Turnovsky (1990), and Giavazzi and Wyplosz (1985) for a further discussion. See also Section 3.5 above for an example of a hysteretic model in discrete time.

international mobility of physical capital–see Bovenberg (1994, p. 122). The investment demand implied by (T3.2) in combination with (13.58) is also iso-elastic:

$$\frac{i(t)}{k(t)} = g(q(t), s_I) \equiv \left(\frac{q(t)}{1 - s_I} \right)^{1/\sigma_I}. \tag{13.59}$$

By inserting (13.59) into (T3.3)–(T3.4) and linearizing, we obtain a simple matrix expression for the investment system:

$$\begin{bmatrix} \dot{k}(t) \\ \dot{q}(t) \end{bmatrix} = \begin{bmatrix} 0 & i^* (1 - s_I)^2 / \left[(q^*)^2 \sigma_I \right] \\ -f''(k^*) & \rho \end{bmatrix} \begin{bmatrix} k(t) - k^* \\ q(t) - q^* \end{bmatrix}, \tag{13.60}$$

where q^* and k^* are steady-state values for, respectively, Tobin's q and the capital intensity. The Jacobian matrix on the right-hand side of (13.60) is denoted by Δ_I and its typical element by δ_{ij}. The investment system is saddle-point stable because Δ_I has a positive trace (equal to ρ) and a negative determinant (equal to $(1 - s_I)^2 i^* f''(k^*) / [(q^*)^2 \sigma_I])$. This implies that the characteristic roots of Δ_I are real, distinct, and opposite in sign. Denoting the stable and unstable roots by, respectively, $-\lambda_1 < 0$ and $\lambda_2 > 0$, it follows from (13.60) that:

$$\lambda_2 - \lambda_1 = \text{tr}(\Delta_I) = \rho \qquad \Leftrightarrow \qquad \lambda_2 = \rho + \lambda_1 > \rho, \tag{13.61}$$

i.e. the unstable root equals the pure rate of time preference (ρ) plus the transition speed in the economy (represented by λ_1). Note that the adjustment speed of the investment system (λ_1) is finite due to the existence of installation costs of investment and the associated short-run immobility of capital.

Intermezzo 13.3

The method of undetermined coefficients in a perfect foresight model.
Here we show how the expressions in (13.62)–(13.63) are derived. In the first step we postulate a trial solution for the capital intensity and Tobin's q:

$$\begin{bmatrix} k(t) - k^* \\ q(t) - q^* \end{bmatrix} = \begin{bmatrix} \pi_{k1} \\ \pi_{q1} \end{bmatrix} e^{-\lambda_1 t} + \begin{bmatrix} \pi_{k2} \\ \pi_{q2} \end{bmatrix} e^{\lambda_2 t}, \tag{a}$$

where π_{ki} and π_{qi} ($i = 1, 2$) are coefficients to be determined, and where $-\lambda_1 < 0$ and $\lambda_2 > 0$ are, respectively, the stable (negative) and unstable (positive) characteristic roots of Δ_I. To eliminate the effects of the unstable root we must set:

$$\begin{bmatrix} \pi_{k2} \\ \pi_{q2} \end{bmatrix} = \begin{bmatrix} 0 \\ 0 \end{bmatrix}. \tag{b}$$

By differentiating (a) with respect to time and noting (b) we obtain:

$$\begin{bmatrix} \dot{k}(t) \\ \dot{q}(t) \end{bmatrix} = -\lambda_1 \begin{bmatrix} \pi_{k1} \\ \pi_{q1} \end{bmatrix} e^{-\lambda_1 t}, \tag{c}$$

where we have also used the fact that $\dot{k}^* = \dot{q}^* = 0$ (constant steady state). By substituting (a)–(c) into (13.60) we obtain:

$$\begin{bmatrix} -(\lambda_1 + \delta_{11}) & -\delta_{12} \\ -\delta_{21} & -(\lambda_1 + \delta_{22}) \end{bmatrix} \begin{bmatrix} \pi_{k1} \\ \pi_{q1} \end{bmatrix} = \begin{bmatrix} 0 \\ 0 \end{bmatrix}, \tag{d}$$

where δ_{ij} represents element (i,j) of the Jacobian matrix Δ_I. Since $-\lambda_1$ is an eigenvalue of Δ_I, the matrix on the left-hand side of (d) is singular, and either row of (d) can be used to solve π_{q1} in terms of π_{k1}. Noting that $\delta_{11} = 0$ we obtain from the first row:

$$\pi_{q1} = -\frac{\lambda_1}{\delta_{12}} \pi_{k1}. \tag{e}$$

Next we exploit the fact that the capital stock is predetermined, i.e. its value at time $t = 0$, denoted by k_0, is given. Substituting this initial condition in the first equation of (a) and noting (b) we obtain:

$$k(0) - k^* = k_0 - k^* = \pi_{k1}. \tag{f}$$

The second equation of (a) in combination with (b) and (e)–(f) yields the solution for Tobin's q on the saddle path:

$$q(0) - q^* = \pi_{q1} = -\frac{\lambda_1}{\delta_{12}} [k_0 - k^*]. \tag{g}$$

By substituting (b), (f)–(g) into (a) the expressions in (13.62)–(13.63) are obtained.

The solution method used here is valid provided the forcing term of the dynamical system is time invariant. This covers both the transition path of an economy which starts outside the steady state and the adjustment path following an unanticipated and permanent shock to the investment subsidy (both are discussed in the text). In the Mathematical Appendix we present a solution method which can handle more general shock patterns.

****

If the initial capital intensity is denoted by k_0, then the system converges to the steady state provided it is on the saddle path. Leaving the technical details of the derivation to Intermezzo 13.3 we find that the solution to (13.60) is:

$$\begin{bmatrix} k(t) - k^* \\ q(t) - q^* \end{bmatrix} = \begin{bmatrix} k_0 - k^* \\ q(0) - q^* \end{bmatrix} e^{-\lambda_1 t}, \tag{13.62}$$

where the initial value of Tobin's q is given by:

$$q(0) = q^* - \frac{\lambda_1}{\delta_{12}} [k_0 - k^*]. \tag{13.63}$$

The solution path is illustrated in Figure 13.3. For the initial capital stock, k_0, Tobin's q is above its equilibrium level and the economy moves gradually from point A towards the steady-state equilibrium at E_0. The expression for the saddle path can be obtained by substituting (13.63) into (13.62):

$$q(t) - q^* = -\frac{\lambda_1}{\delta_{12}} [k(t) - k^*]. \tag{13.64}$$

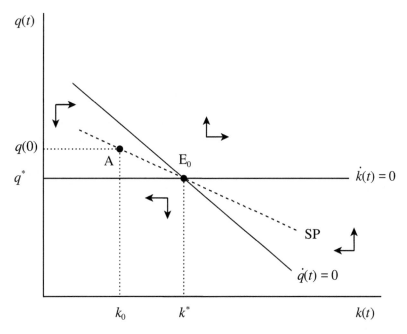

Figure 13.3: Investment in the open economy

Now that we know the dynamic paths for the capital stock and Tobin's q (and thus, by (13.59), the implied path for investment) we can work out the restriction implied by national solvency. First, we linearize the production function, $y(t) = f(k(t))$, and the investment function (13.59) around the steady state:

$$\left[\begin{array}{c} y(t) - y^* \\ i(t) - i^* \end{array} \right] = \left[\begin{array}{cc} f'(k^*) & 0 \\ g^* & k^* g_q^* \end{array} \right] \left[\begin{array}{c} k(t) - k^* \\ q(t) - q^* \end{array} \right], \tag{13.65}$$

where $g^* \equiv g(q^*, s_I)$ and $g_q^* \equiv g_q(q^*, s_I)$. By using (13.62) and (13.64) in (13.65) we find the (approximate) path for $i(t) - y(t)$:

$$\begin{aligned} i(t) - y(t) &= i^* - y^* + k^* g_q^* [q(t) - q^*] + [g^* - f'(k^*)] [k(t) - k^*] \\ &= i^* - y^* - \Omega [k_0 - k^*] e^{-\lambda_1 t}, \end{aligned} \tag{13.66}$$

where $\Omega \equiv f'(k^*) - g^* + \lambda_1 k^* g_q^* / \delta_{12} > 0$. Equation (T3.1) shows that per capita consumption stays constant during the transition, i.e. $c(t) = c^*$. By using this result as well as equation (13.66) in the nation-wide solvency condition (13.57) we obtain the following expression:

$$\begin{aligned} a_{F0} &= \frac{c^*}{\rho} + \int_0^\infty [i(t) - y(t)] e^{-\rho t} dt \\ &= \frac{c^* + i^* - y^*}{\rho} - \Omega [k_0 - k^*] \int_0^\infty e^{-(\rho + \lambda_1)t} dt \\ &= \frac{c^* + i^* - y^*}{\rho} - \frac{\Omega [k_0 - k^*]}{\lambda_2}, \end{aligned} \tag{13.67}$$

where we have used the fact that $\lambda_2 = \rho + \lambda_1$ (see (13.61)) in the final step. It follows from the steady-state version of (13.55) that $\rho a_F^* = c^* + i^* - y^*$ (since $\dot{a}_F^* = 0$) so that

454   FOUNDATIONS OF MODERN MACROECONOMICS, THIRD EDITION

(13.67) can be rewritten as follows:

$$a_{F0} + \frac{\Omega}{\lambda_2}k_0 = a_F^* + \frac{\Omega}{\lambda_2}k^*. \tag{13.68}$$

As Sen and Turnovsky (1990, p. 287) point out, the left-hand side of (13.68) represents the initial value of total resources available to the economy and can thus be interpreted as *national wealth*. National wealth consists of initial non-human wealth, $a_{F0} + k_0$, plus the present value of resources generated by capital accumulation starting from the initial capital stock, k_0.

The striking feature of the open-economy Ramsey-Cass-Koopmans model is that its steady state depends on the initial stock of assets, a_{F0} and k_0. This is the hysteretic property alluded to above. In the steady state we have that $\dot{c}(t) = \dot{q}(t) = \dot{k}(t) = \dot{a}_F(t) = 0$ and the model consists of equation (13.68) as well as:

$$q^* \Phi' \left(\frac{i^*}{k^*} \right) = 1 - s_I, \tag{13.69}$$

$$f'(k^*) = \rho q^* + (1 - s_I)\frac{i^*}{k^*}, \tag{13.70}$$

$$\Phi \left(\frac{i^*}{k^*} \right) = n + \delta, \tag{13.71}$$

$$\rho a_F^* + f(k^*) = c^* + i^*, \tag{13.72}$$

which jointly determine the steady-state values q^*, i^*, k^*, c^*, and a_F^*. Given the structure of the model, only consumption and the net stock of foreign assets display hysteresis and are thus a function of the initial conditions.[14]

13.4.3   Effects of an investment subsidy

We are now in the position to use the model to study the effects of an investment subsidy on the macroeconomy. To keep things simple we restrict attention to the case of an unanticipated and permanent increase in the investment subsidy. It is most convenient to determine the long-run effect first. Equation (13.71) shows that i^*/k^* is constant, so that it follows from (13.69) that q^* is proportional to $(1 - s_I)$. Hence, if s_I is increased, Tobin's q falls in the long run:

$$\frac{dq^*}{ds_I} = -\frac{1}{\Phi'(i^*/k^*)} = -\frac{q^*}{1 - s_I} < 0. \tag{13.73}$$

Equation (13.70) can be used to derive the long-run effect on the stock of capital per worker:

$$\frac{dk^*}{ds_I} = \frac{k^*}{i^*}\frac{di^*}{ds_I} = \frac{1}{f''(k^*)}\left[\rho\frac{dq^*}{ds_I} - \frac{i^*}{k^*} \right] = -\frac{f'(k^*)}{(1 - s_I)f''(k^*)} > 0. \tag{13.74}$$

Hence, investment and the capital stock (both measured per worker) rise equiproportionally in the long run. The national wealth constraint (13.68) shows that the

---

[14]In particular, (13.71) determines i^*/k^* as a function of $n + \delta$, (13.69) then determines q^*, and (13.70) determines k^* (and thus i^*). The only variables remaining to be determined by (13.68) and (13.72) are c^* and a_F^*; only these variables depend on initial conditions, a_{F0} and k_0. Sen and Turnovsky (1990) show that if labour supply is endogenous, the hysteretic property extends to investment and the capital stock also.

composition of wealth changes also, i.e. the increase in the domestic capital stock leads to a reduction in the long-run stock of net foreign assets:

$$\frac{da_F^*}{ds_I} = -\frac{\Omega}{\lambda_2}\frac{dk^*}{ds_I} < 0. \tag{13.75}$$

The net effect on consumption is ambiguous.

The transitional effects of the policy shock can be studied with the aid of Figure 13.4. In that figure, k_0 is the initial capital stock per worker, and the economy is at point A and heading towards the steady state at E_0 (where the steady-state capital stock per worker is k_0^*). Now consider what happens as a result of the subsidy increase. Clearly, the old equilibrium adjustment path from A to E_0 is no longer relevant. What does the new adjustment path look like? The long-run effect on the capital stock is positive (see (13.74)) and saddle-point stability requires that the economy must be on the stable arm of the saddle path. By using the expression for the saddle path (given in (13.64)) we obtain the impact effect for Tobin's q:[15]

$$\begin{aligned}
\frac{dq(0)}{ds_I} &= \frac{dq^*}{ds_I} + \frac{\lambda_1}{\delta_{12}}\frac{dk^*}{ds_I} \\
&= -\frac{q^*}{1-s_I} - \frac{\lambda_1}{\delta_{12}f''(k^*)}\frac{f'(k^*)}{1-s_I} \\
&= -\frac{q^*}{1-s_I} + \frac{1}{\rho+\lambda_1}\frac{f'(k^*)}{1-s_I} \lessgtr 0.
\end{aligned} \tag{13.76}$$

The impact effect on Tobin's q is ambiguous because the first term on the right-hand side is negative whilst the second term is positive. Technically, the ambiguity arises from the fact that both the $\dot{k}(t) = 0$ line and the $\dot{q}(t) = 0$ lines shift as a result of the increase in the investment subsidy. Recall that the $\dot{k}(t) = 0$ line represents points for which the (i/k) ratio is constant. Since an increase in s_I leads to a higher desired (i/k) ratio (see (13.59)), Tobin's q must fall to restore capital stock equilibrium, i.e. the $\dot{k}(t) = 0$ line shifts down. At the same time, the boost in s_I leads to an upward shift in the $\dot{q}(t) = 0$ line.

In Figure 13.4 the new steady-state equilibrium is at E_1 and the saddle path is drawn under the assumption that the capital stock effect is dominated by the effect on Tobin's q (given in (13.76)), so that $dq(0)/ds_I < 0$. At impact the economy jumps from point A to point B, after which gradual adjustment takes place towards the new steady-state equilibrium E_1.

What is the economic intuition behind the ambiguity of the impact effect on Tobin's q? Equation (13.76) shows that the ambiguity arises because $dq(0)/ds_I$ depends among other things on the adjustment speed in the economy, λ_1. If adjustment costs on investment are relatively low ($\sigma_I \approx 0$), then λ_1 is relatively high, physical capital is highly mobile, and installed and new capital goods are close substitutes. The investment subsidy reduces the price of new capital goods and thus also the value of the installed capital stock in that case (Bovenberg, 1993, p. 13). The opposite holds if adjustment costs are severe ($\sigma_I \approx 1$). As the diagram shows, however, regardless of the sign of $dq(0)/ds_I$, net capital accumulation takes place (as B lies above the new $\dot{k}(t) = 0$ line) and the economy moves from B to E_1 over time.

---

[15]We have used equations (13.73) and (13.74) in going from the first to the second line. In going from the second to the third line we have used some results for the characteristic roots, i.e. $\lambda_1\lambda_2 = -f''(k^*)\delta_{12}$ and $\lambda_2 = \rho + \lambda_1$.

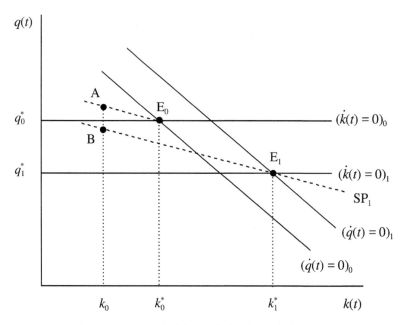

Figure 13.4: An investment subsidy with high mobility of physical capital

13.5   The RCK model with endogenous labour supply

In this section we extend the Ramsey-Cass-Koopmans model by endogenizing the labour supply decision of households. In the model a representative household makes optimal decisions regarding present and future consumption, labour supply, and saving. The representative firm hires the factors of production from the household sector and produces output. The government levies taxes and consumes goods. All agents in the economy operate under perfect foresight. The model can be used to study how the economy reacts to shocks in government spending. In the remainder of this chapter we (a) abstract from population growth and normalize the size of the population to unity, (b) ignore labour-augmenting technological change, and (c) restrict attention to the closed-economy case.[16]

13.5.1   Model elements

The representative agent makes a dynamically optimal decision regarding consumption of goods and leisure both for the present and for the indefinite future. The agent has a time endowment of unity which is allocated over labour, $L(t)$, and leisure, $1 - L(t)$. The agent is infinitely lived and lifetime utility in the planning period, $\Lambda(0)$, is given by the discounted integral of present and future instantaneous utility:

$$\Lambda(0) \equiv \int_0^\infty U(C(t), 1 - L(t)) e^{-\rho t} dt, \tag{13.77}$$

where ρ is the pure rate of time preference ($\rho > 0$), $C(t)$ is consumption, and $U(C(t), 1 - L(t))$ is *instantaneous utility* (or *felicity*) in period t. We assume that the felicity

---

[16]The reader purely interested in the theory of economic growth can skip this section and the next and proceed to Chapter 14. In an exercise to this chapter the model is solved in the presence of population growth and labour-augmenting technological change.

function takes the following form:

$$U(C(t), 1 - L(t)) \equiv \ln \left[C(t)^{\varepsilon} \left[1 - L(t) \right]^{1-\varepsilon} \right], \qquad 0 < \varepsilon < 1. \tag{13.78}$$

Several things are worth noting. First, consumption and leisure both enter felicity in a logarithmic fashion ensuring that preferences are separable in the sense that the marginal felicity of consumption, $U_C(C(t), 1 - L(t)) = \varepsilon/C(t)$, is independent of leisure and the marginal felicity of leisure, $U_{1-L}(C(t), 1 - L(t)) = (1 - \varepsilon)/[1 - L(t)]$, is independent of consumption. Second, the felicity function can be seen as a nested function, i.e. $U(C(t), 1 - L(t)) = \ln u(t)$ with $u(t) \equiv C(t)^{\varepsilon} \left[1 - L(t) \right]^{1-\varepsilon}$. Hence, the "top-level" felicity function is logarithmic, ensuring that the *inter*temporal substitution elasticity equals unity, whilst the "bottom-level" sub-felicity function is of the Cobb-Douglas type, ensuring that the *intra*temporal substitution elasticity also equals unity.

The agent's dynamic budget identity is:

$$\dot{A}(t) \equiv r(t)A(t) + w(t)L(t) - T(t) - C(t), \tag{13.79}$$

where $r(t)$ is the real rate of interest, $A(t)$ is real financial assets, $w(t)$ is the real wage rate, and $T(t)$ is real lump-sum taxes.

The household chooses paths for consumption, labour supply, and assets in order to maximize lifetime utility (13.77) subject to the budget identity (13.79), an asymptotic terminal condition of the form $\lim_{t \to \infty} A(t) \geq 0$, and taking as given the initial level of assets, $A(0)$. The interesting first-order necessary conditions are (see Intermezzo 13.2 or the Mathematical Appendix):

$$\frac{\varepsilon}{C(t)} = \mu(t), \tag{13.80}$$

$$\frac{1 - \varepsilon}{1 - L(t)} = \mu(t)w(t), \tag{13.81}$$

$$\frac{\dot{\mu}(t)}{\mu(t)} = \rho - r(t), \tag{13.82}$$

$$\lim_{t \to \infty} e^{-\rho t} \mu(t) \geq 0, \qquad \lim_{t \to \infty} e^{-\rho t} \mu(t) A(t) = 0, \tag{13.83}$$

where $\mu(t)$ is the co-state variable. By using (13.80) in (13.81)–(13.82) we can eliminate $\mu(t)$ and $\dot{\mu}(t)$ and write the main first-order conditions as follows:

$$\frac{C(t)}{1 - L(t)} \frac{1 - \varepsilon}{\varepsilon} = w(t), \tag{13.84}$$

$$\frac{\dot{C}(t)}{C(t)} = r(t) - \rho. \tag{13.85}$$

Equation (13.84) requires the marginal rate of substitution between leisure and consumption to be equated to the wage rate in each period. This is essentially a static decision which is made in each period. According to (13.84) labour supply depends negatively on consumption and positively on the real wage. The dynamic part of the solution is contained in (13.85) which is the consumption Euler equation. If the real interest rate exceeds (falls short of) the pure rate of time preference, the household chooses an upward (downward) sloping consumption profile over time (see Section 13.1 for further details).

The production function used by the representative firm features the following Cobb-Douglas form:

$$Y(t) = F(K(t), L(t)) \equiv Z_0 K(t)^{\alpha} L(t)^{1-\alpha}, \tag{13.86}$$

where Z_0 is an index of general productivity, $Y(t)$ is aggregate output, and $K(t)$ and $L(t)$ are, respectively, the amounts of capital and labour used in production. In the absence of adjustment costs on investment, the familiar marginal conditions for labour and capital hold (see also equation (13.23) above):

$$F_L(K(t), L(t)) = w(t), \qquad F_K(K(t), L(t)) = r(t) + \delta. \tag{13.87}$$

In view of the fact that both factors are paid their respective marginal products, and the production function exhibits constant returns to scale, excess profits are zero.

Output can be used for private consumption, public consumption, or for investment purposes. Hence, the condition for goods market equilibrium in a closed economy is:

$$Y(t) = C(t) + I(t) + G(t), \tag{13.88}$$

where $I(t)$ is gross investment,

$$I(t) = \dot{K}(t) + \delta K(t), \tag{13.89}$$

and $G(t)$ is government consumption. Finally, the model is completed by the government budget restriction which simply states that public consumption is paid for by lump-sum taxes levied on the representative household:

$$G(t) = T(t). \tag{13.90}$$

For convenience, the complete model has been summarized in Table 13.4. Equations (T4.1), (T4.3), and (T4.7) restate, respectively, equations (13.85), (13.90), and (13.86). Equation (T4.2) is obtained by substituting (13.89) into (13.88). Equation (T4.6) is obtained by slightly rewriting (13.84). Finally, (T4.4)–(T4.5) are obtained by using (13.86) in (13.87). For lack of a better term we refer to the model as the unit-elastic (RCK) model because there are three elasticities that are equal to unity. The felicity function incorporates unitary intertemporal and intratemporal substitution elasticities. And the production function features a unitary intratemporal substitution elasticity between capital and labour.

13.5.2 The phase diagram

The model given in Table 13.4 can be condensed into a non-linear system of differential equations in consumption and the capital stock. To derive this system we first use (T4.4) and (T4.6)–(T4.7) to obtain the relationship describing labour market equilibrium:

$$(1 - \alpha) Z_0 \left(\frac{K(t)}{L(t)} \right)^{\alpha} = \frac{1 - \varepsilon}{\varepsilon} \frac{C(t)}{1 - L(t)}. \tag{13.91}$$

The left-hand side of this expression is the labour demand function whilst the right-hand side in the labour supply function. Equation (13.91) defines an implicit function expressing equilibrium employment in terms of consumption and the capital stock:

$$L(t) \equiv \Psi(C(t), K(t)). \tag{13.92}$$

Table 13.4. The unit-elastic RCK model

$$\frac{\dot{C}(t)}{C(t)} = r(t) - \rho, \tag{T4.1}$$

$$\dot{K}(t) = Y(t) - C(t) - G(t) - \delta K(t), \tag{T4.2}$$

$$G(t) = T(t), \tag{T4.3}$$

$$w(t) = (1 - \alpha)\frac{Y(t)}{L(t)}, \tag{T4.4}$$

$$r(t) + \delta = \alpha\frac{Y(t)}{K(t)}, \tag{T4.5}$$

$$L(t) = 1 - \frac{1 - \varepsilon}{\varepsilon}\frac{C(t)}{w(t)}, \tag{T4.6}$$

$$Y(t) = Z_0 K(t)^\alpha L(t)^{1-\alpha}, \tag{T4.7}$$

Definitions: $Y(t)$ is output, $C(t)$ is private consumption, $L(t)$ is employment, $K(t)$ is the capital stock, $G(t)$ is public consumption, $w(t)$ is the real wage rate, $r(t)$ is the real interest rate, $T(t)$ is the lump-sum tax, ε is a taste parameter for consumption, ρ is the pure rate of time preference, δ is the depreciation rate of capital, Z_0 is a constant, and α is the efficiency parameter of capital. The population is constant and normalized to unity.

The partial elasticities of equilibrium employment with respect to consumption and the capital stock – evaluated around any point (L_0, C_0, K_0) satisfying (13.91) – are given by:

$$\frac{\partial L}{\partial C}\frac{C}{L} \equiv \frac{C_0 \Psi_C (C_0, K_0)}{\Psi (C_0, K_0)} = -\frac{\omega_{LL}}{1 + \alpha \omega_{LL}} < 0, \tag{13.93}$$

$$\frac{\partial L}{\partial K}\frac{K}{L} \equiv \frac{K_0 \Psi_K (C_0, K_0)}{\Psi (C_0, K_0)} = \frac{\alpha \omega_{LL}}{1 + \alpha \omega_{LL}} > 0, \tag{13.94}$$

where ω_{LL} represents the *Frisch elasticity* of labour supply at employment level L_0:

$$\omega_{LL} \equiv \frac{1 - L_0}{L_0} > 0. \tag{13.95}$$

In the second step we use (T4.1)–(T4.2), (T4.5), (T4.7), and (13.92) to obtain the system of differential equations describing the dynamic evolution of the economy:

$$\frac{\dot{C}(t)}{C(t)} = \alpha Z_0 \left(\frac{\Psi (C(t), K(t))}{K(t)}\right)^{1-\alpha} - (\rho + \delta), \tag{13.96}$$

$$\dot{K}(t) = Z_0 K(t)^\alpha \Psi (C(t), K(t))^{1-\alpha} - C(t) - G(t) - \delta K(t). \tag{13.97}$$

In the appendix to this chapter we present the full derivation of the phase diagram for the unit-elastic RCK model. The derivation proceeds under the assumption that government consumption is held constant, i.e. $G(t) = G_0$. The phase diagram is presented graphically in Figure 13.5. The $\dot{K}(t) = 0$ line represents combinations in $(C(t), K(t))$ space for which net investment is zero. For each $(C(t), K(t))$ combination there exists a unique equilibrium employment level. The golden-rule capital

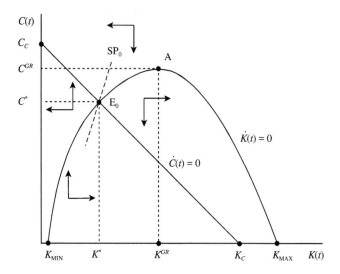

Figure 13.5: Phase diagram of the unit-elastic model

stock is K^{GR} and the associated consumption level is C^{GR} (see point A). For points above (below) the $\dot{K}(t) = 0$ line, consumption is too high (low) and net investment is negative (positive). These dynamic effects have been illustrated with horizontal arrows in Figure 13.5.

The $\dot{C}(t) = 0$ line represents $(C(t), K(t))$ combinations for which consumption is constant over time, i.e. for which the interest rate equals the rate of time preference. Since the interest rate depends on the marginal product of capital, and production features constant returns to scale, consumption equilibrium pins down a unique capital-labour ratio and thus a unique output-capital ratio and real wage rate. It follows (from (T4.6)) that the ratio between consumption and labour supply is constant also. The $\dot{C}(t) = 0$ line is linear and slopes downward. Ceteris paribus the capital stock, an increase (decrease) in consumption decreases (increases) labour supply and equilibrium employment, and decreases (increases) the output-capital ratio and the rate of interest. Hence, consumption falls (rises) at points above (below) the $\dot{C}(t) = 0$ line. This has been indicated with vertical arrows in Figure 13.5.

Since $K_C < K_K$ (see appendix), it follows from Figure 13.5 that the two equilibrium loci intersect only once, at point E_0. The steady-state levels of consumption and the capital stock are, respectively, C^* and K^*. The arrow configuration shows that E_0 is saddle-point stable. The saddle path associated with the steady-state equilibrium E_0, denoted by SP_0, is upward sloping. More formally, local saddle-point stability of the model can be ascertained by linearizing the system around the steady-state point (C^*, K^*). After some manipulation we obtain:

$$\begin{bmatrix} \dot{C}(t) \\ \dot{K}(t) \end{bmatrix} = \Delta \begin{bmatrix} C(t) - C^* \\ K(t) - K^* \end{bmatrix}, \tag{13.98}$$

where the Jacobian matrix Δ (with typical element δ_{ij}) is given by:

$$\Delta \equiv \begin{bmatrix} -\dfrac{(1-\alpha)\omega_{LL}^*}{1+\alpha\omega_{LL}^*}(\rho+\delta) & -\dfrac{1-\alpha}{1+\alpha\omega_{LL}^*}(\rho+\delta)\dfrac{C^*}{K^*} \\[3mm] -\left(\dfrac{C^*}{Y^*}+\dfrac{(1-\alpha)\omega_{LL}^*}{1+\alpha\omega_{LL}^*}\right)\dfrac{Y^*}{C^*} & \left(\dfrac{C^*+G_0}{Y^*}-\dfrac{1-\alpha}{1+\alpha\omega_{LL}^*}\right)\dfrac{Y^*}{K^*} \end{bmatrix}, \qquad (13.99)$$

where ω_{LL}^* is obtained from (13.95) by setting $L_0 = L^* = \Psi(C^*, K^*)$. In an exercise to this chapter the reader is asked to verify that the determinant and trace of the Jacobean are given by:

$$|\Delta| = -\frac{(1-\alpha)(\rho+\delta)}{1+\alpha\omega_{LL}^*} \frac{(1+\omega_{LL}^*)C^*+\omega_{LL}^*G_0}{K^*} < 0, \qquad \mathrm{tr}(\Delta) = \rho > 0. \quad (13.100)$$

Since $|\Delta|$ is equal to the product of the characteristic roots, there is one negative (stable) root and one positive (unstable) root implying saddle-point stability.

13.5.3 Permanent fiscal policy

In this subsection and the next we demonstrate some illustrative properties of the unit-elastic model. Here we start with the easy stuff and study the impact, transitional, and long-run effects of a permanent and unanticipated increase in government consumption.[17] In the next subsection we study how the economy reacts to a temporary fiscal shock. Throughout both subsections we assume that the economy is initially in the steady state and that the government finances its consumption by means of lump-sum taxes—see equation (T4.3).

Although the model in Table 13.4 may look rather complex, it was demonstrated by Baxter and King (1993) that the *long-run* effects of the policy shock can be determined in a relatively straightforward fashion. For that reason we first study the long-run effects, before investigating the somewhat more demanding short-run and transitional effects of fiscal policy.

13.5.3.1 Long-run multipliers

Computation of the long-run "new classical multiplier" is a back-of-the-envelope exercise due to the fact that the economy is structurally characterized by a number of *great ratios* that are independent of public consumption (see Baxter and King, 1993, p. 319). In our model this can be demonstrated as follows. In the steady state, both consumption and the capital stock are constant, i.e. $\dot{C}(t) = \dot{K}(t) = 0$. Equation (T4.1) and (T4.2) in Table 13.4 then imply, respectively, that the real rate of interest and the investment-capital ratio are constant, i.e. $r^* = \rho$ and $(I/K)^* = \delta$. The marginal productivity condition for capital, (T4.5), then pins down the equilibrium capital-output ratio, $\kappa^* \equiv (K/Y)^*$, as a function of structural parameters only ($\kappa^* \equiv \alpha/(\rho+\delta)$). But, since the production function, (T4.7), features constant returns to scale, the equilibrium capital-output also determines a unique capital-labour ratio, $k^* \equiv (K/L)^* = (Z_0\kappa^*)^{1/(1-\alpha)}$. This, in turn, pins down the real wage and thus (by (T4.6)) the ratio between goods and leisure consumption, $(C/(1-L))^*$.

---

[17] A large body of literature studies the effects of fiscal policy in an optimizing equilibrium framework. Pioneering contributions to this branch of the literature were made by Hall (1971, 1980), Barro (1981), Aschauer (1988), and Baxter and King (1993).

The long-run constancy of the various ratios can be exploited to find the long-run effect of an increase in public consumption. By totally differentiating the goods market clearing condition (13.88) around the initial steady state and recalling that government consumption equals G_0, we obtain:

$$\frac{dY(\infty)}{Y^*} = \omega_C^* \frac{dC(\infty)}{C^*} + \omega_I^* \frac{dI(\infty)}{I^*} + \omega_G^* \frac{dG}{G_0}, \tag{13.101}$$

where $\omega_I^* \equiv (I/Y)^* = \delta (K/Y)^* = \delta \kappa^*$, $\omega_C^* \equiv (C/Y)^*$, $\omega_G^* \equiv G_0/Y^*$, and $\omega_C^* + \omega_I^* + \omega_G^* \equiv 1$. Here $dY(\infty)$ represents the ultimate change in output resulting from the fiscal shock, i.e. the difference between the new and the old steady-state output level. Following the shock to public spending, eventually the various ratios will be restored. This implies the following long-run relationships:

$$\frac{dY(\infty)}{Y^*} = \frac{dK(\infty)}{K^*} = \frac{dI(\infty)}{I^*} = \frac{dL(\infty)}{L^*} = -\omega_{LL}^* \frac{dC(\infty)}{C^*}, \tag{13.102}$$

where $\omega_{LL}^* \equiv [1 - L^*]/L^*$. By substituting the relevant results from (13.102) into (13.101) we find an expression for $dY(\infty)/Y^*$ which can be rewritten in a multiplier format:

$$\frac{dY(\infty)}{dG} = \frac{1}{1 - \omega_I^* + \omega_C^*/\omega_{LL}^*} > 0. \tag{13.103}$$

In a similar fashion the long-run multipliers for consumption, investment, and the capital stock can be derived:

$$-1 < \frac{dC(\infty)}{dG} = -\frac{\omega_C^*/\omega_{LL}^*}{1 - \omega_I^* + \omega_C^*/\omega_{LL}^*} < 0, \tag{13.104}$$

$$\frac{dK(\infty)}{dG} = \frac{1}{\delta} \frac{dI(\infty)}{dG} = \frac{\omega_I^*/\delta}{1 - \omega_I^* + \omega_C^*/\omega_{LL}^*} > 0. \tag{13.105}$$

The endogeneity of the labour supply decision plays a crucial role for the new classical multiplier stated in (13.103). Indeed, the higher is the Frisch elasticity of labour supply (ω_{LL}^*), the larger are the long-run effects on output, capital, and investment, and the smaller is the crowding-out effect on consumption.[18]

13.5.3.2   Short-run multipliers

The impact and transitional effects of the fiscal shock can be studied graphically with the aid of Figure 13.6. In this figure, CE_0 is the initial consumption equilibrium line, CSE_0 is the initial capital stock equilibrium line, and E_0 is the initial steady state. As a result of the shock, the CSE line changes to CSE_1. Since lump-sum taxes are used to balance the budget, the position of the CE line is unaffected and the long-run equilibrium shifts from E_0 to E_1 (see (13.103)–(13.105)). At impact, the economy jumps from E_0 to point A on the new saddle path SP_1. Agents cut back consumption of both goods and leisure because they are faced with a higher lifetime tax bill and thus feel poorer. The boost in employment causes an expansion in aggregate output

---

[18]Note that a version of the standard RCK model of Section 13.1 is obtained from the unit-elastic model by setting $\varepsilon = 1$ so that agents derive no felicity from leisure and set $L = 1$ so that $\omega_{LL}^* = 0$. In that case equation (13.102) gives the immediate result that output, investment, and the capital stock are unchanged. Equation (13.104) shows that there is one-for-one crowding out of private by public consumption in that case.

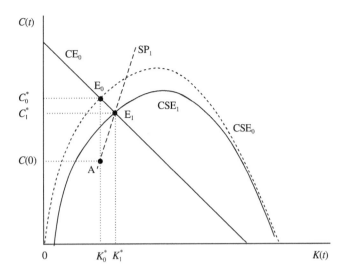

Figure 13.6: Effects of fiscal policy

and an increase in the marginal product of capital, and hence the interest rate, despite the fact that the capital stock is fixed in the short run. The increase in the real interest rate not only results in an upward-sloping time profile for consumption but also creates a boom in saving-investment by the representative household, so that both consumption and the capital stock start to rise over time. This is represented in Figure 13.6 by the gradual movement along the saddle path SP_1 from A to the new equilibrium at E_1. The long-run effect on the capital stock is positive (see (13.105)) and consumption falls. Since the representative agent reacts to the fiscal shock by accumulating a larger capital stock and supplying more labour, steady-state output rises and private consumption crowding out is less than full (see (13.104)).

Though we can get a good feel for the *qualitative* properties of the model by graphical means, such methods are useless to obtain *quantitative* results. For example, it is clear from Figure 13.6 that consumption overshoots its long-run effect at impact and is crowded out $(dC(0)/dG < dC(\infty)/dG < 0)$. It is impossible, however, to deduce how large the overshooting and crowding-out effects are. In order to compute the impact and transitional effects on the economy, the standard practice in the macroeconomic literature is to *linearize* the model around the initial steady state so that it can be analysed more easily.[19] Of course this is exactly the approach we took to prove local stability of the unit-elastic model.

Following a step-wise increase in government consumption from G_0 to $G_0 + dG$ occurring at time $t = 0$, the linearized dynamical system for consumption and capital can be written as:

$$\begin{bmatrix} \dot{C}(t) \\ \dot{K}(t) \end{bmatrix} = \Delta \begin{bmatrix} C(t) - C^* \\ K(t) - K^* \end{bmatrix} - \begin{bmatrix} 0 \\ dG \end{bmatrix}, \tag{13.106}$$

where Δ is the Jacobian matrix given in (13.99). We have already demonstrated that

---

[19]In this chapter we make use of the method of *comparative dynamics*. This method linearizes the non-linear model and tackles the issue of dynamics in the (much easier to analyse) linear world. Intuitively, it is appropriate and gives relatively accurate answers, provided the changes in the forcing terms (the exogenous variables) are not "too large" and the model is not "too non-linear". See also Dotsey and Mao (1992).

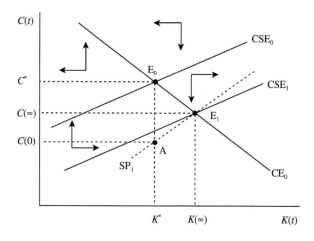

Figure 13.7: Phase diagram of the linearized model

$|\Delta|$ is negative. Denoting the stable root by $-\lambda_1$ (< 0) and the unstable root by λ_2 (> 0) we thus have $|\Delta| = -\lambda_1\lambda_2$. When written in this way, λ_1 also represents the adjustment speed of the economic system (see Section 13.2.2 for details). Furthermore, since $\text{tr}(\Delta) = \lambda_2 - \lambda_1 = \rho$, we easily find that $\lambda_2 = \rho + \lambda_1$.

The linearized model has been illustrated in Figure 13.7. The linearized isocline for consumption is denoted by CE_0 and takes the following form.

$$C(t) = C^* - \frac{\delta_{12}}{\delta_{11}} [K(t) - K^*] , \qquad CE_0, \qquad (13.107)$$

where the δ_{ij} coefficients are the typical elements of Δ given in (13.99). The initial and post-shock linearized isoclines for the capital stock are denoted by, respectively, CSE_0 and CSE_1:

$$C(t) = C^* - \frac{\delta_{22}}{\delta_{21}} [K(t) - K^*] , \qquad CSE_0, \qquad (13.108)$$

$$C(t) = C^* - \frac{\delta_{22}}{\delta_{21}} [K(t) - K^*] + \frac{1}{\delta_{21}} dG, \qquad CSE_1. \qquad (13.109)$$

Note that $\delta_{11} < 0$, $\delta_{12} < 0$, $\delta_{21} < 0$, and $\delta_{22} = \rho - \delta_{11} > 0$ so that CE_0 is downward sloping whilst CSE_0 and CSE_1 are upward sloping (and parallel to each other).

We now return to the fiscal policy experiment. In an exercise to this chapter the reader is asked to verify that as a result of the spending shock the solution paths for consumption and the capital stock take the following form:

$$\begin{bmatrix} C(t) \\ K(t) \end{bmatrix} = \begin{bmatrix} C(0) \\ K^* \end{bmatrix} e^{-\lambda_1 t} + \begin{bmatrix} C(\infty) \\ K(\infty) \end{bmatrix} \left(1 - e^{-\lambda_1 t}\right), \qquad t \geq 0, \qquad (13.110)$$

where $C(0)$, $C(\infty)$, and $K(\infty)$ are given by:

$$C(0) - C^* = \frac{\lambda_2 - \delta_{11}}{\delta_{21}} \frac{dG}{\lambda_2} < 0, \qquad (13.111)$$

$$C(\infty) - C^* = \frac{\delta_{12}}{\lambda_1 \lambda_2} dG < 0, \tag{13.112}$$

$$K(\infty) - K^* = -\frac{\delta_{11}}{\lambda_1 \lambda_2} dG > 0. \tag{13.113}$$

In terms of Figure 13.7 the impact jump in consumption (13.111) is represented by the vertical move from point E_0 to point A directly below it. The transition paths for $C(t)$ and $K(t)$ stated in (13.110) describe all points on the saddle path from A to E_1. Equations (13.110)–(13.113) represent the so-called *impulse-response functions* for consumption and the capital stock with respect to a permanent and unanticipated shock in government consumption which occurs at time $t = 0$. Equation (13.110) shows that the effect of the shock as of time t can be written as the weighted average of the impact effect and the long-run effect with respective time-varying weights $e^{-\lambda_1 t}$ and $1 - e^{-\lambda_1 t}$.

Once the transition paths for consumption and the capital stock are known, the impulse response function for the remaining variables of the model (i.e. $L(t)$, $Y(t)$, $w(t)$, and $r(t)$) can be obtained by employing the following quasi-reduced form expressions:

$$\frac{L(t) - L^*}{L^*} = \frac{\omega_{LL}^*}{1 + \alpha \omega_{LL}^*} \left[\alpha \frac{K(t) - K^*}{K^*} - \frac{C(t) - C^*}{C^*} \right], \tag{13.114}$$

$$\frac{Y(t) - Y^*}{Y^*} = \frac{1}{1 + \alpha \omega_{LL}^*} \left[\alpha(1 + \omega_{LL}^*) \frac{K(t) - K^*}{K^*} - (1 - \alpha)\omega_{LL}^* \frac{C(t) - C^*}{C^*} \right], \tag{13.115}$$

$$\frac{w(t) - w^*}{w^*} = \frac{\alpha}{1 + \alpha \omega_{LL}^*} \left[\frac{K(t) - K^*}{K^*} + \omega_{LL}^* \frac{C(t) - C^*}{C^*} \right], \tag{13.116}$$

$$r(t) - \rho = -\frac{(\rho + \delta)(1 - \alpha)}{1 + \alpha \omega_{LL}^*} \left[\frac{K(t) - K^*}{K^*} + \omega_{LL}^* \frac{C(t) - C^*}{C^*} \right]. \tag{13.117}$$

Since the capital stock is predetermined at the time of the shock ($K(0) = K^*$), the impact effects for employment, output, the wage, and the interest rate are all proportional to $C(0)$. The decrease in consumption thus causes employment, output, and the interest rate to increase and the wage rate to fall.

13.5.3.2.1 Quantitative evidence

Now that the *qualitative* effects of the fiscal shock have been fully characterized analytically, the next question concerns the *quantitative* size of the various effects. In order to cast some light on this issue we must now *calibrate* the model by using information that is more or less plausible for a typical advanced market economy. The calibrated model is then used to compute the various impact, transitional, and long-run effects.

Essentially calibration amounts to choosing the parameters of the theoretical model in such a way that the model replicates certain outcomes about which sufficiently robust information is available. Take, for example, the unit-elastic model given in Table 13.4. The structural parameters appearing in that model are the pure rate of time preference ρ, the rate of depreciation of the capital stock δ, the efficiency parameter of capital α, the preference parameter for consumption ε, and the general productivity parameter Z_0.

Some of these parameters are not hard to guess. For example, under the maintained hypothesis that the economy is at a steady state, it follows from (T4.1) that the real rate of interest must be equal to the rate of pure time preference, i.e. $r^* = \rho$.

King and Rebelo (1999, p. 953) suggest that the average real rate of return to capital in the US has been 6.5% per annum over the period 1948-1986. On a quarterly basis this would give us the estimate $r^* = \rho = (1.065)^{1/4} - 1 = 0.0159$ (1.59% on a quarterly basis). The annual rate of depreciation of the capital stock is set at 10% per annum by King and Rebelo, i.e. $\delta = (1.1)^{1/4} - 1 = 0.0241$. Of course, for buildings this figure is far too high (most buildings last longer than ten years) but for machines (e.g. personal computers) it may be far too low. As an average guess, however, it may not be too widely off the mark. With Cobb-Douglas technology $1 - \alpha$ equals the share of labour income in output (see (T4.4)) which King and Rebelo set equal to two-thirds, i.e. $\alpha = 1/3$ (1999, p. 954). But now that we know ρ and α, we can infer the implied estimate for the equilibrium capital-output ratio from (T4.5), i.e. $(K/Y)^* = \alpha/(\rho + \delta) = \frac{1}{3}/[0.0159 + 0.0241] = 8.33$. By imposing the steady state in (13.89) we obtain the implied investment share of output, i.e. $\omega_I^* \equiv (I/Y)^* = \delta(K/Y)^* = 0.0241 \cdot 8.33 = 0.201$. Baxter and King (1993, p. 320) suggest that the average postwar share of government consumption in output was 20% in the US, i.e. $\omega_G^* = 0.2$. We now have estimates for almost all parameters of interest. By using (T4.6) we observe that the consumption share in output is $\omega_C^* \equiv (C/Y)^* = 1 - \omega_I^* - \omega_G^* = 0.599$. By combining (T4.4) and (T4.6) we derive:

$$\omega_{LL}^* \equiv \left(\frac{1-L}{L}\right)^* = \frac{\omega_C^*}{1-\alpha}\frac{1-\varepsilon}{\varepsilon}, \tag{13.118}$$

so choosing ε implies choosing L^* (and thus ω_{LL}^*) and vice versa. King and Rebelo suggest that 20% of total available time has been dedicated to working in the postwar period in the US, i.e. $L^* = 0.2$ and $\omega_{LL}^* = 4$, so that it follows from (13.118) and the other estimates that $\varepsilon = \omega_C^*/[\omega_C^* + (1-\alpha)\omega_{LL}^*] = 0.183$. Finally, we observe that Z_0 is a "free parameter" in the sense that it merely fixes the scale of the economy. For numerical convenience, we normalize Z_0 such that output is unity in the initial steady state, i.e. we set $Z_0 = (L^*)^{-(1-\alpha)}(K^*)^{-\alpha} = 1.442$.

In summary, we have now calibrated the model using the following values for the *structural parameters*:

$$\begin{aligned} \rho &= 0.0159 \quad \delta = 0.0241 \quad \alpha = 1/3 \\ \varepsilon &= 0.183 \quad Z_0 = 1.442 \quad \omega_G = 0.2. \end{aligned} \tag{13.119}$$

The resulting initial steady state is given by:

$$\begin{aligned} Y^* &= 1 \quad C^* = 0.599 \quad I^* = 0.201 \quad T = G_0 = 0.2 \\ r^* &= 0.0159 \quad L^* = 0.2 \quad K^* = 8.337 \quad w^* = 3.333. \end{aligned} \tag{13.120}$$

Using these calibration values in (13.99) we obtain the implied guess for the Jacobian matrix:[20]

$$\Delta \equiv \begin{bmatrix} -0.04569 & -0.00082 \\ -2.90806 & 0.06156 \end{bmatrix}, \tag{13.121}$$

The characteristic roots of Δ are, respectively, $-\lambda_1 = -0.0646$ and $\lambda_2 = 0.0805$. What do these figures mean? Recall that λ_1 represents the adjustment speed in the economy–see (13.110). Using the reasoning explained in Section 12.3.3, the half-life of the adjustment process in the economy is $t_{1/2} \equiv (1/\lambda_1)\ln 2 = 10.7$. Since we

---

[20]We present the actual numbers here not to test the reader's patience but rather to enable replication and to give a 'feel' for the magnitudes and dimensions involved.

Table 13.5. Government consumption multipliers and elasticities

Variable	Impact effect	Long-run effect
$\frac{dY}{dG}$	1.029	1.054
$\frac{dC}{dG}$	−0.539	−0.158
$\frac{dI}{dG}$	0.568	0.212
$\frac{dK}{K^*} / \frac{dG}{G}$	0	0.211
$\frac{dL}{L^*} / \frac{dG}{G}$	0.309	0.211
$\frac{dr}{r^*} / \frac{dG}{G}$	0.518	0
$\frac{dW}{W^*} / \frac{dG}{G}$	−0.103	0

have calibrated on quarterly observations for the interest rate and the depreciation rate on capital, this figure means, for example, that half of the adjustment in the non-jumping variable (the capital stock) is completed almost eleven quarters after the shock occurred.

Using the information from (13.121) in the various analytical expressions (13.110)–(13.117) we obtain the numerical estimates for the impact and long-run effects on the different variables. These results have been summarized in Table 13.5. There is severe crowding out of private by public consumption at impact. For every €1 of extra government consumption private consumption falls by €0.54 at impact. Because the representative agent cuts back on leisure consumption—by supplying more hours to the labour market—household labour income rises. The additional (saving equals) investment at impact is €0.57 out of every €1 of extra government consumption so that the output multiplier exceeds unity at impact. Let us look at some of the other magnitudes involved. At impact a 1% increase in government spending gives rise to a 0.3% increase in employment and a 0.1% fall in the wage rate. The interest rate rises proportionally by 0.5%, i.e. in absolute terms the interest rate rises by 0.0082 percentage points from 1.587% to 1.595% on a quarterly basis.

In the long run the interest rate, the wage rate, and the capital-labour ratio all return to their respective initial equilibrium values. For a 1% increase in government consumption the capital stock increases by 0.211%. In the long-run *net* investment ceases as the initial investment-capital ratio is restored. Consumption crowding out remains but is less severe than at impact and the output multiplier is a little higher than at impact.

In summary, the results in this subsection show that large output multipliers due to permanent government consumption are quite possible in the representative-agent model. The mechanism behind the multiplier is, however, quite classical and originates from the dynamic interaction of the supply of labour and capital (Baxter and King, 1993, pp. 323–324). The additional lump-sum taxes make people poorer which leads them to increase labour supply both at impact and in the long run. In the long run the capital-labour ratio is restored so that the capital stock rises also. In the short run the strong savings response by households explains why the public consumption shock is accompanied by an investment boom.

13.5.4   Temporary fiscal policy

One of the recurrent themes in the study of fiscal policy is the difference between the effects of temporary and permanent policy. Baxter and King, for example, employ numerical methods to study to what extent the impact multiplier for output depends on the duration for which the fiscal policy impulse is in operation (1993, p. 315). In this subsection we show how a temporary (but unanticipated) fiscal spending shock affects the economy. To keep things simple we assume that the government raises its consumption level unexpectedly at some time $t = 0$ and then gradually lets it fall back to the initial level:

$$G(t) - G_0 = \begin{cases} e^{-\xi_G t} dG & \text{for } t \geq 0 \\ \\ 0 & \text{for } t < 0. \end{cases} \tag{13.122}$$

where $\xi_G > 0$ is the exponential rate at which government consumption returns to its initial level. Clearly, according to (13.122), we have that $G(0) - G_0 = dG > 0$ and $\lim_{t \to \infty} G(t) = G_0$ so the spending shock is temporary.

    The CE line is still as given in (13.107) because lump-sum taxes continue to be used in this experiment. The CSE line (13.109) is changed to:

$$C(t) = C^* - \frac{\delta_{22}}{\delta_{21}} [K(t) - K^*] + \frac{1}{\delta_{21}} e^{-\xi_G t} dG, \qquad \text{CSE}_1(\xi_G t). \tag{13.123}$$

Note that the position of the CSE line depends both on post-shock time t and the persistence parameter (ξ_G). At impact the shock is the same as before but eventually the shock vanishes. Since agents in the economy are assumed to know the path of government consumption (13.122) they will condition their behaviour accordingly and will formulate their plans optimally. Note that ξ_G parameterizes the *persistence* of the shock. For example, if $\xi_G \approx 0$ then the shock is highly persistent and $G(t)$ falls only very slowly towards G_0. In contrast, if ξ_G is large, then $G(t)$ drops off rapidly as time goes by and the shock is very transitory. The time path for $G(t)$ is illustrated in Figure 13.8(a) for three values of ξ_G, namely $\xi_G = 0$ (permanent shock), $\xi_G = 0.02$ (temporary but highly persistent shock), and $\xi_G = 0.10$ (very transitory shock).

    Using the Laplace transform methods explained in the Mathematical Appendix, the perfect foresight solution of the model is obtained:

$$\begin{bmatrix} C(t) \\ K(t) \end{bmatrix} = \begin{bmatrix} C(0) \\ K^* \end{bmatrix} e^{-\lambda_1 t} + \begin{bmatrix} C^* \\ K^* \end{bmatrix} \left(1 - e^{-\lambda_1 t} \right)$$

$$+ \frac{dG}{\lambda_1 (\lambda_2 + \xi_G)} \begin{bmatrix} \delta_{12} \\ -(\delta_{11} + \xi_G) \end{bmatrix} T(\xi_G, \lambda_1, t), \tag{13.124}$$

where the impact effect on consumption, $C(0)$, is:

$$C(0) - C^* = \frac{\lambda_2 - \delta_{11}}{\delta_{21}} \frac{dG}{\lambda_2 + \xi_G} < 0, \tag{13.125}$$

and where $T(\xi_G, \lambda_1, t)$ is a transition term which is defined as follows:

$$T(\xi_G, \lambda_1, t) \equiv \begin{cases} \lambda_1 \dfrac{e^{-\xi_G t} - e^{-\lambda_1 t}}{\lambda_1 - \xi_G} & \text{for } \xi_G \neq \lambda_1 \\ \\ \lambda_1 t e^{-\lambda_1 t} & \text{for } \xi_G = \lambda_1. \end{cases} \tag{13.126}$$

Figure 13.8: Temporary fiscal policy

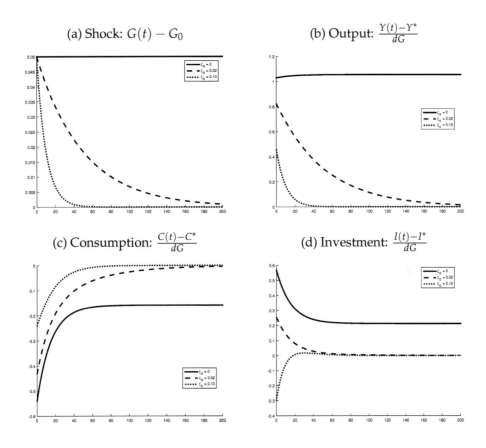

(a) Shock: $G(t) - G_0$

(b) Output: $\frac{Y(t)-Y^*}{dG}$

(c) Consumption: $\frac{C(t)-C^*}{dG}$

(d) Investment: $\frac{I(t)-I^*}{dG}$

Figure 13.8, continued

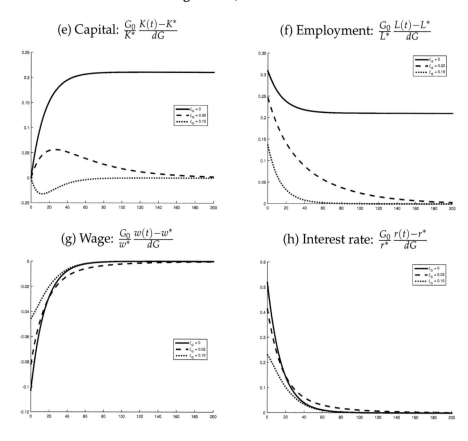

(e) Capital: $\frac{G_0}{K^*}\frac{K(t)-K^*}{dG}$

(f) Employment: $\frac{G_0}{L^*}\frac{L(t)-L^*}{dG}$

(g) Wage: $\frac{G_0}{w^*}\frac{w(t)-w^*}{dG}$

(h) Interest rate: $\frac{G_0}{r^*}\frac{r(t)-r^*}{dG}$

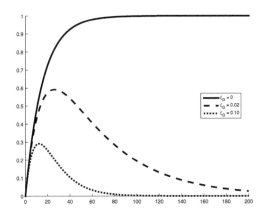

Figure 13.9: The transition function for temporary and permanent shocks

Before developing the economic interpretation of the solutions for consumption and the capital stock, as given in (13.124)–(13.125), it is useful to first look at the shape of the temporary transition term $T(\xi_G, \lambda_1, t)$. In Figure 13.9 we illustrate the shape of this term for a range of values of ξ_G. In this figure, the adjustment speed of the economy is set at the value implied by the calibration, i.e. $\lambda_1 = 0.0646$ (see the text below equation (13.121)).

We observe from Figure 13.9 that, provided ξ_G is strictly positive, the transition term is a non-negative bell-shaped function of time. Furthermore, this term is zero both at the time of the shock ($t = 0$) and in the long run ($t \to \infty$) and features $0 < T(\xi_G, \lambda_1, t) < 1$ for $t \in (0, \infty)$. The lower is the value of ξ_G, the later is the time at which the transition terms reaches its peak and the slower is the decline towards zero as time goes on. In the limiting case, with $\xi_G = 0$, the shock is permanent and the transition term is equal to an adjustment term of the form $A(\lambda_1, t) \equiv 1 - e^{-\lambda_1 t}$. Hence, for $\xi_G = 0$ the transition function is not bell-shaped–see the solid line in Figure 13.9.

We are now in a position to study the intuition behind the macroeconomic effects of a temporary public spending shock. In Figure 13.8 we illustrate the transition paths for output, consumption, and investment in a multiplier format. For the remaining variables the effects are plotted in an elasticity format. The aim is to firmly establish the link between the impulse-response diagrams contained in Figure 13.8 and the analytical results given in (13.124)–(13.125). This task is facilitated by considering the phase diagram presented in Figure 13.10.

In Figure 13.10, CSE_0 and CE_0 are, respectively, the initial capital stock equilibrium and consumption equilibrium curves, and E_0 is the initial equilibrium. The effect of a permanent shock, which was also studied in Figure 13.7, is to shift the CSE curve to CSE_{ps}. The economy adjusts by jumping from E_0 to A_{ps} at impact and by moving gradually along the saddle path, SP_{ps}, from A_{ps} to E_{ps}.

Next we consider what the adjustment path looks like when the shock is temporary. It follows from the comparison of (13.111) and (13.125) that the impact reduction in consumption is larger for a permanent than for a temporary shock. In Figure 13.10 this means that for a temporary shock the economy jumps somewhere along the vertical dashed line through points E_0 and A_{ps}. In order to study the qualitative effects of shock persistence, we consider two particular values for ξ_G, say ξ_G^1 and ξ_G^2,

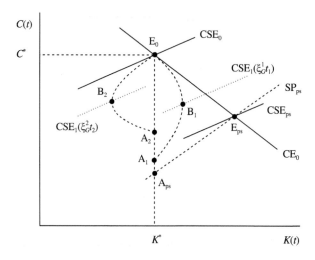

Figure 13.10: Phase diagram for a temporary shock

and we assume that $\zeta_G^1 < \zeta_G^2$, i.e. the shock is relatively more persistent for ζ_G^1. The consumption jumps associated with the two ζ_G values are illustrated in Figure 13.10 by, respectively, points A_1 and A_2.

Consumption falls regardless of the degree of shock persistence. The additional lump-sum taxes make the representative agent poorer as a result of which he cuts back on goods consumption and leisure. This negative human wealth effect is larger the more persistent is the shock. Next we consider whether the agents react to the shock by accumulating or decumulating assets. The diagram in and of itself does not provide an unambiguous answer because it is not a priori clear which region the economy jumps to. This is where the analytical results can provide further guidance.

It follows from the second expression in (13.124) that the impact effect on net investment is given by:[21]

$$\dot{K}(0) = -\frac{\delta_{11} + \zeta_G}{\lambda_2 + \zeta_G}dG = [(\rho + \delta)\eta_{YC} - \zeta_G] \cdot \frac{dG}{\lambda_2 + \zeta_G}, \tag{13.127}$$

where η_{YC} is the (absolute value of the) partial elasticity of output with respect to consumption (obtained from (13.115) above):

$$\eta_{YC} \equiv \left| \frac{\partial Y(t)}{\partial C(t)} \frac{C(t)}{Y(t)} \right| \equiv \frac{(1-\alpha)\omega_{LL}^*}{1 + \alpha\omega_{LL}^*}. \tag{13.128}$$

The impact effect on net investment depends on the interplay of two mechanisms working in opposite directions, namely the labour supply mechanism (parameterized by ω_{LL}^*) and the shock persistence mechanism (parameterized by ζ_G). If the shock is relatively persistent ($\zeta_G^1 < (\rho + \delta)\eta_{YC}$), the labour supply mechanism dominates, the term in square brackets on the right-hand side of (13.127) is positive, and net investment rises at impact ($\dot{K}(0) > 0$). Intuitively, since consumption falls and output increases strongly (because of the large boost in labour supply), the increase

---

[21]This expression is obtained by differentiating the second expression in (13.124) with respect to time and noting that $dT(\zeta_G, \lambda_1, t)/dt = \lambda_1$ for $t = 0$.

in government consumption does not cause any crowding out of private investment. Hence, for $\xi_G^1 < (\rho + \delta)\eta_{YC}$, the transition path at impact is upward sloping–see the dashed line from point A_1 in Figure 13.10. The phase diagram can now be used to characterize the transition path. Over time, the capital stock equilibrium locus starts to shift back towards CSE_0. During the early part of the transition the equilibrium trajectory runs in a north-easterly direction, say from A_1 to B_1 in Figure 13.10. By the time the equilibrium trajectory catches up with the then relevant capital stock equilibrium locus $(CSE_1(\xi_G^1, t_1))$, net capital accumulation ceases, i.e. the trajectory is vertical at point B_1. After that time, the economy returns to the old equilibrium along the trajectory from B_1 to E_0.

If the shock is relatively transient $(\xi_G^2 > (\rho + \delta)\eta_{YC})$, then the persistence mechanism dominates, the term in square brackets on the right-hand side of (13.127) is negative, and net investment falls at impact $(\dot{K}(0) < 0)$. In that case, the economy jumps at impact from E_0 to A_2, after which it moves gradually from A_2 via B_2 to the initial equilibrium E_0. The transition paths for the capital stock and consumption have been illustrated in the time domain and for a range of ξ_G values in Figure 13.8(c) and (e). As is evident from both the phase diagram (Figure 13.10) and the time domain picture (Figure 13.8(c)) the adjustment of consumption is monotonic.

The adjustment paths for employment, wages, output, and the interest rate are obtained by substituting the solutions for consumption and the capital stock, given in (13.124)–(13.125), into the quasi-reduced form expressions (13.114)–(13.117). In a similar fashion, the adjustment path for gross private investment is obtained by using (13.88) and noting (13.122). In panels (b)–(h) of Figure 13.8 we illustrate the paths for output, consumption, gross private investment, the capital stock, employment, wages, and the real interest rate. The dashed and dotted lines represent adjustment paths for temporary shocks. Output jumps up at impact and thereafter monotonically drops back to its initial level. The more transient the shock, the faster is the transition in output. Gross investment jumps up (down) when the shock persistence is high (low) and thereafter returns monotonically to its initial level.

We conclude this section by briefly touching on what has been labelled by Baxter and King (1993) as one of the four classic questions regarding fiscal policy, namely the relationship between policy persistence and the magnitude of impact effects. By using (13.115) and (13.125) and noting that capital is predetermined at impact $(\dot{K}(0) = K^*)$, we find that there exists a simple relationship between the output multiplier for permanent and temporary increases in government consumption in the impact period:

$$\left[\frac{dY(0)}{dG}\right]_{\xi_G > 0} = \frac{\rho + \lambda_1}{\rho + \lambda_1 + \xi_G} \cdot \left[\frac{dY(0)}{dG}\right]_{\xi_G = 0} > 0. \tag{13.129}$$

It follows from (13.129) that the impact multiplier is smaller the less persistent is the shock to government spending, i.e. the higher is ξ_G. We thus confirm analytically the conclusion reached on the basis of numerical simulations by Baxter and King (1993, p. 326).[22] Note also that the closer is the impact effect of a temporary shock to that of a permanent shock, the faster is the inherent speed of adjustment in the economy, i.e. the higher is λ_1.

---

[22]In the classic analyses of Hall (1980) and Barro (1981), exactly the oppostite result holds, i.e. temporary spending shocks have larger effects than permanent ones. The reason for this discrepancy is that these papers do not allow for capital accumulation. See Baxter and King (1993, p. 326).

13.6   The RCK model with search unemployment

Up to this point we have abstracted from one of the key features characterizing advanced economies, namely the existence of unemployment. Indeed, as we showed in Chapter 7 economies such as the United Kingdom and the United States have experienced a long-run unemployment rate of about six percent over the last century or more. In this section we develop a version of the RCK model in which there is a positive equilibrium unemployment rate. More specifically we develop a macroeconomic version of the search and matching model, a simple version of which was studied in Chapter 8 above.[23]

Under the strict (microeconomic) interpretation of the search and matching model, the behaviour of individual workers and single-job firms is analysed. Such individual agents face an inherently stochastic problem, i.e. the worker is either fully employed or seeking a job. Similarly, the firm either has a vacancy or has managed to find a suitable worker. In order to analyse the model at the microeconomic level, it is necessary to solve the stochastic decision making problems faced by workers and firms, using stochastic dynamic programming techniques that are discussed in Part III of this book.

The early macroeconomic literature circumvents many of these complications by embedding individual agents in large groups of similar agents, and studying the behaviour of each group rather than that of the group's individuals. For example, instead of analysing individual workers, it is postulated that the representative household consists of (infinitely) many family members that are each working full time or searching for a job. The family is assumed to pool its income. Because the number of family members is very large, family-wide employment, unemployment, and income are deterministic, so that standard deterministic optimal control techniques can be used to solve the household model. Similarly, by making the large-firm assumption (as in Pissarides, 2000, pp. 68–70), aggregate employment and vacancy flows are rendered deterministic. The discussion presented here is loosely based on Shi and Wen (1997, 1999) and Heijdra and Ligthart (2002).

13.6.1   Model elements

The representative household consists of a large number, N, of identical family members. To cut down on notation, we normalize N to unity. Family members care only about lifetime utility of the household and individual labour income risk is fully insured within the household. Thus, household income is non-stochastic.[24] From the perspective of the planning period $t = 0$, expected lifetime utility of the representative household is given by:

$$\Lambda(0) \equiv \int_0^\infty U(C(t), M(t))e^{-\rho t}dt, \tag{13.130}$$

where ρ is the pure rate of time preference ($\rho > 0$), $C(t)$ is household consumption, and $M(t)$ is household leisure. The household has a time endowment of unity so that leisure is equal to:

$$M(t) \equiv 1 - S(t) - L(t), \tag{13.131}$$

---

[23]The reader purely interested in the theory of economic growth can skip this section and the next and proceed to Chapter 14.

[24]This assumption is quite standard in the macroeconomic literature. See, for example, Andolfatto (1996), Merz (1995), Galí (1996), DenHaan et al. (2000), and Shi and Wen (1997, 1999).

where $S(t)$ is the amount of time the family as a whole spends on searching for jobs at time t (unemployment), and $L(t)$ is the amount of time the family spends working at time t. Just as in the previous section we assume that the felicity function is loglinear in consumption and leisure time:

$$U(C(t), 1 - S(t) - L(t)) \equiv \ln \left[C(t)^\varepsilon \left[1 - S(t) - L(t) \right]^{1-\varepsilon} \right], \qquad 0 < \varepsilon < 1. \quad (13.132)$$

At each instant of time some unemployed household members find a job but some employed members lose their job as idiosyncratic shocks destroy a constant proportion of the pre-existing matches between firms and workers. As a result, the household's stock of employment evolves according to:

$$\dot{L}(t) \equiv f(t)S(t) - \delta_m L(t), \quad (13.133)$$

where $\dot{L}(t) \equiv dL(t)/dt$, $f(t)$ is the job-finding rate (to be determined below), and δ_m is the exogenous job destruction rate (see also Chapter 8). The household's budget identity is:

$$\dot{A}(t) \equiv r(t)A(t) + w(t)L(t) + s_U(t)S(t) - T(t) - C(t), \quad (13.134)$$

where $\dot{A}(t) \equiv dA(t)/dt$, $A(t)$ is the stock of real tangible assets, $r(t)$ is the interest rate, $w(t)$ is the wage rate, $s_U(t)$ is the unemployment benefit (a subsidy on job searching), and $T(t)$ is a lump-sum tax.

The household chooses time paths for consumption, searching time, and tangible assets in order to maximize lifetime utility (13.130) subject to the accumulation identities (13.133)–(13.134) and the definition (13.132). It takes as given its initial stocks of financial assets and employment, $A(0)$ and $L(0)$. The current-value Hamiltonian for the household's optimization problem is:

$$\mathcal{H}_C^H(t) \equiv U(C(t), 1 - S(t) - L(t)) + \xi_A(t) \left[r(t)A(t) + w(t)L(t) \right.$$
$$\left. + s_U(t)S(t) - T(t) - C(t) \right] + \xi_L(t) \left[f(t)S(t) - \delta_m L(t) \right],$$

where $A(t)$ and $L(t)$ are the state variables, $\xi_A(t)$ and $\xi_L(t)$ are the corresponding co-state variables, and $C(t)$ and $S(t)$ are the control variables. The interesting first-order conditions are:

$$\frac{\varepsilon}{C(t)} = \xi_A(t), \quad (13.135)$$

$$\frac{1 - \varepsilon}{1 - S(t) - L(t)} = s_U(t)\xi_A(t) + f(t)\xi_L(t), \quad (13.136)$$

$$\frac{\dot{\xi}_A(t)}{\xi_A(t)} = \rho - r(t), \quad (13.137)$$

$$\dot{\xi}_L(t) = \frac{1 - \varepsilon}{1 - S(t) - L(t)} - w(t)\xi_A(t) + (\rho + \delta_m)\xi_L(t), \quad (13.138)$$

$$\lim_{t \to \infty} \xi_A(t)A(t)e^{-\rho t} = \lim_{t \to \infty} \xi_L(t)L(t)e^{-\rho t} = 0. \quad (13.139)$$

The first-order conditions can be simplified substantially. First, by using (13.135) and its time derivative in (13.137) we obtain the consumption Euler equation determining the optimal time profile of consumption:

$$\frac{\dot{C}(t)}{C(t)} = r(t) - \rho. \quad (13.140)$$

Next we can define the relative (shadow) value of a job by $\eta_L(t) \equiv \xi_L(t)/\xi_A(t)$ and rewrite (13.136) and (13.138) as follows:

$$\frac{1-\varepsilon}{\varepsilon} \frac{C(t)}{1-S(t)-L(t)} = s_U(t) + f(t)\eta_L(t) \ [\equiv w_R(t)], \tag{13.141}$$

$$\dot{\eta}_L(t) = (r(t)+\delta_m)\,\eta_L(t) + \frac{1-\varepsilon}{\varepsilon} \frac{C(t)}{1-S(t)-L(t)} - w(t). \tag{13.142}$$

Equation (13.141) shows that in determining the optimum amount of job search the household ensures that the marginal rate of substitution between consumption and leisure is equated to the reservation wage, $w_R(t)$. The reservation wage itself depends on several factors. By participating in the labour market, rather than enjoying leisure, the household not only receives the unemployment benefit, $s_U(t)$, but also has a non-zero probability, $f(t)$, of locating a job with a pecuniary value of $\eta_L(t)$. Finally, equation (13.142) shows the dynamic path for $\eta_L(t)$, the relative shadow value of a job to the household. Note that by using (13.141), this expression can be rewritten as:

$$\dot{\eta}_L(t) = (r(t)+\delta_m+f(t))\,\eta_L(t) - [w(t)-s_U(t)]. \tag{13.143}$$

By integrating (13.143) and (13.142) we obtain two equivalent expressions for the value of a job in the planning period, $\xi_L(0)$:

$$\eta_L(0) \equiv \int_0^\infty [w(t)-s_U(t)]\, e^{-\int_0^t [r(\tau)+f(\tau)+\delta_m]d\tau}\, dt \tag{13.144}$$

$$= \int_0^\infty [w(t)-w_R(t)]\, e^{-\int_0^t [r(\tau)+\delta_m]d\tau}\, dt. \tag{13.145}$$

Expression (13.144) shows that the value of an additional job at time $t = 0$ equals the present value of the "dividend" earned on the job (equalling the excess of the wage over the unemployment benefit) using $r(\tau)+f(\tau)+\delta_m$ as the instantaneous discount rate in time period τ. An equivalent expression involving the reservation wage is given in (13.145).

Following Pissarides (2000, pp. 68–70) we assume that there is a single very large representative firm which faces certain flows into and out of its labour force. The representative firm is perfectly competitive and uses capital ($K(t)$) and labour ($L(t)$) to produce units of the homogeneous good ($Y(t)$):

$$Y(t) = F(K(t), L(t)), \tag{13.146}$$

where the production function features constant returns to scale. As a result of the matching friction, the firm faces linear costs of adjusting its stock of labour. In order to augment its work force it must post vacancies ($V(t)$) in order to find a worker. The firm's labour force thus changes according to:

$$\dot{L}(t) = q(t)V(t) - \delta_m L(t), \tag{13.147}$$

where $q(t)$ is the instantaneous probability of the firm finding a worker with whom it concludes a deal. In addition to finding new workers at each instant, the firm also loses a given proportion of its work force due to idiosyncratic shocks (see also (13.133) above).

The objective function of the firm is the present value of its cash flow, $FV(0)$:

$$FV(0) = \int_0^\infty \left[Y(t) - cV(t) - w(t)L(t) - I(t) \right] e^{-\int_0^t r(\tau)d\tau} dt, \tag{13.148}$$

where c is the flow cost per vacancy (modelled in terms of lost output), and $I(t)$ is firm investment. The capital stock accumulation identity is given by:

$$\dot{K}(t) = I(t) - \delta_k K(t), \tag{13.149}$$

where δ_k is the depreciation rate. The firm chooses time paths for output, vacancies, investment, the capital stock, and employment in order to maximize (13.148) subject to the production function (13.146) and the accumulation identities for workers (13.147) and capital (13.149), taking as given its initial stocks of labour and capital ($L(0)$ and $K(0)$). The current-value Hamiltonian for the firm's optimization problem is:

$$\mathcal{H}_C^F(t) \equiv F(K(t), L(t)) - cV(t) - w(t)L(t) - I(t)$$
$$+ \mu_L(t) \left[q(t)V(t) - \delta_m L(t) \right] + \mu_K(t) \left[I(t) - \delta_k K(t) \right],$$

where $L(t)$ and $K(t)$ are the state variable, $\mu_L(t)$ and $\mu_K(t)$ are the co-state variables, and $V(t)$ and $I(t)$ are the control variables. The interesting first-order conditions can be written as:

$$\mu_L(t)q(t) = c, \tag{13.150}$$
$$\mu_K(t) = 1, \tag{13.151}$$
$$\dot{\mu}_L(t) = - \left[F_L(K(t), L(t)) - w(t) \right] + (r(t) + \delta_m)\mu_L(t), \tag{13.152}$$
$$\dot{\mu}_K(t) = -F_K(K(t), L(t)) + (r(t) + \delta_k)\mu_K(t), \tag{13.153}$$
$$\lim_{t \to \infty} \mu_L(t)L(t)e^{-\int_0^t r(s)ds} = \lim_{t \to \infty} \mu_K(t)K(t)e^{-\int_0^t r(s)ds} = 0. \tag{13.154}$$

By simplifying these expressions somewhat we find the most important first-order conditions:

$$\mu_L(t) = \frac{c}{q(t)}, \tag{13.155}$$
$$F_K(K(t), L(t)) = r(t) + \delta_k, \tag{13.156}$$
$$\dot{\mu}_L(t) = (r(t) + \delta_m)\mu_L(t) - \left[F_L(K(t), L(t)) - w(t) \right]. \tag{13.157}$$

According to (13.155) the firm sets its vacancies such that the expected cost of recruitment per worker (right-hand side) equals the value to the firm of that worker (left-hand side). Equation (13.156) is the usual expression, calling for an equalization between the marginal product of capital (left-hand side) and the rental rate on capital (right-hand side). Equation (13.157) shows the dynamic path for $\mu_L(t)$, representing the pecuniary value of an additional job to the firm at time t. By integrating (13.157) forward and imposing the terminal condition we obtain:

$$\mu_L(0) = \int_0^\infty \left[F_L(K(t), L(t)) - w(t) \right] e^{-\int_0^t (r(\tau) + \delta_m)d\tau} dt. \tag{13.158}$$

The value of an occupied job to the firm is equal to the present value of the "dividend" it earns on that job, using $r(\tau) + \delta_m$ as the instantaneous discount rate for time period τ. The dividend consists of the excess of labour productivity over the wage (that is, $F_L - w$).

When a job-seeking worker and a firm with a vacancy meet, a pure economic rent is created equal to $\eta_L^i + \mu_L^i$, where the superscript i refers to a particular worker-firm pairing. As in Chapter 8, we assume that this rent is shared across the two parties according to the generalized Nash wage-bargaining solution. The wage in the planning period, $w^i(0)$, is set in such a way that $\Omega_i(0)$ is maximized, i.e.:

$$\max_{w^i(0)} \quad \Omega(0) \equiv \eta_L^i(0)^\beta \mu_L^i(0)^{1-\beta}, \quad 0 < \beta < 1, \tag{13.159}$$

where β and $1 - \beta$ are the bargaining weights of, respectively, the worker and the firm, and where $\eta_L^i(0)$ and $\mu_L^i(0)$ are obtained from, respectively, (13.145) and (13.158) by substituting $w(0) = w^i(0)$. The first-order condition for this maximization problem is given by $\beta \mu_L^i(0) = (1 - \beta) \eta_L^i(0)$. Once a match has been formed wages are continuously renegotiated. Hence, as long as the match persists the wage resulting from this bargaining process can be written in two equivalent ways:[25]

$$w(t) = \beta F_L(K(t), L(t)) + (1 - \beta) w_R(t) \tag{13.160}$$

$$= \beta [F_L(K(t), L(t)) + c\theta(t)] + (1 - \beta) s_U(t). \tag{13.161}$$

Since all worker-firm pairings are identical and wages are renegotiated at each instant, the model is symmetric and the wage does not feature a pairing index i. According to (13.160), the wage equals the weighted average of the marginal product of labour (F_L) and the reservation wage (w_R). Equation (13.161) shows that the wage can also be expressed as a weighted average of the firm's "surplus" ($F_L + c\theta$) and the unemployment benefit. The former consists of not only the marginal product of labour but also includes the search costs that are foregone if the deal is struck ($c\theta$).

For convenience, the complete model has been summarized in Table 13.6. Equations (T6.1), (T6.3), and (T6.6)–(T6.9) restate, respectively, equations (13.140), (13.133), (13.156), (13.141), (13.142) and (13.155). Equation (T6.2) follows from the goods market clearing condition, and (T6.4) is the government budget constraint. Equation (T6.5) is obtained by substituting (13.141) into (13.160). Equation (T6.10) follows from wage bargaining. The expressions in (T6.11)–(T6.12) follow from the Cobb-Douglas matching function, $X(t) = Z_m V(t)^\phi S(t)^{1-\phi}$, and noting that $q(t) \equiv X(t)/V(t)$ and $f(t) \equiv X(t)/S(t)$. Finally, (T6.13) shows that the production function is of the Cobb-Douglas type. The exogenous policy variables are the search subsidy $s_U(t)$ and government consumption $G(t)$. The endogenous variables are output $Y(t)$, consumption $C(t)$, the capital stock $K(t)$, employment $L(t)$, lump-sum taxes $T(t)$, the wage rate $w(t)$, the interest rate $r(t)$, search time $S(t)$, vacancies $V(t)$, the job finding rate $f(t)$, the vacancy filling rate $q(t)$, the worker's job value $\eta_L(t)$, and the firm's job value $\mu_L(t)$. Of the fundamental dynamic variables, $K(t)$ and $L(t)$ are predetermined (sticky) variables whilst $C(t)$ and $\eta_L(t)$ are non-predetermined (jumping) variables.

---

[25] By differentiating the first-order condition with respect to time we find $\beta \dot{\mu}_L^i(t) = (1 - \beta) \dot{\eta}_L^i(t)$. It follows from (13.142) and (13.157) that for this worker-firm pairing we have:

$$\dot{\eta}_L^i(t) = (r(t) + \delta_m) \eta_L^i(t) - \left[w^i(t) - w_R(t) \right],$$

$$\dot{\mu}_L^i(t) = (r(t) + \delta_m) \mu_L^i(t) - \left[F_L(K(t), L(t)) - w^i(t) \right].$$

Using these results we find (13.160). Equation (13.161) is obtained by noting that $w_R = s_U + f\eta_L$, $\beta \mu_L = (1 - \beta) \eta_L$, $\mu_L = c/q$, and $f/q = \theta$.

Table 13.6. The RCK model with search unemployment

$$\frac{\dot{C}(t)}{C(t)} = r(t) - \rho, \tag{T6.1}$$

$$\dot{K}(t) = Y(t) - C(t) - G(t) - cV(t) - \delta_k K(t), \tag{T6.2}$$

$$\dot{L}(t) = f(t)S(t) - \delta_m L(t), \tag{T6.3}$$

$$T(t) = s_U S(t) + G(t), \tag{T6.4}$$

$$w(t) = (1-\alpha)\beta\frac{Y(t)}{L(t)} + (1-\beta)\frac{1-\varepsilon}{\varepsilon}\frac{C(t)}{1-S(t)-L(t)}, \tag{T6.5}$$

$$r(t) + \delta_k = \alpha\frac{Y(t)}{K(t)}, \tag{T6.6}$$

$$\frac{1-\varepsilon}{\varepsilon}\frac{C(t)}{1-S(t)-L(t)} = s_U + f(t)\,\eta_L(t), \tag{T6.7}$$

$$\dot{\eta}_L(t) = (r(t)+\delta_m)\,\eta_L(t) + \frac{1-\varepsilon}{\varepsilon}\frac{C(t)}{1-S(t)-L(t)} - w(t), \tag{T6.8}$$

$$\mu_L(t) = \frac{c}{q(t)}, \tag{T6.9}$$

$$\beta\mu_L(t) = (1-\beta)\eta_L(t), \tag{T6.10}$$

$$f(t) = Z_m\left(\frac{V(t)}{S(t)}\right)^{\phi}, \tag{T6.11}$$

$$q(t) = Z_m\left(\frac{V(t)}{S(t)}\right)^{\phi-1}, \tag{T6.12}$$

$$Y(t) = Z_y K(t)^{\alpha} L(t)^{1-\alpha}. \tag{T6.13}$$

Definitions: $Y(t)$ is output, $C(t)$ is private consumption, $L(t)$ is employment, $K(t)$ is the capital stock, $G(t)$ is public consumption, $w(t)$ is the real wage rate, $r(t)$ is the real interest rate, $S(t)$ is search hours, $V(t)$ is the number of vacancies, $\mu_L(t)$ is the value of a filled job to the firm, $\eta_L(t)$ is the value of a job to the household, $T(t)$ is a lump-sum tax, s_U is the search subsidy, $T(t)$ is the lump-sum tax, $f(t)$ is the job finding rate, $q(t)$ is the vacancy filling rate, c is the cost of maintaining a vacancy, ρ is the pure rate of time preference, δ_k is the depreciation rate of capital, δ_m is the job destruction rate, ϕ is the matching function parameter, ε is the taste parameter for consumption, and α is the efficiency parameter of capital. Z_y and Z_m are constants. The population is constant and normalized to unity.

In the steady state, the policy variables are time-invariant ($s_U(t) = s_{U0}$ and $G(t) = G_0$) and we have $\dot{C}(t) = \dot{K}(t) = \dot{L}(t) = \dot{\eta}_L(t) = 0$. The steady-state equilibrium can be compactly characterized by the following equations:

$$Z_y \left(k^*\right)^{\alpha-1} = \rho + \delta_k, \tag{13.162}$$

$$w^* = \frac{\beta(\rho + \delta_m + f^*)(1-\alpha)Z_y\left(k^*\right)^{\alpha} + (1-\beta)(\rho + \delta_m)s_{U0}}{\rho + \delta_m + \beta f^*}, \tag{13.163}$$

$$\frac{c\theta^*}{f^*} = \frac{(1-\alpha)Z_y\left(k^*\right)^{\alpha} - w^*}{\rho + \delta_m}, \tag{13.164}$$

$$f^* = Z_m\left(\theta^*\right)^{\phi}, \tag{13.165}$$

$$L^*\left[Z_y\left(k^*\right)^{\alpha} - \delta_k k^*\right] = C^* + G_0 + \theta^* S^*, \tag{13.166}$$

$$\frac{1-\varepsilon}{\varepsilon}\frac{C^*}{1-S^*-L^*} = \frac{\beta f^*(1-\alpha)Z_y\left(k^*\right)^{\alpha} + (\rho + \delta_m)s_U}{\rho + \delta_m + \beta f^*}, \tag{13.167}$$

$$f^* S^* = \delta_m L^*. \tag{13.168}$$

The endogenous variables are the capital-labour ratio $k^* \equiv (K/L)^*$, employment L^*, consumption C^*, search time S^*, the labour market tightness indicator $\theta^* \equiv (V/S)^*$, and the wage rate w^*. As usual stars denote steady-state values. The model is block-recursive. Equation (13.162) determines k^*, (13.163)–(13.165) determine (w^*, θ^*, f^*), and (13.166)–(13.168) determine (C^*, L^*, S^*). The unemployment rate follows from (13.171):

$$u^* \equiv \frac{S^*}{S^* + L^*} = \frac{\delta_m}{\delta_m + f^*}. \tag{13.169}$$

13.6.2   Is unemployment efficient?

Before considering the dynamic properties of the model we first investigate the efficiency properties of the decentralized market equilibrium. This task is accomplished as follows. First we compute the social optimum, i.e. the allocation than a benevolent social planner would choose. Next we compare the first-order conditions for the social optimum to those that hold in the decentralized market equilibrium developed above. At time $t = 0$ the social planner chooses paths for private and public consumption, employment, unemployment, investment, vacancies, and the capital stock in order to maximize lifetime utility (13.130), subject to the following constraints:

$$F\left(K(t), L(t)\right) = C(t) + G(t) + I(t) + cV(t), \tag{13.170}$$

$$\dot{K}(t) = I(t) - \delta_k K(t), \tag{13.171}$$

$$\dot{L}(t) = Z_m\left(\frac{V(t)}{S(t)}\right)^{\phi-1} V(t) - \delta_m L(t), \tag{13.172}$$

and taking as given the initial stocks of capital and occupied jobs, $K(0)$ and $L(0)$. Equation (13.170) is the economy-wide resource constraint, stating that total available output (left-hand side) is equal to the sum of privare and public consumption, investment, and recruiting costs (right-hand side). Equation (13.171) is the just the accumulation identity for capital. Finally, equation (13.172) is the accumulation identity for occupied jobs. Like private firms, the planner faces a search friction and must open vacancies in order to augment the stock of filled jobs. Unlike, private firms, however, the social planner takes into account that the probability of filling a vacancy depends on the relative number of vacancies, as measured by the labour market tightness indicator $\theta(t) \equiv V(t)/S(t)$.

The current-value Hamiltonian for the social planner's optimization problem is:

$$\mathcal{H}_C^S(t) \equiv U(C(t), 1 - S(t) - L(t))$$
$$+ \lambda_L(t) \left[Z_m \left(\frac{V(t)}{S(t)} \right)^{\phi-1} V(t) - \delta_m L(t) \right]$$
$$+ \lambda_K(t) \left[F(K(t), L(t)) - C(t) - G(t) - cV(t) - \delta_k K(t) \right],$$

where $L(t)$ and $K(t)$ are the state variables, $\lambda_L(t)$ and $\lambda_K(t)$ are the co-state variables, and $C(t)$, $G(t)$, $S(t)$, and $V(t)$ are the control variables. The first-order conditions can be written as:

$$\lambda_K(t) = \frac{\varepsilon}{C(t)}, \tag{13.173}$$

$$(1 - \phi)\lambda_L(t)Z_m \left(\frac{V(t)}{S(t)} \right)^{\phi} = \frac{1 - \varepsilon}{1 - S(t) - L(t)}, \tag{13.174}$$

$$\phi\lambda_L(t)Z_m \left(\frac{V(t)}{S(t)} \right)^{\phi-1} = c\lambda_K(t), \tag{13.175}$$

and:

$$\dot{\lambda}_L(t) = \frac{1 - \varepsilon}{1 - S(t) - L(t)} + (\rho + \delta_m)\lambda_L(t) - \lambda_K(t)F_L(K(t), L(t)), \tag{13.176}$$

$$\dot{\lambda}_K(t) = [\rho + \delta_k - F_K(K(t), L(t))]\lambda_K(t), \tag{13.177}$$

$$\lim_{t \to \infty} \lambda_L(t)L(t)e^{-\rho t} = \lim_{t \to \infty} \lambda_K(t)K(t)e^{-\rho t} = 0. \tag{13.178}$$

Furthermore, since public consumption is costly but yields no utility, the planner optimally sets $G^s(t) = 0$ where the superscript 's' denotes the socially optimal value. By defining $\eta_L(t) \equiv \lambda_L(t)/\lambda_K(t)$ and simplifying the expressions in (13.173)–(13.178) somewhat, we find the most important first-order conditions for the first-best social optimum:

$$\frac{1 - \varepsilon}{\varepsilon} \frac{C^s(t)}{1 - S^s(t) - L^s(t)} = (1 - \phi)f(\theta^s(t))\eta_L^s(t), \tag{13.179}$$

$$\frac{c}{q(\theta^s(t))} = \phi\eta_L^s(t), \tag{13.180}$$

$$\frac{\dot{C}^s(t)}{C^s(t)} = r^s(t) - \rho, \tag{13.181}$$

$$\dot{\eta}_L^s(t) = (r^s(t) + \delta_m)\eta_L^s(t) + \frac{1 - \varepsilon}{\varepsilon} \frac{C^s(t)}{1 - S^s(t) - L^s(t)}$$
$$- F_L(k^s(t), 1), \tag{13.182}$$

$$r^s(t) = F_K(k^s(t), 1) - \delta_k, \tag{13.183}$$

$$\dot{K}^s(t) = L^s(t)[F_K(k^s(t), 1) - \delta_k k^s(t)] - C^s(t) - c\theta^s(t)S^s(t), \tag{13.184}$$

$$\dot{L}^s(t) = f(\theta^s(t))S^s(t) - \delta_m L^s(t), \tag{13.185}$$

where we have used the fact that $f(\theta(t)) \equiv \theta(t)q(\theta(t)) = Z_m\theta(t)^\phi$ to simplify these expressions.

The market equilibrium is efficient if and only if its first-order conditions exactly match up with the ones for the social optimum as given in (13.179)–(13.185). The corresponding conditions satisfying the market equilibrium are:

$$\frac{1-\varepsilon}{\varepsilon} \frac{C(t)}{1-S(t)-L(t)} = s_U(t) + f(\theta(t))\eta_L(t), \tag{13.186}$$

$$\frac{c}{q(\theta(t))} = \frac{1-\beta}{\beta}\eta_L(t), \tag{13.187}$$

$$\frac{\dot{C}(t)}{C(t)} = r(t) - \rho, \tag{13.188}$$

$$\dot{\eta}_L(t) = (r(t)+\delta_m)\eta_L(t) + \beta\frac{1-\varepsilon}{\varepsilon}\frac{C(t)}{1-S(t)-L(t)}$$
$$- \beta F_L(k(t),1), \tag{13.189}$$

$$r(t) = F_K(k(t),1) - \delta_k, \tag{13.190}$$

$$\dot{K}(t) = L(t)[F_K(k(t),1) - \delta_k k(t)] - C(t) - G(t) - c\theta(t)S(t), \tag{13.191}$$

$$\dot{L}(t) = f(\theta(t))S(t) - \delta_m L(t). \tag{13.192}$$

Comparing the sets of conditions (13.179)–(13.185) and (13.186)–(13.192), we find that they exactly match and the market equilibrium is efficient if and only if the following conditions hold:[26]

$$s_U(t) = G(t) = 0, \qquad 1 - \phi = \beta. \tag{13.193}$$

The first conditions in (13.193) state that the government should not subsidize labour market search or waste output in the form of public consumption. Intuitively, a subsidy of search distorts the labour supply decision in that it artificially raises the reservation wage in the decentralized economy. The second condition (13.193) is called the *Hosios condition* (after Hosios, 1990). It requires the elasticity of the matching function with respect to unemployment ($\eta(\theta) \equiv \frac{\partial X}{\partial S}\frac{S}{X} = 1 - \phi$) to be equal to the bargaining weight of workers (β). With a Cobb-Douglas matching function this elasticity is a constant so that the Hosios condition only holds in the knife-edge case where ϕ happens to be equal to the bargaining weight of firms. In all other cases the decentralized equilibrium in an unmanaged economy (featuring $s_U(t) = G(t) = 0$) is inefficient and the unemployment rate may be too low or too high from a social welfare perspective.

13.6.3 Transitional dynamics

In order to study its dynamic properties it is convenient to condense the model into the following system of non-linear differential equations:

$$\frac{\dot{C}(t)}{C(t)} = \alpha Z_y \left(\frac{K(t)}{L(t)}\right)^{-(1-\alpha)} - (\rho + \delta_k), \tag{13.194}$$

---

[26]First we postulate that $\theta^s(t) = \theta(t)$ and compare (13.179) and (13.186). The marginal rate of substitution is the same for both equilibria provided $s_U(t) = 0$ and $\eta_L^s(t) = \eta_L(t)/(1-\phi)$. Next, we compare (13.180) and (13.187). These expressions coincide provided $\phi/(1-\phi) = (1-\beta)/\beta$. The remaining equivalences follow readily.

$$\dot{K}(t) = Z_y K(t)^\alpha L(t)^{1-\alpha} - C(t) - c\theta(t)S(t) - G(t) - \delta_k K(t), \tag{13.195}$$

$$\dot{L}(t) = Z_m \theta(t)^\phi S(t) - \delta_m L(t), \tag{13.196}$$

$$\dot{\eta}_L(t) = \left[\alpha Z_y \left(\frac{K(t)}{L(t)} \right)^{-(1-\alpha)} + \beta Z_m \theta(t)^\phi - \delta_k + \delta_m \right] \eta_L(t)$$

$$+ \beta \left[s_U(t) - (1-\alpha)Z_y \left(\frac{K(t)}{L(t)} \right)^\alpha \right], \tag{13.197}$$

where $\theta(t)$ and $S(t)$ are given by:

$$\theta(t) = \left(\frac{(1-\beta)Z_m \eta_L(t)}{\beta c} \right)^{1/(1-\phi)}, \tag{13.198}$$

$$S(t) = 1 - L(t) - \frac{1-\varepsilon}{\varepsilon} \frac{C(t)}{s_U(t) + Z_m \theta(t)^\phi \eta_L(t)}. \tag{13.199}$$

In principle it is possible to linearize the model around the steady state and proceed from there. But because there are four dynamic state variables, the dimension is too high for this approach to be analytically tractable. In practice, therefore, a numerical approach is the only avenue left. In the remainder of this subsection we show how the model can be calibrated and simulated with the aid of a simple Matlab program.

Without claiming to parameterize an actual economy we chose the values of the structural parameters as follows. First, in order to facilitate the comparison with the unit-elastic model studied above we use the same values for α, ρ, and δ_k (see (13.119) above). The labour market parameters are taken from Shi and Wen (1999, p. 471) who use the matching function $X = Z_m V^\phi S^{1-\phi}$, and set $Z_m = 1$, $\phi = 0.6$, and $\beta = 0.4$ (the Hosios condition is thus assumed to be satisfied). The job destruction rate is set at five percent per quarter, i.e. $\delta_m = 0.05$. The remainder of the parameters are chosen as follows.

- First, for the given values of ρ, α, and δ_k we compute $\kappa^* \equiv (K/Y)^*$.

- Second, we set the targets $Y^* = 1$, $L^* = 0.2$, and $u^* \equiv (S/(S+L))^* = 0.06$ (a six percent long-run unemployment rate). This gives us K^*, k^*, $F_K(k^*, 1)$, $F_L(k^*, 1)$, f^*, Z_y, and S^*:

$$K^* = \kappa^*, \qquad k^* = \frac{K^*}{L^*} \qquad S^* = \frac{u^* L^*}{1 - u^*}, \qquad f^* = \frac{\delta_m L^*}{S^*}, \qquad Z_y = (K^*)^{-\alpha}(L^*)^{\alpha-1}.$$

- Third, we solve (T6.5), (T6.7) and (T6.8) in steady state for w^*, MRS^*, and η_L^*:

$$w^* = \frac{\beta(\rho + \delta_m + f^*)}{\rho + \delta_m + \beta f^*} F_L(k^*, 1) + \frac{(1-\beta)(\rho + \delta_m)}{\rho + \delta_m + \beta f^*} s_U,$$

$$MRS^* = \frac{\beta f^*}{\rho + \delta_m + \beta f^*} F_L(k^*, 1) + \frac{\rho + \delta_m}{\rho + \delta_m + \beta f^*} s_U,$$

$$\eta_L^* = \frac{\beta}{\rho + \delta_m + \beta f^*} [F_L(k^*, 1) - s_U],$$

where MRS^* is the steady-state marginal rate of substitution between leisure and consumption (the left-hand side of (T6.7)).

- Fourth, by anchoring the initial search subsidy to the marginal product of labour, say $s_U = \zeta F_L(k^*, 1)$ and choosing (somewhat arbitrarily)$\zeta = 0.4$, we obtain values for w^*, MRS^*, and η_L^*. Using (T6.10) we find μ_L^*.

- Fifth, since $q^* = f^*/\theta^*$ we find from (T6.9) that $c\theta^* = f^*\mu_L^*$. Furthermore, since $\theta^* = (f^*)^{1/\phi}$ we can also compute the value for c. By setting $G_0 = 0.2$ (as in (13.120) above) we compute steady-state consumption:

$$C^* = 1 - G_0 - c\theta^* S^* - \delta_k K^*,$$

and solve for ε such that:

$$\frac{1-\varepsilon}{\varepsilon} \frac{C^*}{1 - S^* - L^*} = MRS^*.$$

In summary, the structural parameters are given by:

$$\begin{array}{llll}
\rho = 0.0159 & \delta_k = 0.0241 & \alpha = 1/3 & \delta_m = 0.05 \quad \beta = 0.4 \\
\varepsilon = 0.1944 & Z_y = 1.4420 & Z_m = 1 & \phi = 0.6 \qquad c = 3.7240.
\end{array} \tag{13.200}$$

whilst the resulting initial steady-state is characterized by:

$$\begin{array}{llllll}
Y^* = 1 & C^* = 0.5673 & S^* = 0.0128 & w^* = 3.1249 & \eta_L^* = 2.1097 \\
r^* = 0.0159 & L^* = 0.2 & K^* = 8.3371 & \theta^* = 0.6656 & u^* = 0.06 \quad (13.201) \\
T = G_0 = 0.2 & s_U = 1.3333 & \mu_L^* = 3.1645 & f^* = 0.7833.
\end{array}$$

The parameterized model can be solved by employing the Matlab boundary value problem solver bvp4c which is documented extensively in Shampine et al. (2000) where a number of examples are also found. The mathematical details of this method need not concern us here. But intuitively, bvp4c can solve nonlinear systems of differential equations in the presence of initial and end-point conditions. In the search model employed here the capital stock and employment are predetermined variables for which initial conditions must be specified. In contrast, consumption and the worker's job value are jumping variables for which end-point conditions are relevant. Table 13.7 lists the Matlab program that solves the unemployment model. This program calls two Matlab functions that are listed in Tables 13.8 and 13.9.

Referring to the top-level file Program13_01.m in Table 13.7 the model is solved in the following fashion. First, the structural parameters are packed into a Matlab *structure* called PAR. A Matlab structure is a data construct with named fields, e.g. PAR.alpha contains the value of α and we can refer to PAR.alpha if we need α in computations. Two further structures are defined, namely EXO for the exogenous variables and VAR for the endogenous variables. In the second step the steady-state model is solved. Initial guesses are specified and the Matlab routine fsolve is used to solve the system of equations characterizing the steady state. Note that fsolve calls the Matlab function Function13_01_SS.m that is listed in Table 13.8. By passing PAR and EXO to this function the values of the structural parameters and exogenous variables are "known" to the function. The solutions that are found by fsolve are packed into the VAR structure.

In the third step the transition path is computed using bvp4c. The example considers an economy that is initially in the steady-state equilibrium but is hit by a five-percent reduction in its capital stock. The initial condition is thus $0.95 \cdot K^*$ for capital and L^* for labour. These values are loaded into VAR.Keq0 and VAR.Leq0 respectively. Since we have a strong suspicion that the model is saddle-point stable, we postulate that the long-run equilibrium will be at K^* and L^* and we pack these values into VAR.Keq1 and VAR.Leq1 respectively. Consumption will also returns to its initial steady-state value C^* so we set this value in VAR.Ceq1; an endpoint condition. Now we are ready to rock and roll. The transition paths for consumption, capital, employment, and job value are computed by calling the Matlab function `Function13_01_TP.m` that is listed in Table 13.9.

Referring to Table 13.9 bvp4c proceeds as follows. First, we need to code a Matlab function, called `capck(x,y)` which evaluates the auxiliary equations (13.198)–(13.199) and the differential equations (13.194)–(13.197). See the second page of Table 13.9. Next, we must specify the residual in the boundary conditions. This is done in the Matlab function `bcfun(ya,yb)` where we impose that capital starts in `Keq0` and ends in `Keq1`, labour starts in `Leq0`, and consumption ends in `Ceq1`. Note that `capck(x,y)` is coded in such a way that `y(1)` is consumption, `y(2)` is labour, etcetera. The initial guess to be used by bvp4c is put in a structure called `solinit` which must contain the fields x and y, where `solinit.x` is a guess for the mesh points (in time) and `solinit.y` is a guess for the solution at these mesh points. The helper function bvpinit sets up `solinit` using `linspace(0,400)` for x and a row vector containing guesses for consumption, capital, employment, and job value for y. Finally, the solution is obtained with the instruction `sol=bvp4c(@capck, @bcfun,solinit);`. This returns the ultimate mesh as `sol.x` and the solution as `sol.y`. The command `deval(sol,time);` evaluates the solution sol at the time points in the vector time.

In Figure 13.11 we plot the transition paths for a number of variables. Several things are worth noting. First, as we guessed before, the model is saddle-point stable and all variables return smoothly to their steady-state values. Second, despite the fact that the capital stock and employment are both sluggish variables, transition in output is extremely fast. Third, at the time of the shock search time jumps up causing the unemployment rate to increase dramatically. The feverish search activity leads to a rapid increase in employment, and over time both search time and the unemployment rate fall gradually. Similarly, consumption monotonically rises toward its pre-shock steady-state level. Fourth, at impact the number of vacancies increases sharply. However, because search time rises even more, the labour market tightness indicator falls so it is easy for firms to locate a worker at that time. Finally, note that transition path for $\theta(t)$ (and thus also for the worker's job value, $\eta_L(t)$) is non-monotonic.

13.7 A monetary RCK model

The effects of money on economic growth was studied by inter alia Tobin (1955, 1965), Sidrauski (1967), and Fischer (1979). In this section we present a monetary version of the RCK model. We adopt the money-in-the-utility-function (MIU) approach discussed in Chapter 10 above.

13.7.1 Model elements

The representative household has the following lifetime utility function:

$$\Lambda(0) \equiv \int_0^\infty U\left(C(t), 1 - L(t), m(t)\right) e^{-\rho t} dt, \tag{13.202}$$

where ρ is the pure rate of time preference, $C(t)$ is goods consumption, $L(t)$ is labour supply, and $m(t)$ stands for real money balances defined as $m(t) \equiv M(t)/P(t)$ where $M(t)$ is the nominal money supply and $P(t)$ is the aggregate price level. The felicity function has the usual properties, i.e. marginal felicity is positive but at a diminishing rate: $U_i > 0$ and $U_{ij} < 0$ for $i, j \in \{C, 1 - L, m\}$. Furthermore it is concave (so that indifference curves bulge toward the origin).

Table 13.7. A Matlab file for the Ramsey-Cass-Koopmans model

```
% Ramsey-Cass-Koopmans growth model with search unemployment
%
% Matlab top file:          Program13_01.m
% Matlab functions called:  Function13_01_SS.m (steady-state)
%                           Function13_01_TP.m (transition path)
%

% Parameters as set in equation (13.200)

clear
clf
clc
close all

% Structural parameters
PAR.alpha     = 0.33333;
PAR.epsilon   = 0.19442;
PAR.delta_k   = 0.02411;
PAR.delta_m   = 0.05000;
PAR.rho       = 0.01586;
PAR.phi       = 0.60000;
PAR.beta      = 0.40000;
PAR.Z_y       = 1.44203;
PAR.Z_m       = 1.00000;
PAR.c         = 3.72403;


% Exogenous variables
EXO.G         = 0.20;
EXO.s_U       = 1.33334;
EXO.time      = linspace(0,200,2001); % Post-shock time (for plotting)

% Guesses for equilibrium values of the endogenous varables in base case
C0            =    0.567;
S0            =    0.013;
L0            =    0.200;
K0            =    8.337;
eta_L0        =    2.110;
mu_L0         =    3.165;
theta0        =    0.666;
R0            =    0.016;


% Compute the steady-state equilibrium
x = zeros(8,1);
[x(:,1),fval,exitflag,output] = fsolve(@Function13_01_SS,...
    [C0,S0,L0,K0,eta_L0,mu_L0,theta0,R0]',...
    optimset('MaxFunEvals',1e6,'MaxIter',1000,'TolX',1.0e-8,'TolFun',...
    1.0e-8),PAR,EXO);

fval;
output;
x;
VAR.Cbase     = x(1,1);
VAR.Sbase     = x(2,1);
VAR.Lbase     = x(3,1);
VAR.Kbase     = x(4,1);
VAR.eta_Lbase = x(5,1);
VAR.mu_Lbase  = x(6,1);
VAR.thetabase = x(7,1);
VAR.Rbase     = x(8,1);
```

Table 13.7, continued

```
VAR.Ybase      = PAR.Z_y * VAR.Kbase^PAR.alpha * VAR.Lbase^(1-PAR.alpha);
VAR.Wbase      = PAR.beta *(1-PAR.alpha) * VAR.Ybase / VAR.Lbase ...
   +(1-PAR.beta) * ((1-PAR.epsilon)/PAR.epsilon) * VAR.Cbase ...
   / (1 - VAR.Sbase - VAR.Lbase) ;
VAR.ubase      = 100* VAR.Sbase / (VAR.Sbase+VAR.Lbase);
PAR.om_LLbase = (1 - VAR.Sbase - VAR.Lbase) / (VAR.Sbase+VAR.Lbase) ;
VAR.fbase      = PAR.delta_m * VAR.Lbase/VAR.Sbase;


% Solve the transition path of the model in continuous time using BVP4C
%
% Example: Convergence to the steady state following a five percent
% reduction in the initial capital stock caused by steel-eating mice


VAR.Keq0       = 0.95 * VAR.Kbase;
VAR.Leq0       = VAR.Lbase ;
VAR.Keq1       = VAR.Kbase ;
VAR.Leq1       = VAR.Lbase ;
VAR.Ceq1       = VAR.Cbase ;


[time,Cpath,Kpath,Lpath,etaLpath] = Function13_01_TP(PAR,EXO,VAR) ;

Ypath      = PAR.Z_y * Kpath.^(PAR.alpha) .* Lpath.^(1-PAR.alpha) ;
thetapath = ((1-PAR.beta) * PAR.Z_m * etaLpath / (PAR.beta * PAR.c) ...
           ).^(1/(1-PAR.phi)) ;
Spath      = 1 - Lpath - ((1-PAR.epsilon)/PAR.epsilon) * Cpath  ...
           ./ (EXO.s_U + PAR.Z_m * thetapath.^PAR.phi .* etaLpath) ;
Vpath      = thetapath .* Spath ;
Rpath      = PAR.alpha * (Ypath ./ Kpath) - PAR.delta_k ;
Ipath      = Ypath - Cpath - PAR.c * thetapath .* Spath - EXO.G ;
Wpath      = PAR.beta * (1-PAR.alpha) * Ypath ./Lpath ...
           + ((1-PAR.beta)*(1-PAR.epsilon)/PAR.epsilon) * Cpath ./ ...
           (1 - Spath - Lpath) ;
upath      = Spath ./ (Spath + Lpath);

% Plot some figures, for ezample capital and labour:

figure(1)
hold on
box off
xlim([0,120])
xlabel('post-shock time (quarters)')
ylabel('capital')
plot(time,Kpath,'k','LineWidth',3);
hold off
pause(1)

figure(2)
hold on
box off
xlim([0,120])
xlabel('post-shock time (quarters)')
ylabel('employment')
plot(time,Lpath,'k','LineWidth',3);
hold off
pause(1)
```

Table 13.8. Matlab function to compute the steady state

```
function Result = Function13_01_SS(x,PAR,EXO)

% This function computes the steady-state equilibrium
%
% x(1)      is C
% x(2)      is S
% x(3)      is L
% x(4)      is K
% x(5)      is eta_L
% x(6)      is mu_L
% x(7)      is theta
% x(8)      is r

% Parameter values:
alpha   = PAR.alpha;
epsilon = PAR.epsilon;
delta_k = PAR.delta_k;
delta_m = PAR.delta_m;
rho     = PAR.rho;
phi     = PAR.phi;
beta    = PAR.beta;
Z_y     = PAR.Z_y;
Z_m     = PAR.Z_m;
c       = PAR.c;

% Exogenous variables:
G       = EXO.G;
time    = EXO.time;
s_U     = EXO.s_U;


Result = zeros(size(x));
Result(1) = (x(8)- rho) * x(1) ;
Result(2) = Z_y * x(4)^(alpha) * x(3)^(1-alpha) - x(1) - G ...
    - c * x(7) * x(2) - delta_k * x(4) ;
Result(3) = Z_m * x(7)^phi * x(2) - delta_m * x(3) ;
Result(4) = (x(8) + delta_m) * x(5) + beta ...
    *(s_U + Z_m * x(7)^phi * x(5) - (1-alpha) * Z_y ...
    * x(4)^(alpha) * x(3)^(-alpha) ) ;
Result(5) = (x(8) + delta_m) * x(6) + (1-beta) ...
    *(s_U + Z_m * x(7)^phi * x(5) - (1-alpha) * Z_y ...
    * x(4)^(alpha) * x(3)^(-alpha) ) ;
Result(6) = x(6) - c * x(7)^(1-phi) / Z_m  ;
Result(7) = ((1-epsilon)/epsilon) * x(1)   ...
    -(s_U + Z_m * x(7)^phi * x(5)) * (1 - x(2) - x(3))  ;
Result(8) = x(8) - alpha * Z_y * x(4)^(alpha-1) * x(3)^(1-alpha) ...
    + delta_k ;

end
```

Table 13.9. Matlab function to compute the transition path

```
function [time,Cpath,Kpath,Lpath,etaLpath]=Function13_01_TP(PAR,EXO,VAR)

% Parameter values:
alpha     = PAR.alpha;
epsilon   = PAR.epsilon;
delta_k   = PAR.delta_k;
delta_m   = PAR.delta_m;
rho       = PAR.rho;
phi       = PAR.phi;
beta      = PAR.beta;
Z_y       = PAR.Z_y;
Z_m       = PAR.Z_m;
c         = PAR.c;


% Exogenous variables:
G         = EXO.G;
time      = EXO.time;
s_U       = EXO.s_U;

% Capital and employment
Keq0      = VAR.Keq0;
Keq1      = VAR.Keq1;
Leq0      = VAR.Leq0;
Leq1      = VAR.Lbase;
Ceq1      = VAR.Ceq1;


% Initial consumption and eta_L
Ceq0      = VAR.Cbase;
etaL0     = VAR.eta_Lbase;


solinit   = bvpinit(linspace(0,400),[Ceq0 Keq0 Leq0 etaL0]);
sol       = bvp4c(@capck,@bcfun,solinit);
y         = deval(sol,time);
Cpath     = y(1,:);
Kpath     = y(2,:);
Lpath     = y(3,:);
etaLpath  = y(4,:);
```

Table 13.9, continued

```
% Dynamics of C, K, L, and eta_L

function dydx = capck(x,y)

theta = ((1-beta) * Z_m * y(4) / (beta * c))^(1/(1-phi)) ;
S    = 1 - y(3) - ((1-epsilon)/epsilon) * y(1)   ...
    / (s_U + Z_m * theta^phi * y(4)) ;
dydx(1,1) = (alpha * Z_0 * y(2)^(alpha-1) * y(3)^(1-alpha) ...
    - delta_k - rho) * y(1) ;
dydx(2,1) = Z_0 * y(2)^(alpha) * y(3)^(1-alpha) - y(1) - G ...
    - c * theta * S - delta_k * y(2) ;
dydx(3,1) = Z_m * theta^phi * S - delta_m * y(3) ;
dydx(4,1) = (alpha * Z_0 * y(2)^(alpha-1) * y(3)^(1-alpha) - ...
    delta_k + delta_m) * y(4) + beta ...
    *(s_U + Z_m * theta^phi * y(4) ...
    - (1-alpha) * Z_0 * y(2)^(alpha) * y(3)^(-alpha) );

end


% Boundary conditions

function res = bcfun(ya,yb)
        res = [ya(2) - Keq0
               yb(2) - Keq1
               ya(3) - Leq0
               yb(1) - Ceq1];
end


end
```

Figure 13.11: Transitional dynamics in the RCK unemployment model

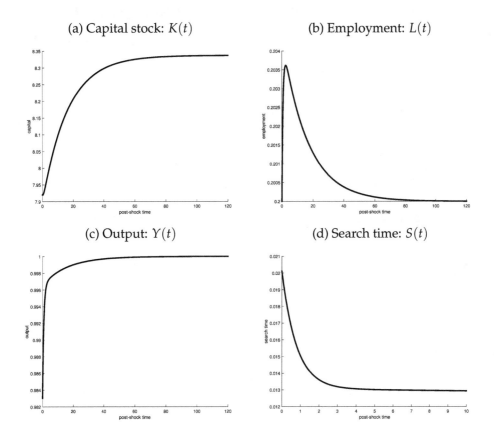

(a) Capital stock: $K(t)$

(b) Employment: $L(t)$

(c) Output: $Y(t)$

(d) Search time: $S(t)$

Figure 13.11, continued

(e) Unemployment rate: $u(t)$ (f) Consumption: $C(t)$

(g) Vacancies: $V(t)$ (h) Tightness: $\theta(t)$

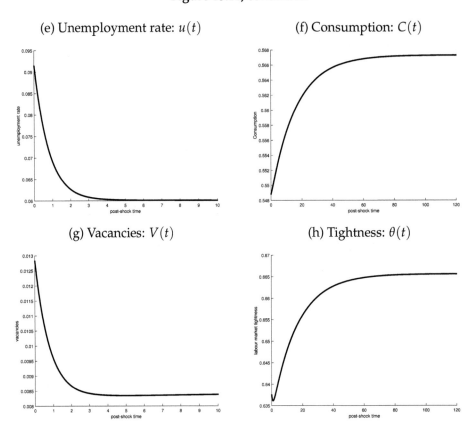

Abstracting from bonds there are two financial assets, namely nominal claims on the capital stock ($V^n(t) = P(t)K(t)$) giving an instantaneous nominal yield equal to $R(t)$ and nominal money balances ($M(t)$) providing a zero nominal yield. Nominal assets, $A^n(t) \equiv M(t) + V^n(t)$, evolve according to:

$$\dot{A}^n(t) = P(t)[R(t)K(t) + w(t)L(t) + Z(t) - C(t)], \qquad (13.203)$$

where $w(t)$ is the real wage rate and $Z(t)$ is real transfers from the government. Accumulation of real financial assets is thus given by:

$$\dot{A}(t) = [R(t) - \pi(t)]A(t) + w(t)L(t) + Z(t) - C(t) - R(t)m(t), \qquad (13.204)$$

where $A(t) \equiv m(t) + K(t)$ and $\pi(t) \equiv \dot{P}(t)/P(t)$ is the rate of price inflation. We observe that the real asset (capital) attracts a real rate of interest $r(t) \equiv R(t) - \pi(t)$. In contrast, because the nominal asset (money) does not pay any interest, $R(t)m(t)$ represents the opportunity cost of holding real money balances.

The household chooses paths for $A(t)$, $C(t)$, $L(t)$, and $m(t)$ in order to maximize lifetime utility (13.202) subject to asset accumulation equation (13.204), taking the initial stock of real assets, $A(0)$, and all goods and factor prices as well as transfers as given. The current-value Hamiltonian for this problem is:

$$\begin{aligned} \mathcal{H}_C \equiv &\, U(C(t), 1 - L(t), m(t)) \\ &+ \lambda(t)[r(t)A(t) + w(t)L(t) + Z(t) - C(t) - R(t)m(t)], \end{aligned}$$

where $C(t)$, $L(t)$, and $m(t)$ are control variables, $A(t)$ is the state variable, and $\lambda(t)$ is the co-state variable. In addition to the transversality condition, $\lim_{t \to \infty} \lambda(t)A(t)e^{-\rho t} = 0$, the first-order conditions are as stated in equations (T10.2) and (T10.4)–(T10.6) in Table 13.10.

Firm behaviour is standard. The objective function is given by:

$$V(0) = \int_0^\infty CF(t)e^{-\int_0^t r(s)ds}dt, \qquad (13.205)$$

where $CF(t)$ is the firm's real net cash flow:

$$CF(t) \equiv F(K(t), L(t)) - w(t)L(t) - I(t), \qquad (13.206)$$

$I(t) \equiv \dot{K}(t) + \delta K(t)$ is gross investment, and $F(K(t), L(t))$ is a neoclassical production (featuring constant returns to scale and positive but diminishing marginal products). In the absence of adjustment costs, value maximization of the firm gives rise to the first-order conditions for capital and labour as reported in equations (T10.7)–(T10.8) in Table 13.10. In addition it is easy to show that the maximized value of the firm equals the capital stock ($V(0) = K(0)$).

In the absence of bonds and taxes, the government budget identity is given in nominal terms by $\dot{M}(t) = P(t)[Z(t) + G_0]$ and in real terms by:

$$\dot{m}(t) + \pi(t)m(t) = Z(t) + G_0, \qquad (13.207)$$

where G_0 is government consumption. The lump-sum transfer ensures that the government budget identity holds at all times. The central bank follows a nominal money growth rule of the form $\dot{M}(t) = \mu M(t)$, where μ is the money growth rate (a policy parameter). In real terms we thus obtain equation (T10.3) in Table 13.10. Finally, in this closed economy the goods market equilibrium condition is given by $Y(t) = C(t) + I(t) + G_0$ which can be combined with the production function and the definition of gross investment to yield equation (T10.1) in Table 13.10.

13.7.2 Equilibrium

The full macroeconomic model is stated in Table 13.10. The endogenous variables are $K(t)$, $C(t)$, $L(t)$, $m(t)$, $\lambda(t)$, $w(t)$, $r(t)$, and $\pi(t)$. The exogenous government policy variables are G_0 and μ. The economic growth properties of the monetary RCK model are quite standard. Provided the model is stable it will converge to a steady state featuring a constant exogenous growth rate equal to zero (as the population is constant here).[27]

Table 13.10. The monetary RCK model

$$\dot{K}(t) = F(K(t), L(t)) - C(t) - \delta K(t) - G_0 \tag{T10.1}$$

$$\frac{\dot{\lambda}(t)}{\lambda(t)} = \rho - r(t) \tag{T10.2}$$

$$\dot{m}(t) = [\mu - \pi(t)] m(t) \tag{T10.3}$$

$$U_C(C(t), 1 - L(t), m(t)) = \lambda(t) \tag{T10.4}$$

$$U_{1-L}(C(t), 1 - L(t), m(t)) = \lambda(t) w(t) \tag{T10.5}$$

$$U_m(C(t), 1 - L(t), m(t)) = \lambda(t) [r(t) + \pi(t)] \tag{T10.6}$$

$$F_K(K(t), L(t)) = r(t) + \delta \tag{T10.7}$$

$$F_L(K(t), L(t)) = w(t) \tag{T10.8}$$

Definitions: $C(t)$ is private consumption, $L(t)$ is employment, $m(t)$ is real money balances, $K(t)$ is the capital stock, G_0 is public consumption, $w(t)$ is the real wage rate, $r(t)$ is the real interest rate, $\pi(t)$ is the rate of price inflation, $\lambda(t)$ is the marginal utility of wealth, ρ is the pure rate of time preference, δ is the depreciation rate of capital, and μ is the growth rate of the nominal money supply. The population is constant and normalized to unity.

13.7.3 Monetary neutrality?

What about the effects of money on this economy? Money is clearly neutral in the sense that a discrete and unanticipated increase in the stock of money has no effect on any real variables. Indeed, such a "helicopter drop" of money balances would leave all endogenous variables unchanged and would merely cause an equiproportional increase in the price level. The additional euro bills would be immediately collected by households who would instantaneously bid up the nominal price level (in their desire to maintain the pre-drop level of real money balances). To destroy neutrality of this kind some kind of nominal price- and/or wage stickiness is required (see Chapter 19).

An alternative neutrality concept asks a different question altogether. Does a change in the *money growth rate* μ affect real variables other than the level of real money balances? This is the concept of monetary superneutrality. The weak version of superneutrality holds if the variables in question are unaffected in the steady state.

[27]The model can be condensed into a fundamental system of differential equations in $K(t)$, $\lambda(t)$, and $m(t)$. This system contains one predetermined variable ($K(t)$) and two non-predetermined"jumping" variables ($\lambda(t)$, and $m(t)$). Conditional on the policy-induced path of the money supply, the price path is obtained by noting that $P(t) \equiv M(t)/m(t)$.

The strong version holds if μ has no influence on these variables during transition also—see Fischer (1979) and Asako (1983).

13.7.3.1   Long-run superneutrality

Denoting steady-state value with star superscripts and asserting stability, the long-run equilibrium is fully characterized by the following set of equations:

$$F_K\left(\kappa^*,1\right) = \rho + \delta, \tag{13.208}$$

$$L^* F(\kappa^*,1) = C^* + \delta\kappa^* L^* + G_0, \tag{13.209}$$

$$\frac{U_{1-L}\left(C^*,1-L^*,m^*\right)}{U_C\left(C^*,1-L^*,m^*\right)} = F_L\left(\kappa^*,1\right), \tag{13.210}$$

$$U_C\left(C^*,1-L^*,m^*\right) = \lambda^*, \tag{13.211}$$

$$U_m\left(C^*,1-L^*,m^*\right) = \lambda^*\left(\rho+\mu\right), \tag{13.212}$$

where $\kappa^* \equiv K^*/L^*$ is the steady-state capital intensity. In the steady-state equilibrium, $\dot{K}(t) = \dot{\lambda}(t) = \dot{m}(t) = 0$, the inflation rate equals $\pi^* = \mu$, and the real interest rate is $r^* = \rho$. It follows from (13.208) that the capital intensity does not depend on the money growth rate μ. This leaves a subsystem of four equations (viz. (13.209)–(13.212)) in four endogenous variables (L^*, C^*, λ^*, and m^*). Long-run superneutrality thus holds provided we can prove that:

$$\frac{dC^*}{d\mu} = \frac{dL^*}{d\mu} = \frac{d\lambda^*}{d\mu} = 0. \tag{13.213}$$

Without further restrictions on the properties of the felicity function we conclude that the subsystem is fully simultaneous ("everything depends on everything") and the results stated in (13.213) do not hold. The money growth rate affects steady-state consumption, employment, and the capital stock.

In a special case, with a felicity function that is *weakly separable* in, on the one hand, consumption and leisure and, on the other hand, money balances, there is long-run superneutrality in the monetary RCK model. Technically weak separability implies that $U_{Cm} = U_{1-L,m} = 0$ so that the subsystem for L^*, C^*, λ^*, and m^* simplifies to:

$$L^* F(\kappa^*,1) = C^* + \delta\kappa^* L^* + G_0, \tag{13.214}$$

$$\frac{U_{1-L}\left(C^*,1-L^*\right)}{U_C\left(C^*,1-L^*\right)} = F_L\left(\kappa^*,1\right), \tag{13.215}$$

$$U_C\left(C^*,1-L^*\right) = \lambda^*, \tag{13.216}$$

$$U_m\left(m^*\right) = \lambda^*\left(\rho+\mu\right). \tag{13.217}$$

The subsystem is recursive: (13.214)–(13.215) jointly determine C^* and L^* independently from μ. For these values of C^* and L^* equation (13.215) determines λ^* (also independently from μ). Finally, equation (13.217) determines m^* as a function of μ.

13.7.3.2   Transitional superneutrality

The monetary RCK model exhibits transitional superneutrality if we can prove that:

$$\frac{dC(t)}{d\mu} = \frac{dK(t)}{d\mu} = \frac{dL(t)}{d\mu} = \frac{d\lambda(t)}{d\mu} = 0 \qquad \text{(for all } t\text{)}. \tag{13.218}$$

It is clear from Table 13.10 that this property does not hold unless further restrictions are imposed on the model. Two special cases for which transitional superneutrality holds can be mentioned.

Case 1 (once again) assumes that preferences are weakly separable in $(C(t), 1 - L(t))$ and $m(t)$ so that the subsystem for $C(t)$, $K(t)$, $L(t)$, and $\lambda(t)$ can be written as:

$$\dot{K}(t) = F(K(t), L(t)) - C(t) - \delta K(t) - G_0, \qquad (13.219)$$

$$\frac{\dot{\lambda}(t)}{\lambda(t)} = \rho + \delta - F_K(K(t), L(t)), \qquad (13.220)$$

$$\lambda(t) = U_C(C(t), 1 - L(t)), \qquad (13.221)$$

$$\frac{U_{1-L}(C(t), 1 - L(t))}{U_C(C(t), 1 - L(t))} = F_L(K(t), L(t)). \qquad (13.222)$$

Since μ and $m(t)$ do not feature in these expressions transitional superneutrality is obvious. Note that for given paths of $\lambda(t)$ and $F_K(K(t), L(t))$, the subsystem for $m(t)$ and $\pi(t)$ consists of:

$$\dot{m}(t) = [\mu - \pi(t)] m(t), \qquad (13.223)$$
$$U_m(m(t)) = \lambda(t) [F_K(K(t), L(t)) - \delta + \pi(t)]. \qquad (13.224)$$

Case 2 was suggested by Asako (1983, p. 1594, fn. 3). Transitional superneutrality holds with non-separable preferences if (a) transfers are—in part—made proportional to real money holdings, $Z(t) = \mu m(t) + \bar{Z}(t)$, **and** (b) households understand this (and thus view μ as an "interest rate" on money balances). In this setting the household budget identity (13.204) changes to:

$$\dot{A}(t) = r(t)A(t) + w(t)L(t) + \bar{Z}(t) - C(t) - [R(t) - \mu] m(t),$$

and the first-order condition for $m(t)$ (given in (T10.6)) is changed to:

$$U_m(C(t), 1 - L(t), m(t)) = \lambda(t) [r(t) + \pi(t) - \mu] = \lambda(t) \left[r(t) - \frac{\dot{m}(t)}{m(t)} \right],$$

where we have used the money growth rule to get from the first to the second expression. Note that the government budget constraint (13.207) is changed to $\bar{Z}(t) = -G_0$.

With these modifications the macroeconomic system is completely independent from the monetary growth rate μ:

$$\dot{K}(t) = F(K(t), L(t)) - C(t) - \delta K(t) - G_0, \qquad (13.225)$$

$$\frac{\dot{\lambda}(t)}{\lambda(t)} = \rho + \delta - F_K(K(t), L(t)), \qquad (13.226)$$

$$\frac{\dot{m}(t)}{m(t)} = F_K(K(t), L(t)) - \delta - \frac{U_m(C(t), 1 - L(t), m(t))}{U_C(C(t), 1 - L(t), m(t))}, \qquad (13.227)$$

$$\lambda(t) = U_C(C(t), 1 - L(t), m(t)), \qquad (13.228)$$

$$\frac{U_{1-L}(C(t), 1 - L(t), m(t))}{U_C(C(t), 1 - L(t), m(t))} = F_L(K(t), L(t)). \qquad (13.229)$$

13.8 Punchlines

In this chapter we augment the Solow-Swan model by getting rid of the Keynesian savings function that many modern macroeconomists find unsatisfactory and ad hoc because it is not based on any microeconomic foundations. The savings decision is endogenized by introducing infinitely-lived dynamically optimizing consumers into the model. This intertemporal optimization approach was pioneered by Frank Ramsey more than eight decades ago and introduced into the macroeconomic growth literature by David Cass and Tjalling Koopmans in the mid 1960s. Optimizing consumers condition their current consumption not on current income, as the Keynesian approach implies, but on a measure of total wealth consisting of the sum of financial and human wealth. The latter is a forward-looking wealth component as it comprises the present value of current and future after-tax wage income, i.e. the value of the consumer's time endowment.

Interestingly, although it takes a radically different approach to the consumption-savings decision the growth properties of the Ramsey-Cass-Koopmans (RCK) model are very similar to those of the Solow-Swan model. Indeed, the long-run growth rate is exogenous and convergence is way too fast for realistic values of the structural parameters. There are some differences between the two models too. In the RCK model there is no oversaving and Ricardian equivalence holds. Furthermore the effects of fiscal policy are quite different as optimizing consumers react not only to current taxes but to the entire rationally expected profile of future taxes.

Because the RCK model has become such a pivotal model in modern macroeconomics we discuss several minor and major extensions to it. In the first extension we build and discuss an RCK model for the small open economy facing an exogenous world interest rate. This model is built on the knife-edge assumption that the impatience parameter of domestic consumers is exactly equal to the world interest rate. This introduces a hysteresis effect in consumption. Furthermore, to limit the degree of international mobility of physical capital, adjustment costs of investment must be postulated for the model to make any sense at all. It turns out that the severity of these adjustment costs (and not aspects of the consumer's willingness to substitute consumption across time) determines the speed of adjustment in the small open economy.

The next three extensions are again based on the closed economy assumption. Since their growth properties are the same as those of the standard RCK model the reader purely interested in economic growth may skip these extensions at first reading. In the first extension we show how the infinitely-lived agent chooses optimal time paths for both consumption and labour supply. To keep the model as simple as possible we assume that the three principal substitution elasticities are all equal to unity. The unit-elastic RCK model is only marginally more complicated than the basic RCK model but it gives some radically different answers to certain questions. For example, in the long run a lump-sum tax-financed increase in useless government consumption leads to an increase in the capital stock (crowding in), equilibrium employment, and output. Consumption is crowded out but by less than one-for-one. For realistic values of the structural parameters the output multiplier even exceeds unity, a result reminiscent of the Haavelmoo multiplier. For the same type of shock the basic RCK model predicts one-for-one crowding out of private by public consumption and no effects on the capital stock and output.

In the penultimate extension to the RCK model we introduce matching frictions in the labour market which give rise to a positive and endogenously determined unemployment rate (as in Chapter 8). Consumer-workers search for jobs and producers post vacancies. Once a match occurs the resulting surplus is divided by the two parties by means of generalized Nash bargaining. The unemployment rate that emerges in the unmanaged economy is typically inefficient because there exist two types of market failure, namely a search externality and a problem of rent-appropriability.

Only if the Hosios condition holds will the market economy produce the efficient unemployment rate.

The final extension deals briefly with the monetary version of the RCK model pioneered by Sidrauski (1967) and developed further by Fischer (1979) and many others. Real money balances are assumed to yield felicity to the household for reasons explained in Chapter 10. Money is neutral in the sense that a once-off change in the money supply merely affects the paths of the price level and the nominal wage rate. The price inflation rate and all real variables are completely unaffected by this monetary impulse. The alternative concept of monetary superneutrality relates to the real effects of the growth rate of the money supply. In the most general version of the model superneutrality fails. If, however, household preferences are weakly separable in consumption-leisure and money then transitional (strong) superneutrality holds. Whilst not very interesting from an economic growth perspective, the monetary RCK model nevertheless forms an important input for the dynamic stochastic general equilibrium (DSGE) approach that is discussed in detail in Chapter 19 below.

The chapter also demonstrates that the analytical analysis of continuous-time models is in some cases quite straightforward but in others completely intractable. In the latter case the use of numerical methods is unavoidable. For the unit-elastic RCK model, for example, analytical results are easy to obtain and a numerical quantification is only needed to get a feel for the magnitude of the different effects. In contrast, in the RCK model with search unemployment, the dimension of the dynamical system is simply too high and the numerical road is the only one available. We develop a simple Matlab program that computes the impulse-response functions for a shock in which part of the capital stock is destroyed. Despite the fact that both the capital stock and employment are sluggish variables, aggregate output rapidly converges to its pre-shock level. As far as the impulse-response functions for the main macroeconomic variables are concerned, matching frictions are not that important because adjustment in the labour market is fast (relative to capital stock adjustment) for realistic parameter values.

Further reading

Key contributions to the optimal growth literature are Ramsey (1928), Cass (1965), and Koopmans (1965, 1967). Spear and Young (2014) provide a fascinating account of the roles played by Cass and Koopmans in the development of what we now call the RCK model. They suggest that the name of Malinvaud should be added to the list in view of his crucial contributions.

For advanced textbook treatments of the optimal growth model, see Takayama (1974, pp. 444–485), Barro and Sala-i-Martin (1995), and Acemoglu (2009). For discussions of the RCK model with endogenous labour supply, see King et al. (1988a) and Baxter and King (1993). Heijdra et al. (2015) study a version of the RCK model with leisure and environmental quality as complements in the felicity function. For the RCK model with search unemployment, see Shi and Wen (1997, 1999), Merz (1995, 1997, 1999), and Andolfatto (1996).

For advanced mathematical discussions of boundary value problems, see Boyce and DiPrima (2005), and Grass et al. (2008).

Appendix: Phase diagram for the unit-elastic RCK model

In this appendix we derive the phase diagram for the unit-elastic RCK model. We drop the superfluous time index where no confusion can arise and hold government consumption constant, i.e. $G(t) \equiv G_0 > 0$.

Employment as a function of the state variables

By using labour demand (T4.4), labour supply (T4.6), and the production function (T4.7), we obtain an expression relating equilibrium employment to consumption and the capital stock ("LME" designates labour market equilibrium).

$$\text{LME:} \qquad \chi(L) \equiv (1-L)L^{-\alpha} = \frac{1-\varepsilon}{\varepsilon(1-\alpha)Z_0}CK^{-\alpha}, \qquad (A13.1)$$

with $\chi'(L) < 0$ and $\chi''(L) > 0$ in the *economically meaningful* interval $L \in [0,1]$. Hence, $\chi(L)$ is as drawn in Figure A13.1. Since $\chi(L)$ is invertible the implicit function $\Psi(C,K)$ mentioned in (13.92) in the text exists:

$$\text{LME:} \qquad L = \Psi(C,K), \qquad (A13.2)$$

with $\Psi_C(C,K) < 0$ and $\Psi_K(C,K) > 0$.

Capital stock equilibrium

Using (T4.7) in (T4.2) we observe that $\dot{K} = 0$ holds if and only if $\delta K + G_0 = F(K,L) - C$. By using (T4.4) and (T4.6), the capital stock equilibrium (CSE) locus ($\dot{K} = 0$) can be written as:

$$\delta K + G_0 = \left[1 - \frac{\varepsilon(1-\alpha)}{1-\varepsilon}\frac{1-L}{L}\right]F(K,L). \qquad (A13.3)$$

We are clearly only interested in positive values of output and capital so that the term in square brackets on the right-hand side of (A13.3) must be non-negative. This furnishes a lower bound for employment:

$$1 > L \geq L_{\text{MIN}} \equiv \frac{\varepsilon(1-\alpha)}{1-\alpha\varepsilon}. \qquad (A13.4)$$

By using L_{MIN} and (T4.7) we can rewrite (A13.3):

$$\text{CSE:} \qquad \phi(K,G_0) \equiv [\delta K + G_0]K^{-\alpha} = \Gamma_0[L - L_{\text{MIN}}]L^{-\alpha} \equiv \xi(L), \qquad (A13.5)$$

where $\Gamma_0 \equiv Z_0 \frac{1-\alpha\varepsilon}{1-\varepsilon}$ is a constant. The functions $\phi(K,G_0)$ and $\xi(L)$ are illustrated in Figure A13.2 using the structural parameters as given in (13.119). The $\phi(K,G_0)$ features a minimum at $K_{\text{crit}} = \alpha G_0/((1-\alpha)\delta)$. Associated with K_{crit} we find $L_{\text{crit}} > L_{\text{MIN}}$ such that $\phi(K_{\text{crit}},G_0) = \xi(L_{\text{crit}})$. For $L = 1$ we find $\xi(1) = Z_0$ so there exist a minimum and a maximum value of the capital stock, such that $\phi(K_{\text{MIN}},G_0) = \phi(K_{\text{MAX}},G_0) = Z_0$. We now have two zeros for the CSE line, i.e. both $(K,L) = (K_{\text{MIN}},1)$ and $(K,L) = (K_{\text{MAX}},1)$ solve equation (A13.3). By using (A13.1) we find the corresponding values for C, i.e. $(C,K,L) = (0,K_{\text{MIN}},1)$ and $(C,K,L) = (0,K_{\text{MAX}}, 1)$ are both zeros for the CSE line. See Figure A13.1. Note that in Figure 13.5 these

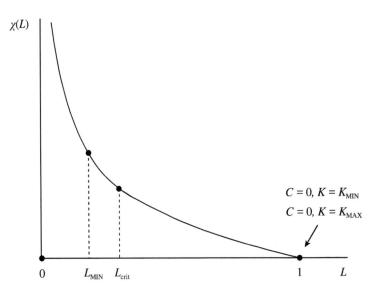

Figure A13.1: The $\chi(L)$ function characterizing labour market equilibrium

Figure A13.2: Constructing the capital isocline

(a) The $\phi(K, G)$ function   (b) The $\xi(L)$ function

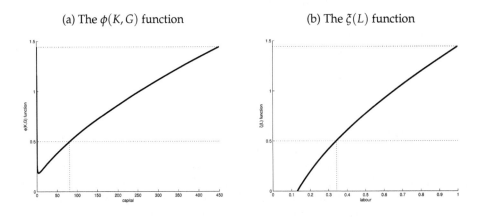

points have been drawn in (C, K) space. Graphically the K isocline can be constructed as follows. By considering all values $K \in [K_{MIN}, K_{MAX}]$ we find the associated $\phi(K, G_0)$ values in panel (a) of Figure A13.2 and the corresponding L values in panel (b) of that figure.

Equation (A13.5) represents an implicit function, $L = \gamma(K)$, over the interval $K \in [K_{MIN}, K_{MAX}]$ relating L and K. In order to compute the slope of this implicit function we totally differentiate (A13.5):

$$\gamma'(K) = \frac{\phi_K(K, G_0)}{\zeta_L(L)} = \frac{K^{-(1+\alpha)} \left[(1-\alpha)\delta K - \alpha G_0 \right]}{\Gamma_0 \gamma(K)^{-(1+\alpha)} \left[(1-\alpha)\gamma(K) + \alpha L_{MIN} \right]}. \tag{A13.6}$$

Since $L \geq L_{MIN} > 0$ the numerator is strictly positive. It follows that $\gamma'(K) < 0$ for $K_{MIN} \leq K < K_{crit}$, $\gamma'(K) = 0$ for $K = K_{crit}$, and $\gamma'(K) > 0$ for $K_{crit} < K < K_{MAX}$.

The slope of the CSE line is computed as follows. We note that for $K \in [K_{MIN}, K_{MAX}]$ the CSE line can be written as:

$$C = Z_0 K^\alpha \gamma(K)^{1-\alpha} - \delta K - G_0, \tag{A13.7}$$

where $L = \gamma(K)$ is the implicit function defined by (A13.5). By taking the derivative of (A13.7) we obtain in a few steps:

$$\left(\frac{dC}{dK} \right)_{\dot{K}=0} = Z_0 \left[\alpha + (1-\alpha)\eta_\gamma(K) \right] \left(\frac{\gamma(K)}{K} \right)^{1-\alpha} - \delta, \tag{A13.8}$$

where $\eta_\gamma(K)$ is the elasticity of the $\gamma(K)$ function:

$$\eta_\gamma(K) \equiv \frac{K\gamma'(K)}{\gamma(K)} = \left(\frac{\gamma(K)}{K} \right)^\alpha \frac{\left[(1-\alpha)\delta K - \alpha G_0 \right]}{\Gamma_0 \left[(1-\alpha)\gamma(K) + \alpha L_{MIN} \right]}. \tag{A13.9}$$

It follows from (A13.8) and (A13.9) that for $K = K_{MIN}$ we have:

$$\eta_\gamma(K_{MIN}) = \frac{1-\varepsilon}{1-\alpha} \left[-\alpha + \frac{\delta}{Z_0} K_{MIN}^{1-\alpha} \right], \tag{A13.10}$$

$$\left(\frac{dC}{dK} \right)_{\dot{K}=0} = \varepsilon \left[\alpha Z_0 K_{MIN}^{\alpha-1} - \delta \right] > 0. \tag{A13.11}$$

It follows that the CSE line is upward sloping at that point (see Figure 13.5).

The *golden-rule point* (for which consumption is at its maximum value) is obtained by setting $dC/dK = 0$ in (A13.8):

$$\left[1 - (1-\alpha) \left[1 - \eta_\gamma(K^{GR}) \right] \right] \frac{Y^{GR}}{K^{GR}} = \delta, \tag{A13.12}$$

where Y^{GR} is given by:

$$Y^{GR} \equiv Z_0 \left[K^{GR} \right]^\alpha \left[\gamma(K^{GR}) \right]^{(1-\alpha)}, \tag{A13.13}$$

and $\eta_\gamma(K)$ is given in (A13.9). The golden rule occurs at point A in Figure 13.5. For points to the right (left) of the golden-rule point, the CSE line is downward (upward) sloping.

The capital stock dynamics follows from (T4.2) in combination with (T4.7) and using the implicit function $L = \gamma(K)$:

$$\dot{K} = Z_0 K^\alpha \gamma(K)^{1-\alpha} - \delta K - C - G_0, \tag{A13.14}$$

from which we derive $\partial \dot{K}/\partial C < 0$. See the horizontal arrows in Figure 13.5.

Consumption equilibrium

The consumption equilibrium (CE) line describes combinations of C and K for which $\dot{C} = 0$. By using (T4.1) (in steady-state format), (T4.5), and (T4.7), we can write the CE line as follows:

$$\text{CE:} \qquad \kappa^* \equiv \left(\frac{K}{Y}\right)^* = \frac{1}{Z_0}(k^*)^{1-\alpha} = \frac{\alpha}{\rho+\delta}, \tag{A13.15}$$

where $k^* \equiv (K/L)^*$ is the steady-state capital intensity and $\kappa^* \equiv (K/Y)^*$ is the steady-state capital-output ratio for which the rate of interest equals the rate of time preference ($r^* = \rho$). It follows from (A13.15) that consumption equilibrium pins down a unique capital-labour ratio, $k^* \equiv (\alpha Z_0/(\rho+\delta))^{1/(1-\alpha)}$. Hence, along the CE locus $L = (1/k^*)K$. By substituting this result into (A13.1) we obtain the expression for the CE line in the (C,K) plane:

$$\begin{aligned}
C &= \frac{\varepsilon(1-\alpha)Z_0}{1-\varepsilon}(k^*)^\alpha [1-L] \\
&= \frac{\varepsilon(1-\alpha)Z_0}{1-\varepsilon}(k^*)^\alpha [1 - \frac{1}{k^*}K] \\
&= (\rho+\delta)\frac{\varepsilon(1-\alpha)}{\alpha(1-\varepsilon)}\left[\left(\frac{\alpha Z_0}{\rho+\delta}\right)^{1/(1-\alpha)} - K\right].
\end{aligned} \tag{A13.16}$$

It follows from (A13.16) that the CE line is linear in K and passes through the coordinates $(C,K) = (0,K_C)$ and $(C,K) = (C_C,0)$ in Figure 13.5:

$$K_C \equiv \left(\frac{\alpha Z_0}{\rho+\delta}\right)^{1/(1-\alpha)}, \qquad C_C \equiv (\rho+\delta)\frac{\varepsilon(1-\alpha)}{\alpha(1-\varepsilon)}K_C. \tag{A13.17}$$

Define $\gamma_0 \equiv G_0/K_{MAX}$. Provided $\gamma_0 < [\rho+\delta(1-\alpha)]/\alpha$, the CE line crosses the K-axis to the left of the K-intercept of the CSE line. To show this result, we note that K_C can be related to K_{MAX} (defined in the text below (A13.5)):

$$\left(\frac{K_C}{K_{MAX}}\right)^{1-\alpha} = \alpha\frac{\gamma_0+\delta}{\rho+\delta}. \tag{A13.18}$$

Provided the condition on γ_0 is satisfied we find that $K_C < K_{MAX}$.

The consumption dynamics can be deduced by noting that (T4.1) can be rewritten in the following fashion:

$$\frac{\dot{C}}{C} = \alpha Z_0 \left(\frac{\Psi(C,K)}{K}\right)^{1-\alpha} - (\rho+\delta). \tag{A13.19}$$

where $\Psi(C,K)$ is defined in (A13.2). It follows readily that:

$$\frac{\partial}{\partial C}\left(\frac{\dot{C}}{C}\right) = \alpha(1-\alpha)Z_0\left(\frac{\Psi(C,K)}{K}\right)^{-\alpha}\frac{\Psi_C(C,K)}{K} < 0, \tag{A13.20}$$

since $\Psi_C(C,K) < 0$. This has been indicated with vertical arrows in Figure 13.5.

Note that Figure 13.5 in the main text is a stylized representation of the phase diagram. Using the structural parameter values given in (13.119) we can compute the corresponding isoclines. See Figure A13.3. In that figure $K_{MIN} = 0.0027$, $K^{GR} = 70.479$, $C^{GR} = 0.8869$ and $K_{MAX} = 449.95$. The calibrated market equilibrium is thus very far from the golden-rule point.

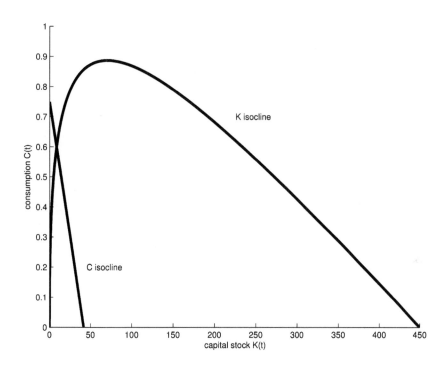

Figure A13.3: Phase diagram of the calibrated unit-elastic model

Chapter 14

Endogenous economic growth

The purpose of this chapter is to discuss the following issues:

1. Under which conditions can long-run endogenous growth emerge?

2. What do we mean by "capital fundamentalism" and what is the role of external effects in this context?

3. How does the purposeful accumulation of human and physical capital contribute to economic growth in the short run and in the long run?

4. What are the effects of research and development and endogenous technical change on economic growth?

14.1   Introduction

The previous two chapters have dealt with the main theories of exogenous economic growth in some detail. As the name already suggests, in exogenous growth models the long-run economic growth rate depends solely on exogenous features of the economy, such as the rates of growth in the population or in labour-augmenting technological change. The objective of this chapter is to move from exogenous to endogenous growth. A model is said to give rise to endogenous growth if it predicts a long-run growth rate which depends on additional features (such as tax or subsidy rates, public infrastructure spending, or private educational decisions) which may be affected by the government or the private sector. The literature on endogenous growth has taken flight during the last two decades and is consequently rather extensive. In this chapter we provide a selective overview of the three main approaches to endogenous growth. The first two approaches reserve a central role to capital accumulation (broadly interpreted) whilst the third approach places research and development (R&D hereafter) activities by firms at the core of the economic growth process. Throughout the chapter we investigate the effects of various government policy instruments on the rate of economic growth. These instruments form the litmus test for the "endogeneity" of the growth rate.

14.2   "Capital-fundamentalist" models

In the previous two chapters we worked exclusively with a production structure satisfying the Inada conditions (See (P2) and (P3) in Chapter 12 for the properties). Although these conditions facilitate the construction of the phase diagrams they are not innocuous (in an economic-theoretic sense) because they imply that economic growth eventually settles down to a particular, exogenously given constant, regardless of household savings plans. In terms of Figure 12.4, the steady-state capital intensity is constant and growth equals the sum of exogenously given population growth and technological progress (see equation (12.17)).

   As was already pointed out in Chapter 12, the Inada conditions have no obvious intrinsic appeal and are certainly difficult to test empirically since they deal with the curvature of the production function for very low and very high levels of capital. For this reason alone, an investigation of the consequences of abandoning (some of) the Inada conditions seems a worthwhile endeavour. As it turns out, this already takes us into the realm of endogenous growth models.

   The key aspect of traditional growth models which ensures that the *growth rate* is reduced as more and more capital is accumulated is the existence of diminishing returns to capital. Indeed, as $k(t)$ rises, the average product of capital falls:

$$\frac{d\left[f(k(t))/k(t)\right]}{dk(t)} = -\frac{\left[f(k(t)) - k(t)f'(k(t))\right]}{k(t)^2} < 0, \tag{14.1}$$

where the term in square brackets denotes the marginal product of labour, which is positive (see (13.24)). It must be stressed that the result stated in (14.1) is not sufficiently strong to ensure the existence of a constant steady-state capital intensity. Indeed, the existence of a steady-state capital intensity requires a much stronger result, namely the equality between $sy(t)/k(t)$ and $(\delta + n)$ in the Solow model. The Inada conditions ensure that this happens. Provided (P2) and (P3) hold, we can derive by l'Hôpital's rule that:

$$\lim_{k(t) \to 0} \frac{f(k(t))}{k(t)} = \lim_{k(t) \to 0} \frac{f'(k(t))}{1} = \infty, \tag{14.2}$$

$$\lim_{k(t) \to \infty} \frac{f(k(t))}{k(t)} = \lim_{k(t) \to \infty} \frac{f'(k(t))}{1} = 0. \tag{14.3}$$

Equations (14.2)–(14.3) show that $sy(t)/k(t)$ goes to zero (infinity) as the capital intensity becomes very large (small). This ensures the existence of a constant steady-state capital-labour ratio and thus a balanced growth path—see Figure 12.4.

14.2.1   Factor substitutability

As was already well known in the 1960s,[1] there are perfectly legitimate production functions which violate the results in (14.2)–(14.3). Consider, for example, the constant elasticity of substitution (CES) production function which takes the following form:

$$F(K(t), N(t)) \equiv Z \cdot \left[\alpha K(t)^{(\sigma_{KL}-1)/\sigma_{KL}} + (1-\alpha)L(t)^{(\sigma_{KL}-1)/\sigma_{KL}}\right]^{\sigma_{KL}/(\sigma_{KL}-1)} \Leftrightarrow$$

$$f(k(t)) \equiv Z \cdot \left[1 - \alpha + \alpha k(t)^{(\sigma_{KL}-1)/\sigma_{KL}}\right]^{\sigma_{KL}/(\sigma_{KL}-1)}, \tag{14.4}$$

---

[1] See e.g. Burmeister and Dobell (1970, pp. 30–36), and indeed Solow (1956).

where Z (> 0) is a constant, representing general productivity, and σ_{KL} (> 0) represents the substitution elasticity between capital and labour. The average product of capital equals:

$$\frac{f(k(t))}{k(t)} = Z \cdot \left[(1-\alpha)k(t)^{(1-\sigma_{KL})/\sigma_{KL}} + \alpha\right]^{\sigma_{KL}/(\sigma_{KL}-1)}. \tag{14.5}$$

It is clear from this expression that two separate cases must be distinguished, depending on the ease with which capital and labour can be substituted in production (relative to the Cobb-Douglas case).

14.2.1.1 Difficult substitution

If substitution is relatively difficult (in the sense that $0 < \sigma_{KL} < 1$) then the average product of capital satisfies:

$$\lim_{k(t) \to 0} \frac{f(k(t))}{k(t)} = Z \cdot \alpha^{\sigma_{KL}/(\sigma_{KL}-1)} > 0, \tag{14.6}$$

$$\lim_{k(t) \to \infty} \frac{f(k(t))}{k(t)} = \lim_{k(t) \to \infty} Z \cdot \left[(1-\alpha)k(t)^{(1-\sigma_{KL})/\sigma_{KL}}\right]^{-\sigma_{KL}/(1-\sigma_{KL})} = 0. \tag{14.7}$$

The average product of capital goes to zero as more and more capital is added but near the origin it attains a finite value, i.e. while (14.3) is still satisfied (14.2) no longer holds. This case has been illustrated in Figure 14.1 for two different savings rates, s_1 and s_2 (with $s_2 > s_1$). For the high savings rate, s_2, the model behaves like a standard Solow-Swan model despite failure of one of the Inada conditions. The intercept with the vertical axis is large enough, $s_2 Z\alpha^{\sigma_{KL}/(\sigma_{KL}-1)} > \delta + n$, thus ensuring that there exists a unique steady state at point E_0 to which convergence is guaranteed. This is not the case for all values of the savings rate. Indeed, for the low savings rate, s_1, the model does not have a steady-state equilibrium at all! The vertical intercept is too small to support net capital accumulation, i.e. $s_1 Z\alpha^{\sigma_{KL}/(\sigma_{KL}-1)} < \delta + n$. An economy characterized with such a low savings rate is unable to accumulate any capital nor would it be able to produce any output (as both product factors are essential in production). Alternatively, consider the case of an economy with a savings rate s_2 that is situated at point B in Figure 14.1. Now suppose that the savings rate drops from s_2 to s_1 so that the economy shifts from point B to point A in Figure 14.1. The new savings rate is too low to ever catch up with required investment and the capital intensity gradually falls to zero.

14.2.1.2 Easy substitution

Matters are radically different if capital can be relatively easily substituted for labour, i.e. if σ_{KL} exceeds unity. In that case, the average product of capital satisfies:

$$\lim_{k(t) \to 0} \frac{f(k(t))}{k(t)} = \lim_{k(t) \to 0} Z \cdot \left[(1-\alpha)k(t)^{-(\sigma_{KL}-1)/\sigma_{KL}}\right]^{\sigma_{KL}/(\sigma_{KL}-1)} = \infty, \tag{14.8}$$

$$\lim_{k(t) \to \infty} \frac{f(k(t))}{k(t)} = Z \cdot \alpha^{\sigma_{KL}/(\sigma_{KL}-1)} > 0. \tag{14.9}$$

The average product of capital starts out very high (as the Inada conditions require) but it approaches a positive limit as more and more capital is added, i.e. (14.3) no

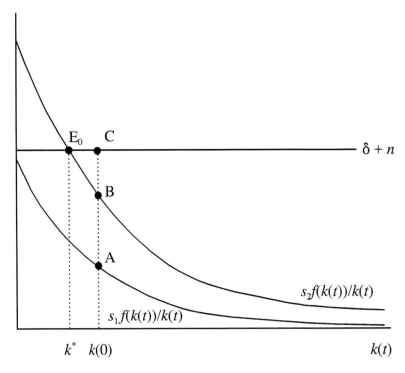

Figure 14.1: Difficult substitution between labour and capital

longer holds. This case has been illustrated in Figure 14.2, again for two values of the savings rate. For the relatively low savings rate, s_1, the model features a unique steady-state capital intensity so that growth is exogenous. In contrast, for the relatively high savings rate, s_2, per capita saving levels out at a rate which is higher than required investment, $s_2 Z \alpha^{\sigma_{KL}/(\sigma_{KL}-1)} > \delta + n$. Starting from an initial value $k(0)$, the capital intensity grows without bounds. Despite the fact that there are diminishing returns to capital, in the long run the production factors are very much alike and substitute well in production ($\sigma_{KL} > 1$). This means that if capital grows indefinitely the constant growth rate of labour never becomes a binding constraint. Relatively scarce labour is simply substituted for capital indefinitely. The long-run "endogenous" growth rate of the capital-labour ratio and the output-labour ratio is:

$$\gamma_k^* \equiv \left(\frac{\dot{k}(t)}{k(t)} \right)^* = s_2 Z \alpha^{\sigma_{KL}/(\sigma_{KL}-1)} - (\delta + n) > 0. \tag{14.10}$$

This growth rate is called "endogenous" because it is affected not only by exogenous parameters (α, δ, σ_{KL}, Z, and n) but also by the savings rate (s_2), a result which is in stark contrast to the predictions of the standard Solow-Swan model discussed in the previous chapter.

It is not difficult to understand that with this kind of labour-substituting endogenous growth, labour becomes less and less important so that, eventually, the income share of capital goes to unity and that of labour goes to zero. This is why this endogenous growth model is an example of the "capital-fundamentalist" class of models (King and Levine, 1994). With $\sigma_{KL} > 1$, labour is not essential in production, and in the limit it is possible to produce output with (almost) only capital. This prediction is, of course, at odds with the stylized facts (SF3) and (SF5), mentioned in Chapter 12.

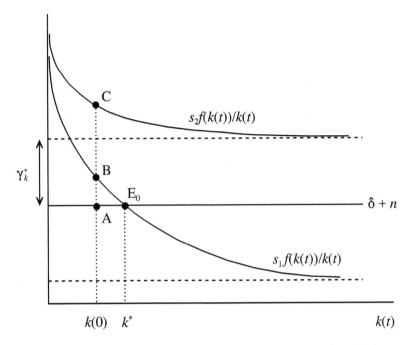

Figure 14.2: Easy substitution between labour and capital

14.2.2 *AK* models

An even more radical example of a capital-fundamentalist model is the so-called "*AK*" model proposed by Paul Romer (1986), Barro (1990), Rebelo (1991), and others. In its most rudimentary form, the *AK* model simply assumes constant returns to scale to (a broad measure of) capital. Hence, the macroeconomic production function is given by:

$$Y(t) = ZK(t), \tag{14.11}$$

where Z denotes general productivity. Equation (14.11) of course clearly violates the Inada conditions.[2] One might be tempted to dismiss this specification out of hand for being blatantly unrealistic, for example, because labour input does not feature in the specification. But such a conclusion would be unwarranted. There are at least two credible microeconomic explanations giving rise to a macroeconomic production function of the form as stated in (14.11). Both explanations acknowledge the existence of diminishing returns to capital at the microeconomic (firm) level, but invoke the existence of external effects which result in constant returns to capital at the macroeconomic level. In the remainder of this section, we assume that the aggregate population (and thus labour supply) is constant and equal to L_0.

14.2.2.1 External effects between firms

Our first *AK* model relies on external effects operating between private firms in the economy. There is a large number of identical, perfectly competitive firms. The

---

[2]The *AK* model derives its name from the usual convention in the literature to denote general productivity by A. Since A denotes financial assets throughout this book, we use the symbol Z for general productivity, but continue to use the generic name, *AK* model.

technology available to firm i is given by:

$$Y_i(t) = F(K_i(t), L_i(t)) \equiv Z(t)K_i(t)^\alpha L_i(t)^{1-\alpha}, \qquad 0 < \alpha < 1, \qquad (14.12)$$

where Y_i, K_i, and L_i, stand for, respectively, output, capital input, and labour input of firm i $(= 1, \cdots, N_0)$, and N_0 is the number of firms (which we assume to be fixed). Z represents the general level of factor productivity which is taken as given by the individual firm. The key thing to note is that the technology (i) features diminishing returns to scale to both factors of production, including capital, and (ii) features constant returns to scale to the production factors jointly. The discounted value of the firm's cash flows is given by:

$$V_i(0) = \int_0^\infty \Big[F(K_i(t), L_i(t)) - w(t)L_i(t) - [1 - s_I(t)] I_i(t) \Big] e^{-R(t)} dt, \qquad (14.13)$$

where $R(t) \equiv \int_0^t r(\tau) d\tau$ is the cumulative discount factor, and $s_I(t)$ is the investment subsidy. Mirroring the analysis in section 13.1.2, we assume that firm i chooses its output and investment plans in order to maximize $V_i(0)$, taking as given the production function (14.12) and the capital accumulation identity, $\dot{K}_i(t) = I_i(t) - \delta K_i(t)$. After some manipulation we find the following marginal productivity conditions for labour and capital:

$$w(t) = F_L(K_i(t), L_i(t)) = (1 - \alpha) Z(t) k_i(t)^\alpha, \qquad (14.14)$$

$$R^K(t) = F_K(K_i(t), L_i(t)) = \alpha Z(t) k_i(t)^{\alpha-1}, \qquad (14.15)$$

where $F_L(K_i(t), L_i(t)) \equiv \partial Y_i(t)/\partial L_i(t)$, $F_K(K_i(t), L_i(t)) \equiv \partial Y_i(t)/\partial K_i(t)$, $k_i(t) \equiv K_i(t)/L_i(t)$ is the capital intensity, and $R^K(t)$ is the rental rate of capital:

$$R^K(t) \equiv (r(t) + \delta) [1 - s_I(t)] + \dot{s}_I(t). \qquad (14.16)$$

The rental rate on each factor is the same for all firms, i.e. they all choose the same capital intensity and $k_i(t) = k(t)$ for all $i = 1, \cdots, N_0$. This is a very useful property of the model because it enables us to aggregate the microeconomic relations to the macroeconomic level (see below).

Following Saint-Paul (1992, p. 1247) and Paul Romer (1989), we assume that the inter-firm externality takes the following form:

$$Z(t) = z_0 K(t)^{1-\alpha}, \qquad (14.17)$$

where z_0 is a positive constant and $K(t) \equiv \sum_i K_i(t)$ is the aggregate capital stock. According to (14.17), total factor productivity depends positively on the aggregate capital stock, i.e. if an individual firm i raises its capital stock, then *all* firms in the economy benefit somewhat as a result because the general productivity indicator rises for all of them. Using (14.17), equations (14.12) and (14.14)–(14.15) can now be rewritten in aggregate terms:

$$Y(t) = Z_0 K(t), \qquad (14.18)$$

$$w(t)L_0 = (1 - \alpha) Y(t), \qquad (14.19)$$

$$R^K(t) = \alpha Z_0, \qquad (14.20)$$

where $Y(t) \equiv \sum_i Y_i(t)$ is aggregate output and $Z_0 \equiv z_0 L_0^{1-\alpha}$ is a positive constant.[3] As was asserted above, the national income share of labour is positive and there are constant returns to capital at the macroeconomic level. Technically the latter result follows from the fact that the exponents for K_i in (14.12) and for K in (14.17) *precisely* add up to unity.

To complete the model, we postulate the existence of an infinitely-lived representative household, which maximizes lifetime utility,

$$\Lambda(0) = \int_0^\infty \left[\frac{C(t)^{1-1/\sigma} - 1}{1 - 1/\sigma} \right] e^{-\rho t} dt, \tag{14.21}$$

subject to a standard asset accumulation identity:

$$\dot{A}(t) = r(t)A(t) + w(t)L_0 - [1 + t_C(t)]C(t) - T(t), \tag{14.22}$$

where σ is the constant intertemporal substitution elasticity (see Chapter 13), t_C is a consumption tax, $T(t)$ is a lump-sum tax (or transfer if it is negative), $A(t)$ represents financial assets, and $r(t)$ is the rate of interest. Using the analytical methods discussed in section 13.1.1, the representative household's Euler equation can be derived:

$$\frac{\dot{C}(t)}{C(t)} = \sigma \left[r(t) - \rho - \frac{\dot{t}_C(t)}{1 + t_C(t)} \right]. \tag{14.23}$$

The model deals with a closed economy and there is no government debt, so the only financial asset which can be accumulated consists of company shares. Since the replacement value of capital equals $1 - s_I$, we thus find that $A(t) = [1 - s_I(t)]K(t)$. The key equations of the basic *AK* growth model have been summarized in Table 14.1.

Table 14.1. An *AK* growth model with inter-firm external effects

$$\dot{C}(t) = \sigma \left[r(t) - \rho - \frac{\dot{t}_C(t)}{1 + t_C(t)} \right] C(t) \tag{T1.1}$$

$$\dot{K}(t) = [(1-g)Z_0 - \delta]K(t) - C(t) \tag{T1.2}$$

$$r(t) = \frac{\alpha Z_0}{1 - s_I(t)} - \frac{\dot{s}_I(t)}{1 - s_I(t)} - \delta \tag{T1.3}$$

Notes: $C(t)$ is consumption, $K(t)$ is the capital stock, $r(t)$ is the interest rate, $t_C(t)$ is the consumption tax, $s_I(t)$ is an investment subsidy, g is the national income share of government consumption, α is the efficiency parameter of capital in the microeconomic production function, ρ is the pure rate of time preference, σ is the intertemporal substitution elasticity, and δ is the depreciation rate of capital.

---

[3] All firms use the same capital intensity $(k_i(t) = k(t))$, so that $Y_i(t) = L_i(t)Z(t)k(t)^\alpha$ and $Y(t) \equiv \sum_i Y_i(t) = L_0 Z(t)k(t)^\alpha$, where $L_0 \equiv \sum_i L_i(t)$ is the labour market clearing condition. Since $K_i(t) = k(t)L_i(t)$, we also find that $Z(t) = z_0 L_0^{1-\alpha} k(t)^{1-\alpha}$ and $K(t) \equiv \sum_i K_i(t) = L_0 k(t)$ or $k(t) = K(t)/L_0$. Combining results we find (14.18). For the wage we find $w(t) = (1-\alpha)Z(t)k(t)^\alpha = (1-\alpha)z_0 L_0^{1-\alpha} k(t) = (1-\alpha)z_0 L_0^{-\alpha} K(t)$, which can be rewritten to get (14.19). Finally, for the rental rate on capital we find $R^K(t) = \alpha Z(t)k(t)^{\alpha-1} = \alpha z_0 L_0^{1-\alpha} = \alpha Z_0$.

Equation (T1.1) just restates (14.23). Equation (T1.2) is the dynamic equation for the capital stock. It is obtained by using the macroeconomic production function (14.18) and noting that $\dot{K}(t) = I(t) - \delta K(t)$ (aggregate capital accumulation identity), $Y(t) = C(t) + G(t) + I(t)$ (national income identity), and $G(t) = gY(t)$, where g is the policy controlled output share of public consumption. Finally, (T1.3) is obtained by substituting (14.20) into (14.16). It is now straightforward to demonstrate the existence of perpetual "endogenous" growth in the model. We focus attention on the case for which both the consumption tax and the investment subsidy are (expected by agents to be) constant over time, i.e. $\dot{t}_C(t) = \dot{s}_I(t) = 0.$[4] In that case the interest rate is constant and the growth rate of consumption is fully determined by (T1.1) and (T1.3):

$$\gamma^* = \frac{\dot{C}(t)}{C(t)} = \sigma \left[\frac{\alpha Z_0}{1 - s_I} - \delta - \rho \right] > 0, \tag{14.24}$$

where we assume that households are relatively patient, i.e. the interest rate exceeds the rate of pure time preference and the growth rate is positive.

With the aid of Figure 14.3 it is possible to prove that the household will maintain a constant ratio between consumption and the capital stock. By defining $\theta(t) \equiv C(t)/K(t)$ (so that $\frac{\dot{\theta}(t)}{\theta(t)} = \frac{\dot{C}(t)}{C(t)} - \frac{\dot{K}(t)}{K(t)}$) and using (T1.1)–(T1.3) we find:

$$\frac{\dot{\theta}(t)}{\theta(t)} = \theta(t) - \theta^*, \tag{14.25}$$

where θ^* is defined as:

$$\theta^* \equiv (1 - g) Z_0 - \delta + \sigma(\rho + \delta) - \frac{\alpha \sigma Z_0}{1 - s_I} > 0. \tag{14.26}$$

Equation (14.25) is an unstable differential equation for which the only economically feasible solution is the steady-state, i.e. $\theta(t) = \theta^*$. But if $\theta(t)$ is constant then it follows that the capital stock, investment, and output, must feature the same growth rate as consumption, i.e. $\gamma^* = \dot{Y}(t)/Y(t) = \dot{K}(t)/K(t) = \dot{I}(t)/I(t)$. The level of the different variables can be determined by using the initial condition regarding the capital stock and noting that $C(0) = \theta^* K(0)$. In the absence of shocks in the interval $(0, t)$, we thus find that $K(t) = K(0) e^{\gamma^* t}$, $C(t) = \theta^* K(t)$, $Y(t) = Z_0 K(t)$, etcetera.

The striking conclusion is that the *growth rate* of the economy can be permanently affected by the investment subsidy, a result which is impossible in the traditional exogenous growth models discussed in the previous chapter. Intuitively, a higher investment subsidy leads to a higher interest rate, a steeper intertemporal consumption profile, and thus a higher rate of capital accumulation in the economy. What happens to the consumption-capital ratio can be gleaned from Figure 14.3. The initial equilibrium is at point E_0, and it follows from (14.26) that $\partial \theta^* / \partial s_I = -\alpha \sigma Z_0 / (1 - s_I)^2 < 0$, i.e. the $\dot{\theta}(t)/\theta(t)$ line shifts to the left, from AA to BB, and the equilibrium consumption-capital ratio falls from θ_0^* to θ_1^*. The increase in the investment subsidy necessitates an increase in the lump-sum tax which makes households poorer.

It follows readily from equation (14.24) that taste parameters also exert a permanent effect on the growth rate of the economy. Hence, an economy populated by

---

[4]The key point to note in Table 14.1 is that the *level* of a time-invariant consumption tax does not influence the growth rate as such a tax does not distort the intertemporal consumption decision.

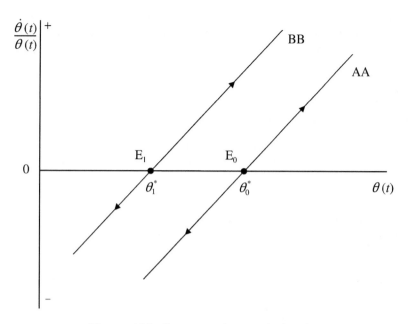

Figure 14.3: Consumption-capital ratio

patient households (a low ρ) or households with a high willingness to substitute consumption intertemporally (a high σ), tends to have a high rate of economic growth. Fiscal policy, consisting of an increase in the share of public consumption, does not affect growth and simply leads to a reduction in the consumption-capital ratio, i.e. $\partial\theta^*/\partial g = -Z_0 < 0$.

A number of further properties of the basic AK model must be pointed out. First, the model will exhibit transitional dynamics if the consumption tax or the investment subsidy are time-varying, since in that case the real interest rate will vary over time and the agents will react to this. Second, the equilibrium in the basic AK model is generally not Pareto-efficient in that the market outcome and the central planning solution do not coincide. Intuitively this result holds because, unlike the central planner, private firms fail to take into account the external effect of their own capital accumulation decision on the general level of productivity facing all firms in the economy. It is left as an exercise to the reader to determine how a subsidy scheme could be used to internalize the externality.

14.2.2.2 External effects between firms and the government

A second version of the AK model was first suggested by Barro (1990). In this model the stock of public infrastructure affects productivity of private firms and thus has an effect on the economic growth rate. In this subsection we discuss a generalized version of Barro's model. The technology facing individual firms is still as given in (14.12) above. The objective function of firm i is given by:

$$V_i(0) = \int_0^\infty \left[(1-t_Y)\, F(K_i(t), L_i(t)) - w(t)L_i(t) - I_i(t)\right] e^{-R(t)} dt, \qquad (14.27)$$

where t_Y is a time-invariant output tax ($0 < t_Y < 1$ and $\dot{t}_Y = 0$). The capital accumulation equation is given by $\dot{K}_i(t) = I_i(t) - \delta_k K_i(t)$, where δ_k stands for the depreciation rate of private capital. As in the previous subsection, firm i chooses paths for capital, employment, and investment which maximize $V_i(0)$ subject to the constraints. After some manipulation we find the following marginal productivity conditions for labour and capital:

$$w(t) = (1 - t_Y) F_L(K_i(t), L_i(t)) = (1 - \alpha)(1 - t_Y) Z(t)k_i(t)^\alpha, \tag{14.28}$$

$$r(t) + \delta_k = (1 - t_Y) F_K(K_i(t), L_i(t)) = \alpha (1 - t_Y) Z(t)k_i(t)^{\alpha-1}, \tag{14.29}$$

where $k_i(t) \equiv K_i(t)/L_i(t)$ is the capital intensity.

In the spirit of Barro (1990), we assume that (14.17) is replaced by:

$$Z(t) = z_0 K_G(t)^{1-\alpha}, \tag{14.30}$$

where $K_G(t)$ is the *stock* of public capital, consisting of infrastructural objects like roads, airports, bridges, and the like.[5] The key idea is that productive public spending affects all producers equally, these services are provided free of charge, and there is no congestion effect. By using (14.30) in (14.12) and (14.28)–(14.29) and aggregating over all firms we obtain the following macroeconomic relationships:

$$Y(t) = Z_0 K(t)^\alpha K_G(t)^{1-\alpha}, \tag{14.31}$$

$$w(t)L_0 = (1 - \alpha)(1 - t_Y) Y(t), \tag{14.32}$$

$$r(t) + \delta_k = \alpha (1 - t_Y) Z_0 \left(\frac{K_G(t)}{K(t)}\right)^{1-\alpha}. \tag{14.33}$$

Several things are worth noting. First, for a constant stock of public capital, the macroeconomic production function (14.31) features diminishing returns to the private capital stock, $K(t)$, because α is less than unity. However, if somehow the government succeeds in maintaining a constant ratio between the public and private stocks of capital, then the model ends up looking very much like a standard AK model and thus will display endogenous growth. Again, what makes this model tick is the fact that the exponents for K in (14.12) and for K_G in (14.30) precisely add up to unity. Second, holding constant the ratio between the two types of capital, the output tax affects the interest rate and thus the rate of growth in the economy.

It remains to flesh out the details of government behaviour. The accumulation identity for the public capital stock is given by:

$$\dot{K}_G(t) = I_G(t) - \delta_g K_G(t), \tag{14.34}$$

where $I_G(t)$ is the flow of public investment, the rate of which is set by the government, and δ_g is the depreciation rate of public capital. In the absence of lump-sum taxes, the static government budget constraint is:

$$t_Y Y(t) = I_G(t) + gY(t), \tag{14.35}$$

where g is the exogenously given national income share of (useless) government consumption ($g < t_Y$). For given values of t_Y and g, it follows from (14.35) that the rate of public investment is proportional to output, i.e. $I_G(t) = (t_Y - g) Y(t)$.

For convenience, the key equations of the model have been summarized in Table 14.2. Since nothing is changed on the household side of the model, the Euler

---

[5]Note that Barro (1990, p. S106), somewhat unrealistically, assumes that the *flow* of public services, rather than the public capital stock itself, enters the production function. We follow Arrow and Kurz (1970) by modelling infrastructure as a stock variable.

Table 14.2. An *AK* growth model with public capital

$$\frac{\dot{C}(t)}{C(t)} = \sigma \left[r(t) - \rho \right] \tag{T2.1}$$

$$\frac{\dot{K}(t)}{K(t)} = (1 - t_Y) Z_0 \left(\frac{K(t)}{K_G(t)} \right)^{\alpha-1} - \frac{C(t)}{K(t)} - \delta_k \tag{T2.2}$$

$$\frac{\dot{K}_G(t)}{K_G(t)} = (t_Y - g) Z_0 \left(\frac{K(t)}{K_G(t)} \right)^{\alpha} - \delta_g \tag{T2.3}$$

$$r(t) = \alpha (1 - t_Y) Z_0 \left(\frac{K(t)}{K_G(t)} \right)^{\alpha-1} - \delta_k \tag{T2.4}$$

Notes: $C(t)$ is consumption, $K(t)$ and $K_G(t)$ are, respectively, the private and public capital stock (featuring respective depreciation rates δ_K and δ_G), $r(t)$ is the interest rate, t_Y is the output tax, g is the national income share of (unproductive) government consumption ($t_Y > g$), α is the efficiency parameter of private capital in the microeconomic production function, ρ is the pure rate of time preference, and σ is the intertemporal substitution elasticity.

---

equation is still of the form given in (14.23) (with $\dot{t}_C(t) = 0$ imposed)—see (T2.1). Equation (T2.2) is obtained by using (14.31), (14.35), the aggregate private capital accumulation expression ($\dot{K}(t) = I(t) - \delta_k K(t)$), and the national income identity ($Y(t) = C(t) + I(t) + gY(t) + I_G(t)$). Ceteris paribus, the output tax exerts a negative influence of the growth rate of private capital in (T2.2). As can be seen from (14.35), the national income share of *total* government spending is equal to t_Y. It follows that only a fraction of total output, $(1 - t_Y) Y$, is available for private consumption and capital accumulation. Next, equation (T2.3) is obtained by using (14.31) and (14.34)–(14.35). The "productive" part of government revenue, $(t_Y - g) Y$, is dedicated to public investment which boosts the growth rate of public capital stock. Finally, equation (T2.4) just restates (14.33).

It can be shown that, given initial conditions for the two capital stocks ($K(0)$ and $K_G(0)$), the model is stable and converges to a balanced growth path. Along this balanced growth path, the interest rate is constant and all macro variables grow at the same endogenous growth rate, γ^*. In the remainder of this subsection we first compute and discuss the asymptotic growth rate. In closing we briefly characterize the nontrivial transitional dynamics of the model.

14.2.2.2.1 Steady-state growth   By definition of the balanced growth path, we find that $[\dot{C}(t)/C(t)]^* = [\dot{K}(t)/K(t)]^* = [\dot{K}_G(t)/K_G(t)]^* = \gamma^*$, and $r^*(t) = r^*$. Using these results in Table 14.2 we find:

$$\gamma^* = \sigma \left[r^* - \rho \right], \tag{14.36}$$

$$\gamma^* = (1 - t_Y) Z_0 (\kappa^*)^{\alpha-1} - \theta^* - \delta_k, \tag{14.37}$$

$$\gamma^* = (t_Y - g) Z_0 (\kappa^*)^{\alpha} - \delta_g, \tag{14.38}$$

$$r^* = \alpha (1 - t_Y) Z_0 (\kappa^*)^{\alpha-1} - \delta_k, \tag{14.39}$$

where $\theta^* \equiv [C(t)/K(t)]^*$ is the private consumption-capital ratio, and $\kappa^* \equiv [K(t)/K_G(t)]^*$ is the ratio between the private and public capital stocks, both measured along the balanced growth path. The model can be analysed graphically with the aid of Figure 14.4. In the top panel, the EE line depicts the steady-state Euler equation (14.36). The GCA line stands for the government capital accumulation line. It is obtained by solving (14.39) for κ^* and substituting the result into (14.38):

$$\gamma^* = (\alpha^\alpha Z_0)^{1/(1-\alpha)} (t_Y - g) \left(\frac{1 - t_Y}{r^* + \delta_k} \right)^{\alpha/(1-\alpha)} - \delta_g, \qquad \text{GCA.} \qquad (14.40)$$

The GCA line is a convex, downward sloping function, relating the steady-state growth rate to the steady-state interest rate and the exogenous policy parameters, t_Y and g. Finally, in the bottom panel of Figure 14.4, the PCA locus represents the private capital accumulation line. It is obtained by using (14.36) and (14.39) in (14.37) and solving for θ^*:

$$\theta^* = \sigma\rho + \frac{(1 - \alpha)\delta_k}{\alpha} + \frac{(1 - \alpha\sigma)r^*}{\alpha}, \qquad \text{PCA.} \qquad (14.41)$$

The PCA line has been drawn under the highly plausible assumption that $\alpha\sigma < 1$.

The initial steady state is at point E_0, where the GCA_0 line intersects the EE line in the top panel. The initial growth rate is γ_0^* whilst the initial interest rate is r_0^*. As is evident from the diagram, the interest rate exceeds the pure rate of time preference ($r_0^* > \rho$) so that the growth rate is strictly positive ($\gamma_0^* > 0$). The steady-state private consumption-capital ratio is θ_0^* as is depicted in the bottom panel. The striking conclusion is that endogenous growth emerges despite the existence of diminishing returns to private capital! Intuitively, by continually increasing the stock of public capital, the government manages to negate the effect of diminishing returns to private capital that would otherwise result from continuing capital accumulation. It is able to do so without ever-increasing (and thus ultimately infeasible) tax rates because the tax base (gross output) grows at the same rate as the private capital stock does.

Now consider the growth effects of various government policies. First, a *decrease* in the share of unproductive government spending, g, rotates the GCA locus (14.40) in a clockwise fashion, say from GCA_0 to GCA_1 in Figure 14.4. The new steady-state equilibrium shifts to E_1, and the interest rate, the growth rate, and the private consumption-capital ratio all rise, i.e. $d\gamma^*/dg < 0$, $dr^*/dg < 0$, and $d\theta^*/dg < 0$. Intuitively, the shock redirects government revenues from unproductive to productive purposes and boosts the rate of growth in the economy.

The effects of an increase in the output tax are more complex because there are offsetting mechanisms at work–see equation (14.40). On the one hand, an increase in t_Y boosts government revenue, increases government capital accumulation, and thus increases growth (upward shift in the GCA curve). On the other hand, however, an increase in t_Y distorts the economic decisions of private agents which leads to a reduction of the tax base (output) and a decrease in public capital accumulation and growth (downward shift in the GCA curve). By differentiating (14.40) with respect to the output tax we find the net effect on the GCA curve:[i]

$$\left(\frac{t_Y - g}{\gamma^* + \delta_g} \cdot \frac{\partial \gamma^*}{\partial t_Y} \right)_{GCA} = 1 - \frac{\alpha}{1 - \alpha} \frac{t_Y - g}{1 - t_Y} \gtrless 0 \text{ for } t_Y \lessgtr 1 - \alpha(1 - g). \qquad (14.42)$$

For low initial tax rates, the revenue effect dominates the tax-base effect and the growth rate increases if the output tax is raised, and vice versa for high tax rates. The growth-maximizing tax rate can be computed by maximizing γ^* with respect to

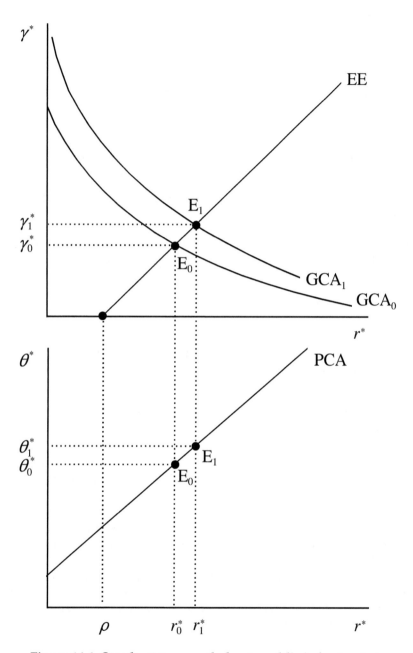

Figure 14.4: Steady-state growth due to public infrastructure

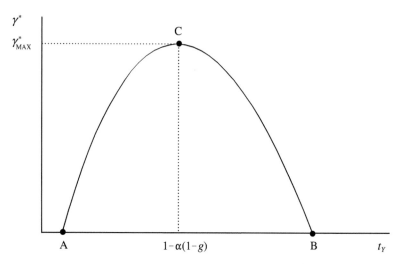

Figure 14.5: Productive government spending and growth

t_Y. It follows readily from (14.36) and (14.42) that $d\gamma^*/dt_Y = (\partial\gamma^*/\partial t_Y)_{GCA} = 0$ for $t_Y = 1 - \alpha(1 - g)$. Indeed, by solving (14.36) for r^* and substituting the result into (14.40) we obtain the implicit equation for γ^*:

$$\gamma^* + \delta_g = (\alpha^\alpha Z_0)^{1/(1-\alpha)} (t_Y - g) \left(\frac{\sigma(1 - t_Y)}{\gamma^* + \sigma(\rho + \delta_k)} \right)^{\alpha/(1-\alpha)}. \tag{14.43}$$

This expression has been plotted in Figure 14.5. Differentiation with respect to γ^* and t_Y yields the slope of the growth line:

$$\frac{t_Y - g}{\gamma^* + \delta_g} \cdot \frac{d\gamma^*}{dt_Y} = \frac{1 - \frac{\alpha}{1-\alpha} \frac{t_Y - g}{1 - t_Y}}{1 + \frac{\alpha}{1-\alpha} \frac{\gamma^* + \delta_g}{\gamma^* + \sigma(\rho + \delta_k)}}. \tag{14.44}$$

In Figure 14.5, the maximum growth rate is at point C, whereas points A and B represent the two values for t_Y for which the growth rate equals zero.

14.2.2.2.2 Transitional dynamics In contrast to our first *AK* model, the public infrastructure model gives rise to non-trivial transitional dynamics because we model public infrastructure as a stock variable and because the rate of public investment is bounded by the available tax revenue (see (14.35) above). As is clear from Table 14.2, the model is fully characterized by two fractions only, namely the private consumption-capital ratio, $\theta(t) \equiv C(t)/K(t)$, and the ratio between the private and public capital stock, $\kappa(t) \equiv K(t)/K_G(t)$. In order to study the dynamic properties of the model, we loglinearize it around the steady-state point (θ^*, κ^*) to obtain:

$$\begin{bmatrix} \dfrac{d\ln\theta(t)}{dt} \\[2ex] \dfrac{d\ln\kappa(t)}{dt} \end{bmatrix} = \Delta \cdot \begin{bmatrix} \ln\theta(t) - \ln\theta^* \\[1ex] \ln\kappa(t) - \ln\kappa^* \end{bmatrix}, \tag{14.45}$$

where Δ is the Jacobian matrix:

$$\Delta \equiv \begin{bmatrix} \theta^* & \dfrac{(1-\alpha)\,(1-\alpha\sigma)\,(r^*+\delta_k)}{\alpha} \\[2ex] -\theta^* & -\dfrac{(1-\alpha)\,(r^*+\delta_k)+\alpha^2\,(\gamma^*+\delta_g)}{\alpha} \end{bmatrix}. \tag{14.46}$$

The determinant of Δ is given by:

$$|\Delta| \equiv -\theta^*\left[\,(1-\alpha)\,\sigma\,(r^*+\delta_k)+\alpha\,(\gamma^*+\delta_g)\,\right] < 0, \tag{14.47}$$

so it follows that the product of the characteristic roots of Δ is negative, i.e. there is one negative (stable root), $-\lambda_1 < 0$, and one positive (unstable) root, $\lambda_2 > 0$, and the model is saddle-path stable. Recall that both capital stocks are predetermined (non-jumping) variables whilst private consumption is a jumping variable. It follows that $\theta(t)$ is a jumping variable (because $C(t)$ is) whilst $\kappa(t)$ is predetermined (because $K(t)$ and $K_G(t)$ are). Given initial values $K(0)$ and $K_G(0)$ (and thus for $\kappa(0) \equiv K(0)/K_G(0)$), the model converges along the saddle path toward the steady-state equilibrium. The transition speed is equal to the absolute value of the stable root, λ_1.

Intermezzo 14.1

Loglinearization of an endogenous growth model. Strangely enough, loglinearization of a non-linear *dynamic* model often confuses students. For that reason we show in detail how we loglinearize the model in Table 14.2. Campbell (1994) and Uhlig (1999) provide further examples. First we note that, by deducting (T2.2) from (T2.1) and (T2.3) from (T2.2), we can rewrite the model as:

$$\frac{d\ln\theta(t)}{dt} = \sigma\,[r(t)-\rho] - (1-t_Y)\,Z_0\kappa(t)^{\alpha-1} + \theta(t) + \delta_k, \tag{a}$$

$$\begin{aligned}\frac{d\ln\kappa(t)}{dt} &= (1-t_Y)\,Z_0\kappa(t)^{\alpha-1} - (t_Y-g)\,Z_0\kappa(t)^{\alpha} \\ &\quad - \theta(t) + \delta_g - \delta_k,\end{aligned} \tag{b}$$

$$r(t) = \alpha\,(1-t_Y)\,Z_0\kappa(t)^{\alpha-1} - \delta_k, \tag{c}$$

where we have used the fact that $d\ln x(t)/dt \equiv \dot{x}(t)/x(t)$. Next, we define the auxiliary variable $\tilde{x}(t)$:

$$a\tilde{x}(t) \equiv \ln\left(\frac{x(t)}{x^*}\right)^a \quad \Leftrightarrow \quad \left(\frac{x(t)}{x^*}\right)^a \equiv e^{a\tilde{x}(t)}, \tag{d}$$

where x^* is the steady-state value for $x(t)$ and a is some scalar. Provided $x(t)$ is near its steady-state value ($x(t)/x^* \approx 1$ and $\tilde{x}(t) \approx 0$) we have $e^{a\tilde{x}(t)} \approx 1 + a\tilde{x}(t)$ so that it follows from (d) that:

$$\left(\frac{x(t)}{x^*}\right)^a \approx 1 + a\tilde{x}(t) \quad \Leftrightarrow \quad a\tilde{x}(t) = \left(\frac{x(t)}{x^*}\right)^a - 1. \tag{e}$$

We now apply these intermediate results to the model. We start with equation (a). In the steady-state, $d\ln\theta(t)/dt = 0$ so:

$$0 = \sigma\,[r^*-\rho] - (1-t_Y)\,Z_0\,(\kappa^*)^{\alpha-1} + \theta^* + \delta_k. \tag{f}$$

Deducting (f) from (a) yields:

$$\frac{d\ln\theta(t)}{dt} = \sigma\left[r(t) - r^*\right] - (1 - t_Y)\, Z_0\left[\kappa(t)^{\alpha-1} - (\kappa^*)^{\alpha-1}\right]$$
$$+ \theta(t) - \theta^*$$
$$= \sigma r^*\left[\frac{r(t)}{r^*} - 1\right] - (1 - t_Y)\, Z_0\,(\kappa^*)^{\alpha-1}\left[\left(\frac{\kappa(t)}{\kappa^*}\right)^{\alpha-1} - 1\right]$$
$$+ \theta^*\left[\frac{\theta(t)}{\theta^*} - 1\right]$$
$$= \sigma r^*\tilde{r}(t) - (\alpha - 1)\left(\frac{r^* + \delta_k}{\alpha}\right)\tilde{\kappa}(t) + \theta^*\tilde{\theta}(t), \tag{g}$$

where we have used (e) (twice for $a = 1$ and once for $a = \alpha - 1$) and noted that it follows from (c) that $(1 - t_Y)\, Z_0\,(\kappa^*)^{\alpha-1} = (r^* + \delta_k)/\alpha$ in the final step. But, in view of the definition of $\tilde{x}(t)$, we can write (g) as:

$$\frac{d\ln\theta(t)}{dt} = \sigma r^*\ln\left(\frac{r(t)}{r^*}\right) + (1 - \alpha)\frac{r^* + \delta_k}{\alpha}\ln\left(\frac{\kappa(t)}{\kappa^*}\right)$$
$$+ \theta^*\ln\left(\frac{\theta(t)}{\theta^*}\right). \tag{h}$$

Following the same approach for equation (b) we find:

$$\frac{d\ln\kappa(t)}{dt} = (1 - t_Y)\, Z_0\,(\kappa^*)^{\alpha-1}\left[\left(\frac{\kappa(t)}{\kappa^*}\right)^{\alpha-1} - 1\right]$$
$$- (t_Y - g)\, Z_0\,(\kappa^*)^{\alpha}\left[\left(\frac{\kappa(t)}{\kappa^*}\right)^{\alpha} - 1\right] - \theta^*\left[\frac{\theta(t)}{\theta^*} - 1\right]$$
$$= -\left[(1 - \alpha)\frac{r^* + \delta_k}{\alpha} + \alpha\left(\gamma^* + \delta_g\right)\right]\ln\left(\frac{\kappa(t)}{\kappa^*}\right)$$
$$- \theta^*\ln\left(\frac{\theta(t)}{\theta^*}\right), \tag{i}$$

where we have used the steady-state relationships $(1 - t_Y)\, Z_0\,(\kappa^*)^{\alpha-1} = (r^* + \delta_k)/\alpha$ and $(t_Y - g)\, Z_0\kappa^* = \gamma^* + \delta_g$ to simplify the expression in the final step. Equation (i) is the second row in (14.45).

Finally, for equation (c) we find:

$$r^*\left[\frac{r(t)}{r^*} - 1\right] = \alpha\,(1 - t_Y)\, Z_0\,(\kappa^*)^{\alpha-1}\left[\left(\frac{\kappa(t)}{\kappa^*}\right)^{\alpha-1} - 1\right]$$
$$r^*\ln\left(\frac{r(t)}{r^*}\right) = (r^* + \delta_k)(\alpha - 1)\ln\left(\frac{\kappa(t)}{\kappa^*}\right). \tag{j}$$

By substituting (j) into (g) we obtain the first row in (14.45).

****

14.3 Human capital formation

In a path-breaking early contribution to the literature, Uzawa (1965) argued that (labour-augmenting) technological progress should not be seen as some kind of "manna from heaven" but instead should be regarded as the outcome of the intentional actions by economic agents employing scarce resources in order to advance the state of technological knowledge. Uzawa (1965) formalized his notions by assuming that all technological knowledge is labour augmenting, i.e. in terms of the aggregate production function (12.11) he sets $Z_K(t) = 1$ for all t and proposes a theory which endogenizes $Z_L(t)$ (and thus its growth rate, n_Z). Uzawa postulates the existence of a broadly defined educational sector which uses labour, $L_E(t)$, in order to augment the state of knowledge in the economy according to the following knowledge production function:

$$\frac{\dot{Z}_L(t)}{Z_L(t)} = \Psi\left(\frac{L_E(t)}{L(t)}\right), \tag{14.48}$$

where $L(t) = L_E(t) + L_P(t)$ is the total labour force, $L_P(t)$ is labour employed in the production of goods, and $\Psi(x)$ satisfies $\Psi'(x) > 0 > \Psi''(x)$ for $0 < x < 1$. The key thing to note in (14.48) is that $\dot{Z}_L(t)$ is linear in $Z_L(t)$, i.e. in the production of new knowledge there are constant returns to existing knowledge. It is clear that there are now two stocks that can be accumulated in this economy, namely the stock of physical capital goods ($K(t)$) and the stock of knowledge ($Z_L(t)$). Uzawa shows how a benevolent social planner would optimally choose these stocks for the special case of a linear felicity function (incorporating an infinite intertemporal substitution elasticity), $U(c(t)) = c(t)$. One of the trade-offs which the planner faces is of course the optimal assignment of labour to the production and educational sectors. By raising the proportion of workers in the educational sector the growth of knowledge will increase but production of goods (and thus the rate of investment) will decrease.

Uzawa's ideas lay dormant for two decades until they were taken up again and extended by Paul Romer (1986), Lucas (1988, 1990b), and Rebelo (1991). The aim of this section is to discuss (a simplified version of) the Lucas model in order to demonstrate that human capital accumulation can serve as the engine of (endogenous) growth.

Lucas (1988) modifies and extends Uzawa's analysis in various directions. First, whereas Uzawa interprets $Z_L(t)$ very broadly as consisting of activities like education, health, construction and maintenance of public goods (1965, p. 18), Lucas adopts a more specific interpretation by interpreting $Z_L(t)$ as human capital. Second, Lucas cites Rosen (1976) whose findings suggests that the empirical evidence on individual earnings is consistent with a knowledge production function that is linear in the stock of knowledge (as in (14.48)).[6] In addition, Lucas assumes that the marginal productivity of labour in the human capital production function is constant, i.e. $\Psi(x) = Z_E x$, where $Z_E > 0$ is a constant index of educational productivity. On the basis of the above considerations, Lucas adopts a specification for the human

---

[6]Despite the fact that in reality people tend to accumulate human capital mainly early on in life, this does not necessarily imply that there are diminishing returns to knowledge accumulation, but it may rather be due to the fact that agents' lives are finite (Lucas, 1988, p. 19). It simply makes no sense for an octogenarian to go to school because the time during which he can cash in on his additional skills is too short for the investment to be worthwhile. Linearity can still hold at the dynastic level provided members of the dynastic family are linked also in terms of their human capital. In Chapter 16 below we discuss a model in which (i) finite-lived agents enjoy full-time education at the start of life, and (ii) there are intergenerational external effects in human capital.

capital accumulation function which we generalize slightly to allow for depreciation:

$$\frac{\dot{H}(t)}{H(t)} = Z_E \cdot \frac{L_E(t)}{L(t)} - \delta_h, \tag{14.49}$$

where δ_h is the depreciation rate of human capital ($\delta_h > 0$). The third modification that Lucas makes is to assume a curved (rather than linear) felicity function. The lifetime utility function for the representative infinitely lived household is thus given by (14.21). The remainder of the model is fairly standard. To keep things simple we abstract from population growth, i.e. $L(t) = L_0$ (a constant). This means that the time constraint can be written as:

$$L_E(t) + L_P(t) = L_0. \tag{14.50}$$

Following Lucas we assume that the aggregate production function for goods is of the Cobb-Douglas form:

$$Y(t) = F(K(t), N_P(t)) = Z_Y N_P(t)^{1-\alpha} K(t)^\alpha, \tag{14.51}$$

where Z_Y is an index of general productivity and $N_P(t)$ is *effective* labour used in goods production, i.e. skill-weighted man-hours:[7]

$$N_P(t) \equiv H(t) L_P(t). \tag{14.52}$$

We are now in a position to solve the model and to demonstrate that it contains a mechanism for endogenous growth. The institutional setting is as follows. Perfectly competitive firms hire capital and labour from the household sector. Households receive rental payments on the two production factors and decide on the optimal accumulation of physical and human capital and the optimal time profile for consumption.

Since technology is linearly homogeneous and competition is perfect it is appropriate to postulate the existence of a representative firm. This firm hires units of labour and capital from the household in order to maximize profit, $\Pi(t) \equiv Y(t) - w(t)L_P(t) - R^K(t)K(t)$, subject to the technology (14.51) and the definition of effective labour (14.52). This yields the familiar expressions for the rental rate on capital $R^K(t)$ and the wage rate $w(t)$:

$$R^K(t) = F_K(K(t), N_P(t)) = \alpha Z_Y k(t)^{\alpha-1}, \tag{14.53}$$

$$w(t) = H(t) F_N(K(t), N_P(t)) = (1-\alpha) Z_Y H(t) k(t)^\alpha, \tag{14.54}$$

where $k(t) \equiv K(t)/N_P(t)$ is the macroeconomic capital intensity of production.[8] Equation (14.53) is the standard condition equating the marginal product of capital to the rental rate. The key thing to note about (14.54) is that, for a given capital intensity, $k(t)$, the wage rate increases as the skill level increases. This gives the household a clear incentive to accumulate human capital. Another important thing to note is that, from the viewpoint of the individual agent described here, the marginal product of effective labour (F_N) is taken as given as it depends on the *aggregate* ratio between physical capital and effective labour.

---

[7]In adopting (14.50)–(14.52) we have simplified the Lucas model by assuming that the population is constant and that there is no external effect of human capital. See Lucas (1988, p. 18) for the latter effect.

[8]Since capital and effective labour receive their respective marginal products, it follows that profit is zero ($\Pi(t) = 0$).

The representative household chooses sequences for consumption and the stocks of physical and human capital in order to maximize lifetime utility (14.21) subject to (i) the time constraint (14.50), (ii) the accumulation identity for physical capital, $\dot{K}(t) = I(t) - \delta_k K(t)$, where $I(t)$ is gross investment in physical capital and δ_k is its depreciation rate, (iii) the accumulation expression for human capital (14.49), and (iv) the budget identity:

$$I(t) + C(t) + T(t) = w(t)L_P(t) + R^K(t)K(t) + s_E w(t)L_E(t), \tag{14.55}$$

where $T(t)$ is a lump-sum tax and s_E is a time-invariant education subsidy received from the government ($\dot{s}_E = 0$).

The current-value Hamiltonian associated with the representative household's decision problem is given by:

$$\mathcal{H}_C(t) = \frac{C(t)^{1-1/\sigma} - 1}{1 - 1/\sigma} + \mu_H(t) \left[Z_E \frac{L_E(t)}{L_0} - \delta_h \right] H(t)$$
$$+ \mu_K(t) \left[\left(R^K(t) - \delta_k \right) K(t) + H(t)F_N(k(t))(L_0 - L_E(t)) \right.$$
$$\left. + s_E H(t)F_N(k(t))L_E(t) - C(t) - T(t) \right], \tag{14.56}$$

where $\mu_K(t)$ and $\mu_H(t)$ are the co-state variables for, respectively, $K(t)$ and $H(t)$. The first-order necessary conditions are:[9]

$$C(t)^{-1/\sigma} = \mu_K(t), \tag{14.57}$$

$$\mu_H(t)\frac{Z_E}{L_0} = \mu_K(t)(1 - s_E)F_N(k(t)), \tag{14.58}$$

$$\frac{\dot{\mu}_K(t)}{\mu_K(t)} = \rho + \delta_k - F_K(k(t)), \tag{14.59}$$

$$\frac{\dot{\mu}_H(t)}{\mu_H(t)} = \rho + \delta_h - Z_E\frac{L_E(t)}{L_0} - \frac{\mu_K(t)}{\mu_H(t)}[L_0 - (1-s_E)L_E(t)]F_N(k(t)), \tag{14.60}$$

$$0 = \lim_{t\to\infty}\mu_K(t)K(t)e^{-\rho t} = \lim_{t\to\infty}\mu_H(t)H(t)e^{-\rho t}, \tag{14.61}$$

where we have used (14.53) to simplify (14.59). Note that (14.61) are the transversality conditions, explained in detail by e.g. Benhabib and Perli (1994, p. 117) and Bond et al. (1996, p. 154). The intuition behind the remaining expressions is as follows. First, according to (14.57) goods must on the margin be equally valuable in their two uses, namely consumption and physical capital accumulation. Similarly, (14.58) says that time must be equally valuable in its two uses, namely the accumulation of physical and human capital (Lucas, 1988, p. 21). The intuition behind (14.59)–(14.60) is best understood by rewriting them slightly and appealing to the fundamental principle of valuation according to which the rate of return on different assets with the same riskiness must be equalized (cf. Miller and Modigliani, 1961, p. 412). For each asset the rate of return can be computed as the sum of dividends plus capital gains divided by the price of the asset. By using (14.59)–(14.60) we find that the rates of return on the two types of assets are given by:

$$\rho = \frac{\dot{\mu}_K(t) + D_K(t)}{\mu_K(t)} = \frac{\dot{\mu}_H(t) + D_H(t)}{\mu_H(t)}, \tag{14.62}$$

---

[9]The first-order conditions are $\partial\mathcal{H}_C/\partial x = 0$ for the control variables ($x \in \{C, L_E\}$) and $-\partial\mathcal{H}_C/\partial x = \dot{\mu}_x - \rho\mu_x$ for the state variables ($x \in \{K, H\}$). The household treats F_N and F_K as given.

where $D_K(t)$ and $D_H(t)$ are "dividend payments" on physical and human capital, respectively:

$$D_K(t) \equiv \mu_K(t) \left[F_K(k(t)) - \delta_k \right], \tag{14.63}$$

$$D_H(t) \equiv \mu_H(t) \left[\frac{Z_E}{1 - s_E} - \delta_h \right], \tag{14.64}$$

where we have used (14.58) to obtain the expression in (14.64). Recall that $\mu_K(t)$ and $\mu_H(t)$ are the imputed shadow prices of the two assets owned by the household. Not surprisingly, as is shown in equation (14.63), $D_K(t)$ represents the imputed value of the net marginal product of physical capital. In (14.64) the "dividend" on human capital, $D_H(t)$, is equal to the subsidy-corrected marginal productivity of educational activities, net of depreciation. The educational subsidy rate features in the expression because an increase in human capital raises the household's wage rate and thus increases the total amount of educational subsidies it receives.

We now have all the ingredients of the model. For convenience we gather the key expressions in Table 14.3. By defining $p(t) \equiv \mu_H(t)/\mu_K(t)$ as the relative shadow price of human capital and using (T3.7), we find that (14.62)–(14.64) can be written as in (T3.1). Equation (T3.2) is the standard Euler equation for consumption. It is obtained by differentiating (14.57) with respect to time, using (14.59), and defining the interest rate as in (T3.7). Equation (T3.3) is the standard expression for net physical capital accumulation, where g represents the exogenous national income share of government consumption. Equation (T3.4) in obtained by using (14.49) and (14.50) and noting that $l_E(t) \equiv L_E(t)/L_0$ is the share of time spent on educational activities. Finally, equation (T3.5) is a slightly rewritten version of (14.58), and (T3.6) provides a definition for the capital intensity.

Given initial conditions for the stocks of physical and human capital ($K(0)$ and $H(0)$), the model is saddle-point stable and converges gradually to a balanced growth path, i.e. the model features nontrivial transitional dynamics. Along the balanced growth path, the interest rate is constant and all macro variables grow at the same endogenous growth rate, γ^*.

14.3.1 Steady-state growth

The first task at hand is to compute and characterize the balanced growth path of the human capital model. We define the consumption-capital ratio as $\theta(t) \equiv C(t)/K(t)$ and the ratio of physical to human capital as $\kappa(t) \equiv K(t)/H(t)$. Along the balanced growth path, consumption and the stocks of physical and human capital all grow at the same exponential growth rate, γ^*, so that $\theta(t) = \theta^*$ and $\kappa(t) = \kappa^*$. Furthermore, the relative price of human capital and the fraction of labour used in education are both constant, i.e. $p(t) = p^*$ and $l_E(t) = l_E^*$. It follows that the capital intensity and the interest rate are also constant, i.e. $k(t) = k^*$ and $r(t) = r^*$. Using these results in the model of Table 14.3, we find that the steady state can be solved recursively.

1. Equation (T3.1) fixes the steady-state interest rate:

$$r^* = \frac{Z_E}{1 - s_E} - \delta_h. \tag{14.65}$$

2. Given r^*, equations (T3.2) and (T3.7) determine, respectively, the growth rate and the capital intensity of production:

$$\gamma^* = \sigma \left[r^* - \rho \right], \tag{14.66}$$

Table 14.3. The Lucas-Uzawa model of growth and human capital accumulation

$$\frac{\dot{p}(t)}{p(t)} = r(t) + \delta_h - \frac{Z_E}{1 - s_E} \qquad \text{(T3.1)}$$

$$\frac{\dot{C}(t)}{C(t)} = \sigma \left[r(t) - \rho \right] \qquad \text{(T3.2)}$$

$$\frac{\dot{K}(t)}{K(t)} = (1 - g) Z_Y k(t)^{\alpha - 1} - \frac{C(t)}{K(t)} - \delta_k \qquad \text{(T3.3)}$$

$$\frac{\dot{H}(t)}{H(t)} = Z_E l_E(t) - \delta_h \qquad \text{(T3.4)}$$

$$p(t) = (1 - s_E)(1 - \alpha) \frac{Z_Y L_0}{Z_E} k(t)^{\alpha} \qquad \text{(T3.5)}$$

$$k(t) \equiv \frac{K(t)}{[1 - l_E(t)] L_0 H(t)} \qquad \text{(T3.6)}$$

$$r(t) \equiv \alpha Z_Y k(t)^{\alpha - 1} - \delta_k \qquad \text{(T3.7)}$$

Notes: $C(t)$ is consumption, $K(t)$ and $H(t)$ are, respectively, the physical and human capital stock (featuring respective depreciation rates δ_k and δ_h), $r(t)$ is the interest rate, $p(t)$ is the relative shadow price of human capital, $l_E(t)$ is the fraction of time spent on education, L_0 is the time endowment, s_E is the educational subsidy, g is the national income share of (un-productive) government consumption, α is the efficiency parameter of physical capital in the production function, ρ is the pure rate of time preference, and σ is the intertemporal substitution elasticity.

$$k^* = \left(\frac{\alpha Z_Y}{r^* + \delta_k} \right)^{1/(1-\alpha)}. \tag{14.67}$$

3. Given γ^* and k^* we find from (T3.3)–(T3.5):

$$\theta^* = \frac{1-g}{\alpha} (r^* + \delta_k) - \gamma^* - \delta_k, \tag{14.68}$$

$$l_E^* = \frac{\gamma^* + \delta_h}{Z_E}, \tag{14.69}$$

$$p^* = (1 - s_E)(1 - \alpha) \frac{Z_Y L_0}{Z_E} (k^*)^\alpha. \tag{14.70}$$

4. Next, given k^* and l_E^* we obtain from (T3.6):

$$\kappa^* = k^* [1 - l_E^*] L_0. \tag{14.71}$$

5. Finally, it remains to be checked that the (common) growth rate given in (14.66) is actually feasible. In view of (T3.4), the maximum growth rate of human capital is equal to $Z_E - \delta_h$ (this rate is attained if the entire labour stock is devoted to educational activities, i.e. $l_E = 1$). Hence, the growth rate in (14.66) is feasible if and only if $\gamma^* < Z_E - \delta_h$. The feasibility requirement thus places an upper limit on the allowable intertemporal substitution elasticity:

$$\sigma < \frac{Z_E - \delta_h}{Z_E / (1 - s_E) - (\rho + \delta_h)}. \tag{14.72}$$

Several features of the steady-state solution are worth emphasizing. First, it follows in a straightforward fashion from (14.65) and (14.66) that the steady-state growth rate depends positively on the education subsidy. Intuitively, an increase in s_I leads to an increase in the fraction of time spent on educational activities which boosts economic growth. Indeed, it is not difficult to verify that $dr^*/ds_E > 0$, $d\gamma^*/ds_E > 0$, $dl_E^*/ds_E > 0$, $dk^*/ds_E < 0$, $d\kappa^*/ds_E < 0$, $dp^*/ds_E < 0$, and $\alpha d\theta^*/ds_E = [1 - g - \alpha\sigma] dr^*/ds_E \gtreqless 0$. Second, useless government consumption only affects the consumption-capital ratio, i.e. $dr^*/dg = d\gamma^*/dg = dl_E^*/dg = dk^*/dg = d\kappa^*/dg = dp^*/dg = 0$ and $d\theta^*/dg = -(r^* + \delta_k)/\alpha < 0$.

14.3.2　Transitional dynamics

We study the dynamic properties of the model by following the approach of Bond et al. (1996). As is clear from Table 14.3, the model is fully characterized by three key variables only, namely the relative shadow price of human capital, $p(t)$, the consumption-capital ratio, $\theta(t) \equiv C(t)/K(t)$, and the ratio between the physical and human capital stock, $\kappa(t) \equiv K(t)/H(t)$. To understand why this is the case, it is useful to note some quasi-reduced-form relationships. First, it follows from (T3.5) that $k(t)$ is an increasing function of both $p(t)$ and s_E:

$$k(t) = \left(\frac{Z_E p(t)}{(1-\alpha) Z_Y L_0 (1 - s_E)} \right)^{1/\alpha} \equiv \Psi[\underset{+}{p(t)}, \underset{+}{s_E}]. \tag{14.73}$$

Second, we find from (T3.6) that $l_E(t)$ depends negatively on $\kappa(t)$ and positively on $k(t)$ (and thus, via (14.73), on $p(t)$ and s_E):

$$l_E(t) = 1 - \frac{\kappa(t)}{L_0 \Psi[p(t), s_E]}. \tag{14.74}$$

Hence, it follows from (14.73) and (14.74) that $k(t)$ and $l_E(t)$ are uniquely determined by the fundamental state variables, $p(t)$ and $\kappa(t)$.

In order to study the dynamic properties of the model, we loglinearize it around the steady-state point (θ^*, κ^*) to obtain:

$$
\begin{bmatrix}
\dfrac{d \ln p(t)}{dt} \\[2mm]
\dfrac{d \ln \theta(t)}{dt} \\[2mm]
\dfrac{d \ln \kappa(t)}{dt}
\end{bmatrix}
= \Delta \cdot
\begin{bmatrix}
\ln p(t) - \ln p^* \\[2mm]
\ln \theta(t) - \ln \theta^* \\[2mm]
\ln \kappa(t) - \ln \kappa^*
\end{bmatrix},
\tag{14.75}
$$

where Δ is the Jacobian matrix:

$$
\Delta \equiv
\begin{bmatrix}
-\dfrac{(1-\alpha)(r^* + \delta_k)}{\alpha} & 0 & 0 \\[3mm]
-\dfrac{(1-\alpha)\sigma(r^* + \delta_k) + Z_E(1 - l_E^*)}{\alpha} & 0 & Z_E(1 - l_E^*) \\[3mm]
-\dfrac{(1-\alpha)(1-g)(r^* + \delta_k) + \alpha Z_E(1 - l_E^*)}{\alpha^2} & -\theta^* & Z_E(1 - l_E^*)
\end{bmatrix}.
\tag{14.76}
$$

The determinant of Δ is given by:

$$
|\Delta| \equiv -\frac{(1-\alpha)(r^* + \delta_k) Z_E(1 - l_E^*)\theta^*}{\alpha} < 0,
\tag{14.77}
$$

so it follows that the product of the characteristic roots of Δ is negative, i.e. there is an odd number of negative roots. To prove saddle-point stability we must prove that there is only one stable root. A little bit of detective work shows that this is indeed the case. Denoting the elements of Δ by δ_{ij}, we find that the characteristic equation of Δ can be written as:

$$
\Phi(s) \equiv |sI - \Delta| = (s - \delta_{11})\left[s^2 - \delta_{33}s - \delta_{23}\delta_{32}\right] = 0.
\tag{14.78}
$$

It follows that δ_{11} is a root of $\Phi(s)$. We denote this negative (stable) root by $-\lambda_1 = -\frac{(1-\alpha)(r^* + \delta_k)}{\alpha}$. The quadratic expression on the right-hand side of (14.78) can be written as $(s - \lambda_2)(s - \lambda_3) = s^2 - (\lambda_2 + \lambda_3)s + \lambda_2\lambda_3$ so that $\lambda_2 + \lambda_3 = \delta_{33} > 0$ and $\lambda_2\lambda_3 = -\delta_{23}\delta_{32} > 0$, i.e. $\lambda_2 > 0$ and $\lambda_3 > 0$. The model is saddle-point stable and features two jumping variables ($p(t)$ and $\theta(t)$) and one predetermined (sticky) variable ($\kappa(t)$). The adjustment speed in the economy is given by λ_1. Given initial values for $K(0)$ and $H(0)$ (and thus for $\kappa(0) \equiv K(0)/H(0)$), the model converges along the saddle path toward the steady-state equilibrium.

14.3.3 Concluding remarks

We have thus demonstrated that endogenous growth can result from the purposeful accumulation of human capital by maximizing agents. No "manna from heaven" assumption is needed to generate this result. The model studied by Lucas (1988) is more complex than the one studied here because he introduces (exogenous) population growth n_L and, more importantly, because he argues that knowledge may have a positive external effect on productivity. Instead of (14.51) he uses the production function $Y(t) = N_P(t)^{1-\alpha}K(t)^\alpha \bar{H}(t)^\beta$, where $\bar{H}(t)$ is the average skill level in society and $\beta > 0$. Intuitively, his formulation attempts to capture the notion that the formation of human capital is, in part, a social activity. Since individual households are infinitesimally small (relative to the economy) they will not recognize the link between their own human capital choice and the resulting level of average economy-wide human capital. As a result, the market economy will not be efficient. Lucas (1990b) uses this extended model to explain why there can be persistent differences in the marginal product of capital across countries even if there are no barriers to international capital flows.

14.4   Endogenous technology

In the previous section we showed that the purposeful accumulation of human capital ("skills") forms the key ingredient of the Lucas-Uzawa theory of economic growth. In this section we briefly review a branch of the (huge) literature in which the purposeful conduct of research and development (R&D) activities forms the key source of growth.[10] In order to demonstrate the key mechanism by which R&D affects economic growth we follow Grossman and Helpman (1991a, chs. 3–4) and Bénassy (1998) by abstracting from physical and human capital altogether. In such a setting all saving by households is directed towards the creation of new technology. We study two types of R&D model. The first model is the expanding input variety (EIV) model. In this model, R&D leads to the creation of additional intermediate inputs that are used by final goods producers. R&D leads to expansion in the "horizontal" direction. The second model is the rising input quality (RIQ) model, in which R&D leads to the development of better-quality versions of already existing productive inputs. Here expansion takes place in the "vertical" direction.

14.4.1   R&D and expanding input variety

The EIV model assumes that there are three production sectors in the economy. The *final goods sector* produces a homogeneous good using varieties of a differentiated intermediate good as productive inputs. Production is subject to constant returns to scale (in these inputs) and perfect competition prevails. The *R&D sector* is also perfectly competitive. In this sector units of labour are used to produce blueprints of new varieties of the differentiated input. Finally, the *intermediate goods sector* is populated by a large number of small firms, each producing a single variety of the differentiated input, who engage in Chamberlinian monopolistic competition (see Chapter 11 for a detailed account of this market structure).

14.4.1.1   Production in the final goods sector

The production function in the final goods sector is given by the following (generalized) Dixit-Stiglitz (1977) form:

$$Y(t) \equiv N(t)^{\eta} \left[N(t)^{-1} \sum_{i=1}^{N(t)} X_i(t)^{1/\mu} \right]^{\mu}, \; \mu > 1, \; 1 \leq \eta \leq 2, \tag{14.79}$$

---

[10]Pioneering contributions to this literature are Paul Romer (1987, 1990), Aghion and Howitt (1992), Segerstrom et al. (1990), Grossman and Helpman (1991a), and Kortum (1997).

where $N(t)$ is the number of different varieties that exist at time t, $X_i(t)$ is input variety i, and μ and η are parameters.[11] Note that, holding constant the number of varieties, doubling all inputs X_i leads to a doubling of output Y in (14.79), i.e. constant returns to scale prevail. The specification in (14.79) implies that, provided $\eta > 1$, there are *returns to specialization* of the form emphasized by Ethier (1982). This can be demonstrated as follows. Suppose that the same amount is used of all inputs (as will indeed be the case in the symmetric equilibrium discussed below), i.e. $X_i(t) = \bar{X}(t)$ for $i = 1, \cdots, N(t)$. Then total output in the final goods sector will be $Y(t) = N(t)^{\eta-1} Z_X L_X(t)$, where $L_X(t) \equiv \sum_i^{N(t)} L_i(t) = N(t)\bar{X}(t)/Z_X$ represents the total amount of labour used up in the intermediate goods sector and Z_X is an exogenous productivity index. Ceteris paribus $L_X(t)$, output in the final goods sector rises with the number of intermediate inputs provided η exceeds unity. By having a larger number of varieties, producers in the final goods sector can adopt a more "round-about" method of production and thus produce more (with the same amount of labour being used indirectly). (Note that the assumption about the upper bound for η is adopted primarily to simplify the exposition in various places.)

The representative producer in the final goods sector minimizes its costs and sets the price of the final good equal to the marginal (equals average) cost of production:

$$P_Y(t) \equiv N(t)^{-\eta} \left[N(t)^{\mu/(1-\mu)} \sum_{i=1}^{N(t)} P_i(t)^{1/(1-\mu)} \right]^{1-\mu}, \tag{14.80}$$

where $P_i(t)$ is the price of input variety i. The cost-minimizing derived demand for input i is given by:

$$\frac{X_i(t)}{Y(t)} = N(t)^{(\eta-\mu)/(\mu-1)} \left(\frac{P_i(t)}{P_Y(t)} \right)^{\mu/(1-\mu)}, \qquad i = 1, \cdots, N(t), \tag{14.81}$$

where $\mu/(1-\mu)$ thus represents the (constant) price elasticity of the demand for variety i.

14.4.1.2   Production in the intermediate goods sector

In the intermediate goods sector there are many monopolistically competitive firms which each hold a blueprint telling them how to produce their own, slightly unique, variety $X_i(t)$. The operating profit of firm i is defined as follows:

$$\Pi_i(t) \equiv P_i(t)X_i(t) - W(t)L_i(t), \tag{14.82}$$

where $W(t)$ is the wage rate (common to all firms in the economy as labour is perfectly mobile) and $L_i(t)$ is the amount of labour used by firm i. Firm i chooses its output level, $X_i(t)$, given the demand for its output (14.81), the production function $X_i(t) = Z_X L_i(t)$, and taking the actions of all other producers in the intermediate goods sector as given. As is familiar from the detailed discussion in Chapter 11,

---

[11] A mathematically correct (but somewhat unintuitive) formulation writes (14.79) as:

$$Y(t) \equiv N(t)^{\eta} \left[N(t)^{-1} \int_0^{N(t)} X_j(t)^{1/\mu} dj \right]^{\mu}, \ \mu > 1, \ 1 \le \eta \le 2,$$

where $N(t)$ now represents the "measure" of products invented before time t. See Paul Romer (1987) and Grossman and Helpman (1991a, p. 45) for details.

the optimal choice of the firm is to set its prices according to a fixed markup over marginal production cost:

$$P_i(t) = \mu \frac{W(t)}{Z_X}, \tag{14.83}$$

where μ thus represents the constant markup.[12] Since all active firms in the intermediate sector possess the same technology and face the same input price and markup, they all choose the same amount of output and charge the same price. Hence, from here on we can suppress the firm subscript, as $X_i(t) = \bar{X}(t)$, $P_i(t) = \bar{P}(t)$, and $\Pi_i(t) = \bar{\Pi}(t)$ for $i = 1, \cdots, N(t)$, and let the barred variables denote the choices of the representative firm in the intermediate sector. By substituting (14.83) into (14.82) and invoking the symmetry results we obtain the following expression for the profit of a representative firm in the intermediate goods sector:

$$\bar{\Pi}(t) = \left[\bar{P}(t) - \frac{W(t)}{Z_X} \right] \bar{X}(t) = \frac{\mu - 1}{\mu} \bar{P}(t) \bar{X}(t). \tag{14.84}$$

14.4.1.3   Production in the R&D sector

In the R&D sector competitive firms use labour (researchers) to produce new blueprints. Since $N(t)$ is the stock of existing blueprints (one blueprint per existing variety), its time rate of change, $\dot{N}(t)$, represents the production of new blueprints (and varieties). It is assumed, following Bénassy (1998) that the production function for new blueprints is given by:

$$\dot{N}(t) = Z_R N(t) L_R(t), \tag{14.85}$$

where $L_R(t)$ is the amount of labour employed in the R&D sector and Z_R is a productivity parameter. By employing more labour in the R&D sector, more new blueprints are produced per unit of time. Furthermore, equation (14.85) incorporates the assumption, due to Paul Romer (1990), that the stock of existing blueprints positively affects the productivity of researchers. R&D researchers are, in a sense, "standing on the shoulders of giants". As Romer puts it, "[t]he engineer working today is more productive because he can take advantage of all the additional knowledge accumulated as design problems were solved during the last 100 years" (1990, pp. S83–84).

   Since the R&D sector is competitive, the price of a new blueprint, $P_N(t)$, is equal to the marginal cost of producing it:

$$P_N(t) = \frac{(1 - s_R) W(t)}{N(t) Z_R}, \tag{14.86}$$

where s_R is a time-invariant wage subsidy received from the government ($\dot{s}_R = 0$). Of course, profits in the R&D sector are zero, i.e. $P_N(t)\dot{N}(t) = (1 - s_R) W(t) L_R(t)$.

---

[12]It is important to distinguish η and μ. The first parameter regulates the strength of the external effect due to specialization, whereas the second parameter measures the degree of substitutability between inputs. Interestingly, in an earlier (February 1975) draft of their classic paper, Dixit and Stiglitz (2004a, pp. 103–107) explicitly consider the case of diversity as a public good, i.e. they distinguish η and μ as in (14.79). In the published version of their paper, however, $\eta = \mu$ is imposed. See Brakman and Heijdra (2004).

14.4.1.4 Household behaviour

It remains to describe the optimal behaviour of the representative, infinitely-lived, household. This household has a utility function as in (14.21) and faces the following budget identity:

$$P_Y(t)C(t) + P_N(t)\dot{N}(t) = W(t)L_0 - T(t) + N(t)\bar{\Pi}(t), \tag{14.87}$$

where L_0 is the exogenous supply of labour of the household and $T(t)$ is the lump-sum tax. Total spending on consumption goods plus investment in new blueprints (left-hand side) equals total after-tax labour income plus the total profits the house-hold receives from firms in the differentiated sector (right-hand side). By using the price of final output as the numeraire ($P_Y(t) = 1$), we obtain the household budget identity in real terms, $C(t) + P_N(t)\dot{N}(t) = W(t)L_0 - T(t) + N(t)\bar{\Pi}(t)$.

The current-value Hamiltonian associated with the representative household's decision problem is given by:

$$\mathcal{H}_C(t) = \frac{C(t)^{1-1/\sigma} - 1}{1 - 1/\sigma} + \mu_N(t)\left[\frac{W(t)L_0 + N(t)\bar{\Pi}(t) - T(t) - C(t)}{P_N(t)}\right], \tag{14.88}$$

where $\mu_N(t)$ is the co-state variable for $N(t)$. The first-order necessary conditions are:

$$C(t)^{-1/\sigma} = \frac{\mu_N(t)}{P_N(t)}, \tag{14.89}$$

$$\frac{\dot{\mu}_N(t)}{\mu_N(t)} = \rho - \frac{\bar{\Pi}(t)}{P_N(t)}. \tag{14.90}$$

By combining these two expressions we obtain the conventional consumption Euler equation:

$$\frac{\dot{C}(t)}{C(t)} = \sigma\left[r(t) - \rho\right], \tag{14.91}$$

where $r(t)$ is the rate of return on blueprints:

$$r(t) = \frac{\bar{\Pi}(t) + \dot{P}_N(t)}{P_N(t)}. \tag{14.92}$$

The return on blueprints is the dividend plus the capital gain expressed in terms of the purchase price of the blueprint.

14.4.1.5 Model closure

The model is closed by two market clearing conditions. The final goods market clears provided output equals consumption:

$$Y(t) = C(t) + G(t), \tag{14.93}$$

where $G(t) \equiv gY(t)$ is useless government consumption, and the national income share of government consumption is time invariant ($\dot{g} = 0$). The government budget constraint is given by $T(t) = G(t) + s_R W(t)L_R(t)$. The labour market equilibrium condition requires the total supply of labour to equal the sum of labour demand in the intermediate and R&D sectors, i.e. $L_X(t) + L_R(t) = L_0$. Since $Z_X L_X(t) =$

$N(t)\bar{X}(t)$ and $Z_R L_R(t) = \dot{N}(t)/N(t)$ we can rewrite this labour market equilibrium condition as:

$$\frac{\dot{N}(t)}{N(t)} = Z_R \left[L_0 - \frac{N(t)\bar{X}(t)}{Z_X} \right], \tag{14.94}$$

where we implicitly assume that the intermediate goods sector is not too large and thus does not absorb all available labour (i.e. the term in square brackets on the right-hand side is strictly positive).

14.4.1.6 Growth

We are now in a position to determine the growth rate in the economy. We follow the solution approach of Bénassy (1998). In the first step, we note a number of intermediate results:

$$\frac{\bar{\Pi}(t)}{P_N(t)} = (\mu - 1)\frac{Z_R}{1 - s_R} L_X(t), \tag{14.95}$$

$$\frac{\dot{P}_N(t)}{P_N(t)} = (\eta - 2)\frac{\dot{N}(t)}{N(t)}, \tag{14.96}$$

$$C(t) = (1 - g) N(t)^{\eta - 1} Z_X L_X(t), \tag{14.97}$$

where we have used the fact that $L_X(t) = N(t)\bar{X}(t)/Z_X$ in various places. Equation (14.95) expresses the real dividend rate on blueprints in terms of the monopoly markup (μ) and the total amount of labour absorbed by the final goods sector. It is obtained by using (14.86) and (14.83) in (14.84) and imposing the symmetry results. Equation (14.96) shows that the capital gains rate on blueprints is proportional to the growth rate of varieties, i.e. the rate of innovation. It is obtained by using (14.83) and (14.80) in (14.86), setting $P_Y(t) = 1$ and imposing symmetry. This yields $P_N(t) = [(1 - s_R) Z_X/(\mu Z_R)]N(t)^{\eta - 2}$ which can be differentiated with respect to time to obtain (14.96). Finally, (14.97) is the goods market clearing condition in the symmetric equilibrium.

In the second step we write the dynamics of the model as follows:

$$\gamma_C(t) = \sigma \left[(\mu - 1)\frac{Z_R}{1 - s_R} L_X(t) + (\eta - 2)\gamma_N(t) - \rho \right], \tag{14.98}$$

$$\gamma_C(t) = (\eta - 1)\gamma_N(t) + \frac{\dot{L}_X(t)}{L_X(t)}, \tag{14.99}$$

$$\gamma_N(t) = Z_R \left[L_0 - L_X(t) \right], \tag{14.100}$$

where we use the conventional notation for growth rates, i.e. $\gamma_x \equiv \dot{x}(t)/x(t)$. Equation (14.98) is the consumption Euler equation. It is obtained by combining (14.91)–(14.92) and (14.95)–(14.96). Equation (14.99) is the logarithmic time derivative of (14.97), noting that $\dot{g} = \dot{Z}_X = 0$. Finally, equation (14.100) is just a rewritten version of (14.94).

In the third step we eliminate $\gamma_N(t)$ and $\gamma_C(t)$ from (14.99) by using (14.98)–(14.100) and obtain a single differential equation for $L_X(t)$:

$$\frac{\dot{L}_X(t)}{L_X(t)} = Z_R \cdot \left[\frac{\sigma (\mu - 1)}{1 - s_R} + \eta - 1 + \sigma(2 - \eta) \right] (L_X(t) - L_X^*), \tag{14.101}$$

where L_X^* is defined as:

$$L_X^* = \frac{[\eta - 1 + \sigma(2 - \eta)]L_0 + \sigma\rho/Z_R}{\sigma(\mu - 1)/(1 - s_R) + \eta - 1 + \sigma(2 - \eta)}. \tag{14.102}$$

The crucial thing to note about this expression is that the coefficient for $L_X(t)$ on the right-hand side is positive, i.e. (14.101) is an unstable differential equation (because $\mu > 1$ and $1 \leq \eta \leq 2$). This, of course, means that the only economically sensible solution is such that $L_X(t)$ jumps immediately to its steady-state value, i.e. $L_X(t) = L_X^*$ for all t.

Since there is no transitional dynamics in $L_X(t)$ (and thus $\dot{L}_X(t) = 0$ for all t) the same holds for the growth rates of the number of varieties and consumption, i.e. $\gamma_N(t) = \gamma_N^*$ and $\gamma_C(t) = \gamma_C^*$. Indeed, by using (14.102) in (14.99) and (14.100) we obtain:

$$\gamma_N^* = \frac{\dfrac{\mu - 1}{1 - s_R}Z_R L_0 - \rho}{\dfrac{\mu - 1}{1 - s_R} + \dfrac{\eta - 1}{\sigma} + (2 - \eta)} > 0, \quad \gamma_C^* = \gamma_Y^* = (\eta - 1)\gamma_N^*, \tag{14.103}$$

where the sign follows from our assumption made in the text below equation (14.94). This expression generalizes the results of Grossman and Helpman (1991a, p. 59), Bénassy (1998, p. 66), and de Groot and Nahuis (1998, p. 293) by incorporating a non-unitary elasticity of intertemporal substitution and by including an R&D subsidy. Like these authors, we find that the rate of innovation increases with the monopoly markup ($d\gamma_N^*/d\mu > 0$) and the size of the labour force ($d\gamma_N^*/dL_0 > 0$) and decreases with the rate of time preference ($d\gamma_N^*/d\rho < 0$). Provided the returns to specialization are operative (so that $\eta > 1$), an increase in the willingness of the representative household to substitute consumption across time raises the rate of innovation ($d\gamma_N^*/d\sigma > 0$). Clearly, of the two government policy instruments, only the investment subsidy affects growth, i.e. $d\gamma_N^*/ds_R > 0$ and $d\gamma_N^*/dg = 0$. Finally, as is evident from (14.103), the growth rate in consumption and output depends critically on whether or not the technology in the final goods sector is characterized by returns from specialization.

14.4.1.7 Efficiency

One of the classic questions in economics concerns the welfare properties of the decentralized market equilibrium. In the context of the R&D model we wish to know whether the market rate of innovation is too high or too low. To study this problem we follow the usual procedure by computing the social optimum and comparing it to the decentralized market equilibrium (with $g = 0$ imposed upfront).

As is pointed out by Bénassy (1998, p. 66), computation of the social optimum is quite a lot easier than that of the market solution because we can impose symmetry upfront and work in terms of aggregates like consumption, the number of firms, and labour used in the intermediate sector. The social planner is assumed to maximize lifetime utility of the representative agent (14.21), subject to the constraints (14.94) and (14.97). By using $L_X(t) = N(t)\bar{X}(t)/Z_X$ in the various expressions we find that the current-value Hamiltonian for the social welfare programme is given by:

$$\mathcal{H}_C(t) = \frac{[N(t)^{\eta - 1}Z_X L_X(t)]^{1 - 1/\sigma} - 1}{1 - 1/\sigma} + \mu_N(t)N(t)Z_R[L_0 - L_X(t)], \tag{14.104}$$

where $\mu_N(t)$ is the co-state variable for $N(t)$. The first-order necessary conditions are given by, respectively, $\partial \mathcal{H}_C / \partial L_X = 0$ and $-\partial \mathcal{H}_C / \partial N = \dot{\mu}_N - \rho \mu_N$:

$$Z_R \mu_N(t) = \frac{Z_X N(t)^{\eta - 2}}{\left[N(t)^{\eta - 1} Z_X L_X(t) \right]^{1/\sigma}}, \tag{14.105}$$

$$\dot{\mu}_N(t) = \rho \mu_N(t) - \frac{(\eta - 1) Z_X L_X(t) N(t)^{\eta - 2}}{\left[N(t)^{\eta - 1} Z_X L_X(t) \right]^{1/\sigma}} - \mu_N(t) Z_R \left[L_0 - L_X(t) \right]. \tag{14.106}$$

By combining these two expressions we obtain (after a number of tedious but straightforward steps) a differential equation in $L_X(t)$:

$$\frac{\dot{L}_X(t)}{L_X(t)} = (\eta - 1) Z_R L_X(t) - (\eta - 1)(1 - \sigma) Z_R L_0 - \sigma \rho. \tag{14.107}$$

Provided there are returns to specialization ($\eta > 1$), the coefficient for $L_X(t)$ on the right-hand side of (14.107) is positive so that the differential equation is unstable and the socially optimal solution is to jump immediately to the steady state ($\dot{L}_X(t) = 0$):

$$L_X^{SO} = (1 - \sigma) L_0 + \frac{\sigma \rho}{(\eta - 1) Z_R}, \tag{14.108}$$

where the superscript "SO" denotes the socially optimal value and we assume implicitly that L_X^{SO} is feasible ($0 < L_X^{SO} < L_0$). The socially optimal rate of innovation associated with (14.108) is:

$$\gamma_N^{SO} \equiv Z_R \left[L_0 - L_X^{SO} \right] = \sigma Z_R L_0 - \frac{\sigma \rho}{\eta - 1} > 0, \quad \gamma_C^{SO} = \gamma_Y^{SO} = (\eta - 1) \gamma_N^{SO}. \tag{14.109}$$

The striking conclusion that can be drawn from (14.109) is that the socially optimal rate of innovation does not depend on the markup (μ) at all but rather on the parameter regulating the returns to specialization (η). This result is obvious when you think of it–in the symmetric equilibrium (14.79) collapses to $Y(t) = N(t)^{\eta - 1} Z_X L_X(t)$ from which we see that the social return to R&D depends critically on $\eta - 1$ (Bénassy, 1998, p. 67).

We can now compare the socially optimal and market rate of innovation (given, respectively, in (14.103) and (14.109)) and answer our question regarding the welfare properties of the decentralized market equilibrium. To keep things simple we set $\sigma = 1$ (logarithmic felicity) for which case $\gamma_N^*(s_R)$ and γ_N^{SO} are:

$$\gamma_N^*(s_R) \equiv \frac{(\mu - 1) Z_R L_0 - \rho (1 - s_R)}{\mu - s_R}, \tag{14.110}$$

$$\gamma_N^{SO} = \frac{(\eta - 1) Z_R L_0 - \rho}{\eta - 1}. \tag{14.111}$$

We consider two cases in turn. In case one, we assume that $s_R = 0$ and use the expressions for $\gamma_N^*(0)$ and γ_N^{SO} to see how the laissez-faire market rate of innovation compares to the socially optimal rate. After some straightforward manipulations we find:

$$\mu \left[\gamma_N^{SO} - \gamma_N^*(0) \right] = Z_R L_0 - \rho \left[\frac{\mu - (\eta - 1)}{\eta - 1} \right]. \tag{14.112}$$

No general conclusion can be drawn from (14.112), and both $\gamma_N^* (0) < \gamma_N^{SO}$ (underinvestment in R&D) and $\gamma_N^* (0) > \gamma_N^{SO}$ (overinvestment in R&D) are distinct possibilities as is the knife-edge case for which the parameters are such that the market yields the correct amount of investment in R&D ($\gamma_N^* (0) = \gamma_N^{SO}$).[13] The literature tends to stress the underinvestment case but that result is not robust as it is based on the implicit assumption that the markup equals the returns to specialization parameter. Indeed, for that special case, $\eta = \mu$, and (14.112) reduces to:

$$\mu \left[\gamma_N^{SO} - \gamma_N^* (0) \right] = Z_R L_0 - \frac{\rho}{\eta - 1} \equiv \gamma_N^{SO} > 0. \tag{14.113}$$

Hence, if $\eta = \mu$ and γ_N^{SO} is positive, the "traditional" result obtains and the market yields too little R&D, and the innovation growth rate is too low (Bénassy, 1998, p. 68; de Groot and Nahuis, 1998, p. 294).[14]

The expressions in (14.110)–(14.111) can also be used to answer a second kind of question, namely for which value of s_R does the market produce the optimal rate of innovation? We return to the general case by allowing η and μ to differ. By equating $\gamma_N^* (s_R)$ and γ_N^{SO} and solving for s_R we find after some tedious but straightforward manipulations:

$$\frac{s_R^*}{1 - s_R^*} = \frac{(\eta - 1) Z_R L_0 - \rho \left[\mu - (\eta - 1) \right]}{\rho (\mu - 1)} = \frac{\mu (\eta - 1)}{\rho (\mu - 1)} \cdot \left[\gamma_N^{SO} - \gamma_N^* (0) \right], \tag{14.114}$$

where s_R^* stands for the optimal R&D subsidy and we have used (14.112) to get to the second expression. Not surprisingly, it is optimal to subsidize (tax) R&D labour if the laissez-faire economy innovates too slowly (quickly) relative to the social optimum.

14.4.1.8 Scale effect

The R&D growth model discussed above predicts that the *scale* of an economy (as parameterized by the size of its labour force, L_0) is an important determinant of that economy's balanced *growth rate*. This so-called *scale effect* is in fact a common feature of many important R&D growth models such as Grossman and Helpman (1991a) and Aghion and Howitt (1992). In an influential paper, Jones (1995) has argued that the prediction of scale effects is easily falsified empirically. In the US, for example, the amount of labour employed in R&D activities grew from 160,000 in 1950 to about 1,000,000 in 1988 whereas total factor productivity growth stayed the same (or even declined somewhat) during that period (Jones, 1995, p. 762). Similar data can be quoted for other industrialized countries such as France, West Germany, and Japan. On the basis of the empirical evidence, Jones concludes that "the assumption embedded in the R&D equation that the growth rate of the economy is proportional to the level of resources devoted to R&D is obviously false" (1995, p. 762).

Jones suggests that, since the R&D equation is clearly the cause of the empirical refutation, it should be replaced by the following specification:

$$\dot{N}(t) = Z_R L_R(t) N(t)^{\phi_1} [\dot{L}_R(t)]^{\phi_2 - 1}, \quad 0 < \phi_1, \phi_2 \leq 1, \tag{14.115}$$

---

[13]Recall that for $\mu > 1$ and $1 < \eta \leq 2$, the term in squares brackets on the right-hand side of (14.112) is positive.

[14]The example in this paragraph serves to demonstrate that, even though the standard Dixit-Stiglitz preferences (for which $\eta = \mu$) are convenient to work with, they are restrictive and may impose too much structure. Ethier (1982) stresses the need to distinguish η and μ. Weitzman (1994) provides some microfoundations for assuming η and μ to be different. Broer and Heijdra (2001) study diversity and markup effects in a traditional exogenous growth model with capital accumulation.

where $\bar{L}_R(t)$ captures an external effect due to unintended duplication of work in the R&D sector. In the symmetric equilibrium $\bar{L}_R(t) = L_R(t)$, and the production of new designs features diminishing returns to labour provided $\phi_2 < 1$. Individual R&D firms, however, take $\bar{L}_R(t)$ as given and operate under the assumption that the R&D production function is linear in $L_R(t)$. Apart from a *duplication externality*, equation (14.115) also features a more general specification of the *knowledge externality* which operates across time via the stock of invented product varieties. Indeed, whereas $N(t)$ enters linearly in the standard R&D equation (14.85), it features in the augmented R&D equation with an exponent ϕ_1 which may or may not equal unity. An attractive feature of the generalized R&D equation (14.115) is that it contains the standard R&D equation (14.85) as a special case. Indeed, if $\phi_1 = \phi_2 = 1$ the duplication externality is absent and the R&D equation is linear in $N(t)$, and the two expressions coincide.

We now demonstrate the implications for economic growth of adopting the more general specification of the R&D function. We generalize our simple R&D model slightly by assuming non-zero population growth. The key ingredients of the model are as follows. The production function for final output is as given in (14.79) except that we follow convention by assuming that the specialization parameter equals the markup ($\eta = \mu$):

$$Y(t) \equiv \left[\sum_{i=1}^{N(t)} X_i(t)^{1/\mu} \right]^{\mu}, \quad \mu > 1. \tag{14.116}$$

The simplifications that result from assuming $\eta = \mu$ are easily incorporated in equations (14.80)–(14.81). Equations (14.82)–(14.84) are unchanged, (14.85) is replaced by (14.115), and (14.86) is replaced by:

$$P_N(t) = \frac{(1 - s_R) w(t)}{Z_R N(t)^{\phi_1}} [\bar{L}_R(t)]^{1-\phi_2}. \tag{14.117}$$

The price of a new design is equal to the *private* marginal cost of producing it. As in our first R&D model, labour is used in both the intermediate goods sector and in the R&D sector. In contrast to what was assumed in that model, the stock of labour is now postulated to grow at a constant exponential rate, i.e. $\dot{L}(t)/L(t) = n_L$. The representative household is assumed to care about its per capita consumption, $c(t) \equiv C(t)/L(t)$, and has the following lifetime utility function:

$$\Lambda(0) = \int_0^\infty \left[\frac{c(t)^{1-1/\sigma} - 1}{1 - 1/\sigma} \right] e^{-\rho t} dt. \tag{14.118}$$

Finally, since the number of family members of the household grows, the budget identity for the household is changed from (14.87) to:

$$L(t)c(t) + P_N(t)\dot{N}(t) = w(t)L(t) - T(t) + N(t)\bar{\Pi}(t), \tag{14.119}$$

where we once again assume that final output is the numeraire commodity (so that $P_Y(t) = 1$). The representative household chooses the optimal per capita consumption path in order to maximize (14.118) subject to (14.119) (plus a solvency condition). The consumption Euler equation that results from this choice problem is given by:

$$\frac{\dot{c}(t)}{c(t)} = \sigma [r(t) - -(\rho + n_L)], \tag{14.120}$$

where the rate of interest ($r(t)$, representing the yield on blueprints) is given by (14.92). The remaining equations of the model are the final goods market clearing condition (14.93) and the labour market condition:

$$L(t) = L_X(t) + L_R(t) = L_X(t) + \left[Z_R^{-1} N(t)^{1-\phi_1} \frac{\dot{N}(t)}{N(t)} \right]^{1/\phi_2}, \tag{14.121}$$

where the second equality uses (14.115) and incorporates the fact that $\bar{L}_R(t) = L_R(t)$ in equilibrium.

Although we could, in principle, retrace the steps leading from the simplified model to the expression in (14.103), we skip the details of dynamic adjustment here and simply compute the steady-state growth rates implied by the augmented model. We are looking for a balanced growth path in which (a) the proportions of labour going into the intermediate and R&D sectors (L_X/L and L_R/L) are both constant, and (b) the proportional rates of growth in $N(t)$, $c(t)$, and $y(t) \equiv Y(t)/L(t)$ are all constant. The steady-state innovation rate is easily found by rewriting (14.115) in steady-state format and substituting $\bar{L}_R = L_R$:

$$[\gamma_N^* \equiv] \left(\frac{\dot{N}(t)}{N(t)} \right)^* = Z_R [N^*(t)]^{\phi_1 - 1} [L_R^*(t)]^{\phi_2}. \tag{14.122}$$

The left-hand side of (14.122) is constant (as γ_N^* is constant). By differentiating the right-hand side of (14.122) with respect to time and noting that $[\dot{L}_R(t)/L_R(t)]^* = n_L$ we obtain $0 = (\phi_1 - 1)\gamma_N^* + \phi_2 n_L$ which can be solved for γ_N^*:

$$\gamma_N^* = \frac{\phi_2 n_L}{1 - \phi_1}. \tag{14.123}$$

By using the steady-state version of (14.116) (and imposing symmetry) we find $Y = N^\mu \bar{X}$ which can be rewritten as $Y/L = Z_X N^{\mu-1} L_X/L$ (where $L_X = N\bar{X}/Z_X$). From this last expression we find:

$$\gamma_y^* = \gamma_Y^* - n_L = (\mu - 1)\gamma_N^*. \tag{14.124}$$

Finally, from the final goods market clearing condition (14.93) we find the growth rate for (per capita) consumption:

$$\gamma_c^* = \gamma_C^* - n_L = \gamma_y^*. \tag{14.125}$$

We reach a rather striking conclusion. By using the R&D equation suggested by Jones (namely equation (14.115)) instead of the standard one (equation (14.85)) we have managed to eliminate the scale effect altogether (compare (14.103) and (14.123)). And it does not stop there: s_R, ρ, σ, and μ ($= \eta$) also no longer have any effect on the rate of innovation! The economy still grows and innovation continues to take place in the modified model but growth is *exogenous*, i.e. it is explained by the rate of population growth just as in the good old Solow model! With a stable population ($n_L = 0$) innovation ceases in the long run because as $N(t)$ rises over time, more and more labour has to be devoted to the R&D sector to sustain a given rate of innovation.

14.4.2 R&D and rising input quality

In our second R&D model, technical progress takes the form of increased quality. The original "quality ladder" approach of Grossman and Helpman (1991b) focuses attention on the case for which the quality of existing *consumer goods* is improved by means of R&D activities. In this version of the model, quality of a good enters the felicity function of households who will always wish to consume units of the state-of-the-art version of any consumption good.

In order to facilitate the comparison with the EIV model of the previous subsection, we follow an alternative approach by assuming that existing *productive inputs* are improved by R&D activities, as in Grossman and Helpman (1991a, p. 116; 1991b, p. 50). The rising input quality (RIQ) model describes an economy with three broadly defined sectors, namely (i) a final goods sector producing a homogeneous product under perfect competition, (ii) an intermediate sector producing inputs under imperfect competition (Bertrand price competition), and (iii) a perfectly competitive R&D sector in which individual entrepreneurs seek to improve input qualities.

14.4.2.1   Production in the final goods sector

We base the discussion of the final goods sector on the behaviour of a single, perfectly competitive, representative firm. The technology in the final goods sector is represented by a Cobb-Douglas production function:

$$Y(t) \equiv Z_Y \prod_{i=1}^{N_0} X_i(t)^{\alpha}, \qquad \alpha \equiv \frac{1}{N_0}, \tag{14.126}$$

where $Y(t)$ is output, Z_Y is an exogenous index of technology, and $X_i(t)$ is the quantity of input i used in production. There is a large (but fixed) number of inputs, which we denote by N_0, so $i = 1, 2, \cdots, N_0$. Since $\alpha \equiv 1/N_0$, it follows that production features constant returns to scale in the inputs.

Input X_i can in principle be produced in different qualities. To capture this notion we define $X_i(t)$ as follows:

$$X_i(t) \equiv \sum_{j=0}^{m_i(t)} Q_{ij} X_{ij}(t), \tag{14.127}$$

where Q_{ij} denotes the quality of input X_{ij}, and j is the indicator for quality, with $j = 0, 1, \cdots, m_i(t)$. The most basic version of input X_{ij} is denoted by X_{i0} and we normalize its quality to unity, i.e. $Q_{i0} = 1$. At the other end of the spectrum, the state-of-the-art version of input X_i at time t is given by $X_{im_i(t)}$, where the value of $m_i(t)$ depends on past R&D innovations. The notion of quality ladders can be illustrated with the aid of Figure 14.6, which depicts the situation in industries $i = 1$ to $i = 7$. Each ladder is drawn as a dashed vertical line, and large solid dots denote the state-of-the-art version, e.g. for industry $i = 1$ we find that at time t there have been 6 successful innovations and $m_1(t) = 6$. In contrast, in industry $i = 6$ there have been no innovations at all and only the basic quality is available at time t, i.e. $m_6(t) = 0$. In principle the ladders grow into the sky, so that there is no maximum attainable quality in any industry. In the simplest version of the quality ladder model, successful innovations increase the quality of an input proportionally, i.e. $Q_{i,j+1} = (1 + \xi) Q_{ij}$ from which we derive that:

$$Q_{ij} \equiv (1 + \xi)^j Q_{i0} = (1 + \xi)^j, \tag{14.128}$$

where ξ is the exogenous quality increment following a successful innovation and we have used the fact that $Q_{i0} = 1$ to get to the second expression. By taking logarithms we thus find that $\ln Q_{ij} / \ln (1 + \xi) = j$. See the vertical axis in Figure 14.6.

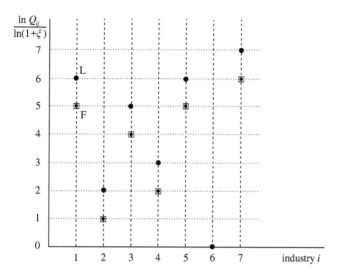

Figure 14.6: Quality ladders

The representative firm minimizes its unit cost of production. It does so by making two choices, namely (a) which quality to purchase of each particular input it wants to use, and (b) which input mix to adopt. We use a two-stage procedure to compute the firm's unit cost function. Since the cost minimization decision is entirely static we drop the time index for now.

14.4.2.1.1 Input quality In choosing the optimal (cost minimizing) quality, the firm solves the following program for each input i:

$$\min_{\{X_{ij}\}} \sum_{j=0}^{m_i} P_{ij} X_{ij} \quad \text{subject to: } X_i = \sum_{j=0}^{m_i} (1+\xi)^j X_{ij}, \quad X_{ij} \geq 0, \qquad (14.129)$$

taking as given the value for X_i and the range of available qualities (m_i). Denoting the Lagrange multiplier of the constraint by μ_X, we find that the first-order Kuhn-Tucker conditions are given by:

$$P_{ij} - \mu_X (1+\xi)^j \geq 0, \quad X_{ij} \geq 0, \quad X_{ij} \cdot \left[P_{ij} - \mu_X (1+\xi)^j \right] = 0. \qquad (14.130)$$

The firm would be equally happy with the different qualities if the quality-corrected price is the same for all qualities, i.e. if $P_{ij} / (1+\xi)^j = P_{ik} / (1+\xi)^k$ for all j and k. Intuitively, for each industry i, quality-weighted inputs are perfect substitutes. However, as we shall see below, the marginal cost of producing inputs X_{ij} is independent of quality, so that ultimately only the state-of-the-art quality will be produced–all other input producers are driven out of the market because their profits will be negative. These "followers" simply cannot compete with the quality "leader". In short, we find that the price of input X_i is equal to the price charged by the state-of-the-art input producer and only that producer's inputs will be used, i.e. $P_i = P_{im_i}$, $X_i = (1+\xi)^{m_i} X_{im_i}$, $X_{im_i} > 0$, and $X_{ij} = 0$ for $j = 0, \cdots, m_i - 1$.

14.4.2.1.2 Input mix In the second step of the minimization problem, the firm minimizes total cost, $\sum_{i=1}^{N_0} P_i X_{im_i}$, subject to the production function (14.126). After

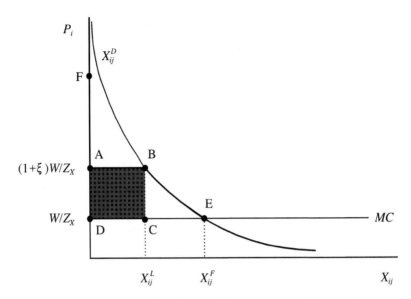

Figure 14.7: Effective demand facing the quality leader

some straightforward manipulations we obtain the total cost function, $TC_Y \equiv UC_Y Y$, where UC_Y is unit cost. But since the firm is perfectly competitive, the sales price of the homogenous good, P_Y, equals unit cost and profits are zero. Reintroducing the time index for future use we find:

$$P_Y(t) = UC_Y(t) \equiv \frac{N_0}{Z_Y} \prod_{i=1}^{N_0} \left(\frac{P_i(t)}{Q_{im_i(t)}} \right)^{\alpha}. \tag{14.131}$$

The derived demand for input X_{im_i} is thus given by:[15]

$$X_{ij}(t) \equiv \frac{\alpha P_Y(t) Y(t)}{P_i(t)}, \qquad \text{for } i = 1, \cdots, N_0, \quad j = m_i(t). \tag{14.132}$$

Because the production function (14.126) is of the Cobb-Douglas form, we obtain the familiar result that cost shares are constant across industries. This is a very convenient assumption which considerably simplifies the analysis to follow (see (14.136)). For future reference, the derived demand for X_{ij} is illustrated—for a given level of aggregate spending ($P_Y Y$)—in Figure 14.7. See the downward sloping curve labelled X_{ij}^D.

14.4.2.2   Production in the intermediate goods sector

Next we consider the input producing sector. As was pointed out above, there are N_0 different inputs and for each input there exists a unique firm which has the ability to produce the state-of-the-art quality. This firm is referred to as the "leader". The production function facing (potential) producers of X_{ij} is given by:

$$X_{ij}(t) = Z_X L_{ij}(t), \tag{14.133}$$

---

[15]Shephard's lemma says that the derived demand for input i is given by the partial derivative of the total cost function with respect to the price of input i, i.e. $X_{im_i} = Y \partial UC_Y / \partial P_i$.

where Z_X is an exogenous productivity index and L_{ij} is the amount of labour used in the production of X_{ij}. The crucial thing to note is that production costs do not depend on the quality of the input that is being produced, i.e. high and low quality producers face the same cost structure. Labour is perfectly mobile across sectors of the economy and fetches a wage rate $W(t)$, i.e. total cost of firm ij is equal to $W(t)X_{ij}(t)/Z_X$ and profit is defined as follows:

$$\Pi_{ij}(t) \equiv \left[P_{ij}(t) - \frac{W(t)}{Z_X}\right] X_{ij}(t). \tag{14.134}$$

The optimal pricing decision of the quality leader in industry i can be studied with the aid of Figure 14.7. It is sufficient to look at the leading firm (for which $j = m_i(t)$) and its immediate predecessor as quality leader (the "follower", whose $j = m_i(t) - 1$). Note that we do not have to consider lower quality producers than the follower because they are even less competitive than the follower. The leader engages in *Bertrand price competition* with the follower and in the optimum will set its price such that the follower is driven out of the market altogether.[16] To see why this is the case, we note that the lowest price the follower can set without incurring losses is given by the marginal cost of production, i.e. $P_i^F = W/Z_X$, $X_{i,m_i-1} = X_{ij}^F$, and $\Pi_i^F = 0$. But the quality leader produces a better version of input X_{ij} and, as we saw above, the purchasers of this input will prefer to buy the higher quality input provided $P_i^L \equiv P_{im_i} \leq (1+\zeta) P_{i,m_i-1} \equiv (1+\zeta) P_i^F$. Hence, the effective demand facing the quality leader is the solid line passing through points E, B, A, and F. It makes no sense for the leader to charge a price in excess of $(1+\zeta) W/Z_X$ because it would lose all its customers to the follower. Similarly, it also makes no sense to charge less than $(1+\zeta) W/Z_X$ because it would leave profit opportunities unused. Using the tie-breaking rule that buyers' indifference between $j = m_i$ and $j = m_i - 1$ results in purchases only from the market leader, it follows that the price set by the quality leader equals:

$$P_i(t) = (1+\zeta) \frac{W(t)}{Z_X}. \tag{14.135}$$

At that price, the quality leader will earn a positive profit equal to:

$$\begin{aligned} \Pi_i(t) &= \left[1 - \frac{W(t)}{P_i(t) Z_X}\right] P_i(t) X_i(t) \\ &= \frac{\zeta}{1+\zeta} \frac{P_Y(t) Y(t)}{N_0} \equiv \Pi^L(t), \end{aligned} \tag{14.136}$$

where we have used equation (14.132) and note that $\alpha = 1/N_0$ to arrive at the second expression. The leader produces a smaller amount of the input than the follower would have done, and thus drives up its price. In Figure 14.7, profit is equal to the shaded area ABCD. The crucial thing to note about (14.136) is that the profit attained by a quality leader is the same no matter which industry the leader is operating in! Similarly, equations (14.132)–(14.133), and (14.135) imply a number of symmetry results:

$$P_i(t) = \bar{P}(t) = (1+\zeta) \frac{W(t)}{Z_X}, \tag{14.137}$$

---

[16]In Figure 14.6, we denote the quality leader in an industry with a solid dot (•) and the follower with a small dot in a box (□). In colloquial terms, the quality leader captures and incarcerates the follower (a former leader) and in the process cuts him/her to size (zero).

$$X_{im_i}(t) = \bar{X}(t) = Z_X \bar{L}(t) = \frac{\alpha P_Y(t) Y(t)}{\bar{P}(t)}, \tag{14.138}$$

$$\sum_{i=1}^{N_0} P_i(t) X_{im_i}(t) = N_0 \bar{P}(t) \bar{X}(t) = P_Y(t) Y(t). \tag{14.139}$$

All quality leaders set the same price, produce the same quantity, and employ the same number of workers. Of course, because $m_i(t)$ will typically not be the same for all industries, it follows from (14.127) that the effective inputs, $X_i(t) \equiv (1 + \xi)^{m_i(t)} \bar{X}(t)$, will not equalize across industries. As Grossman and Helpman put it, progress in each industry i is lumpy and stochastic (1991a, p. 97). However, because there are very many industries (N_0 is large), progress at the aggregate level is smooth and deterministic due to the law of large numbers. We use this result below–see equations (14.152)–(14.154).

14.4.2.3   Production in the R&D sector

The final element of the model concerns the behaviour of innovators in the R&D sector. A successful innovator earns an infinitely-lived patent to produce his particular quality of the input. There is no patent licensing, so the owner of the state-of-the art design is also the unique producer of that particular quality of the input. Of course, the patent becomes valueless once a better-quality version of the same input is developed. Since the current leader does not know when he will be deposed as quality leader, R&D is an inherently risky activity on that account. Furthermore, it is also risky because a given amount of R&D effort may not end up in the development of a new blueprint.

Formally, the R&D activity of innovators looks a lot like the behaviour of a firm (with or without a job vacancy) in a labour market with search frictions that we studied in Chapter 8. We can therefore use the same tools as in Chapter 8 and characterize the risky process of R&D by making use of arbitrage-like equations. We denote the value to the entrepreneur of being a leader in any industry by $V^L(t)$ and of being a follower by $V^F(t)$. An R&D entrepreneur who is not currently a leader in any industry uses $L_R(t)$ units of labour to conduct R&D research. The instantaneous probability of successful innovation is denoted by $\pi(t)$:

$$\pi(t) = Z_R L_R(t), \tag{14.140}$$

where Z_R is an exogenous R&D productivity index. The right-hand side of this expression represents the search intensity. The more labour is employed in R&D, the more intensive is the search, and the higher is the probability that an innovation will actually takes place. The arbitrage equation for a follower can now be written as:

$$r(t) V^F(t) = \dot{V}^F(t) - (1 - s_R) W(t) L_R(t) + \pi(t) \left[V^L(t) - V^F(t) \right], \tag{14.141}$$

where s_R is the R&D subsidy (assumed to be time-invariant, i.e. $\dot{s}_R = 0$). Intuitively, the asset value of being a follower (left-hand side) is equal to the return from the asset (right-hand side). The return consists of capital gains due to revaluation ($\dot{V}^L(t)$) minus the (after-subsidy) wage costs of R&D plus the expected capital gain due to change of status induced by own R&D success ($\pi(t) \left[V^L(t) - V^F(t) \right]$). Under free entry/exit into the R&D activity, the value of being a follower will be driven to zero ($V^F(t) = 0$), so that (14.141) is reduced to $\pi(t) \left[V^L(t) - (1 - s_R) W(t) / Z_R \right] = 0$, where we have used (14.140) to simplify the expression. Provided the R&D intensity is strictly positive ($\pi(t) > 0$), it follows that the value of being a quality leader is equal to:

$$V^L(t) = \frac{(1 - s_R) W(t)}{Z_R}. \tag{14.142}$$

Next we look at the arbitrage equation of a current quality leader:

$$r(t)V^L(t) = \Pi^L(t) + \dot{V}^L(t) - \bar{\pi}(t) \left[V^L(t) - V^F(t) \right], \tag{14.143}$$

where $\bar{\pi}(t)$ stands for the aggregate R&D intensity in the economy. The asset value of being a quality leader (left-hand side) is equal to the return on the asset, consisting of profit receipts plus capital gains due to revaluation ($\Pi^L(t) + \dot{V}^L(t)$) minus the expected capital loss due to status change as a result of R&D successes *of others* ($\bar{\pi}(t) \left[V^L(t) - V^F(t) \right]$). In the symmetric equilibrium we assume that the R&D intensity is the same in all industries, i.e. $\bar{\pi}(t) = \pi(t)$.[17] By also using (14.142) (and its time derivative), and noting that $V^F(t) = 0$ we can simplify (14.143) to obtain:

$$r(t) + \pi(t) = \frac{Z_R \Pi^L(t)}{(1 - s_R) W(t)} + \frac{\dot{W}(t)}{W(t)}. \tag{14.144}$$

14.4.2.4 Consumption and further model details

The representative household has an iso-elastic lifetime utility function as given in (14.21), and the asset accumulation equation is given by:

$$\dot{A}(t) = r(t)A(t) + W(t)L_0 - P_Y(t)C(t) - T(t), \tag{14.145}$$

where L_0 is exogenous labour supply, $P_Y(t)$ is the price of the consumption good (defined in (14.131)), and $T(t)$ is a lump-sum tax.[18] The household maximizes (14.21) subject to (14.145), an initial condition for assets, $A(0)$, and a solvency condition. The household's Euler equation can be written as:

$$\frac{\dot{E}(t)}{E(t)} = \sigma [r(t) - \rho] + (1 - \sigma) \frac{\dot{P}_Y(t)}{P_Y(t)}, \tag{14.146}$$

where $E(t)$ is total expenditure on the consumption good:

$$E(t) \equiv P_Y(t)C(t). \tag{14.147}$$

The equilibrium condition on the market for final goods is given by $Y(t) = C(t) + G(t)$, where $G(t) \equiv gY(t)$ is government consumption. It follows that:

$$(1 - g) P_Y(t)Y(t) = E(t). \tag{14.148}$$

The static government budget constraint is given by:

$$T(t) = gP_Y(t)Y(t) + s_R N_0 W(t) L_R(t), \tag{14.149}$$

---

[17]To be more precise, there is a large number, M_0, of identical potential innovators (households) who each use l_R units of labour and face a probability of success equal to $\pi = Z_R l_R$. The expected total number of innovations is thus equal to $\pi M_0 = Z_R M_0 l_R = Z_R L_R$. By normalizing M_0 to unity there is no need to separately distinguish l_R and L_R. Note finally that quality leaders do not innovate because there is no incentive for them to do so—see Grossman and Helpman (1991b, p. 47).

[18]Equation (14.145) is obtained as follows. First, we note that $A(t) \equiv N_0 V^L(t)$ and $P_Y(t) C(t) + T(t) = N_0 \left[W(t)L(t) + s_R W(t)L_R(t) + \Pi^L(t) \right]$. Next, we find that $\dot{A}(t) \equiv N_0 \dot{V}^L(t)$. By using these results as well as (14.140), (14.142), and (14.143) we obtain (14.145).

and the labour market equilibrium condition is:

$$L_0 = N_0 \left[\bar{L}(t) + L_R(t) \right], \tag{14.150}$$

where L_0 is labour supply and $\bar{L}(t)$ is the amount of labour used in each industry i (see (14.138) above).

14.4.2.5 Growth

We now possess all the ingredients of the model. Following the approach of Grossman and Helpman (1991b, pp. 48–49), we condense the model to two equations in total spending, $E(t)$, and the R&D intensity, $L_R(t)$. Because the steps are non-trivial, we provide some of the details of the derivation. In the first step, we note that equation (14.144), in combination with (14.140), (14.136), and (14.148), can be used to obtain a useful expression for the interest rate:

$$r(t) = \frac{\alpha \xi Z_R}{1 + \xi} \frac{E(t)}{(1 - s_R)(1 - g) W(t)} + \frac{\dot{W}(t)}{W(t)} - Z_R L_R(t), \tag{14.151}$$

where we note that $N_0 = 1/\alpha$. In the second step, we use (14.128) and (14.137) in (14.131) to find an expression for $\ln P_Y(t)$:

$$\ln P_Y(t) = \ln \left(\frac{N_0}{Z_Y} \right) + \ln \bar{P}(t) + \ln \prod_{i=1}^{N_0} (1 + \xi)^{-\alpha m_i(t)}$$

$$= \ln \left(\frac{(1 + \xi) N_0}{Z_Y Z_X} \right) + \ln W(t) - \alpha \ln (1 + \xi) \cdot \sum_{i=1}^{N_0} m_i(t). \tag{14.152}$$

By taking the time derivative of (14.152) we thus obtain:

$$\frac{\dot{P}_Y(t)}{P_Y(t)} \equiv \frac{d \ln P_Y(t)}{dt} = \frac{\dot{W}(t)}{W(t)} - [\alpha \ln (1 + \xi)] \cdot \frac{d}{dt} \sum_i^{N_0} m_i(t). \tag{14.153}$$

Recall that each $m_i(t)$ is a stochastic variable, which may feature an upward jump as a result of R&D activities. The instantaneous probability of such a jump occurring is the same for all $m_i(t)$ and depends on the R&D intensity as stated in (14.140). Since N_0 is assumed to be very large, probabilities and frequencies coincide, so that $\sum_i^{N_0} m_i(t)$ changes smoothly over time according to:

$$\frac{d}{dt} \sum_i^{N_0} m_i(t) = N_0 \pi(t) = N_0 Z_R L_R(t). \tag{14.154}$$

In the third and final step we choose labour as the numeraire and thus set $W(t) = 1$ and $\dot{W}(t) = 0$. The model can now be expressed in a very compact format as:

$$\frac{\dot{E}(t)}{E(t)} = \frac{\alpha \sigma \xi Z_R}{1 + \xi} \frac{E(t)}{(1 - s_R)(1 - g)} - \sigma \rho - \sigma \phi Z_R L_R(t), \tag{14.155}$$

$$L_0 = \frac{E(t)}{(1 + \xi)(1 - g)} + \frac{1}{\alpha} L_R(t), \tag{14.156}$$

where $\phi \equiv 1 + (1/\sigma - 1) \ln (1 + \xi)$ is a composite parameter which we assume to be positive.[19] Equation (14.155) is obtained by (14.151) and (14.153)–(14.154) in (14.146).

---

[19]This is a very mild assumption. For a logarithmic felicity function ($\sigma = 1$) we find that $\phi = 1$. For plausible values of the intertemporal substitution elasticity, $0 < \sigma < 1$, it follows that $\phi > 1$.

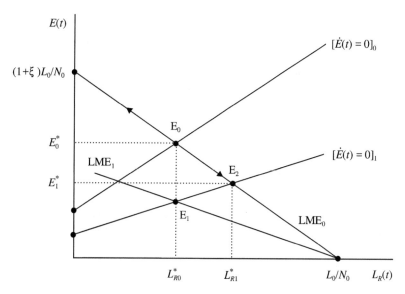

Figure 14.8: Equilibrium in the rising input quality model

Equation (14.156) is the labour market clearing condition (14.150), rewritten by using (14.137)–(14.138) and (14.147)–(14.148).

The dynamic properties of the model can be illustrated with the aid of Figure 14.8. In that figure, LME_0 represents the initial labour market equilibrium condition (14.156). The initial $\dot{E}(t) = 0$ line (labelled $[\dot{E}(t) = 0]_0$) is obtained from (14.155):

$$\frac{\alpha \zeta Z_R}{1 + \zeta} \frac{E(t)}{(1 - s_R)(1 - g)} = \rho + \phi Z_R L_R(t). \tag{14.157}$$

Since ϕ is assumed to be positive, the $[\dot{E}(t) = 0]_0$ is upward sloping and intersects the LME_0 line at point E_0. It follows from (14.155) that $\dot{E}(t) > 0$ (< 0) for points above (below) the $[\dot{E}(t) = 0]_0$ line. This has been indicated with arrows along the LME_0 line. The equilibrium at E_0 is clearly unstable, so the only economically feasible solution is for $E(t)$ to jump to its steady-state value, i.e. there is no transitional dynamics, $E(t) = E^*$, and $L_R(t) = L_R^*$. Solving (14.156)–(14.157) we find:

$$\frac{E^*}{1 - g} = (1 + \zeta) \frac{\phi L_0 + \rho N_0 / Z_R}{\zeta / (1 - s_R) + \phi}, \tag{14.158}$$

$$L_R^* = \frac{\zeta L_0 / [(1 - s_R) N_0] - \rho / Z_R}{\zeta / (1 - s_R) + \phi}, \tag{14.159}$$

where we have also used the fact that $\alpha = 1/N_0$ to simplify the expressions.

How does government policy affect the economy in the RIQ model? Clearly, an increase in the share of government consumption simply leads to crowding out of private consumption but has no effect on the R&D intensity–see (14.158)–(14.159). In terms of Figure 14.8, the $\dot{E}(t) = 0$ locus rotates in a clockwise direction, from $[\dot{E}(t) = 0]_0$ to $[\dot{E}(t) = 0]_1$, and the LME curve rotates counterclockwise from LME_0 to LME_1. The new equilibrium is at E_1, which lies vertically below point E_0. It thus follows that $dL_R^*/dg = 0$ and $dE^*/dg = -E_0^*/(1 - g) < 0$. An increase in the wage subsidy to R&D workers does have a positive effect on the R&D intensity. In terms of Figure 14.8, an increase in s_R rotates the $\dot{E}(t) = 0$ locus in a clockwise direction, from $[\dot{E}(t) = 0]_0$ to $[\dot{E}(t) = 0]_1$, but leaves the LME curve unchanged. The new equilibrium is at point E_2, and we find from (14.158)–(14.159) that $dL_R^* / ds_R > 0$ and $dE^* / ds_R < 0$.

In order to deduce the economic growth properties of the model, we note that $X_i(t) = \bar{X}(t) (1 + \xi)^{m_i(t)}$ and use (14.126) to write the logarithm of output as:

$$\ln Y(t) = \ln Z_Y + \ln \bar{X}(t) + \ln \left[\prod_{i=1}^{N_0} (1 + \xi)^{\alpha m_i(t)} \right]$$

$$= \ln \left(\frac{\alpha Z_Y Z_X}{1 + \xi} \right) + \ln \left(\frac{E^*}{1 - g} \right) + [\alpha \ln (1 + \xi)] \cdot \sum_i^{N_0} m_i(t), \qquad (14.160)$$

where we have used (14.137)–(14.138) and (14.148), and noted that $E(t) = E^*$, to get from the first to the second expression. By taking the time derivative we find the growth rate in aggregate output:

$$\gamma_Y^* \equiv \frac{\dot{Y}(t)}{Y(t)} \equiv \frac{d \ln Y(t)}{dt} = [\alpha \ln (1 + \xi)] \cdot \frac{d}{dt} \sum_i^{N_0} m_i(t)$$

$$= [Z_R \ln (1 + \xi)] \cdot L_R^*, \qquad (14.161)$$

where we have used (14.154) and noted that $L_R(t) = L_R^*$ to get to the final expression. Obviously, consumption grows at the same rate as output, $\gamma_C^* = \gamma_Y^*$, and the final output price falls exponentially, $\gamma_{P_Y}^* = -\gamma_Y^*$. Defining the real wage rate by $w(t) \equiv W(t) / P_Y(t)$ we furthermore find that $\gamma_w^* = \gamma_Y^*$.

The comparative static effects on the economic growth rate can be deduced from (14.161) in combination with (14.159). Obviously, government consumption has no effect on growth ($d\gamma_Y^* / dg = 0$) but the R&D subsidy positively affects the growth rate ($d\gamma_Y^* / ds_R = [Z_R \ln (1 + \xi)] \cdot dL_R^* / ds_R > 0$). Growth depends negatively on the rate of time preference and positively on the intertemporal substitution elasticity ($d\gamma_Y^* / d\rho < 0$ and $d\gamma_Y^* / d\sigma > 0$, with the latter operating via its effect on the composite parameter ϕ). Just as in the standard EIV model discussed in the previous subsection, there is a scale effect in the RIQ model ($d\gamma_Y^* / dL_0 = [Z_R \ln (1 + \xi)] \cdot dL_R^* / dL_0 > 0$). Technically, this scale effect is a direct result from the assumption underlying quality change. Indeed, using (14.128) we find that a successful innovation leads to a constant percentage increase in quality as $\Delta Q_{i,j+1} / Q_{i,j} = \xi$. The instantaneous probability of achieving R&D success itself depends (via (14.140)) on the size of R&D employment. As a result, an increase in the total labour force boosts economic growth because it allows for higher R&D employment. Just as for the EIV model, several authors have suggested ways in which the scale effect can be removed from RIQ-style R&D model—see inter alia Segerstrom (1998), Young (1998), and Jones (1999). Finally, as was already noted by Grossman and Helpman (1991a, p. 98), the RIQ model is isomorphic to the EIV model, in the sense that they give rise to virtually identical qualitative predictions.

14.5 Punchlines

This chapter deals with the recent literature on so-called "endogenous" growth. Three major approaches can be distinguished in this literature. The so-called "capital-fundamentalist" models generate perpetual growth by abandoning one of the key elements of the Solow-Swan model (studied in Chapter 12), namely the assumption that the average product of capital goes to zero as the capital stock gets very large. If it is easy to substitute capital for labour then the average product of capital reaches a finite limiting value. It is possible to produce without any labour at all, and long-run growth depends, among other things, on the savings rate. Similar results are obtained for the AK-model in which labour plays no role at all and production features constant returns to a broad measure of capital.

The second major approach in the endogenous growth literature emphasizes the purposeful accumulation of human capital as the engine of growth. This approach was pioneered by Uzawa in the mid 1960s and further developed by Lucas. The model features infinitely lived households, and technology exhibits constant returns to scale in capital and effective labour. The rate of growth in human capital depends on the fraction of time households spend on educational purposes. Even without population growth, consumption, human and physical capital, and output all grow at the same exponential rate.

The third group of studies in the field of endogenous growth is based on the notion that research and development (R&D) activities by firms constitute the engine of growth in the economy. Studies in this vein abandon the assumption of perfect competition and instead analyse monopolistically competitive firms in the intermediate goods sector. We first study a very simple model of *horizontal input differentiation* (to keep things simple, we abstract from physical and human capital). In this model the R&D sector produces blueprints for new differentiated inputs. In the intermediate goods sector there are many monopolistically competitive firms which each hold a blueprint telling them how to produce their own, slightly unique, input variety. The market for final goods is competitive, but there exists an external effect due to returns to specialization, i.e. a broader range of differentiated inputs raises productivity of final goods producers because a more round-about production process can be adopted. The model features a constant rate of innovation which depends positively on the monopoly markup and the scale of the economy. The scale effect is a problematic feature of many R&D based models because it is easily falsified empirically. Elimination of the scale effect is possible but renders the rate of innovation proportional to the rate of population growth, just as in the standard Solow-Swan model.

The second R&D model is one in which the quality of existing inputs is improved by means of R&D activities, i.e. it describes *vertical input differentiation*. Interestingly, the predictions yielded by the vertical differentiation model are virtually identical in a qualitative sense to those of the horizontal differentiation model.

Further reading

Warsh (2006) presents a highly readable account of the development of the endogenous growth literature. See also the symposium on new growth theory in the Winter 1994 issue of the *Journal of Economic Perspectives*. Important early papers on endogenous growth are by Arrow (1962), Uzawa (1965), Sheshinski (1967), Shell (1967), and Conlisk (1969).

Recent textbooks on economic growth include Barro and Sala-i-Martin (1995), Aghion and Howitt (1998), Gylfason (1999), Jones (2002), Helpman (2004), Weil (2005), and Acemoglu (2009). Key references to the R&D literature are Grossman and Helpman (1991a) and Aghion and Howitt (1998). The classic source on the idea of creative destruction is Schumpeter (1934).

On the human capital approach, see Lucas (1988), Stokey and Rebelo (1995),

Ladrón-de-Guevera et al. (1997, 1999), and Ortigueira and Santos (2002). Lucas (1990a) studies capital taxation in a growth model. Temple (1999) presents a survey of the recent empirical growth literature. See also the articles in Aghion and Durlauf (2005a, 2005b). On the issue of transitional dynamics, see King and Rebelo (1993), Mulligan and Sala-i-Martin (1993), Xie (1994), Benhabib and Perli (1994), and Bond et al. (1996).

For money and endogenous growth, see, for example, Ireland (1994). Key contributions to the literature on public investment include Barro (1981, 1990), Aschauer and Greenwood (1985), Uzawa (1988), Aschauer (1988, 1989), Baxter and King (1993), Glomm and Ravikumar (1994), Turnovsky (1996), Turnovsky and Fisher (1995), and Fisher and Turnovsky (1998). On the scale effect, see Young (1998) and Segerstrom (1998). On R&D and education, see Griliches (2000). Rivera-Batiz and Romer (1991) study the growth effects of economic integration.

In recent years, economists have started to develop growth models in which innovations and technical change are drastic and pervasive (rather than incremental). Key references to this *general purpose technology* (GPT) literature are Bresnehan and Trajtenberg (1995), Helpman and Trajtenberg (1998a, 1998b), and the collection of papers in Helpman (1998).

On directed technological change, see the classic paper by Drandakis and Phelps (1965), and the recent papers by Acemoglu (2002, 2003a, 2003b, 2007), Acemoglu et al. (2006), and Vandenbussche et al. (2006).

Chapter 15

Overlapping generations in continuous time

The purpose of this chapter is to achieve the following goals:

1. To introduce a popular continuous-time overlapping-generations (OLG) model and to show its main theoretical properties.

2. To apply this workhorse model to study fiscal policy, the role of debt, dynamic efficiency, and economic growth.

3. To demonstrate that the model features a plausible type of equilibrium in the context of a small open economy.

4. To extend the continuous-time OLG model to the case of endogenous labour supply, and to conduct a comparative dynamic tax policy experiment; both analytically and numerically.

15.1   Introduction

In this chapter we study one of the "workhorse" models of modern macroeconomics, namely the Blanchard (1985)-Yaari (1965) model of overlapping generations. This model has proved to be quite versatile because it is very flexible and contains the Ramsey-Cass-Koopmans (RCK) model as a special case. The main difference between the Blanchard-Yaari model and the RCK model is that the former distinguishes agents by their date of birth whereas the latter assumes a single representative agent. By incorporating some smart modelling devices, the Blanchard-Yaari model can be solved and analysed at the aggregate macroeconomic level, despite the fact that individual households are heterogeneous.

15.2   Individual behaviour under lifetime uncertainty

15.2.1   Yaari's lessons

One of the great certainties in life–apart from taxes–is death. After that things get fuzzy because nobody knows exactly when the Grim Reaper will make his one and only call. In all consumption models discussed so far in this book, *lifetime uncertainty* has been ignored, however. Indeed, in Chapter 6 we introduced the basic two-period consumption-saving model to illustrate the various reasons for the breakdown of the Ricardian equivalence theorem. But in that model each agent knows exactly that he will only live for two periods. Similarly, in Chapter 13 we explained the Ramsey model in which an infinitely lived representative consumer makes optimal consumption and saving decisions. Again there is no lifetime uncertainty because the agent lives forever in this model.

In a seminal article, Yaari (1965) confronted the issue of lifetime uncertainty in the context of a dynamic consumption-saving model. In doing so, he provided one of the key building blocks of the Blanchard (1985) overlapping-generations model which has become one of the workhorse models of dynamic macroeconomics. Yaari (1965, pp. 139–140) clearly identified the two complications arising in a model with lifetime uncertainty. First, if the agent's time of death, D, is random then so is that agent's lifetime utility function. As a result the agent's decision problem is inherently stochastic, and maximizing lifetime utility makes no sense. Rather, the expected utility hypothesis must be used, and *expected* lifetime utility should be the objective function. Second, the non-negativity constraint on the agent's wealth at the time of death is similarly stochastic as it also depends on the random time of death. In symbols, if $A(t)$ is real assets at time t, then $A(D)$ is stochastic and the solution procedure should ensure that $A(D) \geq 0$ holds with certainty.

Fortunately, Yaari (1965) also proposed appropriate solutions to these two complications. First, though D is a random variable all we need to do to render the expected utility hypothesis operational is to postulate a probability density function for D. Indeed, demographic data can be used to obtain quite detailed estimates of the distribution function for D (see also below). Obviously, no one has a negative expected lifetime and there also seems to be a finite upper limit, $\bar{D}$, beyond which nobody lives. So the density function for D is denoted by $\phi(D)$ and it satisfies:

$$\phi(D) \geq 0 \quad \text{(for all } D \geq 0); \quad \Phi(\bar{D}) = \int_0^{\bar{D}} \phi(D)dD = 1. \tag{15.1}$$

The first property is a general requirement for densities and the second one says that the random variable D lies in the interval $[0, \bar{D}]$ with probability 1 (i.e. $\Pr\{0 \leq D \leq \bar{D}\} = 1$). The cumulative distribution function, $\Phi(x)$, of the random variable D is defined as $\Phi(x) = \Pr\{D \leq x\} = \int_0^x \phi(D)dD$ from which it follows that $d\Phi(x) = \phi(x)dx$, that is, the density function is the derivative of the cumulative distribution function (i.e., $d\Phi(x)/dx = \phi(x)$). In the absence of *mass points*, $\Phi(x)$ is continuous. Figure 15.1 provides an illustration of a stylized cumulative distribution function. In that figure, $\Phi(D_0)$ represents the probability that the agent will expire before or at age D_0. In Figure 15.2 the density function (right axis) as well as the survival probability (left axis) have been illustrated.

The consumer's lifetime utility is given by:

$$\Lambda(D) \equiv \int_0^D U(C(t))e^{-\rho t}dt, \tag{15.2}$$

where $U(C(t))$ is instantaneous utility (or "felicity") at time t, $C(t)$ is private consumption,[1] and ρ is the pure rate of time preference. To keep matters simple, we

---

[1] Labour supply is taken to be inelastically supplied. Hence, the consumption-leisure decision is not part of the consumer's optimization problem. Below this assumption is relaxed.

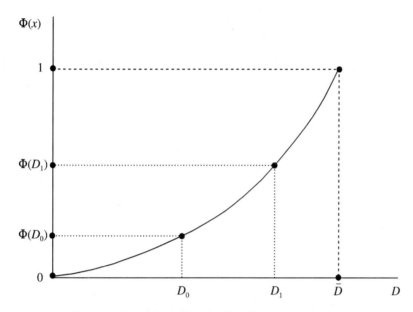

Figure 15.1: Cumulative distribution function

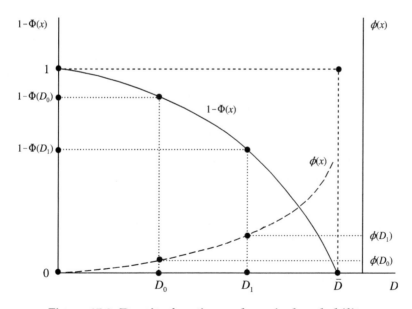

Figure 15.2: Density function and survival probability

assume that the felicity function is iso-elastic:

$$U(C(t)) \equiv \begin{cases} \dfrac{C(t)^{1-1/\sigma} - 1}{1 - 1/\sigma} & \text{for } \sigma > 0, \quad \sigma \neq 1, \\ \ln C(t) & \text{for } \sigma = 1. \end{cases} \tag{15.3}$$

where σ is the intertemporal substitution elasticity. Using (15.1) and (15.2), *expected lifetime utility* can be written as:[2]

$$
\begin{aligned}
E(\Lambda(D)) &\equiv \int_0^{\bar{D}} \phi(D)\Lambda(D)dD \\
&= \int_0^{\bar{D}} \left[\int_t^{\bar{D}} \phi(D)dD \right] U(C(t))e^{-\rho t} dt \\
&= \int_0^{\bar{D}} [1 - \Phi(t)] U(C(t))e^{-\rho t} dt,
\end{aligned}
\tag{15.4}
$$

where $1 - \Phi(t)$ is the probability that the consumer will still be alive at time t:

$$1 - \Phi(t) \equiv \int_t^{\bar{D}} \phi(D)dD. \tag{15.5}$$

The crucial thing to note about (15.4) is that the consumer's objective function is now in a rather standard format. Apart from containing some additional elements ($\bar{D}$ and $\Phi(t)$) resulting from lifetime uncertainty, the expression in (15.4) is very similar to the utility function of the representative consumer (namely equation (13.2) in Chapter 13).

The second complication identified by Yaari (1965) and discussed above can also be easily dealt with. Assume that the household budget identity can be written as follows:

$$\dot{A}(t) = r(t)A(t) + w(t) - C(t), \tag{15.6}$$

where $\dot{A}(t) \equiv dA(t)/dt$, $r(t)$ is the rate of interest, and $w(t)$ is non-interest income, all expressed in real terms (i.e., units of output). Both $r(t)$ and $w(t)$ are known to the consumer as lifetime uncertainty is (by assumption) the only stochastic element in the model. Yaari (1965, pp. 142–143) explains that the time-of-death wealth constraint, $\Pr\{A(D) \geq 0\} = 1$, is then equivalent to:

$$A(\bar{D}) = 0; \qquad C(t) \leq w(t) \text{ whenever } A(t) = 0. \tag{15.7}$$

The intuition behind this result is as follows. We know for sure that the constraint $A(t) \geq 0$ must hold with equality for $t = \bar{D}$, i.e. $A(\bar{D}) = 0$. For other values of t it follows that $A(t) \geq 0$ is equivalent to $\dot{A}(t) = w(t) - C(t) \geq 0$ if $A(t) = 0$, i.e. no dissaving is allowed if no wealth remains. A consumer who owns financial assets $A(0)$ in the planning period ($t = 0$) faces the following lifetime budget constraint (see Intermezzo 13.1 for a detailed derivation):

$$\int_0^{\bar{D}} C(t)e^{-R(0,t)} dt = A(0) + \int_0^{\bar{D}} w(t)e^{-R(0,t)} dt, \tag{15.8}$$

where $R(0,t) \equiv \int_0^t r(s)ds$ is a cumulative interest factor involving the market rate of interest, and we have used the fact that $A(\bar{D}) = 0$. Intuitively, the condition says

---

[2]In going from the first to the second line in (15.4) we have changed the order of integration. See Intermezzo 15.1 for details.

that the present value of the consumption stream must be equal to the sum of initial financial assets plus the present value of current and future non-interest income (i.e. "human wealth"), using the market rate of interest for discounting.

The consumer maximizes expected lifetime utility ($E(\Lambda(D))$ in (15.4)) subject to (15.6), (15.7), and the non-negativity constraint on consumption ($C(t) \geq 0$), and given the initial wealth level ($A(0)$). The interior solution for this optimization problem is summarized by:

$$[1 - \Phi(t)]\, U'(C(t)) = \lambda(t), \tag{15.9}$$

$$\frac{\dot{\lambda}(t)}{\lambda(t)} = \rho - r(t), \tag{15.10}$$

where $\lambda(t)$—the co-state variable associated with (15.6)—represents the expected marginal utility of wealth. Intuitively, (15.9) says that in the interior solution the consumer equates the expected marginal utility of consumption to the expected marginal utility of wealth. Equation (15.10) is the standard expression summarizing the optimal dynamics of the marginal utility of wealth.

By combining (15.9) and (15.10) and noting (15.3) we obtain the household's consumption Euler equation in the presence of lifetime uncertainty:

$$\frac{\dot{C}(t)}{C(t)} = \sigma\left[r(t) - \rho - \mu(t)\right], \tag{15.11}$$

where $\mu(t) \equiv \phi(t)/[1 - \Phi(t)] > 0$ is the so-called "hazard rate" or *instantaneous probability of death* at time t. Compared to the case of an infinitely lived consumer, the hazard rate is the additional term appearing in the Euler equation.[3] This is the *first lesson* from Yaari (1965, p. 143): the uncertainty of survival leads the household to discount the future more heavily, i.e. the subjective discount rate in the presence of lifetime uncertainty is $\rho + \mu(t)$ rather than just ρ. This makes intuitive sense. If there is a positive probability that you will not live long enough to enjoy a given planned future consumption path, then you tend to discount the utility stream resulting from it more heavily. In Figure 15.2, the hazard rate for $x = D_0$ is represented by the ratio $\phi(D_0)/[1 - \Phi(D_0)]$, whilst for $x = D_1$ the hazard rate is $\phi(D_1)/[1 - \Phi(D_1)]$. Clearly, since $\phi(D_1) > \phi(D_0)$ and $1 - \Phi(D_1) < 1 - \Phi(D_0)$, the hazard rate increases with the agent's age.

Up to this point we have studied the consumer's optimal decisions when no insurance possibilities are available. But in reality various forms of life insurance exist, so a relevant question is how this institutional feature would change the consumer's behaviour. Yaari (1965, pp. 140-141) suggests a particular kind of life insurance based on *actuarial notes* issued by the insurance company. An actuarial note can be bought or sold by the consumer and is cancelled upon the consumer's death. The instantaneous rate of interest on such notes is denoted by $r^A(t)$, and non-zero trade in such notes only occurs if $r^A(t)$ exceeds $r(t)$. A consumer who *buys* an actuarial note in fact buys an annuity which stipulates payments to the consumer during life at a rate higher than the rate of interest. Upon the consumer's death the insurance company has no further obligations to the consumer's estate. Reversely, a consumer who *sells* an actuarial note is getting a life-insured loan. During the consumer's life he must pay a higher interest rate on the loan than the market rate of interest but upon death the consumer's estate is held free of any obligations, i.e. the principal does not have to be paid back to the insurance company.

---

[3]In the standard Ramsey model no lifetime uncertainty exists. See e.g. Chapters 13–14.

In order to determine the rate of return on actuarial notes, Yaari makes the (simplest possible) assumption of *actuarial fairness*. To derive the expression for $r^A(t)$ implied by this assumption, consider the case where one euro's worth of actuarial notes is bought at time t. These notes are either redeemed with interest at time $t + dt$ (if the consumer survives) or are cancelled (if the consumer dies between t and $t + dt$). Actuarial fairness then implies:

$$\left[1 + r^A(t)dt\right] \cdot \left(\frac{1 - \Phi(t + dt)}{1 - \Phi(t)}\right) = 1 + r(t)dt, \tag{15.12}$$

where the equality holds as $dt \to 0$. The right-hand side of (15.12) shows the yield if the euro is invested in regular market instruments whereas the left-hand side shows the yield on the actuarial note purchase. The term in round brackets is less than unity and corrects for the fact that the consumer may pass away between t and $t + dt$. Next, we note that (15.12) can be rewritten as:

$$r^A(t) = \frac{1 - \Phi(t)}{1 - \Phi(t + dt)} \cdot r(t) + \frac{\frac{\Phi(t + dt) - \Phi(t)}{dt}}{1 - \Phi(t + dt)}. \tag{15.13}$$

By letting $dt \to 0$, the first term on the right-hand side goes to $r(t)$ and the second approaches $\mu(t) \equiv \phi(t)/[1 - \Phi(t)]$. Hence, we are left with a rather intuitive no-arbitrage equation between the two kinds of financial instruments:

$$r^A(t) = r(t) + \mu(t). \tag{15.14}$$

Up to this point we have been deliberately vague about the age of the individual consumer whose behaviour we are studying. If the consumer is born at time $t = 0$ then t is not only the time index but also stands for the consumer's age. If, on the other hand, the consumer was born at some earlier time $v < 0$ then t is the time index but $u \equiv t - v$ is the age index. In this more general setting the no-arbitrage equation takes the following form:

$$r^A(u) = r(t) + \mu(u). \tag{15.15}$$

In words, at time t an individual of age u receives a yield on actuarial notes equal to the time-dependent interest rate on regular assets *plus* the age-dependent instantaneous mortality rate. As we demonstrate below, a realistic mortality process implies that the instantaneous mortality rate rises with age, i.e. $d\mu(u)/du > 0$. It follows from (15.15) that, holding constant the market interest rate $r(t)$, the annuity rate facing a consumer rises with that consumer's age, i.e. an eighty-year-old person (an *octogenarian*) faces a much higher annuity rate than a twenty-year-old person (a *vicegenarian*) does. The closer the consumer gets to the maximum possible age $\bar{D}$, the higher will be the instantaneous probability of death and thus the higher will be the required excess yield on actuarial notes.

Let us now return to the consumer's choice problem. To economize on notation we assume that the consumer is born at time $t = v = 0$ so we are studying the behavious of an "economic newborn". As Yaari (1965, p. 145) points out, the consumer will always hold his financial assets in the form of actuarial notes, i.e. he will fully insure against the loss of life and the budget identity will be:

$$\dot{A}(t) = r^A(t)A(t) + w(t) - C(t). \tag{15.16}$$

Hence the restriction on the terminal asset position is trivially met as all actuarial notes are automatically cancelled when the consumer dies. The intuition behind this *full-insurance* result is best understood by looking at the two possible cases. If the consumer has positive net assets at any time then they will be held in the form of actuarial notes because these yield the highest return (which is all the consumer is interested in in the absence of a bequest motive). Conversely, if the consumer had negative outstanding net assets in any form other than actuarial notes, he would be violating the constraint on terminal assets mentioned above (i.e. the requirement that $\Pr\{A(D) \geq 0\} = 1$).

We are not out of the forest of complications yet as we also need to ensure that the consumer is unable to beat the system by engaging in unlimited borrowing (sales of actuarial notes) and covering the ever increasing interest payments with yet further borrowings. This prompts the consumer's solvency condition, $\lim_{t \to \bar{D}} A(t) e^{-R^A(0,t)} = 0$, which can be combined with (15.16) to yield the lifetime budget constraint:

$$\int_0^{\bar{D}} C(t) e^{-R^A(0,t)} dt = A(0) + \int_0^{\bar{D}} w(t) e^{-R^A(0,t)} dt, \tag{15.17}$$

where $R^A(0,t) \equiv \int_0^t r^A(s) ds$ is a cumulative interest factor involving the annuity rate of interest. The key difference between the lifetime budget constraints (15.8) and (15.17) lies in the fact that the market rate of interest is used for discounting in the former whereas the rate on actuarial notes is used for discounting in the latter.

The consumer maximizes expected lifetime utility ($E(\Lambda(D))$ in (15.4)) subject to the lifetime budget constraint (15.17) and the non-negativity constraint on consumption ($C(t) \geq 0$). The interior solution to this problem is characterized by the following Euler equation:

$$\frac{\dot{C}(t)}{C(t)} = \sigma[r^A(t) - \rho - \mu(t)] = \sigma[r(t) - \rho], \tag{15.18}$$

where we have used (15.14) in going from the first to the second expression. The striking thing to note about (15.18)–and thus Yaari's *second lesson*–is the fact that the Euler equation with fully insured lifetime uncertainty is identical to the Euler equation when no lifetime uncertainty exists! It should be observed, however, that the consumption levels will differ between the two scenarios as the lifetime consumption possibility frontier will differ between the two cases.

Intermezzo 15.1

Technical results for the Yaari model. In this intermezzo we gather some of the more complicated derivations for the Yaari model. The cumulative distribution function for the random variable D is defined as:

$$\Phi(x) \equiv \int_0^x \phi(D) \, dD, \qquad 0 \leq x \leq \bar{D}, \tag{a}$$

so we find from (15.1) that $\Phi(0) = 0$, $\Phi(\bar{D}) = 1$, and $d\Phi(x) = \phi(x) \, dx$. Intuitively, $\Phi(D_0)$ is the unconditional probability that the agent is no longer alive at age D_0. Its complement, $1 - \Phi(D_0)$, thus represents the unconditional probability that the agent is still alive at age D_0. The probabilities are called *unconditional* because they are taken from the perspective of the beginning of life.

What is the life expectancy of an agent who is still alive at age $D_0 > 0$? The *conditional probability density* function (Ross, 1993, p. 88) is defined as:

$$\phi(D|D \geq D_0) \equiv \frac{\phi(D)}{1 - \Phi(D_0)}, \qquad \text{(for } D_0 \leq D \leq \bar{D}\text{)}, \qquad \text{(b)}$$

where the scaling factor in the denominator corrects for the fact that only values for D exceeding D_0 receive non-zero weight. Clearly we find from (b) that $\int_{D_0}^{\bar{D}} \phi(D|D \geq D_0)\, dD = 1$. The *expected remaining lifetime* (ERL) of an agent of age D_0 is thus given by:

$$
\begin{aligned}
ERL(D_0) &\equiv \int_{D_0}^{\bar{D}} \phi(D|D \geq D_0)\, [D - D_0]\, dD \\
&= \int_{D_0}^{\bar{D}} \frac{\phi(D)}{1 - \Phi(D_0)}\, [D - D_0]\, dD \\
&= \frac{1}{1 - \Phi(D_0)} \cdot \left[\int_{D_0}^{\bar{D}} \phi(D)\, D\, dD - D_0 \int_{D_0}^{\bar{D}} \phi(D)\, dD \right]. \qquad \text{(c)}
\end{aligned}
$$

The first integral on the right-hand side of (c) can be simplified by noting that $\phi(D)\, dD = d\Phi(D)$ so that *integration by parts* gives:

$$
\begin{aligned}
\int_{D_0}^{\bar{D}} \phi(D)\, D\, dD &= \int_{D_0}^{\bar{D}} D\, d\Phi(D) = D\Phi(D) \Big|_{D_0}^{\bar{D}} - \int_{D_0}^{\bar{D}} \Phi(D)\, dD \\
&= \bar{D}\Phi(\bar{D}) - D_0\Phi(D_0) - \int_{D_0}^{\bar{D}} \Phi(D)\, dD. \qquad \text{(d)}
\end{aligned}
$$

The second integral on the right-hand side of (c) is:

$$D_0 \int_{D_0}^{\bar{D}} \phi(D)\, dD = D_0 \int_{D_0}^{\bar{D}} d\Phi(D) = D_0\, [1 - \Phi(D_0)]. \qquad \text{(e)}$$

By using (d)–(e) in (c) and recalling that $\Phi(\bar{D}) = 1$ we thus find that life expectancy is given by:

$$
\begin{aligned}
ERL(D_0) &= \frac{\bar{D} - D_0\Phi(D_0) - \int_{D_0}^{\bar{D}} \Phi(D)\, dD - D_0\, [1 - \Phi(D_0)]}{1 - \Phi(D_0)} \\
&= \frac{1}{1 - \Phi(D_0)} \cdot \int_{D_0}^{\bar{D}} [1 - \Phi(D)]\, dD. \qquad \text{(f)}
\end{aligned}
$$

In the text we often work directly with the instantaneous mortality rate, $\mu(u)$, of an agent with age u (with $0 \leq u \leq \bar{D}$). We know from the text below equation (15.11) that $\mu(u) \equiv \phi(u) / [1 - \Phi(u)]$. Hence, since $\Phi'(u) = \phi(u)$, we can write:

$$\mu(u) = -\frac{d}{du} \ln[1 - \Phi(u)]. \qquad \text{(g)}$$

It thus follows that:

$$-\int_0^{u_0} \mu(u)\,du = \int_0^{u_0} d\ln[1-\Phi(u)] \qquad \Rightarrow$$

$$-M(u_0) = \ln[1-\Phi(u_0)] - \ln[1-\Phi(0)] \qquad \Rightarrow$$

$$e^{-M(u_0)} = 1 - \Phi(u_0), \qquad \text{(h)}$$

where we have used the definition for the *integrated hazard function*, $M(u_0) \equiv \int_0^{u_0} \mu(u)\,du$, and noted that $\Phi(0) = 0$ (so that $\ln[1 - \Phi(0)] = 0$.

The final result to be demonstrated concerns the change in the order of integration that we use in getting from the first to the second line in equation (15.4). By defining the auxiliary function, $g(t) \equiv U(C(t))e^{-\rho t}$, we can write:

$$E(\Lambda(D)) = \int_0^D \phi(D)\left[\int_0^D g(t)\,dt\right]dD$$

$$= \int_0^D \left[\int_0^D \phi(D)g(t)\,dt\right]dD. \qquad \text{(i)}$$

The original region of integration is visualized in Figure A. The inner integral in (i) take all values of t between 0 and D (horizontal shading) whilst the outer integral in (i) takes all values of D between 0 and $\bar{D}$ (vertical shading). It follows that the integration gives rise to the pattern of shading as in Figure A.

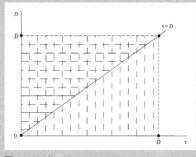
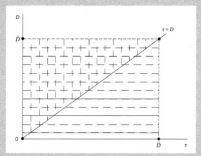

Figure A   Figure B

Changing the order of integration in (i) we get:

$$E(\Lambda(D)) = \int_?^? \left[\int_?^? \phi(D)\,dD\right]g(t)\,dt \qquad \text{(j)}$$

and we need to establish the appropriate region of integration. It is easy to see that the equivalent pattern of shading is obtained in Figure B by ensuring that the inner integral in (j) takes all values of D between t and $\bar{D}$ (vertical shading), and the outer integral in (j) takes all values of t between 0 and $\bar{D}$ (horizontal shading). Using the results in (j) we thus get:

$$E(\Lambda(D)) = \int_0^{\bar{D}} \left[\int_t^{\bar{D}} \phi(D)\,dD\right]g(t)\,dt. \qquad \text{(k)}$$

By using the definition for $g(t)$ and noting that $\int_t^{\bar{D}} \phi(D)\,dD = 1 - \Phi(t)$ we obtain (15.4) in the text.

****

15.2.2 Realistic mortality profile

In this section we visualize the Yaari model with the aid of a realistic mortality process. For expository purposes, and in order to stay as close as possible to the original Yaari setup, we use a demographic parameterization which implies a finite maximum age. Indeed, following Boucekkine et al. (2002), we write the cumulative distribution function as:

$$\Phi(u) \equiv \frac{e^{\eta_1 u} - 1}{\eta_0 - 1}, \qquad \text{for } 0 \le u \le \bar{D} \equiv \frac{\ln \eta_0}{\eta_1}, \tag{15.19}$$

where u is the agent's *economic age*, $\eta_0 > 1$ and $\eta_1 > 0$, and $\bar{D}$ is obtained by noting that $\Phi(\bar{D}) = 1$ (so that $e^{\eta_1 \bar{D}} = \eta_0$). Heijdra and Mierau (2012, p. 884) use mortality data from *biological age* 18 onward for the cohort born in 1960 in the Netherlands to estimate the parameters of this function. They find the following estimates (with t-statistics in brackets) $\hat{\eta}_0 = 122.643$ (11.14) and $\hat{\eta}_1 = 0.0680$ (48.51), implying an estimated maximum economic age of $\bar{D} = 70.75$ years and a life expectancy at birth of 56.62 economic years. In biological years these numbers translate to 88.75 and 74.62. In Figure 15.3 we illustrate the actual and fitted survival fraction.[4] Up to about biological age 85 the fitted curve tracks the data rather well. For ages beyond 85, however, the fit is less impressive because there are some rather sturdy individuals whose mortality process is not captured by the functional form given in (15.19) above.

Using (15.19), we easily find the expressions for the density function and the instantaneous mortality rate:

$$\phi(u) \equiv \frac{d\Phi(u)}{du} = \frac{\eta_1 e^{\eta_1 u}}{\eta_0 - 1}, \qquad \mu(u) \equiv \frac{\phi(u)}{1 - \Phi(u)} = \frac{\eta_1 e^{\eta_1 u}}{\eta_0 - e^{\eta_1 u}}, \tag{15.20}$$

where it must again be noted that these expressions are defined only for $0 < u < \bar{D}$. In Figure 15.4(a) we illustrate the instantaneous mortality rate, $\ln \mu(u)$, using the parameters mentioned above. Not surprisingly, in view of Figure 15.2, the mortality rate increases with age. For low values of u, however, $\mu(u)$ is virtually horizontal, but as u approaches $\bar{D}$, the mortality rate shoots up, becoming infinite at $\bar{D}$ (i.e. $\lim_{u \to \bar{D}} \mu(u) = \infty$).

Figure 15.4(b) depicts the expected remaining lifetime of agents (see Intermezzo 15.1), again using the parameters mentioned above. Whereas life expectancy at birth is 74.62, a surviving 48-year old has an expectancy of 29.6 years, and a surviving 78-year old can expect to live for another 6.7 years. As one gets older, the planning horizon shortens but the expected total length of life increases.

In order to compute individual consumption and asset profiles, we develop a simple numerical version of the Yaari model. We assume that agents start life without any financial assets, $A(0) = 0$, and that they receive a constant wage income

---

[4]The Matlab program used to compute these estimates and to produce the figures can be found on the website for this book, www.heijdra.org/fomm3.

Figure 15.3: Actual and fitted survival fraction for the Dutch cohort born in 1960

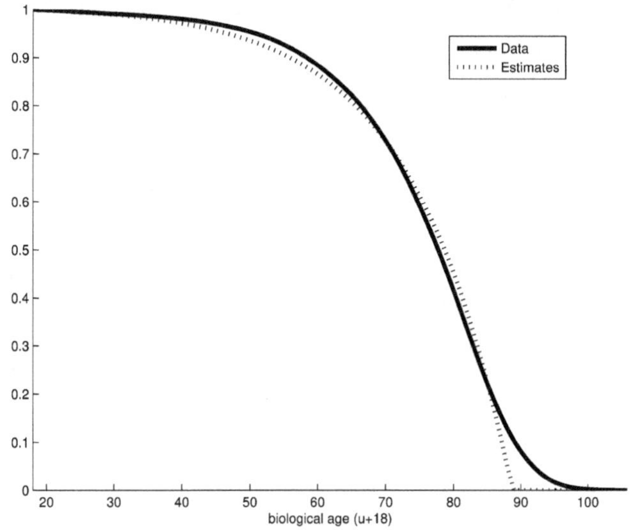

during their entire life, $w = 1$. The interest rate is set at five percent per annum, $r = 0.05$, and the pure rate of time preference is set at $\rho = 0.04$, implying that the agent is relatively patient and will save early on in life. For simplicity, we assume that the felicity function is logarithmic, i.e. we set $\sigma = 1$ in (15.3).

15.2.2.1 Actuarially fair annuities

In the presence of actuarially fair (or *perfect*) annuities, it follows from (15.15) that for an agent of age u, the annuity rate of interest equals $r + \mu(u)$ and (from equation (15.18)) that consumption growth over the life cycle equals $\dot{C}(u)/C(u) = r - \rho > 0$. By using the expressions found in Heijdra and Romp (2008, p. 98), we can write the paths for consumption and assets as:

$$\frac{C(u)}{w} = \frac{\Delta(0,r)}{\Delta(0,\rho)}e^{(r-\rho)u}, \tag{15.21}$$

$$\frac{A(u)}{w} = e^{(r-\rho)u}\frac{\Delta(0,r)}{\Delta(0,\rho)}\Delta(u,\rho) - \Delta(u,r), \tag{15.22}$$

where $\Delta(u,\psi)$ is a *demographic discount function*, the definition and theoretical properties of which can be found in Heijdra and Romp (2008, p. 95). For the demography used here, $\Delta(u,\psi)$ takes the following form (for $0 \leq u \leq \bar{D}$):

$$\Delta(u,\psi) \equiv \frac{e^{\psi u}}{\eta_0 - e^{\eta_1 u}} \cdot \left[\eta_0 \cdot \frac{e^{-\psi u} - e^{-\psi \bar{D}}}{\psi} + \frac{e^{(\eta_1 - \psi)u} - e^{(\eta_1 - \psi)\bar{D}}}{\eta_1 - \psi} \right], \tag{15.23}$$

where ψ is a parameter of the function. It is useful to note that $\Delta(u,\psi)$ is positive, and decreasing in both u and ψ.

Figure 15.4: Features of a realistic mortality profile

(a) Instantaneous mortality rate: $\mu(u)$

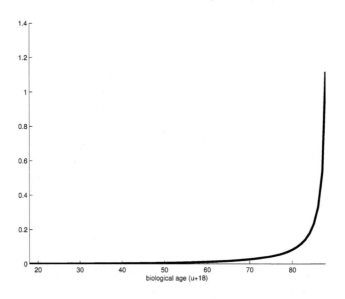

(b) Expected remaining lifetime: $\Delta(u,0)$

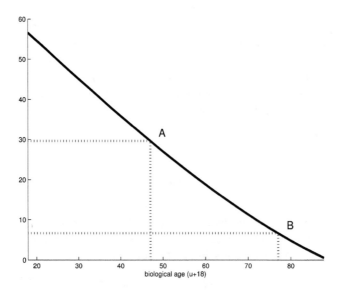

In Figure 15.5(a) the solid line plots the path of consumption with perfect annuities. Not surprisingly, consumption grows monotonically because agents are patient by assumption ($\rho < r$). Early on in life, consumption falls short of wage income ($w = 1$), and agents accumulate financial assets. As a result, in Figure 15.5(b), assets rise initially—see the solid line. Since agents annuitize completely, and thus face the annuity rate, $r + \mu(u)$, it follows from (15.15)–(15.16) that assets rise quite rapidly. Asset holdings peak at about biological age 60, after which they are slowly decumulated. Intuitively, the agent's planning horizon contracts, which leads him to increase the fraction of total wealth that is used for consumption expenditure. Despite the fact that financial assets are run down, the annuity rate of interest increases (ultimately at an increasing rate) thus enabling the agent to finance an ever increasing consumption level (see Heijdra and Romp, 2008, p. 106). Whereas consumption grows monotonically, the profile of financial assets features the classical hump-shaped life-cycle pattern stressed by Modigliani and co-workers.

15.2.2.2 No annuities

In the absence of annuities, agents face the regular interest rate, r, on their savings. Let us first (rather unwisely, as it turns out) ignore the time-of-death wealth constraint (15.7). It follows from (15.11) that agents would choose their consumption growth to satisfy the following Euler equation:

$$\frac{\dot{C}(u)}{C(u)} = r - \rho - \mu(u). \tag{15.24}$$

In view of the fact that r exceeds ρ and $\mu(u)$ is low early on in life (see Figure 15.4(a)), the consumption profile is initially upward sloping. In Figure 15.5(a) the consumption path is shown as the dash-dotted line. As the agent gets older, $\mu(u)$ increases and he effectively becomes more impatient, i.e. consumption growth starts to slow down. Consumption peaks at about economic age $\bar{u} = 40.54$, at which point $r - \rho = \mu(\bar{u})$, and declines thereafter. Since we ignore the time-of-death wealth constraint, consumption falls to zero (at age $u = \bar{D}$) and financial assets become negative before rising back to zero at age $\bar{D}$—see the dash-dotted line in Figure 15.5(b). Since the unrestricted solution violates the time-of-death wealth constraint, it is not the correct optimal consumption-saving plan.

The correct solution to the optimization problem recognizes the fact that—provided he stays alive—the agent must run out of financial assets at some age u^*, which is strictly less than the maximum possible age $\bar{D}$. Once the time-of-death wealth constraint becomes binding, it stays binding, so $A(u) = 0$ and $C(u) = w$ for $u \geq u^*$. It is not difficult to show that u^* is the positive root of:

$$\int_0^{u^*} \frac{1 - \Phi(u)}{1 - \Phi(u^*)} e^{\rho(u^* - u)} du = \frac{e^{ru^*} - 1}{r}, \tag{15.25}$$

whereas, for $0 \leq u \leq u^*$, consumption and assets are given by:

$$\frac{C(0)}{w} = \frac{e^{-(r-\rho)u^*}}{1 - \Phi(u^*)}, \tag{15.26}$$

$$\frac{C(u)}{w} = \frac{1 - \Phi(u)}{1 - \Phi(u^*)} e^{(r-\rho)(u-u^*)}, \tag{15.27}$$

$$\frac{A(u)}{w} = \frac{e^{ru} - 1}{r} - \frac{C(0)}{w} e^{ru} \int_0^u [1 - \Phi(s)] e^{-\rho s} ds. \tag{15.28}$$

Figure 15.5: Life-cycle profiles

(a) Consumption: $C(u)$

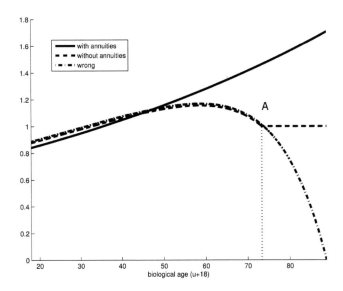

(b) Financial assets: $A(u)$

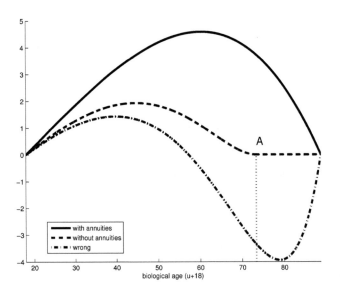

For the demography used here, $u^* = 55.3$, which is quite late in life, given that the life expectancy at birth is 56.6. The optimal consumption and asset profiles are illustrated with dashed lines in Figures 15.5(a) and 15.5(b), respectively. Interestingly, for $0 \leq u \leq u^*$ the consumption paths with and without the time-of-death constraint are very similar, i.e. the dash-dotted line lies virtually on top of the dashed line in Figure 15.5(a). The same does not hold for assets, as is evident from Figure 15.5(b).

15.2.2.3 Lessons

Comparing the case with perfect annuities to that without annuities altogether, several things are worth noting. First, in the absence of annuities both consumption and financial assets display a prominent life-cycle pattern. Second, in the absence of annuities, the time-of-death wealth constraint plays a vital role and ensures that the luck agent runs out of financial assets before the age of certain death. Since assets are positive before hitting the constraint, the model implies the existence of "accidental bequests," i.e. an unplanned inheritance. Third, with actuarially fair annuities consumption grows monotonically but financial assets display a life-cycle pattern as a result of an ever increasing annuity rate of interest. The agent holds positive assets throughout life, but plans to possess zero financial assets at the age of certain death, $\bar{D}$. By design of the annuities, there cannot be any accidental bequests.

15.3 Macroeconomic consequences of lifetime uncertainty

Yaari's crucial insights were more or less ignored for twenty years until Blanchard (1985) made them the core elements of his continuous-time overlapping-generations model. Blanchard simplified the Yaari setup substantially by assuming that (i) the maximum attainable age is infinite ($\bar{D} \to \infty$) and (ii) the probability density function for the consumer's time of death is *exponential*, i.e. $\phi(D)$ in (15.1) is specified as:

$$\phi(D) = \begin{cases} \mu e^{-\mu D} & \text{for } D \geq 0 \\ 0 & \text{for } D < 0 \end{cases}, \tag{15.29}$$

so that $1 - \Phi(t) \equiv \int_t^\infty \phi(D)dD = \phi(t)/\mu$ and $\mu(t) \equiv \phi(t)/[1 - \Phi(t)] = \mu$. Hence, instead of assuming an age-dependent instantaneous death probability—as Yaari did—Blanchard assumes that the hazard rate is constant and independent of the consumer's age; it is as if agents enjoy a life of *perpetual youth*. This approach has several advantages. First and foremost, it leads to optimal consumption rules that are easy to aggregate across households. We are thus able to maintain a high level of aggregation in the model despite the fact that the underlying population of consumers is heterogeneous by age. Second, it follows from (15.29) that the *expected remaining lifetime* of any agent is equal to $1/\mu$. By setting $\mu = 0$, the Blanchard model thus coincides with the representative-agent model studied extensively in Chapters 13–14.[5]

---

[5]Of course, the modelling simplification comes with a price tag. The main disadvantage of assuming a constant instantaneous death probability is that it leads to a consumption model that—like the representative-agent model—is at odds with the typical life-cycle consumption pattern observed in empirical studies.

15.3.1　Individual households

The first task at hand is to derive the expressions for consumption and savings for an individual household at an arbitrary time during its life. Assume that the expected utility function at time t of a consumer born at time $v < t$ is given by $E(\Lambda(v,t))$:

$$
E(\Lambda(v,t)) \equiv \int_t^\infty [1 - \Phi(\tau - t)] \ln C(v,\tau) e^{-\rho(\tau - t)} d\tau
$$
$$
= \int_t^\infty \ln C(v,\tau) e^{-(\rho + \mu)(\tau - t)} d\tau, \tag{15.30}
$$

where we have used the (property of the) exponential distribution in (15.29) to deduce that $1 - \Phi(\tau - t) = e^{-\mu(\tau - t)}$. Furthermore, in going from (15.4) to (15.30) we have assumed a logarithmic felicity function (featuring a unit intertemporal substitution elasticity), and we have added indexes for the agent's date of birth (v) and the time to which the decision problem refers (t). Consequently, $C(v,\tau)$ stands for planned consumption at time τ by an agent born at time v. The agent's budget identity is:

$$
\dot{A}(v,\tau) = [r(\tau) + \mu] A(v,\tau) + w(\tau) - T(\tau) - C(v,\tau), \tag{15.31}
$$

where $r(\tau)$ is the interest rate, $w(\tau)$ is the wage rate, $T(\tau)$ is the lump-sum tax levied by the government, and $A(v,\tau)$ are real financial assets. Equation (15.31) incorporates the Yaari notion of actuarially fair life-insurance contracts and is a straightforward generalization of (15.16) with (15.15) substituted in. Specifically, during life agents receive $\mu A(v,\tau)$ from the life-insurance company but at the time of the agent's death the entire estate $A(v,\tau)$ reverts to that company. To avoid the agent from running a Ponzi game against the life-insurance company, the following *solvency condition* must be obeyed (see also (15.17) above):

$$
\lim_{\tau \to \infty} e^{-R^A(t,\tau)} A(v,\tau) = 0, \qquad R^A(t,\tau) \equiv \int_t^\tau [r(s) + \mu] \, ds. \tag{15.32}
$$

By combining (15.31) and (15.32) the household's lifetime budget restriction is obtained:

$$
A(v,t) + H(t) = \int_t^\infty C(v,\tau) e^{-R^A(t,\tau)} d\tau, \tag{15.33}
$$

where $H(t)$ is the human wealth of the agent consisting of the present value of lifetime after-tax wage income using the annuity factor, $R^A(t,\tau)$, for discounting:

$$
H(t) \equiv \int_t^\infty [w(\tau) - T(\tau)] e^{-R^A(t,\tau)} d\tau. \tag{15.34}
$$

Equation (15.33) is the counterpart to (15.17) above. Intuitively, it says that the present value of the household's consumption plan must be equal to the sum of financial and human wealth.

The consumer maximizes expected lifetime utility (15.30) subject to its lifetime budget restriction (15.33). The Lagrangian for this optimization problem is given by:

$$
\mathcal{L} \equiv \int_t^\infty \ln C(v,\tau) e^{(\rho + \mu)(t - \tau)} d\tau + \lambda(t) \cdot \left[A(v,t) + H(t) - \int_t^\infty C(v,\tau) e^{-R^A(t,\tau)} d\tau \right], \tag{15.35}
$$

where $\lambda(t)$ is the Lagrange multiplier associated with the lifetime budget restriction. The first-order conditions are (15.33) and (for $\tau \geq t$):

$$\frac{1}{C(v,\tau)}e^{-(\rho+\mu)(\tau-t)} = \lambda(t)e^{-R^A(t,\tau)}, \tag{15.36}$$

where the optimized value for $\lambda(t)$ represents the marginal expected lifetime utility of wealth. Intuitively, the optimality condition (15.36) instructs the consumer to plan consumption at each time to be such that the appropriately discounted marginal utility of consumption (left-hand side) and wealth (right-hand side) are equated.[6] For future reference we note that differentiation of (15.36) with respect to τ yields the household's Euler equation:

$$\frac{\dot{C}(v,\tau)}{C(v,\tau)} = r(\tau) - \rho. \tag{15.37}$$

Just as in (15.18) above, the growth rate of individual consumption depends only on the gap between the interest rate and the rate of time preference. The mortality rate does not affect individual consumption growth because of the existence of actuarially fair annuities.

As it turns out, in the macroeconomic OLG model we also need to solve for the consumption *level* in the planning period. By using (15.36) for the planning period ($\tau = t$) we see that $1/C(v,t) = \lambda(t)$. Using this result in (15.36), rearranging, and integrating we can express $C(v,t)$ in terms of total wealth:

$$\int_t^\infty C(v,t)e^{-(\rho+\mu)(\tau-t)}d\tau = \int_t^\infty C(v,\tau)e^{-R^A(t,\tau)}d\tau$$

$$\frac{C(v,t)}{\rho+\mu} \cdot \left[-e^{-(\rho+\mu)(\tau-t)}\right]_t^\infty = A(v,t) + H(t) \qquad \Leftrightarrow$$

$$C(v,t) = (\rho+\mu)\left[A(v,t) + H(t)\right], \tag{15.38}$$

where we have used (15.33) in going from the first to the second line. Optimal consumption in the planning period ($\tau = t$) is proportional to total wealth. The marginal propensity to consume out of total wealth is constant and equal to the "effective" rate of time preference, $\rho + \mu$.

15.3.2 Aggregate households

Now that we know what the consumption decisions for individual households look like, the next task at hand is to describe the demographic structure of the Blanchard model. To keep things simple, Blanchard assumes that at each instant in time a *large* cohort of new agents is born. The size of this cohort of newborns is $P(\tau,\tau) = \beta P(\tau)$, where $P(\tau)$ stands for the aggregate population size at time τ and β is the (crude) birth rate. These newborn agents start their lives without any financial assets as they are unlinked to any existing agents and thus receive no bequests, i.e. $A(\tau,\tau) = 0$. Also to keep things simple, Blanchard assumes that the birth rate is equal to the mortality rate, i.e. $\beta = \mu$. Of course, at each instant in time a fraction of the existing population dies. Since each individual agent faces an instantaneous probability of death equal to μ and the number of agents $P(\tau)$ is large, by the law of large numbers

---

[6]See also the discussion following equation (13.10) and Intermezzo 13.3 above. We could have used the method of optimal control to solve the household's optimization problem.

frequencies and probabilities coincide and the number of deaths at each instant will be equal to $\mu P(\tau)$. Since births and deaths exactly match, the size of the population is constant and can be normalized to unity $(P(\tau) = 1)$.[7]

Another very useful consequence of the large-cohort assumption is that we can exactly trace the size of any particular cohort over time. For example, a cohort born at time v will be of size $\mu e^{-\mu(t-v)}$ at time $t \geq v$, because $\mu[1 - e^{-\mu(t-v)}]$ of the cohort members will have died in the time interval $[v, t]$. Since we know the size of each cohort it is possible to work with aggregate variables. For example, by aggregating the consumption levels of all existing agents in the economy we obtain the following expression for aggregate consumption at time t:

$$C(t) \equiv \mu \int_{-\infty}^{t} e^{-\mu(t-v)} C(v,t) dv. \tag{15.39}$$

Of course, (15.39) is simply a definition and is not of much use in and of itself. But because the optimal consumption rule (15.38) features a propensity to consume out of total wealth which is independent of the generations index v, equation (15.39) gives rise to a very simple aggregate consumption rule:

$$C(t) \equiv \mu \int_{-\infty}^{t} e^{-\mu(t-v)} (\rho + \mu) \left[A(v,t) + H(t) \right] dv$$

$$= (\rho + \mu) \left[\mu \int_{-\infty}^{t} e^{-\mu(t-v)} A(v,t) dv + \mu \int_{-\infty}^{t} e^{-\mu(t-v)} H(t) dv \right]$$

$$= (\rho + \mu) \left[A(t) + H(t) \right], \tag{15.40}$$

where aggregate financial wealth is defined analogously to aggregate consumption (given in (15.39)). It cannot be overemphasized that the aggregation property follows from the assumption that each agent faces a constant instantaneous death probability (see the text below (15.29)). If instead the hazard rate varies with age—as in the Yaari (1965) model—then the optimal household consumption rule no longer features a generation-independent marginal propensity to consume out of total wealth, and exact aggregation is impossible.

What does the aggregate asset accumulation identity look like? By definition we have that $A(t) \equiv \mu \int_{-\infty}^{t} e^{-\mu(t-v)} A(v,t) dv$ from which we derive (by application of Leibniz's rule; see the Mathematical Appendix):

$$\dot{A}(t) = \mu A(t,t) - \mu A(t) + \mu \int_{-\infty}^{t} \dot{A}(v,t) e^{-\mu(t-v)} dv, \tag{15.41}$$

where the first term on the right-hand side represents assets of newborns $(A(t,t) = 0)$, the second term is the wealth of agents who die, and the third term is the change in assets of existing agents. By substituting (15.31) into (15.41) and simplifying we obtain the aggregate asset accumulation identity:

$$\dot{A}(t) = -\mu A(t) + \mu \int_{-\infty}^{t} \left[[r(t) + \mu] A(v,t) + w(t) - T(t) - C(v,t) \right] e^{-\mu(t-v)} dv$$

$$= -\mu A(t) + [r(t) + \mu] A(t) + w(t) - T(t) - C(t)$$

$$= r(t) A(t) + w(t) - T(t) - C(t). \tag{15.42}$$

[7]Net population change can easily be incorporated in the Blanchard model by allowing the birth and death rates to differ—see Buiter (1988) and the exercises to this chapter.

Whereas (fully annuitized) individual wealth attracts the actuarial interest rate, $r(t) + \mu$, for agents that stay alive (see (15.31)), equation (15.42) shows that aggregate wealth accumulates at the rate of interest, $r(t)$. The amount $\mu A(t)$ does not represent aggregate wealth accumulation but is a transfer—via the life-insurance companies—from those who die to those who remain alive.

In the formal analysis of the model it is useful to have an expression for the "aggregate Euler equation". It follows from (15.39) that:

$$\dot{C}(t) = \mu C(t,t) - \mu C(t) + \mu \int_{-\infty}^{t} \dot{C}(v,t) e^{-\mu(t-v)} dv. \tag{15.43}$$

According to (15.38) newborn agents consume a fraction of their human wealth at birth, i.e. $C(t,t) = (\rho + \mu) H(t)$. Equation (15.40) shows that aggregate consumption is proportional to total (human and financial) wealth, i.e. $C(t) = (\rho + \mu) [A(t) + H(t)]$. Finally, as is shown in (15.37), individual households' consumption growth satisfies $\dot{C}(v,\tau)/C(v,\tau) = r(\tau) - \rho$. By using all these results in (15.43) and noting (15.39) we obtain the aggregate Euler equation modified for the existence of overlapping generations of finitely lived agents:

$$\frac{\dot{C}(t)}{C(t)} = r(t) - \rho - \mu(\rho + \mu) \frac{A(t)}{C(t)} \tag{15.44}$$

$$= \frac{\dot{C}(v,t)}{C(v,t)} - \mu \cdot \frac{C(t) - C(t,t)}{C(t)}. \tag{15.45}$$

Equation (15.44) has the same form as the Euler equation for individual households except for the correction term due to the distributional effects caused by the turnover of generations. Optimal consumption *growth* is the same for all generations (since they face the same interest rate) but older generations have a higher consumption *level* than younger generations (since the former generations are wealthier). Since existing generations are continually being replaced by newborns who hold no financial wealth, aggregate consumption growth falls short of individual consumption growth. The correction term appearing on the right-hand side of (15.44) thus represents the difference in average consumption and consumption by newborns, i.e. (15.44) can be re-expressed as in (15.45).

15.3.3 Firms

The production sector is characterized by a large number of firms that produce an identical good under perfect competition. Output, $Y(t)$, is produced according to a linearly homogeneous technology with labour, $L(t)$, and physical capital, $K(t)$, as homogeneous factor inputs which are rented from households:

$$Y(t) = F(K(t), L(t)), \tag{15.46}$$

where $F(\cdot)$ satisfies the usual Inada conditions (see Chapter 12). The stockmarket value of the representative firm is:

$$V(t) = \int_{t}^{\infty} [Y(\tau) - w(\tau) L(\tau) - I(\tau)] e^{-R(t,\tau)} d\tau, \quad R(t,\tau) \equiv \int_{t}^{\tau} r(s) ds, \tag{15.47}$$

where $I(t)$ denotes gross investment. The firm chooses labour and capital in order to maximize (15.47) subject to the production function (15.46) and the capital accumulation constraint:

$$\dot{K}(t) = I(t) - \delta K(t), \tag{15.48}$$

Table 15.1. The Blanchard-Yaari model

$$\dot{C}(t) = [r(t) - \rho] \, C(t) - \mu(\rho + \mu) \, [K(t) + B(t)] \tag{T1.1}$$

$$\dot{K}(t) = Y(t) - C(t) - G(t) - \delta K(t) \tag{T1.2}$$

$$\dot{B}(t) = r(t)B(t) + G(t) - T(t) \tag{T1.3}$$

$$r(t) + \delta = F_K\left(K(t), L(t)\right) \tag{T1.4}$$

$$w(t) = F_L\left(K(t), L(t)\right) \tag{T1.5}$$

$$L(t) = 1 \tag{T1.6}$$

$$Y(t) = F\left(K(t), L(t)\right) \tag{T1.7}$$

Notes: $C(t)$ is private consumption, $G(t)$ is public consumption, $Y(t)$ is output, $K(t)$ is the capital stock, $L(t)$ is employment, $B(t)$ is government debt, $w(t)$ is the wage rate, $T(t)$ is lump-sum taxes, and $r(t)$ is the interest rate. Capital depreciates at a constant rate δ, μ is the death rate (assumed to equal the birth rate), and ρ is the pure rate of time preference.

---

where δ is the constant rate of depreciation of capital. There are no adjustment costs associated with investment. The first-order conditions imply that the marginal productivity of labour and capital equal the producer costs of these factors–see, respectively, equations (T1.4) and (T1.5) in Table 15.1. Finally, we recall from Chapter 13 that the market value of the firm is equal to the replacement value of its capital stock, i.e. $V(t) = K(t)$.

15.3.4 Government and market equilibrium

The government budget identity is given in (T1.3) in Table 15.1. The government consumes $G(t)$ units of the good and levies lump-sum taxes on households $T(t)$. Government debt is $B(t)$ so that $r(t)B(t)$ is interest payments on outstanding debt. Like the private sector, the government must remain solvent and obey a no-Ponzi-game condition:

$$\lim_{\tau \to \infty} e^{-R(t,\tau)} B(\tau) = 0. \tag{15.49}$$

By using (T1.3) and (15.49) the government budget restriction is obtained:

$$B(t) = \int_t^\infty [T(\tau) - G(\tau)] \, e^{-R(t,\tau)} d\tau. \tag{15.50}$$

Intuitively, government solvency means that if there is pre-existing government debt (positive left-hand side) it must be covered in present-value terms by present and future primary surpluses (positive right-hand side).

At each instant in time, factor and goods markets clear instantaneously. In this closed economy households can only accumulate domestic assets so that, as a result, financial market equilibrium requires that $A(t) = K(t) + B(t)$. Wage flexibility ensures that the aggregate supply of labour ($L(t) = 1$) by households matches labour demand by firms. Goods market equilibrium in this closed economy is obtained when the supply of goods equals aggregate demand, which consists of private and public consumption plus investment: $Y(t) = C(t) + I(t) + G(t)$. The key equations of the model have been gathered in Table 15.1.

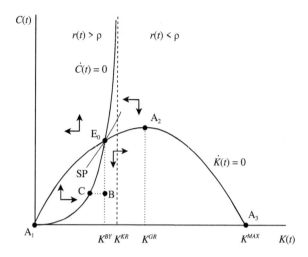

Figure 15.6: Phase diagram of the Blanchard-Yaari model

15.3.5 Phase diagram

In order to illustrate some of the key properties of the model we now derive the phase diagram in Figure 15.6. We assume for simplicity that lump-sum taxes, government consumption, and public debt are all zero in the initial situation ($T(t) = G(t) = B(t) = 0$). The $\dot{K}(t) = 0$ line represents points in (C, K)-space for which the capital stock is in equilibrium. The Inada conditions (see Chapter 12) ensure that it passes through the origin and is vertical there (see point A_1 in Figure 15.6). Golden-rule (GR) consumption occurs at point A_2 where the $\dot{K}(t) = 0$ line reaches its maximum:

$$\left(\frac{dC(t)}{dK(t)}\right)_{\dot{K}(t)=0} = 0: \quad r^{GR} \equiv F_K(K^{GR}, 1) - \delta = 0. \tag{15.51}$$

The maximum attainable capital stock, K^{MAX}, occurs at point A_3, where consumption is zero and total output is used for replacement investment ($F\left(K^{MAX}, 1\right) = \delta K^{MAX}$). For points above (below) the $\dot{K}(t) = 0$ line consumption is too high (too low) to be consistent with a capital stock equilibrium and consequently net investment is negative (positive). This has been indicated by horizontal arrows in Figure 15.6.

The derivation of the $\dot{C}(t) = 0$ line is a little more complex because its position and slope depend on the interplay between effects due to capital scarcity and those attributable to intergenerational-distribution effects. By using (15.44), and setting $\dot{C}(t) = 0$ and $A(t) = K(t)$ (as $B(t) = 0$) we find the mathematical expression for the $\dot{C}(t) = 0$ line:

$$C(t) = \frac{\mu(\rho + \mu)K(t)}{r(t) - \rho}. \tag{15.52}$$

Recall from Chapter 13 that the "Keynes-Ramsey" (KR) capital stock, K^{KR}, is such that the rate of interest equals the exogenously given rate of time preference, i.e. $r^{KR} \equiv F_K(K^{KR}, 1) - \delta = \rho$. Since K^{GR} is associated with a zero interest rate and there are diminishing returns to capital ($F_{KK} < 0$), K^{KR} lies to the left of the golden-rule point as is indicated in Figure 15.6. Furthermore, for points to the left (right) of the dashed line, capital is relatively scarce (abundant), and the interest rate exceeds (falls short of) the pure rate of time preference.

When agents have finite lives ($\mu > 0$) the $\dot{C} = 0$ line is upward sloping because of the turnover of generations. Its slope can be explained by appealing directly to equations (15.44) (with $A = K$ as we set $B = 0$), (15.45), and Figure 15.6. Suppose that the economy is initially on the $\dot{C} = 0$ curve, say at point E_0. Now consider a lower level of consumption, say at point B. With the same capital stock, both points feature the same rate of interest. Accordingly, individual consumption growth, $\dot{C}(v,t)/C(v,t)$ $[= r - \rho]$, coincides at the two points.

Expression (15.45) indicates, however, that aggregate consumption growth depends not only on individual growth but also the *proportional* difference between average consumption and consumption by a newly born generation, i.e. $[C(t) - C(t,t)]/C(t)$. Since newly born generations start without any financial capital, the absolute difference between average consumption and consumption of a newly born household depends on the average capital stock and is thus the same at the two points. Since the level of aggregate consumption is lower at B (than it is at E_0), this point features a larger proportional difference between average and newly born consumption, thereby decreasing aggregate consumption growth (i.e. $\dot{C}(t) < 0$). In order to restore zero growth of aggregate consumption, the capital stock must fall (to point C). The smaller capital stock not only raises individual consumption growth by increasing the rate of interest but also lowers the drag on aggregate consumption growth due to the turnover of generations because a smaller capital stock narrows the gap between average wealth (i.e. the wealth of the generations that pass away) and wealth of the newly born. In summary, for points above (below) the $\dot{C}(t) = 0$ line, the capital-scarcity effect dominates (is dominated by) the intergenerational-redistribution effect, and consumption rises (falls) over time.[8] This is indicated with vertical arrows in Figure 15.6.

In terms of Figure 15.7, steady-state equilibrium is attained at the intersection of the $\dot{K}(t) = 0$ and $\dot{C}(t) = 0$ lines at point E_0. Given the configuration of arrows, it is clear that this equilibrium is saddle-point stable, and that the saddle path, SP, is upward sloping and lies between the two equilibrium loci.

15.4   Basic model properties

15.4.1   Fiscal policy

As a first application of the Blanchard-Yaari model we now consider the effects of a typical fiscal policy experiment, consisting of an unanticipated and permanent increase in government consumption. We abstract from debt policy by assuming that the government balances its budget by means of lump-sum taxes only, i.e. $\dot{B}(t) = B(t) = 0$ and $G(t) = T(t)$ in equation (T1.3). We also assume that the economy is initially in a steady state and that the time of the shock is normalized to $t = 0$.

In terms of Figure 15.7, the $\dot{K}(t) = 0$ line is shifted downward by the amount of the shock dG. In the short run the capital stock is predetermined and the economy jumps from point E_0 to A on the new saddle path SP_1. Over time the economy

---

[8]Since the economy features positive initial assets (as $K > 0$), the $\dot{C} = 0$ line lies to the left of the dashed line representing K^{KR} and approaches this line asymptotically as C gets large (and the intergenerational-redistribution effect gets small). If there is very little capital, the rate of interest is very high and the $\dot{C} = 0$ line is horizontal.

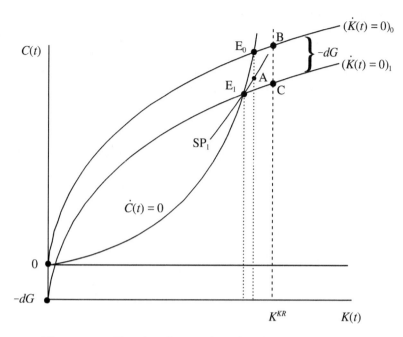

Figure 15.7: Fiscal policy in the Blanchard-Yaari model

gradually moves from A to the new steady-state equilibrium at E_1. As is clear from
the figure, there is less than one-for-one crowding out of private by public consumption in the impact period, i.e. $-1 < dC(0)/dG < 0$. In contrast, there is more than
one-for-one crowding out in the long run, i.e. $dC(\infty)/dG < -1$.

The reason for these crowding-out results is that the change in the lump-sum tax
induces an intergenerational redistribution of resources away from future towards
present generations (Bovenberg and Heijdra, 2002). At impact, all households cut
back on private consumption because the higher lump-sum tax reduces the value
of their human capital. Since households discount present and future tax liabilities
at the annuity rate $(r(\tau) + \mu$, see (15.34)) rather than at the interest rate, existing
households at the time of the shock do not feel the full burden of the additional taxes
and therefore do not cut back their consumption by a sufficient amount. As a result,
private investment is crowded out at impact ($\dot{K}(t) < 0$ at point A) and the capital
stock starts to fall. This in turn puts downward pressure on before-tax wages and
upward pressure on the interest rate so that human capital falls over time. So, future
generations are poorer than newborn generations at the time of the shock because
they have less capital to work with and thus receive lower wages (since $F_{LK} > 0$).

If the birth rate is zero ($\mu = 0$) there is a single infinitely-lived representative consumer and intergenerational redistribution is absent, and the $\dot{C}(t) = 0$ line is vertical
at K^{KR} (where $r^{KR} \equiv F_K(K^{KR}, 1) - \delta = \rho$). Crowding out of consumption is one-for-
one, there is no effect on the capital stock, and thus there is no transitional dynamics.
In terms of Figure 15.7, the only effect on the economy consists of a downward jump
in consumption from point B to point C.

15.4.2   Non-neutrality of government debt

The previous subsection has demonstrated that lump-sum taxes cause intergenerational redistribution of resources in the Blanchard-Yaari model. This suggests that Ricardian equivalence does not hold in this model, i.e. the timing of taxes is not intergenerationally neutral and debt has real effects. Ricardian non-equivalence can be demonstrated by means of some simple "bookkeeping" exercises (see also Section 13.7.3 above). The result that must be proved is that, ceteris paribus the time path of government consumption ($G(\tau)$ for $\tau \geq t$), aggregate consumption ($C(t)$) depends on pre-existing debt ($B(t)$) *and* the time path of taxes ($T(\tau)$ for $\tau \geq t$) (Buiter, 1988, p. 285).

Total consumption is proportional to total wealth (see (15.40)) which can be written as follows:

$$
\begin{aligned}
A(t) + H(t) &\equiv K(t) + B(t) + H(t) \\
&= K(t) + B(t) + \int_t^\infty [w(\tau) - T(\tau)] e^{-R^A(t,\tau)} d\tau \\
&= K(t) + \int_t^\infty [w(\tau) - G(\tau)] e^{-R^A(t,\tau)} d\tau + \Omega(t),
\end{aligned}
\tag{15.53}
$$

where $\Omega(t)$ is defined as:

$$
\Omega(t) \equiv \int_t^\infty [T(\tau) - G(\tau)] e^{-R(t,\tau)} d\tau - \int_t^\infty [T(\tau) - G(\tau)] e^{-R^A(t,\tau)} d\tau. \tag{15.54}
$$

Note that in deriving (15.53), we have used the definition of human wealth (15.34) to go from the first to the second line and the government budget restriction (15.50) to get from the second to the third line. In view of (15.54) it follows that $\Omega(t)$ vanishes *if and only if* the birth rate is zero and $R^A(t,\tau) = R(t,\tau)$. If the birth rate is positive, $\Omega(t)$ is non-zero and Ricardian equivalence does not hold.

Recall that in the Blanchard-Yaari model the birth rate of new generations is equal to the instantaneous death probability facing existing generations. As a result it is not a priori clear which aspect of the model is responsible for the failure of Ricardian equivalence. The analysis of Weil (1989b) provides the strong hint that it is the arrival rate of new generations which destroys Ricardian equivalence (see Section 13.7.3 above). This suggestion was formally demonstrated by Buiter (1988) who integrates and extends the Blanchard-Yaari-Weil models by allowing for differential birth and death rates (β and μ) and labour-augmenting technical change. In his model the population grows at an exponential rate $n \equiv \beta - \mu$. Buiter (1988, p. 285) demonstrates that a zero birth rate ($\beta = 0$) is indeed necessary and sufficient for Ricardian equivalence to hold.

15.4.3   Economic growth

The standard Blanchard-Yaari model is an example of an exogenous growth model, i.e. the capital stock per worker attains a unique steady-state value and, because the population is constant, the steady-state growth rate is equal to zero. It is, however, not difficult to formulate an endogenous growth version of the Blanchard-Yaari model (see Saint-Paul, 1992). Consider for example the case (studied in Section 14.2.2.1 above) in which microeconomic external effects between firms ensure that the macroeconomic production function is linear in the aggregate capital stock. In terms of Table 15.1, equation (T1.7) is replaced by $Y(t) = Z_0 K(t)$, (T1.4) becomes $r(t) + \delta = \alpha Z_0$, and (T1.5) is changed to $w(t) = (1 - \alpha)Y(t)$, where α is the efficiency parameter of capital in the microeconomic production function and Z_0 is a constant technology index.

In the absence of government bonds, the AK-version of the Blanchard-Yaari model thus takes the following form:

$$\frac{\dot{C}(t)}{C(t)} = r(t) - \rho - \mu \left(\rho + \mu \right) \frac{K(t)}{C(t)}, \tag{15.55}$$

$$\frac{\dot{K}(t)}{K(t)} = (1 - g) Z_0 - \frac{C(t)}{K(t)} - \delta, \tag{15.56}$$

$$r(t) = \alpha Z_0 - \delta, \tag{15.57}$$

where we assume that $G(t) = gY(t)$, with g representing a time-invariant fiscal policy parameter ($0 < g < 1$). By defining the aggregate consumption-capital ratio, $\theta(t) \equiv C(t)/K(t)$, we can use (15.55)–(15.57) to derive:

$$\frac{\dot{\theta}(t)}{\theta(t)} = - \left[(1 - \alpha - g) Z_0 + \rho \right] + \theta(t) - \frac{\mu \left(\rho + \mu \right)}{\theta(t)}. \tag{15.58}$$

Equation (15.58) is an unstable differential equation in $\theta(t)$, and the only economically sensible solution is for $\theta(t)$ to coincide with its steady-state value at all times, i.e. $\theta(t) = \theta^*$ for all t. The macroeconomic consumption-capital ratio is constant because it is constant at the individual level also.

In Figure 15.8 we characterize the steady-state consumption-capital ratio and the macroeconomic growth rate. The curve labelled EE_{BY} expresses the growth rate of consumption $\gamma_C(t) \equiv \dot{C}(t)/C(t)$ as a function of $\theta(t)$. The growth expression is obtained by substituting (15.57) into (15.55). Clearly, the EE_{BY} curve features a vertical asymptote for $\theta(t) \to 0$ and a horizontal asymptote for $\theta(t) \to \infty$. Because μ is positive in the Blanchard-Yaari model, EE_{BY} lies below the consumption growth equation for the representative-agent model, EE_{RA}. The EE_{RA} curve itself is horizontal because it does not feature a generational turnover term.

The curve labelled CA_0 is the (initial) capital accumulation locus, expressing $\gamma_K(t) \equiv \dot{K}(t)/K(t)$ as a downward sloping function of $\theta(t)$. The initial equilibrium for the Blanchard-Yaari model is at point E_0, the consumption-capital ratio is θ_0^*, and the growth rate is γ_0^*. In contrast, in the representative-agent model, the equilibrium is at E', a point which features a lower consumption-capital ratio and a higher growth rate. We thus find immediately that the existence of overlapping generations slows down economic growth.

The comparative static effects are also easy to deduce with the aid of Figure 15.8. An increase in the government consumption share, g, moves the capital accumulation locus to the left, from CA_0 to CA_1, and shifts the equilibrium to E_1 in the Blanchard-Yaari model. The increase in taxes prompts agents to reduce their consumption-capital ratios and the growth rate falls. Of course, in the representative-agent model nothing happens to economic growth at all. We leave as an exercise to the reader to show that increases in ρ and μ both lead to a reduction in the rate of growth.

15.4.4   Dynamic efficiency

As is clear from Figure 15.6, the steady-state capital stock in the standard Blanchard-Yaari model is strictly less than the golden rule stock, i.e. $K^{BY} < K^{GR}$, no oversaving

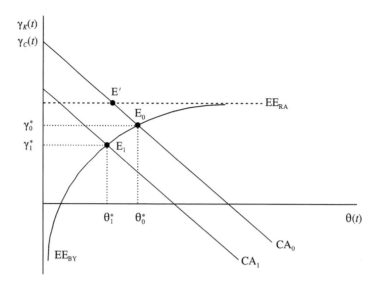

Figure 15.8: Endogenous growth in the Blanchard-Yaari model

takes place, and the Blanchard-Yaari model thus yields a dynamically efficient equilibrium. In its basic form, the model assumes that agents face the same wage income during their entire life, i.e. there is no reason to save early on in life to compensate for low (or absent) wage income during old age.

In this section we augment the Blanchard-Yaari model somewhat by assuming that agents face a downward sloping path of wage income due to the fact that their labour productivity falls with age. In doing so, we introduce a strong motive to save for low income later on in life. Recall that in the standard Blanchard-Yaari model labour supply is exogenous and workers of all ages have the same productivity, i.e. a 60-year old worker produces the same amount of output in a unit of time as his 25-year old colleague does. We now consider what happens if worker productivity is age-dependent. To keep things simple, we assume that agents supply one unit of "raw" labour throughout their lives but that the productivity of their labour declines exponentially with age.

With age-dependent productivity, the aggregate production function (15.46) is replaced by:

$$Y(t) = F(K(t), N(t)), \tag{15.59}$$

where $N(t)$ is the aggregate labour input in *efficiency units*:

$$N(t) \equiv \int_{-\infty}^{t} N(v,t)dv = \int_{-\infty}^{t} E(t-v)L(v,t)dv. \tag{15.60}$$

In this equation, $E(t-v)$ represents the efficiency of a worker of generation v at time t (whose *age* at time t is thus $t-v$), and $L(v,t)$ is the total number of raw labour units supplied by generation-v workers at time t. Since all workers supply one unit of raw labour during life, and generations die at a proportional rate μ, it follows that:

$$L(v,t) = e^{-\mu(t-v)}L(v,v) = \mu e^{-\mu(t-v)}. \tag{15.61}$$

We assume that efficiency falls exponentially with the age of the worker:

$$E(t-v) \equiv \frac{\delta_e + \mu}{\mu} e^{-\delta_e(t-v)}, \tag{15.62}$$

where $\delta_e > 0$ is the proportional rate at which worker productivity declines with age (note that the first term on the right-hand side represents a convenient normalization). According to (15.62), a 20-year old worker is $e^{10\delta_e}$ times as productive as a 30-year old worker. By substituting (15.61)–(15.62) into (15.60) and integrating we derive that the aggregate supply of labour in efficiency units equals unity:

$$N(t) = \int_{-\infty}^{t} \frac{\delta_e + \mu}{\mu} e^{-\delta_e(t-v)} \mu e^{-\mu(t-v)} dv = 1. \tag{15.63}$$

The objective function of the representative firm is changed from (15.47) to:

$$V(t) = \int_{t}^{\infty} \left[F(K(\tau), N(\tau)) - \int_{-\infty}^{\tau} w(v,\tau) L(v,\tau) dv - I(\tau) \right] e^{-R(t,\tau)} d\tau, \tag{15.64}$$

where $N(\tau) \equiv \int_{-\infty}^{t} E(\tau - v) L(v, \tau) dv$ and the capital accumulation constraint is given in (15.48). The firm hires raw units of labour from all age groups in the economy ($L(v, \tau)$) but pays an age-dependent wage ($w(v, \tau)$) because it knows that labour productivity depends on age. The first-order conditions for an optimum are:

$$r(\tau) + \delta = F_K(K(\tau), N(\tau)), \tag{15.65}$$

$$w(\tau) = \frac{w(v, \tau)}{E(\tau - v)} = F_N(K(\tau), N(\tau)). \tag{15.66}$$

Ceteris paribus the aggregate capital-effective-labour ratio ($K(\tau)/N(\tau)$), the wage rate declines with the age of the worker—see equation (15.66). Hence, even in the steady state, households will face a downward-sloping profile of wage income over their lives. Since households want to consume both when they are young and when they are old, they formulate their savings decisions during youth, taking into account that they will have little or no labour income later on in life. As Blanchard (1985, p. 235) points out, a declining path of labour income loosely captures the notion of "saving for retirement".

To keep things simple, we assume that the household has a logarithmic felicity function and maximizes lifetime utility (given in (15.30) above) subject to the budget identity (15.31) (with $w(\tau)$ replaced by $w(v, \tau)$) and the solvency condition (15.32). Abstracting from government taxes and transfers, private consumption in the planning period is:

$$C(v,t) = (\rho + \mu) [A(v,t) + H(v,t)], \tag{15.67}$$

where human wealth, $H(v, t)$ (for $v \leq t$), is now age-dependent:[9]

$$H(v,t) \equiv \int_{t}^{\infty} w(v,\tau) e^{-R^A(t,\tau)} d\tau$$

---

[9]In going from the first to the second line we make use of the fact that $w(v, \tau)$ can be rewritten as:

$$w(v,\tau) = \frac{\delta_e + \mu}{\mu} e^{-\delta_e(\tau - v)} w(\tau),$$

where $w(\tau) = F_N(\cdot, \cdot)$ is the rental rate on efficiency units of labour. To get from the third to the fourth line we have used the definition of $R^A(t, \tau)$ as given in (15.32).

$$= \frac{\delta_e + \mu}{\mu} \cdot \int_t^\infty e^{-\delta_e(\tau - v)} w(\tau) e^{-R^A(t,\tau)} d\tau$$

$$= \frac{\delta_e + \mu}{\mu} \cdot \int_t^\infty e^{-\delta_e(t-v)} w(\tau) e^{-R^A(t,\tau) - \delta_e(\tau - t)} d\tau$$

$$\equiv e^{-\delta_e(t-v)} H(t,t), \tag{15.68}$$

where $H(t,t)$ is the human wealth of a newborn at time t:

$$H(t,t) \equiv \frac{\delta_e + \mu}{\mu} \cdot \int_t^\infty w(\tau) e^{-\int_t^\tau [r(s) + \mu + \delta_e] ds} d\tau. \tag{15.69}$$

Equation (15.68) shows that the human wealth falls with age. For a very old agent, $t - v$ is large, $e^{-\delta_e(t-v)}$ is small, and thus $H(v,t)$ is small also. Equation (15.69) shows that the human wealth of a newborn is the (scaled) present value of wages, using the annuity interest rate *plus* the rate of decline in wages for discounting, i.e. $r(s) + \mu + \delta_e$ features in the discounting factor on the right-hand side. Note finally that, for the case with $\delta_e = 0$, the expressions in (15.68)–(15.69) reduce to (15.34) (with $T(\tau) = 0$ imposed).

Aggregate human wealth in the economy is given by:

$$H(t) \equiv \mu \int_{-\infty}^t e^{\mu(v-t)} H(v,t) dv = H(t,t) \int_{-\infty}^t \mu e^{(\delta_e + \mu)(v-t)} dv$$

$$= \frac{\mu}{\delta_e + \mu} H(t,t)$$

$$= \int_t^\infty w(\tau) e^{-\int_t^\tau [r(s) + \delta_e + \mu] ds} d\tau, \tag{15.70}$$

where we have used (15.69) to arrive at the final expression. The important lesson to be drawn from (15.70) is that the decline in the labour income of individual generations results in a higher discounting of future aggregate labour income in the definition of aggregate human wealth. Not only do current generations face a risk of dying but they also get a smaller share of aggregate wage income as they get older.

In summary, the aggregate household model developed in this subsection is given by:

$$C(t) = (\rho + \mu)[A(t) + H(t)], \tag{15.71}$$

$$\dot{A}(t) = r(t)A(t) + w(t) - C(t), \tag{15.72}$$

$$\dot{H}(t) = [r(t) + \delta_e + \mu] H(t) - w(t). \tag{15.73}$$

By differentiating (15.71) with respect to t and substituting (15.72)–(15.73) as well as (15.71) itself to eliminate $H(t)$ we obtain the Euler equation for aggregate consumption:

$$\frac{\dot{C}(t)}{C(t)} = [r(t) + \delta_e - \rho] - (\delta_e + \mu)(\rho + \mu) \frac{A(t)}{C(t)}. \tag{15.74}$$

This expression reduces to the Euler equation for the standard Blanchard-Yaari model (given in equation (15.44)) if productivity is constant throughout life and $\delta_e = 0$.

The dynamical system characterizing the economy is:

$$\dot{C}(t) = [F_K(K(t), 1) + \delta_e - (\rho + \delta)] C(t) - (\delta_e + \mu)(\rho + \mu) K(t) \tag{15.75}$$

$$\dot{K}(t) = F(K(t), 1) - C(t) - \delta K(t), \tag{15.76}$$

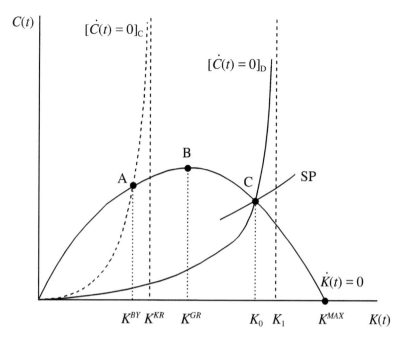

Figure 15.9: Dynamic inefficiency and declining productivity

where we assume that government debt and consumption are both zero ($B(t) = G(t) = 0$). Equation (15.75) is obtained by substituting $A(t) = K(t)$, (15.63), and (15.65) into the aggregate Euler equation (15.74). Equation (15.76) is simply the standard expression for capital accumulation in the absence of government consumption.

Figure 15.9 shows the phase diagram for the model given in (15.75)–(15.76). We make the usual Inada-style assumptions regarding the production function. In Figure 15.9, the $\dot{K}(t) = 0$ line and the dashed $[\dot{C}(t) = 0]_C$ line reproduce the equilibrium loci for the standard Blanchard-Yaari model illustrated in Figure 15.6. Point A is the standard Blanchard-Yaari (BY) equilibrium for which the steady-state capital stock is K^{BY}. The golden-rule capital stock (K^{GR}, for which consumption is at its maximum) is defined in (15.51). Since $K^{BY} < K^{GR}$ the standard Blanchard-Yaari model is *dynamically efficient*. Now consider the effects of declining productivity. It is clear from (15.76) that the $\dot{K}(t) = 0$ line is not affected by δ_e. It follows from (15.75), however, that the $\dot{C}(t) = 0$ line rotates in a clockwise fashion around the origin as δ_e is increased. If δ_e is not very large then the relevant $\dot{C}(t) = 0$ line will intersect the $\dot{K}(t) = 0$ line along the line segment AB and the equilibrium will still be dynamically efficient. There is nothing, however, preventing the occurrence of dynamic inefficiency as depicted in Figure 15.9,[10] where the solid $[\dot{C}(t) = 0]_D$ line intersects the $\dot{K}(t) = 0$ line at point C. The equilibrium at that point is saddle-point stable but there is overaccumulation of capital. Intuitively, because labour income is high early on in life, but falls rapidly with age, agents save a lot during youth as a result of which the aggregate capital stock can become too large.

---

[10]In Figure 15.9, K_1 is such that $r_1 \equiv F_K(K_1, 1) - \delta = \rho - \delta_e$ so a necessary condition for dynamic inefficiency to occur is $\delta_e > \rho$ (so that $r_1 < 0$). Abel et al. (1989) show how to test empirically for dynamic inefficiency. Their results suggest that the US economy is dynamically efficient.

15.4.5   Small open economy

As a final application we now consider how the Blanchard-Yaari approach can be used to model the open economy. In the interest of space we restrict attention to the case of a small open economy in a single-product world in which financial capital is perfectly mobile. Domestic agents can lend to (or borrow from) the rest of the world at an exogenous (and constant) world interest rate, $\bar{r}$. The open economy Blanchard-Yaari model features a well-defined (and non-hysteretic) steady-state because of the existence of the generational turnover effect. Depending on parameter settings, we can distinguish between *creditor nations* (inhabited by relatively patient consumers) and *debtor nations* (with impatient consumers). In the knife-edge case, with the interest rate equalling the pure rate of time preference ($\bar{r} = \rho$), the model is still saddle-point stable. This is in stark contrast with the open economy Ramsey model (see Chapter 13), for which $\bar{r} = \rho$ is not only a necessary existence condition, but also provides the steady state with hysteretic features. Hence, the main conclusion from this section is that the overlapping generations model provides a richer framework to study small open economies.

Just as in the open economy Ramsey-Cass-Koopmans model, adjustment costs on investment are needed to limit the international mobility of physical capital. In order to focus on the key mechanisms, however, we follow Blanchard (1985, pp. 230–231) and abstract from physical capital altogether. The production function is thus given by:

$$Y(t) = Z(t)L(t),$$ (15.77)

where $Z(t)$ is an exogenous (but potentially time-varying) index of technological change. Perfectly competitive firms equate the marginal product of labour to the wage rate, so we find immediately that $w(t) = Z(t)$. Aggregate labour supply is exogenous ($L(t) = 1$) so $Z(t)$ also stands for aggregate output in the economy. In the absence of domestic financial assets (such as government bonds and domestic shares), domestic households can only accumulate foreign assets, the stock of which we denote by $A_F(t)$. The aggregate economy is characterized by the following two equations:

$$\dot{C}(t) = (\bar{r} - \rho)C(t) - \mu(\rho + \mu)A_F(t),$$ (15.78)

$$\dot{A}_F(t) = \bar{r}A_F(t) + Z(t) - C(t),$$ (15.79)

where (15.78) is the aggregate consumption Euler equation and (15.79) is the current account.

In order to study the stability issue, we write the model in a single matrix expression as:

$$\begin{bmatrix} \dot{C}(t) \\ \dot{A}_F(t) \end{bmatrix} = \begin{bmatrix} \bar{r} - \rho & -\mu(\rho + \mu) \\ -1 & \bar{r} \end{bmatrix} \begin{bmatrix} C(t) \\ A_F(t) \end{bmatrix} + \begin{bmatrix} 0 \\ Z(t) \end{bmatrix}.$$ (15.80)

Denoting the Jacobian matrix on the right-hand side by Δ, we easily find that its determinant is equal to:

$$|\Delta| = \bar{r}(\bar{r} - \rho) - \mu(\rho + \mu).$$ (15.81)

For the case with $\mu > 0$, it is easy to demonstrate that, *provided a feasible steady state exists*, it must be saddle-point stable. Indeed, $\dot{C}(t) = 0$ implies that $C = \mu(\rho + \mu)A_F/(\bar{r} - \rho)$ whereas $\dot{A}_F(t) = 0$ implies that $C - \bar{r}A_F = Z_0$ (where Z_0 is the given level of $Z(t)$). Using both results in (15.81) we find that $|\Delta| = -\mu(\rho + \mu)Z_0/C < 0$. Since $|\Delta|$ is the product of the characteristic roots, we thus find that these roots must be of opposite sign, i.e. one is negative (stable) and the other one is positive (unstable). The key thing to note is that we have not assumed anything yet about the sign of $\bar{r} - \rho$!

We can now look at several special cases of the model: (a) the creditor nation ($\bar{r} > \rho$), (b) the debtor nation ($\bar{r} < \rho$), (c) the non-saving nation ($\bar{r} = \rho$), and (d) the representative-agent knife-edge case ($\bar{r} = \rho$ and $\mu = 0$). In each case we study the effects of (permanent or temporary) productivity shocks.

15.4.5.1 Creditor nation ($\bar{r} > \rho$)

The phase diagram for the case of patient domestic agents ($\bar{r} > \rho$) is given in Figure 15.10. It follows from (15.78) that the $\dot{C}(t) = 0$ line is an upward sloping line from the origin:

$$C(t) = \frac{\mu(\rho + \mu)}{\bar{r} - \rho} A_F(t). \tag{15.82}$$

For points above (below) the line, the generational turnover effect is relatively weak (strong) so that consumption rises (falls) over time—see the vertical arrows in Figure 15.10. Similarly, by using (15.79) we find that the $\dot{A}_F(t) = 0$ line is also upward sloping:

$$C(t) = \bar{r}A_F(t) + Z_0, \tag{15.83}$$

where Z_0 is the initial level of $Z(t)$. For points above (below) the line, consumption is relatively high (low), saving is relatively low (high), and the stock of foreign assets falls (rises) over time—see the horizontal arrows in Figure 15.10. If the $\dot{A}_F(t) = 0$ line were steeper than the $\dot{C}(t) = 0$ line, no feasible steady-state equilibrium would exist (the lines would intersect in the third quadrant and consumption would be negative, which is impossible). Hence, the stability condition of the model requires the $\dot{A}_F(t) = 0$ line to be flatter than the $\dot{C}(t) = 0$ line, i.e. $\bar{r} < \mu(\rho + \mu)/(\bar{r} - \rho)$ which is—of course—the result that guarantees saddle-path stability. In terms of Figure 15.10, the steady state is at point E_0, consumption is C_0, and domestic residents have a net claim on the rest of the world, $A_{F0} > 0$.

The effects of an unanticipated and permanent productivity shock are studied in Figure 15.11. At time $t = 0$, $Z(t)$ jumps from Z_0 to Z_1, and the current account locus shifts from $(\dot{A}_F(t) = 0)_0$ to $(\dot{A}_F(t) = 0)_1$. At impact, the stock of net foreign assets is predetermined and the economy jumps from E_0 to point A on the new saddle path, SP_1. During transition, the economy gradually moves from A to the new steady-state equilibrium at E_1. Both consumption and net foreign assets increase in the long run.

What is the economic intuition behind the transitional dynamic effects? The impact effect is easy to understand: all pre-shock agents ($v \leq 0$) experience an equal increase in the level of their human wealth, $H(0)$, which is given by:

$$H(0) \equiv \int_0^\infty Z(\tau)e^{-(\bar{r}+\mu)\tau}d\tau. \tag{15.84}$$

It is easy to verify that, since $dZ(\tau) = dZ$ for $\tau \geq 0$, the impact change in human wealth equals $dH(0) = dZ \cdot \int_0^\infty e^{-(\bar{r}+\mu)\tau}d\tau = dZ/(\bar{r}+\mu)$. We thus find that:

$$\frac{dC(v,0)}{dZ} = (\rho + \mu)\frac{dH(0)}{dZ} = \frac{\rho+\mu}{\bar{r}+\mu} > 0, \tag{15.85}$$

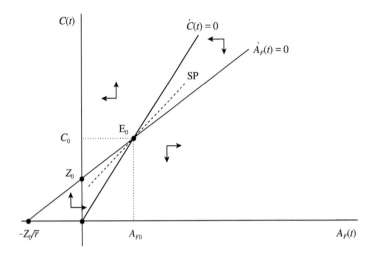

Figure 15.10: A patient small open economy

$$\frac{d\dot{A}_F\left(v,0\right)}{dZ} = 1 - \frac{\rho+\mu}{\bar{r}+\mu} = \frac{\bar{r}-\rho}{\bar{r}+\mu} > 0, \tag{15.86}$$

where we have used (15.31) (with $A = A_F$, $w = Z$, and $T = 0$ imposed), (15.84), (15.38), and (15.40). Pre-shock agents react to the increase in human wealth by increasing both their consumption and their savings rate. During transition, new (wealthier) generations are born who choose higher consumption and saving levels than pre-shock agents did at birth. In fact, it is easy to verify that $dC\left(t,t\right)/dZ = dC\left(v,0\right)/dZ$ and $d\dot{A}_F\left(t,t\right)/dZ = d\dot{A}_F\left(v,0\right)/dZ$ so pre-shock and post-shock generations react in the same way. As a result, both aggregate consumption and net foreign assets rise. Finally, in the new steady-state only post-shock generations remain, which explains why transition is completed at that point.

15.4.5.2 Debtor nation ($\bar{r} < \rho$)

The phase diagram for the debtor nation is given in Figure 15.12. In this case the $\dot{C}(t) = 0$ line is a downward sloping line from the origin because $\bar{r} < \rho$—see equation (15.82). Because net foreign assets are negative in the second quadrant ($A_F\left(t\right) < 0$), the generational turnover term operates in the opposite direction. Aggregate consumption growth *exceeds* individual consumption growth because newborns consume more than older agents in this case. It follows from (15.78) that aggregate consumption rises (falls) over time for points below (above) the $\dot{C}(t) = 0$ locus—see the vertical arrows in Figure 15.12. The model features a unique, saddle-path stable steady state at point E_0. The reader is asked to verify that an unanticipated and permanent productivity increase would move the steady state in a north-westerly direction, say to point E_1. At impact, consumption overshoots its long-run effect.

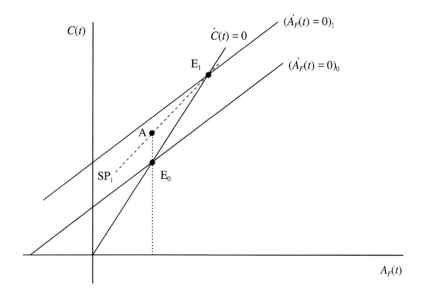

Figure 15.11: A productivity shock

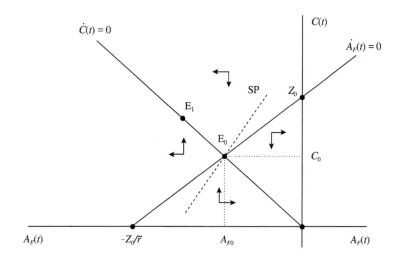

Figure 15.12: An impatient small open economy

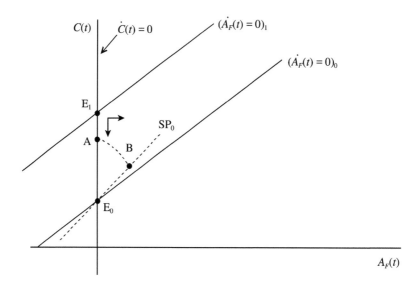

Figure 15.13: A temporary productivity shock in a non-saving nation

15.4.5.3   Non-saving nation ($\bar{r} = \rho$)

The phase diagram for the non-saving nation is given in Figure 15.13. In this case we find from (15.78) that:

$$\dot{C}(t) = -\mu \left(\rho + \mu \right) A_F, \tag{15.87}$$

so the $\dot{C}(t) = 0$ line coincides with the vertical axis. Consumption rises (falls) over time for points to the left (right) of the vertical axis. Of course, as we demonstrated formally above, the model still features a unique steady state (at point E_0) that is saddle-point stable. Both aggregate and individual net foreign assets are zero in the steady state ($A_F(v,0) = A_F(0) = 0$). Because $\bar{r} = \rho$, all agents maintain a time-invariant consumption pattern ($\dot{C}(v,t) = 0$). Facing a constant wage income, they neither save nor dissave.

As is clear from (15.85)–(15.86), an unanticipated and permanent productivity increase induces all pre-shock agents to increase their consumption on a one-for-one basis ($dC(v,0)/dZ = 1$) but has no effect on saving ($d\dot{A}_F(v,0)/dZ = 0$). All post-shock agents are identical to pre-shock agents, so there is no transitional dynamic effect at all. The equilibrium jumps at impact from E_0 to E_1 directly above it.

Next we consider an unanticipated and temporary increase in productivity, i.e. $dZ(t) = dZ$ for $0 \leq t \leq t_E$ and $dZ(t) = 0$ for $t > t_E$. Using the heuristic solution principle (see also Section 4.1.2 above) we deduce that the adjustment path has the following features:

- At time $t = 0$, the current account locus shifts from $(\dot{A}_F(t) = 0)_0$ to $(\dot{A}_F(t) = 0)_1$. The arrows denote the dynamics implied by point E_1. The stock of net foreign assets is predetermined, but there is an jump in aggregate consumption which moves the economy from E_0 to A.

- During the time interval $0 \leq t \leq t_E$ there is a gradual move from A to B. Aggregate consumption falls but net foreign assets increase. The nation is saving temporarily.

- At time $t = t_E$, productivity returns to its former level and the current account locus shifts back to $(\dot{A}_F(t) = 0)_0$, as does the associated saddle path SP_0.

- For $t > t_E$, the economy moves gradually from B to E_0. Both consumption and foreign assets fall during transition. There is no long-run effect of the temporary productivity shock.

The economic intuition behind the adjustment path is easy to deduce. Pre-shock agents ($v \leq 0$) hold no financial assets and change their consumption and savings according to:

$$\frac{dC(v,0)}{dZ} = (\rho + \mu)\frac{dH(0)}{dZ} > 0, \qquad \frac{d\dot{A}_F(v,0)}{dZ} = \frac{dZ(0)}{dZ} - \frac{dC(v,0)}{dZ}. \qquad (15.88)$$

In contrast, post-shock newborns ($v = t > 0$) change their plans according to:

$$\frac{dC(t,t)}{dZ} = (\rho + \mu)\frac{dH(t)}{dZ}, \qquad \frac{d\dot{A}_F(t,t)}{dZ} = \frac{dZ(t)}{dZ} - \frac{dC(t,t)}{dZ}. \qquad (15.89)$$

Given the form of the shock we find that $dZ(\tau)/dZ = 1$ for $0 \leq \tau \leq t_E$ and $dZ(\tau)/dZ = 0$ for $\tau > t_E$. Hence, the human wealth change is given by:[11]

$$\frac{dH(t)}{dZ} = \begin{cases} \dfrac{1 - e^{(\rho+\mu)(t-t_E)}}{\rho + \mu} & \text{for } 0 \leq t \leq t_E \\ 0 & \text{for } t > t_E. \end{cases} \qquad (15.90)$$

Armed with these expressions we see that pre-shock generations benefit the most from the shock, and consequently increase their consumption by the largest amount, i.e. $dC(v,0)/dZ = 1 - e^{-(\rho+\mu)t_E} > 0$ and $d\dot{A}_F(v,0)/dZ = e^{-(\rho+\mu)t_E} > 0$. These generations accumulate net foreign assets because they know that their income is only temporarily higher than before and they want to maintain a time-invariant consumption profile. The assets allow them to do so.

Post-shock generations born in the interval $0 \leq t \leq t_E$ also increase their consumption and savings, though by less than pre-shockers because they face a shorter period of high income, i.e. $dC(t,t)/dZ = 1 - e^{(\rho+\mu)(t-t_E)} > 0$ and $d\dot{A}_F(t,t)/dZ = e^{(\rho+\mu)(t-t_E)} > 0$. This explains why aggregate consumption falls during the transition from A to B. Consumption of newborns is lower than the average consumption in the economy.

Finally, post-shock generations born at time t_E face exactly the same conditions as in the initial steady state, i.e. for them $dC(t,t)/dZ = d\dot{A}_F(t,t)/dZ = 0$. Since both pre-shock generations and post-shock generations born in the interval $0 \leq t \leq t_E$ start to decumulate their financial assets after time t_E, transition from B to E_0 features falling aggregate consumption and financial assets. In the new steady state, the temporary savers have all died off and the economy returns to the initial equilibrium at point E_0.

---

[11]Human wealth at time t is defined as:

$$H(t) \equiv \int_t^\infty Z(\tau)e^{(\bar{r}+\mu)(t-\tau)}d\tau.$$

For the temporary shock we have $dZ(\tau) = dZ$ for $0 \leq \tau \leq t_E$ and $dZ(\tau) = 0$ otherwise. Hence, for $0 \leq t < t_E$ we find that $dH(t)$ is equal to:

$$dH(t) \equiv dZ \cdot \int_t^{t_E} e^{(\bar{r}+\mu)(t-\tau)}d\tau = \frac{dZ}{r^* + \mu} \cdot \left[1 - e^{(\bar{r}+\mu)(t-t_E)}\right].$$

Fot $t \geq t_E$, the shock has already passed and $dH(t) = 0$.

15.4.5.4   Representative-agent model ($\bar{r} = \rho$ and $\mu = 0$)

As a final case we consider the open economy Ramsey model, for which $\mu = 0$ (no new generations and no mortality) and $\bar{r} = \rho$ (knife-edge condition). It follows from (15.78) that the aggregate (and individual) Euler equation is given by $\dot{C}(t) = 0$. In view of (15.80)–(15.81) we find that the model features one positive root ($\lambda_2 = \bar{r} = \rho$) and one zero root ($\lambda_1 = 0$). Clearly we cannot employ our usual graphical apparatus because we are lacking an informative $\dot{C}(t) = 0$ locus in this case. In terms of Figure 15.14, we only have an expression for $\dot{A}_F(t) = 0$ and all we know is that the equilibrium will be somewhere along that locus.

In order to deduce the properties of the model, we first note that the national solvency condition (coinciding in the absence of a government with the household lifetime budget constraint) says:

$$A_{F0} = \int_0^\infty [C(t) - Z(t)] e^{-\rho t} dt, \tag{15.91}$$

where A_{F0} is the initial level of net foreign assets *which may or may not be equal to zero*. The magnitude of A_{F0} is based on decisions that were made in the past! But the representative agent wishes to maintain a flat consumption profile ($\dot{C}(t) = 0$ and $C(t)$ is time-invariant), so (15.91) can be solved for $C(0)$:

$$C(0) = \rho \left[A_{F0} + \int_0^\infty Z(t) e^{-\rho t} dt \right]. \tag{15.92}$$

An unanticipated and permanent productivity increase raises consumption on a one-for-one basis, $dC(0)/dZ = 1$. In Figure 15.14 the current account locus shifts from $(\dot{A}_F(t) = 0)_0$ to $(\dot{A}_F(t) = 0)_1$. If the initial equilibrium happens to be at E_0, where $A_{F0} = 0$, the equilibrium shifts from E_0 to E_1 at impact. (If A_{F0} is non-zero, the initial equilibrium would be located somewhere else along the $(\dot{A}_F(t) = 0)_0$ curve but the effect on consumption would be exactly the same.) Following the jump in consumption, there is no further transitional dynamics at all.

It follows from (15.92) that an unanticipated and temporary productivity shock of the form studied above changes consumption and savings at impact according to:

$$\frac{dC(0)}{dZ} = 1 - e^{-\rho t_E} > 0, \qquad \frac{d\dot{A}_F(0)}{dZ} = e^{-\rho t_E} > 0. \tag{15.93}$$

In terms of Figure 15.14, the economy jumps from E_0 to A at impact. Since A lies to the right of the $(\dot{A}_F(t) = 0)_1$ line, net foreign assets increase because output exceeds consumption, and net exports take place. In the interval $0 \le t \le t_E$, $\dot{A}_F(t)$ is therefore positive but $\dot{C}(t) = 0$ so the economy moves in a horizontal direction from A to B, where it arrives at time t_E. After time t_E, productivity and human wealth are back to their initial levels but consumption is permanently higher despite the fact that the shock was temporary. The higher consumption level can be sustained by the representative agent because he has accumulated net foreign assets, the interest earnings on which can be consumed. The final (hysteretic) steady state is thus at point B.[12]

15.5   Endogenous labour supply

As we have seen throughout the book, an endogenous labour supply response often plays a vital role in various macroeconomic theories. In Chapter 13, for example, it

---

[12]The effects of an unanticipated and *permanent* shock are obtained from (15.93) by setting $t_E \to \infty$.

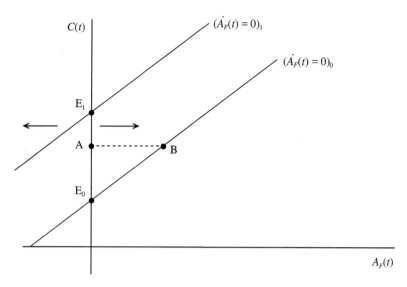

Figure 15.14: A temporary productivity shock in the RA model

was demonstrated that the intertemporal substitutability of household leisure forms one of the key mechanisms determining the impact and long-run effects of fiscal policy. The aim of this section is therefore to extend the basic Blanchard-Yaari model by allowing for an endogenous labour supply decision of the households. We follow Heijdra and Ligthart (2000) by introducing various taxes and assuming simple functional forms for preferences and technology in order to keep the discussion as simple as possible. We analyse the effects of a consumption tax in order to demonstrate some of the key properties of the model.

15.5.1 Model elements

Assume that the (expected-remaining-lifetime) utility function used so far (see (15.30)) is replaced by:

$$E(\Lambda(v,t)) \equiv \int_t^\infty \ln\left(C(v,\tau)^\varepsilon \left[1 - L(v,\tau)\right]^{1-\varepsilon}\right) e^{(\rho+\mu)(t-\tau)} d\tau, \tag{15.94}$$

with $0 < \varepsilon \leq 1$. Leisure is defined as the consumer's time endowment (which is normalized to unity) minus labour supply, $L(v,\tau)$. Note that (15.30) is obtained as a special case of (15.94) by setting $\varepsilon = 1$. Since labour supply is now endogenous and we include various taxes, the agent's budget identity (15.31) is replaced by:

$$\dot{A}(v,\tau) = [r(\tau) + \mu] A(v,\tau) + w(\tau)(1 - t_L) + TR(\tau) - X(v,\tau), \tag{15.95}$$

$$X(v,\tau) \equiv (1 + t_C)C(v,\tau) + w(\tau)(1 - t_L)\left[1 - L(v,\tau)\right], \tag{15.96}$$

where $X(v,\tau)$ represents *full consumption*, i.e. the sum of spending on goods consumption and leisure, t_C is a proportional tax on private consumption, t_L is a proportional tax on labour income, and $TR(\tau)$ are age-independent transfers received from the government. The household's solvency condition is still given by (15.32).

Following Marini and van der Ploeg (1988) we solve the household's optimization problem by using *two-stage budgeting*. We have encountered this technique several times before in this book, albeit in the context of static models—see for example

Chapters 2 and 11. The procedure is, however, essentially the same in dynamic models. Intuitively the procedure works as follows. In the first stage we determine how the consumer chooses an optimal mix of consumption and leisure conditional upon a given level of full consumption $(X(v,\tau))$. Then, in the second stage, we determine the optimal time path for full consumption itself. The procedure is valid provided the utility function is *intertemporally separable*.[13]

In *stage 1* the consumer chooses $C(v,\tau)$ and $1-L(v,\tau)$ in order to maximize instantaneous felicity, $\ln\left[C(v,\tau)^{\varepsilon}[1-L(v,\tau)]^{1-\varepsilon}\right]$, given the restriction (15.96) and conditional upon the level of $X(v,\tau)$. This optimization problem yields the familiar first-order condition calling for the equalization of the marginal rate of substitution between leisure and consumption and the relative price of leisure and consumption:

$$\frac{C(v,\tau)}{1-L(v,\tau)}\frac{1-\varepsilon}{\varepsilon}=w(\tau)\frac{1-t_L}{1+t_C}. \tag{15.97}$$

By substituting (15.97) into (15.96), we obtain expressions for consumption and leisure in terms of full consumption:

$$(1+t_C)C(v,\tau)=\varepsilon X(v,\tau), \tag{15.98}$$
$$w(\tau)(1-t_L)\left[1-L(v,\tau)\right]=(1-\varepsilon)X(v,\tau). \tag{15.99}$$

Since sub-felicity—the term in round brackets in (15.94)—is Cobb-Douglas and thus features a unit substitution elasticity, spending shares on consumption and leisure are constant. To prepare for the second stage we substitute (15.98)–(15.99) into the lifetime utility functional (15.94) to obtain the following expression:

$$E(\Lambda(v,t))\equiv\int_t^{\infty}\left[\ln X(v,\tau)-\ln P_{\Omega}(\tau)\right]e^{(\rho+\mu)(t-\tau)}d\tau, \tag{15.100}$$

where $P_{\Omega}(\tau)$ is a true cost-of-living index relating sub-felicity to full consumption:

$$P_{\Omega}(\tau)\equiv\left(\frac{1+t_C}{\varepsilon}\right)^{\varepsilon}\left(\frac{w(\tau)(1-t_L)}{1-\varepsilon}\right)^{1-\varepsilon}. \tag{15.101}$$

In *stage 2*, the consumer chooses the path of full consumption in order to maximize (15.100) subject to the dynamic budget identity (15.95) and the solvency condition (15.32). This problem is essentially the same as the one that was solved in section 15.3.1 above so it should therefore not surprise the reader that the solution takes the following form:

$$X(v,t)=(\rho+\mu)\left[A(v,t)+H(t)\right], \tag{15.102}$$
$$\frac{\dot{X}(v,\tau)}{X(v,\tau)}=r(\tau)-\rho, \quad(\text{for }\tau\geq t), \tag{15.103}$$
$$H(t)\equiv\int_t^{\infty}\left[w(\tau)(1-t_L)+TR(\tau)\right]e^{-R^A(t,\tau)}d\tau, \tag{15.104}$$

where $R^A(t,\tau)$ is defined in (15.32) above. Equation (15.102) says that full consumption is proportional to total wealth (the sum of financial and human wealth) whereas (15.103) shows that optimal full consumption growth depends on the difference between the interest rate and the pure rate of time preference. Finally, equation (15.104)

---

[13]Preferences are intertemporally separable if the marginal utility of consumption and leisure at time τ only depends on time τ dated variables. Intertemporal separability is commonly assumed in the macro literature and indeed holds for (15.94). See also Deaton and Muellbauer (1980, p. 124).

is the definition of human wealth. It differs from (15.34) because labour income is taxed (at a proportional rate) and because the household receives lump-sum transfers.

By aggregating (15.102) and (15.103) across surviving generations and making use of (15.98)–(15.99), expressions for aggregate consumption growth and labour supply are obtained—see equations (T2.1) and (T2.6) in Table 15.2. Compared to the basic Blanchard-Yaari model we have introduced the following simplifications. First, we abstract from government spending and debt $(G(t) = B(t) = \dot{B}(t) = 0)$ and assume that all tax revenues are rebated to households in a lump-sum fashion. As a result, the government budget identity is static—see (T2.3) in Table 15.2. Second, we have simplified the production structure of the extended model somewhat by assuming a Cobb-Douglas technology—see (T2.7). Using this specification in (T1.4) and (T1.5) yields the expressions (T2.4) and (T2.5), respectively.

Table 15.2. The extended Blanchard-Yaari model

$$\frac{\dot{C}(t)}{C(t)} = r(t) - \rho - \varepsilon\mu(\rho + \mu) \cdot \frac{K(t)}{(1 + t_C)C(t)}, \tag{T2.1}$$

$$\dot{K}(t) = Y(t) - C(t) - \delta K(t) \tag{T2.2}$$

$$TR(t) = t_L w(t)L(t) + t_C C(t) \tag{T2.3}$$

$$r(t) + \delta = \alpha\frac{Y(t)}{K(t)} \tag{T2.4}$$

$$w(t) = (1 - \alpha)\frac{Y(t)}{L(t)} \tag{T2.5}$$

$$w(t)\left[1 - L(t)\right] = \frac{1 - \varepsilon}{\varepsilon}\frac{1 + t_C}{1 - t_L}C(t), \quad 0 < \varepsilon \le 1. \tag{T2.6}$$

$$Y(t) = Z_0 K(t)^\alpha L(t)^{1-\alpha}, \quad 0 < \alpha < 1 \tag{T2.7}$$

Notes: $C(t)$ is consumption, $K(t)$ is the capital stock, $L(t)$ is labour supply, $Y(t)$ is aggregate output, $w(t)$ is the wage rate, $TR(t)$ are lump-sum transfers, and $r(t)$ is the interest rate. There are proportional taxes on consumption (t_C) and on wage income (t_L). Capital depreciates at a constant rate δ, ε is a taste parameter for consumption, ρ is the pure rate of time preference, Z_0 is a constant, α is the efficiency parameter of capital, and μ is the mortality rate (equals birth rate).

15.5.2 Phase diagram

The phase diagram of the model is drawn in Figure 15.15. The endogeneity of the labour supply decision considerably complicates the derivation of the phase diagram. For that reason we report the details of this derivation in a mathematical appendix to this chapter and focus here on a graphical and intuitive discussion.

The capital stock equilibrium locus (CSE) represents the (C, K) combinations for which net investment is zero ($\dot{K}(t) = 0$). Apart from the fact that the model now includes various tax rates and government consumption is set equal to zero, the CSE line is identical to the one discussed in detail in Section 13.3 above. The CSE line is concave and for points above (below) this line consumption is too high (low) and net

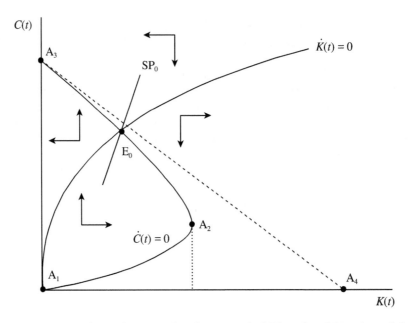

Figure 15.15: Phase diagram for the extended Blanchard-Yaari model

investment is negative (positive).[14]

The consumption equilibrium (CE) locus represents the (C, K) combinations for which *aggregate* consumption is constant ($\dot{C}(t) = 0$). In the representative-agent model of Chapter 13, aggregate and individual consumption coincide, CE is simply the locus of points for which the interest rate equals the rate of time preference ($r = \rho$), and the output-capital ratio is constant (see Chapter 13 for details). For convenience, the CE line for the representative-agent model is included in Figure 15.15—see the dashed line connecting points A_3 and A_4.

In contrast, in the overlapping-generations model, individual and aggregate consumption do not coincide and, as a result, the position and slope of the CE curve are affected by two conceptually distinct mechanisms, namely the *factor scarcity effect* (FS, which explains the slope of the CE curve for the representative-agent model) and the *generational turnover effect* (GT). The interplay between these two effects ensures that CE has the shape of a rather prominent nose. Along the lower branch, $A_1 A_2$, consumption is low, equilibrium employment is close to unity ($L \approx 1$), and CE is upward sloping. In contrast, along the upper branch, $A_2 A_3$, consumption is high, equilibrium employment is low ($L \approx 0$), and CE slopes downward. The dynamic forces at work can be studied by writing (T2.1) as follows:

$$\frac{\dot{C}(t)}{C(t)} = r(t) - \rho - \mu \cdot \frac{C(t) - C(t, t)}{C(t)}$$

$$= r(C(t), K(t)) - \rho - \frac{\mu\varepsilon(\rho + \mu)}{1 + t_C} \cdot \frac{K(t)}{C(t)}, \tag{15.105}$$

where $r(C, K)$ is short-hand notation for the dependence of the real interest rate on consumption and the capital stock. Simple intuitive arguments can be used to motivate the signs of the partial derivatives of the $r(C, K)$ function, which are denoted

---

[14]We have only drawn the upward-sloping part of the CSE line. Recall from Chapter 13 that CSE reaches a maximum for the "golden-rule" capital stock, K^{GR}, and then becomes downward sloping.

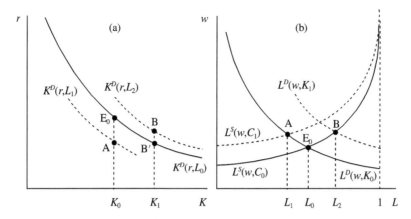

Figure 15.16: Factor markets

by r_C and r_K, respectively. Some simple graphs can clarify matters.

Consider Figure 15.16 which depicts the situation in the rental market for capital and the labour market. In panel (a), the supply of capital is predetermined in the short run—say at K_0. The demand for capital is downward sloping—due to diminishing returns to capital—and depends positively on the employment level—because the two factors are cooperative in production. Panel (b) depicts the situation in the labour market. There are diminishing returns to labour—so labour demand slopes downwards—and additional capital boosts labour demand. The labour supply curve follows from the optimal leisure-consumption choice (T2.6). It slopes upwards because (T2.6) isolates the pure substitution effect of labour supply.[15]

Let us now use Figure 15.16 to deduce the signs of r_C and r_K. Ceteris paribus the capital stock, an increase in consumption shifts labour supply to the left so that the wage rises and employment falls. The reduction in employment shifts the demand for capital to the left so that—for a given inelastic supply of capital—the real interest rate must fall to equilibrate the rental market for capital, i.e. $r_C < 0$. The thought experiment compares points E_0 and A in the two panels.

An increase in capital supply—ceteris paribus consumption—has a *direct effect*, which pushes the interest rate down (a movement along the initial capital demand schedule, $K^D(r, L_0)$ from E_0 to B'), and an *induced effect* operating via the labour market. The boost in K shifts the labour demand curve to the right, leading to an increase in wages and employment and thus (in panel (a)) to an outward shift in the capital demand curve. Although this induced effect pushes the interest rate up somewhat, the direct effect dominates and $r_K < 0$.[16] The comparison is between points E_0 and B in the two panels of Figure 15.16.

We can now study the dynamic forces acting on aggregate consumption along

---

[15]Normally, in static models of labour supply, the income and substitution effects work in opposite directions thus rendering the slope of the labour supply curve ambiguous. Here we do not have this "problem" because the income effect is incorporated in C. Technically speaking, (T2.6) is a so-called *Frisch demand* curve for leisure. See also Judd (1987b).

[16]This assertion follows directly from the *factor price frontier* (FPF) which is obtained by substituting (T2.4) and (T2.5) into (T2.7):

$$1 = \left(\frac{r+\delta}{\alpha}\right)^\alpha \left(\frac{w}{1-\alpha}\right)^{1-\alpha}.$$

The FPF is an inverse relationship between r and w, so if the wage increases then the return to capital must decrease.

the two branches of the CE curve in Figure 15.15. First consider a point on the lower branch of this curve (for which $L \approx 1$). Holding capital constant, an increase in aggregate consumption leads to a small decrease in labour supply[17] and thus a small decrease in the interest rate. At the same time, however, the capital-consumption ratio falls so that aggregate consumption growth increases, i.e. $\dot{C}/C > 0$ for points above the lower branch of CE:

$$\underbrace{\frac{\dot{C}}{C}}_{\uparrow} = \underbrace{r(C,K)}_{\downarrow} - \rho - \frac{\mu\varepsilon(\rho+\mu)}{1+t_C} \cdot \underbrace{\frac{K}{C}}_{\downarrow\downarrow}. \qquad \text{(lower branch of CE)}$$

Now consider a point on the upper branch of the CE curve (for which $L \approx 0$). Ceteris paribus K, a given increase in C has a strong negative effect on labour supply and thus causes a large reduction in the interest rate which offsets the effect operating via the capital-consumption ratio, i.e. $\dot{C}/C < 0$ for points above the upper branch of CE:

$$\underbrace{\frac{\dot{C}}{C}}_{\downarrow} = \underbrace{r(C,K)}_{\downarrow\downarrow} - \rho - \frac{\mu\varepsilon(\rho+\mu)}{1+t_C} \cdot \underbrace{\frac{K}{C}}_{\downarrow}. \qquad \text{(upper branch of CE)}$$

These dynamic effects have been illustrated with vertical arrows in Figure 15.15.

In summary, the CE curve is very similar to the one for the standard Blanchard model with exogenous labour supply (see Figure 15.6) for values of L close to unity (the lower branch in Figure 15.15). At the same time, it is very similar to the CE curve for the representative-agent model with endogenous labour supply for values of L close to zero (compare the upper branch of CE in Figure 15.15 with the dashed line). Put differently, on the lower branch of the CE curve the generational turnover effect dominates whereas on the upper branch the factor scarcity effect dominates.

It follows from the configuration of arrows that the unique equilibrium E_0 in Figure 15.15 is saddle-point stable. Although we have drawn Figure 15.15 such that the equilibrium occurs on the downward-sloping part of the CE curve (for which the factor scarcity effect dominates the generational turnover effect), there is nothing to prevent the opposite occurring, i.e. it is quite possible that the structural parameters are such that E_0 lies on the lower branch of CE.

15.5.3   Raising the consumption tax

We now illustrate how the model can be used for policy analysis. We focus attention on the effects of an unanticipated and permanent increase in the consumption tax, t_C. Using the methods explained in detail in Chapter 13, the model can be linearized along an initial steady state (such as E_0 in Figure 15.15). The resulting expressions are collected in Table 15.3. For convenience, the following notational conventions are used in the table and the remainder of this section. First, for $x \in \{C,K,Y,w,r,L\}$ we

---

[17]Holding constant the tax rates we can use (T2.6) to derive:

$$\frac{dL}{L} = \frac{1-L}{L} \cdot \left[\frac{dw}{w} - \frac{dC}{C}\right].$$

Hence, for $L \approx 1$ ($L \approx 0$) the labour supply curve in Figure 15.16 is relatively steep (flat) and a given change in consumption shifts the curve by a little (a lot). This explains why the parameter $\omega_{LL}^* \equiv (1 - L^*)/L^*$ plays a vital role in the analysis of the loglinearized model below. See also Section 13.5 on this.

define:

$$\tilde{x}(t) \equiv \frac{x(t) - x^*}{x^*}, \qquad \dot{\tilde{x}}(t) \equiv \frac{\dot{x}(t)}{x^*},$$

where starred variables denote the initial steady-state values. Second, for the consumption tax and the lump-sum transfers we use a slightly different notation:

$$\tilde{t}_C \equiv \frac{t_C - t_{C0}}{1 + t_{C0}}, \qquad \widetilde{TR}(t) \equiv \frac{TR(t) - TR^*}{Y^*},$$

where t_{C0} is the initial consumption tax.

Table 15.3. The linearized extended BY model

$$\dot{\tilde{C}}(t) = r^* \tilde{r}(t) + (r^* - \rho)\left[\tilde{C}(t) + \tilde{t}_C - \tilde{K}(t)\right] \tag{T3.1}$$

$$\dot{\tilde{K}}(t) = (\delta/\omega_I^*)\left[\tilde{Y}(t) - \omega_C^* \tilde{C}(t) - \omega_I^* \tilde{K}(t)\right] \tag{T3.2}$$

$$\widetilde{TR}(t) = (1 + t_{C0})\omega_C^*\left[\tilde{t}_C + \frac{t_{C0}}{1 + t_{C0}}\tilde{C}(t)\right] + (1 - \alpha)t_L \tilde{Y}(t) \tag{T3.3}$$

$$r^* \tilde{r}(t) = (r^* + \delta)\left[\tilde{Y}(t) - \tilde{K}(t)\right] \tag{T3.4}$$

$$\tilde{w}(t) = \tilde{Y}(t) - \tilde{L}(t) \tag{T3.5}$$

$$\tilde{L}(t) = \omega_{LL}^*\left[\tilde{w}(t) - \tilde{t}_C - \tilde{C}(t)\right] \tag{T3.6}$$

$$\tilde{Y}(t) = (1 - \alpha)\tilde{L}(t) + \alpha\tilde{K}(t) \tag{T3.7}$$

Definitions: $\omega_C^* \equiv C^*/Y^*$: output share of private consumption; $\omega_I^* \equiv I^*/Y^*$: output share of investment, $\omega_C^* + \omega_I^* = 1$, $\delta/\omega_I^* = Y^*/K^* \equiv (r^* + \delta)/\alpha$; and $\omega_{LL}^* \equiv (1 - L^*)/L^*$: ratio between leisure and labour.

Solving the linearized model is child's play and proceeds along much the same lines as in Chapter 13. First we use (T3.5)–(T3.7) to compute the "quasi-reduced-form" expression for output:

$$\tilde{Y}(t) = \alpha\xi\tilde{K}(t) - (\xi - 1)\left[\tilde{C}(t) + \tilde{t}_C\right], \tag{15.106}$$

where ξ summarizes the intertemporal labour supply effects:

$$1 \leq \xi \equiv \frac{1 + \omega_{LL}^*}{1 + \alpha\omega_{LL}^*} < \frac{1}{\alpha}. \tag{15.107}$$

Second, we use (15.106) in (T3.2) and impose $\dot{\tilde{K}}(t) = 0$ to get the linearized CSE line:

$$\tilde{C}(t) = \frac{\alpha\xi - \omega_I^*}{\omega_C^* + \xi - 1}\tilde{K}(t) - \frac{\xi - 1}{\omega_C^* + \xi - 1}\tilde{t}_C. \tag{15.108}$$

The CSE curve is upward sloping (since $r^* K^*/Y^* = \alpha - \omega_I > 0$ and $\xi \geq 1$) and an increase in the consumption tax shifts the curve down—see the shift from CSE_0 to CSE_1 in Figures 15.17 and 15.18. For a given capital stock, an increase in t_C reduces labour supply, and thus employment and output. To restore capital stock equilibrium, employment and output must return to their former levels, i.e. consumption must fall.

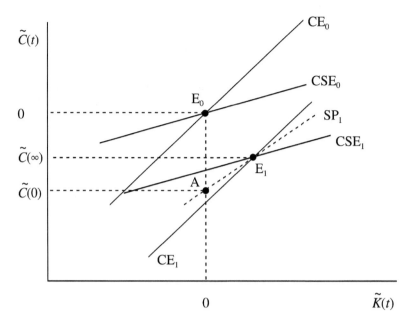

Figure 15.17: Consumption taxation with a dominant GT effect

Finally, we obtain the linearized CE line by substituting (15.106) and (T3.4) into (T3.1) and setting $\dot{\tilde{C}}(t) = 0$:

$$\tilde{C}(t) = -\frac{(r^* + \delta)\,[1 - \alpha\xi] + r^* - \rho}{(\xi - 1)(r^* + \delta) - (r^* - \rho)}\,\tilde{K}(t) - \tilde{t}_C. \tag{15.109}$$

As was apparent from our discussion concerning Figure 15.15 above, the slope of the CE line around the initial steady state is ambiguous and depends on the relative strength of the factor scarcity and generational turnover effects. These two effects show up in the denominator of the coefficient for $\tilde{K}(t)$ on the right-hand side as, respectively, $(\xi - 1)(r^* + \delta)$ (for the FS effect) and $(r^* - \rho)$ (for the GT effect). There are thus two cases of interest. First, if $(r^* - \rho)$ exceeds $(\xi - 1)(r^* + \delta)$ then the GT effect dominates the FS effect, and the linearized CE line is upward sloping as in Figure 15.17. Second, if the reverse holds and $(\xi - 1)(r^* + \delta)$ is larger than $(r^* - \rho)$ then the FS effect dominates the GT effect so that the linearized CE curve is downward sloping as in Figure 15.18.

It turns out that the effect of the consumption tax on the long-run capital stock depends critically on the relative strength of the GT and FS effects. Indeed, by solving (15.108) and (15.109) for $t \to \infty$ we obtain the following expression for the steady-state effect on capital of the consumption tax change:

$$\tilde{K}(\infty) = \omega_C^* \frac{(r^* - \rho) - (\xi - 1)(r^* + \delta)}{\xi(1 - \alpha)\left[(r^* + \delta)\omega_C^* + r^* - \rho\right]}\,\tilde{t}_C. \tag{15.110}$$

If the GT effect is stronger (weaker) than the FS effect, an increase in the consumption tax leads to an increase (decrease) in the long-run capital stock. The intuition behind these results can be explained with the aid of Figures 15.17 and 15.18.

In Figure 15.17 the GT effect is dominant $(r^* - \rho > (\xi - 1)(r^* + \delta))$, the CSE curve shifts down by less than the CE curve does, and the steady state shifts from

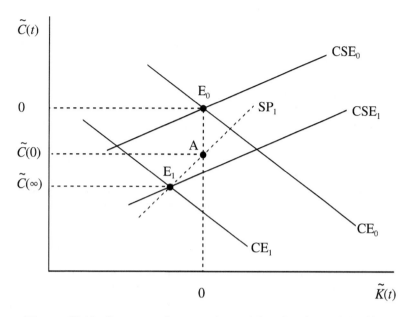

Figure 15.18: Consumption taxation with a dominant FS effect

E_0 to E_1. At impact the tax shock causes a redistribution from old to young existing generations. The old generations are wealthy and thus have a high consumption level, whereas the young generations consume very little and thus face only a small increase in their tax bill. Since the additional tax revenue is recycled to all generations in an age-independent lump-sum fashion, older generations are hit harder by the tax shock than younger generations are and the proportional difference in consumption between the old and young agents falls. In terms of (15.105), $r(t)$ changes hardly at all (because the FS effect is weak) but the generational turnover term, $[C(t) - \tilde{C}(t,t)]/C(t)$, falls so that aggregate consumption growth increases at impact, i.e. $\tilde{C}(0) < 0$ and $\dot{\tilde{C}}(0) > 0$ at point A. The reduction in aggregate consumption outweighs the fall in production (which is slight because labour supply changes by very little), net investment takes place ($\dot{\tilde{K}}(0) > 0$ at point A), and the economy gradually moves from point A to the new steady state in E_1.

Matters are quite different if the FS effect dominates the GT effect, a situation which is depicted in Figure 15.18. Now the downward shift in CE dominates the downward shift in CSE, and the new steady state, E_1, is associated with a lower capital stock. This long-run effect is best understood by noting that with a dominant FS effect, the long-run capital-labour ratio is more or less unchanged. Since the consumption tax reduces labour supply this can only occur if the capital stock falls also.[18] In the impact period the reduction in consumption is dominated by the fall in output, and net investment is negative. At the same time, the reduction in labour supply reduces the capital-labour ratio at impact so that the interest rate falls and the aggregate consumption profile becomes downward sloping. In summary, it follows that both $\dot{\tilde{K}}(0) < 0$ and $\dot{\tilde{C}}(0) < 0$ at point A. Over time, the economy gradually moves from point A to the new steady state at E_1.

---

[18]If the GT effect is absent altogether ($\mu = 0$), the steady-state interest rate equals the rate of time preference ($r = \rho$) and the capital-labour ratio does not change at all. See the discussion surrounding the *great ratios* in Section 13.5 above.

15.5.4   Quantitative evidence

We have demonstrated that the qualitative effects of a consumption tax in the extended BY model depend critically on the relative importance of the GT and FS effects. A simple (rough and ready) calibration exercise suggests that the empirically relevant case is likely to be such that the FS effect is dominant. Consider for this purpose the parameters used to calibrate the unit-elastic RCK model discussed in Chapter 13. In that chapter we used $r^* = 0.0159$ per quarter (6.5% annual rate of interest), $\delta = 0.0241$ (10% per annum), and $\alpha = 1/3$ so that $\kappa^* \equiv (K/Y)^* = \alpha/(r^* + \delta) = 8.33$ and $\omega_I^* = (I/Y)^* = \delta\kappa^* = 0.201$. Since we abstract from government consumption, the steady-state output share of consumption is $\omega_C^* = 1 - \omega_I^* = 0.799$. Just as in Chapter 13, we assume that 20% of available time is used for working, so that $\omega_{LL}^* \equiv (1 - L^*)/L^* = 4$. Using the calibration values of α and ω_{LL}^* in the definition of ξ (given in (15.107) above) we get $\xi = 2.143$ and:

$$(\xi - 1)(r^* + \delta) = 0.0457 \qquad \text{(Calibrated FS effect)}$$

It remains to find a plausible value for $(r^* - \rho)$ in the overlapping generations model. This is where we need more detailed information on the variables affecting the household sector. We assume that the initial tax rates are $t_{C0} = 0.1$ and $t_{L0} = 0.3$. By using (T2.5)–(T2.6) we get the implied value for ε:

$$\varepsilon = \left[1 + \frac{(1 - \alpha)\omega_{LL}^*}{\omega_C^*}\frac{1 - t_{L0}}{1 + t_{C0}}\right]^{-1} = 0.320. \qquad (15.111)$$

From the steady-state version of (T2.1) we can then derive:

$$r^* - \rho = \mu(\rho + \mu)\frac{\varepsilon}{1 + t_C}\frac{\kappa^*}{\omega_C^*} = \mu(\rho + \mu) \times 3.037. \qquad (15.112)$$

This expression still contains two parameters, namely the pure rate of time preference (ρ) and the birth rate (μ), neither of which is directly observable.[19] Recall, however, that in the Blanchard setting $1/\mu$ represents the expected remaining lifetime of all agents. As a result, we do not expect μ to be very high. Suppose that agents have a planning horizon of 200 quarters, so that the implied birth/death rate is $\mu = 0.005$. Plugging this value into (15.112) and recalling that $r^* = 0.0159$ we obtain the implied value for the pure rate of time preference, $\rho = 0.0156$, so that:

$$r^* - \rho = 0.000312. \qquad \text{(Calibrated GT effect)}$$

Hence, for this value of μ the FS effect is much stronger than the GT effect. In Table 15.4 we compute the GT effect for a number of alternative values of μ. The results indicate that the FS effect continues to dominate even for quite high (and unrealistic) values for the birth rate. For example, even if $\mu = 0.04$ so that a household's expected remaining lifetime is only 25 quarters, the FS effect still dominates the GT effect. We conclude that for reasonable parameters the GT effect is quite weak and is dominated by the FS effect.[20]

---

[19]Of course the actual birth and mortality rates in an economy can be observed. It is not possible to directly link actual demographic data to the Blanchard-Yaari model, because in reality (1) the birth and mortality rates are typically not equal, (2) the death hazard is not age-independent, and (3) immigration typically explains part of the population increase.

[20]The fact that the GT effect is of negligible order for plausible birth rates suggests that the extended Blanchard-Yaari model has all the properties of a real business cycle (RBC) model (see Chapter 18). Ríos-Rull (1994) confirms this result using a much more complicated OLG model which is plausibly calibrated for the US economy.

Table 15.4. The birth rate and the GT effect

μ	$1/\mu$	ρ	GT effect	FS effect
0.005	200	0.0156	0.000312	0.0457
0.01	100	0.0151	0.000762	0.0457
0.02	50	0.0138	0.002054	0.0457
0.04	25	0.0098	0.006051	0.0457
0.07229	13.83	0	0.015868	0.0457

Despite the plausible empirical dominance of the FS effect over the GT effect, there are settings in which the overlapping generations feature matters a lot quantitatively. For example, Heijdra and Ligthart (2007) use the OLG model discussed in this section and extend it by incorporating monopolistic competition in the goods market. They use their model to study the dynamic effects of fiscal policy under various government financing scenarios. For a realistic birth-mortality rate, a lump-sum tax financed increase in government consumption increases output, both in the short run and in the long run. The quantitative results are very similar to those obtained for the RA model. The quantitative equivalence between the two models breaks down, however, when bond financing is employed by the government. Indeed, a temporary bond-financed increase in government consumption ends up having quantitatively significant long-run effects in the OLG model and no effect at all in the RA model (see Heijdra and Ligthart, 2007, p. 351). Hence, the failure of Ricardian equivalence that is implied by the OLG model does have quantitative repercussions.

We close this subsection by returning to the issue of consumption taxation in the extended BY model. For small changes in tax rates the qualitative analysis based on the linearized version of the model is adequate and insightful. But what if a government decides to implement a large change in, say, the consumption tax? In such a setting a numerical investigation of the nonlinear model becomes essential. Fortunately, now that the values for the structural parameters have been set, such a simulation exercise is straightforward to conduct using the Matlab boundary value solver bvp4c that was discussed in Chapter 13 above. In Figure 15.19 the transitional dynamic effects of a large consumption tax increase (from $t_{C0} = 0.1$ to $t_{C1} = 0.2$) are illustrated. It is assumed (a) that the system is initially in the steady-state equilibrium (indicated by dashed lines) and (b) that the tax hike is unanticipated and permanent.[21] Just as predicted by the linearized model, the capital stock gradually falls (panel (a)) whilst consumption features a downward jump at impact followed by a further gradual decline (panel (d)). Since employment jumps down at impact (panel (b)) the tax hike leads to an immediate and substantial reduction in output (panel (c)). In the long-run there is a small increase (decrease) in the wage (interest) rate.

---

[21]The Matlab program used to solve the transition paths is available from the website of the book, www.heijdra.org/fomm3.

Figure 15.19: Transitional dynamics in the extended BY model

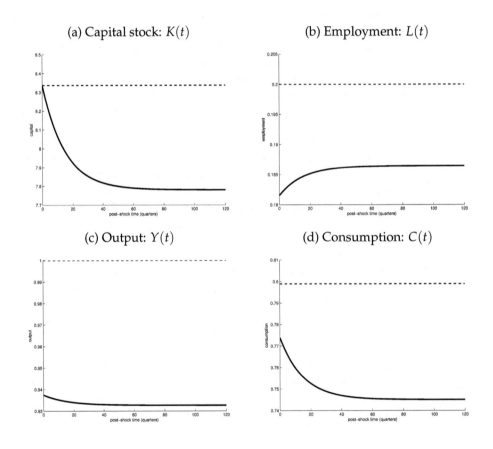

(a) Capital stock: $K(t)$

(b) Employment: $L(t)$

(c) Output: $Y(t)$

(d) Consumption: $C(t)$

Table 15.19, continued

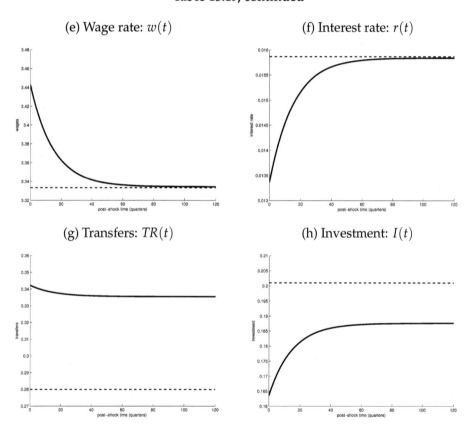

(e) Wage rate: $w(t)$

(f) Interest rate: $r(t)$

(g) Transfers: $TR(t)$

(h) Investment: $I(t)$

15.6 Punchlines

In this chapter we study one of the key models of modern macroeconomics, namely the continuous-time overlapping-generations (OLG) model of Blanchard and Yaari. This model is important not only because it has proved to be quite flexible and easy to work with, but also because it nests the Ramsey-Cass-Koopmans (RCK) model as a special case.

We start the chapter by studying the seminal insights of Yaari who studied optimal consumption behaviour in the presence of lifetime uncertainty. When an agent's lifetime (and thus his planning horizon) is uncertain two complications arise. First, the agent's decision problem becomes inherently stochastic and the expected utility hypothesis must be employed. Second, the non-negativity constraint on the agent's wealth position at the time of death is also stochastic and should be ensured to hold with certainty. Yaari showed that the key implication of uncertain lifetimes is that the instantaneous probability of death (the so-called "death hazard rate") enters the consumption Euler equation of the expected-utility maximizing agent. Intuitively, the uncertainty of survival leads the rational agent to discount the future more heavily.

Yaari makes the analysis of terminal wealth more tractable by postulating the existence of a kind of life insurance based on actuarial notes. Such a note can be bought or sold by the consumer and is cancelled upon the consumer's death. A consumer who *buys* an actuarial note in fact buys an annuity which stipulates payments to the consumer during life at a rate higher than the rate of interest. Upon the consumer's death the insurance company has no further obligations to the consumer's estate. Reversely, a consumer who *sells* an actuarial note is getting a life-insured loan. During the consumer's life he must pay a higher interest rate on the loan than the market rate of interest but upon death the consumer's estate is held free of any obligations, i.e. the principal does not have to be paid back to the insurance company. Under actuarial fairness the rate of return on actuarial notes equals the rate of interest plus the death hazard. Yaari shows that households have the incentive to fully insure against the loss of life. He thus reaches the striking result that, with actuarially fair life insurance, the death hazard drops out of the consumption Euler equation altogether.

Yaari's insights lay dormant for two decades before Blanchard embedded them in his dynamic general equilibrium model with overlapping generations. In order to allow for an aggregate treatment, Blanchard made two modelling choices. First, he assumed that the death hazard is age-independent. This ensures that the optimal decision rules are "linear in the generations index" and can thus be aggregated. Second, he assumed the arrival of large cohorts of newborn agents at each instant. This ensures that frequencies and probabilities coincide. (To ensure a constant population the birth and death rates are assumed to be equal.)

The Blanchard-Yaari (BY) model has a number of important properties. First, the standard RCK model (based on the notion of an infinitely lived representative household) is obtained as a special case of the Blanchard-Yaari model by setting the birth rate equal to zero. Second, the steady-state capital stock is smaller in the BY model than in the RCK model. Due to the turnover of generations, aggregate consumption growth falls short of individual consumption growth. This means that in the steady state the interest rate exceeds the rate of time preference. It also means that the equilibrium is dynamically efficient. Third, fiscal policy, taking the form of a permanent and unanticipated lump-sum tax financed increase in government consumption, causes less (more) than one-for-one crowding out of private consumption in the short (long) run. In the short run, households do not feel the full burden of the additional taxes because they discount present and future tax liabilities at the annuity rather than the market rate of interest. As a result they do not cut back consumption by enough so that private investment is crowded out. In the long run the capital stock and output are smaller, wages are lower, and the interest rate is higher. Intuitively, the shock redistributes resources away from future generations towards present generations. Fourth, Ricardian equivalence does not hold in the BY model. It is the positive birth rate (and not the agents' finite planning horizon) which causes the rejection of Ricardian equivalence. Finally, the BY model provides a richer framework for the study of open economies. We formulate a small open economy version of the model and study the effects on the macroeconomy of a (permanent or temporary) productivity shock. An attractive feature of the open-economy BY model is that it can be used to study both creditor nations (populated by patient citizens) and debtor countries (inhabited by impatient households). (Recall from Section 13.4.1 that in the corresponding RCK model, the steady-state equilibrium only exists for a knife-edge case in which the world interest rate equals the rate of time preference of residents.) As icing on the cake we also formulate and study an endogenous-growth version of the closed-economy BY model.

In the second half of the chapter we show an extension to the BY model in which we endogenize the household's labour supply decision. We use the model to study the effects of an increase in the consumption tax. In the RCK version of the extended model, the tax increase unambiguously leads to a decrease in the long-run capital stock because the household cuts back labour supply. With finite lives, however, the tax redistributes resources from present to future generations which tends to increase the capital stock in the long run. The net effect of the tax shock thus depends on the relative strength of the generational turnover effect vis-à-vis the factor scarcity effect.

Further reading

The Blanchard-Yaari model has been applied in a large number of areas. Open economy models are presented by inter alia Blanchard (1983, 1984), Frenkel and Razin (1986), Buiter (1987), Matsuyama (1987), Giovannini (1988), Heijdra and van der Horst (2000), and Heijdra and Ligthart (2010). The closely related Weil (1989b) model is used for the analysis of tax policy by Bovenberg (1993, 1994) and Nielsen and Sørenson (1991) and for the study of current account dynamics by Obstfeld and Rogoff (1995, pp. 1759–1764).

Alogoskoufis and van der Ploeg (1990) and Saint-Paul (1992) introduce endogenous growth into the model. Weil (1991) and Marini and van der Ploeg (1988) study monetary neutrality. Aschauer (1990) introduces endogenous labour supply in the Blanchard-Yaari model. On public infrastructure, see Heijdra and Meijdam (2002). Marini and Scaramozzino (1995) and Bovenberg and Heijdra (1998, 2002) study environmental issues. Nielsen (1994) and Bettendorf and Heijdra (2006) introduce social security into the model. Gertler (1999) generalizes the model by assuming that workers move into retirement according to a stochastic Poisson process. The International Monetary Fund's MULTIMOD model includes insights from the Blanchard-Yaari framework–see Laxton et al. (1998).

Optimal consumption with and without annuities is studied by Yaari (1965), Barro and Friedman (1977), Levhari and Mirman (1977), Davies (1981), Hurd (1989, 1990), Bütler (2001), and Hansen and Imrohoroglu (2008).

Models with a realistic mortality process include Boucekkine et al. (2002), de la Croix and Licandro (1999), Heijdra and Romp (2008, 2009a, 2009b), d'Albis (2007), and Heijdra and Mierau (2012). On human capital accumulation, see Bils and Klenow (2000), Kalemli-Ozcan et al. (2000), and Heijdra and Reijnders (2016). On annuities, see Sheshinski (2008) for the theory, and Cannon and Tonks (2006) for the practical experience in the UK. Accidental bequests are studied by Kotlikoff and Summers (1981). Kotlikoff and Spivak (1981) show that the family can act as a substitute for missing annuity markets. For adverse selection in annuity markets, see Heijdra and Reijnders (2013).

Appendix: Derivation of the phase diagram

In this appendix we derive the phase diagram for the extended Blanchard-Yaari model with endogenous labour supply and various tax rates (Figure 15.15). In doing so, we follow the general approach discussed in detail in the appendix of Chapter 13. To keep things simple we assume that government consumption is zero. Since the overlapping-generations structure does not affect the functional form for the K-isocline we focus attention to the derivation of the C-isocline. For ease of reference we state a number of useful relationships. First, labour market equilibrium implies:

$$\text{LME:} \qquad \chi(L) \equiv (1-L)L^{-\alpha} = \frac{(1-\varepsilon)(1+t_C)}{\varepsilon(1-\alpha)(1-t_L)Z_0}CK^{-\alpha}. \qquad (A15.1)$$

Note that this expression can be written alternatively as:

$$\frac{1-L}{L} = \frac{(1-\varepsilon)(1+t_C)}{\varepsilon(1-\alpha)(1-t_L)}\frac{C}{Y}. \qquad (A15.2)$$

Second, the capital stock equilibrium condition implies:

$$K^{1-\alpha} = \frac{\varepsilon(1-\alpha)(1-t_L)}{\delta(1-\varepsilon)(1+t_C)}\left(\frac{L-L_{MIN}}{L_{MIN}}\right)Z_0L^{-\alpha}, \qquad (A15.3)$$

where L_{MIN} is given by:

$$L \geq L_{MIN} \equiv \frac{\varepsilon(1-\alpha)(1-t_L)}{\varepsilon(1-\alpha)(1-t_L)+(1-\varepsilon)(1+t_C)}, \qquad 0 < L_{MIN} < 1. \qquad (A15.4)$$

Consumption flow equilibrium

The consumption equilibrium (CE) locus represents points in (C,K)-space for which the aggregate flow of consumption is in equilibrium ($\dot{C} = 0$). By using (T2.1) in steady state, (T2.4), (T2.7), and (A15.2) we can write the CE locus as follows:

$$\mu(\rho+\mu) = \frac{\alpha(1-\alpha)(1-t_L)}{1-\varepsilon}\frac{1-L}{L}y\left[y-y^*\right], \qquad (A15.5)$$

$$y = Z_0\left(\frac{L}{K}\right)^{1-\alpha}, \qquad (A15.6)$$

where $y \equiv Y/K$ is the output-capital ratio and $y^* \equiv (\rho+\delta)/\alpha$. Equations (A15.5)–(A15.6) define consumption flow equilibrium in (K,L)-space.

In the *representative-agent model* (with $\mu = 0$) the CE locus represents points for which $y = y^*$. By using this in (A15.6) and (A15.1) we get after a few steps:

$$\begin{aligned}
C &= \frac{\varepsilon(1-\alpha)(1-t_L)Z_0}{(1-\varepsilon)(1+t_C)}\left(\frac{K}{L}\right)^{\alpha}(1-L) \\
&= \frac{\varepsilon(1-\alpha)(1-t_L)Z_0}{(1-\varepsilon)(1+t_C)}\left(\frac{y^*}{Z_0}\right)^{-\alpha/(1-\alpha)}\left[1-\left(\frac{y^*}{Z_0}\right)^{1/(1-\alpha)}K\right] \\
&= \frac{(\rho+\delta)\varepsilon(1-\alpha)(1-t_L)}{\alpha(1-\varepsilon)(1+t_C)}\left[\left(\frac{\alpha Z_0}{\rho+\delta}\right)^{1/(1-\alpha)}-K\right]. \qquad (A15.7)
\end{aligned}$$

Hence, the CE curve for the RA model (CE^{RA}) is linear and downward sloping—see the dashed line from A_3 to A_4 in Figure 15.15.

For the *overlapping-generations* model the CE line can only be described *parametrically*, i.e. by varying L in the feasible interval $[0,1]$. We first write (A15.5) in a more convenient format:

$$\zeta_0 \left[\equiv \frac{\mu(\rho+\mu)(1-\varepsilon)}{\alpha(1-\alpha)(1-t_L)}\right] = \frac{1-L}{L} y \left[y - y^*\right], \tag{A15.8}$$

where $\zeta_0 > 0$. Solving (A15.8) for the positive (economically sensible) root yields the equilibrium output-capital ratio for the overlapping-generations (OLG) model as a function of L:

$$\frac{y}{y^*} = \frac{1}{2} + \sqrt{\frac{1}{4} + \frac{\zeta_0}{(y^*)^2}\left(\frac{L}{1-L}\right)} \geq 1. \tag{A15.9}$$

Using (A15.9) in (A15.6) yields an expression for the capital-labour ratio:

$$\frac{K}{L} = \left(\frac{Z_0}{y}\right)^{1/(1-\alpha)} = \left(\frac{Z_0}{y^*}\right)^{1/(1-\alpha)} \left[\frac{1}{2} + \sqrt{\frac{1}{4} + \frac{\zeta_0}{(y^*)^2}\left(\frac{L}{1-L}\right)}\right]^{-1/(1-\alpha)}, \tag{A15.10}$$

from which we derive the following limiting results:

$$\lim_{L\to 0} \left(\frac{K}{L}\right) = \left(\frac{Z_0}{y^*}\right)^{1/(1-\alpha)}, \qquad \lim_{L\to 1} \left(\frac{K}{L}\right) = 0. \tag{A15.11}$$

The labour market equilibrium condition (A15.1) yields an expression for consumption:

$$C = \frac{\varepsilon(1-\alpha)(1-t_L)Z_0}{(1-\varepsilon)(1+t_C)} \left(\frac{K}{L}\right)^{\alpha} (1-L), \tag{A15.12}$$

from which we derive the following limiting results:

$$\lim_{L\to 0} C = \frac{\varepsilon(1-\alpha)(1-t_L)Z_0}{(1-\varepsilon)(1+t_C)} \lim_{L\to 0} \left(\frac{K}{L}\right)^{\alpha}$$

$$= \frac{\varepsilon(1-\alpha)(1-t_L)Z_0}{(1-\varepsilon)(1+t_C)} \left(\frac{Z_0}{y^*}\right)^{\alpha/(1-\alpha)}, \tag{A15.13}$$

$$\lim_{L\to 1} C = 0. \tag{A15.14}$$

Hence, the CE line for the OLG model has the same vertical intercept as CE^{RA} as $L \to 0$ and goes through the origin as $L \to 1$.

It is straightforward—though somewhat tedious—to prove that CE^{OLG} is horizontal near the origin (where $L \approx 1$) and downward sloping and steeper than CE^{RA} near the vertical intercept (where $L \approx 0$). Note that the CE^{OLG} is described parametrically by equations (A15.10) and (A15.12). For a given value of L, the first expression yields the corresponding value for K whilst the second expression yields the corresponding value for C.

Figure 15.15 in the text is a stylized representation of the phase diagram. Using the calibration values discussed in section 15.5.4 we obtain the phase diagram for the calibrated model in Figure A15.1. This diagram also shows why the generational turnover effect is as tiny as it is reported to be in Table 15.4.

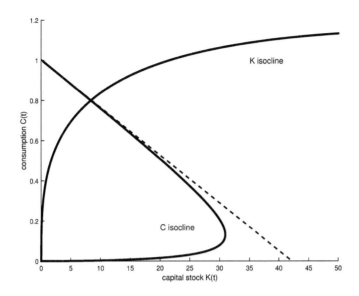

Figure A15.1: Phase diagram of the calibrated extended BY model

Uniqueness

The uniqueness of the equilibrium can be established most easily in the (K, L) plane. First we rewrite (A15.10) as:

$$K^{1-\alpha} = \frac{h(L)}{y^*}, \quad h(L) \equiv L^{1-\alpha} \left[\frac{1}{2} + \sqrt{\frac{1}{4} + \frac{\zeta_0}{(y^*)^2} \left(\frac{L}{1-L} \right)} \right]^{-1}. \quad (A15.15)$$

It is not difficult to show that $h(0) = \lim_{L \to 1} h(L) = 0$, $\lim_{L \to 0} h'(L) = +\infty$, and $\lim_{L \to 1} h'(L) = -\infty$. These properties ensure that the CSE curve (equation (A15.3)) and the CE curve (equation (A15.15)) cross only once, thus determining unique equilibrium values (K^*, L^*). Equilibrium consumption, C^*, then follows from (A15.1), and equilibrium output, Y^*, follows from the production function (T2.7). All other variables are determined uniquely also.

Chapter 16

Overlapping generations in discrete time

The purpose of this chapter is to achieve the following goals:

1. To introduce and study a popular discrete-time overlapping-generations (OLG) model and to show its main theoretical properties.

2. To apply the discrete-time model to study (funded or unfunded) public pension systems; the macroeconomic effects of ageing; and the costs and benefits of annuitization.

3. To extend the model to account for (private versus public) human capital accumulation and public investment.

4. To demonstrate how the model can be used to endogenize the fertility choice made by dynastic households and to re-examine the validity of Ricardian equivalence.

16.1 The Diamond-Samuelson model

As the previous chapter has demonstrated, the continuous-time Blanchard-Yaari framework is quite flexible and convenient and therefore fully deserves its current workhorse status. It yields useful and intuitive macroeconomic results and does so in a simple fashion. This is not to say that the framework has no shortcomings. Indeed, as Blanchard himself points out, the main drawback of the perpetual youth approach is that, though it captures the finite-horizon aspect of life, it fails to account for life-cycle aspects of consumption (1985, p. 224). Indeed, in the standard Blanchard model, a household's age affects the level and composition of its wealth (first aspect) but not its propensity to consume out of wealth (life-cycle aspect). In the absence of a bequest motive and with truly finite lives, one would expect an old agent to have a much higher propensity to consume out of wealth than a young agent, simply because the old agent has a shorter planning horizon (a higher death hazard) than the young agent has (see also Section 16.2.2 above).

A simple model which captures both the finite-horizon and life-cycle aspects of household behaviour was formulated by Diamond (1965) using the earlier insights of Samuelson (1958).[1] The Diamond-Samuelson model is formulated in discrete time and has been *the* workhorse model in various fields of economics for more than half a century. Weil (2008) is a celebratory essay written to commemorate its fiftieth birthday. There are not many models in macroeconomics with that degree of durability. In the remainder of this section we describe (a simplified version of) the Diamond (1965) model in detail.

16.1.1   Households

Individual agents live for two periods. During the first period (their "youth") they work and in their second period (their "old age") they are retired from the labour force. Since they want to consume in both periods, agents save during youth and dissave during old age. We abstract from bequests and assume that the population grows at a constant rate n.

A representative young agent at time t has the following lifetime utility function:

$$\Lambda_t^Y \equiv U(C_t^Y) + \frac{1}{1+\rho} U(C_{t+1}^O), \tag{16.1}$$

where the subscript identifies the time period and the superscript the phase of life the agent is in, with "Y" and "O" standing for, respectively, youth and old age. Hence, C_t^Y and C_{t+1}^O denote consumption by an agent born in period t during youth and old age, respectively, and Λ_t^Y is lifetime utility of a young agent from the perspective of his birth. As usual, $\rho > 0$ captures the notion of pure time preference and we assume that the felicity function, $U(x)$, satisfies Inada-style conditions ($U'(x) > 0 > U''(x)$, $\lim_{x \to 0} U'(x) = +\infty$, and $\lim_{x \to \infty} U'(x) = 0$).

During the first period the agent inelastically supplies one unit of labour and receives a wage w_t which is spent on consumption, C_t^Y, and savings, S_t. In the second period, the agent does not work but receives interest income on his savings, $r_{t+1}S_t$. Principal plus interest are spent on consumption during old age, C_{t+1}^O. The household thus faces the following budget identities:

$$C_t^Y + S_t = w_t, \tag{16.2}$$

$$C_{t+1}^O = (1 + r_{t+1})S_t. \tag{16.3}$$

Since the agents wants to consume in both periods the non-negativity constraint on saving is satisfied ($S_t \geq 0$) and we obtain the consolidated (or lifetime) budget constraint by substituting (16.3) into (16.2):

$$w_t = C_t^Y + \frac{C_{t+1}^O}{1 + r_{t+1}}. \tag{16.4}$$

The young agent chooses C_t^Y and C_{t+1}^O to maximize (16.1) subject to (16.4). The first-order conditions for consumption in the two periods can be combined after which we obtain the familiar consumption Euler equation:

$$\frac{U'(C_{t+1}^O)}{U'(C_t^Y)} = \frac{1 + \rho}{1 + r_{t+1}}. \tag{16.5}$$

---

[1]An even earlier overlapping-generations model was developed by Allais (1947). Unfortunately, due to the non-trivial language barrier, it was not assimilated into the Anglo-Saxon literature.

Together, (16.4)–(16.5) determine implicit functions relating C_t^Y and C_{t+1}^O (and thus S_t) to the variables that are exogenously given to the agents, i.e. w_t and r_{t+1}. The key expression is the savings equation:

$$S_t = S(w_t, r_{t+1}), \tag{16.6}$$

which has the following partial derivatives:

$$0 < S_w \equiv \frac{\partial S}{\partial w_t} = \frac{\theta(C_t^Y)/C_t^Y}{\theta(C_{t+1}^O)/S_t + \theta(C_t^Y)/C_t^Y} < 1, \tag{16.7}$$

$$S_r \equiv \frac{\partial S}{\partial r_{t+1}} = \frac{1 - \theta(C_{t+1}^O)}{(1 + r_{t+1})\left[\theta(C_{t+1}^O)/S_t + \theta(C_t^Y)/C_t^Y\right]} \gtrless 0, \tag{16.8}$$

where the function, $\theta(x) \equiv -xU''(x)/U'(x)$, represents the elasticity of marginal utility evaluated at x. Of course, $\theta(x)$ is positive, given the assumption made regarding $U(x)$ above. Recall from Chapter 13 that the inverse of $\theta(x)$ is the intertemporal substitution elasticity, denoted by $\sigma(x) \equiv 1/\theta(x)$. According to (16.7), an increase in the wage rate increases savings. It follows from (16.2) and (16.3) that both consumption goods are normal, i.e. $\partial C_t^Y/\partial w_t = 1 - \partial S/\partial w_t > 0$ and $\partial C_{t+1}^O/\partial w_t = (1 + r_{t+1})\partial S_t/\partial w_t > 0$. The response of savings with respect to the interest rate is ambiguous as the income and substitution effects work in opposite directions (see Intermezzo 6.1 above). On the one hand an increase in r_{t+1} reduces the relative price of future goods which prompts the agent to substitute future for present consumption and to increase savings. On the other hand, the increase in r_{t+1} expands the budget available for present and future consumption which prompts the agent to increase both present and future consumption and to decrease savings. Equation (16.8) shows that, on balance, if the intertemporal substitution elasticity exceeds (falls short of) unity then the substitution (income) effect dominates and savings depend positively (negatively) on the interest rate:

$$S_r \gtrless 0 \iff \theta(C_{t+1}^O) \lessgtr 1 \iff \sigma(C_{t+1}^O) \equiv \frac{1}{\theta(C_{t+1}^O)} \gtrless 1. \tag{16.9}$$

16.1.2   Firms

The perfectly competitive firm sector produces output, Y_t, by hiring capital, K_t, from the currently old agents, and labour, L_t, from the currently young agents. The production function,

$$Y_t = F(K_t, L_t), \tag{16.10}$$

is linearly homogeneous, and profit maximization ensures that the production factors receive their respective marginal physical products (and that pure profits are zero):

$$w_t = F_L(K_t, L_t), \tag{16.11}$$

$$r_t + \delta = F_K(K_t, L_t), \tag{16.12}$$

where $0 \leq \delta \leq 1$ is the depreciation rate of capital.[2] The crucial thing to note about (16.12) is its timing: capital that was accumulated by the currently old, K_t, commands the rental rate $r_t + \delta$. It follows that the rate of interest upon which the currently young agents base their savings decisions (i.e. r_{t+1} in (16.3)–(16.6)) depends on the *future* capital stock and labour force:

$$r_{t+1} + \delta = F_K(K_{t+1}, L_{t+1}). \tag{16.13}$$

In what follows, we assume that agents are blessed with perfect foresight, i.e. the subjective expectation and actual realisation of r_{t+1} coincide.

Since the labour force grows at a constant rate and we ultimately wish to study an economy which possesses a well-defined steady-state equilibrium, it is useful to rewrite (16.10)–(16.11) and (16.13) in the intensive (per worker) form (see Section 13.1.2 for details):

$$y_t = f(k_t), \tag{16.14}$$
$$w_t = f(k_t) - k_t f'(k_t), \tag{16.15}$$
$$r_{t+1} + \delta = f'(k_{t+1}), \tag{16.16}$$

where $y_t \equiv Y_t / L_t$, $k_t \equiv K_t / L_t$, and $f(k_t) \equiv F(k_t, 1)$.

16.1.3 Market equilibrium

The resource constraint for the economy as a whole can be written as follows:

$$Y_t + (1 - \delta)K_t = C_t + K_{t+1}, \tag{16.17}$$

where C_t represents *aggregate* consumption in period t. Equation (16.17) says that output plus the undepreciated part of the capital stock (left-hand side) can be either consumed or carried over to the next period in the form of capital (right-hand side). Alternatively, (16.17) can be written in a more familiar format as $Y_t = C_t + I_t$ with $I_t \equiv \Delta K_{t+1} + \delta K_t$ representing gross investment.

Aggregate consumption is the sum of consumption by the young and the old agents in period t:

$$C_t \equiv L_{t-1}C_t^O + L_t C_t^Y. \tag{16.18}$$

Since the old, as a group, own the capital stock, their total consumption in period t is the sum of the undepreciated part of the capital stock plus the rental payments received from the firms, i.e. $L_{t-1}C_t^O = (r_t + \delta)K_t + (1 - \delta)K_t$. For each young agent, consumption satisfies (16.2) so that total consumption by the young amounts to: $L_t C_t^Y = w_t L_t - S_t L_t$. By substituting these two results into (16.18), we obtain:

$$C_t = (r_t + \delta)K_t + (1 - \delta)K_t + w_t L_t - S_t L_t$$
$$= Y_t + (1 - \delta)K_t - S_t L_t, \tag{16.19}$$

---

[2]Most authors follow Diamond (1965, p. 1127) by assuming that capital does not depreciate at all ($\delta = 0$). However, since the model divides human life into two periods, each period is quite long (in historical time) and it is thus defensible to assume that capital fully depreciates within the period ($\delta = 1$). Blanchard and Fischer (1989, p. 93) circumvent the choice of δ by assuming that (16.10) is a *net* production function, with depreciation already deducted. In their formulation, δ vanishes from the capital demand equation (16.12).

where we have used the fact that $Y_t = (r_t + \delta)K_t + w_t L_t$ in going from the first to the second line. Output is fully exhausted by factor payments and pure profits are zero.

Finally, by combining (16.17) and (16.19) we obtain the expression linking this period's savings decisions by the young to next period's capital stock:

$$S_t L_t = K_{t+1}. \tag{16.20}$$

Cohorts (and thus the aggregate population) are assumed to grow at a constant rate,

$$L_t = L_0(1+n)^t, \quad n > -1, \tag{16.21}$$

so that (16.20), in combination with (16.6), can be rewritten in the intensive form as:

$$S(w_t, r_{t+1}) = (1+n)k_{t+1}, \tag{16.22}$$

where $k_t \equiv K_t/L_t$ is the capital stock per worker. The capital market is represented by the demand for capital by entrepreneurs (equation (16.16)) and the supply of capital by households (equation (16.22)).

16.1.4 Dynamics and stability

The dynamical behaviour of the economy can be studied by substituting the expressions for w_t and r_{t+1} (given in, respectively, (16.15) and (16.16)) into the capital supply equation (16.22):

$$(1+n)k_{t+1} = S\big(f(k_t) - k_t f'(k_t), f'(k_{t+1}) - \delta\big). \tag{16.23}$$

Equation (16.23) is the *fundamental difference equation* for the capital stock per worker. This expression relates the future to the present capital stock per worker and is thus suitable to study the stability of the model. By totally differentiating (16.23) and gathering terms we obtain:

$$\frac{dk_{t+1}}{dk_t} = \frac{-S_w k_t f''(k_t)}{1 + n - S_r f''(k_{t+1})}, \tag{16.24}$$

where S_w and S_r are given, respectively, in (16.7) and (16.8). We recall from Chapter 3 that local stability requires that the deviations from a steady state must be dampened (and not amplified) over time. Mathematically this means that a steady state is locally stable if $|dk_{t+1}/dk_t| < 1$. It is clear from (16.24) that we are not going to obtain clearcut results on the basis of the most general version of our model. Although we know that the numerator of (16.24) is positive (because $S_w > 0$ and $f'' < 0$), the sign of the denominator is indeterminate (because S_r is ambiguous).

Referring the interested reader to Galor and Ryder (1989) and de la Croix and Michel (2002) for a rigorous analysis of the general case, we take the practical way out by illustrating the existence and stability issues with the *unit-elastic* model. Specifically, we assume that technology is Cobb-Douglas ($Y_t = Z_0 L_t^\alpha L_t^{1-\alpha}$), so that $y_t = Z_0 k_t^\alpha$, and that the felicity function is logarithmic, so that $U(x) = \ln x$ and the intertemporal substitution elasticity is equal to $\sigma(x) = 1/\theta(x) = 1$. With these simplifications imposed the savings function collapses to $S_t = w_t/(2+\rho)$, the wage rate is $w_t = (1-\alpha)Z_0 k_t^\alpha$, and (16.23) becomes:

$$k_{t+1} = g(k_t) \equiv \frac{(1-\alpha)Z_0}{(1+n)(2+\rho)} k_t^\alpha. \tag{16.25}$$

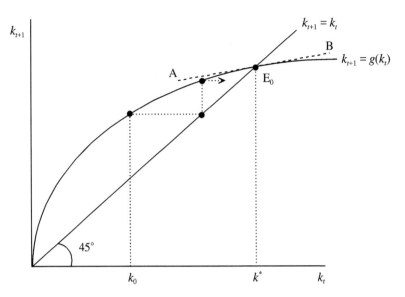

Figure 16.1: The unit-elastic Diamond-Samuelson model

Equation (16.25) has been drawn in Figure 16.1. Since $\lim_{k \to 0} g'(k) = \infty$ and $\lim_{k \to \infty} g'(k) = 0$, the steady state (for which $k_{t+1} = k_t = k^*$ so that $k^* = g(k^*)$) is unique and stable. The diagram illustrates the unique stable trajectory from k_0. The tangent of $g(k_t)$ passing through the steady-state equilibrium point E_0 is the dashed line AB. It follows from the diagram (and indeed from (16.25)) that the unit-elastic Diamond-Samuelson model satisfies the stability condition with a positive slope for $g(k_t)$, i.e. $0 < g'(k^*) < 1$.

16.1.5 Efficiency

It is clear from the discussion surrounding Figure 16.1 that there is a perfectly reasonable setting in which the Diamond-Samuelson model possesses a stable and unique steady-state equilibrium. We now assume for convenience that our most general model also has this property and proceed to study its welfare properties. To keep things simple, and to prepare for the discussion of social security issues below, we restrict attention to a steady-state analysis. Indeed, following Diamond (1965) we compare the market solution to the so-called *optimal golden-age path*.

A golden-age path is such that the capital-labour ratio is constant over time, i.e. $k_{t+1} = k_t = k$. Such a path is called *optimal* if (i) each individual agent has the highest possible utility, and (ii) all agents have the same utility level (Diamond, 1965, p. 1128). Formally, the optimal golden-age path maximizes the lifetime utility of a "representative" individual,

$$\Lambda^Y \equiv U(C^Y) + \frac{1}{1+\rho} U(C^O), \tag{16.26}$$

subject to the economy-wide steady-state resource constraint:[3]

$$f(k) - (n + \delta)k = C^Y + \frac{C^O}{1+n}. \tag{16.27}$$

Note that we have dropped the time subscripts in (16.26)–(16.27) in order to stress the fact that we are looking at a steady-state situation only. An important thing to note about this formulation is the following. In equation (16.26), C^Y and C^O refer, respectively, to consumption during youth and retirement *of a particular individual*. In contrast, in equation (16.27) C^Y and C^O refer to consumption levels of young and old agents, respectively, at a *particular moment in time*. This does, of course, not mean that we are comparing apples and oranges—for the purposes of selecting an optimal golden-age path we can ignore these differences because all individuals are treated symmetrically.

The first-order conditions for the optimal golden-age path consist of the steady-state resource constraint and:

$$\frac{U'(C^O)}{U'(C^Y)} = \frac{1+\rho}{1+n}, \tag{16.28}$$

$$f'(k) = n + \delta. \tag{16.29}$$

Samuelson (1968a) calls these conditions, respectively, the biological-interest-rate consumption golden rule and the production golden rule. Comparing (16.28)–(16.29) with their respective market counterparts (16.5) and (16.16) reveals that they coincide if the market rate of interest equals the rate of population growth:

$$r = f'(k) - \delta = n \qquad \text{(golden rule)}$$

As is stressed by Samuelson (1968a, p. 87) the two conditions (16.28)–(16.29) are analytically independent: even if k is held constant at some suboptimal level, so that production is inefficient as $f'(k) \neq n + \delta$, the optimum consumption pattern must still satisfy (16.28). Similarly, if the division of output among generations is suboptimal (e.g. due to a badly designed pension system), condition (16.28) no longer holds but the optimal k still follows from the production golden rule (16.29).

If the steady-state interest rate is less than the rate of population growth ($r < n$) then there is overaccumulation of capital, k is too high, and the economy is dynamically inefficient. A quick inspection of our unit-elastic model reveals that such a situation is quite possible for reasonable parameter values. Indeed, by computing the steady-state capital-labour ratio from (16.25) and using the result in (16.16) we find that the steady-state interest rate for the unit-elastic model is:

$$r = \frac{\alpha(2+\rho)(1+n)}{1-\alpha} - \delta. \tag{16.30}$$

Blanchard and Fischer (1989, p. 147) suggest the following numbers. Each period of life is 30 years and the capital share is $\alpha = 1/4$. Population grows at 1% per annum so $n = 1.01^{30} - 1 = 0.348$. Capital depreciates at 5% per annum so $\delta = 1 - (0.95)^{30} = 0.785$. With relatively impatient agents, the pure discount rate is 3% percent per annum, so $\rho = (1.03)^{30} - 1 = 1.427$ and (16.30) shows that $r = 0.754$ which exceeds n by quite a margin. With more patient agents, whose pure discount rate is 1% percent per annum, $\rho = (1.01)^{30} - 1 = 0.348$ and $r = 0.269$ which is less than n.

---

[3]The steady-state resource constraint (16.27) is obtained as follows. First, (16.18) is substituted in (16.17) and the resulting expression is divided by L_t. Then (16.14) is inserted, the steady state is imposed ($k_{t+1} = k_t = k$), and all time indexes are dropped.

16.2   Social security and the macroeconomy

In this section we show how the standard Diamond-Samuelson model can be used to study the macroeconomic and welfare effects of old-age pensions. A system of social security was introduced in Germany during the 1880s by Otto von Bismarck, purportedly to stop the increasingly radical working class from overthrowing his conservative regime. It did not help poor Otto—he was forced to resign from office in 1890—but the system he helped create stayed. Especially following the Second World War, most developed countries have similarly adopted social security systems. Typically such a system provides benefit payments to the elderly which continue until the recipient dies.

In the first subsection we show how the method of financing old-age pensions critically determines the effects of such pensions on resource allocation and welfare. In the second subsection we study the effect of the pension system on the retirement decision of households. Finally, in the third subsection we study the effects of a demographic shock, such as an ageing population, on an economy incorporating a non-funded pension system.

16.2.1   Pensions

In order to study the effects of public pensions we must introduce the government into the Diamond-Samuelson model. Assume that, at time t, the government provides lump-sum transfers, Z_t, to old agents and levies lump-sum taxes, T_t, on the young. It follows that the budget identities of a young household at time t are changed from (16.2)–(16.3) to:

$$C_t^Y + S_t = w_t - T_t, \tag{16.31}$$

$$C_{t+1}^O = (1 + r_{t+1})S_t + Z_{t+1}, \tag{16.32}$$

so that the consolidated lifetime budget constraint of such an agent is now:

$$w_t - T_t + \frac{Z_{t+1}}{1 + r_{t+1}} = C_t^Y + \frac{C_{t+1}^O}{1 + r_{t+1}}. \tag{16.33}$$

The left-hand side of (16.33) shows that lifetime wealth consists of after-tax wages during youth plus the present value of pension receipts during old age.

Depending on the way in which the government finances its transfer scheme, we can distinguish two prototypical social security schemes. In a *fully funded* system the government invests the contributions of the young and returns them with interest in the next period in the form of transfers to the then old agents. In such a system we have:

$$Z_{t+1} = (1 + r_{t+1})T_t. \tag{16.34}$$

In contrast, in an unfunded or *pay-as-you-go* (PAYG) system, the transfers to the old are covered by the taxes of the young *in the same period*. Since, at time t, there are L_{t-1} old agents (each receiving Z_t in transfers) and L_t young agents (each paying T_t in taxes) a PAYG system satisfies $L_{t-1}Z_t = L_t T_t$ which can be rewritten by noting (16.21) to:

$$Z_t = (1 + n)T_t. \tag{16.35}$$

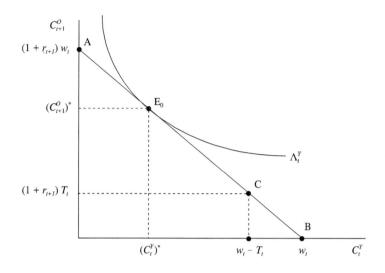

Figure 16.2: Individual effect of a fully-funded pension system

16.2.1.1 Fully funded pensions

A striking property of a fully funded social security system is its neutrality. With this we mean that an economy with a fully funded system is identical in all relevant aspects to an economy without such a system. This important neutrality result can be demonstrated as follows.

First, we note that, by substituting (16.34) into (16.33), the fiscal variables, T_t and Z_{t+1}, disappear from the lifetime budget constraint of the household. Consequently, these variables also do not affect the household's optimal life-cycle consumption plan, i.e. C_t^Y and C_{t+1}^O are exactly as in the pensionless economy described in section 16.1.1 above. It follows, by a comparison of (16.2) and (16.31), that with a fully funded pension system saving plus tax payments are set according to:

$$S_t + T_t = S(w_t, r_{t+1}), \tag{16.36}$$

where $S(w_t, r_{t+1})$ is the same function as the one appearing in (16.6). Matters can be explained further with the aid of Figure 16.2. In the absence of a pension system, the endowment point is at B and the optimal consumption point is at E_0, where there is a tangency between the lifetime budget constraint and an indifference curve. The funded pension system shifts the endowment point to C but leaves the lifetime budget constraint unchanged. Hence, optimal consumption still occurs at E_0.

As a second preliminary step we must derive an expression linking savings of the young to next period's stock of productive capital. The key aspect of a fully funded system is that the government puts the tax receipts from the young to productive use by renting them out in the form of capital goods to firms. Hence, the economy-wide capital stock, K_t, is:

$$K_t = K_t^H + K_t^G, \tag{16.37}$$

where K_t^H and $K_t^G \equiv L_{t-1} T_{t-1}$ denote capital owned by households and the government, respectively. The economy-wide resource constraint is still as given in (16.17) but the expression for total consumption is changed from (16.19) to (see Intermezzo

16.1):

$$C_t = Y_t + (1 - \delta)K_t - L_t(S_t + T_t). \tag{16.38}$$

Finally, by using (16.17), (16.38), and (16.36) we find that the capital market equilibrium condition is identical to (16.22). Since the factor prices, (16.15)–(16.16), are also unaffected by the existence of the social security system, economies with and without such a system are essentially the same. Intuitively, with a fully funded system the household knows that its contributions, T_t, attract the same rate of return as its own private savings, S_t. As a result, the household only worries about its total saving, $S_t + T_t$, and does not care that some of this saving is actually carried out on its behalf by the government.

In closing we note that the neutrality result holds provided the social security system is not too severe, i.e. it should not force the household to save more than it would in the absence of social security. In terms of the model we must have that $T_t \leq (1 + n)k_{t+1}$ (see Blanchard and Fischer, 1989, p. 111). In terms of Figure 16.2 this means that point C must lie to the right of the optimal consumption point E_0.

Intermezzo 16.1

Some tedious but important derivations for the Diamond-Samuelson model. Even though it is only a bookkeeping exercise, the reader may not immediately see how equation (16.38) is derived. Here goes. Consumption by the old agents is $L_{t-1}C_t^O = (r_t + \delta)K_t^H + (1 - \delta)K_t^H + L_{t-1}Z_t$. For young agents we have $L_tC_t^Y = L_t[w_t - S_t - T_t]$ so that aggregate consumption is:

$$\begin{aligned}
C_t &= (r_t + \delta)K_t^H + (1 - \delta)K_t^H + L_{t-1}Z_t + L_t[w_t - S_t - T_t] \\
&= Y_t + (1 - \delta)K_t^H - (r_t + \delta)K_t^G + L_{t-1}Z_t - L_t(S_t + T_t) \\
&= Y_t + (1 - \delta)K_t - L_t(S_t + T_t) + \left[L_{t-1}Z_t - (1 + r_t)K_t^G\right].
\end{aligned}$$

This final expression collapses to (16.38) because the term in square brackets on the right-hand side vanishes, i.e. $L_{t-1}Z_t - (1 + r_t)K_t^G = L_{t-1}[Z_t - (1 + r_t)T_{t-1}] = 0$.

Details concerning equation (16.41): Consumption by the old agents is $L_{t-1}C_t^O = (r_t + \delta)K_t + (1 - \delta)K_t + L_{t-1}Z_t$. For young agents we have $L_tC_t^Y = L_t[w_t - S_t - T_t]$ so that aggregate consumption is:

$$\begin{aligned}
C_t &= (r_t + \delta)K_t + (1 - \delta)K_t + L_{t-1}Z_t + L_t[w_t - S_t - T_t] \\
&= Y_t + (1 - \delta)K_t + [L_{t-1}Z_t - L_tT_t] - L_tS_t.
\end{aligned}$$

This final expression collapses to (16.19) because the term in square brackets on the right-hand side vanishes under the PAYG scheme. Combining (16.17) and (16.19) yields (16.20).

Details concerning Figure 16.4: The fundamental difference equation is obtained by substituting (16.40) into (16.41):

$$(1 + n)k_{t+1} = \frac{w(k_t) - T}{2 + \rho} - \frac{1 + \rho}{2 + \rho}\frac{(1 + n)T}{1 + r(k_{t+1})}.$$

The second term on the right-hand side vanishes as $k_{t+1} \to 0$ (since $r(k_{t+1}) \to +\infty$ in that case). Hence, $w(k_{\text{MIN}}) = T$. For $k_t < k_{\text{MIN}}$ the wage rate is too low ($w(k_t) < T$) and the PAYG scheme is not feasible. By differentiating the fundamental difference equation we obtain:

$$\frac{dk_{t+1}}{dk_t} = \frac{w'(k_t)}{(1+n)\left[2 + \rho + (1+\rho)T\psi(k_{t+1})\right]} \geq 0, \qquad \psi(k_{t+1}) \equiv \frac{-r'(k_{t+1})}{[1 + r(k_{t+1})]^2}.$$

It is straightforward to show that $\psi(k_{t+1}) \to +\infty$ for $k_{t+1} \to 0$, $\psi(k_{t+1}) \to 0$ for $k_{t+1} \to \infty$, $w'(k_t) \to 0$ for $k_t \to \infty$, and $w'(k_{\text{MIN}}) > 0$. It follows that $g(k_t, T)$ is horizontal in $k_t = k_{\text{MIN}}$ (not drawn), is upward sloping for larger values of k_t, and becomes horizontal as k_t gets very large. Provided T is not too large there exist two intersections with the $k_{t+1} = k_t$ line.

Details concerning equation (16.62): Consumption by old agents is $L_{t-1}C_t^O = (r_t + \delta)K_t + (1 - \delta)K_t + (1 + r_t)B_t + L_{t-1}Z_t$. For young agents we have $L_t C_t^Y = L_t\left[w_t - T_t - S_t\right]$ so that aggregate consumption is:

$$\begin{aligned}
C_t &= (r_t + \delta)K_t + (1 - \delta)K_t + (1 + r_t)B_t + L_{t-1}Z_t + L_t\left[w_t - T_t - S_t\right] \\
&= Y_t + (1 - \delta)K_t + \left[(1 + r_t)B_t + L_{t-1}Z_t - L_t T_t\right] - L_t S_t \\
&= Y_t + (1 - \delta)K_t + B_{t+1} - L_t S_t.
\end{aligned}$$

By combining the final expression with the resource constraint (16.17) we obtain (16.62).

****

16.2.1.2   Pay-as-you-go pensions

Under a PAYG system there is a transfer from young to old in each period according to (16.35). Assuming that the contribution rate per person is held constant over time (so that $T_{t+1} = T_t = T$), equation (16.35) implies that $Z_{t+1} = (1+n)T$ so that consolidation of (16.31)–(16.32) yields the following lifetime budget constraint of a young household:

$$\hat{w}_t \equiv w_t - \frac{r_{t+1} - n}{1 + r_{t+1}} \cdot T = C_t^Y + \frac{C_{t+1}^O}{1 + r_{t+1}}. \tag{16.39}$$

This expression is useful because it shows that, ceteris paribus the factor prices, the existence of a PAYG system contracts (expands) the consumption possibility frontier for young agents if the interest rate exceeds (falls short of) the growth rate of the population. Put differently, if $r_{t+1} > n$ ($r_{t+1} < n$) the contribution rate is experienced by the young household as a lump-sum tax (subsidy).

In Figure 16.3 we illustrate the case for which $r_{t+1} > n$. In the absence of the PAYG pension, the lifetime budget constraint is given by the line AB, and the optimal consumption point is at E_0. The PAYG pension moves the endowment point to D which lies vertically below the endowment point for a funded pension (i.e. point C) because the interest rate exceeds the rate of population growth. Hence, the budget constraint under the PAYG system is parallel to but lies below the line AB. Point E_0

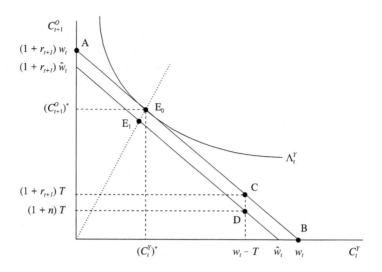

Figure 16.3: Individual effect of a PAYG pension system

is no longer feasible. With homothetic preferences (see Intermezzo 6.1), the optimal consumption point shifts to E_1.

The household maximizes lifetime utility (16.1) subject to its lifetime budget constraint (16.39). Since the rate of return on household saving is r_{t+1}, the consumption Euler equation is still given by (16.5). To keep matters as simple as possible we now restrict attention to the unit-elastic model for which utility is logarithmic (and technology is Cobb-Douglas). In that case, the optimal consumption plan satisfies $C_t^Y = (1+\rho)\hat{w}_t/(2+\rho)$ and $C_{t+1}^O = (1+r_{t+1})\hat{w}_t/(2+\rho)$ and the savings function is:

$$
\begin{aligned}
S_t &= w_t - T - C_t^Y \\
&= w_t - T - \frac{1+\rho}{2+\rho}\left[w_t - \frac{r_{t+1}-n}{1+r_{t+1}}\cdot T\right] \\
&= \frac{w_t}{2+\rho} - \left[1 - \frac{1+\rho}{2+\rho}\frac{r_{t+1}-n}{1+r_{t+1}}\right]\cdot T \equiv S(w_t, r_{t+1}, T).
\end{aligned}
\tag{16.40}
$$

It is easy to verify that the partial derivatives of the savings function satisfy $0 < S_w < 1$, $S_r > 0$, $-1 < S_T < 0$ (if $r_{t+1} > n$), and $S_T < -1$ (if $r_{t+1} < n$).

Since the PAYG pension is a pure transfer from young to co-existing old generations it does not itself lead to the formation of capital in the economy. Since only private saving augments the capital stock, equation (16.20) is still relevant (see Intermezzo 16.1). By combining (16.20) with (16.40) we obtain the expression linking the future capital stock to current saving plans:

$$
S(w_t, r_{t+1}, T) = (1+n)k_{t+1}.
\tag{16.41}
$$

With a Cobb-Douglas technology ($y_t \equiv Z_0 k_t^\alpha$) equations (16.15) and (16.16) reduce to, respectively, $w_t \equiv w(k_t) = (1-\alpha)Z_0 k_t^\alpha$ and $r_{t+1} \equiv r(k_{t+1}) = \alpha Z_0 k_{t+1}^{\alpha-1} - \delta$. By using these expressions in (16.41) we obtain the fundamental difference equation (in implicit form) characterizing the economy under a PAYG system, $k_{t+1} = g(k_t, T)$.

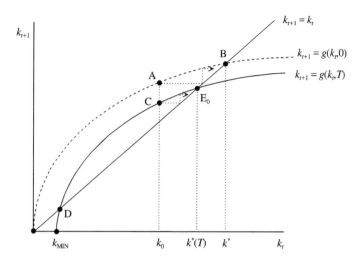

Figure 16.4: PAYG pensions in the unit-elastic model

The partial derivatives of this function are:

$$g_k \equiv \frac{\partial g}{\partial k_t} = \frac{S_w w'(k_t)}{1+n-S_r r'(k_{t+1})} > 0, \tag{16.42}$$

$$g_T \equiv \frac{\partial g}{\partial T} = \frac{S_T}{1+n-S_r r'(k_{t+1})} < 0, \tag{16.43}$$

where S_w and S_r are obtained from (16.40). We illustrate the fundamental difference equation in Figure 16.4 (see Intermezzo 16.1).

In Figure 16.4, the dashed line, labelled "$k_{t+1} = g(k_t, 0)$" characterizes the standard unit-elastic Diamond-Samuelson model without social security, i.e. it reproduces Figure 16.1 and point B is the steady state to which the economy converges in the absence of social security. Suppose now that the PAYG system is introduced at time $t = 0$ when the economy has an initial (non-steady-state) capital-labour ratio of k_0. Members of the old generation at time $t = 0$ cannot believe their luck. They have not contributed anything to the PAYG system but nevertheless receive a pension of $Z = (1+n)T$ (see equation (16.35)). Since the old do not save, this *windfall gain* is spent entirely on additional consumption. Consumption by each old household at time $t = 0$ is now:

$$C_0^O = (1+n)\left[(1+r(k_0))k_0 + T\right], \tag{16.44}$$

and, since k_0 is predetermined, so is the interest rate and $dC_0^O/dT = 1+n > 0$.

In contrast, members of the young generation at time $t = 0$ are affected by the introduction of the PAYG system in a number of different ways. On the one hand, they must pay T in the current period in exchange for which they receive a pension $(1+n)T$ in the next period. Since the wage rate at time $t = 0$, $w(k_0)$, is predetermined, the net effect of these two transactions is to change the value of lifetime resources ($\hat{w}_0$ defined in (16.39)) according to:

$$\frac{\partial \hat{w}_0}{\partial T} = -\frac{r(k_1)-n}{1+r(k_1)} \lessgtr 0, \tag{16.45}$$

where the sign is ambiguous because $r(k_1)$ may exceed or fall short of the population growth rate n. Furthermore, (16.45) is only a partial effect because the interest rate depends on the capital stock in the next period (k_1), which is itself determined by the savings behaviour of the young in period $t = 0$. It follows from (16.41) and (16.43), however, that the total effect of the introduction of the PAYG system is to reduce saving by the young and thus to reduce next period's capital stock, i.e. $dk_1/dT = g_T < 0$. This adverse effect on the capital stock is represented in Figure 16.4 by the vertical difference between points A and C.

As a result of the policy shock, the economy now follows the convergent path from C to the ultimate steady state E_0. It follows from Figure 16.4 that k_t is less than it would have been without the PAYG pension, both during transition and in the new steady state (i.e. the path from C to E_0 lies below the path from A to B). Hence, since $w'(k) > 0$ and $r'(k) < 0$, the steady-state wage is lower and the interest rate is higher than it would have been. The long-run effect on the capital-labour ratio is obtained by using (16.41) and imposing the steady state ($k_{t+1} = k_t$):

$$\frac{dk}{dT} = \frac{g_T}{1 - g_k} < 0, \tag{16.46}$$

where $0 < g_k < 1$ follows from the stability condition.

The upshot of the discussion so far is that, unlike a fully funded pension system, a PAYG system is not neutral but leads to crowding out of capital, a lower wage rate, and a higher interest rate in the long run. Is that good or bad for households? To answer that question we now study the welfare effect on a *steady-state generation* of a change in the contribution rate, T. As in our discussion of dynamic efficiency above we thus continue to ignore transitional dynamics for the time being by only looking at the steady state.

To conduct the welfare analysis we need to utilize two helpful tools, namely the *indirect utility function* and the *factor price frontier*. The indirect utility function is defined in formal terms by:

$$\bar{\Lambda}^Y(w,r,T) \equiv \max_{\{C^Y,C^O\}} \Lambda^Y(C^Y,C^O) \text{ subject to } \hat{w} = C^Y + \frac{C^O}{1+r}, \tag{16.47}$$

where $\Lambda^Y(C^Y,C^O)$ is the direct utility function (i.e. equation (16.1)). The lack of subscripts indicates steady-state values and $\hat{w}$ represents lifetime household resources under the PAYG system:

$$\hat{w} = w - \frac{r-n}{1+r}T. \tag{16.48}$$

For example, for the logarithmic felicity function (employed regularly in this chapter) the indirect utility function takes the following form:

$$\bar{\Lambda}^Y = \omega_0 + \frac{2+\rho}{1+\rho}\ln\hat{w} + \frac{1}{1+\rho}\ln(1+r), \tag{16.49}$$

where ω_0 is a constant.[4]

---

[4]The explicit functional form of the indirect utility is obtained by plugging the optimal consumption levels, as chosen by the household, back into the direct utility function (16.1). The reader should verify the properties stated in (16.50)–(16.52).

The indirect utility function (16.47) has a number of properties which will prove to be very useful below:

$$\frac{\partial \bar{\Lambda}^Y}{\partial w} = \frac{\partial \Lambda^Y}{\partial C^Y} > 0, \tag{16.50}$$

$$\frac{\partial \bar{\Lambda}^Y}{\partial r} = \frac{S}{1+r} \frac{\partial \Lambda^Y}{\partial C^Y} > 0, \tag{16.51}$$

$$\frac{\partial \bar{\Lambda}^Y}{\partial T} = -\frac{r-n}{1+r} \frac{\partial \Lambda^Y}{\partial C^Y} \lessgtr 0. \tag{16.52}$$

These properties are derived as follows. We start with the identity:

$$\bar{\Lambda}^Y(w,r,T) \equiv \Lambda^Y \left[C^Y(w,r,T), C^O(w,r,T) \right], \tag{16.53}$$

where $C^i(w,r,T)$ are the optimal consumption levels during the two periods of life. By using this identity, differentiating (16.53) with respect to w, and noting that $\partial \Lambda^Y / \partial C^O = (\partial \Lambda^Y / \partial C^O) / (1+r)$ we obtain:

$$\frac{\partial \bar{\Lambda}^Y}{\partial w} = \frac{\partial \Lambda^Y}{\partial C^Y} \left[\frac{\partial C^Y}{\partial w} + \frac{1}{1+r} \frac{\partial C^O}{\partial w} \right]. \tag{16.54}$$

It follows from the constraint in (16.47) that the term in square brackets is equal to unity. Using the same steps we obtain for $\partial \bar{\Lambda}^Y / \partial r$:

$$\frac{\partial \bar{\Lambda}^Y}{\partial r} = \frac{\partial \Lambda^Y}{\partial C^Y} \left[\frac{\partial C^Y}{\partial r} + \frac{1}{1+r} \frac{\partial C^O}{\partial r} \right] = \frac{\partial \Lambda^Y}{\partial C^Y} \left[\frac{C^O - (1+n)T}{(1+r)^2} \right]. \tag{16.55}$$

Using $C^O - (1+n)T = (1+r)S$ we obtain (16.51). Finally, we obtain for $\partial \bar{\Lambda}^Y / \partial T$:

$$\frac{\partial \bar{\Lambda}^Y}{\partial T} = \frac{\partial \Lambda^Y}{\partial C^Y} \left[\frac{\partial C^Y}{\partial T} + \frac{1}{1+r} \frac{\partial C^O}{\partial T} \right] = -\frac{r-n}{1+r} \frac{\partial \Lambda^Y}{\partial C^Y}, \tag{16.56}$$

where the final result follows from the constraint in (16.47).

According to (16.50)–(16.51), steady-state welfare depends positively on both the wage rate and the interest rate. Since we saw above that the wage falls ($dw/dT = w'(k)dk/dT < 0$) but the interest rate rises ($dr/dT = r'(k)dk/dT > 0$) in the long run, the effects of factor prices on welfare work in opposite directions even in the absence of a PAYG system (if $T = 0$).

But both w and r depend on the capital-labour ratio (as in the standard neoclassical model) and are thus not independent of each other. By exploiting this dependency we obtain the factor price frontier, $w_t = \phi(r_t)$, which has a very useful property:

$$w_t = \phi(r_t), \qquad \frac{dw_t}{dr_t} \equiv \phi'(r_t) = -k_t. \tag{16.57}$$

The slope of the factor price frontier is obtained as follows. In general, by differentiating (16.15) and (16.16) (for r_t) we get $dr_t = f''(k_t)dk_t$ and $dw_t = -k_t f''(k_t)dk_t$ so that $dw_t/dr_t = -k_t$. From this it follows that $d^2w_t/dr_t^2 = -dk_t/dr_t = -1/f''(k_t).$[5]

---

[5]The factor price frontier for the Cobb-Douglas technology is given by:

$$w - (1-\alpha)z_0^{1/(1-\alpha)} \left(\frac{\alpha}{r+\delta} \right)^{\alpha/(1-\alpha)},$$

where the reader should verify the property stated in (16.57).

We now have all the necessary ingredients to perform our welfare analysis. By differentiating the indirect utility function (16.47) with respect to T we obtain in a few steps:

$$
\begin{aligned}
\frac{d\bar{\Lambda}^Y}{dT} &= \frac{\partial\bar{\Lambda}^Y}{\partial w}\frac{dw}{dT} + \frac{\partial\bar{\Lambda}^Y}{\partial r}\frac{dr}{dT} + \frac{\partial\bar{\Lambda}^Y}{\partial T} \\
&= \frac{\partial\Lambda^Y}{\partial C^Y}\cdot\left(\frac{dw}{dT} + \frac{S}{1+r}\cdot\frac{dr}{dT} - \frac{r-n}{1+r}\right) \\
&= -\frac{r-n}{1+r}\frac{\partial\Lambda^Y}{\partial C^Y}\cdot\left[1 + k\cdot\frac{dr}{dT}\right] \gtreqless 0 \qquad \text{for } r \lesseqgtr n,
\end{aligned}
\tag{16.58}
$$

where we have used (16.48) and (16.50)–(16.52) in going from the first to the second line and (16.57) as well as $S = (1+n)k$ in going from the second to the third line. The term in square brackets on the right-hand side of (16.58) shows the two channels by which the PAYG pension affects welfare. The first term is the partial equilibrium effect of T on lifetime resources and the second term captures the general equilibrium effects that operate via factor prices.

The expression in (16.58) is important because it illustrates in a transparent fashion the intimate link that exists between, on the one hand, the steady-state welfare effect of a PAYG pension and, on the other hand, the dynamic (in)efficiency of the initial steady-state equilibrium. If the economy happens to be in the golden-rule equilibrium (so that $r = n$) then it follows from (16.58) that a *marginal* change in the PAYG contribution rate has no effect on steady-state welfare (i.e. $d\bar{\Lambda}^Y/dT = 0$ in that case). Since the yield on private saving and the PAYG pension are the same in that case, a small change in T does not produce a first-order welfare effect on steady-state generations despite the fact that it causes crowding out of capital (see (16.46)) and thus an increase in the interest rate (since $r'(k) < 0$).

Matters are different if the economy is initially not in the golden-rule equilibrium (so that $r \neq n$) because the capital crowding out does produce a first-order welfare effect in that case. For example, if the economy is initially dynamically inefficient ($r < n$), then an increase in the PAYG contribution rate actually raises steady-state welfare! The intuition behind this result, which was first demonstrated in the pensions context and with a partial equilibrium model by Aaron (1966), is as follows. In a dynamically inefficient economy there is oversaving by the young generations as a result of which the market rate of interest is low. By raising T the young partially substitute private saving for saving via the PAYG pension. The latter has a higher yield than the former because the biological interest rate, n, exceeds the market interest rate, r. The reduction in the capital stock lowers the wage but this adverse effect on welfare is offset by the increase in the interest rate in a dynamically inefficient economy. To put it bluntly, capital crowding out is beneficial in such an economy.

16.2.1.3   Equivalence PAYG and deficit financing government debt

As was shown by Auerbach and Kotlikoff, a PAYG social security scheme can also be reinterpreted as a particular kind of government debt policy (1987, pp. 149–150). In order to demonstrate this equivalency result, we now introduce government debt into the model. This model extension also allows us to further clarify the link between the pension insights of Aaron (1966) and the macroeconomic effects of debt as set out by Diamond (1965).

Assume that the government taxes the young generations, provides transfers to the old generations, and issues one-period (indexed) debt which yields the same rate of interest as capital. Ignoring government consumption, the government budget identity is now:

$$B_{t+1} - B_t = r_t B_t + L_{t-1} Z_t - L_t T_t, \tag{16.59}$$

where B_t is the stock of public debt at the beginning of period t. Interest payments on existing debt $(r_t B_t)$ plus transfers to the old are covered by the revenues from the tax on the young and/or additional debt issues $(B_{t+1} - B_t)$.

Because government debt and private capital attract the same rate of return, the household is indifferent about the *composition* of its savings over these two assets. Consequently, the young choose consumption in the two periods and *total* saving in order to maximize lifetime utility (16.1) subject to the budget identities (16.31) and (16.32). The savings function that results takes the following form:

$$S_t = S(\hat{w}_t, r_{t+1}), \tag{16.60}$$

where $\hat{w}_t$ is given by the left-hand side of (16.33) which is reproduced here for convenience:

$$\hat{w}_t = w_t - T_t + \frac{Z_{t+1}}{1 + r_{t+1}}. \tag{16.61}$$

It remains to derive the expression linking private savings plans and aggregate capital formation. There are L_t young agents who each save S_t so that aggregate saving is $S_t L_t$. Saving can be in the form of private capital or public debt. Hence the capital market equilibrium condition is now (see Intermezzo 16.1):

$$L_t S_t = B_{t+1} + K_{t+1}. \tag{16.62}$$

We are now in the position to present an important equivalence result which was proved inter alia by Wallace (1981), Sargent (1987a), and Calvo and Obstfeld (1988). Buiter and Kletzer state the equivalence result as follows: "...any equilibrium with government debt and deficits can be replicated by an economy in which the government budget is balanced period-by-period (and the stock of debt is zero) by appropriate age-specific lump-sum taxes and transfers" (1992, pp. 27–28). A corollary of the result is that if the policy maker has access to unrestricted age-specific taxes and transfers then public debt is redundant in the sense that it does not permit additional equilibria to be supported (1992, p. 28).

The model developed in this subsection is fully characterized (for $t \geq 0$) by the following equations:

$$C_t^O = (1 + r(k_t))(1 + n)(k_t + b_t) + Z_t, \tag{16.63}$$

$$U'(C_t^Y) = \frac{1 + r(k_{t+1})}{1 + \rho} U'(C_{t+1}^O), \tag{16.64}$$

$$w(k_t) - T_t - C_t^Y = (1 + n)[k_{t+1} + b_{t+1}], \tag{16.65}$$

$$(1 + n)b_{t+1} = (1 + r(k_t))b_t + \frac{Z_t}{1 + n} - T_t, \tag{16.66}$$

where $b_t \equiv B_t / L_t$ is government debt per worker and where k_0 and b_0 are both given. Equation (16.63) is consumption of an old household, (16.64) is the consumption Euler equation for a young household (see also (16.5)), (16.65) is (16.31) combined with (16.62), and (16.66) is the government budget identity (16.59) expressed in per-worker form. Finally, we have substituted the rental expressions $w_t = w(k_t)$ and $r_t = r(k_t)$ in the various equations (see equations (16.15) and (16.16) above).

The first thing we note is that the fiscal variables only show up in two places in the dynamical system. In (16.63) there is a resource transfer from the government to each old household (Γ_t^{GO}) consisting of debt service and transfers:

$$\Gamma_t^{GO} \equiv (1 + r(k_t))(1 + n)b_t + Z_t. \qquad \text{(government to old)}$$

Similarly, in (16.65) there is a resource transfer from each young household to the government (Γ_t^{YG}) in the form of purchases of government debt plus taxes:

$$\Gamma_t^{YG} \equiv (1 + n)b_{t+1} + T_t. \qquad \text{(young to government)}$$

Since there are L_{t-1} old and L_t young households, the net resource transfer to the government is $L_t \Gamma_t^{YG} - L_{t-1} \Gamma_t^{GO} = 0$, where the equality follows from the government budget constraint (16.66). Hence, in the absence of government consumption, what the government takes from the young it must give to the old. Put differently, once you know Γ_t^{YG} you also know $\Gamma_t^{GO} \equiv (1 + n)\Gamma_t^{YG}$ and the individual components appearing in the government budget identity (such as b_{t+1}, b_t, Z_t, and T_t) are irrelevant for the determination of the paths of consumption and the capital stock (Buiter and Kletzer, 1992, p. 17).

The equivalence result is demonstrated by considering two paths of the economy which, though associated with different paths for bonds, taxes, and transfers, nevertheless give rise to the same paths for the real variables, namely the capital stock and consumption by the young and the old. For the reference path, the sequence $\{\hat{b}_t, \hat{Z}_t, \hat{T}_t\}_{t=0}^{\infty}$ gives rise to a sequence for the real variables denoted by $\{\hat{C}_t^Y, \hat{C}_t^O, \hat{k}_t\}_{t=0}^{\infty}$ given k_0 and b_0. We can then show that for any other debt sequence $\{\check{b}_t\}_{t=1}^{\infty}$ we can always find sequences for taxes and transfers $\{\check{Z}_t, \check{T}_t\}_{t=0}^{\infty}$ such that the resulting sequences for the real variables are the same as in the reference path, i.e. $\{\hat{C}_t^Y\}_{t=0}^{\infty} = \{\check{C}_t^Y\}_{t=0}^{\infty}$, $\{\hat{C}_t^O\}_{t=0}^{\infty} = \{\check{C}_t^O\}_{t=0}^{\infty}$, and $\{\hat{k}_t\}_{t=0}^{\infty} = \{\check{k}_t\}_{t=0}^{\infty}$.

The key ingredient of the proof is to construct the alternative path such that the resource transfers from the young to the government (Γ_t^{YG}) and from the government to the old (Γ_t^{GO}) are the same for the two paths. These requirements give rise to the following expressions:

$$\hat{Z}_t - \check{Z}_t = (1 + n)\left[(1 + r(\check{k}_t))\check{b}_t - (1 + r(\hat{k}_t))\hat{b}_t\right], \qquad (16.67)$$

$$\check{b}_{t+1} - \hat{b}_{t+1} = \frac{1}{1 + n}\left[\hat{T}_t - \check{T}_t\right]. \qquad (16.68)$$

By using (16.67) in (16.63) and (16.68) in (16.65) we find that these equations solve for the same real variables. As a result, the Euler equation (16.64) is the same for both paths. Obviously the government budget identity still holds. Finally, if the reference path satisfies the government solvency condition (see Intermezzo 16.2) then so will the alternative path.

As a special case of the equivalence result we can take as the reference path the PAYG system (studied above), which has $\hat{b}_t = 0$, $\hat{T}_t = T$, and $\hat{Z}_t = (1 + n)T$ for all t. One (of many) alternative paths is the deficit path in which there are only taxes on the young generations, i.e. $\check{Z}_t = 0$, $\check{b}_t = (1 + n)T/(1 + r_t)$, and $\check{T}_t = T - (1 + n)\check{b}_{t+1}$ for all t.

16.2.1.4 From PAYG to a funded system

In the previous subsection we have established the equivalence between traditional deficit financing and a PAYG social security system. As a by-product of the analysis there we showed how public debt affects the equilibrium path of the economy. In this section we continue our analysis of the welfare effects of a PAYG system, first without and then with bond policy.

Up to this point we have only unearthed the welfare effect of a PAYG system on steady-state generations (see (16.58)) and we have ignored the initial conditions facing the economy, i.e. we have not yet taken into account the costs associated with the transition from the initial growth path to the golden-rule path. As both Diamond (1965, pp. 1128–1129) and Samuelson (1975b, p. 543) stress, ignoring transitional welfare effects is not a very good idea.

As we argued above, the introduction of a PAYG system (or the expansion of a pre-existing one) affects different generations differently. The welfare of old generations at the time of the shock unambiguously rises because of the windfall gain the shock confers on them. From the perspective of their last period of life, they gain utility to the tune of $U'(C_1^O)dC_0^O/dT = (1+n)U'(C_1^O) > 0$ (see (16.44)). The welfare effect on generations born in the new steady state is ambiguous as it depends on whether or not the economy is dynamically efficient (see (16.58)). In a dynamically inefficient economy, $r < n$, all generations, including those born in the new steady state, gain from the pension shock. Intuitively, the PAYG system acts like a "chain letter" system which ensures that each new generation passes resources to the generation immediately preceding it. In such a situation a PAYG system which moves the economy in the direction of the golden-rule growth path is surely "desirable" for society as a whole.

Intermezzo 16.2

Government solvency condition under perfect foresight. The government budget identity (16.59) can be written in per-worker format as:

$$b_t = \frac{b_{t+1} + ps_t}{1 + \bar{r}_t}, \tag{a}$$

where $1 + \bar{r}_t \equiv (1 + r_t)/(1 + n)$ is the net interest factor and $ps_t \equiv [T_t - Z_t/(1+n)]/(1+n)$ is the primary surplus. Of course, (a) can also be used for future periods. For example, for b_{t+1} and b_{t+2} we obtain:

$$b_{t+1} = \frac{b_{t+2} + ps_{t+1}}{1 + \bar{r}_{t+1}}, \qquad b_{t+2} = \frac{b_{t+3} + ps_{t+2}}{1 + \bar{r}_{t+2}}. \tag{b}$$

By repeated substitution of b_{t+1}, b_{t+2}, etcetera into (a) we obtain after $T - 1 \ (\geq 2)$ such substitutions:

$$
\begin{aligned}
b_t = b_{t+T} \cdot & \left[\frac{1}{1 + \bar{r}_t} \frac{1}{1 + \bar{r}_{t+1}} \cdots \frac{1}{1 + \bar{r}_{t+T-1}} \right] + \frac{ps_t}{1 + \bar{r}_t} \\
& + \frac{ps_{t+1}}{(1 + \bar{r}_t)(1 + \bar{r}_{t+1})} \\
& + \cdots + \frac{ps_{t+T-1}}{(1 + \bar{r}_t)(1 + \bar{r}_{t+1}) \cdots (1 + \bar{r}_{t+T-1})}.
\end{aligned}
\tag{c}
$$

The term in square brackets on the right-hand side is the cumulative discount factor applied to b_{t+T}. Equation (c) can be written in short-hand notation as:

$$b_t = b_{t+T} \cdot \left[\prod_{i=0}^{T-1} \frac{1}{1+\bar{r}_{t+i}} \right] + \sum_{\tau=0}^{T-1} ps_{t+\tau} \cdot \left[\prod_{i=0}^{\tau} \frac{1}{1+\bar{r}_{t+i}} \right]. \qquad \text{(d)}$$

The government solvency condition is:

$$\lim_{T \to \infty} b_{t+T} \cdot \left[\prod_{i=0}^{T-1} \frac{1}{1+\bar{r}_{t+i}} \right] = 0. \qquad \text{(e)}$$

Imposing (e) in (d) we obtain the government budget constraint:

$$b_t = \sum_{\tau=0}^{\infty} ps_{t+\tau} \cdot \left[\prod_{i=0}^{\tau} \frac{1}{1+\bar{r}_{t+i}} \right]. \qquad \text{(f)}$$

To the extent that there is a positive government debt at time t, it must be covered in present-value terms by primary surpluses.

****

As Abel et al. (1989) suggest, however, actual economies are not likely to be dynamically inefficient. If the economy is dynamically efficient, so that $r > n$, then it follows from, respectively, (16.44) and (16.58) that whilst an increase in T still makes the old initial generation better off, it leaves steady-state generations worse off than they would have been in the absence of the shock. Since some generations gain and other lose out, it is no longer obvious whether a pension-induced move in the direction of the golden-rule growth path is "socially desirable" at all.

There are two ways in which the concept of social desirability, which we have deliberately kept vague up to now, can be made operational. The first approach, which was pioneered by Bergson (1938) and Samuelson (1947), makes use of a so-called *social welfare function*. In this approach, a functional form is typically postulated which relates an indicator for social welfare (*SW*) to the welfare levels experienced by the different generations. Using our notation, an example of a social welfare function would be:

$$SW_t = \Omega(\Lambda_{t-1}^Y, \Lambda_t^Y, ..., \Lambda_\infty^Y). \qquad (16.69)$$

Once a particular form for the social welfare function is adopted, the social desirability of different policies can be ranked. If policy A is such that it yields a higher indicator of social welfare than policy B, then it follows that policy A is *socially preferred* to policy B (i.e. $SW_t^A > SW_t^B$). Note that, depending on the form of the social welfare function $\Omega(\cdot)$, it may very well be the case that some generations are worse off under policy A than under policy B despite the fact that A is socially preferred to B. What the social welfare function does is establish marginal rates of substitution between lifetime utility levels of different generations (i.e. $(\partial\Omega/\partial\Lambda_{t-1}^Y)/(\partial\Omega/\partial\Lambda_t^Y)$, etc.).[6]

The second approach to putting into operation the concept of social desirability makes use of the concept of *Pareto-efficiency*. Recall that an allocation of resources in

---

[6] Applications of the social welfare function approach are given in Sections 16.4.1 and 16.4.2 below.

the economy is called Pareto-optimal (or Pareto-efficient) if there is no other feasible allocation which (i) makes no individual in the economy worse off and (ii) makes at least one individual strictly better off than he or she was. Similarly, a policy is called *Pareto-improving* vis-à-vis the initial situation if it improves welfare for at least one agent and leaves all other agents equally well off as in the status quo.

Recently, a number of authors have applied the Pareto-criterion to the question of pension reform. Specifically, Breyer (1989) and Verbon (1989) ask themselves the question whether it is possible to abolish a pre-existing PAYG system (in favour of a fully funded system) in a Pareto-improving fashion in a dynamically efficient economy. This is a relevant question because in such an economy, steady-state generations gain if the PAYG system is abolished or reduced (since r exceeds n, it follows from equation (16.58) that $d\Lambda^Y/dT < 0$ in that case) but the old generation at the time of the policy shock loses out (see (16.44)). This generation paid into the PAYG system when it was young in the expectation that it would receive back $1 + n$ times its contribution during old age. Taken in isolation, the policy shock is clearly not Pareto-improving.

Of course, bond policy constitutes a mechanism by which the welfare gains and losses of the different generations can be redistributed. This is the case because it breaks the link between the contributions of the young ($L_t T_t$) and the pension receipts by the old in the same period ($L_{t-1} Z_t$)—compare (16.35) and (16.59). The key issue is thus whether it is possible to find a bond path such that the reduction in the PAYG contribution is Pareto-improving. As it turns out, no such path can be found. It is thus not possible to compensate the old generation at the time of the shock without making at least one future generation worse off (Breyer, 1989, p. 655).

16.2.2 PAYG pensions and endogenous retirement

In a very influential article, Feldstein (1974) argued that a PAYG system not only affects a household's savings decisions (as is the case in the model studied up to this point) but also its decision to retire from the labour force. We now augment the model in order to demonstrate the implications for allocation and welfare of endogenous retirement. Following the literature, we capture the notion of retirement by assuming that labour supply during the first period of life is endogenous. To keep the model as simple as possible, we continue to assume that households do not work at all during the second period of life. To bring the model closer to reality, we assume furthermore that the contribution to the PAYG system is levied in the form of a proportional tax on labour income and that the pension is *intragenerationally fair*, i.e. in principle an agent who would work a lot during youth would get a higher pension during old age than an agent who would be lazy during youth. Agents are assumed to be identical, however, so we can focus from the outset on the symmetric equilibrium in which members of the same cohort all behave in the same way. Within the augmented model it is possible that the PAYG system distorts the labour supply decisions by households.

16.2.2.1 Households

The lifetime utility function of a (representative) young agent who is born at time t is given in general form by:

$$\Lambda_t^Y \equiv \Lambda^Y(C_t^Y, C_{t+1}^O, 1 - N_t), \tag{16.70}$$

where N_t is labour supply ($1 - N_t$ is leisure) and $\Lambda^Y(\cdot)$ satisfies the usual Inada-style conditions. The agent faces the following budget identities:

$$C_t^Y + S_t = w_t N_t - T_t, \tag{16.71}$$

$$C_{t+1}^O = (1 + r_{t+1}) S_t + Z_{t+1}, \tag{16.72}$$

where T_t and Z_{t+1} are defined as follows:

$$T_t = t_L w_t N_t, \tag{16.73}$$

$$Z_{t+1} = \left[t_L w_{t+1} \overline{NL}_{t+1} \right] \cdot \frac{N_t}{\overline{NL}_t}, \tag{16.74}$$

where t_L is the labour income tax ($0 < t_L < 1$) and $\overline{NL}_t$ stands for *aggregate* labour supply in period t. According to (16.73), the individual agent's contribution to the PAYG system is equal to a proportion of his labour income, where the proportional tax, t_L, is assumed to be the same for all individuals and constant over time. Equation (16.74) shows that the pension is intragenerationally fair (as in Breyer and Straub, 1993, p. 81). The term in square brackets on the right-hand side of (16.74) is the total tax revenue that is available for pension payments in the next period. Each agent gets a share of this revenue that depends on his *relative* labour supply effort during youth (given by $N_t / \overline{NL}_t$).

Each household is fully aware of the features of the pension system (as formalized in (16.73)–(16.74)) so that the consolidated lifetime budget constraint, upon which the household bases its decisions, is given by:

$$C_t^Y + \frac{C_{t+1}^O}{1 + r_{t+1}} = w_t N_t - t_L \cdot \left[1 - \frac{w_{t+1} \overline{NL}_{t+1}}{w_t (1 + r_{t+1}) \overline{NL}_t} \right] w_t N_t$$

$$\equiv (1 - t_{Et}) w_t N_t, \tag{16.75}$$

where t_{Et} is the (potentially time-varying) effective tax rate on labour:

$$t_{Et} \equiv t_L \cdot \left[1 - \frac{w_{t+1}}{w_t} \frac{\overline{NL}_{t+1}}{\overline{NL}_t} \frac{1}{1 + r_{t+1}} \right]. \tag{16.76}$$

The key thing to note about (16.75) is that in the current setting the household's pension depends not only on future wages but also on the aggregate supply of labour *by future young agents*. To solve its optimization problem, the household must thus form expectations regarding these variables, and, as usual, by suppressing the expectations operator we have implicitly assumed in (16.75) that the agent is blessed with perfect foresight.

Assuming an interior optimum, the first-order conditions for consumption during the two periods and labour supply are:

$$\frac{\partial \Lambda^Y}{\partial C_{t+1}^O} = \frac{1}{1 + r_{t+1}} \frac{\partial \Lambda^Y}{\partial C_t^Y}, \tag{16.77}$$

$$\frac{\partial \Lambda^Y}{\partial (1 - N_t)} = (1 - t_{Et}) w_t \frac{\partial \Lambda^Y}{\partial C_t^Y}. \tag{16.78}$$

Equation (16.77) is the familiar consumption Euler equation in general functional form. The optimal labour supply decision is characterized by (16.78) in combination with (16.76). Equation (16.78) is the usual condition calling for an equalization of the after-effective-tax wage rate and the marginal rate of substitution between leisure and consumption during youth. Equation (16.76) shows to what extent the PAYG system has the potential to distort the labour supply decision. It is not the *statutory* tax rate, t_L, which determines whether or not the labour supply decision is distorted but rather the *effective* tax rate, t_{Et}. By paying the PAYG premium during youth one obtains the right to a pension. Ceteris paribus labour supply, the effective tax rate may actually be negative, i.e. it may in fact be an employment subsidy (Breyer and Straub, 1993, p. 82).

Since all agents of a particular generation are identical in all aspects we can now simplify the model by imposing symmetry. In the symmetric equilibrium we have $\overline{NL}_t = N_t L_t$, and $\overline{NL}_{t+1} = N_{t+1} L_{t+1}$. With a constant growth rate of the population ($L_{t+1} = (1+n)L_t$) equation (16.76) thus simplifies to:

$$t_{Et} \equiv t_L \cdot \left[1 - \frac{w_{t+1}}{w_t} \frac{N_{t+1}}{N_t} \frac{1+n}{1+r_{t+1}} \right] = \frac{t_L}{1+r_{t+1}} \cdot \left[r_{t+1} - \frac{\Delta \overline{WI}_{t+1}}{\overline{WI}_t} \right], \qquad (16.79)$$

where $\overline{WI}_t \equiv w_t N_t L_t$ is total wage income in period t and $\Delta \overline{WI}_{t+1} \equiv \overline{WI}_{t+1} - \overline{WI}_t$. We find that the pension system acts like an employment subsidy (and $t_{Et} < 0$) if the so-called *Aaron condition* holds, i.e. if the growth of total wage income exceeds the rate of interest (Aaron, 1966).

In the symmetric equilibrium, equations (16.75)–(16.78) define the optimal values of C_t^Y, C_{t+1}^O, and N_t as a function of the variables that are exogenous to the representative agent (w_t, r_{t+1}, and t_{Et}). We write these solutions as $C_t^Y = C^Y(w_t^N, r_{t+1})$, $C_{t+1}^O = C^O(w_t^N, r_{t+1})$, and $N_t = N(w_t^N, r_{t+1})$, where $w_t^N \equiv w_t(1 - t_{Et})$. The (partial-equilibrium) effect of a change in the statutory tax rate, t_L, on the household's labour supply decision can thus be written in elasticity format as:

$$\frac{t_L}{N} \frac{\partial N}{\partial t_L} = -\varepsilon_{wN}^N \cdot \frac{t_{Et}}{1 - t_{Et}}, \qquad \varepsilon_{wN}^N \equiv \frac{w_t^N}{N} \frac{\partial N}{\partial w_t^N}, \qquad (16.80)$$

where ε_{wN}^N is the uncompensated elasticity of labour supply. It follows from (16.80) that the effect of the contribution rate on labour supply is ambiguous for two reasons. First, it depends on whether the Aaron-condition is satisfied ($t_{Et} < 0$) or violated ($t_{Et} > 0$). Second, it also depends on the sign of ε_{wN}^N. We recall that $\varepsilon_{wN}^N > 0$ (< 0) if the substitution effect in labour supply dominates (is dominated by) the income effect. If the labour supply is upward sloping and the Aaron condition is satisfied then, for given factor prices, an increase in the statutory tax rate increases labour supply.

16.2.2.2 The macroeconomy

We must now complete the description of the model and derive the fundamental difference equation for the economic system. We follow the approach of Ihori (1996, pp. 36–37). With endogenous labour supply, the number of young agents (L_t) no longer coincides with the amount of labour used in production ($L_t N_t$). By redefining the capital-labour ratio as $k_t \equiv K_t/(L_t N_t)$, however, the expressions for the wage and the interest rate are still as in (16.15)–(16.16) and the factor price frontier is still as given in (16.57). Current savings leads to the formation of capital in the next period, i.e. $L_t S_t = K_{t+1}$. In terms of the redefined capital-labour ratio we get:

$$S_t = (1+n)N_{t+1}k_{t+1}. \qquad (16.81)$$

To characterize this fundamental difference equation we note that the labour supply and savings equations can be written in general functional form as:

$$N_t = N(w_t(1 - t_{Et}), r_{t+1}), \tag{16.82}$$

$$S_t = \frac{C^O(w_t(1 - t_{Et}), r_{t+1}) - (1 + n)t_L w_{t+1} N_{t+1}}{1 + r_{t+1}} \tag{16.83}$$

$$\equiv S(w_t(1 - t_{Et}), r_{t+1}, t_L w_{t+1} N_{t+1}). \tag{16.84}$$

By using these expressions in (16.81) we obtain the following expression:

$$S(w_t(1 - t_{Et}), r_{t+1}, t_L w_{t+1} N_{t+1}) = (1 + n)N(w_{t+1}(1 - t_{Et+1}), r_{t+2})k_{t+1}. \tag{16.85}$$

Clearly, since $w_t = w(k_t)$ and $r_t = r(k_t)$, this expression contains the terms k_t, k_{t+1}, and k_{t+2} so one is tempted to conclude that it is a second-order difference equation in the capital stock. As Breyer and Straub (1993, p. 82) point out, however, the presence of future pensions introduces an infinite regress into the model, i.e. since t_{Et} depends on N_{t+1} (see (16.79)), it follows that t_{Et+1} depends on N_{t+2} which itself depends on k_{t+2}, k_{t+3}, and t_{Et+2}. As a result, (16.85) depends on the entire sequence of present and future capital stocks, $\{k_{t+\tau}\}_{\tau=0}^{\infty}$, so that, even though we assume perfect foresight, the model has a continuum of equilibria.[7] Since we assume that the population growth rate is constant, however, we can skip over the indeterminacy issue by first studying the steady state.

16.2.2.3 The steady state

We study two pertinent aspects of the steady state. First, we show how the endogeneity of labour supply affects the welfare effect of the PAYG pension. Second, we show that in the unit-elastic model the pension crowds out capital in the long run. As before, the long-run welfare analysis makes use of the indirect utility function which is now defined as follows:

$$\bar{\Lambda}^Y(w, r, t_L) \equiv \max_{\{C^Y, C^O, N\}} \Lambda^Y(C^Y, C^O, 1 - N)$$

$$\text{subject to: } wN\left[1 - t_L\frac{r - n}{1 + r}\right] = C^Y + \frac{C^O}{1 + r}. \tag{16.86}$$

(The constraint is obtained from (16.75) and (16.76) by noting that in the steady state we have $w_t = w$, $N_t = N$, $r_{t+1} = r$, and $\overline{NL}_{t+1} = (1 + n)\overline{NL}_t$.) Retracing our earlier derivation we can deduce the following properties of the indirect utility function:

$$\frac{\partial \bar{\Lambda}^Y}{\partial w} = N\frac{\partial \Lambda^Y}{\partial C^Y}\left[1 - t_L\frac{r - n}{1 + r}\right], \tag{16.87}$$

$$\frac{\partial \bar{\Lambda}^Y}{\partial r} = \frac{S}{1 + r}\frac{\partial \Lambda^Y}{\partial C^Y}, \tag{16.88}$$

$$\frac{\partial \bar{\Lambda}^Y}{\partial t_L} = -\frac{r - n}{1 + r}wN\frac{\partial \Lambda^Y}{\partial C^Y}. \tag{16.89}$$

---

[7]Indeterminacy and multiple equilibria are quite common phenomena in overlapping-generations models of the Diamond-Samuelson type. Azariadis (1993) gives a general discussion. Reichlin (1986) and Nourry (2001) deal specifically with the case of endogenous labour supply. See also Woodford (1984).

The total effect of a marginal change in the statutory tax rate on steady-state welfare is now easily computed:

$$
\begin{aligned}
\frac{d\bar{\Lambda}^Y}{dt_L} &= \frac{\partial \bar{\Lambda}^Y}{\partial w}\frac{dw}{dt_L} + \frac{\partial \bar{\Lambda}^Y}{\partial r}\frac{dr}{dt_L} + \frac{\partial \bar{\Lambda}^Y}{\partial t_L} \\
&= \frac{\partial \Lambda^Y}{\partial C^Y} \cdot \left(N\left(1 - t_L\frac{r-n}{1+r}\right)\frac{dw}{dt_L} + \frac{S}{1+r}\frac{dr}{dt_L} - \frac{r-n}{1+r}wN \right) \\
&= -N \cdot \frac{r-n}{1+r} \cdot \frac{\partial \Lambda^Y}{\partial C^Y} \cdot \left[w + (1 - t_L)k \cdot \frac{dr}{dt_L} \right],
\end{aligned}
\tag{16.90}
$$

where we have used (16.87)–(16.89) in going from the first to the second line and (16.57) and (16.81) in going from the second to the third line. There are two noteworthy conclusions that can be drawn on the basis of (16.90). First, if the economy is initially in the golden-rule equilibrium ($r = n$), then a marginal change in t_L does not produce a first-order welfare effect on steady-state generations. Intuitively, the labour supply decision is not distorted because the effective tax on labour is zero in that case ($t_E = t_L(r-n)/(1+r) = 0$). Second, if the economy is not in the golden-rule equilibrium ($r \neq n$), then the sign of the welfare effect is determined by the sign of the term in square brackets on the right-hand side of (16.90). Just as for the case with lump-sum contributions (see (16.58)), the PAYG pension affects welfare through lifetime resources (the first term within the square brackets) and via factor prices (the second composite term). It turns out, however, that with endogenous labour supply the sign of dr/dt_L (and thus the sign of $d\bar{\Lambda}^Y/dt_L$) is ambiguous (Ihori, 1996, p. 237).

Matters are simplified quite a lot if Cobb-Douglas preferences are assumed, i.e. if (16.70) is specialized to:

$$
\Lambda_t^Y \equiv \ln C_t^Y + \lambda_C \ln(1 - N_t) + \frac{1}{1+\rho}\ln C_t^O,
\tag{16.91}
$$

where ρ is the rate of time preference and λ_C (≥ 0) regulates the strength of the labour supply effect. The following solutions for the decision variables are then obtained by maximizing (16.91) subject to (16.75):

$$
C_t^Y = \frac{1+\rho}{2+\rho+\lambda_C(1+\rho)}w_t^N,
\tag{16.92}
$$

$$
C_{t+1}^O = \frac{1+r_{t+1}}{2+\rho+\lambda_C(1+\rho)}w_t^N,
\tag{16.93}
$$

$$
N_t = \frac{2+\rho}{2+\rho+\lambda_C(1+\rho)},
\tag{16.94}
$$

where $w_t^N \equiv w_t(1 - t_{Et})$ is the effective after-tax wage. In the unit-elastic model, consumption during youth and old age are both normal goods (i.e. depend positively on w_t^N) and labour supply is constant because income and substitution effects cancel out. Since the current workers know that future workers will also supply a fixed amount of labour ($N_{t+1} = N_t = N$), the expression for the after-tax wage simplifies to:

$$
w_t^N \equiv w_t(1 - t_{Et}) \equiv w_t\left[1 - t_L\left(1 - \frac{w_{t+1}}{w_t}\frac{1+n}{1+r_{t+1}}\right)\right].
\tag{16.95}
$$

Note furthermore that in (16.92) the presence of pension payments during old age ensures that consumption during youth depends negatively on the interest rate—via the effective tax rate—despite the fact that logarithmic preferences are used. According to (16.93) old-age consumption depends positively on the interest rate and negatively (positively) on the tax rate if the Aaron condition $t_{Et} > 0$ is violated (holds; $t_{Et} < 0$). Finally, in (16.94) the standard model is recovered by setting $\lambda_C = 0$, in which case labour supply is exogenous and equal to unity.

We can now determine the extent to which capital is crowded out by the PAYG system. In view of (16.93) and (16.95), the fundamental difference equation for the model (16.85) can be written as follows:

$$(1+n)k_{t+1} = (1-t_L)\frac{w_t}{2+\rho} - t_L(1+n)\frac{1+\rho}{2+\rho}\frac{w_{t+1}}{1+r_{t+1}}. \tag{16.96}$$

Since $w_t = w(k_t)$ and $r_t = r(k_t)$, equation (16.96) constitutes a first-order difference equation in the capital-labour ratio. Hence, in the unit-elastic model the indeterminacy of the transition path (that was mentioned in the text below equation (16.85)) disappears because the uncompensated labour supply elasticity is zero.

The stability condition and the long-run effect of the PAYG system on the capital-labour ratio are derived in the usual manner by finding the partial derivatives of the implicit function, $k_{t+1} = g(k_t, t_L)$, around the steady state (in which $k_{t+1} = k_t = k$). After some manipulation we obtain:

$$g_k \equiv \frac{\partial k_{t+1}}{\partial k_t} = \frac{(1-t_L)w'(k)}{(1+n)(2+\rho)\left[1 + t_L\frac{1+\rho}{2+\rho}\frac{(1+r)w'(k)-wr'(k)}{(1+r)^2}\right]} > 0, \tag{16.97}$$

$$g_t \equiv \frac{\partial k_{t+1}}{\partial t_L} = -\frac{w[1+r+(1+\rho)(1+n)]}{(1+r)(1+n)(2+\rho)\left[1 + t_L\frac{1+\rho}{2+\rho}\frac{(1+r)w'(k)-wr'(k)}{(1+r)^2}\right]} < 0. \tag{16.98}$$

Since g_k is positive (as $w'(k) > 0 > r'(k)$), stability requires it to be less than unity ($0 < g_k < 1$). As a result, the long-run effect on the capital-labour ratio is unambiguously negative in the unit-elastic model:

$$\frac{dk}{dt_L} = \frac{g_t}{1-g_k} < 0. \tag{16.99}$$

16.2.2.4 Welfare effects

We are now in the position to compare and contrast the key results of this subsection to those that hold when labour supply is exogenous and the pension contribution is levied in a lump-sum fashion (see subsection 16.2.1.2). At first view, the assumption of a distorting pension contribution does not seem to change the principal conclusions very much—at least in the unit-elastic model. In both cases, the PAYG contribution leads to long-run crowding out of the capital-labour ratio (compare (16.46) and (16.99)) and a reduction (increase) in steady-state welfare for a dynamically efficient (inefficient) economy (compare (16.58) and (16.90)). Intuitively, this similarity is only moderately surprising in view of the fact that in the unit-elastic model (optimally chosen) labour supply is constant (see (16.94)).

There is a very important difference between the two cases, however, because the pension contribution, t_L, itself causes a distortion of the labour supply decision of households which is absent if the contribution is levied in a lump-sum fashion. The resulting loss to the economy of using a distorting rather than a non-distorting tax is often referred to as the *deadweight loss* (or burden) of the distorting tax (Diamond and McFadden, 1974, p. 5). Following Diamond and McFadden we define

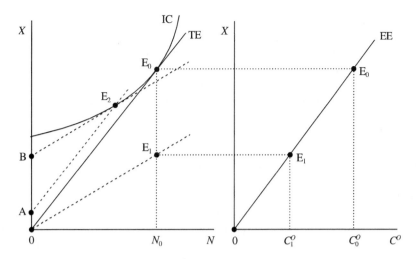

Figure 16.5: Deadweight loss of taxation

the deadweight loss (DWL) associated with t_L as the difference between, on the one hand, the income one must give a young household to restore it to its pre-tax utility level and, on the other hand, the tax revenue collected from it (1974, p. 5).

In Figure 16.5 we illustrate the DWL of the pension contribution for a steady-state generation in the unit-elastic model. We hold factor prices (w and r) constant and assume that the economy is dynamically efficient ($r > n$). We follow the approach of Belan and Pestieau (1999) by solving the model in two stages. In the first stage we define lifetime income as:

$$X \equiv wN \left[1 - t_L \frac{r - n}{1 + r}\right] \equiv wN(1 - t_E), \tag{16.100}$$

and let the household choose current and future consumption in order to maximize:

$$\ln C^Y + \frac{1}{1 + \rho} \ln C^O, \tag{16.101}$$

subject to the constraint $C^Y + C^O/(1 + r) = X$. This yields the following expressions:

$$C^Y = \frac{1 + \rho}{2 + \rho} X, \qquad C^O = \frac{1 + r}{2 + \rho} X. \tag{16.102}$$

In the right-hand panel of Figure 16.5 the line EE relates old-age consumption to lifetime income. In that panel the value of consumption during youth can be deduced from the fact that it is proportional to lifetime income.

By substituting the expressions (16.102) into the utility function (16.91) we obtain:

$$\Lambda^Y \equiv \frac{2 + \rho}{1 + \rho} \ln X + \lambda_C \ln(1 - N) + \ln \left[\frac{1 + \rho}{2 + \rho} \left(\frac{1 + r}{2 + \rho}\right)^{1/(1+\rho)}\right], \tag{16.103}$$

In the second stage, the household chooses its labour supply and lifetime income in order to maximize (16.103) subject to (16.100). The solution to this second-stage problem is, of course, that N takes the value indicated in (16.94) and X follows from the constraint. The second-stage optimization problem is shown in the left-hand panel of Figure 16.5. In that panel, TE represents the budget line (16.100) in the absence of taxation ($t_E = 0$). The indifference curve which is tangent to the pre-tax budget line is given by IC and the initial equilibrium is at E_0. In the right-hand panel E_0 on the EE line gives the corresponding optimal value for old-age consumption.

Now consider what happens if a positive effective tax is levied ($t_E > 0$). Nothing happens in the right-hand panel but in the left-hand panel the budget line rotates in a counter-clockwise fashion. The new budget line is given by the dashed line from the origin. We know that in the unit-elastic model income and substitution effects in labour supply cancel out so that labour supply does not change (see (16.94)). Hence, the new equilibrium is at E_1 in the two panels. By shifting the new budget line in a parallel fashion and finding a tangency along the pre-tax indifference curve we find that the pure substitution effect of the tax change is given by the shift from E_0 to E_2 (the income effect is thus the shift from E_2 to E_1). Hence, the vertical distance 0B represents the income one would have to give the household to restore it to its pre-tax indifference curve. We call this hypothetical transfer TR_0. What is the tax revenue which is collected from the agent? To answer that question we draw a line that is parallel to the pre-tax budget line, through the compensated point E_2. This line has an intercept with the vertical axis at point A. We now have two expressions for lines that both pass through the compensated point E_2, namely $X = w(1 - t_E)N + TR_0$ and $X = wN + TR_0 - T$, where T is the vertical distance AB in Figure 16.5. By deducting the two lines we find that $T = t_E wN$ so that AB represents the tax revenue collected from the agent. Since the required transfer is 0B the DWL of the tax is given by the distance 0A.

16.2.2.5 Reform

As a number of authors have pointed out, the distorting nature of the pension system has important implications for the possibility of designing Pareto-improving reform (see e.g. Homburg, 1990, Breyer and Straub, 1993, and the references to more recent literature in Belan and Pestieau, 1999). Recall from the discussion at the end of section 16.2.1.4 that a Pareto-improving transition from PAYG to a fully funded system is not possible in the standard model because the resources cannot be found to compensate the old generations at the time of the reform without making some future generation worse off. Matters are different if the PAYG system represents a distorting system. In that case, as Breyer and Straub (1993) point out, *provided lump-sum (nondistorting) contributions can be used during the transition phase,* a gradual move from a PAYG to a fully funded system can be achieved in a Pareto-improving manner. Intuitively, by moving from a distortionary to a non-distortionary scheme, additional resources are freed up which can be used to compensate the various generations (Belan and Pestieau, 1999).[8] Of course, this type of argument has only limited practical relevance. Indeed, it begs the question why, if non-distortionary taxes are available, the government used the distortionary tax in the first place.

---

[8]The distortive nature of the PAYG scheme does not have to result from endogenous labour supply. Demmel and Keuschnigg (2000), for example, assume that union wage-setting causes unemployment which is exacerbated by the pension contribution. Efficiency gains then materialize because pension reform reduces unemployment. In a similar vein, Belan et al. (1998) use a Paul Romer-style (1986, 1989) endogenous growth model and show that reform may be Pareto-improving because it helps to internalize a positive externality in production. See also Corneo and Marquardt (2000).

Table 16.1. Age composition of the population

	1950	1990	2025
World			
0–19	44.1	41.7	32.8
20–65	50.8	52.1	57.5
65+	5.1	6.2	9.7
OECD			
0–19	35.0	27.2	24.8
20–64	56.7	59.9	56.6
65+	8.3	12.8	18.6
US			
0–19	33.9	28.9	26.8
20–65	57.9	58.9	56.0
65+	8.1	12.2	17.2

16.2.3   The macroeconomic effects of ageing

Up to this point we have assumed that the rate of population growth is constant and equal to n (see equation (16.21) above). This simplifying assumption of course means that the age composition of the population is constant also. A useful measure to characterize the economic impact of demography is the so-called (old-age) *dependency ratio*, which is defined as the number of retired people divided by the working-age population. In our highly stylized two-period overlapping-generations model the number of old and young people at time t are, respectively, L_{t-1} and $L_t = (1+n)L_{t-1}$ so that the dependency ratio is $1/(1+n)$.

Of course, as all members of the baby-boom generation will surely know, the assumption of a constant population composition, though convenient, is not a particularly realistic one. Table 16.1, which is taken from Weil (1997, p. 970), shows that significant demographic changes have taken place between 1950 and 1990 and are expected to take place between 1990 and 2025.

The figures in Table 16.1 graphically illustrate that throughout the world, and particularly in the group of OECD countries and in the US, the proportion of young people (0–19 years of age) is on the decline whilst the fraction of old people (65 and over) steadily increases. Both of these phenomena are tell-tale signs of an ageing population.

In this subsection we show how the macroeconomic effects of demographic composition changes can be analysed with the aid of a simple overlapping-generations model. We only stress some of the key results, especially those relating to the interaction between demography and the public pension system. The interested reader is referred to Weil (1997) for an excellent survey of the literature on the economics of ageing.

In the absence of immigration from abroad (or emigration out of the country), population ageing can result from two distinct sources, namely a decrease in *fertility* and a decrease in *mortality*. In the two-period overlapping-generations model used so far the length of life is exogenously fixed but we can nevertheless capture the notion of ageing by reducing the rate of population growth, n.[9] In order to study the effects on allocation and welfare of such a demographic shock we first reformulate the model of subsection 16.2.1.2 in terms of a variable growth rate of the population, n_t. Hence, instead of (16.21) we use:

$$L_t = (1+n_t)L_{t-1}. \tag{16.104}$$

Assuming a constant contribution rate per person ($T_t = T$), the pension at time t equals $Z_t = (1+n_t)T$. Redoing the derivations presented in subsection 16.2.1.2 yields the following fundamental difference equation of the model:

$$S(w_t, r_{t+1}, n_{t+1}, T) = (1+n_{t+1})k_{t+1}, \tag{16.105}$$

where the savings function is the same as in (16.40) but with n_{t+1} replacing n. Ceteris paribus, saving by the young depends negatively on the (expected) rate of population growth, n_{t+1}, because the pension they receive when old depends on it (as $Z_{t+1} = (1+n_{t+1})T$). An anticipated reduction in fertility reduces the expected pension and lifetime income, and causes the agent to cut back on both present and future consumption and to increase saving. Hence, $S_n \equiv \partial S/\partial n_{t+1} < 0$. The right-hand side of (16.105) shows that a decrease in the population growth rate makes it possible to support a higher capital-labour ratio for a given amount of per capita saving.

Following the solution method discussed in subsection 16.2.1.2, we can derive that (16.105) defines an implicit function, $k_{t+1} = g(k_t, n_{t+1})$, with partial derivatives $0 < g_k < 1$ (see equation (16.42)) and $g_n < 0$:

$$g_n \equiv \frac{\partial g}{\partial n_{t+1}} = \frac{S_n - k_{t+1}}{1 + n_{t+1} - S_r r'(k_{t+1})} < 0. \tag{16.106}$$

It follows that a permanent reduction in the population growth rate, say from n_0 to n_1, gives rise to an increase in the long-run capital stock, i.e. $dk/dn = g_n/(1-g_k) < 0$, where $k = k_{t+1} = k_t$. The transition path of the economy to the steady state is illustrated in Figure 16.6. In that figure, the dashed line labelled "$k_{t+1} = g(k_t, n_0)$" reproduces the initial transition path with social security in Figure 16.4. The reduction in fertility boosts saving at impact so that, if the economy starts out with a capital stock k_0, the new transition path is the dotted line from B to the new equilibrium at E_1. During transition the wage rate gradually rises and the interest rate falls. The intuition behind the long-run increase in the capital-labour ratio is straightforward. As a result of the demographic shock there are fewer young households, who own no assets, and more old households, who own a lot of assets which they need to provide income for their retirement years (Auerbach and Kotlikoff, 1987, p. 163).

The effect of a permanent reduction in fertility on steady-state welfare can be computed by differentiating the indirect utility function (16.47) with respect to n, using (16.50)–(16.51) and (16.57), and noting that $\partial \bar{\Lambda}^Y/\partial n = T \left(\partial \bar{\Lambda}^Y/\partial C^Y \right)/(1+r)$:

$$\begin{aligned} \frac{d\bar{\Lambda}^Y}{dn} &= \frac{\partial \bar{\Lambda}^Y}{\partial w}\frac{dw}{dn} + \frac{\partial \bar{\Lambda}^Y}{\partial r}\frac{dr}{dn} + \frac{\partial \bar{\Lambda}^Y}{\partial n} \\ &= \frac{\partial \Lambda^Y}{\partial C^Y} \cdot \left(\frac{dw}{dn} + \frac{S}{1+r}\frac{dr}{dn} + \frac{T}{1+r} \right) \\ &= \frac{\partial \Lambda^Y}{\partial C^Y} \cdot \left[-k\frac{r-n}{1+r} \cdot \frac{dr}{dn} + \frac{T}{1+r} \right] \gtrless 0. \end{aligned} \tag{16.107}$$

[9]The length of life can be made stochastic, as in Chapter 15, by assuming that the probability of surviving into the second phase of life is between zero and one. See Section 16.3 below for such a model.

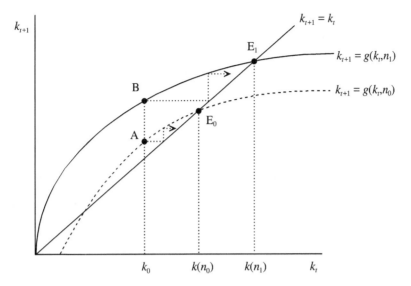

Figure 16.6: The effects of ageing

In a dynamically efficient economy (for which $r > n$ holds) there are two effects which operate in opposite directions. The first term in square brackets on the right-hand side of (16.107) represents the effect of fertility on the long-run interest rate. Since $dr/dn = r'(k)dk/dn > 0$, a fall in fertility raises long-run welfare on that account. The second term in square brackets on the right-hand side of (16.107) is the PAYG-yield effect. If fertility falls so does the rate of return on the PAYG contribution. Since the yield effect works in the opposite direction to the interest rate effect, the overall effect of a fertility change is ambiguous. If the PAYG contribution is very small ($T \approx 0$) and the economy is not close to the golden-rule point ($r \gg n$), then a drop in fertility raises long-run welfare.

Although our results are based on a highly stylized (and perhaps oversimplified) model, they nevertheless seem to bear some relationship to reality. Indeed, Auerbach and Kotlikoff (1987, ch. 11) simulate a highly detailed computable general equilibrium model for the US economy and find qualitatively very similar results: wages rise, the interest rate falls, and long-run welfare increases strongly (see their Table 11.3). In their model, households live for 75 years, labour supply is endogenous, productivity is age-dependent, households' retirement behaviour is endogenous, taxes are distorting, and demography is extremely detailed.

16.3   The tragedy of annuitization

In Chapter 15 we studied the microeconomic and macroeconomic effects of lifetime uncertainty in the context of a continuous-time model. One of the lessons from Yaari (1965) turned out to be the private desirability of annuitization. Intuitively, an individual who faces lifetime uncertainty and has no voluntary bequest motives wants to fully annuitize his wealth (if positive) or take out life-insured loans (if he wants to borrow funds). The availability of such insurance instruments leads to an expansion of the choice set available to the consumer and thus to an increase in utility.

In this section we investigate the private and social desirability of annuitization in the context of a simple Diamond-Samuelson model. As it turns out, opening up a perfect annuity market offering actuarially fair rates may lead to a decrease in the welfare level of future generations. Heijdra et al. (2014) label this "a tragedy of annuitization".

To keep things simple we structure the exposition on a simplified version of the model discussed in Heijdra et al. (2014). Expected lifetime utility of a young agent at time t is given by:

$$E_t \Lambda_t^Y = \ln C_t^Y + \frac{1-\pi}{1+\rho} \ln C_{t+1}^O, \tag{16.108}$$

where E_t is the expectations operator and π is the probability of dying after the first period. The felicity function is logarithmic implying a unitary intertemporal substitution elasticity. In the absence of annuity markets the agent faces the following budget identities:

$$C_t^Y + S_t = w_t + Z_t, \tag{16.109}$$
$$C_{t+1}^O = (1 + r_{t+1}) S_t, \tag{16.110}$$

where Z_t are transfers received from the government during youth. The consolidated lifetime budget constraint is obtained by eliminating S_t from (16.109)–(16.110):

$$w_t + Z_t = C_t^Y + \frac{C_{t+1}^O}{1 + r_{t+1}}. \tag{16.111}$$

The present value of consumption equals the sum of wage income plus lump-sum transfers.

The optimal choices made during youth are given by:

$$C_t^Y = \frac{1+\rho}{2+\rho-\pi} [w_t + Z_t], \tag{16.112}$$

$$\frac{C_{t+1}^O}{1 + r_{t+1}} = S_t = \frac{1-\pi}{2+\rho-\pi} [w_t + Z_t]. \tag{16.113}$$

Several things are worth noting. First, the individual consumes a constant fraction of income during its youth and saves the rest. Second, the optimal amount of savings is independent of the interest rate. This is a direct consequence of the fact that the felicity function is logarithmic and there is no second period non-asset income—see Intermezzo 6.1.

The link between saving by the young and the future capital intensity is still given by $(1+n)k_{t+1} = S_t$. Furthermore, factor prices are determined as in equations (16.15)–(16.16) above. To keep the model simple we assume a Cobb-Douglas production function, $y_t = Z_0 k_t^\alpha$. Finally, the assets of those who die after the first period of life are not wasted but are collected by the government and disbursed among the young. Hence the fact that there are *accidental bequests* explains why transfers to the young are positive in a world without annuitization opportunities:

$$\pi(1 + r_t) K_t = L_t Z_t. \tag{16.114}$$

At time t the old generation owns the interest-rate inclusive capital stock, $(1+r_t)K_t$. A fraction π of the old generation has died, however, so the left-hand side represents the total amount of accidental bequests.

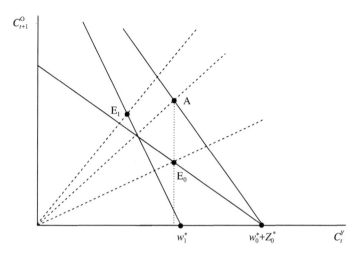

Figure 16.7: Impact and long-run effect of opening an annuity market

The fundamental difference equation for the capital intensity in the absence of longevity risk insurance and with transfers accruing to the young is given by:

$$(1+n)k_{t+1} = \frac{1-\pi}{2+\rho-\pi}\left[(1-\alpha(1-\pi))Z_0 k_t^{\alpha} + \pi(1-\delta)k_t\right]. \tag{16.115}$$

It is easy to show that this difference equation is stable and features a unique steady-state capital intensity, k_0^*. As a result the steady-state wage and interest rate are given by $w_0^* = (1-\alpha)Z_0(k_0^*)^{\alpha}$ and $r_0^* = \alpha Z_0(k_0^*)^{\alpha-1} - \delta$ whilst transfers amount to $Z_0^* = \pi(1+r_0^*)k_0^*$. In terms of Figure 16.7 the individual optimum is at point E_0 where there is a tangency between an indifference curve (not drawn to avoid cluttering the diagram) and the budget constraint.

Next we ask ourselves the following question. What happens if a *perfect* annuity market is opened up at time t, i.e. one offering actuarially fair annuities? Clearly the old at that time no longer save (and cannot borrow because there is no third period of life). So they have no need for annuities. The shock-time young, however, will fully annuitize. To see why this is so note that the actuarially fair annuity rate is:

$$1 + r_{t+1}^A = \frac{1+r_{t+1}}{1-\pi}, \tag{16.116}$$

from which it follows that $r_{t+1}^A > r_{t+1}$. Savings will attract a higher yield when fully annuitized.

The consolidated lifetime budget constraint for the young at time t is thus:

$$w_t + Z_t = C_t^Y + \frac{1-\pi}{1+r_{t+1}}C_{t+1}^O, \tag{16.117}$$

where it must be noted that they still get the accidental bequests *and* obtain a higher rate of interest on their assets. Optimal youth consumption C_t^Y and S_t are unaffected but old-age consumption changes to:

$$\frac{C_{t+1}^O}{1+r_{t+1}} = \frac{1}{2+\rho-\pi}\left[w_t + Z_t\right]. \tag{16.118}$$

In terms of Figure 16.7 the optimal consumption choice of a shock-time young individual moves from point E_0 to point A. At shock time the wage rate and transfers are both predetermined but the choice set is nevertheless expanded as the budget line rotates in a clockwise fashion. The shock-time young are clearly benefiting from the opening up of a perfect annuity market!

But now things start to unravel. Because the shock-time young fully annuitize they do not leave accidental bequests if they die after the first period as their assets accrue to the life-insurance companies in that unfortunate case. Hence the young from time $t+1$ onward no longer get bequests so the budget line starts to shift in, i.e. $Z_{t+\tau} = 0$ for $\tau = 1, 2, 3, \ldots$. But that is not all that happens over time. If the young no longer receive transfers then this will affect their savings plans and this will give rise to general equilibrium effects on the capital intensity causing factor prices to change.

Figure 16.8: Introducing a perfect annuity market

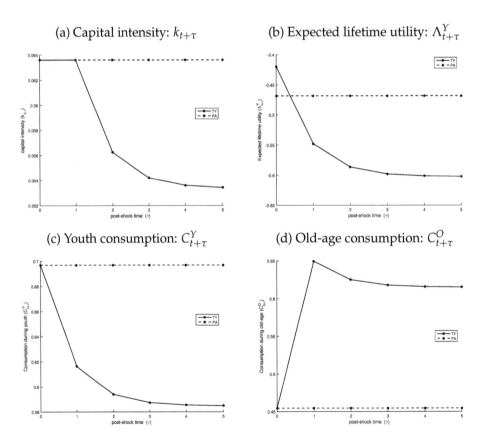

(a) Capital intensity: $k_{t+\tau}$

(b) Expected lifetime utility: $\Lambda_{t+\tau}^Y$

(c) Youth consumption: $C_{t+\tau}^Y$

(d) Old-age consumption: $C_{t+\tau}^O$

Notes: The Matlab program used to produce these figures, Program16_01.m, is available on the website www.heijdra.org/fomm3. Each period represents forty years. The parameters are $\pi = \alpha = 0.3$, $\delta = 0.9158$ (6% annual), $\rho = 4.1517$ (4.14% annual), $n = 0.4889$ (1% annual), and $Z_0 = 2.2854$. The pre-shock steady state features $y_0^* = 1$, $k_0^* = 0.0636$, and $r_0^* = 3.8010$ (4% annual).

The capital intensity evolves as follows. First, the shock-time young do not change their savings plans, so $k_{t+1} = k_0^*$. Second, the fundamental difference equation under annuitization for $\tau = 2, 3, \ldots$ is:

$$(1+n)k_{t+\tau} = \frac{1-\pi}{2+\rho-\pi}(1-\alpha)Z_0 k_{t+\tau-1}^\alpha. \tag{16.119}$$

The transitional effects of the introduction of a perfect annuity market have been illustrated in Figure 16.8. The capital intensity falls monotonically from $t+2$ onward to reach a permanently lower steady-state level after about five periods. Youth consumption falls from $t+1$ onward as this is the first young cohort confronted with the loss of transfers. Old-age consumption overshoots due to the old-age consumption binge of the shock-time young who—in a sense—get to have their cake (transfers via unintended bequests) and eat it (annuitize). The most interesting piece of information is found in Figure 16.8(b). In terms of expected lifetime utility, the shock-time old are unaffected, the shock-time young benefit, but all future young generations are worse off as a result of the annuitization opportunities. This is what Heijdra et al. (2014) call the *tragedy of annuitization*. The addition of a previously unavailable insurance market makes future generations worse off. The microeconomic choices made in the new steady state can be explained with the aid of Figure 16.7. There the new steady-state wage rate is w_1^* and the annuity rate of interest is $(1+r_1^*)/(1-\pi)$. The budget line is steeper than before the shock but the pre-shock optimal point E_0 is no longer feasible.

The intuition behind the tragedy of annuitization is straightforward. Private annuities recycle assets of unlucky (deceased) individuals to the lucky (surviving) members of their own cohort who just consume the extra resources. This is an intragenerational transfer. In contrast, unintended bequests that are channelled to the young via transfers amount to an intergeneral transfer from dissavers to savers. Note that the paradoxical result is obtained despite the fact that the economy is dynamically efficient (and $r_t > n$ holds throughout the transition).

16.4 Further applications of the DS model

16.4.1 Human capital accumulation

16.4.1.1 Human capital and growth

Following the early contributions by Arrow (1962) and Uzawa (1965), a number of authors have drawn attention to the importance of human capital accumulation for the theory of economic growth. The key papers that prompted the renewed interest in human capital in the 1980s are Paul Romer (1986) and Lucas (1988). In this subsection we show how the Diamond-Samuelson overlapping-generations model can be extended by including the purposeful accumulation of human capital by households. We show how this overlapping-generations version of the celebrated Lucas (1988) model can give rise to endogenous growth in the economy (see also Section 14.3 above).

As in the standard model, we continue to assume that households live for two periods, but we deviate from the standard model by assuming that the household works full-time during the second period of life and divides its time between working and training during youth. Following Lucas (1988) human capital is equated to the worker's level of skill at producing goods. We denote the human capital of worker i at time t by H_t^i and assume that producers can observe each worker's skill level and will thus pay a skill-dependent wage (just as in the continuous-time model discussed in Chapter 14 above).

The lifetime utility function of a young agent who is born at time t is given in general terms by:

$$\Lambda_t^{Y,i} \equiv \Lambda^Y \left(C_t^{Y,i}, C_{t+1}^{O,i} \right). \tag{16.120}$$

This expression incorporates the notion that the household does not value leisure and attaches no utility value to training *per se*. The household is thus only interested in improving its skills because it will improve its income later on in life. The budget identities facing the agent are:

$$C_t^{Y,i} + S_t^i = w_t H_t^i N_t^i, \tag{16.121}$$

$$C_{t+1}^{O,i} = (1 + r_{t+1}) S_t^i + w_{t+1} H_{t+1}^i, \tag{16.122}$$

where w_t denotes the going wage rate for an efficiency unit of labour at time t, and N_t^i is the amount of time spent working (rather than training) during youth. Since the agent has one unit of time available in each period we have by assumption that $N_{t+1}^i = 1$ (there is no third period of life so there is no point in training during the second period). The amount of training during youth is denoted by E_t^i and equals:

$$E_t^i = 1 - N_t^i \geq 0. \tag{16.123}$$

To complete the description of the young household's decision problem we must specify how training augments the agent's skills. As a first example of a *training technology* we consider the following specification:

$$H_{t+1}^i = G(E_t^i) H_t^i, \tag{16.124}$$

where $G' > 0 \geq G''$ and $G(0) = 1$. This specification captures the notion that there are positive but non-increasing returns to training in the production of human capital and that zero training means that the agent keeps his initial skill level. Just as in the Lucas (1988) model, the training function is linear in human capital.

The household chooses $C_t^{Y,i}$, $C_{t+1}^{O,i}$, S_t^i, N_t^i, and E_t^i in order to maximize lifetime utility $\Lambda_t^{Y,i}$ (given in (16.120)) subject to the constraints (16.121)–(16.123), and given the training technology (16.124), the expected path of wages w_t, and its own initial skill level H_t^i. The optimization problem can be solved in two steps. In the first step the household chooses its training level, E_t^i, in order to maximize its lifetime income, LI_t^i, i.e. the present value of wage income:

$$LI_t^i(E_t^i) \equiv H_t^i \cdot \left[w_t(1 - E_t^i) + \frac{w_{t+1} G(E_t^i)}{1 + r_{t+1}} \right]. \tag{16.125}$$

The first-order condition for this optimal human capital investment problem, taking account of the inequality constraint (16.123) explicitly, is:

$$\frac{dLI_t^i}{dE_t^i} = H_t^i \cdot \left[-w_t + \frac{w_{t+1} G'(E_t^i)}{1 + r_{t+1}} \right] \leq 0, \quad E_t^i \geq 0, \quad E_t^i \cdot \frac{dLI_t^i}{dE_t^i} = 0. \tag{16.126}$$

This expression shows that it may very well be in the best interest of the agent not to pursue any training at all during youth. Indeed, this no-training solution will hold if the first inequality in (16.126) is strict. Since there are non-increasing returns to training (so that $G'(0) \geq G'(E_t^i)$ for $E_t^i \geq 0$) we derive the following implication from (16.126):

$$G'(0) < \frac{w_t(1 + r_{t+1})}{w_{t+1}} \quad \Rightarrow \quad E_t^i = 0. \tag{16.127}$$

If the training technology is not very productive to start with ($G'(0)$ low), then the corner solution will be selected.

An internal solution with a strictly positive level of training is such that $dLI_t^i / dE_t^i = 0$. After some rewriting we obtain the investment equation in arbitrage format:

$$E_t^i > 0 \Rightarrow \quad r_{t+1} = \frac{w_{t+1}G'(E_t^i) - w_t}{w_t}. \tag{16.128}$$

This expression shows that in the interior optimum the agent accumulates physical and human capital such that their respective yields are equalized. By investing in physical capital during youth the agent receives a net yield of r_{t+1} during old age (left-hand side of (16.128)). By working a little less and training a little more during youth, the agent gives up w_t but upgrades his human capital and gains $w_{t+1}G'(E_t^i)$ during old age. Expressed in terms of the initial investment (foregone wages in the first period) we get the net yield on human capital (right-hand side of (16.128)).

In the second step of the optimization problem the household chooses consumption for the two periods and its level of savings in order to maximize lifetime utility (16.120) subject to its lifetime budget constraint:

$$C_t^{Y,i} + \frac{C_{t+1}^{O,i}}{1 + r_{t+1}} = LI_t^i, \tag{16.129}$$

where LI_t^i is now maximized lifetime income. The savings function which results from this stage of the optimization problem can be written in general form as:

$$S_t^i = S\left(r_{t+1}, (1 - E_t^i)w_t H_t^i, w_{t+1}H_{t+1}^i\right). \tag{16.130}$$

In order to complete the description of the decision problem of household i we must specify its initial level of human capital at birth, i.e. H_t^i in the training technology (16.124). Following Azariadis and Drazen (1990, p. 510) we assume that each household born in period t "inherits" (is born with) the average stock of currently available knowledge at that time, i.e. $H_t^i = H_t$ on the right-hand side of (16.124). From this final assumption it follows that all individuals in the model face the same interest rate and learning technology so that they will choose the same consumption, saving, and investment plans. We can thus drop the individual index i from here on and study the symmetric equilibrium.

We assume that there is no population growth and normalize the size of the young and old population cohorts to unity ($L_{t-1} = L_t = 1$). Total labour supply in efficiency units is defined as the sum of efficiency units supplied by the young and the old, i.e. $N_t = (1 - E_t)H_t + H_t$. For convenience we summarize the key expressions of the (simplified) Azariadis-Drazen model in Table 16.2.

Equation (T2.1) relates saving by the representative young household to next period's stock of physical capital. Note that the capital-labour ratio is defined in terms of efficiency units of labour, i.e. $k_t \equiv K_t / N_t$. With this definition, the expressions for the wage rate and the interest rate are, respectively (T2.2) and (T2.3). Equation (T2.4)

Table 16.2. Growth, human capital, and overlapping generations

$$N_{t+1}k_{t+1} = S(r_{t+1}, (1 - E_t)w_t H_t, w_{t+1}H_{t+1}) \tag{T2.1}$$

$$r_{t+1} + \delta = f'(k_{t+1}) \tag{T2.2}$$

$$w_t = f(k_t) - k_t f'(k_t) \tag{T2.3}$$

$$N_t = (2 - E_t)H_t \tag{T2.4}$$

$$1 + r_{t+1} = \frac{w_{t+1}}{w_t} G'(E_t) \tag{T2.5}$$

$$H_{t+1} = G(E_t)H_t, \tag{T2.6}$$

Notes: N_t is efficiency units of labour, k_t is the physical capital intensity in production, r_t is the interest rate, E_t is time spent on training, w_t is the wage rate, H_t is the stock of human capital, δ is the depreciation rate of physical capital, and $G(E_t)$ is the training function.

is labour supply in efficiency units, (T2.5) is the investment equation for human capital (assuming an internal solution), and (T2.6) is the accumulation for aggregate human capital in the symmetric equilibrium.

It is not difficult to show that the model allows for endogenous growth in the steady state. On the steady-state growth path the capital-labour ratio, the wage rate, the interest rate, and the proportion of time spent training during youth, are all constant over time (i.e. $k_t = k$, $w_t = w$, $r_t = r$, and $E_t = E$). The remaining variables grow at a common growth rate $\gamma \equiv G(E) - 1$, i.e. $\Delta H/H = \Delta K/K = \Delta N/N = \gamma$. Referring the reader for a general proof to Azariadis (1993, p. 231), we demonstrate the existence of a unique steady-state growth path for the unit-elastic model for which technology is Cobb-Douglas ($y_t = Z_0 k_t^\alpha$) and the utility function (16.120) is loglinear ($\Lambda_t^Y = \ln C_t^Y + (1/(1+\rho)) \ln C_{t+1}^O$). For the unit-elastic case the savings function can be written as:

$$S_t = \left[\frac{1}{2+\rho}(1 - E_t)w_t - \frac{1+\rho}{2+\rho}\frac{w_{t+1}G(E_t)}{1+r_{t+1}} \right] H_t. \tag{16.131}$$

By using (16.131), (T2.4), and (T2.6) in (T2.1) and imposing the steady state we get an implicit relationship between E and k for which savings equals investment:

$$(2+\rho)\frac{k}{w(k)} = \frac{1}{2-E}\left[\frac{1-E}{G(E)} - \frac{1+\rho}{1+r(k)} \right], \tag{16.132}$$

where $r(k) \equiv \alpha Z_0 k^{\alpha-1} - \delta$ and $w(k) \equiv (1-\alpha)Z_0 k^\alpha$. Similarly, by using (T2.2) and (T2.4) in the steady-state we get a second expression, again relating E and k, for which the rates of return on human and physical capital are equalized:

$$G'(E) = 1 + r(k). \tag{16.133}$$

The joint determination of E and k in the steady-state growth path is illustrated in the upper panel of Figure 16.9. The portfolio-balance (PB) line (16.133) is upward sloping because both the production technology and the training technology exhibit diminishing returns ($r'(k) = f''(k) < 0$ and $G''(E) < 0$). The savings-investment (SI) line (16.132) is downward sloping with a Cobb-Douglas technology. The right-hand side of (16.132) is downward sloping in both k and E. With Cobb-Douglas technology we have that $k/w(k) = k^{1-\alpha}/((1-\alpha)Z_0)$ which ensures that the left-hand side of (16.132) is increasing in k. Together these results imply that SI slopes down. In the upper panel the steady state is at E_0. In the bottom panel we relate the equilibrium growth rate to the level of training.

The *engine of growth* in the Azariadis-Drazen model is clearly the training technology (T2.6) which ensures that a given steady-state *level* of training allows for a steady-state *rate of growth* in the stock of human capital. Knowledge and technical skills are *disembodied*, i.e. they do not die with the individual agents but rather they are passed on in an automatic fashion to the newborns. The newborns can then add to the stock of knowledge by engaging in training. It should be clear that endogenous growth would disappear from the model if skills were *embodied* in the agents themselves. In that case young agents would have to start all over again and "re-invent the wheel" the moment they are born.

16.4.1.2 Human capital and education

Whilst it is undoubtedly true that informal social interactions can give rise to the transmission of knowledge and skills (as in the Azariadis-Drazen (1990) model) most developed countries have had formal educational systems for a number of centuries. A striking aspect of these systems is that they are compulsory, i.e. children up to a certain age are forced by law to undergo a certain period of basic training. This prompts the question why the adoption of compulsory education has been so widespread, even in countries which otherwise strongly value their citizens' right to choose.

Eckstein and Zilcha (1994) have recently provided an ingenious answer to this question which stresses the role of parents in the transmission of human capital to their offspring. They use an extended version of the Azariadis-Drazen model and show that compulsory education may well be welfare-enhancing to the children if the parents do not value the education of their offspring to a sufficient extent. The key insight of Eckstein and Zilcha (1994) is thus that there may exist a significant *intra-family* external effect which causes parents to underinvest in their children's human capital. Note that such an effect is not present in the Azariadis-Drazen model because in that model the agent *himself* bears the cost of training during youth and reaps the benefits during old age.

We now develop a simplified version of the Eckstein-Zilcha model to demonstrate their important underinvestment result. We assume that all agents are identical. The representative parent consumes goods during youth and old age (C_t^Y and C_{t+1}^O, respectively), enjoys leisure during youth (M_t), is retired during old age, and has $1+n$ children during the first period of life. Fertility is exogenous so that the number of children is exogenously given ($n \geq 0$). There are L_t young agents at time t. The lifetime utility function of the young agent at time t is given in general form as:

$$\Lambda_t^Y \equiv \Lambda^Y(C_t^Y, C_{t+1}^O, M_t, O_{t+1}), \tag{16.134}$$

where $O_{t+1} \equiv (1+n)H_{t+1}$ represents the total human capital of the agent's offspring. Since the agent has $1+n$ kids, each child gets H_{t+1} in human capital (knowledge) from its parent. There is no formal schooling system so the parent cannot purchase education services for its offspring in the market. Instead, the parent must spend (part of its) leisure time during youth to educate its children and the training

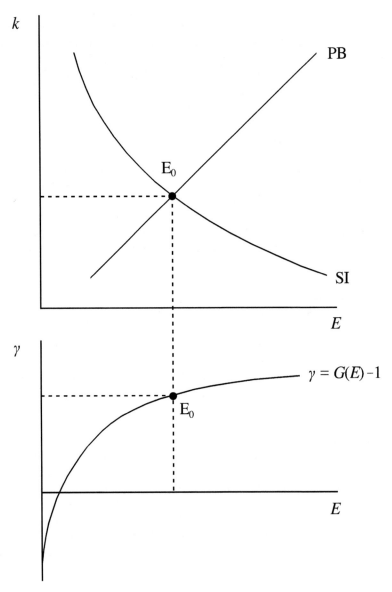

Figure 16.9: Endogenous growth due to human capital formation

function is given by:

$$H_{t+1} = G(E_t)H_t^\beta, \tag{16.135}$$

where E_t is the educational effort per child, $G(\cdot)$ is the training curve (satisfying $0 < G(0) \le 1$, $G(1) > 1$, and $G' > 0 \ge G''$), and $0 < \beta \le 1$. Equation (16.135) is similar in format to (T2.6) but its interpretation is different. In (T2.6) H_{t+1} and E_t are chosen by and affect the same agent. In contrast, in (16.135) the parent chooses H_{t+1} and E_t and the consequences of this choice are felt by both the parent and his/her offspring.

The agent has two units of time available during youth, one of which is supplied inelastically to the labour market (Eckstein and Zilcha, 1994, p. 343), and the other of which is spent on leisure and educational activities:

$$M_t + (1+n)E_t = 1. \tag{16.136}$$

The household's consolidated budget constraint is of a standard form:

$$C_t^Y + \frac{C_{t+1}^O}{1 + r_{t+1}} = w_t H_t, \tag{16.137}$$

where the left-hand side represents the present value of consumption and the right-hand side is labour income. Competitive firms hire capital, K_t, and efficiency units of labour, $N_t \equiv L_t H_t$, from the households, and the aggregate production function is $Y_t = F(K_t, N_t)$. The wage and interest rate then satisfy, respectively, $w_t = F_N(K_t, N_t)$ and $r_t + \delta = F_K(K_t, N_t)$.

The representative parent chooses C_t^Y, C_{t+1}^O, M_t, E_t, and H_{t+1} in order to maximize lifetime utility (16.134) subject to the training technology (16.135), the time constraint (16.136), and the consolidated budget constraint (16.137). By substituting the constraints into the objective function and optimizing with respect to the remaining choice variables (C_t^Y, C_{t+1}^O, and E_t) we obtain the following first-order conditions:

$$\frac{\partial \Lambda^Y / \partial C_t^Y}{\partial \Lambda^Y / \partial C_{t+1}^O} = 1 + r_{t+1} \tag{16.138}$$

$$\frac{\partial \Lambda^Y}{\partial O_t} G'(E_t) H_t^\beta - \frac{\partial \Lambda^Y}{\partial M_t} < 0 \quad \Longrightarrow \quad E_t = 0, \tag{16.139}$$

$$\frac{\partial \Lambda^Y}{\partial O_t} G'(E_t) H_t^\beta - \frac{\partial \Lambda^Y}{\partial M_t} = 0 \quad \Longleftarrow \quad E_t > 0. \tag{16.140}$$

Equation (16.138) is the standard consumption Euler equation, which we encountered time and again, and (16.139)–(16.140) characterizes the optimal educational activities of the parent. The left-hand side appearing in (16.139)–(16.140) represents the net marginal benefit of child education. If the (marginal) costs outweigh the benefits this term is negative and the parent chooses not to engage in educational activities at all (see (16.139)). Conversely, a strictly positive (interior) choice of E_t implies that the net marginal benefit of child education is zero. In the remainder we assume that conditions are such that $E_t > 0$ is chosen by the representative parent.

A notable feature of the parent's optimal child education rule (16.140) is that it only contains the costs and benefits as they accrue to the parent. But if a child receives a higher level of human capital from its parents, then it will have a higher labour income and will thus be richer and enjoy a higher level of welfare. By assumption, however, the parent only cares about the level of education it passes on to its children and therefore disregards any welfare effects that operate directly on its offspring. This is the first hint of the under-investment problem. Loosely put, by disregarding some of the positive welfare effects its own educational activities have on its children, the parent does not provide "enough" education.

As was explained above, in our discussion regarding pension reform, there are several ways in which we can tackle the efficiency issue of under-investment in a more formal manner. One way would be to look for Pareto-improving policy interventions. For example, in the present context one could investigate whether a system of financial transfers to parents could be devised which (a) would induce parents to raise their child-educational activities and (b) would make no present or future generation worse off and at least one strictly better off. If such a transfer system can be found we can conclude that the status quo is inefficient and that there is underinvestment.

An alternative approach, one which we pursue here, makes use of a social welfare function. Following Eckstein and Zilcha (1994, pp. 344–345) we postulate a specific form for the social welfare function (16.69) which is linear in the lifetime utilities of present and future agents:

$$SW_0 \equiv \sum_{t=0}^{\infty} \lambda_t \Lambda_t^Y = \sum_{t=0}^{\infty} \lambda_t \Lambda^Y (C_t^Y, C_{t+1}^O, M_t, O_{t+1}), \tag{16.141}$$

where SW_0 is social welfare in the planning period ($t = 0$), and $\{\lambda_t\}_{t=0}^{\infty}$ is a positive monotonically decreasing sequence of weights attached to the different generations, which satisfies $\sum_{t=0}^{\infty} \lambda_t < \infty$.[10] In the social optimum, the social planner chooses sequences for consumption ($\{C_t^Y\}_{t=0}^{\infty}$ and $\{C_{t+1}^O\}_{t=0}^{\infty}$), the stocks of human and physical capital ($\{K_{t+1}\}_{t=0}^{\infty}$ and $\{H_{t+1}\}_{t=0}^{\infty}$), and the educational effort ($\{E_t\}_{t=0}^{\infty}$) in order to maximize (16.141) subject to the training technology (16.135), the time constraint (16.136), and the following resource constraint:

$$C_t^Y + \frac{C_t^O}{1+n} + (1+n)k_{t+1} = F(k_t, H_t) + (1-\delta)k_t, \tag{16.142}$$

where $k_t \equiv K_t / L_t$ is capital per worker.

The Lagrangian associated with the social optimization problem is given by:

$$\mathcal{L}_0 \equiv \sum_{t=0}^{\infty} \lambda_t \Lambda^Y (C_t^Y, C_{t+1}^O, M_t, (1+n)H_{t+1})$$

$$+ \sum_{t=0}^{\infty} \mu_t^R \left[F(k_t, H_t) + (1-\delta)k_t - C_t^Y - \frac{C_t^O}{1+n} - (1+n)k_{t+1} \right]$$

$$+ \sum_{t=0}^{\infty} \mu_t^T [1 - M_t - (1+n)E_t] + \sum_{t=0}^{\infty} \mu_t^H \left[G(E_t) H_t^\beta - H_{t+1} \right], \tag{16.143}$$

where μ_t^R, μ_t^T, and μ_t^H are the Lagrange multipliers associated with, respectively, the resource constraint, the time constraint, and the training technology.

After some manipulation we find the following first-order conditions for the social optimum for $t = 0, ..., \infty$:

$$\frac{\partial \mathcal{L}_0}{\partial C_t^Y} = \lambda_t \frac{\partial \Lambda^Y}{\partial C_t^Y} - \mu_t^R = 0, \tag{16.144}$$

---

[10] An often used weighting scheme sets $\lambda_t \equiv (1+\lambda)^{-t}$ with $\lambda > 0$ representing the constant rate at which the social planner discounts lifetime utility of future generations. Obviously, for this scheme we find that $\sum_{t=0}^{\infty} \lambda_t = (1+\lambda)/\lambda$.

$$\frac{\partial \mathcal{L}_0}{\partial C^O_{t+1}} = \lambda_t \frac{\partial \Lambda^Y}{\partial C^O_{t+1}} - \frac{\mu^R_{t+1}}{1+n} = 0, \tag{16.145}$$

$$\frac{\partial \mathcal{L}_0}{\partial M_t} = \lambda_t \frac{\partial \Lambda^Y}{\partial M_t} - \mu^T_t = 0, \tag{16.146}$$

$$\frac{\partial \mathcal{L}_0}{\partial E_t} = -(1+n)\mu^T_t + \mu^H_t G'(E_t) H^\beta_t = 0, \tag{16.147}$$

$$\frac{\partial \mathcal{L}_0}{\partial H_{t+1}} = (1+n)\lambda_t \frac{\partial \Lambda^Y}{\partial O_t} + \mu^R_{t+1} F_N(k_{t+1}, H_{t+1})$$
$$- \mu^H_t + \beta \mu^H_{t+1} G(E_{t+1}) H^{\beta-1}_{t+1} = 0, \tag{16.148}$$

$$\frac{\partial \mathcal{L}_0}{\partial k_{t+1}} = -(1+n)\mu^R_t + \mu^R_{t+1} [F_K(k_{t+1}, H_{t+1}) + 1 - \delta] = 0. \tag{16.149}$$

By combining (16.144)–(16.145) and (16.149) we obtain the socially optimal consumption Euler equation:

$$(1+n)\frac{\mu^R_t}{\mu^R_{t+1}} = \frac{\partial \Lambda^Y(\hat{x}_t)/\partial C^Y_t}{\partial \Lambda^Y(\hat{x}_t)/\partial C^O_{t+1}} = F_K(\hat{k}_{t+1}, \hat{H}_{t+1}) + 1 - \delta \quad [\equiv 1 + \hat{r}_{t+1}], \tag{16.150}$$

where $x_t \equiv (C^Y_t, C^O_{t+1}, M_t, O_{t+1})$ and hats ("$\hat{\ }$") denote socially optimal values, e.g. $\hat{r}_{t+1}$ represents the socially optimal interest rate. Similarly, by using (16.144) for period $t+1$ and (16.145) we obtain an expression determining the socially optimal division of consumption between old and young agents living at the same time:

$$\frac{\lambda_{t+1}}{\lambda_t} = (1+n)\frac{\partial \Lambda^Y(\hat{x}_t)/\partial C^O_{t+1}}{\partial \Lambda^Y(\hat{x}_{t+1})/\partial C^Y_{t+1}}. \tag{16.151}$$

This expression shows that, by adopting a particular sequence of generational weights $\{\lambda_t\}_{t=0}^\infty$, the social planner in fact chooses the generational consumption profile between the young and the old (see Calvo and Obstfeld, 1988, p. 417).

Finally, by using (16.145)–(16.147), and (16.151) in (16.148) we can derive the following expression:

$$\frac{\partial \Lambda^Y(\hat{x}_t)}{\partial M_t} = G'(\hat{E}_t)\hat{H}^\beta_t \cdot \frac{\partial \Lambda^Y(\hat{x}_t)}{\partial O_t}$$
$$+ G'(\hat{E}_t)\hat{H}^\beta_t \cdot \frac{\partial \Lambda^Y(\hat{x}_t)}{\partial C^O_{t+1}} \cdot F_N(\hat{k}_{t+1}, \hat{H}_{t+1})$$
$$+ G'(\hat{E}_t)\hat{H}^\beta_t \cdot \frac{\beta(1+n)\hat{H}_{t+2}}{G'(\hat{E}_{t+1})\hat{H}^{1+\beta}_{t+1}} \cdot \frac{\partial \Lambda^Y(\hat{x}_t)/\partial C^O_{t+1}}{\partial \Lambda^Y(\hat{x}_{t+1})/\partial C^Y_{t+1}} \cdot \frac{\partial \Lambda^Y(\hat{x}_{t+1})}{\partial M_{t+1}}. \tag{16.152}$$

In the social optimum the marginal social cost of educational activities (left-hand side of (16.152)) should be equated to the marginal social benefits of these activities (right-hand side of (16.152)). The marginal social costs are just the value of leisure time of the parent, but the marginal social benefits consist of three terms. All three terms on the right-hand side of (16.152) (written on separate lines to facilitate interpretation) contain the expression $G'(\hat{E}_t)\hat{H}^\beta_t$, which represents the marginal product of time spent on educational activities in the production of human capital (see

(16.135)). The first line on the right-hand side of (16.152) is the "own" effect of educational activities on the parent's utility. This term also features in the first-order condition for the privately optimal (internal) child-education decision, namely (16.140). The second and third lines show the additional effects that the social planner takes into account in determining the optimal level of child education. The second line represents the effect of the parent's decision on the children's earnings: by endowing each child with more human capital they will have a higher skill level and will thus command a higher wage. The third line represents the impact of the parent's investment on the children's incentives to provide education for their own children (i.e. the parent's grandchildren).

Eckstein and Zilcha are able to prove that (a) the competitive allocation is suboptimal, and (b) that under certain reasonable assumptions regarding the lifetime utility function there is underinvestment of human capital. Intuitively, this result obtains because the parents ignore some of the benefits of educating their children (1994, pp. 345–346). To internalize the externality in the human capital investment process, the policy maker would need to construct a rule such that the parent's decision regarding educational activities would take account of the effect on the children's wages and education efforts. As Eckstein and Zilcha argue, it is not likely that such a complex rule can actually be instituted in the real world. For that reason, the institution of compulsory education, which is practicable, may well achieve a welfare improvement over the competitive allocation because it imposes a minimal level of educational activities on parents (1994, pp. 341, 346).

Intermezzo 16.3

Dynamic consistency of the social planner. There are some subtle issues that must be confronted when using a social welfare function like (16.141). If we are to attach any importance to the social planning exercise we must assume that either one of the following two situations holds:

Commitment the policy maker only performs the social planning exercise once and can credibly commit never to re-optimize. Economic policy is a one-shot event and no further restrictions on the generational weights are needed.

Consistency the policy maker can re-optimize at any time but the generational weights are such that the socially optimal plan is dynamically consistent, i.e. the mere evolution of time itself does not make the planner change his mind.

This intermezzo shows how dynamic consistency can be guaranteed in the absence of credible commitment. We study dynamic consistency in the context of the standard Diamond-Samuelson model. The social welfare function in the planning period 0 is given in general terms by:

$$SW_0 \equiv \lambda_{0,-1}\Lambda^Y(C^Y_{-1}, C^O_0) + \sum_{\tau=0}^{\infty} \lambda_{0,\tau}\Lambda^Y(C^Y_\tau, C^O_{\tau+1}), \qquad (a)$$

where $\lambda_{0,\tau}$ is the weight that the planner in time 0 attaches to the lifetime utility of the generation born in period τ (for $\tau = -1, 0, 1, 2, ...$). The social planner chooses sequences for consumption during youth and old age ($\{C_\tau^Y\}_{\tau=0}^\infty$ and $\{C_\tau^O\}_{\tau=0}^\infty$) and the capital stock ($\{k_{\tau+1}\}_{\tau=0}^\infty$) in order to maximize social welfare (a) subject to the resource constraint:

$$C_\tau^Y + \frac{C_\tau^O}{1+n} + (1+n)k_{\tau+1} = f(k_{\tau+1}) + (1-\delta)k_\tau, \tag{b}$$

and taking the initial capital stock, k_0, as given. Obviously, since the past cannot be undone, consumption during youth of the initially old generation (C_{-1}^Y) is also taken as given. After some straightforward computations we find the following first-order conditions characterizing the social optimum:

$$\frac{\partial \Lambda^Y(\hat{x}_\tau)/\partial C_\tau^Y}{\partial \Lambda^Y(\hat{x}_\tau)/\partial C_{\tau+1}^O} = f'(\hat{k}_{\tau+1}) + 1 - \delta, \tag{c}$$

$$\frac{\partial \Lambda^Y(\hat{x}_\tau)/\partial C_\tau^Y}{\partial \Lambda^Y(\hat{x}_{\tau-1})/\partial C_\tau^O} = \frac{(1+n)\lambda_{0,\tau-1}}{\lambda_{0,\tau}}, \quad \tau = 0,1,2,\dots. \tag{d}$$

where $x_\tau \equiv (C_\tau^Y, C_{\tau+1}^O)$ and hats denote socially optimal values.

Now consider a planner who performs the social planning exercise at some later planning period $t > 0$. The social welfare function in planning period t is:

$$SW_t \equiv \lambda_{t,t-1}\Lambda^Y(C_{t-1}^Y, C_t^O) + \sum_{\tau=t}^\infty \lambda_{t,\tau}\Lambda^Y(C_\tau^Y, C_{\tau+1}^O), \tag{e}$$

where $\lambda_{t,\tau}$ is the weight that the planner in time t attaches to the lifetime utility of the generation born in period τ (for $\tau = t-1, t, t+1, t+2, \dots$). The social planner chooses sequences for consumption during youth and old age ($\{C_\tau^Y\}_{\tau=t}^\infty$ and $\{C_\tau^O\}_{\tau=t}^\infty$) and the capital stock ($\{k_{\tau+1}\}_{\tau=t}^\infty$) in order to maximize social welfare (e) subject to the resource constraint (b). The (interesting) first-order conditions consist of (c) and:

$$\frac{\partial \Lambda^Y(\hat{x}_\tau)/\partial C_\tau^Y}{\partial \Lambda^Y(\hat{x}_{\tau-1})/\partial C_\tau^O} = \frac{(1+n)\lambda_{t,\tau-1}}{\lambda_{t,\tau}}, \quad \tau = t, t+1, t+2, \dots \tag{f}$$

The crucial thing to note is that conditions (d) and (f) overlap for the time interval $\tau = t, t+1, t+2, \dots$. The sequences $\{C_\tau^Y\}_{\tau=0}^{t-1}$, $\{C_\tau^O\}_{\tau=0}^{t-1}$, and $\{k_{\tau+1}\}_{\tau=0}^{t-1}$ are chosen by the planner at time 0 but taken as given ("water under the bridge") by the planner at time t. But the sequences $\{C_\tau^Y\}_{\tau=t}^\infty$, $\{C_\tau^O\}_{\tau=t}^\infty$, and $\{k_{\tau+1}\}_{\tau=t}^\infty$ are chosen by both planners. Unless the planner at time 0 can commit to his plan (and thus can stop any future planner from re-optimizing the then relevant social welfare function), the sequences chosen by the planners at time 0 and at time t will not necessarily be the same. If they are not the same we call the social plan dynamically inconsistent (see Chapter 9).

Following the insights of Strotz (1956), Burness (1976) has derived conditions on the admissible pattern of generational weights, $\lambda_{t,\tau}$, that ensure that the optimal social plan is dynamically consistent. Comparing (d) and (f) reveals that dynamic consistency requires the following condition to hold for any planning period t:

$$\frac{\lambda_{t,\tau-1}}{\lambda_{t,\tau}} = \frac{\lambda_{0,\tau-1}}{\lambda_{0,\tau}}, \quad \tau = t, t+1, t+2, \dots \tag{g}$$

Condition (g) means that $\lambda_{t,\tau}$ must be multiplicatively separable in time (τ) and the planning date (t), i.e. it must be possible to write $\lambda_{t,\tau} = g(t)\lambda_\tau$, where g is some function of t. A simple example of such a multiplicatively separable function is:

$$\lambda_{t,\tau} = \left(\frac{1}{1+\lambda}\right)^{\tau-t}, \tag{h}$$

where $\lambda > 0$ is the planner's constant discount rate. By using (h) we normalize the weight attached to the young in the planning period to unity ($\lambda_{t,t} = 1$). It follows necessarily, that in order to preserve dynamic consistency, there must be reverse discounting applied to the old generation in the planning period. Indeed, the dynamic consistency requirement (g) combined with (h) implies $\lambda_{t,\tau-1}/\lambda_{t,\tau} = 1+\lambda$ so that $\lambda_{t,t-1} = (1+\lambda)\lambda_{t,t} = 1+\lambda$. Calvo and Obstfeld (1988) apply this notion of reverse discounting in the context of the Blanchard-Yaari model of overlapping generations.

****

16.4.2 Public investment

At least since the seminal work by Arrow and Kurz (1970), macroeconomists have known that the stock of public infrastructure is an important factor determining the productive capacity of an economy. In this subsection we show how productive public capital can be introduced into the Diamond-Samuelson model. We show how the dynamic behaviour of the economy is affected if the government adopts a constant infrastructural investment policy. Finally, we study how the socially optimal capital stock can be determined. To keep things simple we assume that labour supply is exogenous, and that the government has access to lump-sum taxes. We base our discussion in part on Azariadis (1993, pp. 336–340).

Prototypical examples of government capital are objects like roads, bridges, airports, hospitals, etc., which all have the stock dimension. Just as with the private capital stock, the public capital stock is gradually built up by means of infrastructural investment and gradually wears down because depreciation takes place. Denoting the stock of government capital by G_t we have:

$$G_{t+1} - G_t = I_t^G - \delta_g G_t, \tag{16.153}$$

where I_t^G is infrastructural investment and $0 < \delta_g < 1$ is the depreciation rate of public capital. Assuming that the population grows at a constant rate (as implied by

(16.21)), the stock of public capital per worker evolves according to:

$$(1+n)g_{t+1} = i_t^G + (1-\delta_g)g_t, \tag{16.154}$$

where $g_t \equiv G_t/L_t$ and $i_t^G \equiv I_t/L_t$.

We assume that public capital enters the production function of the private sector, i.e. instead of (16.10) we have:

$$Y_t = F(K_t, L_t, g_t), \tag{16.155}$$

where we assume that $F(\cdot)$ is linearly homogeneous in the *private* production factors, K_t and L_t. This means that we can express output per worker ($y_t \equiv Y_t/L_t$) as follows:

$$y_t = f(k_t, g_t), \tag{16.156}$$

where $k_t \equiv K_t/L_t$ and $f(k_t, g_t) \equiv F(K_t/L_t, 1, g_t)$. We make the following set of assumptions regarding technology:

$$f_k \equiv \frac{\partial f}{\partial k_t} > 0, \quad f_g \equiv \frac{\partial f}{\partial g_t} > 0, \tag{P1}$$

$$f_{kk} \equiv \frac{\partial^2 f}{\partial k_t^2} < 0, \quad f_{gg} \equiv \frac{\partial^2 f}{\partial g_t^2} < 0, \tag{P2}$$

$$f(0, g_t) = f(k_t, 0) = 0, \tag{P3}$$

$$f_{kg} \equiv \frac{\partial^2 f}{\partial k_t \partial g_t} > 0, \tag{P4}$$

$$f_g - k f_{kg} > 0. \tag{P5}$$

Private and public capital both feature positive (property (P1)) but diminishing marginal productivity (property (P2)). Both types of capital are essential in production, i.e. output is zero if either input is zero (property (P3)). Finally, properties (P4)–(P5) ensure that public capital is complementary with both private capital and labour. This last implication can be seen by noting that perfectly competitive firms hire capital and labour according to the usual rental expressions $r_t + \delta_k = F_K(K_t, L_t, g_t)$ and $w_t = F_L(K_t, L_t, g_t)$. These can be expressed in the intensive (per-worker) form as:

$$r_t = r(k_t, g_t) \equiv f_k(k_t, g_t) - \delta_k, \tag{16.157}$$

$$w_t = w(k_t, g_t) \equiv f(k_t, g_t) - k_t f_k(k_t, g_t), \tag{16.158}$$

where $0 < \delta_k < 1$ is the depreciation rate of the private capital stock. We can deduce from properties (P1)–(P5) that $r_k \equiv \partial r/\partial k_t < 0$ and $w_k \equiv \partial w/\partial k_t > 0$ (as in the standard model) and $r_g \equiv \partial r/\partial g_t > 0$ and $w_g \equiv \partial w/\partial g_t > 0$ (public capital positively affects both the interest rate and the wage rate). To illustrate the key properties of the model we shall employ a simple Cobb-Douglas production function below of the form $Y_t = Z_0 K_t^\alpha L_t^{1-\alpha} g_t^\eta$, with $0 < \eta < 1 - \alpha < 1$. This function satisfies properties (P1)–(P5) and implies $w(k_t, g_t) = (1-\alpha)Z_0 k_t^\alpha g_t^\eta$ and $r(k_t, g_t) = \alpha Z_0 k_t^{\alpha-1} g_t^\eta - \delta_k$.

To keep things simple, we assume that the representative young agent has the following lifetime utility function:

$$\Lambda_t^Y = \ln C_t^Y + \frac{1}{1+\rho} \ln C_{t+1}^O. \tag{16.159}$$

The budget identities facing the household are:

$$C_t^Y + S_t = w_t - T_t^Y, \tag{16.160}$$

$$C_{t+1}^O = (1 + r_{t+1})S_t - T_{t+1}^O, \tag{16.161}$$

where T_t^Y and T_{t+1}^O are lump-sum taxes paid by the agent during youth and old age respectively. The consolidated budget constraint is:

$$\hat{w}_t \equiv w_t - T_t^Y - \frac{T_{t+1}^O}{1 + r_{t+1}} = C_t^Y + \frac{C_{t+1}^O}{1 + r_{t+1}}, \tag{16.162}$$

where $\hat{w}_t$ is after-tax non-interest lifetime income. The optimal household choices are $C_t^Y = c\hat{w}_t$ and $C_{t+1}^O/(1 + r_{t+1}) = (1 - c)\hat{w}_t$, where $c \equiv (1 + \rho)/(2 + \rho)$ is a constant. The savings function can then be written as follows:

$$S_t \equiv S(w_t, r_{t+1}, T_t^Y, T_{t+1}^O) = (1 - c)\left(w_t - T_t^Y\right) + \frac{cT_{t+1}^O}{1 + r_{t+1}}. \tag{16.163}$$

It follows that, ceteris paribus, lump-sum taxes during youth reduce private saving whilst taxes during old age increase saving. As before, private saving by the young is next period's stock of private capital, i.e. $L_t S_t = K_{t+1}$. In the intensive form we have:

$$S_t = (1 + n)k_{t+1}. \tag{16.164}$$

The government budget constraint is very simple and states that government infrastructural investment (I_t^G) is financed by tax receipts from the young and the old, i.e. $I_t^G = L_t T_t^Y + L_{t-1} T_t^O$ which can be written in per capita form as:

$$i_t^G = T_t^Y + \frac{T_t^O}{1 + n}. \tag{16.165}$$

We now have a complete description of the economy. The key expressions are the accumulation identity for the public capital stock (16.154), the government budget constraint (16.165), and the accumulation expression for private capital (16.164). The latter can be written in the following format by using (16.157), (16.158), and (16.163) in (16.164):

$$(1 + n)k_{t+1} = (1 - c)\left[w(k_t, g_t) - T_t^Y\right] + \frac{cT_{t+1}^O}{1 + r(k_{t+1}, g_{t+1})}. \tag{16.166}$$

Once a path for public investment *and* a particular financing method are chosen, (16.154) and (16.166) describe the dynamical evolution of, respectively, the public and private capital stocks. We derive the phase diagram for the case of Cobb-Douglas technology and a constant public investment policy (so that $i_t^G = i^G$ for all t) financed by taxes on only the young generations (so that $T_t^Y = i^G$ and $T_t^O = 0$ for all t). The consequences of alternative assumptions regarding financing are left as an exercise for the reader.

The phase diagram has been drawn in Figure 16.10. The GE line is the graphical representation of (16.154) for the constant public investment policy $i_t^G = i^G$, i.e. along the line we have $g_{t+1} = g_t$. The GE line is horizontal and defines a unique steady-state equilibrium value for the stock of public capital equal to $g = i^G/(n + \delta_g)$. The dynamic path for public capital is derived from the rewritten version of (16.154):

$$g_{t+1} - g_t = \frac{i^G - (n + \delta_g)g_t}{1 + n} = -\frac{n + \delta_g}{1 + n}[g_t - g], \tag{16.167}$$

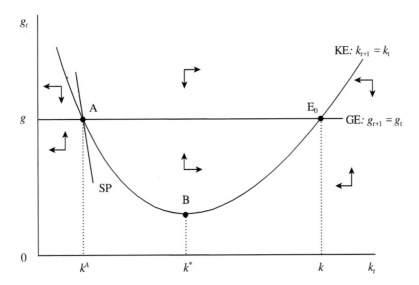

Figure 16.10: Public and private capital

from which we conclude that for points above (below) the GE line, $g_t > g$ ($< g$) and the public capital stock falls (rises) over time, $g_{t+1} < g_t$ ($> g_t$). This (stable) dynamic pattern has been illustrated with vertical arrows in Figure 16.10.

The KE line in Figure 16.10 is the graphical representation of (16.166), with the constant investment policy and the financing assumption both substituted in and imposing the steady state, $k_{t+1} = k_t$. For the Cobb-Douglas technology, the KE line has the following form:

$$g_t^\eta = \frac{(1+n)}{(1-\alpha)(1-c)Z_0}\left[k_t^{1-\alpha} + i^G \frac{1-c}{1+n}k_t^{-\alpha}\right], \tag{16.168}$$

from which we derive that $\lim_{k_t \to 0} g_t^\eta = \lim_{k_t \to \infty} g_t^\eta = \infty$ and that g_t reaches its minimum value along the KE curve at point B where $k_t = k^*$:

$$k^* \equiv i^G \frac{1-c}{1+n}\frac{\alpha}{1-\alpha}. \tag{16.169}$$

Hence, the KE line is as drawn in Figure 16.10. There are two steady-state equilibria (at A and E_0, respectively). The dynamic path of the private capital stock is obtained by rewriting (16.166) as:

$$k_{t+1} - k_t = \frac{1-c}{1+n}\left[(1-\alpha)Z_0 k_t^\alpha g_t^\eta - i^G\right] - k_t, \tag{16.170}$$

and noting that $\partial[k_{t+1} - k_t]/\partial g_t > 0$. Since the wage rate increases with public capital and future consumption is a normal good, private saving increases with g_t. Hence, the capital stock is increasing (decreasing) over time for points above (below) the KE line. These dynamic forces have been illustrated with horizontal arrows in Figure 16.10.

It follows from the configuration of arrows (and from a formal local stability analysis of the linearized model) that the low-private-capital equilibrium at A is a saddle point whereas the high-private-capital equilibrium at E_0 is a stable node. For the latter equilibrium it holds that, regardless of the initial stocks of private and public capital, provided the economy is close enough to E_0 it will automatically return to E_0.

What about the steady-state equilibrium at A? Is it stable or unstable? In the typical encounters that we have had throughout this book with two-dimensional saddle-point equilibria, we called such equilibria stable because there always was one predetermined and one non-predetermined variable. By letting the non-predetermined variable jump onto the saddle path, stability was ensured. For example, in Chapter 4 we studied Tobin's q theory of private investment and showed that K and q are, respectively, the predetermined and jumping variables. In the present application, however, both K and G are predetermined variables so neither can jump. Only if the initial stocks of private and public capital by pure coincidence happen to lie on the saddle path (SP in Figure 16.10), will the equilibrium at A eventually be reached given the constant investment policy employed by the government. Appealing to the Samuelsonian correspondence principle we focus attention in the remainder of this subsection on the truly stable equilibrium at E_0.

Now consider what happens if the government increases its public investment. It follows from, respectively (16.167) and (16.168), that both the GE and KE lines shift up. Clearly, the higher public investment level will lead to a higher long-run stock of public capital, i.e. $dg/di^G = 1/(n + \delta_g) > 0$. The long-run effect on the private capital stock is ambiguous and depends on the relative scarcity of public capital. By imposing the steady state in (16.170) and differentiating we obtain:

$$\left[1 - \frac{1-c}{1+n} w_k\right] \frac{dk}{di^G} = \frac{1-c}{1+n} \left[w_g \frac{dg}{di^G} - 1\right], \tag{16.171}$$

where the term in square brackets on the left-hand side is positive because the model is outright stable around the initial steady-state equilibrium E_0.[11] The first term in the square brackets on the right-hand side represents the positive effect of the investment increase on the pre-tax wage of the young households whilst the second term is the negative tax effect. Since $w_g = \eta w/g$, $w = (1-\alpha)y$, and $g = i^G/(n + \delta_g)$, it follows from (16.171) that the steady-state private capital stock rises (falls) as a result of the shock if $i^G/y < \eta(1-\alpha)$ $(> \eta(1-\alpha))$, i.e. if public capital is initially relatively scarce (abundant).

16.4.2.1   Modified golden rules

Now that we have established the macroeconomic effects of public capital, we can confront the equally important question regarding the socially optimal amount of public infrastructure. Just as in the previous subsection on education, we study this issue by computing the public investment plan that a social planner would choose. Following Calvo and Obstfeld (1988, p. 414) and Diamond (1973, p. 219) we assume

---

[11]Recall that for a constant level of public capital, the model is stable provided the following stability condition is satisfied around the initial steady state, E_0:

$$0 < \frac{\partial k_{t+1}}{\partial k_t} \equiv \frac{1-c}{1+n} w_k < 1.$$

that the social welfare function takes the following Benthamite form:[12]

$$SW_0 \equiv \left(\frac{1+n}{1+\rho_{sp}}\right)^{-1} \Lambda^Y(C_{-1}^Y, C_0^O) + \sum_{t=0}^{\infty} \left(\frac{1+n}{1+\rho_{sp}}\right)^t \Lambda^Y(C_t^Y, C_{t+1}^O), \quad (16.172)$$

where we assume that $\rho_{sp} > n$ to ensure that the infinite sum appearing on the right-hand side of (16.172) converges. Equation (16.172) is a special case of the expression used in Intermezzo 16.3 with the generational weight set equal to $\lambda_{0,t} \equiv [(1+n)/(1+\rho_{sp})]^t$. This means that the social planner discounts the lifetime utility of generations at a constant rate ρ_{sp} which may or may not be equal to the rate employed by the agents to discount their own periodic utility (namely ρ). The social planner chooses sequences for consumption for young and old agents ($\{C_t^Y\}_{t=0}^{\infty}$ and $\{C_t^O\}_{t=0}^{\infty}$), and the per capita stocks of public and private capital ($\{g_{t+1}\}_{t=0}^{\infty}$ and $\{k_{t+1}\}_{t=0}^{\infty}$), in order to maximize (16.172) subject to the following resource constraint:

$$C_t^Y + \frac{C_t^O}{1+n} + (1+n)[k_{t+1} + g_{t+1}] = f(k_t, g_t) + (1-\delta_k)k_t + (1-\delta_g)g_t, \quad (16.173)$$

and taking as given k_0 and g_0. The Lagrangian associated with the social optimization problem is given by:

$$\begin{aligned}
\mathcal{L}_0 &\equiv \left(\frac{1+n}{1+\rho_{sp}}\right)^{-1} \Lambda^Y(C_{-1}^Y, C_0^O) + \sum_{t=0}^{\infty} \left(\frac{1+n}{1+\rho_{sp}}\right)^t \Lambda^Y(C_t^Y, C_{t+1}^O) \\
&+ \sum_{t=0}^{\infty} \mu_t^R \Big[f(k_t, g_t) + (1-\delta_k)k_t + (1-\delta_g)g_t \\
&\quad - C_t^Y - \frac{C_t^O}{1+n} - (1+n)[k_{t+1} + g_{t+1}] \Big],
\end{aligned} \quad (16.174)$$

where μ_t^R is the Lagrange multiplier associated with the resource constraint.

After some manipulation we find the following first-order conditions for the social optimum for $t = 0, ..., \infty$:

$$\frac{\partial \mathcal{L}_0}{\partial C_t^Y} = \left(\frac{1+n}{1+\rho_{sp}}\right)^t \frac{\partial \Lambda^Y(x_t)}{\partial C_t^Y} - \mu_t^R = 0, \quad (16.175)$$

$$\frac{\partial \mathcal{L}_0}{\partial C_t^O} = \left(\frac{1+n}{1+\rho_{sp}}\right)^{t-1} \frac{\partial \Lambda^Y(x_{t-1})}{\partial C_t^O} - \frac{\mu_t^R}{1+n} = 0, \quad (16.176)$$

$$\frac{\partial \mathcal{L}_0}{\partial g_{t+1}} = -(1+n)\mu_t^R + \mu_{t+1}^R [f_g(k_{t+1}, g_{t+1}) + 1 - \delta_g] = 0, \quad (16.177)$$

$$\frac{\partial \mathcal{L}_0}{\partial k_{t+1}} = -(1+n)\mu_t^R + \mu_{t+1}^R [f_k(k_{t+1}, g_{t+1}) + 1 - \delta_k] = 0, \quad (16.178)$$

where $x_t \equiv (C_t^Y, C_{t+1}^O)$. By combining (16.175)–(16.178) to eliminate the Lagrange multipliers we find some intuitive expressions characterizing the social optimum:

$$\frac{\partial \Lambda^Y(\hat{x}_t)/\partial C_t^Y}{\partial \Lambda^Y(\hat{x}_t)/\partial C_{t+1}^O} = f_k(\hat{k}_{t+1}, \hat{g}_{t+1}) + 1 - \delta_k = f_g(\hat{k}_{t+1}, \hat{g}_{t+1}) + 1 - \delta_g, \quad (16.179)$$

---

[12]This name for the social welfare function derives from the classical economist Jeremy Bentham (1748–1832) who argued that "it is the greatest happiness of the greatest number that is the measure of right and wrong" (quoted by Harrison, 1987, p. 226). This explains why the rate of population growth enters (16.172).

$$\frac{\partial \Lambda^Y(\hat{x}_t)/\partial C_t^Y}{\partial \Lambda^Y(\hat{x}_{t-1})/\partial C_t^O} = 1 + \rho_{sp}, \tag{16.180}$$

where hatted variables once again denote socially optimal values. The first equality in (16.179) is the socially optimal consumption Euler equation calling for an equalization of, on the one hand, the marginal rate of substitution between present and future consumption and, on the other hand, the socially optimal gross interest factor, $1 + \hat{r}_{t+1}$, where $\hat{r}_{t+1} \equiv f_k(\hat{k}_{t+1}, \hat{g}_{t+1}) - \delta_k$. The second equality in (16.179) says that the socially optimal stock of public capital per worker should be such that the yields on private and public capital are equalized, i.e. $\hat{g}_{t+1}$ should be set in such a way that $\hat{r}_{t+1}^G = \hat{r}_{t+1}$, where $\hat{r}_{t+1}^G \equiv f_g(\hat{k}_{t+1}, \hat{g}_{t+1}) - \delta_g$. Finally, equation (16.180) determines the socially optimal *intra*temporal division of consumption. Its intuitive meaning, and especially the interplay between the agent's and the planner's discount rate, can best be understood by considering intertemporally separable preferences (which have been used throughout this chapter). By postulating $\Lambda_t^Y(x_t) \equiv U(C_t^Y) + (1+\rho)^{-1}U(C_{t+1}^O)$ we can rewrite (16.180) in terms of the agent's felicity function ($U(\cdot)$) and the pure rate of time preference (ρ):

$$\frac{U'(\hat{C}_t^Y)}{U'(\hat{C}_t^O)} = \frac{1 + \rho_{sp}}{1 + \rho}. \tag{16.181}$$

It follows from (16.181) that if the planner's discount rate exceeds (falls short of) the agent's rate of time preference, $\rho_{sp} > \rho \ (< \rho)$, then the social planner ensures that $U'(\hat{C}_t^Y)$ exceeds (falls short of) $U'(\hat{C}_t^O)$, and thus (since $U'' < 0$) that $\hat{C}_t^Y$ falls short of (exceeds) $\hat{C}_t^O$. If $\rho_{sp} = \rho$, the planner chooses the egalitarian solution ($\hat{C}_t^O = \hat{C}_t^Y$).

Intermezzo 16.4

Calvo-Obstfeld two-step procedure. Calvo and Obstfeld (1988) have shown that with intertemporally separable preferences, the social planning problem can be solved in two stages. In the first stage, the planner solves a static problem and in the second stage a dynamic problem is solved. Their procedure works as follows. Aggregate consumption at time τ, expressed per worker, is defined as:

$$C_\tau \equiv C_\tau^Y + \frac{1}{1+n}C_\tau^O. \tag{a}$$

With intertemporally separable preferences (and ignoring a constant like $U(C_{t-1}^Y)$) the social welfare function in period t can be rewritten as:

$$\begin{aligned}
SW_t &\equiv \frac{1 + \rho_{sp}}{(1+n)(1+\rho)} U\left(C_t^O\right) \\
&\quad + \sum_{\tau=t}^{\infty} \left(\frac{1+n}{1+\rho_{sp}}\right)^{\tau-t} \cdot \left(U\left(C_\tau^Y\right) + \frac{1}{1+\rho}U\left(C_{\tau+1}^O\right)\right) \\
&= \sum_{\tau=t}^{\infty} \left(\frac{1+n}{1+\rho_{sp}}\right)^{\tau-t} \cdot \left[U\left(C_\tau^Y\right) + \frac{1 + \rho_{sp}}{(1+n)(1+\rho)}U\left(C_\tau^O\right)\right],
\end{aligned} \tag{b}$$

where the term in square brackets in (b) now contains the weighted felicity levels of old and young agents living in the same time period. The special treatment of period-t felicity of the old is to preserve dynamic consistency (see the Intermezzo above). We can now demonstrate the two-step procedure.

In the first step, the social planner solves the static problem of dividing a given level of aggregate consumption, C_τ, over the generations that are alive at that time:

$$\bar{U}(C_\tau) \equiv \max_{\{C_\tau^Y, C_\tau^O\}} \left[U\left(C_\tau^Y\right) + \frac{1+\rho_{sp}}{(1+n)(1+\rho)} U\left(C_\tau^O\right) \right], \quad \text{s.t. (a), (c)}$$

where $\bar{U}(C_\tau)$ is the (indirect) social felicity function. The first-order condition associated with this optimization problem is:

$$\frac{U'(C_\tau^Y)}{U'(C_\tau^O)} = \frac{1+\rho_{sp}}{1+\rho}, \tag{d}$$

which is the same as (16.181). Furthermore, by differentiating (c) and using (a) and (d) we find the familiar envelope property:

$$\bar{U}'(C_\tau) \equiv \frac{d\bar{U}(C_\tau)}{dC_\tau} = U'(C_\tau^Y). \tag{e}$$

For the special case of logarithmic preferences, for example, individual felicity is $U(x) \equiv \ln x$ and the social felicity function would take the following form:

$$\bar{U}(C_\tau) = \ln \left[\frac{(1+n)(1+\rho)C_\tau}{(1+n)(1+\rho)+1+\rho_{sp}} \right]$$

$$+ \frac{1+\rho_{sp}}{(1+n)(1+\rho)} \ln \left[\frac{(1+n)(1+\rho_{sp})C_\tau}{(1+n)(1+\rho)+1+\rho_{sp}} \right]$$

$$\equiv \omega_0 + \frac{(1+n)(1+\rho)+1+\rho_{sp}}{(1+n)(1+\rho)} \ln C_\tau. \tag{f}$$

In the second step the social planner chooses sequences of aggregate consumption and the two types of capital in order to maximize social welfare:

$$SW_t = \sum_{\tau=t}^{\infty} \left(\frac{1+n}{1+\rho_{sp}} \right)^{\tau-t} \bar{U}(C_\tau), \tag{g}$$

subject to the initial conditions (k_t and g_t given) and the resource constraint:

$$C_\tau + (1+n)\left[k_{\tau+1} + g_{\tau+1}\right] = f(k_\tau, g_\tau) + (1-\delta_k)k_\tau + (1-\delta_g)g_\tau, \tag{h}$$

where we have used (a) in (16.173) to get (h). Letting μ_τ^R denote the Lagrange multiplier for the resource constraint in period τ we obtain the following first-order conditions:

$$\frac{(1+n)\mu_\tau^R}{\mu_{\tau+1}^R} = f_k(k_{t+1}, g_{t+1}) + 1 - \delta_k = f_g(k_{t+1}, g_{t+1}) + 1 - \delta_g, \tag{i}$$

$$\mu_\tau^R = \left(\frac{1+n}{1+\rho_{sp}}\right)^{\tau-t} \bar{U}'(C_\tau). \tag{j}$$

By using (j) for period $\tau+1$ and noting (d) and (e) we find that (i) coincides with (16.179).

****

We now return to the general first-order conditions (16.179)–(16.180) and study the steady state. In the steady state we have $C_t^Y = C^Y, C_t^O = C^O, k_t = k, g_t = g$, and $\hat{x}_t = \hat{x}$ for all t so that (16.179)–(16.180) simplify to:

$$\frac{\partial \Lambda^Y(\hat{x})/\partial C_t^Y}{\partial \Lambda^Y(\hat{x})/\partial C_t^O} = 1 + \rho_{sp}, \tag{16.182}$$

$$[\hat{r} \equiv] f_k(k,g) - \delta_k = \rho_{sp} = f_g(k,g) - \delta_g \, [\equiv \hat{r}_G]. \tag{16.183}$$

Equation (16.182) calls for an optimal division of consumption over the young and the old. The first equality in (16.183) is the *modified golden rule* (MGR) equating the steady-state yield on the private capital stock (the steady-state rate of interest) to the rate of time preference of the social planner. There is an important difference between this version of the MGR and the one encountered in Chapter 13 in the context of the Ramsey representative-agent model. In the OLG setting, the planner's rate of time preference features in the MGR whereas in the Ramsey model the representative agent's own rate of time preference is relevant (compare (16.183) with (13.28)).

The second equality in (16.183) is a modified golden rule for public capital that was initially derived by Pestieau (1974). It calls for an equalization of the public rate of return and the planner's rate of time preference. The two equalities in (16.183) together determine the optimal per worker stocks of public and private capital. For example, for Cobb-Douglas technology we have $y_t = Z_0 k_t^\alpha g_t^\eta$ (with $\eta < 1 - \alpha$) so that $k/y = \alpha/(\rho_{sp} + \delta_k), g/y = \eta/(\rho_{sp} + \delta_g)$. It follows from these results that output per worker is:

$$y = \left[Z_0 \left(\frac{k}{y}\right)^\alpha \left(\frac{g}{y}\right)^\eta\right]^{1/(1-\alpha-\eta)} = \left[Z_0 \left(\frac{\alpha}{\rho_{sp} + \delta_k}\right)^\alpha \left(\frac{\eta}{\rho_{sp} + \delta_g}\right)^\eta\right]^{1/(1-\alpha-\eta)} \tag{16.184}$$

Now that we have characterized the necessary conditions for the steady-state social optimum, a relevant question concerns the *decentralization* of this optimum. Can the policy maker devise a set of policy tools in such a way that the private sector choices concerning consumption and private capital accumulation coincide exactly with their respective values in the social optimum? The answer is affirmative provided the policy maker has access to the right kind of policy instruments. In the present context, for example, the first-best social optimum can be mimicked in the market place if (i) the level of public investment (and thus the public capital stock) is chosen to be consistent with (16.183), and (ii) there are age-specific lump-sum taxes available (see Pestieau, 1974 and Ihori, 1996, p. 114). The latter instrument is needed to ensure that the market replicates the socially optimal mix of consumption by the young and the old (cf. (16.182)).

16.4.3 Endogenous fertility

Up to this point in the book we have assumed that the rate of population growth is exogenous. This does not mean, of course, that economists have not proposed any theories endogenizing the growth rate of the population. Following the pioneering contributions by Becker (1960, 1991), Becker and Barro (1988), and Barro and Becker (1989), a huge literature has emerged on the economic theory of fertility. The objective of this subsection is to provide a brief introduction to this literature, focussing on those aspects most relevant to macroeconomics, namely the determination of the population growth rate and the failure of Ricardian equivalence. Our discussion is based on a simplified version of Lapan and Enders (1990).

At each moment in time there exists a large number of dynastic families. Members of each family live for two period, namely youth and adulthood. During youth, an agent makes no economic decisions, i.e. he is fully dependent on the parent. During adulthood, an agent (a) inherits wealth from its parent, (b) inelastically supplies a unit of labour and receives a wage income, (c) decides on consumption, (d) decides on the number of children, and (e) decides on the bequest to be granted to each child. As Barro and Becker (1989, p. 482) point out, this population structure simplifies matters substantially because it ignores the life-cycle aspects of individual behaviour. Each child is treated symmetrically and we ignore the integer constraint on the number of children. Procreation is sexless, i.e. "...[N]ot wishing to model the actual mechanics of the fertility process, we assume that each single individual, like an amoeba, can have children" (Lapan and Enders, 1990, p. 228). Children are born at the beginning of their parents' adult period.

16.4.3.1 Individual adults

At time t there are L_t adults, that can each be seen as the head of a dynasty. Lifetime utility, Λ_t^i, of adult i is given by:

$$\Lambda_t^i \equiv U(c_t^i, n_t^i) + \xi \Lambda_{t+1}^i, \qquad 0 < \xi < 1, \tag{16.185}$$

where ξ is the altruism parameter (see also Section 6.1.4 above), c_t^i is consumption by the adult, n_t^i is the number of children, and Λ_{t+1}^i is the (maximized) utility enjoyed by a representative child. The agent's budget constraint is given by:

$$(1 + r_t) a_t^i + w_t = c_t^i + tax_t^i + n_t^i \left[\bar{c} + a_{t+1}^i \right], \tag{16.186}$$

where r_t is the real interest rate, a_t^i is the bequest received at the beginning of adulthood, w_t is the wage rate, tax_t^i is the lump-sum tax, $\bar{c}$ is the cost of raising a child, and a_{t+1}^i is the bequest granted to each child at the end of life.

Provided bequests remain operative ($a_{t+\tau}^i > 0$, for all $\tau = 1, 2, \cdots$), all members of this dynasty are effectively linked to each other. As a result, the model can be solved "as if" the adult in period t is an infinitely lived agent. Indeed, by iterating (16.185) forward in time, we obtain an alternative expression for lifetime utility of the adult:

$$\Lambda_t^i \equiv \sum_{\tau=0}^{\infty} \xi^\tau U(c_{t+\tau}^i, n_{t+\tau}^i). \tag{16.187}$$

Dynastic utility is thus given by the infinite sum of felicities enjoyed by the current and all future adults, using the altruism parameter, ξ, for discounting. The adult in period t chooses paths for $c^i_{t+\tau}$, $n^i_{t+\tau}$, and $a^i_{t+\tau+1}$ (for $\tau = 0, 1, 2, \cdots$) in order to maximize (16.187) subject to a sequence of periodic budget constraints like (16.186), taking as given factor prices, taxes, and the initial bequest received, a^i_t. The Lagrangian for this problem is given by:

$$\mathcal{L}^i_t \equiv \sum_{\tau=0}^{\infty} \xi^\tau U(c^i_{t+\tau}, n^i_{t+\tau}) + \sum_{\tau=0}^{\infty} \xi^\tau \lambda^i_{t+\tau} \left[(1 + r_{t+\tau}) a^i_{t+\tau} + w_{t+\tau} \right.$$

$$\left. - c^i_{t+\tau} - tax^i_{t+\tau} - n^i_{t+\tau} \left[\bar{c} + a^i_{t+\tau+1} \right] \right], \tag{16.188}$$

where $\lambda^i_{t+\tau}$ is the Lagrange multiplier for the budget constraint in period $t + \tau$, in the optimum representing the marginal utility of wealth in that period. The first-order conditions for an interior solution are:

$$\frac{\partial \mathcal{L}_t}{\partial c^i_{t+\tau}} = 0: \quad U_c(c^i_{t+\tau}, n^i_{t+\tau}) = \lambda^i_{t+\tau}, \tag{16.189}$$

$$\frac{\partial \mathcal{L}_t}{\partial n^i_{t+\tau}} = 0: \quad U_n(c^i_{t+\tau}, n^i_{t+\tau}) = \lambda^i_{t+\tau} \left[\bar{c} + a^i_{t+\tau+1} \right], \tag{16.190}$$

$$\frac{\partial \mathcal{L}_t}{\partial a^i_{t+\tau+1}} = 0: \quad \xi \lambda^i_{t+\tau+1} (1 + r_{t+\tau+1}) = \lambda^i_{t+\tau} n^i_{t+\tau}, \tag{16.191}$$

$$\frac{\partial \mathcal{L}_t}{\partial \lambda^i_{t+\tau}} = 0: \quad (1 + r_{t+\tau}) a^i_{t+\tau} + w_t = c^i_{t+\tau} + tax^i_{t+\tau}$$

$$+ n^i_{t+\tau} \left[\bar{c} + a^i_{t+\tau+1} \right], \tag{16.192}$$

where U_c and U_n denote the marginal utility of, respectively, consumption and offspring. Equation (16.189) shows that in each period the marginal utility of consumption is equated to the marginal utility of wealth. Similarly, equation (16.190) shows that in each period the marginal utility of children is equated to the marginal utility cost of producing these children. The total pecuniary cost per child is given by the direct cost of raising it, $\bar{c}$, plus the bequest to be granted to each child, $a^i_{t+\tau+1}$. Equation (16.191) shows that the optimal bequest is set such that the marginal utility of making the bequest (left-hand side) is equal to its marginal cost (right-hand side), both from the perspective of the parent (the donor). Finally, equation (16.192) is simply the budget constraint for period $t + \tau$.

By using (16.189) in (16.191) and (16.190), respectively, we obtain:

$$\frac{U_c(c^i_{t+\tau+1}, n^i_{t+\tau+1})}{U_c(c^i_{t+\tau}, n^i_{t+\tau})} = \frac{n^i_{t+\tau}}{\xi [1 + r_{t+\tau+1}]}, \tag{16.193}$$

$$\frac{U_n(c^i_{t+\tau}, n^i_{t+\tau})}{U_c(c^i_{t+\tau}, n^i_{t+\tau})} = \bar{c} + a^i_{t+\tau+1}. \tag{16.194}$$

Equation (16.193) is dynamic and shows that the optimal profile of marginal utility of consumption in adjacent periods is dictated by a term involving the interest rate on productive assets, $r_{t+\tau+1}$, the biological interest rate (chosen by the agent), $n^i_{t+\tau}$, and the altruism parameter, ξ. Equation (16.194) is static, and shows that the marginal rate of substitution between children and consumption (left-hand side) is equated to the total cost per child (right-hand side).

Finally, we note that there are two financial assets in this (closed) economy, namely claims on the capital stock and government bonds. Since these assets are perfect substitutes they attract the same rate of return. Financial wealth of person i can thus be written as:

$$a_{t+\tau}^i = k_{t+\tau}^i + b_{t+\tau}^i, \tag{16.195}$$

where $k_{t+\tau}^i$ and $b_{t+\tau}^i$ denote, respectively, capital and bonds owned by person i at time $t + \tau$.

16.4.3.2 Aggregate behaviour

Since there are L_t adults in period t, the number of adults one period later will equal $L_{t+1} \equiv \sum_{i=1}^{L_t} n_t^i = \bar{n}_t L_t$, where $\bar{n}_t \equiv \sum_{i=1}^{L_t} n_t^i / L_t$ is the average number of children born in period t. Population growth between periods t and $t+1$ will thus be equal to $\Delta L_{t+1} / L_t = \bar{n}_t - 1$.

The government issues one-period debt which yields the same rate of interest as the physical capital stock. The government budget identity in aggregate terms in given by:

$$B_{t+1} = (1 + r_t) B_t + G_t - TAX_t, \tag{16.196}$$

where $B_t \equiv \sum_{i=1}^{L_t} b_t^i$ is the aggregate stock of debt at the beginning of period t, G_t is aggregate government consumption, and $TAX_t \equiv \sum_{i=1}^{L_t} tax_t^i$ is aggregate tax revenue. By dividing both sides of this expression by L_t, we obtain an expression for the evolution of government debt per adult:

$$\bar{n}_t b_{t+1} = (1 + r_t) b_t + g_t - tax_t, \tag{16.197}$$

where $b_t \equiv B_t / L_t$, $g_t \equiv G_t / L_t$, $tax_t \equiv TAX_t / L_t$, and we note that $L_{t+1} / L_t = \bar{n}_t$.

At time t the total capital stock available for production purposes is given by $K_t \equiv \sum_{i=1}^{L_t} k_t^i$, and there are L_t working-age (adult) persons. Output is given by $Y_t = F(K_t, L_t)$, where the production function has the usual features (see (16.10) above). With perfectly competitive producers, factor prices satisfy $w_t = F_L(K_t, L_t)$ and $r_t + \delta = F_K(K_t, L_t)$. In the intensive form, therefore, the expressions (16.14)–(16.16) are still valid:

$$y_t = f(k_t), \tag{16.198}$$
$$w_t = f(k_t) - k_t f'(k_t), \tag{16.199}$$
$$r_{t+1} + \delta = f'(k_{t+1}), \tag{16.200}$$

where $y_t \equiv Y_t / L_t$, $k_t \equiv K_t / L_t$, and $f(k_t) \equiv F(k_t, 1)$.

16.4.3.3 Ricardian equivalence revisited

Before analysing the general form of the model, we briefly revisit the issue of Ricardian equivalence. As was pointed out by Lapan and Enders (1990, p. 231), the Ricardian equivalence theorem is valid in a *very special case* of the model, namely one in which the following conditions are all satisfied:

(a) The chain of bequests is unbroken, i.e. $a_{t+\tau}^i > 0$ for all τ and i. This ensures that each dynasty is effectively infinitely lived.

(b) Fertility is not a choice variable but is exogenously given, i.e. $n_{t+\tau}^i = n_0$, where n_0 is exogenous (and assumed to be constant for notational convenience).

(c) The government does not engage in redistribution between dynasties, i.e. $tax_{t+\tau}^i$ $= tax_{t+\tau}$ for all i and τ, so that the government solvency condition implies (at the individual and per capita level) that:

$$b_t^i = b_t = \sum_{\tau=0}^{\infty} n_0^\tau R_{t-1,\tau} \left[tax_{t+\tau} - g_{t+\tau} \right], \qquad R_{t-1,\tau} \equiv \prod_{s=0}^{\tau} \frac{1}{1+r_{t+s}}, \quad (16.201)$$

where $R_{t-1,\tau}$ is a cumulative discount factor involving the market rate of interest. In the aggregate—per capita—form, government solvency requires the present value of primary surpluses to be equal to the pre-existing debt at time t. With a symmetric fiscal treatment of dynasties, per capita and individual debt coincide.

As a consequence of condition (b), equation (16.194) is no longer relevant. Individual behaviour is fully characterized by the following equations:

$$\frac{U_c(c_{t+\tau+1}^i, n_0)}{U_c(c_{t+\tau}^i, n_0)} = \frac{n_0}{\xi \left[1 + r_{t+\tau+1} \right]}, \quad (16.202)$$

$$(1+r_{t+\tau}) a_{t+\tau}^i + w_{t+\tau} = c_{t+\tau}^i + tax_{t+\tau} + n_0 \left[\bar{c} + a_{t+\tau+1}^i \right], \quad (16.203)$$

$$n_0 b_{t+\tau+1}^i = (1+r_{t+\tau}) b_{t+\tau}^i + g_{t+\tau} - tax_{t+\tau}, \quad (16.204)$$

where factor prices obey (16.199) and (16.200). These expressions are obtained from, respectively, (16.193), (16.192), and (16.197). By noting (16.195), however, equations (16.203)–(16.204) can be combined into a single expression:

$$(1+r_{t+\tau}) k_{t+\tau}^i + w_{t+\tau} = c_{t+\tau}^i + g_{t+\tau} + n_0 \left[\bar{c} + k_{t+\tau+1}^i \right]. \quad (16.205)$$

The particular time path of taxes is completely irrelevant to agent i. Of course, the time path of government consumption does affect real plans of the agent but that path is held constant in the Ricardian tax cut experiment.

With endogenous fertility condition (b) is not satisfied and consequently debt will no longer be neutral. In technical terms, behaviour at the individual level in period t is characterized by:

$$\frac{U_c(c_{t+1}^i, n_{t+1}^i)}{U_c(c_t^i, n_t^i)} = \frac{n_t^i}{\xi \left[1 + r_{t+1} \right]}, \quad (16.206)$$

$$\frac{U_n(c_t^i, n_t^i)}{U_c(c_t^i, n_t^i)} = \bar{c} + k_{t+1}^i + b_{t+1}, \quad (16.207)$$

$$(1+r_{t+\tau}) k_t^i + w_t = c_t^i + g_t + \left(n_t^i - \bar{n}_t \right) b_{t+1} + n_t^i \left[\bar{c} + k_{t+1}^i \right]. \quad (16.208)$$

The first two expressions are obtained in a straightforward way from, respectively (16.193)–(16.194) and (16.195). The third is obtained by substituting the per capita debt path (16.197) into the individual budget constraint (16.203) and noting (16.195) and (16.201). Future debt appears in two places in these first-order conditions. First, it features on the right-hand side of (16.207) and thus affects the relative price of children. Second, it appears on the right-hand side in the budget constraint (16.208). As Lapan and Enders (1990, p. 231–232) point out, there exists a kind of "fiscal external effect" in the sense that an increase in economy-wide average fertility, $\bar{n}_t$, reduces the tax burden of individual agents (who treat $\bar{n}_t$ parametrically). Free riding on child production by others thus explains that children will be underproduced (and fertility will be too low) in the presence of public debt.

16.4.3.4   Steady-state equilibrium

In the symmetric equilibrium we assume that all agents are alike to that we can dispense with the index i. In the steady state, we also have that $k_{t+1} = k_t = k$, $b_{t+1} = b_t = b$, $c_{t+1} = c_t = c$, and $n_{t+1} = n_t = n$. The macroeconomic steady-state equilibrium is thus described by the following set of equations:

$$n = \xi \left[1 + f'(k) - \delta \right], \tag{16.209}$$

$$\frac{U_n(c,n)}{U_c(c,n)} = \bar{c} + k + b, \tag{16.210}$$

$$f(k) + (1 - \delta) k = c + g + n \left[\bar{c} + k \right], \tag{16.211}$$

where we have used the fact that $f(k) = (r + \delta) k + w$ in (16.211). It is possible to derive the comparative static effects for n, k, and c with respect to $\bar{c}$, b, and ξ, using a homothetic utility function featuring a non-zero substitution elasticity, σ. Here we simplify matters, however, and visualize the comparative static effects in the unit-elastic version of the model, i.e. we assume that the production function is Cobb-Douglas, $y_t = Z_0 k_t^\alpha$ (with $0 < \alpha < 1$), and we postulate a loglinear felicity function, $U(c_t, n_t) = \varepsilon \ln c_t + (1 - \varepsilon) \ln n_t$ (with $0 < \varepsilon < 1$). The unit-elastic model is given by:

$$n = \xi \left[1 - \delta + \alpha Z_0 k^{\alpha-1} \right], \tag{16.212}$$

$$c = \frac{\varepsilon}{1 - \varepsilon} n \left[\bar{c} + k + b \right], \tag{16.213}$$

$$c = Z_0 k^\alpha + (1 - \delta) k - n \left[\bar{c} + k \right] - g. \tag{16.214}$$

Figure 16.11 depicts the steady-state equilibrium in (n, k)-space. In the figure, the EC line represents the efficiency condition (16.212). It is downward sloping and features a horizontal asymptote at $n_0 \equiv \xi (1 - \delta) > 0$. The upward sloping line labelled BC represents the budget constraint. It is obtained by substituting (16.213) into (16.214):

$$Z_0 k^\alpha + (1 - \delta) k = \frac{n}{1 - \varepsilon} \left[\bar{c} + k + \varepsilon b \right] + g. \tag{16.215}$$

For $k = 0$, n reaches its minimum value, $n_{MIN} \equiv - (1 - \varepsilon) g / (\bar{c} + \varepsilon b) < 0$ and $n = 0$ for $k = k_0$, where k_0 is implicitly defined by $g = Z_0 k_0^\alpha + (1 - \delta) k_0$. Finally, BC reaches a horizontal asymptote at $n_1 \equiv (1 - \varepsilon) (1 - \delta)$. Provided n_1 exceeds $n_0 (1 - \varepsilon > \xi)$, there is a unique equilibrium at point E_0, where BC and EC intersect, $k = k^*$, and $n = n^*$.

An increase in $\bar{c}$ or b rotates the BC line in a clockwise fashion around point A and shifts the equilibrium to point E_1. Hence, $dn/d\bar{c} < 0$, $dn/db < 0$, $dk/d\bar{c} > 0$, and $dk/db > 0$. These effects are intuitively obvious. An increase in the rearing cost per child reduces the demand for children. Similarly, an increase in debt results in a higher tax rate which leads to a reduction in fertility. An increase in (useless) government consumption leads to a downward shift in the BC curve and again shifts the equilibrium to point E_1, i.e. $dn/dg < 0$ and $dk/dg > 0$. The agent substitutes capital for kids because of the increased tax.

16.5   Punchlines

In this chapter we study the discrete-time overlapping-generations model that was developed by Diamond and Samuelson. Just as in the Blanchard-Yaari model (studied in the previous chapter), the demographic structure of the population plays a

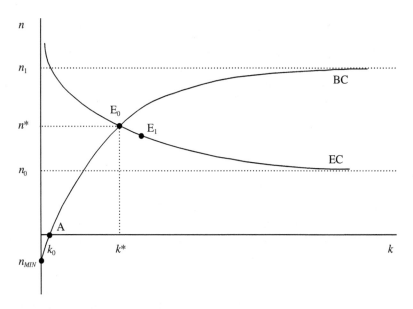

Figure 16.11: Steady-state fertility rate and capital intensity

central role in the Diamond-Samuelson model. One of the attractive features of the model is its ability to capture the life-cycle aspects of economic behaviour in an analytically tractable fashion. Because of its flexibility and simplicity, the model has played a central role during the last four decades in such diverse fields as macroeconomics, monetary theory, public finance, international economics, and environmental economics.

We start this chapter by formulating a simplified version of the Diamond-Samuelson model featuring time-separable preferences. In this model households live for two periods, called "youth" and "old age" respectively. They consume during both periods of life but they work only during youth, when they inelastically supply one unit of labour. Young households save part of their labour income in order to finance their consumption during old age (life-cycle saving). In the basic model there is no public debt and household saving takes the form of capital formation. This means that saving by the young in one period equals the capital stock available for production in the next period. Perfectly competitive firms use capital and labour to produce the homogeneous good. The model has a well-defined steady state provided the relevant stability condition is satisfied. There is a distinct possibility of oversaving occurring. Indeed, if the households are relatively patient, and thus have a low rate of time preference, they may well save too much for retirement and thus accumulate too much capital and render the steady state dynamically inefficient.

We next apply the basic model to study the macroeconomic and welfare effects of old-age pensions. Two prototypical pension systems are distinguished, namely the *fully funded* system and the *pay-as-you-go* (PAYG) system. In a fully funded system the government taxes the young, invests the tax receipts in the capital market, and returns principal plus interest to the old in the form of a pension in the next period. The fully funded system is neutral and does not affect consumption, capital, factor prices, or welfare. Intuitively, the household knows that its pension contributions during youth attract the same rate of return as its own private savings. The household therefore does not care that some of its saving is actually carried out on its behalf by the government.

Matters are different under a PAYG system. In such a system the taxes levied on the young are used to finance the pension payments to the old living in the same period. The yield that the household earns on its pension contributions is not the market rate of interest (as in the fully funded system) but rather the rate of population growth. The PAYG system is not neutral. Indeed, the introduction of such a system (or the expansion of an existing one) crowds out capital, lowers the wage rate, and increases the interest rate. Steady-state welfare decreases (increases) if the economy is dynamically efficient (inefficient), i.e. if the interest rate exceeds (falls short of) the rate of population growth. Intuitively, in a dynamically efficient (inefficient) economy, crowding out of capital reduces (increases) the welfare of the generations born in the new steady-state.

Two further aspects of the PAYG system are discussed. First, a PAYG system can be reinterpreted as a particular kind of debt policy. Second, in a dynamically efficient economy it is impossible to abolish a pre-existing PAYG system (in favour of a fully funded system) in a Pareto-improving fashion. Intuitively, it is not possible in the standard model to compensate the old generation at the time of the policy initiative without making at least one other (present or future) generation worse off. (Pareto-improving reform may be possible, however, if the reform reduces a pre-existing distortion in the economy. We consider the particular example where labour supply is endogenous and the pension contribution is distorting.)

The basic model can also be used to study the macroeconomic effects of population ageing. A useful measure to characterize the economic impact of demography is the dependency ratio, which is defined as the number of retired people divided by the working-age population. A reduction in the growth rate of the population leads to an increase in the dependency ratio. Under a PAYG system an anticipated reduction in fertility reduces expected pensions and lifetime income, and causes households to increase saving. As a result, the long-run capital-labour ratio rises.

Next we welcome the reader deeper into to the weird and wonderful world of overlapping generations economics by discussing the so-called tragedy of annuitization. To quote Weil (2008, p. 115): "...all is not well in the best of market economies: with overlapping generations, even absent the usual suspects such as distortions and market failures, a competitive equilibrium need not be Pareto efficient." In a world with uninsured longevity risk insurance people leave unintended bequests upon their death. If these bequests are recycled to the young (who will end up saving part of these extra resources), then opening up a perfect annuity market offering actuarially fair rates will benefit the shock-time young but may lead to a decrease in the welfare level of all future generations. This paradoxical result follows not from a pre-existing dynamic inefficiency but rather from the fact that annuities are intragenerational transfers between dissavers whilst unintended bequests are intergenerational transfers from dissavers to saver.

In the second half of the chapter we consider a number of further applications of the Diamond-Samuelson model. In the first extension we introduce human capital into the model and study the implications for economic growth. Young agents are born with the average stock of currently available knowledge and can spend time during youth engaged in training. Provided the training technology is sufficiently productive, the young choose to accumulate human capital. In the aggregate this mechanism provides the engine of growth for the economy.

Next we augment the human capital model by assuming that the parent must choose the level of training of its offspring. If the parent derives utility from the human capital of its offspring then it is quite possible that the parent will not devote the socially optimal amount of time on training its children. Intuitively, the underinvestment result follows from the fact that the parent fails to take into account all welfare effects (on its children and grandchildren) of its training efforts. In such a situation it may well be socially optimal to have a system of mandatory public education.

In the second extension we show how public infrastructure can be introduced into the overlapping generations model. We show how public investment affects the macroeconomy and derive simple modified-golden-rule expressions calling for an equalization of the rate of return on public and private capital and the social planner's rate of time preference.

Finally, in the third extension we show how the fertility decision of dynastic families can be endogenized. Ricardian equivalence does not hold in this model. There exists a fiscal external effect which enables each dynastic family to free-ride on child production by other families. As a result, from a societal point of view, fertility will be too low in the presence of public debt.

Further reading

A highly readable introduction to the literature on the Diamond-Samuelson model is Weil (2008). For very advanced surveys of the overlapping generations model, see Geanakoplos (2008b) and Geanakoplos and Polemarchakis (1991). Classic papers on pensions are Samuelson (1975a, 1975b) and Feldstein (1974, 1976, 1985, 1987). In recent years a large literature has been developed on the issue of pension system reform. See Diamond (1997, 1999), Feldstein (1997, 1998), and Sinn (2000). For surveys on the economic effects of ageing, see Bosworth and Burtless (1998) and Lee (2016).

The Diamond-Samuelson model has been generalized in a number of directions. Barro (1974) studies intergenerational linkages. Jones and Manuelli (1992) consider the growth effects of finite lives. Tirole (1985) and O'Connell and Zeldes (1988) consider the possibility of asset bubbles. Grandmont (1985) presents a model exhibiting endogenous business cycles. Michel and de la Croix (2000) study the model properties under both myopic foresight and perfect foresight. Bierwag et al. (1969) show that a full set of age-specific taxes renders debt policy redundant. Abel (1986) and Zilcha (1990, 1991) introduce uncertainty into the model. On intergenerational risk sharing, see Gordon and Varian (1988). Barro and Becker (1989) present a model of endogenous fertility. For applications of endogenous fertility models, see Wildasin (1990), Zhang (1995), Robinson and Srinivasan (1997), and Nerlove and Raut (1997). Galor (1992) and Nourry (2001) study a two-sector version of the Diamond-Samuelson model.

On endogenous fertility models, see Becker and Lewis (1973), Razin and Ben-Zion (1975), Eckstein and Wolpin (1985), Becker and Barro (1988), Barro and Becker (1989), Becker et al. (1990), Wildasin (1990), Lapan and Enders (1990), and Zhang (2003, 2006). There is also the survey by Nerlove and Raut (1997).

The Diamond-Samuelson model has been applied in a large number of fields. For public finance applications, see Auerbach (1979a), Kotlikoff and Summers (1979), and Ihori (1996). On the economics of education, see Loury (1981), Glomm and Ravikumar (1992), Zhang (1996), Buiter and Kletzer (1993), and Kaganovich and Zilcha (1999). Environmental policy applications include Howarth (1991, 1998), Howarth and Norgaard (1990, 1992), John and Pecchenino (1994), John et al. (1995), and Mourmouras (1993).

On accidental bequests, see Abel (1985), Kotlikoff and Summers (1981), Kotlikoff and Spivak (1981), Eckstein et al. (1985a, 1985b), and Sheshinski and Weiss (1981). On endogenous labour supply, see Reichlin (1986), Nourry (2001), Cazzavillan and

Pintus (2004), Nourry and Venditti (2006), and Nishimura and Venditti (2007). A general survey of the literature is de la Croix and Michel (2002) For the human capital and development literature, see the survey by Galor (2005) in the *Handbook of Economic Growth*. For adverse selection and the benefits of mandatory annuitization, see Heijdra and Reijnders (2012) and the references therein. On pensions and intergenerational risk sharing, see Gordon and Varian (1988), Bohn (2009), Demange (2002), Ball and Mankiw (2007), and Bovenberg and Uhlig (2008).

Part III

Stochastic general equilibrium macroeconomics

Chapter 17

Decision making in a stochastic environment

The purpose of this chapter is to achieve the following goals:

1. Explain the nature of sequential decision problems facing individuals or the social planner.

2. Introduce the method of dynamic programming and to illustrate this method using simple deterministic and stochastic toy models featuring either finite or infinite planning horizons.

3. Explain the concept of complete contingent-claim markets (Arrow-Debreu securities).

4. Explain how under complete markets it is possible to aggregate heterogeneous agents in such a way that it looks as if the economy is populated by the "representative consumer".

17.1 Introduction

Throughout the book we have studied how individuals and firms make decisions in a forward-looking fashion. For example, in the Ramsey-Cass-Koopmans (RCK) model individuals decide on current and future consumption and asset holdings, taking as given (a) the expected path of factor prices and government taxes and transfers, and (b) the initial stock of assets in their possession in the planning period. As time evolves the consumer continuously makes such dynamic decisions. Up to this point we have ignored stochastic shocks that may affect economic decision makers. The aim of this chapter is to study sequential decision making in a stochastic environment. In doing so we pave the way for the final two chapters of the book dealing, respectively, with real and monetary business cycle models. From here on attention is restricted to discrete-time models.

17.2 Dynamic programming in a deterministic world

In this section we introduce the method of dynamic programming in a deterministic setting. Rather than jumping in at the deep end attention is focused on a number of simple consumption-savings examples. Once these examples are well understood, the nontrivial step from a deterministic to a stochastic world (in the next section) becomes a lot easier.

17.2.1   Finite planning horizon

Consider an individual who lives for three periods and has the following lifetime utility function:

$$\Lambda_1 \equiv U(C_1) + \beta U(C_2) + \beta^2 U(C_3),$$ (17.1)

where C_t is consumption in period t, $\beta \equiv 1/(1+\rho)$ is the discount factor due to impatience (ρ is the rate of time preference, $\rho > 0$), and $U(x)$ is a felicity function satisfying $U'(x) > 0, U''(x) < 0$, and the usual Inada style condition $\lim_{x \to 0} U'(x) = +\infty$. To keep the discussion as simple as possible we assume that the felicity function is logarithmic:

$$U(C_t) = \ln C_t,$$ (17.2)

so that the intertemporal substitution elasticity is equal to unity.

Financial asset accumulation proceeds according to:

$$A_{t+1} = (1 + r_t)A_t + w_t - C_t,$$ (17.3)

where r_t and w_t denote, respectively, the interest rate and wage in period t, and A_t is assets at the start of period t. The consumer owns an initial stock of financial assets A_1 at time $t = 1$ (savings from the past). The agent chooses C_t and A_{t+1} for $t \in \{1,2,3\}$ taking as given (a) initial assets A_1 and (b) the paths of factor prices r_t and w_t. Since the world ends for this consumer at the end of period $t = 3$ there is a terminal constraint of the form:

$$A_{t+4} \geq 0.$$ (17.4)

17.2.1.1   Traditional solution method

The traditional approach solves the consumer's problem by postulating the Lagrangian:

$$
\begin{aligned}
\mathcal{L}_1 \equiv\ & U(C_1) + \beta U(C_2) + \beta^2 U(C_3) \\
& + \lambda_1 \left[(1+r_1)A_1 + w_1 - C_1 - A_2 \right] \\
& + \lambda_2 \left[(1+r_2)A_2 + w_2 - C_2 - A_3 \right] \\
& + \lambda_3 \left[(1+r_3)A_3 + w_3 - C_2 - A_4 \right],
\end{aligned}
$$

where λ_t is the Lagrange multiplier, and deriving the first-order necessary conditions for consumption:

$$\frac{\partial \mathcal{L}_1}{\partial C_1} = U'(C_1) - \lambda_1 = 0,$$ (17.5)

$$\frac{\partial \mathcal{L}_1}{\partial C_2} = \beta U'(C_2) - \lambda_2 = 0,$$ (17.6)

$$\frac{\partial \mathcal{L}_1}{\partial C_3} = \beta^2 U'(C_3) - \lambda_3 = 0,$$ (17.7)

and for assets:

$$\frac{\partial \mathcal{L}_1}{\partial A_2} = -\lambda_1 + (1 + r_2)\lambda_2 = 0, \tag{17.8}$$

$$\frac{\partial \mathcal{L}_1}{\partial A_3} = -\lambda_2 + (1 + r_3)\lambda_3 = 0, \tag{17.9}$$

$$\frac{\partial \mathcal{L}_1}{\partial A_4} = -\lambda_3 \leq 0, \qquad A_4 \geq 0, \qquad A_4 \frac{\partial \mathcal{L}_1}{\partial A_4} = 0, \tag{17.10}$$

where we must use the Kuhn-Tucker conditions for final assets—see also Section 6.1.4.

Since the Lagrange multipliers are strictly positive, $\lambda_t > 0$, we immediately find from (17.10) that the consumer will exhaust all his financial assets during the last period of life:

$$A_4^* = 0, \tag{17.11}$$

where the star designates the *optimum choice* for A_4. The consolidated lifetime budget constraint is thus given by:

$$(1 + r_1)A_1 + H_1 = C_1 + \frac{C_2}{1 + r_2} + \frac{C_3}{(1 + r_2)(1 + r_3)}, \tag{17.12}$$

where H_1 is human wealth:

$$H_1 \equiv w_1 + \frac{w_2}{1 + r_2} + \frac{w_3}{(1 + r_2)(1 + r_3)}. \tag{17.13}$$

The present value of lifetime consumption (right-hand side of (17.12)) is equal to the total amount of wealth that the consumer has at time $t = 1$ (left-hand side of (17.12)).

To derive the optimal consumption plans we first derive the consumption Euler equations by eliminating the Lagrange multipliers, i.e. by substituting (17.8)–(17.9) in (17.5)–(17.7):

$$U'(C_1^*) = \beta(1 + r_2)U'(C_2^*), \tag{17.14}$$
$$U'(C_2^*) = \beta(1 + r_3)U'(C_3^*). \tag{17.15}$$

For the logarithmic felicity function (17.2) these conditions simplify to $C_{t+1}^* = \beta(1 + r_{t+1})C_t^*$ (for $t \in \{1, 2\}$). By using these expressions in the lifetime budget constraint (17.12) we obtain the optimal consumption levels:

$$C_1^* = \frac{(1 + r_1)A_1 + H_1}{1 + \beta + \beta^2}, \tag{17.16}$$

$$\frac{C_2^*}{1 + r_2} = \beta \frac{(1 + r_1)A_1 + H_1}{1 + \beta + \beta^2}, \tag{17.17}$$

$$\frac{C_3^*}{(1 + r_2)(1 + r_3)} = \beta^2 \frac{(1 + r_1)A_1 + H_1}{1 + \beta + \beta^2}. \tag{17.18}$$

The optimal asset levels follow readily:

$$A_2^* = (1 + r_1)A_1 + w_1 - C_1^*, \tag{17.19}$$
$$A_3^* = (1 + r_2)A_2 + w_2 - C_2^*, \tag{17.20}$$

$$A_4^* = 0. \tag{17.21}$$

Of course these expressions are not very surprising. Indeed, as we have seen time and again throughout the book, for a logarithmic felicity function spending shares are constant which is exactly what (17.16)–(17.18) show.

For future reference we present some numerical results for a parameterized version of the three-period model in Table 17.1. The parameters are chosen as follows. We assume that each period is 25 years, and that the individual starts life without any financial assets, i.e. $A_1 = 0$. The wage rate and interest rate are both constant over time, i.e. $r_t = r$ and $w_t = w$. Output per worker is normalized to unity so that with a capital share of $\alpha = 0.3$ the wage rate is equal to $w = 0.7$. Under the assumption that the annual interest rate is 4 percent and the annual rate of time preference is 3 percent we find $r = 1.6658$ and $\beta = 0.4776$. Panel (a) of Table 17.1 shows that the consumer is a strong saver in the first two periods and a dissaver in the final period.

There is an alternative way of writing down the solutions which gives us a first glance at *policy functions*. Consider the consumer who has a in assets in period $t = 1$. What does he choose for current consumption and next period's assets? To answer this question there is no need to redo the optimization problem because we already know the solutions. Indeed, by substituting a for A_1 in (17.16) and (17.19) we find:

$$\hat{C}_1 = \mathbf{C}_1(a; r_1, r_2, r_2, w_1, w_2, w_3)$$

$$\equiv \frac{1}{1+\beta+\beta^2}\left[(1+r_1)a + w_1 + \frac{w_2}{1+r_2} + \frac{w_3}{(1+r_2)(1+r_3)}\right], \tag{17.22}$$

and:

$$\hat{A}_2 = (1+r_1)a + w_1 - \hat{C}_1$$

$$= \mathbf{A}_1^+(a; r_1, r_2, r_3, w_1, w_2, w_3)$$

$$\equiv \frac{\beta(1+\beta)}{1+\beta+\beta^2}\left[(1+r_1)a + w_1\right] - \frac{1}{1+\beta+\beta^2}\left[\frac{w_2}{1+r_2} + \frac{w_3}{(1+r_2)(1+r_3)}\right], \tag{17.23}$$

where the hats designate *conditionally optimal* choices. In words, the policy function $\mathbf{C}_1(a; \cdot)$ in (17.22) gives the choice for current consumption in period 1 (hence the subscript) if he has a in assets at the start of that period. Hence, if $a = A_1$ then it follows readily that $C_1^* = \mathbf{C}_1(A_1; \cdot)$. If $a < A_1$ the conditionally optimal solution is feasible but suboptimal and if $a > A_1$ the conditionally optimal solution is infeasible as the consumer does not possess that much in financial assets.

In a similar fashion, the policy function $\mathbf{A}_1^+(a; \cdot)$ in (17.23) represents the conditionally optimal choice that the agents makes in period 1 (hence the subscript) about the level of assets he want to carry over to the next period (hence the superscript '+'). It should now be obvious to the reader that $A_2^* = \mathbf{A}_1^+(a; \cdot)$ for $a = A_1$ only.[1]

Now consider the consumer with a in assets in period $t = 2$. What does he choose for C_2 and A_3? The answer is obtained by maximizing $\ln C_2 + \beta \ln C_3$ subject to:

$$(1+r_2)a + w_2 + \frac{w_3}{1+r_3} = C_2 + \frac{C_3}{1+r_3},$$

---

[1] The literature often uses a slightly different notation to indicate future values, e.g. if a denotes current assets then a' represents future assets—see for example Stokey and Lucas (1989, ch. 9) and Adda and Cooper (2003). Like Cai and Judd (2010) we prefer to use the plus superscript notation in which a^+ denotes future assets. We have used prime accents throughout the book to denote derivatives.

Table 17.1. Some numerical examples

(a) Deterministic choices:

Consumption:	C_1^*	0.6221
	C_2^*	0.7920
	C_3^*	1.0084
Assets:	A_2^*	0.0779
	A_3^*	0.1157
	A_4^*	0.0000

(b) Sequential stochastic choices:

Choices made in period 1:

Consumption:	C_1^*	0.6165
Assets:	A_2^*	0.0835

Choices made in period 2:

Consumption:	$C_2^*(e_1)$	0.6591
	$C_2^*(e_2)$	0.7982
	$C_2^*(e_3)$	0.9411
Assets:	$A_3^*(e_1)$	0.0884
	$A_3^*(e_2)$	0.1243
	$A_3^*(e_3)$	0.1564

Choices made in period 3:

Consumption:	$C_3^*(e_1, e_1)$	0.7607
	$C_3^*(e_1, e_2)$	0.9357
	$C_3^*(e_2, e_1)$	0.8564
	$C_3^*(e_2, e_2)$	1.0314
	$C_3^*(e_2, e_3)$	1.2064
	$C_3^*(e_3, e_2)$	1.1171
	$C_3^*(e_3, e_3)$	1.2921
Assets:	$A_4^*(e_i, e_j)$	0.0000

Notes: Initial financial assets are $A_1 = 0$, initial human wealth is $H_1 = 1.0611$, the wage rate is $w_t = w = 0.7$, the interest rate is $r_t = r = 1.6658$, and the discount factor is $\beta = 0.4776$. The Matlab program Program17_01.m is available from the website of the book, http://www.heijdra.org/fomm3. In the table $C_2^*(e_i)$ stands for optimal consumption in period 2 when $\eta_2 = e_i$. Similarly, $C_3^*(e_i, e_j)$ is consumption in period 3 when $(\eta_2, \eta_3) = (e_i, e_j)$. The Markov process for labour productivity is visualized in Figure 17.2. It features three states: $e_1 = 0.75$, $e_2 = 1.00$, and $e_3 = 1.25$.

which gives the policy functions:

$$\hat{C}_2 = \mathbf{C}_2(a; r_2, r_3, w_2, w_3)$$
$$\equiv \frac{1}{1+\beta} \left[(1+r_2)a + w_2 + \frac{w_3}{1+r_3} \right], \tag{17.24}$$

and:

$$\hat{A}_3 = (1+r_2)a + w_2 - \hat{C}_1$$
$$= \mathbf{A}_2^+ (a; r_2, r_3, w_2, w_3)$$
$$\equiv \frac{\beta}{1+\beta} \left[(1+r_2)a + w_2 \right] - \frac{1}{1+\beta} \frac{w_3}{1+r_3}. \tag{17.25}$$

Obviously, $\hat{C}_2 = C_2^*$ and $\hat{A}_3 = A_3^*$ if and only if $a = A_2^*$, i.e. $C_2^* = \mathbf{C}_2(A_2^*; \cdot)$ and $A_3^* = \mathbf{A}_2^+(A_2^*; \cdot)$.

Finally, consider the consumer who has a in assets in period $t = 3$. What does he choose for C_3 and A_4? The answer is obtained by maximizing $\ln C_3$ subject to $(1+r_3)A_3 + w_3 = C_3 + A_4$ and $A_4 \geq 0$. We easily find that:

$$\hat{C}_3 = \mathbf{C}_3(a; r_3, w_3) \equiv (1+r_3)a + w_3 \tag{17.26}$$
$$\hat{A}_4 = \mathbf{A}_3^+ (a; r_3, w_3) \equiv 0. \tag{17.27}$$

Just as before, $\hat{C}_3 = C_3^*$ if and only if $a = A_3^*$, i.e. so that $C_3^* = \mathbf{C}_3(A_3^*; \cdot)$. Unlike what we found before, however, $\hat{A}_4 = A_4^* = 0$ regardless of a, i.e. the consumer will always deplete resources completely in the final period of life.

The sceptical reader may feel that this way of looking at the consumer's decisions over time is unnecessarily complicated. Indeed, it is easy to find the optimal consumption and asset holdings in one go as we saw in the derivation of (17.16)–(17.21). And for this particular example the sceptical reader is absolutely right. For other, more complicated cases the "brute-force" direct method may, however, be unpractical or far too complex. One thing we note in our example is that the decision in the final period is rather simple. This simplicity of this sub-problem—deciding about C_3 and A_4 conditional on something—is what the method of dynamic programming exploits.

17.2.1.2   Dynamic programming

> PRINCIPLE OF OPTIMALITY. An optimal policy has the property that whatever the initial state and decision are, the remaining decisions must constitute an optimal policy with regard to the state resulting from the first decision. (Bellman, 1957, p. 83)

Intuitively, the method of dynamic programming solves a complex multi-stage problem by breaking it up into a number of smaller subproblems. In particular the method computes a number of value functions which depend on the state variable at each time. To demonstrate how Bellman's method works we return to the decision problem of the consumer who lives for three periods.

We start at the end of life and work back to the first period. The last decision is made at the start of period $t = 3$. As we already saw in the previous subsection, the consumer who has a in assets at the start of the period will choose $\hat{C}_3 = \mathbf{C}_3(a; r_3, w_3)$

and $\hat{A}_4 = A_3^+(a; r_3, w_3) \equiv 0$. By substituting the consumption choice into the felicity function we obtain the value function for period $t = 3$ in terms of a:

$$V_3(a) \equiv U(C_3(a; r_3, w_3)) = \ln\left[(1 + r_3)a + w_3\right]. \tag{17.28}$$

For future reference we note that this value function is differentiable and features the following derivative:

$$V_3'(a) = (1 + r_3)U'(C_3(a; r_3, w_3)) = \frac{1 + r_3}{C_3(a; r_3, w_3)}, \tag{17.29}$$

where we have used (17.26).

Now let us see what the individual decides in period $t = 2$. The objective is to maximize remaining lifetime utility, $V_2 \equiv U(C_2) + \beta U(C_3)$, subject to the budget constraint, $A_3 = (1 + r_2)A_2 + w_2 - C_2$. In period 2 the consumer decides on current consumption and the amount of assets to carry over into the third period, which we denote by c and a^+. But we know from the first step that the choice of a^+ will ensure that the value function in period 3 is equal to $V_3(a^+)$. Hence, the choice problem in period 2 can be stated as follows:

$$V_2(a) = \max_{c, a^+} \quad U(c) + \beta V_3(a^+)$$

$$\text{subject to:} \quad a^+ = (1 + r_2)a + w_2 - c. \tag{17.30}$$

Equation (17.30) is usually referred to as the *Bellman equation*, after its inventor. It is a recursive relationship relating value functions across time. In words, the value function in period 2 is equal to the felicity level given by the optimal consumption choice plus the discounted continuation value of the level of assets induced by that consumption choice. Since we know that $V_3(\cdot)$ is differentiable the maximization problem on the right-hand side of (17.30) is easily seen to feature the following first-order condition:

$$U'(c) = \beta V_3'((1 + r_2)a + w_2 - c). \tag{17.31}$$

This is an implicit relationship between c and a, the solution of which gives the policy function $C_2(a, r_2, w_2)$. The policy function for a^+ follows from the constraint, $A_2^+(a, r_2, w_2) = (1 + r_2)a + w_2 - C_2(a, r_2, w_2)$.

For the logarithmic felicity function (17.2) equation (17.31) simplifies to:

$$\frac{1}{c} = \frac{\beta(1 + r_3)}{(1 + r_3)[(1 + r_2)a + w_2 - c] + w_3}. \tag{17.32}$$

By solving for $c = C_2(a; \cdot)$ we find:

$$C_2(a; \cdot) \equiv \frac{1}{1 + \beta}\left[(1 + r_2)a + w_2 + \frac{w_3}{1 + r_3}\right], \tag{17.33}$$

and:

$$A_2^+(a; \cdot) = (1 + r_2)a + w_2 - C_2(a; \cdot)$$

$$= \frac{\beta}{1 + \beta}[(1 + r_2)a + w_2] - \frac{1}{1 + \beta}\frac{w_3}{1 + r_3}, \tag{17.34}$$

where we use the notational convenience to write $C_2(a; r_2, w_2, r_3, w_3)$ as $C_2(a; \cdot)$ and $A_2^+(a; r_2, w_2, r_3, w_3)$ as $A_2^+(a; \cdot)$. But once we know these policy functions, we also know the value function for period 2! Indeed, by substituting (17.33) and (17.34) into (17.30) we find:

$$V_2(a) \equiv U(\mathbf{C}_2(a; \cdot)) + \beta V_3(\mathbf{A}_2^+(a; \cdot)), \tag{17.35}$$

which simplifies for the logarithmic felicity function to:

$$V_2(a) = \ln\left(\frac{\beta^\beta}{(1+\beta)^{1+\beta}}\right) + \beta \ln(1+r_3) + (1+\beta) \ln\left[(1+r_2)a + w_2 + \frac{w_3}{1+r_3}\right]. \tag{17.36}$$

In equation (17.29) above we found that there is an intimate relationship between the derivative of the value function, $V_3'(a)$, and marginal utility, $U'(\mathbf{C}_3(a; \cdot))$. This is not a coincidental result. In fact it results from the envelope theorem and is often referred to as the Benveniste-Scheinkman theorem (after its inventors in a dynamic programming setting)—see Benveniste and Scheinkman (1979). To show the result for the second period we use (17.35) to find:

$$V_2'(a) \equiv U'(\mathbf{C}_2(a; \cdot)) \frac{d\mathbf{C}_2(a; \cdot)}{da} + \beta V_3'(\mathbf{A}_2^+(a; \cdot)) \left[(1+r_2) - \frac{d\mathbf{C}_2(a; \cdot)}{da}\right]$$

$$= \left[U'(\mathbf{C}_2(a; \cdot)) - \beta V_3'(\mathbf{A}_2^+(a; \cdot))\right] \frac{d\mathbf{C}_2(a; \cdot)}{da} + \beta(1+r_2) V_3'(\mathbf{A}_2^+(a; \cdot))$$

$$= (1+r_2) U'(\mathbf{C}_2(a; \cdot)), \tag{17.37}$$

where we have used the first-order condition (17.31) to simplify the expression.

In period $t = 1$ the choice problem can be stated as follows:

$$V_1(a) = \max_{c, a^+} \quad U(c) + \beta V_2(a^+)$$

$$\text{subject to:} \quad a^+ = (1+r_1)a + w_1 - c. \tag{17.38}$$

The first-order condition for the maximization problem is given by:

$$U'(c) = \beta V_2'((1+r_1)a + w_1 - c), \tag{17.39}$$

which simplifies for the logarithmic felicity function to:

$$\frac{1}{c} = \frac{\beta(1+\beta)}{(1+r_1)a + w_1 + \frac{w_2}{1+r_2} + \frac{w_3}{(1+r_2)(1+r_3)}}, \tag{17.40}$$

where we have used (17.36) to compute $V_2'(a^+)$. By solving (17.40) for $c = \mathbf{C}_2(a, r_2, w_2)$ we find:

$$\mathbf{C}_1(a; \cdot) \equiv \frac{1}{1+\beta+\beta^2}\left[(1+r_1)a + w_1 + \frac{w_2}{1+r_2} + \frac{w_3}{(1+r_2)(1+r_3)}\right], \tag{17.41}$$

and:

$$\mathbf{A}_1^+(a; \cdot) = (1+r_1)a + w_1 - \mathbf{C}_1(a, \cdot)$$

$$= \frac{\beta(1+\beta)}{1+\beta+\beta^2}[(1+r_1)a + w_1] - \frac{1}{1+\beta+\beta^2}\left[\frac{w_2}{1+r_2} + \frac{w_3}{(1+r_2)(1+r_3)}\right], \tag{17.42}$$

where the dot in $\mathbf{C}_1(a;\cdot)$ and $\mathbf{A}_1^+(a;\cdot)$ is short-hand for the entire sequence of interest rates and wages $(r_1, r_2, r_3, w_1, w_2, w_3)$. By substituting the policy functions into the first-period Bellman equation (17.38) we obtain:

$$V_1(a) = U(\mathbf{C}_1(a;\cdot)) + \beta V_2(\mathbf{A}_1^+(a;\cdot)), \tag{17.43}$$

which simplifies for the logarithmic felicity function to:

$$V_1(a) = -(1+\beta+\beta^2)\ln(1+\beta+\beta^2) + \beta(1+2\beta)\ln\beta$$
$$+ (1+\beta(1+\beta))\ln\left[(1+r_1)a + w_1 + \frac{w_2}{1+r_2} + \frac{w_3}{(1+r_2)(1+r_3)}\right]$$
$$+ \beta(1+\beta)\ln(1+r_2) + \beta^2\ln(1+r_3). \tag{17.44}$$

Before delivering the *coup de grace* it may be useful to summarize what we have achieved up to this point. We have computed the policy functions for consumption, $\mathbf{C}_t(a;\cdot)$, for future assets, $\mathbf{A}_t^+(a;\cdot)$, and the value functions, $V_t(a)$, all in terms of a. In words, the expression for the value function in the initial period, $V_1(a)$, states the lifetime utility level that the individual attains if he has financial assets a in the first period. Since we in fact assume that the agent has A_1 in assets, we thus find the actual level of lifetime utility by substituting $a = A_1$ into equation (17.44). Note that $V_1(A_1)$ is the maximum attainable utility level, i.e. it is based on optimal plans during life. But once we know the "initial condition" for this individual —namely that $a = A_1$ in the first period—we also know that optimal consumption in the first period will be $C_1^* = \mathbf{C}_1(A_1;\cdot)$, whilst optimal assets at the start of the second period will be $A_2^* = \mathbf{A}_1^+(A_1;\cdot)$. Obviously, in the second period we find that $C_2^* = \mathbf{C}_2(A_2^*;\cdot)$ and $A_3^* = \mathbf{A}_2^+(A_2^*;\cdot)$, whilst in the third period we find $C_3^* = \mathbf{C}_3(A_3^*;\cdot)$ and $A_4^* = \mathbf{A}_3^+(A_3^*;\cdot) = 0$.

For convenience we visualize the value functions $V_t(a)$ as well as the policy functions for consumption $\mathbf{C}_t(a)$ and next-period's financial assets $\mathbf{A}_t^+(a)$ in Figure 17.1. As is to be expected the value functions are increasing in the asset level a. Note that $V_1(0)$ represents the lifetime utility level attained by the consumer as the initial condition is such that $a = A_1 = 0$. The optimal consumption choice in period 1 is on the solid policy function in panel (b) for the point where $a = 0$, i.e. $C_1^* = \mathbf{C}_1(0)$. In a similar fashion we find $A_2^* = \mathbf{A}_1^+(0)$ which lies on the solid policy function in panel (c). By setting $a = A_2^*$ in the policy functions $\mathbf{C}_2(a)$ and $\mathbf{A}_1^+(0)$ we find C_2^* and A_3^*. These points are located on the dashed policy functions in panels (b) and (c).

Schematically the method of dynamic programming in a T-period finite horizon setting thus proceeds as follows:

- Compute the value function for the final period, $V_T(a)$, as well as the policy functions, $\mathbf{C}_T(a)$ and $\mathbf{A}_T^+(a)$.

- Use the Bellman equation to compute $V_{T-1}(a)$ and the policy functions $\mathbf{C}_{T-1}(a)$ and $\mathbf{A}_{T-1}^+(a)$. Continue this step until $V_1(a)$, $\mathbf{C}_1(a)$ and $\mathbf{A}_1^+(a)$ are obtained.

- Impose the initial condition, $a = A_1$ and iterate forward in time to compute the optimal choices, $C_1^* = \mathbf{C}_1(A_1)$, $A_2^* = \mathbf{A}_1^+(A_1)$, $C_2^* = \mathbf{C}_2(A_2^*)$, $A_3^* = \mathbf{A}_2^+(A_2^*)$, $\ldots$, $C_T^* = \mathbf{C}_T(A_T^*)$, $A_{T+1}^* = \mathbf{A}_T^+(A_T^*) = 0$.

17.2.2 Infinite planning horizon

As we have seen throughout the book, a large part of modern macroeconomics is based on the notion of an infinitely-lived representative consumer. How can we use

Figure 17.1: Value functions and policy functions: Deterministic case

(a) Value functions: $V_t(a)$

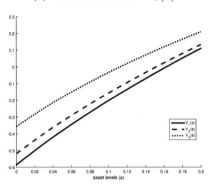

(b) Policy function for consumption: $\mathbf{C}_t(a)$

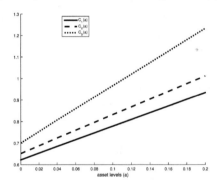

(c) Policy function for next period's assets: $\mathbf{A}_t^+(a)$

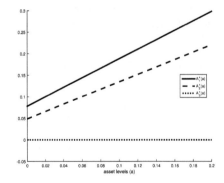

the method of dynamic programming when there is no finite horizon, and there is no final-period value function that can be computed? Just as in the previous section we demonstrate the dynamic programming method by using a simple consumption savings example. This example is also discussed in a slightly different form by Sargent (1987a, p. 22).

The infinitely-lived consumer has a lifetime utility of the form:

$$\Lambda_1 \equiv \sum_{t=1}^{\infty} \beta^{t-1} U(C_t),$$
(17.45)

where the felicity function is given in (17.2) above. Financial assets accumulate according to:

$$A_{t+1} = (1 + r_t) A_t + w_t - C_t,$$
(17.46)

where A_t denotes assets at the start of period t. By defining the primary surplus $S_t \equiv w_t - C_t$ and iterating the asset accumulation equation for T period we find:

$$\frac{A_T}{(1 + r_2) \cdots (1 + r_{T-1})} = (1 + r_1) A_1 + S_1 + \frac{S_2}{1 + r_2} + \cdots + \frac{S_{T-1}}{(1 + r_2) \cdots (1 + r_{T-1})}.$$
(17.47)

By imposing the solvency condition,

$$\lim_{T \to \infty} \frac{A_T}{(1 + r_2) \cdots (1 + r_{T-1})} = 0,$$
(17.48)

we obtain the lifetime budget constraint for the infinitely-lived consumer:

$$\sum_{t=1}^{\infty} R_{0,t-1} C_t = (1 + r_1) A_1 + \sum_{t=1}^{\infty} R_{0,t-1} w_t,$$
(17.49)

where $R_{0,t-1}$ is a cumulative discount factor:

$$R_{0,t-1} \equiv \begin{cases} 1 & \text{for } t = 1 \\ \prod_{s=1}^{t-1} \frac{1}{1 + r_{s+1}} & \text{for } t = 2, 3, \ldots. \end{cases}$$
(17.50)

Rather than going through the straightforward but tedious Lagrangian approach we use the method of dynamic programming right from the start to solve this problem. Obviously, since there is no final period, we cannot start by computing $V_T(a)$. Instead we postulate the Bellman equation for period t as:

$$V_t(a) = \max_{c, a^+} U(c) + \beta V_{t+1}(a^+)$$

$$\text{subject to:} \quad a^+ = (1 + r_t) a + w_t - c.$$
(17.51)

The first-order condition for c is:

$$U'(c) = \beta V'_{t+1}((1 + r_t) a + w_t - c).$$
(17.52)

In principle we could solve (17.52) for $c = C_t(a)$, $A_t^+(a) = (1 + r_t) a + w_t - C_t(a)$, and find:

$$V_t(a) = U(C_t(a)) + \beta V_{t+1}(A_t^+(a)).$$
(17.53)

But we do not know the functional form of $V'_{t+1}(a^+)$ so this seems to be a dead end. Recall, however, that the Benveniste-Scheinkman theorem furnishes a link between the derivative of the value function and marginal utility. Indeed, by differentiating (17.53) with respect to a we find:

$$
\begin{aligned}
V'_t(a) &= U'(\mathbf{C}_t(a))\frac{d\mathbf{C}_t(a)}{da} + \beta V'_{t+1}(\mathbf{A}^+_t(a))\left[(1+r_t) - \frac{d\mathbf{C}_t(a)}{da}\right] \\
&= \left[U'(\mathbf{C}_t(a)) - \beta V'_{t+1}(\mathbf{A}^+_t(a))\right]\frac{d\mathbf{C}_t(a)}{da} + \beta(1+r_t)V'_{t+1}(\mathbf{A}^+_t(a)) \\
&= (1+r_t)U'(\mathbf{C}_t(a)),
\end{aligned}
\tag{17.54}
$$

where we have used the first-order condition (17.52) to simplify the expression. By induction we thus find that $V'_{t+1}(a^+) = (1+r_{t+1})U'(c^+)$ where $c^+ = \mathbf{C}_{t+1}(a^+)$, so that the expression in (17.52) can be rewritten as $U'(c) = \beta(1+r_{t+1})U'(c^+)$. Put differently, consumption in adjacent periods will be related according to the usual Euler equation:

$$
U'(C_t) = \beta(1+r_{t+1})U'(C_{t+1}),
\tag{17.55}
$$

which simplifies for the logarithmic felicity function to:

$$
\frac{C_{t+1}}{C_t} = \beta(1+r_{t+1}).
\tag{17.56}
$$

The Euler equation is a vital piece of information which allows us to compute the optimal solutions for current and future consumption without any further need for value functions or policy functions.

Note that future consumption can be expressed conditional on current consumption as:

$$
C_t = \beta^{t-1}(1+r_2)(1+r_3)\cdots(1+r_t)C_1,
\tag{17.57}
$$

which allows us to compute:

$$
\sum_{t=1}^{\infty} R_{0,t-1}C_t = C_1 + \beta C_1 + \beta^2 C_1 + \cdots = \frac{C_1}{1-\beta}.
\tag{17.58}
$$

By substituting (17.58) into the lifetime budget constraint (17.49) we obtain the expression for optimal consumption in the first period and assets in the second period:

$$
C^*_1 = (1-\beta)\left[(1+r_1)A_1 + \sum_{t=1}^{\infty} R_{0,t-1}w_t\right],
\tag{17.59}
$$

$$
A^*_2 = (1+r_1)A_1 + w_1 - C^*_1.
\tag{17.60}
$$

The solutions for C^*_t and A^*_{t+1} for $t = 2,3,\dots$ are obtained by using (17.57) and iterating the asset accumulation equation (17.60) forward in time. Expressed in terms of policy functions, it is not hard to derive that:

$$
\mathbf{C}_t(a) \equiv (1-\beta)\left[(1+r_t)a + H_t\right],
\tag{17.61}
$$

$$
\mathbf{A}^+_t(a) \equiv (1+r_t)a + w_t - \mathbf{C}_t(a),
\tag{17.62}
$$

where H_t is human wealth at time t:

$$
H_t \equiv w_t + \frac{w_{t+1}}{1+r_{t+1}} + \frac{w_{t+2}}{(1+r_{t+1})(1+r_{t+2})} + \cdots
\tag{17.63}
$$

With logarithmic utility the agent consumes a constant fraction of total wealth, consisting of the sum of interest-inclusive financial wealth plus human wealth.

17.3   Dynamic programming in a stochastic world

Whereas the traditional and dynamic programming methods are both feasible in a deterministic world the same does not hold in a stochastic setting. Indeed, the true power of the dynamic programming method becomes apparent when confronting optimal sequential choices under risk and uncertainty. In many cases the dynamic programming method turns out to be "the only game in town". We again build up this section by means of a sequence of simple example problems.

17.3.1   Finite planning horizon

We return to the three-period consumption-savings model but postulate that the agent faces idiosyncratic labour productivity risk. Since future income is risky, the consumer's objective function is expected utility at birth which we write as:

$$E_1[\Lambda_1] = U(C_1) + \beta E_1[U(C_2)] + \beta^2 E_1[U(C_3)], \tag{17.64}$$

where the felicity function is given in (17.2) above, and $E_1[\cdot]$ is the expectation operator conditional on information available at time $t = 1$.

We assume that labour income is stochastic and postulate that financial assets accumulate according to:

$$A_{t+1} = (1 + r_t)A_t + \eta_t w_t - C_t, \tag{17.65}$$

where η_t is a stochastic variable representing labour productivity risk. Both r_t and w_t are taken as given and η_t is a random variable for which nature draws realizations over time. Since the world ends for this consumer at the end of period $t = 3$ there is a terminal constraint of the form:

$$A_{t+4} \geq 0. \tag{17.66}$$

To keep things simple we make the following assumptions regarding the stochastic process for η_t:

1. At birth the agent has an average productivity level, $\eta_1 = e_2 = 1$.

2. For later periods, η_t follows a three state stationary Markov scheme, i.e. $\eta_t \in \{e_1, e_2, e_3\}$.

3. The transition probabilities are defined as:

$$p_{ij} = \text{Prob}(\eta_{t+1} = e_j | \eta_t = e_i). \tag{17.67}$$

   In words, p_{ij} is the probability that the productivity state will be e_j in the next period given that it is e_i in the current period. For obvious reasons it must be the case that $\sum_{j=1}^{3} p_{ij} = 1$.

4. The transition matrix is defined as:

$$P \equiv \begin{bmatrix} p_{11} & p_{12} & p_{13} \\ p_{21} & p_{22} & p_{23} \\ p_{31} & p_{32} & p_{33} \end{bmatrix}. \tag{17.68}$$

We assume that $0 < p_{ij} < 1$ so there are no absorbing states (states that one cannot escape from anymore). Since p_{13} and p_{31} are both positive, spectacular reversals of fortune in both directions are possible.

We visualize the labour productivity process in Figure 17.2. The three possible states are depicted as boxes labelled "good" ($\eta_t = e_3$), "average" ($\eta_t = e_2$), and "bad" ($\eta_t = e_1$) whilst the dashed arrows indicate the possible flows between states over time. The probabilities next to the dashed arrows are the transition probabilities.

Since we assume that the agent starts in the average state, $\eta_1 = e_2$, we immediately find that the initial unconditional probability distribution of η_1 is trivial:

$$\pi_1 \equiv \begin{bmatrix} \pi_{11} \\ \pi_{12} \\ \pi_{13} \end{bmatrix} = \begin{bmatrix} 0 \\ 1 \\ 0 \end{bmatrix}. \tag{17.69}$$

In words this expression says that the consumer experiences $\eta_1 = e_2$ for sure because $\pi_{12} = 1$.

To obtain the next period's unconditional probability distribution of η_2 we use the result that $\pi_2' = \pi_1' P$, where P is given in (17.68) above. We thus find:

$$\pi_2 \equiv \begin{bmatrix} \pi_{21} \\ \pi_{22} \\ \pi_{23} \end{bmatrix} = \begin{bmatrix} p_{21} \\ p_{22} \\ 1 - p_{21} - p_{22} \end{bmatrix}. \tag{17.70}$$

From the perspective of period $t = 1$ ('unconditionally') the consumer assigns probability π_{2j} to being in state j in period $t = 2$.

Finally, the unconditional probability distribution of η_3 is determined by $\pi_3' = \pi_2' P$:

$$\pi_3 \equiv \begin{bmatrix} \pi_{31} \\ \pi_{32} \\ \pi_{33} \end{bmatrix} = \begin{bmatrix} p_{21}(p_{11} + p_{22}) + p_{23}p_{31} \\ p_{12}p_{21} + p_{22}^2 + p_{23}p_{32} \\ p_{13}p_{21} + p_{23}(p_{22} + p_{33}) \end{bmatrix}. \tag{17.71}$$

Again the interpretation of π_{3j} is that in period $t = 1$ the consumer assigns probability π_{3j} to being in state j in period $t = 3$.

17.3.1.1 Traditional solution method

What is the optimal consumption level in the first period? Under the assumption that the consumer understands the features of the stochastic process for η_t and has perfect foresight concerning the interest rates and wage rates (no aggregate uncertainty), the decision maker will know that expected utility can be written in terms of asset levels:

$$\begin{aligned} E_1[\Lambda_1] &= U((1+r_1)A_1 + e_2 w_1 - A_2) \\ &+ \beta \Big[\pi_{21} U((1+r_2)A_2 + e_1 w_2 - A_3) + \pi_{22} U((1+r_2)A_2 + e_2 w_2 - A_3) \\ &\quad + \pi_{23} U((1+r_2)A_2 + e_3 w_2 - A_3) \Big] \\ &+ \beta^2 \Big[\pi_{31} U((1+r_3)A_3 + e_1 w_3 - A_4) + \pi_{32} U((1+r_3)A_3 + e_2 w_3 - A_4) \\ &\quad + \pi_{33} U((1+r_3)A_3 + e_3 w_3 - A_4) \Big]. \end{aligned} \tag{17.72}$$

Note that (17.72) is obtained by using (17.65) to eliminate C_t (for $t \in \{1, 2, 3\}$, and by using the unconditional probabilities π_{2j} and π_{3j} stated in (17.70) and (17.71).

Since A_1 and the paths of r_t and w_t are given, and nature draws realizations for η_2 and η_3, the only choice variables are A_2, A_3, and A_4. We can make short shrift

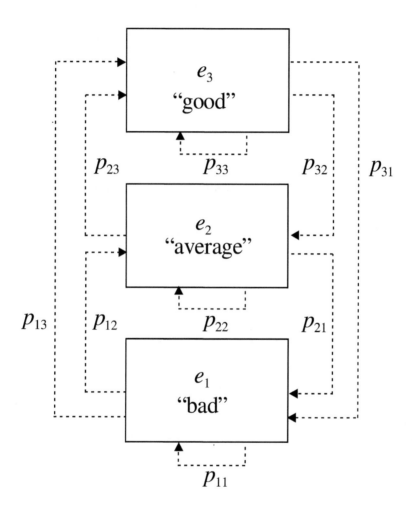

Figure 17.2: Markov process for labour productivity

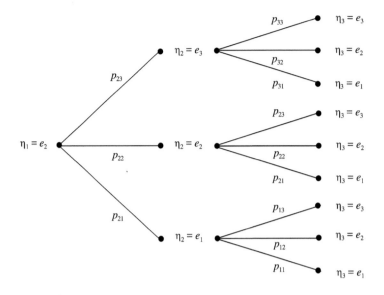

Figure 17.3: Labour productivity over the life cycle

concerning the optimal choice of A_4, since the Kuhn-Tucker conditions amount to:

$$\frac{\partial E_1[\Lambda_1]}{\partial A_4} = -\beta^2 \Big[\pi_{31} U'((1+r_3)A_3 + e_1 w_3 - A_4)$$

$$+ \pi_{32} U'((1+r_3)A_3 + e_2 w_3 - A_4)$$

$$+ \pi_{33} U'((1+r_3)A_3 + e_3 w_3 - A_4) \Big] < 0,$$

$$A_4 \geq 0, \qquad A_4 \frac{\partial E_1[\Lambda_1]}{\partial A_4} = 0. \tag{17.73}$$

Since $\partial E_1[\Lambda_1]/\partial A_4$ is strictly negative, it is never (under no state of the world) optimal to end up with unused financial resources. Hence, $A_4^* = 0$ just as in the deterministic case.

This leaves the more interesting first-order conditions for A_2 and A_3. For the former we find:

$$\frac{\partial E_1[\Lambda_1]}{\partial A_2} = -U'((1+r_1)A_1 + w_1 - A_2)$$

$$+ \beta(1+r_2) \Big[\pi_{21} U'((1+r_2)A_2 + e_1 w_2 - A_3)$$

$$+ \pi_{22} U'((1+r_2)A_2 + e_2 w_2 - A_3)$$

$$+ \pi_{23} U'((1+r_2)A_2 + e_3 w_2 - A_3) \Big] = 0, \tag{17.74}$$

whilst for the latter we obtain:

$$\frac{\partial E_1[\Lambda_1]}{\partial A_3} = -\beta \Big[\pi_{21} U'((1+r_2)A_2 + e_1 w_2 - A_3) + \pi_{22} U'((1+r_2)A_2 + e_2 w_2 - A_3)$$

$$+ \pi_{23} U'((1+r_2)A_2 + e_3 w_2 - A_3) \Big]$$

$$+ \beta^2(1+r_3)\Big[\pi_{31}U'((1+r_3)A_3 + e_1w_3) + \pi_{32}U'((1+r_3)A_3 + e_2w_3)$$

$$+ \pi_{33}U'((1+r_3)A_3 + e_3w_3)\Big] = 0. \tag{17.75}$$

Two things are worth noting. First, equations (17.74)–(17.75) represent two equations in two unknowns which can in principle be solved for A_2^* and A_3^* in terms of the parameters of the problem (i.e., r_2, r_3, w_2, w_3, e_j, and p_{ij}). Second, even for the very simple logarithmic felicity function (17.2) no analytical solutions can be obtained. Numerically it is easy to solve (17.74)–(17.75) for A_2^* and A_3^*. This gives us two points on the policy functions:

$$A_2^* = \mathbf{A}_1^+(A_1, e_2), \tag{17.76}$$
$$C_1^* = \mathbf{C}_1(A_1, e_2) = (1+r_1)A_1 + e_2w_1 - \mathbf{A}_1^+(A_1, e_2), \tag{17.77}$$

where we have already substituted the initial conditions, namely that initial assets are given by A_1 and initial labour productivity is $\eta_1 = e_2$.

In period $t = 2$, the consumer has $A_2^* = \mathbf{A}_1^+(A_1, e_2)$ in financial assets for sure but he enters the risky part of life as nature reveals the realization of η_2. If the agent gets $\eta_2 = e_i$ then expected utility from the perspective of period $t = 2$ is given by:

$$E_2[\Lambda_2(A_2^*, e_i)] = U((1+r_2)A_2^* + e_iw_2 - A_3) + \beta \sum_{j=1}^{3} p_{ij}U((1+r_3)A_3 + e_jw_3), \tag{17.78}$$

where we have already incorporated the fact that $A_4^* = 0$. The only choice variable is A_3 for which we find the following first-order condition:

$$\frac{dE_2[\Lambda_2(A_2^*, e_i)]}{dA_3} = -U'((1+r_2)A_2^* + e_iw_2 - A_3)$$

$$+ \beta(1+r_3) \sum_{j=1}^{3} p_{ij}U'((1+r_3)A_3 + e_jw_3) = 0. \tag{17.79}$$

Numerically, equation (17.79) can easily be solved for A_3^*. This gives us the points on the policy functions if the state is (A_2^*, e_i):

$$A_3^* = \mathbf{A}_2^+(A_2^*, e_i), \tag{17.80}$$
$$C_2^* = \mathbf{C}_2(A_2^*, e_i) = (1+r_2)A_2 + e_iw_2 - \mathbf{A}_2^+(A_2, e_i). \tag{17.81}$$

Finally, in period $t = 3$, the consumer has $A_3^* = \mathbf{A}_2^+(A_2, e_i)$ in financial assets and the value of $\eta_3 = e_j$ is revealed. The optimal choices are trivial:

$$C_3^* = \mathbf{C}_3(A_3^*, e_j) = (1+r_3)A_3^* + e_jw_3, \tag{17.82}$$
$$A_4^* = \mathbf{A}_3^+(A_3^*, e_j) = 0. \tag{17.83}$$

The upshot of this discussion is twofold. First, it is feasible though tedious to compute the optimal choices in the traditional manner by repeatedly solving a maximization problem involving expected remaining lifetime utility. Second, it is clear that with idiosyncratic labour productivity risk of the Markov form, the state vector in a particular period consists of assets at the start of the period as well as the productivity indicator for that period. Armed with this knowledge we can proceed to solve the model with the method of dynamic programming.

17.3.1.2   Dynamic programming

Just as in the deterministic case we start at the end of life and work back to the first period. The last decision is made at the start of period $t = 3$. The consumer who has a in assets and labour productivity η will choose c and a^+ in order to maximize $U(c)$ subject to $a^+ = (1 + r_3)a + \eta w_3 - c$. This results in the following policy functions:

$$\mathbf{C}_3(a, \eta; r_3, w_3) \equiv (1 + r_3)a + \eta w_3, \tag{17.84}$$

$$\mathbf{A}_3^+(a, \eta; r_3, w_3) = 0, \tag{17.85}$$

and the value function for period $t = 3$:

$$V_3(a, \eta) \equiv U(\mathbf{C}_3(a, \eta; r_3, w_3)) = \ln\left[(1 + r_3)a + \eta w_3\right], \tag{17.86}$$

where we have used (17.2) in getting to the final expression. For future reference we note that:

$$V_3'(a, \eta) \equiv (1 + r_3)U'(\mathbf{C}_3(a, \eta; \cdot)) = \frac{1 + r_3}{(1 + r_3)a + \eta w_3}. \tag{17.87}$$

It must be stressed that, since η has three possible realizations, there are three each of the $V_3(a, \eta)$ and $V_3'(a, \eta)$ functions that must be computed (see more on this below).

For period $t = 2$ we write the Bellman equation as:

$$V_2(a, \eta) = \max_{c, a^+} \quad U(c) + \beta E_{\eta^+ | \eta}\left[V_3(a^+, \eta^+)\right]$$

$$\text{subject to:} \quad a^+ = (1 + r_2)a + \eta w_2 - c, \tag{17.88}$$

where $E_{\eta^+ | \eta}[\cdot]$ stands for the conditional expectations operator so that $E_{\eta^+ | \eta}[V_3(a^+, \eta^+)]$ stands for:

$$E_{\eta^+ | \eta}\left[V_3(a^+, \eta^+)\right] = \sum_{j=1}^{3} p_{ij} V_3(a^+, \eta_j), \tag{17.89}$$

where we let $\eta = e_i$ and $\eta^+ = e_j$. Since the expectations operator is a linear operator—it is just a weighted average of $V_3(a^+, \eta_j)$ functions—it is easy to see that the first-order condition for c is given by:

$$U'(c) = \beta E_{\eta^+ | \eta}\left[V_3'(a^+, \eta^+)\right] = \beta \sum_{j=1}^{3} p_{ij} V_3'(a^+, \eta_j). \tag{17.90}$$

In principle we can solve (17.90) for the policy function $c = \mathbf{C}_2(a, \eta; \cdot)$ but it is clear that a closed-form analytical solution cannot be obtained even for the logarithmic felicity function (17.2). Indeed, by setting $\eta = e_i$ and $\eta^+ = e_j$ we easily find that (17.90) reduces to:

$$\frac{1}{c} = \beta(1 + r_3) \sum_{j=1}^{3} \frac{p_{ij}}{(1 + r_3)a^+ + e_j w_3}$$

$$= \beta \sum_{j=1}^{3} \frac{p_{ij}}{(1 + r_2)a + e_i w_2 - c + e_j \frac{w_3}{1 + r_3}}, \tag{17.91}$$

where we have used (17.87) and the definition of a^+ to obtain the final expression. The only way to compute $c = \mathbf{C}_2(a, \eta; \cdot)$ and $\mathbf{A}_2^+(a, \eta; \cdot) \equiv (1 + r_2)a + \eta w_2 - \mathbf{C}_2(a, \eta; \cdot)$ is thus by employing numerical means.

The value function in the second period is given by:

$$V_2(a, \eta) = U(\mathbf{C}_2(a, \eta; \cdot)) + \beta E_{\eta^+ | \eta}[V_3(\mathbf{A}_2^+(a, \eta; \cdot), \eta^+)], \tag{17.92}$$

which can be differentiated with respect to a to obtain the Benveniste-Scheinkman result in a stochastic setting:

$$V_2'(a, \eta) \equiv U'(\mathbf{C}_2(a, \eta; \cdot)) \frac{d\mathbf{C}_2(a, \eta; \cdot)}{da}$$
$$+ \beta E_{\eta^+ | \eta} \left[V_3'(\mathbf{A}_2^+(a, \eta; \cdot), \eta^+) \left((1 + r_2) - \frac{d\mathbf{C}_2(a, \eta; \cdot)}{da} \right) \right]$$
$$= (1 + r_2)U'(\mathbf{C}_2(a, \eta; \cdot)), \tag{17.93}$$

where we have used the first-order condition (17.90) to simplify the expression.

Finally, for period $t = 1$ we write the Bellman equation as:

$$V_1(a, \eta) = \max_{c, a^+} \quad U(c) + \beta E_{\eta^+ | \eta} \left[V_2(a^+, \eta^+) \right]$$
$$\text{subject to:} \quad a^+ = (1 + r_1)a + \eta w_1 - c, \tag{17.94}$$

which gives the first-order condition:

$$U'(c) = \beta E_{\eta^+ | \eta} \left[V_2'(a^+, \eta^+) \right], \tag{17.95}$$

the policy functions $\mathbf{C}_1(a, \eta; \cdot)$ and $\mathbf{A}_1^+(a, \eta; \cdot)$, and the value function:

$$V_1(a, \eta) = U(\mathbf{C}_1(a, \eta; \cdot)) + \beta E_{\eta^+ | \eta} \left[V_2(\mathbf{A}_2^+(a, \eta; \cdot), \eta^+) \right]. \tag{17.96}$$

As we saw in Section 17.2, in the deterministic consumption-savings model the consumption Euler equation plays an important role—see for example the discussion surrounding equation (17.55) above. It is not difficult to see that in a stochastic setting some version of the Euler equation should be operative on the background. Indeed, by combining (17.87) and (17.90) we find that:

$$U'(\mathbf{C}_2(a, \eta; \cdot)) = \beta(1 + r_3)E_{\eta^+ | \eta} \left[U'(\mathbf{C}_3(a^+, \eta^+; \cdot)) \right], \tag{17.97}$$

whilst (17.93) and (17.95) give:

$$U'(\mathbf{C}_1(a, \eta; \cdot)) = \beta(1 + r_2)E_{\eta^+ | \eta} \left[U'(\mathbf{C}_2(a^+, \eta^+; \cdot)) \right]. \tag{17.98}$$

Equations (17.97) and (17.98) are examples of *stochastic consumption Euler equations*. In each period the consumer chooses current consumption in such a way that its marginal utility is equated to the conditional expectation of next period's marginal utility of consumption times a term correcting for impatience and the relative intertemporal price of future consumption.[2]

Unfortunately the stochastic Euler equations are not quite as useful here as they are in a deterministic setting. Indeed, to solve the consumer's choice problem we must compute the policy functions and value functions numerically. In Figure 17.4 we plot the value functions that are computed using the parameters mentioned in Table 17.1. A selection of policy functions are depicted in Figure 17.5. In schematic terms the Matlab program that is used to compute these value and policy functions proceeds as follows.

---

[2]For example, in period $t = 1$ the price of current consumption C_1 is unity and the intertemporal price of future consumption C_2 is $1/(1 + r_2)$. Hence, the relative price of current consumption equals $1 + r_2$.

Figure 17.4: Value functions: Stochastic case

(a) Value functions for period $t = 1$: $V_1(a, e_2)$

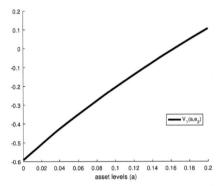

(b) Value functions for period $t = 2$: $V_2(a, \eta)$

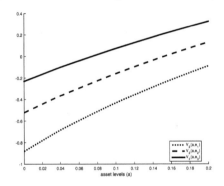

(c) Value functions for period $t = 3$: $V_3(a, \eta)$

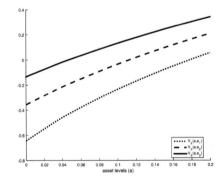

Figure 17.5: Policy functions: Stochastic case

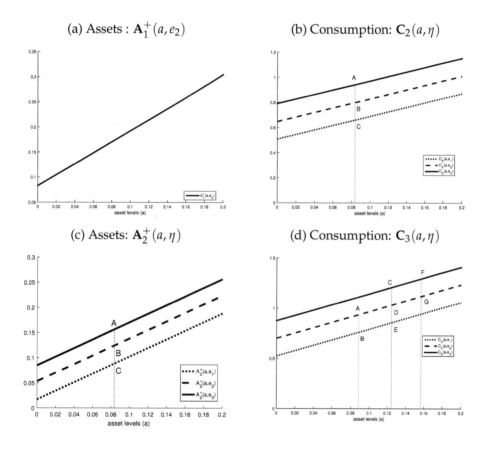

(a) Assets : $\mathbf{A}_1^+(a, e_2)$

(b) Consumption: $\mathbf{C}_2(a, \eta)$

(c) Assets: $\mathbf{A}_2^+(a, \eta)$

(d) Consumption: $\mathbf{C}_3(a, \eta)$

- **Step 1**. In the mathematical derivations a is a continuous variable but the computer cannot work with these directly. For this reason we set up a grid of discrete values for a (labelled a_k) that is sufficiently wide and has a large (but not too large) number of points in it. From the deterministic model we know that assets vary within the interval $[0,0.20]$ so we set `avals =linspace(0,0.20, 201);`. Hence, $a_1 = 0$, $a_2 = 0.001,\ldots$, $a_{201} = 0.20$ (the step size is 0.001 and there are 201 grid points).

- **Step 2**. For each a_k compute the value functions for the final period using the expression in equation (17.86). This gives us three vectors with "data points", $V_3(a_k,e_j) = (1+r)a_k + e_j w$. These value functions have been plotted in Figure 17.4(c).

- **Step 3**. For each possible e_i use equation (17.91) to solve for the policy function for consumption. For each a_k value and case e_i the Matlab routine `fsolve` can be used to solve a nonlinear equation of the form:

$$\frac{1}{c_{ik}} = \beta \sum_{j=1}^{3} \frac{p_{ij}}{(1+r_2)a_k + e_i w - c_{ik} + e_j \frac{w}{1+r}}.$$

This gives us the policy functions $c_{ik} = \mathbf{C}_2(a_k,e_i)$ and $\mathbf{A}_2^+(a_k,e_i) = (1+r)a_k + e_i w - \mathbf{C}_2(a_k,e_i)$.

- **Step 4**. Use these policy functions in (17.92) to obtain the value functions:

$$V_2(a_k,e_i) = \ln \mathbf{C}_2(a_k,e_i) + \beta \sum_{j=1}^{3} p_{ij} \log\left[(1+r)\mathbf{A}_2^+(a_k,e_i) + e_j w\right].$$

These functions have been plotted in Figure 17.4(b).

- **Step 5**. Observe from the figure that the $V_2(a_k,e_i)$ are very smooth, i.e. they do not feature sharp kinks or veer off to infinity. This implies that for each e_i we can create a function $\bar{V}_2(a,e_i)$ by interpolating the observations on $V_2(a_k,e_i)$. The crux is that in the interpolated function a can vary continuously. We use the Matlab routine `interp1` with the option `'spline'` to compute the $\bar{V}_2(a,e_i)$ functions.

- **Step 6**. Since the agent starts with $\eta_1 = e_2$ for sure, we note from (17.96) that we only need to compute $V_1(a_k,e_2)$. For each a_k value we get Matlab to compute the corresponding c_{2k} value which minimizes the following function:

$$\Phi(c_{2k},a_k) \equiv -\log(c_{2k}) - \beta \sum_{j=1}^{3} p_{2j}\bar{V}_2((1+r)a_k + e_2 w - c_{2k},e_j).$$

(The minus sign is used on the right-hand side to turn a maximization problem into a minimization problem.) We use the Matlab minimization routine `fminsearch` to find the policy functions $c_{2k} = \mathbf{C}_1(a_k,e_2)$ and $\mathbf{A}_1^+(a_k,e_2) = (1+r)a_k + e_2 w - \mathbf{C}_1(a_k,e_2)$. The latter is depicted in Figure 17.5(a). The minimization routine also gives the value of the objective function at the optimum so we easily obtain $V_1(a_k,e_2) = -\Phi(c_{2k},a_k)$. The value function has been plotted in Figure 17.4(a).

Armed with Figures 17.4 and 17.5 as well as Table 17.1 we can now explain how the agent makes sequential choices over his life. The consumer starts for sure with the average productivity level e_2 in the first period, $\eta_1 = e_2$, and has no financial assets initially, $A_1 = 0$. From Figure 17.5(a) we find that the optimal amount of assets at the start of period 2 is given by $A_2^* = A_1^+(0, e_2) = 0.0835$ where the numerical result is taken from Table 17.1. From period $t = 2$ onward, nature places the agent on a sequence of value and policy functions. Figure 17.5(b) shows the optimal second-period consumption choices for the three possible productivity states, e_1, e_2, and e_3. From the perspective of period $t = 1$ the agent assigns probabilities p_{21}, p_{22}, and p_{23} of getting, respectively, productivity levels e_1, e_2, and e_3 in the second period. This gives the three optimal consumption points A, B, and C. In Table 17.1(b) the three consumption values are stated as $C_2^*(e_1) = 0.6591$, $C_2^*(e_2) = 0.7982$, and $C_2^*(e_2) = 0.9411$. Obviously, if the agent is lucky (and jumps to a higher than average productivity level) he will be wealthier and part of the extra resources will be consumed immediately. The remaining part will be saved. This explains the different values for $A_3^*(e_i)$ in Table 17.1. Note that in Figure 17.5(c) the choices for $A_3^*(e_i)$ are obtained by evaluating the policy functions for $a = A_2^*$. This gives points A to C in the figure.

At the start of period $t = 3$ the realization for η_3 is revealed. Since there are three possible asset levels at the start of that period, there are seven possible optimal consumption points. These have been marked from A to G in Figure 17.5(d). In Table 17.1 the optimal consumption levels have been stated in short-hand notation as $C_3^*(e_i, e_j)$. So depending on the luck of the draw, there is a wide range of optimal consumption levels that the consumer can end up enjoying in the third period of life. For this reason the "uninsured idiosyncratic risk model" developed here can easily be used to explain why consumption and wealth holdings are so unequal at later ages even if all consumers are identical at birth.[3]

17.3.2 Infinite planning horizon

We defer the treatment of the infinite-horizon stochastic consumption-saving problem to the Manual. Instead we illustrate some features of decision making in an infinite-horizon stochastic environment by looking at the stochastic version of the Ramsey-Cass-Koopmans model (the deterministic version of which was covered in a continuous-time setting in Chapter 13). Starting with the seminal contribution by Brock and Mirman (1972) the optimal stochastic growth model has been extensively studied in the literature. It also forms the backbone of the material in Chapters 18 and 19.

Here we focus on the social planning solution. There is a large population of identical consumers. The population size is constant and normalized to unity. The benevolent social planner maximizes the utility function of the representative consumer. The objective function is thus:

$$\Omega_0 \equiv E_0 \left[\sum_{t=0}^{\infty} \beta^t U(C_t) \right], \tag{17.99}$$

where C_t is consumption and β is the discount factor due to impatience ($0 < \beta < 1$). The felicity function has the usual properties, i.e. $U'(x) > 0$, $U''(x) < 0$, and

---

[3]Even though (expected) human wealth is the same with and without income risk, first-period saving is higher in the risky case—compare the entries for A_2^* in Table 17.1. This is an example of precautionary saving. See Carroll and Kimball (1996, 2001) and Kimball and Weil (2009) on this.

$\lim_{x \to 0} U'(x) = +\infty$. The macroeconomic resource constraint is given by:

$$C_t + K_{t+1} = Z_t F(K_t, 1) + (1 - \delta) K_t, \tag{17.100}$$

where $F(K_t, 1)$ is the production function, K_t is the capital stock at the start of period t, and δ is the depreciation rate of capital ($0 < \delta < 1$). The random technology shock is given by Z_t. We define the history of all technology shocks that have occurred at or before time t by h^t:

$$h^t \equiv (Z_0, Z_1, \ldots, Z_t). \tag{17.101}$$

In the most general case the optimal plans that the social planner formulates at time t will depend on the entire vector h^t. If we assume that the stochastic process has the Markov property, however, then Z_t is all the planner needs to know to make optimal plans at time t. Finally, we note that there are two constraints, namely (a) consumption must be non-negative $C_t \geq 0$ and (b) at time $t = 0$ the existing capital stock is given (K_0 is fixed) and Z_0 is known.

17.3.2.1   Traditional approach

The traditional approach to solve the social planning problem exploits the Markov assumption for the technology shocks and writes the Lagrangian at time $t = 0$ as:

$$
\begin{aligned}
\mathcal{L}_0 = {} & U(Z_0 F(K_0, 1) + (1 - \delta) K_0 - K_1) \\
& + \beta E_{Z_1 | Z_0} \left[U(Z_1 F(K_1, 1) + (1 - \delta) K_1 - K_2) \right] \\
& + \beta^2 E_{Z_2 | Z_0} \left[U(Z_2 F(K_2, 1) + (1 - \delta) K_2 - K_3) \right] + \ldots,
\end{aligned}
$$

where the expectation operator $E_{Z_{t+1} | Z_t} [\phi(Z_{t+1})]$ stands for the conditional expectation of $\phi(Z_{t+1})$ given Z_t. Note that we have substituted the expressions for consumption in periods 0, 1, and 2. Since K_0 is predetermined, the only choice that is made and executed at time $t = 0$ is the one about K_1. The first-order necessary condition is given by:

$$
\begin{aligned}
\frac{\partial \mathcal{L}_0}{\partial K_1} = {} & -U'(Z_0 F(K_0, 1) + (1 - \delta) K_0 - K_1) \\
& + \beta E_{Z_1 | Z_0} \left[U'(Z_1 F(K_1, 1) + (1 - \delta) K_1 - K_2) \cdot \left(Z_1 F_K(K_1, 1) + 1 - \delta \right) \right] = 0,
\end{aligned}
$$

where $F_K(K_1, 1)$ is the marginal product of capital when the stock equals K_1. Substituting back the expressions for C_0 and C_1 we find that the optimal plan concerning K_1 is characterized by:

$$U'(C_0) = \beta E_{Z_1 | Z_0} \left[U'(C_1) \cdot \left(Z_1 F_K(K_1, 1) + 1 - \delta \right) \right]. \tag{17.102}$$

Here is the intuition: by slightly increasing K_1 the planner foregoes some felicity at time $t = 0$ (left-hand side) but expects to gain future felicity (discounted for impatience) as a result of the investment (right-hand side). In the optimum the costs and expected benefits of investing are equalized. Note that for any arbitrary period t the social optimum is characterized by the corresponding stochastic Euler equation:

$$U'(C_t) = \beta E_{Z_{t+1} | Z_t} \left[U'(C_{t+1}) \cdot \left(Z_{t+1} F_K(K_{t+1}, 1) + 1 - \delta \right) \right]. \tag{17.103}$$

How would one derive this expression with dynamic programming?

17.3.2.2 Dynamic programming

Because of the Markov assumption regarding the technology shocks we can solve the social planning exercise with the aid of dynamic programming. At time t the control variable is consumption for that time period, C_t, whilst the state variables are the capital stock and the technology indicator, K_t and Z_t. Many writers express the Bellman equation as:

$$V(K_t, Z_t) = \max_{C_t, K_{t+1}} U(C_t) + \beta E_{Z_{t+1}|Z_t} \left[V(K_{t+1}, Z_{t+1}) \right]$$

$$\text{subject to } K_{t+1} = Z_t F(K_t, 1) + (1 - \delta) K_t - C_t.$$

Note that the value function does not depend on time itself because the horizon is infinite and the problem is recursive—see for example Sydsæter et al. (2008, pp. 458–464) on this. Using the notation employed in this chapter, however, we prefer to write the Bellman equation as follows:

$$V(K, Z) = \max_{C, K^+} U(C) + \beta E_{Z^+|Z} \left[V(K^+, Z^+) \right]$$

$$\text{subject to } K^+ = Z F(K, 1) + (1 - \delta) K - C. \tag{17.104}$$

The first-order necessary condition for the maximization problem on the right-hand side is:

$$U'(C) = \beta E_{Z^+|Z} \left[\frac{\partial V(K^+, Z^+)}{\partial K^+} \right]. \tag{17.105}$$

Using the Benveniste-Scheinkman theorem results in:

$$\frac{\partial V(K, Z)}{\partial K} = \beta E_{Z^+|Z} \left[\frac{\partial V(K^+, Z^+)}{\partial K^+} \cdot \left(Z F_K(K, 1) + 1 - \delta \right) \right]$$

$$= \left(Z F_K(K, 1) + 1 - \delta \right) \cdot U'(C), \tag{17.106}$$

where we have used (17.105) to get from the first to the second line. Leading (17.106) by one period gives:

$$\frac{\partial V(K^+, Z^+)}{\partial K^+} = \left(Z^+ F_K(K^+, 1) + 1 - \delta \right) \cdot U'(C^+). \tag{17.107}$$

Finally, by combining (17.105) and (17.107) we obtain the stochastic Euler equation:

$$U'(C) = \beta E_{Z^+|Z} \left[\left(Z^+ F_K(K^+, 1) + 1 - \delta \right) \cdot U'(C^+) \right]. \tag{17.108}$$

Apart from the difference in notation, (17.108) and (17.103) are identical. Much of Chapters 18 and 19 will make use of (17.108) in some form or another. There it will also be shown how models containing a stochastic Euler equation can be solved (approximately) to obtain the policy functions $\mathbf{C}(K, Z)$ and $\mathbf{K}^+(K, Z)$.

17.4 Complete markets and Arrow-Debreu securities

Up to this point attention has been focused largely on the study of individual behaviour under risk. In this section we take the next step and study the way in which a tractable aggregate model can be constructed in a situation where individuals are faced with (and need to make decisions in) an inherently stochastic world. The key concept that is introduced here is that of complete markets in dated contingent claims—so-called Arrow-Debreu securities. To explain matters further we develop a simple example of a multi-period endowment economy inhabited by a large number of individuals. The example is a simplified version of the model formulated by Ljungqvist and Sargent (2012, ch. 8).

17.4.1 Model

Consider a dynamic endowment economy featuring a time horizon denoted by T (which may or may not be infinite). There are I agents indexed by $i = 1, \ldots, I$, and in each period $t = 0, 1, \ldots, T$ there is a realization of a some stochastic event $s_t \in \mathcal{S}$. We assume that any trading among individuals occurs after s_0 is revealed, i.e. the initial state is a certainty. We define the history of stochastic events up to and including period t by the vector $h^t \in \mathcal{H}^t$:

$$h^t \equiv (s_0, s_1, \ldots, s_t). \tag{17.109}$$

It easily follows from (17.109) that $h^t = (h^{t-1}, s_t)$. We assume that h^t is publicly and perfectly observable by all agents. We denote the unconditional probability of observing h^t by $\pi_t(h^t)$. Probabilities add to unity, i.e. $\sum_{h^t \in \mathcal{H}^t} \pi_t(h^t) = 1$. Under the Markov assumption we find furthermore that:

$$\pi_t(h^t) = \pi(s_t|s_{t-1})\pi(s_{t-1}|s_{t-2}) \ldots \pi(s_1|s_0),$$
$$\pi_t(h^t|h^\tau) = \pi(s_t|s_{t-1})\pi(s_{t-1}|s_{t-2}) \ldots \pi(s_{\tau+1}|s_\tau).$$

Before continuing it is useful to note that $\mathcal{H}^t$, denoting the set of all possible histories at time t, typically becomes very large as time evolves. For example, even with a low-dimensional three-state Markov process (such that $s_t \in (s^a, s^b, s^c)$) $\mathcal{H}^t$ gets large very rapidly, i.e. $\mathcal{H}^0 = \{s_0\}$, $\mathcal{H}^1 = \{(s_0, s^a), (s_0, s^b), (s_0, s^c)\}$, $\mathcal{H}^2 = \{(s_0, s^a, s^a), (s_0, s^a, s^b), (s_0, s^a, s^c), (s_0, s^b, s^a), (s_0, s^b, s^b), (s_0, s^b, s^c), (s_0, s^c, s^a), (s_0, s^c, s^b), (s_0, s^c, s^c)\}$, etcetera.[4]

The endowment of the non-storable commodity for agent i depends on s_t and is denoted by $y^i(s_t)$. Consumption of agent i at time t under history h^t is denoted by $c_t^i(h^t)$. At time $t = 0$ each agent i chooses a life-time consumption plan denoted by $c^i = \{c_t^i(h^t)\}_{t=0}^\infty$. The (expected) utility function of agent i is given by:

$$\Lambda(c^i) \equiv E_0 \left[\beta^t U(c_t^i) \right] = \sum_{t=0}^T \sum_{h^t \in \mathcal{H}^t} \beta^t U(c_t^i(h^t)) \pi_t(h^t), \tag{17.110}$$

where β is the discount rate due to impatience (such that $0 < \beta < 1$). Note that (17.110) implies that individuals have the same degree of impatience, feature the same felicity function $U(x)$, and assign the same probabilities to future histories. As usual we assume that felicity satisfies Inada style conditions, i.e. $U'(x) > 0$, $U''(x) < 0$, and $\lim_{x \to \infty} U'(x) = +\infty$.

As the commodity is non storable by assumption, the economy-wide resource constraint (for all $t = 0, 1, \ldots, T$ and $h^t \in \mathcal{H}^t$) is given by:

$$\sum_{i=1}^I c_t^i(h^t) = \sum_{i=1}^I y_t^i(h^t). \tag{17.111}$$

---

[4]Of course s_0 must itself assume one of the three possible values.

Depending on the size of the aggregate endowment (right-hand side) individuals can attempt to trade among each other and thus react optimally to the fact that they live in a stochastic environment.

17.4.2   Pareto optimal allocation

In this subsection we study how a social planner would allocate risk in the endowment economy introduced above. In particular we compute the set of Pareto optimal allocations by using the approach pioneered by Negishi (1960).

The objective function of the social planner is given by:

$$\Omega_0 \equiv \sum_{i=1}^{I} \lambda_i \Lambda(c^i), \tag{17.112}$$

where λ_i is the time-invariant Pareto weight that the planner assigns to agent i. Obviously every agent matters to the planner ($\lambda_i > 0$) and by normalization one can always ensure that the weights add up to unity ($\sum_{i=1}^{I} \lambda_i = 1$).

The social planner chooses $c^i = \{c_t^i(h^t)\}_{t=0}^{\infty}$ for all i in order to maximize Ω_0 subject to the resource constraints (17.111). The Lagrangian for this planning problem is:

$$\mathcal{L}_0 \equiv \sum_{t=0}^{T} \sum_{h^t \in \mathcal{H}^t} \left[\sum_{i=1}^{I} \lambda_i \beta^t U(c_t^i(h^t)) \pi_t(h^t) + \mu_t(h^t) \sum_{i=1}^{I} \left(y_t^i(h^t) - c_t^i(h^t) \right) \right],$$

where $\mu_t(h^t)$ is the Lagrange multiplier for the resource constraint at time t and history h^t. The first-order necessary condition for $c_t^i(h^t)$ can be written as:

$$\beta^t U'(c_t^i(h^t)) \pi_t(h^t) = \frac{\mu_t(h^t)}{\lambda_i}. \tag{17.113}$$

Note that (17.113) must hold for each t, h^t, and i. Comparing a benchmark individual—say agent 1—with any other agent i we easily obtain from (17.113) that for given t and h^t:

$$\frac{U'(c_t^i(h^t))}{U'(c_t^1(h^t))} = \frac{\lambda_1}{\lambda_i}. \tag{17.114}$$

This expression is alternately referred to as the Borch (1962) condition—after one of its earliest expositors—or the efficient risk sharing condition.

Recall that the felicity function satisfies $U''(x) < 0$ so that the marginal felicity function can be inverted. Hence it is possible to express $c_t^i(h^t)$ in terms of $c_t^1(h^t)$ and λ_1/λ_i. Indeed, by using (17.114), taking $U'(c_t^1(h^t))$ to the other side, and inverting the marginal felicity function of person i we find:

$$c_t^i(h^t) = U'^{-1}(\lambda_1 U'(c_t^1(h^t))/\lambda_i). \tag{17.115}$$

By substituting (17.115) into the resource constraint (17.111) we obtain:

$$\sum_{i=1}^{I} U'^{-1}(\lambda_1 U'(c_t^1(h^t))/\lambda_i) = \sum_{i=1}^{I} y_t^i(h^t). \tag{17.116}$$

The key thing to note is that (17.116) is an implicit equation determining $c_t^1(h^l)$ as a function of the aggregate realized endowment at time t (right-hand side). To further clarify this point consider the example with two agents ($I = 2$) and a logarithmic felicity function ($U(x) = \ln x$). It is easy to show that for a such an endowment economy efficient risk sharing results in:

$$c_t^1(h^t) = \lambda_1 \sum_{i=1}^{I} y_t^i(h^t), \qquad c_t^2(h^t) = (1 - \lambda_1) \sum_{i=1}^{I} y_t^i(h^t). \tag{17.117}$$

17.4.3 Decentralization with Arrow-Debreu securities

In the previous subsection we characterized the set of Pareto optimal risk-sharing allocations in the endowment economy. In this subsection we study how the Pareto optimal allocation can be decentralized, i.e. replicated in a competitive market equilibrium. The crucial insight into this nontrivial question was provided by Arrow (1953) and Debreu (1959): the Pareto optimal equilibrium can be decentralized provided the securities market is *complete*, i.e. individuals are able to trade a (potentially huge) set of claims on period t consumption contingent on history h^t with each other.[5]

With the aid of our simple endowment economy the Arrow-Debreu approach can be easily demonstrated. The structure of the contingent claims market is as follows. At time $t = 0$ agents trade claims to consumption at all times $t > 0$ contingent on all possible histories h^t. Trading occurs at all nodes $h^t \in \mathcal{H}^t$ because the agents do not know which histories will actually materialize. After time $t = 0$ no further trades occur.[6] We let $q_t^0(h^t)$ denote the price of claims on period t consumption contingent on history h^t.

In the presence of contingent claims, individual i's lifetime budget constraint can be written as:

$$\sum_{t=0}^{T} \sum_{h^t \in \mathcal{H}^t} q_t^0(h^t) c_t^i(h^t) = \sum_{t=0}^{T} \sum_{h^t \in \mathcal{H}^t} q_t^0(h^t) y_t^i(h^t). \tag{17.118}$$

Intuitively, total spending on consumption goods (left-hand side) must equal the total value of the endowment for each person i. Individual i chooses $c^i \equiv \{c_t^i(h^t)\}_{t=0}^{\infty}$ in order to maximize (17.110) subject to (17.118). The Lagrangian for this maximization problem is:

$$\mathcal{L}_0^i \equiv \sum_{t=0}^{T} \sum_{h^t \in \mathcal{H}^t} \left[\beta^t U(c_t^i(h^t)) \pi_t(h^t) + \zeta_i q_t^0(h^t) \left(y_t^i(h^t) - c_t^i(h^t) \right) \right],$$

where ζ_i is the Lagrange multiplier for the lifetime budget constraint faced by agent i. The first-order necessary condition for $c_t^i(h^t)$ is:

$$\beta^t U'(c_t^i(h^t)) \pi_t(h^t) = \zeta_i q_t^0(h^t). \tag{17.119}$$

To characterize the decentralized equilibrium a bit further we first note that for agent 1 and any other agent i we obtain from (17.119) that:

$$\frac{U'(c_t^i(h^t))}{U'(c_t^1(h^t))} = \frac{\zeta_i}{\zeta_1}. \tag{17.120}$$

---

[5] As is noted by Wilson (2008), the assumption of market completeness "...strains the credibility of the model by requiring an unrealistic number of goods to be simultaneously exchanged". When there are not enough Arrow-Debreu securities the setting is one of *incomplete markets*.

[6] Ljungqvist and Sargent (2012, ch. 8) also study the sequential model in which only one-period ahead state-contingent claims are available. This model supports the same equilibrium allocations.

The ratio of marginal utilities for any two individuals is constant for all t and h^t. We can thus express $c_t^i(h^t)$ in terms of $c_t^1(h^t)$ and ζ_i/ζ_1 by inverting the marginal felicity function of person i:

$$c_t^i(h^t) = U'^{-1}(\zeta_i U'(c_t^1(h^t))/\zeta_1). \tag{17.121}$$

Substituting (17.121) into the resource constraint gives:

$$\sum_{i=1}^{I} U'^{-1}(\zeta_i U'(c_t^1(h^t))/\zeta_1) = \sum_{i=1}^{I} y_t^i(h^t). \tag{17.122}$$

Just as in the planning optimum, $c_t^1(h^t)$ depends only on the aggregate realized endowment at time t (right-hand side). Put differently, individual consumption is perfectly correlated with the aggregate endowment (Ljungqvist and Sargent, 2012, p. 261). For the two-person logarithmic felicity case we find that (17.122) implies:

$$c_t^1(h^t) = \frac{\zeta_2}{\zeta_1+\zeta_2}\sum_{i=1}^{I} y_t^i(h^t), \qquad c_t^2(h^t) = \frac{\zeta_1}{\zeta_1+\zeta_2}\sum_{i=1}^{I} y_t^i(h^t), \tag{17.123}$$

Intuitively, a "lucky individual" is somebody who at time $t=0$ expects the economy to evolve in such a way that the value of the lifetime endowment is high (Mother Nature has stacked the deck in favour of such a person). For such an individual the marginal utility of endowment income (ζ_i) is relatively low. Hence, if person 1 is the lucky individual then it follows that $\zeta_2 > \zeta_1$ and that $c_t^1(h^t) > c_t^2(h^t)$.

Going back to the general case we are now in the position to demonstrate the full force of the Negishi (1960) insight. Indeed, by comparing (17.115)–(17.116) and (17.121)–(17.122) we find that the competitive risk-sharing equilibrium allocation is Pareto optimal with weights such that $\lambda_i = 1/\zeta_i$. In other words, as Negishi puts it:

> ...a competitive equilibrium is a maximum point of a social welfare function which is a linear combination of utility functions of consumers, with the weights in the combination in inverse proportion to the marginal utilities of income. (1960, p. 92)

Note that, in view of the inverse relationship between λ_i and ζ_i, a "lucky individual" (as defined above) gets a larger weight in the social welfare function than a less lucky person gets.

Negishi's equivalence result can be exploited further. Indeed by setting $\lambda_i = 1/\zeta_i$ in (17.113) and comparing the resulting expression with (17.119) we find that the shadow prices of the social planning problem equals the contingent price, i.e. $\mu_t(h^t) = q_t^0(h^t)$.

Finally, we note that for a given process generating the stochastic events and the endowment incomes depending on them, the competitive risk-sharing equilibrium can be computed by using the so-called Negishi algorithm—see Ljungqvist and Sargent (2012, p. 260). In the context of our model it works as follows. The task at hand is to find ζ_i/ζ_1 for $i=1,2,\ldots,I$. This is done iteratively in a number of steps:

1 Keep ζ_1 fixed and postulate guesses for the other ζ_i parameters. Solve (17.121) and (17.122) for candidate allocations, c^i for $i=1,2,\ldots,I$.

2 Compute $q_t^0(h^t)$ by using (17.119) for any household i (does not matter which one).

3 For all $i = 1, 2, \ldots, I$ check the budget constraint (17.118) and:

- for all i who are overspending their endowment, raise the guess for ζ_i;
- for all i who are underspending their endowment, lower the guess for ζ_i.

4 Iterate over steps 1–3 until convergence is obtained.

17.4.3.1 Some two-person examples

We close the section on the competitive risk-sharing equilibrium with two prototypical examples. Both examples are very specific in the sense that there are only two individuals in the endowment economy under consideration ($I = 2$).

Special Case #1 abstracts from aggregate risk and thus zooms in on idiosyncratic risk. In particular we follow Ljungqvist and Sargent (2012, p. 262) and assume that the stochastic events are such that $s_t \in [0, 1]$ and that the endowments are given by:

$$y_t^1(h^t) = s_t, \qquad y_t^2(h^t) = 1 - s_t.$$

There is no aggregate risk because total endowment income is constant for each t and h^t, i.e. $\sum_{i=1}^{2} y_t^i(h^t) = 1$.

What are the features of the competitive risk-sharing equilibrium? We first note that (17.122) simplifies to:

$$\sum_{i=1}^{2} U'^{-1}(\zeta_2 U'(c_t^1(h^t))/\zeta_1) = 1, \tag{17.124}$$

which implies that $c_t^1(h^t) = \bar{c}^1$ and thus $c_t^2(h^t) = \bar{c}^2$ (both constant over time and across histories). By using the first-order condition (17.119) and exploiting the constancy of $\bar{c}^i$ we find:

$$q_t^0(h^t) = \frac{\beta^t U'(\bar{c}^i)\pi_t(h^t)}{\zeta_i}. \tag{17.125}$$

By substituting (17.125) into the budget identity of person i (given in (17.118) above) we obtain:

$$0 = \frac{U'(\bar{c}^i)}{\zeta_i} \sum_{t=0}^{T} \sum_{h^t \in \mathcal{H}^t} \beta^t \pi_t(h^t) \left[\bar{c}^i - y_t^i(h^t) \right],$$

or (since $U'(\bar{c}^i)/\zeta_i > 0$ and probabilities add up to unity):

$$\bar{c}^i = (1 - \beta) \sum_{t=0}^{T} \sum_{h^t \in \mathcal{H}^t} \beta^t \pi_t(h^t) y_t^i(h^t). \tag{17.126}$$

There is perfect consumption smoothing over time and across histories. Even though individual endowment incomes fluctuate randomly each individual can completely insure against this idiosyncratic risk.

Special Case #2 abstracts from idiosyncratic risk and zooms in on aggregate risk. Following Altug and Labadie (2008, pp. 137–138) we assume that endowment incomes are given by:

$$y_t^1(h^t) = \alpha s_t, \qquad y_t^2(h^t) = (1 - \alpha)s_t,$$

with $0 < \alpha < 1$. There is no idiosyncratic risk: if s_t is low (high) then endowment income is low (high) for both individuals. Of course, there is aggregate risk because $\sum_{i=1}^{2} y_t^i(h^t) = s_t$ and s_t fluctuates randomly over time.

Intuitively one expects that aggregate risk cannot be insured, and that is what the competitive risk-sharing model says. Indeed, by using (17.121)–(17.122) we find that:

$$c_t^2(h^t) = U'^{-1}(\zeta_2 U'(c_t^1(h^t))/\zeta_1), \qquad (17.127)$$
$$c_t^1(h^t) + c_t^2(h^t) = s_t. \qquad (17.128)$$

Both consumption levels are stochastic. Efficient risk sharing results in shifting the risk to those who can best bear it. Note finally that for a logarithmic felicity function we get (17.123) again.

17.5 Constructing the representative agent

In the previous section we discovered that, under complete contingent-claim markets, risk sharing is efficient and there is full insurance. This property of the Arrow-Debreu model provides a rationale for the "representative-agent" assumption. Indeed, as is shown inter alia by Obstfeld and Rogoff (1996, pp. 292–293), under quite general conditions regarding preferences one can construct a fictional "representative agent" and ignore the underlying heterogeneity of individuals when interested in macroeconomic issues.

This convenient feature of the complete-markets approach can be demonstrated with the aid of our simple endowment model. In what follows we set $q_0^0(h^0) = q_0^0(s_0) = 1$ as the numeraire. This means that the price system is expressed in units of period 0 goods. To keep things simple we assume a logarithmic felicity function, $U(x) = \ln x$. It follows from (17.119) that:

$$\zeta_i = \frac{1}{c_0^i(s_0)} = \frac{\beta^t \pi_t(h^t)}{q_t^0(h^t) c_t^i(h^t)}, \qquad (17.129)$$

where we have used the fact that $\pi_t(h^0) = \pi_t(s_0) = 1$ and $c_0^i(h^0) = c_0^i(s_0)$ to obtain the first equality. The individual Euler equation is thus:

$$\frac{c_t^i(h^t)}{c_0^i(s_0)} = \frac{\beta^t \pi_t(h^t)}{q_t^0(h^t)}. \qquad (17.130)$$

The right-hand side of this expression is the same for all $i = 1, 2, \ldots, I$. Hence, the aggregate Euler equation can be written as:

$$\frac{C_t(h^t)}{C_0(s_0)} = \frac{\beta^t \pi_t(h^t)}{q_t^0(h^t)}, \qquad (17.131)$$

where aggregate consumption, $C_t(h^t)$, is defined as:

$$C_t(h^t) \equiv \sum_{i=1}^{I} c_t^i(h^t). \qquad (17.132)$$

Next we consider the "representative agent" who has a utility function which depends on aggregate consumption and takes the following form:

$$\Lambda(C) \equiv E_0 \left[\beta^t U(C_t) \right] = \sum_{t=0}^{T} \sum_{h^t \in \mathcal{H}^t} \beta^t \ln C_t(h^t) \pi_t(h^t). \tag{17.133}$$

The economy-wide budget constraint facing the representative agent is obtained by summing (17.118) over all individuals $i = 1, 2, \ldots, I$:

$$\sum_{t=0}^{T} \sum_{h^t \in \mathcal{H}^t} q_t^0(h^t) C_t(h^t) = \sum_{t=0}^{T} \sum_{h^t \in \mathcal{H}^t} q_t^0(h^t) Y_t(h^t), \tag{17.134}$$

where $Y_t(h^t)$ is the aggregate endowment:

$$Y_t(h^t) \equiv \sum_{i=1}^{I} y_t^i(h^t). \tag{17.135}$$

The fictional representative agent chooses $C_t(h^t)$ in order to maximize (17.133) subject to (17.134). The Lagrangian for this optimization problem is:

$$\mathcal{L} \equiv \sum_{t=0}^{T} \sum_{h^t \in \mathcal{H}^t} \left[\beta^t \ln C_t(h^t) \pi_t(h^t) + \zeta q_t^0(h^t) \left(Y_t(h^t) - C_t(h^t) \right) \right],$$

where ζ is the Lagrange multiplier for the aggregate budget constraint. The first-order necessary condition for $C_t(h^t)$ is:

$$\beta^t \frac{\pi_t(h^t)}{C_t(h^t)} = \zeta q_t^0(h^t). \tag{17.136}$$

It is easy to see that (17.136) implies (17.131). Hence, we obtain exactly the same solution for $C_t(h^t)$ as before by letting the fictional agent do the utility maximization. In words, the economy's aggregate consumption $C_t(h^t)$ behaves *as if* chosen by a representative consumer with a logarithmic felicity function defined over aggregate consumption, $C_t(h^t)$, who owns the economy's total endowment $Y_t(h^t)$.

17.6　Punchlines

This chapter introduces a number of methods and concepts that will be used in the next two chapters. We start by looking at a simple deterministic utility maximization problem in which an individual has to decide about consumption and saving in a three-period setting. We first solve this problem with the traditional (Lagrangian) method and subsequently show that it can also be solved in a sequential fashion by making use of the method of dynamic programming (DP hereafter). Intuitively, the DP method solves a complex multi-period (or multi-stage) problem by breaking it up into a number of smaller subproblems. Crucial objects appearing in the DP method are the value function, the Bellman equation, and policy functions. The deterministic three-period consumption model is simple enough to provide explicit closed-form expressions for value- and policy functions so that they are less abstract to the novice reader.

　Next we generalize the deterministic consumption-saving problem somewhat by assuming that the planning horizon is infinite. Although this problem can still be solved with traditional methods we directly proceed to the DP approach to find the key first-order condition—the consumption Euler equation—and to characterize the solution.

The true power of the DP method lies in its use for analysing and solving stochastic decision problems. In such a setting the traditional approach is either clumsy or infeasible. In many cases the DP method turns out to be "the only game in town". We again proceed by means of a sequence of simple toy problems. In the first of these, we return to the three-period utility maximization problem but augment it by assuming that labour income is stochastic—say due to idiosyncratic productivity shocks. To keep the analysis simple we assume that the productivity shocks are generated by a Markov process. We explain such processes in some detail and show how the expected-utility maximization problem can be solved with traditional (clumsy) means and with the method of DP. To aid in the interpretation of the results we show some simple simulations. Depending on the luck of the draw, there is a wide range of optimal consumption levels that the consumer can end up enjoying in the third period of life. For this reason the "uninsured idiosyncratic risk model" developed here can easily be used to explain why consumption and wealth holdings are so unequal at later ages even if all consumers are identical at birth.

In the final application of sequential decision making tools we introduce and analyse a stochastic version of the Ramsey-Cass-Koopmans model. To prepare for the next two chapters we restrict attention to the social planning solution. If productivity shocks follow a Markov process then both the Lagrangian method and the DP method can be used to derive the key first-order condition—the stochastic consumption Euler equation.

In the penultimate section of this chapter we study an endowment economy featuring a full set of dated contingent claims—the so-called Arrow-Debreu securities. We demonstrate a result first discovered by Borch (1962), namely that in a complete-markets setting risk sharing is efficient. By using the methods suggested by Negishi (1960) it is shown that the competitive risk-sharing equilibrium is Pareto efficient and is identical to the social planning solution that can be obtained by using a Negishi-type social welfare function. In such a social welfare function utility of person i is weighted by the inverse of the marginal utility of endowment income for that person.

In the final section of the chapter we show that there exists an important aggregation result in complete-markets economies. Indeed, under quite general conditions regarding preferences one can construct a fictional "representative agent" and ignore the underlying heterogeneity of individuals when interested in macroeconomic issues.

Further reading

On the theory of dynamic programming every serious student should read the Preface of Bellman (1957) at least once in order to get a very clear introduction about what this method is all about. An early economic application of dynamic programming is found in Samuelson (1969a). Rust (2008) gives an accessible overview covering the modern literature on dynamic programming. Textbook treatments of various degrees of complexity are Ross (1983), Dixit (1990, ch. 11), Sydsæter et al. (2008), Stachurski (2009), Adda and Cooper (2003), Wälde (2011), Ljungqvist and Sargent (2012), and Miao (2014). Very good textbooks on the economics of risk and uncertainty are Gollier (2001) and Bikhchandani et al. (2013).

Most dynamic programming applications can only be solved numerically and a large literature in computational economics has emerged over the last decades. A very gentle and accessible introduction to dynamic programming (using Matlab implementations) is provided by Femminis (2016). The novice computer programmer will learn enough from this 'how-to' manual to be able to access the more advanced sources. Excellent survey articles and books are Judd (1998), Miranda and Fackler (2002), Judd et al. (2003), Heer and Maussner (2009), and Cai and Judd (2010). Sargent and Stachurski (2015) discuss dynamic programming applications and implement these using the Python computer language. Fehr and Kindermann (2017) is highly recommended as it provides a nice and accessible introduction to various programming problems (including dynamic programming). It also explains and supplies sample Fortran programs.

On Arrow-Debreu securities, see Arrow (1953, 1964, 1970) and Debreu (1959, ch. 7). The interested reader may also wish to read Düppe and Weintraub (2014) on the genesis of the Arrow-Debreu model (and the forgotten contribution by McKenzie), and Geanakoplos (2008a) for a compact survey. Kehoe (1990) is quite instructive and includes overlapping-generations models. Kirman (1992) is very critical of the concept of the representative agent. See Majumdar and Radner (2008) on uncertainty and sequential general equilibrium. On incomplete markets, good places to start reading are Wilson (2008) and Magill and Quinzii (2008).

Macroeconomic implementations of the idiosyncratic risk model in the closed economy are plentiful. The classic contributions are Aiyagari (1994), Bewley (1977), and Huggett (1993, 1997). A good survey article is Heathcote et al. (2009). A recent application of the idiosyncratic risk model to study loan system reform is Heijdra et al. (2017).

Chapter 18

Dynamic Stochastic General Equilibrium—New Classical models

The purpose of this chapter is to achieve the following goals:

1. To turn the Ramsey-Cass-Koopmans model with endogenous labour supply (studied in Chapter 13) into a prototypical real business cycle (RBC) model by reformulating it in discrete time and by assuming that the economy is hit by stochastic technology shocks.

2. To analyse the theoretical properties of the RBC model by means of its impulse-response functions.

3. To study the quantitative performance of the RBC model by showing how well it can be made to fit real world data.

4. To briefly discuss some of the extensions that have been proposed in recent years to improve the model's empirical performance.

18.1 The Lucas research programme

One of the lasting contributions of the rational expectations revolution of the 1970s (see Chapter 5) has been a methodological one. Throughout the 1950s and 1960s macroeconomists engaged in a huge model construction programme in which the insights of the IS-LM model and its refinements were estimated by econometric means. These macroeconometric models were quite popular in both public and private sectors because they could be used for prediction and simulation purposes. Two developments occurred in the early 1970s which led to a drastic reduction in the popularity of these models. First, a lot of the macroeconometric models then in use included a relatively poorly specified supply side and consequently were ill equipped to predict the effects of the various oil price shocks that occurred at the time. Of course, this criticism is not deadly *per se* as macroeconometric models can be (and indeed, have been) re-specified to better deal with shocks affecting the supply side of the economy.

A second—potentially much more lethal—criticism was raised by Lucas (1976). The so-called *Lucas critique* was briefly discussed above—see Chapter 5. Loosely put, it states that macroeconometric models that are not based on a consistent set of optimizing foundations are *non-structural* and cannot be used for policy evaluation. The reason is that the estimated parameters of the model's equations are mixtures of structural and policy parameters and are therefore not invariant across different policy regimes (see Chapter 5 for a simple example of this point). To avoid the critique that now carries his name, Lucas (1980, 1987) argued forcefully and eloquently that macroeconomists should build structural models, i.e. models that are based on optimizing behaviour of the various agents in the economy. In doing so he proposed what Christiano, Eichenbaum, and Evans (1999) have labelled the *Lucas (research) programme*.

As Lucas (1980, p. 696–697) argues, well-articulated structural models are of necessity unrealistic and artificial. They should be tested "as useful imitations of reality by subjecting them to shocks for which we are fairly certain how actual economies ...would react. The more dimensions on which the model mimics the answers actual economies give to simple questions, the more we trust its answers to harder questions." He goes on to argue that:

> On this general view of the nature of economic theory then, a "theory" is not a collection of assertions about the behavior of the actual economy but rather an explicit set of instructions for building a parallel or analogue system—a mechanical, imitation economy. A "good" model, from this point of view, will not be exactly more "real" than a poor one, but will provide better imitations. (1980, p. 697)

In a seminal paper, Kydland and Prescott (1982) accepted the challenge posed by Lucas and his co-workers by building a full-scale structural model with maximizing agents doing as well as they can in a world in which technology is subject to stochastic shocks. Their model can be seen as the starting point of the real business cycle (RBC) research programme (see also Long and Plosser (1983) and Prescott (1986)). As their testing procedure they ask themselves the following question: can shocks to productivity explain fluctuations in actual economies using a model that is plausibly calibrated, i.e. that uses parameter estimates that are not inconsistent with micro observations (Kydland and Prescott, 1982, p. 1359)? The performance of the model is not gleaned by estimating its equations econometrically and testing its implied restrictions. Indeed, as Kydland and Prescott (1982, p. 1360) suggest, the model would undoubtedly have been rejected statistically both because of measurement problems and because of its abstract nature. Instead, the model is tested by comparing *model-generated* and *actual* statistics characterizing fluctuations in the economy. "Failure of the theory to mimic the behavior of the post-war US economy with respect to these stable statistics ... would be ground for its rejection."

The aim of this chapter is to illustrate to what extent RBC models have been successful in passing the tests proposed by Kydland and Prescott (1982). Since the Kydland-Prescott model is rather complex, we start our assessment with a much simpler RBC model based on Prescott (1986). It is shown that even this relatively simple model does surprisingly well in mimicking the fluctuations in the US economy. At the end of the chapter we show some deficiencies of the simple model as well as some of the possible extensions that can potentially fix them.[1]

---

[1] Of necessity, our discussion of the RBC methodology is far from complete. The interested reader is referred to Plosser (1989), Danthine and Donaldson (1993), Stadler (1994), Cooley (1995), King and Rebelo (1999), Rebelo (2005), and especially McCandless (2008) for much more extensive surveys of the literature.

18.2   Building the unit-elastic RBC model

The model constructed in section 13.5 can be viewed as a deterministic version of an RBC model. To turn that model into a conventional RBC model we must reformulate it in discrete time, introduce a stochastic technology shock, and derive the rational expectations solution for the loglinearized version of the model.

In much of the early RBC literature attention was restricted to competitive models without distortions (like tax rates, useless government consumption, etc.) or externalities (like congestion, pollution, etc.). As Prescott (1986, p. 271) argues, the advantage of working with such models is that the competitive equilibrium is Pareto optimal and unique. The solution algorithm can then exploit this equivalence between the decentralized market outcome and the social planning problem by solving the latter (easy) problem rather than the former (more difficult) problem. Here we do not pursue this approach because we wish to emphasize the link with the theoretical framework used throughout the book. As a result of this, we need to spell out the decentralized economy. (An additional advantage of doing so is that distortions, such as taxes, are easily introduced in, and analysed with, the model.) The approach adopted here is loosely based on Brock and Turnovsky (1981) and its discrete-time counterpart due to Altug and Labadie (2008, ch. 10).

18.2.1   Households

There is a large number of identical households. Each individual household is infinitely small and is a price taker on all markets in which it operates. By normalizing the population size to unity we can develop the argument on the basis of a single representative agent. The representative household is infinitely lived and has an objective function based on expected lifetime utility. Denoting the planning period by t, expected lifetime utility, $E_t \Lambda_t$, is given by:

$$E_t \Lambda_t \equiv E_t \sum_{\tau=t}^{\infty} U(C_\tau, 1 - L_\tau) \left(\frac{1}{1+\rho} \right)^{\tau-t}, \tag{18.1}$$

where E_t is the (conditional) expectations operator, $U(C_\tau, 1 - L_\tau)$ is the felicity function, C_τ and $1 - L_\tau$ are, respectively, consumption and leisure in period τ, and $1/(1+\rho)$ is the discounting factor due to time preference. To keep things simple we assume that the felicity function is loglinear, implying that both the *intra*temporal and *inter*temporal substitution elasticities are equal to unity:

$$U(C_\tau, 1 - L_\tau) \equiv \varepsilon \ln C_\tau + (1 - \varepsilon) \ln[1 - L_\tau]. \tag{18.2}$$

Equations (18.1) and (18.2) are the discrete-time analogues to, respectively, (13.77) and (13.78) modified for the existence of uncertainty. The notation for the expectation operator, E_t, indicates that the household bases its decisions on information available at time t.

The household receives wage, interest, and dividend payments from the firm sector, pays lump-sum taxes to the government, and uses its after-tax income for consumption and savings purposes. The budget identity is given in discrete time (for $\tau = t, t+1, t+2, ...$) by:

$$C_\tau + p_\tau S_{\tau+1} + B_{\tau+1} = w_\tau L_\tau + (1 + r^c_{\tau-1})B_\tau + S_\tau(p_\tau + D_\tau) - T_\tau, \tag{18.3}$$

where w_τ is the wage rate, T_τ is the lump-sum tax, and S_τ and B_τ denote, respectively, the number of shares and single-period corporate bonds owned at the start of period τ. Corporate bonds pay a risk-free interest rate $r_{\tau-1}^c$ (whose value is determined in period $\tau - 1$), dividends are given by D_τ, and the stock market price of shares at time τ is p_τ.

The household chooses sequences for consumption, labour supply, share holdings and corporate bonds $\{C_\tau, L_\tau, S_{\tau+1}, B_{\tau+1}\}_t^\infty$ in order to maximize expected utility (18.1) subject to (18.3), taking as given its initial share and bond holdings (S_t and B_t). In addition, the household treats as given the paths of prices (w_τ and p_τ), the corporate bond rate (r_τ^c), and dividends (D_τ).

For the planning period t the first-order conditions for this optimization problem can be written in general terms as (see Intermezzo 18.1):

$$U_C(C_t, 1 - L_t) = \frac{1}{w_t} U_{1-L}(C_t, 1 - L_t), \tag{18.4}$$

$$U_C(C_t, 1 - L_t) = E_t \left[\frac{1 + r_t^c}{1 + \rho} U_C(C_{t+1}, 1 - L_{t+1}) \right], \tag{18.5}$$

$$U_C(C_t, 1 - L_t) = E_t \left[\frac{1 + r_{t+1}^e}{1 + \rho} U_C(C_{t+1}, 1 - L_{t+1}) \right], \tag{18.6}$$

where $U_C(\cdot)$ and $U_{1-L}(\cdot)$ denote the marginal felicity of, respectively, consumption and leisure, and r_{t+1}^e is the net yield on equity shares which is defined as:

$$r_{t+1}^e \equiv \frac{p_{t+1} - p_t + D_{t+1}}{p_t}. \tag{18.7}$$

The expression in (18.4) implies that the household chooses consumption and leisure in such a way that the marginal rate of substitution between the two is equated to the wage rate. Note that the expectations operator does not feature in this expression. As Mankiw et al. (1985, p. 231) explain, this is the case because (18.4) is a purely static condition as the household knows the wage rate at time t and simply chooses the optimal mix of consumption and leisure appropriately.

Equations (18.5)–(18.6) characterize the optimal portfolio investment decisions by the household. Intuitively, these expressions says that it is optimal for the household to equalize its marginal felicity in the planning period to the *expected* marginal utility in the next period discounted for impatience. Since the corporate bond rate is risk free (as r_t^c is known in period t), equation (18.5) can be rewritten as follows:

$$1 = (1 + r_t^c) E_t [\mathcal{R}_{t,t+1}], \tag{18.8}$$

where $\mathcal{R}_{t,s}$ is the *stochastic discount factor* which is defined in general terms as:

$$\mathcal{R}_{t,s} \equiv \left(\frac{1}{1 + \rho} \right)^{s-t} \frac{U_C(C_s, 1 - L_s)}{U_C(C_t, 1 - L_t)}, \qquad \text{for } s \geq t. \tag{18.9}$$

Equation (18.6) is a little more complicated because the net yield on equity shares is a random variable (r_{t+1}^e is **not** known in period t). By owning one share which costs p_t, the household is entitled to next period's dividend plus next period's share price. But the future payoff $p_{t+1} + D_{t+1}$ is stochastic (as a result of technology shocks). Rewriting (18.6) by using (18.7) and (18.9) gives the first-order condition for equity shares in the form of an *asset pricing condition* (Cochrane, 2005, ch. 1):

$$p_t = E_t [(p_{t+1} + D_{t+1}) \mathcal{R}_{t,t+1}]. \tag{18.10}$$

When viewed in this form, it is clear that the current price of shares equals the expected gross payoff weighted by the stochastic discount factor. Since all households are identical the stochastic discount factor is the same for everybody and we can solve the expectational difference equation (18.10) to obtain:

$$p_t = E_t \left[\sum_{i=1}^{\infty} D_{t+i} \mathcal{R}_{t,t+i} \right], \tag{18.11}$$

where we assume that $\lim_{i\to\infty} E_t [p_{t+i} \mathcal{R}_{t,t+i}] = 0$ (see Intermezzo 18.2 for the derivation). The current price of equity shares equals the expected present value of dividend payments using the relevant stochastic discount factor for discounting.

Intermezzo 18.1

Optimal household and firm decisions under uncertainty. The easiest way to find the first-order conditions for the household's decision problem makes use of the Lagrangian methods used throughout much of this book (see also Chow (1997)). The Lagrangian expression is:

$$\mathcal{L}_t^H \equiv E_t \sum_{\tau=t}^{\infty} \left(\frac{1}{1+\rho} \right)^{\tau-t} \left[U(C_\tau, 1 - L_\tau) + \lambda_\tau \big[w_\tau L_\tau + (1 + r_{\tau-1}^c) B_\tau \right.$$

$$\left. + S_\tau (p_\tau + D_\tau) - T_\tau - C_\tau - p_\tau S_{\tau+1} - B_{\tau+1} \big] \right],$$

where λ_τ is the Lagrange multiplier for the budget identity in period τ. Assuming an interior solution the first-order conditions for this problem (for $\tau = t, t+1, t+2, ...$) are:

$$\frac{\partial \mathcal{L}_t^H}{\partial C_\tau} = \left(\frac{1}{1+\rho} \right)^{\tau-t} E_t \left[U_C(C_\tau, 1 - L_\tau) - \lambda_\tau \right] = 0, \tag{a}$$

$$\frac{\partial \mathcal{L}_t^H}{\partial L_\tau} = \left(\frac{1}{1+\rho} \right)^{\tau-t} E_t \left[-U_{1-L}(C_\tau, 1 - L_\tau) + \lambda_\tau w_\tau \right] = 0, \tag{b}$$

$$\frac{\partial \mathcal{L}_t^H}{\partial B_{\tau+1}} = \left(\frac{1}{1+\rho} \right)^{\tau-t} E_t \left[-\lambda_\tau + \frac{\lambda_{\tau+1}}{1+\rho} (1 + r_\tau^c) \right] = 0, \tag{c}$$

$$\frac{\partial \mathcal{L}_t^H}{\partial S_{\tau+1}} = \left(\frac{1}{1+\rho} \right)^{\tau-t} E_t \left[-\lambda_\tau p_\tau + \frac{\lambda_{\tau+1}}{1+\rho} (p_{\tau+1} + D_{\tau+1}) \right] = 0. \tag{d}$$

For the planning period, the expression in (a) implies that $\lambda_t = U_C(C_t, 1 - L_t)$. But when period $t+1$ comes around the household will set $\lambda_{t+1} = U_C(C_{t+1}, 1 - L_{t+1})$. Using this result in (c)–(d) and noting the definition of the yield on equity (18.7) we find the expressions in (18.5)–(18.6).

To derive the same first-order condition with the method of dynamic programming requires a bit more work. In the planning period B_t and S_t are given state variables. By defining the artificial control variable, $X_t \equiv S_{t+1}$, we have two transition equations:

$$B_{t+1} = w_t L_t + (1 + r_{t-1}^c) B_t + S_t (p_t + D_t) - C_t - p_t X_t - T_t, \tag{e}$$

$$S_{t+1} = X_t. \tag{f}$$

The value function for the household is:

$$V_t^H(B_t, S_t) \equiv \max_{\{C_t, L_t, X_t\}} \quad U(C_t, 1 - L_t) + \beta E_t \left[V_{t+1}^H(B_{t+1}, S_{t+1}) \right]$$

$$\text{subject to (e) and (f).} \tag{g}$$

Performing the maximization on the right-hand side gives the first-order conditions:

$$U_C(C_t, 1 - L_t) = \beta E_t \left[\frac{\partial V_{t+1}^H(B_{t+1}, S_{t+1})}{\partial B_{t+1}} \right], \tag{h}$$

$$U_{1-L}(C_t, 1 - L_t) = \beta w_t E_t \left[\frac{\partial V_{t+1}^H(B_{t+1}, S_{t+1})}{\partial B_{t+1}} \right], \tag{i}$$

$$\beta p_t E_t \left[\frac{\partial V_{t+1}^H(B_{t+1}, S_{t+1})}{\partial B_{t+1}} \right] = \beta E_t \left[\frac{\partial V_{t+1}^H(B_{t+1}, S_{t+1})}{\partial S_{t+1}} \right]. \tag{j}$$

Differentiating the value function (g) with respect to B_t and S_t gives:

$$\frac{\partial V_t^H(B_t, S_t)}{\partial B_t} = \beta E_t \left[\frac{\partial V_{t+1}^H(B_{t+1}, S_{t+1})}{\partial B_{t+1}} (1 + r_{t-1}^c) \right]$$

$$= (1 + r_{t-1}^c) U_C(C_t, 1 - L_t), \tag{k}$$

$$\frac{\partial V_t^H(B_t, S_t)}{\partial S_t} \equiv \beta E_t \left[\frac{\partial V_{t+1}^H(B_{t+1}, S_{t+1})}{\partial B_{t+1}} (p_t + D_t) \right]$$

$$= (p_t + D_t) U_C(C_t, 1 - L_t), \tag{l}$$

where we have used (h) to get from the first to the second expression in both cases. Using (k)–(l) for period $t + 1$ and substituting the resulting expressions in (h) and (j) gives the first-order conditions that are reported in the text (viz. (18.5)–(18.6)).

The value function for the firm is:

$$V_t^F(K_t) \equiv \max_{\{L_t, I_t\}} \quad F(K_t, L_t, Z_t) - w_t L_t - I_t + E_t \left[V_{t+1}^F(K_{t+1}) \mathcal{R}_{t,t+1} \right]$$

$$\text{subject to } K_{t+1} = I_t + (1 - \delta) K_t. \tag{m}$$

The first-order conditions for the maximization on the right-hand side are:

$$F_L(K_t, L_t, Z_t) = w_t, \tag{n}$$

$$1 = E_t \left[\frac{\partial V_{t+1}^F(K_{t+1})}{\partial K_{t+1}} \mathcal{R}_{t,t+1} \right]. \tag{o}$$

The envelope result gives:

$$\frac{\partial V_t^F(K_t)}{\partial K_t} = F_K(K_t, L_t, Z_t) + (1 - \delta) E_t \left[\frac{\partial V_{t+1}^F(K_{t+1})}{\partial K_{t+1}} \mathcal{R}_{t,t+1} \right]$$

$$= F_K(K_t, L_t, Z_t) + 1 - \delta, \tag{p}$$

where we have used (o) to get to the final expression. Using (p) for period $t+1$ and substituting the resulting expressions in (o) gives us (18.17) in the text. Note finally that (n) is the same as (18.16).

****

18.2.2 Firms

The representative firm is perfectly competitive and produces homogeneous output, Y_τ, by using its capital stock, K_τ, and by renting labour, L_τ, from the household sector. The production function is linearly homogeneous in capital and labour and features a unit elasticity of substitution:

$$Y_\tau = F(Z_\tau, K_\tau, L_\tau) \equiv \Omega_0 Z_\tau K_\tau^\alpha L_\tau^{1-\alpha}, \quad 0 < \alpha < 1, \tag{18.12}$$

where Z_τ is the state of general technology at time τ and Ω_0 is a scaling constant used in the numerical computations.

Given the household portfolio investment behaviour (as characterized by (18.8) and (18.10)), the objective function of the firm in the planning period t takes the following form (see Intermezzo 18.2 for the nontrivial derivation of this expression):

$$V_t = CF_t + E_t \left[\sum_{\tau=t+1}^{\infty} CF_\tau \mathcal{R}_{t,\tau} \right], \tag{18.13}$$

where $\mathcal{R}_{t,\tau}$ is the stochastic discount factor (defined in (18.9) above) and CF_τ is the net cash flow:

$$CF_\tau \equiv F(K_\tau, L_\tau, Z_\tau) - w_\tau L_\tau - I_\tau. \tag{18.14}$$

As usual, I_τ is gross investment which affects next period's capital stock according to:

$$K_{\tau+1} = I_\tau + (1 - \delta)K_\tau, \tag{18.15}$$

where δ is the depreciation rate (such that $0 < \delta < 1$). At time t the firm chooses sequences for investment and labour demand $\{I_\tau, L_\tau\}_t^\infty$ in order to maximize the value of the firm (18.13) subject to (18.15), taking as given its initial capital stock (K_t). In addition, the firm treats as given the paths of wages and the stochastic discount factor (w_τ and $\mathcal{R}_{t,\tau}$). For the planning period ($\tau = t$) the first-order conditions can be summarized by (see Intermezzo 18.1):

$$w_t = F_L(Z_t, K_t, L_t), \tag{18.16}$$

$$1 = E_t \left[\left(F_K(Z_{t+1}, K_{t+1}, L_{t+1}) + 1 - \delta \right) \mathcal{R}_{t,t+1} \right]. \tag{18.17}$$

Competitive labour demand is such that the wage rate is equalized to the marginal product of labour. By defining the real interest rate, $r_\tau \equiv F_K(Z_\tau, K_\tau, L_\tau) - \delta$, noting the definition of $\mathcal{R}_{t,t+1}$ and incorporating the felicity function (18.2) we can rewrite (18.17) to obtain the discrete-time consumption Euler equation:

$$\frac{\varepsilon}{C_t} = E_t \left[\frac{1+r_{t+1}}{1+\rho} \frac{\varepsilon}{C_{t+1}} \right]. \tag{18.18}$$

Intuitively (18.18) says that along the optimal path the representative household cannot change his/her expected lifetime utility by consuming a little less and investing a little more in period t, and consuming the additional resources thus obtained in period $t+1$. The left-hand and right-hand sides of (18.18) represent, respectively, the (marginal) utility cost of giving up present consumption and the expected utility gain of future consumption (Mankiw et al., 1985, p. 231).

Intermezzo 18.2

Deriving the firm's objective function. The firm's objective function as stated in (18.13) is derived as follows. The exposition here closely follows Altug and Labadie (2008, pp. 264–265). The firm's net cash flow is given by:

$$CF_t = F(K_t, L_t, Z_t) - w_t L_t - I_t. \tag{a}$$

The firm can finance its investment spending in three ways, namely by issuing bonds, emitting new shares, or by means of retained earnings. This gives:

$$I_t = B_{t+1} + p_t(S_{t+1} - S_t) + RE_t. \tag{b}$$

Retained earnings equal gross operating surplus $(F(K_t, L_t, Z_t) - w_t L_t)$ minus the sum of dividend payments plus interest payments on existing corporate debt:

$$RE_t = F(K_t, L_t, Z_t) - w_t L_t - S_t D_t - (1 + r_{t-1}^c) B_t. \tag{c}$$

By using (b)–(c) in (a) we get:

$$CF_t = S_t D_t + (1 + r_{t-1}^c) B_t + p_t(S_t - S_{t+1}) - B_{t+1}. \tag{d}$$

The *ex-dividend* value of the firm is defined as:

$$V_t^g = B_{t+1} + p_t S_{t+1}, \tag{e}$$

whilst the value of the firm at the start of period t is given by:

$$V_t = CF_t + V_t^g. \tag{f}$$

Using the household's first-order conditions for corporate bonds and equity shares (given in (18.8) and (18.10)) to write:

$$B_{t+1} = E_t \left[(1 + r_t^c) B_{t+1} \mathcal{R}_{t,t+1} \right], \tag{g}$$

$$p_t S_{t+1} = E_t \left[(p_{t+1} + D_{t+1}) S_{t+1} \mathcal{R}_{t,t+1} \right]. \tag{h}$$

By using (g)–(h) in (e) we obtain the following expression for the ex-dividend value of the firm:

$$V_t^g = E_t \left[\left((1 + r_t^c) B_{t+1} + (p_{t+1} + D_{t+1}) S_{t+1} \right) \mathcal{R}_{t,t+1} \right]. \tag{i}$$

By adding and subtracting $p_{t+1} S_{t+2}$ and B_{t+2} from the right-hand side and noting (d)–(e) we find the fundamental expectational difference equation for V_t^g:

$$V_t^g = E_t \left[\left(CF_{t+1} + V_{t+1}^g \right) \mathcal{R}_{t,t+1} \right]. \tag{j}$$

By solving this equation forward in time we obtain:

$$V_t^g = E_t \left[\sum_{i=1}^{\infty} CF_{t+i} \mathcal{R}_{t,t+i} \right], \tag{k}$$

where we have used the fact that the stochastic discount factor satisfies $\prod_{j=1}^{i} \mathcal{R}_{t+j-1,t+j} = \mathcal{R}_{t,t+i}$ and we assume that $\lim_{i \to \infty} E_t \left[V_{t+i}^g \mathcal{R}_{t,t+i} \right] = 0$. By substituting (k) into (f) we obtain the firm's objective function (18.13).

Equation (18.11) is obtained by solving (18.10) forward in time (noting the property of the stochastic discount factor mentioned above) and assuming that $\lim_{i \to \infty} E_t \left[p_{t+i} \mathcal{R}_{t,t+i} \right] = 0$.

****

The remainder of the model is quite standard. For future reference we state the basic RBC model in Table 18.1. The government is assumed to finance its consumption with lump-sum taxes—see equation (T1.8). The model features Ricardian equivalence so the introduction of government debt is not very interesting. Finally, the goods market clearing condition is given in each period by equation (T1.5).

18.3 Model analysis

Comparing the discrete-time model of Table 18.1 to the continuous-time model (stated in Table 13.4) reveals the close connection between the two models. Apart from the fluctuating technology term appearing in the discrete-time model, the only significant difference between the two models lies in the consumption Euler equation. In the continuous time model agents are blessed with perfect foresight and thus actual consumption growth ($\dot{C}(t)/C(t)$) appears in the Euler equation—see equation (13.85). In contrast, in the discrete-time model the representative household does not know the future interest rate (r_{t+1}) because future general technology (Z_{t+1}) is stochastic. As a result, the expectations operator features in the Euler equation (T1.2).

18.3.1 Loglinearized model

We follow Campbell (1994) by looking for analytical solutions to the loglinearized model. The advantage of this approach is that it allows us to study the economic

Table 18.1. The basic RBC model

$$K_{t+1} = I_t + (1 - \delta)K_t \tag{T1.1}$$

$$\frac{\varepsilon}{C_t} = E_t \left[\frac{1 + r_{t+1}}{1 + \rho} \frac{\varepsilon}{C_{t+1}} \right] \tag{T1.2}$$

$$w_t = (1 - \alpha) \frac{Y_t}{L_t} \tag{T1.3}$$

$$r_t + \delta = \alpha \frac{Y_t}{K_t} \tag{T1.4}$$

$$Y_t = C_t + I_t + G_t \tag{T1.5}$$

$$L_t = 1 - \frac{1 - \varepsilon}{\varepsilon} \frac{C_t}{w_t} \tag{T1.6}$$

$$Y_t = \Omega_0 Z_t K_t^\alpha L_t^{1-\alpha} \tag{T1.7}$$

$$T_t = G_t \tag{T1.8}$$

Definitions: Y_t is output, C_t is private consumption, L_t is employment, K_t is the capital stock, G_t is public consumption, w_t is the real wage rate, r_t is the real interest rate, T_t is the lump-sum tax, ε is a taste parameter for consumption, ρ is the pure rate of time preference, δ is the depreciation rate of capital, Z_t is a stochastic technology index, Ω_0 is a scaling constant, and α is the efficiency parameter of capital. The population is constant and normalized to unity.

---

mechanisms behind our simulation results in a straightforward fashion. The loglinearized model is reported in Table 18.2. We loglinearize the model around the steady state featuring a constant level of government consumption G_0 and use the notation $\tilde{x}_t \equiv \ln[x_t/x^*]$, where x^* is the steady-state value of x_t. Intermezzo 18.3 provides some details of the loglinearization for those in need.

Intermezzo 18.3

Linearization of nonlinear stochastic systems. The model of Table 18.1 is loglinearized around an initial steady state featuring a constant public consumption level G_0. We first define the variable $\tilde{x}_t$:

$$\tilde{x}_t \equiv \ln \left(\frac{x_t}{x^*} \right) \quad \Leftrightarrow \quad \frac{x_t}{x^*} \equiv e^{\tilde{x}_t}, \tag{a}$$

where x^* is the steady-state value for x_t. Provided x_t is near its steady-state value ($x_t/x^* \approx 1$ and $\tilde{x}_t \approx 0$) we have $e^{\tilde{x}_t} \approx 1 + \tilde{x}_t$ so that it follows from (a) that:

$$\frac{x_t}{x^*} \approx 1 + \tilde{x}_t. \tag{b}$$

We now apply these intermediate results to the unit-elastic model. In the RBC model there are three "basic types" of equations, namely dynamic equations (like (T1.1) and (T1.2)), equations that need no approximation

Table 18.2. The loglinearized model

$$\tilde{K}_{t+1} - \tilde{K}_t = \delta \left[\tilde{I}_t - \tilde{K}_t \right] \tag{T2.1}$$

$$E_t \tilde{C}_{t+1} - \tilde{C}_t = \frac{\rho}{1+\rho} E_t \tilde{r}_{t+1} \tag{T2.2}$$

$$\tilde{w}_t = \tilde{Y}_t - \tilde{L}_t \tag{T2.3}$$

$$\rho \tilde{r}_t = (\rho + \delta) \left[\tilde{Y}_t - \tilde{K}_t \right] \tag{T2.4}$$

$$\tilde{Y}_t = \omega_C^* \tilde{C}_t + \omega_I^* \tilde{I}_t + \omega_G^* \tilde{G}_t \tag{T2.5}$$

$$\tilde{L}_t = \omega_{LL}^* \left[\tilde{w}_t - \tilde{C}_t \right] \tag{T2.6}$$

$$\tilde{Y}_t = \tilde{Z}_t + \alpha \tilde{K}_t + (1 - \alpha) \tilde{L}_t \tag{T2.7}$$

$$\tilde{I}_t = \tilde{G}_t \tag{T2.8}$$

Definitions: $\omega_G^* \equiv G_0/Y^*$: output share of public consumption; $\omega_C^* \equiv (C/Y)^*$: output share of private consumption; $\omega_I^* \equiv (I/Y)^*$: output share of investment, $\omega_C^* + \omega_I^* + \omega_G^* = 1$, $\delta/\omega_I^* = (Y/K)^* \equiv (\rho + \delta)/\alpha$. $\omega_{LL}^* \equiv (1 - L^*)/L^*$: ratio between leisure and labour. $\tilde{x}(t) \equiv \ln[x(t)/x^*]$. Stars designate steady-state values.

because they are multiplicative and thus loglinear (like (T1.3), (T1.4), and (T1.7)), and linear equations (like (T1.5)).

Consider first a dynamic equation like (T1.1). We obtain in a few steps:

$$\frac{K_{t+1}}{K^*} = \left(\frac{I}{K} \right)^* \frac{I_t}{I^*} + (1 - \delta) \frac{K_t}{K^*}$$

$$1 + \tilde{K}_{t+1} \approx \delta \left[1 + \tilde{I}_t \right] + (1 - \delta) \left[1 + \tilde{K}_t \right]$$

$$\tilde{K}_{t+1} - \tilde{K}_t \approx \delta \left[\tilde{I}_t - \tilde{K}_t \right],$$

where we have used (b) (plus the steady-state relation $I^* = \delta K^*$) in going from the first to the second line.

Next we consider an equation like (T1.7). By taking logarithms on both sides we get:

$$\ln Y_t = \ln \Omega_0 + \ln Z_t + \alpha \ln K_t + (1 - \alpha) \ln L_t. \tag{c}$$

In the steady state we have:

$$\ln Y^* = \ln \Omega_0 + \ln Z^* + \alpha \ln K^* + (1 - \alpha) \ln L^*. \tag{d}$$

Deducting (d) from (c) and noting the definitions of $\tilde{Y}_t$, $\tilde{K}_t$, and $\tilde{L}_t$ we obtain the desired expression:

$$\tilde{Y}_t = \tilde{Z}_t + \alpha \tilde{K}(t) + (1 - \alpha) \tilde{L}(t).$$

Third, we consider a linear equation like (T1.5). We derive in a few steps:

$$\frac{Y_t}{Y^*} = \left(\frac{C}{Y} \right)^* \frac{C_t}{C^*} + \left(\frac{I}{Y} \right)^* \frac{I_t}{I^*} + \left(\frac{G_0}{Y^*} \right) \frac{G_t}{G_0}$$

$$1 + \tilde{Y}_t \approx \left(\frac{C}{Y}\right)^* [1 + \tilde{C}_t] + \left(\frac{I}{Y}\right)^* [1 + \tilde{I}_t] + \left(\frac{G_0}{Y^*}\right) [1 + \tilde{G}_t]$$

$$\tilde{Y}_t \approx \omega_C^* \tilde{C}_t + \omega_I^* \tilde{I}_t + \omega_G^* \tilde{G}_t.$$

We have used (b) in going from the first to the second line. In going from the second to the third line, we use the definitions for ω_C^*, ω_I^*, and ω_G^* (stated in Table 18.2).

Finally, consider an equation like (T1.6) which is loglinear in consumption, the wage rate, and leisure (but not in labour). Of course, we obtain in a straightforward fashion that $\tilde{w}_t + \widetilde{[1 - L_t]} = \tilde{C}_t$. But in the rest of the model we work with $\tilde{L}_t$. Using (b) we can relate $\tilde{L}_t$ and $\widetilde{[1 - L_t]}$:

$$\widetilde{1 - L_t} \equiv \ln\left(\frac{1 - L_t}{1 - L^*}\right) \approx \frac{[1 - L_t] - [1 - L^*]}{1 - L^*} = -\frac{L_t - L^*}{1 - L^*}$$

$$\tilde{L}_t \equiv \ln\left(\frac{L_t}{L^*}\right) \approx \frac{L_t - L^*}{L^*},$$

from which it follows that $\widetilde{[1 - L_t]} = -[1/\omega_{LL}^*]\tilde{L}_t$, where ω_{LL}^* is defined in Table 18.2.

****

The derivation of the loglinearized Euler equation (T2.2) from its level counterpart (T1.2) is not straightforward and warrants some further comment. First we note that (T1.2) can be rewritten as:

$$1 = E_t\left[\frac{1 + r_{t+1}}{1 + \rho} \frac{C_t}{C_{t+1}}\right]. \tag{18.19}$$

By definition we have that $(1 + r_{t+1})/(1 + \rho) = \exp[\widetilde{1 + r_{t+1}}]$, $C_t/C^* = e^{\tilde{C}_t}$ and $C_{t+1}/C^* = e^{\tilde{C}_{t+1}}$ so we can rewrite (18.19) in a number of steps:

$$1 = E_t\left[e^{(\widetilde{1 + r_{t+1}}) + \tilde{C}_t - \tilde{C}_{t+1}}\right]$$

$$= E_t\left[1 + (\widetilde{1 + r_{t+1}}) + 1 + \tilde{C}_t - 1 - \tilde{C}_{t+1}\right],$$

$$0 = E_t\left[\frac{\rho}{1 + \rho}\tilde{r}_{t+1} + \tilde{C}_t - \tilde{C}_{t+1}\right]. \tag{18.20}$$

In going from the first to the second line we have used the approximation $e^{\tilde{x}_t} \approx 1 + \tilde{x}_t$, and in going from the second to the third line we relate $\widetilde{1 + r_{t+1}}$ to $\tilde{r}_{t+1}$.[2]

---

[2] An alternative derivation, mentioned by Campbell (1994, p. 469) and Uhlig (1999, p. 33), is due to Hansen and Singleton (1983, p. 253). (See also Attanasio, 1999, p. 768.) Under the assumption that C_{t+1}/C_t and $1 + r_{t+1}$ are jointly distributed lognormally with a constant variance-covariance matrix, (18.19) can be rewritten as:

$$E_t \ln(1 + r_{t+1}) = E_t \ln[C_{t+1}/C_t] + \ln(1 + \rho) - \frac{\sigma^2}{2},$$

where σ^2 is the (constant) variance of $\ln[(C_t/C_{t+1})(1 + r_{t+1})]$. The σ^2 term is subsequently ignored by Campbell (1994) and Uhlig (1999).

As was the case for the deterministic continuous-time model of section 13.5, the stochastic discrete-time model of Table 18.2 can best be solved by first condensing it. This procedure yields a system of stochastic difference equations in the key dynamic variables $\tilde{K}_t$ and $\tilde{C}_t$, of which the former is a predetermined variable and the latter is a jumping variable.

By using labour demand (T2.3), labour supply (T2.6), and the production function (T2.7), we solve for the equilibrium levels of employment $\tilde{L}_t$, wages $\tilde{w}_t$, and output $\tilde{Y}_t$, *conditional* upon $\tilde{K}_t$, $\tilde{C}_t$, *and* the existing state of general productivity $\tilde{Z}_t$:

$$(1 - \alpha)\tilde{L}_t = (\phi - 1)\left[\tilde{Z}_t + \alpha\tilde{K}_t - \tilde{C}_t\right], \tag{18.21}$$

$$(1 - \alpha)\tilde{w}_t = (1 - \alpha\phi)\left[\tilde{Z}_t + \alpha\tilde{K}_t\right] + (\phi - 1)\alpha\tilde{C}_t, \tag{18.22}$$

$$\tilde{Y}_t = \phi\left[\tilde{Z}_t + \alpha\tilde{K}_t\right] - (\phi - 1)\tilde{C}_t, \tag{18.23}$$

where ϕ is defined as:

$$\phi \equiv \frac{1 + \omega_{LL}^*}{1 + \alpha\omega_{LL}^*}. \tag{18.24}$$

Since $\omega_{LL}^* > 0$ we easily find that $1 < \phi < 1/\alpha$ and thus that $\alpha < \alpha\phi < 1$. Ceteris paribus consumption and capital, a higher than average level of general productivity ($\tilde{Z}_t > 0$) implies that labour demand is higher than average. As a result, employment, wages, and output are also higher than average.

By using (18.23) in (T2.5) and (T2.4), respectively, we obtain the relevant expressions for investment $\tilde{I}_t$ and the interest rate $\tilde{r}_t$:

$$\omega_I^*\tilde{I}_t = \alpha\phi\tilde{K}_t - (\omega_C^* + \phi - 1)\tilde{C}_t + \phi\tilde{Z}_t - \omega_G^*\tilde{G}_t, \tag{18.25}$$

$$\frac{\rho}{\rho + \delta}\tilde{r}_t = -(1 - \alpha\phi)\tilde{K}_t - (\phi - 1)\tilde{C}_t + \phi\tilde{Z}_t. \tag{18.26}$$

General productivity affects investment and the interest rate positively because, ceteris paribus, output and capital productivity are both higher than average if $\tilde{Z}_t > 0$. By leading (18.26) by one period and taking expectations we obtain the following expression:

$$\frac{\rho}{\rho + \delta}E_t\tilde{r}_{t+1} = -(1 - \alpha\phi)\tilde{K}_{t+1} - (\phi - 1)E_t\tilde{C}_{t+1} + \phi E_t\tilde{Z}_{t+1}. \tag{18.27}$$

Since investment is known in period t, the household knows exactly what next period's capital stock will be. Hence, the *actual* future capital stock ($\tilde{K}_{t+1}$) features in (18.27). Furthermore, the household must form expectations regarding next period's general productivity level ($E_t\tilde{Z}_{t+1}$) and labour supply. The latter effect explains why $E_t\tilde{C}_{t+1}$ enters in (18.27).

Finally, by using (18.25) in (T2.1) and (18.27) in (T2.2) we obtain the following expression for the (condensed) dynamic system of stochastic difference equations:

$$\begin{bmatrix} \tilde{K}_{t+1} - \tilde{K}_t \\ E_t\tilde{C}_{t+1} - \tilde{C}_t \end{bmatrix} = \Delta \begin{bmatrix} \tilde{K}_t \\ \tilde{C}_t \end{bmatrix} + \begin{bmatrix} \gamma_t^K \\ \gamma_t^C \end{bmatrix}, \tag{18.28}$$

where $\Delta \equiv \Theta^{-1}\Delta^*$ is the Jacobian matrix, and Δ^* and Θ are defined, respectively, as:

$$\Delta^* \equiv \begin{bmatrix} y^*(\alpha\phi - \omega_I^*) & -y^*(\omega_C^* + \phi - 1) \\ -\zeta(1 - \alpha\phi) & -\zeta(\phi - 1) \end{bmatrix}, \qquad \Theta \equiv \begin{bmatrix} 1 & 0 \\ -\delta_{21}^* & 1 \end{bmatrix}. \tag{18.29}$$

Here δ_{ij}^* is the typical element of Δ^* and ζ is given by:

$$0 < \zeta \equiv \frac{\rho + \delta}{1 - \delta + \phi(\rho + \delta)} < 1. \tag{18.30}$$

In equation (18.28) the time-varying shock terms are given by γ_t^K and γ_t^C:

$$\begin{bmatrix} \gamma_t^K \\ \gamma_t^C \end{bmatrix} \equiv \Theta^{-1} \begin{bmatrix} y^* \left(\phi \tilde{Z}_t - \omega_G^* \tilde{G}_t \right) \\ \phi \zeta E_t \tilde{Z}_{t+1} \end{bmatrix} = \begin{bmatrix} y^* \left(\phi \tilde{Z}_t - \omega_G^* \tilde{G}_t \right) \\ \delta_{21}^* y^* \left(\phi \tilde{Z}_t - \omega_G^* \tilde{G}_t \right) + \phi \zeta E_t \tilde{Z}_{t+1} \end{bmatrix}. \tag{18.31}$$

A number of things should be noted about the dynamical system defined in (18.28). First, the determinants of Δ and Δ^* are identical.[3] It is straightforward to verify that $|\Delta|$ equals:

$$|\Delta| = |\Delta^*| = -\zeta y^* \left[\omega_G^*(\phi - 1) + \phi \omega_C^*(1 - \alpha) \right] < 0. \tag{18.32}$$

Second, since the determinant is the product of the characteristic roots it follows from (18.32) that the system in (18.28) possesses one negative characteristic root, denoted by $-\lambda_1 < 0$, and one positive characteristic root which we denote by $\lambda_2 > 0$. If, in addition, the parameters of the problem are such that $\lambda_1 < 1$ it follows that the system is saddle-point stable.[4]

Checking saddle-point stability is thus more involved in a discrete-time setting than in a continuous-time context. With continuous time, the only thing that must be checked is the *sign* of the characteristic roots. In contrast, with discrete time, the *magnitude* of the roots matters, i.e. one must check whether they are inside or outside the unit circle. Note that (18.28) is conventionally written as:

$$\begin{bmatrix} \tilde{K}_{t+1} \\ E_t \tilde{C}_{t+1} \end{bmatrix} = \bar{\Delta} \begin{bmatrix} \tilde{K}_t \\ \tilde{C}_t \end{bmatrix} + \begin{bmatrix} \gamma_t^K \\ \gamma_t^C \end{bmatrix}, \tag{18.33}$$

where $\bar{\Delta} \equiv I + \Delta$ has characteristic roots $\bar{\lambda}_1 \equiv 1 - \lambda_1$ and $\bar{\lambda}_2 \equiv 1 + \lambda_2$. A stable (unstable) root satisfies $|\bar{\lambda}_i| < 1$ ($|\bar{\lambda}_i| > 1$). Saddle-point stability thus obtains provided $|1 - \lambda_1| < 1$ and $|1 + \lambda_2| > 1$. Since $\lambda_2 > 0$ the second condition is satisfied so there is one unstable root. To verify the first condition we write the determinant of $|\bar{\Delta}|$ as:

$$|\bar{\Delta}| = (1 + \delta_{11}^*)(1 + \delta_{22}^*) = \bar{\lambda}_1 \bar{\lambda}_2 > 0,$$

where the sign follows from the fact that δ_{11}^* and δ_{22}^* can be rewritten in terms of structural parameters as:

$$\delta_{11}^* = \alpha y^* \left(\phi - \frac{\delta}{\rho + \delta} \right) > 0, \quad 1 + \delta_{22}^* = \frac{1 + \rho}{1 - \delta + \phi(\rho + \delta)} > 0.$$

Hence $\bar{\lambda}_1$ and $\bar{\lambda}_2$ are both positive, i.e. $0 < \lambda_1 < 1$ and $\lambda_2 > 1$.

---

[3]Denoting the typical elements of Δ and Δ^* by, respectively, δ_{ij} and δ_{ij}^* we find:

$$\Delta \equiv \Theta^{-1} \Delta^* = \begin{bmatrix} \delta_{11}^* & \delta_{12}^* \\ \delta_{21}^*(1 + \delta_{11}^*) & \delta_{22}^* + \delta_{12}^* \delta_{21}^* \end{bmatrix}.$$

From matrix algebra we know that the subtraction of a multiple of any row from another row leaves the determinant unchanged, so it follows that $|\Delta| = |\Delta^*|$. See Section A.2.4 of the Mathematical Appendix.

[4]See Azariadis (1993, pp. 39 and 62–67) for a very thorough discussion of stability issues in the discrete-time case.

18.3.2   The shock process

Our description of the unit-elastic RBC model is completed once particular specifications are adopted for the exogenous variables, $\tilde{Z}_t$ and $\tilde{G}_t$. To keep things simple, we assume that government consumption is constant, so that $\tilde{G}_t = 0$ for all t, and that the technology shock takes the following first-order autoregressive form:

$$\ln Z_t = \alpha_Z + \xi_Z \ln Z_{t-1} + \eta_t, \qquad 0 \leq \xi_Z < 1, \tag{18.34}$$

where α_Z is a constant, ξ_Z is the autoregressive parameter, and η_t is a stochastic "innovation" term. The parameter ξ_Z parameterizes the persistence in the productivity term—the closer ξ_Z is to unity, the higher is the degree of persistence. It is assumed that the innovation term, η_t, is identically and independently distributed with mean zero and variance σ_η^2. In the absence of stochastic shocks, technology would settle in a steady state for which $(1 - \xi_Z) \ln Z^* = \alpha_Z$. Since, by definition, we have that $\tilde{Z}_t \equiv \ln [Z_t / Z^*]$, equation (18.34) can be rewritten as follows:

$$\tilde{Z}_t = \xi_Z \tilde{Z}_{t-1} + \eta_t. \tag{18.35}$$

Recall that agents must form an expectation at time t about technology in the next period $(E_t \tilde{Z}_{t+1})$ in order to forecast the interest rate featuring in their Euler equation $(E_t \tilde{r}_{t+1}$, see (18.27)). Since agents are aware of the shock process for technology (given in (18.35)) they will use this information to compute their forecast, i.e. they will base their decisions on the forecast $E_t \tilde{Z}_{t+1} = \xi_Z \tilde{Z}_t$ (since $E_t \eta_{t+1} = 0$ this is the best they can do).

The model is now fully specified and consists of (18.28), (18.31), and (18.35). There exist several methods that can be used to solve for the rational expectations solution of the model. Campbell (1994, pp. 470–472), for example, uses the method of undetermined coefficients. Intuitively, this method works as follows. First, we guess a solution for consumption in terms of the state variables $(\tilde{K}_t, \tilde{Z}_t)$ and unknown parameters (π_{ck}, π_{cz}) of the form $\tilde{C}_t = \pi_{ck}\tilde{K}_t + \pi_{cz}\tilde{Z}_t$. Next, we use all the structural information contained in the model plus the assumption of rational expectations in order to relate the unknown coefficients to the structural parameters of the model. Another method is due to Blanchard and Kahn (1980)—see Uhlig (1999, pp. 54–56) for an example.

18.3.3   Impulse-response functions

In the appendix to this chapter we work out the general rational expectations solution of the model in terms of its state variables, following the approach suggested by Campbell (1994). Here, we focus directly on the impulse-response functions for the different variables. The advantage of doing so is twofold. First, it facilitates the comparison with the analytical discussion in section 13.5 above. Second, the impulse-response functions nicely visualize the key properties of our prototypical RBC model, especially those related to the degree of persistence of the shock.

We compute the impulse-response functions as follows. We normalize the time of the shock at $t = 0$, and assume that $\eta_0 > 0$ and $\eta_t = 0$ for $t = 1, 2, \ldots$. Assuming that technology was at its steady-state level in the previous period $(\tilde{Z}_{-1} = 0)$ we can use (18.35) to solve for the implied path of $\tilde{Z}_t$ that results from the innovation at time $t = 0$:

$$\tilde{Z}_t = \xi_Z^t \cdot \eta_0. \tag{18.36}$$

By using (18.36) in (18.31) (and recalling that $\tilde{G}_t = 0$ and $E_t \tilde{Z}_{t+1} = \xi_Z \tilde{Z}_t$) we find that the shock term affecting the dynamical system takes the following, time-varying, form:

$$\begin{bmatrix} \gamma_t^K \\ \gamma_t^C \end{bmatrix} \equiv \phi \Gamma^{-1} \begin{bmatrix} y^* \tilde{Z}_t \\ \zeta \xi_Z \tilde{Z}_t \end{bmatrix} = \phi \begin{bmatrix} y^* \\ \zeta [\xi_Z - y^* [1 - \alpha \phi]] \end{bmatrix} \eta_0 \xi_Z^t. \tag{18.37}$$

It follows from (18.37) that the productivity shock directly affects the dynamics of both the capital stock and consumption. For $0 \leq \xi_Z < 1$, the shock eventually dies out as time goes by, i.e. $\gamma_{K\infty} = \gamma_{C\infty} = 0$. The innovation therefore does not have a long-run effect in that case but the impact and transition results are non-zero. In the appendix to this chapter we derive the impulse-response function for the capital stock and consumption:

$$\begin{bmatrix} \tilde{K}_t \\ \tilde{C}_t \end{bmatrix} = \begin{bmatrix} 0 \\ \tilde{C}_0 \end{bmatrix} (1 - \lambda_1)^t + \begin{bmatrix} y^* [(1 - \xi_Z)(1 - \zeta(\phi - 1)) + \xi_Z \zeta \omega_C^*] \\ \zeta \xi_Z [1 - \xi_Z + (1 - \omega_I) y^*] \end{bmatrix}$$
$$\times \frac{\phi \eta_0}{\lambda_2 + 1 - \xi_Z} T_t(\xi_Z, 1 - \lambda_1), \tag{18.38}$$

where the impact jump in consumption is given by:

$$\tilde{C}_0 = \frac{\lambda_2 + \zeta [(1 - \xi_Z)(\phi - 1) - \xi_Z \omega_C^*]}{\omega_C^* + \phi - 1} \frac{\phi \eta_0}{\lambda_2 + 1 - \xi_Z}, \tag{18.39}$$

and $T_t(\alpha_1, \alpha_2)$ is a non-negative bell-shaped term (defined for for $t = 0, 1, 2, \cdots$):

$$T_t(\alpha_1, \alpha_2) \equiv \begin{cases} \dfrac{\alpha_1^t - \alpha_2^t}{\alpha_1 - \alpha_2} & \text{for } \alpha_1 \neq \alpha_2 \\ t\alpha_1^{t-1} & \text{for } \alpha_1 = \alpha_2. \end{cases} \tag{18.40}$$

Although these expressions look rather forbidding, it turns out that quite a lot can be understood about them by first focusing on some special cases that have received a lot of attention in the literature. In doing so we are able to demonstrate the crucial role of shock persistence in the unit-elastic RBC model.

18.3.3.1 A purely temporary shock ($\xi_Z = 0$)

We follow King and Rebelo (1999, pp. 964–967) by first considering the effects of a purely transitory productivity shock. In terms of our model this means that the shock displays no serial correlation at all (i.e. $\xi_Z = 0$ in (18.35)) and we study the response of the system to a technology shock of the form $\tilde{Z}_0 = \eta_0$ and $\tilde{Z}_t = 0$ for $t = 1, 2, \ldots$. Clearly, such a shock has no long-run effect on the macroeconomy as technology only deviates in the impact period from its steady-state level. The impact effect on consumption, and thus on the other variables, is, however, non-zero. Indeed, by setting $\xi_Z = 0$ in (18.39) we obtain the expression for the consumption jump with a purely transitory shock:

$$\tilde{C}_0 = \frac{\phi [\lambda_2 + \zeta(\phi - 1)] \eta_0}{(1 + \lambda_2) [\omega_C^* + \phi - 1]} > 0. \tag{18.41}$$

Intuitively, consumption rises in the impact period because the technology shock, brief though it may be, makes the agent a tiny bit richer. Since leisure, like consumption, is a normal good, the shock also causes a small wealth effect in labour supply. In

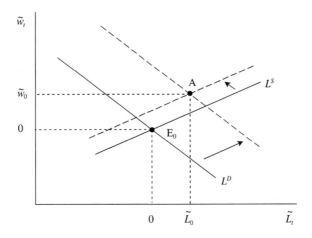

Figure 18.1: A shock to technology and the labour market

terms of Figure 18.1 the labour supply curve shifts up and to the left (from the solid to the dashed line). At the same time, however, the shock raises labour productivity and thus labour demand. Hence, even though the capital stock is predetermined in the impact period, the labour demand curve shifts up and to the right. As is clear from the diagram, the impact effect on the wage rate is unambiguously positive, but the impact effect on employment appears to be ambiguous as it depends on the relative magnitudes of the labour supply and demand effects.

By using (18.41) and $\tilde{Z}_0 = \eta_0$ in (18.21)–(18.23) we obtain the following analytical expressions for $\tilde{L}_0$, $\tilde{w}_0$, and $\tilde{Y}_0$:

$$\tilde{L}_0 = \frac{\phi - 1}{1 - \alpha} \left[1 - \frac{\phi \left[\lambda_2 + \zeta(\phi - 1) \right]}{(1 + \lambda_2) \left[\omega_C^* + \phi - 1 \right]} \right] \eta_0, \tag{18.42}$$

$$\tilde{w}_0 = \frac{1 - \alpha\phi}{1 - \alpha} \eta_0 + \frac{(\phi - 1)\alpha}{1 - \alpha} \tilde{C}_0 > 0, \tag{18.43}$$

$$\tilde{Y}_0 = \frac{(1 + \lambda_2)\omega_C^* + (\phi - 1) \left[1 - \zeta(\phi - 1) \right]}{(1 + \lambda_2) \left[\omega_C^* + \phi - 1 \right]} \phi\eta_0 > 0. \tag{18.44}$$

For realistic calibrations of the model the labour-demand effect dominates the labour-supply effect, so that employment increases in the impact period as illustrated in Figure 18.1. The wage rate increases at impact regardless of the parameter values as the labour-demand and supply effects work in the same direction. Finally, despite the fact that the employment effect is ambiguous in general, the output effect is unambiguously positive.[5] Since output rises and capital is predetermined at impact, the immediate effect on the interest rate is positive (see e.g. (T2.4)). Finally, the impact effect on investment is obtained by using (18.41) and setting $\tilde{Z}_0 = \eta_0$ and $\tilde{G}_t = 0$ in

---

[5]The sign of the output effect follows in a straightforward fashion from the fact that ζ, defined in (18.30), satisfies $0 < \zeta(\phi - 1) < 1$. This can be seen by noting that $\zeta > 0$, $\phi > 1$, and:

$$1 - \zeta(\phi - 1) = \frac{1 + \rho}{1 - \delta + \phi(\rho + \delta)} > 0.$$

(18.25). After some manipulation we obtain:

$$\tilde{I}_0 = \frac{1 - \zeta(\phi - 1)}{\omega_I^* (1 + \lambda_2)} \phi \eta_0 > 0, \tag{18.45}$$

where the sign follows from the fact that $0 < \zeta(\phi - 1) < 1$ (see footnote 5).

By substituting $\xi_Z = 0$ into (18.38) and (18.40) (and noting (18.45)) we find the transition paths for the capital stock and consumption:

$$\begin{bmatrix} \tilde{K}_t \\ \tilde{C}_t \end{bmatrix} = \begin{bmatrix} \dfrac{\delta}{1 - \lambda_1} \tilde{I}_0 \\ \tilde{C}_0 \end{bmatrix} (1 - \lambda_1)^t, \quad \text{for } t = 1, 2, 3, ... \tag{18.46}$$

In Figure 18.2 we plot the impulse-response functions for the purely transitory shock, using the calibration values discussed above (see (13.119) above). There is no long-run effect on productivity, so there is no long-run effect on the other variables either. Productivity is higher only in the impact period, $t = 0$. One period after the shock has occurred, technology is back to its steady-state level (as $\tilde{Z}_t = 0$ for $t = 1, 2, ...$).

The intuition behind the impact effects is as follows. As a result of the shock ($\tilde{Z}_0 = 0.01$; a 1% increase), agents are a tiny little bit wealthier and thus increase consumption somewhat, i.e. $\tilde{C}_0 > 0$ (an increase close to 0.14%). The agents wish to smooth consumption, however, so they also increase their saving-investment at impact, i.e. $\tilde{I}_0 > 0$ (close to a 10% increase). There is a strong incentive to work hard when productivity is high, so the tiny income effect is dominated by the large substitution effect and labour supply increases sharply at impact, i.e. $\tilde{L}_0 > 0$ (almost 1.5% increase). Together with the impact shock in productivity, the labour supply expansion produces a large increase in output, $\tilde{Y}_0 > 0$ (about a 2% increase). Because employment is high, capital is relatively scarce and the real interest rate rises sharply.[6]

It follows from (18.46) that the economy has a slightly higher capital stock in period 1 (since $\tilde{K}_1 = \delta \tilde{I}_0 > 0$) which is gradually run down over time. Consumption also gradually returns to its initial steady-state value. As the simulations confirm, investment and employment fall below their respective steady-state levels during transition ($\tilde{I}_t < 0$ and $\tilde{L}_t < 0$ for $t = 1, 2, \ldots$). The real interest rate also falls below its steady-state level in period $t = 1$ after which it gradually returns to this level. Since $\tilde{r}_t < 0$ for $t = 1, 2, \ldots$, it is optimal for the household to choose a downward-sloping consumption profile.

In summary, for a purely temporary shock the following key features stand out. First, the substitution effect in labour supply is dominant and produces a large employment effect in the impact period. Second, the transitional effects on consumption and the capital stock are small because the shock itself is only small from a lifetime perspective. Third, apart from scaling, the output response looks virtually identical to the impulse. In colloquial terms, the model itself does not seem to "do very much to the shock". This disappointing feature of the model is called its *lack of propagation* (see below).

18.3.3.2   A permanent shock ($\xi_Z = 1$)

The second special case that can be distinguished assumes that the technology shocks are permanent, i.e. the technology process (18.35) features a unit root ($\xi_Z = 1$). The

---

[6]King and Rebelo (1999, pp. 966–967) incorrectly argue that the interest rate falls in the impact period. Since output rises and the capital stock is unchanged at impact, it must be the case that the interest rate rises at impact also.

Figure 18.2: Purely transitory productivity shock

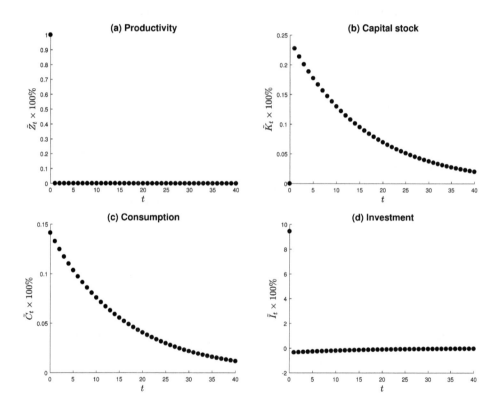

Figure 18.2, continued

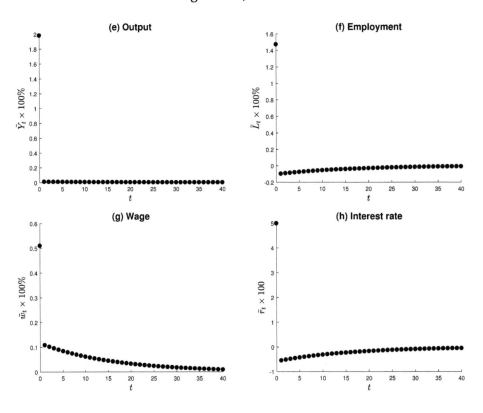

impact effect on consumption is obtained from (18.39):

$$\tilde{C}_0 = \frac{\phi \left[\lambda_2 - \zeta \omega_C^*\right] \eta_0}{\lambda_2 \left[\omega_C^* + \phi - 1\right]} > 0. \tag{18.47}$$

Consumption rises at impact because the permanent technology shock makes the representative agent wealthier. By substituting (18.47) into (18.21)–(18.23) we obtain the impact effects for employment, the wage, and output:

$$\tilde{L}_0 = \frac{\phi - 1}{1 - \alpha} \left[1 - \frac{\phi \left[\lambda_2 - \zeta \omega_C^*\right]}{\lambda_2 \left[\omega_C^* + \phi - 1\right]}\right] \eta_0, \tag{18.48}$$

$$\tilde{w}_0 = \frac{1 - \alpha\phi}{1 - \alpha} \eta_0 + \frac{(\phi - 1)\alpha}{1 - \alpha} \tilde{C}_0 > 0, \tag{18.49}$$

$$\tilde{Y}_0 = \frac{\lambda_2 + \zeta(\phi - 1)}{\lambda_2 \left[\omega_C^* + \phi - 1\right]} \phi \omega_C^* \eta_0 > 0. \tag{18.50}$$

As for the purely temporary shock, the employment effect is ambiguous in general but positive for realistic calibrations. The wage rate rises unambiguously as does output. Finally, the impact effect on investment is obtained by using (18.47) and setting $\tilde{Z}_0 = \eta_0$ and $\tilde{G}_t = 0$ in (18.25):

$$\tilde{I}_0 = \frac{\zeta \phi \omega_C^* \eta_0}{\omega_I^* \lambda_2} > 0. \tag{18.51}$$

By setting $\xi_Z = 1$ in (18.38) and (18.40) we obtain analytical expressions for the transition paths of the capital stock and consumption:

$$\begin{bmatrix} \tilde{K}_t \\ \tilde{C}_t \end{bmatrix} = \begin{bmatrix} 0 \\ \tilde{C}_0 \end{bmatrix} (1 - \lambda_1)^t + \begin{bmatrix} \tilde{K}_\infty \\ \tilde{C}_\infty \end{bmatrix} \left[1 - (1 - \lambda_1)^t\right], \tag{18.52}$$

where $\tilde{C}_0$ is given in (18.47) above, and $\tilde{K}_\infty$ and $\tilde{C}_\infty$ are given by:

$$\tilde{K}_\infty = \frac{\omega_C^*}{1 - \omega_I^*} \tilde{C}_\infty = \frac{\phi \omega_C^* \eta_0}{\omega_G^*(\phi - 1) + \phi \omega_C^*(1 - \alpha)} > 0. \tag{18.53}$$

As equation (18.52) shows, $\tilde{K}_t$ and $\tilde{C}_t$ (and thus all other variables also) can be written as the weighted average of the relevant impact and long-run effects. The transition speed of the economy, $(1 - \lambda_1)$, determines the time-varying weights. With a permanent productivity shock both consumption and the capital stock increase in the long run—see (18.53). The intuition behind this result follows readily from the steady-state constancy of the great ratios (see also above). Imposing the steady state in equations (T2.1)–(T2.2) (and ignoring the expectations operator) we find $\tilde{I}_\infty = \tilde{K}_\infty$ and $\tilde{r}_\infty = 0$. But this implies, by (T2.4), that $\tilde{Y}_\infty = \tilde{K}_\infty$, and by (T2.3) and (T2.7) that $\tilde{K}_\infty - \tilde{L}_\infty = \tilde{w}_\infty = (1/(1 - \alpha))\tilde{Z}_\infty$, where $\tilde{Z}_\infty = \eta_0$. With constant government spending ($\tilde{G}_t = 0$), the steady-state versions of (T2.5) and (18.23) can be solved for $\tilde{C}_\infty$ and $\tilde{Y}_\infty$:

$$\tilde{Y}_\infty = \frac{\omega_C^*}{\omega_C^* + \omega_G^*} \tilde{C}_\infty = \frac{\phi \omega_C^* \tilde{Z}_\infty}{\omega_G^*(\phi - 1) + \phi \omega_C^*(1 - \alpha)} > 0, \tag{18.54}$$

and (T2.6) can be solved for $\tilde{L}_\infty$:

$$\tilde{L}_\infty = \frac{\tilde{Y}_\infty - \tilde{C}_\infty}{1 + \omega_{LL}^*} = -\frac{\omega_G^*}{\omega_C^* + \omega_G^*} \frac{\tilde{C}_\infty}{1 + \omega_{LL}^*} \le 0. \tag{18.55}$$

In the long run a permanent productivity improvement makes the representative agent wealthier which prompts him to increase consumption. The investment-capital ratio and the output-capital ratio are unchanged but the capital-labour ratio rises as does the real wage. In the absence of government consumption ($w_G^* = 0$) the income and substitution effects in labour supply exactly cancel out and employment is unchanged (see (18.55)). With positive government consumption the income effect dominates the substitution effect and labour supply goes down (i.e. the household consumes more leisure).

In Figure 18.3 we present the impulse-response functions for the permanent shock, again using the calibration values discussed above (see (13.119) above). Following their initial jumps, consumption and the wage both gradually increase further during transition. Investment and employment both overshoot their respective long-run levels. Though the impact effect on employment is positive, employment falls in the long run because the calibration is based on a positive share of government consumption (see (18.55)). The real interest jumps up at impact and gradually returns to its initial level. This explains why the time profile of consumption is upward sloping.

In summary, for a purely permanent shock the following key features stand out. First, there is a long-run effect on productivity and thus also on most macroeconomic variables. The great ratios explain why output, consumption, the capital stock, and investment increase in the long run and employment falls (provided $w_G^* > 0$). Second, the substitution effect in labour supply is countered by a large income effect so the transitional effects on employment are small. Third, the effects on consumption and the capital stock are large because the shock itself is substantial from a lifetime perspective. Fourth, just as for the purely temporary shock, the output response looks virtually identical to the impulse (*lack of propagation* again).

18.3.3.3   A realistic shock

Now that we have discussed the impulse-response functions for purely transitory and permanent technology shocks, we can proceed and study the reaction of the economy to *realistic* productivity shocks. The seminal work by Solow (1957) has been used by RBC proponents to estimate the nature of technological change. Solow (1957) tried to determine how much of economic growth can be accounted for by fluctuations in the production factors capital and labour. He found that the unexplained part of output growth (later termed the *Solow residual* in his honour) accounted for approximately half of the growth of output in the US since the 1870s (Stadler, 1994, p. 1753). It was shown by Prescott (1986) that data on the Solow residual can be used to recover an estimate for the persistence parameter (ξ_Z) and the standard deviation of the innovation term (denoted by σ_η). King and Rebelo (1999, pp. 952–953) explain in detail how this can be done.[7] They use quarterly data for the US and obtain the following estimates for these parameters: $\xi_Z = 0.979$ and

---

[7]In the context of our (simple) model the procedure would work as follows. First, we take logarithms of (18.12) to derive the estimate for the Solow residual:

$$\ln SR_t \equiv \ln Y_t - \ln \Omega_0 - (1 - \alpha) \ln L_t - \alpha \ln K_t = \ln Z_t.$$

Hence, in our model the Solow residual is equal to the general productivity index Z_t. By using this result in (18.34) one obtains an equation which can be estimated empirically:

$$\ln SR_t = \alpha_Z + \xi_Z \ln SR_{t-1} + \eta_t.$$

The procedure of King and Rebelo (1999) is a little more complicated because they also allow for labour-augmenting technological change.

Figure 18.3: Permanent productivity shock

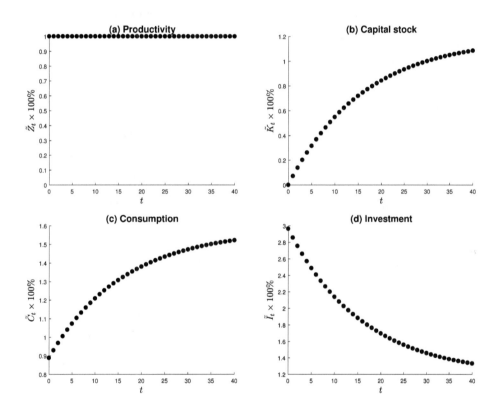

Figure 18.3, continued

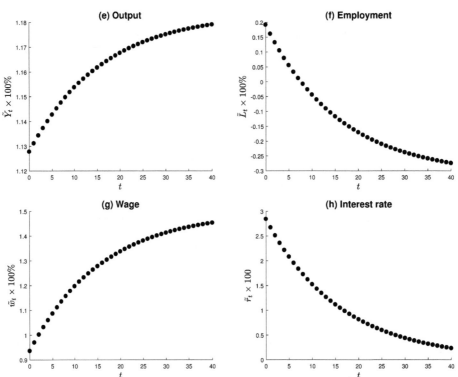

Figure 18.4: Temporary productivity shock

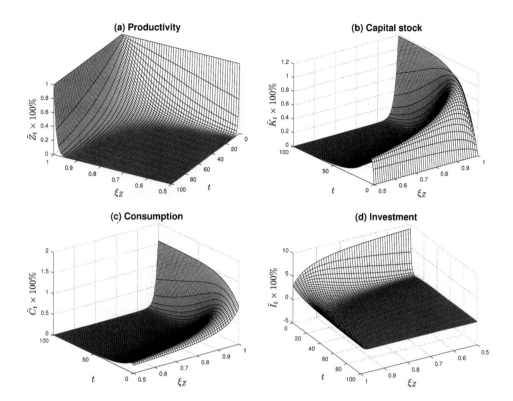

$\sigma_\eta = 0.0072$. The key thing to note is that the technology shock displays a very high degree of persistence, i.e. ξ_Z is very close to unity!

In Figure 18.4 we present impulse-response functions for all macroeconomic variables using the calibration values discussed above (see (13.119) above). Instead of focusing on one particular estimate for the persistence parameter, we show these impulse-response functions for a range of values of ξ_Z which includes both King and Rebelo's estimate and the unit-root case (i.e. $0.5 \leq \xi_Z \leq 1$ in these figures).

As King and Rebelo (1999, p. 969) point out, the shape of each impulse-response function is very sensitive to ξ_Z for the high-persistence case (i.e. if ξ_Z is near unity). Hence, impulse responses associated with, respectively, $\xi_Z = 0.979$ and $\xi_Z = 1$, are very different in shape. In contrast, for relatively transient shocks this non-linearity does not show up in Figure 18.4, i.e. impulse responses for $\xi_Z = 0.5$ and $\xi_Z = 0.7$ look very much alike. Intuitively, the non-linearity in the high-persistence case is due to the fact that permanent shocks cause non-zero long-run effects whilst transitory shocks (no matter how persistent they are) do not.

18.3.3.4 Lack of propagation

Perhaps the most important (and somewhat disappointing) feature of the unit-elastic RBC model is its *lack of internal propagation*, a point first made in a more general setting by Cogley and Nason (1995). For example, as is clear from Figure 18.2, the

Figure 18.4, continued

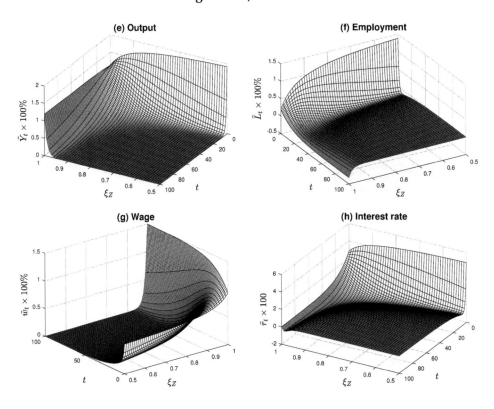

Table 18.3. The unit-elastic RBC model

x_t:	(a) US economy		(b) Model economy I		(c) Model economy II	
	$\text{std}(x_t)$	$\text{cor}(x_t, Y_t)$	$\text{std}(x_t)$	$\text{cor}(x_t, Y_t)$	$\text{std}(x_t)$	$\text{cor}(x_t, Y_t)$
Y_t	1.76		1.35		1.76	
C_t	1.29	0.85	0.42	0.89	0.51	0.87
I_t	8.60	0.92	4.24	0.99	5.71	0.99
K_t	0.63	0.04	0.36	0.06	0.47	0.05
L_t	1.66	0.76	0.70	0.98	1.35	0.98
Y_t/L_t	1.18	0.42	0.68	0.98	0.50	0.87

impulse-response function of output looks virtually identical to the exogenous productivity shock itself. Although it is impossible to see in the figure, there is some transitional dynamics in output after period $t = 1$ but it is of a very small magnitude. Exactly the same result is found in Figures 18.3 (which deals with permanent shocks) and 18.4 (which illustrates temporary shocks). For this reason, research has focused in recent years on ways to improve the internal propagation mechanism of the model. Some of this literature will be discussed briefly below.

18.3.4 Correlations

As was pointed out in the introduction to this section, most RBC modellers follow the suggestion by Kydland and Prescott (1982) and evaluate the usefulness of their model by judging how well the model-generated data match the data for an actual economy. The typical approach is to compute actual and model-generated moments for a number of key variables (King and Rebelo, 1999, p. 956). Usually the moments of interest are the *variances* (or standard deviations) of output, consumption, investment, capital, labour, and productivity. Often the contemporaneous *correlations* between output and the other variables are also compared.[8]

In Table 18.3 we show the results that were computed by Hansen (1985) for the US economy. In this table, $\text{std}(x_t)$ and $\text{cor}(x_t, Y_t)$ are, respectively, the (asymptotic) standard deviation of x_t and the contemporaneous correlation between x_t and Y_t. In panel (a) of Table 18.3 the indicators for the US economy are reported. The following regularities can be distinguished (Stadler, 1994, pp. 1751–1752). First, investment is much more volatile than output, i.e. the standard deviation of investment is $\text{std}(I_t) = 8.60$ which far exceeds the standard deviation of output which equals $\text{std}(Y_t) = 1.76$. Second, consumption is somewhat less volatile than output ($\text{std}(C_t) = 1.29$). Third, the capital stock is much less volatile than both consumption and output ($\text{std}(K_t) = 0.63$). Fourth, employment is approximately as volatile as output ($\text{std}(L_t) = 1.66$). Fifth, productivity is less volatile than output ($\text{std}(Y_t/L_t) = 1.18$). Sixth, all variables are positively correlated with output, although the correlation is rather weak for the capital stock.

In panel (b) of Table 18.3 the model-generated standard deviations and correlations are reported. Hansen (1985, pp. 319–320) uses the unit-elastic model to generate these results and employs the following calibration parameters: $\omega_G^* = 0$, $\alpha = 0.36$, $\rho = 0.01$, $\delta = 0.025$, and $\varepsilon = 1/3$. These parameters imply: $y^* = (\rho + \delta)/\alpha = 0.097$, $\omega_I^* = \delta/y^* = 0.257$, $\omega_C^* = 1 - \omega_I^* = 0.743$, and (by (13.118))

---

[8]In the appendix to this chapter we show how these various indicators can be computed for the theoretical model without having to use statistical simulation methods.

$\omega_{LL}^* = 2.321$. The persistence parameter and standard deviation of the technology shock (η_t in (18.35)) are set at, respectively, $\xi_Z = 0.95$ and $\sigma_\eta = 0.00712$.

A comparison of panels (a) and (b) reveals that the model captures the facts that consumption is less and investment is more volatile than aggregate output. It also matches the output correlations of consumption, investment, capital, and employment quite well but it overpredicts the correlation between output and productivity. Given the extremely simple structure of the unit-elastic model, the match between actual and model-generated moments is quite impressive. As we shall document in Section 18.4 below, however, a number of empirical facts are not well captured by the unit-elastic RBC model.

18.3.5   A detour: Dynare comes to the rescue

Up to this point we have used a rather analytical approach to investigate the properties of the unit-elastic RBC model. Whilst this approach has the advantage of allowing a close inspection of the key mechanisms present in the model, it has a disadvantage in that it is very time-consuming. Indeed, under the analytical approach the researcher needs to take the following steps:

- Loglinearize the model around a steady state.

- Investigate (local) stability of the loglinearized model.

- Solve the linear system of difference equations under rational expectations.

- Study the effects productivity shocks.

- Compute theoretical moments for the different variables.

In addition to being time-consuming the analytical approach quickly becomes infeasible for more complicated RBC models. For this reason most economists restrict attention to purely numerical implementations of their preferred RBC model. As was pointed out in Section 5.4.2 above, Dynare is a very useful (and free-of-charge) software package that can do all the hard and tedious work for you at lightning speed.

In Table 18.4 we give an example of a Dynare model file that can handle the basic unit-elastic RBC model. The model file is called `Program18_01.mod` as is indicated in the commented line at the top. As was explained in Section 5.4.2 above, the model file contains several blocks of statements. Block 1 defines the endogenous and exogenous variables whilst Block 2 provides the values for the structural parameters (α, δ, Ω_0, ε, ρ, σ_η, and ξ_Z). Note that we use the same parameter values for α, δ, Ω_0, ε, and ρ as were used in Chapter 13 (see (13.119)). In Block 3 we formulate the model in a format that Dynare can work with. The key thing to remember is that Dynare must be "told" that the capital stock is a predetermined variable by representing K_t in the program by k(-1). This means, of course, that k in the program represents K_{t+1}.

In Block 4 the actual computations are done. The Dynare command `steady` computes the deterministic steady state, using the starting values stated between the commands `initval` and `end`. Because the model is nonlinear Dynare must be provided with starting values for the endogenous variables, i.e. the model will not run without values for $K0$, $C0$, $L0$, etcetera. Furthermore, the command `check` computes the characteristic roots of the Jacobian matrix (ξ_1 and ξ_2). In between the commands `shocks` and `end` we specify the stochastic process for the shock term (η_t). The statement var eta = sigma_eta^2; means that we set the standard deviation of η_t equal to σ_η. The last command in Block 4 is stoch_simul(order = 1). As the name suggests it solves the stochastic rational expectations model using a first-order linearization technique. The interested reader is invited to run Program18_01.mod and to observe the huge amount of results that are computed in a few seconds.

Table 18.4. A Dynare model file for the basic RBC model

```
% Basic RBC model
%
% Dynare model file: Program18_01.mod
%


%-----------------------------------------------------------------
% 0. Housekeeping
%-----------------------------------------------------------------

close all;

%-----------------------------------------------------------------
% 1. Defining variables
%-----------------------------------------------------------------

var Y C K I L W R Z;
varexo G eta;

parameters Omega_0 alpha epsilon delta xi_Z rho sigma_eta;

%-----------------------------------------------------------------
% 2. Calibration
%-----------------------------------------------------------------

alpha     = 0.333333333333333;
delta     = 0.024113689084445;
Omega_0   = 1.442032886235652;
epsilon   = 0.183413993147403;
rho       = 0.015868284782784;
sigma_eta = 0.0015;
xi_Z      = 0.95;


% Guess for the initial steady state

Y0            = 1;
K0            = 8.337;
C0            = 0.599;
I0            = 0.201;
L0            = 0.200;
W0            = 3.333;
R0            = rho;
```

18.4 Extending the model

Despite its impressive performance in some dimensions, a number of empirical facts are not well captured by the unit-elastic RBC model. Following Stadler (1994, pp. 1757–1761) we focus on some stylized facts about the labour market which the model is unable to mimic. These are:

Table 18.4, continued

```
%----------------------------------------------------------------
% 3. Model
%----------------------------------------------------------------

model;
  K = I + (1 - delta)*K(-1);
  (1/C) = ((1 + R(+1))/(1+rho)) * (1/C(+1)) ;
  W = (1 - alpha) * Y / L;
  R = alpha * Y / K(-1) - delta;
  Y = C + I + G ;
  W * (1 - L) = ((1 - epsilon)/epsilon) * C;
  Y = Omega_0 * exp(Z) * K(-1)^(alpha) * L^(1-alpha);
  Z = xi_Z * Z(-1) + eta;
end;

%----------------------------------------------------------------
% 4. Computation
%----------------------------------------------------------------

initval;
  K   = K0;
  C   = C0;
  L   = L0;
  I   = I0;
  Y   = Y0;
  W   = W0;
  R   = R0;
  Z   = 0;
  eta = 0;
  G   = 0.2;
end;

shocks;
var eta = sigma_eta^2;
end;

steady;

stoch_simul(order = 1);
```

- Employment variability puzzle.

- Productivity puzzle.

- Absence of unemployment.

In the remainder of this section we first explain briefly what is meant by these troublesome features of the RBC model. Next, we discuss how RBC modellers have attempted to enrich the model in order to bring it in closer line with reality. Here we focus attention on just some of the many ways in which RBC modellers have responded to the various puzzles discussed above.[9]

18.4.1 Employment variability puzzle

As is clear from column (a) in Table 18.3, in the US employment and output are almost equally variable ($\text{std}(Y_t) = 1.76$ which is close to $\text{std}(L_t) = 1.66$), and employment is strongly procyclical ($\text{cor}(L_t, Y_t) = 0.76$). The basic model in column (b) predicts a much higher correlation between employment and output, i.e. $\text{cor}(L_t, Y_t) = 0.98$ which substantially exceeds the observed correlation of 0.76. In contrast, the basic model underpredicts the variability of employment by quite a bit, $\text{std}(L_t) = 0.70$ which falls short of the observed value of 1.66 by quite a margin.

In Figure 18.5 we attempt to graphically visualize the contemporaneous correlations implied by the basic RBC model.[10] The top panel depicts the short-run labour market whilst the bottom panel illustrates the short-run production function. Steady-state schedules for labour demand, labour supply, and output are denoted by, respectively, L_n^D, L_n^S, and Y_n. The subscript n can be understood as denoting "normal" productivity. If there is a positive productivity shock, at impact labour demand shifts to L_h^D (direct productivity effect), and labour supply shifts to L_h^S (wealth effect), where the subscript h denotes "higher than normal" productivity. Equilibrium employment increases as does the real wage. In the bottom panel, the short-run production function shifts to Y_h, and equilibrium output increases both because of the direct effect and because of the induced employment expansion.

In a similar fashion, a negative productivity shock (lower than normal productivity, subscripted by l) shifts labour demand to L_l^D, labour supply to L_l^S, and the short-run production function to Y_l. Employment, the real wage, and output are lower than normal in this situation. Connecting the three types of equilibria (low, normal, and high), we find that CWL in the top panel visualizes the positive correlation between the wage rate and employment, whilst CYL in the bottom panel visualizes the correlation between employment and output.

Armed with Figure 18.5 we understand immediately why $\text{cor}(w_t, L_t)$, $\text{cor}(L_t, Y_t)$, and $\text{std}(w_t)$ are high in the model, whilst $\text{std}(L_t)$ is low. These results can be attributed to a large extent by the steep slope of the labour supply curve.

How can the employment variability puzzle be resolved? Clearly, one would observe a more realistic correlation between real wages and employment if the labour supply curve were relatively flat. There are several ways to get this. First, there may be strong intertemporal substitution effects in labour supply, but this is rejected by the econometric evidence to date (Card, 1994). Second, the dominant RBC solution

---

[9]Stadler (1994), Hansen and Wright (1994), King and Rebelo (1999), Rebelo (2005), and McCandless (2008) discuss many other model extensions that have been proposed in the RBC literature over the past three decades.

[10]This way to visualize correlations and variability is not rigorous. It ignores, for example, the fact that there is transitional dynamics as a result of each innovation.

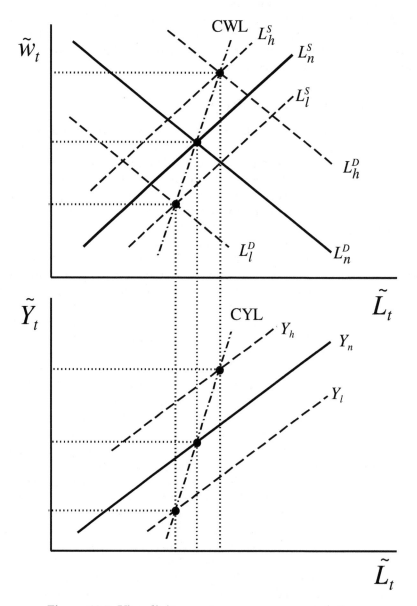

Figure 18.5: Visualizing contemporaneous correlations

to the employment variability puzzle is provided by Hansen (1985) who incorporated the insights of Rogerson (1988) into an RBC model. His argument makes use of the fact that in reality about two thirds of the variation of total hours worked is due to movements into and out of employment, whilst only one third is explained by variation in the number of hours worked. Hansen (1985) assumes that the length of the working week is constant: you either have a job and work for, say, 40 hours per week, or you do not work at all. This non-convexity in the form of *indivisible labour* (IL) ensures that workers wish to work as much as possible when wages are high. Hansen shows that even if individual agents have a zero intertemporal labour supply elasticity, the aggregate economy behaves as if the (average) "representative agent" has an infinite intertemporal labour supply elasticity. Individual households do not choose the number of working hours per period, but rather the probability of working. Who actually works is determined by a lottery. There is a contract between the firm and a household that specifies that the household must work $\bar{L}$ hours with probability π_t in period t. The firm provides complete insurance to the worker and the lottery contract is traded, so that each household gets the same amount from the firm, regardless of whether it works or not in any particular period. Actual per capita employment in period t will be $L_t = \pi_t \bar{L}$, and each household gets paid as if it worked L_t hours in period t.

The IL model is obtained by replacing (18.2) by a felicity function that is linear in labour supply:

$$U(C_\tau, L_\tau) \equiv \varepsilon \ln C_\tau - (1 - \varepsilon) L_\tau. \tag{18.56}$$

With this modification, the consumption Euler equation continues to be given by (T1.2) but leisure drops out of equation (T1.6) which becomes:

$$\frac{w_t}{C_t} = \frac{1 - \varepsilon}{\varepsilon}. \tag{18.57}$$

In the IL model, consumption is proportional to the wage, i.e. the labour supply equation is horizontal. In terms of the loglinearized model of Table 18.2, equation (T2.6) is replaced by $\tilde{w}_t = \tilde{C}_t$. Hence, in formal terms, the IL model is a special case of the model presented in Table 18.2 with $\omega_{LL}^* \to \infty$.

In Figure 18.6 we visualize the contemporaneous correlations implied by the IL model. Labour demand and the short-run production function are both unchanged and we leave out labels to avoid cluttering the diagram unnecessarily. Labour supply is horizontal but its position depends on the level of consumption—see equation (18.57). Normal labour supply is given by L_n^S. If productivity is high, consumption is high (wealth effect) and the wage rate restoring labour market equilibrium is also higher than normal though less so than in the basic RBC model. As a result, the employment expansion is higher than in the basic RBC model. A similar pattern occurs for lower than normal productivity.

By tracing the three types of equilibria (low, normal, high productivity) we find CWL_1 in the top panel and CYL_1 in the bottom panel. Note that CWL_0 and CYL_0 depict the correlations for the basic model that we deduced in Figure 18.6. We find immediately that compared to the basic model, the IL model predicts higher values for $\text{std}(L_t)$ and $\text{std}(Y_t)$ and lower values for $\text{cor}(w_t, L_t)$ and $\text{cor}(L_t, Y_t)$.

That our intuitive visualization approach captures the essence of what is going on in the simulation model is confirmed by the results reported in Table 18.3. In panel (c) of that table we show the results that were obtained by Hansen's (1985) calibration of the IL model. With the exception of ε (and thus ω_{LL}^*) the calibration parameters are

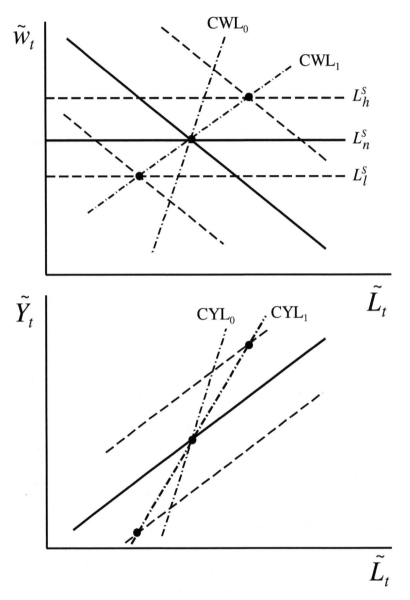

Figure 18.6: Lottery model and contemporaneous correlations

the same as for panel (b). The parameter ε is chosen such that employed individuals spend 53 percent of their time endowment on work, i.e. $\bar{L} = 0.53$ (Hansen, 1985, p. 320).[11] This yields the value of $\varepsilon = 0.381$. It is clear from Table 18.3 that the IL model provides a much better match between the model-generated and actual variability of employment than the standard model does.[12] By incorporating the assumption of indivisible labour in the unit-elastic model, the model-generated standard deviation of employment rises from $\text{std}(L_t) = 0.70$ (in panel (b)) to $\text{std}(L_t) = 1.35$ (in panel (c)), a value that is close to the observed variability of 1.66%. Because it largely solves the employment variability puzzle, Hansen's approach has become standard practice in the RBC literature.

18.4.2 Productivity puzzle

Column (a) in Table 18.3 shows that the correlation between labour productivity and output is modest, i.e. $\text{cor}(Y_t/L_t, Y_t) = 0.42$. Both the basic model (column (b)) and Hansen's IL model (column (c)), however, predict much higher values for this correlation (0.98 and 0.87, respectively). Although the IL model reduces the predicted correlation somewhat, it does not do so to a sufficient extent. Since technology is represented by a Cobb-Douglas production function in both RBC models, the real wage is proportional to productivity (see (T2.3) above). It thus follows that both models generate wage fluctuations that are much more procyclical than is consistent with reality. In reality, wages are only mildly procyclical. In addition, the correlation between the real wage and employment is virtually zero, i.e. $\text{cor}(w_t, L_t) \approx 0$.

One would be tempted to use efficiency wage theory to explain the low variability of the real wage rate one observes in reality, but this does not seem to solve the excessive fluctuations in wages in RBC models. Gomme (1999) develops an RBC model incorporating the shirking model of efficiency wages (see also Section 7.4 above). In such a model, the real wage does not clear the labour market but rather is used to induce high effort by the workers. He demonstrates that this model also predicts a very high correlation between the real wage and output. Why is this so? A positive technology shock shifts labour demand to the right, just as in the standard RBC model. In the efficiency-wage RBC model, such a shock also shifts the incentive-compatibility (IC) constraint (the no-shirking condition) to the left as a result of an income effect. Indeed, the IC constraint acts like a kind of labour supply curve and the model performs more or less like a standard RBC model.

A potentially more fruitful approach to resolving the productivity puzzle is to introduce additional stochastic shocks into the model. This is, for example, the approach pursued by Christiano and Eichenbaum (1992) who allow government consumption shocks to influence the labour market via the labour supply curve. Without going into the details of their model, the essence of the two-shock approach can

---

[11]By manipulating (18.57) we find that the value of ε can be written as follows:

$$\varepsilon = \left[1 + \frac{(1-\alpha)}{\bar{L}\omega_C^*}\right]^{-1}.$$

Since ω_C^* and α are known, the value of ε is readily obtained from this expression.

[12]Note that the actual and model-generated standard deviation of output are the same in panels (a) and (c) of Table 18.3. This cannot be counted as a success for the unit-elastic model because it is a feature of the calibration procedure. The standard deviation of the productivity shock (σ_η) is chosen such that the variation in aggregate output is perfectly matched (Hansen, 1985, p. 320). In a model with divisible labour (given in panel (b)) a larger standard deviation of the innovation term is needed to match the observed standard deviation of output.

be explained with the aid of Figure 18.6. Recall that CWL_1 visualizes the contemporaneous correlation between the real wage and employment. Resolving the productivity puzzle means finding a way to flatten the CWL curve somehow. If shocks to government consumption are such that the horizontal shifts of the supply curve are dampened somewhat, then clearly a flatter CWL is obtained, the variability of the real wage is reduced, and employment variability is increased.

RBC theorists have also proposed alternative mechanisms by which the (effective) labour supply shifts are dampened. Examples that are found in the literature include the existence of nominal wage contracts, taste shocks, labour hoarding by firms, and the existence of a non-market production sector that is also subject to technology shocks (see Stadler, 1994, pp. 1759–1761). In home production models, for example, households divide their labour over market and non-market activities. If market productivity rises, agents not only intertemporally substitute labour, but also shift labour intratemporally from the non-market to the market sector.

18.4.3   Unemployment

Since there is no unemployment in the unit-elastic model, all variation in employment is explained by fluctuations in the supply of labour by the representative household. In reality, however, about two thirds of the variation in hours is due to movements into (and out of) employment and only one third is explained by variation in the number of hours worked per employed worker (Stadler, 1994, p. 1758).

Over the last three decades, many authors have introduced equilibirum unemployment into the RBC framework by making use of the search-theoretic approach of Diamond, Mortensen, and Pissarides (see Chapters 8 and 13).[13] In an early contribution, Andolfatto (1996, p. 113) shows that the introduction of labour market search into an RBC model leads to three major improvements. First, the model is able to predict that labour hours fluctuate more than wages. Second, the model predicts a lower correlation between labour hours and productivity. Third, the model predicts a more realistic impulse-response function for output. DenHaan et al. (2000) generalize the RBC model with search unemployment by introducing endogenous job destruction and costly capital mobility.

In recent years, however, a number of authors have argued that the search and matching RBC model has its own set of empirical problems. Indeed, Shimer (2005, 2010) and Costain and Reiter (2008) have argued that *the* central variables in the model—unemployment and vacancies—are much more volatile in reality than in conventionally calibrated search and matching models with Nash-bargained wages. In response to this criticism, however, Hagedorn and Manovskii (2008) show that the search and matching model can be salvaged when a different calibration procedure is used. No consensus has emerged to date. Interestingly, both Hall (2005) and Shimer (2010) strongly argue in favour of introducing some kind of wage rigidity. And that is, of course, what we called the Holy Grail of Macroeconomics in Chapter 7.

18.5   Punchlines

This chapter deals with the most important theme that has kept most new classical economists busy over the last three decades, namely the equilibrium approach to

---

[13]See, e.g. Andolfatto (1996), Merz (1995, 1997, 1999), and Cole and Rogerson (1999). Section 13.6 provides details of a deterministic dynamic search model that can easily be adapted to study productivity shocks.

real business cycles (RBC). The RBC methodology builds on and extends the insights that were obtained as a result of the rational expectations revolution of the 1970s. In order to discuss the equilibrium approach to business cycles, we start this chapter by extending the deterministic Ramsey model with endogenous labour supply (that was studied in detail in Chapter 13) in two directions. First, we incorporate the notion that households and firms are living in an inherently stochastic world. Second, we recast it in discrete time thus making it relatively straightforward to incorporate uncertainty.

The chapter focuses on technology shocks but other shocks can easily be added to the model. By introducing a stochastic process for general productivity, and imposing the assumption of rational expectations we obtain a prototypical RBC model. We study the properties of the so-called unit-elastic RBC model by computing the analytical impulse-response functions for the different macroeconomic variables. The degree of persistence of the technology shock exerts a critical influence on the shape of the impulse-response functions.

For a purely transitory technology shock, consumption, employment, investment, and output all rise in the impact period. The employment response is explained not so much by the wealth effect (which is rather weak) but rather by the incentive to substitute labour supply across time. The technology shock makes it attractive to work in the current period because the current wage is high relative to future wages. After technology has returned to its initial level, capital and consumption gradually fall back over time.

With a permanent productivity shock, consumption, capital, output, investment, and the real wage all rise in the long run. In the absence of government consumption (and the concomitant lump-sum taxes), employment stays the same because the income and substitution effects of the wage change cancel out. With positive lump-sum taxes the former dominates the latter effect and employment falls. The intuition behind the long-run results is provided by the constancy of a number of great ratios. Consumption jumps up at impact and thereafter increases further during transition.

Next we study the impulse-response functions for a "realistic" shock persistence parameter. Most RBC modellers use the so-called Solow residual to obtain an estimate for this persistence parameter. The typical finding is that productivity shocks (thus measured) are very persistent, i.e. the persistence parameter is close to (but strictly less than) unity.

An important, somewhat disappointing, feature of the unit-elastic RBC model is its lack of internal propagation. For all cases considered, the impulse-response function for output is virtually identical to the exogenous technology shock itself. The lack of propagation plagues not just the unit-elastic model but many other RBC models as well. For this reason, one of the currently active areas of research in the RBC literature concerns the development of models with stronger and more realistic internal propagation mechanisms.

It is standard practice to evaluate the quantitative performance of a given RBC model in terms of the quality of the match it provides between model-generated and actual data. Typically, the statistics of interest are the standard deviations (and correlations with aggregate output) of some key macroeconomic variables. Despite its simplicity, the unit-elastic model is able to capture quite a few features of the real world data. For example, it correctly predicts that investment is more and consumption is less volatile than aggregate output. It also matches the output correlations of consumption, investment, capital, and employment quite closely. There are also a number of empirical facts that are difficult or impossible to reconcile with the unit-elastic model. For that reason a huge literature has emerged over the last three decades which aims to improve the empirical fit of RBC models.

Perhaps the most important contribution of the RBC approach is a methodological one. Recall that in the traditional macroeconometric approach, weakly founded relationships were typically estimated with the aid of time series data. RBC modellers have largely abandoned the macroeconometric approach and have instead forged a link with micro-founded stochastic computable equilibrium models. Attention has shifted from estimation to simulation. The approach has proved to be quite flexible. RBC models now exist which include alternative market structures (on goods and labour markets), price and wage stickiness (see Chapter 19), open-economy features, different types of stochastic shocks, and heterogeneous households. The broad range of applications indicates that the RBC methodology has received widespread acceptance from classical and Keynesian economists alike.

Further reading

Pioneering contributions to the real business cycle (RBC) approach were made by Kydland and Prescott (1982), Long and Plosser (1983), and Prescott (1986). Some of the most important early articles on the RBC approach have been collected in Miller (1994). For survey articles, see King et al. (1987, 1988a, 1988b), McCallum (1989b), Plosser (1989), Eichenbaum (1991), Danthine and Donaldson (1993), Campbell (1994), Stadler (1994), Cooley (1995), King and Rebelo (1999), and Rebelo (2005). The Nobel Prize Lecture by Prescott (2006) is required reading for any student of the RBC approach. Altug and Young (2015) summarizes a panel discussion marking the 30th anniversary of the RBC approach featuring its key contributors.

Early critics of the approach are Summers (1986) and Mankiw (1989). For a discussion on the method of calibration, see Kydland and Prescott (1996), Hansen and Heckman (1996), Sims (1996), and Gomme and Rupert (2009). Watson (1993) suggests measures-of-fit for calibrated models. Cogley and Nason (1995) and Rotemberg and Woodford (1996) document the weak propagation mechanisms of a number of standard RBC models.

There is a huge and growing literature on various labour market aspects. The intertemporal substitution mechanism is studied in detail by Hall (1991, 1997) and Mulligan (1999). On family labour supply, see Cho and Rogerson (1988) and Cho and Cooley (1994). Nominal wage contracts are studied by Cho and Cooley (1995) and Huang and Liu (2002).

On search unemployment, see among others Andolfatto (1996), Merz (1995, 1997, 1999), Cole and Rogerson (1999), DenHaan et al. (2000), Shimer (2005, 2010), Hall (2005), Costain and Reiter (2008), Hagedorn and Manovskii (2008), and Christiano et al. (2016). Gertler and Trigari (2009) introduce staggered wage setting. Nakajima (2012) allows for incomplete markets and self-insurance. Rogerson et al. (2005) present an extensive literature survey of the search literature. Efficiency wage theories are used by Danthine and Donaldson (1990), Kimball (1994), Georges (1995), and Gomme (1999).

Early papers on the macroeconomic effects of government purchases, using a deterministic approach, include Foley and Sidrauski (1971), Hall (1971), Miller and Upton (1974), Barro (1981), and Aschauer (1988). More recent stochastic models include Cassou and Lansing (1998) (on public infrastructure), Christiano and Eichenbaum (1992), McGrattan (1994), Braun (1994), Jonsson and Klein (1996), and Canton (2001). Edelberg et al. (1999) study the empirical effects of a shock to government purchases.

Key articles on home production are Benhabib et al. (1991) and Greenwood and Hercowitz (1991). Models with distorting taxes are presented by Greenwood and Huffman (1991) and McGrattan (1994). Ljungqvist and Uhlig (2000) introduce habit formation in household consumption. Studies focusing on firm investment include Greenwood, Hercowitz, and Huffman (1988) and Gilchrist and Williams (2000). Models including a monopolistically competitive goods market are formulated by Bénassy (1996a), Hornstein (1993), Chatterjee and Cooper (2014), Rotemberg and Woodford (1992, 1996), Devereux et al. (1996a, 1996b), Heijdra (1998), and Galí (1999). Rotemberg (2008) introduces imperfect competition on the goods market in a model with search unemployment and allows for changes in market power.

RBC methods have also been used to explain the Great Depression of the 1930s—see the collection of essays in Kehoe and Prescott (2007). This literature is not uncontroversial —see the critical book review of Kehoe and Prescott (2007) by the economic historian Peter Temin (2008).

Galí and Rabanal (2004) argue that there is little evidence that technology shocks are important determinants of the business cycle. Chari, Kehoe and McGrattan (2007) strongly disagree. On changes in expectations ('news') as determinants of the business cycle, see Beaudry and Portier (2007), and Beaudry et al. (2011). An insightful discussion on asset pricing is found in Blanchard and Fischer (1989, ch. 10). Also useful on asset pricing in a macroeconomic context are Jermann (1998), and Altug and Labadie (2008).

Appendix: On the unit-elastic RBC model

In this appendix we derive some technical results for the unit-elastic RBC model used in this chapter.

A.1 Derivation of (18.38)–(18.39)

We compute the impulse-response function associated with the innovation η_0 by solving the following system:

$$\begin{bmatrix} \tilde{K}_{t+1} - \tilde{K}_t \\ \tilde{C}_{t+1} - \tilde{C}_t \end{bmatrix} = \Delta \begin{bmatrix} \tilde{K}_t \\ \tilde{C}_t \end{bmatrix} + \begin{bmatrix} \gamma_t^K \\ \gamma_t^C \end{bmatrix}, \tag{A18.1}$$

where the shock vector is given in (18.37). The key thing to note is that (A18.1) is the deterministic counterpart to (18.28). The expectations operator, E_t, can be dropped from (18.28) when we compute the impulse-response function because we have already incorporated the rational expectations assumption by substituting the path for $\tilde{Z}_t$ that results from the innovation η_0 into the shock term.

In the Mathematical Appendix we show how a system like (A18.1) can be solved with the aid of the z-transform method. Assuming that Δ possesses real characteristic roots, $-1 < -\lambda_1 < 0$ and $\lambda_2 > 0$, the general solution of (A18.1) is:

$$[z - (1 - \lambda_1)] \begin{bmatrix} \mathcal{Z}\{\tilde{K}_t, z\} \\ \mathcal{Z}\{\tilde{C}_t, z\} \end{bmatrix} = \begin{bmatrix} \mathcal{Z}\{\gamma_t^K, z\} \\ z\tilde{C}_0 + \mathcal{Z}\{\gamma_t^C, z\} \end{bmatrix} \tag{A18.2}$$

$$+ \frac{\text{adj}\Lambda(\lambda_2) \begin{bmatrix} \mathcal{Z}\{\gamma_t^K, z\} - \frac{z}{1+\lambda_2}\mathcal{Z}\{\gamma_t^K, 1+\lambda_2\} \\ \mathcal{Z}\{\gamma_t^C, z\} - \frac{z}{1+\lambda_2}\mathcal{Z}\{\gamma_t^C, 1+\lambda_2\} \end{bmatrix}}{z - (1 + \lambda_2)},$$

where $\Lambda(\lambda_2) \equiv \lambda_2 I - \Delta$ and we have used the fact that capital cannot jump at impact (i.e. $\tilde{K}_0 = 0$). The impact jump in consumption ($\tilde{C}_0$) is:

$$\tilde{C}_0 = -\frac{\mathcal{Z}\{\gamma_t^C, 1+\lambda_2\}}{1+\lambda_2} - \frac{\lambda_2 - \delta_{22}}{\delta_{12}} \left[\frac{\mathcal{Z}\{\gamma_t^K, 1+\lambda_2\}}{1+\lambda_2} \right] \tag{A18.3}$$

The shock term (18.37) can be written in general format as:

$$\begin{bmatrix} \gamma_t^K \\ \gamma_t^C \end{bmatrix} = \begin{bmatrix} \gamma_K \\ \gamma_C \end{bmatrix} \xi_Z^t, \qquad \begin{bmatrix} \gamma_K \\ \gamma_C \end{bmatrix} \equiv \phi \begin{bmatrix} y^* \\ \zeta[\xi_Z - y^*[1-\alpha\phi]] \end{bmatrix} \eta_0. \tag{A18.4}$$

The z-transform for γ_t^i can then be written as:

$$\mathcal{Z}\{\gamma_t^i, z\} = \gamma^i \frac{z}{z - \xi_Z}, \qquad i \in \{K, C\}. \tag{A18.5}$$

Using (A18.5) in (A18.3) we obtain the following expression for $\tilde{C}_0$:

$$\tilde{C}_0 = -\frac{\gamma^C}{\lambda_2 + (1 - \xi_Z)} - \frac{\lambda_2 - \delta_{22}}{\delta_{12}} \frac{\gamma^K}{\lambda_2 + (1 - \xi_Z)}. \tag{A18.6}$$

By substituting γ^C and γ^K in (A18.6) we obtain equation (18.39) in the text. We derive from (A18.5) that:

$$\frac{\mathcal{Z}\{\gamma_t^i, z\} - \frac{z}{1+\lambda_2}\mathcal{Z}\{\gamma_t^i, 1+\lambda_2\}}{z - (1+\lambda_2)} = -\frac{\gamma^i}{1 + \lambda_2 - \xi_Z} \frac{z}{z - \xi_Z}, \tag{A18.7}$$

so that (A18.2) can be rewritten as:

$$
\begin{bmatrix} \mathcal{Z}\{\tilde{K},z\} \\ \mathcal{Z}\{\tilde{C},z\} \end{bmatrix} = \begin{bmatrix} 0 \\ \tilde{C}_0 \end{bmatrix} \frac{z}{z-(1-\lambda_1)} + \begin{bmatrix} \delta_{22}+(1-\xi_Z) & -\delta_{12} \\ -\delta_{21} & \delta_{11}+(1-\xi_Z) \end{bmatrix}
$$
$$
\times \frac{1}{\lambda_2+(1-\xi_Z)} \begin{bmatrix} \gamma^K \\ \gamma^C \end{bmatrix} \frac{z}{(z-\xi_Z)[z-(1-\lambda_1)]}. \tag{A18.8}
$$

We recognize that $\mathcal{Z}^{-1}\{z/(z-\alpha)\} = \alpha^t$ and $\mathcal{Z}^{-1}\{z/[(z-\alpha_1)(z-\alpha_2)]\} = T_t(\alpha_1,\alpha_2)$, where $T_t(\cdot)$ is a temporary bell-shaped transition term:

$$
T_t(\alpha_1,\alpha_2) \equiv \begin{cases} \dfrac{\alpha_1^t-\alpha_2^t}{\alpha_1-\alpha_2} & \text{for } \alpha_1 \neq \alpha_2 \\ t\alpha_1^{t-1} & \text{for } \alpha_1 = \alpha_2, \end{cases} \tag{A18.9}
$$

with $\alpha_i \neq 0$ (see Ogata, 1995, p. 30). A result we use in the analysis of permanent shocks is that $T_t(1,\alpha_2) = (1-\alpha_2)^{-1}A_t(\alpha_2)$, where $A_t(\alpha_2) \equiv 1-\alpha_2^t$ is a discrete-time adjustment term. For purely transitory shocks we have:

$$
T_t(0,\alpha_2) \equiv \begin{cases} 0 & \text{for } t=0 \\ \alpha_2^{t-1} & \text{for } t=1,2,\dots. \end{cases} \tag{A18.10}
$$

(Note that in the text we combine (A18.9) and (A18.10) into (18.40).) By inverting (A18.8) we find the solution in the time domain:

$$
\begin{bmatrix} \tilde{K}_t \\ \tilde{C}_t \end{bmatrix} = \begin{bmatrix} 0 \\ \tilde{C}_0 \end{bmatrix} (1-\lambda_1)^t + \begin{bmatrix} \delta_{22}+(1-\xi_Z) & -\delta_{12} \\ -\delta_{21} & \delta_{11}+(1-\xi_Z) \end{bmatrix}
$$
$$
\times \frac{1}{\lambda_2+(1-\xi_Z)} \begin{bmatrix} \gamma^K \\ \gamma^C \end{bmatrix} T_t(\xi_Z,1-\lambda_1). \tag{A18.11}
$$

By simplifying (A18.11) somewhat we find the equation (18.38) in the text.

A.2 Method of undetermined coefficients

In this subsection we show how the unit-elastic RBC model can be solved using the method of undetermined coefficients. Following Campbell (1994, p. 470), we conjecture the following trial solution:

$$
\tilde{C}_t = \pi_{ck}\tilde{K}_t + \pi_{cz}\tilde{Z}_t, \tag{A18.12}
$$

where π_{ck} and π_{cz} are coefficients to be determined. By substituting (A18.12) in the system (18.28) we obtain:

$$
\begin{bmatrix} 1 & 0 \\ \theta_{21} & 1 \end{bmatrix} \begin{bmatrix} \tilde{K}_{t+1} \\ \pi_{ck}\tilde{K}_{t+1}+\xi_Z\pi_{cz}\tilde{Z}_t \end{bmatrix} = \begin{bmatrix} 1+\delta_{11}^* & \delta_{12}^* \\ 0 & 1+\delta_{22}^* \end{bmatrix} \begin{bmatrix} \tilde{K}_t \\ \pi_{ck}\tilde{K}_t+\pi_{cz}\tilde{Z}_t \end{bmatrix}
$$
$$
+ \begin{bmatrix} y^* \\ \xi\xi_Z \end{bmatrix} \phi\tilde{Z}_t, \tag{A18.13}
$$

where δ_{ij}^* are the elements of Δ^* (defined in (18.29)) and we have used the fact that $E_tC_{t+1} = \pi_{ck}\tilde{K}_{t+1}+\pi_{cz}E_t\tilde{Z}_{t+1}$ and $E_t\tilde{Z}_{t+1} = \xi_Z\tilde{Z}_t$. The system in (A18.13) gives two expressions for $\tilde{K}_{t+1}$ in terms of $\tilde{K}_t$ and $\tilde{Z}_t$ which must hold for all $(\tilde{K}_t,\tilde{Z}_t)$ combinations. By eliminating $\tilde{K}_{t+1}$ from (A18.13) we find:

$$
0 = \left[1+\delta_{11}^* + \delta_{12}^*\pi_{ck} - (1+\delta_{22}^*)\frac{\pi_{ck}}{\theta_{21}+\pi_{ck}}\right] \tilde{K}_t \tag{A18.14}
$$

$$+ \left[\delta_{12}^{*} \pi_{cz} + \phi y^{*} - \frac{(1 - \xi_Z + \delta_{22}^{*}) \pi_{cz} + \phi \zeta \xi_Z}{\theta_{21} + \pi_{ck}} \right] \tilde{Z}_t.$$

We use π_{ck} to ensure that the term in square brackets in front of $\tilde{K}_t$ is zero. After some manipulation we find the following quadratic function in π_{ck}:

$$\delta_{12} \pi_{ck}^2 + (\delta_{11} - \delta_{22}) \pi_{ck} - \delta_{21} = 0, \tag{A18.15}$$

where δ_{ij} are the elements of Δ ($\delta_{11} = \delta_{11}^{*}$, $\delta_{12} = \delta_{12}^{*}$, $\delta_{21} = -\theta_{21} \delta_{11}^{*} + \delta_{21}^{*} = -\theta_{21}(1 + \delta_{11}^{*})$, and $\delta_{22} = -\theta_{21} \delta_{12}^{*} + \delta_{22}^{*}$). Given saddle path stability, we solve (A18.15) for the positive root:[14]

$$\pi_{ck} = \frac{-(\delta_{11} - \delta_{22}) - \sqrt{(\delta_{11} - \delta_{22})^2 + 4 \delta_{12} \delta_{21}}}{2 \delta_{12}} > 0. \tag{A18.16}$$

(Note also that $\delta_{12} \pi_{ck} = \delta_{22} - \lambda_2$.) For this value of π_{ck}, the term in square brackets in front of $\tilde{Z}_t$ in (A18.14) can be put to zero by the appropriate choice of π_{cz}:

$$\pi_{cz} = \frac{\phi \left[\zeta \xi_Z - (\theta_{21} + \pi_{ck}) y^{*} \right]}{\delta_{12} \pi_{ck} - \delta_{22} - (1 - \xi_Z)} > 0. \tag{A18.17}$$

Once we know the coefficients π_{ck} and π_{cz}, we obtain the solution for $\tilde{K}_{t+1}$ by using either row of (A18.13):

$$\tilde{K}_{t+1} = \pi_{kk} \tilde{K}_t + \pi_{kz} \tilde{Z}_t, \tag{A18.18}$$

where $\pi_{kk} \equiv 1 + \delta_{11} + \delta_{12} \pi_{ck}$ and $\pi_{kz} \equiv \delta_{12} \pi_{cz} + \phi y^{*}$. (Note also that $\pi_{kk} = 1 - \lambda_1$.)

A.3 Computing correlations

In order to judge the empirical performance of the unit-elastic RBC model we can compute various correlations that are implied by the theoretical model. We approach the problem from an analytical viewpoint in order to stress the link with the rational expectations literature discussed in Chapter 5. We start by computing the statistical properties of the capital stock. We derive from (A18.18) that:

$$E \left[\tilde{K}_{t+1} - E\tilde{K}_{t+1} \right]^2 = \pi_{kk}^2 E \left[\tilde{K}_t - E\tilde{K}_t \right]^2 + \pi_{kz}^2 E\tilde{Z}_t^2 + 2\pi_{kk}\pi_{kz} E \left[\tilde{K}_t - E\tilde{K}_t \right] \tilde{Z}_t \Leftrightarrow$$
$$\text{var}(\tilde{K}_{t+1}) = \pi_{kk}^2 \text{var}(\tilde{K}_t) + \pi_{kz}^2 \text{var}(\tilde{Z}_t) + 2\pi_{kk}\pi_{kz}\text{cov}(\tilde{K}_t, \tilde{Z}_t), \tag{A18.19}$$

where we have used the fact that $E\tilde{Z}_t = 0$. Since $\tilde{Z}_t$ is covariance stationary,[15] the same holds for $\tilde{K}_t$ (and all other endogenous variables). Hence, $\text{var}(\tilde{K}_{t+1}) = \text{var}(\tilde{K}_t)$ and equation (A18.19) can be simplified to:

$$(1 - \pi_{kk}^2)\text{var}(\tilde{K}_{t+1}) = \pi_{kz}^2 \text{var}(\tilde{Z}_t) + 2\pi_{kk}\pi_{kz}\text{cov}(\tilde{K}_t, \tilde{Z}_t). \tag{A18.20}$$

---

[14]The sign of π_{ck} follows from saddle-point stability. First, we note that the discriminant in (A18.16) can be written as $(\delta_{11} - \delta_{22})^2 + 4\delta_{12}\delta_{21} = (\delta_{11} + \delta_{22})^2 - 4|\Delta| > 0$, where the sign follows from the fact that $|\Delta| < 0$. Hence, the roots are real and distinct. Next we note that $\delta_{12}\delta_{21} = -\theta_{21}\delta_{12}^{*}(1 + \delta_{11}^{*}) > 0$. Hence, the discriminant is larger than $(\delta_{11} - \delta_{22})$ so that (A18.15) has one positive and one negative root. The positive root must be selected in order to ensure that the steady state is stable, i.e. that π_{kk} in (A18.18) lies between zero and one (see also Campbell, 1994, pp. 471–472).

[15]A stochastic process, $\{x_t\}$, is covariance stationary if the mean is independent of time and the sequence of autocovariance matrices, $E(x_{t+j} - Ex_{t+j})(x_t - Ex_t)^T$ depends only on j but not on t. See Ljungqvist and Sargent (2012, p. 45) and Patterson (2000, ch. 3).

It is straightforward to derive from (18.35) that:

$$
\begin{aligned}
\text{var}(\tilde{Z}_t) &\equiv E\tilde{Z}_t^2 = E\left[\zeta_Z^2\tilde{Z}_{t-1}^2 + 2\zeta_Z Z_{t-1}\eta_t + \eta_t^2\right] \\
&= \zeta_Z^2\text{var}(\tilde{Z}_{t-1}) + \sigma_\eta^2 \quad \Rightarrow
\end{aligned}
$$

$$
\text{var}(\tilde{Z}_t) = \frac{\sigma_\eta^2}{1 - \zeta_Z^2}, \tag{A18.21}
$$

where σ_η^2 is the (constant) variance of the innovation term (i.e. $\sigma_\eta^2 \equiv E(\eta_t^2)$) and we have used covariance stationarity of the shock process (so that $\text{var}(\tilde{Z}_t) = \text{var}(\tilde{Z}_{t-1})$). Similarly, we find:

$$
\text{cov}(\tilde{Z}_t, \tilde{Z}_{t-j}) \equiv E\tilde{Z}_t\tilde{Z}_{t-j} = \zeta_Z^j\text{var}(\tilde{Z}_t). \tag{A18.22}
$$

Next we use (A18.18) to write $\tilde{K}_t$ in terms of $\tilde{Z}_{t-j}$ terms:

$$
\begin{aligned}
\tilde{K}_t &= \lim_{T\to\infty} \pi_{kk}^T\tilde{K}_{t-T} + \pi_{kz}\left[\tilde{Z}_{t-1} + \pi_{kk}\tilde{Z}_{t-2} + \pi_{kk}^2\tilde{Z}_{t-3} + \ldots\right] \\
&= \pi_{kz}\sum_{j=1}^{\infty}\pi_{kk}^{j-1}\tilde{Z}_{t-j}, \tag{A18.23}
\end{aligned}
$$

where we have used the fact that (A18.18) is a stable difference equation so that $\pi_{kk}^T\tilde{K}_{t-T}$ goes to zero as T becomes large. By using (A18.22) and (A18.23) we find the expression for $\text{cov}(\tilde{K}_t, \tilde{Z}_t)$:

$$
\begin{aligned}
\text{cov}(\tilde{K}_t, \tilde{Z}_t) &\equiv E\left[\tilde{K}_t - E\tilde{K}_t\right]\tilde{Z}_t = \pi_{kz}\sum_{j=1}^{\infty}\pi_{kk}^{j-1}E\tilde{Z}_t\tilde{Z}_{t-j} \\
&= \pi_{kz}\sum_{j=1}^{\infty}\pi_{kk}^{j-1}\zeta_Z^j\text{var}(\tilde{Z}_t) = \zeta_Z\pi_{kz}\text{var}(\tilde{Z}_t)\sum_{j=1}^{\infty}(\zeta_Z\pi_{kk})^{j-1} \\
&= \frac{\zeta_Z\pi_{kz}}{1 - \zeta_Z\pi_{kk}}\text{var}(\tilde{Z}_t). \tag{A18.24}
\end{aligned}
$$

By substituting (A18.22) and (A18.24) into (A18.20) we obtain the final expression for the variance of the capital stock:

$$
\text{var}(\tilde{K}_{t+1}) = \frac{1 + \zeta_Z\pi_{kk}}{1 - \zeta_Z\pi_{kk}}\frac{\pi_{kz}^2}{1 - \pi_{kk}^2}\text{var}(\tilde{Z}_t). \tag{A18.25}
$$

It follows from (A18.18) that:

$$
\begin{aligned}
\text{cov}(\tilde{K}_{t+1}, \tilde{K}_t) &\equiv E\left[\tilde{K}_{t+1} - E(\tilde{K}_{t+1})\right]\left[\tilde{K}_t - E(\tilde{K}_t)\right] \\
&= \pi_{kk}\text{var}(\tilde{K}_{t+1}) + \pi_{kz}\text{cov}(\tilde{K}_t, \tilde{Z}_t) \\
&= \frac{\zeta_Z + \pi_{kk}}{1 - \zeta_Z\pi_{kk}}\frac{\pi_{kz}^2}{1 - \pi_{kk}^2}\text{var}(\tilde{Z}_t). \tag{A18.26}
\end{aligned}
$$

Now that we have expressions for $\text{var}(\tilde{K}_t)$, $\text{var}(\tilde{Z}_t)$, and $\text{cov}(\tilde{K}_t, \tilde{Z}_t)$, the variances and covariances of all remaining variables are easily obtained. For consumption, for example, we derive from (A18.12):

$$
\text{var}(\tilde{C}_t) = \pi_{ck}^2\text{var}(\tilde{K}_t) + \pi_{cz}^2\text{var}(\tilde{Z}_t) + 2\pi_{ck}\pi_{cz}\text{cov}(\tilde{K}_t, \tilde{Z}_t), \tag{A18.27}
$$

$$\text{cov}(\tilde{C}_t, \tilde{K}_t) = \pi_{ck}\text{var}(\tilde{K}_t) + \pi_{cz}\text{cov}(\tilde{K}_t, \tilde{Z}_t). \tag{A18.28}$$

By using (A18.12) in (18.21)–(18.26) we can write employment, wages, output, investment, and the interest rate in terms $\tilde{K}_t$ and $\tilde{Z}_t$ and derive expressions similar to (A18.27)–(A18.28) for these variables. For output, for example, we find the following expression:

$$\tilde{Y}_t = \pi_{yk}\tilde{K}_t + \pi_{yz}\tilde{Z}_t, \tag{A18.29}$$

where $\pi_{yk} \equiv \alpha\phi - (\phi - 1)\pi_{ck}$ and $\pi_{yz} \equiv \phi - (\phi - 1)\pi_{cz}$. Equation (A18.29) is useful to compute the covariances of the different variables with output. For example, it follows from (A18.12) and (A18.29) that $\text{cov}(\tilde{C}_t, \tilde{Y}_t)$ is:

$$\text{cov}(\tilde{C}_t, \tilde{Y}_t) = \pi_{ck}\pi_{yk}\text{var}(\tilde{K}_t) + \left[\pi_{ck}\pi_{yz} + \pi_{cz}\pi_{yk}\right]\text{cov}(\tilde{K}_t, \tilde{Z}_t)$$
$$+ \pi_{cz}\pi_{yz}\text{var}(\tilde{Z}_t). \tag{A18.30}$$

Similarly, we derive from (A18.29) that $\text{cov}(\tilde{K}_t, \tilde{Y}_t)$ is:

$$\text{cov}(\tilde{K}_t, \tilde{Y}_t) = \pi_{yk}\text{var}(\tilde{K}_t) + \pi_{yz}\text{cov}(\tilde{K}_t, \tilde{Z}_t). \tag{A18.31}$$

Similar expressions for the other variables are easily found. Finally, note that in the text we report correlation coefficients. These are defined as follows:

$$\text{cor}(x_t, y_t) = \frac{\text{cov}(x_t, y_t)}{[\text{var}(x_t)\text{var}(y_t)]^{1/2}}. \tag{A18.32}$$

Chapter 19

Dynamic Stochastic General Equilibrium—New Keynesian models

The purpose of this chapter is to achieve the following goals:

1. To introduce monetary features into the dynamic stochastic general equilibrium (DSGE) model discussed in the previous chapter.

2. To incorporate a micro-based theory of monopolistic competition and price stickiness into the model.

3. To study the key features of a special case—the canonical New Keynesian model which abstracts from capital accumulation.

4. To calibrate and simulate the general version of the New Keynesian DSGE model and to demonstrate its key properties with the aid of its impulse-response functions.

5. To discuss some of the reasons why some Classical and Keynesian economists dislike the current crop of models.

19.1 Introduction

When the narrator of this lengthy textbook was himself in graduate school during the early 1980s Olivier Blanchard (1981) published a paper which can be seen as the high watermark of the ad hoc IS-LM approach. The fixed-price version of this model was studied in detail (and in a continuous-time setting) in Chapter 4 above. Re-expressed in discrete time the sticky-price version of the model can be characterized by the following set of equations:

$$y_t^d = \varepsilon_q q_t + \varepsilon_y y_{t-1}, \tag{19.1}$$

$$y_t - y_{t-1} = \phi_y \left[y_t^d - y_{t-1} \right], \tag{19.2}$$

$$q_t = \frac{d_t + q_{t+1}}{1 + r_t}, \tag{19.3}$$

$$d_t = \alpha_0 + \alpha_y y_t, \tag{19.4}$$

$$m_0 - p_t = y_t - \lambda R_t, \tag{19.5}$$

$$R_t = r_t + p_{t+1} - p_t, \tag{19.6}$$

$$p_t - p_{t-1} = \phi_p \left[p^f - p_{t-1} \right], \tag{19.7}$$

where y_t^d is goods demand, y_t is output, q_t is Tobin's q, d_t is dividends to share holders, m_0 is the exogenous nominal money supply, p_t is the price level, R_t is the nominal interest rate, and r_t is the real interest rate. All variables except the interest rates and Tobin's q are measured natural logarithms. Equation (19.1) shows that goods demand is positively affected by Tobin's q via investment ($\varepsilon_q > 0$), and by production (and thus income) in the previous period via consumption ($0 < \varepsilon_y < 1$). Equation (19.2) shows that production is a sluggish variable in the sense that demand increases are first met out of inventory decumulation and only lead to higher production later on. Stability of the adjustment process is ensured by assuming that the adjustment parameter satisfies $0 < \phi_y < 1$. Equation (19.3) is an arbitrage equation stating that the real rate of return on shares must equal the real rate of interest on single-period bonds. According to (19.3) real dividend payments are an increasing function of output ($\alpha_y > 0$). Equation (19.5) is a loglinear money demand equation which is downward sloping in the nominal interest rate ($\lambda > 0$) and features a unitary income elasticity. The expression in (19.6) shows that the nominal interest rate equals the real interest rate plus the anticipated inflation rate. Finally, in equation (19.7) p^f denotes the hypothetical price level that would be attained for a given money supply m_0 if output is at its full employment level $\bar{y}$ and the dynamic system is in the steady state, i.e.:

$$q^* = \frac{(1 - \varepsilon_y)\bar{y}}{\varepsilon_q}, \qquad r^* = \frac{\alpha_0 + \alpha_y \bar{y}}{q^*}, \qquad p^f = m_0 - \bar{y} + \lambda r^*, \tag{19.8}$$

where stars denote steady-state values. Note that in (19.7) it is assumed that the actual price level only gradually adjusts to the flex-price price level p^f, i.e. the adjustment parameter ϕ_p satisfies $0 < \phi_p < 1$.

Blanchard uses the model to study inter alia the effects of stepwise changes in the money supply under perfect foresight. The outcome of this exercise is not of premier importance here. The real question is, why did economists abandon stylized models such as the one formulated above? What is "wrong" with Blanchard's model? New Classical economists would point out that the model lacks microeconomic foundations, that reality is better characterized by stochastic rational expectations models, and that prices are perfectly flexible. New Keynesian economists largely agree with the first two points but disagree with the third. Price- and/or wage stickiness is a fact of life according to these economists and must be included in a micro-based model of the monetary macro-economy. This chapter presents a brief introduction to the New Keynesian DSGE model which can be seen as the natural successor to Blanchard's ad hoc dynamic IS-LM model.

19.2   Building an MBC model

In this section we construct a basic New Keynesian dynamic stochastic general equilibrium (DSGE) model to be used (in various forms) throughout the remainder of this chapter. The model can be seen as an RBC model (see Chapter 18) appended with some monetary features and imperfect price adjustment. An alternative name for the model constructed here could thus be the monetary business cycle (MBC) model even though this terminology has not gained widespread currency in the literature.

Basic as it is, the MBC model developed here draws together a large number of components that were discussed in earlier parts of the book. Some of these main features are:

- Just as in Chapter 18 we postulate the existence of an infinitely-lived representative individual who makes decisions in a stochastic environment.

- Just as in Section 13.7 we assume that the household derives felicity from holding real money balances. The so-called money-in-the-utility-function approach is adopted.

- Just as in Section 14.4 we assume that the final good is produced in a perfectly competitive sector which uses differentiated inputs produced by monopolistic competitors in the intermediate goods sector. To capture input differentiation we utilize the Dixit-Stiglitz approach discussed in Chapters 11 and 14.

- Just as in Section 11.3.3 we capture the notion of price adjustment costs by adopting the Calvo pricing model which assumes that a monopolistically competitive firm can only change its price if it receives a "green light" from Mother Nature. In case it gets a "red light" it must honour its previously determined price level.

Armed with this long list of things to remember we can now start building the basic DSGE model.

19.2.1   Firms

There are two production sectors in the economy. The final goods sector is perfectly competitive and it uses inputs produced by monopolistically competitive producers in the intermediate goods sector. The output of the final goods sector is consumed by households or the government and is used to augment the physical capital stock.

19.2.1.1   Production in the final goods sector

The representative firm in the final goods sector produces a homogeneous good using varieties of a differentiated intermediate good as productive inputs. Production is subject to constant returns to scale (in these inputs) and perfect competition prevails. The number of inputs is constant (as there is no entry into or exit from the input-producing sector). Using the continuum approach to product differentiation (see Intermezzo 19.1) we write the aggregate production function as:

$$Y_t = \left[\int_0^1 Y_t(i)^{1-1/\theta} \, di \right]^{1/(1-1/\theta)}, \qquad 1 < \theta \ll \infty, \tag{19.9}$$

where Y_t is homogeneous output, $Y_t(i)$ is the quantity of input i used in production, and θ is the substitution elasticity between any two inputs $Y_t(i)$ and $Y_t(j)$ (for $i \neq j$). Since θ is close to but strictly greater than unity the inputs are close but imperfect substitutes for each other. Denoting the price of input i by $P_t(i)$ we find that the unit-cost function is:

$$UC_t \equiv \left[\int_0^1 P_t(i)^{1-\theta}\, di \right]^{1/(1-\theta)}. \tag{19.10}$$

In the absence of fixed costs, unit cost equals marginal cost. Perfect competition in the final goods sector thus results in:

$$P_t = UC_t. \tag{19.11}$$

For future reference we note that the derived demand function for input variety i can be written as:

$$Y_t(i) = Y_t \left(\frac{P_t(i)}{P_t} \right)^{-\theta}. \tag{19.12}$$

Intermezzo 19.1

The continuum approach to product differentiation. Interestingly enough the first discussion paper version of the famous Dixit-Stiglitz model that appeared in 1974 used the continuum approach to product differentiation—see Dixit and Stiglitz (2004a, p. 72). They dropped it from the 1975 version (as well as the published one) because they had found that it led to "unnecessary confusion" on the part of a lot of readers—see Dixit and Stiglitz (2004b, p. 92). Presumably because the profession had tooled up sufficiently by then, the continuum approach was re-introduced into the literature in the late 1980s by inter alia Paul Romer (1987) and Grossman and Helpman (1991a, p. 45). Since we employ the continuum approach throughout this chapter and we definitely wish to avoid confusion it is useful to quickly review it.

Infinitesimally small firms in the differentiated sector are labelled by the index $i \in [0,1]$. Since all firms have the same size they all receive the same weight in the CES aggregate function (19.9). The representative firm in the final goods sector is a perfectly competitive cost minimizer. Hence, given the input prices $P_t(i)$, the factors of production $Y_t(i)$ are chosen such that a given amount of Y_t is produced at minimum cost. More formally the cost function is defined as:

$$TC\,(P_t(i), Y_t) \equiv \min_{\{Y_t(i)\}} \int_0^1 P_t(i) Y_t(i)\, di \quad \text{subject to:}$$

$$Y_t = \left[\int_0^1 Y_t(i)^{1-1/\theta}\, di \right]^{1/(1-1/\theta)}. \tag{a}$$

The Lagrangian for this minimization problem is:

$$\mathcal{L} \equiv \int_0^1 P_t(i) Y_t(i)\, di + \lambda_t \left[Y_t - \left[\int_0^1 Y_t(i)^{1-1/\theta}\, di \right]^{1/(1-1/\theta)} \right],$$

and the first-order necessary conditions are (for all $Y_t(i)$ such that $i \in [0,1]$):

$$\frac{\partial \mathcal{L}}{\partial Y_t(i)} = P_t(i) - \lambda_t \left[\int_0^1 Y_t(i)^{1-1/\theta} di \right]^{1/(1-1/\theta)-1} Y_t(i)^{-1/\theta} = 0. \quad \text{(b)}$$

We note from the definition of Y_t that:

$$\left[\int_0^1 Y_t(i)^{1-1/\theta} di \right]^{1/(1-1/\theta)-1} = \left[\int_0^1 Y_t(i)^{1-1/\theta} di \right]^{1/(\theta-1)} = Y_t^{1/\theta}, \quad \text{(c)}$$

so that the expressions in (b) can be written as $P_t(i) = \lambda_t \left(Y_t / Y_t(i) \right)^{1/\theta}$ or:

$$Y_t(i) = Y_t \left(\frac{\lambda_t}{P_t(i)} \right)^\theta. \quad \text{(d)}$$

By substituting (d) into the production function (19.9) and solving for λ_t we find in a number of steps:

$$Y_t^{1-1/\theta} = \int_0^1 Y_t(i)^{1-1/\theta} di$$

$$= Y_t^{1-1/\theta} \lambda_t^{\theta-1} \int_0^1 P_t(i)^{1-\theta} di \quad \Rightarrow$$

$$\lambda_t = \left[\int_0^1 P_t(i)^{1-\theta} di \right]^{1/(1-\theta)} \equiv UC_t, \quad \text{(e)}$$

where UC_t is the unit cost function. By substituting (e) into (d) we obtain the derived demand curve for input i:

$$Y_t(i) = Y_t \left(\frac{P_t(i)}{UC_t} \right)^{-\theta}. \quad \text{(f)}$$

Note that total cost is given by:

$$TC(P_t(i), Y_t) = \int_0^1 P_t(i) Y_t(i) di = \int_0^1 P_t(i) Y_t \left(\frac{P_t(i)}{UC_t} \right)^{-\theta} di$$

$$= Y_t UC_t^\theta \int_0^1 P_t(i)^{1-\theta} di = UC_t Y_t. \quad \text{(g)}$$

There are no fixed costs so unit cost equals marginal cost in the final goods sector. With perfect competition prevailing in that sector we find that $P_t = UC_t$.

****

19.2.1.2 Production in the intermediate goods sector

The intermediate goods sector is populated by a large number of small firms, each producing a single variety of the differentiated input. Firms engage in Chamberlinian monopolistic competition (see Chapter 11 for a detailed account of this market structure). Since all firms in the sector are assumed to be identical we focus on the decisions made by firm i.

Firm i believes that it is too small to affect the overall market outcome, i.e. in setting its price $P_t(i)$ it takes the prices charged by other firms (as well as aggregate demand) as given. In formal terms it assumes that $\partial P_t(j)/\partial P_t(i) = 0$ for $j \neq i$ and that $\partial Y_t/\partial P_t(i) = 0$. The firm rents capital and labour from the household and faces a fixed cost in the form of "overhead labour". The production function is given by:

$$Y_t(i) = F(K_t(i), Z_t(L_t(i) - \bar{L})) \equiv K_t(i)^\alpha [Z_t(L_t(i) - \bar{L})]^{1-\alpha}, \tag{19.13}$$

where $K_t(i)$ and $L_t(i)$ denote the amounts of capital and labour, respectively, $\bar{L}$ is overhead labour (so that $L_t(i) - \bar{L}$ is the number of production workers), and Z_t is a labour-augmenting technological shock term (which is stochastic and common to all firms in the sector). The second expression in (19.13) shows that the technology is of the Cobb-Douglas type with the capital coefficient such that $0 < \alpha < 1$.

Firm i faces perfectly competitive input markets because capital and labour are assumed to be perfectly mobile across firms. This ensures that at any time t there exist common nominal rental rates, which we denote by R_t^K for capital and W_t for labour. At each moment in time the firm chooses its input mix in order to minimize total factor cost, $R_t^K K_t(i) + W_t L_t(i)$, subject to the production function (19.13). This results in:

$$TC_t(i) = MC_t Y_t(i) + W_t \bar{L}, \tag{19.14}$$

$$MC_t \equiv \left(\frac{R_t^K}{\alpha}\right)^\alpha \left(\frac{W_t}{(1-\alpha)Z_t}\right)^{1-\alpha}, \tag{19.15}$$

where $TC_t(i)$ is total cost, MC_t is marginal cost, and $W_t \bar{L}$ is fixed cost. To produce anything at all the firm must hire $\bar{L}$ overhead workers. Variable cost is given by $MC_t Y_t(i)$ and depends on the firm's output. Note that marginal and fixed cost are the same for all firms in the intermediate goods sector. The derived demands for the two production factors are obtained by employing Shephard's lemma:

$$K_t(i) = \frac{\partial TC_t(i)}{\partial R_t^K} = \frac{\alpha}{R_t^K} MC_t Y_t(i), \tag{19.16}$$

$$L_t(i) = \frac{\partial TC_t(i)}{\partial W_t} = \bar{L} + \frac{1-\alpha}{W_t} MC_t Y_t(i). \tag{19.17}$$

In order to prepare for things to come we first study the price-setting decision of firm i in the hypothetical case where it faces no price adjustment costs at all. In this flex-price scenario the choice facing the firm is static. Nominal profit of the firm is defined as follows:

$$NP_t(i) \equiv P_t(i) Y_t(i) - TC_t(i),$$

$$= [P_t(i) - MC_t] Y_t \left(\frac{P_t(i)}{P_t}\right)^{-\theta} - W_t \bar{L}, \tag{19.18}$$

where we have used the demand function (19.12) and the cost function (19.14) to arrive at the second expression.

Firm i chooses its price $P_t(i)$ in order to maximize nominal profit $NP_t(i)$, taking as given the "macroeconomic variables" (P_t, W_t, MC_t, and Y_t). The first-order condition for this problem is:

$$\frac{dNP_t(i)}{dP_t(i)} = Y_t \left(\frac{P_t(i)}{P_t} \right)^{-\theta} \left[1 - \theta \frac{P_t(i) - MC_t}{P_t(i)} \right] = 0.$$

By setting the term in square brackets equal to zero we obtain the usual result that the firm sets its (flex-price) optimal price equal to a fixed gross markup times marginal cost:

$$P_t^f(i) = \frac{\theta}{\theta - 1} MC_t. \tag{19.19}$$

At that price the firm's flex-price output level is $Y_t^f(i) = Y_t (P_t^f(i) / P_t)^{-\theta}$ whilst its flex-price profit level is:

$$NP_t^f(i) \equiv P_t^f(i) Y_t^f(i) - TC_t(i)$$

$$= \frac{1}{\theta - 1} MC_t Y_t^f(i) - W_t \bar{L}. \tag{19.20}$$

Since θ is greater than unity it follows from (19.19) that the gross markup is greater than one so that the firm more than covers its variable production cost. This explains why nominal profit is increasing in the firm's output level in (19.20).

In the presence of price adjustment costs the choice facing the firm is a dynamic one. Following much of the New Keynesian literature Calvo pricing is used (see Section 11.3.3 for a discussion of its basic principles). The main features of the pricing approach are as follows. In each period a fraction $1 - \zeta$ of firms receive a green light from nature and get to charge a new price, $P_t(i) = P_t^n(i)$. The remaining fraction ζ of firms receive a red light and must charge their old price.

To derive the firm's pricing decision when it receives a green light we first write nominal profit at some future time $t + \tau$ from the perspective of time t as follows:

$$NP_{t+\tau}(i) = [P_t(i) - MC_{t+\tau}] Y_{t+\tau} \left(\frac{P_t(i)}{P_{t+\tau}} \right)^{-\theta} - W_{t+\tau} \bar{L}$$

$$\equiv \Phi(P_t(i), X_{t+\tau}), \tag{19.21}$$

where $X_{t+\tau}$ is the vector of macroeconomic variables (expressed in nominal terms) that are taken as given by the firm:

$$X_{t+\tau} \equiv (P_{t+\tau}, Y_{t+\tau}, W_{t+\tau}, MC_{t+\tau}). \tag{19.22}$$

The nominal value of a firm that has just received a green light and decides on $P_t(i)$ is given by:

$$V_t^0(i) \equiv \Phi(P_t(i), X_t) + E_t \left[\sum_{\tau=1}^{\infty} \zeta^\tau \mathcal{N}_{t,t+\tau} \Phi(P_t(i), X_{t+\tau}) + \dots \right], \tag{19.23}$$

where $\mathcal{N}_{t,s}$ is the *nominal* stochastic discount factor used for discounting *nominal* profits:

$$\mathcal{N}_{t,s} \equiv \left(\frac{1}{1+\rho} \right)^{s-t} \frac{U_C(C_s, 1 - L_s, M_{s+1}/P_s)}{U_C(C_t, 1 - L_t, M_{t+1}/P_t)} \frac{P_t}{P_s}, \qquad s \geq t. \tag{19.24}$$

In equation (19.24) $U_C(\cdot)$ is the marginal felicity of consumption (see more on this below). Note that in equation (19.23) we have only written out the terms involving the choice variable of the green-light firm in period t ($P_t(i)$). Below we explain why profits are discounted with the nominal stochastic discount factor.

The firms sets $P_t^n(i)$ in order to maximize $V_t^0(i)$. We show in Intermezzo 19.2 that the solution for this problem is:

$$P_t^n(i) = P_t^n = \frac{\theta}{\theta-1} \frac{P_t^\theta Y_t MC_t + E_t\left[\sum_{\tau=1}^\infty \zeta^\tau \mathcal{N}_{t,t+\tau} P_{t+\tau}^\theta Y_{t+\tau} MC_{t+\tau}\right]}{P_t^\theta Y_t + E_t\left[\sum_{\tau=1}^\infty \zeta^\tau \mathcal{N}_{t,t+\tau} P_{t+\tau}^\theta Y_{t+\tau}\right]}. \tag{19.25}$$

Several things are worth noting in this expression. First, since firms face the same macroeconomic environment every green-light firm sets the same price! This symmetry property is convenient because it facilitates the computation of aggregates later on. Second, if firms would get a green light in every period for sure (so that $\zeta = 0$) then equation (19.25) would reduce to $P_t^n(i) = P_t^n = \frac{\theta}{\theta-1} MC_t$ which is—of course—the flex-price solution stated in (19.19). Third, in the general case (with $0 < \zeta < 1$) the new price $P_t^n(i)$ depends in a complicated way on the current and expected future macroeconomic environment. The new price is explicitly forward looking.

Intermezzo 19.2

Some derivations for the New Keynesian DSGE model. The price set by a green-light firm (19.25) is derived as follows. The first-order necessary condition for maximizing $V_t^0(i)$ by choice of $P_t(i)$ is:

$$\frac{dV_t^0(i)}{dP_t(i)} = E_t \sum_{\tau=0}^\infty \zeta^\tau \mathcal{N}_{t,t+\tau} \frac{\partial \Phi(P_t(i), X_{t+\tau})}{\partial P_t(i)} = 0. \tag{a}$$

We use (19.21) to deduce that:

$$\frac{\partial \Phi(P_t(i), X_{t+\tau})}{\partial P_t(i)} = P_t(i)^{-\theta} P_{t+\tau}^\theta Y_{t+\tau} \left[1 - \theta \frac{P_t(i) - MC_{t+\tau}}{P_t(i)}\right]$$

$$= (1-\theta) P_t(i)^{-\theta} P_{t+\tau}^\theta Y_{t+\tau} \left[1 - \frac{\theta}{\theta-1} \frac{MC_{t+\tau}}{P_t(i)}\right]. \tag{b}$$

By substituting (b) into (a) (and eliminating $1-\theta$) we obtain:

$$0 = E_t \sum_{\tau=0}^\infty \zeta^\tau \mathcal{N}_{t,t+\tau} P_t(i)^{-\theta} P_{t+\tau}^\theta Y_{t+\tau} \left[1 - \frac{\theta}{\theta-1} \frac{MC_{t+\tau}}{P_t(i)}\right]. \tag{c}$$

The expression in (c) can be written as:

$$\Xi_D P_t(i)^{-\theta} = \frac{\theta}{\theta-1} \Xi_N P_t(i)^{-(1+\theta)}, \tag{d}$$

with:

$$\Xi_D \equiv E_t \left[\sum_{\tau=0}^\infty \zeta^\tau \mathcal{N}_{t,t+\tau} P_{t+\tau}^\theta Y_{t+\tau}\right], \tag{e}$$

$$\Xi_N \equiv E_t \left[\sum_{\tau=0}^{\infty} \zeta^{\tau} \mathcal{N}_{t,t+\tau} P_{t+\tau}^{\theta} Y_{t+\tau} MC_{t+\tau} \right]. \tag{f}$$

Finally, by substituting (e)–(f) in (d) and simplifying we obtain the expression for $P_t^n(i)$:

$$P_t^n(i) = \frac{\theta}{\theta - 1} \frac{E_t \left[\sum_{\tau=0}^{\infty} \zeta^{\tau} \mathcal{N}_{t,t+\tau} P_{t+\tau}^{\theta} Y_{t+\tau} MC_{t+\tau} \right]}{E_t \left[\sum_{\tau=0}^{\infty} \zeta^{\tau} \mathcal{N}_{t,t+\tau} P_{t+\tau}^{\theta} Y_{t+\tau} \right]}. \tag{g}$$

In (19.25) we have slightly rewritten (g) to facilitate its interpretation.

The relationship between the alternative output measure Y_t^a and aggregate factor supplies in (19.44) is derived as follows. Recall that for each firm i we have:

$$\frac{W_t}{R_t^K} = \frac{(1-\alpha)MC_t \frac{Y_t(i)}{L_t(i) - \bar{L}}}{\alpha MC_t \frac{Y_t(i)}{K_t(i)}} = \frac{1-\alpha}{\alpha} \frac{K_t(i)}{L_t(i) - \bar{L}}. \tag{h}$$

Hence, at both firm and aggregate level we have:

$$\frac{K_t}{L_t - \bar{L}} = \frac{K_t(i)}{L_t(i) - \bar{L}} = \Gamma_t \quad \left[\equiv \frac{\alpha}{1-\alpha} \frac{W_t}{R_t^K} \right]. \tag{i}$$

The alternative quantity index for aggregate output can now be computed as:

$$Y_t^a \equiv \int_0^1 Y_t(i) di = \int_0^1 K_t(i)^{\alpha} \left[Z_t \left(L_t(i) - \bar{L} \right) \right]^{1-\alpha} di$$

$$= Z_t^{1-\alpha} \int_0^1 \left[\Gamma_t \left(L_t(i) - \bar{L} \right) \right]^{\alpha} \left[L_t(i) - \bar{L} \right]^{1-\alpha} di$$

$$= Z_t^{1-\alpha} \Gamma_t^{\alpha} \int_0^1 \left(L_t(i) - \bar{L} \right) di = Z_t^{1-\alpha} \Gamma_t^{\alpha} (L_t - \bar{L}). \tag{j}$$

By using the fact that $\Gamma_t = K_t / (L_t - \bar{L})$ in (j) we obtain (19.44) in the text. To derive (19.46) we substitute the demand for variety i (stated in equation (19.12)) into the definition of Y_t^a:

$$Y_t^a \equiv \int_0^1 Y_t(i) di = Y_t P_t^{\theta} \int_0^1 P_t(i)^{-\theta} di. \tag{k}$$

By using the definition for P_t^a from (19.45) in (k) we find (19.46).

****

19.2.1.3   The aggregate price level

It remains to derive an expression for the aggregate price level P_t. In view of (19.10)–(19.11) we know that:

$$P_t^{1-\theta} \equiv \int_0^1 P_t(i)^{1-\theta}\, di. \tag{19.26}$$

At time t a fraction $1 - \zeta$ of firms in the intermediate goods sector obtain a green light and set the price according to equation (19.25). Hence, a component of P_t consists of the prices newly set in period t:

$$P_t^{1-\theta} \equiv (1-\zeta)(P_t^n)^{1-\theta} + \int_{1-\zeta}^1 P_t(i)^{1-\theta}\, di. \tag{19.27}$$

The second expression on the right-hand side represent the component of P_t resulting from prices set in the past (i.e., P_{t-s}^n for $s = 1, 2, \ldots$). The law of large numbers says that $(1-\zeta)\zeta^s$ is the fraction of firms which determined its new price s periods before period t. Hence, we know exactly the weights that should be given to prices set in previous periods: $\zeta(1-\zeta)$ is the weight for P_{t-1}^n, $\zeta^2(1-\zeta)$ is the weight for P_{t-2}^n, etcetera. We thus obtain from (19.27) that:

$$P_t^{1-\theta} = (1-\zeta)\left[(P_t^n)^{1-\theta} + \zeta(P_{t-1}^n)^{1-\theta} + \zeta^2(P_{t-2}^n)^{1-\theta} + \ldots \right]. \tag{19.28}$$

It follows from (19.28) that the lagged price level can be written as:

$$\zeta P_{t-1}^{1-\theta} = (1-\zeta)\left[\zeta(P_{t-1}^n)^{1-\theta} + \zeta^2(P_{t-2}^n)^{1-\theta} + \zeta^3(P_{t-3}^n)^{1-\theta} + \ldots \right]. \tag{19.29}$$

Hence, $P_{t-1}^{1-\theta}$ shares all but one of the terms appearing in $P_t^{1-\theta}$. By using (19.29) in (19.28) and taking the exponent to the other side we finally obtain a relationship for the current aggregate price level:

$$P_t = \left[(1-\zeta)(P_t^n)^{1-\theta} + \zeta P_{t-1}^{1-\theta} \right]^{1/(1-\theta)}. \tag{19.30}$$

The current price level is a CES aggregate of the price set by current green-light firms and the lagged aggregate price level. As we saw in a much simpler context in Section 11.3.3 the current price level contains both a backward-looking term (P_{t-1}) and a forward-looking term (P_t^n).

19.2.2   Households

Just as in the previous chapter, there is a large number of identical households. Each individual household is infinitely small and is a price taker on all markets in which it operates. By normalizing the population size to unity we can develop the argument on the basis of a single representative agent. The representative household is infinitely lived and has an objective function based on expected lifetime utility. Denoting the planning period by t, expected lifetime utility, $E_t \Lambda_t$, is given by:

$$E_t \Lambda_t \equiv E_t \sum_{\tau=t}^{\infty} U(C_\tau, 1 - L_\tau, M_{\tau+1}/P_\tau)\left(\frac{1}{1+\rho}\right)^{\tau-t}, \tag{19.31}$$

where $U(C_\tau, 1 - L_\tau, M_{\tau+1}/P_\tau)$ is the felicity function, C_τ is consumption, $1 - L_\tau$ is leisure, and $1/(1+\rho)$ is the discounting factor due to time preference (with $\rho > 0$).

We assume that real money balances provide utility to the household for reasons explained in Section 13.7 above. As far as timing is concerned, M_τ denotes nominal money balances held at the start of period τ so we assume that end-of-period real balances enter the felicity function. To keep things simple we assume that the felicity function is loglinear, implying that both the *intra*temporal and *inter*temporal substitution elasticities are equal to unity:

$$U(C_\tau, 1 - L_\tau, M_{\tau+1}/P_\tau) \equiv \varepsilon_c \ln C_\tau + \varepsilon_l \ln (1 - L_\tau) + \varepsilon_m \ln \left(\frac{M_{\tau+1}}{P_\tau} \right), \quad (19.32)$$

with $0 < \varepsilon_c, \varepsilon_l, \varepsilon_m < 1$ and $\varepsilon_c + \varepsilon_l + \varepsilon_m = 1$. The felicity function is weakly separable in consumption, leisure, and real money balances implying that money is superneutral in a model with perfectly flexible prices and nominal wages (see Section 13.7).

In order to simplify the exposition somewhat we assume that households are the direct owners of the capital stock and thus make the capital accumulation decision and derive income from renting out their capital stock to firms in the intermediate goods sector. The household also engages in portfolio investments by purchasing risk-free government bonds, by holding money balances, and by buying equity shares in firms in the intermediate goods sector.

The household's periodic budget identity (in nominal terms) is given by:

$$P_\tau [C_\tau + I_\tau] + M_{\tau+1} + B_{\tau+1} + \sum_{s=0}^{\infty} Q_\tau^s S_{\tau+1}^s = W_\tau L_\tau + R_\tau^K K_\tau + (1 + R_{\tau-1}) B_\tau$$

$$+ \sum_{s=0}^{\infty} X_\tau^s S_\tau^s + M_\tau - P_\tau T_\tau, \quad (19.33)$$

where P_τ is the price level, I_τ is gross investment, M_τ is cash balances at the start of period τ, B_τ is the nominal value of the stock of single-period bonds available at the start of period τ, $R_{\tau-1}$ is the (risk-free) nominal interest rate received on such bonds, Q_τ^i is the nominal price of share type i in period τ, S_τ^s is the number of shares of type s held at the start of period τ, X_τ^s is the payoff from such shares (see below), W_τ is the nominal wage rate, R_τ^K is the nominal rental rate on capital, K_τ is the stock of capital available at the start of period τ, and $P_\tau T_\tau$ is the nominal lump-sum tax. Note that—in principle—there are infinitely many firm types, i.e. $s = 0, 1, \ldots$, where firm type $s = 0$ is a green-light firm in period t, $s = 1$ is a firm which had a green light in period $t - 1$ (but a red light in period t), etcetera. The law of motion for the capital stock is given by:

$$K_{\tau+1} = I_\tau + (1 - \delta) K_\tau, \quad (19.34)$$

where δ is the depreciation rate of capital ($0 < \delta < 1$).

The household chooses sequences for consumption, labour supply, investment, single-period bonds, share purchases, money balances, and the capital stock $\{C_\tau, L_\tau, I_\tau, B_{\tau+1}, S_{\tau+1}^s, M_{\tau+1}, K_{\tau+1}\}_{\tau=t}^{\infty}$ in order to maximize expected utility (19.31) subject to (19.33)–(19.34) and taking its initial stocks, B_t, S_t^s, M_t, and K_t as given. In addition, the household treats as given the paths of prices and rental rates (P_τ, Q_τ^s, W_τ, and R_τ^K), the bond rate (R_τ), payoffs (X_τ^s), and taxes (T_τ).

For the planning period t the key first-order conditions for this optimization problem can be obtained by using the insights from Intermezzo 18.1. Just as in the standard RBC model of Chapter 18 the optimal static choice regarding consumption and leisure is such that the marginal rate of substitution between leisure and consumption is equated to the real wage rate:

$$\frac{U_{1-L}(C_t, 1 - L_t, M_{t+1}/P_t)}{U_C(C_t, 1 - L_t, M_{t+1}/P_t)} = \frac{W_t}{P_t}. \tag{19.35}$$

Furthermore, the first-order condition for optimal investment gives the consumption Euler equation for the representative household:

$$1 = E_t \left[\frac{r_{t+1}^K + 1 - \delta}{1 + \rho} \frac{U_C(C_{t+1}, 1 - L_{t+1}, M_{t+2}/P_{t+1})}{U_C(C_t, 1 - L_t, M_{t+1}/P_t)} \right], \tag{19.36}$$

where $r_{t+1}^K \equiv R_{t+1}^K/P_{t+1}$ is the next period's real rental rate on capital. Optimal purchases of the risk-free nominal bond result in:

$$1 = E_t \left[(1 + R_t) \mathcal{N}_{t,t+1} \right], \tag{19.37}$$

where $\mathcal{N}_{t,t+1}$ is the nominal stochastic discount factor defined in (19.24) above. Note that the interest factor $1 + R_t$ can be taken out of the expectations operator because its value is known to the investor at time t. We thus have the usual result that the risk-free gross interest rate satisfies $1 + R_t = 1/E_t \left[\mathcal{N}_{t,t+1} \right]$ (Cochrane, 2005, p. 11).

The first-order condition for nominal money balances is given by:

$$1 = \frac{U_{M/P}(C_t, 1 - L_t, M_{t+1}/P_t)}{U_C(C_t, 1 - L_t, M_{t+1}/P_t)} + E_t \left[\mathcal{N}_{t,t+1} \right]. \tag{19.38}$$

As was pointed out in Section 10.4 above, money provides not only direct felicity (captured by the first term on the right-hand side) but also acts as a store of value (second term). By using the expression for the risk-free interest rate from (19.37) we can rewrite (19.38) in a more intuitive form as:

$$\frac{U_{M/P}(C_t, 1 - L_t, M_{t+1}/P_t)}{U_C(C_t, 1 - L_t, M_{t+1}/P_t)} = \frac{R_t}{1 + R_t}. \tag{19.39}$$

Optimal demand for real money balances is such that the marginal rate of substitution between such balances and consumption is equated to the nominal interest factor on the right-hand side of (19.39).

The final (and most complicated) first-order condition is the one for optimal share purchases:

$$Q_t^s = E_t \left[\mathcal{N}_{t,t+1} X_{t+1}^s \right], \tag{19.40}$$

where X_{t+1}^s is the one-period payoff to purchasing a share in firm type s in period t. What is this payoff and why is it uncertain at time t? Assume that the investor purchases a share in a period-t green-light firm, i.e. $Q_t^0 = E_t \left[\mathcal{N}_{t,t+1} X_{t+1}^0 \right]$. Whilst the firm has a green light in period t there are two possible outcomes for the next period. With probability $1 - \zeta$ it will have a green light again in period $t + 1$ so that the payoff to the investor will be $Q_{t+1}^0 + NP_{t+1}^0$, where Q_{t+1}^0 is the share price for green-light firms and NP_{t+1}^0 is nominal profit of such a firm (both in period $t + 1$). With probability ζ, however, the firm gets a red light in period $t + 1$ so that the payoff to the investor will be $Q_{t+1}^1 + NP_{t+1}^1$, where Q_{t+1}^1 and NP_{t+1}^1 denote the share price and nominal profit level of type $s = 1$ firms in period $t + 1$. Since the household is ultimately interested in what he or she can consume as a result of the payoff, the nominal stochastic discount factor is applied in the expression in (19.40). To answer the question at the start of this paragraph, the payoff is stochastic both because there are technology shocks affecting all firms *and* because the firm may change type between periods t and $t+1$. To summarize we note that for a firm of type s in period t the share price satisfies:

$$Q_t^s = E_t \left[\mathcal{N}_{t,t+1} \left[(1-\zeta)(Q_{t+1}^0 + NP_{t+1}^0) + \zeta(Q_{t+1}^{s+1} + NP_{t+1}^{s+1}) \right] \right]. \tag{19.41}$$

No matter how long a red-light firm has been in this sorry state there is always hope in the form of a non-zero probability of switching to the green-light status in the next period.

19.2.3 Macroeconomic equilibrium

In this section we tie up some loose ends and define the macroeconomic equilibrium model using the functional forms for household preferences and the technology in the intermediate goods sector (as stated in, respectively, (19.32) and (19.13)). For convenience the equations defining the macroeconomic equilibrium have been gathered in Table 19.1.

Equation (T1.1) restates (19.34), and (T1.2) is the final goods market clearing condition for a closed economy. Equations (T1.3)–(T1.6) are obtained from, respectively, (19.37), (19.36), (19.39), and (19.35) by using the logarithmic felicity function (19.32) and noting (19.24). Equations (T1.7)–(T1.8) are obtained by aggregating (19.16)–(19.17) over all firms in the intermediate sector (using the definition of Y_t^a) and by expressing the result in real terms. Equation (T1.9) is obtained from (19.25) by using the definition of the nominal stochastic discount factor from (19.24). Finally, equation (T1.10) just restates (19.30).

The remaining equations in Table 19.1 deal with the loose ends mentioned above. Since primary factors are used in the intermediate goods sector only, the equilibrium conditions in the rental markets for labour are given by:

$$L_t = \int_0^1 L_t(i)di, \tag{19.42}$$

$$K_t = \int_0^1 K_t(i)di, \tag{19.43}$$

where L_t is total employment and K_t is the capital stock. It turns out to be convenient to define an alternative output measure which can be tied directly to the aggregate factor supplies. The alternative output index is defined as:

$$Y_t^a \equiv \int_0^1 Y_t(i)di = K_t^\alpha \left[Z_t (L_t - \bar{L}) \right]^{1-\alpha}, \tag{19.44}$$

where the final expression is derived in Intermezzo 19.2. Note that the expression in (19.44) differs from the true aggregate production function (19.9) in that it treats any two inputs $Y_t(i)$ and $Y_t(j)$ as if they are perfect substitutes whereas (19.9) says that they are not. But by defining the alternative price index:

$$P_t^a \equiv \left[\int_0^1 P_t(i)^{-\theta} di \right]^{-1/\theta}, \tag{19.45}$$

we nevertheless find that Y_t and Y_t^a are related to each other according to the following expression:

$$Y_t = \left(\frac{P_t^a}{P_t}\right)^\theta Y_t^a. \tag{19.46}$$

Note that (19.44) and (19.46) have been restated in (T1.11) and (T1.13) respectively. The recursive relationship for P_t^a in (T1.12) is obtained by repeating the steps leading to (19.30) above.

The nominal government budget identity is given by:

$$B_{t+1} + M_{t+1} = (1 + R_{t-1}) B_t + M_t + P_t(G_t - T_t). \tag{19.47}$$

Together with an assumption regarding the money supply and a government solvency condition the macroeconomic equilibrium is determined. We implicitly assume that the lump-sum tax ensures government solvency. Since the model features Ricardian equivalence the timing of taxation does not matter.

19.3 The canonical New Keynesian DSGE model

The model given in Table 19.1 is an example of a unit-elastic MBC model with sticky prices. It shares all non-monetary features with the basic RBC model studied in Chapter 18. Hence it is clear that both the labour supply elasticity and the capital accumulation mechanism play a crucial role in the MBC model also. Interestingly most of the New Keynesian DSGE literature has chosen to ignore the capital accumulation mechanism by focusing on a much simpler version of the MBC model which abstracts from physical capital altogether—see for example Galí (2015, ch. 3). We study such a simplified model in the section (but we return to the more general model in Section 19.4 below).

The canonical New Keynesian DSGE model is obtained from Table 19.1 by adopting the following simplifying assumptions. First, there is no role for physical capital, i.e. $\alpha = 0$ and $K_t = I_t = 0$ for all t. Second, there is no government consumption, so that output is equal to private consumption, $Y_t = C_t$ for all t. Third, there is no trend in the nominal money supply and the deterministic steady state is characterized by zero price inflation.

By imposing these simplifications the model of Table 19.2 is obtained. Several things are worth noting in the comparison between this model and its more general parent in Table 19.1. First, in the absence of physical capital real marginal cost is equal to the productivity-weighted real wage rate. Second, since consumption equals output both drop out of the pricing equation (T2.5). Third, since nominal government bonds are the only interest-yielding investment instruments to the households, the expected real interest rate on such bonds enters the Euler equation (T2.1). Whereas the nominal interest rate on bonds is known at time t, the future price level is not, so the real rate of interest is uncertain.

Despite all these simplifications the model is still rather complex! This is to a large extent a result of the pricing friction that is incorporated. Indeed, with the Calvo mechanism in place we need to keep track of three different prices (P_t^n, P_t^a, and P_t) and two different output measures (Y_t^a and Y_t). It is impossible to make any analytical progress with the model expressed in levels. But as we saw in a related context in the previous chapter, a more tractable model is obtained by linearizing the equations appearing in Table 19.2 around a deterministic steady state assuming that the unconditional mean of the technology shock is equal to unity ($EZ_t = 1$).

Table 19.1. The basic MBC model

$$K_{t+1} = I_t + (1 - \delta)K_t \tag{T1.1}$$

$$Y_t = C_t + I_t + G_t \tag{T1.2}$$

$$\frac{\varepsilon_c}{C_t} = E_t \left[\frac{1 + R_t}{1 + \rho} \frac{\varepsilon_c}{C_{t+1}} \frac{P_t}{P_{t+1}} \right] \tag{T1.3}$$

$$\frac{\varepsilon_c}{C_t} = E_t \left[\frac{1 + r_{t+1}^K - \delta}{1 + \rho} \frac{\varepsilon_c}{C_{t+1}} \right] \tag{T1.4}$$

$$\frac{M_{t+1}}{P_t} = \frac{\varepsilon_m}{\varepsilon_c} C_t \frac{1 + R_t}{R_t} \tag{T1.5}$$

$$L_t = 1 - \frac{\varepsilon_l}{\varepsilon_c} \frac{C_t}{w_t} \tag{T1.6}$$

$$w_t = (1 - \alpha) \, mc_t \, \frac{Y_t^a}{L_t - \bar{L}} \tag{T1.7}$$

$$r_t^K = \alpha \, mc_t \, \frac{Y_t^a}{K_t} \tag{T1.8}$$

$$P_t^n = \frac{\theta}{\theta - 1} \frac{E_t \left[\sum_{\tau=0}^{\infty} \left(\frac{\zeta}{1+\rho} \right)^\tau C_{t+\tau}^{-1} P_{t+\tau}^\theta Y_{t+\tau} mc_{t+\tau} \right]}{E_t \left[\sum_{\tau=0}^{\infty} \left(\frac{\zeta}{1+\rho} \right)^\tau C_{t+\tau}^{-1} P_{t+\tau}^{\theta-1} Y_{t+\tau} \right]} \tag{T1.9}$$

$$P_t = \left[(1 - \zeta) \left(P_t^n \right)^{1-\theta} + \zeta P_{t-1}^{1-\theta} \right]^{1/(1-\theta)} \tag{T1.10}$$

$$Y_t^a = K_t^\alpha \left[Z_t (L_t - \bar{L}) \right]^{1-\alpha} \tag{T1.11}$$

$$P_t^a = \left[(1 - \zeta) \left(P_t^n \right)^{-\theta} + \zeta \left(P_{t-1}^a \right)^{-\theta} \right]^{-1/\theta} \tag{T1.12}$$

$$Y_t = \left(\frac{P_t^a}{P_t} \right)^\theta Y_t^a \tag{T1.13}$$

Definitions: Y_t is output, C_t is private consumption, L_t is employment, K_t is the capital stock, $w_t \equiv W_t/P_t$ is the real wage rate, $r_t^K \equiv R_t^K/P_t$ is the real rental rate on capital, $mc_t \equiv MC_t/P_t$ is real marginal cost, P_t is the price level, P_t^n is the price set by green-light firms, Y_t^a is an alternative output measure, P_t^a is an alternative price index, R_t is the rate of interest on risk-free bonds, and I_t is gross investment. The exogenous variables are the nominal money supply M_{t+1}, government consumption G_t, and the technology shock Z_t. The structural parameters are ε_c, ε_l, ε_m, ρ, δ, ζ, θ, $\bar{L}$, and α.

Table 19.2. A minimal New Keynesian DSGE model

$$\frac{1}{Y_t} = \frac{1 + R_t}{1 + \rho} E_t \left[\frac{1}{Y_{t+1}} \frac{P_t}{P_{t+1}} \right] \tag{T2.1}$$

$$\frac{M_{t+1}}{P_t} = \frac{\varepsilon_m}{\varepsilon_c} Y_t \frac{1 + R_t}{R_t} \tag{T2.2}$$

$$L_t = 1 - \frac{\varepsilon_l}{\varepsilon_c} \frac{Y_t}{w_t} \tag{T2.3}$$

$$mc_t = \frac{w_t}{Z_t} \tag{T2.4}$$

$$P_t^n = \frac{\theta}{\theta - 1} \frac{E_t \left[\sum_{\tau=0}^{\infty} \left(\frac{\zeta}{1+\rho} \right)^{\tau} P_{t+\tau}^{\theta} mc_{t+\tau} \right]}{E_t \left[\sum_{\tau=0}^{\infty} \left(\frac{\zeta}{1+\rho} \right)^{\tau} P_{t+\tau}^{\theta-1} \right]} \tag{T2.5}$$

$$P_t = \left[(1 - \zeta) (P_t^n)^{1-\theta} + \zeta P_{t-1}^{1-\theta} \right]^{1/(1-\theta)} \tag{T2.6}$$

$$Y_t^a = Z_t (L_t - \bar{L}) \tag{T2.7}$$

$$P_t^a = \left[(1 - \zeta) (P_t^n)^{-\theta} + \zeta \left(P_{t-1}^a \right)^{-\theta} \right]^{-1/\theta} \tag{T2.8}$$

$$Y_t = \left(\frac{P_t^a}{P_t} \right)^{\theta} Y_t^a \tag{T2.9}$$

Definitions: Y_t is output, L_t is employment, $w_t \equiv W_t / P_t$ is the real wage rate, $mc_t \equiv MC_t / P_t$ is real marginal cost, P_t is the price level, P_t^n is the price set by green-light firms, Y_t^a is an alternative output measure, P_t^a is an alternative price index, and R_t is the rate of interest on risk-free bonds. The exogenous variables are the nominal money supply M_t and the technology shock Z_t. The structural parameters are ε_c, ε_l, ε_m, ρ, ζ, $\bar{L}$, and θ.

19.3.1 Preliminary steps (without apologies)

Since the linearization of the model is Table 19.2 is far from trivial we show some details here. We adopt the following notation:

- Deterministic steady-state values are denoted with stars.

- For output, employment, prices, real wages, and the money supply we use the following definition:

$$\tilde{x}_t \equiv \frac{x_t - x^*}{x^*}. \tag{19.48}$$

- For the interest rate we use a slightly alternative definition:

$$\tilde{R}_t \equiv \frac{R_t - \rho}{1 + \rho}. \tag{19.49}$$

The deterministic steady state has the following features. First, it incorporates the assumption that the unconditional mean of Z_t equals $EZ_t = Z^* = 1$. Second, there is no real growth so $Y_t^* = Y^*$, $w_t^* = w^*$, etcetera. Third, there is zero money growth so $P_{t+1}^* = P_t^* = P^*$ and the deterministic steady-state inflation rate is zero, $\pi^* = 0$. Fourth, from the (deterministic) Euler equation we find that in this zero-inflation world the nominal interest rate equals the pure rate of time preference:

$$\frac{\varepsilon_c}{Y_t^*} = \frac{1 + R_t^*}{1 + \rho} \frac{\varepsilon_c}{Y_{t+1}^*} \frac{P_t^*}{P_{t+1}^*} \quad \Leftrightarrow \quad 1 = \frac{1 + R_t^*}{1 + \rho} \quad \Leftrightarrow \quad R_t^* = \rho. \tag{19.50}$$

Fifth, it follows from (T2.5)–(T2.6) and (T2.8) that $P^* = (P^a)^* = (P^n)^*$ and from (T2.5) we thus get that the steady-state real wage is constant:

$$w^* \equiv \frac{W^*}{P^*} = \frac{\theta - 1}{\theta}. \tag{19.51}$$

Finally, in the calibration exercise below it will prove useful to note a number of steady-state relationships. From (T2.7) and (T2.9) we find that:

$$Y^* = (Y^a)^* = L^* - \bar{L}, \tag{19.52}$$

whilst from (T2.2)–(T2.3) we obtain:

$$\frac{M_0}{P^*} = \frac{\varepsilon_m}{\varepsilon_c} Y^* \frac{1 + \rho}{\rho}, \qquad \frac{\varepsilon_l}{1 - L^*} = \frac{\varepsilon_c}{Y^*} w^*, \tag{19.53}$$

where M_0 is the given level of the money supply.

Armed with this notation and these steady-state results we can linearize the model in Table 19.2 by performing first-order Taylor approximations on its defining equations. Recall that $R^* = \rho$ and $\pi^* = 0$. We drop the expectations operator from (T2.1) and start with the (deterministic) Euler equation (in terms of output):

$$\frac{1}{Y_t} = \frac{1 + R_t}{1 + \rho} \frac{1}{Y_{t+1}} \frac{1}{1 + \pi_{t+1}}, \tag{19.54}$$

where future inflation, π_{t+1}, is defined as:

$$\frac{P_{t+1}}{P_t} = \frac{P_t + \Delta P_{t+1}}{P_t} = 1 + \pi_{t+1}. \tag{19.55}$$

A first-order approximation of the left-hand side of (19.54) gives:

$$\frac{1}{Y_t} \approx \frac{1}{Y^*} - \left(\frac{1}{Y^*}\right)^2 [Y_t - Y^*] = \frac{1 - \tilde{Y}_t}{Y^*}, \tag{19.56}$$

whilst approximating the right-hand side yields:

$$\frac{1 + R_t}{1 + \rho} \frac{1}{Y_{t+1}} \frac{1}{1 + \pi_{t+1}} \approx \frac{1}{Y^*} \left[1 + \tilde{R}_t - \tilde{Y}_{t+1} - \pi_{t+1}\right], \tag{19.57}$$

where we have used the definition for $\tilde{Y}_t$ and $\tilde{Y}_{t+1}$. Finally, by combining (19.56) and (19.57), simplifying, and putting the expectations operator back in we obtain one of the key equations underlying the New Keynesian DSGE model:

$$\tilde{Y}_t = E_t \tilde{Y}_{t+1} - \left[\tilde{R}_t - E_t \pi_{t+1}\right]. \tag{19.58}$$

Equation (19.58) is often referred to as the dynamic IS curve (DIS hereafter) although its foundations are completely at odds with those underlying the "old-fashioned" IS curve of the IS-LM model. In the canonical model the DIS curve says something about saving (consuming in this period or the next one) but is silent about investment as capital is absent from the model.

Next we turn to the money demand equation (T2.2). For a given money stock $M_t = M_0$ the left-hand side can be approximated by:

$$\frac{M_{t+1}}{P_t} \approx \frac{M_0}{P^*} \left[1 + \tilde{M}_{t+1} - \tilde{P}_t\right],$$

whilst for the right-hand side we find:

$$\frac{\varepsilon_m}{\varepsilon_c} Y_t \frac{1 + R_t}{R_t} \approx \frac{\varepsilon_m}{\varepsilon_c} Y^* \frac{1 + \rho}{\rho} \left[1 + \tilde{Y}_t - \frac{\tilde{R}_t}{\rho}\right].$$

Combining these results and simplifying we obtain:

$$\tilde{M}_{t+1} - \tilde{P}_t = \tilde{Y}_t - \frac{\tilde{R}_t}{\rho}. \tag{19.59}$$

Continuing our linearization we observe that equations (T2.3)–(T2.4), (T2.7), and (T2.9) do not pose very challenging tasks. By applying the rules of first-order linearization we easily find:

$$\tilde{L}_t = \frac{1 - L^*}{L^*} \left[\tilde{w}_t - \tilde{Y}_t\right], \tag{19.60}$$

$$\widetilde{mc}_t = \tilde{w}_t - \tilde{Z}_t, \tag{19.61}$$

$$\tilde{Y}_t^a = \frac{L^*}{L^* - \bar{L}} \tilde{L}_t + \tilde{Z}_t, \tag{19.62}$$

$$\tilde{Y}_t = \tilde{Y}_t^a + \theta \left(\tilde{P}_t^a - \tilde{P}_t\right), \tag{19.63}$$

Expressions like (T2.6) and (T2.8) are a little tricker. We start by rewriting (T2.6) as:

$$P_t^{1-\theta} = (1 - \zeta)(P_t^n)^{1-\theta} + \zeta P_{t-1}^{1-\theta}. \tag{19.64}$$

Since $P_t^* = (P_t^n)^* = P_{t-1}^* = P^*$ the left-hand side of (19.64) can be approximated by:

$$P_t^{1-\theta} \approx (P^*)^{1-\theta} \left[1 + (1 - \theta)\tilde{P}_t\right],$$

whilst the right-hand side gives:

$$(1 - \zeta)\,(P_t^n)^{1-\theta} + \zeta P_{t-1}^{1-\theta} \approx (1 - \zeta)(P^*)^{1-\theta}\left[1 + (1 - \theta)\tilde{P}_t^n\right]$$
$$+ \zeta(P^*)^{1-\theta}\left[1 + (1 - \theta)\tilde{P}_{t-1}\right].$$

Combining results yields the final expression:

$$\tilde{P}_t = (1 - \zeta)\tilde{P}_t^n + \zeta\tilde{P}_{t-1}. \tag{19.65}$$

In a similar fashion we can find that the linearized version of (T2.8) is:

$$\tilde{P}_t^a = (1 - \zeta)\tilde{P}_t^n + \zeta\tilde{P}_{t-1}^a. \tag{19.66}$$

Since (19.65) and (19.66) depend in the same way on $\tilde{P}_t^n$ and feature the same lag structure we find that $\tilde{P}_t = \tilde{P}_t^a$ for all t (and thus that $\tilde{Y}_t = \tilde{Y}_t^a$).

As always we have saved the best for last. At least the hardest one! As it turns out it is most convenient to rewrite (T2.5) in *relative* terms first by dividing both sides by the current price level P_t:

$$p_t^n = \frac{\theta}{\theta - 1} \frac{E_t\left[\sum_{\tau=0}^{\infty}\left(\frac{\zeta}{1+\rho}\right)^\tau p_{t+\tau}^\theta mc_{t+\tau}\right]}{E_t\left[\sum_{\tau=0}^{\infty}\left(\frac{\zeta}{1+\rho}\right)^\tau p_{t+\tau}^{\theta-1}\right]}, \tag{19.67}$$

where $p_t^n \equiv P_t^n/P_t$ and $p_{t+\tau} \equiv P_{t+\tau}/P_t$ denote, respectively, the relative new price and the relative price in period $t + \tau$. Next, we drop the expectations operator E_t and write (19.67) as:

$$\Xi_D\, p_t^n = \frac{\theta}{\theta - 1}\, \Xi_N, \tag{19.68}$$

where Ξ_D and Ξ_N are defined as:

$$\Xi_D \equiv \sum_{\tau=0}^{\infty}\left(\frac{\zeta}{1+\rho}\right)^\tau p_{t+\tau}^{\theta-1}, \qquad \Xi_N \equiv \sum_{\tau=0}^{\infty}\left(\frac{\zeta}{1+\rho}\right)^\tau p_{t+\tau}^\theta mc_{t+\tau}. \tag{19.69}$$

For future reference we note that $(p_t^n)^* = p_{t+\tau}^* = 1$ so that:

$$\Xi_D^* \equiv \sum_{\tau=0}^{\infty}\left(\frac{\zeta}{1+\rho}\right)^\tau = \frac{1+\rho}{1-\zeta+\rho}, \qquad \Xi_N^* \equiv \sum_{\tau=0}^{\infty}\left(\frac{\zeta}{1+\rho}\right)^\tau mc^* = \Xi_D^*\, mc^*.$$

We reach our goal in four steps. In step 1 we linearize the left-hand side of (19.68) to obtain:

$$\Xi_D\, p_t^n \approx \Xi_D^* + \Xi_D^*\tilde{p}_t^n + (\theta - 1)\sum_{\tau=0}^{\infty}\left(\frac{\zeta}{1+\rho}\right)^\tau \tilde{p}_{t+\tau}, \tag{19.70}$$

whilst for the right-hand side we find:

$$\Xi_N \approx \Xi_N^* + \theta\, mc^* \sum_{\tau=0}^{\infty}\left(\frac{\zeta}{1+\rho}\right)^\tau \tilde{p}_{t+\tau} + mc^* \sum_{\tau=0}^{\infty}\left(\frac{\zeta}{1+\rho}\right)^\tau \widetilde{mc}_{t+\tau}. \tag{19.71}$$

In step 2 we substitute (19.70)–(19.71) into (19.68), use the definitions for Ξ_N^* and Ξ_D^*, and simplify to obtain:

$$\tilde{p}_t^n = \frac{1-\zeta+\rho}{1+\rho}\left[\sum_{\tau=0}^{\infty}\left(\frac{\zeta}{1+\rho}\right)^\tau \tilde{p}_{t+\tau} + \sum_{\tau=0}^{\infty}\left(\frac{\zeta}{1+\rho}\right)^\tau \widetilde{mc}_{t+\tau}\right]. \tag{19.72}$$

In step 3 we note that $\tilde{p}_t^n \equiv \tilde{P}_t^n - \tilde{P}_t$, $\tilde{p}_{t+\tau} \equiv \tilde{P}_{t+\tau} - \tilde{P}_t$, and put E_t back in:

$$\tilde{P}_t^n = \frac{1-\zeta+\rho}{1+\rho} E_t \left[\sum_{\tau=0}^{\infty} \left(\frac{\zeta}{1+\rho} \right)^{\tau} \left[\tilde{P}_{t+\tau} + \widetilde{mc}_{t+\tau} \right] \right]. \tag{19.73}$$

We note that (19.73) can be written recursively as:

$$\tilde{P}_t^n = \frac{1-\zeta+\rho}{1+\rho} \left[\tilde{P}_t + \widetilde{mc}_t \right] + \frac{\zeta}{1+\rho} E_t \left[\tilde{P}_{t+1}^n \right]. \tag{19.74}$$

In step 4 we use (19.65) to eliminate $\tilde{P}_t^n$ and $\tilde{P}_{t+1}^n$ from (19.74):

$$\frac{\tilde{P}_t - \zeta \tilde{P}_{t-1}}{1-\zeta} = \frac{1-\zeta+\rho}{1+\rho} \left[\tilde{P}_t + \widetilde{mc}_t \right] + \frac{\zeta}{1+\rho} E_t \left[\frac{\tilde{P}_{t+1} - \zeta \tilde{P}_t}{1-\zeta} \right]. \tag{19.75}$$

By using the approximations $\pi_t = \tilde{P}_t - \tilde{P}_{t-1}$ and $\pi_{t+1} = \tilde{P}_{t+1} - \tilde{P}_t$ we easily find that (19.75) can be rewritten as:

$$\tilde{\pi}_t = \frac{1-\zeta}{\zeta} \frac{1-\zeta+\rho}{1+\rho} \widetilde{mc}_t + \frac{1}{1+\rho} E_t \tilde{\pi}_{t+1}. \tag{19.76}$$

Equation (19.76) is often referred to as the New Keynesian Phillips curve (NKPC hereafter). Note that A.W. Phillips would certainly not recognize (19.76) as a relationship worthy of his name. Indeed, the traditional Phillips curve is an inverse relationship between unemployment and inflation in an economy. And the model developed here does not feature unemployment.

That expectations regarding prices affect the location of the Phillips curve is the well-known lesson we learnt from Friedman and Phelps in the 1960s. Indeed, the ad hoc expectations-augmented Phillips curve typically relates inflation to Okun's output gap (OOG), i.e. the difference between actual and potential output (named after Arthur Okun). It turns out that in our micro-founded model we can relate mc_t to an OOG-like measure. This measure is obtained by comparing equilibrium output in the sticky-price economy under consideration to the hypothetical flex-price solution for output. For our model this relationship is given by:

$$\widetilde{mc}_t = \frac{1-\bar{L}}{1-L^*} \left[\tilde{Y}_t - \tilde{Y}_t^f \right], \tag{19.77}$$

where $\tilde{Y}_t^f = \tilde{Z}_t$ is the flex-price perturbation in output (equalling the perturbation in the technology level). If output exceeds its potential level, $\tilde{Y}_t > \tilde{Y}_t^f$, then real marginal cost rises. Ceteris paribus expected inflation, it follows from (19.76) that actual inflation rises.

The expression in (19.77) is derived as follows. In the hypothetical flex-price economy ($\zeta = 0$), all firms set the same price ($P_t^n = P_t = P_t^a = \frac{\theta}{\theta-1} MC_t = \frac{\theta}{\theta-1} \frac{W_t}{Z_t}$), the real wage rate $w_t^f \equiv \frac{\theta-1}{\theta} Z_t$ is lower than Z_t, and flex-price output and employment satisfy:

$$Y_t^f = Z_t \left(L_t^f - \bar{L} \right), \qquad \frac{\varepsilon_l}{1-L_t^f} = \frac{\varepsilon_c}{Y_t^f} w_t^f,$$

or:

$$Y_t^f = \frac{\varepsilon_c(1-\bar{L})}{\varepsilon_l \frac{\theta}{\theta-1} + \varepsilon_c} Z_t, \qquad L_t^f = \bar{L} + \frac{\varepsilon_c(1-\bar{L})}{\varepsilon_l \frac{\theta}{\theta-1} + \varepsilon_c}. \tag{19.78}$$

Flex-price output is proportional to the technology indicator so that:

$$\tilde{Y}_t^f = \tilde{Z}_t. \tag{19.79}$$

With perfectly flexible prices output fluctuates one-for-one with the random technology shocks just as in the typical RBC model. This is, of course, not surprising in view of the fact that the flex-price MBC model is an RBC model.

For an economy characterized by sticky-prices ($0 < \zeta < 1$) it is not possible to obtain analytical expressions for the equilibrium levels of output and employment but we do know that in proportional rates of change perturbations in these variables are related according to:

$$\tilde{Y}_t = \tilde{w}_t - \frac{L^*}{1 - L^*}\tilde{L}_t, \tag{19.80}$$

$$\tilde{Y}_t = \tilde{Z}_t + \frac{L^*}{L^* - \bar{L}}\tilde{L}_t. \tag{19.81}$$

Note that (19.80) is the linearized labour supply equation and (19.81) is the linearized production function. By solving for $\tilde{w}_t$ in terms of $\tilde{Z}_t$ and $\tilde{Y}_t$ we find:

$$\tilde{w}_t = \tilde{Y}_t + \frac{L^* - \bar{L}}{1 - L^*}\left[\tilde{Y}_t - \tilde{Z}_t\right]. \tag{19.82}$$

By using (19.82) in (19.61) and noting (19.79) we find (19.77).

19.3.2 Stability

It was a lot of work but we got something worthwhile in return. By means of first-order linearization the model of Table 19.2 has been condensed into three key equations plus a definition:

$$\tilde{Y}_t = E_t\tilde{Y}_{t+1} - \left[\tilde{R}_t - E_t\pi_{t+1}\right], \tag{19.83}$$

$$\pi_t = \gamma\left[\tilde{Y}_t - \tilde{Z}_t\right] + \frac{1}{1 + \rho}E_t\pi_{t+1}, \tag{19.84}$$

$$\tilde{M}_{t+1} - \tilde{P}_t = \tilde{Y}_t - \frac{\tilde{R}_t}{\rho}, \tag{19.85}$$

$$\pi_t \equiv \tilde{P}_t - \tilde{P}_{t-1}, \tag{19.86}$$

where γ is a composite parameter:

$$\gamma \equiv \frac{1 - \zeta}{\zeta}\frac{1 - \zeta + \rho}{1 + \rho}\frac{1 - \bar{L}}{1 - L^*} > 0. \tag{19.87}$$

Equations (19.83) and (19.85) just restate, respectively, (19.58) and (19.59) whilst the expression in (19.86) links inflation with price levels. Equation (19.84) is obtained by substituting (19.77) in (19.76) and noting (19.79).

Let us start by assuming that monetary policy is of the traditional type, i.e. the Central Bank sets the nominal money supply and lets the nominal interest rate equilibrate the money market. In such a setting the endogenous variables appearing in (19.83)–(19.85) are output $\tilde{Y}_t$, the nominal interest rate $\tilde{R}_t$, inflation π_t, and the current price level $\tilde{P}_t$. The exogenous variables are the money supply $\tilde{M}_{t+1}$ and the technology shock $\tilde{Z}_t$. The predetermined variable is the lagged price level, $\tilde{P}_{t-1}$.

To investigate the stability properties of the model it is convenient to cast it in the form suggested by Blanchard and Kahn (1980). In the Blanchard-Kahn (BK) form the system is written in a particular way in terms of forward-looking and backward-looking variables—see Intermezzo 19.3. In the context of our model we know that $\pi_t \equiv \tilde{P}_t - \tilde{P}_{t-1}$ and we must somehow impose that $\tilde{P}_{t-1}$ is a predetermined (backward-looking) variable. We do so by defining an auxiliary variable, $\widetilde{LP}_t \equiv \tilde{P}_{t-1}$. Using this variable it follows that $\widetilde{LP}_{t+1} = \tilde{P}_t$ so that we can write equation (19.86) as:

$$\widetilde{LP}_{t+1} = \pi_t + \widetilde{LP}_t. \tag{19.88}$$

By solving (19.85) for $\tilde{R}_t$, substituting the result in (19.83), and using (19.88) and (19.84) we can write the system as:

$$\Gamma \begin{bmatrix} E_t \widetilde{LP}_{t+1} \\ E_t \tilde{Y}_{t+1} \\ E_t \tilde{\pi}_{t+1} \end{bmatrix} = \Delta^* \begin{bmatrix} \widetilde{LP}_t \\ \tilde{Y}_t \\ \pi_t \end{bmatrix} + \begin{bmatrix} 0 \\ -\rho \tilde{M}_{t+1} \\ \gamma(1+\rho)\tilde{Z}_t \end{bmatrix}, \tag{19.89}$$

where Γ, Γ^{-1}, and Δ^* are defined as:

$$\Gamma \equiv \begin{bmatrix} 1 & 0 & 0 \\ -\rho & 1 & 1 \\ 0 & 0 & 1 \end{bmatrix}, \quad \Gamma^{-1} \equiv \begin{bmatrix} 1 & 0 & 0 \\ \rho & 1 & -1 \\ 0 & 0 & 1 \end{bmatrix}, \quad \Delta^* \equiv \begin{bmatrix} 1 & 0 & 1 \\ 0 & 1+\rho & 0 \\ 0 & -\gamma(1+\rho) & 1+\rho \end{bmatrix}.$$

Hence (19.89) can be expressed in the BK form as:

$$\begin{bmatrix} E_t \widetilde{LP}_{t+1} \\ E_t \tilde{Y}_{t+1} \\ E_t \tilde{\pi}_{t+1} \end{bmatrix} = \Delta \begin{bmatrix} \widetilde{LP}_t \\ \tilde{Y}_t \\ \pi_t \end{bmatrix} + \begin{bmatrix} 0 \\ -\rho \tilde{M}_{t+1} - \gamma(1+\rho)\tilde{Z}_t \\ \gamma(1+\rho)\tilde{Z}_t \end{bmatrix}, \tag{19.90}$$

where $\Delta \equiv \Gamma^{-1}\Delta^*$ is defined as:

$$\Delta \equiv \begin{bmatrix} 1 & 0 & 1 \\ \rho & (1+\gamma)(1+\rho) & -1 \\ 0 & -\gamma(1+\rho) & 1+\rho \end{bmatrix}. \tag{19.91}$$

Now that we have recast the system in the BK format we can apply Proposition 1 from Intermezzo 19.3 and conclude that the system features a unique solution for output, inflation, and the price level *if and only if* the Jacobian matrix Δ features two roots outside the unit circle (because $\tilde{Y}_t$ and $\tilde{\pi}_t$ are jumping variables) and one root inside the unit circle (because $\widetilde{LP}_t$ is a predetermined variable).

To check whether the root condition is satisfied we write the characteristic equation of Δ as:

$$\Psi(s) \equiv |sI - \Delta| = [s - (1+\rho)]\,\Phi(s), \tag{19.92}$$

where $\Phi(s)$ is given by:

$$\begin{aligned} \Phi(s) &\equiv (s-1)(s-(1+\gamma)(1+\rho)) - \gamma(1+\rho) \\ &= s^2 - [1 + (1+\gamma)(1+\rho)]s + 1 + \rho. \end{aligned} \tag{19.93}$$

It follows from (19.92) that the system has one unstable root for sure, say:

$$\lambda_3 = 1+\rho > 0. \tag{19.94}$$

To check the remaining characteristic roots we note that $\Phi(s)$ can be written as:

$$\Phi(s) = (s - \lambda_1)(s - \lambda_2)$$
$$= s^2 - (\lambda_1 + \lambda_2)s + \lambda_1\lambda_2 \tag{19.95}$$

so it follows (from the comparison of (19.93) and (19.95)) that:

$$\lambda_1 + \lambda_2 = 1 + (1 + \gamma)(1 + \rho) > 2, \quad \lambda_1\lambda_2 = 1 + \rho > 1. \tag{19.96}$$

The sum and product of the roots are both positive so we know that $\lambda_1 > 0$ and $\lambda_2 > 0$ for sure. Using (19.95) and (19.96) to compute $\Phi(1)$ results in:

$$\Phi(1) = (1 - \lambda_1)(1 - \lambda_2)$$
$$= 1 - [1 + (1 + \gamma)(1 + \rho)] + 1 + \rho$$
$$= -\gamma(1 + \rho) < 0. \tag{19.97}$$

Hence, λ_1 and λ_2 are not only both positive but they also lie on either side of unity, say:

$$0 < \lambda_1 < 1, \quad \lambda_2 > 1. \tag{19.98}$$

The canonical model is saddle-path stable when the money supply acts as the policy variable. The nominal interest rate is endogenous in that case and fluctuations in it will guarantee stability. Matters may not be so straightforward if the monetary policy maker wishes to set nominal interest rates.

Intermezzo 19.3

Blanchard-Kahn stability and existence conditions. To investigate stability of the rational expectations model the technique proposed by Blanchard and Kahn (1980) is particularly convenient. To illustrate their method we write the dynamic system in general as:

$$\begin{bmatrix} B_{t+1} \\ E_t F_{t+1} \end{bmatrix} = \Delta \begin{bmatrix} B_t \\ F_t \end{bmatrix} + \Psi X_t, \tag{a}$$

where B_t is an $(n_b \times 1)$ vector of predetermined (backward-looking) variables, F_t is an $(n_f \times 1)$ vector of non-predetermined (forward-looking) variables, X_t is a $(k \times 1)$ vector of exogenous variables, Δ is an $(n_b + n_f) \times (n_b + n_f)$ matrix of coefficients, and Ψ is an $(n_b + n_f) \times k$ matrix of coefficients.

Blanchard and Kahn prove the following propositions:

- **B-K Proposition 1**: If the number of eigenvalues of Δ outside the unit circle (say n_f') is equal to the number of non-predetermined variables (n_f) then there exists a unique solution.

- **B-K Proposition 2**: If n_f' exceeds n_f there no solution.

- **B-K Proposition 3**: If n_f' falls short of n_f there is an infinity of solutions ("indeterminacy").

Blanchard and Kahn also provide explicit expressions for the solution paths in the case for which B-K Proposition 1 holds (i.e. if $n'_f = n_f$) but we do not use their expressions here.

****

19.3.3 Interest rate setting, instability, and Taylor rules

Up to this point we have adopted the traditional approach by assuming that monetary policy is conducted by means of changes in the nominal money supply. In reality, however, Central Banks typically set interest rates in order to achieve their policy aims. In the context of our canonical model (given in equations (19.83)–(19.86) above) this means that the interest rate $\tilde{R}_t$ becomes the policy variable whilst the nominal money supply $\tilde{M}_{t+1}$ is endogenously (and residually) determined by (19.85).

With the interest rate as the policy variable, the canonical model is fully characterized by:

$$\tilde{Y}_t = E_t \tilde{Y}_{t+1} - \left[\tilde{R}_t - E_t \pi_{t+1}\right], \tag{19.99}$$

$$\pi_t = \gamma \left[\tilde{Y}_t - \tilde{Z}_t\right] + \frac{1}{1+\rho} E_t \pi_{t+1}. \tag{19.100}$$

The endogenous variables are output $\tilde{Y}_t$ and inflation π_t. The exogenous variables are the nominal interest rate $\tilde{R}_t$ and the technology shock $\tilde{Z}_t$. There is no predetermined variable in this system: given the lagged price $\tilde{P}_{t-1}$ the current price follows once π_t is known (as $\pi_t \equiv \tilde{P}_t - \tilde{P}_{t-1}$). Is the model still saddle-path stable under this type of monetary policy?

Following similar steps as before we can deduce the BK format of the model. First we use (19.99)–(19.100) to obtain:

$$\Gamma \left[\begin{array}{c} E_t \tilde{Y}_{t+1} \\ E_t \tilde{\pi}_{t+1} \end{array} \right] = \Delta^* \left[\begin{array}{c} \tilde{Y}_t \\ \tilde{\pi}_t \end{array} \right] + \left[\begin{array}{c} \tilde{R}_t \\ \gamma (1+\rho) \tilde{Z}_t \end{array} \right], \tag{19.101}$$

where Γ, Γ^{-1}, and Δ^* are given by:

$$\Gamma \equiv \left[\begin{array}{cc} 1 & 1 \\ 0 & 1 \end{array} \right], \qquad \Gamma^{-1} \equiv \left[\begin{array}{cc} 1 & -1 \\ 0 & 1 \end{array} \right], \qquad \Delta^* \equiv \left[\begin{array}{cc} 1 & 0 \\ -\gamma (1+\rho) & 1+\rho \end{array} \right]. \tag{19.102}$$

It follows that equation (19.101) can be expressed in the BK form as:

$$\left[\begin{array}{c} E_t \tilde{Y}_{t+1} \\ E_t \tilde{\pi}_{t+1} \end{array} \right] = \Delta \left[\begin{array}{c} \tilde{Y}_t \\ \tilde{\pi}_t \end{array} \right] + \left[\begin{array}{c} \tilde{R}_t - \gamma (1+\rho) \tilde{Z}_t \\ \gamma (1+\rho) \tilde{Z}_t \end{array} \right], \tag{19.103}$$

where $\Delta \equiv \Gamma^{-1} \Delta^*$ is defined as:

$$\Delta \equiv \left[\begin{array}{cc} 1+\gamma (1+\rho) & -(1+\rho) \\ -\gamma (1+\rho) & 1+\rho \end{array} \right]. \tag{19.104}$$

Since output and inflation are jumping variables, stability holds if and only if the Jacobian matrix Δ features two unstable roots, i.e. both λ_1 and λ_2 must lie outside the unit circle. Our usual trick can be used to establish the signs and magnitude of the characteristic roots. The characteristic equation of Δ is:

$$\Phi(s) = s^2 - [1 + (1+\gamma)(1+\rho)] s + 1 + \rho,$$

and it is easy to verify that:

$$\lambda_1 + \lambda_2 = 1 + (1+\gamma)(1+\rho) > 2, \qquad \lambda_1 \lambda_2 = 1 + \rho > 1.$$

By computing $\Phi(1)$ we find:

$$\begin{aligned} \Phi(1) &= (1 - \lambda_1)(1 - \lambda_2) \\ &= 1 - [2 + \rho + \gamma(1+\rho)] + 1 + \rho = -\gamma(1+\rho) < 0, \end{aligned}$$

which implies that both roots are positive and lie on either side of unity, say:

$$0 < \lambda_1 < 1, \qquad \lambda_2 > 1. \tag{19.105}$$

The root condition is clearly not satisfied as there are two non-predetermined variables and only one root outside the unit circle. Proposition 3 from Intermezzo 19.3 implies that there exist infinitely many solutions—the model suffers from *indeterminacy*. The economic lesson is that using the nominal interest rate as a policy variable induces indeterminacy in an economy that is stable if the Central Bank would just control the money supply. Loosely put, the intuition behind this result is as follows. Assume that expected future inflation rises ($E_t \tilde{\pi}_{t+1} \uparrow$). Since $\tilde{R}_t$ does not react to this change the real interest rate falls. This prompts an increase in output via the dynamic IS curve (19.99) ($\tilde{Y}_t \uparrow$). But this output change in turn boosts current inflation via the New Keynesian Phillips curve (19.100) and ($\tilde{\pi}_t \uparrow$). A self-fulfilling increase in inflation emerges: if the public thinks the inflation rate will rise then it will.

The indeterminacy problem arises because the interest rate set by the Central Bank is independent of the state of the economy, i.e. we have implicitly assumed that the Central Bank uses a passive policy rule (PPR hereafter) like:

$$\tilde{R}_t = \tilde{U}_t, \qquad \text{PPR}, \tag{19.106}$$

where $\tilde{U}_t$ is an exogenously given stationary stochastic process. In reality policy makers may not be that passive. To see if it could help eliminate indeterminacy let us try a feed-back policy rule (FPR hereafter) that chokes off the inflation spiral mentioned above:

$$\tilde{R}_t = \delta_\pi \pi_t + \tilde{U}_t, \qquad \delta_\pi > 0, \qquad \text{FPR}_1. \tag{19.107}$$

There is some hope such a rule may do the job as an increase in inflation will result in an increase in the nominal interest rate. To see whether this hunch works we write the system consisting of (19.99)–(19.100) and (19.107) in the form of (19.103) and find that element $(1,2)$ of Δ^* in (19.102) changes from 0 to δ_π and Δ becomes:

$$\Delta \equiv \begin{bmatrix} 1 + \gamma(1+\rho) & \delta_\pi - (1+\rho) \\ -\gamma(1+\rho) & 1 + \rho \end{bmatrix}. \tag{19.108}$$

We easily find that the characteristic roots satisfy:

$$\lambda_1 + \lambda_2 = 2 + \rho + \gamma(1+\rho) > 2, \qquad \lambda_1 \lambda_2 = (1+\rho)[1 + \delta_\pi \gamma] > 1 + \rho,$$

whilst the characteristic equation evaluated at $s = 1$ gives:

$$\Phi(1) = (1 - \lambda_1)(1 - \lambda_2) = (\delta_\pi - 1)\gamma(1 + \rho).$$

Provided the feedback coefficient exceeds unity ($\delta_\pi > 1$) we find that $\Phi(1) > 0$ so that both roots are larger than unity, i.e.:

$$\lambda_1 > 1, \qquad \lambda_2 > 1. \tag{19.109}$$

The root condition is clearly satisfied because we have two non-predetermined variables and two characteristic roots outside the unit circle. Proposition 1 from Intermezzo 19.3 implies that there exist unique solution paths for output and inflation. The economic lesson is that a feed-back policy rule such as FPR_1 eliminates indeterminacy provided $\delta_\pi > 1$. This is called the *Taylor principle* after John B. Taylor (1993) who was one of the first economists to stress that the interest rate rule should react more than one-for-one to inflation. Intuitively, under this rule an increase in inflation prompts a change in the nominal interest rate large enough to cause an increase in the *real* interest rate.

As the icing of the cake, let us try a more complicated feedback rule that responds both to inflation and to output:

$$\tilde{R}_t = \delta_\pi \pi_t + \delta_y \tilde{Y}_t + \tilde{U}_t, \qquad \delta_\pi, \delta_y > 0, \qquad \text{FPR}_2. \tag{19.110}$$

This is an example of a *Taylor rule*, and empirically such a rule seems to have been followed by many Central Banks in the world. To see how this policy rule works we write the system consisting of (19.99)–(19.100) and (19.110) in the form of (19.103) and find that element $(1,1)$ of Δ^* in (19.102) changes from 1 to $1 + \delta_y$ whilst (just as before) element $(1,2)$ of that matrix changes from 0 to δ_π. As a result Δ becomes:

$$\Delta \equiv \begin{bmatrix} 1 + \delta_y + \gamma(1+\rho) & \delta_\pi - (1+\rho) \\ -\gamma(1+\rho) & 1+\rho \end{bmatrix}. \tag{19.111}$$

We easily find that:

$$\lambda_1 + \lambda_2 = 2 + \delta_y + \rho + \gamma(1+\rho) > 2, \qquad \lambda_1 \lambda_2 = (1+\rho)\left[1 + \delta_y + \delta_\pi \gamma\right] > 1 + \rho,$$

and that:

$$\Phi(1) = (1 - \lambda_1)(1 - \lambda_2) = \rho \delta_y + (\delta_\pi - 1)\gamma(1+\rho). \tag{19.112}$$

The stability condition is that $\Phi(1) > 0$ so that (19.109) holds. In view of (19.112) we conclude that, since $\delta_y > 0$ we now have that $\delta_\pi > 1$ is no longer a necessary condition for determinacy. Even if δ_π falls short of unity, the model is still determinate provided δ_y is large enough.

19.4　Back to the general case

The canonical New Keynesian DSGE model is quite useful in that its basic mechanism are quite transparent and it allows us to analytically investigate stability issues arising from the particular form of the monetary policy rules. Of course the canonical model has severe limitations, the most important of which is the absence of capital accumulation effects in response to economic shocks. And in Chapter 18 we saw that the capital accumulation mechanism is a very important component of DSGE models of the New Classical type.

In this section we return to the general New Keynesian DSGE model given in Table 19.1. Compared to the canonical model this model not only includes capital as a productive factor but also allows government consumption to be non-zero. To solve the model we could of course proceed along the lines of the previous section and linearize the model around a deterministic steady state. Here, however, we follow the numerical Dynare route that we also took in Chapter 18 for the New Classical DSGE model.

19.4.1 Calibration

We postulate that the deterministic steady state has the following features:

- All prices are constant: $P_t^* = P_{t-1}^* = (P_t^a)^* = (P_{t-1}^a)^* = P^*$.

- The output measures coincide: $Y_t^* = (Y_t^a)^* = Y^*$.

- Capital and consumption are constant over time: $K_{t+1}^* = K_t^* = K^*$ and $C_{t+1}^* = C_t^* = C^*$.

- The money supply and government consumption are both constant: $M_{t+1} = M_0$ and $G_t = G_0$.

Imposing these features on the model in Table 19.1 gives the following representation of the deterministic steady state:

$$I^* = \delta K^*, \tag{19.113}$$

$$Y^* = C^* + I^* + G_0, \tag{19.114}$$

$$R^* = \rho, \tag{19.115}$$

$$\left(r^K\right)^* = \rho + \delta, \tag{19.116}$$

$$\frac{M_0}{P^*} = \frac{\varepsilon_m}{\varepsilon_c} C^* \frac{1 + R^*}{R^*}, \tag{19.117}$$

$$L^* = 1 - \frac{\varepsilon_l}{\varepsilon_c} \frac{C^*}{w^*}, \tag{19.118}$$

$$w^* = (1 - \alpha) \, mc^* \frac{Y^*}{L^* - \bar{L}}, \tag{19.119}$$

$$\left(r^K\right)^* = \alpha \, mc^* \frac{Y^*}{K^*}, \tag{19.120}$$

$$mc^* = \frac{\theta - 1}{\theta}, \tag{19.121}$$

$$Y^* = \Omega_0 \, (K^*)^\alpha \, (L^* - \bar{L})^{1-\alpha}, \tag{19.122}$$

where Ω_0 is a calibration parameter that we have included in order to obtain a convenient scaling of steady-state output (this constant is introduced by writing (19.13) as $Y_t(i) = \Omega_0 K_t(i)^\alpha \, [Z_t(L_t(i) - \bar{L})]^{1-\alpha}$).

The structural parameters affecting the deterministic steady state of the model are δ, ρ, ε_c, ε_l, ε_m, α, Ω_0, $\bar{L}$, and θ. We choose these parameters such that a plausible steady state is obtained. (Though ζ is crucially important outside the steady state it does not feature in (19.113)–(19.122).)

We proceed with an example calibration. DSGE models are typically calibrated in a quarterly fashion. Assume that the steady-state nominal (and real) interest rate is four percent per annum, so $1 + R^a = 1.04$. On a quarterly basis we would thus get $R^* = (1 + R^a)^{1/4} - 1 = 0.00985$. Since $R^* = \rho$ in this model we have pinned down one of the structural parameters. The annual rate of depreciation of the capital stock δ^a is set at ten per annum i.e. $\delta = (1 - \delta^a)^{1/4} - 1 = 0.0260$. This pins down the second structural parameter. Recall that $\frac{\theta}{\theta - 1}$ is the steady-state markup of price over marginal cost. A reasonable range of values for that markup is between 1.2 and 1.3 (implying some monopoly power but not an outrageous amount). Selecting the highest value we get a value for $\theta = 13/3$. In view of (19.121) this value of θ also fixes the level of steady-state real marginal cost:

$$mc^* = \frac{1}{1.3} = 0.7692.$$

Setting the efficiency parameter of capital equal to the conventional value, $\alpha = 1/3$, we find from (19.116) and (19.120) that:

$$\frac{K^*}{Y^*} = \frac{\alpha \, mc^*}{\rho + \delta} = 7.1524.$$

We normalize output to unity by choice of Ω_0, so $Y^* = 1$, $K^* = 7.1524$, and $I^* = \delta K^* = 0.1859$. If the government consumption share of output is set at twenty percent we find that $G_0 = 0.2$ and (from (19.114)) $C^* = 0.6141$.

Of the structural parameters mentioned above we still need to assign value to the taste parameters (ε_c, ε_l, and ε_m) and the returns-to-scale parameter ($\bar{L}$). People have 24 hours of time per day of which they typically work 8 hours (and consume the rest in the form of active or passive leisure). We thus want to get a steady-state such that $(1 - L^*)/L^* = 2$ or $L^* = \frac{1}{3}$. Assume that a fraction ϕ of employment consists of overhead labour ("useless managers"), i.e. $\bar{L} = \phi L^*$. We set $\phi = 0.1$ so overhead labour plays a modest role in the steady state.[1] From (19.119) we find that the steady-state real wage rate equals:

$$w^* = \frac{(1 - \alpha) \, mc^*}{1 - \phi} \frac{Y^*}{L^*} = 1.7094.$$

By using (19.118) we find that the target for steady-state employment is provided by the relative taste coefficient for leisure, $\varepsilon_l/\varepsilon_c$, which satisfies the following equality:

$$\eta_l \equiv \frac{\varepsilon_l}{\varepsilon_c} = \frac{w^*[1 - L^*]}{C^*} = 1.8558.$$

To ensure consistency we set Ω_0 equal to:

$$\Omega_0 = Y^* (K^*)^{-\alpha} ((1 - \phi)L^*)^{\alpha - 1} = 1.1582.$$

We can normalize the nominal price such that $P^* = 1$ and set $M_0 = 1$. By using money demand (19.117) we find that the relative taste coefficient for money balances, $\varepsilon_m/\varepsilon_c$, must satisfy:

$$\eta_m \equiv \frac{\varepsilon_m}{\varepsilon_c} = \frac{R^*}{1 + R^*} \frac{M_0}{P^* C^*} = 0.0159.$$

---

[1] Modest from the perspective of an academic economist working in the Dutch public university system!

Since the taste coefficients themselves add up to unity, $1 = \varepsilon_c + \varepsilon_l + \varepsilon_m$, we find that the calibration is consistent provided:

$$\varepsilon_c = \frac{1}{1 + \eta_l + \eta_m} = 0.3482, \qquad \varepsilon_l = \eta_l \varepsilon_c = 0.6462, \qquad \varepsilon_m = \eta_m \varepsilon_c = 0.0055.$$

Even though we do not need it to calibrate the steady-state, in the computations of the transition paths a value for ζ is required. Following Bernanke et al. (1999) we assume that the probability that a firm does not change its price in a given quarter is 75 percent, i.e. our structural parameter is set at $\zeta = 0.75$. The average period between adjustments is thus four quarters.

19.4.2 Computation

Now that we have a plausible calibration for the deterministic steady state we can once again ask Dynare to do all the difficult stuff for us, i.e. to compute the short-run dynamic adjustments that occur in the stochastic version of the model.

Glancing at the structure of the model in Table 19.1, however, there seems to be a rather complicated expression that Dynare may not be able to handle, namely the equation for price set by green-light firms:

$$P_t^n = \frac{\theta}{\theta - 1} \frac{E_t \left[\sum_{\tau=0}^{\infty} \left(\frac{\zeta}{1+\rho} \right)^\tau C_{t+\tau}^{-1} P_{t+\tau}^\theta Y_{t+\tau} mc_{t+\tau} \right]}{E_t \left[\sum_{\tau=0}^{\infty} \left(\frac{\zeta}{1+\rho} \right)^\tau C_{t+\tau}^{-1} P_{t+\tau}^{\theta-1} Y_{t+\tau} \right]}. \tag{19.123}$$

How on earth are we going to enter infinitely many leading terms (such as C_{t+1}, C_{t+2}, etc.) into a Dynare model file of finite size? The answer is that we have no need to do so because we can quite easily derive a recursive expression for (19.123). Note that (19.123) can be written as:

$$P_t^n \equiv \frac{\theta}{\theta - 1} \frac{\Xi_{N,t}}{\Xi_{D,t}}, \tag{19.124}$$

where $\Xi_{D,t}$ and $\Xi_{N,t}$ are defined as:

$$\Xi_{D,t} \equiv E_t \left[\sum_{\tau=0}^{\infty} \left(\frac{\zeta}{1+\rho} \right)^\tau C_{t+\tau}^{-1} P_{t+\tau}^{\theta-1} Y_{t+\tau} \right], \tag{19.125}$$

$$\Xi_{N,t} \equiv E_t \left[\sum_{\tau=0}^{\infty} \left(\frac{\zeta}{1+\rho} \right)^\tau C_{t+\tau}^{-1} P_{t+\tau}^\theta Y_{t+\tau} mc_{t+\tau} \right]. \tag{19.126}$$

It is easy to see that $\Xi_{D,t}$ can be written recursively as:

$$\Xi_{D,t} \equiv C_t^{-1} P_t^{\theta-1} Y_t + E_t \left[\sum_{\tau=1}^{\infty} \left(\frac{\zeta}{1+\rho} \right)^\tau C_{t+\tau}^{-1} P_{t+\tau}^{\theta-1} Y_{t+\tau} \right]$$

$$= C_t^{-1} P_t^{\theta-1} Y_t + \frac{\zeta}{1+\rho} E_t \left[\Xi_{D,t+1} \right]. \tag{19.127}$$

Hence, $\Xi_{D,t}$ consists of the current contribution made to it in period t (first term on the right-hand side) plus the expected value of $\Xi_{D,t+1}$ discounted by the impatience-weighted probability of getting a red light ($\zeta/(1+\rho)$). Similarly, the recursive relationship for $\Xi_{N,t}$ is given by:

$$\Xi_{N,t} = C_t^{-1} P_t^\theta Y_t mc_t + \frac{\zeta}{1+\rho} E_t \left[\Xi_{N,t+1} \right]. \tag{19.128}$$

The key thing to note is that (19.127) and (19.128) are forward-looking expectational difference equations expressed in a format that Dynare can handle.

In Table 19.3 we show an example Dynare model file implementing the general MBC model of Table 19.1. The model file is called Program19_01.mod as is indicated in the commented line at the top. As was explained in Section 18.3.5 above, the model file contains several blocks of statements. Block 1 defines the endogenous and exogenous variables, Block 2 provides the values for the structural parameters and gives guesses for the steady-state equilibrium values, Block 3 states the model in a format that Dynare can work with, and Block 4 performs the computations. Note that the Dynare implementation considers the nominal money supply to be exogenously fixed and assumes that the technology terms can be written as $Z_t = e^{\tilde{Z}_t}$ where $\tilde{Z}_t$ follows an AR1 process:

$$\tilde{Z}_t = \xi_Z \tilde{Z}_{t-1} + \eta_t, \qquad 0 < \xi_Z < 1. \tag{19.129}$$

In the Manual the reader is asked to verify that the Dynare program actually runs correctly and that the model is saddle-path stable. In addition the reader is asked to introduce a Taylor rule into the model and to investigate the stability properties of the model.

19.4.3 Visualizing some shocks

In this subsection we visualize some of the properties of the general MBC model of Table 19.1. Just as in Section 18.3.3 we do so by studying the theoretical impulse-response functions. We consider three types of shocks, namely a productivity shock, a money supply shock, and a public consumption shock.

19.4.3.1 Productivity shock

We compute the impulse-response functions as follows. Productivity proceeds according to (19.129). We normalize the time of the shock at $t = 0$, and assume that $\eta_0 > 0$ and $\eta_t = 0$ for $t = 1, 2, \ldots$ Assuming that technology was at its steady-state level in the previous period ($\tilde{Z}_{-1} = 0$) we set η_0 such that $Z_0 = 1.01$ (a one-percent impact jump in productivity). We assume that the shock displays a lot of persistence, i.e. $\xi_Z = 0.95$. The time path for $\tilde{Z}_t$ is illustrated in panel (a) of Figure 19.1.

We compute the transition paths for the different variables by conducting a deterministic simulation with Dynare.[2] For ease of comparison the response functions in panels (b)–(h) are drawn for the sticky-price case (featuring $\zeta = 0.75$ and marked with solid dots) and the flexible-price case (with $\zeta = 0$, marked with open dots).

The case with perfectly flexible prices is easy to understand. At impact ($t = 0$) productivity increases by one percent (panel (a)) and labour demand shifts out. The representative agent is a bit wealthier, increases both consumption (panel (e)) and saving. Labour supply is reduced somewhat but in net terms both employment (panel (c)) and the real wage rate (panel (f)) increase. Despite the fact that the capital stock is predetermined at impact, output increases (panel (d)). The additional household saving results in an increase in the capital stock during the early phase of transition (panel (b)). As a result of the technology shock the aggregate price levels falls initially but is eventually restored to its old equilibrium level (see panel (g)).

---

[2]The programs used to compute the transition paths are available from the website for the book: www.heijdra.org/fomm3.

Table 19.3. A Dynare model file for the general MBC model

```
% Basic MBC model
%
% Dynare model file: Program19_01.mod
%
% Ben J. Heijdra
% Groningen, July 29, 2016

%------------------------------------------------------------
% 0. Housekeeping
%------------------------------------------------------------

close all;

%------------------------------------------------------------
% 1. Defining variables
%------------------------------------------------------------

var Y Ya K L C w rk R mc P Pa Pn XI_N XI_D Ztilde;
varexo G M_0 eta;

parameters alpha delta rho Omega_0 theta epsilon_c epsilon_l
epsilon_m zeta Lbar xi_Z sigma_eta;

%------------------------------------------------------------
% 2. Calibration
%------------------------------------------------------------


alpha     = 0.333333333333333;
delta     = 0.025996253574703;
rho       = 0.009853406548969;
Omega_0   = 1.158161294323214;
theta     = 4.333333333333333;
epsilon_c = 0.348223238919264;
epsilon_l = 0.646243623572566;
epsilon_m = 0.005533137508169;
zeta      = 0.75;
Lbar      = 0.033333333333333;
xi_Z      = 0.95;
sigma_eta = 0.0015;

% Guess for the initial steady state


Y0        = 1.0000;
K0        = 7.1524;
L0        = 0.3333;
C0        = 0.6141;
w0        = 1.7094;
rk0       = 0.0358;
R0        = rho;
mc0       = 0.7692;
P0        = 1.0000;
XI_N0     = 4.8682;
XI_D0     = 6.3287;
```

Table 19.3, continued

```
%------------------------------------------------------------
% 3. Model
%------------------------------------------------------------

model;
  K = Y - C - G + (1 - delta) * K(-1);
  (1/C) = ((1 + R)/(1+rho)) * (P/P(+1))  * (1/C(+1)) ;
  (1/C) = ((1 + rk(+1) - delta)/(1+rho)) * (1/C(+1)) ;
  M_0 / P = (epsilon_m/epsilon_c) * C * (1 + 1/R) ;
  w * (1 - L) = (epsilon_l /epsilon_c) * C;
  w = (1 - alpha) * mc *  Ya / (L - Lbar) ;
  rk = alpha * mc *  Ya / K(-1) ;
  Pn = (theta/(theta-1)) * XI_N / XI_D ;
  XI_N = P^theta * Y * mc / C + (zeta/(1+rho)) * XI_N(+1) ;
  XI_D = P^(theta-1) * Y / C  + (zeta/(1+rho)) * XI_D(+1) ;
  P^(1-theta) = (1-zeta) * Pn^(1-theta) + zeta * P(-1)^(1-theta) ;
  Pa^(-theta) = (1-zeta) * Pn^(-theta)  + zeta * P(-1)^(-theta) ;
  Ya = Omega_0 * exp((1-alpha)*Z) * K(-1)^(alpha) * (L - Lbar)^(1-alpha);
  Y = (Pa/P)^theta * Ya ;
  Ztilde = xi_Z * Ztilde(-1) + eta;
end;


%------------------------------------------------------------
% 4. Computation
%------------------------------------------------------------

initval;
  Y       = Y0;
  Ya      = Y0;
  K       = K0;
  L       = L0;
  C       = C0;
  w       = w0;
  R       = R0;
  mc      = mc0;
  P       = P0;
  Pn      = P0;
  Pa      = P0;
  XI_N    = XI_N0;
  XI_D    = XI_D0;
  Ztilde = 0;
  eta     = 0;
  G       = 0.2;
  M_0     = 1.0;
end;

steady;

shocks;
var eta = sigma_eta^2;
end;

stoch_simul(order = 2);
```

Figure 19.1: Transitory productivity shock

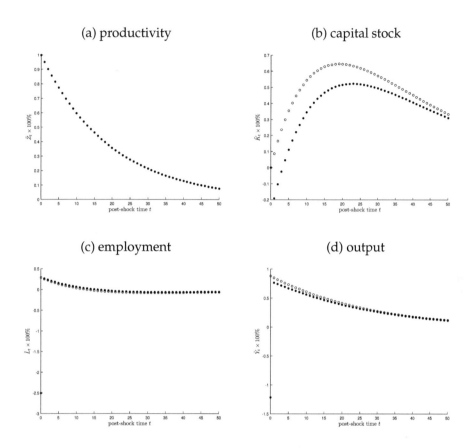

(a) productivity

(b) capital stock

(c) employment

(d) output

In conclusion, the MBC model with perfectly flexible prices gives us the same conclusions that an RBC model would provide us with. The only additional feature of the MBC model is that nominal values (such as P_t, W_t, and MC_t) are determined endogenously.

Matters are quite different for the sticky-price model, especially so at impact. Indeed, at the time of the shock, consumption still increases (though by less than with perfect price flexibility) so ceteris paribus real wages labour supply is reduced on that account (wealth effect). In addition, however, seventy-five percent of firms face a red light and are thus unable to lover the price for their product. The remaining twenty-five percent indeed lower their price because they know labour productivity is temporarily higher than normal. On balance, however, for the calibration used here labour demand shifts to the left and both employment and the real wage rate fall at impact (see panels (c) and (f)). The red-light firms face a large cut in the demand for their product and cut production and their demand for labour accordingly. At impact aggregate output falls by more than one percent (panel (d)).

Figure 19.1 Continued

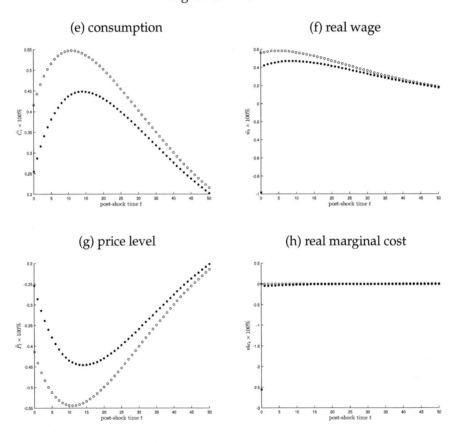

(e) consumption

(f) real wage

(g) price level

(h) real marginal cost

19.4.3.2 Money supply shock

The next shock we consider is a change in the nominal money supply. Indeed, we write $M_{t+1} = e^{\tilde{M}_{t+1}}$ and assume that $\tilde{M}_{t+1}$ follows an AR1 process:

$$\tilde{M}_{t+1} = \xi_M \tilde{M}_t + \eta_t, \qquad 0 < \xi_M < 1,$$

where ξ_M is the persistence parameter and η_t is the innovation term featuring a zero mean and a constant variance σ_η^2. Just as for the productivity shock we normalize the time at which the shock occurs to $t = 0$, assume that $\tilde{M}_0 = 0$, and let $\eta_0 = 0.09531$ and $\eta_t = 0$ for $t = 1, 2, \ldots$. In the simulations we assume a lot of persistence by setting $\xi_M = 0.95$. The resulting time path for M_{t+1} is depicted in panel (a) of Figure 19.2. The impact jump in the level of the money supply is ten percent (as $e^{\eta_0} - 1 = 0.10$).

Again the response functions are drawn for the sticky-price case (featuring $\zeta = 0.75$ and marked with solid dots) and the flexible-price case (with $\zeta = 0$ marked with open dots). Not surprisingly, for the flexible-price case the monetary shock has no effect on the capital stock, employment, output, real factor prices, and real marginal cost. The price level is affected on a one-for-one basis as can be seen in panel (g) of Figure 19.2. Money is neutral.

Just as for the productivity shock, matters are quite different for the sticky-price model, especially in the impact period. Indeed, at the time of the shock both employment (panel (c)) and consumption (panel (e)) increase substantially. Despite the fact that the capital stock is predetermined output rises by more than eight percent at impact (panel (d)). Twenty-five percent of firms are able to set a new (and higher) price but the red light firms must honour their old prices (set in the past). As a result the aggregate price level increases but less than under full price flexibility (see panel (g)). Since the nominal wage rate is perfectly flexible in our model, the real wage rate increases by almost seven percent at impact (panel (f)).

In the impact period households also increase savings so that next period's capital stock is higher by almost 1.2 percent. Over time this capital stock is run down gradually as is illustrated in panel (b). As can be seen from panel (e) consumption also returns gradually to its deterministic steady-state level. Interestingly there is almost no transitional dynamics in the remaining real variables. One period after the shock output, employment, real factor prices, and real marginal cost all more or less returns to their respective deterministic steady-state values.

In summary, just as in the ad hoc Blanchard model of Section 19.1 money is clearly not neutral in the sticky-price model. A money supply shock causes huge employment and output effects at impact and relatively modest transitional effects on consumption and the capital stock. It must be stressed that these results were obtained in a model with a relatively high degree of price stickiness, i.e. only twenty-five percent of firms are facing a green light in any period. Furthermore, just as in the canonical New Keynesian DSGE model (of Table 19.2) traditional monetary policy (here taking the form of an increase in the money supply) does not give rise to macroeconomic instability.

19.4.3.3 Government consumption shock

The final shock we consider is a change in government consumption. As before we write $G_t = e^{\tilde{G}_t}$ and assume that $\tilde{G}_t$ follows an AR1 process:

$$\tilde{G}_t = \xi_G \tilde{G}_{t-1} + \eta_t, \qquad 0 < \xi_G < 1,$$

Figure 19.2: Transitory money supply shock

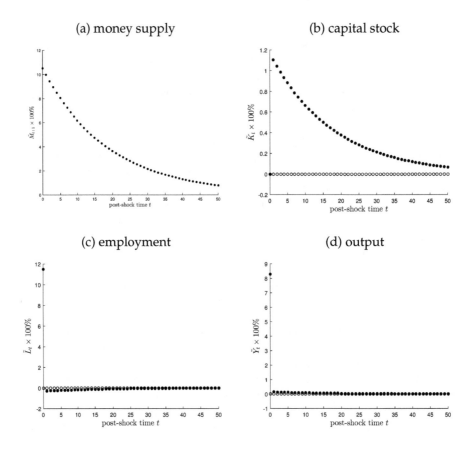

Figure 19.2, continued

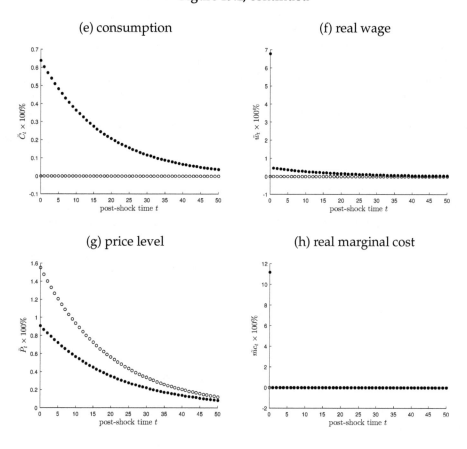

(e) consumption

(f) real wage

(g) price level

(h) real marginal cost

where ξ_G is the persistence parameter and η_t is the innovation term featuring a zero mean and a constant variance σ_η^2. Just as for the previous two shocks we normalize the time at which the shock occurs to $t = 0$, assume that $\tilde{G}_0 = 0$, and let $\eta_0 = 0.09531$ and $\eta_t = 0$ for $t = 1, 2, \ldots$. In the simulations we assume a lot of persistence by setting $\xi_G = 0.95$. The resulting time path for G_t is depicted in panel (a) of Figure 19.3. The impact jump in the level of government consumption is ten percent (as $e^{\eta_0} - 1 = 0.10$).

The response functions have been drawn in panels (b)–(h), again with solid dots representing the sticky-price case (featuring $\zeta = 0.75$) and open dots showing the flexible-price case (with $\zeta = 0$). The results for the flex-price model are familiar to readers of the previous chapter. The temporary shock causes temporary increases in employment, output, and the price level. Consumption falls at impact and is gradually and monotonically restored to its deterministic steady-state level. The adjustment path for the capital stock is non-monotonic.

Just as for the previous two shocks matters are quite different for the sticky-price model, especially in the impact period. Indeed, at the time of the shock both employment (panel (c)) and output (panel (d)) increase substantially. Twenty-five percent of firms are able to set a new (and higher) price but the red light firms must honour their old prices (set in the past). As a result the aggregate price level increases but less than under full price flexibility (see panel (g)). Since the nominal wage rate is perfectly flexible in our model, the real wage rate increases by almost four-and-a-half percent at impact (panel (f)).

In the impact period households also increase savings so that next period's capital stock is higher by almost 0.8 percent. Over time this capital stock is run down gradually as is illustrated in panel (b). As can be seen from panel (e) consumption also returns gradually to its deterministic steady-state level. Interestingly there is almost no transitional dynamics in the remaining real variables (relative to the huge impact effects). One period after the shock output, employment, real factor prices, and real marginal cost all more or less returns to their respective deterministic steady-state values.

In summary, in the sticky-price model a fiscal policy shock causes huge employment and output effects at impact. Indeed, the output multiplier at impact is equal to 3.53 whereas it is equal to 0.49 in the flex-price model.

19.5 Estimation rather than calibration

In the previous section we have analysed a relatively simple New Keynesian DSGE model featuring sticky prices and flexible wages. The simulations were based on a loosely calibrated version of the model. It must be stressed that nowadays a pure calibration approach is no longer deemed appropriate. Indeed, the second wave of MBC models try to directly estimate as many as possible of the structural coefficients and only use calibration if estimation is not feasible.

The earliest and most famous examples of this estimation-cum-calibration approach are the contributions by Smets and Wouters (2003, 2007) and Christiano et al. (2005). Since these papers are landmarks in the development of the New Keynesian DSGE approach the remainder of this section discusses the punchlines from Christiano et al. (2005). They pose themselves the following question: "Can models with moderate degrees of nominal rigidities generate inertial inflation and persistent output movements in response to monetary policy shocks?" (Christiano et al., 2005, p. 2). Not surprisingly, their answer is in the affirmative.

Figure 19.3: Transitory government consumption shock

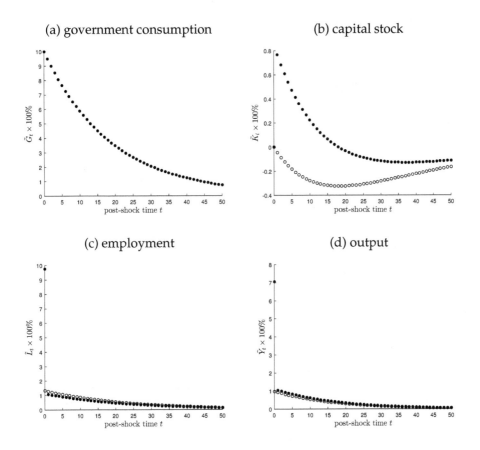

(a) government consumption

(b) capital stock

(c) employment

(d) output

Figure 19.3, continued

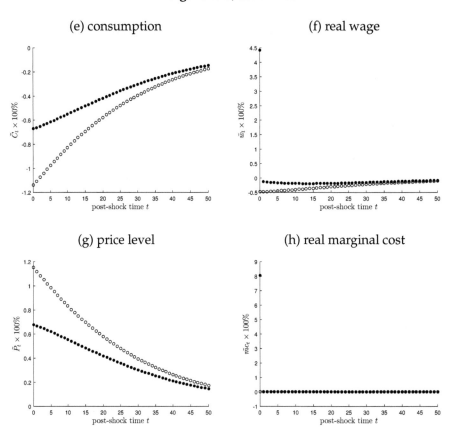

19.5.1 Model features

Compared to our general MBC model Christiano et al. (2005) need to change some features and add others. In what follows we give a stylized account of the main additional features not found in our general MBC model:

Additional Feature (AF1): Calvo-style pricing of labour.

Additional Feature (AF2): Habit formation in the agent's preferences for consumption.

Additional Feature (AF3): Adjustment costs of investment.

Additional Feature (AF4): Variable utilization rate of the capital stock.

Additional Feature (AF5): Firms borrow working capital to pay workers upfront.

Additional Feature (AF6): The lagged inflation rate is used for indexation purposes by red-light firms and workers.

Let us now briefly look at some of these added features, using the notation adopted in this chapter. On (AF1). Calvo pricing of labour is modelled in an analogous fashion to stickiness of goods prices. It is assumed that each household supplies a slightly unique variety of labour, $L_t(j)$, which it sells at a nominal wage $W_t(j)$. A representative, perfectly competitive firm buys all types of labour and transforms it into homogeneous (standardized) labour L_t according to a CES aggregation function:

$$L_t = \left[\int_0^1 L_t(j)^{1-1/\theta_l} \, dj \right]^{1/(1-1/\theta_l)}, \qquad 1 < \theta_l \ll \infty, \tag{19.130}$$

where θ_l measures the ease with which labour types can be substituted. Labour types are employed such that the wage bill is minimized for a given amount of L_t. This ensures that the aggregate wage rate (i.e., the unit cost of standardized labour) is given by:

$$W_t \equiv \left[\int_0^1 W_t(j)^{1-\theta_l} \, dj \right]^{1/(1-\theta_l)}, \tag{19.131}$$

and the derived demand for labour of type j is:

$$L_t(j) = L_t \left(\frac{W_t(j)}{W_t} \right)^{-\theta_l}. \tag{19.132}$$

Note that each labour supplier possesses a little bit of market power because θ_l is assumed to be close to unity.

On (AF2), habit formation in preferences is included by assuming that the felicity function takes the following form:

$$U(C_t, 1 - L_t, m_t) \equiv \varepsilon_c \ln \left[C_t - \beta C_{t-1} \right] - \varepsilon_l L_t^2 + \varepsilon_m \frac{m_t^{1-1/\sigma} - 1}{1 - 1/\sigma}, \tag{19.133}$$

with $\varepsilon_c > 0$, $\varepsilon_l > 0$, and $\varepsilon_m > 0$. Several features are worth noting. First, it is not C_t itself which provides the household with felicity in period t, but rather C_t in reference to weighted consumption in period $t-1$. For $\beta > 0$ there is habit formation in consumption preferences. Second, felicity is quadratic in the hours of time that are supplied to the labour market. Third, felicity depends on current real cash balances, i.e. $m_t \equiv M_t/P_t$, so the stock of money held at the start of period t yields felicity.

On (AF3), adjustment costs of investment are incorporated in the model by postulating that the law of motion for the capital stock is given by:

$$K_{t+1} = \left[1 - \Phi\left(\frac{I_t}{I_{t-1}}\right)\right] I_t + (1-\delta) K_t, \tag{19.134}$$

where the $\Phi(x)$ function captures the notion of installation costs. The key features of this function are that $\Phi(1) = \Phi'(1) = 0$ and $\Phi''(1) > 0$. Note that (19.134) differs from the usual adjustment cost specification in the sense that $\Phi(x)$ depends on the relative investment rate (I_t/I_{t-1}) rather than the investment-capital ratio (I_t/K_t).

On (AF4), a variable utilization rate of the capital stock is modelled in the following fashion. Capital services, K_t^s, are defined as:

$$K_t^s \equiv u_t K_t, \tag{19.135}$$

where u_t is the utilization rate and K_t is the existing stock of capital. By adjusting u_t a given stock of capital can be utilized less or more intensively. Whereas the capital stock is by its nature a predetermined variable, capital services are not. It is assumed that a more intensive utilization rate increases costs. To capture the utilization rate mechanism the household's nominal budget identity is affected on both sides:

$$W_t L_t + R_t^K u_t K_t + \ldots = P_t \left[C_t + I_t + \Gamma(u_t) K_t\right] + \ldots, \tag{19.136}$$

where $\Gamma(u_t)$ represents the cost of setting the utilization rate u_t. The $\Gamma(x)$ function is increasing and convex, i.e. $\Gamma'(x) > 0$, and $\Gamma''(x) > 0$. On the left-hand side of (19.136) the utilization rate appears because capital services (and not the capital stock itself) yield rental payments. On the right-hand side of (19.136) the utilization rate appears because it affects costs.

On (AF6), the lagged inflation rate is used for indexation purposes by red-light firms and workers. Whereas we have abstracted from an underlying positive inflation rate throughout this chapter, New Keynesian DSGE researchers typically include a constant core inflation rate π^* in their models. Christiano et al. (2005) augment this feature by assuming that the core inflation rate is not constant but time-varying and equal to the lagged actual inflation rate. Indeed, it is assumed that the typical red-light firm sets its price according to:

$$P_t(i) = (1 + \pi_{t-1}) P_{t-1}(i), \tag{19.137}$$

where $P_{t-1}(i)$ is the price it charged last quarter. Similarly, a worker facing a red light sets his wage rate according to:

$$W_t(j) = (1 + \pi_{t-1}) W_{t-1}(j). \tag{19.138}$$

19.5.2 Model calibration and estimation

Christiano et al. (2005, pp. 15–17) adopt the following 3-step approach to calibration cum estimation. They consider three groups of structural parameters. The first group of structural parameters is calibrated in the standard way (conform the example shown above).

The second group of parameters characterize the form of the monetary policy rule which they write as:

$$\mu_t = \mu + \theta_0 \varepsilon_t + \theta_1 \varepsilon_{t-1} + \theta_2 \varepsilon_{t-2} + \dots, \tag{19.139}$$

where where μ_t is the growth rate in the nominal money supply. To obtain estimates for this policy rule they adopt a two-step procedure. In the first step they estimate the impulse response functions of eight key macroeconomic variables to a monetary policy shock using an identified VAR specification. In the second step they use the estimated VAR coefficients to obtain estimates for the θ_i parameters.

The third group of parameters are estimated such that the distance between the model-generated and empirical impulse-response functions is minimized.

19.5.3 Main findings

Referring the interested reader to the paper itself for details, the main findings reported by Christiano et al. (2005) are as follows. First, the average period between price adjustments is about two quarters whilst for wage adjustments it is three quarters. This represents the 'moderate degree of nominal rigidity' they were looking for in the first place. The model accounts quantitatively for the estimated response functions to a policy shock.

Second, of the two nominal frictions contained in the model it is the sluggishness of nominal wages which is the most important one. A model with only nominal wage contracts does almost as well as the full model. In contrast, a model with only price rigidities performs badly. This last feature was also noted by Chari et al. (2000) who argued that staggered price setting alone cannot generate business cycle fluctuations.

Third, the effects of nominal frictions depends a lot on how the real side of the economy is modelled. If the additional features (AF2)–(AF5) are dropped from the model then the estimated model implies very infrequent occurrences of green lights in goods and labour markets. The model fails in the sense that the nominal rigidities are no longer 'moderate' and thus must be considered implausible.

Fourth, additional feature (AF4)—capturing variable capital utilization—is important to get a good fit for the estimated model. Intuitively this feature dampens fluctuations in the rental rate on capital and thus on marginal costs and prices.

Fifth, additional features (AF2)–(AF3)—capturing investment adjustment costs and habit formation in consumption—are mainly important to account for the macroeconomic variables other than inflation and output.

Sixth, in the absence of the working capital assumption—additional feature (AF5) —the average duration of price contracts becomes unrealistically large.

Seventh, the model contains a strong internal propagation mechanism. The lack of propagation was an oft-heard criticism of New Classical DSGE models—see Chapter 18 for examples.

19.6 Critics

The landmark contributions by Smets and Wouters (2003, 2007) and Christiano et al. (2005) have given rise to a veritable tsunami of New Keynesian DSGE models. There even exists an internet depository of models (coordinated and kept up to date by Volker Wieland and co-workers) which contains links to software implementations of a large number of New Keynesian DSGE models. See:

http://www.macromodelbase.com/.

This is not to say that the New Keynesian DSGE models have met with universal acceptance by macroeconomists. In the remainder of this section we discuss some of the main critics. Interestingly, criticism is quite diverse and comes from New Classical and New Keynesian economists alike.[3] Even though New Classicals and New Keynesians both dislike (features of) the New Keynesian DSGE approach, their reasoning is quite different.

19.6.1   New Classical critics

In a provocatively titled contribution, Chari et al. (2009) (CKM hereafter) argue that "New Keynesian models are not yet useful for policy analysis." The use of the word "yet" of course suggests that they think there is still hope that such models will become useful in the future. Interestingly CKM aim their arrows of destruction not so much at the Christiano et al. (2005) paper discussed in some detail above. Instead they target their critique almost exclusively at Smets and Wouters (2007). The central premise of CKM is as follows.

> Macroeconomists have largely converged on methods, model design, reduced-form shocks, and principles of policy advice. Our main disagreements today are implementing the methodology. Some think New Keynesian models are ready to be used for quarter-to-quarter quantitative policy advice. We do not. (2009, p. 242)

So why are CKM so unhappy with the New Keynesian DSGE models? Like true adherents of the Lucas research program they argue that serious policy analysis can only be conducted with a microeconomically founded structural model "with primitive, interpretable shocks that are invariant to the policy interventions being considered" (2009, p. 242). Furthermore, they argue that the aim of the policy analyst is "... to keep a macro model simple, [and to] keep the number of its parameters small and well motivated by micro facts ..." (2009, p. 243). Parsimony is thus more important to CKM than a good fit with the macroeconomic data.

In their desire to fit the macro data closely, CKM argue, New Keynesian economists use too many "free parameters" and fail to subject their models to the "discipline of microeconomic evidence". Put differently, New Keyesian economists add shocks that are what CKM call "dubiously structural". As examples of such dubiously structural shocks in the Smets and Wouters model, CKM mention shocks to wage markups, to price markups, to exogenous government spending, and to risk premia.

As examples of further dubious features of not only Smets and Wouters (2007) but also Christiano et al. (2005), Chari et al. (2009, pp. 261–264) mention the backward indexation of prices (as in (19.137) above) and the specification of the Taylor rule.

With non-structural—reduced-form—shocks multiple structural explanations can be formulated that give rise to drastically different policy implications. For example, a labour wedge (defined as the difference between the real wage and the MRS between leisure and consumption) constitutes a reduced-form shock. CKM discuss two (what they call) structural explanations. The first assumes that government policy

---

[3] A more traditional Keynesian critique is provided by Nobel Laureate Paul Krugman (2009) in his Op-Ed column in the *New York Times Magazine* entitled "How did economists get it so wrong?" This piece has led to a polemical discussion between Krugman and Cochrane (2011). Also see Buiter (2009) for a traditional Keynesian criticism of the DSGE approach. It is fair to say that both Krugman and Buiter are dismissive of the DSGE approach in general. Cochrane sees Keynesian economics as a waste of two decades or so. See also Paul Romer (forthcoming) on the trouble with macroeconomics.

toward trade unions is the source of the labour wedge. The policy recommendation in this case would be to bust the unions. The second structural explanation assumes that the labour wedge results from stochastic taste-for-leisure shocks. In this case the policy advice would be to adopt a laissez faire attitude.

19.6.2 New Keynesian critics

We started this chapter with an ad hoc IS-LM type model by Blanchard (1981) which represented the state of the art in Keynesian macroeconomics in the early 1980s. It is therefore particularly interesting to take notice of Blanchard's views on New Keynesian DSGE models. In a recent policy brief for the Peterson Institute for International Economics, Blanchard asks himself the question "Do DSGE models have a future?" (2016, p. 1). His answer is unambiguous: "I see the current DSGE models as seriously flawed, but they are eminently improvable and central to the future of macroeconomics" (2016, p. 1). At first viewing, it seems that Blanchard agrees with CKM on this point.

So what are the features of the New Keynesian DSGE models that Blanchard finds objectionable? Again referring the interested readers to the paper itself for details, his main points of criticism are as follows. First, the models are based on unappealing assumptions. For example, aggregate demand is just a rewritten version of the stochastic consumption Euler equation which is strongly at odds with empirical evidence. Furthermore, by introducing backward-looking indexation of prices and wages (as in (19.137)–(19.138)) price and wage inflation become more sluggish than it would otherwise be. But this is almost a one-liner. The modeller introduces an ad hoc feature and lo and behold it helps to fit the data.

Second, Blanchard also does not like the standard methods of calibration-estimation (as sketched above). As he points out, "In many cases, the choice to rely on a standard set of parameters is simply a way of shifting blame for the choice of parameters to previous researchers" (2016, p. 2). To paraphrase: if he can get away with it then so can I. As was pointed out much earlier by the Nobel Laureates Lars Peter Hansen and James Heckman (1996), the empirical foundations of the calibration approach are much less robust than its practitioners want you to believe. See also Browning et al. (1999) on this.

Third, even though the New Keynesian DSGE models are microeconomically founded so that welfare effects can be computed, such effects are typically unconvincing. The reason is that these welfare effects depend critically on the different frictions that are introduced into the model. And these frictions (such as Calvo pricing) are typically modelled in a way that is analytically tractable rather than economically plausible.

Fourth, Blanchard argues that DSGE models are bad communication devices. To put it more bluntly, DSGE models tend to be black boxes and one cannot readily see which feature of the complicated model is responsible for which model outcome.

In summary, Blanchard accepts the need for microeconomic foundations—"where else to start from?" —but also argues that the DSGE approach should become less imperialistic.

> Models can also differ in their degree of simplicity. Not all models have to be explicitly microfounded. While this will sound like a *plaidoyer pro domo*, I strongly believe that ad hoc macro models, from various versions of the IS-LM to the Mundell-Fleming model, have an important role to play in relation to DSGE models. They can be useful upstream, before

DSGE modelling, as a first cut to think about the effects of a particular distortion or a particular policy. They can be useful downstream, after DSGE modelling, to present the major insight of the model in a lighter and pedagogical fashion. (2016, p. 3)

Blanchard is by no means the only Keynes-inspired critic of the DSGE approach. Kiyotaki (2011) criticizes the approach—as used by New Keynesians and New Classicals alike—because financial frictions such as credit constraints are typically ignored. Markets are assumed to be more perfect than they are in reality. Kiyotaki's argument runs as follows. First, in the prototypical DSGE framework firms and individuals are heterogeneous but to render the quantitative analysis tractable it is assumed that markets are complete. By this it is meant that "...there exists a complete set of Arrow Securities so that state-contingent claims to goods and factors of production for every possible future state can be traded at the initial period" (2011, p. 196). With complete markets heterogeneity of firms and individuals does not matter because we can always study the aggregate economy with the constructs of the representative agent and the representative firm—See Chapter 17 on this. This is in fact what we have done implicitly in Chapters 18 and 19.

Second, Kiyotaki argues, in such a *complete markets economy* (CME), credit is just a frictionless exchange between future and present goods. It is always enforced by an auctioneer who has the authority and ability to enforce all contracts costlessly. In reality such an auctioneer is absent and we are forced to enter the realm of the *incomplete markets economy* (IME): borrowers might default, creditors require collateral, and agent heterogeneity becomes crucial again.

Of course there is an inherent problem with the incomplete market paradigm. Whereas these is typically only one way to write down the conditions characterizing a complete markets economy, there are many ways in which to formulate an incomplete markets economy, depending on which frictions one wishes to emphasize. In a series of papers, Kiyotaki and Moore (2005, 2012) stress the importance of credit constraints. They also argue that credit market imperfections exacerbate the effects of shocks. Similar conclusions are reached by Bernanke et al. (1999) and Gertler and Karadi (2011).

19.7   Punchlines

This chapter documents some of the developments in New Keynesian economics over the last two decades or so. We start by introducing money into a dynamic stochastic general equilibrium (DSGE) model. To keep things simple we adopt the money-in-the-utility-function approach. In the presence of a nominal anchor (the money supply) nominal goods and factor prices are determined within the model and we can distinguish between nominal and real interest rates as price inflation may be non-zero.

In the absence of frictions money is neutral. To render money non-neutral New Keynesians incorporate a microeconomically founded theory of price (and wage) stickiness into their models. In the chapter we use the parable of Calvo pricing to capture price stickiness. In the Calvo approach monopolistically competitive firms can only change their optimal (profit-maximizing) price if they receive a 'green light' from Mother Nature. If they receive a 'red light' they must continue to supply their product at the price set in the past.

A special case of the New Keynesian DSGE model is obtained by abstracting from capital accumulation and by assuming that government consumption is zero. This model can be linearized around the deterministic steady state after which we can characterize the economy with only three equations. The first of these is a rewritten version of the stochastic consumption Euler equation but is called the dynamic IS (DIS) curve by the New Keynesians. The second equation is a rewritten version of the aggregate price equation (a complicated weighted average of the newly set price level by green-light firms and lagged past prices). New Keynesians call this the New Keynesian Phillips curve (NKPC). The third equation is the money market equilibrium condition (MME).

Under traditional monetary policy—with the Central Bank controlling the money supply—the stochastic equilibrium process for output and inflation is stable. Following stochastic shocks, with a given money supply the nominal interest rate maintains equilbrium in the money market and inflation and output remain stochastically stable. In contrast, if the Central Bank controls the nominal interest rate (rather than the monetary aggregate) without incorporating feed-back effects (a passive policy rule) the economy is unstable. An active policy rule, such as the Taylor rule, restores stochastic stability by ensuring that increases in inflation lead to a more than one-for-one increase in the nominal interest rate and a reduction in the real interest rate (thus choking off the instability that occurs under a passive interest rate setting rule).

Next we return to the general New Keynesian DSGE model with an endogenous capital stock and show how it can be calibrated and then simulated with the aid of Dynare. Price stickiness matters to the shape of the impulse-response functions for productivity-, monetary-, and government-consumption shocks. Especially at impact the fact that a significant fraction of firms face a red light makes a big difference when comparing the sticky-price and flex-price solutions.

We finish the chapter by showing how the New Keynesian DSGE model can be fleshed out by combining calibration and estimation techniques. In addition we review the main points of criticism that have been aimed at the current crop of New Keynesian DSGE models. Both New Classicals and New Keynesians dislike certain features of these models. Some more traditional Keynesians go even further and reject the DSGE approach in its entirety. The debate between New Classicals and (New) Keynesians reminds this commentator of the age-old debate between Keynesian and Classical economists! So in that sense nothing has changed over the last fifty years or so.

Further reading

The "bible" of the New Keynesian DSGE approach is the monograph by Woodford (2003). This book is certainly not easy to read but it contains a very thorough discussion of the core of the DSGE approach. A more accessible treatment can be found in the book by Galí (2015). See also Galí and Gertler (2007) and Galí (2015).

A textbook treatment of monetary economics is provided by Walsh (2010). This book is best read after you have gained a basic understanding of the techniques and issues that are relevant in the field. If you want an overview of recent micro-founded work there is no better source than the brand new handbooks edited by Friedman and Woodford. At first reading the key chapters are Gertler and Kiyotaki (2011), Galí (2011), and Woodford (2011). Surveys of the older literature on monetary economics can be found in the handbooks edited by Friedman and Hahn (1990a, 1990b).

Our basic DSGE model makes use of insights from Yun (1996), Bernanke et al. (1999), Ireland (2004a,b), and Christiano et al. (2011). For New Keynesian DSGE models with unemployment, see Galí et al. (2012). On Taylor rules, see Taylor (1993),

Orphanides (2008), and Davig and Leeper (2007). Altug and Labadie (2008) discuss monetary issues with (in)complete markets. For optimal monetary policy under price stickiness, see Schmitt-Grohé and Uribe (2004). The continuous-time approach to monetary economics that was started by Brock (1975), has been making a come-back in recent years, see Brunnermeier and Sannikov (2014),

For a comparison of different price adjustment cost models, see Ascari and Rossi (2012). See also Dotsey et al. (1999) on Calvo pricing. For New Keynesian models with capital accumulation, see Carlstrom and Fuerst (2005), Dupor (2001) in continuous time, Huang and Meng (2007), Kurozumi and Van Zandweghe (2008), and Xiao (2008).

For computational aspects, see McCandless (2008) and Schmidt and Wieland (2013). For a collection of New Keynesian DSGE models and comparative model analysis, see Wieland et al (2012a, 2012b).

In the wake of the financial crisis a large number of popular science books have come on the market. The ones I like particularly are the following. John Quiggin's (2010) book on dead ideas that refuse to die (including the efficient markets hypothesis). Paul Krugman's (2012) passionate plea for old-fashioned Keynesian policies. Justin Fox (2009) on the myth of the rational market. It contains a critical review of the academic field of finance (on which micro-based monetary theory draws rather heavily). I also like Cassidy (2010) on market failures in general.

Mathematical Appendix

A.1 Introduction

In this Mathematical Appendix we give a brief overview of the main techniques that are used in this book. In order to preserve space, for most cases we simply state the results and refer the interested reader to various sources—of differing levels of sophistication—where the mathematical background for these results is explained in more detail. The transform methods used in sections A.6.1 and A.7.2 are explained in more detail because they are somewhat unfamiliar to most economists. Klein (1998), Simon and Blume (1994), and Pemberton and Rau (2001) are all good single-volume sources for the mathematical techniques employed in this book, both in terms of coverage and the level of sophistication. Sydsæter et al. (2000) is a very convenient reference book describing most of the tricks used by economists.

A.2 Matrix algebra

A.2.1 General

A *matrix* is a rectangular array of numbers a_{ij} where $i = 1, 2, ..., m$ is the row index and $j = 1, 2, ..., n$ is the column index. A matrix of dimension m by n thus has m rows and n columns:

$$
\underset{m \times n}{A} \equiv \begin{bmatrix} a_{11} & a_{12} & \cdots & a_{1n} \\ a_{21} & a_{22} & \cdots & a_{2n} \\ \vdots & \vdots & \ddots & \vdots \\ a_{m1} & a_{m2} & \cdots & a_{mn} \end{bmatrix}. \tag{A.1}
$$

If $m = n = 1$ then A is a *scalar*, if $m = 1$ and $n > 1$ it is *row vector*, and if $n = 1$ and $m > 1$ it is a *column vector*. If $m = n$ then the matrix A is *square* and we call the diagonal containing the elements $a_{11}, a_{22}, ..., a_{nn}$ the *principal diagonal*. There are a number of special matrices. The *zero matrix* contains only elements equal to zero ($a_{ij} = 0$ for $i = 1, 2, ..., m$ and $j = 1, 2, ..., n$). The *identity matrix*, I_n, is a square n by n matrix with ones on the principal diagonal and zeros elsewhere.

A.2.2 Addition, subtraction, multiplication

Two matrices A and B can be added if and only if they have the same dimension. If A has elements $[a_{ij}]$ and B has elements $[b_{ij}]$ then the matrix $C \equiv A + B$ is obtained by adding corresponding elements:

$$
A + B = C, \quad \text{with } c_{ij} = a_{ij} + b_{ij}, \tag{A.2}
$$

for $i = 1, 2, ..., m$ and $j = 1, 2, ..., n$. Subtracting matrices works the same way:

$$A - B = D, \qquad \text{with } d_{ij} = a_{ij} - b_{ij}, \tag{A.3}$$

for $i = 1, 2, ..., m$ and $j = 1, 2, ..., n$.

Matrices can be multiplied by a scalar, k, by multiplying all elements of the matrix by that scalar, i.e. $B \equiv kA$ then $b_{ij} \equiv ka_{ij}$ for $i = 1, 2, ..., m$ and $j = 1, 2, ..., n$. Some rules and properties follow immediately (k and l are both scalars):

$$\begin{aligned}
kA &= Ak, \\
k(A + B) &= kA + kB, \\
(k + l)A &= kA + lA, \\
(kl)A &= k(lA), \\
(-1)A &= -A, \\
A + (-1)B &= A - B.
\end{aligned} \tag{A.4}$$

Two matrices can be multiplied if they are *conformable* for that operation. The matrix product AB is defined if the column dimension of the matrix on the left (matrix A) is the same as the row dimension of the matrix on the right (the B matrix). If A is m by r and B is r by n then by this rule AB is m by n and is defined as follows:

$$AB = C, \qquad c_{ij} = \sum_{k=1}^{r} a_{ik} b_{kj}, \tag{A.5}$$

for $i = 1, 2, ..., m$ and $j = 1, 2, ..., n$. Unless $m = n$ the product BA is not defined. Even if BA is defined it is not equal to AB in general. So premultiplying B by A (yielding AB) does not give the same matrix in general as premultiplying A by B (an operation yielding BA). Some properties of matrix multiplication are the following (A, B, and C are conformable matrices, 0 is the zero matrix, and k is a scalar):

$$\begin{aligned}
A(B + C) &= AB + AC, \\
(A + B)C &= AC + BC, \\
A(BC) &= (AB)C, \\
k(AB) &= A(kB), \\
A0 &= 0A = 0, \\
AI &= IA = A.
\end{aligned} \tag{A.6}$$

A.2.3 Transposition

The *transpose* of matrix A is denoted by A^T (or sometimes by A'). It is obtained by interchanging the rows and columns of matrix A. Hence, if A is m by n and $B \equiv A^T$ then B is n by m and $b_{ij} \equiv a_{ji}$. Some properties of transposes are:

$$\begin{aligned}
(A^T)^T &= A, \\
(kA)^T &= kA^T, \\
(A + B)^T &= A^T + B^T, \\
(AB)^T &= B^T A^T.
\end{aligned} \tag{A.7}$$

A.2.4 Square matrices

In this subsection we gather the key results pertaining to square matrices (for which the row and column dimensions are the same). The *trace* of the n by n matrix A, denoted by $\mathrm{tr}(A)$, is the sum of the elements on its principal diagonal:

$$\mathrm{tr}(A) \equiv \sum_{i=1}^{n} a_{ii}. \tag{A.8}$$

The following properties can be derived:

$$\begin{aligned}
\mathrm{tr}(I_n) &= n, \\
\mathrm{tr}(0) &= 0, \\
\mathrm{tr}(A^T) &= \mathrm{tr}(A), \\
\mathrm{tr}(AA^T) &= \mathrm{tr}(A^T A) = \sum_{i=1}^{n} \sum_{j=1}^{n} a_{ij}^2, \\
\mathrm{tr}(kA) &= k\,\mathrm{tr}(A), \\
\mathrm{tr}(AB) &= \mathrm{tr}(BA).
\end{aligned} \tag{A.9}$$

The *determinant* of a square matrix A, denoted by $|A|$ (sometimes by $\det(A)$) is a unique scalar associated with that matrix. For a two-by-two matrix the determinant is:

$$A \equiv \begin{bmatrix} a_{11} & a_{12} \\ a_{21} & a_{22} \end{bmatrix}, \qquad |A| \equiv a_{11}a_{22} - a_{12}a_{21}. \tag{A.10}$$

For a three-by-three matrix the determinant can be computed as follows:

$$\begin{aligned}
|A| &\equiv \begin{vmatrix} a_{11} & a_{12} & a_{13} \\ a_{21} & a_{22} & a_{23} \\ a_{31} & a_{32} & a_{33} \end{vmatrix} = a_{11} \begin{vmatrix} a_{22} & a_{23} \\ a_{32} & a_{33} \end{vmatrix} - a_{12} \begin{vmatrix} a_{21} & a_{23} \\ a_{31} & a_{33} \end{vmatrix} + a_{13} \begin{vmatrix} a_{21} & a_{22} \\ a_{31} & a_{32} \end{vmatrix} \\
&= a_{11}\left[a_{22}a_{33} - a_{23}a_{32}\right] - a_{12}\left[a_{21}a_{33} - a_{23}a_{31}\right] + a_{13}\left[a_{21}a_{32} - a_{22}a_{31}\right] \\
&= a_{11}a_{22}a_{33} - a_{11}a_{23}a_{32} - a_{12}a_{21}a_{33} + a_{12}a_{23}a_{31} + a_{13}a_{21}a_{32} - a_{13}a_{22}a_{31}.
\end{aligned} \tag{A.11}$$

We have computed $|A|$ by going along the first row and seeking two-by-two determinants associated with each element on that first row. For element a_{11} we find the associated two-by-two determinant by deleting the row and column in which a_{11} is located. The resulting two-by-two determinant is called the *minor* of element a_{11}. In a similar fashion, the minor of element a_{12} is found by deleting row 1 and column 2 from the original determinant, and the minor of a_{13} is obtained by deleting row 1 and column 3 from the original determinant. Denoting the minor of element a_{ij} by $|M_{ij}|$ we can define the *cofactor* of that element by $|C_{ij}| = (-1)^{i+j}|M_{ij}|$. A cofactor is a minor with a sign in front of it. The sign is determined as follows: if the sum of the row and column indices $(i+j)$ is even, then the sign is positive and the cofactor is equal to the minor. Conversely, if $i+j$ is uneven, then the cofactor is minus the minor. Using these definitions we can now see that the determinant of the three-by-three matrix in (A.11) can be written as: $|A| \equiv a_{11}|C_{11}| + a_{12}|C_{12}| + a_{13}|C_{13}| = \sum_{j=1}^{3} a_{1j}|C_{1j}|$. Of course, we could have computed $|A|$ by going along row 2 ($|A| = \sum_{j=1}^{3} a_{2j}|C_{2j}|$) or row 3 ($|A| = \sum_{j=1}^{3} a_{3j}|C_{3j}|$) or by going along any of the columns of the original determinant ($|A| = \sum_{i=1}^{3} a_{ij}|C_{ij}|$ for $j=1,2,3$). It is not difficult to verify that in each case we would have found the same value for $|A|$.

The procedure we have just followed to compute $|A|$ is called a *Laplace expansion*. The Laplace expansion of an n by n matrix is given by:

$$|A| = \sum_{i=1}^{n} a_{ij}|C_{ij}|, \quad \text{for } j = 1, ..., n, \quad \text{(column expansion)} \tag{A.12}$$

$$= \sum_{j=1}^{n} a_{ij} \left| C_{ij} \right|, \quad \text{for } i = 1, ..., n, \quad \text{(row expansion)}. \tag{A.13}$$

The determinant has a number of useful properties (k is a scalar):

$$
\begin{aligned}
|I| &= 1, \\
|0| &= 0, \\
|A| &= \left| A^T \right|, \\
|A| &= (-1)^n |-A| = k^{-n} |kA|, \\
|AB| &= |BA|.
\end{aligned} \tag{A.14}
$$

- If any row (column) is a non-trivial linear combination of all the other rows (columns) of A then $|A| = 0$.

- If B results from A by interchanging two rows (or columns) then $|B| = -|A|$.

- If B results from A by multiplying one row (or one column) by k then $|B| = k|A|$.

- The addition (subtraction) of a multiple of any row to (from) another row leaves $|A|$ unchanged.

- The addition (subtraction) of a multiple of any column to (from) another column leaves $|A|$ unchanged.

The *adjoint matrix* of matrix A is denoted by $\text{adj}A$. It is defined as the transposed matrix of cofactors:

$$
\text{adj}A \equiv
\begin{bmatrix}
|C_{11}| & |C_{12}| & \cdots & |C_{1n}| \\
|C_{21}| & |C_{22}| & \cdots & |C_{2n}| \\
\vdots & \vdots & \ddots & \vdots \\
|C_{n1}| & |C_{n2}| & \cdots & |C_{nn}|
\end{bmatrix}^T
. \tag{A.15}
$$

If $|A| \neq 0$ then the matrix A is *non-singular* and possesses a unique *inverse*, denoted by A^{-1}:

$$A^{-1} = \frac{1}{|A|} \text{adj}A. \tag{A.16}$$

If the matrix A has an inverse it follows that $A^{-1}A = AA^{-1} = I$.

Intermezzo A.1

Matrix inversion. For example, let A be:

$$A \equiv \begin{bmatrix} 1 & 2 \\ 3 & 4 \end{bmatrix},$$

then we find by applying the rules that $|A| = 4 - 6 = -2$ (non-singular matrix) so that the inverse matrix exists and is equal to:

$$A^{-1} = \frac{1}{-2} \begin{bmatrix} 4 & -2 \\ -3 & 1 \end{bmatrix} = \begin{bmatrix} -2 & 1 \\ \frac{3}{2} & -\frac{1}{2} \end{bmatrix}.$$

To check that we have not made any mistakes we compute AA^{-1} and $A^{-1}A$ (both should equal the identity matrix).

$$AA^{-1} = \begin{bmatrix} 1 & 2 \\ 3 & 4 \end{bmatrix} \begin{bmatrix} -2 & 1 \\ \frac{3}{2} & -\frac{1}{2} \end{bmatrix}$$

$$= \begin{bmatrix} 1 \cdot -2 + 2 \cdot \frac{3}{2} & 1 \cdot 1 + 2 \cdot -\frac{1}{2} \\ 3 \cdot -2 + 4 \cdot \frac{3}{2} & 3 \cdot 1 + 4 \cdot -\frac{1}{2} \end{bmatrix} = \begin{bmatrix} 1 & 0 \\ 0 & 1 \end{bmatrix},$$

$$A^{-1}A = \begin{bmatrix} -2 & 1 \\ \frac{3}{2} & -\frac{1}{2} \end{bmatrix} \begin{bmatrix} 1 & 2 \\ 3 & 4 \end{bmatrix}$$

$$= \begin{bmatrix} -2 \cdot 1 + 1 \cdot 3 & -2 \cdot 2 + 1 \cdot 4 \\ \frac{3}{2} \cdot 1 - \frac{1}{2} \cdot 3 & \frac{3}{2} \cdot 2 - \frac{1}{2} \cdot 4 \end{bmatrix} = \begin{bmatrix} 1 & 0 \\ 0 & 1 \end{bmatrix}.$$

****

Assuming that the indicated inverses exist (and the matrices A and B are thus non-singular), we find the following properties:

$$\begin{aligned} I^{-1} &= I, \\ (A^{-1})^{-1} &= A, \\ (A^T)^{-1} &= (A^{-1})^T, \\ (AB)^{-1} &= B^{-1}A^{-1}, \\ |A^{-1}| &= |A|^{-1}. \end{aligned} \tag{A.17}$$

A.2.5 Cramer's Rule

Suppose we have a linear system of n equations in n unknowns:

$$\begin{aligned} a_{11}x_1 + a_{12}x_2 + \cdots + a_{1n}x_n &= b_1, \\ a_{21}x_1 + a_{22}x_2 + \cdots + a_{2n}x_n &= b_2, \\ &\vdots \\ a_{n1}x_1 + a_{n2}x_2 + \cdots + a_{nn}x_n &= b_n, \end{aligned} \tag{A.18}$$

where a_{ij} are the coefficients, b_i are the exogenous variables, and x_i are the endogenous variables. We can write this system in the form of a single matrix equation as:

$$Ax = b, \tag{A.19}$$

where A is an n by n matrix, and x and b are n by 1 (column) vectors:

$$A \equiv \begin{bmatrix} a_{11} & a_{12} & \cdots & a_{1n} \\ a_{21} & a_{22} & \cdots & a_{2n} \\ \vdots & \vdots & \ddots & \vdots \\ a_{n1} & a_{n2} & \cdots & a_{nn} \end{bmatrix}, \quad x \equiv \begin{bmatrix} x_1 \\ x_2 \\ \vdots \\ x_n \end{bmatrix}, \quad b \equiv \begin{bmatrix} b_1 \\ b_2 \\ \vdots \\ b_n \end{bmatrix}. \tag{A.20}$$

Provided the coefficient matrix A is non-singular (so that $|A| \neq 0$) the solution of the matrix equation is:

$$x = A^{-1}b. \tag{A.21}$$

Instead of inverting the entire matrix A we can find the solutions for individual variables by means of *Cramer's Rule* (which only involves determinants):

$$x_j = \frac{|A_j|}{|A|}, \quad \text{for } j = 1, 2, ..., n, \tag{A.22}$$

where $|A_j|$ is the determinant of the matrix A_j which is obtained by replacing column j of A by the vector of exogenous variables, for example A_1 is:

$$A_1 \equiv \begin{bmatrix} b_1 & a_{12} & a_{13} & \cdots & a_{1n} \\ b_2 & a_{22} & a_{23} & \cdots & a_{2n} \\ \vdots & \vdots & \vdots & \ddots & \vdots \\ b_n & a_{n2} & a_{n3} & \cdots & a_{nn} \end{bmatrix}. \tag{A.23}$$

If the vector b consists entirely of zeros we call the system *homogeneous*. If $|A| \neq 0$ then the unique solution to the matrix equation is the trivial one: $x = A^{-1}b = 0$. The only way to get a non-trivial solution to a homogeneous system is if the coefficient matrix is singular, i.e. if $|A| = 0$. In that case Cramer's Rule cannot be used. An infinite number of solutions nevertheless exist (including the trivial one) in that case. Take, for example, the following homogeneous system:

$$\begin{bmatrix} 1 & 2 \\ 2 & 4 \end{bmatrix} \begin{bmatrix} x_1 \\ x_2 \end{bmatrix} = \begin{bmatrix} 0 \\ 0 \end{bmatrix}. \tag{A.24}$$

Clearly, $|A| = 4 - 4 = 0$ so the system is singular (row 2 is two times row 1). Nevertheless, both the trivial solution ($x_1 = x_2 = 0$) and an infinite number of non-trivial solutions (any combination for which $x_1 + 2x_2 = 0$) exist. Intuitively, we have infinitely many solutions because we have a single equation but two unknowns.

A.2.6 Characteristic roots and vectors

A characteristic vector of an n by n matrix A is a non-zero vector x which, when premultiplied by A yields a multiple of the same vector:

$$Ax = \lambda x, \tag{A.25}$$

where λ is called the *characteristic root* (or *eigenvalue*) of A. By rewriting equation (A.25) we find:

$$(A - \lambda I)x = 0, \tag{A.26}$$

which constitutes a homogeneous system of equations which has non-trivial solutions provided the determinant of its coefficient matrix, $A - \lambda I$, is zero:

$$\Phi(\lambda) \equiv |A - \lambda I| = 0. \tag{A.27}$$

Note that $\Phi(\lambda)$ is called the *characteristic equation* of A. For a 2 by 2 matrix the characteristic equation can be written as:

$$\Phi(\lambda) \equiv |A - \lambda I| = \begin{vmatrix} a_{11} - \lambda & a_{12} \\ a_{21} & a_{22} - \lambda \end{vmatrix} = (\lambda - a_{11})(\lambda - a_{22}) - a_{12}a_{21}$$

$$= \lambda^2 - (a_{11} + a_{22})\lambda + a_{11}a_{22} - a_{12}a_{21}$$

$$= \lambda^2 - \text{tr}(A)\lambda + |A| = 0, \qquad (\text{A.28})$$

where $\text{tr}(A)$ and $|A|$ are, respectively, the trace and the determinant of matrix A. Hence, for such a matrix the characteristic equation is quadratic in λ and thus possesses two roots:

$$\lambda_{1,2} = \frac{\text{tr}(A) \pm \sqrt{[\text{tr}(A)]^2 - 4|A|}}{2}. \qquad (\text{A.29})$$

These roots are distinct if the discriminant, $[\text{tr}(A)]^2 - 4|A|$, is non-zero. They are real (rather than complex) if the discriminant is positive (this is certainly the case if $|A| < 0$). For an n by n matrix the characteristic equation is an n-th order polynomial with n roots, $\lambda_1, \lambda_2, ..., \lambda_n$, which may not all be distinct or real. Some properties of characteristic roots are:

$$\begin{aligned} \sum_{i=1}^{n} \lambda_i &= \text{tr}(A), \\ \prod_{i=1}^{n} \lambda_i &= |A|. \end{aligned} \qquad (\text{A.30})$$

Associated with each characteristic root is a *characteristic vector* (or *eigenvector*), which is unique up to a constant. The characteristic vector $x^{(i)}$ associated with λ_i solves (A.26). If a matrix has distinct characteristic roots then it can be *diagonalized* as follows:

$$P^{-1}AP = \Lambda \quad \Leftrightarrow \quad A = P\Lambda P^{-1}, \qquad (\text{A.31})$$

where P is the matrix with the characteristic vectors, $x^{(i)}$, as columns and Λ is the diagonal matrix with characteristic roots, λ_i, on the principal diagonal. Diagonalization is useful in the context of difference and differential equations—see Section 2.2 and below.

Intermezzo A.2

Eigenvalues, eigenvectors, and matrix diagonalization. Suppose that A is defined as:

$$A = \begin{bmatrix} 6 & 10 \\ -2 & -3 \end{bmatrix}.$$

The characteristic equation is $\lambda^2 - 3\lambda + 2 = (\lambda - 1)(\lambda - 2) = 0$ so that the characteristic roots are $\lambda_1 = 1$ and $\lambda_2 = 2$. The characteristic vector associated with λ_1 is obtained by noting from (A.26) that:

$$(\lambda_1 I - A)x = 0$$

$$\left(\begin{bmatrix} 1 & 0 \\ 0 & 1 \end{bmatrix} - \begin{bmatrix} 6 & 10 \\ -2 & -3 \end{bmatrix} \right) \begin{bmatrix} x_1 \\ x_2 \end{bmatrix} = \begin{bmatrix} 0 \\ 0 \end{bmatrix}$$

$$\begin{bmatrix} -5 & -10 \\ 2 & 4 \end{bmatrix} \begin{bmatrix} x_1 \\ x_2 \end{bmatrix} = \begin{bmatrix} 0 \\ 0 \end{bmatrix}.$$

Any solution for which $2x_1 + 4x_2 = 0$ will do. Hence, by setting $x_1 = c$ (a non-zero constant) we find that $x_2 = -c/2$ so that the characteristic vector associated with λ_1 is:

$$x^{(1)} \equiv \begin{bmatrix} c \\ -c/2 \end{bmatrix}.$$

Similarly, for $\lambda_2 = 2$ we find:

$$(\lambda_2 I - A)x = 0$$

$$\left(\begin{bmatrix} 2 & 0 \\ 0 & 2 \end{bmatrix} - \begin{bmatrix} 6 & 10 \\ -2 & -3 \end{bmatrix} \right) \begin{bmatrix} x_1 \\ x_2 \end{bmatrix} = \begin{bmatrix} 0 \\ 0 \end{bmatrix}$$

$$\begin{bmatrix} -4 & -10 \\ 2 & 5 \end{bmatrix} \begin{bmatrix} x_1 \\ x_2 \end{bmatrix} = \begin{bmatrix} 0 \\ 0 \end{bmatrix}.$$

Any combination for which $2x_1 + 5x_2 = 0$ will do. Hence, the characteristic vector associated with λ_2 is:

$$x^{(2)} \equiv \begin{bmatrix} c \\ -2c/5 \end{bmatrix}.$$

In the example matrix we have:

$$P \equiv \begin{bmatrix} c & c \\ -c/2 & -2c/5 \end{bmatrix} \quad \text{and} \quad \Lambda \equiv \begin{bmatrix} 1 & 0 \\ 0 & 2 \end{bmatrix},$$

from which we verify the result:

$$P\Lambda P^{-1} = \frac{10}{c^2} \begin{bmatrix} c & c \\ -c/2 & -2c/5 \end{bmatrix} \begin{bmatrix} 1 & 0 \\ 0 & 2 \end{bmatrix} \begin{bmatrix} -2c/5 & -c \\ c/2 & c \end{bmatrix}$$

$$= 10 \begin{bmatrix} 1 & 1 \\ -1/2 & -2/5 \end{bmatrix} \begin{bmatrix} 1 & 0 \\ 0 & 2 \end{bmatrix} \begin{bmatrix} -2/5 & -1 \\ 1/2 & 1 \end{bmatrix}$$

$$= 10 \begin{bmatrix} 1 & 2 \\ -1/2 & -4/5 \end{bmatrix} \begin{bmatrix} -2/5 & -1 \\ 1/2 & 1 \end{bmatrix} = 10 \begin{bmatrix} 3/5 & 1 \\ -1/5 & -3/10 \end{bmatrix}$$

$$= A.$$

It works!

****

A.2.7   Literature

Basic: Klein (1998, chs. 4–5), Chiang (1984, chs. 4–5), Sydsæter and Hammond (1995, chs. 12–14). Intermediate: Intriligator (1971, appendix B), Kreyszig (1999, chs. 6–7), and Strang (1988). Advanced: Ayres (1974), Lancaster and Tismenetsky (1985), and Ortega (1987).

A.3   Implicit function theorem

A.3.1   Single equation

Throughout the text we make extensive use of the implicit function trick. For example, in Chapter 1 (equation (1.4)) we find that the short-run profit maximizing demand for labour is such that the marginal product of labour is equal to the real wage rate:

$$F_N(N, \bar{K}) = w, \tag{A.32}$$

where $F(N, \bar{K})$ is a constant-returns-to-scale production function, $F_N(N, \bar{K}) \equiv \partial F(N, \bar{K})/ \partial N$ is the marginal product of labour, $\bar{K}$ is the fixed capital stock, and w is the real wage rate. Mathematically, equation (A.32) constitutes a relationship between N, $\bar{K}$, and w. All the equation says is that these three variables are related to each other. An economist, however, typically wants to know, for example, how labour demand N depends on w and $\bar{K}$. The way to squeeze out the desired information (and the key to the implicit function trick) is to totally differentiate (A.32) with respect to all its arguments:

$$F_{NN}dN + F_{NK}d\bar{K} = dw. \tag{A.33}$$

If we want to know how N depends on w we keep $\bar{K}$ constant ($d\bar{K} = 0$) and rewrite (A.33) as:

$$F_{NN}\partial N = \partial w \qquad \Leftrightarrow \qquad \frac{\partial N}{\partial w} = \frac{1}{F_{NN}}, \tag{A.34}$$

where we use ∂ instead of d because this is a *partial* effect of w on N (since $\bar{K}$ is held constant). Similarly, by holding w constant (and setting $dw = 0$) we can obtain the partial effect of $\bar{K}$ on N from (A.33):

$$F_{NN}\partial N = -F_{NK}\partial \bar{K} \qquad \Leftrightarrow \qquad \frac{\partial N}{\partial \bar{K}} = -\frac{F_{NK}}{F_{NN}}. \tag{A.35}$$

This trick is great! What it tells us is that (A.32) apparently defines an *implicit function* between N and $(w, \bar{K})$ whose partial derivatives are given by, respectively (A.34) and (A.35). Of course, (A.32) also implies an implicit function relating $\bar{K}$ to (w, N) and another one relating w to $(\bar{K}, N)$, and we can find the partial derivatives of these implicit functions in the same way. But economically, the one we were looking for was the implicit function relating labour demand to w and $\bar{K}$. Let us now generalize the trick somewhat.

Suppose we have the following equation relating the endogenous variable of interest, y, to one or more exogenous variables, x_i:

$$F(y, x_1, x_2, ..., x_m) = 0. \tag{A.36}$$

Assume that (a) F has continuous partial derivatives (denoted by $F_y \equiv \partial F/\partial y$, $F_j \equiv \partial F/\partial x_j$ for $j = 1, 2, ..., m$) and (b) $F_y \neq 0$ around a point (y^0, x_j^0) which satisfies (A.36). Then according to the *implicit function theorem*, there exists an m-dimensional neighbourhood of (x_j^0) in which y is an implicitly defined function of the exogenous variables:

$$y = f(x_1, x_2, ..., x_m). \tag{A.37}$$

The implicit function is continuous and has continuous partial derivatives, denoted by $f_j \equiv \partial f/\partial x_j$, which can be computed as follows:

$$\frac{\partial y}{\partial x_j} = f_j = -\frac{F_j}{F_y}, \quad \text{for } j = 1, 2, ..., m. \tag{A.38}$$

As an example, consider $F(y,x) = y^2 + x^2 - 9$. We find that $F_y = 2y$ and $F_x = 2x$, so that $\partial y/\partial x = -F_x/F_y = -x/y$ provided $y \neq 0$. Note that $F(y,x) = 0$ defines a circle around the origin with a ray of length 3. Evaluated at a particular point on the circle, say $y_0 = 1$ and $x_0 = +\sqrt{8}$, we know from the implicit function rule that $\partial y/\partial x = -F_x/F_y = -x_0/y_0 = -\sqrt{8}$ at that point.

A.3.2 System of equations

Next we consider the system of n equations in n endogenous variables $(y_1, y_2, ..., y_n)$:

$$
\begin{aligned}
F^1(y_1, y_2, ..., y_n; x_1, x_2, ..., x_m) &= 0, \\
F^2(y_1, y_2, ..., y_n; x_1, x_2, ..., x_m) &= 0, \\
&\vdots \quad = \quad \vdots, \\
F^n(y_1, y_2, ..., y_n; x_1, x_2, ..., x_m) &= 0.
\end{aligned}
\tag{A.39}
$$

We assume that (a) the functions F^i all have continuous partial derivatives with respect to all y_i and x_j and (b) at a point $(y_i^0; x_j^0)$ the following determinant (of the *Jacobian matrix*) is non-zero:

$$
|J| \equiv
\begin{vmatrix}
\partial F^1/\partial y_1 & \partial F^1/\partial y_2 & \cdots & \partial F^1/\partial y_n \\
\partial F^2/\partial y_1 & \partial F^2/\partial y_2 & \cdots & \partial F^2/\partial y_n \\
\vdots & \vdots & \ddots & \vdots \\
\partial F^n/\partial y_1 & \partial F^n/\partial y_2 & \cdots & \partial F^n/\partial y_n
\end{vmatrix}
\neq 0.
\tag{A.40}
$$

Then, according to the *generalized implicit function theorem* there exists an m-dimensional neighbourhood of (x_j^0) in which the variables y_i are implicitly defined functions of the exogenous variables:

$$
\begin{aligned}
y_1 &= f^1(x_1, x_2, ..., x_m), \\
y_2 &= f^2(x_1, x_2, ..., x_m), \\
&\vdots \quad = \quad \vdots, \\
y_n &= f^n(x_1, x_2, ..., x_m).
\end{aligned}
\tag{A.41}
$$

These implicit functions are continuous and have continuous partial derivatives, denoted by $f_j^i \equiv \partial f^i/\partial x_j$, which can be computed as follows:

$$
\frac{\partial y_i}{\partial x_j} = f_j^i = \frac{|J_j^i|}{|J|}, \quad \text{for } i = 1, 2, ..., n,
\tag{A.42}
$$

where J_j^i is the matrix obtained by replacing column i of matrix J by the following vector of partial derivatives:

$$
\begin{bmatrix}
-\partial F^1/\partial x_j \\
-\partial F^2/\partial x_j \\
\vdots \\
-\partial F^n/\partial x_j
\end{bmatrix}.
\tag{A.43}
$$

Intermezzo A.3

Generalized implicit function theorem: a macroeconomic application.
As an example, consider the IS-LM model:

$$Y = C(Y - T(Y)) + I(R) + G_0,$$
$$M_0 = L(R, Y),$$

where Y is output, C is consumption, I is investment, R is the interest rate, T is taxes. The endogenous variables are R and Y and the exogenous variables are government consumption G_0 and the money supply M_0. By differentiating with respect to G_0 we get:

$$\begin{bmatrix} 1 - C_{Y-T}(1 - T_Y) & -I_R \\ L_Y & L_R \end{bmatrix} \begin{bmatrix} \partial Y / \partial G_0 \\ \partial R / \partial G_0 \end{bmatrix} = \begin{bmatrix} 1 \\ 0 \end{bmatrix}.$$

The Jacobian determinant is:

$$|J| \equiv L_R [1 - C_{Y-T}(1 - T_Y)] + I_R L_Y < 0,$$

where the sign follows from the fact that both money demand and investment depend negatively on the interest rate ($L_R < 0$ and $I_R < 0$), the marginal propensity to consume and the marginal tax rate are between zero and unity (so that $0 < C_{Y-T}(1 - T_Y) < 1$), and money demand depends positively on output ($L_Y > 0$). By Cramer's Rule we get the partial derivatives:

$$\frac{\partial Y}{\partial G_0} = \frac{1}{|J|} \begin{vmatrix} 1 & -I_R \\ 0 & L_R \end{vmatrix} = \frac{L_R}{L_R [1 - C_{Y-T}(1 - T_Y)] + I_R L_Y} > 0$$

$$\frac{\partial R}{\partial G_0} = \frac{1}{|J|} \begin{vmatrix} 1 - C_{Y-T}(1 - T_Y) & 1 \\ L_Y & 0 \end{vmatrix}$$

$$= \frac{-L_Y}{L_R [1 - C_{Y-T}(1 - T_Y)] + I_R L_Y} > 0.$$

These expressions, of course, accord with intuition (see also Section 1.2.3 above).

****

A.3.3   Literature

Basic: Klein (1998, pp. 239–245), Chiang (1984, ch. 8), and Sydsæter and Hammond (1995, pp. 591–593). Advanced: de la Fuente (2000, ch. 5).

A.4   Static optimization

A.4.1   Unconstrained optimization

Suppose we wish to find an optimum (minimum or maximum) of the following function:

$$y = f(x), \tag{A.44}$$

where we assume that this function is continuous and possesses continuous derivatives. The necessary condition for a (relative) extremum of the function at point $x = x_0$ is

$$f'(x_0) = 0. \tag{A.45}$$

To test whether $f(x)$ attains a relative maximum or a relative minimum at $x = x_0$ we compute the second derivative. The second-order sufficient condition is:

$$\text{if } f''(x_0) \begin{Bmatrix} < \\ > \end{Bmatrix} 0, \quad f(x_0) \text{ is a relative } \begin{Bmatrix} \text{maximum} \\ \text{minimum} \end{Bmatrix}. \tag{A.46}$$

Now suppose that the function depends on n arguments (choice variables):

$$y = f(x_1, x_2, ..., x_n), \tag{A.47}$$

where $f(\cdot)$ is continuous and possesses continuous derivatives. The first-order necessary conditions for a relative extremum are:

$$f_i = 0, \quad i = 1, 2, ..., n, \tag{A.48}$$

where $f_i \equiv \partial f / \partial x_i$ are the partial derivatives of $f(\cdot)$ with respect to x_i. To study the second-order sufficient conditions we define the *Hessian matrix* of second-order derivatives, H:

$$\underset{n \times n}{H} \equiv \begin{bmatrix} f_{11} & f_{12} & \cdots & f_{1n} \\ f_{21} & f_{22} & \cdots & f_{2n} \\ \vdots & \vdots & \ddots & \vdots \\ f_{n1} & f_{n2} & \cdots & f_{nn} \end{bmatrix}, \tag{A.49}$$

where $f_{ii} \equiv \partial^2 f / \partial x_i^2$ and $f_{ij} \equiv \partial^2 f / \partial x_i \partial x_j$ are second-order partial derivatives. By Young's theorem we know that $f_{ij} = f_{ji}$ so the Hessian matrix is symmetric. We define the following set of leading principal minors of H, i.e. the sub-determinants along the main diagonal:

$$|H_1| \equiv f_{11}, \quad |H_2| \equiv \begin{vmatrix} f_{11} & f_{12} \\ f_{21} & f_{22} \end{vmatrix}, ..., |H_n| \equiv \begin{vmatrix} f_{11} & f_{12} & \cdots & f_{1n} \\ f_{21} & f_{22} & \cdots & f_{2n} \\ \vdots & \vdots & \ddots & \vdots \\ f_{n1} & f_{n2} & \cdots & f_{nn} \end{vmatrix}. \tag{A.50}$$

Then, provided the first-order conditions hold at a point $(x_1^0, x_2^0, .., x_n^0)$, the second-order sufficient condition for $f(x_i^0)$ to be a relative maximum is:

$$|H_1| < 0, |H_2| > 0, ..., (-1)^n |H_n| > 0, \tag{A.51}$$

whilst for a relative minimum the second-order sufficient condition is:

$$|H_1|, |H_2|, ..., |H_n| > 0. \tag{A.52}$$

See Chiang (1984, pp. 337–353) for the relation between concavity-convexity of $f(\cdot)$ and the second-order conditions.

A.4.2 Equality constraints

We focus on the case with multiple choice variables and a single equality constraint. As in the unconstrained case, the objective function is given by (A.47). The constraint is given by:

$$g(x_1, x_2, ..., x_n) = c, \tag{A.53}$$

where c is a constant. We assume that $g(\cdot)$ is continuous and possesses continuous derivatives. The *Lagrangian* is defined as follows:

$$\mathcal{L} \equiv f(x_1, x_2, ..., x_n) + \lambda \left[c - g(x_1, x_2, ..., x_n) \right], \tag{A.54}$$

where λ is the Lagrange multiplier. The first-order necessary conditions for an extremum are:

$$
\begin{aligned}
\mathcal{L}_i &= 0, \quad i = 1, 2, ..., n, \\
\mathcal{L}_\lambda &= 0,
\end{aligned}
\tag{A.55}
$$

where $\mathcal{L}_i \equiv \partial \mathcal{L} / \partial x_i$ and $\mathcal{L}_\lambda \equiv \partial \mathcal{L} / \partial \lambda$ are the partial derivatives of the Lagrangian with respect to x_i and λ, respectively. To study the second-order conditions we formulate a so-called *bordered Hessian matrix*, denoted by $\bar{H}$:

$$
\underset{(n+1) \times (n+1)}{\bar{H}} \equiv
\begin{bmatrix}
0 & g_1 & g_2 & \cdots & g_n \\
g_1 & f_{11} & f_{12} & \cdots & f_{1n} \\
g_2 & f_{21} & f_{22} & \cdots & f_{2n} \\
\vdots & \vdots & \vdots & \ddots & \vdots \\
g_n & f_{n1} & f_{n2} & \cdots & f_{nn}
\end{bmatrix}.
\tag{A.56}
$$

The bordered Hessian consists of the ordinary Hessian but with the borders made up of the derivatives of the constraint function (g_i). We define the following set of principal minors of $\bar{H}$:

$$
|\bar{H}_2| \equiv
\begin{vmatrix}
0 & g_1 & g_2 \\
g_1 & f_{11} & f_{12} \\
g_2 & f_{21} & f_{22}
\end{vmatrix}, ..., |H_n| \equiv
\begin{vmatrix}
0 & g_1 & g_2 & \cdots & g_n \\
g_1 & f_{11} & f_{12} & \cdots & f_{1n} \\
g_2 & f_{21} & f_{22} & \cdots & f_{2n} \\
\vdots & \vdots & \vdots & \ddots & \vdots \\
g_n & f_{n1} & f_{n2} & \cdots & f_{nn}
\end{vmatrix}.
\tag{A.57}
$$

Then provided the first-order conditions hold at a point $(x_1^0, x_2^0, ..., x_n^0)$ the second-order sufficient conditions for $f(x_i^0)$ to be a relative constrained maximum are:

$$(-1)^k |\bar{H}_k| > 0, \; k = 2, ..., n, \tag{A.58}$$

whilst the second-order conditions for a relative constrained minimum are:

$$|\bar{H}_k| < 0, \; k = 2, ..., n. \tag{A.59}$$

If there are multiple constraints then additional Lagrange multipliers are added to the Lagrangian (one per constraint) and the first-order condition for each Lagrange multiplier, λ_j, takes the form $\mathcal{L}_{\lambda_j} \equiv \partial \mathcal{L} / \partial \lambda_j = 0$. See Chiang (1984, pp. 385–386) for the appropriately defined bordered Hessian for the multi-constraint case.

A.4.2.1 Interpretation of the Lagrange multiplier

We now return to the single constraint case in order to demonstrate the interpretation of the Lagrange multiplier in the optimum. Using the superscript "0" to denote optimized values, we can write the optimized value of the Lagrangian as:

$$\mathcal{L}^0 \equiv f(x_1^0, x_2^0, ..., x_n^0) + \lambda^0 \left[c - g(x_1^0, x_2^0, ..., x_n^0) \right]. \tag{A.60}$$

Next, we ask the question what happens if the constraint is changed marginally. Obviously, both λ^0 and x_i^0 are expected to change if c does. Differentiating (A.60) we get:

$$\frac{d\mathcal{L}^0}{dc} = \sum_{i=1}^{n} \mathcal{L}_i \cdot \frac{dx_i^0}{dc} + \mathcal{L}_\lambda \cdot \frac{d\lambda^0}{dc} + \lambda^0 \cdot \frac{dc}{dc} = \lambda^0, \tag{A.61}$$

where we have used the necessary conditions for an optimum ($\mathcal{L}_\lambda = \mathcal{L}_i = 0$ for $i = 1, 2, ..., n$) to get from the first to the second equality. Recall that the constraint holds with equality ($c = g(\cdot)$) so that λ^0 measures the effect of a small change in c on the optimized value of the objective function $f(\cdot)$. For example, if the objective function is utility and c is income, then λ^0 is the marginal utility of income.

A.4.3 Inequality constraints

We now briefly study some key results from non-linear programming. We first look at the simplest case with non-negativity constraints on the choice variables. Then we take up the more challenging case of general inequalities. We focus on first-order conditions and ignore some of the subtleties involved (like constraint qualifications and second-order conditions).

A.4.3.1 Non-negativity constraints

Suppose that the issue is to maximize a function $y = f(x)$ subject only to the non-negativity constraint $x \geq 0$. There are three situations which can arise. These have been illustrated in Figure A.1 which is taken from Chiang (1984, p. 723).

Panel (a) shows the case we have studied in detail above—see section A.4.1. The function attains a maximum for a strictly positive value of x. We call this an *interior solution* because the solution lies entirely within the feasible region (and not on a boundary). The constraint $x \geq 0$ is *non-binding* and the first-order condition is as before:

$$f'(x_0) = 0. \qquad\qquad \text{(interior solution)}$$

Panels (b) and (c) deal with two types of *boundary solutions*. In panel (b) the function happens to attain a maximum for $x = x_0 = 0$, i.e. exactly on the boundary of the feasible region. In panel (b) we thus have:

$$f'(x_0) = 0 \text{ and } x_0 = 0. \qquad\qquad \text{(boundary solution)}$$

Finally, in panel (c) we also have a boundary solution but one for which the function $f(x)$ continues to rise for negative (infeasible) values of x. Hence, at that point we have:

$$f'(x_0) < 0 \text{ and } x_0 = 0. \qquad\qquad \text{(boundary solution)}$$

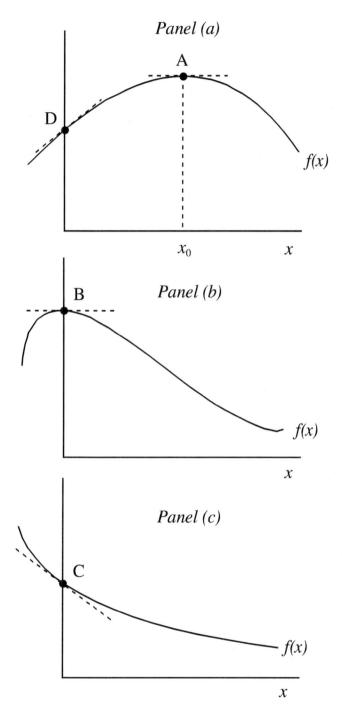

Figure A.1: Non-negativity constraints

These three conditions, covering the interior solution and both types of boundary solutions, can be combined in a single statement:

$$f'(x_0) \leq 0, \quad x_0 \geq 0, \quad x_0 f'(x_0) = 0. \tag{A.62}$$

There are two key things to note about this statement. First, as is evident from Figure A.1, we can safely exclude the case of $f'(x_0) > 0$ from consideration. If $f'(x_0) > 0$ even for $x_0 = 0$ then this can never be a maximum as raising x by a little would also raise the objective function (see point D in panel (a)). The second key result concerns the third condition in (A.62), saying that at least one of x_0 or $f'(x_0)$ must be zero.

When there are n choice variables the problem becomes one of choosing x_i ($i = 1, 2, ..., n$) in order to maximize $f(x_1, x_2, ..., x_n)$ subject to the non-negativity constraints $x_i \geq 0$ ($i = 1, 2, ..., n$). The first-order conditions associated with this problem are straightforward generalizations of (A.62):

$$f_i \leq 0, \quad x_i \geq 0, \quad x_i f'(x_i) = 0, \quad i = 1, 2, ..., n. \tag{A.63}$$

A.4.3.2 General inequality constraints

Suppose that the objective function is given by (A.47), the non-negativety constraints are $x_i \geq 0$, and the set of non-linear constraints is given by:

$$\begin{aligned} g^1(x_1, x_2, ..., x_n) &\leq c_1, \\ g^2(x_1, x_2, ..., x_n) &\leq c_2, \\ \vdots \quad &\leq \quad \vdots \\ g^m(x_1, x_2, ..., x_n) &\leq c_m, \end{aligned} \tag{A.64}$$

where c_j are constants and the $g^j(\cdot)$ functions are continuous and possess continuous derivatives ($j = 1, 2, ..., m$). The Lagrangian associated with the problem is:

$$\mathcal{L} \equiv f(x_1, x_2, ..., x_n) + \sum_{j=1}^{m} \lambda_j \left[c_j - g^j(x_1, x_2, ..., x_n) \right], \tag{A.65}$$

where λ_j is the Lagrange multiplier associated with the inequality constraint $c_j \geq g^j(\cdot)$. The first-order conditions for a constrained maximum are:

$$\begin{aligned} \mathcal{L}_i \leq 0 \quad x_i \geq 0 \quad x_i \mathcal{L}_i = 0 \quad i = 1, 2, ..., n, \\ \mathcal{L}_{\lambda_j} \geq 0 \quad \lambda_j \geq 0 \quad \lambda_j \mathcal{L}_{\lambda_j} = 0 \quad j = 1, 2, ..., m, \end{aligned} \tag{A.66}$$

where $\mathcal{L}_i \equiv \partial \mathcal{L} / \partial x_i$ and $\mathcal{L}_{\lambda_j} \equiv \partial \mathcal{L} / \partial \lambda_j$.

For a minimization problem, the Lagrangian is the same as before but the first-order conditions are:

$$\begin{aligned} \mathcal{L}_i \geq 0 \quad x_i \geq 0 \quad x_i \mathcal{L}_i = 0 \quad i = 1, 2, ..., n, \\ \mathcal{L}_{\lambda_j} \leq 0 \quad \lambda_j \geq 0 \quad \lambda_j \mathcal{L}_{\lambda_j} = 0 \quad j = 1, 2, ..., m. \end{aligned} \tag{A.67}$$

We refer the reader to Chiang (1984, pp. 731–755) for a detailed discussion of second-order conditions and the restrictions that the constraint functions must satisfy (the so-called constraint qualification proviso).

A.4.4 Literature

Basic: Klein (1998, chs. 9–11), Chiang (1984, chs. 9–12, 21), and Sydsæter and Hammond (1995, chs. 17–18). Intermediate: Dixit (1990, chs. 2–8) and Intriligator (1971, chs 2–4). Advanced: de la Fuente (2000, chs. 7–8).

A.5 Single differential equations

In this section we show how to solve the most commonly encountered differential equations. We follow standard procedure in the economics literature by using the Newtonian 'dot' notation to indicate derivatives with respect to time, i.e. $\dot{y}(t) \equiv dy(t)/dt$ and $\ddot{y}(t) \equiv d^2y(t)/dt^2$ etc.

A.5.1 First-order (constant coefficients)

A.5.1.1 Homogeneous

Suppose we have the following differential equation in $y(t)$:

$$\dot{y}(t) + ay(t) = 0, \tag{A.68}$$

where a is a constant. This is called a *homogeneous* differential equation because the constant on the right-hand side is zero. To solve this equation, we must find a path for $y(t)$, such that the exponential rate of growth in $y(t)$ is constant, i.e. $\dot{y}(t)/y(t) = -a$. Since growth must be exponential it is logical to try a solution of the exponential type:

$$y(t) = Ae^{\alpha t}, \tag{A.69}$$

where $A \neq 0$ and α are constants to be determined. Clearly the trial solution must solve (A.68). This implies that:

$$\alpha Ae^{\alpha t} + aAe^{\alpha t} = 0$$
$$(\alpha + a)\,Ae^{\alpha t} = 0 \quad \Rightarrow \quad \alpha = -a, \tag{A.70}$$

where the result follows from the fact that $Ae^{\alpha t} \neq 0$. Suppose we are also given an initial value for $y(t)$, say $y(0) = y_0$ (a constant). Then it follows from our trial solution, $y(t) = Ae^{-at}$, that $y(0) = A = y_0$ (since $e^{-at} = 1$ for $t = 0$) so that the full solution of the homogeneous differential equation is:

$$y(t) = y_0 e^{-at}. \tag{A.71}$$

A.5.1.2 Non-homogeneous

Now suppose that the differential equation is non-homogeneous:

$$\dot{y}(t) + ay(t) = b, \qquad y(t) \neq 0, \tag{A.72}$$

where $b \neq 0$. We look for the solution in two steps. First we find the *complementary function*, $y_C(t)$, which is the path for $y(t)$ which solves the homogeneous part of the differential equation. Next, we find the so-called *particular solution*, $y_P(t)$, to the general equation. By adding the complementary function and the particular solution we obtain the general solution. In case we want to impose an initial condition this can be done after the general solution is found.

Since the complementary function solves the homogeneous part of the differential equation it makes sense to try $y_C(t) = Ae^{-at}$. The particular integral is found by trial and error starting with the simplest possible case. Try $y_P(t) = k$ (a constant) and substitute it in the differential equation:

$$\dot{y}_P(t) + ay_P(t) = b$$

$$0 + ak = b \quad \Rightarrow \quad k = \frac{b}{a} \quad \text{(for } a \neq 0\text{)}. \tag{A.73}$$

Hence, provided $a \neq 0$, our simplest trial solution works and the general solution is given by:

$$y(t) \, [= y_C(t) + y_P(t)] = Ae^{-at} + \frac{b}{a} \quad \text{(for } a \neq 0\text{)}. \tag{A.74}$$

If we have the initial condition $y(0) = y_0$ (as before) then we find that $A = y_0 - b/a$.

What if $a = 0$? In that case the complementary function is $y_C(t) = Ae^{-0t} = A$, a constant, so it makes no sense to assume that the particular solution is also a constant. Instead we guess that $y_P(t) = kt$ (a time trend). Substituting it in the differential equation (A.68) (with $a = 0$ imposed) we obtain:

$$\dot{y}_P(t) + ay_P(t) = b \quad \Rightarrow \quad k = b \text{ (for } a = 0\text{)}. \tag{A.75}$$

Hence, the trial works and the general solution is:

$$y(t) = A + bt, \quad \text{(for } a = 0\text{)}. \tag{A.76}$$

(Imposing the initial condition $y(0) = y_0$ we obtain that $A = y_0$.) The thing to note about the general solution is that we could have obtained it by straightforward integration. Indeed, by rewriting (A.72) and setting $a = 0$ we get $dy(t) = bdt$ which can be integrated:

$$\int dy(t) = \int bdt \quad \Rightarrow y(t) = A + bt, \tag{A.77}$$

where A is the constant of integration. Of course, equations (A.76) and (A.77) are the same but in the derivation of the latter no inspired guessing is needed.

A.5.2   First-order (variable coefficients)

Assume that the differential equation has the following form:

$$\dot{y}(t) + a(t)y(t) = b(t), \tag{A.78}$$

where a and b are now both functions of time. Though the expression does not have constant coefficients it is nevertheless linear in the unknown function $y(t)$ and its time derivative $\dot{y}(t)$. This linearity property makes the solution relatively straightforward. We first solve the homogeneous equation for which $b(t) \equiv 0$. Assuming that $a(t)$ is continuous and $y(t) \neq 0$ we can rewrite equation (A.78) as:

$$\frac{dy(t)/dt}{y(t)} = -a(t), \tag{A.79}$$

from which we conclude that:

$$\ln|y(t)| = A - \int a(t)dt, \tag{A.80}$$

where we have used the fact that $\int dy(t)/y(t) = \ln|y(t)|$ and where A is the constant of integration. Assuming that $y(t) > 0$, as is often the case in economic applications, we find that the general solution for $y(t)$ is:

$$y(t) = Ae^{-\int a(t)dt}. \tag{A.81}$$

The non-homogeneous equation (A.78) can also be solved readily because it possesses an *integrating factor*, $e^{F(t)}$, where $F(t)$ is given by:

$$F(t) \equiv \int a(t)dt. \tag{A.82}$$

First we note the following result:

$$\frac{d}{dt}\left[e^{F(t)}y(t)\right] = e^{F(t)}\dot{y}(t) + y(t)e^{F(t)}\dot{F}(t) = e^{F(t)}\left[\dot{y}(t) + a(t)y(t)\right], \tag{A.83}$$

where we have used the fact that $\dot{F}(t) = a(t)$. Next, by multiplying both sides of (A.78) by the integrating factor $e^{F(t)}$ and using (A.83) we obtain:

$$\frac{d}{dt}\left[e^{F(t)}y(t)\right] = b(t)e^{F(t)}. \tag{A.84}$$

Finally, by integrating both sides of (A.84) we obtain:

$$e^{F(t)}y(t) = A + \int b(t)e^{F(t)}dt \implies$$

$$y(t) = e^{-F(t)}\left[A + \int b(t)e^{F(t)}dt\right], \tag{A.85}$$

where A is again the constant of integration.

A.5.3 Leibnitz's rule

In the text we occasionally make use of *Leibnitz's rule* for differentiation under the integral sign (Spiegel, 1974, p. 163). Suppose that the function $f(x)$ is defined as follows:

$$f(x) \equiv \int_{u_1(x)}^{u_2(x)} g(t,x)dt, \qquad a \leq x \leq b. \tag{A.86}$$

Then, if (i) $g(t,x)$ and $\partial g/\partial x$ are continuous in both t and x (in some region including $u_1 \leq t \leq u_2$ and $a \leq x \leq b$) and (ii) $u_1(x)$ and $u_2(x)$ are continuous and have continuous derivatives (for $a \leq x \leq b$), then df/dx is given by:

$$\frac{df(x)}{dx} = \int_{u_1(x)}^{u_2(x)} \frac{\partial g(t,x)}{\partial x}dt + g(u_2,x)\frac{du_2}{dx} - g(u_1,x)\frac{du_1}{dx}. \tag{A.87}$$

Often u_1 and/or u_2 are constants so that one or both of the last two terms on the right-hand side of (A.87) vanish. See also Sydsæter and Hammond (1995, pp. 547–549) for examples of Leibnitz's rule.

A.5.4 Literature

Basic: Klein (1998, ch. 14), Chiang (1984, chs. 13–15), Sydsæter and Hammond (1995, ch. 21). Intermediate: Apostol (1967, ch. 8), Kreyszig (1999, chs. 1–5), Boyce and DiPrima (2005), and de la Fuente (2000, chs. 9–11).

A.6   Systems of differential equations

The main purpose of this section is to demonstrate how useful Laplace transform techniques can be to (macro) economists. Whilst the technique is not much more difficult than the method of comparative statics—that most students are familiar with—it enables one to study thoroughly (the properties of) low-dimensional[1] dynamic models in an analytical fashion.

A.6.1   The Laplace transform

The Laplace transform is a tool used extensively in engineering contexts and a very good source is the engineering mathematics textbook by Kreyszig (1999). The Laplace transform is extremely useful for solving (systems of) differential equations. Intuitively, the method works in three steps: (i) the difficult problem is transformed into a simple problem, (ii) we use (matrix) algebra to solve the simple problem, and (iii) we invert ("transform back") the solution obtained in step (ii) to obtain the ultimate solution of our hard problem. Instead of having to work with difficult operations in calculus we work with algebraic operations on transforms. This is why the Laplace transform technique is called *operational calculus*.

The major advantage of the Laplace transform technique lies in the ease with which time-varying shocks can be studied. In economic terms this makes it very easy to identify the propagation mechanism that is contained in the economic model. As we demonstrate in Chapter 18 this is important, for example, in models in the real business cycle (RBC) tradition.

Suppose that $f(t)$ is a function defined for $t \geq 0$. Then we can define the Laplace transform of that function as follows:[2]

$$\mathcal{L}\{f,s\} \equiv \int_0^\infty e^{-st} f(t) dt. \tag{A.88}$$

In economic terms $\mathcal{L}\{f,s\}$ is the discounted present value of the function $f(t)$, from present to the indefinite future, using s as the discount rate. Clearly, provided the integral on the right-hand side of (A.88) exists, $\mathcal{L}\{f,s\}$ is well-defined and can be seen as a function of s.

Here are some simple examples. Suppose that $f(t) = 1$ for $t \geq 0$. What is $\mathcal{L}\{f,s\}$? We use the definition in (A.88) to get:

$$\mathcal{L}\{f,s\} = \mathcal{L}\{1,s\} = \int_0^\infty 1 \cdot e^{-st} dt = -\frac{1}{s} e^{-st} \Big|_0^\infty = \frac{1}{s},$$

for $s > 0$. We have found our first Laplace transform, i.e. $\mathcal{L}\{1,s\} = 1/s$. Despite the ease with which it was derived, the transform of unity, $\mathcal{L}\{1,s\}$, is an extremely useful one to remember. Let us now try to find a more challenging one. Suppose that $f(t) = e^{at}$ for $t \geq 0$. What is $\mathcal{L}\{f,s\}$? We once again use the definition in (A.88) and get:

$$\mathcal{L}\{f,s\} = \mathcal{L}\{e^{at},s\} = \int_0^\infty e^{at} e^{-st} dt = \int_0^\infty e^{-(s-a)t} dt$$

---

[1] By "low dimensional" we mean that the characteristic polynomial of the Jacobian matrix of the system must be of order four or less. For such polynomials closed-form solutions for the roots are available. For higher-order polynomials Abel's theorem proves that finite algebraic formulae do not exist for the roots. See the amusing historical overview of this issue in Turnbull (1988, pp. 114–115).

[2] Some authors prefer to use the notation $F(s)$ for the Laplace transform of $f(t)$. Yet others use notation similar to ours but suppress the s argument and write $\mathcal{L}\{f\}$ for the Laplace transform of $f(t)$. We adopt our elaborate notation since we shall need to evaluate the transforms for particular values of s below.

Table A.1. Commonly used Laplace transforms

$f(t)$	$\mathcal{L}\{f,s\}$	valid for:
1	$\frac{1}{s}$	$s > 0$
t	$\frac{1}{s^2}$	$s > 0$
$\frac{t^{n-1}}{(n-1)!}$	$\frac{1}{s^n}$	$n = 1, 2, ...; s > 0$
e^{at}	$\frac{1}{s-a}$	$s > a$
te^{at}	$\frac{1}{(s-a)^2}$	$s > a$
$\frac{t^{n-1}e^{at}}{(n-1)!}$	$\frac{1}{(s-a)^n}$	$n = 1, 2, ...; s > a$
$\frac{e^{at}-e^{bt}}{a-b}$	$\frac{1}{(s-a)(s-b)}$	$s > a, s > b, a \neq b$
$\frac{ae^{at}-be^{bt}}{a-b}$	$\frac{s}{(s-a)(s-b)}$	$s > a, s > b, a \neq b$
$\mathcal{U}(t - a) \equiv \begin{cases} 0 & \text{for } 0 \leq t < a \\ 1 & \text{for } t > a \end{cases}$	$\frac{e^{-as}}{s}$	

$$= -\frac{1}{s-a}e^{-(s-a)t}\Big|_0^\infty = \frac{1}{s-a},$$

provided $s > a$ (otherwise the integral does not exist and the Laplace transform is not defined).

So now we have found our second Laplace transform and in fact we already possess the two transforms used most often in economic contexts. Of course there are very many functions for which the technical work has been done already by others and the Laplace transforms are known. In Table A.1 we show a list of commonly used transforms. Such a table is certainly quite valuable but even more useful are the *general properties* of Laplace transforms which allow us to work with them in an algebraic fashion. Let us look at some of the main properties.

Property 1 *Linearity. The Laplace transform is a linear operator. Hence, if the Laplace transforms of $f(t)$ and $g(t)$ both exist, then we have for any constants a and b that:*

$$\mathcal{L}\{af + bg, s\} = a\mathcal{L}\{f, s\} + b\mathcal{L}\{g, s\}. \tag{P1}$$

The proof is too obvious to worry about.

The usefulness of (P1) is easily demonstrated: it allows us to deduce more complex transforms from simple transforms. Suppose that we are given a Laplace transform and want to figure out the function in the time domain which is associated with it. Assume that $\mathcal{L}\{f, s\} = \frac{1}{(s-a)(s-b)}$, $a \neq b$. What is $f(t)$? We use the method of partial fractions to split up the Laplace transform:

$$\frac{1}{(s-a)(s-b)} = \frac{1}{a-b}\left[\frac{1}{s-a} - \frac{1}{s-b}\right]. \tag{A.89}$$

Now we apply (P1) to equation (A.89)—which is in a format we know—and derive:

$$\mathcal{L}\{f, s\} = \frac{1}{a-b}\left[\frac{1}{s-a} - \frac{1}{s-b}\right] = \frac{1}{a-b}\left[\mathcal{L}\{e^{at}, s\} - \mathcal{L}\{e^{bt}, s\}\right], \tag{A.90}$$

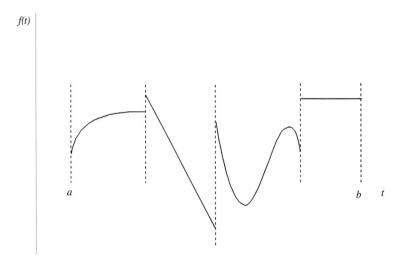

Figure A.2: Piecewise continuous function

where we have used Table A.1 to get to the final expression. But (A.90) can now be inverted to get our answer:

$$f(t) = \frac{e^{at} - e^{bt}}{a - b}. \tag{A.91}$$

This entry is also found in Table A.1.

But we have now performed an operation (inverting a Laplace transform) for which we have not yet established the formal validity. Clearly, going from (A.91) to (A.90) is valid but is it also allowed to go from (A.90) to (A.91), i.e. is the Laplace transform unique? The answer is "no" in general but "yes" for all cases of interest. Kreyszig (1999, p. 256) states the following sufficient condition for existence.

Property 2 *Existence. (P2) Let $f(t)$ be a function that is piecewise continuous on every finite interval in the range $t \geq 0$ and satisfies:*

$$|f(t)| \leq M e^{\gamma t},$$

for all $t \geq 0$ and for some constants γ and M. Then the Laplace transform exists for all $s > \gamma$.

With "piecewise continuous" we mean that, on a finite interval $a \leq t \leq b$, $f(t)$ is defined on that interval and is such that the interval can be subdivided into finitely many sub-intervals in each of which $f(t)$ is continuous and has finite limits (Kreyszig, 1999, p. 255). Figure A.2 gives an example of a piecewise continuous function. The requirement mentioned in the property statement is that $f(t)$ is of exponential order γ as $t \to \infty$. Functions of exponential order cannot grow in absolute value more rapidly than $M e^{\gamma t}$ as t gets large. But since M and γ can be as large as desired the requirement is not much of a restriction (Spiegel, 1965, p. 2).

Armed with these results we derive the next properties. The first one says that discounting very heavily will wipe out the integral (and thus the Laplace transform) of any function of exponential order. The second one settles the uniqueness issue.

Property 3 *If $\mathcal{L}\{f, s\}$ is the Laplace transform of $f(t)$, then:*

$$\lim_{s \to \infty} \mathcal{L}\{f, s\} = 0. \tag{P3}$$

Property 4 *Unique inversion [Lerch's theorem]. (P4) If we restrict ourselves to functions $f(t)$ which are piecewise continuous in every finite interval $0 \le t \le N$ and of exponential order for $t > N$, then the inverse Laplace transform of $\mathcal{L}\{f, s\}$, denoted by $\mathcal{L}^{-1}\{\mathcal{L}\{f, s\}\} = f(t)$, is unique.*

Let us now push on and study one more property that will prove rather useful later on.

Property 5 *Transform of a derivative. If $f(t)$ is continuous for $0 \le t \le N$ and of exponential order γ for $t > N$ and $f'(t)$ is piecewise continuous for $0 \le t \le N$ then:*

$$\mathcal{L}\{\dot{f}, s\} = s\mathcal{L}\{f, s\} - f(0), \tag{P5}$$

for $s > \gamma$.

PROOF: Note that we state and prove the property for the simple case with $f(t)$ continuous for $t \ge 0$. Then we have by definition:[3]

$$\mathcal{L}\{\dot{f}, s\} = \int_0^\infty e^{-st} \dot{f}(t)dt$$

$$= e^{-st}f(t)\big|_0^\infty + s\int_0^\infty e^{-st}f(t)dt$$

$$= \lim_{t \to \infty} e^{-st}f(t) - f(0) + s\mathcal{L}\{f, s\}.$$

But for $s > \gamma$ the discounting by s dominates the exponential order of $f(t)$ so that $\lim_{t \to \infty} e^{-st}f(t) = 0$ and the result follows.

Of course, we can use (P5) repeatedly. For second- and third-order time derivatives of $f(t)$ we obtain:

Property 6

$$\mathcal{L}\{\ddot{f}, s\} = s\mathcal{L}\{\dot{f}, s\} - \dot{f}(0) = s\left[s\mathcal{L}\{f, s\} - f(0)\right] - \dot{f}(0), \tag{P6}$$
$$\mathcal{L}\{\dddot{f}, s\} = s^3\mathcal{L}\{f, s\} - s^2 f(0) - s\dot{f}(0) - \ddot{f}(0).$$

We can now illustrate the usefulness of the properties deduced so far and introduce the three-step procedure mentioned above (on page 816) by means of the following prototypical example.

A.6.2   Simple applications

Suppose we have the following differential equation:

$$\ddot{y}(t) + 4\dot{y}(t) + 3y(t) = 0, \tag{A.92}$$

which must be solved subject to the initial conditions:

$$y(0) = 3, \quad \dot{y}(0) = 1. \tag{A.93}$$

Here goes the three-step procedure:

Step 1: Set up the subsidiary equation. By taking the Laplace transform of (A.92) and noting (P6) we get:

$$\mathcal{L}\{\ddot{y}, s\} + 4\mathcal{L}\{\dot{y}, s\} + 3\mathcal{L}\{y, s\} = 0 \iff$$

---

[3] We use integration by parts, i.e. $\int u\,dv = uv - \int v\,du$, and set $u = e^{-st}$ and $v = f(t)$.

$$\left[s^2 \mathcal{L}\{y,s\} - sy(0) - \dot{y}(0) \right] + 4 \left[s\mathcal{L}\{y,s\} - y(0) \right] + 3\mathcal{L}\{y,s\} = 0 \Leftrightarrow$$
$$\left[s^2 + 4s + 3 \right] \mathcal{L}\{y,s\} = (s+4)y(0) + \dot{y}(0). \tag{A.94}$$

By substituting (A.93) in (A.94) we obtain the *subsidiary equation* of the differential equation including its initial conditions.

$$\left[s^2 + 4s + 3 \right] \mathcal{L}\{y,s\} = 3s + 13. \tag{A.95}$$

Step 2: Solve the subsidiary equation. We now do the easy stuff of algebraically manipulating the expression (A.95) in s-space. We notice that the quadratic on the left-hand side of (A.95) can be written as $s^2 + 4s + 3 = (s+1)(s+3)$ so we can solve for $\mathcal{L}\{y,s\}$ quite easily:[4]

$$\begin{aligned} \mathcal{L}\{y,s\} &= \frac{3s+13}{(s+1)(s+3)} = \frac{3(s+1)+10}{(s+1)(s+3)} \\ &= \frac{3}{s+3} + \frac{10}{(s+1)(s+3)} \\ &= \frac{3}{s+3} + \frac{10}{3-1} \left[\frac{1}{s+1} - \frac{1}{s+3} \right] \\ &= \frac{5}{s+1} - \frac{2}{s+3}. \end{aligned} \tag{A.96}$$

Step 3: Invert the transform to get the solution of the given problem. We have now written the (Laplace transform of the) solution in terms of known transforms. Inversion of (A.96) is thus straightforward and results in:

$$y(t) = \mathcal{L}^{-1}\left\{ \mathcal{L}\{y,s\} \right\} = 5\mathcal{L}^{-1}\left\{ \frac{1}{s+1} \right\} - 2\mathcal{L}^{-1}\left\{ \frac{1}{s+3} \right\} = 5e^{-t} - 2e^{-3t}. \tag{A.97}$$

Of course we could have obtained this solution quite easily using the standard techniques so for this simple example the Laplace transform technique is not that useful. It has some value added but not a lot. The thing to note, however, is that the method is essentially unchanged for much more complex problems. We now study two such cases.

Assume that the differential equation (A.92) is replaced by:

$$\ddot{y}(t) + 4\dot{y}(t) + 3y(t) = g(t), \tag{A.98}$$

where $g(t)$ is some (piecewise continuous) *forcing function* which is time-dependent and has a unique Laplace transform $\mathcal{L}\{g,s\}$. The initial conditions continue to be as given in (A.93). Using the same procedure as before we derive the solution of the subsidiary equation in terms of the Laplace transforms:

$$\underbrace{\mathcal{L}\{y,s\}}_{\text{output}} = \underbrace{\frac{3s+13}{(s+1)(s+3)}}_{\text{initial conditions}} + \underbrace{\frac{\mathcal{L}\{g,s\}}{(s+1)(s+3)}}_{\text{input}}. \tag{A.99}$$

---

[4]We show the trivial steps leading to the final result in order to demonstrate that the algebra involved in s-space is indeed trivial. In general, the work involved in step 2 of the procedure is always easier than tackling the problem directly in t-space.

The first term on the right-hand side is the same as before (see (A.96)) and results from the initial conditions of the problem. The second term on the right-hand side represents the influence of the time-varying forcing term. Two further things must be noted about equation (A.99). First, the expression is perfectly general. A whole class of shock terms can be used in (A.99) to solve for $y(t)$ after inversion. Second, it should be noted that all of the model's dynamic properties are contained in the quadratic function appearing in the denominator. In fact, $H(s) \equiv \frac{1}{(s+1)(s+3)}$ is often referred to as the *transfer function* in the engineering literature since it transfers the shock (the "input") to the variable of interest (the "output")—see for example Boyce and DiPrima (2005, p. 350). The inverse of $H(s)$, denoted by $h(t) \equiv \mathcal{L}^{-1}\{H(s)\}$, is called the *impulse response function* of the system.

A.6.3   Systems of differential equations

The transform method is equally valuable for systems of differential equations. Suppose that the dynamic model is given in matrix form by:

$$\begin{bmatrix} \dot{K}(t) \\ \dot{Q}(t) \end{bmatrix} = \Delta \begin{bmatrix} K(t) \\ Q(t) \end{bmatrix} + \begin{bmatrix} g_K(t) \\ g_Q(t) \end{bmatrix}, \tag{A.100}$$

where Δ is the two-by-two Jacobian matrix with typical element δ_{ij}, and $g_i(t)$ are (potentially time-varying) shock terms. Note that a system like (A.100) occurs quite regularly in analytical low-dimensional macro models.

By taking the Laplace transform of (A.100), and noting property (P5) we get:

$$\begin{bmatrix} s\mathcal{L}\{K,s\} - K(0) \\ s\mathcal{L}\{Q,s\} - Q(0) \end{bmatrix} = \Delta \begin{bmatrix} \mathcal{L}\{K,s\} \\ \mathcal{L}\{Q,s\} \end{bmatrix} + \begin{bmatrix} \mathcal{L}\{g_K,s\} \\ \mathcal{L}\{g_Q,s\} \end{bmatrix} \Leftrightarrow$$

$$\Lambda(s) \begin{bmatrix} \mathcal{L}\{K,s\} \\ \mathcal{L}\{Q,s\} \end{bmatrix} = \begin{bmatrix} K(0) + \mathcal{L}\{g_K,s\} \\ Q(0) + \mathcal{L}\{g_Q,s\} \end{bmatrix}, \tag{A.101}$$

where $\Lambda(s) \equiv sI - \Delta$ is a two-by-two matrix depending on s and the elements of Δ. We know from matrix algebra that the inverse of this matrix, $\Lambda(s)^{-1}$, can be written as:

$$\Lambda(s)^{-1} = \frac{1}{|\Lambda(s)|} \text{adj}\Lambda(s), \tag{A.102}$$

where $\text{adj}\Lambda(s)$ is the adjoint matrix (see above in section A.2.4) of $\Lambda(s)$ and $|\Lambda(s)|$ is the determinant of $\Lambda(s)$. For the simple two-by-two model $\text{adj}\Lambda(s)$ and $|\Lambda(s)|$ are:

$$\text{adj}\Lambda(s) \equiv \begin{bmatrix} s - \delta_{22} & \delta_{12} \\ \delta_{21} & s - \delta_{11} \end{bmatrix}, \tag{A.103}$$

and:

$$\begin{aligned} |\Lambda(s)| &= (s - \delta_{11})(s - \delta_{22}) - \delta_{12}\delta_{21} \\ &= s^2 - (\delta_{11} + \delta_{22})s + \delta_{11}\delta_{22} - \delta_{12}\delta_{21} \\ &= s^2 - s\,\text{tr}(\Delta) + |\Delta|, \end{aligned} \tag{A.104}$$

where $\text{tr}(\Delta)$ and $|\Delta|$ are, respectively, the trace and the determinant of the matrix Δ. The quadratic equation in (A.104) can be factored as follows:

$$|\Lambda(s)| = (s - \lambda_1)(s - \lambda_2), \tag{A.105}$$

where λ_1 and λ_2 are the characteristic roots of the matrix Δ:

$$\lambda_{1,2} = \frac{\text{tr}(\Delta) \pm \sqrt{[\text{tr}(\Delta)]^2 - 4|\Delta|}}{2}. \tag{A.106}$$

Before going on we note—by comparing (A.104) and (A.105)—that for the two-by-two case we have:

$$\text{tr}(\Delta) = \lambda_1 + \lambda_2, \quad |\Delta| = \lambda_1 \lambda_2, \tag{A.107}$$

i.e. the sum of the characteristic roots equals the trace of the Jacobian matrix Δ and the product of these roots equals the determinant of this matrix. This property is often very useful for deducing the signs of these roots. It is not difficult to see why this is so by looking at (A.106). We note that the roots are real (imaginary) if $[\text{tr}(\Delta)]^2 > (<) \, 4|\Delta|$ and that they are distinct provided $[\text{tr}(\Delta)]^2 \neq 4|\Delta|$. Also, if $\text{tr}(\Delta) > 0$ there must be at least one positive root. Finally, if $|\Delta| < 0$ there is exactly one positive (unstable) and one negative (stable) real characteristic root.[5]

Let us now consider the two cases encountered most often in the economics literature for which the roots are real and distinct, i.e. $[\text{tr}(\Delta)]^2 > 4|\Delta|$.

A.6.3.1 Both roots negative ($\lambda_1, \lambda_2 < 0$)

We can use (A.101), (A.102), and (A.105) to derive the following expression in Laplace transforms:

$$\begin{bmatrix} \mathcal{L}\{K,s\} \\ \mathcal{L}\{Q,s\} \end{bmatrix} = \frac{\text{adj}\Lambda(s) \begin{bmatrix} K(0) + \mathcal{L}\{g_K, s\} \\ Q(0) + \mathcal{L}\{g_Q, s\} \end{bmatrix}}{(s - \lambda_1)(s - \lambda_2)}, \tag{A.108}$$

which is in the same format as equation (A.99), with $H(s) \equiv \text{adj}\Lambda(s)/[(s - \lambda_1)(s - \lambda_2)]$ acting as the transfer function. To solve the model for particular shocks it is useful to re-express the transfer function. We note that for the two-by-two case $\text{adj}\Lambda(s)$ has the following properties:

$$\text{adj}\Lambda(s) = \text{adj}\Lambda(\lambda_i) + (s - \lambda_i)I, \qquad (i = 1, 2), \tag{A.109}$$

$$I = \frac{\text{adj}\Lambda(\lambda_1) - \text{adj}\Lambda(\lambda_2)}{\lambda_1 - \lambda_2},$$

where the second result follows from the first. We can now perform a partial fractions expansion of the transfer matrix:

$$\frac{\text{adj}\Lambda(s)}{(s - \lambda_1)(s - \lambda_2)} = \frac{\text{adj}\Lambda(s)}{\lambda_1 - \lambda_2} \left[\frac{1}{s - \lambda_1} - \frac{1}{s - \lambda_2} \right]$$

$$= \frac{1}{\lambda_1 - \lambda_2} \left[\frac{\text{adj}\Lambda(s)}{s - \lambda_1} - \frac{\text{adj}\Lambda(s)}{s - \lambda_2} \right]$$

$$= \frac{1}{\lambda_1 - \lambda_2} \left[I + \frac{\text{adj}\Lambda(\lambda_1)}{s - \lambda_1} - I - \frac{\text{adj}\Lambda(\lambda_2)}{s - \lambda_2} \right]$$

---

[5]These characteristic roots are going to show up in exponential functions, $e^{\lambda_i t}$, in the solution of the (system of) differential equation(s). If the root is positive (negative) $e^{\lambda_i t} \to \infty \, (\to 0)$ as $t \to \infty$ so positive (negative) roots are unstable (stable). The knife-edge case of a zero root is also stable as $e^{0t} = 1$ for all t. See section A.6.4 below.

$$= \frac{1}{\lambda_1 - \lambda_2} \left[\frac{\text{adj}\Lambda(\lambda_1)}{s - \lambda_1} - \frac{\text{adj}\Lambda(\lambda_2)}{s - \lambda_2} \right]. \tag{A.110}$$

By using (A.110) in (A.108) we obtain the following general expression in terms of the Laplace transforms:

$$\left[\begin{array}{c} \mathcal{L}\{K,s\} \\ \mathcal{L}\{Q,s\} \end{array} \right] = \frac{1}{\lambda_1 - \lambda_2} \left[\frac{\text{adj}\Lambda(\lambda_1)}{s - \lambda_1} - \frac{\text{adj}\Lambda(\lambda_2)}{s - \lambda_2} \right] \left[\begin{array}{c} K(0) + \mathcal{L}\{g_K,s\} \\ Q(0) + \mathcal{L}\{g_Q,s\} \end{array} \right]. \tag{A.111}$$

Suppose that the shocks are step functions and satisfy $g_i(t) = g_i$ for $i = K, Q$ and $t \geq 0$. The Laplace transform for such step functions is $\mathcal{L}\{g_i, s\} = g_i/s$ which can be substituted in (A.111). After some manipulation we obtain the following result:

$$\left[\begin{array}{c} \mathcal{L}\{K,s\} \\ \mathcal{L}\{Q,s\} \end{array} \right] = \left[\frac{B}{s - \lambda_1} + \frac{I - B}{s - \lambda_2} \right] \left[\begin{array}{c} K(0) \\ Q(0) \end{array} \right]$$
$$- \left[\frac{B}{\lambda_1} \cdot \frac{-\lambda_1}{s(s - \lambda_1)} + \frac{I - B}{\lambda_2} \cdot \frac{-\lambda_2}{s(s - \lambda_2)} \right] \left[\begin{array}{c} g_K \\ g_Q \end{array} \right], \tag{A.112}$$

where $B \equiv \text{adj}\Lambda(\lambda_1)/(\lambda_1 - \lambda_2)$ and $I - B \equiv -\text{adj}\Lambda(\lambda_2)/(\lambda_1 - \lambda_2)$ are weighting matrices.[6] The expression is now in terms of known Laplace transforms so that inversion is child's play:

$$\left[\begin{array}{c} K(t) \\ Q(t) \end{array} \right] = \left[Be^{\lambda_1 t} + (I - B)e^{\lambda_2 t} \right] \left[\begin{array}{c} K(0) \\ Q(0) \end{array} \right]$$
$$- \left[\frac{B}{\lambda_1} \left(1 - e^{\lambda_1 t} \right) + \frac{I - B}{\lambda_2} \left(1 - e^{\lambda_2 t} \right) \right] \left[\begin{array}{c} g_K \\ g_Q \end{array} \right]. \tag{A.113}$$

Equation (A.113) constitutes the full solution of the problem. It yields impact, transition, and long-run results of the shock. To check that we have done things correctly we verify that we can recover from (A.113) the initial conditions by setting $t = 0$ and the long-run steady state by letting $t \to \infty$. The first result is obvious: for $t = 0$ we have that $e^{\lambda_i t} = 1$ so that $K(t) = K(0)$ and $Q(t) = Q(0)$. Similarly, for $t \to \infty$, $e^{\lambda_i t} \to 0$ (since both roots are stable) and we get from (A.113):

$$\left[\begin{array}{c} K(\infty) \\ Q(\infty) \end{array} \right] = - \left[\frac{B}{\lambda_1} + \frac{I - B}{\lambda_2} \right] \left[\begin{array}{c} g_K \\ g_Q \end{array} \right] = \frac{-\text{adj}\Lambda(0)}{-\lambda_1 \lambda_2} \left[\begin{array}{c} g_K \\ g_Q \end{array} \right]$$
$$= \frac{\text{adj}\Delta}{-|\Delta|} \left[\begin{array}{c} g_K \\ g_Q \end{array} \right] = -\Delta^{-1} \left[\begin{array}{c} g_K \\ g_Q \end{array} \right], \tag{A.114}$$

which is the same solution we would have obtained by substituting the permanent shock in (A.100) and imposing the steady state. So at least the initial and ultimate effects check out!

We could have checked our results also by working directly with the solution in terms of Laplace transforms (i.e. (A.111) in general and (A.112) for the particular shocks). We need the following two properties to do so.

---

[6] These weighting matrices also satisfy:

$$\frac{B}{\lambda_1} + \frac{I - B}{\lambda_2} = \frac{\text{adj}\Lambda(0)}{-\lambda_1 \lambda_2} = \frac{\text{adj}\Delta}{\lambda_1 \lambda_2} = \Delta^{-1}.$$

These results are used below. Note that we have used the fact that $\text{adj}\Lambda(0) = \text{adj}(-\Delta) = (-1)^{n-1}\text{adj}\Delta$, where n is the order of Δ ($n = 2$ here). See Lancaster and Tismenetsky (1985, p. 43).

Property 7 *If the indicated limits exist then the initial-value theorem says:*

$$\lim_{t\to 0} f(t) = \lim_{s\to\infty} s\mathcal{L}\{f,s\}, \tag{P7a}$$

and the final-value theorem says:

$$\lim_{t\to\infty} f(t) = \lim_{s\to 0} s\mathcal{L}\{f,s\}. \tag{P7b}$$

PROOF: See Spiegel (1965, p. 20).

Applying Property (P7a) directly to (A.112) we obtain:

$$\lim_{s\to\infty}\begin{bmatrix} s\mathcal{L}\{K,s\} \\ s\mathcal{L}\{Q,s\} \end{bmatrix} = \begin{bmatrix} B\underbrace{\lim_{s\to\infty}\frac{s}{s-\lambda_1}}_{=1} + (I-B)\underbrace{\lim_{s\to\infty}\frac{s}{s-\lambda_2}}_{=1} \end{bmatrix}\begin{bmatrix} K(0) \\ Q(0) \end{bmatrix}$$

$$-\begin{bmatrix} \frac{B}{\lambda_1}\underbrace{\lim_{s\to\infty}\frac{-\lambda_1 s}{s(s-\lambda_1)}}_{=0} + \frac{I-B}{\lambda_2}\underbrace{\lim_{s\to\infty}\frac{-\lambda_2 s}{s(s-\lambda_2)}}_{=0} \end{bmatrix}\begin{bmatrix} g_K \\ g_Q \end{bmatrix}$$

$$= [B+I-B]\begin{bmatrix} K(0) \\ Q(0) \end{bmatrix} = \begin{bmatrix} K(0) \\ Q(0) \end{bmatrix}.$$

Similarly, applying Property (P7b) to (A.112) we get:

$$\lim_{s\to 0}\begin{bmatrix} s\mathcal{L}\{K,s\} \\ s\mathcal{L}\{Q,s\} \end{bmatrix} = \begin{bmatrix} B\underbrace{\lim_{s\to 0}\frac{s}{s-\lambda_1}}_{=0} + (I-B)\underbrace{\lim_{s\to 0}\frac{s}{s-\lambda_2}}_{=0} \end{bmatrix}\begin{bmatrix} K(0) \\ Q(0) \end{bmatrix}$$

$$-\begin{bmatrix} \frac{B}{\lambda_1}\underbrace{\lim_{s\to 0}\frac{-\lambda_1 s}{s(s-\lambda_1)}}_{=1} + \frac{I-B}{\lambda_2}\underbrace{\lim_{s\to 0}\frac{-\lambda_2 s}{s(s-\lambda_2)}}_{=1} \end{bmatrix}\begin{bmatrix} g_K \\ g_Q \end{bmatrix}$$

$$= -\begin{bmatrix} \frac{B}{\lambda_1} + \frac{I-B}{\lambda_2} \end{bmatrix}\begin{bmatrix} g_K \\ g_Q \end{bmatrix} = \begin{bmatrix} K(\infty) \\ Q(\infty) \end{bmatrix}.$$

A.6.3.2   Roots alternate in sign ($\lambda_1 < 0 < \lambda_2$)

A situation which occurs quite regularly in dynamic macro models is one in which the Jacobian matrix Δ in (A.100) has one negative (stable) root and one positive (unstable) root. The way to check for such saddle-point stability is either by means of (A.106) or (A.107). From (A.106) we observe that if $|\Delta| < 0$ then we have distinct and real roots for sure since $\sqrt{(\text{tr}\Delta)^2 - 4|\Delta|} > 0$. Also, since $|\Delta| = \lambda_1\lambda_2 < 0$ it must be the case that $\lambda_1 < 0 < \lambda_2$. Of course we also see this directly from (A.107).

The beauty of the Laplace transform technique is now that (A.108) is still appropriate and just needs to be solved differently. Let us motivate the alternative solution method heuristically by writing (A.108) as follows:

$$(s-\lambda_1)\begin{bmatrix} \mathcal{L}\{K,s\} \\ \mathcal{L}\{Q,s\} \end{bmatrix} = \frac{\text{adj}\Lambda(s)\begin{bmatrix} K(0) + \mathcal{L}\{g_K,s\} \\ Q(0) + \mathcal{L}\{g_Q,s\} \end{bmatrix}}{s-\lambda_2}. \tag{A.115}$$

In a two-by-two saddle-point stable system there is one predetermined and one non-predetermined (or "jumping") variable so we need to supply only one initial condition (and not two as before). Let us assume that K is the predetermined variable (the value of which is determined in the past, e.g. a stock of human or physical capital, assets, etc.) so that $K(0)$ is given. But then Q is the non-predetermined variable (e.g. a (shadow) price) so we must somehow figure out its initial condition.[7] It is clear from (A.115) how we should do this.

Note that the instability originates from the unstable root λ_2. For $s = \lambda_2$ we have that the denominator on the right-hand side of (A.115) is zero. The only way we can still obtain bounded (and thus economically sensible) solutions for $\mathcal{L}\{K, s\}$ and $\mathcal{L}\{Q, s\}$ is if the numerator on the right-hand side of (A.115) is also zero for $s = \lambda_2$, i.e. if:

$$\text{adj}\Lambda(\lambda_2) \begin{bmatrix} K(0) + \mathcal{L}\{g_K, \lambda_2\} \\ Q(0) + \mathcal{L}\{g_Q, \lambda_2\} \end{bmatrix} = \begin{bmatrix} 0 \\ 0 \end{bmatrix}. \tag{A.116}$$

All except one of the variables appearing in (A.116) are determined so $Q(0)$ must be such that (A.116) holds. At first view it appears as if (A.116) represents two equations in one unknown but that is not the case. A theorem from matrix algebra says that, since $\Lambda(\lambda_2)$ is of rank 1 so is $\text{adj}\Lambda(\lambda_2)$.[8] So, in fact, we can use either row of (A.116) to compute $Q(0)$:

$$\begin{bmatrix} 0 \\ 0 \end{bmatrix} = \begin{bmatrix} \lambda_2 - \delta_{22} & \delta_{12} \\ \delta_{21} & \lambda_2 - \delta_{11} \end{bmatrix} \begin{bmatrix} K(0) + \mathcal{L}\{g_K, \lambda_2\} \\ Q(0) + \mathcal{L}\{g_Q, \lambda_2\} \end{bmatrix} \implies$$

$$Q(0) = -\mathcal{L}\{g_Q, \lambda_2\} - \frac{\lambda_2 - \delta_{22}}{\delta_{12}} \cdot [K(0) + \mathcal{L}\{g_K, \lambda_2\}] \tag{A.117}$$

$$= -\mathcal{L}\{g_Q, \lambda_2\} - \frac{\delta_{21}}{\lambda_2 - \delta_{11}} \cdot [K(0) + \mathcal{L}\{g_K, \lambda_2\}]. \tag{A.118}$$

We next use (A.109), (A.115), and (A.116) to get:

$$(s - \lambda_1) \begin{bmatrix} \mathcal{L}\{K, s\} \\ \mathcal{L}\{Q, s\} \end{bmatrix} = \frac{\text{adj}\Lambda(\lambda_2) \begin{bmatrix} K(0) + \mathcal{L}\{g_K, s\} \\ Q(0) + \mathcal{L}\{g_Q, s\} \end{bmatrix}}{s - \lambda_2} + \begin{bmatrix} K(0) + \mathcal{L}\{g_K, s\} \\ Q(0) + \mathcal{L}\{g_Q, s\} \end{bmatrix}$$

$$= \begin{bmatrix} K(0) + \mathcal{L}\{g_K, s\} \\ Q(0) + \mathcal{L}\{g_Q, s\} \end{bmatrix} + \text{adj}\Lambda(\lambda_2) \begin{bmatrix} \frac{\mathcal{L}\{g_K, s\} - \mathcal{L}\{g_K, \lambda_2\}}{s - \lambda_2} \\ \frac{\mathcal{L}\{g_Q, s\} - \mathcal{L}\{g_Q, \lambda_2\}}{s - \lambda_2} \end{bmatrix}, \tag{A.119}$$

where we have used (A.116) in the last step. Note that in (A.119) all effects of the unstable root have been incorporated and only the stable dynamics remains (represented by the term involving $s - \lambda_1$).

Suppose again that the shocks satisfy $g_i(t) = g_i$ for $i = K, Q$ and $t \geq 0$ so that $\mathcal{L}\{g_i, s\} = g_i/s$ and:

$$\frac{\mathcal{L}\{g_i, s\} - \mathcal{L}\{g_i, \lambda_2\}}{s - \lambda_2} = \frac{\frac{g_i}{s} - \frac{g_i}{\lambda_2}}{s - \lambda_2} = -\frac{g_i}{s\lambda_2}.$$

---

[7] Of course, economic theory suggests which variables are predetermined and which ones are not.

[8] In general, if the n-square matrix Λ has distinct eigenvalues its eigenvectors are linearly independent and the rank of $\Lambda(\lambda_i) \equiv \lambda_i I - \Delta$ is $n - 1$ (Ayres, 1974, p. 150). Furthermore, for any n-square matrix A of rank $n - 1$ we have that $\text{adj}A$ is of rank 1 (Ayres, 1974, p. 50).

By using these results in (A.119) we obtain the full solution of the saddle-point stable model:

$$(s - \lambda_1) \begin{bmatrix} \mathcal{L}\{K, s\} \\ \mathcal{L}\{Q, s\} \end{bmatrix} = \begin{bmatrix} K(0) \\ Q(0) \end{bmatrix} - \frac{1}{\lambda_2} [\text{adj}\Lambda(\lambda_2) - \lambda_2 I] \begin{bmatrix} g_K \\ g_Q \end{bmatrix} \frac{1}{s} \iff$$

$$\begin{bmatrix} \mathcal{L}\{K, s\} \\ \mathcal{L}\{Q, s\} \end{bmatrix} = \begin{bmatrix} K(0) \\ Q(0) \end{bmatrix} \frac{1}{s - \lambda_1} - \frac{\text{adj}\Lambda(0)}{-\lambda_1 \lambda_2} \begin{bmatrix} g_K \\ g_Q \end{bmatrix} \frac{-\lambda_1}{s(s - \lambda_1)}$$

$$= \begin{bmatrix} K(0) \\ Q(0) \end{bmatrix} \frac{1}{s - \lambda_1} + \begin{bmatrix} K(\infty) \\ Q(\infty) \end{bmatrix} \frac{-\lambda_1}{s(s - \lambda_1)}, \qquad (A.120)$$

where we have used (A.109) and the result in footnote 6, and where $Q(0)$ is obtained by substituting the shock terms in either (A.117) or (A.118). By inverting (A.120) we obtain the solution in the time dimension.

$$\begin{bmatrix} K(t) \\ Q(t) \end{bmatrix} = \begin{bmatrix} K(0) \\ Q(0) \end{bmatrix} e^{\lambda_1 t} + \begin{bmatrix} K(\infty) \\ Q(\infty) \end{bmatrix} \left(1 - e^{\lambda_1 t}\right). \qquad (A.121)$$

The key point to note is that the stable root determines the speed of transition between the respective impact and long-run results.

A.6.4 Hysteretic models

We now consider a special class of models that have the *hysteresis* property. With hysteresis we mean a system whose steady state is not given, but can wander about and depends on the past path of the economy. Mathematically, this property implies that the Jacobian matrix of a continuous-time system has, apart from some "regular" (non-zero) eigenvalues, a zero eigenvalue.[9] Hysteretic systems are important in macroeconomics because they allow us to depart from the rigid framework of equilibrium, ahistorical, economics. Put differently: history matters in such systems.

In the remainder of this section we show that the Laplace transform methods studied above can easily be applied in low-dimensional hysteretic models also. We restrict attention to the two cases encountered most frequently in the economics literature, namely two-dimensional models with both roots non-positive and non-negative, respectively.

A.6.4.1 Non-positive roots ($\lambda_1 < 0 = \lambda_2$)

Suppose that the matrix Δ in (A.100) satisfies $|\Delta| = \lambda_1 \lambda_2 = 0$ and $\text{tr}(\Delta) = \lambda_1 + \lambda_2 < 0$ so that the system has a zero root and is hysteretic, i.e. $\lambda_1 = \text{tr}(\Delta) < 0$ and $\lambda_2 = 0$. Clearly, since $|\Delta| = 0$, the inverse matrix Δ^{-1} does not exist and we cannot compute the long-run results of a shock by imposing the steady state in (A.100) and inverting Δ. However, the derivations leading from (A.108) to (A.111) are all still valid even for $\lambda_2 = 0$, i.e. the general solution in Laplace transforms is:

$$\begin{bmatrix} \mathcal{L}\{K, s\} \\ \mathcal{L}\{Q, s\} \end{bmatrix} = \left[\frac{B}{s - \lambda_1} + \frac{I - B}{s} \right] \begin{bmatrix} K(0) + \mathcal{L}\{g_K, s\} \\ Q(0) + \mathcal{L}\{g_Q, s\} \end{bmatrix}, \qquad (A.122)$$

where $B \equiv \text{adj}\Lambda(\lambda_1)/\lambda_1$ and $I - B \equiv -\text{adj}\Lambda(0)/\lambda_1$ are weighting matrices. Now assume that there is a *temporary* shock, i.e. $g_i(t) = g_i e^{-\xi_i t}$ for $i = K, Q, \xi_i > 0$, and

---

[9]Note that in a discrete-time setting a model displays hysteresis if it contains a unit root. Amable et al. (1994) argue that it is inappropriate to equate zero-root (or unit-root) dynamics with "true" hysteresis. Strong hysteresis is a much more general concept in their view and they suggest that zero-root dynamics at best captures some aspects of this concept.

$t \geq 0$. In a non-hysteretic model such a temporary shock has no effect in the long run as the system will eventually just return to its initial steady state which is uniquely determined by the long-run values of the shock terms.

In stark contrast, in a hysteretic model, a temporary shock does have permanent effects. In order to demonstrate this result we first substitute $\mathcal{L}\{g_i, s\} = g_i/(s + \xi_i)$ into (A.122):

$$\begin{bmatrix} \mathcal{L}\{K, s\} \\ \mathcal{L}\{Q, s\} \end{bmatrix} = \begin{bmatrix} \dfrac{B}{s - \lambda_1} + \dfrac{I - B}{s} \end{bmatrix} \begin{bmatrix} K(0) + g_K/(s + \xi_K) \\ Q(0) + g_Q/(s + \xi_Q) \end{bmatrix}. \tag{A.123}$$

Equation (A.123) constitutes the full solution for $K(t)$ and $Q(t)$ once the (history-determined) initial conditions are plugged in. Using the final-value theorem (P8) we derive from (A.123):

$$\lim_{s \to 0} \begin{bmatrix} s\mathcal{L}\{K, s\} \\ s\mathcal{L}\{Q, s\} \end{bmatrix} = \begin{bmatrix} B \underbrace{\lim_{s \to 0} \dfrac{s}{s - \lambda_1}}_{=0} + (I - B) \underbrace{\lim_{s \to 0} \dfrac{s}{s}}_{=1} \end{bmatrix} \begin{bmatrix} K(0) + \lim_{s \to 0} \dfrac{g_K}{s + \xi_K} \\ Q(0) + \lim_{s \to 0} \dfrac{g_Q}{s + \xi_Q} \end{bmatrix}$$

$$= \dfrac{\text{adj}\Delta}{\lambda_1} \begin{bmatrix} K(0) + g_K/\xi_K \\ Q(0) + g_Q/\xi_Q \end{bmatrix} = \begin{bmatrix} K(\infty) \\ Q(\infty) \end{bmatrix}, \tag{A.124}$$

where we have used the fact that $\text{adj}\Lambda(0) = -\text{adj}\Delta$ in going from the first to the second line. Equation (A.124) shows that the hysteretic system does not return to its initial state following the temporary shock. It is not unstable, however, because it does settle down in a new "steady state" (for which $\dot{K}(\infty) = \dot{Q}(\infty) = 0$) but the position of this new steady state depends on the entire path of the shock terms, i.e. in our example on ξ_K and ξ_Q. The ultimate steady state is thus "path dependent" which explains why another term for hysteresis is *path dependency*.

Intermezzo A.4

Pegging the nominal interest rate. Giavazzi and Wyplosz (1985, p. 355) give a simple example of a hysteretic system. Consider the following simple macroeconomic model:

$$m(t) - p(t) = ay(t) - bi_0 \tag{LM}$$
$$i_0 = r(t) + \dot{p}(t) \tag{Fisher}$$
$$y(t) = y_0^D(t) - \eta r(t) \tag{IS}$$
$$\dot{y}(t) = \theta[\bar{y}_0 - y(t)], \tag{AS}$$

where m, y, $\bar{y}$, and p are, respectively, the money supply, actual output, full employment output, and the price level (all in logarithms), r and i are the real and nominal interest rate, respectively, and y_0^D represents the exogenous elements of aggregate demand. The monetary authority uses monetary policy to peg the nominal interest rate (at $i(t) = i_0$) so the LM curve residually determines the money supply. By combining the Fisher relation with the IS curve we obtain $\dot{p}(t) = (1/\eta)[y(t) - y_0^D(t)] + i_0$. By differentiating this expression and the AS curve—keeping the other exogenous variables constant—we obtain the system in the required format:

$$
\begin{bmatrix} d\dot{p}(t) \\ d\dot{y}(t) \end{bmatrix} = \begin{bmatrix} 0 & 1/\eta \\ 0 & -\theta \end{bmatrix} \begin{bmatrix} dp(t) \\ dy(t) \end{bmatrix} + \begin{bmatrix} -(1/\eta)dy_0^D(t) \\ 0 \end{bmatrix},
$$

where the Jacobian matrix has characteristic roots $\lambda_1 = -\theta$ and $\lambda_2 = 0$ and it is assumed that both p and y are predetermined variables (so that $dp(0) = dy(0) = 0$). Now consider the effects of a temporary boost in aggregate demand, i.e. $dy_0^D(t) = e^{-\xi_D t}$ for $\xi_D > 0$ and $t \geq 0$. Using the methods developed in this subsection we derive:

$$
\begin{bmatrix} \mathcal{L}\{dp, s\} \\ \mathcal{L}\{dy, s\} \end{bmatrix} = \begin{bmatrix} -1/(\eta\xi_D) \\ 0 \end{bmatrix} \left(\frac{1}{s} - \frac{1}{s + \xi_D} \right).
$$

Despite the fact that the shock is purely transitory it has a permanent effect on the price level.

****

A.6.4.2 Non-negative roots ($\lambda_1 = 0 < \lambda_2$)

We now assume that Δ in (A.100) satisfies $|\Delta| = \lambda_1 \lambda_2 = 0$ and $\text{tr}(\Delta) = \lambda_1 + \lambda_2 > 0$ so that $\lambda_1 = 0$ and $\lambda_2 = \text{tr}(\Delta) > 0$. For this hysteretic case the analysis in subsection A.6.3.2 is relevant. The general solution in Laplace transforms is obtained by setting $\lambda_1 = 0$ in (A.119):

$$
s \begin{bmatrix} \mathcal{L}\{K, s\} \\ \mathcal{L}\{Q, s\} \end{bmatrix} = \begin{bmatrix} K(0) + \mathcal{L}\{g_K, s\} \\ Q(0) + \mathcal{L}\{g_Q, s\} \end{bmatrix} + \text{adj}\Lambda(\lambda_2) \begin{bmatrix} \frac{\mathcal{L}\{g_K, s\} - \mathcal{L}\{g_K, \lambda_2\}}{s - \lambda_2} \\ \frac{\mathcal{L}\{g_Q, s\} - \mathcal{L}\{g_Q, \lambda_2\}}{s - \lambda_2} \end{bmatrix}. \quad \text{(A.125)}
$$

Let us once again assume that the shock is temporary and has a Laplace transform $\mathcal{L}\{g_i, s\} = g_i/(s + \xi_i)$ for $i = K, Q$ so that:

$$
\frac{\mathcal{L}\{g_i, s\} - \mathcal{L}\{g_i, \lambda_2\}}{s - \lambda_2} = \frac{-g_i}{(\lambda_2 + \xi_i)(s + \xi_i)}. \quad \text{(A.126)}
$$

Equation (A.125) can then be rewritten as:

$$
s \begin{bmatrix} \mathcal{L}\{K, s\} \\ \mathcal{L}\{Q, s\} \end{bmatrix} = \begin{bmatrix} K(0) + g_K/(s + \xi_K) \\ Q(0) + g_Q/(s + \xi_Q) \end{bmatrix} - \text{adj}\Lambda(\lambda_2) \begin{bmatrix} \frac{g_K}{(\lambda_2 + \xi_K)(s + \xi_K)} \\ \frac{g_Q}{(\lambda_2 + \xi_Q)(s + \xi_Q)} \end{bmatrix}, \quad \text{(A.127)}
$$

where $Q(0)$ follows from either (A.117) or (A.118). By using the final-value theorem (P8) in (A.127) we derive the hysteretic result:[10]

$$
\lim_{s \to 0} s \begin{bmatrix} \mathcal{L}\{K, s\} \\ \mathcal{L}\{Q, s\} \end{bmatrix} = \begin{bmatrix} K(0) + g_K/\xi_K \\ Q(0) + g_Q/\xi_Q \end{bmatrix} - \text{adj}\Lambda(\lambda_2) \begin{bmatrix} \frac{g_K}{\xi_K(\lambda_2 + \xi_K)} \\ \frac{g_Q}{\xi_Q(\lambda_2 + \xi_Q)} \end{bmatrix}
$$

---

[10]In going from the first to the second line we use (A.116), note that (A.109) implies $\lambda_2 I = \text{adj}\Lambda(\lambda_2) - \text{adj}\Lambda(0)$, and recall that $\text{adj}\Lambda(0) = -\text{adj}\Delta$.

$$= \frac{\text{adj}\Delta}{\lambda_2} \left[\begin{array}{c} K(0) + g_K/\xi_K \\ Q(0) + g_Q/\xi_Q \end{array} \right] = \left[\begin{array}{c} K(\infty) \\ Q(\infty) \end{array} \right]. \qquad (A.128)$$

As in the outright stable case (see (A.124)) parameters of the shock path determine the ultimate long-run result.

Intermezzo A.5

Current account dynamics. Consider the simple representative-agent model of a small open economy suggested by Blanchard (1985, p. 230). There is no capital and labour supply is exogenously fixed (at unity) so that output, Y, and the wage rate, $W = Y$, are exogenous. The model is:

$$\dot{C}(t) = [r(t) - \alpha] C(t)$$
$$\dot{F}(t) = r(t)F(t) + W(t) - C(t),$$

where F is net foreign assets, and C and r are, respectively, consumption and the exogenous interest rate. As is well known, a steady state only exists in this model if the steady-state interest rate equals the rate of time preference, i.e. if $r(t) = \alpha$. After loglinearizing the model around an initial steady state we obtain:

$$\left[\begin{array}{c} \dot{\tilde{F}}(t) \\ \dot{\tilde{C}}(t) \end{array} \right] = \left[\begin{array}{cc} \alpha & -\alpha(1 + \omega_F) \\ 0 & 0 \end{array} \right] \left[\begin{array}{c} \tilde{F}(t) \\ \tilde{C}(t) \end{array} \right] + \left[\begin{array}{c} \omega_F \\ 1 \end{array} \right] \alpha \tilde{r}(t),$$

where $\omega_F \equiv \alpha F/Y = C/Y - 1$ is the initial share of foreign asset income in national output, $\dot{\tilde{F}}(t) \equiv \alpha d\dot{F}/Y$, and $\tilde{F}(t) \equiv \alpha dF/Y$. The Jacobian matrix on the right-hand side has characteristic roots $\lambda_1 = 0$ and $\lambda_2 = \alpha$ and it is assumed that F is the predetermined variable and C is the jumping variable. Now consider a temporary change in the world interest rate, $\tilde{r}(t) = e^{-\xi_R t}$ for $\xi_R > 0$ and $t \geq 0$. By using (A.117) and making the obvious substitutions we obtain the jump in consumption:

$$\tilde{C}(0) = -\frac{\alpha}{(\alpha + \xi_R)(1 + \omega_F)} < 0.$$

In a similar fashion, the long-run results can be obtained by using (A.128):

$$\left[\begin{array}{c} \tilde{F}(\infty) \\ \tilde{C}(\infty) \end{array} \right] = \left[\begin{array}{cc} 0 & 1 + \omega_F \\ 0 & 1 \end{array} \right] \left[\begin{array}{c} \alpha \omega_F/\xi_R \\ \tilde{C}(0) + \alpha/\xi_R \end{array} \right]$$

$$= \left[\begin{array}{c} 1 + \omega_F \\ 1 \end{array} \right] \left(\frac{\alpha [\alpha + \omega_F(\alpha + \xi_R)]}{\xi_R(\alpha + \xi_R)(1 + \omega_F)} \right).$$

In the impact period the household cuts back consumption to boost its savings. In the long run both consumption and net foreign assets are higher than in the initial steady state (provided $\omega_F > -\alpha/(\alpha + \xi_R)$ in the initial steady state).

****

A.6.5   Literature

The most accessible intermediate sources to the Laplace transform method are to be found in the engineering literature. Kreyszig (1999, ch. 5) and Boyce and DiPrima (2005, ch. 6) are particularly illuminating. An advanced and encyclopedic source on Laplace transforms is Spiegel (1965). Judd (1982, 1985, 1987a, 1987b) was the first to apply the method to saddle-point stable perfect foresight models, and to note the close link with welfare evaluations along the transition path.

A.7   Difference equations

Although continuous-time models are quite convenient to work with, economists often work with models formulated in discrete time. Most RBC models fall under this category as does the class of overlapping-generations models in the Samuelson (1958)-Diamond (1965) tradition. In this section we briefly introduce the z-transform method. This method plays the same role in discrete-time models that the Laplace transform method performs in continuous-time models. In order to avoid unnecessary duplication, only the basic elements of the z-transform are introduced. The student should be able to "translate" the insights obtained above to the discrete-time setting after reading this section. Extremely lucid expositions of the z-transform method are Ogata (1995) and Elaydi (1996). Meijdam and Verhoeven (1998) apply the techniques in an economic setting.

A.7.1   Basic methods

The basic first-order linear difference equation takes the following form:

$$y_{t+1} + ay_t = b, \tag{A.129}$$

where a and b are constant parameters. If $b = 0$ ($\neq 0$) the equation is homogeneous (non-homogeneous). Equation (A.129) can be seen as the discrete-time counterpart to (A.68). Just as for the continuous case we can solve the difference equation in two steps. In step 1 we solve the complementary function, y_t^C, which solves the homogeneous part of (A.129). In step 2 we then look for the particular solution, y_t^P. The general solution is then given by $y_t = y_t^C + y_t^P$.

To solve the homogeneous part of the difference equation we are looking for a function for which $y_{t+1}/y_t = -a$ which suggests that a good trial solution is $y_t^C = A\alpha^t$. Substituting this trial in (A.129) and setting $b = 0$ we obtain $A\alpha^t [\alpha + a] = 0$ or $\alpha = -a$. Hence, the complementary function is:

$$y_t^C = A(-a)^t. \tag{A.130}$$

To find the particular solution we first try the simplest possible guess, $y_t^P = k$ (a constant). Substituting this trial solution into (A.129) we find $(1 + a)k = b$ which can be solved for k provided $a \neq -1$: $k = b/(1 + a)$. The general solution of the difference equation is thus:

$$y_t = A(-a)^t + \frac{b}{1+a} \qquad \text{(for } a \neq -1\text{)}. \tag{A.131}$$

This expression is the discrete time counterpart to (A.74).

Whereas a zero coefficient necessitates a different trial for the particular solution in the continuous time case, the same holds for the discrete-time case when the coefficient is minus unity. If $a = -1$ we use the trial solution $y_t^P = kt$, after which we find that $k = b$ so that the general solution is:

$$y_t = A + bt \qquad \text{(for } a = -1\text{)}. \tag{A.132}$$

Initial conditions can be imposed just as for the continuous-time case. Suppose that y_0 is some given constant. Then we obtain from (A.131) that $A = y_0 - b/(1+a)$ and from (A.132) that $A = y_0$.

Just as in the continuous-time case, there exists a very convenient transformation method for solving difference equations. We now briefly explain how this z-transform method works.

A.7.2   The z-transform

Suppose we have a discrete-time function, f_t, which satisfies $f_t = 0$ for $t = -1, -2, \dots$. The (one-sided) z-transform of the function is then defined as follows:[11]

$$\mathcal{Z}\{f_t, z\} \equiv \sum_{t=0}^{\infty} f_t z^{-t}. \tag{A.133}$$

Provided the sum on the right-hand side converges, $\mathcal{Z}\{f_t, z\}$ exists and can be seen as a function of z. The region of convergence is determined as follows. Suppose that f_t satisfies:

$$\lim_{t \to \infty} \left| \frac{f_{t+1}}{f_t} \right| = R. \tag{A.134}$$

Then the infinite sum in (A.133) converges provided:

$$\lim_{t \to \infty} \left| \frac{f_{t+1} z^{-(t+1)}}{f_t z^{-t}} \right| < 1, \tag{A.135}$$

and diverges if the inequality is reversed. Together, (A.134) and (A.135) imply that (A.133) converges—and $\mathcal{Z}\{f_t, z\}$ exists—in the region $|z| > R$ ("heavy discounting"). In the region $|z| < R$, on the other hand, discounting is "light" and $\mathcal{Z}\{f_t, z\}$ does not exist. R is referred to as the *radius of convergence* of $\mathcal{Z}\{f_t, z\}$.

Here are some examples. Suppose that $f_t = 1$ for $t = 0, 1, 2, \dots$ (and $f_t = 0$ otherwise). Then $\mathcal{Z}\{f_t, z\}$ is:

$$\mathcal{Z}\{f_t, z\} \equiv \mathcal{Z}\{1, z\} = \sum_{t=0}^{\infty} \left(1 \times z^{-t}\right) = 1 + (1/z) + (1/z)^2 + \dots$$

$$= \frac{1}{1 - 1/z} = \frac{z}{z - 1},$$

provided $|z| > 1$ (recall that $\sum_{t=0}^{\infty} a^t = 1/(1-a)$ iff $|a| < 1$). Now a slightly harder one: suppose that $f_t = a^t$ for $t = 0, 1, 2, \dots$ (and $f_t = 0$ otherwise). Then $\mathcal{Z}\{f_t, z\}$ is:

$$\mathcal{Z}\{f_t, z\} \equiv \mathcal{Z}\{a^t, z\} = \sum_{t=0}^{\infty} a^t z^{-t} = 1 + (a/z) + (a/z)^2 + \dots$$

---

[11] By comparing (A.88) and (A.133) we cannot help but notice the close relation that exists between the Laplace transform and the z-transform. Indeed, assuming that $f(t)$ in (A.88) is continuous we obtain by discretizing $\mathcal{L}\{f, s\} = \sum_{t=0}^{\infty} e^{-st} f_t$. By setting $z = e^s$ we obtain (A.133). See also Elaydi (1996, p. 254).

Table A.2. Commonly used z-transforms

f_t	$\mathcal{Z}\{f,z\}$	valid for:
$\mathcal{D}_t \equiv \begin{cases} 1 & \text{for } t=0 \\ 0 & \text{for } t=1,2,... \end{cases}$	1	
1	$\frac{z}{z-1}$	$\lvert z \rvert > 1$
t	$\frac{z}{(z-1)^2}$	$\lvert z \rvert > 1$
a^t	$\frac{z}{z-a}$	$\lvert z \rvert > \lvert a \rvert$
a^{t-1}	$\frac{1}{z-a}$	$\lvert z \rvert > \lvert a \rvert$
ta^{t-1}	$\frac{z}{(z-a)^2}$	$\lvert z \rvert > \lvert a \rvert$
$\frac{a^t - b^t}{a-b}$	$\frac{z}{(z-a)(z-b)}$	$\lvert z \rvert > \lvert a \rvert,\ \lvert z \rvert > \lvert b \rvert,\ a \neq b$

$$= \frac{1}{1 - a/z} = \frac{z}{z-a},$$

provided $\lvert z \rvert > \lvert a \rvert$.

In Table A.2 we have gathered some often-used z-transforms. The student should verify that both the form of each transform and its associated radius of convergence are correct.

The z-transform has a number of properties which allow us to perform algebraic calculations with them. The most important of these are the following. Notice that in each case we assume that f_t possesses a z-transform and that $f_t = 0$ for $t = -1, -2, \dots$.

Property 8 *Multiplication by a constant. (P8) If $\mathcal{Z}\{f,s\}$ is the z-transform of f_t then $\mathcal{Z}\{af,z\} = a\mathcal{Z}\{f,z\}$.*

Property 9 *If f_t and g_t both have a z-transform then we have for any constants a and b that:*

$$\mathcal{Z}\{af + bg, z\} = a\mathcal{Z}\{f,z\} + b\mathcal{Z}\{g,z\}. \tag{P9}$$

Property 10 *Left-shifting.*

$$\mathcal{Z}\{f_{t+1}, z\} = z\mathcal{Z}\{f_t, z\} - zf_0, \tag{P10}$$

$$\mathcal{Z}\{f_{t+2}, z\} = z\mathcal{Z}\{f_{t+1}, z\} - zf_1 = z^2\mathcal{Z}\{f_t, z\} - z^2 f_0 - zf_1 \tag{P11}$$

$$\dots,$$

$$\mathcal{Z}\{f_{t+k}, z\} = z^k\mathcal{Z}\{f_t, z\} - \sum_{r=0}^{k-1} z^{k-r} f_r. \tag{P12}$$

Property 11 *Initial-value and final-value theorems:*

$$\lim_{\lvert z \rvert \to \infty} \mathcal{Z}\{f_t, z\} = f_0, \tag{P13}$$

$$\lim_{z \to 1}(z-1)\mathcal{Z}\{f_t, z\} = \lim_{t \to \infty} f_t. \tag{P14}$$

A.7.3 Simple application

Suppose we wish to solve the following difference equation:

$$x_{t+2} + 3x_{t+1} + 2x_t = 0, \ x_0 = 0, \ x_1 = 1. \tag{A.136}$$

By using properties (P10) and (P11) we obtain the subsidary equation in a few steps:

$$0 = \left[z^2 \mathcal{Z}\{x_t, z\} - z^2 x_0 - z x_1 \right] + 3 \left[z \mathcal{Z}\{x_t, z\} - z x_0 \right] + 2\mathcal{Z}\{x_t, z\} \Leftrightarrow$$

$$\left(z^2 + 3z + 2 \right) \mathcal{Z}\{x_t, z\} = z^2 x_0 + z x_1 + 3 z x_0 = z \Leftrightarrow$$

$$\mathcal{Z}\{x_t, z\} = \frac{z}{(z+1)(z+2)} = \frac{z}{z+1} - \frac{z}{z+2}. \tag{A.137}$$

Inverting (A.137) yields the solution in the time domain:

$$x_t = (-1)^t - (-2)^t, \tag{A.138}$$

for $t = 0, 1, 2, \ldots$..

This example is—of course—rather unexciting apart from the fact that it gives us a hint as to the stability properties of difference equations. Asymptotic stability of (a system of) difference equations is obtained if the roots lie inside the unit circle, i.e. terms like $\frac{z}{z+a}$ are (un) stable if $|a| < 1$ ($|a| > 1$).

A.7.4 The saddle-path model

We now consider the following system of difference equations (by analogy with (A.100)):

$$\left[\begin{array}{c} K_{t+1} - K_t \\ Q_{t+1} - Q_t \end{array} \right] = \Delta \left[\begin{array}{c} K_t \\ Q_t \end{array} \right] + \left[\begin{array}{c} g_{K,t} \\ g_{Q,t} \end{array} \right], \tag{A.139}$$

where $g_{K,t}$ and $g_{Q,t}$ are shock terms (possessing a z-transform) and Δ has typical element δ_{ij}. Taking the z-transform of (A.139) yields:

$$\Lambda(z-1) \left[\begin{array}{c} \mathcal{Z}\{K_t, z\} \\ \mathcal{Z}\{Q_t, z\} \end{array} \right] = \left[\begin{array}{c} z K_0 + \mathcal{Z}\{g_{K,t}, z\} \\ z Q_0 + \mathcal{Z}\{g_{Q,t}, z\} \end{array} \right], \tag{A.140}$$

where $\Lambda(z-1) \equiv (z-1)I - \Delta$. We assume that the characteristic roots of Δ are both real and that $-1 < \lambda_1 < 0$ and $\lambda_2 > 0$.[12] As before, K_t is deemed to be predetermined (so that K_0 is given) whilst Q_t is a non-predetermined variable (so that Q_0 can jump). Since $\Lambda(z-1)^{-1} = \text{adj}\Lambda(z-1)/[(z-(1-\lambda_1))(z-(1+\lambda_2))]$ we can rewrite (A.140) as:

$$[z - (1 - \lambda_1)] \left[\begin{array}{c} \mathcal{Z}\{K_t, z\} \\ \mathcal{Z}\{Q_t, z\} \end{array} \right] = \frac{\text{adj}\Lambda(z-1) \left[\begin{array}{c} z K_0 + \mathcal{Z}\{g_{K,t}, z\} \\ z Q_0 + \mathcal{Z}\{g_{Q,t}, z\} \end{array} \right]}{z - (1 + \lambda_2)}. \tag{A.141}$$

To ensure saddle-point stability the denominator and numerator on the right-hand side of (A.141) must both go to zero as z goes to $1 + \lambda_2$. This furnishes the expression for Q_0:

$$\text{adj}\Lambda(\lambda_2) \left[\begin{array}{c} (1 + \lambda_2)K_0 + \mathcal{Z}\{g_{K,t}, 1 + \lambda_2\} \\ (1 + \lambda_2)Q_0 + \mathcal{Z}\{g_{K,t}, 1 + \lambda_2\} \end{array} \right] = \left[\begin{array}{c} 0 \\ 0 \end{array} \right]. \tag{A.142}$$

---

[12] We write the system in a form which emphasizes the close analogy with (A.100). Of course, we can also re-express (A.139) as:

$$\left[\begin{array}{c} K_{t+1} \\ Q_{t+1} \end{array} \right] = \Delta^* \left[\begin{array}{c} K_t \\ Q_t \end{array} \right] + \left[\begin{array}{c} g_{K,t} \\ g_{Q,t} \end{array} \right],$$

where $\Delta^* \equiv I + \Delta$. The characteristic roots of Δ^* and Δ are related according to $\lambda_i^* = 1 + \lambda_i$. Azariadis (1993, p. 65) gives the conditions for saddle-point stability.

By rewriting (A.142) we finally obtain:

$$Q_0 = -\frac{\mathcal{Z}\{g_{Q,t}, 1+\lambda_2\}}{1+\lambda_2} - \left(\frac{\lambda_2 - \delta_{22}}{\delta_{12}}\right)\left[K_0 + \frac{\mathcal{Z}\{g_{K,t}, 1+\lambda_2\}}{1+\lambda_2}\right] \tag{A.143}$$

$$= -\frac{\mathcal{Z}\{g_{Q,t}, 1+\lambda_2\}}{1+\lambda_2} - \left(\frac{\delta_{21}}{\lambda_2 - \delta_{11}}\right)\left[K_0 + \frac{\mathcal{Z}\{g_{K,t}, 1+\lambda_2\}}{1+\lambda_2}\right]. \tag{A.144}$$

Similarly, the general expression for the solution can be written as:

$$[z - (1+\lambda_1)]\begin{bmatrix} \mathcal{Z}\{K_t, z\} \\ \mathcal{Z}\{Q_t, z\} \end{bmatrix} = \begin{bmatrix} zK_0 + \mathcal{Z}\{g_{K,t}, z\} \\ zQ_0 + \mathcal{Z}\{g_{Q,t}, z\} \end{bmatrix}$$

$$+ \frac{\text{adj}\Lambda(\lambda_2)\begin{bmatrix} \mathcal{Z}\{g_{K,t}, z\} - \left(\frac{z}{1+\lambda_2}\right)\mathcal{Z}\{g_{K,t}, 1+\lambda_2\} \\ \mathcal{Z}\{g_{Q,t}, z\} - \left(\frac{z}{1+\lambda_2}\right)\mathcal{Z}\{g_{Q,t}, 1+\lambda_2\} \end{bmatrix}}{z - (1+\lambda_2)}, \tag{A.145}$$

where the analogy with (A.119) should be obvious. In the Appendix to Chapter 18 equations (A.143)–(A.145) are used to solve the impulse-response functions for the unit-elastic RBC model with technology shocks.

A.7.5   Literature

Basic: Klein (1998, ch. 13), Chiang (1984, chs. 16–17), Sydsæter and Hammond (1995, ch. 20). Intermediate: de la Fuente (2000, chs. 9–11). Advanced: Azariadis (1993), Elaydi (1996), and Ogata (1995).

A.8   Dynamic optimization in continuous time

In this section we present some of the key results from optimal control theory as they are used in this book. We start by forging the link between the static Lagrangian method and the dynamic Optimum Principle, using the insights of Intriligator (1971, pp. 346–348) and Chiang (1992, pp. 177–181). We focus attention on maximization problems in continuous time and ignore second-order conditions. (Of course, in all applications discussed in the text, these glossed-over second-order conditions are indeed fulfilled.) Discrete-time problems are solved in the text by making use of the Lagrangian methods discussed above in this appendix.

A.8.1   From Lagrange to the Optimum Principle

We start with a very basic dynamic optimization problem, involving the optimal consumption and saving plans of a finitely-lived agent. This agent has the following objective function:

$$\Lambda(t_0) \equiv \int_{t_0}^{t_1} U(C(t)) \cdot e^{\rho(t_0 - t)} dt, \tag{A.146}$$

where $\Lambda(t_0)$ is (remaining-) lifetime utility, t_0 is the planning period, t_1 is the planning horizon (say, the agent's time of death), $U(\cdot)$ is the felicity function, $C(t)$ is the flow of consumption at time t, and ρ is the pure rate of time preference. As usual, the felicity function features positive but diminishing marginal utility of consumption, i.e. $U'(\cdot) > 0 > U''(\cdot)$.

Next we turn to the constraints faced by this agent. We assume that financial assets, $A(t)$, evolve over time according to the following budget identity:

$$\dot{A}(t) = r(t)A(t) + W(t) - C(t), \tag{A.147}$$

where $\dot{A}(t) \equiv dA(t)/dt$, $r(t)$ is the interest rate, and $W(t)$ is wage income. Both $r(t)$ and $W(t)$ are taken as given by the agent but may vary over time. Simply put, equation (A.147) says that any unconsumed income is added to financial assets (i.e., is saved). The second constraint faced by the agent is the terminal condition, which says that the agent wants to end up with zero financial wealth at the time of death:

$$A(t_1) = 0. \tag{A.148}$$

Third, there is an initial condition which says that assets in the planning period are equal to whatever the agent owns at that time (A_0):

$$A(t_0) = A_0, \tag{A.149}$$

where A_0 is a predetermined variable at time t_0 (the past cannot be undone). Finally, there are no borrowing constraints, so $A(t)$ may be negative for some $t < t_1$.

The optimization problem is as follows. The agent must choose a time path for $C(t)$ and $A(t)$ for $t_0 \leq t \leq t_1$ such that (A.146) is maximized subject to the constraints (A.148)–(A.149). Let us first try to solve this problem using the Lagrangian method discussed above. In the first step we define the Lagrangian:

$$\mathcal{L}(t_0) \equiv \int_{t_0}^{t_1} U(C(t)) \cdot e^{\rho(t_0-t)} dt + \int_{t_0}^{t_1} \lambda(t) \cdot \left[r(t)A(t) + W(t) - C(t) - \dot{A}(t) \right] dt, \tag{A.150}$$

where $\lambda(t)$ is the Lagrange multiplier for the budget identity at time t, and we note that the term in square brackets is simply a rewritten version of the constraint (A.147). We can rewrite (A.150) somewhat to obtain:

$$\mathcal{L}(t_0) \equiv \int_{t_0}^{t_1} \left[U(C(t)) \cdot e^{\rho(t_0-t)} + \lambda(t) \cdot \left[r(t)A(t) + W(t) - C(t) \right] \right] dt$$

$$- \int_{t_0}^{t_1} \lambda(t) \dot{A}(t) dt$$

$$= \int_{t_0}^{t_1} \mathcal{H}(t, C(t), A(t), \lambda(t)) dt - \int_{t_0}^{t_1} \lambda(t) \dot{A}(t) dt, \tag{A.151}$$

where the $\mathcal{H}(\cdot)$ function is defined as follows:

$$\mathcal{H}(t, C(t), A(t), \lambda(t)) \equiv U(C(t)) \cdot e^{\rho(t_0-t)} + \lambda(t) \cdot \left[r(t)A(t) + W(t) - C(t) \right]. \tag{A.152}$$

This still does not look like a standard (static) Lagrangian problem because $\dot{A}(t)$ still features on the right-hand side of (A.152). Using integration by parts, however, we can write:

$$- \int_{t_0}^{t_1} \lambda(t) \dot{A}(t) dt = -\lambda(t)A(t) \Big|_{t_0}^{t_1} + \int_{t_0}^{t_1} A(t) \dot{\lambda}(t) dt$$

$$= \lambda(t_0) A(t_0) - \lambda(t_1) A(t_1) + \int_{t_0}^{t_1} A(t) \dot{\lambda}(t) \, dt. \quad \text{(A.153)}$$

By substituting (A.153) into (A.151) we thus obtain the ultimate expression for the Lagrangian which no longer involves $\dot{A}(t)$:

$$\mathcal{L}(t_0) \equiv \int_{t_0}^{t_1} \left[\mathcal{H}(t, C(t), A(t), \lambda(t)) + A(t) \dot{\lambda}(t) \right] dt$$
$$+ \lambda(t_0) A(t_0) - \lambda(t_1) A(t_1), \quad \text{(A.154)}$$

where we recall that $A(t_1) = 0$.

In the next step we consider the following variational experiment. Denote the optimal, utility-maximizing, paths for $C(t)$ and $A(t)$ by, respectively, $\bar{C}(t)$ and $\bar{A}(t)$. Consider neighbouring solutions for $C(t)$ and $A(t)$ taking the following form:

$$C(t) = \bar{C}(t) + \varepsilon z_1(t), \quad \text{(A.155)}$$
$$A(t) = \bar{A}(t) + \varepsilon z_2(t), \quad \text{(A.156)}$$

where $z_1(t)$ ($\neq 0$) is the *perturbation path* for $C(t)$ and $z_2(t)$ is the corresponding perturbation path for $A(t)$. Note that the latter perturbation path is induced by (a) the perturbation path for $C(t)$ and (b) the dynamic path for $A(t)$ (stated in equation (A.147) above). We can now rewrite (A.154) for the neighbouring solution as:

$$\mathcal{L}(\varepsilon, t_0) \equiv \int_{t_0}^{t_1} \left[\mathcal{H}(t, \bar{C}(t) + \varepsilon z_1(t), \bar{A}(t) + \varepsilon z_2(t), \lambda(t)) \right.$$
$$\left. + \dot{\lambda}(t) [\bar{A}(t) + \varepsilon z_2(t)] \right] dt + \lambda(t_0) A(t_0) - \lambda(t_1) A(t_1), \quad \text{(A.157)}$$

where we have already incorporated the fact that the perturbation path for $A(t)$ must be consistent with both (A.148) and (A.149), i.e. $\bar{A}(t_0) = A(t_0)$ so that $z_2(t_0) = 0$ and $\bar{A}(t_1) = A(t_1) = 0$ so that $z_2(t_1) = 0$. Other than at time t_0 and t_1, we have that $z_2(t) \neq 0$.

If, as we asserted, $\bar{C}(t)$ and $\bar{A}(t)$ are indeed the optimal solution paths, then it must be the case that $d\mathcal{L}(\varepsilon, t_0)/d\varepsilon = 0$ for $\varepsilon = 0$. By taking the derivative, we find:

$$\frac{d\mathcal{L}(\varepsilon, t_0)}{d\varepsilon} = \int_{t_0}^{t_1} \left[\frac{\partial \mathcal{H}(\cdot)}{\partial C(t)} z_1(t) + \left[\frac{\partial \mathcal{H}(\cdot)}{\partial A(t)} + \dot{\lambda}(t) \right] z_2(t) \right] dt. \quad \text{(A.158)}$$

It thus follows that $d\mathcal{L}(\varepsilon, t_0)/d\varepsilon = 0$ if and only if all terms on the right-hand side of (A.158) are equal to zero for all non-zero perturbation paths, i.e. it must be the case that the optimal solutions satisfy:

$$\frac{\partial \mathcal{H}(t, C(t), A(t), \lambda(t))}{\partial C(t)} = 0, \quad \text{(A.159)}$$

$$-\frac{\partial \mathcal{H}(t, C(t), A(t), \lambda(t))}{\partial A(t)} = \dot{\lambda}(t), \quad \text{(A.160)}$$

plus, of course, the original constraint (A.147) which we can write as:

$$\frac{\partial \mathcal{H}[t, C(t), A(t), \lambda(t)]}{\partial \lambda(t)} = \dot{A}(t). \quad \text{(A.161)}$$

Congratulations! If you have followed us up to this point, you have now derived the first-order necessary conditions associated with the *method of optimal control*! To prepare for the discussion to follow, we now introduce some concepts and nomenclature from the optimal control literature:

- The $\mathcal{H}(\cdot)$ function defined in (A.152) above is called the *Hamiltonian* function associated with the dynamic optimization problem.

- The variable whose path can be chosen freely at each moment in time is called the *control variable*. In the problem studied here, $C(t)$ is the control variable.

- The variable whose path results dynamically from the path of the control variable is called the *state variable*. In the problem studied here, $A(t)$ is the state variable. The equation that postulates the time path for the state variable is called the *state equation*. Here, equation (A.147) is the state equation. The best way to recognize the state variable in particular applications is to look for the state equation.

- The Lagrange multiplier that is attached to the state variable is called the *co-state variable*. In the problem studied here, $\lambda(t)$ is the co-state variable.

Now that we have had a first glance at the method of optimal control, the remainder of this section discusses some of the key results used throughout the book. From here on we focus on the case in which the planning horizon is infinite, i.e. $t_1 \to \infty$. We first study the unconstrained case for which there are no restrictions on the control variable(s). Next we briefly show how (in)equality constraints can be imposed on the control variable(s).

A.8.2 Unconstrained

The proto-typical infinite-horizon optimal control problem encountered in economics takes the following form. The objective function is defined as:

$$\Psi(t_0) = \int_{t_0}^{\infty} \Phi(x(t), u(t), t) \cdot e^{\rho(t_0 - t)} dt, \tag{A.162}$$

where t_0 is the planning period, $x(t)$ is the state variable, $u(t)$ is the control variable, $e^{\rho(t_0 - t)}$ is the discount factor, and t is time. The state and control variable are related according to the following *state equation*:

$$\dot{x}(t) = f(x(t), u(t), t). \tag{A.163}$$

The state equation thus describes the (equation of) motion of the state variable. The initial condition for the state variable is given by:

$$x(0) = x_0, \tag{A.164}$$

where x_0 is a given constant (e.g. the accumulated stock of some resource). In most optimal control problems studied in the text, the terminal value of the state variable can be freely chosen but is subject to a lower limit. For example, a household's asset holdings or a firm's capital stock cannot become negative *in the limit*. We thus write the terminal condition as:

$$\lim_{t \to \infty} x(t) \geq x_{min}, \tag{A.165}$$

where x_{min} is the exogenously given lower bound on the state variable (typically $x_{min} = 0$). The objective is to find a time path for the control variable, $u(t)$ for $t \in [t_0, \infty)$, such that the objective function (A.162) is maximized given the state equation (A.163), the initial condition (A.164), and the terminal condition (A.165).

To solve this problem one formulates a *Hamiltonian* function which takes the following form:

$$\mathcal{H} \equiv \Phi(x(t), u(t), t)e^{\rho(t_0-t)} + \lambda(t) \cdot f(x(t), u(t), t), \tag{A.166}$$

where $\lambda(t)$ is the co-state variable which plays the role similar to the Lagrange multiplier encountered in static optimization problems. The Maximum Principle furnishes the following conditions (for $t \in [t_0, \infty)$):

$$\frac{\partial \mathcal{H}}{\partial u(t)} = 0, \tag{A.167}$$

$$\dot{x}(t) = \frac{\partial \mathcal{H}}{\partial \lambda(t)}, \qquad x(0) = x_0, \tag{A.168}$$

$$\dot{\lambda}(t) = -\frac{\partial \mathcal{H}}{\partial x(t)}, \tag{A.169}$$

$$\lim_{t\to\infty} \lambda(t) \geq 0, \qquad \lim_{t\to\infty} \lambda(t) \cdot [x(t) - x_{\min}] = 0. \tag{A.170}$$

The first condition says that the control variable should be chosen such that the Hamiltonian is maximized, the second condition gives the equation of motion for the state variable, whilst the third equation gives the equation of motion for the co-state variable. Finally, the expressions in (A.170) constitute the *transversality condition* (Chiang, 1992, p. 241). It is very much like a complementary slackness condition. Recall that $\lambda(t)$ is the shadow value of the state variable $x(t)$. If it turns out that $\lim_{t\to\infty} x(t) > x_{\min}$, then the second expression in (A.170) implies that $\lim_{t\to\infty} \lambda(t) = 0$. Intuitively, if in the limit the state strictly exceeds its minimum allowable level, then it must be the case that this final state variable is worthless. Vice versa, if it turns out that $\lim_{t\to\infty} \lambda(t) > 0$, then it must be the case that $\lim_{t\to\infty} x(t) = x_{\min}$, i.e. it is not optimal to end up with more than the bare minimum of a valued state variable.

An equivalent way of solving the same problem is to work with the *current-value Hamiltonian*, which is defined as follows:

$$\mathcal{H}_C \left[\equiv \mathcal{H}e^{\rho(t-t_0)}\right] = \Phi(x(t), u(t), t) + \mu(t) \cdot f(x(t), u(t), t), \tag{A.171}$$

where $\mu(t) \equiv \lambda(t)e^{\rho(t-t_0)}$ is the redefined co-state variable. The first-order conditions expressed in terms of the current-value Hamiltonian are:

$$\frac{\partial \mathcal{H}_C}{\partial u(t)} = 0, \tag{A.172}$$

$$\dot{x}(t) = \frac{\partial \mathcal{H}_C}{\partial \mu(t)}, \tag{A.173}$$

$$\dot{\mu}(t) - \rho\mu(t) = -\frac{\partial \mathcal{H}_C}{\partial x(t)}, \tag{A.174}$$

$$\lim_{t\to\infty} e^{\rho(t_0-t)}\mu(t) \geq 0, \qquad \lim_{t\to\infty} e^{\rho(t_0-t)}\mu(t) \cdot [x(t) - x_{\min}] = 0. \tag{A.175}$$

In many applications of optimal control techniques (e.g. the firm's investment decision), the discount term in (A.162) is not $e^{\rho(t_0-t)}$ but rather takes the form $e^{-R(t_0,t)}$, where $R(t_0, t) \equiv \int_{t_0}^{t} r(s)\,ds$. In such a case we define $\mathcal{H}_C \equiv \mathcal{H}e^{R(t_0,t)}$, $\mu(t) \equiv \lambda(t)e^{R(t_0,t)}$, and change (A.174) to:

$$\dot{\mu}(t) - r(t)\mu(t) = -\frac{\partial \mathcal{H}_C}{\partial x(t)}, \tag{A.176}$$

where we have used the fact that $dR(t_0, t)/dt = r(t)$. In (A.175) we use $e^{-R(t_0,t)}$ instead of $e^{\rho(t_0-t)}$.

If there are n state variables and m controls then the same methods carry over except, of course, that $x(t) \equiv (x_1(t), ..., x_n(t))$ and $u(t) \equiv (u_1(t), ..., u_m(t))$ must be interpreted as vectors, and the set of conditions is suitably expanded:

$$\frac{\partial \mathcal{H}_C}{\partial u_j(t)} = 0, \tag{A.177}$$

$$\dot{x}_i(t) = \frac{\partial \mathcal{H}_C}{\partial \mu_i(t)}, \tag{A.178}$$

$$\dot{\mu}_i(t) - \rho\mu_i(t) = -\frac{\partial \mathcal{H}_C}{\partial x_i(t)}, \tag{A.179}$$

$$\lim_{t\to\infty} e^{\rho(t_0-t)}\mu_i(t) \geq 0, \qquad \lim_{t\to\infty} e^{\rho(t_0-t)}\mu_i(t) \cdot [x_i(t) - x_{i,\min}] = 0, \tag{A.180}$$

where $\mu_i(t)$ is the co-state variable corresponding to the state variable $x_i(t)$, $j = 1, ..., m$, and $i = 1, ..., n$.

A.8.3 (In)equality constraints

Suppose the problem is as in (A.162)–(A.165) but that there is an additional constraint in the form of:

$$g(x(t), u(t), t) \leq c, \tag{A.181}$$

where c is some constant. Suppose furthermore that there is a non-negativity constraint on the control variable, i.e. $u(t) \geq 0$ is required (for example, consumption or leisure cannot become negative). The way to deal with these inequalities is to form the following current-value Lagrangian:

$$\mathcal{L}_C = \Phi(x(t), u(t), t) + \mu(t) \cdot f(x(t), u(t), t) + \theta(t) \cdot [c - g(x(t), u(t), t)], \tag{A.182}$$

where $\theta(t)$ is the Lagrange multiplier associated with the inequality constraint (A.181). The first-order conditions are now:

$$\frac{\partial \mathcal{L}_C}{\partial u(t)} \leq 0, \quad u(t) \geq 0, \quad u(t)\frac{\partial \mathcal{L}_C}{\partial u(t)} = 0, \tag{A.183}$$

$$\frac{\partial \mathcal{L}_C}{\partial \theta(t)} \geq 0, \quad \theta(t) \geq 0, \quad \theta(t)\frac{\partial \mathcal{L}_C}{\partial \theta(t)} = 0, \tag{A.184}$$

$$\dot{x}(t) = \frac{\partial \mathcal{L}_C}{\partial \mu(t)}, \tag{A.185}$$

$$\dot{\mu}(t) - \rho\mu(t) = -\frac{\partial \mathcal{L}_C}{\partial x(t)}. \tag{A.186}$$

Equation (A.183) gives the Kuhn-Tucker conditions taking care of the non-negativity constraint on the control variable. The second equation gives the Kuhn-Tucker conditions for the inequality constraint (A.181). Finally, (A.185) and (A.186) give the laws of motion of, respectively, the state variable and the co-state variable. The transversality condition is again given by (A.175).

A.8.4 Second-order conditions

The second-order sufficient conditions are given by Chiang (1992, p. 290).

A.8.5   Literature

Basic: Klein (1998, ch. 15) and Chiang (1992). Intermediate: Dixit (1990, chs 10–11), Intriligator (1971, chs. 11–14), Léonard and Long (1992), and de la Fuente (2000, chs. 12–13). Advanced: Kamien and Schwartz (1991), Seierstad and Sydsæter (1987), and Chow (1997).

Bibliography

Aaron, H. J. (1966). The social insurance paradox. *Canadian Journal of Economics and Political Science*, 32:371–374.

Abel, A. B. (1981). A dynamic model of investment and capacity utilization. *Quarterly Journal of Economics*, 96:379–403.

Abel, A. B. (1982). Dynamic effects of permanent and temporary tax policies in a q model of investment. *Journal of Monetary Economics*, 9:353–373.

Abel, A. B. (1985). Precautionary savings and accidental bequests. *American Economic Review*, 75:777–791.

Abel, A. B. (1986). Capital accumulation and uncertain lifetimes with adverse selection. *Econometrica*, 54:1079–1097.

Abel, A. B. (1990). Consumption and investment. In Friedman, B. M. and Hahn, F. H., editors, *Handbook of Monetary Economics*. North-Holland, Amsterdam.

Abel, A. B. and Bernanke, B. S. (2005). *Macroeconomics*. Addison Wesley, Boston, MA, fifth edition.

Abel, A. B., Dixit, A. K., Eberly, J. C., and Pindyck, R. S. (1996). Options, the value of capital, and investment. *Quarterly Journal of Economics*, 111:753–777.

Abel, A. B. and Eberly, J. C. (1994). A unified model of investment under uncertainty. *American Economic Review*, 84:1369–1384.

Abel, A. B., Mankiw, N. G., Summers, L. H., and Zeckhauser, R. (1989). Assessing dynamic efficiency: Theory and evidence. *Review of Economic Studies*, 56:1–19.

Acemoglu, D. (2002). Technical change, inequality, and the labor market. *Journal of Economic Literature*, 40:7–72.

Acemoglu, D. (2003a). Labor- and capital-augmenting technical change. *Journal of the European Economic Association*, 1:1–37.

Acemoglu, D. (2003b). Patterns of skill premia. *Review of Economic Studies*, 70:199–230.

Acemoglu, D. (2007). Equilibrium bias of technology. *Econometrica*, 75:1371–1409.

Acemoglu, D. (2009). *Introduction to Modern Economic Growth*. Princeton University Press, Princeton, NJ.

Acemoglu, D., Zilibotti, F., and Aghion, P. (2006). Distance to frontier, selection, and economic growth. *Journal of the European Economic Association*, 4:37–74.

Adda, J. and Cooper, R. W. (2003). *Dynamic Economics: Quantitative Methods and Applications*. MIT Press, Cambridge, MA.

Adjemian, S., Bastani, H., Juillard, M., Karamé, F., Mihoubi, F., Perendia, G., Pfeifer, J., Ratto, M., and Villemot, S. (2011). Dynare: Reference manual, version 4. Dynare Working Papers 1, CEPREMAP, Paris.

Aghion, P. and Durlauf, S. N., editors (2005a). *Handbook of Economic Growth*, volume 1A. North-Holland, Amsterdam.

Aghion, P. and Durlauf, S. N., editors (2005b). *Handbook of Economic Growth*, volume 1B. North-Holland, Amsterdam.

Aghion, P. and Howitt, P. (1992). A model of growth through creative destruction. *Econometrica*, 60:323–351.

Aghion, P. and Howitt, P. (1998). *Endogenous Growth Theory*. MIT Press, Cambridge, MA.

Aiyagari, S. R. (1994). Uninsured idiosyncratic risk and aggregate saving. *Journal of Political Economy*, 109:659–684.

Akerlof, G. and Yellen, J. (1985a). Can small deviations from rationality make significant differences to economic equilibria? *American Economic Review*, 75:708–721.

Akerlof, G. and Yellen, J. (1985b). A near-rational model of the business cycle with wage and price inertia. *Quarterly Journal of Economics, Supplement*, 100:823–838.

Akerlof, G. A. and Yellen, J. L., editors (1986). *Efficiency Wage Models of the Labor Market*. Cambridge University Press, Cambridge.

Albis, H. d' (2007). Demographic structure and capital accumulation. *Journal of Economic Theory*, 132:411–434.

Alesina, A. and Grilli, V. (1992). The European central bank: Reshaping monetary politics in Europe. In Canzoneri, M., Grilli, V., and Masson, P., editors, *Establishing a Central Bank. Issues in Europe and Lessons from the US*. Cambridge University Press, Cambridge.

Allen, R. G. D. (1967). *Macro-Economic Theory: A Mathematical Treatment*. Macmillan, London and Basingstoke.

Alogoskoufis, G. and Ploeg, F. van der (1990). Endogenous growth and overlapping generations. Discussion Paper 9072, CentER, Tilburg University.

Altug, S. and Labadie, P. (2008). *Asset Pricing for Dynamic Economies*. Cambridge University Press, Cambridge.

Altug, S. and Young, W. (2015). Real business cycles after three decades: A panel discussion with Edward Prescott, Finn Kydland, Charles Plosser, Thomas Cooley, and Gary Hansen. *Macroeconomic Dynamics*, 19:425–445.

Amable, B., Henry, J., Lordon, F., and Topol, R. (1994). Strong hysteresis versus unit-root dynamics. *Economics Letters*, 44:43–47.

Andolfatto, D. (1996). Business cycles and labor market search. *American Economic Review*, 86:112–132.

Angeletos, G.-M., Laibson, D., Repetto, A., Tobacman, J., and Weinberg, S. (2001). The hyperbolic consumption model: Calibration, simulation, and empirical evaluation. *Journal of Economic Perspectives*, 15:47–68.

Aoki, M. (1981). *Dynamic Analysis of Open Economies*. Academic Press, New York.

Apostol, T. M. (1967). *Calculus*, volume I. John Wiley, New York, second edition.

Argy, V. and Salop, J. (1979). Price and output effects of monetary and fiscal policy under flexible exchange rates. *IMF Staff Papers*, 26:224–256.

Argy, V. and Salop, J. (1983). Price and output effects of monetary and fiscal expansion in a two-country world under flexible exchange rates. *Oxford Economic Papers*, 35:228–246.

Armington, P. S. (1969). A theory of demand for products distinguished by place of production. *IMF Staff Papers*, 16:159–178.

Arrow, K. J. (1953). Le rôle des valeurs boursières pour la repartition la meilleure des risques. *Econometrie*, 11:41–47. Colloques Internationaux du Centre Nationale de la Recherche Scientifique. English translation in Arrow (1964).

Arrow, K. J. (1959). Towards a theory of price adjustment. In Abramovitz, M. et al., editors, *The Allocation of Economic Resources*. Stanford University Press, Stanford, CA.

Arrow, K. J. (1962). The economic implications of learning by doing. *Review of Economic Studies*, 29:155–173.

Arrow, K. J. (1964). The role of securities in the optimal allocation of risk-bearing. *Review of Economic Studies*, 31:91–96.

Arrow, K. J. (1965). *Aspects of the Theory of Risk-Bearing*. Yrjö Jahnssonin Säätio, Helsinki.

Arrow, K. J. (1970). *Essays in the Theory of Risk-Bearing*. North-Holland, Amsterdam.

Arrow, K. J. and Kurz, M. (1970). *Public Investment, the Rate of Return, and Optimal Fiscal Policy*. Johns Hopkins Press, Baltimore, MD.

Asako, K. (1983). The utility function and the superneutrality of money on the transition path. *Econometrica*, 51:1593–1596.

Ascari, G. and Rossi, L. (2012). Trend inflation and firms price-setting: Rotemberg versus Calvo. *Economic Journal*, 122:1115–1141.

Aschauer, D. (1988). The equilibrium approach to fiscal policy. *Journal of Money, Credit, and Banking*, 20:41–62.

Aschauer, D. A. (1989). Is public expenditure productive? *Journal of Monetary Economics*, 23:177–200.

Aschauer, D. A. (1990). Finite horizons, intertemporal substitution, and fiscal policy. *Public Finance Quarterly*, 18:77–91.

Aschauer, D. A. and Greenwood, J. (1985). Macroeconomic effects of fiscal policy. *Carnegie-Rochester Conference Series on Public Policy*, 23:91–138.

Atkinson, A. B. (1994). The distribution of the tax burden. In Quigley, J. M., editor, *Modern Public Finance*, pages 13–57. Harvard University Press, Cambridge, MA.

Atkinson, A. B. and Stern, N. H. (1974). Pigou, taxation, and public goods. *Review of Economic Studies*, 41:119–128.

Atkinson, A. B. and Stiglitz, J. E. (1980). *Lectures on Public Economics*. McGraw-Hill, New York.

Attanasio, O. P. (1999). Consumption. In Taylor, J. B. and Woodford, M., editors, *Handbook of Macroeconomics*, volume 1B. North-Holland, Amsterdam.

Attfield, C. L. F., Demery, D., and Duck, N. W. (1985). *Rational Expectations in Macroeconomics*. Basil Blackwell, Oxford.

Auerbach, A. J. (1979a). The optimal taxation of heterogeneous capital. *Quarterly Journal of Economics*, 94:589–612.

Auerbach, A. J. (1979b). Wealth maximization and the cost of capital. *Quarterly Journal of Economics*, 93:433–446.

Auerbach, A. J. and Kotlikoff, L. J. (1987). *Dynamic Fiscal Policy*. Cambridge University Press, Cambridge.

Axelrod, R. (1984). *The Evolution of Cooperation*. Basic Books, New York.

Ayres, F. (1974). *Theory and Problems of Matrices*. McGraw-Hill, New York.

Azariadis, C. (1975). Implicit contracts and underemployment equilibria. *Journal of Political Economy*, 83:1183–1202.

Azariadis, C. (1981). Implicit contracts and related topics: A survey. In Hornstein, Z., Grice, J., and Webb, A., editors, *The Economics of the Labour Market*. Her Majesty's Stationary Office, London.

Azariadis, C. (1993). *Intertemporal Macroeconomics*. Basil Blackwell, Oxford.

Azariadis, C. and Drazen, A. (1990). Threshold externalities in economic development. *Quarterly Journal of Economics*, 105:501–526.

Azariadis, C. and Stiglitz, J. E. (1983). Implicit contracts and fixed price equilibria. *Quarterly Economic Journal, Supplement*, 98:1–22.

Backus, D. and Driffill, J. (1985). Inflation and reputation. *American Economic Review*, 75:530–538.

Bailey, M. J. (1956). The welfare costs of inflationary finance. *Journal of Political Economy*, 64:93–110.

Ball, L. and Mankiw, N. G. (2007). Intergenerational risk sharing in the spirit of Arrow, Debreu, and Rawls, with applications to social security design. *Journal of Political Economy*, 115:523–547.

Ball, L., Mankiw, N. G., and Romer, D. (1988). The new Keynesian economics and the output-inflation trade-off. *Brookings Papers on Economic Activity*, Issue 1:1–65.

Ball, L. and Romer, D. (1990). Real rigidities and the non-neutrality of money. *Review of Economic Studies*, 57:183–203.

Barro, R. J. (1974). Are government bonds net wealth? *Journal of Political Economy*, 82:1095–1117.

Barro, R. J. (1976). Rational expectations and the role of monetary policy. *Journal of Monetary Economics*, 2:1–32.

Barro, R. J. (1977). Long-term contracting, sticky prices, and monetary policy. *Journal of Monetary Economics*, 3:305–316.

Barro, R. J. (1979). On the determination of the public debt. *Journal of Political Economy*, 87:940–971.

Barro, R. J. (1981). Output effects of government purchases. *Journal of Political Economy*, 89:1086–1121.

Barro, R. J. (1989). The Ricardian approach to budget deficits. *Journal of Economic Perspectives*, 3:37–54.

Barro, R. J. (1990). Government spending in a simple model of endogenous growth. *Journal of Political Economy*, 98:S103–S125.

Barro, R. J. and Becker, G. S. (1989). Fertility choice in a model of economic growth. *Econometrica*, 57:481–501.

Barro, R. J. and Friedman, J. W. (1977). On uncertain lifetimes. *Journal of Political Economy*, 85:843–849.

Barro, R. J. and Gordon, D. B. (1983a). A positive theory of monetary policy in a natural rate model. *Journal of Political Economy*, 91:589–610.

Barro, R. J. and Gordon, D. B. (1983b). Rules, discretion, and reputation in a model of monetary policy. *Journal of Monetary Economics*, 12:101–120.

Barro, R. J. and Sala-i-Martin, X. (1995). *Economic Growth*. McGraw-Hill, New York.

Barsky, R. B., Mankiw, N. G., and Zeldes, S. P. (1986). Ricardian consumers with Keynesian propensities. *American Economic Review*, 76:676–691.

Batina, R. G. and Ihori, T. (2000). *Consumption Tax Policy and the Taxation of Capital Income*. Oxford University Press, Oxford.

Baumol, W. (1952). The transactions demand for cash: An inventory theoretic approach. *Quarterly Journal of Economics*, 67:545–556.

Baumol, W. J. (1959). *Economic Dynamics: An Introduction*. Macmillan, New York, second edition.

Baxter, M. and King, R. G. (1993). Fiscal policy in general equilibrium. *American Economic Review*, 83:315–334.

Bean, C. R. (1994). European unemployment: A survey. *Journal of Economic Literature*, 32:573–619.

Beaudry, P., Dupaigne, M., and Portier, F. (2011). Modeling news-driven international business cycles. *Review of Economic Dynamics*, 14:72–91.

Beaudry, P. and Portier, F. (2007). When can changes in expectations cause business cycle fluctuations in neo-classical settings? *Journal of Economic Theory*, 135:458–477.

Becker, G. S. (1960). An economic analysis of fertility. In Roberts, G. B., editor, *Demographic and Economic Change in Developed Countries*. Princeton University Press for the National Bureau of Economic Research, Princeton, NJ.

Becker, G. S. (1991). *A Treatise on the Family*. Harvard University Press, Cambridge, MA, enlarged edition.

Becker, G. S. and Barro, R. J. (1988). A reformulation of the economic theory of fertility. *Quarterly Journal of Economics*, 103:1–25.

Becker, G. S. and Lewis, H. G. (1973). On the interaction between the quantity and quality of children. *Journal of Political Economy*, 81:S279–S288.

Becker, G. S., Murphy, K. M., and Tamura, R. (1990). Human capital, fertility, and economic growth. *Journal of Political Economy*, 98:S12–S37.

Belan, P., Michel, P., and Pestieau, P. (1998). Pareto improving social security reform. *Geneva Papers on Risk and Insurance Theory*, 23:119–125.

Belan, P. and Pestieau, P. (1999). Privatizing social security: A critical assessment. *Geneva Papers on Risk and Insurance Theory*, 24:114–130.

Bellman, R. E. (1957). *Dynamic Programming*. Princeton University Press, Princeton, NJ. Reprinted by Dover Publications, New York.

Benassi, C., Chirco, A., and Colombo, C. (1994). *The New Keynesian Economics*. Basil Blackwell, Oxford.

Bénassy, J.-P. (1991a). Monopolistic competition. In Hildenbrand, W. and Sonnenschein, H., editors, *Handbook of Mathematical Economics*, volume IV. North-Holland, Amsterdam.

Bénassy, J.-P. (1991b). Optimal government policy in a macroeconomic model with imperfect competition and rational expectations. In Barnett, W. et al., editors, *Equilibrium Theory and Applications*. Cambridge University Press, Cambridge.

Bénassy, J.-P. (1993a). Imperfect competition and the suboptimality of rational expectations. *European Economic Review*, 37:1315–1330.

Bénassy, J.-P. (1993b). Non-clearing markets: Microeconomic concepts and macroeconomic applications. *Journal of Economic Literature*, 31:732–761.

Bénassy, J.-P. (1996a). Monopolistic competition, increasing returns to specialisation and output persistence. *Economics Letters*, 52:187–191.

Bénassy, J.-P. (1996b). Taste for variety and optimum production patterns in monopolistic competition. *Economics Letters*, 52:41–47.

Bénassy, J.-P. (1998). Is there always too little research in endogenous growth with expanding product variety? *European Economic Review*, 42:61–69.

Benhabib, J. and Farmer, R. E. A. (1994). Indeterminacy and increasing returns. *Journal of Economic Theory*, 63:19–41.

Benhabib, J. and Perli, R. (1994). Uniqueness and indeterminacy: Transitional dynamics in a model of endogenous growth. *Journal of Economic Theory*, 63:113–142.

Benhabib, J., Rogerson, R., and Wright, R. (1991). Homework in macroeconomics: Household production and aggregate fluctuations. *Journal of Political Economy*, 99:1166–1187.

Benveniste, L. M. and Scheinkman, J. A. (1979). On the differentiability of the value function in dynamic models of economics. *Econometrica*, 47:727–732.

Bergson, A. (1938). A reformulation of certain aspects of welfare economics. *Quarterly Journal of Economics*, 42:310–334.

Bernanke, B. S., Gertler, M., and Gilchrist, S. (1999). The financial accelerator in a quantitative business cycle framework. In Taylor, J. B. and Woodford, M., editors, *Handbook of Macroeconomics*, volume 1B. North-Holland, Amsterdam.

Bernheim, B. D. (1987). Ricardian equivalence: An evaluation of theory and evidence. *Macroeconomics Annual*, 2:263–304.

Bernheim, B. D. (1989). A neoclassical perspective on budget deficits. *Journal of Economic Perspectives*, 3:55–72.

Bernheim, B. D. and Bagwell, K. (1988). Is everything neutral? *Journal of Political Economy*, 96:308–338.

Bettendorf, L. J. H. and Heijdra, B. J. (2006). Population ageing and pension reform in a small open economy with non-traded goods. *Journal of Economic Dynamics and Control*, 30:2389–2424.

Bewley, T. (1977). The permanent income hypothesis: A theoretical formulation. *Journal of Economic Theory*, 16:252–292.

Bewley, T. (1980). The optimum quantity of money. In Kareken, J. H. and Wallace, N., editors, *Models of Monetary Economies*. Federal Reserve Bank of Minneapolis, Minneapolis.

Bierwag, G. O., Grove, M. A., and Khang, C. (1969). National debt in a neoclassical growth model: Comment. *American Economic Review*, 59:205–210.

Bikhchandani, S., Hirshleifer, J., and Riley, J. G. (2013). *The Analytics of Uncertainty and Information*. Cambridge University Press, Cambridge, second edition.

Bils, M. and Klenow, P. J. (2000). Does schooling cause growth? *American Economic Review*, 90:1160–1183.

Binmore, K. and Dasgupta, P., editors (1987). *The Economics of Bargaining*. Basil Blackwell, Oxford.

Blanchard, O. J. (1981). Output, the stock market, and interest rates. *American Economic Review*, 71:132–143.

Blanchard, O. J. (1983). Debt and the current account in Brazil. In Aspe Armella, P., Dornbusch, R., and Obstfeld, M., editors, *Financial Policies and the World Capital Market: The Problem of Latin American Countries*. University of Chicago Press, Chicago.

Blanchard, O. J. (1984). Current and anticipated deficits, interest rates and economic activity. *European Economic Review*, 25:7–27.

Blanchard, O. J. (1985). Debts, deficits, and finite horizons. *Journal of Political Economy*, 93:223–247.

Blanchard, O. J. (1990). Why does money affect output? A survey. In Friedman, B. M. and Hahn, F. H., editors, *Handbook of Monetary Economics*, volume II. North-Holland, Amsterdam.

Blanchard, O. J. (2000). What do we know about macroeconomics that Fisher and Wicksell did not? *Quarterly Journal of Economics*, 115:1375–1409.

Blanchard, O. J. (2006). *Macroeconomics*. Prentice-Hall, Upper Saddle River, NJ, fourth edition.

Blanchard, O. J. (2016). Do DSGE models have a future? Policy Brief 16-11, Peterson Institute for International Economics, Washington, DC. See https://piie.com/system/files/documents/pb16-11.pdf.

Blanchard, O. J., Amighini, A., and Giavazzi, F. (2013). *Macroeconomics: A European Perspective*. Pearson Education, Harlow, United Kingdom, second edition.

Blanchard, O. J. and Diamond, P. (1989). The Beveridge curve. *Brookings Papers on Economic Activity*, 1:1–76.

Blanchard, O. J. and Diamond, P. (1994). Ranking, unemployment duration, and wages. *Review of Economic Studies*, 61:417–434.

Blanchard, O. J. and Fischer, S. (1989). *Lectures on Macroeconomics*. MIT Press, Cambridge, MA.

Blanchard, O. J. and Kahn, C. M. (1980). The solution of linear difference models under rational expectations. *Econometrica*, 48:1305–1311.

Blanchard, O. J. and Kiyotaki, N. (1987). Monopolistic competition and the effects of aggregate demand. *American Economic Review*, 77:647–666.

Blinder, A. S. and Solow, R. M. (1973). Does fiscal policy matter? *Journal of Public Economics*, 2:319–337.

Blinder, A. S. and Solow, R. M. (1976a). Does fiscal policy matter? A correction. *Journal of Public Economics*, 5:183–184.

Blinder, A. S. and Solow, R. M. (1976b). Does fiscal policy still matter? A reply. *Journal of Monetary Economics*, 2:501–510.

Boeri, T. and Ours, J. van (2013). *The Economics of Imperfect Labor Markets*. Princeton University Press, Princeton, NJ, second edition.

Bohn, H. (2009). Intergenerational risk sharing and fiscal policy. *Journal of Monetary Economics*, 56:805–816.

Bond, E. W., Wang, P., and Yip, C. K. (1996). A general two-sector model of endogenous growth with human and physical capital: Balanced growth and transitional dynamics. *Journal of Economic Theory*, 68:149–173.

Booth, A. L. (1995). *The Economics of the Trade Union.* Cambridge University Press, Cambridge.

Borch, K. (1962). Equilibrium in a reinsurance market. *Econometrica*, 30:424–444.

Bosworth, B. and Burtless, G., editors (1998). *Aging Societies: The Global Dimension.* Brookings Institution Press, Washington.

Boucekkine, R., Croix, D. de la, and Licandro, O. (2002). Vintage human capital, demographic trends, and endogenous growth. *Journal of Economic Theory*, 104:340–375.

Bovenberg, A. L. (1993). Investment-promoting policies in open economies: The importance of intergenerational and international distributional effects. *Journal of Public Economics*, 51:3–54.

Bovenberg, A. L. (1994). Capital taxation in the world economy. In Ploeg, F. van der, editor, *Handbook of International Macroeconomics*. Basil Blackwell, Oxford.

Bovenberg, A. L. and Heijdra, B. J. (1998). Environmental tax policy and intergenerational distribution. *Journal of Public Economics*, 67:1–24.

Bovenberg, A. L. and Heijdra, B. J. (2002). Environmental abatement and intergenerational distribution. *Environmental and Resource Economics*, 23:45–84.

Bovenberg, A. L. and Uhlig, H. (2008). Pension systems and the allocation of macroeconomic risk. In Reichlin, L. and West, K., editors, *NBER International Seminar on Macroeconomics 2006*, pages 241–323. University of Chicago Press, Chicago.

Boyce, W. E. and DiPrima, R. C. (2005). *Elementary Differential Equations and Boundary Value Problems.* Wiley, New York, eighth edition.

Brakman, S. and Heijdra, B. J., editors (2004). *The Monopolistic Competition Revolution in Retrospect.* Cambridge University Press, Cambridge.

Branson, W. H. (1972). *Macroeconomic Theory and Policy.* Harper and Row, New York.

Branson, W. H. and Rotemberg, J. J. (1980). International adjustment with wage rigidity. *European Economic Review*, 13:309–332.

Braun, R. A. (1994). Tax disturbances and real economic acticity in the postwar United States. *Journal of Monetary Economics*, 33:441–462.

Bresnehan, T. F. and Trajtenberg, M. (1995). General purpose technologies: 'Engines of growth'? *Journal of Econometrics*, 65:83–108.

Breyer, F. (1989). On the intergenerational Pareto efficiency of pay-as-you-go financed pension systems. *Journal of Institutional and Theoretical Economics*, 145:643–658.

Breyer, F. and Straub, M. (1993). Welfare effects of unfunded pension systems when labor supply is endogenous. *Journal of Public Economics*, 50:77–91.

Brinkley, D. (2003). *Wheels for the World: Henry Ford, His Company, and a Century of Progress.* Viking-Penguin, New York.

Brock, W. A. (1975). A simple perfect foresight monetary model. *Journal of Monetary Economics*, 1:133–150.

Brock, W. A. and Mirman, L. J. (1972). Optimal growth and uncertainty: The discounted case. *Journal of Economic Theory*, 4:479–513.

Brock, W. A. and Turnovsky, S. J. (1981). The analysis of macroeconomic policies in perfect foresight equilibrium. *International Economic Review*, 22:179–209.

Broer, D. P. and Heijdra, B. J. (2001). The investment tax credit under monopolistic competition. *Oxford Economic Papers*, 53:318–351.

Browning, M., Hansen, L. P., and Heckman, J. J. (1999). Micro data and general equilibrium models. In Taylor, J. B. and Woodford, M., editors, *Handbook of Macroeconomics*, volume 1A. North-Holland, Amsterdam.

Brunnermeier, M. K. and Sannikov, Y. (2014). A macroeconomic model with financial frictions. *American Economic Review*, 104:379–421.

Buchanan, J. M. (1976). Barro on the Ricardian Equivalence Theorem. *Journal of Political Economy*, 84:337–342.

Buiter, W. H. (1980). The macroeconomics of Dr. Pangloss. *Economic Journal*, 90:34–50.

Buiter, W. H. (1985). A guide to public sector debt and deficits. *Economic Policy*, 1:13–79.

Buiter, W. H. (1987). Fiscal policy in open, interdependent economies. In Razin, A. and Sadka, E., editors, *Economic Policy in Theory and Practice*. Macmillan, London.

Buiter, W. H. (1988). Death, productivity growth and debt neutrality. *Economic Journal*, 98:279–293.

Buiter, W. H. (1990). *Principles of Budgetary and Financial Policy*. Harvester Wheatsheaf, New York.

Buiter, W. H. (2009). The unfortunate uselessnes of most 'state of the art' academic monetary economics. Blog on *Financial Times* website: http://blogs.ft.com/maverecon.

Buiter, W. H. and Kletzer, K. M. (1992). Government solvency, Ponzi finance and the redundancy and usefulness of public debt. Working Paper 4076, NBER, Cambridge, MA.

Buiter, W. H. and Kletzer, K. M. (1993). Permanent international productivity growth differentials in an integrated global economy. *Scandinavian Journal of Economics*, 95:467–493.

Buiter, W. H. and Kletzer, K. M. (1998). Government solvency, Ponzi finance and the redundancy and usefulness of public debt. In Brakman, S., Ees, H. van, and Kuipers, S., editors, *Market Behaviour and Macroeconomic Modelling*, pages 275–307. Macmillan, London.

Buiter, W. H. and Miller, M. (1981). Monetary policy and international competitiveness: The problems of adjustment. *Oxford Economic Papers, Supplement*, 33:143–175.

Buiter, W. H. and Miller, M. (1982). Real exchange rate overshooting and the output cost of bringing down inflation. *European Economic Review*, 33:143–175.

Bulow, J. and Summers, L. H. (1986). A theory of dual labor markets with applications to industrial policy, discrimination, and Keynesian unemployment. *Journal of Labor Economics*, 4:376–414.

Burda, M. and Wyplosz, C. (2005). *Macroeconomics: A European Text*. Oxford University Press, Oxford, fourth edition.

Burmeister, E. and Dobell, A. R. (1970). *Mathematical Theories of Economic Growth*. Macmillan, London.

Burness, H. S. (1976). A note on consistent naive intertemporal decision making and an application to the case of uncertain lifetime. *Review of Economic Studies*, 43:547–549.

Burrows, P. and Hitiris, T. (1974). *Macroeconomic Theory: A Mathematical Introduction*. John Wiley, London.

Bütler, M. (2001). Neoclassical life-cycle consumption: A textbook example. *Economic Theory*, 17:209–221.

Caballero, R. J. (1999). Aggregate investment. In Taylor, J. B. and Woodford, M., editors, *Handbook of Macroeconomics*, volume 1B. North-Holland, Amsterdam.

Caballero, R. J. and Leahy, J. V. (1996). Fixed costs: The demise of marginal q. Working Paper 5508, NBER, Cambridge, MA.

Cahuc, P., Carcillo, S., and Zylberberg, A. (2014). *Labor Economics*. MIT Press, Cambridge, MA, second edition.

Cai, Y. and Judd, K. L. (2010). Stable and efficient computational methods for dynamic programming. *Journal of the European Economic Association*, 8:626–634.

Calmfors, L. and Driffill, J. (1988). Centralisation of wage bargaining. *Economic Policy*, 6:14–61.

Calvo, G. A. (1982). Staggered contracts and exchange rate policy. In Frenkel, J., editor, *Exchange Rates and International Economics*. University of Chicago Press, Chicago.

Calvo, G. A. (1983). Staggered prices in a utility-maximizing framework. *Journal of Monetary Economics*, 12:383–398.

Calvo, G. A. (1987). Real exchange rate dynamics with nominal parities, structural change and overshooting. *Journal of International Economics*, 22:141–155.

Calvo, G. A. and Obstfeld, M. (1988). Optimal time-consistent fiscal policy with finite lifetimes. *Econometrica*, 56:411–432.

Calvo, G. A. and Végh, C. A. (1994). Stabilization dynamics and backward-looking contracts. *Journal of Development Economics*, 43:59–84.

Campbell, J. Y. (1994). Inspecting the mechanism: An analytical approach to the stochastic growth model. *Journal of Monetary Economics*, 33:463–506.

Cannon, E. and Tonks, I. (2006). Survey of annuity pricing. Research Report 318, Department for Work and Pensions, Corporate Document Services, Leeds.

Canton, E. (2001). Fiscal policy in a stochastic model of endogenous growth. *Economic Modelling*, 18:19–47.

Card, D. (1994). Intertemporal labour supply: An assessment. In Sims, C., editor, *Advances in Econometrics: Sixth World Congress*, volume II. Cambridge University Press, Cambridge.

Carlin, W. and Soskice, D. (2006). *Macroeconomics: Imperfections, Institutions, and Policies*. Oxford University Press, Oxford.

Carlstrom, C. T. and Fuerst, T. S. (2005). Investment and interest rate policy: A discrete-time analysis. *Journal of Economic Theory*, 123:4–20.

Carroll, C. D. and Kimball, M. S. (1996). On the concavity of the consumption function. *Econometrica*, 64:981–992.

Carroll, C. D. and Kimball, M. S. (2001). Liquidity constraints and precautionary saving. Working Paper 8496, NBER, Cambridge, MA.

Cass, D. (1965). Optimum growth in an aggregative model of capital accumulation. *Review of Economic Studies*, 32:233–240.

Cass, D. and Yaari, M. E. (1966). A re-examination of the pure consumption loans model. *Journal of Political Economy*, 74:353–367.

Cassidy, J. (2010). *How Markets Fail: The Logic of Economic Calamities*. Penguin, London.

Cassou, S. P. and Lansing, K. J. (1998). Optimal fiscal policy, public capital, and the productivity slowdown. *Journal of Economic Dynamics and Control*, 22:911–935.

Cazzavillan, G. and Pintus, P. A. (2004). Robustness of multiple equilibria in OLG economies. *Review of Economic Dynamics*, 7:456–475.

Chadha, B. (1989). Is increased price flexibility stabilizing? *Journal of Money, Credit, and Banking*, 21:481–497.

Chamley, C. (1985). On a simple rule for the optimal inflation rate in second best taxation. *Journal of Public Economics*, 26:35–50.

Chari, V. V., Christiano, L. J., and Kehoe, P. J. (1996). Optimality of the Friedman rule in economies with distorting taxes. *Journal of Monetary Economics*, 37:203–223.

Chari, V. V., Kehoe, P. J., and McGrattan, E. R. (2000). Sticky price models of the business cycle: Can the contract multiplier solve the persistence problem? *Econometrica*, 68:1151–1179.

Chari, V. V., Kehoe, P. J., and McGrattan, E. R. (2007). Business cycle accounting. *Econometrica*, 75:781–836.

Chari, V. V., Kehoe, P. J., and McGrattan, E. R. (2009). New Keynesian models: Not yet useful for policy analysis. *American Economic Journal: Macroeconomics*, 1:242–266.

Chatterjee, S. and Cooper, R. W. (2014). Entry, exit, product variety and the business cycle. *Economic Inquiry*, 52:1466–1484.

Chiang, A. C. (1984). *Fundamental Methods of Mathematical Economics*. McGraw-Hill, New York, third edition.

Chiang, A. C. (1992). *Elements of Dynamic Optimization*. McGraw-Hill, New York.

Cho, J. O. and Cooley, T. F. (1994). Employment and hours over the business cycle. *Journal of Economic Dynamics and Control*, 18:411–432.

Cho, J. O. and Cooley, T. F. (1995). The business cycle with nominal contracts. *Economic Theory*, 6:13–33.

Cho, J. O. and Rogerson, R. (1988). Family labor supply and aggregate fluctuations. *Journal of Monetary Economics*, 21:233–245.

Chow, G. C. (1997). *Dynamic Economics: Optimization by the Lagrange Method*. Oxford University Press, New York and Oxford.

Christiano, L. J. and Eichenbaum, M. S. (1992). Current real-business-cycle theories and aggregate labour-market fluctuations. *American Economic Review*, 82:430–450.

Christiano, L. J., Eichenbaum, M. S., and Evans, C. L. (1999). Monetary policy shocks: What have we learned and to what end? In Taylor, J. B. and Woodford, M., editors, *Handbook of Macroeconomics*, volume 1B. North-Holland, Amsterdam.

Christiano, L. J., Eichenbaum, M. S., and Evans, C. L. (2005). Nominal rigidities and the dynamic effects of a shock to monetary policy. *Journal of Political Economy*, 113:1–45.

Christiano, L. J., Eichenbaum, M. S., and Trabandt, M. (2016). Unemployment and business cycles. *Econometrica*, 84:1523–1569.

Christiano, L. J., Trabandt, M., and Walentin, K. (2011). DSGE models for monetary policy analysis. In Friedman, B. M. and Woodford, M., editors, *Handbook of Monetary Economics*, volume 3A. North-Holland, Amsterdam.

Chung, J. W. (1994). *Utility and Production Functions*. Basil Blackwell, Oxford.

Clarida, R., Galí, J., and Gertler, M. (1999). The science of monetary policy: A new Keynesian perspective. *Journal of Economic Literature*, 37:1661–1707.

Clower, R. W. (1967). A reconsideration of the microfoundations of monetary theory. *Western Economic Journal*, 6:1–8.

Cochrane, J. H. (2005). *Asset Pricing*. Princeton University Press, Princeton, NJ, revised edition.

Cochrane, J. H. (2011). How did Paul Krugman get it so wrong? *Economic Affairs*, 31:36–40.

Cogley, T. and Nason, J. M. (1995). Output dynamics in real-business-cycle models. *American Economic Review*, 85:492–511.

Cole, H. L. and Rogerson, R. (1999). Can the Mortensen-Pissarides matching model match the business-cycle facts? *International Economic Review*, 40:933–959.

Conlisk, J. (1969). A neoclassical growth model with endogenously positioned technological change frontier. *Economic Journal*, 79:348–362.

Cooley, T. F. (1995). *Frontiers of Business Cycle Research*. Princeton University Press, Princeton, NJ.

Cooper, R. N. (1968). *The Economics of Interdependence*. McGraw-Hill, New York.

Cooper, R. W. (1999). *Coordination Games: Complementarities and Macroeconomics*. Cambridge University Press, Cambridge.

Cooper, R. W. and John, A. (1988). Coordinating coordination failures in Keynesian models. *Quarterly Journal of Economics*, 103:441–464.

Corneo, G. and Marquardt, M. (2000). Public pensions, unemployment insurance, and growth. *Journal of Public Economics*, 75:293–311.

Costain, J. S. and Reiter, M. (2008). Business cycles, unemployment insurance, and the calibration of matching models. *Journal of Economic Dynamics and Control*, 32:1120–1155.

Croix, D. de la, and Licandro, O. (1999). Life expectancy and endogenous growth. *Economics Letters*, 65:255–263.

Croix, D. de la, and Michel, P. (2002). *A Theory of Economic Growth: Dynamics and Policy in Overlapping Generations*. Cambridge University Press, Cambridge.

Cross, R., editor (1988). *Unemployment, Hysteresis and the Natural Rate Hypothesis*. Basil Blackwell, Oxford.

Cukierman, A. (1992). *Central Bank Strategy, Credibility, and Independence: Theory and Evidence*. MIT Press, Cambridge, MA.

Cukierman, A. and Meltzer, A. H. (1986). A theory of ambiguity, credibility, and inflation under discretion and asymmetric information. *Econometrica*, 54:1099–1128.

Danthine, J. P. and Donaldson, J. B. (1990). Efficiency wages and the business cycle puzzle. *European Economic Review*, 34:1275–1301.

Danthine, J. P. and Donaldson, J. B. (1993). Methodological and empirical issues in real business cycle theory. *European Economic Review*, 37:1–35.

Danziger, L. (1999). A dynamic economy with costly price adjustment. *American Economic Review*, 89:878–901.

Davies, G. (1994). *A History of Money: From Ancient Times to the Present Day*. University of Wales Press, Cardiff.

Davies, J. B. (1981). Uncertain lifetime, consumption, and dissaving in retirement. *Journal of Political Economy*, 89:561–577.

Davig, T. and Leeper, E. M. (2007). Generalizing the Taylor Principle. *American Economic Review*, 97:607–635.

Davis, S. J., Haltiwanger, J. C., and Schuh, S. (1996). *Job Creation and Destruction*. MIT Press, Cambridge, MA.

Deaton, A. (1992). *Understanding Consumption*. Oxford University Press, Oxford.

Deaton, A. and Muellbauer, J. (1980). *Economics and Consumer Behavior*. Cambridge University Press, Cambridge.

Debreu, G. (1959). *Theory of Value: An Axiomatic Analysis of Economic Equilibrium*. Yale University Press, New Haven.

DeCanio, S. J. (1979). Rational expectations and learning from experience. *Quarterly Journal of Economics*, 93:47–57.

Demange, G. (2002). On optimality in intergenerational risk sharing. *Economic Theory*, 20:1–27.

Demmel, R. and Keuschnigg, C. (2000). Funded pensions and unemployment. *FinanzArchiv*, 57:22–38.

Den Haan, W., Ramey, G., and Watson, J. (2000). Job destruction and propagation of shocks. *American Economic Review*, 90:482–498.

Devereux, M. B., Head, A. C., and Lapham, B. J. (1996a). Aggregate fluctuations with increasing returns to specialisation and scale. *Journal of Economic Dynamics and Control*, 20:627–656.

Devereux, M. B., Head, A. C., and Lapham, B. J. (1996b). Monopolistic competition, increasing returns, and the effects of government spending. *Journal of Money, Credit, and Banking*, 28:233–253.

Diamond, P. A. (1965). National debt in a neoclassical growth model. *American Economic Review*, 55:1126–1150.

Diamond, P. A. (1973). Taxation and public production in a growth setting. In Mirrlees, J. A. and Stern, N. H., editors, *Models of Economic Growth*. Macmillan, London.

Diamond, P. A. (1982a). Aggregate demand management in search equilibrium. *Journal of Political Economy*, 90:881–894.

Diamond, P. A. (1982b). Wage determination and efficiency in search equilibrium. *Review of Economic Studies*, 49:217–227.

Diamond, P. A. (1984a). Money in search equilibrium. *Econometrica*, 52:1–20.

Diamond, P. A. (1984b). *A Search-Equilibrium Approach to the Micro Foundations of Macroeconomics*. MIT Press, Cambridge, MA.

Diamond, P. A. (1997). Macroeconomic aspects of social security reform. *Brookings Papers on Economic Activity*, 2:1–87.

Diamond, P. A., editor (1999). *Issues in Privatizing Social Security*. MIT Press, Cambridge, MA.

Diamond, P. A. and Fudenberg, D. (1989). Rational expectations business cycles in search equilibrium. *Journal of Political Economics*, 97:606–619.

Diamond, P. A. and Fudenberg, D. (1991). Rational expectations business cycles in search equilibrium: A correction. *Journal of Political Economics*, 99:218–219.

Diamond, P. A. and McFadden, D. L. (1974). Some uses of the expenditure function in public finance. *Journal of Public Economics*, 3:3–21.

Dixit, A. K. (1990). *Optimization in Economic Theory*. Oxford University Press, Oxford, second edition.

Dixit, A. K. (1996). *The Making of Economic Policy: A Transaction-Cost Perspective*. MIT Press, Cambridge, MA.

Dixit, A. K. and Pindyck, R. S. (1994). *Investment under Uncertainty*. Princeton University Press, Princeton, NJ.

Dixit, A. K. and Stiglitz, J. E. (1977). Monopolistic competition and optimum product diversity. *American Economic Review*, 67:297–308.

Dixit, A. K. and Stiglitz, J. E. (2004a). Monopolistic competition and optimum product diversity (February 1975). In Brakman, S. and Heijdra, B. J., editors, *The Monopolistic Competition Revolution in Retrospect*. Cambridge University Press, Cambridge.

Dixit, A. K. and Stiglitz, J. E. (2004b). Monopolistic competition and optimum product diversity (May 1974). In Brakman, S. and Heijdra, B. J., editors, *The Monopolistic Competition Revolution in Retrospect*. Cambridge University Press, Cambridge.

Dixon, H. D. (1987). A simple model of imperfect competition with Walrasian features. *Oxford Economic Papers*, 39:134–160.

Dixon, H. D. and Hansen, C. T. (1999). A mixed industrial structure magnifies the importance of menu costs. *European Economic Review*, 43:1475–1499.

Dixon, H. D. and Lawler, P. (1996). Imperfect competition and the fiscal multiplier. *Scandinavian Journal of Economics*, 98:219–231.

Dixon, H. D. and Rankin, N., editors (1995). *The New Macroeconomics, Imperfect Markets and Policy Effectiveness*. Cambridge University Press, Cambridge.

Dorfman, R. (1969). An economic interpretation of optimal control theory. *American Economic Review*, 59:817–831.

Dornbusch, R. (1976a). Expectations and exchange rate dynamics. *Journal of Political Economy*, 84:1161–1176.

Dornbusch, R. (1976b). The theory of flexible exchange rate regimes and macroeconomic policy. *Scandinavian Journal of Economics*, 78:255–275.

Dotsey, M., King, R. G., and Wolman, A. L. (1999). State-dependent pricing and the general equilibrium dynamics of money and output. *Quarterly Journal of Economics*, 114:655–690.

Dotsey, M. and Mao, C. S. (1992). How well do linear approximation methods work? The production tax case. *Journal of Monetary Economics*, 29:25–58.

Drandakis, E. M. (1963). Factor substitution in the two-sector growth model. *Review of Economic Studies*, 30:217–228.

Drandakis, E. M. and Phelps, E. S. (1965). A model of induced invention, growth and distribution. *Economic Journal*, 76:823–840.

Drazen, A. (2000). *Political Economy in Macroeconomics*. Princeton University Press, Princeton, NJ.

Drazen, A. and Helpman, E. (1990). Inflationary consequences of anticipated macro-economic policies. *Review of Economic Studies*, 57:147–164.

Drèze, J. and Modigliani, F. (1972). Consumption decisions under uncertainty. *Journal of Economic Theory*, 5:308–335.

Dunlop, J. (1944). *Wage Determination under Trade Unions*. Macmillan, New York.

Dupor, B. (2001). Investment and interest rate policy. *Journal of Economic Theory*, 98:85–113.

Düppe, T. and Weintraub, E. R. (2014). *Finding Equilibrium: Arrow, Debreu, McKenzie and the Problem of Scientific Credit*. Princeton University Press, Princeton, NJ.

Eckstein, Z., Eichenbaum, M. S., and Peled, D. (1985a). The distribution of wealth and welfare in the presence of incomplete annuity markets. *Quarterly Journal of Economics*, 100:789–806.

Eckstein, Z., Eichenbaum, M. S., and Peled, D. (1985b). Uncertain lifetimes and the welfare enhancing properties of annuity markets and social security. *Journal of Public Economics*, 26:303–326.

Eckstein, Z. and Wolpin, K. I. (1985). Endogenous fertility and optimal population size. *Journal of Public Economics*, 27:93–106.

Eckstein, Z. and Zilcha, I. (1994). The effects of compulsory schooling on growth, income distribution and welfare. *Journal of Public Economics*, 54:339–359.

Edelberg, W., Eichenbaum, M. S., and Fisher, J. D. M. (1999). Understanding the effects of a shock to government purchases. *Review of Economic Dynamics*, 2:166–206.

Eichenbaum, M. S. (1991). Real business-cycle theory: Wisdom or whimsey? *Journal of Economic Dynamics and Control*, 15:607–626.

Einzig, P. (1949). *Primitive Money in Its Ethnological, Historical and Economic Aspects*. Eyre and Spottiswood, London.

Eisner, R. and Strotz, R. H. (1963). Determinants of business investment. In Commission on Money and Credit, editor, *Impacts of Monetary Policy*. Prentice-Hall, Englewood Cliffs, NJ.

Elaydi, S. N. (1996). *An Introduction to Difference Equations*. Springer, New York.

Ethier, W. J. (1982). National and international returns to scale in the modern theory of international trade. *American Economic Review*, 72:389–405.

Evans, G. W. and Honkapohja, S. (2001). *Learning and Expectations in Macroeconomics*. Princeton University Press, Princeton, NJ.

Farber, H. S. (1986). The analysis of union behavior. In Ashenfelter, O. and Layard, R., editors, *Handbook of Labor Economics*, volume 1. North-Holland, Amsterdam.

Favero, C. and Hendry, D. F. (1992). Testing the Lucas critique: A review. *Econometric Reviews*, 11:265–306.

Feenstra, R. C. (1986). Functional equivalence between liquidity costs and the utility of money. *Journal of Monetary Economics*, 17:271–291.

Fehr, H. and Kindermann, F. (2017). *Introduction to Computational Economics using Fortran*. Oxford University Press, Oxford. Supporting website: `http://fabian-kindermann.de/compecon/`.

Feldstein, M. S. (1974). Social security, induced retirement, and aggregate capital accumulation. *Journal of Political Economy*, 82:905–926.

Feldstein, M. S. (1976). Social security and saving: The extended life cycle theory. *American Economic Review, Papers and Proceedings*, 66:77–86.

Feldstein, M. S. (1985). The optimal level of social security benefits. *Quarterly Journal of Economics*, 100:303–320.

Feldstein, M. S. (1986). Supply side economics: Old truths and new claims. *American Economic Review, Papers and Proceedings*, 76:26–30.

Feldstein, M. S. (1987). Should social security benefits be means tested? *Journal of Political Economy*, 95:468–484.

Feldstein, M. S. (1988). The effects of fiscal policies when incomes are uncertain: A contradiction to Ricardian equivalence. *American Economic Review*, 78:14–23.

Feldstein, M. S. (1997). Transition to a fully funded pension system: Five economic issues. Working Paper 6149, NBER, Cambridge, MA.

Feldstein, M. S., editor (1998). *Privatizing Social Security*. University of Chicago Press, Chicago.

Femminis, G. (2016). From simple growth to numerical simulations: A primer in dynamic programming. Working Paper 50, Università Cattolica del Sacro Cuoro, Milan, Italy.

Ferguson, C. E. (1969). *The Neoclassical Theory of Production and Distribution*. Cambridge University Press, Cambridge.

Fischer, S. (1974). Money in the production function. *Economic Inquiry*, 12:518–533.

Fischer, S. (1977). Long-term contracts, rational expectations, and the optimal money supply rule. *Journal of Political Economy*, 85:191–205.

Fischer, S. (1979). Capital accumulation on the transition path in a monetary optimizing model. *Econometrica*, 47:1433–1439.

Fischer, S. (1980a). Dynamic inconsistency, cooperation, and the benevolent dissembling government. *Journal of Economic Dynamics and Control*, 2:93–107.

Fischer, S., editor (1980b). *Rational Expectations and Economic Policy*. University of Chicago Press, Chicago.

Fisher, I. (1913). *The Purchasing Power of Money*. Macmillan, New York. Reprinted by Augustus M. Kelley, Fairfield, NJ, 1985.

Fisher, I. (1930). *The Theory of Interest*. Macmillan, New York. Reprinted by Augustus M. Kelley, Fairfield, NJ, 1986.

Fisher, L. A. and Kingston, G. H. (2004). Theory of tax smoothing in the small open economy. *Economics Letters*, 85:1–7.

Fisher, L. A. and Kingston, G. H. (2005). Joint implications of consumption and tax smoothing. *Journal of Money, Credit, and Banking*, 37:1101–1119.

Fisher, W. H. and Turnovsky, S. J. (1998). Public investment, congestion, and private capital accumulation. *Economic Journal*, 108:399–413.

Fleming, J. M. (1962). Domestic financial policies under fixed and flexible exchange rates. *IMF Staff Papers*, 9:369–379.

Foley, D. K. and Sidrauski, M. (1971). *Monetary and Fiscal Policy in a Growing Economy*. Macmillan, London.

Fox, J. (2009). *The Myth of the Rational Market*. Harper, New York.

Frederick, S., Loewenstein, G., and O'Donoghue, T. (2002). Time discounting and time preference: A critical review. *Journal of Economic Literature*, 40:351–401.

Frenkel, J. A. and Razin, A. (1986). Fiscal policies in the world economy. *Journal of Political Economy*, 34:564–594.

Frenkel, J. A. and Razin, A. (1987). The Mundell-Fleming model: A quarter century later. *IMF Staff Papers*, 34:567–620.

Friedman, B. M. (1979). Optimal expectations and the extreme information assumption of 'rational expectations' macromodels. *Journal of Monetary Economics*, 5:23–41.

Friedman, B. M. and Hahn, F. H., editors (1990a). *Handbook of Monetary Economics*, volume I. North Holland, Amsterdam.

Friedman, B. M. and Hahn, F. H., editors (1990b). *Handbook of Monetary Economics*, volume II. North Holland, Amsterdam.

Friedman, B. M. and Woodford, M., editors (2011a). *Handbook of Monetary Economics*, volume 3A. North Holland, Amsterdam.

Friedman, B. M. and Woodford, M., editors (2011b). *Handbook of Monetary Economics*, volume 3B. North Holland, Amsterdam.

Friedman, M. (1968). The role of monetary policy. *American Economic Review*, 58:1–17.

Friedman, M. (1969). *The Optimal Quantity of Money and Other Essays*. Aldine, Chicago.

Frydman, R. and Phelps, E. S., editors (1983). *Individual Forecasting and Aggregate Outcomes*. Cambridge University Press, Cambridge.

Fuente, A. de la (2000). *Mathematical Methods and Models for Economists*. Cambridge University Press, Cambridge.

Gahvari, F. (1988). Lump-sum taxation and the superneutrality and optimum quantity of money in life cycle growth models. *Journal of Public Economics*, 36:339–367.

Galí, J. (1996). Unemployment in dynamic general equilibrium models. *European Economic Review*, 40:839–845.

Galí, J. (1999). Technology, employment, and the business cycle: Do technology shocks explain aggregate fluctuations? *American Economic Review*, 89:249–271.

Galí, J. (2011). Monetary policy and unemployment. In Friedman, B. M. and Woodford, M., editors, *Handbook of Monetary Economics*, volume 3A. North-Holland, Amsterdam.

Galí, J. (2015). *Monetary Policy, Inflation, and the Business Cycle*. Princeton University Press, Princeton, NJ, second edition.

Galí, J. and Gertler, M. (2007). Macroeconomic modeling for monetary policy evaluation. *Journal of Economic Perspectives*, 21:25–45.

Galí, J. and Rabanal, P. (2004). Technology shocks and aggregate fluctuations: How well does the Real Business Cycle model fit postwar U.S. data? *NBER Macroeconomics Annual*, 19:225–288.

Galí, J., Smets, F., and Wouters, R. (2012). Unemployment in an estimated New Keynesian model. *NBER Macroeconomics Annual*, 26:329–360.

Galor, O. (1992). A two-sector overlapping-generations model: A global characterization of the dynamical system. *Econometrica*, 60:1351–1386.

Galor, O. (2005). From stagnation to growth: Unified growth theory. In Aghion, P. and Durlauf, S. N., editors, *Handbook of Economic Growth*. North-Holland, Amsterdam.

Galor, O. and Ryder, H. E. (1989). Existence, uniqueness, and stability of equilibrium in an overlapping-generations model with productive capital. *Journal of Economic Theory*, 49:360–375.

Gärtner, M. (2016). *Macroeconomics*. Prentice-Hall, Harlow, United Kingdom, fifth edition.

Geanakoplos, J. D. (2008a). Arrow-Debreu model of general equilibrium. In Durlauf, S. N. and Blume, L. E., editors, *The New Palgrave: A Dictionary of Economics*. Palgrave Macmillan, London, second edition.

Geanakoplos, J. D. (2008b). Overlapping generations models of general equilibrium. In Durlauf, S. N. and Blume, L. E., editors, *The New Palgrave: A Dictionary of Economics*. Palgrave Macmillan, London, second edition.

Geanakoplos, J. D. and Polemarchakis, H. M. (1991). Overlapping generations. In Hildenbrand, W. and Sonnenschein, H., editors, *Handbook of Mathematical Economics*, volume IV. North-Holland, Amsterdam.

Georges, C. (1995). Adjustment costs and indeterminacy in perfect foresight models. *Journal of Economic Dynamics and Control*, 19:39–50.

Gertler, M. (1999). Government debt and social security in a life-cycle model. *Carnegie-Rochester Series on Public Policy*, 50:61–117.

Gertler, M. and Karadi, P. (2011). A model of unconventional monetary policy. *Journal of Monetary Economics*, 58:17–34.

Gertler, M. and Kiyotaki, N. (2011). Financial intermediation and credit policy in business cycle research. In Friedman, B. M. and Woodford, M., editors, *Handbook of Monetary Economics*, volume 3B. North-Holland, Amsterdam.

Gertler, M. and Trigari, A. (2009). Unemployment fluctuations with staggered Nash wage barganing. *Journal of Political Economy*, 117:38–86.

Ghosh, A. R. (1995). Intertemporal tax smoothing and the government budget surplus: Canada and the United States. *Journal of Money, Credit, and Banking*, 27:1033–1045.

Giavazzi, F. and Wyplosz, C. (1985). The zero root problem: A note on the dynamic determination of the stationary equilibrium in linear models. *Review of Economic Studies*, 52:353–357.

Gilchrist, S. and Williams, J. C. (2000). Putty-clay and investment: A business cycle analysis. *Journal of Political Economy*, 108:928–960.

Giovannini, A. (1988). The real exchange rate, the capital stock, and fiscal policy. *European Economic Review*, 32:1747–1767.

Glomm, G. and Ravikumar, B. (1992). Public versus private investment in human capital: Endogenous growth and income inequality. *Journal of Political Economy*, 100:818–834.

Glomm, G. and Ravikumar, B. (1994). Public investment in infrastructure in a simple growth model. *Journal of Economic Dynamics and Control*, 18:1173–1187.

Gollier, C. (2001). *The Economics of Risk and Time*. MIT Press, Cambridge, MA.

Gomme, P. (1999). Shirking, unemployment and aggregate fluctuations. *International Economic Review*, 40:3–21.

Gomme, P. and Rupert, P. (2009). Theory, measurement and calibration of macroeconomic models. *Journal of Monetary Economics*, 54:460–497.

Goodfriend, M. and King, R. G. (1997). The new neoclassical synthesis and the role of monetary policy. *Macroeconomics Annual*, 12:231–283.

Gordon, R. H. and Varian, H. R. (1988). Intergenerational risk sharing. *Journal of Public Economics*, 37:185–202.

Gordon, R. J., editor (1974). *Milton Friedman's Monetary Framework: A Debate with His Critics*. University of Chicago Press, Chicago.

Gordon, R. J. (1990). What is New-Keynesian economics? *Journal of Economic Literature*, 28:1115–1171.

Gottfries, N. and Horn, H. (1987). Wage formation and the persistence of unemployment. *Economic Journal*, 97:877–884.

Gould, J. P. (1968). Adjustment costs in the theory of investment of the firm. *Review of Economic Studies*, 35:47–55.

Grandmont, J.-M. (1985). On endogenous competitive business cycles. *Econometrica*, 53:995–1045.

Grass, D., Caulkins, J. P., Feichtinger, G., Tragler, G., and Behrens, D. A. (2008). *Optimal Control of Nonlinear Processes*. Springer, Berlin.

Gray, J. A. (1976). Wage indexation: A macroeconomic approach. *Journal of Monetary Economics*, 2:221–235.

Gray, J. A. (1978). On indexation and contract length. *Journal of Political Economy*, 86:1–18.

Greenwood, J. and Hercowitz, Z. (1991). The allocation of capital and time over the business cycle. *Journal of Political Economy*, 99:1188–1214.

Greenwood, J., Hercowitz, Z., and Huffman, G. W. (1988). Investment, capacity utilization, and the real business cycle. *American Economic Review*, 78:402–417.

Greenwood, J. and Huffman, G. W. (1991). Tax analysis in a real business cycle model: On measuring Harberger triangles and Okun gaps. *Journal of Monetary Economics*, 27:167–190.

Griliches, Z. (2000). *R & D, Education, and Productivity: A Retrospective*. Harvard University Press, Cambridge, MA.

Groot, H. L. F. de, and Nahuis, R. (1998). Taste for diversity and the optimality of economic growth. *Economics Letters*, 58:291–295.

Grossman, G. M. and Helpman, E. (1989). Product development and international trade. *Journal of Political Economy*, 97:1261–1283.

Grossman, G. M. and Helpman, E. (1990). Comparative advantage and long-run growth. *American Economic Review*, 80:796–815.

Grossman, G. M. and Helpman, E. (1991a). *Innovation and Growth in the Global Economy*. MIT Press, Cambridge, MA.

Grossman, G. M. and Helpman, E. (1991b). Quality ladders in the theory of growth. *Review of Economic Studies*, 58:43–61.

Grossman, S. J. and Stiglitz, J. E. (1980). On the impossibility of informationally efficient markets. *American Economic Review*, 70:393–408.

Gylfason, T. (1999). *Principles of Economic Growth*. Oxford University Press, Oxford.

Haavelmoo, T. (1945). Multiplier effects of a balanced budget. *Econometrica*, 13:311–318.

Hacche, G. (1979). *The Theory of Economic Growth: An Introduction*. Macmillan, London.

Hagedorn, M. and Manovskii, I. (2008). The cyclical behavior of equilibrium unemployment and vacancies revisited. *American Economic Review*, 98:1692–1706.

Hall, R. E. (1971). The dynamic effects of fiscal policy in an economy with foresight. *Review of Economic Studies*, 38:229–244.

Hall, R. E. (1980). Labor supply and aggregate fluctuations. *Carnegie-Rochester Series on Public Policy*, 12:7–33.

Hall, R. E. (1991). Substitution over time in consumption and work. In McKenzie, L. W. and Zamagni, S., editors, *Value and Capital Fifty Years Later*. Macmillan, London.

Hall, R. E. (1997). Macroeconomic fluctuations and the allocation of time. *Journal of Labor Economics*, 15:S223–S250.

Hall, R. E. (2005). Employment fluctuations with equilibrium wage stickiness. *American Economic Review*, 95:50–65.

Hall, R. E. (2009). Reconciling cyclical movements in the marginal value of time and the marginal product of labor. *Journal of Political Economy*, 117:281–323.

Hamberg, D. (1971). *Models of Economic Growth*. Harper and Row, New York.

Hamermesh, D. S. (1993). *Labor Demand*. Princeton University Press, Princeton, NJ.

Hamermesh, D. S. and Pfann, G. A. (1996). Adjustment costs in factor demand. *Journal of Economic Literature*, 34:1264–1292.

Hansen, G. D. (1985). Indivisible labour and the business cycle. *Journal of Monetary Economics*, 16:309–327.

Hansen, G. D. and İmrohoroğlu, S. (2008). Consumption over the life cycle: The role of annuities. *Review of Economic Dynamics*, 11:566–583.

Hansen, G. D. and Wright, R. (1994). The labor market in real business cycle theory. In Miller, P. J., editor, *The Rational Expectations Revolution: Readings from the Front Line*. MIT Press, Cambridge, MA.

Hansen, L. P. and Heckman, J. J. (1996). The empirical foundations of calibration. *Journal of Economic Perspectives*, 10:87–104.

Hansen, L. P. and Singleton, K. J. (1983). Stochastic consumption, risk aversion, and the temporal behavior of asset returns. *Journal of Political Economics*, 91:249–265.

Harris, C. and Laibson, D. (2001). Dynamic choices of hyperbolic consumers. *Econometrica*, 69:935–957.

Harris, C. and Laibson, D. (2003). Hyperbolic discounting and consumption. In Dewatripont, M., Hansen, L. P., and Turnovsky, S. J., editors, *Advances in Economics and Econometrics: Theory and Applications*, volume I. Cambridge University Press, Cambridge.

Harris, C. and Laibson, D. (2013). Instantaneous gratification. *Quarterly Journal of Economics*, 128:205–248.

Harrison, R. (1987). Jeremy Bentham. In Eatwell, J., Milgate, M., and Newman, P., editors, *The New Palgrave: A Dictionary of Economics*. Macmillan, London.

Hart, O. D. (1982). A model of imperfect competition with Keynesian features. *Quarterly Journal of Economics*, 97:109–138.

Hayashi, F. (1982). Tobin's marginal q and average q: A neoclassical interpretation. *Econometrica*, 50:213–224.

Heathcote, J., Storesletten, K., and Violante, G. L. (2009). Quantitative macroeconomics with heterogeneous households. *Annual Review of Economics*, 1:319–354.

Heer, B. and Maussner, A. (2009). *Dynamic General Equilibrium Modeling: Computational Methods and Applications*. Springer, Berlin, second edition.

Heijdra, B. J. (1998). Fiscal policy multipliers: The role of market imperfection and scale economies. *International Economic Review*, 39:659–696.

Heijdra, B. J., Heijnen, P., and Kindermann, F. (2015). Optimal pollution taxation when leisure and environmental quality are complements. *De Economist*, 163:95–122.

Heijdra, B. J., Kindermann, F., and Reijnders, L. S. M. (2017). Life in shackles? The quantitative implications of reforming the educational loan system. *Review of Economic Dynamics*, 24.

Heijdra, B. J. and Ligthart, J. E. (1997). Keynesian multipliers, direct crowding out, and the optimal provision of public goods. *Journal of Macroeconomics*, 19:803–826.

Heijdra, B. J. and Ligthart, J. E. (2000). The dynamic macroeconomic effects of tax policy in an overlapping generations model. *Oxford Economic Papers*, 52:677–701.

Heijdra, B. J. and Ligthart, J. E. (2002). The hiring subsidy *cum* firing tax in a search model of unemployment. *Economics Letters*, 75:97–108.

Heijdra, B. J. and Ligthart, J. E. (2007). Fiscal policy, monopolistic competition, and finite lives. *Journal of Economic Dynamics and Control*, 31:325–359.

Heijdra, B. J. and Ligthart, J. E. (2009). Labor tax reform, unemployment, and search. *International Tax and Public Finance*, 16:82–104.

Heijdra, B. J. and Ligthart, J. E. (2010). The transitional dynamics of fiscal policy in small open economies. *Macroeconomic Dynamics*, 14:1–28.

Heijdra, B. J., Ligthart, J. E., and Ploeg, F. van der (1998). Fiscal policy, distortionary taxation, and direct crowding out under monopolistic competition. *Oxford Economic Papers*, 50:79–88.

Heijdra, B. J. and Meijdam, A. C. (2002). Public investment and intergenerational distribution. *Journal of Economic Dynamics and Control*, 26:707–735.

Heijdra, B. J. and Mierau, J. O. (2012). The individual life-cycle, annuity market imperfections and economic growth. *Journal of Economic Dynamics and Control*, 36:876–890.

Heijdra, B. J., Mierau, J. O., and Reijnders, L. S. M. (2014). The tragedy of annuitization: Longevity risk in general equilibrium. *Macroeconomic Dynamics*, 18:1607–1634.

Heijdra, B. J. and Reijnders, L. S. M. (2012). Adverse selection in private annuity markets and the role of mandatory social annuitization. *De Economist*, 160:311–337.

Heijdra, B. J. and Reijnders, L. S. M. (2013). Economic growth and longevity risk with adverse selection. *De Economist*, 161:69–97.

Heijdra, B. J. and Reijnders, L. S. M. (2016). Human capital accumulation and the macroeconomy in an ageing society. *De Economist*, 164:297–334.

Heijdra, B. J. and Romp, W. E. (2008). A life-cycle overlapping-generations model of the small open economy. *Oxford Economic Papers*, 60:89–122.

Heijdra, B. J. and Romp, W. E. (2009a). Human capital formation and macroeconomic performance in an ageing small open economy. *Journal of Economic Dynamics and Control*, 33:53–64.

Heijdra, B. J. and Romp, W. E. (2009b). Retirement, pensions, and ageing. *Journal of Public Economics*, 93:586–604.

Heijdra, B. J. and Horst, A. van der (2000). Taxing energy to improve the environment: Efficiency and distributional effects. *De Economist*, 148:45–69.

Heijdra, B. J. and Ploeg, F. van der (1996). Keynesian multipliers and the cost of public funds under monopolistic competition. *Economic Journal*, 106:1284–1296.

Helpman, E., editor (1998). *General Purpose Technologies and Economic Growth*. MIT Press, Cambridge, MA.

Helpman, E. (2004). *The Mystery of Economic Growth*. Harvard University Press, Cambridge, MA.

Helpman, E. and Trajtenberg, M. (1998a). Diffusion of general purpose technologies. In Helpman, E., editor, *General Purpose Technologies and Economic Growth*, pages 85–119. MIT Press, Cambridge, MA.

Helpman, E. and Trajtenberg, M. (1998b). A time to sow and a time to reap: Growth based on general purpose technologies. In Helpman, E., editor, *General Purpose Technologies and Economic Growth*, pages 55–83. MIT Press, Cambridge, MA.

Hicks, J. R. (1937). Mr Keynes and the Classics: A suggested interpretation. *Econometrica*, 5:147–159.

Hirshleifer, J. and Riley, J. G. (1992). *The Analytics of Uncertainty and Information*. Cambridge University Press, Cambridge.

Hoel, M. (1990). Efficiency wages and income taxes. *Journal of Economics*, 51:89–99.

Homburg, S. (1990). The efficiency of unfunded pension systems. *Journal of Institutional and Theoretical Economics*, 146:640–647.

Homer (1946). *The Odyssey*. Penguin, Harmondsworth. Edition used: E.V. Rieu, Ed.

Hoover, K. D., editor (1992). *The New Classical Macroeconomics*. Edward Elgar, Aldershot.

Hornstein, A. (1993). Monopolistic competition, increasing returns to scale, and the importance of productivity shocks. *Journal of Monetary Economics*, 31:299–316.

Hosios, A. J. (1990). On the efficiency of matching and related models of search and unemployment. *Review of Economic Studies*, 57:279–298.

Howarth, R. B. (1991). Intergenerational competitive equilibria under technological uncertainty and an exhaustible resource constraint. *Journal of Environmental Economics and Management*, 21:225–243.

Howarth, R. B. (1998). An overlapping generations model of climate-economy interactions. *Scandinavian Journal of Economics*, 100:575–591.

Howarth, R. B. and Norgaard, R. B. (1990). Intergenerational resource rights, efficiency, and social optimality. *Land Economics*, 66:1–11.

Howarth, R. B. and Norgaard, R. B. (1992). Environmental valuation under sustainable development. *American Economic Review, Papers and Proceedings*, 82:473–477.

Howitt, P. (1985). Transaction costs in the theory of unemployment. *American Economic Review*, 75:88–100.

Hoy, M., Livernois, J., McKenna, C., Rees, R., and Stengos, T. (2011). *Mathematics for Economists*. MIT Press, Cambridge, MA, third edition.

Huang, C.-H. and Lin, K. S. (1993). Deficits, government expenditures, and tax smoothing in the United States: 1929-1988. *Journal of Monetary Economics*, 31:317–339.

Huang, K. X. D. and Liu, Z. (2002). Staggered price setting, staggered wage-setting, and business cycle persistence. *Journal of Monetary Economics*, 49:405–433.

Huang, K. X. D. and Meng, Q. (2007). Capital and macroeconomic instability in a discrete-time model with forward-looking interest rate rules. *Journal of Economic Dynamics and Control*, 31:2802–2826.

Huggett, M. (1993). The risk-free rate in heterogeneous-agent incomplete-insurance economies. *Journal of Economic Dynamics and Control*, 17:953–969.

Huggett, M. (1997). The one-sector growth model with idiosyncratic shocks: Steady states and dynamics. *Journal of Monetary Economics*, 39:385–403.

Hurd, M. D. (1989). Mortality risk and bequests. *Econometrica*, 57:779–813.

Hurd, M. D. (1990). Research on the elderly: Economic status, retirement, and consumption and saving. *Journal of Economic Literature*, 28:565–637.

Ihori, T. (1996). *Public Finance in an Overlapping Generations Economy*. Macmillan Press, London.

Inada, K.-I. (1963). On a two-sector model of economic growth: Comments and a generalisation. *Review of Economic Studies*, 30:119–127.

Inada, K.-I. (1964). On the stability of growth in two-sector models. *Review of Economic Studies*, 31:127–142.

Intriligator, M. D. (1971). *Mathematical Optimization and Economic Theory*. Prentice Hall, Englewood Cliffs, NJ.

Ireland, P. N. (1994). Money and growth: An alternative approach. *American Economic Review*, 84:47–65.

Ireland, P. N. (2004a). Money's role in the Monetary Business Cycle model. *Journal of Money, Credit, and Banking*, 36:969–983.

Ireland, P. N. (2004b). Technology shocks in the New Keynesian model. *Review of Economics and Statistics*, 86:923–936.

Jermann, U. J. (1998). Asset prices in production economies. *Journal of Monetary Economics*, 41:257–275.

Jevons, W. S. (1875). *Money and the Mechanism of Exchange*. King, London.

John, A. and Pecchenino, R. A. (1994). An overlapping generations model of growth and the environment. *Economic Journal*, 104:1393–1410.

John, A., Pecchenino, R., Schimmelpfennig, D., and Schreft, S. (1995). Short-lived agents and the long-lived environment. *Journal of Public Economics*, 58:127–141.

Jones, C. I. (1995). R & D-based models of economic growth. *Journal of Political Economy*, 103:759–784.

Jones, C. I. (1999). Growth; With or without scale effects? *American Economic Review, Papers and Proceedings*, 89:139–144.

Jones, C. I. (2002). *Introduction to Economic Growth*. W.W. Norton, New York and London, second edition.

Jones, L. E. and Manuelli, R. E. (1992). Finite lifetimes and growth. *Journal of Economic Theory*, 58:171–197.

Jones, R. A. (1976). The origin and development of media of exchange. *Journal of Political Economy*, 84:757–775.

Jonsson, G. and Klein, P. (1996). Stochastic fiscal policy and the Swedish business cycle. *Journal of Monetary Economics*, 38:245–268.

Judd, K. L. (1982). An alternative to steady-state comparisons in perfect foresight models. *Economics Letters*, 10:55–59.

Judd, K. L. (1985). Short-run analysis of fiscal policy in a simple perfect foresight model. *Journal of Political Economy*, 93:298–319.

Judd, K. L. (1987a). Debt and distortionary taxation in a simple perfect foresight model. *Journal of Monetary Economics*, 20:51–72.

Judd, K. L. (1987b). The welfare cost of factor taxation in a perfect-foresight model. *Journal of Political Economy*, 95:675–709.

Judd, K. L. (1998). *Numerical Methods in Economics*. MIT Press, Cambridge, MA.

Judd, K. L. (1999). Optimal taxation and spending in general competitive growth models. *Journal of Public Economics*, 71:1–26.

Judd, K. L., Kubler, F., and Schmedders, K. (2003). Computational methods for dynamic equilibria with heterogeneous agents. In Dewatripont, M., Hansen, L. P., and Turnovsky, S. J., editors, *Advances in Economics and Econometrics: Theory and Applications*, volume III. Cambridge University Press, Cambridge.

Kaganovich, M. and Zilcha, I. (1999). Education, social security, and growth. *Journal of Public Economics*, 71:289–309.

Kahn, R. F. (1931). The relation of home investment to unemployment. *Economic Journal*, 41:173–198.

Kaldor, N. (1961). Capital accumulation and economic growth. In Lutz, F. A. and Hague, D. C., editors, *The Theory of Capital*, pages 177–222. St Martin's Press, New York.

Kalemli-Ozcan, S., Ryder, H. E., and Weil, D. N. (2000). Mortality decline, human capital investment, and economic growth. *Journal of Development Economics*, 62:1–23.

Kamien, M. I. and Schwartz, N. L. (1991). *Dynamic Optimization: The Calculus of Variations and Optimal Control in Economics and Management*. North-Holland, Amsterdam, second edition.

Katz, L. F. (1986). Efficiency wage theories: A partial evaluation. *NBER Macroeconomics Annual*, 1:235–290.

Kehoe, T. J. (1990). Intertemporal general equilibrium models. In Hahn, F. H., editor, *The Economics of Missing Markets, Information, and Games*, pages 363–393. Oxford University Press, Oxford.

Kehoe, T. J. and Prescott, E. C., editors (2007). *Great Depressions of the Twentieth Century*. Federal Reserve Bank of Minneapolis, Minneapolis.

Kennan, J. (1979). The estimation of partial adjustment models with rational expectations. *Econometrica*, 47:1441–1455.

Keynes, J. M. (1930). *A Treatise on Money*. Macmillan, London.

Keynes, J. M. (1936). *The General Theory of Employment, Interest, and Money*. Macmillan, London.

Keynes, J. M. (1937). The general theory of employment. *Quarterly Journal of Economics*, 51:209–223.

Killingsworth, M. R. and Heckman, J. J. (1986). Female labor supply: A survey. In Ashenfelter, O. and Layard, R., editors, *Handbook of Labor Economics*. North-Holland, Amsterdam.

Kimball, M. S. (1994). Labor-market dynamics when unemployment is a worker discipline device. *American Economic Review*, 84:1045–1059.

Kimball, M. S. and Weil, P. (2009). Precautionary saving and consumption smoothing across time and possibilities. *Journal of Money, Credit and Banking*, 41:245–284.

King, R. G. and Levine, R. (1994). Capital fundamentalism, economic development and economic growth. *Carnegie-Rochester Series on Public Policy*, 40:259–292.

King, R. G., Plosser, C. I., and Rebelo, S. (1987). Production, growth and business cycles: Technical appendix. Working paper, University of Rochester, Rochester, NY. Published in *Computational Economics*, 2002, 20:87-116.

King, R. G., Plosser, C. I., and Rebelo, S. (1988a). Production, growth and business cycles I: The basic neoclassical model. *Journal of Monetary Economics*, 21:195–232.

King, R. G., Plosser, C. I., and Rebelo, S. (1988b). Production, growth and business cycles II: New directions. *Journal of Monetary Economics*, 21:309–341.

King, R. G. and Rebelo, S. (1993). Transitional dynamics and economic growth in the neoclassical model. *American Economic Review*, 83:908–931.

King, R. G. and Rebelo, S. (1999). Resuscitating real business cycles. In Taylor, J. B. and Woodford, M., editors, *Handbook of Macroeconomics*, volume 1B. North-Holland, Amsterdam.

King, R. G. and Watson, M. W. (1998). The solution of singular linear difference systems under rational expectations. *International Economic Review*, 39:1015–1026.

King, R. G. and Watson, M. W. (2002). System reduction and solution algorithms for singular linear difference systems under rational expectations. *Computational Economics*, 20:57–86.

King, R. G. and Wolman, A. L. (1996). Inflation targeting in a St. Louis model of the 21st century. Working Paper 5507, NBER, Cambridge, MA.

King, R. G. and Wolman, A. L. (1999). What should the monetary authority do when prices are sticky? In Taylor, J. B., editor, *Monetary Policy Rules*. University of Chicago Press, Chicago.

Kingston, G. H. (1984). Efficient timing of income taxes. *Journal of Public Economics*, 24:271–280.

Kingston, G. H. (1991). Should marginal tax rates be equalized through time? *Quarterly Journal of Economics*, 106:911–924.

Kirman, A. P. (1992). Whom or what does the representative individual represent? *Journal of Economic Perspectives*, 6:117–136.

Kiyotaki, N. (1988). Multiple expectational equilibria under monopolistic competition. *Quarterly Journal of Economics*, 103:695–713.

Kiyotaki, N. (2011). A perspective on modern business cycle theory. *Federal Reserve Bank of Richmond Economic Quarterly*, 97:195–208.

Kiyotaki, N. and Moore, J. (2005). Liquidity and asset prices. *International Economic Review*, 46:317–349.

Kiyotaki, N. and Moore, J. (2012). Liquidity, business cycles, and monetary policy. Working Paper 17934, NBER, Cambridge, MA.

Kiyotaki, N. and Wright, R. (1993). A search-theoretic approach to monetary economics. *American Economic Review*, 83:63–77.

Klamer, A. (1984). *The New Classical Macroeconomics*. Wheatsheaf, Brighton, United Kingdom.

Klein, M. W. (1998). *Mathematical Methods for Economics*. Addison Wesley, Reading, MA.

Klein, P. (2000). Using the generalized Schur form to solve a multivatiate linear rational expectations model. *Journal of Economic Dynamics and Control*, 24:1405–1423.

Klein, P. (2008). Time consistency of monetary and fiscal policy. In Durlauf, S. N. and Blume, L. E., editors, *The New Palgrave: A Dictionary of Economics*. Palgrave Macmillan, London, second edition.

Koopmans, T. C. (1965). On the concept of optimal economic growth. In *The Econometric Approach to Development Planning*. Rand-McNally, Chicago.

Koopmans, T. C. (1967). Intertemporal distribution and 'optimal' aggregate economic growth. In *Ten Economic Studies in the Tradition of Irving Fisher*. Wiley, New York.

Kortum, S. S. (1997). Research, patenting, and technological change. *Econometrica*, 65:1389–1419.

Koskela, E. and Vilmunen, J. (1996). Tax progression is good for employment in popular models of trade union behaviour. *Labour Economics*, 3:65–80.

Kotlikoff, L. J. and Spivak, A. (1981). The family as an incomplete annuities market. *Journal of Political Economy*, 89:372–391.

Kotlikoff, L. J. and Summers, L. H. (1979). Tax incidence in a life cycle model with variable labor supply. *Quarterly Journal of Economics*, 94:705–718.

Kotlikoff, L. J. and Summers, L. H. (1981). The role of intergenerational transfers in aggregate capital accumulation. *Journal of Political Economy*, 89:706–732.

Kotlikoff, L. J. and Summers, L. H. (1987). Tax incidence. In Auerbach, A. J. and Feldstein, M., editors, *Handbook of Public Economics*, volume I. North-Holland, Amsterdam.

Kreyszig, E. (1999). *Advanced Engineering Mathematics*. John Wiley, New York, eighth edition.

Krugman, P. R. (1994). *Peddling Prosperity: Economic Sense and Nonsense in the Age of Diminished Expectations*. W.W. Norton, New York and London.

Krugman, P. R. (2009). How did economists get it so wrong? *New York Times Magazine*. http://www.nytimes.com/2009/09/06/magazine/06Economic-t.html.

Krugman, P. R. (2012). *End This Depression Now!* W.W. Norton, New York.

Kurozumi, T. and Van Zandweghe, W. (2008). Investment, interest rate policy, and equilibrium stability. *Journal of Economic Dynamics and Control*, 32:1489–1516.

Kydland, F. E. and Prescott, E. C. (1977). Rules rather than discretion: The inconsistency of optimal plans. *Journal of Political Economy*, 85:473–491.

Kydland, F. E. and Prescott, E. C. (1982). Time to build and aggregate fluctuations. *Econometrica*, 50:1345–1370.

Kydland, F. E. and Prescott, E. C. (1996). The computational experiment: An econometric tool. *Journal of Economic Perspectives*, 10:69–85.

Ladrón-de-Guevara, A., Ortigueira, S., and Santos, M. S. (1997). Equilibrium dynamics in two-sector models of endogenous growth. *Journal of Economic Dynamics and Control*, 21:115–143.

Ladrón-de-Guevara, A., Ortigueira, S., and Santos, M. S. (1999). A two-sector model of endogenous growth with leisure. *Review of Economic Studies*, 66:609–631.

Laibson, D. (1997). Golden eggs and hyperbolic discounting. *Quarterly Journal of Economics*, 112:443–477.

Laibson, D., Repetto, A., and Tobacman, J. (2003). A debt puzzle. In Aghion, P., Frydman, R., Stiglitz, J., and Woodford, M., editors, *Knowledge, Information, and Expectations in Modern Macroeconomics: In Honor of Edmund S. Phelps*. Princeton University Press, Princeton, NJ.

Laidler, D. (1991). *The Golden Age of the Quantity Theory*. Philip Alland, New York.

Lancaster, P. and Tismenetsky, M. (1985). *The Theory of Matrices*. Academic Press, San Diego, CA, second edition.

Lapan, H. E. and Enders, W. (1990). Endogenous fertility, Ricardian equivalence, and debt management policy. *Journal of Public Economics*, 41:227–248.

Laxton, D., Isard, P., Faruqee, H., Prasad, E., and Turtelboom, B. (1998). *MULTI-MOD Mark III: The Core Dynamic and Steady-State Models*. International Monetary Fund, Washington, DC.

Layard, R., Nickell, S., and Jackman, R. (2005). *Unemployment: Macroeconomic Performance and the Labour Market*. Oxford University Press, Oxford, second edition.

Lee, R. (2016). Macroeconomics, aging and growth. Working Paper 22310, NBER, Cambridge, MA.

Léonard, D. and Long, N. V. (1992). *Optimal Control Theory and Static Optimization in Economics*. Cambridge University Press, Cambridge.

Leontief, W. (1946). The pure theory of the guaranteed annual wage contract. *Journal of Political Economy*, 54:76–79.

Levhari, D. and Mirman, L. J. (1977). Savings and consumption with an uncertain horizon. *Journal of Political Economy*, 85:265–281.

Levy, D., Bergen, M., Dutta, S., and Venable, R. (1997). The magnitude of menu costs: Direct evidence from large U.S. supermarket chains. *Quarterly Journal of Economics*, 112:791–825.

Lindbeck, A. and Snower, D. J. (1988). *The Insider-Outsider Theory of Employment and Unemployment*. MIT Press, Cambridge, MA.

Lipman, B. L. and Pesendorfer, W. (2013). Temptation. In Acemoglu, D., Arellano, M., and Dekel, E., editors, *Advances in Economics and Econometrics*, volume I: Economic Theory. Cambridge University Press, Cambridge.

Liviatan, N. (1984). Tight money and inflation. *Journal of Monetary Economics*, 13:5–15.

Ljungqvist, L. and Sargent, T. J. (2012). *Recursive Macroeconomic Theory*. MIT Press, Cambridge, MA, third edition.

Ljungqvist, L. and Uhlig, H. (2000). Tax policy and aggregate demand management under catching up with the Joneses. *American Economic Review*, 90:356–366.

Long, J. B. and Plosser, C. I. (1983). Real business cycles. *Journal of Political Economy*, 91:39–69.

Loury, G. C. (1981). Intergenerational transfers and the distribution of earnings. *Econometrica*, 49:843–867.

Lucas, R. E. (1967). Adjustment costs and the theory of supply. *Journal of Political Economy*, 75:321–334.

Lucas, R. E. (1972). Expectations and the neutrality of money. *Journal of Economic Theory*, 4:103–124. Reprinted in: Lucas (1981).

Lucas, R. E. (1973). Some international evidence on the output-inflation tradeoffs. *American Economic Review*, 63:326–334. Reprinted in: Lucas (1981).

Lucas, R. E. (1976). Econometric policy analysis: A critique. *Carnegie-Rochester Conference on Public Policy*, 1:19–46. Reprinted in: Lucas (1981).

Lucas, R. E. (1980). Methods and problems in business cycle theory. *Journal of Money, Credit, and Banking*, 12:696–715. Reprinted in: Lucas (1981).

Lucas, R. E. (1981). *Studies in Business-Cycle Theory*. MIT Press, Cambridge, MA.

Lucas, R. E. (1987). *Models of Business Cycles*. Basil Blackwell, Oxford.

Lucas, R. E. (1988). On the mechanics of economic development. *Journal of Monetary Economics*, 22:3–42.

Lucas, R. E. (1990a). Supply-side economics: An analytical review. *Oxford Economic Papers*, 42:293–316.

Lucas, R. E. (1990b). Why doesn't capital flow from rich to poor countries? *American Economic Review, Paper and Proceedings*, 80:92–96.

Lucas, R. E. and Sargent, T. J., editors (1981). *Rational Expectations and Econometric Practice*. George Allen & Unwin, London.

Lucas, R. E. and Stokey, N. L. (1983). Optimal fiscal and monetary policy in an economy without capital. *Journal of Monetary Economics*, 12:55–93.

McCallum, B. T. (1980). Rational expectations and macroeconomic stabilization policy: An overview. *Journal of Money, Credit, and Banking*, 12:716–746.

McCallum, B. T. (1983a). The liquidity trap and the Pigou effect: A dynamic analysis with rational expectations. *Economica*, 50:395–405.

McCallum, B. T. (1983b). On non-uniqueness in rational expectations models: An attempt at perspective. *Journal of Monetary Economics*, 11:139–168.

McCallum, B. T. (1983c). The role of overlapping-generations models in monetary economics. *Carnegie-Rochester Conference Series on Public Policy*, 18:9–44.

McCallum, B. T. (1989a). *Monetary Economics: Theory and Policy*. Macmillan, New York.

McCallum, B. T. (1989b). Real business cycle models. In Barro, R. J., editor, *Modern Business Cycle Theory*. Basil Blackwell, Oxford.

McCallum, B. T. (1998). Solutions to linear rational expectations models: A compact exposition. *Economics Letters*, 61:143–147.

McCallum, B. T. (1999). Roles of the minimal state variable criterion in rational expectations models. Working Paper 7087, NBER, Cambridge, MA.

McCallum, B. T. and Goodfriend, M. S. (1987). Demand for money: Theoretical studies. In Eatwell, J., Milgate, M., and Newman, P., editors, *The New Palgrave: A Dictionary of Economics*. Macmillan, London.

McCandless, G. T. (2008). *The ABCs of RBCs*. Harvard University Press, Cambridge, MA.

McDonald, I. M. and Solow, R. M. (1981). Wage bargaining and employment. *American Economic Review*, 71:896–908.

McDonald, I. M. and Solow, R. M. (1985). Wage and employment in a segmented labor market. *Quarterly Journal of Economics*, 100:1115–1141.

McGrattan, E. R. (1994). The macroeconomic effects of distortionary taxation. *Journal of Monetary Economics*, 33:573–601.

Machin, S. and Manning, A. (1999). The causes and consequences of longterm unemployment in Europe. In Ashenfelter, O. and Card, D., editors, *Handbook of Labor Economics*, volume 3C. North-Holland, Amsterdam.

Maddock, R. and Carter, M. (1982). A child's guide to rational expectations. *Journal of Economic Literature*, 20:39–51.

Magill, M. and Quinzii, M. (2008). General equilibrium with incomplete markets. In Durlauf, S. N. and Blume, L. E., editors, *The New Palgrave: A Dictionary of Economics*. Palgrave Macmillan, London, second edition.

Majumdar, M. and Radner, R. (2008). Uncertainty and general equilibrium. In Durlauf, S. N. and Blume, L. E., editors, *The New Palgrave: A Dictionary of Economics*. Palgrave Macmillan, London, second edition.

Mankiw, N. G. (1985). Small menu costs and large business cycles: A macroeconomic model of monopoly. *Quarterly Journal of Economics*, 100:529–539.

Mankiw, N. G. (1987). The optimal collection of seigniorage: Theory and evidence. *Journal of Monetary Economics*, 20:327–341.

Mankiw, N. G. (1988). Imperfect competition and the Keynesian cross. *Economics Letters*, 26:7–13.

Mankiw, N. G. (1989). Real business cycles: A new Keynesian perspective. *Journal of Economic Perspectives*, 3:79–90.

Mankiw, N. G. (2007). *Macroeconomics*. Worth Publishers, New York, sixth edition.

Mankiw, N. G. and Romer, D., editors (1991). *New Keynesian Economics*. MIT Press, Cambridge, MA.

Mankiw, N. G., Romer, D., and Weil, D. N. (1992). A contribution to the empirics of economic growth. *Quarterly Journal of Economics*, 107:407–437.

Mankiw, N. G., Rotemberg, J. J., and Summers, L. H. (1985). Intertemporal substitution in macroeconomics. *Quarterly Journal of Economics*, 100:225–251.

Mankiw, N. G. and Whinston, M. D. (1986). Free entry and social inefficiency. *Rand Journal of Economics*, 17:48–58.

Manning, A. (1987). An integration of trade union models in a sequential bargaining framework. *Economic Journal*, 97:121–139.

Marini, G. and Scaramozzino, P. (1995). Overlapping generations and environmental control. *Journal of Environmental Economics and Management*, 29:64–77.

Marini, G. and Ploeg, F. van der (1988). Monetary and fiscal policy in an optimising model with capital accumulation and finite lives. *Economic Journal*, 98:772–786.

Marschak, J. (1953). Economic measurement for policy and prediction. In Hood, W. C. and Koopmans, T. C., editors, *Studies in Econometric Method*. Wiley, New York.

Matsuyama, K. (1987). Current account dynamics in a finite horizon model. *Journal of International Economics*, 23:299–313.

Matsuyama, K. (1995). Complementarities and cumulative processes in models of monopolistic competition. *Journal of Economic Literature*, 33:701–729.

Meade, J. A. (1961). *A Neo-Classical Theory of Economic Growth*. George Allen & Unwin, London.

Meijdam, A. C. and Verhoeven, M. J. (1998). Comparative dynamics in perfect-foresight models. *Computational Economics*, 12:115–124.

Menger, C. (1892). On the origin of money. *Economic Journal*, 2:239–255.

Merton, R. C. (1971). Optimum consumption and portfolio rules in a continuous-time model. *Journal of Economic Theory*, 3:373–413. Reprinted in: Merton, *Continuous-Time Finance*. Oxford: Basil Blackwell, 1990.

Merz, M. (1995). Search in the labor market and the real business cycle. *Journal of Monetary Economics*, 36:269–300.

Merz, M. (1997). A market structure for an environment with heterogeneous job-matches, indivisible labour and persistent unemployment. *Journal of Economic Dynamics and Control*, 21:853–872.

Merz, M. (1999). Heterogeneous job-matches and the cyclical behavior of labor turnover. *Journal of Monetary Economics*, 43:91–124.

Miao, J. (2014). *Economic Dynamics in Discrete Time*. MIT Press, Cambridge, MA.

Michel, P. and Croix, D. de la (2000). Myopic and perfect foresight in the OLG model. *Economics Letters*, 67:53–60.

Miller, M. H. (1977). Debt and taxes. *Journal of Finance*, 32:261–275.

Miller, M. H. and Modigliani, F. (1961). Dividend policy, growth, and the valuation of shares. *Journal of Business*, 34:411–433.

Miller, M. H. and Orr, D. (1966). A model of the demand for money by firms. *Quarterly Journal of Economics*, 79:413–435.

Miller, M. H. and Upton, C. W. (1974). *Macroeconomics: A Neoclassical Introduction*. University of Chicago Press, Chicago.

Miller, P. J., editor (1994). *The Rational Expectations Revolution: Readings from the Front Line*. MIT Press, Cambridge, MA.

Miranda, M. J. and Fackler, P. L. (2002). *Applied Computational Economics and Finance*. MIT Press, Cambridge, MA.

Mitchell, B. R. (1998a). *International Historical Statistics: Europe, 1750-1993*. Macmillan, London.

Mitchell, B. R. (1998b). *International Historical Statistics: The Americas, 1750-1993.* Macmillan, London.

Modigliani, F. (1944). Liquidity preference and the theory of interest and money. *Econometrica,* 12:45–88.

Modigliani, F. and Miller, M. H. (1958). The cost of capital, corporation finance and the theory of investment. *American Economic Review,* 48:261–297.

Molana, H. and Moutos, T. (1992). A note on taxation, imperfect competition, and the balanced-budget multiplier. *Oxford Economic Papers,* 44:68–74.

Mortensen, D. T. (1978). Specific capital and labor turnover. *Bell Journal of Economics,* 9:572–586.

Mortensen, D. T. (1982a). The matching process as a noncooperative bargaining game. In McCall, J. J., editor, *The Economics of Information and Uncertainty.* University of Chicago Press, Chicago.

Mortensen, D. T. (1982b). Property rights and efficiency in mating, racing, and related games. *American Economic Review,* 72:968–979.

Mortensen, D. T. (1986). Job search and labor market analysis. In Ashenfelter, O. and Layard, R., editors, *Handbook of Labor Economics.* North-Holland, Amsterdam.

Mortensen, D. T. (1989). The persistence and indeterminacy of unemployment in search equilibrium. *Scandinavian Journal of Economics,* 91:347–370.

Mortensen, D. T. and Pissarides, C. A. (1994). Job creation and job destruction in the theory of unemployment. *Review of Economic Studies,* 61:397–415.

Mortensen, D. T. and Pissarides, C. A. (1999a). Job reallocation, employment fluctuations and unemployment. In Taylor, J. B. and Woodford, M., editors, *Handbook of Macroeconomics,* volume 1B. North-Holland, Amsterdam.

Mortensen, D. T. and Pissarides, C. A. (1999b). New developments in models of search in the labor market. In Ashenfelter, O. and Card, D., editors, *Handbook of Labor Economics,* volume 3B. North-Holland, Amsterdam.

Mortensen, D. T. and Pissarides, C. A. (2001). Taxes, subsidies and equilibrium labor market outcomes. Discussion Paper 2989, CEPR, London.

Mourmouras, A. (1993). Conservationist government policies and intergenerational equity in an overlapping generations model with renewable resources. *Journal of Public Economics,* 51:249–268.

Mueller, D. C. (1989). *Public Choice II.* Cambridge University Press, Cambridge.

Mulligan, C. B. (1999). Microfoundations and macro implications of indivisible labor. Working Paper 7116, NBER, Cambridge, MA.

Mulligan, C. B. and Sala-i-Martin, X. (1993). Transitional dynamics in two-sector models of endogenous growth. *Quarterly Journal of Economics,* 108:739–773.

Mundell, R. A. (1968). *International Economics.* Macmillan, New York.

Muth, J. F. (1961). Rational expectations and the theory of price movements. *Econometrica,* 29:315–335.

Nakajima, M. (2012). Business cycles in the equilibrium model of labor market search and self-insurance. *International Economic Review*, 53:399–431.

Negishi, T. (1960). Welfare economics and existence of an equilibrium for a competitive economy. *Metroeconomica*, 12:92–97.

Nerlove, M. and Raut, L. K. (1997). Growth models with endogenous population: A general framework. In Rosenzweig, M. R. and Stark, O., editors, *Handbook of Population and Family Economics*. North-Holland, Amsterdam.

Neumann, J. von, and Morgenstern, O. (1944). *Theory of Games and Economic Behavior*. Princeton University Press, Princeton, NJ.

Ng, Y.-K. (1982). Macroeconomics with non-perfect competition. *Economic Journal*, 90:598–610.

Nickell, S. J. (1986). Dynamic models of labour demand. In Ashenfelter, O. and Layard, R., editors, *Handbook of Labor Economics*, volume 1. North-Holland, Amsterdam.

Nickell, S. J. and Layard, R. (1999). Labor market institutions and economic performance. In Ashenfelter, O. and Card, D., editors, *Handbook of Labor Economics*, volume 3C. North-Holland, Amsterdam.

Niehans, J. (1978). *The Theory of Money*. Johns Hopkins, Baltimore, MD.

Nielsen, S. B. (1994). Social security and foreign indebtedness in a small open economy. *Open Economies Review*, 5:47–63.

Nielsen, S. B. and Sørensen, P. B. (1991). Capital income taxation in a growing open economy. *European Economic Review*, 34:179–197.

Nishimura, K. and Venditti, A. (2007). Indeterminacy in discrete-time infinite-horizon models with non-linear utility and endogenous labor. *Journal of Mathematical Economics*, 43:446–476.

Nourry, C. (2001). Stability of equilibria in the overlapping generations model with endogenous labour supply. *Journal of Economic Dynamics and Control*, 25:1647–1663.

Nourry, C. and Venditti, A. (2006). Overlapping generations model with endogenous labor supply: General formulation. *Journal of Optimization Theory and Applications*, 128:355–377.

Obstfeld, M. and Rogoff, K. (1995). The intertemporal approach to the current account. In Grossman, G. M. and Rogoff, K., editors, *Handbook of International Economics*, volume 3. North-Holland, Amsterdam.

Obstfeld, M. and Rogoff, K. (1996). *Foundations of International Macroeconomics*. MIT Press, Cambridge, MA.

O'Connell, S. A. and Zeldes, S. P. (1988). Rational Ponzi games. *International Economic Review*, 29:431–450.

O'Donoghue, T. and Rabin, M. (1999). Doing it now or later. *American Economic Review*, 89:103–124.

O'Driscoll, G. P. (1977). The Ricardian Nonequivalence Theorem. *Journal of Political Economy*, 85:207–210.

OECD (2001). *OECD Economic Outlook*. Organisation for Economic Co-operation and Development, Paris. (Volume 69, June).

OECD (2006). *Labour Force Statistics, 1985-2006*. Organisation for Economic Co-operation and Development, Paris.

OECD (2015). *Labour Force Statistics, 2014*. Organisation for Economic Co-operation and Development, Paris.

Ogata, K. (1995). *Discrete-Time Control Systems*. Prentice Hall, Upper Saddle River, NJ, second edition.

Orphanides, A. (2008). Taylor rules. In Durlauf, S. N. and Blume, L. E., editors, *The New Palgrave: A Dictionary of Economics*. Palgrave Macmillan, London, second edition.

Ortega, J. M. (1987). *Matrix Theory: A Second Course*. Plenum Press, New York.

Ortigueira, S. and Santos, M. S. (2002). Equilibrium dynamics in a two-sector model with taxes. *Journal of Economic Theory*, 105:99–119.

Oswald, A. J. (1982). The microeconomic theory of the trade union. *Economic Journal*, 97:269–283.

Oswald, A. J. (1985). The economic theory of trade unions: An introductory survey. *Scandinavian Journal of Economics*, 87:160–193.

Parkin, M. (1986). The output-inflation trade-off when prices are costly to change. *Journal of Political Economy*, 94:200–224.

Patinkin, D. (1987). Walras's law. In Eatwell, J., Milgate, M., and Newman, P., editors, *The New Palgrave: A Dictionary of Economics*. Macmillan, London.

Patterson, K. (2000). *An Introduction to Applied Econometrics: A Time Series Approach*. Macmillan, London.

Peleg, B. and Yaari, M. E. (1973). On the existence of a consistent course of action when tastes are changing. *Review of Economic Studies*, 40:391–401.

Pencavel, J. (1986). Labor supply of men: A survey. In Ashenfelter, O. and Layard, R., editors, *Handbook of Labor Economics*. North-Holland, Amsterdam.

Pencavel, J. (1991). *Labor Markets under Trade Unionism: Employment, Wages, and Hours*. Blackwell, Oxford.

Persson, T. and Tabellini, G. (1989). *Macroeconomic Policy, Credibility and Politics*. Harwood, London.

Persson, T. and Tabellini, G., editors (1994a). *Monetary and Fiscal Policy, I: Credibility*. MIT Press, Cambridge, MA.

Persson, T. and Tabellini, G. (1994b). Representative democracy and capital taxation. *Journal of Public Economics*, 55:53–70.

Persson, T. and Tabellini, G. (2000). *Political Economics: Explaining Economic Policy*. MIT Press, Cambridge, MA.

Pesaran, M. H. (1987). *The Limits to Rational Expectations*. Basil Blackwell, Oxford.

Pestieau, P. M. (1974). Optimal taxation and discount rate for public investment in a growth setting. *Journal of Public Economics*, 3:217–235.

Petrongolo, B. and Pissarides, C. A. (2001). Looking into the black box: A survey of the matching function. *Journal of Economic Literature*, 39:390–431.

Phelps, E. S. (1967). Phillips curves, expectations of inflation and optimal unemployment over time. *Economica*, 34:254–281.

Phelps, E. S. (1972). *Inflation Policy and Unemployment Theory*. Norton, New York.

Phelps, E. S. (1973). Inflation in theory of public finance. *Scandinavian Journal of Economics*, 75:67–82.

Phelps, E. S. (1978). Disinflation without recession: Adaptive guideposts and monetary policy. *Weltwirtschaftliches Archiv*, 100:783–809.

Phelps, E. S. et al., editors (1970). *Microeconomic Foundations of Employment and Inflation Theory*. Macmillan, London.

Phelps, E. S. and Pollak, R. A. (1968). On second-best national saving and game-equilibrium growth. *Review of Economic Studies*, 35:185–199.

Phelps, E. S. and Taylor, J. B. (1977). Stabilizing powers of monetary policy under rational expectations. *Journal of Political Economy*, 85:163–317.

Pissarides, C. A. (1990). *Equilibrium Unemployment Theory*. Basil Blackwell, Oxford.

Pissarides, C. A. (1994). Search unemployment with on-the-job search. *Review of Economic Studies*, 61:457–475.

Pissarides, C. A. (2000). *Equilibrium Unemployment Theory*. MIT Press, Cambridge, MA, second edition.

Pissarides, C. A. (2001). The economics of search. In *International Encyclopedia of the Social and Behavioral Sciences*, pages 13760–13768. North-Holland, Amsterdam.

Pissarides, C. A. (2011). Equilibrium in the labor market with search frictions. *American Economic Review*, 101:1092–1105.

Ploeg, F. van der (1995). Political economy of monetary and budgetary policy. *International Economic Review*, 36:427–439.

Plosser, C. I. (1989). Understanding real business cycles. *Journal of Economic Perspectives*, 3:51–77.

Pollak, R. A. (1968). Consistent planning. *Review of Economic Studies*, 35:201–208.

Poole, W. (1970). Optimal choice of monetary policy instruments in a simple stochastic macro model. *Quarterly Journal of Economics*, 84:197–216.

Poterba, J. M., Rotemberg, J., and Summers, L. H. (1986). A tax-based test for nominal rigidities. *American Economic Review*, 76:659–675.

Pratap, R. (2017). *Getting Started with MATLAB: A Quick Introduction for Scientists and Engineers*. Oxford University Press, Oxford, seventh edition.

Pratt, J. W. (1964). Risk aversion in the small and in the large. *Econometrica*, 32:122–136.

Prescott, E. C. (1977). Should control theory be used for economic stabilization? *Carnegie-Rochester Conference Series on Public Policy*, 7:13–38.

Prescott, E. C. (1986). Theory ahead of business cycle measurement. *Federal Reserve Bank of Minneapolis Quarterly Review*, 10:9–22. Reprinted in: Miller (1994).

Prescott, E. C. (2006). Nobel lecture: The transformation of macroeconomic policy and research. *Journal of Political Economy*, 114:203–235.

Quiggin, J. (2010). *Zombie Economics: How Dead Ideas Still Walk Among Us*. Princeton University Press, Princeton, NJ.

Raff, D. M. G. and Summers, L. H. (1987). Did Henry Ford pay efficiency wages? *Journal of Labor Economics*, 57:S57–S86.

Ramsey, F. P. (1927). A contribution to the theory of taxation. *Economic Journal*, 37:47–61.

Ramsey, F. P. (1928). A mathematical theory of savings. *Economic Journal*, 38:543–559.

Razin, A. and Ben-Zion, U. (1975). An intergenerational model of population growth. *American Economic Review*, 66:923–933.

Rebelo, S. (1991). Long-run policy analysis and long-run growth. *Journal of Political Economy*, 99:500–521.

Rebelo, S. (2005). Real business cycle models: Past, present, and future. *Scandinavian Journal of Economics*, 107:217–238.

Reichlin, R. (1986). Equilibrium cycles in an overlapping generations economy with production. *Journal of Economic Theory*, 40:89–102.

Ricardo, D. (1817). *On the Principles of Political Economy and Taxation*. John Murray, London. Edition used: Sraffa, P., editor, *The Works and Correspondence of David Ricardo*, volume I. Cambridge: Cambridge University Press, 1951.

Ríos-Rull, J. V. (1994). On the quantitative importance of market completeness. *Journal of Monetary Economics*, 34:463–496.

Rivera-Batiz, L. A. and Romer, P. M. (1991). Economic integration and endogenous growth. *Quarterly Journal of Economics*, 106:531–555.

Roberts, J. M. (1995). New Keynesian economics and the Phillips curve. *Journal of Money, Credit, and Banking*, 27:975–984.

Robinson, J. A. and Srinivasan, T. N. (1997). Long-term consequences of population growth: Technological change, natural resources, and the environment. In Rosenzweig, M. R. and Stark, O., editors, *Handbook of Population and Family Economics*. North-Holland, Amsterdam.

Rogerson, R. (1988). Indivisible labor, lotteries and equilibrium. *Journal of Monetary Economics*, 21:3–16.

Rogerson, R., Shimer, R., and Wright, R. (2005). Search-theoretic models of the labor market: A survey. *Journal of Economic Literature*, 43:959–988.

Rogoff, K. (1985). The optimal degree of commitment to an intermediate monetary target. *Quarterly Journal Economics*, 100:1169–1190.

Romer, D. (1986). A simple general equilibrium version of the Baumol-Tobin model. *Quarterly Journal of Economics*, 101:663–686.

Romer, D. (1987). The monetary transmission mechanism in a general equilibrium version of the Baumol-Tobin model. *Journal of Monetary Economics*, 20:105–122.

Romer, D. (2012). *Advanced Macroeconomics*. McGraw-Hill, New York, fourth edition.

Romer, P. M. (1986). Increasing returns and long-run growth. *Journal of Political Economy*, 94:1002–1037.

Romer, P. M. (1987). Growth based on increasing returns due to specialization. *American Economic Review, Papers and Proceedings*, 77:56–62.

Romer, P. M. (1989). Capital accumulation in the theory of long-run growth. In Barro, R. J., editor, *Modern Business Cycle Theory*, pages 51–127. Basil Blackwell, Oxford.

Romer, P. M. (1990). Endogenous technological change. *Journal of Political Economy*, 98:S71–S101.

Romer, P. M. (forthcoming). The trouble with macroeconomics. *The American Economist*.

Rosen, S. (1976). A theory of life earnings. *Journal of Political Economy*, 84:545–567.

Rosen, S. (1985). Implicit contracts: A survey. *Journal of Economic Literature*, 23:1144–1175.

Ross, S. M. (1983). *Introduction to Stochastic Dynamic Programming*. Academic Press, San Diego, CA.

Ross, S. M. (1993). *Introduction to Probability Models*. Academic Press, San Diego, CA, fifth edition.

Rotemberg, J. J. (1982). Monopolistic price adjustment and aggregate output. *Review of Economic Studies*, 49:517–531.

Rotemberg, J. J. (1987). The New Keynesian microfoundations. *NBER Macroeconomics Annual*, 2:69–104.

Rotemberg, J. J. (2008). Cyclical wages in a search-and-bargaining model with large firms. In Reichlin, L. and West, K., editors, *NBER International Seminar on Macroeconomics 2006*, pages 65–114. University of Chicago Press, Chicago.

Rotemberg, J. J. and Woodford, M. (1992). Oligopolistic pricing and the effects of aggregate demand on economic activity. *Journal of Political Economy*, 100:1153–1207.

Rotemberg, J. J. and Woodford, M. (1996). Real-business-cycle models and forecastable movements in output, hours, and consumption. *American Economic Review*, 86:71–89.

Rotemberg, J. J. and Woodford, M. (1999). Interest-rate rules in an estimated sticky price model. In Taylor, J. B., editor, *Monetary Policy Rules*. University of Chicago Press, Chicago.

Roubini, N. (1988). Current account and budget deficits in an intertemporal model of consumption and taxation smoothing: A solution to the Feldstein-Horioka puzzle? Working Paper 2773, NBER, Cambridge, MA.

Rust, J. (2008). Dynamic programming. In Durlauf, S. N. and Blume, L. E., editors, *The New Palgrave: A Dictionary of Economics*. Palgrave Macmillan, London, second edition.

Saint-Paul, G. (1992). Fiscal policy in an endogenous growth model. *Quarterly Journal of Economics*, 107:1243–1259.

Saint-Paul, G. (1996). *Dual Labor Markets: A Macroeconomic Perspective*. MIT Press, Cambridge, MA.

Saint-Paul, G. (2000). The "new political economy": Recent books by Drazen and Persson and Tabellini. *Journal of Economic Literature*, 38:915–925.

Samuelson, P. A. (1947). *Foundations of Economic Analysis*. Harvard University Press, Cambridge, MA.

Samuelson, P. A. (1958). An exact consumption-loan model of interest with or without the social contrivance of money. *Journal of Political Economics*, 66:467–482.

Samuelson, P. A. (1965). Proof that properly anticipated prices fluctuate randomly. *Industrial Management Review*, 6:41–49.

Samuelson, P. A. (1968a). The two-part golden rule deduced as the asymptotic turnpike of catenary motions. *Western Economic Journal*, 6:85–89.

Samuelson, P. A. (1968b). What classical and neoclassical monetary theory really was. *Canadian Journal of Economics*, 1:1–15.

Samuelson, P. A. (1969a). Lifetime portfolio selection by dynamic stochastic programming. *Review of Economics and Statistics*, 51:239–246.

Samuelson, P. A. (1969b). Nonoptimality of money holding under laissez faire. *Canadian Journal of Economics*, 2:303–308.

Samuelson, P. A. (1975a). The optimum growth rate for population. *International Economic Review*, 16:531–538.

Samuelson, P. A. (1975b). Optimum social security in a life-cycle growth model. *International Economic Review*, 16:539–544.

Sandmo, A. (1969). Capital risk, consumption, and portfolio choice. *Econometrica*, 37:586–599.

Sandmo, A. (1970). The effect of uncertainty on saving decisions. *Review of Economic Studies*, 37:353–360.

Sandmo, A. (1977). Portfolio theory, asset demand and taxation: Comparative statics with many assets. *Review of Economic Studies*, 44:369–379.

Sargent, T. J. (1973). Rational expectations, the real rate of interest, and the natural rate of unemployment. *Brookings Papers on Economic Activity*, 2:169–183.

Sargent, T. J. (1987a). *Dynamic Macroeconomic Theory*. Harvard University Press, Cambridge, MA.

Sargent, T. J. (1987b). *Macroeconomic Theory*. Academic Press, Boston, second edition.

Sargent, T. J. (1993). *Rational Expectations and Inflation*. Harper Collins College Publishers, New York, second edition.

Sargent, T. J. (2001). Comment on 'Fiscal consequences for Mexico of adopting the dollar'. *Journal of Money, Credit and Banking*, 33:617–625.

Sargent, T. J. and Stachurski, J. (2015). Quantitative economics with Python. Download from `http://quant-econ.net/`.

Sargent, T. J. and Wallace, N. (1975). Rational expectations, the optimal monetary instrument, and the optimal money supply rule. *Journal of Political Economy*, 83:241–254.

Sargent, T. J. and Wallace, N. (1976). Rational expectations and the theory of economic policy. *Journal of Monetary Economics*, 2:169–183.

Sargent, T. and Wallace, N. (1982). The real-bills doctrine versus the quantity theory: A reconsideration. *Journal of Political Economics*, 90:1212–1236.

Sargent, T. J. and Wallace, N. (1993). Some unpleasant monetarist arithmetic. In Sargent, T., editor, *Rational Expectations and Inflation*. Harper Collins, New York, second edition.

Sato, R. (1963). Fiscal policy in a neoclassical growth model: An analysis of time required for equilibrating adjustment. *Review of Economic Studies*, 30:16–23.

Saving, T. R. (1971). Transactions costs and the demand for money. *American Economic Review*, 61:407–420.

Scarth, W. M. (1988). *Macroeconomics: An Introduction to Advanced Methods*. Harcourt Brace Jovanovich, Toronto.

Schmidt, S. and Wieland, V. (2013). The New Keynesian approach to dynamic general equilbrium modeling: Models, methods, and macroeconomic policy evaluation. In Dixon, P. B. and Jorgenson, D. W., editors, *Handbook of Computable General Equilibrium Modeling*. North-Holland, Amsterdam.

Schmitt-Grohé, S. and Uribe, M. (2004). Optimal fiscal and monetary policy under sticky prices. *Journal of Economic Theory*, 114:198–230.

Schumpeter, J. A. (1934). *The Theory of Economic Development*. Harvard University Press, Cambridge, MA. Reprinted by Transaction Publishers, New Brunswick, NJ, 1983.

Seater, J. J. (1993). Ricardian equivalence. *Journal of Economic Literature*, 31:142–190.

Segerstrom, P. S. (1998). Endogenous growth without scale effects. *American Economic Review*, 88:1290–1310.

Segerstrom, P. S., Anant, T. C. A., and Dinopoulos, E. (1990). A Schumpeterian model of the product life cycle. *American Economic Review*, 80:1077–1091.

Seierstad, A. and Sydsæter, K. (1987). *Optimal Control Theory with Economic Applications*. North-Holland, Amsterdam.

Sen, P. and Turnovsky, S. J. (1990). Investment tax credit in an open economy. *Journal of Public Economics*, 42:277–299.

Shampine, L. F., Kierzenka, J., and Reichelt, M. W. (2000). Solving boundary value problems for ordinary differential equations in Matlab with **bvp4c**. (Downloadable from the Matlab website).

Shapiro, C. (1989). Theories of oligopoly behavior. In Schmalensee, R. and Willig, R. D., editors, *Handbook of Industrial Organization*, volume II. North-Holland, Amsterdam.

Shapiro, C. and Stiglitz, J. E. (1984). Equilibrium unemployment as a worker discipline device. *American Economic Review*, 74:433–444.

Sheffrin, S. M. (1996). *Rational Expectations*. Cambridge University Press, Cambridge, second edition.

Shell, K. (1967). A model of inventive activity and capital accumulation. In Shell, K., editor, *Essays on the Theory of Optimal Economic Growth*. MIT Press, Cambridge, MA.

Sheshinski, E. (1967). Optimal accumulation with learning by doing. In Shell, K., editor, *Essays on the Theory of Optimal Economic Growth*. MIT Press, Cambridge, MA.

Sheshinski, E. (1978). A model of social security and retirement decisions. *Journal of Public Economics*, 10:337–360.

Sheshinski, E. (2008). *The Economic Theory of Annuities*. Princeton University Press, Princeton, NJ.

Sheshinski, E. and Weiss, Y. (1981). Uncertainty and optimal social security systems. *Quarterly Journal of Economics*, 96:189–206.

Sheshinski, E. and Weiss, Y., editors (1993). *Optimal Pricing, Inflation, and the Cost of Price Adjustnent*. MIT Press, Cambridge, MA.

Shi, S. and Wen, Q. (1997). Labor market search and capital accumulation: Some analytical results. *Journal of Economic Dynamics and Control*, 21:1747–1776.

Shi, S. and Wen, Q. (1999). Labor market search and the dynamic effects of taxes and subsidies. *Journal of Monetary Economics*, 43:457–495.

Shiller, R. J. (1978). Rational expectations and the dynamic structure of macroeconomic models: A critical review. *Journal of Monetary Economics*, 4:1–44.

Shimer, R. (2005). The cyclical behavior of equilibrium unemployment and vacancies. *American Economic Review*, 95:25–49.

Shimer, R. (2010). *Labor Markets and Business Cycles*. Princeton University Press, Princeton, NJ.

Shleifer, A. (1986). Implementation cycles. *Journal of Political Economy*, 94:1163–1190.

Sidrauski, M. (1967). Rational choice and patterns of growth in a monetary economy. *American Economic Review*, 57:534–544.

Silberberg, E. (1987). Envelope theorem. In Eatwell, J., Milgate, M., and Newman, P., editors, *The New Palgrave: A Dictionary of Economics*. Macmillan, London.

Silvestre, J. (1993). The market-power foundations of macroeconomic policy. *Journal of Economic Literature*, 31:105–141.

Simon, C. P. and Blume, L. (1994). *Mathematics for Economists*. W.W. Norton, New York & London.

Sims, C. A. (1996). Macroeconomics and methodology. *Journal of Economic Perspectives*, 10:105–120.

Sinn, H.-W. (1987). *Capital Income Taxation and Resource Allocation*. North-Holland, Amsterdam.

Sinn, H.-W. (2000). Why a funded pension system is useful and why it is not useful. *International Tax and Public Finance*, 7:389–410.

Smets, F. and Wouters, R. (2003). An estimated dynamic general equilibrium model of the euro area. *Journal of the European Economic Association*, 1:1123–1175.

Smets, F. and Wouters, R. (2007). Shocks and frictions in U.S business cycles: A Bayesian DSGE approach. *American Economic Review*, 97:586–606.

Snowdon, B., Vane, H., and Wynarczyk, P. (1994). *A Modern Guide to Macroeconomics*. Edward Elgar, Aldershot.

Solow, R. M. (1956). A contribution to the theory of economic growth. *Quarterly Journal of Economics*, 70:65–94.

Solow, R. M. (1957). Technical change and the aggregate production function. *Review of Economics and Statistics*, 39:312–320.

Solow, R. M. (1961). Note on Uzawa's two-sector model of economic growth. *Review of Economic Studies*, 29:48–50.

Solow, R. M. (1979). Another possible source of wage stickiness. *Journal of Macroeconomics*, 1:79–82.

Solow, R. M. (1986). Monopolistic competition and the multiplier. In Heller, W. P., Starr, R. M., and Starrett, D. A., editors, *Equilibrium Analysis: Essays in Honour of Kenneth J. Arrow, Vol. II*. Cambridge University Press, Cambridge.

Solow, R. M. (1998). *Monopolistic Competition and Macroeconomic Theory*. Cambridge University Press, Cambridge.

Solow, R. M. (1999). Neoclassical growth theory. In Taylor, J. B. and Woodford, M., editors, *Handbook of Macroeconomics*, volume 1A. North-Holland, Amsterdam.

Spear, S. E. and Young, W. (2014). Optimum savings and optimal growth: The Cass-Malinvaud-Koopmans nexus. *Macroeconomic Dynamics*, 18:215–243.

Spence, M. (1976). Product selection, fixed costs, and monopolistic competition. *Review of Economic Studies*, 43:217–235.

Spiegel, M. R. (1965). *Laplace Tranforms*. McGraw-Hill, New York.

Spiegel, M. R. (1974). *Advanced Calculus*. McGraw-Hill, New York.

Stachurski, J. (2009). *Economic Dynamics: Theory and Computation*. MIT Press, Cambridge, MA.

Stadler, G. W. (1994). Real business cycles. *Journal of Economic Literature*, 32:1750–1783.

Startz, R. (1989). Monopolistic competition as a foundation for Keynesian macroeconomic models. *Quarterly Journal of Economics*, 104:737–752.

Stiglitz, J. E. (1986). Theories of wage rigidity. In Butkiewicz, J. L., Koford, K. J., and Miller, J. B., editors, *Keynes' Economic Legacy: Contemporary Economic Theories*. Praeger, New York.

Stokey, N. L. and Lucas, R. E. (1989). *Recursive Methods in Economic Dynamics*. Harvard University Press, Cambridge, MA.

Stokey, N. L. and Rebelo, S. (1995). Growth effects of flat-rate taxes. *Journal of Political Economy*, 103:519–550.

Strang, G. (1988). *Linear Algebra and Its Applications*. Harcourt Brace Jovanovich, San Diego, CA, third edition.

Strotz, R. H. (1956). Myopia and inconsistency in dynamic utility maximization. *Review of Economic Studies*, 23:165–180.

Summers, L. H. (1981). Taxation and corporate investment: A q-theory approach. *Brookings Papers on Economic Activity*, 1:67–140.

Summers, L. H. (1986). Some skeptical observations on real business cycle theory. *Federal Reserve Bank of Minneapolis Quarterly Review*, 10:23–27. Reprinted in: Miller (1994).

Summers, L. H. (1988). Relative wages, efficiency wages and unemployment. *American Economic Review, Papers and Proceedings*, 78:383–388.

Swan, T. W. (1956). Economic growth and capital accumulation. *Economic Record*, 32:334–361.

Sydsæter, K. and Hammond, P. J. (1995). *Mathematics for Economic Analysis*. Prentice-Hall, Englewood Cliffs, NJ.

Sydsæter, K., Hammond, P. J., Seierstad, A., and Strøm, A. (2008). *Further Mathematics for Economic Analysis*. Prentice-Hall, Englewood Cliffs, NJ, second edition.

Sydsæter, K., Strøm, A., and Berck, P. (2000). *Economists' Mathematical Manual*. Springer, Berlin, third edition.

Takayama, A. (1974). *Mathematical Economics*. Dryden Press, Hinsdale, IL.

Taylor, J. B. (1979). Staggered wage setting in a macro model. *American Economic Review*, 69:108–113.

Taylor, J. B. (1980). Aggregate dynamics and staggered contracts. *Journal of Political Economy*, 88:1–17.

Taylor, J. B. (1986). New econometric approaches to stabilization policy in stochastic models of macroeconomic fluctuations. In Griliches, Z. and Intriligator, M. D., editors, *Handbook of Econometrics*, volume III. North-Holland, Amsterdam.

Taylor, J. B. (1993). Discretion versus policy rules in practice. *Carnegie-Rochester Conference Series on Public Policy*, 39:195–214.

Temin, P. (2008). Real business cycle views of the great depression and recent events. *Journal of Economic Literature*, 46:669–684.

Temple, J. (1999). The new growth evidence. *Journal of Economic Literature*, 37:112–156.

Tirole, J. (1985). Asset bubbles and overlapping generations. *Econometrica*, 53:1499–1528.

Tobin, J. (1955). A dynamic aggregative model. *Journal of Political Economy*, 63:103–115.

Tobin, J. (1956). The interest elasticity of the transactions demand for cash. *Review of Economics and Statistics*, 38:241–247.

Tobin, J. (1958). Liquidity preference as behavior towards risk. *Review of Economic Studies*, 25:65–86.

Tobin, J. (1965). Money and economic growth. *Econometrica*, 33:671–684.

Tobin, J. (1969). A general equilibrium approach to monetary theory. *Journal of Money, Credit, and Banking*, 1:15–29.

Tobin, J. and Buiter, W. H. (1976). The long-run effects of fiscal and monetary policy on aggregate demand. In Stein, J., editor, *Monetarism*. North-Holland, Amsterdam.

Treadway, A. B. (1969). On rational entrepreneurial behaviour and the demand for investment. *Review of Economic Studies*, 36:227–239.

Trejos, A. and Wright, R. (1995). Search, bargaining, and prices. *Journal of Political Economy*, 103:118–141.

Turnbull, H. W. (1988). The great mathematicians. In Newman, J. R., editor, *The World of Mathematics*. Tempus Books, Redmond, WA.

Turnovsky, S. J. (1977). *Macroeconomic Analysis and Stabilization Policies*. Cambridge University Press, Cambridge.

Turnovsky, S. J. (1995). *Methods of Macroeconomic Dynamics*. MIT Press, Cambridge, MA.

Turnovsky, S. J. (1996). Optimal tax, debt, and expenditure policies in a growing economy. *Journal of Public Economics*, 60:21–44.

Turnovsky, S. J. and Brock, W. A. (1980). Time consistency and optimal government policies in perfect foresight equilibrium. *Journal of Public Economics*, 13:183–212.

Turnovsky, S. J. and Fisher, W. H. (1995). The composition of government expenditure and its consequences for macroeconomic performance. *Journal of Economic Dynamics and Control*, 19:747–786.

Uhlig, H. (1999). A toolkit for analysing nonlinear dynamic stochastic models easily. In Marimon, R. and Scott, A., editors, *Computational Methods for the Study of Dynamic Economies*, pages 30–61. Oxford University Press, Oxford.

Uzawa, H. (1961). On a two-sector model of economic growth. *Review of Economic Studies*, 29:40–47.

Uzawa, H. (1963). On a two-sector model of economic growth, II. *Review of Economic Studies*, 30:105–118.

Uzawa, H. (1965). Optimum technical change in an aggregative model of economic growth. *International Economic Review*, 6:18–31.

Uzawa, H. (1988). On the economics of social overhead capital. In Uzawa, H., editor, *Preference, production, and capital*. Cambridge University Press, Cambridge.

Vandenbussche, J., Aghion, P., and Meghir, C. (2006). Growth, distance to frontier and composition of human capital. *Journal of Economic Growth*, 11:97–127.

Varian, H. R. (1992). *Microeconomic Analysis*. W. W. Norton, New York, third edition.

Verbon, H. A. A. (1989). Conversion policies for public pension plans in a small open economy. In Gustafsson, B. A. and Klevmarken, N. A., editors, *The Political Economy of Social Security*. North-Holland, Amsterdam.

Viner, J. (1931). Cost curves and supply curves. *Zeitschrift für Nationalökonomie*, 3:23–46. Reprinted with supplementary note in: G.J. Stigler and K.E. Boulding, editors, *Readings in Price Theory*. London: George Allen & Unwin, 1953.

Wälde, K. (2011). *Applied Intertemporal Optimization, Edition 1.1.* Mainz University Gutenberg Press, Download from www.waelde.com/aio.

Wallace, N. (1980). The overlapping generations model of fiat money. In Kareken, J. H. and Wallace, N., editors, *Models of Monetary Economies*. Federal Reserve Bank of Minneapolis, Minneapolis.

Wallace, N. (1981). A Modigliani-Miller theorem for open-market operations. *American Economic Review*, 71:267–274.

Walsh, C. E. (2010). *Monetary Theory and Policy*. MIT Press, Cambridge, MA, third edition.

Wan, H. Y. (1971). *Economic Growth*. Harcourt Brace Jovanovich, New York.

Warsh, D. (2006). *Knowledge and the Wealth of Nations*. W.W. Norton, New York.

Watson, M. W. (1993). Measures of fit for calibrated models. *Journal of Political Economy*, 101:1011–1041.

Weil, D. N. (1997). The economics of population aging. In Rosenzweig, M. and Stark, O., editors, *Handbook of Population and Family Economics*. North-Holland, Amsterdam.

Weil, D. N. (2005). *Economic Growth*. Addison Wesley, Boston.

Weil, P. (1989a). Increasing returns and animal spirits. *American Economic Review*, 79:889–894.

Weil, P. (1989b). Overlapping families of infinitely-lived agents. *Journal of Public Economics*, 38:183–198.

Weil, P. (1991). Is money net wealth? *International Economic Review*, 37:37–53.

Weil, P. (2008). Overlapping generations: The first jubilee. *Journal of Economic Perspectives*, 22:115–134.

Weiss, A. (1991). *Efficiency Wages: Models of Unemployment, Layoffs, and Wage Dispersion*. Oxford University Press, Oxford.

Weitzman, M. L. (1982). Increasing returns and the foundation of unemployment theory. *Economic Journal*, 92:787–804.

Weitzman, M. L. (1984). *The Share Economy: Conquering Stagflation*. Harvard University Press, Cambridge, MA.

Weitzman, M. L. (1994). Monopolistic competition with endogenous specialization. *Review of Economic Studies*, 61:57–80.

Wicksell, K. (1935). *Lectures on Political Economy*, volume II. George Routledge and Sons, London. Reprinted by Augustus M. Kelley, Fairfield, NJ, 1978.

Wieland, V., Cwik, T., Müller, G. L., Schmidt, S., and Wolters, M. (2012a). A new comparative approach to macroeconomic modeling and policy analysis. *Journal of Economic Behavior and Organization*, 83:523–541.

Wieland, V., Cwik, T., Müller, G. L., Schmidt, S., and Wolters, M. (2012b). A new comparative approach to macroeconomic modeling and policy analysis. Working Paper 49, Institute for Monetary and Financial Stability, Johann Wolfgang Goethe University, Frankfurt am Main.

Wildasin, D. E. (1990). Non-neutrality of debt with endogenous fertility. *Oxford Economic Papers*, 42:414–428.

Wilson, C. (2008). Incomplete markets. In Durlauf, S. N. and Blume, L. E., editors, *The New Palgrave: A Dictionary of Economics*. Palgrave Macmillan, London, second edition.

Woodford, M. (1984). Indeterminacy of equilibrium in the overlapping generations model: A survey. (May 1984 draft available on Woodford's website).

Woodford, M. (1990). The optimum quantity of money. In Friedman, B. M. and Hahn, F. H., editors, *Handbook of Monetary Economics*, volume II. North-Holland, Amsterdam.

Woodford, M. (1999). Revolution and evolution in twentieth-century macroeconomics. Presented at a conference, *Frontiers of the Mind in the Twenty-First Century*, U.S. Library of Congress, Washington D.C., June.

Woodford, M. (2003). *Interest and Prices: Foundations of a Theory of Monetary Policy*. Princeton University Press, Princeton, NJ.

Woodford, M. (2011). Optimal monetary stabilization policy. In Friedman, B. M. and Woodford, M., editors, *Handbook of Monetary Economics*, volume 3A. North-Holland, Amsterdam.

Xiao, W. (2008). Increasing returns and the design of interest rate rules. *Macroeconomic Dynamics*, 12:22–49.

Xie, D. (1994). Divergence in economic performance: Transitional dynamics with multiple equilibria. *Journal of Economic Theory*, 63:97–112.

Yaari, M. E. (1965). Uncertain lifetime, life insurance, and the theory of the consumer. *Review of Economic Studies*, 32:137–150.

Young, A. (1998). Growth without scale effects. *Journal of Political Economy*, 106:41–63.

Yun, T. (1996). Nominal price rigidity, money supply endogeneity, and business cycles. *Journal of Monetary Economics*, 37:345–370.

Zhang, J. (1995). Social security and endogenous growth. *Journal of Public Economics*, 58:185–213.

Zhang, J. (1996). Optimal public investments in education and endogenous growth. *Scandinavian Journal of Economics*, 98:387–404.

Zhang, J. (2003). Optimal debt, endogenous fertility, and human capital externalities in a model with altruistic bequests. *Journal of Public Economics*, 87:1825–1835.

Zhang, J. (2006). Second-best public debt with human capital externalities. *Journal of Economic Dynamics and Control*, 30:347–360.

Zilcha, I. (1990). Dynamic efficiency in overlapping generations models with stochastic production. *Journal of Economic Theory*, 52:364–379.

Zilcha, I. (1991). Characterizing efficiency in stochastic overlapping generations models. *Journal of Economic Theory*, 55:1–16.

Index